The Oxford Annotated Mishnah

A New Translation of the Mishnah With Introductions and Notes

Volume III

EDITED BY
Shaye J. D. Cohen
Robert Goldenberg
Hayim Lapin

UNIVERSITY PRESS

Great Clarendon Street, Oxford, OX2 6DP,
United Kingdom

Oxford University Press is a department of the University of Oxford.
It furthers the University's objective of excellence in research, scholarship,
and education by publishing worldwide. Oxford is a registered trade mark of
Oxford University Press in the UK and in certain other countries

First Edition published in 2022

Published in the United States of America by Oxford University Press
198 Madison Avenue, New York, NY 10016, United States of America

British Library Cataloguing in Publication Data
Data available

Library of Congress Control Number: 2020946217

ISBN 978–0–19–284614–3 (Pack)
ISBN 978–0–19–923970–2 (Vol I)
ISBN 978–0–19–284612–9 (Vol II)
ISBN 978–0–19–284613–6 (Vol III)

Printed and bound by
CPI Group (UK) Ltd, Croydon, CR0 4YY

Contents

List of Figures

THE MISHNAH

ORDER OF QODASHIM
and
ORDER OF TOHOROT

ORDER OF QODASHIM

Tractate Zevahim

Aryeh Cohen

Introduction

Overview

Tractate *Zevahim* ("Offerings") covers the primary forms of animal sacrifice. Some topics (grain offerings, bird offerings, the daily offerings) are addressed in greater detail in other tractates (*Menahot, Qinnim, Tamid*) but are discussed in our tractate as well.

Structure and Organization of the Tractate

Zevahim consists of fourteen chapters. Broadly speaking, the first five deal with the sacrificing of cattle, with intention—improper designation of the sacrifice, or intention at the time of the offering to handle the sacrifice in some prohibited way—playing a central role. Chapter 5 delineates the proper locations and procedures for the major groups of sacrifices of these animals. Chapters 6 through 7 turn to the slaughter and offering of bird offerings. While there are issues particular to birds, this section also discusses intention, with 6:7 largely reproducing 1:4 and 2:2–5.

The next section, *Zevahim* 8:1–10:6, addresses topics arising from the sacrifice itself. Chapter 8 deals with animals of differing status that became intermingled; or blood or sacrificial parts that became intermingled (a characteristically mishnaic concern). Chapter 9 deals with the questions of material that was placed on the altar but should not have been, and of offerings that had been placed on the altar and flew off. The first part of chapter 10 discusses precedence among sacrifices.

In *Zevahim* 10:7–12:6 the tractate turns to the handling of the meat and animal parts after sacrifice at the altar, discussing eating (10:7–8, 12:1–4), cleansing textiles that were stained with blood (11:1–5), utensils used in cooking the meat (11:5–8), and the disposal of sacrificial remains (12:5–6).

Chapter 13 delineates the prohibition of offering sacrifices outside the Temple, and analyzes the liability for this act. This leads to a discussion of invalid sacrifices (14:1–3). Finally, the tractate outlines a history of the sacrificial cult from before the building of the Tabernacle in the desert to the building of the Jerusalem Temple (14:4–8).

Main Ideas

Among the main legal issues discussed in the tractate are boundaries in time, boundaries in space, and boundaries between persons. Some offerings could only be brought at particular times, and if they were permitted to be eaten, could only be eaten within the delimited time. Among other discussions, chapters 13 and 14 discuss the biblical prohibition of sacrifice outside the Sanctuary. Finally, although slaughter can be carried out "by anyone," all the other sacrificial acts can be performed only by a pure *kohen*, or priest, and the flesh of those sacrifices that are eaten by priests must also be eaten in a state of purity.

The one issue that occupies more space in the tractate than any other is intention. A particular concern is maintenance of the proper intention while performing the sacrifice, eating the meat, or offering its blood. Indeed, the Mishnah transforms biblical *piggul*, "abomination," from a consequence of leaving sacrificial meat beyond its appropriate time (Leviticus 7:18, 19:17), to the consequence of intending at the time of sacrifice to eat it after its time (2:3). The emphasis on intention affects the language of the tractate. The Mishnah repeatedly uses the shorthand of doing something "outside its time" or "outside its place" when what is meant is performing a sacrificial act with the intention of eating it outside the approved time or place (e.g. 2:3–4).

Another important theme is the centrality of blood; even if the animal has been slaughtered correctly and its meat has been placed correctly on the altar, the manipulation of the blood determines the efficacy of the sacrifice (2:4–7). Finally, the discussion of bird offerings makes a sharp distinction between the act of killing birds for sacrificial purposes ("pinching the neck") and for lay purposes ("slaughtering with a knife"), as in 13:7.

Relationship to Scripture

The main legal concepts and terminology draw on the Torah, particularly the outline of the sacrifices in Leviticus 1–7. The categorization of sacrifices into types (whole burnt and well-being offerings; purgation, guilt, and thanksgiving offerings); the distinct procedures for cattle, bird, and grain; the rules governing the collection and sprinkling of the blood; the rules governing the handling of the limbs, innards, meat, and skin of the sacrifice; the avoidance of *piggul* ("abomination") and *notar* ("remnant"); and the requirement of offering in the Temple alone (Leviticus 17:4–5; Deuteronomy 12:5)—all these ultimately derive from the biblical text, even if in rabbinic hands the rules are sometimes transformed and creatively interpreted.

Special Notes for the Reader

In addition to the Kaufmann (**K**) and Parma (**P**) manuscripts, in the translation and annotations I also cite variants from Vatican Hebrew Ms 120–121 (identified as **V**) and the Munich Manuscript of the Babylonian Talmud (**M**), as well as the textual evidence of the traditional commentaries.

Tractate Zevahim

Chapter One

1:1–4 *Inappropriate Intentions for Passover and Purgation Offerings*

I All animal offerings offered without their proper designation are valid,
but they do not fulfill the owners' obligations,
except for the Passover offering and the purgation offering:
the Passover offering at its appropriate time;
the purgation offering at any time.
R. Eliezer says:
Even the guilt offering—
the Passover offering at its appropriate time;
the purgation offering and the guilt offering at any time.
R. Eliezer said:
The purgation offering comes to expiate for[1] a sin
and the guilt offering comes to expiate for a sin.
Just as the purgation offering is invalid without its appropriate designation,
so too the guilt offering is invalid without its appropriate designation.

[1] Here and in the following instance, lit. "on, for."

1:1–4 The passages in this chapter address two principles. First, sacrifices should be "designated" (lit. "in the name of"), offered with the proper intention. Second, that an offering might be valid as an offering, yet not be valid for the purpose for which it was offered. The Mishnah repeatedly works through the rules stated in the opening statement of 1:1.

1:1 *except for the Passover offering and the purgation offering*, when slaughtered without proper designation. In these two cases the sacrifices are invalid even as generic offerings (see *Pesahim* 5:4).

Passover... at its appropriate time: When a Passover offering is brought on the fourteenth of Nisan without the proper designation it is not valid at all. At other times of the year, if a Passover offering is offered without a proper designation it remains a valid offering.

The same is true of a *purgation offering* (often called "sin offering"), *at any time* of the year: if it is offered without the intention that it be a purgation offering, it is completely invalid as an offering.

R. Eliezer adds the guilt offering to the list of exceptions. His second statement adds the rationale: analogy with the purgation (or "sin") offering.

2 Yose b. Honi says:
[All animals] that are slaughtered with the designation of Passover offering
or with the designation of purgation offering,
are invalid.
Simeon brother of Azariah says:
If one slaughters them with a designation of higher sanctity than they have[2]—
they are valid;
with a designation of lower sanctity than they have[3]—
they are invalid.
How?
Offerings of the highest sanctity that were slaughtered
with the designation of offerings of lesser sanctity are invalid.
Offerings of lesser sanctity that were slaughtered
with the designation of offerings of the highest sanctity are valid.
The firstborn and tithed [animals] that were slaughtered
with the designation of offerings of well-being are valid.
Offerings of well-being that were offered
with the designation of firstborn or tithed [animals] are invalid.

3 The Passover offering that one slaughtered on the morning of the fourteenth of [Nisan]
without the appropriate designation,
R. Joshua deems it valid, as if it was slaughtered on the thirteenth.
Ben Betera deems it invalid, as if it had been slaughtered *in the evening*.
Simeon b. Azzai said:
I have received a tradition from seventy-two elders
on the day they seated R. Eleazar b. Azariah in the assembly,

[2] Lit. "in the name of one higher than they." [3] Lit. "in the name of one lower than they."

1:2 *Yose b. Honi* is in dispute with the anonymous first ruling of 1:1: any offering erroneously designated as a Passover or purgation offering is invalid.

with a designation of higher…lower sanctity: As exemplified below, if one incorrectly designated a sacrifice as one that had higher sanctity, it is valid as an offering; as one that had lower sanctity, it has no validity.

Offerings of the highest…lesser sanctity: See chapter 5 for this classification.

firstborn and tithed [animals] and *offerings of well-being* are all "offerings of lesser sanctity," but well-being offerings have a higher sanctity than the first two.

1:3 *morning of the fourteenth of [Nisan]*: The proper time for the Passover was the afternoon of the fourteenth of Nisan. The dispute centers on whether slaughter in the morning also constitutes "at its appropriate time" (1:1).

as if it was slaughtered on the thirteenth, and not at a time when it could have been a Passover offering. Therefore, it is valid as an offering though not as a Passover offering.

in the evening: Exodus 12:6, the time for the sacrifice of the Passover. Ben Betera treats the whole day as appropriate (*as if…slaughtered in the evening*). Consequently, it is an otherwise valid Passover sacrifice except that it lacks proper designation and therefore is completely invalid.

the day they seated R. Eleazar b. Azariah in the assembly: The incident in question is reported in both Talmudim in tractate *Berakhot*. See also *Yadayim* 3:5.

that all the offerings that are eaten that were offered with improper designations—
are valid,
but they do not fulfill the requirements of their owners,[4]
with the exception of the Passover offering and the purgation offering.
Ben Azzai only added the whole burnt offering,
and Sages did not agree with him.

4 The Passover offering and the purgation offering
that were slaughtered without the appropriate designation;
or if he received, conveyed, or sprinkled [the blood] without its proper designation,
or with its proper designation and without its proper designation,
or without its proper designation and with its proper designation,
they are invalid.
How is "with its proper designation and without its proper designation"
[to be understood]?
With the designation of a Passover offering
and with the designation of an offering of well-being.
How is "without its proper designation and with its proper designation"
[to be understood]?
With the designation of an offering of well-being
and with the designation of a Passover offering.
For an offering is invalidated by four things:
(1) slaughter, (2) receiving, (3) conveying, and (4) sprinkling.
R. Simeon deems valid in the case of conveying.
For R. Simeon[5] would say:
An offering is impossible[6] without slaughtering, without receiving, and without sprinkling.
However, it is possible without conveying the blood:
One might slaughter beside the altar and sprinkle the blood.
R. Eliezer[7] says:
When one conveys in a place where there is a need to convey,
[inappropriate] intention[8] can invalidate.
In a place where there is no need to convey,
[inappropriate] intention does not invalidate.

[4] **M** lacks this line. [5] Some witnesses lack "R. Simeon." [6] Heb. "It is impossible."
[7] Some witnesses: "Eleazar." [8] Lit. "thought," and so throughout.

offerings that are eaten: This excludes the whole burnt offering, which is totally consumed on the altar.

1:4 The mishnah now extends the discussion beyond slaughter and asks about the consequences of having a single offering receive different designations at different times.

received the blood, *conveyed* it to the altar, and *sprinkled* the blood on the altar. These are all essential elements in a proper sacrifice.

For an offering is invalidated by four things, if not performed with the proper designation.

R. Eliezer: The reading "Eleazar" (see n. 7) makes sense, in that it makes the speaker a contemporary of R. Simeon.

intention: Lit. "thought."

Chapter Two

2:1 *Inappropriate Persons, Misplaced Actions*

2 All animal offerings for which the one who received was:
a nonpriest,[9]
an *onen*,
a *tevul yom*,
lacking vestments,[10]
lacking atonement,
one whose hands and feet are unwashed,
uncircumcised,
impure,
sitting,
standing on utensils,[11]
on an animal,
on his fellow's legs—
he has invalidated it.
If he received with his left hand, he invalidated it.
R. Simeon deems it valid.
If the blood spilled on to the floor and he collected it,[12] it is invalid.

[9] Lit. "stranger." [10] **M** lacks "lacking vestments."
[11] **K**: "standing on utensils atop utensils." **M** lacks "standing," so that the text reads "sitting on utensils."
[12] **M** lacks "and he collected it."

2:1 *received* the blood.

nonpriest: Lit. "stranger, foreigner."

onen: A direct relative of the dead in the interval before the burial.

tevul yom: One who has ritually immersed, but must now wait for sundown to become pure. See *Tevul Yom*, introduction.

lacking vestments: An ordinary priest must wear four items. a tunic, breeches, a sash, and a turban. The high priest must wear another four items: the diadem, the breastplate, the *ephod*, and the robe (see Leviticus 8:7).

lacking atonement: Anyone who incurred certain types of impurity (childbirth, skin affliction, etc.) and is now pure but has not yet offered the sacrifices necessary to effect atonement (see *Keritot* 2:1). A priest in this status is ineligible to perform these rituals.

standing on utensils: The floor of the sanctuary itself sanctifies the ritual and therefore the priest must stand on the floor.

applied the blood: The Mishnah uses two word groups for the putting of blood on the altar and elsewhere. One is based on the root *ntn* (which also has the meaning "give"), here translated with "apply" and related forms. The other is the root *nzy* ("spray" or "sprinkle"). *Zevahim* often uses the two as synonyms but there may be a technical distinction with "apply" referring to the end result (i.e. the blood ends up here or there, two or four times, etc.) and "sprinkle" to the specific manner (e.g. sprinkling as opposed to pouring).

If he applied it on the ramp,
or not in the direction of the foundation of the altar,[13]
if he applied the blood that is to be applied below, above,
or if he applied the blood that is to be applied above, below,
that which is to be applied inside, outside;
that which is to be applied outside, inside—
it is invalid but there is no *karet*.

2:2–5 *Inappropriate Intentions during the Offering*

2 One who slaughters an offering,
intending to sprinkle its blood outside, or part of its blood outside;[14]
to burn its innards outside, or some of its innards outside;
to eat its flesh outside or an olive's bulk of its flesh outside;
or to eat an olive's bulk of the skin of the fat-tail outside—
it is invalid but there is no *karet*.
To sprinkle its blood on the morrow or part of its blood on the morrow;
to burn its innards on the morrow or some of its innards on the morrow;
to eat its flesh on the morrow or an olive's bulk of its flesh on the morrow;
or to eat an olive's bulk of the skin of the fat-tail on the morrow—
it is *piggul* and one is liable for *karet*.
3 This is the general rule:
One who slaughters,

[13] Heb. "of the foundation." [14] **K** lacks "or part of its blood outside."

ramp: There is a ramp on the southern side of the altar that leads to the top of the altar where the offerings are burnt. See *Middot* 3:3.

not in the direction of the foundation: See 5:8 and *Middot* 3:1. The blood was not applied to the right part of the altar.

above... below the halfway mark (a "red thread") of the altar, *Middot* 3:1. The blood of the animal purgation offering and the bird whole burnt offering are sprinkled above the halfway mark while the blood of the rest of the offerings are sprinkled below.

outside... inside: The former refers to blood sprinkled on the altar in the "Court of the Priests"; the latter to that sprinkled in the interior of the Temple (*Middot* 5:1–2).

there is no karet: They are not *piggul*, as described in 2:2.

2:2 In the Torah, *piggul* ("abomination") is used to describe sacrificial meat that is eaten after the designated time (Leviticus 7:17–20, 19:7). The Mishnah makes intention to eat it after the time central to the definition.

to sprinkle its blood outside: In the first set of examples, the invalidating intention is to perform an act *outside* the Temple precinct. There is no *piggul*, and no punishment (*karet* "extirpation") in these cases.

skin of the fat-tail: The fat-tail is burnt on the altar, but its skin is permissible to the priests.

To sprinkle its blood on the morrow, etc.: In the second set of cases, the intention is to perform the act after the appointed time. This results in *piggul*, and the priest receives a penalty of *karet*.

and who receives,
and who conveys,
and who sprinkles,
intending to eat that which is normally eaten,
or to burn that which is normally burnt—
If the intention is directed outside[15] its place—
it is invalid but there is no *karet*;
if outside its time—
it is *piggul* and one is liable for *karet*,
so long as he offered the permitting element as commanded.

4 How is "he offered the permitting element as commanded"
[to be understood]?
If one slaughtered in silence; and received, conveyed, and sprinkled
[intending to eat it] outside its time;
or if one slaughtered [intending to eat it] outside its time,
but received, conveyed, and sprinkled in silence;
or if one slaughtered, received, conveyed, and sprinkled
[intending to eat it] outside its time—
this is one who "offered the permitting element as commanded."
How is it not "he offered the permitting element as commanded"?
If one slaughtered [intending to burn it] outside its place,
and received, conveyed, and sprinkled [intending to eat it] outside its time;
of if one slaughtered [intending to eat it] outside its time,
and received, conveyed, and sprinkled [intending to eat it] outside its appointed place;
or if one slaughtered, received, conveyed, and sprinkled
[intending to burn it] outside its appointed place;
the Passover offering and the purgation offering
that were slaughtered without the appropriate designation,

[15] "If... outside": Heb. "outside."

2:3 *receives... conveys... sprinkles*: These three actions all relate to the blood. The term for sprinkling the blood here is neither of the ones discussed in the annotations to 2:1, but *zrq*, meaning "throw" or "cast."

normally eaten: The parts of the animal that are eaten.

normally burnt: Those portions usually offered on the altar. See 3:3.

outside its place. The priest intended to eat the priestly portion (Leviticus 6:22, 7:6) or to burn the parts that should be offered on the altar outside of the Temple confines.

"*the permitting element*": The offering of the blood, which makes the sacrifice ready for eating or burning.

2:4 *How is*, etc.: Explains the qualification at the end 2:3. In the first part of the passage, the blood was handled without any other invalidating intention than to eat it outside its proper time or *in silence* (without expressing any invalidating intention at all). Consequently, the intention to eat the sacrifice *outside its time* makes it *piggul*.

How is it not, etc.: In this second part, some other disqualifying intention caused the sacrifice to be invalid, so the blood work was not performed *as commanded*, and it does not become *piggul*.

Passover... purgation offering: These are exceptional in that they are invalid if not slaughtered for their designated purpose (1:1). This wrong intention disqualifies the sacrifice and it does not then become *piggul*.

and one received, conveyed, and sprinkled [intending to eat them] outside their time;
or one slaughtered [intending to eat them] outside their time,
and received, conveyed, and sprinkled without the appropriate designation;
or one slaughtered, received, conveyed, and sprinkled without the appropriate designation:
this is one who has not "offered the permitting element as commanded."

5 Intention to eat an olive's bulk outside and an olive's bulk the next day;
an olive's bulk the next day and an olive's bulk outside;
half an olive's bulk outside and half an olive's bulk the next day;
half an olive's bulk the next day and half an olive's bulk outside—
it is invalid, but there is no *karet.*
R. Judah said:
This is the general rule:
If the intention regarding the time precedes the intention regarding the place—
it is *piggul*, and one is liable for *karet*;
if the intention regarding the place precedes the intention regarding the time—
it is invalid, but there is no *karet*;
but the Sages say:
Both are invalid, but there is no *karet.*
To eat half an olive's bulk [of offering] and to burn half an olive's bulk—
it is valid,
for eating and burning do not join.

Chapter Three

3:1–2 *Actions Done by Those Who Are Not Supposed to Do Them*

3 Any of those who are invalid who slaughtered,
their slaughtering is valid.
For slaughtering is valid whether by nonpriests, by women, by slaves,

2:5 *an olive's bulk*: Frequently, the minimum threshold for laws involving foodstuffs.

no karet: The general principle is the same as in 2:4. Intention to eat *outside its place* invalidates the sacrifice but does not make one liable for *karet*; intending to eat beyond *its* appropriate *time* makes it *piggul* and makes one liable for *karet*. This passage adds the idea that if one errs in intention on both accounts, place is the decisive criterion and therefore there is no *piggul*.

R. Judah, in contrast to what precedes, asks which intention was first.

To eat... to burn half an olive's bulk: Both with incorrect intentions; neither amount is sufficient to disqualify but together they would be.

do not join: To eat and to burn on the altar are two different ritual activities and the two half-olives do not combine to make up a disqualifying amount.

3:1 *invalid*: Not eligible to serve in the Temple.

nonpriests: Lit. "strangers" or "aliens." See 2:1 above.

or by those who are impure,[16]
even in regard to offerings of the highest sanctity,
so long as those who are impure do not touch the animal's flesh.
Therefore, they invalidate offerings by intention.
And if any of them received the blood [intending]
outside its time or outside its appointed place—
if there is still life's blood, a valid person must go back to receive it.
2 If a valid person received and gave it to an invalid person,
[the latter] must return it to the valid person.
If he received with his right hand and then placed it in his left hand,
he must return it to his right hand.
If he received the blood in a sanctified utensil and placed it in an ordinary utensil,
he must return it to the sanctified utensil.
If the blood spilled from the utensil on to the floor and he collected it, it is valid.
If he sprinkled it on the ramp, not in the direction of the foundation of the altar;
if he applied the blood that is to be applied below, above;
or if he applied the blood that is to be applied above, below;
that which is to be applied inside, outside;
that which is to be applied outside, inside—
if there is still life's blood,
a valid person must go back to receive it.

3:3–6 *Slaughtering with Inappropriate Intention*

3 One who slaughters the offering:
intending to eat something that is not typically eaten,
or to burn something that is not typically burnt—
it is valid.
R. Eliezer deems it invalid.
To eat something that is typically eaten,

[16] **K, P** lack "those who are impure."

life's blood: Blood that issues at the moment of death, which is the blood that effects atonement.

go back to receive it: A priest is not needed to slaughter an animal for sacrifice. However, from the receiving of the blood and onward, a priest is required. Further, only a person who can do a specific service can invalidate that service. Here, paradoxically, an invalid person has performed an invalid operation that does not invalidate the offering if a valid person repeats the act.

3:2 *If he sprinkled it on the ramp*: See above 2:1. The subject of this sentence is ambiguous. Some commentators read this sentence as a continuation of the first line of this mishnah—that is, that a valid priest gave the blood to an invalid person who then performed these mistaken rituals. For the rest of the blood related issues discussed see 2:1.

3:3 *not typically eaten... not typically burnt*: That is, with the intention to eat or burn it beyond the appropriate time or outside the appointed place. See 2:3.

it is valid: Since the slaughterer's intentions are anomalous when compared with the average person, they are not considered powerful enough to invalidate the sacrifice.

or to burn something that is typically burnt,
less than an olive's bulk—
it is valid.
To eat half an olive's bulk of offering and to burn half an olive's bulk—
it is valid,
for eating and burning do not join.

4 If one slaughters an offering:
intending to eat an olive's bulk
of the hide,
or of the soup,
or of the sediment on the sides of the pot,
or of the remnants of the meat stuck to the hide,
or of the bones,
or of the tendons,
or of the hooves,
or of the horns,
outside its time or outside its place—[17]
it is valid,
and one is not liable on their account for *piggul*, remnant, or impurity.

5 One who slaughters a sanctified animal,
intending to eat the fetus or the fetal sac outside the sanctuary—
has not made it *piggul*.
One who pinches the neck of turtle doves
in order to eat their eggs outside the sanctuary,
has not made it *piggul*.
The milk of the offerings and eggs of the turtle doves,
one is not liable on their account for *piggul*, remnant, or impurity.

6 If one slaughtered intending to leave its blood or its innards for the morrow,
or to remove them outside the sacred precinct,
R. Judah deems it invalid,

[17] "Outside its time or outside its place" is lacking in the manuscripts.

eating and burning do not join: See 2:5.

3:4 These are things that are not normally eaten by a person. Therefore, intentions about them do not harm the validity of the sacrifice and there is no culpability.

and one is not liable: If, in fact, the sacrifice was *piggul* or leftover (remnant) or impure (or the priest was impure when he ate it), one is not liable for eating these substances since they are not typically eaten.

remnant: Sacrificial meat that has not been eaten in its appropriate time.

3:5 *fetus...fetal sac*: As in 3:4, these are not typically eaten (see *Hullin* 4:7). In addition (as below), they are not intrinsically part of the slaughtered animal.

pinches the neck of turtle doves: To slaughter them. See Leviticus 1:14–15, below 6:4ff.

milk, eggs: These are not intrinsic parts of the animal that was slaughtered, even if found within the carcass.

and the Sages deem it valid.
In order to apply the blood on the ramp,
or not in the direction of the foundation of the altar,
to apply the blood that is to be applied below, above;
or apply the blood that is to be applied above, below;
to apply that which is to be applied inside, outside,
and to apply that which is to be applied outside, inside;
that impure persons would eat it,
or that impure persons would offer it;
that uncircumcised persons would eat it,
or that uncircumcised persons would offer it;
in order to break the bones of a Passover offering, or eat from it raw;
in order to mix its blood with the blood of invalid offerings—
it is valid,
since [inappropriate] intention invalidates only cases of
outside the appropriate time and outside the appointed place,
or the case of a Passover offering and a purgation offering without their proper designations.

Chapter Four

4:1–2 *Rules Involving the Sprinkling of Blood*

4 The House of Shammai say:
All offerings whose blood is applied[18] on the outer altar,

[18] Lit. "All that are applied."

3:6 *Sages deem it valid*: The Sages draw a distinction between intending to sprinkle the blood or burn the innards on the morrow and intending to just leave it sitting until the next day. Similarly, they draw a distinction between intending to sprinkle the blood outside the sacred precinct and just removing the blood outside the sacred precinct with no intention of sprinkling. *R. Judah* does not draw such a distinction and therefore invalidates the offering.

on the ramp... inside: See above 2:1.

break the bones of a Passover offering, or eat from it raw: See Exodus 12:9, *Pesahim* 7:11.

Passover offering and a purgation offering without their proper designations: See above 1:1.

4:1 The dispute between the Hillelites and the Shammaites is embedded in the discussion of the status of a sacrifice if a priest, for whatever reason, has only sprinkled the blood once. In general, it still atones—that is, it still accomplishes its sacrificial function. This is derived from a midrashic reading of Deuteronomy 12:27: *and of your other sacrifices, the blood shall be poured out on the altar of the Lord your God*. The *House of Shammai* and the *House of Hillel* disagree over whether this rule applies also to the purgation offering.

whose blood is applied: For the terminology, see the annotation to 2:1.

on the outer altar: There are two altars in the Temple, an inner, smaller altar also referred to as the golden altar, used for incense, and a larger, outer altar, where animal sacrifices were offered. See Exodus 27:1–8; 30:1–10; and e.g. *Yoma* 5:5–6.

if he applies only once—
it atones;
and for a purgation offering—
two applications.
But the House of Hillel say:
Even a purgation offering whose blood is applied only once atones.
Therefore, if he applied the first appropriately
and the second intending to act[19] outside its time—
it atones.
If he applied the first intending to act outside its time
and the second intending to act outside its place—
it is *piggul*, and one is liable for *karet* for it.

2 All offerings whose blood is applied[20] on the inner altar,
if he had omitted one of the gifts—
it does not atone.
Therefore, if he applied all of them appropriately and one inappropriately,
it is invalid, but there is no *karet*.

4:3–5 *More Laws of Piggul*

3 These are the parts of the offering for which one does not become liable for *piggul*:
the handful,
the frankincense,
the aromatic incense,

[19] Here and below: the words "intending to act" are taken to be implied.
[20] Lit. "All that are applied."

For the offerings *whose blood is applied on the outer altar*, see 5:3–8; the offerings discussed require differing numbers of applications.

applied the first intending…its time: Analogously, in this second case, the first sprinkling of blood was definitive, making the sacrifice *piggul*. The transgressive second sprinkling cannot ameliorate the transgression of the first sprinkling.

4:2 *inner altar*: For the offerings whose blood is offered on this altar see 5:1–2. Unlike 4:1, failure to complete any of these blood offerings invalidates the whole offering, so unless all of the offerings were made with the intention to act outside the mandated time, there is no *piggul*.

4:3 The principle underlying this passage is only stated at the end. One can only be culpable with respect to *piggul* for an item that another item permitted to be sanctified or offered on the altar. The items listed here are generally themselves "permitters," not elements permitted by another. If while offering them one had intention to act outside the time, the sacrifice itself is *piggul*. However, eating the *handful* itself or the other elements listed does not make one culpable for *piggul*.

handful: Of a grain offering (the remainder is eaten by the priests); see *Menahot* 2:1.

frankincense: A handful of which was offered with the grain offering; Leviticus 2:2; and see *Menahot* 2:1.

aromatic incense: The incense that is part of the daily service of the Temple, accompanying the continual offering, *Tamid* 5:4–5.

the grain offering of the priests,
the grain offering that accompanies libations,[21]
the grain offering of the anointed priest,
the blood,
and the libations that are offered by themselves—
the words of R. Meir.
But the Sages say:
Even those that are offered together with the animal.
The *log* of oil of one with *tsara'at*—
R. Simeon says:
One is not liable for *piggul* on account of it.
R. Meir says:
One is liable for *piggul* on account of it,
since the blood of the guilt offering permits it to be offered.[22]
Any sanctified item that has elements that permit it,
whether to a person or to the altar,
one is liable for *piggul* on its account.

4 The whole burnt offering—
its blood permits its flesh to the altar,
and its hide to the priests.
A whole burnt offering of a bird—
its blood permits its flesh to the altar.
A purgation offering of a bird—
its blood permits its flesh to the priests.

[21] Present in **K**, **P**; some medieval commentators delete this line.

[22] Lit. "permits it."

grain offering of the priests: When a priest offers a grain offering as a free-will offering (based on Leviticus 6:16), it is entirely burnt; nothing is kept off the altar, so there is no "permitter."

grain offering that accompanies libations: Offerings were accompanied by libations of wine as well as grain offerings. See Numbers 15:4–10; 15:24; 28:1–29:39.

grain offering of the anointed priest: Leviticus 6:12–15, understood to be offered daily by the high priest. This too is completely burnt on the altar, so again there is no "permitter."

blood: In the Mishnah's system of offerings, blood is the primary "permitter" (2:3).

libations... by themselves: Lit. "that come by themselves," that are brought as offerings in their own right rather than as accompaniments to animal offerings.

log of oil: Brought at the end of the impurity of the one with *tsara'at*: Leviticus 14:10, 21. The dispute partially specifies the rule: for R. Simeon, the oil has no permitter; according to R. Meir it does.

4:4 *whole burnt offering*: For the hide, see Leviticus 7:8.

of a bird: Leviticus 1:14–17.

bulls that are burnt include the bull of the Day of Atonement, the bull brought by the high priest for the forgetting of a law (Horayot 2:2), and the bull brought in the name of all of Israel or a specific tribe for acting incorrectly based on a mistaken ruling by the high court (Leviticus 4:1–12, 13–21; 16:6).

goats: Leviticus 16:5; Numbers 15:24.

The bulls that are burnt and the goats that are burnt—
their blood permits their innards to be offered.
R. Simeon says:
Any offering whose blood is not sprinkled upon the outer altar[23]
like an offering of well-being—
one is not liable for *piggul* on account of it.

5 The offerings of the gentiles—
one is not liable on their account for *piggul*, remnant, or impurity.
One who slaughters them outside the sacred precincts is not liable—
the words of R. Meir;[24]
R. Yose deems liable.
Those parts of the offering[25] for which one is not liable due to *piggul*,
one is liable on their account for remnant and impurity,
except blood.
R. Simeon says:
When it is a thing that is normally eaten.
However, for things like the firewood, the frankincense, or the spices—
one is not liable for impurity.

4:6 *The Necessary Intentions for an Offering*

6 An offering that is offered is designated in six respects:
(1) the offering;[26]
(2) the one who is offering;
(3) the divine Name;
(4) to be burnt on the altar;
(5) the odor;
(6) the pleasure.

[23] Lit. "Any that is not on the outer altar."
[24] Some manuscripts of both the Mishnah and Talmud have "Simeon."
[25] Heb. "Those things."
[26] Phrase absent in **K**.

that are burnt: That is, burnt outside of Jerusalem. Leviticus 4:12 mandates that certain purgation offerings be burnt outside the Israelite encampment in the desert. The Babylonian Talmud identifies outside the camp with outside of Jerusalem. The goats burnt outside of Jerusalem are the scapegoat of the Day of Atonement service (Leviticus 16:10, 21–22) and the purgation offering for the worship of idolatry.

one is not liable for piggul: The Torah prohibits *piggul* in the context of the sacrifice of well-being (Leviticus 7:18) and therefore all offerings, in order to be covered by this prohibition, must be similar to the well-being offering in that their blood must be sprinkled on the outer altar.

4:5 *offerings of gentiles*: Whole burnt offerings brought by gentiles are valid, but the rules of *piggul* and other disqualifications do not apply to them.

piggul, remnant, or impurity: See 3:4.

R. Meir: See n. 24.

Those parts: Listed above in 4:3.

The purgation offering and the guilt offering are designated for the specific sin.
R. Yose said:
Even if one did not have any of these designations,
it is valid;
for it is a decree[27] of the court that the intention follows the officiant.

Chapter Five

5:1–5 *The Proper Location for Offerings of the Highest Sanctity*

5 What is the location of offerings?
Offerings of the highest sanctity—
their slaughtering is to the north [of the altar].
The bull and the goat of the Day of Atonement—
their slaughtering is to the north,
and the collecting of their blood in service utensils is to the north,
and their blood requires sprinkling on the space between the poles,
and on the curtain,
and on the golden altar.
Omission of any of these applications invalidates.
He would pour the remnants of the blood on the western base of the outer altar.
If he did not apply it, he did not disqualify it.
2 The bulls that are burnt and the goats that are burnt,
their slaughtering is to the north [of the altar],

[27] Lit. "condition."

4:6 *the intention follows the officiant*: The person bringing the offering need not have the proper intention (except where that person does the slaughtering, 3:1). The person who carries out the individual ritual acts is the one who needs to have the proper intention.

5:1 *Offerings of the highest sanctity*: This sentence is an introduction to the chapter, which then explicates which offerings are "of the highest sanctity."

The bull and the goat of the Day of Atonement: See Leviticus 16 and *Yoma* 4:2–3, 5:3–6.

to the north: See Leviticus 1:11 explicitly, and Leviticus 6:18 and 7:2, which refer to the slaughtering place of the whole burnt offering.

between the poles: These were on either side of the ark and used for carrying in the desert (Exodus 25:14). The Mishnah assumes that the poles project backward toward the rear of the Temple and forward toward the front. See also *Yoma* 5:1–4.

and on the curtain: The curtain that separated the Holy from the Holy of Holies (Exodus 26:31–33).

the golden altar: The "inner altar" of 4:2.

invalidates: In other words, the priest has to perform every one of the three sprinklings of the blood. Compare above, 4:2.

5:2 *that are burnt*: That is, burnt outside of Jerusalem. See note to 4:4 above.

and the collection of their blood in service utensils is to the north,
and their blood requires sprinkling on the curtain,
and on the golden altar.
Omission of any of these applications invalidates.
He would pour the remnants of the blood on the western base of the outer altar.
If he did not apply it, he did not disqualify it.
These and those are burnt on the ash heap.

3 Individual and communal purgation offerings.
These are the communal purgation offerings:
the goats of the new moon and the festivals—
their slaughtering is to the north,
and the collecting of their blood in service utensils is to the north,
and their blood requires application four times at the four corners.
How?[28]
He would go up the ramp, and turn towards the walkway.
He would come to the southeastern corner, then the northeastern,
then the northwest, then the southwest.
He would pour the remnants of the blood on the southern base of the outer altar.
And they are eaten within the hangings, by male priests, in any manner of preparation,
for one day and one night until midnight.

4 The whole burnt offering,
which is of the highest sanctity,
its slaughtering is to the north,
and the collecting of its blood in service utensils is to the north,
its blood requires application twice, which is actually four times,
and it requires flaying, cutting into pieces, and burning it completely.

5 Offerings of well-being of the community and guilt offerings—
(these are the guilt offerings:
the guilt offering for robbery,

[28] V lacks "How?"

These and those: The sacrifices of 5:1 and 5:2.

are burnt on the ash heap: See Leviticus 4:12, 6:4: the Torah designates *a clean place, outside the camp*. The Mishnah is alluding to a specific location in the environs of Jerusalem. See 8:4.

5:3 *walkway*: This traced the perimeter of the altar. See *Middot* 3:1, and the introduction to that tractate.

The *ramp* extends to the south. From the top of the ramp the priest turns right to the *southeastern corner* and progresses counterclockwise around the altar.

within the hangings: That is, within the sacred space marked out in the description of the Tabernacle (Exodus 27:9–16; 6:18–19).

any manner of preparation: As opposed to the Passover offering that is eaten roasted only. See 5:8.

5:4 *which is actually four times*: The priest stops at two corners and sprinkles blood, so that all four sides are sprinkled.

5:5 *offerings ... of the community*: The two sheep brought on the Festival of Weeks: see Leviticus 23:19.

robbery: Leviticus 5:21–25.

the guilt offering for sacrilege,
the guilt offering for a designated slave woman,
the guilt offering of a *nazir*,
the guilt offering of a person with *tsara'at*,
and the offering for uncertain guilt)—
their slaughtering is to the north,
and the collecting of their blood in service utensils is to the north,
their blood requires application twice, which is actually four times,
and they are eaten within the hangings by male priests, in any manner of preparation,
for one day and one night until midnight.

5:6–8 *The Proper Location for Offerings of Lesser Sanctity*

6 The thank offering and the ram of the *nazir*,
which are offerings of lesser sanctity—
their slaughtering is any place in the Temple Court,
their blood requires application twice, which is actually four times,
they are eaten throughout the city,
by any person,
in any manner of preparation,
for a day and a night until midnight.
That which is removed from the offerings[29] is like the offerings themselves,
except that that which is removed is eaten only by priests, their wives, their children,
and their slaves.
7 Offerings of well-being,
which are offerings of lesser sanctity—

[29] Here and the following, for "the offerings," Hebrew has "them."

sacrilege: Leviticus 5:13–15.

designated slave woman: See Leviticus 19:20–21. In the Mishnah's understanding, the Torah speaks of a man who had sexual relations with a slave woman who had been assigned ("designated") to another man, but has neither been married to the man to whom she had been designated nor set free. See *Keritot* 2:5.

of a nazir: Brought by a *nazir* after having broken his vow through contact with the dead. See Numbers 6:9–12, and *Nazir* introduction.

tsara'at: usually translated "leprosy" or "skin affliction. " See Leviticus chapters 13–14 and tractate *Nega'im*.

the offering for uncertain guilt: This type of sacrifice is brought in a case in which a person is not sure that he or she transgressed (Leviticus 5:17–18).

which is actually four times: See note to 5:4.

within the hangings: See above 5:3 and Leviticus 7:1–2.

5:6 *the ram of the nazir*: The purgation offering that the *nazir* brings at the end of his tenure. See Numbers 6:13–21, and *Nazir* introduction.

which is actually four times: See note to 5:4.

That which is removed from the offerings: The portion set aside for the priests (the thigh and breast) follows the same rules as the portion given to nonpriests.

their slaughtering is any place in the Temple Court,
their blood requires application blood twice, which is actually four times,
and they are eaten throughout the city,
by any person, in any manner of preparation,
for two days and one night.
That which is removed from the offerings[30] is like the offerings themselves,
except that that which is removed is eaten only by priests, their wives, their children,
and their slaves.

8 The firstlings, the tithe, and the Passover offering,
which are offerings of lesser sanctity—
their slaughtering is any place in the Temple Court,
their blood requires application once,
as long as it is in the direction of the foundation of the altar.[31]
Scripture[32] differentiated with respect to their eating.
The firstlings are eaten by the priests;
the tithe by any person,
and they are eaten throughout the city,
by any person,[33]
in any manner of preparation,
for two days and one night.
The Passover offering is only eaten at night,
and it is eaten only until midnight,[34]
and it is eaten only by those subscribed to it,
and it is eaten only roasted.

[30] Here and the following, for "the offerings," Hebrew has "them."
[31] "Of the altar" added for clarity.
[32] Heb. "it."
[33] Some witnesses lack this phrase. See annotations.
[34] **V** lacks "and it is only eaten until midnight."

5:7 *which is actually four times*: See note to 5:4.

5:8 *foundation of the altar*: A foundation layer jutted out along the northern and western sides of the altar; see *Middot* 3:1.

firstling of the "pure" animals (which is sacrificed). Numbers 18:15–18.

tithe: The animal tithe, which was brought to Jerusalem and offered as a sacrifice. This interpretation combines Leviticus 27:32 with Deuteronomy 12:5–6.

by any person: The second occurrence of this phrase is omitted in some witnesses (see n. 33) and deleted by some commentaries on the grounds that this should refer to all the sacrifices mentioned at the beginning of the passage, but the firstling could be eaten only by priests.

The Passover offering: The regulations for the Passover offering are described in Exodus 12. See also *Pesahim* introduction.

Chapter Six

6:1–3 *The Proper Location for Grain and Bird Offerings*

6 The offerings of the highest sanctity that were slaughtered on top of the altar—
R. Yose says:
It is as if they were slaughtered to the north.
R. Yose b. Judah says:
From the halfway point of the altar and toward the north is like the north;
from the halfway point and to the south is like the south.
The handfuls were taken from the grain offerings at any place in the Temple Court
and are eaten within the hangings,
by the male priests,
in any manner of preparation,
for a day and a night until midnight.

2 The purgation offering of a bird was performed
on the southwest[35] corner of the altar.
It was valid in any place, but this was its place.
That corner served for three things below and three above.
Below:
(1) the purgation offering of a bird,
(2) the bringing near, and
(3) the remnants of the blood.
Above:
(1) the libation of the water, and
(2) of the wine, and
(3) the burnt offering of a bird when there were too many in the east.

[35] V: "south."

6:1 *on top of the altar*: Instead of their proper location, to the north of the altar: 5:1.

From the halfway point: R. Yose b. Judah still requires the slaughter to have been on the northern side of the altar.

The handfuls were taken: The priestly act of taking a handful of the grain offering is ritually analogous to the act of slaughtering an animal offering. See Leviticus 2:2 and *Menahot* 1.

6:2 *three things below... and three above*: See 2:1.

bringing near: The bringing of the grain offering to the altar before a part of it was burnt on the altar, Leviticus 2:8.

remnants of the blood: See above 5:3. According to *Middot* 3:2–3 there was a drain at the southwest corner of the altar.

libation of the water: During the Festival of Sukkot, a special libation of water was brought to the Temple. See *Sukkah* 4:9.

libation... of the wine: Any wine libation.

burnt offering of a bird: See 6:5.

3 All who ascend to the altar,
ascend the ramp on the right side, circle the altar, and descend on the left side,
except the one who ascends for any of these three things,
who would ascend and then turn on their heels and descend.

6:4–6 *Bird Offerings: Sacrificial Procedures*

4 The purgation offering of a bird—
how was it done?
He would pinch the head at the nape of the neck without severing it
and sprinkle its blood on the wall of the altar.
The remains of the blood would be drained on the altar base.
The altar consumed only the blood,
the whole of it is the priests'.
5 The whole burnt offering of a bird—
how was it done?
He would ascend the ramp and turn to the walkway.
Arriving at the southeastern corner,
he would pinch the head at the nape of the neck and sever it,
and drain the blood on the wall of the altar.
He would take the head,
and squeeze the place that had been pinched against the altar,
cover it with salt,
and throw it on the flames.
He would take the body,
and remove the crop and the feathers and the part of the gut that comes out with them,
and throw them on the ash pile.
He would split it without severing it;
and if he severed it, it is valid.
He would cover it with salt,
and throw it on the flames.
6 If he did not remove the crop
or the feathers
or the part of the gut that comes out with them,
or did not cover it with salt—

6:3 *these three things* that were labeled "above" in 6:2.

ascend and then turn on their heels and descend: This is because the right side of the ramp leads directly to the southeast corner. The priest turns left at the top of the ramp and walks to the southwest corner where he does the service and then returns the way he came. The priest does not circle the altar so that the smoke does not defile the wine and so that the sacrificial bird does not suffocate.

6:4 Birds were sacrificed either as purgation offerings or whole burnt offerings. The *purgation offering* was always paired with a whole burnt offering, but a single bird could be offered as a whole burnt offering (*Menahot* 12:5, *Qinnim* 1:1).

6:5 *walkway*: See 5:3.

if he deviated in anything after he drained the blood—
it is valid.
If he severed the head of the purgation offering,
or did not sever that of the burnt offering—
it is invalid.
If he drained the blood of the head,
but did not drain the blood of the body—
it is invalid.
If he drained[36] the blood of the body,
but did not drain the blood of the head—
it is valid.

6:7 *Bird Offerings: Inappropriate Intentions*

7 A purgation offering of a bird that was pinched at the nape of the neck
without[37] its proper designation,
or its blood was drained without its proper designation,
or with its proper designation and then without its proper designation,
or without its proper designation and then with its proper designation—
it is invalid.
A whole burnt offering of a bird is valid,
but it did not fulfill its owners' obligation.
The rule is the same for a purgation offering of a bird or for a whole burnt offering of a bird
that was pinched,
or its blood was drained,
intending to eat that which is normally eaten,
or to burn that which was normally burnt,
outside the appointed place—
it is invalid, but there is no *karet*;
beyond its time—
it is *piggul*, and he is liable for *karet*,
so long as he offered the permitting element as commanded.

[36] **K, P** lack "If he drained." [37] **V** lacks the word "without."

6:6 *after he drained the blood*: As with sacrifices involving cattle, the blood offering determines the acceptability and validity of the sacrifice. After the blood has been offered, the omission of an element does not disqualify the sacrifice.

severed the head: See 6:5.

6:7 Our passage largely repeats 1:4 and 2:2–5 with specific application to the bird offerings.

A whole burnt offering... did not fulfill its owners' obligation: A bird can take one of two designations. If it is a purgation offering and some sacrificial act took place without the correct designation it is invalid, but if it is a whole burnt offering then it is valid. See 1:1.

How is "he offered the permitting element as commanded"
[to be understood]?
If one pinched the nape of the neck in silence;
and drained the blood [intending] outside its time;
or if one pinched the nape of the neck [intending] outside its time,
but drained the blood in silence;
or if one pinched the nape of the neck and drained the blood
[intending] outside its time;
this is one who "offered the permitting element as commanded."
How is it not "he offered the permitting element as commanded"?
If one pinched the nape of the neck [intending] outside its place,
and drained the blood [intending] outside its time;
or if one pinched the nape of the neck [intending] outside its time,
and drained the blood [intending] outside its place;
or if one pinched the nape of the neck and drained the blood
[intending] outside its place;
the purgation offering that one pinched at the nape of the neck
without the appropriate designation,
and one drained the blood [intending] outside its time;
or one pinched the nape of the neck [intending] outside its time,
and drained the blood without the appropriate designation;
or one pinched the nape of the neck and drained the blood without the appropriate designation,
this is one who has not "offered the permitting element as commanded."
Intention to eat an olive's bulk outside and an olive's bulk the next day;
an olive's bulk the next day and an olive's bulk outside;
half an olive's bulk outside and half an olive's bulk the next day;
half an olive's bulk the next day and half an olive's bulk outside—
it is invalid but there is no *karet*.
R. Judah said:
This is the general rule:
If the intention regarding the time precedes the intention regarding the place—
it is *piggul*, and one is liable for *karet*;
and if the intention regarding the place precedes the intention regarding the time—
it is invalid, but there is no *karet*.
But the Sages say:
Both are invalid, but there is no *karet*.
To eat half an olive's bulk and to burn half an olive's bulk—
it is valid,
for eating and burning do not join.

Chapter Seven

7:1–4 *Bird Offerings: Sprinkling the Blood*

7 A purgation offering of a bird whose blood offering[38] he performed below,
according to the practice of a purgation offering
with the designation of a purgation offering—
it is valid.
According to the practice of a purgation offering
with the designation of a whole burnt offering;
or according to the practice of a whole burnt offering
with the designation of a purgation offering;
or according to the practice of a whole burnt offering
with the designation of a whole burnt offering—
it is invalid.
If he performed it above according to the practice of any of these
it is invalid.

2 A whole burnt offering of a bird whose blood offering he performed above,
according to the practice of a whole burnt offering
with the designation of a whole burnt offering—
it is valid;
according to the practice of a whole burnt offering
with the designation of a purgation offering—
it is valid,
but it did not fulfill its owners' obligation.
According to the practice of a purgation offering
with the designation of a whole burnt offering,
or according to the practice of a purgation offering
with the designation of a purgation offering—
it is invalid;
If he performed the blood offering below according to the practice of any of these
it is invalid.

[38] Here and through 7:4, "whose blood offering" added for clarity.

7:1 *purgation offering... below*: This is the proper place to perform the blood ritual for the purgation offering.

with the designation of a whole burnt offering: Since the intention was not correct, in the case of a purgation offering it is invalid (1:1).

according to the practice of a whole burnt offering: In these two cases, the priest has offered the sacrifice either following the wrong procedure or with a disqualifying intention or both.

above according to the practice of any of these: In this circumstance even the purgation offering with the designation of a purgation offering would be invalid, since the blood was offered in the wrong place (2:1).

7:2 The outcomes in this passage differ from those in 7:1, since a whole burnt offering offered with the wrong designation remains valid (1:1).

3 None of these conveys impurity upon swallowing,
and one is liable for sacrilege for them,
except for the purgation offering of a bird
whose blood offering he performed below,
according to the practice of a purgation offering
with the designation of a purgation offering.
4 A whole burnt offering of a bird
[whose blood offering] he performed below,
according to the practice of a purgation offering
with the designation of a purgation offering:
R. Eliezer says:
One is liable for sacrilege for it;
R. Joshua says:
One is not liable for sacrilege for it.
R. Eliezer said:
If in the case of a purgation offering,
offered with the proper designation,
one is not liable for sacrilege,
but when he changed its designation,
he is liable for sacrilege,
then in the case of a whole burnt offering,
for which one is liable for sacrilege
when offered with the proper designation,
does not logic require that when he changed its designation
he should be liable for sacrilege?
R. Joshua said to him:
No. You have made this comparison[39] to a case of a purgation offering

[39] Here and below, lit. "If you have said."

7:3 *None of these*: Even though they are invalid.

impurity upon swallowing: The carcass of a kosher bird conveys impurity when eaten, that is, its presence in the eater's mouth renders him impure. However, these birds, although it is forbidden to eat them, have been properly killed and so do not have the status of carcass. See *Tohorot* 1:1.

sacrilege: Making profane use of any object dedicated to the Temple.

except for: In general, sacrilege does not apply to any dedicated object that already has a permitted use. A *purgation offering* that has been properly carried out may now be eaten by the priests and so is no longer subject to the law of sacrilege, and likewise does not convey impurity upon swallowing.

7:4 The sacrifice was originally intended as a whole burnt offering but performed entirely as a purgation offering. According to *R. Eliezer* it remains a whole burnt offering and *one is liable to sacrilege for it* because it has no other permitted use. According to *R. Joshua* it is a purgation offering and is not subject to *sacrilege* because it is permitted to priests. The debate that follows turns on the question of what known case is most like the current one.

R. Eliezer said: A purgation offering is not liable to sacrilege since the priests eat it, but a whole burnt offering starts out liable to sacrilege since no one will ever eat it. Therefore, if a purgation offering is in essence turned into a whole burnt offering it should acquire that liability and become subject to sacrilege.

R. Joshua rejects this reasoning, since in his opinion the changing of the designation in the two cases has different consequences with respect to sacrilege.

where he changed its designation to a burnt offering,
in which he changed its designation to something
for which one is liable for sacrilege;
but can you then conclude thus[40] regarding a case of a burnt offering
whose intention was changed to a purgation offering,
in which he changed its designation to something
for which one is not liable for sacrilege?
R. Eliezer said to him:
Now, the case of offerings of the highest sanctity
that were slaughtered to the south
with the designation of offerings of lesser sanctity
will prove my point,
for he changed their designation to something
for which one is not liable for sacrilege,
and yet one is liable for their sacrilege;
so too, do not be surprised at the whole burnt offering,
where even though he changed its designation to something
for which one is not liable for sacrilege,
one is still liable for sacrilege.
R. Joshua said to him:
No. You have made this comparison to a case of offerings of the highest sanctity
that were slaughtered to the south
with the designation of offerings of lesser sanctity,
in which he changed its designation to something
that has circumstances of both prohibition and permission,
but can you then conclude thus in a case of a whole burnt offering
where he changed its designation to something that has only circumstances of permission?

7:5–6 *Bird Offerings: Additional Rules Regarding Pinching the Neck*

5 If he pinched the nape of its neck with his left hand
or at night,
if he slaughtered nonsacral [birds] inside the sanctuary
or dedicated ones outside—
they do not convey impurity upon swallowing.
If he pinched the nape of the neck with a knife,

[40] Here and below, lit. "Will you say?"

R. Eliezer said to him: We now compare our case to one where *offerings of the highest sanctity... were slaughtered to the south with the designation of offerings of lesser sanctity*: In such cases, the change of designation to a sacrifice that is not liable to sacrilege still leaves the sacrifice liable to sacrilege (see above 5:1, *Me'ilah* 1:1).

R. Joshua again objects to the comparison. Sacrifices of lesser sanctity have *circumstances of both prohibition and permission*. Their meat is eaten and is not subject to sacrilege, but the parts that are burnt are liable for sacrilege. However, a bird purgation sacrifice has no such corresponding parts that are liable to sacrilege. It has only circumstances of permission, so the question of sacrilege should never come up at all.

or pinched the nape of the neck of nonsacral [birds] inside
or dedicated ones outside,
turtle doves that had not reached the proper age,
doves that had passed the proper age,
one whose wing was dried out,
whose eye was blinded,
whose leg was cut off,
it conveys impurity upon swallowing.
This is the general rule:
Any offerings that became invalid in the sanctuary
do not convey impurity upon swallowing;
if their invalidation was not in the sanctuary,
they convey impurity upon swallowing.
All those who are invalid to slaughter who pinched the nape of the neck of a bird—
their pinching is invalid,
and the offerings do not convey impurity upon swallowing.

6 If one pinched the nape of the neck and it was found to be *terefah*,
R. Meir says:
It does not convey impurity upon swallowing.
R. Judah says:
It does convey impurity upon swallowing.
R. Meir said:
If in the case of an animal's carcass,
which makes one impure through touching or carrying,
where slaughtering it purifies its *terefah* body from its impurity;
in the case of a bird's carcass,
which does not make one impure through touching or carrying,
does not logic demand that slaughter should purify
its *terefah* body from its impurity?
Just as we find in the case of an animal's slaughter that it validates it for eating,
and purifies its *terefah* body from its impurity,
so, too, pinching the nape of the neck,
which validates it for eating,
should purify its defectively slaughtered body from its impurity.
R. Yose says:
It is sufficient that it be like an animal carcass,
where slaughter purifies but not pinching the nape of the neck.

7:5 *proper age*: Yellow feathers disqualified both types of birds. Turtle doves were thought to lose their yellow feathers at some point and were not valid for sacrifice until that point. The feathers of doves were thought to become yellow and were only valid until that point (see *Hullin* 1:5).

7:6 *terefah*: Lit. "torn apart," as opposed to *nevelah* "carcass" (see Leviticus 7:24), an animal that has died naturally. In the Mishnah, *terefah* usually means meat or fowl that upon examination after slaughter appears to have been diseased or deformed (*Hullin* 3:1–4; for the consequences of improper slaughter, see 2:4). An important distinction in practice is that the *nevelah* conveys impurity, while *terefah* does not.

R. Meir and *R. Judah* dispute whether proper pinching of a bird that turned out to be *terefah* yields a *nevelah* or not. Note again the dialectical discussion. *R. Meir* compares to the slaughter of an animal; *R. Judah* to the fact that the bird has been pinched (for sacrifice) and not slaughtered (for common use) at all.

Chapter Eight

8:1–3 *Intermingling Animals Before They Are Offered*

8 All [animals designated for] offerings that became intermingled with purgation offerings that were awaiting death,
or with an ox that was to be stoned,
even one in ten thousand—
they all must die.
If they became intermingled with an ox used in commission of a sin,
or[41] that killed a person upon the testimony of only one witness,
or upon the testimony of the owners alone;
one penetrating or penetrated in bestiality,
or set aside for idolatry,
or worshiped,
or used as payment for a prostitute,
or used as payment for a dog,
or a forbidden mixed breed,
or a *terefah*,
or one born of a caesarean section—
they must graze until they acquire a defect.
Then they are to be sold,
and one brings an offering of the same type
from the proceeds of the most expensive of those animals.

[41] **P**: "and"; **K** lacks any conjunction.

8:1 *intermingled*: The consequences of mixing items of different statuses is very characteristic of the Mishnah. See e.g. *Qinnim*.

purgation offerings that were awaiting death: That is, purgation offerings that can no longer be sacrificed and must be left to graze until they die. For these see *Temurah* 2:2.

ox that was to be stoned: An ox that fatally gored a human. Exodus 21:28.

they all must die: They cannot be brought to the altar.

used in commission of a sin: The sin is not specified. The commentaries read this as introducing the list of cases below. In any case all of the following were permitted for common use but could not be offered on the altar.

or upon the testimony of the owners alone: The ox could only be put to death on the basis of valid testimony of two witnesses.

payment for a prostitute... payment for a dog: Deuteronomy 23:19.

terefah: The Talmud and commentaries ask how an animal that was known to be *terefah* if slaughtered could not be distinguished from the sacrificial animal that was confused with it.

until they acquire a defect: Once all have become defective, they may be put to nonsacral use.

offering of the same type: That is, if it was a purgation offering, then they must bring a replacement purgation offering.

If it was intermingled with unblemished, nonsacral animals—
the nonsacral animals are to be sold
for the needs of those offering that type of offering.

2 Sanctified animals that became intermingled with others of the same type,
this one is to be offered for someone,
and this one is to be offered for someone.[42]
Sanctified animals that became intermingled with others of different types,
they must graze until they acquire a defect.
Then they are sold,
and one brings an offering of this type
from the proceeds of the most expensive of those animals,
and one brings an offering of that type
from the proceeds of the most expensive of those animals,
and the difference must be paid out of pocket.
If they were intermingled with a firstborn or a tithed animal—
they must graze until they acquire a defect
and then may be eaten like a firstborn or a tithed animal.
All offerings can become intermingled save for a purgation offering with a guilt offering.

3 If a guilt offering became intermingled with an offering of well-being—
they must graze until they acquire a defect.[43]
R. Simeon says:

[42] **K**, **P** have "for something"; **K** has only the first occurrence of this phrase.
[43] "They... defect" absent in **K**, **P**.

unblemished, nonsacral animals: Unlike the preceding, these animals can be brought as a sacrifice. As a result, we do not need to wait until defects arises.

for the needs of those offering that type of offering: For example, if the animal that mixed with the others was to have been a whole burnt offering, all the animals must be sold to persons wishing to offer such a sacrifice.

8:2 *offered for someone*: See n. 42. This phrase is fraught with translation and interpretation problems. Beyond the textual issues, there is a debate amongst the commentators whether the sacrificial intention should be stated as written here (i.e. for a particular person) or for its (unidentified) owner, or, perhaps, it should be offered without the dedicatory mention at all. Finally, Maimonides writes that this only applies to sacrifices that are brought by women since those sacrifices do not need to be dedicated by the placing on of the hands of the one offering the sacrifice. However, in regard to sacrifices in which the placing on of hands is required, this rule is not applicable since a specific dedication is necessary (see *Menahot* 9:7ff).

one brings an offering of this type: The value of the animals is assessed and the price of the most expensive animal is used for the replacement of all the animals. Since the total spent on sacrifices is greater than the worth of the animals, a loss is incurred.

the difference must be paid out of pocket: Lit. "he must lose the extra from his house."

eaten like a firstborn or a tithed animal: See above 1:2 and 5:8. Unlike most dedicated animals, if these develop a blemish they are not redeemed and replaced, but slaughtered and eaten, the former by the priests, and the latter by the lay owners.

a purgation offering with a guilt offering: Since a guilt offering is from male animals while a purgation offering is of female animals, they can be distinguished easily.

8:3 *they must graze... defect*: R. Simeon holds that it is better to consider both guilt offerings, in order to err on the side of strictness. The Sages respond that this could cause the offering of well-being to become invalid (guilt offerings have a shorter time limit), and therefore we follow the rule that we do not cause holy things to come to be invalidated.

Both are to be slaughtered to the north of the altar,
and eaten according to the rules of the most stringent among them.
They said to him:
One does not cause sacred offerings to become invalid.

8:3 cont.–5 *Intermingled Parts or Limbs*

If pieces of offerings were intermingled,
whether offerings of the highest sanctity with offerings of lesser sanctity,
or those to be eaten within one day with those to be eaten within two days,[44]
they must be eaten according [to the rules of] the most stringent among them.
4 If the limbs of a purgation offering became intermingled
with the limbs of a whole burnt offering,
R. Eliezer says:
He must place them both on top of the altar,
and I consider the purgation offering meat on top of the altar as if it were wood.
But the Sages say:
They must be left to spoil and then go to the place of burning.
5 If limbs were intermingled with the limbs of blemished animals,
R. Eliezer says:
If he has offered the head of one of the offerings, then all the heads must be offered.
If the thighs of one of them, then all the thighs must be offered.
But the Sages say:
Even if all of them had been offered save one—
that one must go to the place of burning.

[44] **V** adds "and a night."

slaughtered to the north of the altar: Guilt offerings must be slaughtered to the north of the altar (above 5:5) and offerings of well-being can be slaughtered anywhere in the sanctuary (5:7). So, as long as they are slaughtered to the north of the altar, the proper procedure has been followed for both the guilt and the well-being offering.

the most stringent among them: That is as guilt offerings, which are governed by more stringent rules.

One does not cause sacred offerings to become invalid: Lit. "we do not bring holy things to the place of invalidation." Meat from a well-being offering may be eaten until the end of the next day, while guilt offerings cannot be eaten after the first night. After those respective deadlines leftover meat becomes invalid and must be taken away and burnt. If a well-being offering is treated like a guilt offering its deadline arrives a day sooner, and there is greater danger that its meat will become forbidden and have to be burnt. That is the meaning of the Sages' response to R. Simeon.

8:4 *as if it were wood*: i.e. merely wood: the purgation offering meat is burnt on the altar, but I do not consider it a whole burnt offering.

the place of burning: This was one of the locations where disqualified sacrificial meat could be taken and incinerated.

8:5 *R. Eliezer* treats the offered head as if it was the invalid one, and the remaining ones as if they were valid. *The Sages* require the potentially invalid offering to be treated as invalid.

8:6–12 *Intermingling of Sacrificial Blood*

6 If sacrificial blood was intermingled with water:
if it retains the look of blood—
it is valid.
If it was intermingled with wine—
we consider the wine as if it were water.
If it was intermingled with the blood of a domestic animal
or with the blood of a wild animal—
we consider the blood as water.
R. Judah says:
Blood does not invalidate blood.
7 If it became mingled with the blood of invalid animals,
it must be poured into the gutter.
If it mixed with the blood that drained,
it must be poured into the gutter;
R. Eliezer deems it valid.
If he did not take counsel and applied the blood—
it is valid.
8 Blood of unblemished animals[45] intermingled with the blood of blemished animals—
it must be poured into the gutter;
a cup of blood intermingled with cups from blemished animals,
R. Eliezer says:
If he offered one cup, all the cups must be offered.
But the Sages say:
Even if all of them had been offered save one, that one must be poured into the gutter.
9 Blood that is to be applied below mixed with that to be applied above:

[45] The manuscripts do not have "unblemished animals."

8:6 *If sacrificial blood was intermingled with water*: The water accidentally spilled into the blood. Compare *Hullin* 6:5.

we consider the wine as if it were water: We approximate whether that much water in the blood would have nullified the bloody appearance.

with the blood of a domestic animal: Specifically, a nonsacrificial animal.

Blood does not invalidate blood: Whatever the proportions, the nonsacral blood cannot nullify the sacral. Since the mixture still contains sacral blood, it can used for sprinkling.

8:7 *gutter*: See *Middot* 3:2–3.

blood that drained: Blood that issues from the cut throat but after the moment of death (see annotation to 3:1 above). Only the blood that emerges with the cut was considered "life blood," and only this blood could effect atonement.

8:8 *blemished animals*: That were not valid for burning on the altar. The rest of the passage follows 8:5.

8:9 *Blood that is to be applied below…applied above*: The blood of the animal purgation offering or of the bird burnt offering is applied above the halfway mark of the altar while the blood of the rest of the offerings is applied below. See above 2:1.

R. Eliezer says:
He must apply it above,
and I consider what was supposed to be applied below but applied above
as if it were water,
and he must once again apply below.
But the Sages say:
They are to be poured into the gutter.
If he did not take counsel and applied the blood, it is valid.

10 Blood to be applied once intermingled with blood to be applied once
it must be applied once;
to be applied four times with that to be applied four times,
it must be applied four times.
To be applied four times with that to be applied once:
R. Eliezer says:
It must be applied four times.
R. Joshua says:
It must be applied once.
R. Eliezer said to him:
In this case, he is transgressing the prohibition against *subtracting*.
R. Joshua said to him:
In this case, he is transgressing the prohibition against *adding*.
R. Eliezer said to him:
The prohibition against *adding* is only stated in regard to the blood when it is by itself.
R. Joshua said:
The prohibition against *subtracting* is only stated in regard to the blood when it is by itself.
R. Joshua further said:
When you applied the blood,
you transgressed the prohibition against *adding*,
and you performed an act with your hand.
When you did not apply,
you transgressed the prohibition against *subtracting*,
but you did not perform an act with your hand.

11 Blood to be applied inside intermingled with that to be applied outside—
it must be poured into the gutter;
if he applied it outside and then returned and applied it inside—

I consider: See above 8:4.

as if it were water: As merely water, not inappropriately offered blood.

he must once again apply below: in the end blood was applied above and below, and some of the blood was appropriately applied and some was inappropriately applied both above and below.

8:10 *it must be applied once*: See chapter 5 above for discussion of which offerings require what number of applications of their blood.

the prohibition against subtracting... adding: Deuteronomy 4:2.

8:11 *Blood to be applied inside*: The blood of the bull and the goat for the Day of Atonement and bulls and goats that are burnt. See above 5:1–2.

it is valid;
inside and then returned and applied it outside—
R. Aqiva deems it invalid,
and the Sages deem it valid.
For R. Aqiva would say:
Any blood that enters the Holy to atone is invalid.
And the Sages say:
This applies only to purgation offerings.
R. Eliezer says:
Even guilt offerings,
as it is said: *The guilt offering is like the purgation offering.*

12 Blood of a purgation offering that he received in two cups,
if one of them went outside the sacred precincts—
the one inside is valid;
if one entered the sanctuary—
R. Yose the Galilean deems valid the one remaining outside the sanctuary;[46]
but the Sages deem it invalid.
R. Yose the Galilean said:
If in the case where intention renders invalid, outside,
the law[47] did not treat the blood that remained like that which went out,
in a case where intention does not render invalid, inside,
does not logic require that that the law should not treat the remainder like that which went in?
If the blood went into the sanctuary to atone,
even though it did not atone—
it is invalid—
the words of R. Eliezer.[48]
R. Simeon says:
Only once it atones.
R. Judah says:

[46] Heb. "the exterior one." [47] Lit. "it," perhaps "the priest." [48] **K**, **P**: "Eleazar."

Any blood that enters the Holy to atone is invalid to atone on the outside altar. Therefore if the priest first applied it inside, even the part of the mixed blood that needed to be applied outside is no longer valid to be applied outside.

The guilt offering is like the purgation offering: Leviticus 7:7.

8:12 *the case where intention renders invalid, outside*: If one had intention to eat the sacrifice outside the sanctuary it would be invalid; but if one cup of blood went out, the other remains valid.

like the blood *which went out*: i.e. invalid.

a case where intention does not render invalid, inside: If one had intention to eat the sacrifice inside the sanctuary, it would not render the sacrifice invalid. Does it not follow that if a cup went inside the sanctuary, the other should remain valid?

even though it did not atone: it was not yet sprinkled.

R. Eliezer or *Eleazar* (see n. 48) and *R. Judah* debate whether the cup that went in is invalidated just for having been brought into the Temple, or whether it had to have been offered.

If it was brought into the sanctuary unintentionally—
it is valid.
Of all the cases of invalid blood that were applied on the altar,
the diadem only propitiates for the impure,
for the diadem propitiates for the impure
but does not propitiate for that which went out of the sacred precincts.

Chapter Nine

9:1–7 *Rules Concerning the Altar*

9 The altar sanctifies that which is appropriate to it.
R. Joshua says:
Anything that is appropriate to the flames,
if it went up [to the altar]—
it may not descend,
as it is said: *It is the whole burnt offering over its flame on the altar.*
Just as *the whole burnt offering,*
which is appropriate for the flames,
if it went up [to the altar] it may not descend,
so too anything that is appropriate for the flames—
if it went up it may not descend.
Rabban Gamaliel says:
Anything that is appropriate for the altar,
if it went up, it may not descend,
as it is said: *It is the whole burnt offering over its flame on the altar.*
Just as the burnt offering,
which is appropriate for the altar,
if it went up, it may not descend,
so too anything that is appropriate for the altar—
if it went up, it may not descend.
The only difference between the words of Rabban Gamaliel and the words of R. Joshua is blood and libations,
for Rabban Gamaliel says that they do not descend,
and R. Joshua says they descend.

for the diadem propitiates: The high priest's diadem propitiates for any accidental impurity of the offerings that were placed on the altar. See Exodus 28:38.

9:1 *that which is appropriate to it*: If something that in general is appropriate or worthy to be sacrificed is placed on the altar, even if it is not at that moment an offering, it is not removed from the altar.

It is the whole burnt offering: Leviticus 6:2.

R. Joshua says they descend: Since blood and libations are not burnt on the altar but sprinkled on the sides or in the gutter of the altar.

R. Simeon says:
If the offering is valid but the libations are invalid,
or the libations are valid but the offering is invalid,
and even if both are invalid—
the offering is not removed,
but the libations descend.

2 And these, if they went up [to the altar], may not descend:
that which was left overnight,
or impure,
or went out of the sacred precincts,
or were slaughtered intending[49] an act outside its time or outside its place,
or were received by invalid priests,[50]
or they sprinkled the blood.
R. Judah says:
That which was slaughtered at night,
whose blood was spilled,
whose blood was taken outside the hangings—
if it went up, it must descend.
R. Simeon says:
It does not descend.[51]
For R. Simeon would say:
Anything whose invalidation was in the sacred precincts,
the sacred precincts accept it;
if its invalidation was not in the sacred precincts,
the sacred precincts do not accept it.

3 These, their invalidation was not in the sacred precincts:
an animal penetrating or penetrated in bestiality,
or set aside for idolatry,
or worshiped,
or used as payment for a prostitute,
or used as payment for a dog,
or was a forbidden mixed breed,
or a *terefah*,
or born of a caesarean section
or those that are blemished.

[49] As elsewhere in the tractate, lit. "slaughtered outside its time or outside its place"; intention is implied.

[50] Lit. "which invalid ones received."

[51] **K, P**: "for it became invalid in the sanctuary."

9:2 *left overnight*: Was not offered on the same day the slaughter took place.

sprinkled the blood: Or invalid priests sprinkled the blood.

whose blood was spilled: See 2:1.

whose invalidation was in the sacred precincts: Some commentators understand this phrase to mean that it became invalid after it was slaughtered. Others, literally after it was brought into the Temple Court.

9:3 For this list see 8:1, 14:2.

R. Aqiva deems valid those that are blemished.
R. Hananiah[52] the Prefect of the Priests says:
Father would push the blemished animals off the altar.

4 Just as
if they went up they do not descend,
so too
if they descended, they may not go up [again].
All animals that went up to the top of the altar alive, must descend.
A whole burnt offering that went up to the top of the altar alive, must descend.
If it was slaughtered at the top of the altar—
it must be skinned and divided on the spot.

5 And these, if they went up must[53] descend:
the meat of the offerings of highest sanctity,
and the meat of offerings of lesser sanctity,
the surplus of the *omer*,
the two breads,
and the showbread,
the remainder of grain offerings,
and the incense offering.
The wool on the heads of lambs,
the hair in the beard of goats;
the bones, and the sinews, and the horns, and the hooves—
when they are attached they go up,
as it is said: *And the priest shall turn it all to smoke on the altar.*
If they were separated from the animal offering,

[52] Or "Hanina." [53] K: "not."

R. Aqiva... blemished: That is, such animals need not be removed from the altar. The Talmud understands this to refer to specific defects such as on the eye, which are not considered disqualifying in bird offerings and which are therefore considered as lower-level blemishes in other animals. Offerings with more serious blemishes would need to be removed from the altar.

9:4 *slaughtered at the top of the altar*: Not in its proper location. See chapter 5.

9:5 *highest sanctity*: See chapter 5 and the annotation to 5:1 for the distinction between offerings that are of the highest sanctity and those which are of lesser sanctity. In both cases the meat of the sacrifices is meant to be eaten and not burnt upon the altar.

the omer... grain offering: These offerings too are intended to be eaten.

omer: This is the offering that is brought from the first grain cut according to rabbinic tradition on the second day of Passover. A sheaf of grain is brought to the sanctuary and ground into flour. Only a small portion of that is burnt on the altar and the rest, *the surplus of the omer*, is available to be eaten. See Leviticus 23:10–14, *Menahot* 10:3–5.

the two breads: See Leviticus 23:17.

the showbread: See Leviticus 24:5–9.

and the incense offering: This is not intended for the exterior altar at all but only for the interior altar (4:1).

wool... hooves: These are not intended to be eaten or to be offered on the altar.

And the priest shall turn it all: Leviticus 1:9.

they are not placed upon the altar,
as it is said: *And you shall perform your whole burnt offerings, the meat and the blood.*
6 Any of these that flew off the altar, he may not return them.[54]
So too, a coal that flew off the altar.
Limbs that flew off the altar:
prior to midnight—
he returns them, and one is liable for sacrilege for them;
after midnight—
he does not return them, and one is not liable for sacrilege for them.
7 Just as the altar sanctifies that which is appropriate to it,
so too the ramp [of the altar] sanctifies.
Just as the altar and the ramp sanctify that which is appropriate to them,
so too the utensils sanctify.
The utensils for the liquids sanctify the liquids,
and the measuring utensils for the dry ingredients sanctify the dry ingredients.
The utensils for the liquids do not sanctify the dry ingredients,
neither do the measuring utensils for the dry ingredients sanctify the liquids.
Sacred utensils that were punctured:
if they can still be put to use for the purpose for which they were intended while whole—
they sanctify;
if not—
they do not sanctify.
All of these sanctify only in the sacred precincts.

Chapter Ten

10:1–6 *Rules of Precedence of Offerings*

10 Anything that is more frequent than another takes precedence over the other.
Continual offerings take precedence over the additional offerings.

[54] K: "it may not return."

And you shall perform your whole burnt offerings: Deuteronomy 12:27.

9:6 *liable for sacrilege*: Since they are suitable to be returned to the altar, their nonsacral use is sacrilege.

9:7 The ramp and the utensils are assimilated to the holiness of the altar itself.

the liquids: Blood, water, or oil.

the dry ingredients: The flour.

punctured: Puncturing can make the object no longer a "vessel." Compare *Kelim* 3:3.

10:1 *Anything that is more frequent*: See *Horayot* 3:6. Precedence here is sequential: they go first.

the additional offerings: The additional offerings are those listed in the following sentence plus the additional offerings for the annual festivals. See Numbers 28–29.

The additional offerings for the Sabbath take precedence over
the additional offerings for the New Moon.
The additional offerings for the New Moon take precedence over
the additional offerings for[55] the New Year.
As it is said: *Beside the whole burnt offering of the morning, which is for a continual burnt offering, you shall perform these.*

2 That which is holier takes precedence over others.
The blood of a purgation offering precedes the blood of a whole burnt offering,
since the former[56] invokes divine compassion.[57]
The limbs of a whole burnt offering precede
the portions of the purgation offering that are burned,
since the former are consumed totally in the flames.
A purgation offering precedes a guilt offering,
since the blood of the former is applied upon the four corners and the foundation.
A guilt offering precedes a thank offering and the ram of a *nazir*,
since the former is an offering of the highest sanctity.
A thank offering and the ram of the *nazir* precede an offering of well-being,
since they are eaten on one day and require bread.
An offering of well-being precedes a firstborn,
since the former needs four applications, and the placing on of hands,
and libations and waving the chest and thigh.

3 A firstborn precedes animal tithes,
since [the former's] sanctity was from the womb and it is eaten by the priests.
Tithes precede bird offerings,
since [the former] is an animal offering and has elements that are of the highest sanctity,
namely its blood and the portions that are burned.

4 Bird offerings precede grain offerings,
since [the former] are blood offerings.
The grain offering of a sinner precedes a free-will grain offering,
since [the former] comes as the result of a sin.

[55] **K, P** add "the holiday of."
[56] "The former" added for clarity, here and below.
[57] Lit. "makes willing/makes acceptance."

Beside the whole burnt offering: Numbers 28:23.

10:2 *That which is holier*: *Horayot* 3:6.

portions…that are burned: That is, the parts of the animal such as the fat of the tail and the fat around the kidneys.

A purgation offering precedes a guilt offering, etc.: For these sacrifices see the annotations to 5:2–8.

10:3 *precedes animal tithes*: See 5:8.

precede bird offerings: See 6:2.

10:4 *grain offerings*: See 6:1.

[the former] are blood offerings: The commentaries say that this means that they afford greater atonement.

The purgation offering of a bird precedes the whole burnt offering of a bird.
So too when they are dedicated.[58]

5 All the purgation offerings listed in the Torah precede all the guilt offerings,
except for the guilt offering of one with *tsara'at*,
since [the latter] comes to make him fit.[59]
All the guilt offerings listed in Torah come at the age of two years
and must be worth two *sheqel*,
save for the guilt offering of the *nazir* and the guilt offering of one with *tsara'at*,
which come at the age of one year and need not be worth two *sheqel*.

6 Just as they have precedence in offering, so too do they have precedence in eating:
yesterday's offering of well-being and today's offering of well-being—
yesterday's takes precedence;
yesterday's offering of well-being and today's purgation offering or guilt offering—
yesterday's offering of well-being takes precedence—
the words of R. Meir;[60]
the Sages say:
The purgation offering takes precedence,
since it is of the highest sanctity.

10:7–8 *Consuming Sacred Foodstuffs*

7 In regard to all of these, the priests are allowed to vary the manner in which they eat them.
They may eat them roasted, boiled, or cooked,
and they may spice them with nonsacral spices[61] or *terumah* spices—
the words of R. Simeon.
R. Meir says:
He may not spice them with *terumah* spices,
so as not to cause the *terumah* to be invalidated.

[58] **V** lacks "So too when they are dedicated" and adds "The purgation offering of an animal precedes the burnt offering of an animal."

[59] **K**: "For making fit"; **M**: "In order to make fit. " See annotations.

[60] **V** lacks "the words of R. Meir."

[61] **K** lacks "nonsacral spices."

So too when they are dedicated: This refers only to the last statement. When a person dedicates two birds—one for a purgation offering and one as a burnt offering—the person must dedicate the bird for a purgation offering prior to the bird for a burnt offering.

10:5 *[the latter] comes to make him fit*: The sacrifice either completes his purification, or it allows him to bring offerings to the Temple.

worth two sheqel: See Leviticus 5:15: *as you value them in sheqel according to the sheqel of the sanctuary*. The Hebrew is in the plural, and, as is often the case, the plural is taken to mean a minimum of two. The *sheqel of the sanctuary* is usually understood to correspond to the Tyrian standard, which was twice the weight of the conventional standard used in the Mishnah (*Ketubbot* 5:9).

10:7 *In regard to all of these*: The above sacrifices that are eaten.

not to cause the terumah *to be invalidated*: Because the sacrifice must be eaten within a certain amount of time, by using spices from *terumah* one is causing otherwise permissible *terumah* to become prohibited.

8 Said R. Simeon:
If you see oil being divided in the Temple Court,[62] you need not ask what it is.
Rather: it is the remains of the flat cakes of the Israelites' grain offerings,
and of the *log* of oil of one with *tsara'at*.
If you see oil placed upon the flames of the altar, you need not ask what it is.
Rather: it is the remains of the flat cakes[63] of the priests' grain offerings,
or the grain offering of the anointed priest,
for no one donates oil by itself.
R. Tarfon says:
One may donate oil by itself.

Chapter Eleven

11:1–5 *Laundering Blood off the Priests' Garments*

11 If the blood of a purgation offering sprayed[64] on a garment,
in this case, it must be laundered.
Even though the verse only refers to the parts of the offering that are eaten,
as it is said: *In a holy place it shall be eaten—*
both the purgation offering that is eaten
and the one whose blood is offered within require laundering of the blood,[65]
as it is said: *The instruction for the purgation offering,*
the same teaching for all the purgation offerings.
2 The blood of an invalid purgation offering does not require washing,

[62] V lacks "in the Temple Court." [63] V: "leftovers" instead of "flat cakes."
[64] K: "was put, applied," also in 11:3.
[65] Lit. "both the one eaten and the one internal require laundering."

10:8 *oil being divided*: For the priests to consume.

the Israelites' grain offerings: See *Menahot* 6:3.

log of oil of one with tsara'at: Leviticus 14:10.

the priests' grain offerings: The priests' grain offerings are wholly burnt on the altar and are not eaten by the priests. See *Menahot* 6:2.

11:1 *it must be laundered*: See Leviticus 6:20. This immediately follows an instruction about eating the sacrifice.

In a holy place it shall be eaten: Leviticus 6:19. The Mishnah acknowledges that the explicit instruction appears to assume a sacrifice that is eaten.

The instruction for the purgation offering: Leviticus 6:18. This verse introduces instructions for the purgation offering. The Mishnah therefore applies the requirement of washing that follows to all types of purgation offering, and not only to those eaten.

11:2 *invalid purgation offering*: The phrase *of its blood* in Leviticus 6:20 is taken to exclude sacrifices that were not valid.

whether or not it ever had a period of validity.
Which had a period of validity?
One that was left overnight,
or became impure,
or went out of the sacred precincts.
And which had no period of validity?
One that was slaughtered [with the intention of performing a ritual act]
outside its time or outside its place,
or one that invalid persons received or sprinkled[66] its blood.

3 If blood sprayed from the neck onto the garment,
it does not require laundering;
from the corner of the altar, or the base,
it does not require laundering.
If it spilled on the floor and he collected it,
it does not require laundering.
Only blood that was received in a utensil
and is suitable for sprinkling requires laundering.
If it sprayed[67] on the skin of an offering before it was skinned,
it does not require laundering;
if after it was skinned,
it requires laundering—
the words of R. Judah.
R. Eliezer[68] says:
Even once it was removed it does not require laundering.
The only things that require laundering are:
the place of the blood,
on something susceptible to impurity,
and suitable to be laundered.

4 The rule is one and the same for cloth, sackcloth, and hide:
they require laundering[69] in a holy place.

[66] **V** lacks "or sprinkled." [67] **K**: "put" or "applied" as above.
[68] **K**, **P**: "Eleazar." [69] Manuscripts add "the washing must be."

period of validity: The Mishnah here distinguishes between sacrifices that became invalidated and those that were invalid from the outset. There is no legal consequence discussed here, but compare similar language used for levirate marriage (*Yevamot* 8:4) and nonsacral slaughter (*Hullin* 4:4).

left overnight, etc.: See 9:2.

11:3 For the classification of blood that does or does not require laundering, compare 2:2, 3:2.

the place of the blood: That is, the place on the garment that was stained by the blood, not the whole garment.

susceptible to impurity: Things that have been fashioned into "vessels" or tools rather than raw materials. See *Kelim*, introduction.

suitable to be laundered: As opposed to wooden vessels, which cannot merely be washed but must be scraped (Leviticus 15:12). Alternatively, "laundering" implies certain kinds of materials (cloth, sackcloth, hide, 11:4) and not others.

11:4 *cloth, sackcloth, and hide*: For cleansing these (in a different context), see Leviticus 11:32.

a holy place: Leviticus 6:20, taken to mean the sanctuary.

The breaking of an earthenware utensil must be in a holy place.
The scouring and washing of a copper utensil must be in a holy place.[70]
This is a stringency of a purgation offering as against [other] offerings of the highest sanctity.

5 A garment that was removed outside the hangings—
he enters and launders in a holy place.
If it became impure outside the hangings,
he tears it, then he enters, and he launders it in a holy place.

11:5 cont.–8 *Cleaning Utensils*

An earthenware utensil that was removed outside the hangings—
he enters, and he breaks it in a holy place.
If it became impure outside the sanctuary,
he pierces it, and he enters, and he breaks it in a holy place.

6 A copper utensil that was removed outside the hangings—
he enters, and scours and rinses it in a holy place.
If it became impure outside of the sanctuary, he diminishes it,
and he enters and scours and rinses it in a holy place.

7 The rule is one and the same whether he cooked in it or poured boiling liquid:
whether in the case of offerings of highest sanctity or those of lesser sanctity—
they require scouring and rinsing.
R. Simeon says:
Offerings of lesser sanctity do not require scouring and rinsing.
R. Tarfon says:
If he started to cook with the utensil on a pilgrimage festival,
he continues to cook with it throughout the festival.
But the Sages say:

[70] **K, P** lack this rule.

breaking of an earthenware utensil: In which the purgation offering is cooked. Leviticus 6:21.

11:5 *garment*: The garment is stained with sacrificial blood and must be laundered in the sacred precincts. If it became impure outside the sacred precincts it cannot be returned there. The solution is to perform an act that removes the status of "garment" from it, which also has the effect of purifying it (*Kelim* 27:12). The garment can then be returned to the Temple precincts and dealt with.

earthenware utensil: The analogous problem and solution apply to pottery, which must be broken rather than laundered.

11:6 *he diminishes it*. As in 11:5, by making a hole in it. *Kelim* 14:1 discusses the size of holes that "purify" metal vessels.

scours and rinses it: See Leviticus 6:21. Commentators explain that scouring is the operation in which all foodstuff is removed from the vessel while rinsing follows that and involves flushing with water.

11:7 *require scouring and rinsing*: See 11:6. Even in an earthenware vessel. Only the purgation offering requires breaking the vessel.

throughout the festival: That is, without any need to scour or rinse between cooking. Some commentators believe that this only implies one day at a time, and that at the end of a day scouring and rinsing is required since leaving fat or other detritus of the food on the vessel overnight, and then cooking with the vessel on

The time for scouring and rinsing is up to the time of eating.
Scouring and rinsing is done in the manner of scouring a cup,
and rinsing is done in the manner of rinsing a cup.
Scouring [is to be done] with hot water,[71] and rinsing with cold water.
The spit and the grill are scalded with hot water.
8 If he cooked both sacred offerings and nonsacral food in it
or food of the highest sanctity and of lesser sanctity,
if there is enough of [the holier] to impart a taste,
in this case, those foods bound by less stringent rules are eaten[72]
according to the more stringent rules,
but the utensils do not require scouring and rinsing,
and they do not invalidate by touch.
If a flat cake from one offering touched an [invalid] flat cake,[73]
or a piece from one offering touched a piece from an [invalid] offering[74]—
neither the whole flat cake nor the whole of the pieces[75] are prohibited;
but only the place where it absorbed.

Chapter Twelve

12:1–4 *Who May Partake of the Offerings?*

12 A *tevul yom* and one lacking atonement
do not take a portion of the offerings to eat in the evening.

[71] Some versions have "scouring and rinsing with cold water."
[72] **V** adds "and they require scouring and rinsing and are invalidated by touch, if there is no trace of the taste the foodstuffs bound by a less stringent rule are not eaten."
[73] Lit. "A flat cake that touched a flat cake."
[74] Lit. "and a piece [that touched] a piece."
[75] **K**, **P**: "piece."

the morrow, is abrogating the prohibition against eating an offering beyond its time. Others take this literally, as applying to the entire length of the festival.

up to the time of eating: While it is still permitted to eat the sacrifice (one or two days and a night, depending on the sacrifice). Alternatively, one must wash immediately upon finishing eating.

11:8 *less stringent rules... more stringent rules*: Lit. "If there is that in them that gives off taste, in that case, the lesser are eaten as the more stringent." That is, if some of the meat may only be eaten by priests then only priests can eat all of it.

do not require scouring and rinsing: Perhaps in accordance with the view of R. Simeon in 11:7: the pots are treated as pots that were used to cook sacrifices of lesser sanctity. (The Talmud emends this passage to require scouring and rinsing except where there was not enough of the more stringent to impart a taste.)

do not invalidate by touch: If the mixture came into contact with other sacred food, it does not invalidate.

absorbed: The point of contact where they transferred taste from one to another.

12:1 *tevul yom... lacking atonement*: See 2:1.

take a portion... to eat in the evening: In both cases, both would be eligible to eat in the evening. However, at the time of the distribution they are still not eligible.

An *onen* may touch [the offering],
but he may not offer,
and he may not take a portion to eat in the evening.
Those with blemishes,
whether permanent blemishes or passing blemishes,
may take a portion and eat,
but they may not offer.
Anyone who is not appropriate for the Temple service may not take a portion of the meat,
and anyone who does not have a portion in the meat does not have one in the hides.
Even one who is impure at the time of the sprinkling of the blood,
but pure at the time of the burning of the fats,
does not take a portion of the meat.
As it is said: *He of the sons of Aaron who offers the blood*
and the fat of the offering of well-being shall get the right thigh as his portion.

2 Any [offering] whose meat the altar did not acquire,
the priests did not acquire its hide,
as it is said: *A man's whole burnt offering*:
a whole burnt offering that was offered for a man.
A whole burnt offering that was slaughtered without the proper designation,
even though it did not fulfill its owners' obligation,
its hide belongs to the priests.
The rule is one and the same for the whole burnt offering of a man
or the whole burnt offering of a woman—
their hides go to the priests.

3 The hides of offerings of lesser sanctity belong to their owners;
the hides of offerings of highest sanctity belong to the priests.
[This results from] an argument of lesser and greater.

onen may touch: See 2:1. Although not impure (so that his touch does not disqualify), the priest who is an *onen* may not take part in the cult or get a distribution.

blemishes: See Deuteronomy 23:2.

not appropriate for the Temple service: As the commentaries note, if this does not conflict with the rule for the blemished priest earlier in this mishnah, then the blemished priest, who cannot offer sacrifices, is an exception to the current rule.

in the hides: Leviticus 7:8.

He of the sons of Aaron: Leviticus 7:33.

12:2 *the altar did not acquire*: If, for example, it became invalid before the sprinkling of the blood, the meat would not be burnt upon the altar.

A man's whole burnt offering: Leviticus 7:8. The sacrifice has to have been successfully offered on the altar for the man. Since whole burnt offerings that are *slaughtered without the proper designation* remain valid (1:1), the hides go to the priests despite the fact that *it did not fulfill its owners' obligation.*

12:3 *offerings of lesser sanctity*: See 5:5–8. By contrast, the whole burnt offering mentioned in 12:2 is an offering of the highest sanctity (5:4).

argument of lesser and greater: A formal principle for comparing rules of greater and lesser stringency. The goal of the argument is to prove that while Scripture only states that the hides of whole burnt offerings go to the priests (Leviticus 7:8), in fact, the hides of other sacrifices also go to the priests.

If, in the case of a whole burnt offering,
where the priests do not acquire its meat,
they do acquire its hide,
offerings of the highest sanctity,
where they do acquire their meat,
does not logic require that they acquire their hide?
We cannot argue: The altar will disprove it,[76]
for the altar does not ever acquire the hide.

4 All offerings that became invalidated prior to their skinning,
their hides do not go to the priests;
after their skinning, their hides go to the priests.
R. Hananiah[77] the Prefect of the Priests said:
In all my days, I never saw a hide taken to the place of burning.
R. Aqiva said:
From his words we learn that if one skins a firstling and it is found to be *terefah*—
the priests may benefit from its hide.
But the Sages say:
"We have not seen"[78] is not a proof;
rather, it is taken to the place of burning.

12:5–6 *The Burning of Sacrificial Remains*

5 Bulls that are burnt and goats that are burnt:
when they are burnt as commanded—
they are burnt in the ash heap,
and they make clothes impure;
if they are not burnt as commanded—

[76] **P**: "The altar does not prove"; **K** (perhaps erroneously): "The altar has no proof."
[77] Or "Hanina." [78] **V**: "I have not seen."

We cannot argue...disprove it: Presumably, this statement responds to an argument that has been raised. The altar "acquires" the flesh of the sacrifice but not its skin, so one might have objected that the altar shows that it is an expected outcome for sacrifices that the flesh is acquired but not the hide. However, the Mishnah says, this is an inappropriate comparison, since *the altar does not ever acquire the hide*: we need to compare our case to one where the hide could be acquired.

12:4 *R. Hananiah the Prefect of the Priests*: Cf. 9:3; the tradition also appears in *Eduyot* 2:2. Here, he attests to his own knowledge of Temple times.

the place of burning: See above 8:4 and annotations there.

firstling: A firstborn animal must be sacrificed (above 1:2, 5:8). Since here the animal is found to be *terefah* one would imagine that like the flesh, the hide could not be used by the priests. R. Aqiva concludes from the testimony of R. Hananiah that the actual practice was otherwise. Based on the Talmud, the commentaries apply this even to animals that were blemished and could be slaughtered by lay persons outside the Temple.

12:5 *Bulls...goats that are burnt*: 5:1–2. See *Temurah* 7:5–6.

ash heap: This is one of the three places for burning once-sacred materials. The *ash heap* is outside of Jerusalem opposite the eastern entrance to the Temple. See above 5:2.

make clothes impure: Leviticus 16:28 is taken to imply that priest's clothing and any clothing that he contacts become impure.

they are burnt on the Temple Mount,
and they do not make clothes impure.

6 They would carry them out on poles.
When the first porters exited the wall of the Temple Court
and the latter had not yet exited,
the former make clothing impure while the latter do not
until they exit;
once they have both exited, they both make clothing impure.
R. Simeon says:
Neither these nor those[79] make clothing impure
until the fire has caught the major part of the offerings.
Once the meat is burnt, the one who burns it no longer makes clothing impure.

Chapter Thirteen

13:1–3 *Animal Sacrifices Inside and Outside the Temple*

13 1 One who slaughters and offers[80] outside [the Temple precincts]
is liable for both the slaughter and the offering.
R. Yose the Galilean says:
If he slaughtered inside and offered outside—
he is liable;
if he slaughtered outside and offered outside—
he is exempt,
for he only offered an invalid thing.

[79] **K**: "they do not" for "neither these nor those."

[80] Lit. "brings up"; so too throughout 13:1.

not burnt as commanded: If something has happened to them to invalidate them prior to the burning.

do not make clothes impure: Since it is not the final burning of a valid sacrifice carried out according to the commandment.

12:6 *R. Simeon* differs from the preceding tradition and limits impurity only to the burning itself.

Once the meat is burnt: The period during which a priest who deals with the animal transmits impurity to clothing only lasts until the meat is "burnt." According to the commentaries this is when the surfaces of the pieces are seared.

13:1 *offers*: Lit. "sends up." See e.g. Joshua 22:23, 1 Samuel 10:8.

liable: That is, he has committed a transgression.

R. Yose the Galilean: The anonymous opinion treats the slaughter and offering as two distinct acts, each with penalties for performing them outside the sanctuary. R. Yose the Galilean examines the circumstances of each. In his second case, *he slaughtered outside and offered outside*, the sacrifice was invalidated by slaughtering outside the sanctuary, so the sacrifice was invalid at the moment of offering and is subject to only one penalty.

They said to him:
Even if he slaughtered inside and offered outside,
since he took it outside, he invalidated it.

2 One who, while impure, ate
either of a pure offering or of an impure offering—
he is liable.
R. Yose the Galilean says:
One who is impure who ate pure offering—
he is liable;
one who is pure who ate impure offering—
he is exempt,
for he has only eaten an impure thing.
They said to him:
Even one who is impure who ate pure offering,
since he touched it he made it impure.
One who is pure who ate impure offering is exempt,
for he is only liable for his bodily impurity.

3 Slaughtering is more stringent than offering,[81]
and offering is more stringent than slaughtering.[82]
Slaughtering is more stringent:[83]
for one who slaughters for a layperson outside the sacred precincts is liable,
but one who offers for a layperson is exempt.

[81] Lit. "bringing up," here and throughout 13:3.
[82] **V** lacks this line.
[83] **K** lacks "slaughtering is more stringent."

They said: On first reading, the anonymous Sages here seem to extend the argument: one is even exempt for bringing the properly slaughtered sacrifice outside for offering, since it was invalidated before being offered by the very act of bringing it outside. R. Yose the Galilean ruled that one is liable, since it was still valid at the moment it was offered. However, see the next comment and 13:2.

since he took it outside, he invalidated it: The commentaries understand this as if it reads "even though he took it out and invalidated it," nevertheless the priest who offered it outside is liable.

13:2 This passage is structured in parallel to 13:1.

One who, while impure: Specifically, a priest.

R. Yose the Galilean considers a sacrifice that has become impure to have been invalidated, so the eating of an impure sacrifice does not incur a penalty.

They said: On its surface, "they" appear to be deeming an impure person who ate pure sacrificial meat exempt, which appears to go against Leviticus 16:19, 20. Perhaps, then, the anonymous Sages are making the counterargument that by this same logic an impure person who ate pure sacrificial meat, whom R. Yose the Galilean holds liable, should be exempt as well.

since... he made it impure: See 13:1.

his bodily impurity: He is only liable when his bodily impurity causes impurity to the sacrifice.

13:3 *slaughters... offers for a layperson outside the sacred precincts*: Although there is some discrepancy among the commentaries, the consensus seems to be that the situation is one of nonidolatrous sacrifice.

for a layperson may mean in honor or in the name of that person and not in the name of God; alternatively, for a lay person to eat. In Leviticus 17:5 the slaughtering outside the sanctuary is specifically said to be "to the Lord."

Offering is more stringent:
Two who held the knife and slaughtered—
are exempt;
if they held a limb and offered it—
they are liable.
If one offered and again offered and again offered—
he is liable for each and every offering—
the words of R. Simeon.
R. Yose says:
He is only liable for one.[84]
and he is only liable when he offered it[85] on the top of the altar.
R. Simeon says:
Even if he offered on a boulder or a rock, he is liable.

13:4–6 *Inside and Outside*

4 The rule is one and the same for valid offerings
or invalid offerings whose invalidation was in the sanctuary:
if he offered them outside [the sacred precincts]—
he is liable.
One who offers an olive's bulk of a whole burnt offering
and of the innards[86] that are burnt on the altar
outside [the sacred precincts]—
he is liable.
One who offered an olive's bulk of:
the handful,
the frankincense,
the aromatic incense,
the grain offering of priests,
the grain offering of the anointed priest,
or the grain offering offered with libations
outside [the sacred precincts]—
he is liable.
R. Eliezer exempts unless one offers the whole of it.
In regard to all of them:

[84] **K** lacks "He…for one." [85] Lit. "brought it up."
[86] Some witnesses read "of its innards"; compare 13:5.

Two who held the knife…held a limb: The slaughter is invalid if done by two people.

13:4 *invalidation was in the sanctuary*: That is, they are of the category of things that if they "were placed on the altar they are not removed" as defined above 9:2.

an olive's bulk of a whole burnt offering and of the innards: The simplest reading is that these are alternative to one another ("or an olive's bulk"). However, most commentators follow the Talmud in seeing the point of the Mishnah to stress that one is liable for offering an olive's bulk of these items combined. See n. 86.

the handful, etc. See 4:3. The discussion here revolves around whether there is a complete act of offering for which one would be liable.

if he offered them inside
and left over an olive's bulk and offered that outside—
he is liable.
In regard to all of them:
if they lacked even the smallest amount from an olive's bulk
and he offered them outside—
he is exempt.

5 One who offers sacred offerings and their innards
outside [the sacred precincts]—
he is liable.
A grain offering from which the handful has not been separated,
and he offered it outside—
he is exempt.
If he took a handful of it,
and the handful fell back into it,
and then the grain offering was offered outside—
he is liable.

6 The handful and the frankincense,
one of which was offered outside [the sacred precincts]—
he is liable.
R. Eleazar exempts until he has offered both.[87]
If he offered one inside and one outside—
he is liable.
Two utensils of frankincense, one of which was offered outside—
he is liable.
R. Eleazar exempts until he has offered both.[88]
If he offered one inside and one outside—
he is liable.
One who sprinkles a small amount of the blood outside—
is liable.
R. Eleazar says:
Even one who pours the Festival water outside during the Festival is liable.
R. Nehemiah says:

[87] Lit. "the second." [88] Lit. "the second."

13:5 *offerings and their innards*: With their innards, which needed to be offered on the altar, still attached. Although they have not been detached, this counts as offering them outside and *he is liable*.

grain offering…separated: The situation is analogous to that of the animal offering above. In this first instance the portion to be burnt was not yet designated by taking a handful. In the second instance, where *he took a handful of it and the handful fell back into it*, the portion to be burnt was "attached" to the rest of the grain offering as in the case of the animal. For the remixing of the handful with the rest of the offering, see *Menahot* 3:3.

13:6 As in 13:4, the question is what constitutes a complete, and therefore punishable, act of offering (now, specifically the grain offering).

Festival water: See 6:2 and the annotation there.

Remnants of the blood that he offered outside—
he is liable.[89]

13:7 *Bird Offerings Inside and Outside the Temple*

7 One who pinches the neck of the bird offering inside
and offered it outside—
he is liable.
If he pinched its neck outside
and offered it outside—
he is exempt.
One who slaughters a bird inside
and offered it outside—
he is exempt.
If he slaughtered it outside
and offered it outside—
he is liable.
One finds that the manner that makes it valid inside makes it exempt outside;
the manner that makes it valid outside makes it exempt inside.
R. Simeon says:
Anything for which one is held liable outside,
one is held liable for that which is like it inside,
when he then offered it outside,
except for one who slaughters inside and offers outside.

13:8 *Blood Inside and Outside the Temple*

8 The purgation offering whose blood he received in one cup—
if he applied it outside,

[89] **V** lacks "R. Nehemiah says... he is liable."

remnants of the blood: See 5:1–3. The commentaries note that this view is contrary to the rule at the end of 5:1 that failure to dispose of the blood does not prevent the successful completion of the sacrifice.

13.7 Bird offerings differ from other animal sacrifices, in that sacrificial birds are killed only by pinching, and nonsacrificial birds are killed only by cutting the neck. Thus if he *pinched its neck outside* or *slaughtered it inside* but he *offered it outside* the killing was invalid, thus he is exempt for the offering.

One finds: Derives a general rule that summarizes the preceding.

makes it exempt: If he performed the killing of the animal by pinching outside or slaughtering inside and then offered the animal outside, he would be exempt.

R. Simeon: The commentaries follow the Talmud, which finds this passage somewhat difficult. However, the Talmud does initially assume that *R. Simeon* differs from the preceding view regarding a bird pinched outside and offered outside.

The exception noted by *R. Simeon* appears to conflict with the view of R. Yose the Galilean in 13:1.

13.8 The Mishnah now turns to the blood offering itself.

in one cup, and made the offering inside and outside from the same vessel.

and then returned and applied it inside;
or inside and then returned
and applied it outside—
he is liable,
for the whole of it is valid to be brought[90] inside the sanctuary.
If he received the blood in two cups
and applied both inside—
he is exempt.
If he applied both outside—
he is liable.
If he applied one inside
and then one outside—
he is exempt.
One outside and then one inside—
he is liable for the outside application,
and the inside application atones.
To what is this similar?
To one who separated his purgation offering and it was lost,
then he separated another in its place,
and subsequently the first one was found.
And now, both are present.[91]
If he slaughtered both inside—
he is exempt.
If he slaughtered both outside—
he is liable.
One inside and one outside—
he is exempt.
One outside and one inside—
he is liable for the one on the outside,
and the one on the inside atones.
Just as its blood exempts its flesh,
so too, the blood exempts the flesh of its fellow.

[90] **K** lacks "to be brought."

[91] Lit. "both are standing."

the whole of it was at one point *valid to be* offered: For the expression *valid to be brought inside* see the rule of R. Simeon in 14:1.

in two cups: If the first is offered inside the second no longer has a purpose, so offering it outside does not make one liable. If the first was offered outside one is liable, but the second is still effective.

To one who separated his purgation offering: See *Me'ilah* 1:2. According to *Temurah* 4:3, when two animals are present in this way, one slaughters one, and the other must be left to die since it no longer has a sacrificial purpose.

so too, the blood exempts the flesh of its fellow: The blood offering of one of the sacrifices exempts the meat of both animals from sacrilege, even though the meat of the second is still prohibited.

Chapter Fourteen

14:1–3 *Invalid Offerings*

14 The purgation-offering heifer that one burnt[92] outside of its enclosure,
and likewise the scapegoat that he offered outside—
he is exempt,
for it is said: *and does not bring it to the entrance of the Tent of Meeting*—
anything that is not valid to come into the entrance of the Tent of Meeting,
one is not liable for it.

2 An animal penetrating or penetrated in bestiality,
or set aside for idolatry,
or worshiped,
or used as payment for a prostitute,
or used as payment for a dog,
or was a forbidden mixed breed,
or one that was *terefah*,
or one born of a caesarean section—
that he offered outside,
he is exempt,
as it is said: *before the Lord's Tabernacle*:
anything that is not appropriate before the Lord's Tabernacle, one is not liable for it.
Animals with blemishes:
whether those with permanent blemishes or those with passing blemishes
that he offered outside—
he is exempt.
R. Simeon says:

[92] V, Rashi: "slaughtered" instead of "burnt."

14:1 *The purgation-offering heifer*: The red heifer whose ashes are used in the purification of corpse impurity. See *Parah*, introduction.

its enclosure: Lit. "winepress," the place designated for the burning of the heifer, *Parah* 3:10.

the scapegoat: Leviticus 16:8–10. Rather than casting it out, someone slaughtered it as a sacrifice *outside* the sanctuary.

for it is said: Leviticus 17:4.

valid to come into the entrance: Neither the heifer nor the goat are offerings of this type.

14.2 *An animal…caesarean section*: See the list in 8:1, 9:3.

before the Lord's Tabernacle: Leviticus 17:4. The preceding animals are not valid to come into the Tabernacle as sacrifices.

In the cases that follow, the anonymous rulings are that one who offers the animals in question outside the sanctuary is exempt because the animal is not a valid sacrifice, while *R. Simeon* rules that in a case where the animal might in the future be a valid sacrifice one transgresses.

Animals with blemishes: 12:2.

Those with permanent blemishes—
he is exempt;
those with passing blemishes—
he transgresses[93] a prohibition.
Turtle doves that had not reached the proper age,
or doves that had passed the proper age—
that he offered outside,
he is exempt.
R. Simeon says:
Doves that had passed the proper age,
he is exempt;
turtle doves that had not reached the proper age—
it is under a prohibition.
An animal and its offspring,
or one whose time had not yet come,
he is exempt.
R. Simeon says:
In this case, it is under a prohibition.
For R. Simeon would say:
Any animal that it would be appropriate to bring in the future,
in such a case, it is under a prohibition,
and does not carry *karet*;
but the Sages say:
Anything that does not carry *karet*,
is not under a prohibition.

3 "Whose time had not yet come":
whether in respect of itself,[94] or its owner.
What is "whose time had not yet come in respect of its owner"?
A *zav*,
or a *zavah*,
or one who has given birth,

[93] The manuscripts lack the phrase "he transgresses."

[94] Lit. "in its body."

Turtle doves . . . doves: 7:5.

its offspring: Lit. "it with its young," a reference to the prohibition in Leviticus 22:28. The issue here is whether, having temporarily invalidated the animal or its offspring by slaughtering the other, one is liable for slaughtering the remaining animal outside.

whose time had not yet come: An animal (excluding birds) that is less than eight days old. See Exodus 22:29.

R. Simeon . . . Sages: Generalizing a rule from the above cases: according to *R. Simeon*, if at some future point the animal might be a valid sacrifice, offering it outside the sanctuary is prohibited, but (since it is not valid now) does not result in *karet*. *The Sages* rule that if there is no *karet* then slaughtering the animal outside the sanctuary does not transgress a prohibition.

14:3 *time had not yet come*: Repeated from 14:2.

of itself: As above: an animal that was too young to be sacrificed.

zav . . . zavah, etc.: All of these are required to bring sacrifices upon purification. *Zav . . . zavah*: Leviticus 15:14, 29; *one who has given birth*: Leviticus 12:6; *one with tsara'at*: Leviticus 14:10.

or one with *tsara'at*
who offered their purgation offering or their guilt offering outside—
they are exempt;
their whole burnt offerings, or their offerings of well-being outside,
they are liable.
One who offers from the meat of a purgation offering,
from the meat of a guilt offering,
from the meat of an offering of the highest sanctity,
from the meat of an offering of lesser sanctity,
the surplus of the *omer*,
the two breads,
the showbread,
the remainder of the grain offering,
or pours the oil,
or mixes the flour with oil,
or breaks the grain offering into bits,
or salts it,[95]
or waves it,
or lays it out,
or orders the table,
or readies the lampstand,
or took a handful,
or received the blood
outside—
he is exempt.
One is not liable for these:
for being a nonpriest,[96]
nor for impurity,
nor for lacking vestments,
nor for nonwashing[97] of hands and feet.

[95] V lacks "or salts it." [96] Lit. "foreignness." [97] Lit. "washing."

who offered their purgation offering or their guilt offering outside, they are exempt: These people are still impure or are still (in the case of the one with *tsara'at*) under the ban. These offerings are not valid at all and are considered profane animals that may be slaughtered outside.

their whole burnt offerings, or their offerings of well-being outside, they are liable: These may be brought as free-will offerings at any time, so if the *zav*, etc. slaughtered such a sacrifice outside the sanctuary he or she would be liable.

from the meat of a purgation offering: These are eaten and not put on the altar.

surplus of the omer... of the grain offering: See 9.5. These too are eaten by the priests.

pours the oil... lays it out: Operations having to do with a grain offering that are not the core of the offering itself.

orders the table: Lays the showbread out on the Temple table. *Menahot* 11:4–9.

readies the lampstand: Prepares the wicks each morning. *Tamid* 3:9.

he is exempt: For all of the above if one performed them outside the sanctuary. The person who did so is not liable to a sacrifice or *karet* for performing sacrifices outside the sanctuary.

impurity: Performing any of the above when impure.

lacking vestments... nonwashing of hands and feet: See 2:1.

14:4–8 *From Tabernacle to Temple*

4 Until the Tabernacle was established,
high places were permitted,
and the service was performed by the firstborn.
Once the Tabernacle was established,
the high places became prohibited,
and the service was performed by the priests.
Offerings of the highest sanctity were eaten within the hangings [of the Tabernacle];
offerings of lesser sanctity, throughout the Israelite camp.
5 When they came to Gilgal,
the high places became permitted.
Offerings of the highest sanctity were eaten within the hangings;
offerings of lesser sanctity, anywhere.
6 When they came to Shiloh,
the high places became prohibited.
There was no roof, only a building of stone below and skins above.
It was *the abode.*
Offerings of the highest sanctity were eaten within the hangings;
offerings of lesser sanctity and the second tithe,
were eaten any place from which one could see it.
7 When they came to Nob and Gibeon,
the high places became permitted.
Offerings of the highest sanctity were eaten within the hangings;
offerings of lesser sanctity, in any of the Israelite cities.

14:4–8 The Mishnah lays out a kind of history of sacrifice and sacrificial places from the Exodus to the building of Solomon's Temple in Jerusalem. Until the building of the Temple there were alternating periods during which sacrifice was permitted outside a single central shrine.

14:4 *Until the Tabernacle was established*: In the desert, prior to entering into Canaan.

Offerings... were eaten within the hangings: This is the expression used in 5:3, 5:6, 6:1.

offerings of lesser sanctity: In 5:6–8 the expression is "throughout the city."

14:5 *came to Gilgal*: Joshua 5:8–11.

high places became permitted, despite the fact that there was a shrine at Gilgal.

14:6 *Shiloh*: Joshua 18:1–10.

no roof: The Mishnah describes a structure covered by the Tabernacle coverings.

the abode: A reference to Deuteronomy 12:9: *For you have not come as yet to the alloted abode that the Lord your God is giving you*. The rabbis understood the phrase *alloted abode* as referring to two places: Shiloh and the Temple in Jerusalem.

the second tithe: Second tithe is mentioned here and not previously since there was no obligation to separate second tithe prior to Shiloh. In other respects, the situation is similar to that in the desert after the Tabernacle.

14:7 *Nob and Gibeon*: In rabbinic usage, this refers to the period from the death of Eli the high priest and the loss of the Ark to the Philistines in 1 Samuel 4 through Saul's destruction of Nob in 1 Samuel 22 and the death of Samuel. David brought the Ark to Jerusalem in 2 Samuel 6.

8 When they came to Jerusalem
the high places became prohibited,
and they were never again permitted.
And this was *the allotment.*
Offerings of the highest sanctity were eaten within the hangings;
offerings of lesser sanctity and the second tithe inside the wall [of Jerusalem].

14:9–10 *Tabernacle, High Places, and Temple*

9 All offerings that one dedicated at a time when the high places were prohibited,
and offered outside at the time when the high places were prohibited,
in this case, they involve a positive commandment and a prohibition,
and one is liable for *karet* for them.
If one dedicated them at a time that high places were permitted,
and offered them at a time when the high places were prohibited,
in this case, they involve a positive commandment and a prohibition,
but one is not liable for *karet* for them.
If one dedicated at a time when the high places were prohibited,
and one offered them at a time when the high places were permitted,
in this case, they involve a positive commandment, but not a prohibition.
10 These are the sacred offerings that are offered in the Tabernacle:
offerings that were dedicated for the Tabernacle.
Offerings for the community were offered in the Tabernacle,
but individual offerings at the high places.
Individual offerings that were dedicated for the Tabernacle,
let them be offered at the Tabernacle;
but if one offered them at a high place—
one is exempt.
What distinguishes high places of individuals from high places of the community?
Laying on of hands,

14:8 *and they were never again permitted*: The founding of the Jerusalem Temple permanently centralized the cult and made other cult places prohibited.

the allotment: See Deuteronomy 12:9, cited above in note to 14:6.

14:9 When high places were permitted, offering sacrifices "outside" did not transgress a prohibition.

a positive commandment: Leviticus 17:5: *and bring them to the Lord, to the entrance of the Tent of Meeting.*

a prohibition: Deuteronomy 12:13.

liable for karet: Leviticus 17:4.

not liable for karet: *Karet* only applies when one made the dedication while the high places were prohibited.

14:10 *offered in the Tabernacle*: Offered at the Tabernacle only, even at a time when sacrificial sites were permitted.

high places of the community: Gilgal, Nob, Gibeon. The features that follow took place at the public cult site but not at private ones.

Laying on of hands: Leaning on the sacrifice. See *Menahot* 9:7–9.

slaughtering in the north,
applying the blood around the altar,
waving,
and bringing near.
(R. Judah says:
There is no grain offering in a high place.)
And priesthood,
priestly vestments,
utensils of the service,
pleasing odor,
division of blood,
washing of hands and feet.
However, the time,
remnant,
and impurity—
these are the same in both.

slaughtering in the north: 5:1–5.

applying the blood around: 5:4.

waving, and bringing near: Part of the offering of grain. See *Menahot* 5:5–6.

R. Judah adds another aspect of sacrifice that was not part of worship in private high places.

pleasing odor: A biblical expression that frequently describes the scent of the sacrifices before the deity. See e.g. Genesis 8:21, Leviticus 17:6.

division of blood between the upper and lower part of the altar. See 2:1, *Middot* 3:1.

the time: Presumably, intention to perform a sacrificial act outside of its appropriate time, resulting in *piggul*.

Tractate Menahot

Dvora Weisberg

Introduction

Overview

The title *Menahot* refers to the offerings called *minhah* in the Torah (Leviticus 2:1–14, 6:7–11). These were sacrificial offerings of grain that might be brought on their own or as a supplement to an animal offering.

Structure and Organization of the Tractate

Menahot follows tractate *Zevahim* and has parallels to it, insofar as the four steps in presenting a grain offering correspond to the four steps in presenting an animal offering. Moreover, both animal offerings and grain offerings may be rendered invalid by the same acts or intentions. The most significant parallels are found to *Menahot* 1:1 (*Zevahim* 1:1, 1:4); *Menahot* 1:2 (*Zevahim* 2:1); *Menahot* 1:3–4 (*Zevahim* 2:2–5); and *Menahot* 3:1 (*Zevahim* 3:3).

The tractate has thirteen chapters. The first section of the tractate (1:1–3:4) focuses on actions that invalidate a grain offering. The tractate then considers the relationship of each component of an offering or of a ritual act to the others (3:5–4:4). In some cases, the absence of one component negates the entire offering or ritual; in others, a ritual or offering may be effective without all of its components. The tractate then turns to the preparation and consumption of grain offerings and other breads brought to the Temple (5:1–7:2). Chapter 8 discusses the proper sources for agricultural products used in the Temple, while chapter 9 discusses measurements of foodstuffs and aspects of presenting offerings. The tenth chapter deals with the *omer*, the offering of new grain brought to the Temple after the beginning of Passover. Chapter 11 focuses on the showbread and the two loaves brought on the Festival of Weeks. The final chapters of the tractate discuss the proper fulfillment of vows to bring voluntary offerings.

Main Ideas

The ritual surrounding the presentation of a grain offering consisted of four steps, parallel to the four steps involved in the presentation of an animal offering. The officiating priest took a handful of the grain offering and placed it in a Temple vessel. He then conveyed it to the altar and burnt it. In most cases, the remainder of the grain offering was consumed by the priests in the Temple precincts.

Throughout the tractate, the Mishnah refers to the practice of burning components of grain offerings on the altar, the last of the four steps that make the offering acceptable and allow the priests to consume the remaining portion of the grain offering (1:1, 1:3-4, 2:1, etc.). The verb used is *qtr*, as distinct from the verbs *srf* and *b'r*, the more common Hebrew verbs for "to burn." The verb *qtr* is also used, both in the Hebrew Bible and in the Mishnah, for the burning of incense as part of a Temple ritual. With the exception of *Menahot* 3:4, which uses a form of the verb *srf*, the verb translated as "burn" in this tractate is always a form of *qtr*, and refers to the ritualized burning of either grain or incense.

A primary concern of these chapters is incorrect designation (believing the offering is for one purpose when in fact it was brought for another) or improper intention (with a mind to eat part of the residue of the grain offering or burn the portion that is intended for the altar outside of the Temple precincts). As with animal sacrifices, in the first case the offering does not fulfill its purpose, although it is valid. In the latter case, improper intention may result in it being invalid (*pasul*) or even desecrated (*piggul*), and anyone who eats it is subject to extirpation (*karet*), a punishment imposed by God rather than a human court. The concern with intention is one of the Mishnah's most distinctive innovations in sacrificial law. Intention is also a major theme in tractate *Zevahim*.

Relationship to Scripture

All of the offerings described in the tractate are mentioned in the Torah, as are the steps taken in the rituals surrounding the offerings.

The Torah discusses two major types of grain offerings. One type is a grain offering that accompanies an animal sacrifice, as follows:

a. voluntary whole burnt offerings and offerings of well-being (Numbers 15:3–13)
b. daily offerings and additional offerings (Numbers 28:3–31).
c. the bull brought when the community sinned unknowingly (Numbers 15:24)
d. the offering of the *nazir* (Numbers 6:14–20)
e. the *omer* offering (Leviticus 23:13)
f. the offering of two loaves of bread (Leviticus 23:17–22)
g. the purification offerings of the one with *tsara'at* (Leviticus 14:10–32)

The offering was made of fine flour and oil; a libation of wine was also included with all of these offerings, except for the bull brought in response to communal sin and the offerings of those with *tsara'at*.

The second type of grain offering is a freestanding offering. Some grain offerings are voluntary, while others are mandated for specific occasions. Four types of voluntary grain offerings are enumerated in Leviticus 2. Grain offerings might also be offered to replace required sacrifices when the person bringing the offering had insufficient funds for the more costly animal or bird offering (Leviticus 5:11). "A grain offering of jealousy" was brought by a woman whose husband suspected her of adultery and took her to the Temple for an ordeal that tested her chastity (Numbers 5). *Menahot* also discusses several other offerings that were made of grain including the showbread (Exodus 25:30), the bread brought with the thank offering (Leviticus 7), and the *omer* (Leviticus 23:9–14).

Tractate Menahot

Chapter One

1:1–3:4 *Actions and Intentions That Invalidate a Grain Offering*

1 All grain offerings from which a handful was taken without their proper designation are valid,
but they do not fulfill the owners' obligation,
except for the sinner's grain offering and the grain offering of jealousy.
The sinner's grain offering and the grain offering of jealousy
from which a handful was taken
without their proper designation,
or which was placed in the utensil or conveyed or burnt
without their proper designation,
or with their proper designation and without their proper designation,
or without their proper designation and with their proper designation—
are invalid.
How is "with their proper designation and without their proper designation"

1:1 *from which a handful was taken*: The taking of a handful of the grain and offering it on the altar is the central cultic act of the grain offering (Leviticus 2:2, 9).

without their proper designation: The officiating priest acts with the belief that the offering is for a purpose other than that intended by the owner. The opening words of this mishnah are almost identical to those of *Zevahim* 1:1. Close parallels are found several times in these two tractates between the laws surrounding grain offerings and those regulating sacrifices.

are valid: May be offered on the altar and consumed by the priests.

but they do not fulfill the owners' obligation: The person who brought the offering must bring another to fulfill the purpose for which he intended the incorrectly designated one.

except for: These are invalid when offered under an incorrect designation.

the sinner's grain offering: Brought in expiation of a sin by a person who could not afford an animal or bird offering (Leviticus 5:11).

the grain offering of jealousy: Brought by a woman suspected of adultery (see *Sotah*, introduction and 2:1; Numbers 5:11–31). The name here reflects the jealousy that causes the husband to subject his wife to the ordeal.

the sinner's grain offering...from which a handful was taken: Compare *Zevahim* 1:4.

with...and without their proper designation: The priest's awareness of the type of offering shifts during the ritual, from the correct awareness to a mistaken belief about the purpose of the offering, or vice versa.

to be understood?
As a sinner's grain offering and then as a voluntary grain offering.
How is "without their proper designation and with their proper designation"
[to be understood]?
As a voluntary grain offering and then as a sinner's grain offering.

2 The law is one and the same for a sinner's grain offering
and any grain offering from which a handful was taken by:
a nonpriest,
an *onen*,
a *tevul yom*,
one lacking vestments,
one lacking atonement,
one whose hands and feet are unwashed,
one uncircumcised,
impure,
sitting,
standing on utensils,
on an animal,
or on his fellow's feet—
he has invalidated it.
If he took a handful with the left hand, he has invalidated it.
Ben Betera says:
Let him put it back, and then take a handful with the right hand.
If he took a handful and it included a pebble, a grain of salt, or a sliver of frankincense,
he has invalidated it,
for they said:

1:2 Compare *Zevahim* 2:1.

nonpriest: Lit. "foreigner."

an onen: A mourner before the burial. Priests are forbidden to officiate while awaiting the funeral of a close relative for whom they are expected to mourn.

a tevul yom: His purification is incomplete until the end of the day and he may not officiate. See *Tevul Yom*, introduction, and Leviticus 22:7.

lacking vestments: A priest must wear the prescribed vestments when officiating; omission of any of the vestments renders his service invalid.

one lacking atonement: Immersion has taken place but some part of the purification ritual has not been performed.

with the left hand: The right hand is preferred for ritual acts unless otherwise specified.

a sliver of frankincense: Frankincense was a key component of many *minhah* offerings (cf. e.g. Leviticus 2:1–2, 15–16; 6:8; and below, 5:3). The frankincense was laid on the offering and produced a "pleasing odor" when the designated portion of the offering was burnt on the altar (Leviticus 2:2). Frankincense is a whitish resin produced by the species of tree known as *Boswellia*. It is a solid substance that was applied to the *minhah* in small amounts.

for they said: A rabbinic tradition. With respect to what has just been said, it is taken to mean that a pebble or some other foreign object makes the handful "lacking." Some commentaries consider the foreign substance to be separating the handful into two.

A handful that is overmuch or lacking is invalid.
How much is overmuch?
When he took an overflowing handful.
And lacking?
When he took it with his fingertips.
How must he do it?
He stretches his fingers over his palm.

3 If he put in too much or too little oil,
or too little frankincense—
it is invalid.
One who takes a handful of a grain offering intending:
to eat the remnants outside,
or an olive's bulk of the remnants outside,
to burn the handful outside,
or an olive's bulk of the handful outside,
or to burn the frankincense outside—
it is invalid, but there is no *karet*.
To eat the remnants the next day,
or an olive's bulk of the remnants the next day,
to burn the handful the next day,
or an olive's bulk of the handful the next day,
or to burn the frankincense the next day—
it is *piggul*, and one is liable for *karet*.
This is the general rule:

1:3 *One who takes...*: *Zevahim* 2:2.

intending to eat: Offerings must be consumed within a certain timeframe and in specific places. If the priest enacts the ritual correctly, but intends to eat portions in the wrong place, the offering becomes invalid. A greater violation is an intention to eat the offering after the permitted time.

remnants: The portion of the grain offering that remains after the handful has been taken and burnt. In most cases, this remaining portion may be eaten by the priests in the Temple precincts and within a fixed period of time.

outside: The *minhah*, as an offering of the highest sanctity, must be consumed within the Temple precincts. Cf. *Zevahim* 14 and *Middot*, introduction.

karet: "Extirpation," from the Hebrew root, *krt*, to cut off. This punishment, incurred by anyone who eats or burns a portion of a grain offering after the permitted time, is in the hands of God. The exact nature of the punishment is unclear and is the subject of discussion by many commentators. See introduction to *Keritot*.

there is no karet: Although the offering has been desecrated and should be burnt, one who eats it does not incur extirpation.

the next day: The handful taken from the grain offering is burnt that day, and the remnants, the portions consumed by the priests, must be eaten that day.

piggul: Lit. "abomination." The designation of some offerings as *piggul* is based on biblical verses (Leviticus 7:18; 19:7), where it refers to parts of the sacrifices left beyond the appropriate time. The Mishnah makes intention at the time of the offering to eat the sacrificial food or to perform a subsequent cultic act after the correct time central to the definition. See *Zevahim* introduction.

the general rule: *Zevahim* 2:3.

Anyone who takes a handful,
puts it in a utensil,
conveys it, or burns it,
intending to eat something that is typically eaten,
or to burn something that is typically burned,
if intending outside its proper place—
it is invalid, but there is no *karet*;
outside its proper time—
it is *piggul*, and one is liable for *karet*,
so long as he offered the permitting element as commanded.
How is "he offered the permitting element as commanded"
[to be understood]?
If he took the handful in silence,
and placed it in the utensil, conveyed it,
and burnt it intending to perform an act[1] outside its proper time,
or he took the handful intending to perform an act outside its proper time,
and placed it in the utensil, conveyed it,[2] and burnt it in silence,
or he took a handful, placed it in the utensil, conveyed it,
and burnt it intending to perform an act outside its proper time—
this is one who "offered the permitting element as commanded."

4 How is "he did not offer the permitting element as commanded"
[to be understood]?
If he took a handful intending to perform an act outside its proper place,
and placed it in the utensil, conveyed it, and burnt it
intending to perform an act outside its proper time;
or he took the handful intending to perform an act outside its proper time,
and placed it in the utensil, conveyed it, and burnt it
intending to perform an act outside its proper place;
or he took a handful, placed it in the utensil, conveyed it, and burnt it
intending to perform an act outside its proper place;
the sinner's grain offering and the grain offering of jealousy

[1] Here and below: "intending to perform an act" added for clarity.
[2] **K** lacks "and burnt it . . . conveyed it," probably due to scribal error.

so long as he offered the permitting element: The steps of the ritual that allow portions of the offering to be consumed were otherwise performed properly. For grain offerings this is the offering of the handful of grain. The rule means that if everything else was *as commanded*, and the only disqualifier was offering the handful with the intention "to perform a cultic act outside the permitted time," *piggul* results.

How is "he offered the permitting?" Zevahim 2:4.

in silence: Without contemplating anything that would render the offering invalid.

1:4 Compare *Zevahim* 2:5.

How is "he did not . . . as commanded?" In the following cases, the offering of the handful (the *permitting element*) was disqualified by the intention to do something outside the proper location. Since its *permitting element* was not *as commanded*, it does not become *piggul* due to intention involving time.

the sinner's grain offering and the grain offering of jealousy: Because offering these *without their proper designation* invalidates them, for these two types of sacrifices this too prevents them from becoming *piggul* due to intention involving time.

from which he took a handful without their proper designation,
and then placed it in a utensil, conveyed it, and burnt it
intending to perform an act outside its proper time,
or he took a handful intending to perform an act outside its proper time,
and then placed it in a utensil, conveyed it, and burnt it
without their proper designation,
or he took a handful, placed it in a utensil, conveyed it,
and burnt it without the proper designation—
this is one "who did not offer the permitting element as commanded."
Intending to eat an olive's bulk outside and an olive's bulk the next day,
an olive's bulk the next day and an olive's bulk outside,
half an olive's bulk outside and half an olive's bulk the next day,
or half an olive's bulk the next day and half an olive's bulk outside,
it is invalid, but there is no *karet.*
R. Judah said:
This is the general rule:
If the intention regarding the time precedes the intention regarding the place,
it is *piggul,* and one is liable for *karet,*
but if the intention regarding the place preceded the intention regarding the time,
it is invalid, but there is no *karet.*
But the Sages say:
Both are invalid, but there is no *karet.*
To eat half an olive's bulk and to burn half an olive's bulk, it is valid,
for eating and burning do not join.

Chapter Two

2 One who takes a handful of a grain offering
intending to eat the remnants or to burn the handful the next day—
R. Yose agrees that this is *piggul* and they are liable for *karet.*
To burn its frankincense the next day—
R. Yose says:
It is invalid,[3] but there is no *karet,*

[3] **K, P**: "It is *piggul.*"

an olive's bulk: This is the amount of food that is significant for performing rituals or engendering liability. At issue here is whether there were two separate inappropriate intentions each directed to a ritually significant bit of the offering. The first, anonymous view (so too the Sages below) rules that *intending... outside* invalidates the sacrifice, so it cannot become *piggul.*

R. Judah asks which one came first.

for eating and burning do not join: Although the intention in both cases was the same disqualifying intention, it was directed at two distinct cultic acts, so the two half-amounts do not combine to make up a disqualifying amount.

but the Sages say:
It is *piggul*, and they are liable for *karet*.
They said to him:
How is this different from a sacrifice?
He said to them:
A sacrifice: its blood, and flesh, and the portions offered on the altar are all of a kind,
while the frankincense is not of the [same kind as the] grain offering.
2 If he slaughtered the two lambs
intending to eat one of the loaves the next day,
or burned two dishes of frankincense
intending to eat one of the rows
[of showbread] the next day[4]—
R. Yose says:
The loaf or the row of showbread that he was thinking of is *piggul*,
and they are liable for *karet*,
and the other is invalid, but there is no *karet*,
but the Sages say:
Both are *piggul*, and they are liable for *karet*.
If one of the loaves or one of the rows of showbread becomes impure—
R. Judah says:
Both of them must be taken out to the place of burning,
for a communal offering cannot be divided,
but the Sages say:
The impure one remains impure, but the pure one may be eaten.
3 The thank offering can render the bread *piggul*,
but the bread cannot render the thank offering *piggul*.
How?

[4] **K** lacks "the next day."

2:1 *while the frankincense is not of the [same kind as the] grain offering*: Although frankincense may be required for some grain offerings, it is not of the substance of the flour the way blood and flesh are parts of the animal. As a result, according to R. Yose, intention to *burn its frankincense the next day* does not make the offering *piggul*. (This may be related to his view of parts of sacrifices in 2:2.)

2:2 *the two lambs*: Brought on the Festival of Weeks. See Leviticus 23:19–20.

one of the loaves: Two loaves of bread were brought with the lambs on the Festival of Weeks. See Leviticus 23:17.

frankincense: Brought with the showbread. See Leviticus 24:7.

rows: Heb. "orders." The arrangement of the showbread on the Temple Table. See Leviticus 24:6–8.

For *R. Yose* the parts of a grain offering can become *piggul* leaving the rest valid.

If one of the loaves . . . becomes impure: An analogous dispute about impurity.

2:3 Intention regarding the grain portion of an animal offering can only make that portion *piggul*. Intention regarding the animal portion disqualifies all of it.

The thank offering: Leviticus 7:12–13. This offering is brought with unleavened loaves, flat cakes, and leavened bread.

If one slaughters the thank offering,
intending to eat from it the next day—
it and the bread are *piggul*;
to eat from the bread the next day—
the bread is *piggul*, but the thank offering is not *piggul*.
The lambs can render the bread *piggul*,
but the bread cannot render the lambs *piggul*.
How?
If one slaughters the lambs,
intending to eat from them the next day—
they and the bread are *piggul*;
intending to eat from the bread the next day—
the bread is *piggul*, but the lambs are not *piggul*.

4 The sacrifice can render the libations *piggul*
once the latter are sanctified in the utensil—
the words of R. Meir,
but the libations cannot render the sacrifice *piggul*.
How?
If one slaughters the sacrifice intending to eat from it the next day—
it and its libations are *piggul*.
To offer the libations the next day—
the libations are *piggul*, but the sacrifice is not *piggul*.

5 If one rendered the handful *piggul* but not the frankincense,
or the frankincense but not the handful—
R. Meir says:
The offering is *piggul*, and they are liable for *karet*,
but the Sages say:
There is no *karet* until he renders the entire permitting element *piggul*.
The Sages agree with R. Meir in the case of the sinner's grain offering
or the grain offering of jealousy,

The lambs: See 2:2.

2:4 *the libations*: Some animal offerings were accompanied by grain offerings as well as libations of wine. This type of grain offering is known as "a grain offering of libations." The word *libations* here refers to both the grain offering and the wine.

once the latter are sanctified in the utensil: Until they are in the offering vessel, they are not impacted by the status of the sacrifice. With the exception of this apparently parenthetical qualification, the logic of 2:4 follows that of 2:3.

2:5 The previous two paragraphs focused on offerings that involve both an animal component and a grain component. This mishnah opens with a discussion of the relationship between multiple components of the grain offering itself. It then returns to the discussion of the connection between animal and grain components of an offering.

rendered the handful piggul but not the frankincense: R. Meir allows either element to disqualify the whole. The Sages only deem the offering *piggul* if both are made invalid by intention. Compare 2:1.

For *permitting element*, see 1:3. Here, the issue is whether the permitting element is itself divided.

The Sages agree: These two grain offerings are not accompanied by frankincense.

that if he rendered the handful *piggul*,
the offering is *piggul*, and one is liable for *karet*,
for the burning of the handful makes it permissible to eat the grain offering.[5]
If he slaughtered one of the lambs intending to eat the two loaves the next day,
or burnt one of the measures intending to eat the two portions the next day—
R. Meir says:
It is *piggul*, and they are liable for *karet*,
but the Sages say:
It is not *piggul*[6] until he renders the entire permitting element *piggul*.
If he slaughtered one of the lambs intending to eat from it the next day—
it is *piggul*, and its fellow is valid;
to eat from the other the next day—
both are valid.

Chapter Three

3 One who takes a handful of a grain offering,
intending to eat something that is not typically eaten,
or to burn something that is not typically burnt,
it is valid.
R. Eliezer deems it invalid.
To eat something that is typically eaten
or to burn something that is typically burnt—
less than an olive's bulk,
the offering is valid.
To eat half an olive's bulk and to burn half an olive's bulk,
the offering is valid,

[5] "Burning of," "to eat the meal offering" added for clarity.

[6] **K**, **P**: "There is no *piggul*."

the burning of the handful makes it permissible: Only after a handful of the grain offering is burnt are the priests permitted to eat the residue.

slaughtered one of the lambs: See 2:2. Only part of the slaughter was done with disqualifying intention to consume all of the grain offering.

measures: Dishes of frankincense.

R. Meir again views the partial disqualification to make the whole *piggul*. *The Sages* require the *entire permitting element*, that is, the slaughter, etc., of both animals or the burning of both bowls of frankincense, to be performed with the wrong intention to make the sacrifice *piggul*.

slaughtered one of the lambs: Here the distinction is between the intention during slaughter regarding the animal being slaughtered and intention regarding the other animal.

3:1 See *Zevahim* 2:3.

intending to eat: With the intention to eat or burn the sacrificial product beyond its proper time or place.

it, the offering, *is valid*: The intention has no impact, since it involved something that is not usually done.

because eating and burning do not join.

2 If he did not:
pour oil on the offerings,
mix,
break up,
salt,
wave,
or bring it near,
or if he broke it up into many pieces,
or he did not anoint them—
they are valid.
If a handful from this offering was intermingled
with a handful from another,
or with a priest's grain offering,
or with the grain offering of the anointed priest,
or with the grain offering that accompanies libations—
it is valid.
R. Judah says:
With the grain offering of the anointed priest
or the grain offering that accompanies libations—
it is invalid,
for the former is a thick mixture while the latter is a thin mixture,
and the former will absorb oil from the latter.

3 Two grain offerings

because eating and burning do not join: See above, 1:4.

3:2 Although the acts listed here are required, their absence does not disqualify the sacrifices.

If he did not pour oil on the offerings: See Leviticus 2:1 and below, 6:3.

mix: The oil with the flour of the offering. See Leviticus 2:4 and below, 6:3.

break up: Some offerings were broken into small pieces. See Leviticus 2:6 and below 6:4.

salt: Grain offerings were salted (Leviticus 2:13).

wave: See Leviticus 8:27 and below, 5:6.

or bring it near: See below, 5:6.

or he did not anoint them: See Leviticus 2:4.

priest's grain offering: Brought by each priest when he begins his service. There is no biblical source for this custom.

the anointed priest: The high priest, who is anointed at his consecration ceremony (Leviticus 8:12). Although Leviticus 6:13 refers to a grain offering brought when the high priest is anointed, the verse includes the word "regular," which led the Sages to rule that the offering was to be made on a daily basis.

grain offering that accompanies libations: Grain offerings were brought, together with libations of wine, with certain sacrifices. See Numbers 15:4–10; 15:24; and 28.

the former will absorb oil from the latter: The voluntary grain offering of the commoner will absorb the excess oil of the other grain offering and become too thin, and leave the other offering too thick.

3:3 Compare the discussion of intermingled sacrifices in *Zevahim* 8.

from which handfuls had not been taken and that were intermingled—
if one can take a handful from each by itself—
they are valid;
but if not—
they are invalid.
A handful that was mixed with [another] grain offering
from which a handful had not been taken,
he should not burn it;
and if he burnt it—
that from which a handful was taken
fulfilled the owners' obligation;
but that from which a handful was not taken
did not fulfill the owners' obligation.
If a handful was mingled with its own remnants,
or with the remnants of another grain offering,
he may not burn it,
but if he burnt it,
the grain offering fulfilled the owners' obligation.
If the handful became impure and he offered it,
the diadem propitiates;
If he went out [of the Temple precincts] and offered it,
the diadem does not propitiate,
for the diadem propitiates for the impure,
but not for that which goes out.
4 If its remnants became impure,
if its remnants were burnt,
or if its remnants were lost—
according to the view[7] of R. Eliezer,
[the handful] is valid,
but according to the view[8] of R. Joshua,
it is invalid.
If it was not placed in a utensil of service,
it is invalid.
R. Simeon deems it valid.
If the handful was burnt in two parts,
it is valid.

[7] Lit. "According to the measure of." Cf. *Hullin* 2:6.

[8] Lit. "According to the measure of."

if one can take a handful from each by itself: The two offerings are still more or less distinct.

he should not burn: One may not burn the mixture.

if he burnt it: Burning the mixture inevitably burns the handful, so the offering from which it was taken is valid.

did not fulfill the owners' obligation: The offering is invalid without the removal and burning of the handful designated for the altar.

the diadem propitiates: The diadem worn by the high priest atones for the sin of offerings brought in impurity (see Exodus 28:36–38).

3:4 *in two parts*: Lit. "twice." According to commentators, the case is one in which the handful is divided into two parts and each is burnt separately.

3:5–4:4 *The Relationship of a Part to the Whole*

5 The handful—
[omission of] a minority prevents the fulfillment of the majority.
The one-tenth of an *ephah*—
a minority prevents the fulfillment of the majority.
Wine—
a minority prevents the fulfillment of the majority.
Oil—
a minority prevents the fulfillment of the majority.
The flour or the oil prevent the fulfillment of one another.
The handful and the frankincense prevent the fulfillment of one another.
6 The two goats of the Day of Atonement—
prevent the fulfillment of one another.
The two lambs of the Festival of Weeks—
prevent the fulfillment of one another.
The two loaves—
prevent the fulfillment of one another.
The two rows—
prevent the fulfillment of one another.
The two dishes of frankincense—
prevent the fulfillment of one another.
The rows and the utensils—
prevent the fulfillment of one another.
The two types in connection with the *nazir*,
the three in connection with the red heifer,

3:5 *Menahot* 3:5–7 deals with rituals and items that are indispensable to successful completion of the ritual; without these, the entire object or ritual is invalid. *Menahot* 4:1–4 deals with situations in which a missing part does not invalidate an object or ritual.

a minority prevents the fulfillment of the majority: The handful must be complete to be ritually efficacious. The same is true of all of the items in this passage; each must be a full measure for the ritual to be efficacious. The amounts or numbers stipulated in the Bible must be present for a ritual to be valid.

prevent the fulfillment of one another: Both must be completed; neither is valid without the other also being present.

3:6 *Menahot* 3:6–7 feature a repeating structure. Each act or ritual mentioned involves multiple elements; and the absence of one element renders the others ineffective or inadequate to work the ritual.

two goats of the Day of Atonement: Leviticus 16:5–9.

two loaves: Of Shavu'ot (Pentecost, Festival of Weeks) (2:2).

two rows of bread; *two dishes* of frankincense. Required for the showbread (2:2).

The rows and utensils: The failure to set out the showbread or the frankincense properly disqualifies the other.

The *nazir* brings two types of bread with his sacrifice. See Numbers 6:15 and above, 3:6.

red heifer: Burnt with cedar wood, hyssop, and crimson stuff. The ashes of the heifer were used in purification from corpse impurity. See Numbers 19:5–6 and *Parah*, introduction.

the four in connection with the thank offering,
the four in connection with the *lulav*,
the four in connection with one who has *tsara'at*—
prevent the fulfillment of one another.
The seven sprinklings of the red heifer—
prevent the fulfillment of one another.
The seven sprinklings between the poles,
and on the curtain,
and on the gold altar—
prevent the fulfillment of one another.

7 The seven branches of the lampstand—
[omission of] one prevents the fulfillment of the others.
Its seven lamps—
one prevents the fulfillment of the others.
The two sections in the *mezuzah*—
one prevents the fulfillment of the other;
even a single letter prevents the fulfillment of them.
The four sections in *tefillin*—
one prevents the fulfillment of the other;
even a single letter prevents the fulfillment of them,
The four fringes—
one prevents the fulfillment of the others,
since the four of them constitute a single commandment.
R. Ishmael said:
The four of them constitute four commandments.

thank offering: This offering includes four types of bread. See Leviticus 7:12–13.

the four in connection with the lulav: The four are held together during the festival of Sukkot: palm, myrtle, willow, and citron. See Leviticus 24:40 and *Sukkah* 3.

one who has tsara'at: Commonly translated "leper." The sacrifice involves two birds, cedar wood, hyssop, and crimson stuff. See Leviticus 14:4 and *Nega'im* 14:1.

red heifer: Numbers 19:4; see *Parah* 12.

poles of the Ark... *curtain*... *gold altar*: These are part of the rite on the Day of Atonement (Leviticus 16:14–15).

3:7 The discussion shifts from rituals to objects with multiple parts.

The seven branches of the lampstand... *Its seven lamps*: Exodus 25:31–37.

The two sections of Deuteronomy 6:4–9 and 11:13–21. The *mezuzah* is a capsule placed in or on the doorpost and contains the text of these two sections written on parchment.

single letter: Lit. "a single writing."

four sections in tefillin: Deuteronomy 6:4–9 and 11:13–21 as in the *mezuzah*, as well as Exodus 13:10–13, and 11–16. *Tefillin* are leather boxes with scriptural portions inside, worn on the head and on the arm; often rendered "phylacteries."

The four fringes, or *tsitsit*. Attached to the corners of a garment and worn in fulfillment of Numbers 15:37–39. In keeping with Numbers 15:38, the fringes included a single strand of blue.

four commandments: Each is distinct and independent, so lacking one fringe does not prevent the completion of the others.

Chapter Four

4 [Omission of] the blue does not prevent fulfillment of the white,
nor does the white prevent fulfillment of the blue.
The *tefillin* of the hand does not prevent fulfillment of the head,
nor does that of the head prevent fulfillment of the hand.
The flour and the oil do not prevent fulfillment of the wine,
nor does the wine prevent fulfillment of them.
Applications of blood on the outer altar do not[9] prevent the others.
2 The bulls, the rams, and the lambs do not prevent one another;
R. Simeon says:
If they had many[10] bulls, but they did not have sufficient libations,
they should bring one bull and its libations,
but they should not offer all of them without libations.
3 [Omission of] the bull, the rams, the lambs, and the goat
does not prevent fulfillment of the bread,
nor does the bread prevent fulfillment of them.
The bread prevents fulfillment of the lambs,
but the lambs do not prevent fulfillment of the bread—
the words of R. Aqiva.
Simeon b. Nanas said:

[9] **L** lacks "not." [10] **K** lacks "many."

4:1–4 discuss elements of sacrifice and sacred objects that do not prevent fulfillment of the commandment. Although less tightly composed than 3:6–7, this section has repeating phrases that link the cases (as well as the statements of R. Simeon in 4:2–4). It also refers to some of the same cases discussed in 3:6–7.

4:1 *blue…white*, of the *tsitsit* or "fringes" (3:7). Fringes that are wholly white or wholly blue do not invalidate the performance of the commandment.

The tefillin of the hand: See 3:7. If one wears only one *tefillah*, he has still performed a commandment.

flour…oil…wine: For wine brought with grain offerings see 3:2.

Applications of blood: Lit. "puttings," "givings." See *Zevahim* 5:3–7, and, for this rule, 4:1.

outer altar: See *Tamid* introduction.

4:2 *The bulls, the rams, and the lambs*: Offered on the New Moon and the festivals (Numbers 28:11ff. and Leviticus 23:18).

R. Simeon says: He believes that each bull must be offered with its libations and grain offerings. It is therefore preferable to offer one bull with the accompanying components than to offer many without the prescribed libations and grain offerings.

4:3 *the bull, the rams, the lambs, and the goat*: Offered on the Festival of Weeks with the loaves (Leviticus 23:17–19 and above, 3:6).

The bread prevents fulfillment of the lambs: Two additional animals brought together with the loaves (Leviticus 23:20).

It is not so; rather,
the lambs prevent fulfillment of the bread,
but the bread does not prevent fulfillment of the lambs,
for we find that when Israel was in the wilderness for forty years
they offered lambs without bread;
so too here they may offer lambs without bread.
R. Simeon said:
The *halakhah* follows Ben Nanas, but not for the reason he gave.
For everything that is mentioned in Numbers[11] was offered in the wilderness,
but not everything that was mentioned in Leviticus[12] was offered in the wilderness;
when they came to the Land, they offered these and those.
Why do I say that they may offer lambs without bread?
Because the lambs are permitting elements for themselves, without the bread,[13]
but as for the bread without the lambs,
I have no permitting elements for it.

4 [Omission of] continual offerings does not prevent fulfillment of the additional offerings,
nor do the additional offerings prevent fulfillment of the continual offerings,
nor does one of the additional offerings prevent fulfillment of another.
If they did not offer the lamb in the morning, they may offer it in the afternoon.
R. Simeon said:
When?
At a time when they are under duress or make an error,
but if they intentionally did not offer the lamb in the morning,
they may not offer the one in the afternoon.
If they did not burn the incense in the morning, they may burn it in the afternoon.
R. Simeon said:
All of the incense is burnt in the afternoon.

[11] Lit. "The Fifth of the Censuses." [12] Lit. "Law of the Priests."
[13] **K** lacks "the bread;" **P** lacks "without the bread."

they offered lambs without bread: Based on an interpretation of Leviticus 23:17, *You shall bring from your settlements two loaves*, Simeon b. Nanas claims that bread was not part of the offerings made before the Israelites entered the land of Canaan.

not for the reason he gave: Since there were different sacrificial practices before and after entering the land, practice in the wilderness is not evidence for later practice.

Because the lambs are permitting elements for themselves: Once the blood of an offering is dashed on the altar, the meat may be eaten. There is no ritual offering connected with the loaves and thus they may not be eaten unless the blood of the accompanying lambs has been offered. For *permitting elements* see 1:3.

4:4 *continual offerings*: The sacrifices offered daily, in the morning and the afternoon. *Tamid*, introduction, and Numbers 28:3–8.

the additional offerings: Offered on the Sabbath, New Moons, and festivals.

they may offer it in the afternoon: Failure to sacrifice the daily offering of the morning does not impact the second daily offering, the one sacrificed in the afternoon. This dispute between the anonymous first view in the Mishnah and R. Simeon reflects differing views on whether the two daily offerings of lambs or incense are indispensable to each other, the theme running through this section.

For they dedicate the gold altar only through the incense,
and the altar of the burnt offering only through the morning continual offering,
and the table only through the weekly showbread,
and the lampstand only through its seven lamps in the afternoon.

4:5 *The Daily Grain Offering of the High Priest*

5 The cakes of the high priest are not brought separately;
rather he brings a full tenth and divides it in half,
and offers half in the morning and half in the afternoon.
And if a priest offered half in the morning and died,
and they appoint another priest in his place—
the latter does not bring the remaining half-tenth from his house,
nor the half-tenth of the first priest;
rather he brings a full tenth,
and divides it in half,
and offers half,
and the remaining half is destroyed.
Thus two halves are offered and two halves are destroyed.
If they did not appoint another priest,
from whose property was the twilight portion offered?
R. Simeon[14] says:
From that of the community.
R. Judah[15] says:
From that of the heirs,
and it was offered whole.

[14] K: "R. Judah." [15] K: "R. Simeon."

For they dedicate: The acts listed here "dedicate" the Temple vessels for their use that day; that is, these are the first uses of these vessels during that period. Therefore, these acts must be performed if additional offerings or acts are to take place afterward. The relationship between this statement and the views expressed earlier in the passage are not entirely clear. It appears to explain why if incense was not brought in the morning, it is nonetheless brought in the afternoon: it is the afternoon offering that "dedicates" the incense altar. However, by the same logic, if the continual offering of the morning was not brought, the altar was never dedicated for the day, and one cannot bring the afternoon offering (apparently, in accord with neither the anonymous first view nor R. Simeon above).

4:5 *The cakes of the high priest*: Offered daily (Leviticus 6:13–15). See annotation to *anointed priest*, 3:2.

rather he brings a full tenth of an *ephah*. Leviticus 6:13 speaks of the priest bringing one tenth of an *ephah*, rather than two half-tenths. This is taken to mean that a whole measure of grain is brought and subsequently divided.

that of the heirs: Of the deceased high priest. The assumption appears to be that the heirs of the last high priest continue to owe the obligation of bringing the sacrifice. By contrast, in the absence of a high priest, R. Simeon holds the entire community responsible for this obligation.

whole: There was no high priest to divide it so the grain offering of the high priest was offered whole.

Chapter Five

5:1–9 *Grain Offerings*

5 All grain offerings are offered unleavened,
except for the leavened cakes of the thank offering and the two loaves,
which are leavened.
R. Meir says:
The leaven[16] for them is set aside from them and causes them to rise.
R. Judah says:
But that is not the best way;[17]
Rather, leaven is brought and placed in the measure,
and the measure is then filled with flour.
They said to him:
But that would result in a lesser or greater measure.
2 All grain offerings are kneaded in tepid water,
and he watches them so that they do not become leavened.
If the remnants became leavened,
he transgresses a negative commandment,
as it is said: *No grain offering that you offer to the Lord shall be made with leaven.*
And one is liable for its kneading,
rolling,
and baking.

[16] **K** adds "an olive-sized bit."
[17] **K** has "attached" instead of "best," resulting from transposition of two letters.

5:1 *unleavened*: See Leviticus 2:11.

leavened cakes: Brought with the thank offering, 7:1 below, and Leviticus 7:13.

two loaves: See Leviticus 23:17 and *Menahot* 2:2, 3:6, and 11.

The leaven for them is set aside from them: The proper amount of flour is measured, and then a portion is taken, made into dough, and leavened, then that fermented dough is used to raise the rest of the dough. The intention is to ensure that the amount of flour does not exceed the amount specified in the Torah.

R. Judah says: He proposes a better way to ensure the proper amount of flour in the offering. The dispute is not about what actually happened but what should have been done.

lesser or greater measure: The strength of and the amount of moisture of the "starter" placed in the measuring utensil impacts its volume and that of the flour in it, which affects whether the full measure is attained or exceeded.

5:2 *No grain offering*: Leviticus 2:11.

liable for its kneading, rolling, and baking: If the dough becomes leavened, any and each of these acts becomes a transgression.

3 There are [grain offerings] that require:
oil and frankincense,
oil but not frankincense,
frankincense but not oil,
and neither oil nor frankincense.
These require oil and frankincense:
the fine-flour grain offering,
the grain offering on a griddle,
the grain offering in a pan,
the loaves,
the flat cakes,
the grain offering of priests,
the grain offering of the anointed priest,
the grain offering of gentiles,
the grain offering of women,
and the *omer*.
The grain offering for libations requires oil,
but does not require frankincense.
The showbread requires frankincense,
but does not require oil.
The two loaves,
the sinner's grain offering,
and the grain offering of jealousy—
neither oil nor frankincense.
4 And he is liable for the oil by itself and for the frankincense by itself.
If he applied oil,

5:3 *There are [grain offerings]*: Compare 5:5–6.

the fine-flour grain offering: Leviticus 2:1.

the grain offering on a griddle... the flat cakes: Leviticus 2:4–7. The rabbis derived the requirement for frankincense on these offerings from Leviticus 2:1.

the grain offering of priests: The previous offerings mentioned in this mishnah if brought by a priest.

the grain offering of the anointed priest: See 4:5.

the grain offering of gentiles: Voluntary offerings were accepted from non-Jews.

the grain offering of women: Offerings brought by women were subject to the same requirements as those brought by men.

the omer: A measure of new grain brought after Passover. See chapter 10.

The grain offering for libations: See above, 3:2. These were brought with animal sacrifices, and required oil and no frankincense.

showbread: The loaves arrayed on the Table in the Temple; Leviticus 24:5–9 and *Menahot* 11.

two loaves: See Leviticus 23:17 and *Menahot* 2:2; 3:6; and 11.

sinner's grain offering and the grain offering of jealousy: See 1:1.

5:4 *liable for the oil by itself and for the frankincense by itself*: If one puts both substances into a grain offering requiring neither, one has committed two transgressions.

he makes it invalid;
frankincense,
he should pluck it off.
If he applied oil to the remnants,
he has not transgressed a negative commandment.
If he put utensil on top of utensil,
he has not made it invalid.

5 There are [grain offerings] that require:
presentation but not waving,
waving but not presentation,
presentation and waving,[18]
and neither waving nor presentation.
These require presentation but do not require waving:
the fine-flour grain offering,
the grain offering on a griddle,
the grain offering in a pan,
the loaves,
the flat cakes,
the grain offering of priests,
the grain offering of the anointed priest,
the grain offering of gentiles,
the grain offering of women,
and the grain offering of the sinner.
R. Simeon says:
The grain offering of priests and the grain offering of the anointed priest—
they do not have presentation,
because there is no handful taken from them,[19]
and any time there is no handful taken,[20]
there is no presentation.

6 These require waving but do not require presentation:
the *log* of oil for the one with *tsara'at* and his guilt offering,

[18] **P** lacks "presentation and waving." [19] **K**, **P**: "because there is no waving."
[20] **K**, **P**: "there is no waving."

utensil on top of utensil: A vessel containing oil or frankincense atop a vessel containing the grain offering. This does not count as an application of oil.

5:5 *There are [grain offerings]*: Cf. 5:3–4.

waving: The procedure for ceremonial waving is described in 5:6.

presentation: The offering is presented to the priest who then takes it to the altar (Leviticus 2:8).

fine-flour grain offering…sinner: For this list, see 5:3.

R. Simeon: See 6:4. The reading found in **K** and **P** (see n. 19) links the absence of presentation to the absence of waving. This is problematic, since the earlier part of the passage claims there are offerings that require presentation without waving.

5:6 *the one with tsara'at*: Leviticus 14:12.

and the firstfruits in accordance with the words of R. Eliezer b. Jacob,
the innards of an individual's offerings of well-being,
their breast and thigh—
whether of men or of women of Israel, but not of others—
the two loaves,
and the two lambs of the Festival of Weeks.
How does he perform it?
He places the two loaves on top of the two lambs[21] and places his hands underneath,
moving back and forth, up and down,
as it is said, *which was waved and lifted.*
Waving was done on the east,
and presentation on the west,
and waving precedes presentation.
The *omer* and the grain offering of jealousy require waving and presentation.
The showbread and the grain offering for libations,
neither waving nor presentation.

7 R. Simeon says:
Three kinds of offerings[22] require three commanded acts—
each requires two but lacks the third[23]—
and they are:
(1) individual offerings of well-being,
(2) communal offerings of well-being,
and (3) the guilt offering of the one with *tsara'at.*
Individual sacrifices of well-being require:

[21] K adds "and the breast and thigh on top of them, and the two kidneys and the protuberances of the liver on top of them. If there is bread, he places the bread."
[22] Heb. "Three kinds."
[23] Lit. "Two for each and every one, and the third does not apply to them."

firstfruits in accordance with...: That is, R. Eliezer b. Jacob requires waving of the firstfruits (as at *Bikkurim* 3:6), although others do not.

innards: The portions of the offering of well-being offered on the altar. See Leviticus 7:30.

breast and thigh: Portions of the well-being offering given to the priest, Leviticus 7:31–34.

others: Non-Jews.

How does he perform the waving?

which was waved and lifted: Exodus 29:27.

east... west: Sides of the altar. See introduction and chapter 3 of *Middot*, and *Zevahim* 5.

omer: See 10:1–9 and "Money, Weights, and Measures."

grain offering of jealousy: See 1:1.

5:7 *Three kinds... third*: Between them, the three types of offerings have three required acts, but no one type has all three: laying of hands, waving the offering while it is alive, waving the sacrifice after slaughter.

individual offerings of well-being: Leviticus 3.

communal offerings of well-being: Leviticus 23:19–20.

the guilt-offering of one with tsara'at: Leviticus 14:12.

the laying on of hands while living,
waving when slaughtered,
but no waving while living.
Communal sacrifices of well-being require:
waving while living and when slaughtered,
but no laying on of hands.
The guilt offering of the one with *tsara'at* requires:
laying on of hands and waving while living,
but no waving when slaughtered.

8 One who says: "I hereby pledge a grain offering on a griddle,"[24]
may not bring it in a pan;
"In a pan,"
he may not bring it on a griddle.
What is the difference between a griddle and a pan?
Only that a pan has a cover and a griddle does not—
the words of R. Yose the Galilean.
R. Hananiah[25] b. Gamaliel says:
A griddle is deep and its contents move,
while the pan is flat and its contents are hard.

9 One who says: "I hereby pledge an offering in an oven,"[26]
may not bring:
one baked in a stove,
or baked on hot bricks,
or baked in the kettles of nomads.[27]
R. Judah says:
If he wants, he may bring one baked in a stove.
"I hereby pledge[28] a grain offering that is baked,"
he may not bring half in loaves and half in flat cakes.
R. Simeon permits it,
since it is one offering.

[24] Lit. "One on a griddle is upon me."
[25] **K**: "R. Nehemiah b. Gamaliel."
[26] Lit. "One in an oven is upon me."
[27] Lit. "Arabs."
[28] Lit. "Is upon me."

5:8 *"I hereby pledge"*: The expression (see n. 24) implies a vow to bring a sacrifice of the kind specified. See *Nedarim*, introduction.

and its contents move: The contents soak in the oil at the bottom of the griddle and have the consistency of a batter. The explanation, that contents on a griddle move (*rohashim*) is either a pun or an etymological note on the word for griddle (*marheshet*).

5:9 *"I hereby pledge"*: See 5:8.

stove: A small oven that holds only one pot.

bricks: Or tiles.

kettles of nomads: See *Kelim* 5:10.

nomads: Lit. "Arabs." The term "Arab" had varied meanings in both Jewish and non-Jewish sources of this period.

half in loaves and half in flat cakes: This is prohibited because all ten portions (6:5) should be the same.

R. Simeon permits it: Since Leviticus 2:4 mentions both loaves and flat cakes in discussing a baked offering.

Chapter Six

6:1–5 *Consumption of Grain Offerings*

6 These are the grain offerings that have a handful taken,
and whose remnants belong to the priests:
the fine-flour grain offering,
the grain offering in a pan,
the grain offering on a griddle,
the loaves,
the flat cakes,
grain offerings of gentiles,
grain offerings of women,
the *omer*,
the sinner's grain offering,
and the grain offering of jealousy.
R. Simeon says:
The sinner's grain offering of a priest:
a handful was taken,
and the handful and the remnants were each offered separately.
2 The grain offering of priests,
the grain offering of the anointed priest,
and the grain offering with libations—
go entirely to the altar,
and none to the priests.
In this, the power of the altar is greater than the power of the priests.
The two loaves and the showbread go entirely to the priests,
and none to the altar.
In this, the power of the priests is greater than the power of the altar.
3 All grain offerings made in a utensil require three applications of oil:
(1) pouring,
(2) mixing,

6:1 *fine-flour grain offering... jealousy*: For this list, see 5:3.

the sinner's grain offering of a priest: If a priest is required to bring a grain offering for a sin. According to R. Simeon, priests cannot eat the residue of a grain offering brought by a priest. The residue must be burnt but should not be burnt together with the handful. Compare R. Simeon in 5:3.

6:2 *grain offering of priests... to the altar*: See Leviticus 6:15; Numbers 15:4–10.

power of the altar: The altar's "claim" to the products of the sacrifice: since these sacrifices are entirely consumed on the altar, the *power of the altar is greater*. In what follows, there are two cases in which *the power of the priests is greater*. These are all situations in which the "claims" of the priests and the altar are absolute, in contrast to the many instances in which each party receives a portion of the offering.

6:3 *pouring*: See Leviticus 2:6.

mixing: See Leviticus 2:5.

and (3) applying oil in the utensil before they are made.
As loaves they are mixed with oil—[29]
the words of Rabbi;
but the Sages say:
While fine flour.
Loaves require mixing,
and those in the form of flat cakes are anointed.
How does he anoint them?
In the shape of [the Greek letter] *chi*.
The remainder of the oil can be eaten by the priests.

4 All grain offerings made in a utensil must be broken into pieces.
An Israelite's grain offering—
he folds it over once and then again,[30]
and divides it.
The grain offering of priests—
he folds it over once and then again,
but does not divide it.
The grain offering of the anointed priest—
he would not fold over.[31]
R. Simeon says:
The grain offering of priests and that of the anointed priest
have no breaking into pieces,
because no handful was taken from them,
and any offering from which a handful is not taken is not broken into pieces.[32]
And all of the pieces are the size of an olive's bulk.

5 All grain offerings require:
three hundred of rubbing
and five hundred of pounding.
Rubbing and pounding are done to wheat.
R. Yose says:
Even[33] to dough.

[29] Lit. "And the loaves, he mixes them." [30] Lit. "folds it once into two and two into four."
[31] **K**, **P**: "he would fold over."
[32] **P**: "any offering which was not broken into pieces did not have a handful taken from it."
[33] **P** lacks "even."

applying: Derived from Leviticus 2:7.

Rabbi: When the title is used without a proper name, it refers to Rabbi Judah the Patriarch.

[the Greek letter] chi: For the use of Greek letters cf. *Sheqalim* 3:2.

6:4 *once and then again*: See n. 30. This is understood as fulfilling Leviticus 2:6, which requires that the grain offering prepared on a griddle be "broken into bits." The rabbis based the requirement for four parts on the verse's inclusion of a verb and noun with the same root.

R. Simeon says: The grain offerings of priests are wholly burned on the altar; therefore no handful is taken.

6:5 *Rubbing...pounding*: Abrading or working with the hand, and pounding with the palm of the hand or a utensil. The commentators assume these acts are performed on the grain, presumably to remove the husks. R. Yose associates these acts with dough, presumably to shape it.

All grain offerings come in batches of ten,
except for the showbread and the cakes of the high priest,
which come in batches of twelve—
the words of R. Judah.
R. Meir says:
All come in batches of twelve,
except for the loaves of the thank offering and those for the *nazir*,
which come in batches of ten.

6:6–7 *Sifting the Grain Offerings*

6 The *omer* was one tenth derived from three *se'ah*;
the two loaves, two tenths derived from three *se'ah*;
the showbread, twenty-four tenths derived from twenty-four *se'ah*.
7 [Grain for] the *omer* was sifted in thirteen sifters,
the two loaves in twelve,
and the showbread in eleven.
R. Simeon says:
There was no fixed number;
rather, one would bring fine flour sifted as much as needed,
as it is said: *You shall take fine flour and bake it*[34]—
it should be sifted as much as needed.

Chapter Seven

7:1–2 *The Composition of Grain Offerings and Breads*

7 The bread that accompanied the thank offering consisted of[35] five Jerusalemite *se'ah*,

[34] **K** adds "two piles."
[35] Heb. "The thank offering would come."

All grain offerings… ten: That is, offerings that are brought as formed loaves or cakes.

nazir: Numbers 6:15 and above, 3:6.

6:6 *omer*: See: 10:1–9.

one tenth derived from three se'ah: Through a process of sifting (6:7).

se'ah: The *omer* was one-thirtieth of the volume of the *se'ah*.

the two loaves, two tenths: See Leviticus 23:17.

the showbread, twenty-four tenths: See Leviticus 24:5.

6:7 *You shall take fine flour and bake it*: Leviticus 24:5. R. Simeon understands the verse to require that the flour be sifted until it is sufficiently fine, rather than indicating a fixed number of siftings.

which are six wilderness *se'ah*:
this is two *ephah*—
an *ephah* being three *se'ah*—
which is twenty tenths-of-*ephah*—
ten for what is leavened and ten for what is unleavened.
Ten for what is leavened—
a tenth-of-*ephah*[36] for each loaf.
And ten for what is unleavened—
and there are three kinds of unleavened offering:
(1) loaves,
(2) flat cakes,
and (3) soaked cakes.
There were thus three and a third[37] tenths-of-*ephah* for each type,
three loaves to a tenth.
According to the Jerusalem measure, there were thirty *qav*—
fifteen for that which was leavened and fifteen for that which was unleavened.
Fifteen for what is leavened—
one and a half *qav* for each loaf.
And fifteen for what is unleavened—
and there are three kinds of unleavened offering:
(1) loaves,
(2) flat cakes,
and (3) soaked cakes.
There were thus five[38] *qav* for each type,
two loaves to a *qav*.

2 The bread brought with the consecration offering was[39] similar
to the unleavened portion of the thank offering:
loaves,
flat cakes,
and soaked cakes.
The bread brought with the *nazir*'s offering

[36] K: "ten." [37] K: "three." [38] K lacks "five." [39] Heb. "The consecration would come."

7:1 The compressed wording makes the beginning of this mishnah difficult to translate literally. The passage presents two calculations, using two different sets of measurements. The first is based on the wilderness standard, i.e. the one used by the Torah for the Israelites in the wilderness, which has *ephah*, divided into *se'ah* as well as tenths. The second is the Jerusalem measure, which is the system of measurement the Mishnah uses conventionally. This system has a larger *se'ah*, divided into *qav*.

According to the *wilderness* standard two *ephah* = six *se'ah* = twenty tenths-of-*ephah*. According to the *Jerusalem measure*, that same *ephah* = five larger *se'ah* [each twenty percent larger than the smaller *se'ah*] = thirty *qav*. Each *qav* is two-thirds of a tenth-of-*ephah*.

an ephah being three se'ah, according to the wilderness *se'ah*.

twenty tenths-of-ephah: The measure is called *isaron*, "tenth."

leavened…unleavened: See 5:1.

7:2 *the consecration*: Of Aaron and his sons as priests. See Leviticus 8:2, 26.

soaked cakes: Cakes soaked in oil.

was[40] similar to two parts of the thank offering:
loaves and flat cakes,
but no soaked cakes.
There were thus ten *qav* using the Jerusalem measure,
which is six tenths-of-*ephah* and two thirds.[41]
And he would take a tenth of each as *terumah*,
as it is written:
From this he shall offer one of each kind of offering as terumah to the Lord—
one—he should not take a broken one,
of each kind of offering—
that each offering should be equal,
and that one should not take from one offering for another;
it shall go to the priest who dashes the blood of the offering of well-being—
and the remainder shall be eaten by the owners.[42]

7:3–4 *Grain Offerings and Bread Brought with Animal Offerings*

3 If one slaughters the thank offering inside
and its bread is outside the wall—
the bread is not sanctified.
If he slaughtered it before the crust of the bread formed in the oven,
even if all but one of them formed a crust—
the bread is not sanctified.
If he slaughtered it intending outside its time or outside its place,
the bread is sanctified.
If he slaughtered it and it was found to be *terefah*,
the bread is not sanctified.
If he slaughtered it and it was discovered to be blemished,
R. Eliezer says:
It is sanctified;
but the Sages say:
It is not sanctified.

[40] Heb. "The *nazir*'s would come." [41] Perhaps "and two additions"? [42] K: "the priests."

which is six...: According the units of the wilderness measure (7:1).

And he would take...from each: Lit. "from all of them." This returns to the thank offering.

terumah: A portion set aside for the priest.

From this he shall offer: Leviticus 7:14.

7:3 *inside...outside*: See *Zevahim* 13:1–14:2.

intending outside its time or...place: Intending to perform an essential ritual act outside the proper time or space. See 1:3–4 and the passages from *Zevahim* cited there.

found to be terefah: An animal whose slaughtering itself was defective, or which was found after slaughtering to have disqualifying injuries or disease. See *Zevahim* 7:6, 9:2–3; *Hullin* 2:3.

If he slaughtered it without its proper designation,
and likewise the ram of consecration,
and likewise the two sheep of the Festival of Weeks without their proper designation—
the bread is not sanctified.

4 Libations that were sanctified through a utensil,
and then the sacrifice was found to be invalid—
if there is another sacrifice at hand,
they should offer them with it;
but if not—
they are made invalid through being left overnight.
The offspring of a thank offering,
or an animal exchanged for it,
or one who sets aside an animal as a thank offering and it was lost,
and he designates another in its place[43]—
none of these require bread,
as it is said: *He shall offer together with the sacrifice of thanksgiving unleavened cakes*—
the thank offering requires bread,
but neither its offspring,
nor that which is exchanged for it,
nor its substitute
requires bread.

7:5–6 *The Fulfillment of a Vow to Bring an Offering*

5 One who says:
"I hereby pledge a thank offering,"

[43] **K** lacks "as a thank offering . . . designates."

proper designation: See 1:1–2, and the passages from *Zevahim* cited there.

7:4 *Libations*: Grain offerings brought with liquid libations.

sanctified in the utensil: Above, 2:4.

offer them with it: Offer the libations and grain offerings with the other sacrifice.

they are made invalid: The grain offering cannot be eaten unless the sacrifice it accompanies is offered. Therefore in this case, the grain offering must left to become invalid.

being left overnight: Grain offerings can be consumed only on the day they are offered. The next day, anything that remains of the offering must be burnt.

offspring: The mother of the offspring was already dedicated as a sacrifice when this animal was born, so it was born in a state of dedication.

an animal exchanged for it: If the dedicator states the intention to substitute an animal for one he has already designated as an offering, both become dedicated property (Leviticus 27:9–10; *Temurah*, introduction).

lost, and subsequently found. The original animal retains its sacred status.

He shall offer together with the sacrifice of thanksgiving unleavened cakes: Leviticus 7:12.

7:5 *"I hereby pledge"*: For the expression see 5:7. The principle, spelled out in 7:6, is that obligatory sacrifices (and vows are considered a sacrifice for which one has obligated oneself) may be brought exclusively from

must bring it and its bread from nonsacral property;
"A thank offering from nonsacral property and its bread from tithes"—
he must bring its bread from nonsacral property;
"A thank offering from tithes and its bread from nonsacral property"—
he may bring;
"A thank offering and its bread from tithes,"
he may bring.
But he may not bring it from wheat that is second tithe,
only from coins of second tithe.

6 From what biblical verse do we learn[44] that one who says:
"I hereby pledge a thank offering,"
may only bring it from nonsacral property?
Since it is said:
And you shall sacrifice a Passover offering from herds or cattle to the Lord your God—
but is not the Passover offering brought only from sheep or goats?
If so, why does it say, *herds or cattle*?
To make an analogy between any animal
that is brought from herds or cattle
and the Passover offering:
just as the Passover offering, which is an obligatory offering,
may be brought only from nonsacral property,
so too any obligatory offering
may be brought only from nonsacral property.
Therefore, one who says:
"I hereby pledge a thank offering,"[45]
Or "I hereby pledge a well-being offering,"
since they are obligatory offerings,
they may only be brought from nonsacral property.[46]
And all libations may be brought only from nonsacral property.

[44] Lit. "whence." [45] **K** lacks "Therefore, one who says, "I hereby pledge a thank offering."
[46] **P** lacks this sentence.

unsanctified property. This mishnah considers cases when the one making the offering specifies the source of parts of the sacrifice as *tithe*.

"*its bread from tithes...from nonsacral property*": Because the bread is brought on account of the *thank offering*, it, like the offering, must still come from nonsacral property despite the specification of the one making the offering.

The *tithe* referred to here is the one described in Deuteronomy 14:22–26, known as the second tithe. It was to be brought to Jerusalem and eaten there. See *Ma'aser Sheni*, introduction.

"*thank offering from tithes... bread from nonsacral property*": Since the one making the offering specified *nonsacral* grain for the *bread*, *he may bring* the bread as specified.

only from coins of second tithe: In the case where the bread could come as second *tithes*, the person must use not use actual second-tithe grain, but funds from the redemption of second tithes (Deuteronomy 14:24–26). In this way, both the animal and the grain would be bought with second tithe funds.

7:6 *And you shall sacrifice a Passover offering*: Deuteronomy 16:2. The exegesis on the verse focuses on the seemingly unnecessary mention of cattle. This word, argues the exegete, is included to draw a parallel between the Passover offering and all other obligatory offerings, proving that all such offerings, like the Passover offering, must come from unconsecrated property.

since they are obligatory: They become obligatory as the result of the person's vow.

Chapter Eight

8:1–3 *Proper Sources for Foodstuffs Used in Offerings*

8 All offerings, communal and individual,
may come from the Land or outside the Land,
from produce new or old,
except for the *omer* and the two loaves,
which may come only from new and from the Land.
And all of them must come from choice produce.
What is choice?
Mikhmas and Mezonihah are the foremost choice[47] for fine flour.
The second to these: Hafarayim in the Valley.
All lands are valid,
but they used to bring it from these.
2 One does not bring grain from fields that require fertilizer,[48]
nor from fields that require watering,
nor from fields that contain trees,
but if he brought—
it is valid.
How does he do it?
He plows it one year,
and in the following year, sows it seventy days before Passover,
and it produces a great deal of fine flour.
How does he check it?
The treasurer puts his hand into it;
if he discovered particles,
it is unfit until it was sifted,

[47] Lit. "alpha." [48] Lit. "dung fields."

8:1 *offerings*: Grain offerings.

the Land: The ritual borders of Israel. See Numbers 34:1–15; and *Shevi'it* 6:1; *Hallah* 4:8.

new or old: Produce of the most recent harvest, or that of previous years.

omer (5:3)…*two loaves* (2:2): The *omer* permitted the new grain to be used.

Mikhmas: A town in the territory of Benjamin, north of Jerusalem. See 1 Samuel 13.

Mezonihah: Zanoah, a town in the territory of Judah, southwest of Jerusalem. See Joshua 15:34.

the foremost choice: The Mishnah here uses *alpha*, the first letter of the Greek alphabet to indicate "A-list" produce.

Hafarayim: In the territory of Issachar, in the Lower Galilee. See Joshua 19:19.

8:2 *How does he do it?* Prepare a field to grow grain that will produce fine flour for the Temple.

He plows it one year, but leaves the field unplanted.

check it: The flour.

and if there were worms—
it is unfit.
3 Tekoa is the foremost choice[49] for oil.
Abba Saul says:
Second to it is Regev on the other side of the Jordan.
All lands are valid,
but they used to bring it from these.
One does not bring oil from fields that require fertilizer,[50]
nor from fields that require watering,
nor from trees that had other plants sown among them,
but if he brought—
it is valid.
One does not bring oil made from unripe olives,
and if he brought it—
it is invalid.
One does not bring oil from shriveled olives that were soaked in water,
nor from pickled olives,
nor from overcooked olives,
and if he brought it—
it is invalid.

8:4–5 *Preparation of Oil for Temple Use*

4 There are three grades of olive,
and each has three grades of oil.[51]
The first grade of olive:
He gathers from the top of the tree,
crushes them,
and puts them in a basket—
R. Judah says:
Around the sides of the basket—
this is the first grade of oil.
He presses them under the beam—
R. Judah says:
Under stones—
this is the second grade of oil.

[49] Lit. "alpha." [50] Lit. "dung fields." [51] Heb. "three olives," "three oils."

8:3 *Tekoa*: A town between Jerusalem and Hebron. See 2 Samuel 14:2.

Regev: Possibly the Argov region in Transjordan. See Deuteronomy 3:4.

shriveled olives that were soaked in water: To extract the oil.

8:4 *three grades of olive . . . three grades of oil*: A total of nine grades of oil based on the quality of the olives and on process.

puts them in a basket: The oil drips from the olives in the basket into a collecting basin.

He grinds and presses them again,
this is the third grade of oil.
The first grade of oil was for the lampstand,
and the rest for grain offerings.
The second grade of olive:
He lays the olives on the top of the roof,
crushes them,
and puts them in a basket.
R. Judah says:
Around the sides of the basket—
this is the first grade of oil.
He presses them under the beam—
R. Judah says:
Under stones—
this is the second grade of oil.
He grinds and presses them again—
this is the third grade of oil.
The first grade of oil was for the lampstand,
and the rest were for grain offerings.
The third grade of olive:
He stores them in containers inside the house until they ripen,
then brings them up and dries them on the roof,
then crushes them,
and puts them in the basket—
R. Judah says:
Around the sides of a basket—
this is the first grade of oil.
He presses them under the beam—
R. Judah says:
Under stones—
this is the second grade of oil.
One grinds and presses them again—
this is the third grade of oil.
The first grade of oil was for the lampstand,
and the rest were for grain offerings.

5 The first grade of oil produced from the first grade of olives[52]—
there is nothing better than this.
The second from the first
and the first from the second
are equal in quality.
The third from the first,
the second from the second,
and the first from the third
are equal in quality.
The third from the second
and the second from the third are equal in quality.
The third from the third—

[52] Heb. "The first from the first" as below.

there is nothing worse than this.
Logic requires that the grain offerings too require the purest oil:
inasmuch as the lampstand,
whose oil[53] is not for eating,
requires the finest oil,
does not logic require that the grain offerings,
whose oil[54] is for eating,
require the finest oil?
Therefore Scripture teaches: *Clear oil of beaten olives for lighting*—
and not clear oil of beaten olives for grain offerings

8:6–7 *Preparation of Wine for Temple Use*

6 From where would they bring the wine?
Qarutim and Hatulim are the foremost choices[55] for wine.
Second to these are Bet Rimah and Bet Lavan in the hills,
and Kfar Signa in the valley.
All lands are valid,
but they used to bring it from these.
One does not bring it from fields that required fertilizer,[56]
nor from fields that required watering,
nor from fields in which other species were planted among the vines,
but if one did so—
it is valid.
One does not bring wine from sun-baked grapes,
but if he brought it—
it is valid.
One does not bring old wine—
these are the words of Rabbi,[57]
but the Sages deem it valid.
One does not bring sweet,
smoked,

[53] Lit. "which is." [54] Lit. "which is." [55] Lit. "alpha."
[56] Lit. "dung fields." [57] **P**: "R. Meir."

8:5 *Logic requires*: The principle of "lesser and greater." The point is that logic alone would lead to the wrong conclusion and we need the rule of Scripture.

Clear oil of beaten olives for lighting: Exodus 27:20. Scripture specified clear oil for lighting only.

8:6 *Qarutim and Hatulim*: Two towns in Judah.

Bet Rimah and Bet Lavan: In Judah, southwest of Shiloh.

Kfar Signa: In the Lower Galilee near Sepphoris.

but if one did so—it is valid: Some wines are deemed less choice than others, and as such are not the preferred choices for Temple use. However, if used, they are valid.

sweet, smoked, or boiled wine: These wines are invalid in all cases, possibly because the flavor comes not from the grapes but from another source.

or boiled wine,
and if he brought it—
it is invalid.
One does not bring from trellised vines,
but only from vines on the ground
and from tended vineyards.

7 They did not collect it in large vats,
but in small jars.
And he does not fill the jars up to their rims,
so that its fragrance would spread.
And he does not bring wine from its rim because of the scum,
nor from its bottom because of the sediments;
rather, he brings it from middle of the middle-third.
How does he inspect it?
The treasurer would sit with a reed in his hand;
he would toss out the froth and then tap it with the reed.
R. Yose b. Judah says:
Wine that produces scum is unfit,
as it is written: *And they and their grain offerings shall be to you without blemish*
and *they and their libations shall be to you without blemish.*

Chapter Nine

9:1–3 *Liquid and Dry Measures in the Temple*

9 There were two dry measures in the Temple:
(1) a tenth and
(2) a half-tenth.
R. Meir said:

vines on the ground and from tended vineyards: Which were thought to produce better wine.

8:7 *so that its fragrance would spread*: The fragrance would fill the empty space in the vessel, ensuring that it would remain in the vessel and improve the wine, rather than escape.

toss out the froth and then tap it with the reed: To indicate that the jar should be sealed back up. The description is not entirely clear, but one may assume that the wine was being drained by a bunghole in the side. As soon as the froth (from the top) started draining, the attendant would tap.

And they and their grain offerings: Numbers 28:23.

they and their libations: Numbers 28:31.

9:1 *tenth*: Biblical *issaron*, a tenth of an *ephah* (7:1).

The second *tenth*. R. Meir derives the existence of a second tenth measure from the repetition of *a tenth* in Numbers 28:29. One held a tenth only when overflowing, while the other held a tenth even when not filled to the top.

(1) a tenth,
(2) a tenth,[58] and
(3) a half-tenth.
For what was the tenth used?
It was used to measure all grain offerings.
One did not use a measure containing three tenths for a bull
or a measure containing two tenths for a ram;[59]
rather one measures them by tenths.
For what was the half-tenth used?
It was used to measure[60] the cakes[61] of the high priest,
half in the morning and half in the afternoon.

2 There were seven liquid measures in the Temple:
(1) a *hin*,
(2) a half-*hin*,
(3) a third of a *hin*, and
(4) a quarter-*hin*;
(5) a *log*,
(6) a half-*log*, and
(7) a quarter-*log*.
R. Eleazar b. Zadok says:
There were marks on the *hin*:
up to here for a bull,
up to here for a ram,
up to here for a lamb.
R. Simeon says:
There was no *hin* measure, for what would it be used for?[62]
Rather, there was an additional measure of a *log* and a half,
which was used to measure the grain offering of the high priest,
a *log* and a half in the morning and a *log* and a half in the afternoon.

3 For what was the quarter-*log* measure used?
For the quarter-*log* of water for the one with *tsaraʾat*,
and the quarter-*log* of oil for the *nazir*.
For what was the half-*log* measure used?

[58] **K** lacks this second "a tenth." [59] Lit. "With one of three . . . with one of two . . ."
[60] **K, P**: "divide." [61] **K, P**: "grain offering." [62] **K** lacks "for what would it be used for."

rather one measures them by tenths: Rather than employing a variety of measuring utensils, they measured out multiple measures of a tenth, possibly because of the repeated use of the word "tenth" in the Bible.

9:2 *bull*: Half a *hin*. Numbers 28:14.

ram: A third of a *hin*. Numbers 28:14.

lamb: A quarter of a *hin*. Numbers 28:14.

There was no hin measure: There was no point in having such a measuring utensil in the Temple, since no offering required precisely one *hin* of liquid.

9:3 *one with tsaraʾat*: See 5:6. No measure of water is given in Leviticus 14:5.

nazir: See 3:6. No measure of oil is given at Numbers 6:15.

For the half-*log* of water for the woman suspected of adultery,
and the half-*log* of oil for the thank offering.
And the *log* was used to measure oil for all grain offerings.
Even if a grain offering was sixty tenths,
sixty individual *log* were placed on it.
R. Eliezer b. Jacob says:
Even if a grain offering was sixty tenths,
it only required one *log*,
as it is written: *For a grain offering and a log of oil.*
Six for a bull,
four for a ram,
three for a lamb,
three and a half for the lampstand—a half-*log* for each lamp.

9:4–5 *Preparation of Libations and Grain Offerings*

4 One may intermingle:
the grain offerings brought with libations[63] of rams
with those brought with the libations of bulls;
the grain offerings brought with libations of lambs[64]
with those brought with the libations of other lambs;
the grain offering brought with libations of an individual
with those of the community;
or those of one day
with those of the previous day.
But the grain offering brought with libations of lambs
may not be intermingled with those of bullocks or rams.
If each was stirred separately and then they were intermingled,
they are valid;
If they were intermingled before they were stirred,
it is invalid.
The lamb brought with the *omer*—
even though its grain offering is doubled,
its libations are not doubled.

[63] Here and below: for "grain offerings brought with libations," Hebrew has only "libations."
[64] **K**: "rams."

woman suspected of adultery: The *sotah*; above, 1:1. No measure of oil is given at Numbers 5:17.

thank offering: Leviticus 7:12, which does not mention what measure of oil should be used.

sixty tenths: See 12:4.

sixty individual log were placed on it, using the one-*log* measure.

For a grain offering and a log of oil: Leviticus 14:21: thus, only one *log*.

9:4 *intermingle*: Grain offerings with flour and oil in the same proportion could be mixed together since the prescribed consistency of each grain offering would be maintained. Cf. 3:2–3. For the problem of the intermingling of other sacrificial stuff see *Zevahim* 8.

5 All the measures in the Temple were heaped up,
except for that of the high priest,
which was heaped up into itself.
The liquid measures—their overflow is sacral;
but dry measures—their overflow is nonsacral.
R. Aqiva says:
Liquid measures are sacral, thus their overflow is sacral;
dry measures are nonsacral, thus their overflow is nonsacral.
R. Yose says:
Not because of that, but because what is in the liquid measure is stirred up
while what is in the dry measure is not stirred up.

9:6–9 *Requirements of Various Offerings*

6 All offerings of the community and of the individual require libations,
except for:
the firstborn,
the tithe,
the Passover offering,
the purgation offering,
and the guilt offering;
except that the purgation offering of the one with *tsara'at*
and his guilt offering require libations.

9:5 *All the measures in the Temple were heaped up*: The material in the measuring utensil was not leveled; the measures were generous.

heaped up into itself: A larger utensil was always used to measure out ingredients for this offering so it was automatically generous.

sacral: Overflow could be used only for Temple rituals.

nonsacral: Overflow could be used for profane purposes.

R. Aqiva... R. Yose: These rabbis explain the earlier rule rather than disputing the rule itself.

Liquid measures are sacral: The vessels themselves are sanctified inside and out by anointing; therefore the overflow, which has come into contact with the outside of the vessels, is also sanctified.

stirred up... not stirred up: Liquids that overflow are all deemed to have come into contact with the inside of the sanctifying vessel. Meal that overflows is deemed to have remained outside the vessel.

9:6 *except*: Because these are not in the category of voluntary offerings. See Numbers 15:3.

firstborn: Deuteronomy 15:19.

tithe: Deuteronomy 14:23.

Passover offering: Deuteronomy 16:1–2.

purgation offering: Leviticus 4.

guilt offering: Leviticus 5.

except that... require libations: Leviticus 14:10–19.

7 No communal offerings require the laying on of hands,
except for the bull that is brought for any of the commandments,
and the scapegoat.
R. Simeon says:
Even[65] the goats for idolatry.
All offerings of an individual require the laying on of hands, except for:
the firstborn,
the tithe,
and the Passover offering.
The heir may perform the laying on of hands and bring libations,
and is liable if he substitutes [the animals].
8 All may perform the laying on of hands,
except for the deaf-mute,
the legally incompetent,
a minor,
the blind,
a gentile,
a slave,
an agent,
and a woman.
Laying on of hands is a residue of a commandment,
with both hands on the head.

[65] **K** lacks "even."

9:7 *the laying on of hands*: The laying of the owner's hands on the head of the sacrifice before slaughter (Leviticus 1:4).

bull that is brought for any of the commandments: Leviticus 4:13–15.

the scapegoat: Offered on the Day of Atonement. See Leviticus 16:6–10; *Yoma*, introduction and 6:2.

the goats for idolatry: Numbers 15:24–26.

firstborn ... Passover offering. See 9:6.

The heir: If the dedicant died before these actions took place, the heir may complete them.

substitutes: See n. 65. The reference is to the rule that one may not substitute one animal for another once it has been dedicated, and the consequence of this is that both become designated as offerings. See Leviticus 27:9–10, 32–3; *Temurah*, introduction.

9:8 *deaf-mute ... legally incompetent ... minor*: These three categories are regarded as lacking the power to form legal intent. See *Bava Qamma* 4:4; 8:4; *Shevu'ot* 6:4.

blind: The rabbis link all laying on of hands to that done by the elders when the community sins (Leviticus 4:15). Because the elders are associated with the Sanhedrin, and a blind man could not sit in the Sanhedrin, the blind were not permitted to lay hands on their offerings.

gentile: Leviticus 1:2 speaks of *the sons of Israel* and then of the laying on of hands.

slave ... agent: The words *his hand* in Leviticus 1:4 are understood to exclude laying on of hands by the slave or agent of the man offering the sacrifice. This is an exception to the Mishnah's general rule of agency.

woman: Leviticus 1:2 uses the term *the sons of Israel*, here understood to exclude women.

a residue of a commandment: Its omission does not invalidate the offering.

Slaughtering is done where the laying on of hands is done,
and occurs immediately after the laying on of hands.

9 The laying on of hands is stricter than waving,
waving than the laying on of hands.
One may wave on behalf of a group,
but one may not lay on hands on behalf of a group.
Waving is stricter:
in that waving applies to offerings of an individual and offerings of the community,
to living and slaughtered animals,
and to animate and inanimate objects,
which is not the case for the laying on of hands.

Chapter Ten

10:1–10 *The Omer*

10 R. Ishmael says:
The *omer* was brought on the Sabbath from three *se'ah*,
and on a weekday from five;
but the Sages say:
The rule is the same on the Sabbath and on a weekday:
it was brought from three.
R. Hananiah the Prefect of the Priests says:
On the Sabbath it was cut by one person,
with one scythe,
and into one container;
and on a weekday by three,
into three containers,
and with three scythes;
but the Sages say:
The rule is the same on the Sabbath and on a weekday:
By three,
into three containers,
and with three scythes.

Slaughtering is done...: See *Zevahim* 5:1–6 for the location of sacrifices.

9:9 *which is not the case for the laying on of hands*, which applies only to individual offerings and to live animals

10:1 *The omer*: The measure of barley brought on the sixteenth of Nisan (the second day of Passover) to mark the beginning of the harvest (Leviticus 23:9–14).

on the Sabbath: R. Ishmael and R. Hananiah limit labor that is usually forbidden on the Sabbath but is necessary to bring the *omer*.

2 The commandment is that the *omer* come from nearby.
If the barley close to Jerusalem had not ripened,
they may bring it from any place.
It once happened that it was brought from Gagot Tsrifin,[66]
and the two loaves from the valley of Ein Sokher.

3 How would they do it?
The agents of the court would go out on the eve of the festival
and make sheaves still rooted in the ground,
so that it would be easy to cut.
And all of the adjacent towns gathered there,
so that it would be cut with great fanfare.
When it grew dark, he said to them: "Has the sun set?"
They said: "Yes."
"Has the sun set?"
They said: "Yes."
"This scythe?"
They said: "Yes."
"This scythe?"
They said: "Yes."
"This container?"
They said: "Yes."
"This container?"
They said: "Yes."
On the Sabbath, he asked them: "On this Sabbath?"
They said: "Yes."
"On this Sabbath?"[67]
They said: "Yes."
"Shall I reap?"
They said: "Reap."
"Shall I reap?"
They said: "Reap."
Three times about each thing,
and they would say: "Yes, yes, yes."
Why was all this done?
Because of the Boethusians, who said:

[66] Alt. "Ganot Tsrifim."

[67] The repetition of the Sabbath question and response is lacking in **P**.

10:2 *Gagot Tsrifin*: Near Lod. Lit. "the roofs of Tsrifim" (or "huts"); the variant, "Ganot Tsrifim," means the gardens of Tsrifim.

two loaves: See 2:2.

Ein Sokher: Near Shechem.

10:3 *the eve of the festival*: Of Passover.

When it grew dark: On the evening of the sixteenth of Nisan.

Boethusians: The Sadducees or another group that rejected the rabbis' reading of Leviticus 23:11.

The *omer* is not reaped at the close of the festival.
4 They would reap it,
and place it in the baskets,
and bring it to the Temple Court.
They would toast it in the flame,
to fulfill the commandment that it be parched—
the words of R. Meir.
But the Sages say:
They would beat it with reeds[68] and stalks of plants so the grain would not be crushed;
then they would place it in a tube,
and the tube was pierced with holes so the flame would affect all of it.
They would spread it out[69] in the Temple Court and the wind would blow on it.
They would place it on the grist-grinders' mills and bring forth a tenth,
which would be sifted thirteen times.
The remainder could be redeemed and eaten by anyone.
It was subject to the dough offering,
but exempt from tithes.
R. Aqiva deems it subject to the dough offering and tithes.
He came to the tenth,
he would take oil and frankincense,
pour and mix,
wave and bring near,
take the handful and burn,
and the remainder was eaten by the priests.
5 Once the *omer* had been offered,
they would go out and find the marketplace of Jerusalem
full of flour and parched grain—
which was without the approval of the Sages—
the words of R. Meir;
R. Judah says:

68 **K** lacks "reeds."
69 **K** reverses two letters of "they spread it out" and thus reads "they slaughtered it."

The omer is not reaped at the close of the festival: The rabbis interpreted Leviticus 23:11 *the day after the Sabbath* as meaning the day after the first day of the festival of Passover. They also understood Leviticus 23:15 as mandating that the reaping of the *omer* take place at night. Others read the word *Sabbath* literally and thought the *omer* should be offered the day after the Sabbath following the first day of Passover.

10:4 *the commandment that it be parched*: Leviticus 23:14. R. Meir holds that the stalks must be parched. The Sages hold that the *omer* is not roasted until it is processed into grain. The description of roasting in the tube is part of the Sages' understanding of this roasting.

reed... tube: Both words for types of reeds or stalks.

thirteen times: See 6:7.

dough offering: See Numbers 15:17–21; *Hallah*, introduction.

came to the tenth: The priest; we return to the description of the ritual.

10:5 *without the approval of the Sages*: The grain in the market had been reaped and ground before the *omer* was offered, raising concerns lest new produce be eaten before the offering.

They acted with the approval of the Sages.
Once the *omer* was offered,
new produce could be eaten.
Those far away were permitted from midday onward.
Once the Temple was destroyed,
Rabban Yohanan b. Zakkai decreed that new produce was forbidden
throughout the day of waving.
R. Judah said:
Is it not forbidden according to the Torah?
As it is written: *Until that very day.*
Why were those far away permitted from midday onward?
Because they knew the court would not be lax about offering it.

6 The *omer* made new produce[70] permissible throughout the country,
and the two loaves [made new produce permissible] in the Temple.
They did not[71] bring grain offerings,
firstfruits,
or grain offerings accompanying animal offerings
before the *omer*,
and if they did so,
it is invalid.
Before the two loaves—
he may not bring,
but if he brought,
it is valid.

7 Wheat,
barley,
spelt,
rye,
or oats—
are subject to the dough offering,
and combine together,
and are forbidden as new produce before Passover,

[70] Heb. "it." [71] Or "one may not."

far away from Jerusalem. *From midday onward*: On the assumption that the *omer* had already been offered in Jerusalem by then.

Until that very day: Leviticus 23:14. Seemingly R. Judah understands this verse to include all of *that very day* in the prohibition. See the commentaries for extensive discussion of this exposition.

10:6 *the two loaves*: Only after this offering, brought on the Festival of Weeks seven weeks after Passover, could grain offerings from new grain be offered in the Temple. See Numbers 28:26; the ruling is based on interpretation of the word "new" in the verse.

They did not bring grain offerings…: From newly harvested produce.

10:7 *Wheat…oats*: These five types are all considered grain by the Mishnah.

combine together: If dough is made from two or more of these grains, the dough is subject to the dough offering if the total amount of flour used meets the requirements for dough offering, even if the amount of each species alone does not.

and may not be reaped before the *omer*.
If they have taken root before the *omer*,
the *omer* makes them permissible,
but if not,
they are forbidden until the next year's *omer*.

8 One reaps fields requiring watering in the valleys
[before the *omer* is brought],
but one may not stack it.
The people of Jericho reap with the approval of the Sages,
and stack without the approval of the Sages,
but the Sages did not protest against them.
He may reap for fodder and feed it to animals.
R. Judah says:
When?
When he began to reap before it reached a third of its growth.
R. Simeon says:
One may reap and feed animals,
even after it reaches a third.

9 One may reap:
for seedlings,
or for a place of mourning,
or neglect of the house of study.
He does not make them into bundles;
rather he leaves it in small piles.
The commandment is that the *omer* be brought from standing grain;
if none can be found,
it may be brought from sheaves.
The commandment is that it be brought from fresh grain;
if none can be found,
it may be brought from dried grain.
The commandment is that it be reaped at night;
if it is reaped in the daytime,
it is valid.
And it supersedes the Sabbath.

10:8 *may not stack*: Stacking is regarded as the final step of harvesting and thus should not take place before the *omer* is brought.

for fodder: One may harvest unripe grain (subject to the limitations below) to use as feed. R. Simeon allows the farmer to continue to use produce even if the grain is more mature, as long as it is for fodder rather than human consumption.

10:9 *a place of mourning*: To clear a place for a funeral procession to stop on its way to burial.

neglect of the house of study: One may reap early to create opportunity for the study of Torah.

Chapter Eleven

11:1–4 *Making the Various Breads and Grain Offerings*

11 The two loaves are kneaded separately
and baked separately.
The showbread is kneaded separately
and baked in pairs.
And he would make them in a form,
and when he removed them from the oven,
he would place them in a form so they would not be ruined.
2 The rule is the same for the two loaves and the showbread:
they are kneaded and shaped outside
and baked inside,
and they do not supersede the Sabbath.
R. Judah says:
All of the work is done inside.
R. Simeon says:
Always be accustomed to saying:
The two loaves and the showbread are valid when made in the Temple Courts
and valid when made in Bet Pagi.
3 The cakes of the high priest—
are kneaded, shaped,[72] and baked inside,
and making them supersedes the Sabbath.
Grinding and sifting flour for them do not supersede the Sabbath.
R. Aqiva stated a general principle:
Any work that can be done on the eve of the Sabbath does not supersede the Sabbath,
and that cannot be done on the eve of the Sabbath supersedes the Sabbath.

[72] **K, P** lack "shaped."

11:1 *two loaves...showbread*: See 2:2 and the biblical verses cited there.

The two loaves are kneaded separately: To ensure that each was made of the precise measure of flour prescribed.

11:2 *outside...inside*: Of the Temple Court.

do not supersede the Sabbath: See *Shabbat* 7:2, and cf. *Menahot* 10:2 and below.

Always be accustomed to saying: This is an unusual way to introduce an alternative position. It appears only a few times in rabbinic literature, all quoting this statement of R. Simeon. The phrase might indicate a correction of another Sage, rather than a disagreement.

Bet Pagi: A place near Jerusalem (Bethphage in the New Testament). R. Simeon was of the opinion that the two loaves and the showbread could be made outside the Temple precincts. The reason for the dispute with R. Judah is not clear.

11:3 *Any work...supersedes the Sabbath*: See *Shabbat* 19:1. Even when fulfillment of a commandment requires performing labor on the Sabbath, R. Aqiva permits only those acts that cannot be done in advance. Any work that could be done before the Sabbath must be done then.

4 All grain offerings:
what is done inside is in a consecrating utensil;
what is done outside is not in a consecrating utensil.[73]
How?
The length of the two loaves is seven handbreadths,[74]
its width four,
and its horns four fingerbreadths.
The length of the showbread is ten,
its width five,
and its horns seven fingerbreadths.
R. Judah says:
So you do not make a mistake: *Zayin-Dalet-Dalet, Yod-Heh-Zayin.*
Ben Zoma says:
And you shall place the showbread on the table before me always[75]—
it should have a face.

11:5–9 *The Showbread*

5 The table is ten [handbreadths] long and five wide;
the showbread is ten long and five wide.
He places it lengthwise along the width of the table
and folds it—
two and a half on this side, and two and a half on this side—

[73] Lit. "have making/performance in a utensil inside, and do not have making/performance in a utensil outside."

[74] Here and below, "handbreadths" added for clarity.

[75] **K** lacks "before Me always."

11:4 *inside…outside*: Of the Temple Court.

in a consecrating utensil: See 1:1 and 2:4.

How? Generally introduces an explication of the preceding rule or expression. Here, the Mishnah returns to the procedures for baking the loaves (11:1).

horns: Small pieces of dough resembling the horns of the altar were placed on the corners of the bread.

Zayin-Dalet-Dalet, Yod-Heh-Zayin: A mnemonic for the measurements of the two types of bread. The letters represent numbers, so 7–4–4 and 10–5–7.

And you shall place the showbread on the table before me always: Exodus 25:30. "Showbread" can be translated literally "bread of the face."

it should have a face: It should be symmetrical.

11:5 The next mishnah describes a superstructure built over the table to hold the loaves of showbread in two vertical stacks. Here the text describes the size of the loaves of bread relative to the surface of the table.

ten [handbreadths]: The table was two cubits by one cubit (Exodus 25:23). The dispute of R. Judah and R. Meir turns on whether the cubit in the desert was five or six handbreadths.

folds it: Lit. "doubles." The bread is folded into a U-shape with the two ends pointed upward. In the view of *R. Judah*, this would make a loaf that *filled the width of the table*. On this view, the second loaf of a pair (the corresponding loaf in the second stack) would take up the other half of the table's area.

so its length fills the width of the table—
the words of R. Judah.
R. Meir says:
The table is twelve handbreadths long and six wide;
the showbread was ten long and five wide;
he places it lengthwise along the width of the table
and folds it—
two on one side and two on the other side—
leaving a space of two[76] in the middle,
so the wind might blow between them.
Abba Saul says:
There they would place the two dishes of frankincense for the showbread.
They said to him:
It already has been said: *Upon each row you shall place pure frankincense!*
He said to them:
And it has already been said: *Next to it, the tribe of Manasseh!*

6 There were four gold inserts split at the top on which they supported the showbread,
two for one arrangement and two for the other;
and twenty-eight staves, like half a hollow reed,
fourteen for one arrangement and fourteen for the other.
Neither the setting up of the staves nor the removal supersedes the Sabbath;
rather, he goes in on the eve of the Sabbath
and removes them
and lays them along the length of the table.
All of the utensils that were in the Temple—
they are laid out so that their length was parallel to the length of the sanctuary.

[76] **K** lacks "of two."

In the view of *R. Meir*, the folds would leave a space of one handbreadth on either side. Since the table was twelve handbreadths long and the bread five wide, there would also be a space of two handbreadths *in the middle*, between the two loaves.

There they would place: In the two-handbreadth space left between the breads according to R. Meir.

Upon (Heb. *al*) *each row you shall place pure frankincense*: Leviticus 24:7.

Next to it, the tribe of Manasseh: Numbers 2:20. Abba Saul points out that in this verse *al* cannot mean "upon" but must mean "near." Therefore it may mean "near" in Leviticus 24:7.

11:6 The description of the laying out of the showbread is obscure.

four gold inserts: These were places on the floor at the corners of the table, to support the staves, in two vertical *arrangements*.

staves: Lit. "reeds."

half a hollow reed: Each was a hollow half-cylinder. There were twelve loaves offered (Leviticus 24:5–8), in their forms (*Menahot* 11:2). Somehow the twenty-eight "reeds" supported twelve loaves in two vertical columns.

the Sabbath: The bread was changed on the Sabbath (see 11:7), but the labor of dismantling the superstructure and reassembling it could not be done on the Sabbath itself. The disassembly was done on Friday; the new assembly is not described.

All of the utensils . . . parallel to the length of the sanctuary: Everything was set out east to west.

7 There were two tables in the porch on the inside near the doorway of the sanctuary, one marble and one gold.
They place the showbread on the marble table when it is brought in,
and on the gold one when it is taken out,
for we increase holiness rather than decrease it.
And there is one of gold inside on which there is always showbread.
Four priests go in,
two with the two arrangements in their hands[77]
and two with the two dishes in their hands.
Four priests precede them,
two to remove the two portions
and two to remove the two dishes.
Those bringing in[78] stand in the north facing south,
and those removing stand in the south facing north.
These pull out, while these put in, filling up the space as it opened,
as it is said: *Before me always*.
R. Yose says:
Even if these were removed completely and then placed,
it would constitute *always*.
They went out and put the old bread[79] on the gold table in the porch.
They burned the dishes of incense,
and the loaves are distributed among the priests.
If the Day of Atonement falls on the Sabbath,
the loaves are distributed in the evening.
If it falls on the eve of the Sabbath,
the goat of the Day of Atonement is eaten in the evening;[80]
The Babylonians eat it raw since their constitutions are strong.

[77] **K** reads "in judgment," resulting from the transposition of two letters. [78] **P** reads "entering."
[79] Heb. "it." [80] **P** lacks "in the evening."

11:7 *two tables in the porch*: These do not derive from the Torah, and served for the laying out of the showbread before and after it was formally presented "inside."

for we increase holiness rather than decrease it: And the gold table was holier than the marble one.

two with the two arrangements for the current week. The six loaves would be arranged in a vertical column.

two dishes: Containing the frankincense.

two to remove the previous week's showbread.

filling up the space as it opened: Lit. "[the displacement of] a handbreadth of this one corresponding to [the displacement of] a handbreadth of this one."

Before me always: Exodus 25:30.

in the evening: At the conclusion of the Day of Atonement.

goat of the Day of Atonement: See Numbers 29:11.

in the evening: After the Day of Atonement ended and at the beginning of the Sabbath.

Babylonians: Priests of Babylonian origin, perhaps on pilgrimage. This sentence should perhaps be read as explaining the preceding. Since neither on the Day of Atonement nor on the Sabbath could the animal be cooked, only Babylonian priests would eat it, because they would eat it raw.

8 If he set out the bread on the Sabbath,
and the dishes of frankincense after the Sabbath,
and burned the dishes of frankincense on the Sabbath,
it is invalid,
but one is not liable for *piggul*,
remnant,
or impurity.
If he set out the loaves and the dishes on the Sabbath,
and he burned the dishes of frankincense after the Sabbath,
it is invalid,
but one is not liable for *piggul*,
remnant,
or impurity.
If he set out the loaves and the dishes after the Sabbath[81]
and he burned the dishes of frankincense on the Sabbath,
it is invalid.[82]
How is he to act?
He leaves it until the following Sabbath,[83]
for even if it is on the table for many[84] days,
it does not matter.

9 The two loaves are eaten no fewer than two and no more than three days [after baking].
How?
If they are baked on the eve of the festival and eaten on the festival,

[81] **K**: "on the Sabbath." [82] **K**, **P** lack "it is invalid."
[83] **K** lacks "following." [84] **K**, **P** lack "many."

11:8 *after the Sabbath*: The showbread with the frankincense was to be offered *each Sabbath* (Leviticus 24:8). The Mishnah assumes that these must be set out for a full seven days. In the first situation, the frankincense was only set out for six days. In the second, the frankincense was set out only one day (or left out for an extra day and thus invalidated). In both cases, the offering of the showbread was properly set out but then invalidated, because the frankincense was put out for too short or too long a time. In the third case the bread was not offered on its proper day, and so was never sanctified.

not liable: This is the reading found in printed editions and manuscripts of the Mishnah and preferred by most commentators. Maimonides claims that if the frankincense is burned after the Sabbath one is culpable for the stated categories, suggesting he had a text that read "he is liable."

piggul: If the priest handling an offering intends to eat it after the prescribed time, the offering becomes desecrated. See 1:3.

remnant: If an offering is not eaten within the prescribed time; it must be burned but a person who eats it is not subject to *karet*. See 1:3.

impurity: The prescription against eating from an offering while in a state of ritual impurity. See *Zevahim* 2:1.

How is he to act with respect to bread and frankincense offered after the Sabbath in order to make them valid?

He leaves it: They leave the bread in place for another week. The new Sabbath sanctifies it, and it is valid at the conclusion of that new week.

11:9 In counting, the Mishnah here counts any part of a day as a day.

two loaves: See 2:2, brought on the festival of Festival of Weeks (Shavu'ot).

that is two days.
If the festival falls on the day after the Sabbath,
that is three days.
The showbread is eaten no fewer than nine and no more than eleven days [after baking].
How?
If it is baked on the eve of the Sabbath and eaten on the Sabbath:
nine days.
If a festival falls on the eve of the Sabbath,
that is ten days.
If it is the two days of the New Year,
it is eaten after eleven days.
And it does not supersede the Sabbath or a festival.
Rabban Simeon b. Gamaliel says in the name of R. Simeon son of the Prefect:
It supersedes a festival,
but not the fast day.

Chapter Twelve

12:1 *Redemption of Dedicated Items*

12 Grain offerings and libations that became impure—
before they were sanctified in a utensil,
they may be redeemed;
once they were sanctified in a utensil,
they may not be redeemed.
Birds, wood, frankincense, and sacred utensils may not be redeemed,
for nothing is said [in the Torah] except animals.

the day after the Sabbath: Baking the loaves was prohibited on the Sabbath, so the bread was baked on Friday, adding a third day.

eaten on the Sabbath: The following Sabbath.

does not supersede the Sabbath or a festival: This explains why additional days are added to the eating: one had to allow an additional day for most festivals and two days for the New Year.

According to *Rabban Simeon b. Gamaliel...in the name of R. Simeon the Prefect*, we do not have to allow extra days for festivals.

the fast day: The Day of Atonement.

12:1 *may be redeemed*: May be exchanged for money that then takes on the sanctity of the redeemed object.

for nothing is said [in the Torah] except animals: When Leviticus 27:11–13 discusses redeeming dedicated items it speaks only of animals.

12:2–4 *Voluntary Offerings That Do Not Correspond to the Statement of Dedication: Grain Offerings*

2 One who said: “I hereby pledge [a grain offering made] on a griddle,”
but brought one in a pan;
“In a pan,”
but brought on a griddle—
what he brought he brought,
but he has not fulfilled his obligation.
“To bring this on a griddle,”
but brought it in a pan;
“In a pan,”
but brought it on a griddle—
it is invalid.
“I hereby pledge to bring two tenths in one utensil,”
but brought it in two utensils;
“In two utensils,”
but brought it in one—
what he brought he brought,
but he has not fulfilled his obligation.
“To bring these in one utensil,”
but brought it in two;
“In two utensils,”
and brought it in one—
it is invalid.
“I hereby pledge to bring two tenths in one utensil,”
and he brought it in two,
and they said to him:
“You vowed: In one utensil.”
If he offered it in one utensil—
they are valid;
if in two—
they are invalid.[85]
“I pledge two tenths in two utensils,”
and he brought it in one,
and they said to him:
“You vowed: In two utensils.”

[85] In **K** and **P**, this rule and the following appear in reverse order.

12:2 *“I hereby pledge”*: See 5:8.

what he brought he brought, but he has not fulfilled his obligation: The offering is regarded as a valid free-will offering, but he must also bring the offering he promised in order to fulfill his original vow.

it is invalid: Because the flour was not used in the manner he set forth in his vow.

two tenths: Flour in the amount of two-tenths of an *ephah* (see 7:1).

and they said to him: If someone reminds him of his original declaration and he then acts in accord with the declaration, the offering is valid; if not, it is invalid.

If he offered it in two utensils—
they are valid;
if he put them in one utensil—
it is like two grain offerings that were mixed together.

3 "I hereby pledge a grain offering of barley"—
he must bring one of wheat;
"Of flour"—
he must bring one of fine flour;
"Without oil or frankincense"—
he must bring one with oil and frankincense;
"A half-tenth"—
he must bring one of a full tenth;
"One and a half tenth"—
he must bring one of two tenths.
R. Simeon exempts,
because he did not act in the manner of those who make voluntary offerings.

4 A person may designate a voluntary grain offering of sixty tenths and bring it in one utensil.
If he said: "I hereby pledge sixty-one"—
he may bring sixty in one utensil and one in another utensil,
for on the first day of the Festival that falls on the Sabbath
the community brings sixty and one,
and it is enough for an individual that his offering be one less than that of the community.
R. Simeon said:
But some of these are for bulls and some of these are for lambs,
and they are not stirred with oil together!
Rather up to sixty they can be stirred with oil together.
They said to him:
Sixty are stirred with oil together, but sixty-one are not stirred with oil together?

like two grain offerings that were mixed together: See 3:3: if the possibility exists to offer a handful from each original offering, the offerer may do so.

12:3 *he must bring one of wheat*: In each of the five cases enumerated here, the person commits to something that is not a valid offering. For the requirements of a valid grain offering, see Leviticus 2:1–7 and *Menahot* 3:5. His words are taken as a commitment that must be fulfilled by bringing a valid offering.

R. Simeon treats the declaration as nonbinding since it did not describe a valid offering.

12:4 *sixty... sixty-one...*: No grain offering may be composed of more than sixty measures of flour.

the Festival: The Festival of Sukkot (Booths). See *Sukkah*, introduction. The maximum number of mandatory grain offerings of the community is sixty-one.

it is enough: The amount brought on the Festival less one is an appropriate ceiling.

But some... together: The grain offerings brought by the community on Sukkot are of different types, and cannot be mixed with oil together (9:4), so they prove nothing about this case.

up to sixty they can be stirred: R. Simeon gives a practical reason: it is possible to successfully mix up to sixty tenths with oil, but more than that amount cannot be mixed well. Thus no grain offering may be more than sixty tenths.

They said to him: The interlocutors object that the difference between sixty and sixty-one is not significant if the reason is the possibility of mixing.

He said to them:
It is so with all measures set by the Sages:
forty *se'ah*, he may immerse;
but in forty *se'ah* less a *qartov*, he may not immerse.
A person may not designate a voluntary offering of one *log*,
two,
or five,
but may designate a voluntary offering of three,
or four,
or six,
or more than six.

12:5 *Voluntary Offerings That Do Not Correspond to the Statement of Dedication: Wine and Oil*

5 One may designate voluntary offerings of wine,
but not of oil—
the words of R. Aqiva.
R. Tarfon says:
One may designate voluntary offerings of oil.
R. Tarfon said:
Just as we find in the case of wine,
that it may be brought as an obligatory offering or a voluntary offering,
so too in the case of oil,
it may be brought as an obligatory offering or a voluntary offering.
R. Aqiva said to him:
No, if you say this of wine,
which can be brought as an obligatory offering on its own,
will you say it also of oil,
which cannot be brought as an obligatory offering on its own?
Two may not designate a voluntary offering of one tenth,
but they may designate a voluntary whole burnt offering or offering of well-being,
and in the case of a bird, even a single pigeon.

It is so with all measures set by the Sages: If a ritual requires a fixed measure, whether minimum or maximum, that measure must be adhered to, whether or not a lesser or greater measure might be handled or might fulfill the desired act.

forty se'ah, he may immerse: Immersion in a minimum of forty *se'ah* of water is required to remove many forms of ritual impurity. See *Miqva'ot*, introduction.

qartov: A small liquid measure, 1/64 of a *log*.

one log…or more than six: Only the latter are mentioned in connection with libations. See Numbers 28:14.

12:5 *wine…oil*: Wine may be used as a libation without flour or oil, but oil is never used on its own.

Just as we find…so too…: R. Tarfon bases his ruling on a similarity between wine and oil; both can be brought for voluntary and obligatory offerings. This justifies allowing oil, like wine, to be offered alone.

Two may not: From the specification *nefesh* ("soul" or person) in Leviticus 2:1.

Chapter Thirteen

13:1–9 *Voluntary Offerings That Do Not Correspond to the Statement of Dedication: Indeterminate Sacrificial Dedications*

13 "I hereby pledge a tenth"—
he must bring one tenth.
"Tenths"—
he must bring two tenths.
"I specified an amount, but I do not know how much I specified"—
he must bring sixty tenths.
"I hereby pledge a grain offering"—
he may bring whichever kind he wishes.
R. Judah says:
Let him bring a grain offering of fine flour,
since it is the distinctive kind among grain offerings.
2 "A grain offering"
or "A type of grain offering"—
he must bring one;
"Grain offerings"
or "Types of grain offerings"—
he must bring two.[86]
"I specified, but I do not know which type I specified"—
he must bring all five types.
"I specified a grain offering[87] of a number of tenths,
but I do not know how many[88] I specified"—
he must bring a grain offering of sixty tenths.

[86] **P**: "sixty." [87] **P**: "grain offerings." [88] Lit. "what."

13:1–8 deal with situations when the person vowing to bring an offering is not clear as to his intentions. The language that opens each unit, "I hereby pledge," indicates a vow.

13:1 *"I hereby pledge a tenth"*: Grain offerings were measured in tenths of an *ephah* of flour, with one tenth being the smallest possible offering.

"*Tenths*": The vow is nonspecific and is determined to be the smallest amount he could have meant when using the plural.

"*but I do not know*": He does not remember what amount he pledged.

sixty tenths: The largest amount possible for a single grain offering. See 12:4.

the distinctive kind: When the term *minhah* is used in the Torah without any other explanation, it refers to an offering of fine flour (Leviticus 2:1).

13:2 *all five types*: Enumerated in Leviticus 2. This ensures he brings the offering he specified.

Rabbi[89] says:
He must bring grain offerings of tenths, from one to sixty.
3 "I hereby pledge wood"—
he must bring no fewer than two sticks;
"Frankincense"—
he must bring no less than a handful.
There are five rules involving handfuls:[90]
(1) one who says: "I hereby pledge frankincense" must bring no less than a handful;
(2) one who offers a voluntary grain offering must bring with it a handful of frankincense;
(3) one who offers a handful outside is liable;
(4, 5) and the two dishes require two handfuls each.
4 "I hereby pledge gold"—
he must bring no less than a gold *dinar*;
"Silver"—
he must bring no less than a silver *dinar*;
"Copper"—
he must bring no less than the value of a silver *ma'ah*;
"I specified an amount but I do not know how much I specified"—
he brings until he says: "This is not what I intended."
5 "I hereby pledge wine"—
he must bring no less than three *log*;
"Oil"—
he must bring no less than a *log*.
Rabbi says:
"Three *log*."
"I specified, but I do not know how much[91] I specified"—
he must bring the amount brought on the day of the most offerings.
6 "I hereby pledge a whole burnt offering"—

[89] **K**: "R. Judah." [90] Lit. "five kinds of handfuls." [91] Lit. "what."

grain offerings of tenths, from one to sixty: Since he does not remember what he specified, he must bring sixty offerings of different sizes, so that one of them will fulfill his vow.

13:3 *no fewer than two sticks*: The word *wood* in the declaration is in the plural.

outside: Of the Temple Court.

two dishes: Of frankincense, brought with the showbread.

13:4 *"This is not what I intended"*: This assumes that although he may not remember what he agreed to bring, he can be certain he did not intend to bring this large an amount.

13:5 *three log*: The smallest amount required for a libation. See 9:3.

log: See: 9:3.

Rabbi requires the minimum amount that can be brought in a private dedication according to 12:3.

the day of the most offerings: The first day of Sukkot coinciding with the Sabbath, 12:4.

13:6 *"burnt offering"*: See Leviticus 1.

he must bring a lamb.
R. Eleazar b. Azariah says:
Or a pigeon or a dove.
“I specified an offering of cattle, but I do not know what I specified”—
he must bring a bull and a calf;
“Of grazing animals, but I do not know what I specified”—
he must bring a bull,
a calf,
a ram,
a kid,
and a lamb.
“I specified but I do not know what I specified”—
he must add to these a pigeon or a dove.

7 “I hereby pledge a thank offering or offerings of well-being”—
he must bring a lamb.
“I specified an offering from cattle, but I do not know which I specified”—
he must bring
a bull and a cow,
a calf and a heifer;
“Of grazing animals, but I do not know which I specified”—
he must bring
a bull and a cow,
a young bull,
a young cow,
a ram,
a ewe,
a male kid and a female kid,
a male goat and a female goat,
a young ram and a young ewe.

8 “I hereby pledge an ox”—
he must bring it and its libations to the value of a hundred *dinar*;
“A calf”—
he must bring it and its libations to the value of five *sela*;
“A ram”—
he must bring it and its libations to the value of two *sela*;

a lamb: The least expensive grazing animal that may be used as a burnt offering.

Or a pigeon or a dove: The least expensive animal offering.

a bull…a lamb…add to these a pigeon or a dove: By bringing all of these, he ensures that he has indeed brought the animal he specified.

13:7 *“thank offering…offering of well-being”* See Leviticus 3 and Leviticus 7:11–15.

13:8 *to the value of a hundred*: These amounts are not spelled out in the Torah. Some commentators explain that these amounts are part of the oral tradition, others believe that they reflect the average cost of these items during the time the Mishnah was compiled.

“*An ox valued at a hundred*”: The Mishnah considers cases where the dedicator committed to the minimal value for the animal alone.

"A lamb"—
he must bring it and its libations[92] to the value of a *sela*;
"An ox valued at a hundred *dinar*"—
he must bring one valued at a hundred apart from its libations;
"A young bull valued at five"—
he must bring one valued at five apart from its libations;
"A ram valued at two"—
he must bring one valued at two apart from its libations;
"A lamb valued at a *sela*"—
he must bring one valued at a *sela* apart from its libations.
"An ox valued at a hundred,"
and he brought two valued together at a hundred—
he has not fulfilled his obligation,
even if this one is valued at a hundred less a *dinar*
and this one is valued at a hundred less a *dinar*.
"A black one,"
but brought a white one;
"A white one,"
but brought a black one;
"A large one,"
but brought a small one—
he has not fulfilled his obligation;
"A small one,"
but brought a large one—
he has fulfilled his obligation.
Rabbi says:
He has not fulfilled his obligation.

9 "This ox shall be a whole burnt offering,"
and it became blemished—
if he wants, he may bring two worth its value.
"These oxen shall be whole burnt offerings,"
and they became blemished—
if he wants, he may bring one worth their value.
Rabbi forbids.
"This ram shall be a whole burnt offering,"

[92] **K** lacks "and its libations."

"*An ox*"... *and he brought two*: The obligation can only be met by a single ox valued at a *maneh* or more.

"*A black one*": Since the actual animal did not comply with the specification, the dedicator has not met fulfilled the obligation.

Rabbi says: Although the offering is larger than the one he vowed to bring, it is not what he committed to, and therefore does not fulfill his vow.

13:9 *if he wants, he may bring two worth its value*: Unlike previous cases, in this situation, the presenter has fulfilled his vow, since it is no fault of his that the animal he designated became blemished. He may therefore bring more than one animal, as long as he matches the value of the original animal.

Rabbi forbids: Insisting that the man must bring animals similar to those he designated.

and it became blemished—
if he wants, he may bring a lamb worth the value of the ram.
"This lamb shall be a whole burnt offering,"
and it became blemished—
if he wants, he may bring a ram worth the value of the lamb.
Rabbi forbids.
One who says: "One of my lambs is hereby dedicated for an offering,"
or "One of my oxen is hereby dedicated for an offering":
if he has two—
the larger[93] one is dedicated;
if three—
the middling one is dedicated.
"I specified, but I do not know which one I specified,"
or he said: "My father told me but I do not know which"[94]—
the larger of them is dedicated.

13:10 *Voluntary Offerings That Do Not Correspond to the Statement of Dedication: Temples Other Than Jerusalem*

10 "I hereby pledge a whole burnt offering"—
he must offer it in the Temple;
and if he offers it in Bet Honyo,[95]
he has not fulfilled his obligation.
"That I will offer it in Bet Honyo"—
he may offer it in the Temple,
but if he offers it in Bet Honyo,
he has fulfilled his obligation.
R. Simeon says:
This is not a whole burnt offering.
"I will be a *nazir*"—
he must shave in the Temple,
and if he shaves in Bet Honyo,
he has not fulfilled his obligation.
"I will shave in Bet Honyo"—
he may shave in the Temple,
but if he shaves in Bet Honyo,

[93] **K, P**: "the smaller." [94] **K, P** lack "but I do not know which."
[95] **K, P**: "Bet Nehonyon" throughout.

13:10 *Bet Honyo*: Lit. "house of Honyo" (Onias in Greek sources), a Jewish temple in Egypt, built in the second century BCE, and destroyed in 73 CE by the Romans. This mishnah debates whether or not the worship in Bet Honyo was idolatry. The first view expressed in the Mishnah did not regard worship there as idolatry, while R. Simeon did.

This is not a whole burnt offering: Because it was made in connection with Bet Honyo, it is not a valid vow and the animal is not consecrated.

"*nazir*": See Numbers 6:1–21 and above, 3:6.

he has fulfilled his obligation.
R. Simeon says:
He is not a *nazir*.
The priests who served in Bet Honyo may not serve in the Temple in Jerusalem,
and there is no need to say if they offered[96] to something else,
as it is written: *However, they would not ascend to the altar of the Lord in Jerusalem,*
but they ate unleavened bread along with their kinsmen—
they are thereby treated as blemished priests:
they may take portions of the offerings and eat them,[97]
but they may not bring offerings.

13:11 *Concluding Homily*

11 It is said regarding an animal offering:
An offering by fire of pleasing odor,
and regarding a bird offering:
An offering by fire of pleasing odor,[98]
and regarding a grain offering:
An offering by fire of pleasing odor,
to teach that it is the same whether one brings a larger or smaller offering,
provided that a person's intention is directed toward God.

[96] "If they offered" added for clarity. [97] Lit. "they divide and eat." [98] **K** lacks this sentence.

something else: Bet Honyo is acknowledged to be dedicated to the God of Israel; it follows that if one was a priest to other gods, he would not be able to serve.

However, they would not ascend: 2 Kings 23:9. This reference to priests who had served at *bamot* (raised platforms or shrines) outside Jerusalem is offered as proof that a priest at Bet Honyo forfeits his eligibility to serve in the Jerusalem Temple, while retaining the right to partake of sacrificial food.

blemished priests: Leviticus 21:21–23.

13:11 *An offering by fire of pleasing odor*: Leviticus 1:9 (animal offering); 1:17 (bird offering); 2:2 (grain offering).

Tractate Hullin

Jordan D. Rosenblum

Introduction

Overview

Hullin, or "nonsacral things," discusses nonsacral animal slaughter, as opposed to sacrificial slaughter (dealt with in *Zevahim*). Deuteronomy 12 makes an allowance for nonsacral slaughter: it may occur outside of the Jerusalem Temple, in a noncultic setting, provided that one pours the animal's blood upon the ground. This allowance forms the basis for tractate *Hullin*.

While there are many rules for sacrificial slaughter in the Hebrew Bible, there are significantly fewer regulations concerning noncultic slaughter. In addition to the provision of the pouring of blood found in Deuteronomy 12, the only other major relevant legislation relates to prohibited and permitted animals (Leviticus 11; Deuteronomy 14); the avoidance of the sciatic nerve (Genesis 32); the prohibition against slaughtering a parent and its offspring on the same day (Leviticus 22:28); the requirement to send away a mother bird before taking her eggs or chicks (Deuteronomy 22:6–7); and the prohibition against cooking a kid in its mother's milk (Exodus 23:19; 34:26; Deuteronomy 14:21). In *Hullin*, the rabbis expand this biblical legislation, thus developing an elaborate system for animal slaughter and ingestion.

Structure and Organization of the Tractate

While the main focus of *Hullin* is nonsacral animal slaughter, there are occasional interludes that address Temple matters (1:5–6; 10–11). Although the Temple had been destroyed in 70 CE, the rabbis preserved such practices, as they understood them, in anticipation of a future time when the Temple would be rebuilt and appropriate sacrifice would recommence.

The basic structure of the tractate is as follows: chapters 1–2 address slaughtering procedure; chapter 3 surveys indications that an animal is invalid or valid (that is, impermissible or permissible); chapters 4–5 discuss the rules associated with slaughtering a pregnant animal and slaughtering an animal and its offspring on the same day; chapter 6 explores the requirement to cover an animal's blood after its slaughter; chapters 7–8 address the prohibitions against consuming the sciatic nerve, against mixing milk and meat, and against consuming blood and fat; chapter 9 discusses food and impurity issues; chapters 10–11 discuss priestly gifts; and chapter 12 addresses the biblical commandment to send away the mother bird before taking her chicks or eggs from her nest.

Main Ideas

There are two important slaughter-related terms vital for understanding *Hullin*. In the Hebrew Bible, *nevelah* (carcass) is a technical term for an animal that has died a natural death, and *terefah* (lit. "torn") refers to an animal killed by another animal. However, in rabbinic texts, *nevelah*, represented by "carcass" in the translation, refers to an animal that has been improperly slaughtered, while *terefah* refers to an animal that has been properly slaughtered but is declared invalid for another reason (see 2:4). Since this tractate is concerned with valid, nonsacral animal slaughter, these terms are often used to determine whether an animal or an act of slaughter is valid or invalid.

Further, knowledge of animal physiology and biology (to the extent that they were understood at that time) is assumed by the tractate. To help the reader, terms are generally rendered in the appropriate modern anatomical nomenclature.

Finally, several passages about slaughtering procedure imply knowledge that is only specified and/or worked out in later commentaries. Most of this information is supplied in the annotations. However, it will help the reader to know that the Talmud lists five invalidating acts of slaughter: (1) slicing either above or below a prescribed limit (see 1:3); (2) pressing into the neck (see 2:3); (3) pausing in the midst of slaughtering (see 2:3); (4) tearing (see 2:4); and (5) burrowing (see 2:4). Since proper rabbinic slaughter requires a continuous stroke in the appropriate anatomical location with a smooth blade, these five acts are deemed to invalidate the animal.

Special Notes for the Reader

In addition to the standard traditional texts (e.g. Tosefta, Talmud) and commentaries (e.g. Rashi), the modern Hebrew commentary of Hanoch Albeck (*Shishah Sidrei Mishnah*) was consulted. To better understand modern, ultra-Orthodox interpretations (especially pertinent for a tractate with such importance for modern practice), Artscroll's Mishnah and Talmud editions were consulted. Samantha Morello, DVM, answered technical questions related to animal physiology.

Further, English translations by Herbert Danby and Jacob Neusner were consulted. Much of the biblical animal nomenclature was based on Jacob Milgrom's translations in his Anchor Bible (*AB*) commentary *Leviticus 1–16*.

Tractate Hullin

Chapter One

1:1–4 *Valid Animal Slaughter*

1 All may slaughter, and their slaughter is valid,
except for a deaf-mute, one who is legally incompetent, or a minor,
lest they ruin the meat in their act of slaughtering.
But all of these who slaughter while others observe them,
their slaughter is valid.
An animal slaughtered by a gentile is carcass,
and it imparts impurity by carriage.
One who slaughters at night,
and so too a blind person who slaughters—
his slaughter is valid.
One who slaughters on the Sabbath or on the Day of Atonement,
even though he becomes liable for death—
his slaughter is valid.

1:1 *Hullin* begins by discussing various rules concerning valid animal slaughter, including who, with what, and how one may slaughter. Many of these issues will be expanded upon later on in the tractate.

All may slaughter: All Jews.

deaf-mute... legally incompetent... minor: The concern here is that they possess neither the ability nor the knowledge to produce valid slaughter.

But all of these: So long as they are observed to ensure that they follow proper procedure, then their slaughter is valid. The Tosefta allows blind people and minors to slaughter, so long as they know how to do so properly.

by a gentile is carcass: An animal that died without slaughter is *carcass* (Hebrew, *nevelah*), which is neither to be consumed nor touched by Israelites (e.g. Leviticus 11:39–40). If a gentile slaughters, it is considered a natural act, meaning that no actual—or valid—slaughter has occurred.

slaughters at night: Since darkness and blindness prevent one from seeing the actual act, one might have thought that the slaughter is not valid.

liable for death: One may not slaughter on either of these holidays. Intentionally slaughtering an animal on the Sabbath is punished by stoning and on the Day of Atonement is punished by extirpation (*karet*). The concept here is that, although the slaughter constitutes a serious transgression, the act itself is valid and the meat can be consumed by others.

2 One who slaughters with a hand sickle, with a flint, or with a reed—
his slaughter is valid.
All may slaughter.
And at any time they may slaughter.
And with anything they may slaughter,
except for a reaping sickle, saw, teeth, or fingernails—
because they choke.
One who slaughters with a reaping sickle in a forward motion:
the House of Shammai deem it invalid,
but the House of Hillel deem it valid.
But if they filed down its teeth, then, it is like a knife.
3 One who slaughters at the top cartilage ring of the trachea[1]
and leaves in it a thread's breadth of its whole circumference—
his slaughter is valid.
R. Yose b. Judah says:
A thread's breadth of the greater part of its circumference.
4 One who slaughters at the sides—
his slaughter is valid;
one who pinches at the sides—
his act of pinching is invalid.
One who slaughters at the back of the neck—

[1] "top . . . trachea": Heb. "the ring."

1:2 *teeth*: Teeth anchored into the jawbone of a dead animal.

they choke: Valid animal slaughter requires a precise severing of the trachea (discussed in detail, below).

forward motion: Lit. "in the direction of its motion." According to Rashi, this type of sickle has its teeth facing the handle and sharply angled inwards, so it would perform the proper cut only going forward, but would tear when going backwards.

House of Shammai: The Talmud is unsure what precise issue is at stake in this dispute.

like a knife: Filing down the reaping sickle's teeth renders it equivalent to a knife, which is a valid implement for slaughter.

1:3 *ring*: Valid slaughter requires extensive knowledge of animal physiology. According to tradition, the top cartilage ring (known as the "great ring") is the cricoid cartilage.

thread's breadth: When slaughtering an animal, there are upper and lower limits of the throat that one cannot incise above or below. (See the discussion in the introduction.) This case addresses the upper limit. So long as there remains a part of the ring the entire length of its circumference—even if only the length of a single thread—then one has cut within the prescribed limit and one's slaughter is valid.

greater part: Provided that most of its circumference remains, then the slaughter is valid.

1:4 *at the sides*: Rather than at the middle of the throat.

pinches at the sides: Pinching is a sacrificial method for slaughtering bird offerings. According to Leviticus 5:8, pinching must occur opposite the back of the neck, which explains why this mishnah invalidates an act of pinching from the side. Further, Leviticus 5:8 mandates that the head not be completely separated.

at the back of the neck: One who slaughters at the nape of the neck will sever the neck bone first. As a result, the animal will immediately be *terefah*. Valid slaughter requires that the two major organs of the throat (the trachea and esophagus) be severed. However, this can only occur on a valid animal, which is not the case here, since, by the time these organs would be cut, the animal is already *terefah*.

his slaughter is invalid;
one who pinches at the back of the neck—
his act of pinching is valid.
One who slaughters from the throat—
his slaughter is valid;
one who pinches from the throat—
his act of pinching is invalid,[2]
for the whole back of the neck is valid for pinching,
and the whole throat is valid for slaughter.
It thus emerges that what is valid with regard to slaughter
is invalid with regard to pinching;
what is valid with regard to pinching
is invalid with regard to slaughter.

1:5–6 *Various Ritual Matters*

5 What is valid with regard to turtle doves
is invalid with regard to pigeons;
what is valid with regard to pigeons
is invalid with regard to turtle doves.
The beginning of the yellowing in both turtle doves and pigeons[3] is invalid.
6 What is valid with regard to the heifer

[2] **P**, **K** lack this entire phrase; in **K** it appears in the margin.
[3] Lit. "in this one and in that one."

pinches at the back: Since the biblical procedure of pinching a bird requires a priest to pinch its neck, the usual procedure for valid slaughter (i.e. cutting the organs of the throat) does not apply. Hence, the animal would not be *terefah* and would be permissible.

the whole back of the neck: So long as one slaughters within the prescribed upper and lower limits, then the entire front of the neck is valid for slaughter and the entire back is valid for pinching.

It thus emerges: This sentence seems redundant, although the Talmud attempts to explain what it adds. Possibly because of this seeming redundancy, as well as similar phrasing, **K** and **P** place this sentence at the beginning of 1:5.

1:5 The topic switches to various ritual matters (sacrificial animals, purity, and tithing) discussed in similar phrasing.

turtle doves: Turtle doves and pigeons are the only two birds acceptable for biblical sacrifice (e.g. Leviticus 1:14). According to the Talmud, turtle doves may be offered only after they have reached maturity, while pigeons may be offered only before they reach maturity. Thus, when one is eligible, the other is ineligible.

yellowing: According to the Talmud, when these birds transition to maturity, their feathers turn yellow. This serves as a physical marker of a liminal stage of development: it is neither minor nor adult. At this moment, the pigeon is presumed to be too old for sacrifice and the turtle dove is presumed to be too young.

1:6 *heifer*: A red heifer is a key component of the biblical ritual for the removal of corpse impurity (see Numbers 19; and *Parah*).

is invalid with regard to the calf;
what is valid with regard to the calf
is invalid with regard to the heifer.
What is valid with regard to priests
is invalid with regard to Levites;
what is valid with regard to Levites
is invalid with regard to priests.
What is pure with regard to earthenware utensils
is impure with regard to all [other] utensils;
what is pure with regard to all utensils
is impure with regard to earthenware utensils.
What is pure with regard to wooden utensils
is impure with regard to metal utensils;
what is pure with regard to metal utensils
is impure with regard to wooden utensils.
What is liable with regard to bitter almonds
is exempt with regard to sweet;
what is liable with regard to sweet,
is exempt with regard to bitter.

calf: The calf is the "broken-neck calf" (see 5:3). If a murdered corpse is found in the open field and the murderer is unknown, a problem arises: blood pollutes the Land of Israel and this pollution can only be removed by shedding the murderer's blood (see Numbers 35:33–34). To address this situation, Deuteronomy 21:1–9 mandates a procedure for purging Israel of this pollution involving the breaking of a calf's neck.

valid with regard to the calf: Each ritual mandates that the animal is killed in its own precise (and contradictory) manner: the calf by breaking the neck and the heifer by slaughter. Thus the procedure for one would invalidate the other, and one cannot substitute the method of killing without invalidating the ritual itself.

valid with regard to priests: In addition to serving different functions in the Temple, priests and Levites also have different requirements. Two facts are relevant for the present case. (1) Levites have a mandatory retirement age of fifty (see Numbers 8:23–26), though priests have no such limit; and (2) priests are disqualified if they have certain blemishes or physical deformities (see Leviticus 21:16–24), though Levites have no such condition.

What is pure: In both biblical and rabbinic literature, there is a complicated binary system of purity and impurity. See the tractates in the Order of Purities (*Tohorot*).

earthenware utensils: An earthenware utensil does not contract impurity if an impure person or object comes into contact with its exterior surface. All other utensils contract impurity in this circumstance. On the other hand, if an impure person or object enters the internal space of a non-earthenware utensil without actually touching it, then that utensil remains pure. In this circumstance an earthenware vessel would become impure.

wooden utensils: According to the Talmud, a wooden utensil that is unfinished (i.e. lacking finishing touches but still functional) can be rendered impure; this does not apply to metal utensils. On the other hand, a wooden utensil that is flat, and hence lacks a cavity, does not become impure, unlike metal utensils.

bitter almonds: Apparently, the rule is about tithing and *terumah* (on these rules, see *Ma'aserot* and *Terumah*, introductions). According to a tannaitic tradition in the Babylonian Talmud, bitter almonds are consumed when they are small (when they are less bitter) and sweet almonds are consumed when they are large (when they taste best). As such, each type of almond is subject to tithes when it is considered edible.

1:7 *Miscellaneous Rules about Changing Circumstances*

7 Grapeskin wine:
until it has fermented—
it may not be purchased with tithe money,
and it invalidates the immersion pool;[4]
once it has fermented—
it may be purchased with tithe money,
and it does not invalidate the immersion pool.
Brothers who are partners:
when they are liable for an exchange fee—
they are exempt from the animal tithe;
but when they are liable for the animal tithe—
they are exempt from the exchange fee.
Wherever there is a right of sale there is no fine;
but wherever there is a fine there is no right of sale.
Wherever there is a right of refusal there is no *halitsah*;

[4] **K**, **P** lack the clause about the immersion pool both here and in the sentence that follows.

1:7 A common pattern continues here, wherein the same person or thing is compared in two different states.

Grapeskin wine: An inferior-quality wine made by steeping grapeskins or other grape refuse in water and then fermenting it. This same ruling appears almost verbatim in *Ma'aser Sheni* 1:3; see also *Ma'aserot* 5:6.

tithe money: Specifically "second tithe," see *Ma'aser Sheni*, which must be eaten in Jerusalem, or redeemed for money, and the money spent on food in Jerusalem (see Deuteronomy 14:12–26). This is an issue here because fermented grapeskin wine is classed as a food that one may acquire with second-tithe money, while unfermented grapeskin wine is classified as merely water.

immersion pool: Heb. *miqveh*. If an immersion pool has less than forty *se'ah* of naturally collected water, then adding a small amount of drawn water invalidates it. Since unfermented grapeskin wine is equivalent to water, then it would invalidate the *miqveh* (*Miqva'ot* 7:2). However, fermented grapeskin wine is "wine" and has different rules (see *Miqva'ot* 7:2–5).

Brothers who are partners: Brothers who form a business partnership, handling together the estate they inherited from their deceased father. If they separated the estate and then formed their partnership, they are required to pay the surcharge (*qalbon*, Greek *kollybos*, "exchange fee") for paying a single *sheqel* for the two of them. (See *Sheqalim* 1:6–7; our passage is paralleled at 1:7 and *Bekhorot* 9:3.) However, they are not obligated to pay the animal tithe (Leviticus 27:32), from which the rabbis exempt animals owned in partnership. On the other hand, if the estate was not divided, it is subject to the animal tithe, but not the surcharge (since the estate is still considered property of the father, who can pay a *sheqel* for his sons, without incurring the surcharge).

right of sale: A father's right to sell his minor daughter (conventionally, from birth until the age of twelve and the appearance of two pubic hairs) as a maidservant, Exodus 21:7–11.

fine: The payment that the seducer pays to the father of a young woman (conventionally, during the six months following the end of minority); Exodus 22:15–16 and Deuteronomy 22:28–29. The rabbis understood the fine to apply to a young woman and not to a minor. Thus, when one's daughter is a minor, she is eligible for the right of sale, but not subject to the fine; and when she is a young woman, she is subject to the fine, but not to the right of sale. (This interpretation is clearer in the parallel in *Ketubbot* 3:8.)

right of refusal: When a mother or brother have married off a minor girl, in a case where her father is deceased, the girl has the right of refusal while a minor (*Yevamot* 13:1–5).

but wherever there is *halitsah* there is no right of refusal.
Wherever there is a sounding of the *shofar* there is no *havdalah*;
but wherever there is *havdalah* there is no sounding of the *shofar*.
A[5] festival day that coincides with the Sabbath eve—
they sound the *shofar* but do not recite *havdalah*;
for the day after the Sabbath—
they recite *havdalah* but do not sound the *shofar*.
How do they recite the *havdalah*?
"[Blessed are You . . .] who distinguishes between holy and holy."
R. Dosa says:
"Who distinguishes between more holy and less holy."

Chapter Two

2:1–10 *Slaughtering Procedure*

2 One who slaughters [by cutting through one organ] for a bird,
or two for a domestic animal,

[5] **K, P**: "How? A festival day..."

halitsah: The brother of a man who died childless must either engage in a levirate marriage with the widow, or release her through a rite involving the removing of the levir's shoe, or *halitsah*. See Deuteronomy 25:5–9 and *Yevamot*, introduction. According to *Yevamot* 12:4, neither a minor boy nor minor girl can participate in a valid *halitsah* ceremony.

sounding: Blowing a horn made from a ram or goat for ritual purposes. *Sukkah* 5:5 describes the rules for blowing the *shofar* to announce the arrival of the festival.

havdalah: Lit. "separation/distinction," the blessing recited at the end of Sabbath to demarcate sacred time from profane time. While the *shofar* may not be sounded on the Sabbath, it may be sounded on a festival day. Further, the Mishnah does not appear to know about the apparently later custom of reciting *havdalah* at the conclusion of a festival day (already known in the Talmud). Therefore, the *shofar* may be sounded on a festival day, but *havdalah* is not recited; on the Sabbath, the opposite is true.

Sabbath eve: Friday night, as the Jewish Sabbath goes from sundown Friday night until sundown Saturday night. The day after the Sabbath is therefore Sunday.

How do they recite the havdalah? When the festival day coincides with the day after the Sabbath.

between holy and holy: The usual *havdalah* blessing distinguishes "between holy and profane." The discussion here is about how to phrase a prayer that distinguishes between two, albeit unequal, times of holiness. R. Dosa suggests that the blessing be worded so as to reflect this inequality.

2:1 *[one organ] for a bird, or two for a domestic animal*: One must cut through both the esophagus and the trachea if slaughtering a domestic animal, but need only cut one of those two organs if slaughtering a bird. Thus, the rules for slaughtering fowl are more lenient than for domestic animals. In general, a permissible domestic animal (*behemah*) is a ruminant, ungulate, and domesticated quadruped that can be either large (e.g. cows, oxen) or small (e.g. goats, sheep).

his slaughter is valid;
and the greater part of one, counts as the whole.[6]
R. Judah says:
Not until he cuts through the veins.
Half of one of a bird, or one and a half of a domestic animal,
his slaughter is invalid;
the greater part of one of a bird,
or the greater part of two of a domestic animal,
his slaughter is valid.

2 One who slaughters two heads at once,
his slaughter is valid.
Two who are holding the knife and slaughtering—
even one above and the other below[7]—
their slaughter is valid.

3 If he chopped off the head with a single stroke—
it is[8] invalid.
If he was slaughtering and chopped off the head with a single stroke:
if the knife is the length of the width of a neck—
it is valid.
If he was slaughtering and chopped off two heads with a single stroke:

[6] Lit. "is like it." [7] **K, P**: "one from above them and the other from below them."
[8] **P**: "his slaughter is invalid."

greater part: So long as the majority of an organ is severed, then it is equivalent to the entire organ being cut through.

veins: Specifically of a bird. Since the ruling regarding fowl is more lenient, R. Judah states that valid slaughter of a bird requires one to severe its neck veins (probably the jugular vein, though perhaps also or instead the carotid arteries).

half of one: Half is not the *greater part*, and hence one has not severed enough of the required organ(s) to result in valid slaughter.

the greater part: This clause repeats a rule stated above in this mishnah.

2:2 *two heads at once*. Two animals are standing side-by-side and the slaughterer severs the two organs of each of their throats in a single motion. This scenario and the one that follows is more likely academic than practical.

above...below: The question here is whether two slaughterers, apparently holding the same knife, can effect valid slaughter. According to Rashi the knife was held at an angle. The Talmud adds that this mishnah could refer to two people holding two distinct knives, one cutting higher up on the throat and the other cutting lower.

2:3 On the invalidating acts of slaughter mentioned in 2:3–4, see the introduction.

chopped... invalid: Since the animal is decapitated by pressing and not the proper cutting motion.

slaughtering and chopped: He used the proper motion, but the head was nevertheless severed. As specified below, slaughter properly involves forward ("going") and backward ("coming") strokes.

the width of a neck: If the knife is too short, slaughter that results in decapitation would involve pressing and be invalid; but if the knife is the length of the neck's width (or, according to the Talmud, two neck widths), it is valid.

two heads: Two animals are standing side-by-side and the slaughterer acts in a single cutting motion (cf. 2:2).

if the knife is the length of the width of one neck—
it is valid.
When does this apply?
When he made a forward stroke but not a backward stroke,
made a backward stroke but not a forward stoke.
But if he made a forward and a backward stroke,
however short it was, even with a scalpel—
it is valid.
If a knife fell and slaughtered,
even though it slaughtered according to proper procedure—
it is invalid;
as it is said: *And you shall slaughter... and you shall eat*:
That which you slaughter, you may eat.
If the knife fell and he picked it up;
his clothes[9] fell and he picked them up;
he whetted the knife;
he became fatigued, and his fellow came and slaughtered:
if he paused long enough to slaughter,[10]—
it is invalid.
R. Simeon says:
If one paused long enough to examine.
4 If he slaughtered the esophagus but [merely] cut the trachea,
or slaughtered the trachea but cut the esophagus,[11]
or slaughtered one of [the organs] and waited until it died,
or burrowed the knife under the second and severed it—

[9] Or "utensils." [10] **K, P** add "one [animal]."
[11] The Vilna edition of the Talmud (32a) reads: "or tore open the trachea and afterwards slaughtered [by cutting through] the esophagus," though some commentators delete "afterwards."

When does this apply? When do these rules regarding knife length apply?

however short it was: This phrase could refer either to the length of the stroke or of the knife.

fell and slaughtered: If a knife happened to fall and, in doing so, properly slaughtered an animal.

And you shall slaughter... and you shall eat: Deuteronomy 12:21. The Mishnah reads "you" as requiring a human agent to effect valid slaughter. The Tosefta applies this same logic to the slaughter of a non-Jew, an ape, or the animal itself (i.e. carcass).

knife fell... came and slaughtered: Several cases of pausing in the midst of slaughtering, which renders the slaughter invalid. The Talmud debates the precise length of the pause that renders the slaughter invalid.

examine: Most commentators suggest that R. Simeon's statement refers to one pausing to examine the slaughtering knife. However, it could refer to pausing to inspect the animal (see also Tosefta).

2:4 The following cases involve a slaughterer who properly severs only one throat organ.

esophagus but [merely] cut the trachea: Later commentators associate this with the invalidating act of tearing (see introduction).

waited until it died: The slaughterer severs one of the two organs but then waits until the animal dies before severing the other one.

burrowed the knife: On burrowing, see the introduction. In this case, the first organ of the throat is properly cut, but the second organ is severed (and not torn) when the slaughterer thrusts the knife under it and severs it from back to front.

R. Yeshevav says:
It is carcass;
R. Aqiva says:
It is *terefah.*
R. Yeshevav stated a general rule in the name of R. Joshua:
Whatever became invalid through its slaughtering—
it is carcass;
whatever is slaughtered properly, but another matter caused it to become invalid—
it is *terefah.*
And R. Aqiva conceded to him.
5 One who slaughters a domestic animal, a wild animal, or fowl,
and blood did not flow forth from them—
they are valid;
and they may be eaten with impure hands,
since they have not been made susceptible to impurity by the blood.
R. Simeon says:
They have been made susceptible by the act of slaughtering.
6 One who slaughters an animal that is at the point of death—
Rabban Simeon b. Gamaliel[12] says:
So long as[13] it jerks a foreleg and a hindleg;
R. Eliezer says:
It is sufficient if it spurts;

[12] **K**, **P**: "Rabban Gamaliel." [13] Lit. "until."

carcass ... terefah: According to R. Yeshevav, a half-act is tantamount to a natural death; hence, the animal is carcass. For R. Aqiva, a half-act constitutes an act of defective slaughter; hence, the animal is *terefah*. The distinction has purity implications. Carrying carcass imparts impurity (see 1:1), while carrying an animal *terefah* does not.

rule: This general rule establishes definitions for these two categories: carcass (*nevelah*) is an improperly slaughtered animal and an animal *terefah* is one that was properly slaughtered, but due to another reason (chapter 3), is considered invalid.

2:5 *flow forth from them*: Even if blood did not flow from the neck where one severed the two throat organs, it is still a valid slaughter. However, one must still drain the animal's blood (see 2:9).

impure hands: In the Mishnah, hands that have come into contact with low-level impurity can convey impurity also to foodstuffs that have been moistened. See Leviticus 11:34 and *Makhshirin* introduction and 6:4–8. (This is particular concern in the case of sacrificial meat and *terumah*, but can apply more broadly.)

by the blood: Since no blood flowed, the carcass of the animal is not susceptible to impurity.

R. Simeon argues that the act of slaughter itself makes the animal susceptible to impurity because just as slaughter renders the animal "food" (it is no longer subject to the Noahide law prohibiting the consumption of the limb of a living animal), so too does it render it "food," in that it is susceptible to impurity (Rashi).

2:6 *point of death*: Valid slaughter cannot be performed on a dead animal; therefore, this mishnah asks how near to death an animal can be and still be considered alive enough for the purposes of valid slaughter.

So long as it jerks: The slaughter is invalid, unless the animal when it was slaughtered was able to jerk its limbs.

spurts: This is considered sufficient proof that the animal is alive at the moment of slaughter.

R. Simeon says:
Even one who slaughters at night,
and the next day rises early[14] and finds the walls full of blood—
it is valid,
for it spurted;
and as in accordance with R. Eliezer.
But the Sages say:
So long as it jerks either a foreleg, or a hindleg,
or unless it wags its tail;
the law is the same for a small domestic animal
and a large domestic animal.
A small domestic animal that stretched out its foreleg
but did not retract—
it is invalid,
since this is only[15] the expiration of life.
When does this apply?
When it was presumed to be at the point of death;
but if it was presumed to be healthy, even if it does not have one of these signs, it is valid.

7 One who slaughters for a gentile—
his slaughter is valid;
but R. Eliezer invalidates.
R. Eliezer said:
Even if he slaughtered it so that the gentile might eat from its midriff, it is invalid,
since the unexpressed[16] intention of a gentile is for idolatry.

[14] **K, P**: "and at dawn arises." [15] **K, P** lack "only." [16] **K, P** lack "unexpressed."

walls full of blood: The Talmud explains that "walls" here refers to the walls of the throat adjacent to the incision.

in accordance with R. Eliezer: One who slaughters at night might not see if the animal's blood had spurted at the moment of slaughter. However, if there is evidence that the animal's blood spurted, then the slaughter would comply with R. Eliezer's opinion.

the Sages say: An animal is valid so long as it can jerk either a front or back limb, or wag its tail. This is more lenient than Rabban Simeon b. Gamaliel, who requires both a front and back limb (although he does not mention its tail), but more stringent than R. Eliezer, who only requires spurted blood.

expiration of life: The jerking is merely a death spasm. However, if it retracts its foreleg, then its final movement is not just a death spasm, but a sign of sufficient vitality; hence the slaughter would be valid in the case of foreleg contraction.

2:7 *slaughters for a gentile*: Underlying this mishnah is the question: what is the status of an animal owned by a gentile and slaughtered by a Jew on the gentile's behalf? We have already learned that an animal slaughtered by a gentile is carcass (1:1).

midriff: Lit. "courtyard of the liver." While Rashi says this refers to the diaphragm, it more likely refers to the lobe of the liver. The issue at hand is whether a Jew who has slaughtered an animal for a gentile who only wants one specific portion of the body may then partake of the rest of the animal.

unexpressed intention of a gentile: The rationale for R. Eliezer's opinion: a gentile's intention is always presumed to be idolatrous. Thus, even if a Jew slaughters the animal, this unstated intention invalidates the animal for Jewish consumption and benefit (see *Avodah Zarah* 2:3).

R. Yose said:
The matter is one of lesser and greater:
if in a case where intention invalidates—
with regard to sanctified animals—
everything depends only on the one who performs the ritual act,
does not logic require[17] that in a case where intention does not invalidate—
with regard to nonsacral animals—
that everything depends only on the one who slaughters?

8 One who slaughters designating it for mountains,
designating it for hills,
designating it for seas,
designating it for rivers,
designating it for wilderness—
his slaughter is invalid.
Two who are holding the knife and slaughtering:
one designating it for any of these, and the other designating it for a valid thing—
their slaughter is invalid.

9 One may not slaughter either into seas,
or into rivers, or into utensils;
but one may slaughter into a pool[18] of water,
or on a boat on top of utensils.
One may not slaughter over a pit under any circumstances;[19]

[17] **K**, **P** lack "does not logic require."
[18] **K**, **P** read *ogel* ("reservoir") instead of *uga* ("pool").
[19] **K**, **P** lack "under any circumstances."

lesser and greater: Heb. *qal va-homer*, a mode of inference.

everything depends…ritual act: Only the intention of the actual slaughterer (and not the animal's owner) can invalidate sacrificial slaughter (see *Zevahim* 4:6). This is the "greater" case in the inference from greater to lesser.

who slaughters: In the less serious case of nonsacrificial slaughter, the intention of the slaughterer alone should determine whether the animal is valid.

2:8 *for mountains*: If the worship of nature is the slaughterer's intent, then the resulting slaughter is considered idolatrous, and hence invalid. On the worship of natural objects, see *Avodah Zarah* 3:5.

Two who are holding the knife: See 2:2. So long as one of the actual slaughterers has an improper intent, then the entire slaughter is invalid.

2:9 *into seas*: Giving the appearance that one is worshipping natural objects, which invalidates the slaughter (2:7).

or into utensils: Because one might think that the slaughterer is collecting the blood for use in idolatrous rites.

pool of water: Some sort of small cavity or reservoir, perhaps round in shape. This might be distinguished from an empty utensil, into which one may not allow the blood to drain.

on a boat on top of utensils: If onboard a ship, how does one both keep the ship clean from blood and adhere to rabbinic slaughtering procedure? By pouring blood on top of an overturned utensil, from which the blood may pour into the sea, the slaughterer indicates that the animal is not part of an idolatrous ritual. At the same time, the slaughterer complies with rabbinic law by not directly pouring the blood into either the sea or the utensil.

pit under any circumstances: The concern here, and in what follows, is that one would appear to mimic heretical practice by slaughtering into a pit. It offers a leniency in one's home (a trench that the blood can

but one[20] makes a pit in his house, so that the blood may collect into it;
in the marketplace one may not do so,
so that one does not imitate the heretics.
10 One who slaughters:
designating it a whole burnt offering,
designating it an animal sacrifice,[21]
designating it a suspended guilt offering,
designating it a Passover offering,
designating it a thank offering—
his slaughter is invalid;
but R. Simeon declares it valid.
Two are holding a knife and slaughtering:
one designating it any one of these, and the other for the sake of a valid thing—
their slaughter is invalid.
One who slaughters:
designating it a purgation offering,
designating it an unconditional guilt offering,
designating it a firstborn,
designating it a tithe,

[20] **K**, **P** add "a person, he..." [21] **K**, **P**: "peace offering" (*shelamim*).

drain into after spilling on the floor). This leniency allows one to maintain a clean home, while not publicly imitating heretical slaughtering procedure.

imitate the heretics: Since heretics were understood to slaughter animals and collect the blood in a pit or trench, then rabbinic Jews must distinguish themselves by abstaining from this practice.

2:10 *One who slaughters* a nonsacral domestic animal outside the Temple, which the slaughterer wishes to designate as an offering. However, the animal has not been properly consecrated prior to the slaughter. On offering sacral animals outside the Temple, see *Zevahim* 13:1.

whole burnt offering: e.g. Leviticus 1.

animal sacrifice: According to **K** and **P**, this is an offering of well-being (e.g. Leviticus 7:11–36).

suspended guilt offering: An offering that one must bring if one may have unintentionally violated a law whose punishment is extirpation (*karet*); e.g. Leviticus 5:17–19; *Keritot* 4:1–3.

Passover offering: e.g. Deuteronomy 16:1–7.

thank offering. A type of well-being offering (e.g. Leviticus 7:12–15).

R. Simeon declares it valid: It seems that the preceding rule that the slaughter is invalid is due to the appearance that one was offering a consecrated sacrifice outside the Temple. R. Simeon rejects this view.

Two: See 2:8.

purgation offering: e.g. Leviticus 4:1–5:13. As above, the Mishnah refers to one who performs nonsacral slaughter outside the Temple, but designates the animal a sacral offering at the time of the slaughtering. The obligation to bring any of the offerings mentioned in this second list would be a matter of public knowledge. Therefore, there is no concern that others seeing the slaughter would think that he is truly offering sacrifice outside the Temple.

unconditional guilt offering: See *Zevahim* 5:5.

firstborn: e.g. 4:2; 10:2–3; Numbers 18:15–18.

tithe: The animal tithe, see 1:7; 10:2; Leviticus 27:32.

designating it a substitute offering—
his slaughter is valid.
This is the rule:
Anything that can be offered as a vow or a free-will offering:
one who slaughters with its proper designation—
it is prohibited;[22]
but anything that is not offered as a vow or a free-will offering—
one who slaughters with its proper designation—
it is valid.

Chapter Three

3:1–5 *Invalidating Defects on an Animal*

3 These are *terefah* among domestic animals:
one whose esophagus is pierced;
or one whose trachea is torn;
the membrane of the brain is pierced;
the heart is pierced into its chamber;
the spine is broken and its cord is severed;
the liver is removed and nothing whatsoever remains of it;
the lung is pierced;
or deficient;
R. Simeon says:
Not until it is pierced into the bronchial tubes;

[22] **K**, **P**: "invalid."

substitute offering: See Leviticus 27:10 and *Temurah*.

rule: Since concerns about public misperception only apply to offerings brought in fulfillment of a vow or as a free-will offering, only these are invalid if one designated the slaughter in this way. The Talmud argues that the wording of this general rule includes cases that might otherwise have not been considered applicable.

prohibited: See n. 22.

3:1–5 The defects that invalidate animals. These defects are unrelated to an animal's slaughter (discussed above in chapters 1–2). Rather, these defects are those discovered on the animal in a postslaughter inspection. The presumption throughout is that the slaughter procedure was valid.

3:1 This mishnah lists eighteen defects that result in a domestic animal being *terefah*.

brain…liver: In these cases, the invalidating act is considered fully completed, hence the animal is *terefah*. Contrast 3:2, in which these acts are considered only partially completed, hence the animal is deemed valid.

the lung is pierced; or deficient: The Talmud asks: what is the difference between these two terms? what is meant by "deficient"?

bronchial tubes: Located inside of the lung. As there are many bronchi in the lungs, the Talmud states that these refer to the primary bronchi.

the abomasum is pierced;
the gallbladder is pierced;
the intestines are pierced;
the inner rumen is pierced;
or the greater part of the outer is torn;
R. Judah says:
For a large animal, it is a handbreadth,
for a small animal, it is the greater part.
The omasum
or the reticulum are pierced to the outside.
It fell from the roof;
most of its ribs are broken;
or it is mauled by a wolf.
R. Judah says:
One mauled by a wolf, in the case of a small animal;
and one mauled by a lion, in the case of a large animal;
one mauled by a hawk, in the case of small fowl;
and one mauled by a falcon,[23] in the case of large fowl.
This is the rule:
[If] any animal with a similar defect could not live, it is *terefah*.

[23] Following **K**, **P**, which have *gaz*, "falcon" instead of *gas*, "large."

abomasum: Also called the maw; the fourth and final stomach of a ruminant.

gallbladder: Though connected to the liver, the gallbladder is a separate organ.

inner rumen: The rumen, or paunch, is the first stomach in a ruminant.

outer: In contrast to the inner rumen, where if *any* part is pierced then it is *terefah*, the majority of the outer rumen must be torn for the domestic animal to be *terefah*.

large... small animal: The differences in size refer to the physical size of the domestic animal and not to different species. Depending on the domestic animal's size, a handbreadth tear might amount to more or less than the majority of its outer rumen. Thus, the operating rule is that whichever is smaller, the handbreadth or the majority, is the determining factor in its status.

omasum: The third stomach in a ruminant.

reticulum: The second stomach in a ruminant. Since the reticulum and the omasum are joined, if the domestic animal is pierced at the place where the stomachs join, it is not deemed pierced "to the outside" and is not *terefah* (see 3:2). However, if it is pierced anywhere else on these stomachs, then it is *terefah*.

most of its ribs: According to the Talmud, there are twenty-two ribs (modern animal science counts differently), and twelve constitutes a majority.

falcon: The reading of the manuscripts is preferred. Although the taxonomic nomenclature is uncertain, this term clearly refers to a large bird of prey.

similar defect: Since the animal under consideration has already been slaughtered, one must ask what effect such a defect would have in a living animal to determine the status of the slaughtered animal. Since this general rule seems unnecessary after such a long and specific list of defects, the Talmud uses it to derive seven other defects that render a domestic animal *terefah*.

2 And these are valid among domestic animals:
the trachea is pierced or is slit.
How much may be missing?
Rabban Simeon b. Gamaliel says:
As much as an Italian *issar*.
The skull is broken through, but the membrane of the brain is not pierced;
the heart is pierced, but not into its chamber;
the spine is broken, but its cord is not severed;
the liver is removed, but an olive's bulk of it remains;[24]
the omasum or the reticulum are pierced one into the other;
the spleen is removed;
the kidneys are removed;
the lower jaw is removed;
its uterus is removed;
one with a lung dried by an act of heaven.[25]
One which is flayed—
R. Meir deems it valid;
but the Sages deem it invalid.
3 These are *terefah* among fowl:
one whose esophagus is pierced;
one whose trachea is torn;
a weasel struck it on its head, in a place that renders it *terefah*;
the gizzard is pierced;

[24] **K**, **P**: "but any at all remains of it." [25] **K**, **P** add "it is valid."

3:2 *these are valid*: Even if an animal possesses these defects, it is still deemed valid. Many of the defects are variants of those in 3:1.

trachea is pierced or is slit: As opposed to "torn" (1:3).

Italian issar: A Roman coin (from *assarius*, or *as*).

olive's bulk: A common minimum measurement in rabbinic literature.

one into the other: Instead of to the outside (see 3:1), the hole is at the place where the second and third stomachs join.

spleen is removed: However, according to the Talmud, if the spleen is present but pierced, then the animal is *terefah*.

lower jaw is removed: The Talmud debates the meaning of this, since the lower jaw would need to be removed in such a way so as to leave the vital organs of the throat intact.

uterus is removed: Cf. *Bekhorot* 4:4.

lung dried by an act of heaven: Since both the meaning and the means of distinguishing lungs dried by heavenly (i.e. thunder, lightning) and nonheavenly (i.e. human, animal) acts are unclear, the Talmud seeks to elucidate this phrase.

One which is flayed: An animal that has lost its hide.

3:3 According to the Talmud, all of the defects that render a domestic animal *terefah* (see 3:1) are likewise applicable to fowl. Therefore, this mishnah discusses laws that are specific to fowl (e.g. regarding the gizzard).

esophagus…trachea…: The first two rules about the esophagus and the trachea appear verbatim in 3:1.

place that renders it terefah: As in 3:2, the brain's membrane must be pierced for an animal to be *terefah*; simply cracking the skull does not invalidate it.

the intestines are pierced.
If it fell into the fire and its internal organs are scorched—
if they are green, they are invalid;
if they are red—
they are valid.
If he trampled it or knocked it against the wall,
or a domestic animal crushed it,
but it flutters and[26] it remains alive for twenty-four hours and then he slaughtered it—
it is valid.

4 These are valid among fowl:
the trachea is pierced or is slit;
a weasel struck it on its head, in a place that does not render it[27] *terefah*;
the crop is pierced;
Rabbi[28] says:
Even if it is removed;
the intestines protrude but are not pierced;
its wings are broken;
its legs are broken;[29]
its wing feathers are plucked.
R. Judah says:
If the down is removed, it is invalid.

[26] **K, P**: "if." [27] **K, P** lack "on its head . . . it." [28] **K**: "R. Meir."
[29] **P** reverses the order of the statements about "wings" and "legs"; **K** lacks "its legs are broken."

intestines: Perhaps repeated here (cf. 3:1) because of the particular ruling regarding fowl intestines in 3:4.

internal organs: Usually the term *bnei me'ayim* is translated "intestines"; however, "internal organs" is preferable here for two reasons: (1) this chapter has consistently used a more specific term (*dakkin*) for intestines; and (2) a flaming fowl would scorch (and hence shrivel) more than a single organ. The broader term, therefore, conveys the fact that this ruling probably refers to the viscera in general rather than just the intestines (cf. Tosefta).

green . . . red . . .: Red is the natural hue of fowl bowels. Hence, if the flames turn them green, then the fowl is invalid; if the fowl escapes before its bowels are damaged to the point of changing color, then it remains valid.

trampled: Since the action immediately below is ascribed to a domestic animal, the agent of action here is most likely human.

knocked: Since the root *t-r-f* is the same as for *terefah*, perhaps this is a pun, wherein one that he "knocked" (*terafah*) is valid (and hence, not "*terefah*").

3:4 *These are valid*: Even if a fowl possesses these defects, it is still deemed valid.

Rabbi: The Mishnah's redactor, R. Judah the Patriarch.

intestines protrude: Unlike in 3:3, where we translated *bnei me'ayim* as "internal organs," here the standard translation of "intestines" seems warranted, as 3:1 and 3:3 also discuss pierced intestines. The use of the term here is probably influenced by 3:3. Further, this is the term used in *Zevahim* 6:5, which describes the burnt offering of fowl and mandates the removal of its crop, plumage, and intestines. In our present mishnah, we also learn the rules concerning a pierced crop and removed plumage.

wings are broken: Probably referring to the bones of the wing (Rashi).

legs are broken: See 4:6.

5 One that has congestion of the blood;
or has inhaled smoke;
or has been sickened by cold;[30]
or that has eaten oleander;
or that has eaten chicken feces;
or that has drunk contaminated[31] water,
it is valid.[32]
If it ate deadly poison, or a snake bit it,
it is permissible in regard to being *terefah*,
but it is forbidden in regard to endangering life.

3:6–7 *Edible Birds and Locusts*

6 The signs of the domestic animal and wild animal were stated in the Torah,
but the signs of the fowl were not stated.
However, the Sages have said:
Any fowl that mauls is impure;
any that has an extra toe, and a crop, and whose gizzard can be peeled is pure.
R. Eleazar b. Zadok says:
Any fowl that parts its feet is impure.

[30] **K, P** lack this phrase, perhaps due to haplography with the previous participle.
[31] Lit. "bad" or "evil." [32] **K**: "it is invalid."

3:5 Ailments that, though they may harm the entire animal and not just particular body parts (as discussed above in 3:1–4), do not render it *terefah*.

congestion of the blood: Some sort of disorder that sickens the animal due to an increase in its blood.

oleander: Large doses of oleander are toxic to both humans and animals.

it is valid: Since there is no reason to declare the animal *terefah*, it is valid. However, the rules for an animal at the point of death (2:6) would still apply.

snake bit it: Cf. *Terumot* 8:6.

3:6–7 Leviticus 11 and Deuteronomy 14 list a variety of animals that can and cannot be consumed. For domestic animals, water creatures, and winged swarming creatures, criteria for inclusion and exclusion are provided; for fowl, no criteria are provided, only a list of prohibited animals; and for small land animals, the entire category—without exception—is prohibited.

3:6 *signs*: The signs that indicate whether an animal is valid. Domesticated and wild animals must be ruminants and have split hooves (e.g. Leviticus 11:2–3). Fowl lack any explicit criteria (e.g. Leviticus 11:13–19).

the Sages have said: The Sages offer rules for inclusion and exclusion of fowl. The language here is pure/impure, following biblical language for permitted and prohibited animals. If it is not a bird of prey and has three common characteristics cited below, then it is acceptable for ingestion.

extra toe: According to Rashi, this is the toe that is behind the other toes, a common anatomical feature of birds.

gizzard can be peeled: The lining of the gizzard can be peeled away from the underlying muscle.

parts its feet: That parts the toes on its feet evenly (i.e. two in the front and two in the back; cf. Tosefta). In contrast, parted hooves mark a domestic animal as pure.

7 And among locusts:
any that have four legs, four wings, and jointed legs,
and whose wings cover the greater part of it.
R. Yose says:
And its name is "locust."
And among fish:
Any that have fins and scales.
R. Judah says:
Two scales and one fin.
And which are scales?
Those that are permanent.
And the fins?
Those with which it swims.

Chapter Four

4:1–7 *Slaughtering a Pregnant Animal*

4 A domestic animal that is in hard labor:
and the fetus put forth its foreleg and retracts it—
it is permitted for consumption.[33]
If it put forth its head, even though it retracted it—
in this case, it is as one that has been born.
One who cuts off part of the fetus that is in her womb—

[33] **K, P** lack "for consumption."

3:7 *locusts*: While in the Hebrew Bible *hagavim* means "grasshoppers," the rabbis use it as the generic term for all locusts. A common source of protein in antiquity, locusts were roasted, boiled, salted, or brined.

four legs, etc.: The first three rules for permissibility follow biblical law for winged swarming creatures (Leviticus 11:20–23). The fourth rule is derived by the rabbis from the biblical criteria.

name is "locust": In addition to the above-stated criteria, a winged swarming creature must be commonly called (and hence classified as) "locust" in order to be valid. Due to taxonomic uncertainty, Ashkenazic communities follow rulings that prohibit all locusts; however, some Middle Eastern communities do consume them.

fins and scales: Leviticus 11:9–12. Since neither the minimum number nor the precise definition of either are provided in the Bible, the Mishnah clarifies potential ambiguities.

4:1 *put forth its head*: A similar test for birth also applies to humans. See *Niddah* 3:5.

one that has been born: At this point, it is deemed an offspring not a fetus. Thus, it would require proper slaughter if alive and would be *terefah* if dead.

cuts off part of the fetus: Presumably, to help a dam in distress. If the dam is properly slaughtered, then the part of the fetus that remains inside the dam is valid (and would not violate the Noahide law prohibiting consuming the limb from a living animal). On rabbinic law regarding cutting a fetus in a human womb during hard labor, see *Oholot* 7:6.

it is permitted for consumption;
part of the [dam's] spleen or kidneys—
it is forbidden for consumption.
This is the rule:
Something that is from its body is forbidden;
[but] that which is not from its body is permitted.

2 A domestic animal that is delivering its firstborn in hard labor:
he may cut off each limb and throw it to the dogs.
If the greater part of it came forth—
in this case, it must be buried,
and she is exempt[34] from the firstborn.

3 A domestic animal whose fetus died in her womb,
and the shepherd put in his hand and touched it:
whether an impure domestic animal or a pure domestic animal—
he is pure.
R. Yose the Galilean says:
In the case of an impure animal, he is impure;
and in the case of a pure animal, he is pure.
A woman whose fetus died in her womb,
and the midwife put in her hand and touched it,
the midwife is impure with seven-day impurity,
but the woman is pure until the fetus emerges.

[34] Due to metathesis, **K** reads "becomes *terefah*."

spleen or kidneys: The rule refers to the dam's organs: if one cut off part of her spleen or kidneys, they may not be eaten. Though the dam would be valid with its spleen or kidneys removed (see 3:2), if one cuts part of them off while she is still alive, both the removed part and that which remains inside the dam are classified as a limb from a living animal, and are forbidden. Cf. 9:7.

rule: A piece cut off of the dam's body is considered a limb from a living animal and is forbidden. However, the fetus is not considered her body.

4:2 *each limb*: As each limb emerges, it may be cut off. Until the greater part emerges in a single mass, the animal has not been "born."

it must be buried: In the second case, one dismembers it after the greater part has emerged. At this point, the animal is considered "born," and thus cannot be fed to the dogs and must be buried.

exempt from the firstborn: A subsequent live birth would no longer be considered a firstborn (see 2:10; 10:2–3; Numbers 18:15).

4:3 *whether an impure…or pure domestic animal*: Animal carcasses (i.e. animals killed by a means other than valid slaughter) convey impurity. However, the fetus is not considered a dead animal on its own, since its mother's proper slaughter can validate it (see 4:1).

R. Yose the Galilean argues that this only applies to a "pure" (i.e. permitted) animal, in contrast to an impure animal, which would convey impurity. According to the Talmud, R. Yose's argument is based on an interpretation of Leviticus 5:2.

woman whose fetus: This case is discussed here because it raises analogous issues regarding the purity status of a human who comes into contact with a dead fetus.

seven-day impurity: She is deemed to have touched a corpse (see Numbers 19:11). However, the mother does not contract impurity until the fetus emerges from her body. See further *Oholot* 7:4–6. On the postpartum impurity associated with birthing a living child, see Leviticus 12.

4 A domestic animal that is in hard labor,
and the fetus puts forth its foreleg and one cuts it off,
and afterward one slaughters its mother—
the meat is pure.
If he slaughtered its mother,
and afterward cuts it off—
the meat is [in the status of] that which has touched carcass—
the words of R. Meir.
But the Sages say:
[In the status of] that which has touched a *terefah* that has been slaughtered.
Just as we find with regard to a *terefah*,
that the slaughter of the domestic animal renders it pure,
so too the slaughter of the domestic animal[35] renders pure the severed limb![36]
R. Meir said to them:
No. If the slaughter of a domestic animal *terefah* renders it pure,
it does so to something that is its own body;
should it render pure the limb,[37]
which is something that is not its own body?
From where do we know concerning a *terefah* that its slaughter[38] renders it pure?
An impure domestic animal is forbidden for consumption;
so too[39] an animal *terefah* is forbidden for consumption:
just as an impure domestic animal,
its slaughter does not render it pure,
so too a *terefah*,
should not its slaughter fail to render it pure?
No. Although you said this in regard to an impure domestic animal,

[35] **P**: "its mother." [36] **K, P**: "the fetus." [37] **K, P**: "the fetus."
[38] **K** adds "does not." [39] **K, P**: "and."

4:4 *meat is pure*: The severed limb is impure, but the remaining meat that came into contact with it becomes pure after its mother is properly slaughtered (see the rule in 4:1). On purity issues involving limbs, see 9:7 and *Oholot* 1:7–8.

touched carcass: If the mother is slaughtered and then the foreleg, which is outside the womb, is severed, the foreleg is now considered a limb from a living animal and, according to R. Meir, conveys the impurity of having touched carcass to the remaining meat of the fetus, since the fetus came into contact with it.

Just as we find: A formula introducing an inferential argument. The Sages explain their ruling that just as slaughtering an animal that would have died by itself gives it the status of *terefah*, which is not impure, as opposed to carcass, which is impure, so too should the slaughter prevent the detached limb from transmitting impurity. (In either case, eating the meat of the fetus is prohibited.) Cf. *Zevahim* 7:6 (which also cites R. Meir).

No. If the slaughter...: R. Meir disagrees based on logic: slaughtering a dam found to be *terefah* does not convey impurity, while leaving it to die on its own it would, because the status of *its own body* is affected by the slaughter; however, this change in status should not extend to the detached limb of the fetus, since it is not part of the dam's *own body*.

From where do we know: This term usually introduces scriptural support for a ruling (e.g. 9:5; *Shabbat* 9:1–4). Here, however, no direct scriptural prooftext appears. The expression introduces the Sages' reply to R. Meir, which continues to up to *Take for yourself* below.

which never had a moment of permissibility,
can you say this in regard to a domestic animal *terefah*,
that does have a moment of permissibility?
Take for yourself what you have brought!
Indeed, that which is born *terefah* from the womb, from where do we know it?
No. Although you said this in regard to an impure domestic animal,
none of whose kind is subject to slaughter,
can you say this in regard to a *terefah* domestic animal,
whose kind is subject to slaughter?
A live eight-months' birth:
its slaughter does not render it pure,
since none of its kind is subject to slaughter.

5 One who slaughters a domestic animal,
and finds in it an eight-months' fetus, alive or dead,
or a dead nine-months' birth,
one may tear it open, but must remove its blood.
If he found a live nine-months' birth,
it requires slaughter,[40]
and he is liable with regard to *It and its offspring*—
the words of R. Meir.

[40] **P** adds "because it was not."

moment of permissibility: An impure animal, such as a pig, is never permitted even if slaughtered. A slaughtered permitted animal that was deemed *terefah*, on the other hand, is born valid and later becomes invalid due to physical defects (chapter 3). Surely, we cannot derive from an impure animal the consequences of slaughter for pure animals.

Take for yourself what you have brought! A response in support of R. Meir. Retract what you have said, since your argument has a logical flaw. While slaughter prevents the animal from being impure, your argument does not prove that the fetus is made pure.

Indeed…from where do we know it? R. Meir might say: on the argument provided above, the fetus in this case, too, never had a moment of permissibility, and should not be purified.

whose kind is subject to slaughter: An unborn fetus of a permitted animal is of a kind that is subject to the laws of slaughter. This reflects a variant of the Sages' argument above.

live eight-months' birth: A full-term (and hence, eligible for slaughter) animal must gestate for nine months (4:5). Even if born alive, an eight-months' birth is considered unviable, and thus is ineligible for slaughter. This case appears here because it presents an exception to the previously stated law (in that it is both a pure animal and categorically ineligible for slaughter).

4:5 *tear it open*: Since neither a live eight-months' birth (see 4:4) nor a dead eight- or nine-months' birth are viable, they may be torn open rather than properly slaughtered and still be valid for consumption.

must remove its blood: e.g. Deuteronomy 12:23–25.

It and its offspring: Leviticus 22:28. The verse prohibits killing a dam and its offspring on the same day (also see 5:1–3, 5). Since a live nine-months' birth is considered viable, it requires slaughter and would violate a biblical mandate if slaughtered on that same day. The Sages disagree with R. Meir on the grounds that, until the fetus is actually born, it is part of the dam; as such, slaughtering the dam would render its fetus pure and exempt it from the requirement of having its own slaughter (and, logically, the biblical prohibition). R. Simeon of Shezur states that the animal remains in this status throughout the course of its entire life.

But the Sages say:
Its mother's slaughter renders it pure.
R. Simeon of Shezur says:
Even if it became an eight-year-old[41] and plows the field—
its mother's slaughter renders it pure.
If he tore the mother[42] open and found in it a live nine-months' fetus—
it requires slaughter,
since its mother was not slaughtered.

6 A domestic animal, whose hindlegs were cut off:
below the joint—
it is valid;
above the joint—
it is invalid.
And so too if the juncture of the sinews is removed.
If the bone was broken:
if most of the meat remains—
its slaughter renders it pure;
but if not[43]—
its slaughter does not render it pure.

7 One who slaughters a domestic animal and finds in it an afterbirth—
one with robust sensibilities may eat it;
and it does not impart impurity,
neither food impurity nor carcass impurity.

[41] **K, P**: "five-year-old." [42] For "the mother," Hebrew has "her."
[43] **K, P**: "if most of the flesh does not remain."

tore the mother open: If one cut open the dam (either alive or dead but not properly slaughtered), then the dam has not been properly slaughtered. Thus, the loophole for exempting the live nine-months' birth from slaughter does not apply.

4:6 While this mishnah does not discuss a pregnant animal, it is included here because it addresses severing an animal's hindlegs, which relates to the removal of the limbs of an animal or its fetus, mentioned earlier in this chapter. As these defects would render it *terefah*, this mishnah might have better fit in chapter 3.

the joint: A domestic animal's leg has six joints. The Talmud debates to which joint this refers.

juncture of the sinews: If removed, the animal is invalid. The Talmud debates this precise anatomical identification.

bone was broken: If an animal's hindleg was broken such that it is not *terefah*, it does not convey impurity and slaughtering it makes the limb valid for consumption, provided that the majority of the meat surrounding the fracture remains intact. Otherwise, the limb would be prohibited on account of being "a limb from a living animal."

4:7 *finds in it an afterbirth*: By slaughtering a dam, her afterbirth (like the fetus inside her) becomes valid for ingestion. One who is not a squeamish eater may ingest it (cf. *Avodah Zarah* 2:5; *Menahot* 11:7).

neither food impurity, nor carcass impurity: Since the afterbirth is not considered an actual food, it neither imparts food impurity (as does a standard foodstuff), nor carcass impurity (if the dam is carcass, its afterbirth is not affected, as it is not considered part of the dam's body). On these categories, see 9:1.

If he had this in mind—
it imparts food impurity but not carcass impurity.
An afterbirth that has partially emerged is forbidden for consumption;
it is a sign of an offspring in a woman,
and a sign of an offspring in a domestic animal.
A domestic animal delivering its firstborn that miscarried an afterbirth—
one may throw it to the dogs;
but if it was a sacral animal, one must bury it.
And one neither buries it at a crossroads,
nor hangs it on a tree,
because of the prohibition of the ways of the Amorite.

Chapter Five

5:1–5 *Slaughtering a Domestic Animal and Its Offspring on the Same Day*

5 *It and its offspring* applies
whether in the Land and outside the Land,
in the time of the Temple and not in the time of the Temple,
to nonsacral animals and offerings.
How?

had this in mind: If the slaughterer intended to eat any afterbirth found in it, the intention to eat the afterbirth now classifies it as food (with the result that it imparts impurity; see *Uqtsin* 3:1). This does not change its classification vis-à-vis the dam's body, so it does not impart carcass impurity.

afterbirth that has partially emerged: If any of the afterbirth exited the dam's body prior to her slaughter, then the entire afterbirth is invalid, perhaps due to concerns that either the fetus' head (4:1) or the majority of its body (4:2) may have emerged.

sign of an offspring: By partially emerging from a female body, the afterbirth is a sign that one has given birth and, in the case of a woman, is subject to postpartum impurity (see 4:3; Leviticus 12; *Niddah* 3), and in the case of an animal, is rendered invalid for consumption because it might have been born (cf. *Bekhorot* 3:1), which means the dam's slaughter would not render it permitted.

miscarried: If a dam's first pregnancy results in a miscarriage, then the laws associated with its firstborn do not apply (e.g. 4:2). However, if the dam has been consecrated, then one must treat the afterbirth with the respect owed to a consecrated domestic animal.

ways of the Amorite: This phrase (which also appears in *Shabbat* 6:10) designates practices that were deemed to be characteristic of the pre-Israelite peoples of Canaan, and hence prohibited. Perhaps the practices are intended to prevent future miscarriages.

5:1 *It and its offspring*: Leviticus 22:28, prohibiting killing a dam and its offspring on the same day (also see 4:5).

the Land: Israel. On which laws apply only to Israel or to both Israel and abroad, see *Qiddushin* 1:9.

offerings: Sacral animals.

How? 5:1–2 provides twelve examples of how these rules apply. Throughout 5:1–2, when the Mishnah speaks of permissibility, it refers to the animals; and when it speaks of liability, it is refers to the slaughterers.

One who slaughters *It and its offspring*:
nonsacral animals, outside [the Temple Court]—
both of them are valid,
but the second incurs the forty stripes;
offerings, outside—
the first is liable for *karet*,
and both of them are invalid,
and both of them incur the forty stripes;
nonsacral animals, inside—
both of them are invalid,
and the second incurs the forty stripes;
offerings, inside—
the first is valid and is exempt,
but the second incurs the forty stripes and is invalid;
2 A nonsacral animal and an offering outside—
the first is valid and is exempt,
but the second incurs the forty stripes and is invalid;
an offering and a nonsacral animal outside—
the first is liable for *karet* and is invalid,
but the second is valid,
and both of them incur the forty stripes;
a nonsacral animal and an offering inside—
both of them are invalid,
and the second incurs the forty stripes;
an offering and a nonsacral animal, inside—
the first is valid and exempt,

nonsacral animals, outside: Since these animals are eligible for slaughter, and the biblical ban is not violated until the second animal is slaughtered, it is only at that point that the slaughterer is liable to punishment.

forty stripes: Deuteronomy 25:3. For the general procedure for administering stripes, see *Makkot* 3:10–14, which reduces the number to thirty-nine. Though the slaughterer is punished, both animals are valid (cf. slaughter on Sabbath/Day of Atonement, discussed in 1:1).

offerings, outside: Consecrated animals must be slaughtered within the Temple Court; failure to do so results not only in the invalidation of the animals, but more seriously in extirpation (*karet*; see Leviticus 17:3–4). Since the second animal is now ineligible for sacrifice, as the parent or offspring of an animal just slaughtered, extirpation no longer applies, as this penalty only results from the improper offering of an animal eligible for sacrifice (cf. *Zevahim* 14:2).

both of them incur the forty stripes: The first slaughterer is punished because of slaughtering an offering outside the Temple Court (see *Makkot* 3:2) and the second one because of *It and its offspring*.

nonsacral animals, inside: One cannot derive benefit from nonsacral animals offered in the Temple Court (cf. *Qiddushin* 2:9). Nevertheless, the second slaughterer violates the biblical ban of *It and its offspring*.

offerings, inside: The first animal is valid and its slaughterer is exempt from punishment because it is the appropriate animal offered in the appropriate place. Because the second was not eligible for slaughter, it is an invalid sacrifice in addition to *It and its offspring*.

5:2 *A nonsacral animal and an offering*: In the next four examples, each animal has a different status (e.g. an unconsecrated dam and her consecrated offspring). However, the logic and legal principles for assessing the results of each slaughter is similar to that discussed in 5:1.

but the second incurs the forty stripes and is invalid;
nonsacral animals, outside and inside—
the first is valid and exempt,
but the second incurs the forty stripes and is invalid;
offerings, outside and inside—
the first is liable for *karet*,
and both are invalid,
and both of them incur the forty stripes;
nonsacral animals, inside and outside—
the first is invalid and exempt,
but the second incurs the forty stripes and is valid;
offerings, inside and outside—
the first is valid and exempt,
but the second incurs the forty stripes and is invalid.

3 One who slaughters, and it is found to be *terefah*,
one who slaughters for idolatry,
or one who slaughters a heifer of the purgation offering,
or an ox that is to be stoned,
or a calf whose neck is to be broken—
R. Simeon exempts;
but the Sages deem liable.[44]
One who slaughters and it became carcass by his hand,
or one who stabs or who tears—
is exempt from *It and its offspring*.
Two who bought a cow and its offspring:

[44] In **K**, **P**, the order is reversed and it is R. Meir who declares liable.

outside and inside... inside and outside: Four examples where the animals have the same status, but the first is slaughtered *outside* and the second *inside* or the first *inside* and the second *outside*. Compare the logic here to 5:1.

5:3 *One who slaughters*: Each of these cases describes a slaughtered animal whose meat is ineligible for ingestion.

found to be terefah: See chapter 3.

for idolatry... broken: One may not derive benefit from idol meat (e.g. *Avodah Zarah* 2:3). The red heifer is burned to ash and not consumed (see 1:6; Numbers 19; and *Parah*). The ox is sentenced to stoning because it killed a person (Exodus 21:28); on the calf, see 1:6. Benefit from the last two is prohibited.

exempts from violating *It and its offspring*. R. Simeon holds that since the previous cases do not result in meat valid for ingestion, their slaughter does not transgress the biblical ban (cf. *Bava Qamma* 7:2); the Sages disagree (cf. 6:2, where the Sages hold the opposite view; however, see n. 44).

carcass by his hand: One renders it carcass due to improper slaughter (see 2:4).

exempt from It and its offspring: Leviticus 22:28. Since none of these animals are valid for ingestion, the biblical ban is not violated.

Two who bought: Two separate people purchase a dam and her offspring. The first buyer has the right to slaughter his animal first; the second buyer must wait until the following day. However, if the second buyer slaughters first—even though he violates protocol—the act is allowed and the first buyer must wait one day.

whoever bought first may slaughter first;
but if the second preceded—
he has obtained the privilege of doing so.
One who slaughtered a cow and afterward[45] its two offspring—
he incurs eighty stripes;
If he slaughtered its two offspring and afterward slaughtered it—
he incurs the forty stripes;[46]
if he slaughtered it, its daughter, and its daughter's daughter—
he incurs eighty stripes;
if he slaughtered it and its daughter's daughter, and afterward slaughtered its daughter—
he incurs the forty stripes;
Symmachus says in the name of R. Meir:
He incurs eighty stripes.
At four times of the year, one who sells a domestic animal to his fellow must inform him:
"I sold its mother for slaughter," "I sold its daughter for slaughter"—
(1) the eve of the final[47] festival day of the Festival;
(2) the eve of the first festival day of Passover;
(3) the eve of the Festival of Weeks;
(4) and the eve of the New Year.
And, according to the opinion of R. Yose the Galilean:
Also on the eve of the Day of Atonement in the Galilee.
R. Judah said:
When?
When there is no interval of time;
but if there is an interval of time—
one does not need to inform him.
But R. Judah agrees that if one sells the mother to a bridegroom
and the daughter to a bride—
one must inform,
since it is known that both will slaughter on the same day.

[45] **K, P** lack "and afterward." [46] **K** has, erroneously, "If one slaughtered it, he incurs forty stripes."
[47] **P**: "first," corrected to "final" in the margin.

eighty stripes: The slaughterer receives one set of the forty stripes for each offspring.

afterward slaughtered it: When the offspring are slaughtered, the dam is alive and therefore no violation has occurred. Once the cow herself is slaughtered, *It and its offspring* has been transgressed and one incurs the penalty.

four times of the year: Usually, a seller need not note prior to the sale whether the mother/offspring was sold on the same day. On these four occasions, however, there is a presumption that both purchasers intend to slaughter their animals immediately for their festival-day feasts, therefore transgressing *It and its offspring*.

interval of time: At least one day.

on the same day: Though one may have sold them on separate days, the presumption is that the bridal couple will slaughter on the same day for their wedding feast.

4 At these four times they make the butcher slaughter against his will.
Even if it is an ox worth one thousand *dinar*,[48]
and the buyer had only a single *dinar*—
they compel him to slaughter.
Therefore, if it dies, the loss falls to the buyer.[49]
But on the other days of the year, it is not so;
therefore, if it dies, the loss falls to the seller.[50]

5 The *one day* that is stated regarding *It and its offspring*
means the day together with the preceding night.
This was expounded by Simeon b. Zoma:[51]
It is stated regarding the Creation account: *one day*;
and it is stated regarding *It and its offspring*: *one day*.
Just as the *one day* that is stated regarding the Creation account
means the day together with the preceding night,
so too the *one day* that is stated regarding *It and its offspring*
means the day together with the preceding night.

Chapter Six

6:1–7 *Covering the Blood*

6 Covering the blood applies in the Land and outside the Land,
in the time of the Temple and not in the time of the Temple,

[48] **P**: "one thousand *zuz dinar*" (a *zuz* is equivalent to a *denarius*).
[49] Lit. "it died for the buyer." [50] Lit. "it died for the seller." [51] **K**: "R. Simeon b. Zoma."

5:4 Though this mishnah does not address the laws of *It and its offspring*, it continues the discussion from the previous mishnah.

these four times: See 5:3.

single dinar: Due to the importance of these occasions, the butcher must slaughter the animal, even if the customer acquires only a small amount of the meat and the butcher cannot secure customers for the remaining meat.

loss falls to the buyer: While the butcher is compelled to slaughter the animal, in the event that the animal dies prior to slaughter, the butcher need not issue the buyer a refund.

Loss falls to the seller. On all other days, the butcher is neither compelled to sell nor exempt from refunding the buyer.

5:5 *one day*: Leviticus 22:28 prohibits slaughtering *It and its offspring* "in one day." The implication of this mishnah is that one who slaughters the dam at night cannot slaughter her offspring until the following night; however, one who slaughters the dam during the day may slaughter her offspring at nightfall.

Creation account: one day: Genesis 1:5 is the basis for defining *one day* as from sundown to sundown.

6:1–7 Leviticus 17:13 commands Israelites and resident outsiders who hunt wild animals and fowl to pour out their blood and cover it with earth. This chapter discusses the rules associated with this command.

6:1 *Covering the blood applies*, etc.: For the categories (the form of this mishnah), see 5:1.

to nonsacral animals but not to sacral animals;
and it applies to wild animals and fowl, captive or not captive;
and it applies to a *koy*, because it is of uncertain classification.
And one may not slaughter it on a festival;
but if they slaughtered it, they do not cover its blood.

2 One who slaughters, and it is found to be *terefah*,
or one who slaughters for idolatry,
or one who slaughters nonsacral animals inside [the Temple Court],
or offerings outside,
or a wild animal or fowl that are to be stoned—
R. Meir deems liable,
but the Sages exempt.
One who slaughters, and it becomes carcass by his hand,
one who stabs
or one who tears—
he is exempt from covering.

3 A deaf-mute, one who is legally incompetent, or a minor slaughtered,
while others observe them—
they are liable to cover;
all by themselves—
they are exempt from covering.
And so too regarding *It and its offspring*:
If they slaughtered while others observe them—
it is forbidden to slaughter after them;

not to sacral animals: Since only domestic animals (which are exempt, see below) and fowl (which are sacrificed via pinching, see 1:4, and thus not subject to covering the blood) are offered as consecrated animals, this law would not apply.

wild animals and fowl: In accordance with Leviticus 17:13.

captive: Though Leviticus 17:13 discusses hunting these animals, this law applies even when they are in captivity.

koy: An animal of uncertain taxonomy, sometimes classified as domesticated, and other times as undomesticated (see *Bikkurim* 2:8–11). Since it might be a wild animal, one should cover its blood.

festival: Covering blood on a festival day involves the potential to violate festival-day rules (see *Betsah* 1:2); thus, one should not risk violating these prohibitions for a *koy*, an animal to whom it is uncertain whether these rules even apply.

6:2 *found to be terefah*: This mishnah asks whether the law of covering blood applies to animals ineligible for consumption. On defects that render an animal *terefah*, see 3:1–4. Several of these categories are discussed regarding *It and its offspring* in 5:1, and especially 5:3 (where the logic behind the difference of rabbinic opinion is explained). On stoning a fowl, see *Eduyot* 6:1.

it becomes carcass: Cf. 5:3.

6:3 *deaf-mute… observe them*: According to 1:1, such slaughter is valid; therefore, their supervisors are obligated to cover the blood (cf. 6:4). If they were not supervised (*all by themselves*), then their slaughter is invalid and does not require covering.

It and its offspring: See chapter 5.

forbidden to slaughter after them: Since their supervised slaughter is valid, then if they slaughter a dam/offspring, one could not slaughter the offspring/dam on the same day without violating the biblical ban.

all by themselves—
R. Meir permits slaughtering after them;
but the Sages forbid.
But they agree that if one slaughtered, he does not incur the forty stripes.
4 If he slaughtered a hundred wild animals in one place—
a single covering for all of them;
a hundred fowl in one place—
a single covering for all of them;
a wild animal and fowl in one place—
a single covering for all of them.[52]
R. Judah says:
If he slaughtered a wild animal—
he covers, and afterward he may slaughter the fowl.
If he slaughtered and did not cover, and another observed him—
the latter is liable to cover.
If he covered it, and it became uncovered—
he is exempt from covering;
if the wind covered it—
he is liable to cover.
5 Blood that was mixed with water:
if it has the appearance of blood—
one is liable to cover.
If it was mixed with wine—
they consider the wine as water.[53]
If it was mixed with the blood of a domestic animal
or the blood of a wild animal—
they regard it as if it is water.
R. Judah says:
Blood does not nullify blood.
6 Blood that splatters or that remains on the knife—
one is liable to cover.[54]

[52] **K** lacks "for all of them"; however, it has, then deletes, an extra "for all of them" in the previous sentence. **P** lacks this entire sentence, but it appears in the margin.

[53] **K** has "If it was mixed with blood, they regard it as if it is water."

[54] **P** lacks "to cover."

6:5 Parallel to *Zevahim* 8:6. This mishnah addresses the rules regarding blood becoming mixed with another liquid prior to covering it.

wine: Since the colors of blood and red wine are indistinguishable, the matter is decided based on whether an amount of water equal to that of the wine would, when mixed with the same amount of blood, require covering the mixture.

wild animal: Heb. *hayyah*, either "wild animal" or "living animal." Since a wild animal's blood requires covering, *hayyah* here perhaps signifies that the blood comes from a live animal, most likely that of a living wild animal.

Blood does not nullify blood: While water or wine can potentially nullify blood in regard to the obligation to cover it, the same substance cannot do so.

6:6 *Blood that splatters*: One must cover any blood that splatters outside of the pit into which one slaughters (see 2:9) or on a wall (see 2:6), or that remains on the knife after slaughter.

R. Judah said:
When?
If it is the only blood there;
but if there is blood there other than it—
one is exempt from covering.

7 With what may one cover and with what may one not cover?
They may cover with fine dung or with fine sand,
with lime or with powdered clay,
or with brick or with the plug of a jar that have been crushed.
But they may not cover with coarse dung or coarse sand,
or with brick or the plug of a jar that have not been crushed;
nor may they invert a utensil over it.
Rabban Simeon b. Gamaliel stated a rule:
Something in which one can grow plants,
one may cover with it;
but that in which one cannot grow plants,
one may not cover with it.

Chapter 7

7:1–6 *Prohibition against Consuming the Sciatic Nerve*

7 [The prohibition of] the sciatic nerve applies in the Land and outside the Land,
in the time of the Temple and not in the time of the Temple,
to nonsacral animals but not to sacral animals;
and it applies to a domestic animal and a wild animal,
on the right thigh and on the left thigh.
But it does not apply to fowl,
since it does not have a *hollow*.
And it applies to a fetus.

only blood there: One must cover splattered blood or what remains on the knife only if there is no other blood from the slaughtered animal with which to fulfill one's obligation.

6:7 Leviticus 17:13 commands blood to be covered with earth (*afar*). This mishnah defines what substances count as "earth" for the purposes of fulfilling this commandment. These substances are those that are considered most earthlike.

invert a utensil: Covering the blood with a bowl (or similar utensil) does not fulfill this commandment, since it must be absorbed into the substance.

7:1–6 The prohibition of consuming the sinew of the thigh, or sciatic nerve, is stated in Genesis 32:23–33.

applies: For the categories and form of this mishnah cf. 5:1, 6:1.

hollow: Genesis 32:33 specifies that the sciatic nerve is *on the hollow of the thigh*.

fetus: Heb. *shelil*, a different term than in chapter 4.

R. Judah says:
It does not apply to a fetus.
And its fat is permitted.
And[55] butchers are not trusted concerning the sciatic nerve—
the words of R. Meir;
but the Sages say:
They are trusted concerning it and concerning the fat.

2 A person may send to a gentile a thigh with the sciatic nerve inside it,
since its place is known.
One who removes the sciatic nerve must remove all of it.
R. Judah says:
Sufficient to fulfill with it the commandment of removal.

3 One who eats an olive's bulk of the sciatic nerve—
incurs the forty stripes.
If he ate it, and it does not contain an olive's bulk—
he is liable.
If he ate an olive's bulk from this thigh, and an olive's bulk from that—
he incurs eighty stripes.
R. Judah says:
He only incurs the forty stripes.

4 A thigh with which the sciatic nerve was cooked:
if there is in it a sufficient amount to impart flavor—

[55] **K**, **P** lack "and."

its fat: On forbidden fat, see 8:6. The Talmud debates whether this refers to the fat of the fetus or of the sciatic nerve.

butchers are not trusted: To remove the sciatic nerve, since it is difficult to do so. However, the Sages trust butchers to remove both the sciatic nerve and forbidden fat (see Leviticus 3:17; 7:23). The extent of this removal is debated in 7:2.

7:2 *may send to a gentile*: Although prohibited from eating it, Jews may derive benefit from the sciatic nerve (e.g. by giving it to gentiles, who are allowed to eat it).

its place is known: So there is no danger that one will eat it at some later point (commentaries).

commandment of removal: According to the Talmud, removing the entire sciatic nerve is a rabbinic enactment, whereas removing only the surface—and not digging deep into the meat—is the biblical requirement.

7:3 *forty stripes*: Above 5:1.

and it does not contain an olive's bulk: The entire sciatic nerve amounted to less than an olive's bulk; one is still liable for punishment for eating it in its entirety.

from this thigh…from that: If one eats an olive's bulk portion from both the right and left thighs of the same animal.

7:4 The sciatic nerve must be removed prior to cooking. The Mishnah now discusses the case in which it was not.

impart flavor: The test of "imparting flavor" appears below (7:5; 8:3, 5) and in other tractates. This principle allows for a small amount of a prohibited or prohibiting substance to be present with a permitted food. Most of these mixtures eventually fall under the principle that any substance less than one-sixtieth of the total volume is nullified. One issue addressed not in the Mishnah but in the Talmud is who exactly tastes the food to decide if it imparts flavor.

in this case, it is forbidden.
How do they measure it?
Like meat with turnips.

5 A sciatic nerve that was cooked with other sinews:
if one can recognize it—
[the others are prohibited if] it imparts flavor;
but if not,[56] all of them are forbidden;
and the broth is forbidden if it imparts flavor.[57]
And so too a piece of carcass
and so too a piece of impure fish, that was cooked with other pieces of the same:
if one can recognize them—
[the others are forbidden] if it imparts flavor;
but if not—
all of them are forbidden;
and the broth is forbidden if there is a sufficient amount to impart flavor.

6 It applies to a pure animal, but it does not apply to an impure animal.
R. Judah says:
Also for an impure animal.
R. Judah said:
Was not the sciatic nerve forbidden from the time of the sons of Jacob,
yet an impure domestic animal was still permitted to them?
They said to him:
At Sinai it was said, but it was written in its present place.

[56] K, P: "but if one cannot recognize it."
[57] K has (then deletes): "sciatic nerve" and lacks the remaining section of this mishnah.

meat with turnips: Since the sciatic nerve and the meat might not taste noticeably different, then the test is whether an amount of meat corresponding to the sciatic nerve would impart its flavor to turnips in the amount of the thigh meat.

7:5 *if one can recognize it*: If the sciatic nerve is distinguishable, then one removes it and the rest is prohibited using the test of *a sufficient amount to impart flavor.*

And so too: The previously stated laws apply to other food mixtures wherein prohibited food is mixed with permitted food of the same type.

all of them are forbidden: When the prohibited substance is unrecognizable and thus cannot be removed, the entire foodstuff is forbidden.

7:6 *It applies to a pure animal*, etc.: 7:1, above.

from the time of the sons of Jacob: The law, which appears in Genesis and relates to the Patriarch Jacob, predates the giving of the Torah; at that time, the prohibition of impure animals was not yet in effect.

Sinai: Supporters of the former statement argue that the prohibition of the sciatic nerve was given on Mount Sinai. When the Torah was written, however, this legislation was recorded alongside the story of Jacob/Israel in Genesis 32:33. The sciatic prohibition therefore only appears to predate that of the impure animal.

Chapter Eight

8:1–5 *Prohibition against Mixing Milk and Meat*

8 All meat is forbidden to be cooked with milk,
except for the meat of fish and locusts.
And it is forbidden to bring it up with cheese on the table,
except for the meat of fish and locusts.
One who vows to abstain from meat is permitted the meat of fish and locusts.
Fowl may go up with cheese on the table, but it may not be eaten—[58]
the words of the House of Shammai;
but the House of Hillel says:
It may neither go up, nor may it be eaten.
R. Yose said:
This is one of the lenient rulings of the House of Shammai and the stringent rulings of the House of Hillel.
Regarding which table did they speak?
Regarding a table that one eats upon;
but regarding a table upon which one arranges the food—
one may place one beside the other and does not scruple.
2 A person may wrap meat and cheese in one cloth,
provided that they do not touch one another.
Rabban Simeon b. Gamaliel says:
Two guests may eat on one table,

[58] **P** lacks "but it may not be eaten."

8:1 Three times the Hebrew Bible declares *You shall not cook a kid in its mother's milk* (Exodus 22:30; 23:19; Deuteronomy 14:21). The rabbis understand the biblical legislation as a general prohibition against cooking *any* meat with *any* milk. Doing so raises many legal questions, only some of which are addressed in this chapter.

fish and locusts: These animals are not considered "meat" in regard to this law. See 8:4.

bring it up with cheese on the table: Meat and cheese on the same table present two potential problems: one might forget and accidentally eat them together; and the hot meat might come into contact with the cheese and hence *cook* together.

One who vows: For such vows, see e.g. *Nedarim* 3:6–11, and *Nedarim*, introduction.

Fowl: The applicability of this biblical prohibition to fowl (which has no milk) is debated even in the Mishnah (see 8:4).

House of Shammai…House of Hillel: Usually, the Hillelites are more lenient than the Shammaites (see *Eduyot* 5:2, which includes a parallel to this mishnah); this case is one of the exceptions.

Regarding which table: These rules only apply to a table upon which one eats and not to a side table upon which one arranges the cooked dish (for which the previously stated concerns would not apply, commentaries).

8:2 *guests*: More precisely, lodgers at an inn. These travelers will not share food since they are strangers, so they may occupy the same table without concern (cf. 8:1).

this one meat and that one cheese,
and they do not scruple.

3 A drop of milk that fell on a piece of meat:
if there is in it a sufficient amount to impart flavor to that piece—
it is forbidden.[59]
If he stirred the pot,
if there is in it a sufficient amount to impart flavor to that pot—
it is forbidden.[60]
The udder:
he tears it open and removes its milk.
If he did not tear it open, he did not transgress on its account.
The heart:
He tears it open and removes its blood.
If he did not tear it open, he did not transgress on its account.
One who brings up fowl with cheese on the table
does not transgress a negative commandment.

4 Meat of a pure domestic animal in milk of pure domestic animal—
it is forbidden to cook, and it is forbidden to derive benefit.
Meat of a pure domestic animal in milk of an impure domestic animal,
or meat of an impure domestic animal in milk of a pure domestic animal—
it is permitted to cook, and it is permitted to derive benefit.
R. Aqiva says:
Wild animal and fowl are not prohibited by the Torah,[61]
as it is said: *You shall not cook a kid in its mother's milk*,
three times, to exclude
(1) the wild animal,
(2) fowl, and

[59] **K, P** lack "it is forbidden." [60] **K, P** lack "it is forbidden." [61] Lit. "are not from the Torah."

8:3 *drop of milk*: Since the biblical ban concerns *cooking* meat and milk, what happens if a drop of milk falls into a boiling pot of meat? Two cases are considered: the milk drop falls on one piece; the milk drop is mixed in with the entire contents of the pot of meat.

impart flavor: See 7:4.

udder . . . heart: Both of these organs present interesting cases: the udder is meat and contains milk; and the heart contains blood. In both cases, the milk/blood is allowed only if the organ is whole.

remove its blood: This phrase also appears in 4:5. On the permissibility of eating blood in certain organs (including the heart), see *Keritot* 5:1.

fowl with cheese: This mishnah appears to consider the prohibition against consuming fowl with cheese to be a rabbinic enactment and not a negative commandment from the Hebrew Bible (see 8:1, 4). Consequently the restriction on having both on a table is eased.

8:4 *permitted to cook*: The prohibition against cooking milk and meat together only applies to permitted animals. One may cook and derive benefit from a mixture involving an invalid animal, but may not consume it.

by the Torah: The mixing of wild animal/fowl meat and cheese are not biblical prohibitions.

three times: Exodus 22:30; 23:19; and Deuteronomy 14:21. According to R. Aqiva, each time this phrase appears, it teaches that a separate category of animals is excluded from the biblical prohibition of mixing.

(3) the impure domestic animal.[62]
R. Yose the Galilean says:
It is said: *You shall not eat any carcass*,
and it is said: *You shall not cook a kid in its mother's milk*:
that which is forbidden on account of carcass it is forbidden to cook in milk.
Fowl, which is forbidden[63] on account of carcass:
might one conclude that it is forbidden to cook in milk?
Scripture says, *in its mother's milk*, to exclude fowl, which has no mother's milk.

5 Milk in the abomasum[64] of an animal carcass belonging to a gentile—
in this case, this is forbidden.
One who curdles milk with the skin of the abomasum of a permissible animal:
if there is[65] sufficient amount to impart flavor—
in this case, this is forbidden.
A permissible animal that suckled from a *terefah*—
the milk in its abomasum is forbidden;
a *terefah* that suckled from a permissible animal—
the milk in its abomasum is permitted, because it is collected in its belly.

8:6 *Contrasting the Prohibitions against Consuming Blood and Fat*

6 A greater stringency applies to fat than to blood,
and a greater stringency applies to blood than to fat.

62 **P** begins this list with "domestic animal," but a later hand correctly suggests deleting it.
63 **K** lacks "forbidden."
64 Hebrew has only: "The abomasum." So too below in this mishnah.
65 **K, P** insert "in it."

You shall not eat any carcass: R. Yose connects carcass with the milk and meat prohibition because Deuteronomy 14:21 begins with these words and concludes with the prohibition against cooking a kid in its mother's milk.

no mother's milk: R. Yose the Galilean's midrash means that the prohibition would apply to the wild animal (which R. Aqiva excludes). However, according to R. Yose, Scripture explicitly excludes fowl from this prohibition with the words *its mother's milk*.

8:5 This mishnah examines whether the use of animal products in cheese production results in a violation of mixing meat and milk.

the abomasum: Rennet, an enzyme that causes milk to curdle into cheese, was derived from two sources in antiquity: the congealed milk in an animal's abomasum (see 3:1); or the lining of the abomasum (discussed immediately below). Here, as in 1:1, the Mishnah equates an animal slaughtered by a gentile with carcass. However, in the next clauses, milk in the animal's stomach is not considered part of the animal itself. On that logic, such rennet should not be considered carcass (cf. *Avodah Zarah* 2:5; and Tosefta, which retracts this ruling).

collected in its belly: In both cases, the criterion is the source of the milk: if it originates with a permissible animal, it is permitted; otherwise, it is prohibited.

8:6 Leviticus 7:22–27 prohibits the consumption of certain fats and blood. However, different laws apply to each animal product.

A greater stringency applies to fat,[66]
since fat is subject to the law of sacrilege,
and one is liable on its account for *piggul*, remnant, and impurity,
which is not the case with blood.
And a greater stringency applies to blood,[67]
since the [prohibition of] blood applies to a domestic animal,
to a wild animal, and to a fowl,
whether impure or pure;
but [the prohibition of] fat applies only to a pure domestic animal alone.

Chapter Nine

9:1–8 *Impurity Transmitted by Foodstuffs*

9 The hide, the broth, the sediment, the flayed-off meat, the bones, the sinews, the horns, and hooves
combine to impart food impurity,
but not carcass impurity.
Likewise, one who slaughters an impure domestic animal for a gentile,
and it is convulsing,
it transmits food impurity,
but does not transmit carcass impurity until it dies, or until he chops off its head.
[Scripture has prescribed] more cases of transmitting food impurity
than it prescribed transmitting carcass impurity.
R. Judah says:
The flayed-off meat that was collected together:
if there is an olive's bulk in one place, he is liable on its account.
2 These are things whose skins are like their meat:

[66] **K, P** lack "A greater stringency applies to fat." [67] **P** has "blood alone."

sacrilege: The misuse of sacred property. Leviticus 5:15–16. The law extends even to accidental misuse.

piggul, remnant, and impurity: Cf. *Zevahim* 3:4; 4:5; *Me'ilah* 3:3. *Piggul* refers to a sacrifice that one intends at the time of sacrifice to consume beyond its allotted time; *remnant*, to the portions of a sacrifice that remain after the allotted time, which must be burned (e.g. Leviticus 7:15–18); and *impurity* to the prohibition against eating consecrated food while impure (e.g. Leviticus 7:20).

blood: Leviticus 7:23–27 bans all blood, but only the fat of domestic animals. See *Keritot* 5:1.

9:1 *food impurity*: An egg's bulk of a substance conveys impurity to food.

carcass impurity: An olive's bulk of carcass conveys impurity: see Leviticus 11:39–40 and *Tohorot* 1:4.

9:2 An animal's skin in its natural state is distinct from an animal's skin that has been processed into leather.

skins are like their meat: They are deemed equivalent regarding impurity. Unlike other hides (cf. 9:1), the skins of these animals are soft, and thus similar to their meat. If their skins were *not* deemed like their meat,

the skin of a human, the skin of a domestic pig—
R. Yose says:
also the skin of the wild pig—
the skin of the hump of a young camel,
the skin of the head of a young calf,
the skin of the hooves,
the skin of the genitals,
the skin of the fetus,
the skin beneath the fat-tail,
and the skin of the gecko, the spotted lizard, the lizard, and the skink.
R. Judah says:
The lizard is like the rat.
And all of them that have been tanned
or trodden upon sufficiently for tanning
are pure,
except for the skin of a human.
R. Yohanan b. Nuri[68] says:
The eight creeping animals have skins.

3 One who flays a domestic animal or a wild animal[69]—
pure or impure,
small or large:
for a spread—
an amount sufficient to grasp;
and for a flask—
until one flays the breast;[70]

[68] **P** lacks "b. Nuri," but it appears in the margin.
[69] **K** includes "fowl." [70] **K**, **P**: "until one removes all of the breast."

then they would not convey carcass impurity (or in the case of humans, corpse impurity), so long as no meat was attached to the skin.

skin of the genitals: Lit. "house of shame," which Rashi understands as referring specifically to female genitalia.

skin of the fetus: A dead fetus in the womb of a dead dam. See chapter 4.

gecko, etc.: These comprise four of the eight creeping animals forbidden in Leviticus 11:29–30. R. Judah excludes the lizard, while R. Yohanan b. Nuri excludes all eight. Since their precise taxonomy is unknown, we follow Jacob Milgrom's translations.

tanned: Once any of these hides (except for that of a human) have been either tanned or trodden upon (which begins the tanning process), then the rules of leather products—rather than animal skins—apply.

have skins: R. Yohanan b. Nuri deems the skins of all eight creeping animals to be like the hides discussed in 9:1, and therefore their skins are *not* like their meat.

9:3 This mishnah discusses the point in the process of flaying an animal at which its hide ceases to impart impurity.

spread...flask: One uses the hide to make a bedspread or tablecloth, as opposed to e.g. a wineskin. In both cases, when one has separated the amount specified, the hide ceases to be merely a "handle" to work the hide from the meat, and is deemed disconnected to the animal itself in regard to transmitting impurity.

One who flays from the hindleg upward:
all of it is connected for impurity,
to contract impurity and to convey impurity.
The skin on the neck:
R. Yohanan b. Nuri[71] says:
It is not connected;
but the Sages say:
It is connected, until one flays all of it.

4 A hide that has an olive's bulk of meat on it:
one who touches a shred that protrudes from it,
or a hair opposite it—
is impure.
If there were on it two half-olive's bulks—
it conveys impurity by carriage, but not by contact—[72]
the words of R. Ishmael.
R. Aqiva says:
Neither by contact, nor by carriage.
But R. Aqiva agrees that if he stuck two half-olive's bulks with a twig and moved them, then he is impure.[73]
Then why does R. Aqiva deem pure in regard to the hide?
Because the hide nullifies them.

5 The marrowbone of a corpse and the marrowbone of sacral animals:
one who touches them,
whether they are closed or perforated—
is impure.
The marrowbone of carcass and the marrowbone of a creeping animal:

[71] **P** lacks "b. Nuri." [72] **K**, **P**: "by contact, but not by carriage." [73] **K**: "it is all pure."

flays from the hindleg upward: In order to make a flask. In the previous case, the animal is flayed from the neck downward, and the breast is flayed close to the beginning of the process. When one starts from the hindleg, the hide is deemed connected to the flesh until one has flayed the entire breast.

on the neck: The delicate skin on the neck is treated as not connected at all, according to R. Yohanan b. Nuri; apparently because it can be easily peeled away by hand.

9:4 *olive's bulk of* carcass *meat* attached to a hide.

a shred that protrudes from the meat side and the *hair* is from the hide where the hide connects to the meat. In both instances, one is not directly contacting an olive's bulk of meat.

two half-olive's bulks: Since one olive's bulk of meat is required to impart impurity, one who carries such a hide would carry an entire olive's bulk, even if the one who contacts it would only touch a half-olive's bulk. For R. Ishmael, this is a sufficient amount to transmit impurity by carrying.

R. Aqiva agrees: If one uses a twig to connect two half-olive's bulk pieces of meat, they are deemed connected and impart impurity by carriage. However, if it is the hide that connects them, according to R. Aqiva *the hide nullifies them*, so they are considered part of the hide itself.

9:5 *closed*: So that the marrow itself remains within the bone.

or perforated: So that the marrow can be touched. On defilement from human bones, see Numbers 19:16; and on consecrated animals that are *piggul* or remnant, see *Pesahim* 10:9.

carcass… creeping animal: The meat, which includes the marrow but not the bones of such animals, transmits impurity. If it is *at all perforated* there is the possibility of coming into contact with the marrow.

one who touches them,
closed—
they are pure;
perforated at all—
they impart impurity by contact.
Whence do we learn also [impurity] by carriage?
Scripture teaches, *one who touches* and *one who carries*.
That which comes into the category of impurity by[74] contact,
comes into the category of impurity by carriage;
that which does not come into the category of impurity by contact,
does not come into the category of impurity by carriage.

6 The egg of a creeping animal in which the embryo has formed is pure;
if it is at all perforated—
it is impure.
A mouse[75] that is half-flesh and half-dirt:
one who touches the flesh is impure;
the dirt, is pure.
R. Judah says:
Even one who touches the dirt that is opposite the flesh is impure.

7 The limb and the meat that dangle on a domestic animal
impart food impurity in their place,
but they require preparation.
If the domestic animal has been slaughtered—
they are prepared by its blood—
the words of R. Meir;
but R. Simeon says:
They have not been prepared.
If the domestic animal died:

[74] Here and below: "impurity by" added for clarity.

[75] **K**, **P**: "creeping animal."

one who touches and one who carries: Leviticus 11:39–40. This midrash reasons that since the Torah connects the cases of *one who touches* and *one who carries* carcass, then anything that falls into the former category also falls into the latter category. Carcass bones in any state should therefore impart impurity by contact and by carriage. This midrash does not apply to creeping animals (see *Kelim* 1:1), and carrying their closed bones does not impart impurity.

9:6 *egg*: Since one cannot touch the embryo and the eggshell does not impart impurity, it is pure.

mouse: This creature was thought to be created from the earth. If it died while half-formed, then it would be half-flesh and half-earth, which is the case presently discussed.

9:7 *dangle*: The limb (meat, sinew, and bone) or meat that hang loosely from an animal's body. Once severed from the body, they impart carcass impurity. Cf. 9:1; *Keritot* 3:8.

they require preparation: Solid foods must first come into contact with liquid in order to become susceptible to impurity. See further, 2:5.

domestic animal died: By a means other than valid slaughter. This mishnah is based on a general principle that "death effects falling off," whereby if an animal dies by a means other than valid slaughter, its dangling parts are deemed as if they fell off prior to its death. Accordingly, dangling *meat* is not inherently impure (it is not deemed to be carcass) and requires preparation if it is to be made impure. A dangling *limb* is also not carcass (since it is deemed to have fallen off before the animal died), but it is treated as a limb from a living

the meat requires preparation;
the limb imparts impurity as a limb from a living animal,
but it does not impart impurity as a limb from a carcass—
the words of R. Meir;
But R. Simeon deems it pure.

8 The limb and the meat that dangle on a human are pure.
If the human died, the meat is pure;
the limb imparts impurity as a limb from a living animal,
but it does not impart impurity as a limb from a corpse—
the words of R. Meir;
But R. Simeon declares it pure.

Chapter Ten

10:1–11:2 *Gifts Owed to Priests*

10 The *shoulder*, the *two cheeks*, and the *abomasum* apply:
in the Land and outside the Land,
in the time of the Temple and not in the time of the Temple,
to nonsacral animals but not to sacral animals.
For logic might have led to the following conclusion:
If nonsacral animals,
which are not liable for the breast and the thigh,
are liable for the gifts,
does not logic require that sacral animals,
which are liable for the breast and the thigh,
should be liable for the gifts?
Scripture teaches: *And I gave them to Aaron the Priest and to his sons as a due forever*;

animal, with its own impure status. On these issues, cf. *Eduyot* 6:3; *Oholot* 2:1. R. Simeon's ruling is puzzling, so the Talmud attempts to explain his logic.

9:8 This mishnah raises similar issues to the previous one. On the impurity of flesh and limbs of a human corpse, see e.g. 9:5, 7; *Eduyot* 6:2–3; and *Oholot* 1:6–8.

10:1 *shoulder*, etc.: The priests' due from slaughtered animals prescribed in Deuteronomy 18:3.

apply: On the formula and the categories, see 5:1.

the breast and the thigh: Given to the priests from offerings of well-being (Leviticus 7:31–34) and thus not applicable to nonsacral animals.

the gifts: The Mishnah's shorthand for the shoulder, the two cheeks, and the abomasum.

Scripture teaches: On this formula, see 9:5.

And I gave: Leviticus 7:34. Scripture prevents one from reaching a seemingly logical, though incorrect, conclusion. In Leviticus 7:34, the word *them* limits the application of this rule to the breast and the thigh only. The gifts are therefore excluded.

He[76] has only what is spoken of in the passage.

2 All sacred offerings whose permanent blemish preceded their consecration,
and they were redeemed:
are liable for the firstborn and the gifts,
and they become nonsacral animals that may be shorn and worked,
and their offspring and their milk are permitted after their redemption,
and one who slaughters them outside [the Temple Court] is exempt,
and they do not effect substitution,
and if they died, they may be redeemed,
except for the firstborn and the tithe.
All whose consecration preceded their blemish, or whose temporary blemish preceded their consecration,
and afterward developed a permanent blemish[77] and were redeemed:
they are exempt from the firstborn and the gifts,
and they do not become nonsacral animals that may be shorn and worked,
and their offspring and their milk are forbidden after their redemption,
and one who slaughters them outside is liable,
and they effect substitution,
and if they died, they must be buried.

3 A firstborn [animal] that was mingled with a hundred:
If a hundred slaughter them all—
they exempt them all;
one slaughters them all—
they exempt one animal for him.
One who slaughters for a priest or a gentile is exempt from the gifts;
and one who forms a partnership with them must mark it;

[76] **K**, **P**: "You."
[77] **K**, **P** have "with respect to their consecration."

10:2 Parallel to *Bekhorot* 2:2–3. This mishnah appears here because it mentions the gifts addressed in 10:1. Offerings must be unblemished. If they are blemished, they may be redeemed for money, which can then be used to purchase unblemished animals. In the first case discussed here, a permanent blemish preceded the animal's consecration. The animal thus never had sacrificial status. In the second case, the animal did attain and retains its sacrificial status, even if the animal cannot be sacrificed.

firstborn: See 2:10; 4:2; Numbers 18:15–18.

outside: Cf. *Zevahim* 14:2.

substitution: See Leviticus 27:10; *Temurah* 1:2. If the animal had sacrificial status, and one tried to substitute another for it both it and the substitute would be sanctified.

tithe: The animal tithe (see 1:7; 2:10; and Leviticus 27:32).

they do not become nonsacral animals: Cf. *Temurah* 2:3.

10:3 *firstborn*: In this case, the firstborn is blemished. As such, it cannot be offered as a sacrifice, but a priest may eat or sell it.

a hundred: If 101 different slaughterers slaughter 101 animals, any of which might have been the firstborn; they are *all* deemed *exempt* from the gifts of 10:1.

one slaughters: Only one can have been exempt from the gifts.

mark it: In order to distinguish this animal as belonging to a partnership.

but if he said: "Except for the gifts"—
he is exempt from the gifts.[78]
If he said:[79] "Sell me the intestines of a cow,"
and among them were the gifts—
he must give them to the priest, but he does not deduct from the price;
if he bought them from him by weight—
he must give them to the priest, and he does deduct from the price.
4 A convert who converted and owned a cow:
if it was slaughtered before he converted, he is exempt;
after he converted, he is liable;
if it is in doubt, he is exempt,
since the one who would take from his fellow bears the burden of proof.
What is the *shoulder*?
From the knee joint to the shoulder blade of the foreleg;
and this is also [the shoulder of] the *nazir*.
And the corresponding part in the hindleg is the thigh.
R. Judah says:
The thigh is from the knee joint to the fleshy part of the hindleg.
What is the *cheek*?
From the joint of the jaw to the thyroid cartilage.

[78] **K** lacks "he is exempt from the gifts," but adds it in the margin. "He said" is only written once.
[79] **K**, **P**: "to him."

Except for the gifts: A priest or gentile sells an animal, stipulating that the sale excludes the portions of the gifts, to a regular Jew. The buyer is exempt from the gifts, since they were not part of the sale (and hence, still belong to the seller).

If he said: A nonpriest said to a butcher. In the first case, where the intestines are purchased as a whole unit, one of the three gifts (the abomasum) is included in the intestines, which must be given to the priest, though it does not reduce the price that the butcher can demand. In the second case, where the intestines are purchased by weight, the cost of the abomasum must be deducted from the purchase price, since cost is directly correlated with the amount available for use.

10:4 The discussion of slaughter by a convert turns on whether the slaughter took place before or after his conversion.

doubt: If his status at the time of his cow's slaughter is uncertain.

one who would take: A regular expression in the Mishnah for assigning the burden of proof.

shoulder... cheek: See 10:1; Deuteronomy 18:3.

knee joint: On the difficulty of identifying an animal's leg joints, see 4:6.

nazir: See Numbers 6:19; *Nazir*.

thigh: See 10:1.

R. Judah: R. Judah argues that the thigh of the hindleg only refers to the tibia, and not to the tibia and the femur.

joint of the jaw: Cf. *Nega'im* 10:9.

Chapter Eleven

11 1 *The first of the fleece* applies:
in the Land[80] and outside the Land,
in the time of the Temple and not in the time of the Temple,
to nonsacral animals but not to sacral animals.
A greater stringency applies to the *shoulder*, the *two cheeks*, and the *abomasum* than to *the first of the fleece*,
since the *shoulder*, the *two cheeks*, and the *abomasum* apply:
to cattle and flocks, whether many or few,
but *the first of the fleece* only applies to sheep,
and only applies when they are many.
2 And how much is "many"?
The House of Shammai say:
Two sheep,
as it is said: *A man shall nourish a young cow and two sheep.*
But the House of Hillel say:
Five,
as it is said: *And five dressed sheep.*
R. Dosa b. Harqinas says:[81]
Five sheep,
each shorn of a hundred and a half are liable to *the first of the fleece*;
but the Sages say:
Five sheep,
shorn in any amount.
And how much do they give him?
The weight of five *sela* in Judaea,
which are ten *sela* in the Galilee,
bleached and not dirty,

[80] **K** lacks "in the Land."
[81] **K, P** have "the words of R. Dosa" at the end of the statement. Cf. *Eduyot* 3:3.

11:1 This chapter continues the discussion about gifts owed to priests by focusing on *the first of the fleece* (Deuteronomy 18:4).

applies: See 5:1.

the shoulder: See 10:1 and Deuteronomy 18:3.

only applies: Based on the wording of Deuteronomy 18:4 and further explained below, in 11:2.

11:2 *A man shall nourish*: Isaiah 7:21.

five dressed sheep: 1 Samuel 25:18. Both Hillel and Shammai reference biblical texts found outside the Torah.

R. Dosa accepts the House of Hillel, but the necessary amount of fleece is now defined. Cf. the parallel in *Eduyot* 3:3.

And how much do they give him? This question concerns the case where one has shorn more than the minimum amount and wants to give the extra to multiple priests, so how much fleece must each priest receive?

sela: The Galilean version of this coin weighed half the amount of the Judaean *sela* (cf. *Ketubbot* 5:9).

enough with which to make a small garment,
as it is said: *You shall give to him*:
that there be in it enough for a gift.
If he did not manage to give it to him before he dyed it—
he is exempt;[82]
if bleached it, but did not dye it—
he is liable.
One who buys the fleece of a gentile's sheep is exempt from *the first of the fleece*.
One who buys the fleece of his fellow's sheep:[83]
if the seller retained some—
the seller is obligated;
if he did not retain some[84]—
the buyer is obligated.
If he had two kinds, dark ones and white ones:
if he sold him the dark ones but not the white ones,
the males but not the females—
this one gives for himself, and that one gives for himself.

Chapter Twelve

12:1–5 *Sending Away the Mother from the Bird's Nest*

12 Sending away from the nest applies:
in the Land and outside the Land,
in the time of the Temple and not in the time of the Temple,
to nonsacral animals but not to sacral animals.
A greater stringency applies to covering the blood than to sending away from the nest,

[82] **P** has "from *the first of the fleece*." The words "One who buys the fleece of his fellow's sheep" were added, then deleted in this manuscript.
[83] **K**: "goat." [84] **K, P**: "And if not."

You shall give to him: Deuteronomy 18:4. The minimum amount given to each priest should be enough to constitute a gift. According to the Talmud, this is the amount needed to make a belt.

did not manage to give it: Dyeing is considered to alter the fleece in that it is no longer deemed the same thing; bleaching does not result in a similar transformation.

One who buys: Since Deuteronomy 18:4 speaks of *your sheep*, the mishnah discusses cases where one buys the fleece prior to its shearing, but not the sheep itself. If he buys the fleece from a *fellow* Jew, then his sheep would be obligated for *the first of the fleece*, whereas a gentile's sheep would not. Further, because both the Jewish seller and the Jewish buyer would be obligated, it matters if the seller purchased all or only some of the fleece, since the obligation would remain for *all* of the fleece.

12:1 This chapter discusses the biblical mandate to send away a mother bird from her nest before taking her young or her eggs (Deuteronomy 22:6–7).

applies: On this formula, see 5:1.

covering the blood: See 6:1.

since covering the blood applies to a wild animal and a fowl,
captive or not captive;
but the sending away from the nest only applies to fowl,
and it only applies to that which is not captive.
What is "that which is not captive"?
For example, geese or chickens that nested in the orchard;
but if they nested in the house,
and so too Herodian doves—
one is exempt from sending away.

2 An impure bird—one is exempt from sending away.
An impure bird that sits on the eggs of a pure bird,
or a pure bird that sits on the eggs of an impure bird—
one is exempt from sending away.
A male partridge:
R. Eliezer deems one liable;
but the Sages exempt.

3 If she was hovering:
when her wings touch the nest—
he is liable to send away;
her wings do not touch the nest—
he is exempt from sending away.
If there is there only one chick or one egg—
he is liable to send away,[85]
as it is said: *a nest*:
a nest of any kind.
If there were there fledglings or spoiled eggs—
he is exempt from sending away,
as it is said: *And the mother sitting on the chicks or on the eggs*:
just as the chicks are viable, so too the eggs must be viable;
spoiled eggs are excluded;
and just as the eggs need their mother, so too the chicks need their mother,
thus fledglings are excluded.
If he sent her away and she returned, sent her away and she returned,

[85] **K** lacks "to send away."

nested in the orchard: Fowl that literally flee the coop and now reside in the wild.

Herodian doves: A domesticated dove reportedly bred by Herod. Cf. *Shabbat* 24:3.

12:2 *male partridge*: Thought to sit on eggs, derived by some from Jeremiah 17:11.

12:3 *hovering*: Since Deuteronomy 22:6 specifically refers to the dam sitting, what then is the law if she is hovering?

a nest: Deuteronomy 22:6. The word *nest* means any kind of nest, regardless of the number of chicks or eggs contained therein.

spoiled eggs: Infertile eggs (Rashi).

And the mother: Deuteronomy 22:6. Due to the repetition of *chicks* and *eggs* in this verse, the mishnah argues that both categories must be comparable for the law to apply.

even four or five times—
he is liable,
as it is said: *You shall surely send away.*[86]
If he said: "I hereby take the mother and send away the young"—
he is liable to send away,
as it is said: *You shall surely send away the mother.*[87]
If he took the young and returned them to the nest,
and afterward the mother returned to them—
he is exempt from sending away.

4 One who takes a mother sitting on young:
R. Judah says:
One incurs stripes, and is not liable to send her away.
But the Sages say:
He is liable to send her away, and does not incur stripes.
This is the rule:
Any negative commandment that has in it a positive commandment,
one does not incur stripes[88] on account of it.

5 One may not take a mother sitting on young
even to purify the one with *tsara'at*.
Now, if concerning an easy commandment,
[whose economic cost] is about an *issar*,
the Torah said, *in order that it may go well for you and you may prolong your days*,
how much the more so concerning the difficult commandments that are in the Torah!

[86] **K** continues the quote: "*the mother*."
[87] **P** continues the quote: "*but the young you may take for yourself*"; **K** adds this in abbreviated form.
[88] **K, P**: "one is not liable"

You shall surely: Deuteronomy 22:7, quoted twice in this passage. In the first case, the repetition of the verb *send away* indicates that one must continue to do so as many times as the mother returns before one is allowed to remove the chicks or eggs. In the second case, the fact that the verse specifies *the mother* indicates that, even if one only wants the dam, one is still obligated to send her away from her nest.

took the young and returned them: By taking the chicks or eggs, one has acquired them. If he places them back in the nest, presumably for further motherly nurturing, they still remain his property. Since one must send away the mother when taking *her* chicks or eggs, this rule no longer applies to them, as they are no longer hers.

12:4 See the parallel in *Makkot* 3:4.

stripes: Corporal punishment for transgressing a negative commandment. See *Makkot* 3:10–14.

rule: Taking the mother bird sitting upon her young transgresses a negative commandment, but sending away the mother is a positive commandment (lit. a "rise and do"). If a negative commandment has a means to fix the transgression thereof, then one does not receive corporal punishment. *R. Judah* allows one to keep the bird having already taken the birds there was no mechanism to fix it, but *the Sages* hold that sending away the bird is the positive mechanism for doing so.

12:5 *purify*: To purify the person afflicted with skin disease (*tsara'at*), Leviticus 14:4–7 mandates a ritual involving two birds.

issar: By sending away the mother bird, one loses her worth, which is only a small amount.

the Torah said: Deuteronomy 22:7.

how much the more so: A *qal va-homer* argument (see 2:7).

Tractate Bekhorot

Chaya Halberstam

Introduction

Overview

Tractate *Bekhorot*, "firstborns," treats the laws of firstborn (male) animals and humans.

Structure and Organization of the Tractate

Tractate *Bekhorot* considers three principal topics: (1) the status of firstborn male offspring among both animals and humans (chapters 1 through 5, and 8); (2) blemishes that render animals unfit for the altar and priests unfit for service (chapters 6 and 7); and (3) the animal tithe (chapter 9).

Summary of Legal Contents and Their Biblical Foundations

Firstborn males, both animal and human, belong to God (in most cases, i.e. dedicated to the Temple: Exodus 13:1–2, 11–16; Exodus 22:29–30; Exodus 34:19; Numbers 3:12–13; Number 8:16–19; Numbers 18:15–19; Deuteronomy 15:19–23; Nehemiah 10:36–37).

Chapters 1 through 3 cover the rules for firstborn animals, "pure" and "impure." Firstborn male domesticated animals , which are considered consecrated to God, may not be worked, shorn, or slaughtered. Pure unblemished male firstborns were to be offered as Temple sacrifices. Impure male firstborns must be killed and buried (Exodus 13:13), or redeemed with another pure animal which may be offered as a Temple sacrifice (Exodus 34:20).

In the post-Temple time of the Mishnah, when ritual sacrifice was not an option, firstborn pure animals would have to be left untouched until they acquired a blemish which would disqualify them from the altar, as would the pure animals used for redemption of impure firstborns. Once they acquired blemishes, they still belonged to the priest, but the priest could then slaughter and eat (or otherwise derive benefit from) these firstborn animals without the need for a Temple sacrifice.

Chapters 4 through 6 focus on how to establish whether a firstborn is actually blemished. The first issue is one of authority: who is trusted to identify disqualifying blemishes? The second is how to identify the blemishes that disqualify; these are delineated in chapter 6. The Mishnah then takes up the conceptually related topic of blemishes that render priests unfit for service.

Human male firstborns are also considered consecrated to God and must be redeemed by way of five silver *sheqel* (Numbers 3:47). Inheritance law also pertains to firstborn male humans, who are biblically mandated to receive a double portion of the father's estate (Deuteronomy 21:17). Chapter 8 delineates the criteria by which to distinguish between those firstborns that need to be redeemed and those that are to receive a double portion as inheritance.

Finally, chapter 9 discusses the procedure for determining the animal tithe (Leviticus 27:32) in which every tenth animal in the herd or flock must be consecrated to materially support the priestly class. It is unlikely that the animal tithe was performed in the rabbinic era. Questions raised by the Mishnah regarding this tithe are how exactly to determine the limits of one herd or flock, which animals are exempt from the tithe, and what to do in cases of miscounting.

Relationship of Rabbinic Law to Biblical Law

In the Hebrew Bible, the repeated idea that firstborn males belong to God establishes a firm hierarchy between humans and the deity; it is also linked to the slaying of the firstborn sons of the Egyptians during the Exodus narrative, suggesting that firstborn sons of Israel would belong to God in a kind of exchange (Numbers 3:13). Similarly, the requirement of the animal tithe derives from Leviticus 27:32, which states that every tenth animal of the flock or herd belongs to the Lord. The Mishnah offers a less robust concept of firstborns "belonging" to God than does the Pentateuch. The Mishnah's categorizations and questions suggest that the rabbis viewed the issue of whether a particular firstborn should be given to the priest more as a property dispute between priests and lay Israelites than an issue of sacred, ontological status. For example, in one case in which the firstborn status of an animal cannot be determined conclusively, R. Aqiva uses the principle "the one who would take from his fellow bears the burden of proof" (2:7; cf. *Bava Metsi'a* 3:11), a rabbinic expression of the idea that "possession is nine-tenths of the law."

As for the blemishes that render animals unfit for the altar and priests unfit for Temple service, the Mishnah relies on two biblical passages: Leviticus 22:21–25, on blemished animals, and Leviticus 21:17–23, on priests. Each passage provides a list of disqualifying imperfections. It is apparent that the rabbis were uncertain about the precise meaning of these biblical terms: on occasion, the Mishnah asks "what is a [biblical term]?" and provides multiple rabbinic options that often do not have the hallmarks of homiletic interpretation. The Mishnah does, however, also take advantage of midrashic hermeneutics to link certain physical imperfections to biblical verses (7:2, 5).

The elaboration, expansion, and precision around blemishes in the Mishnah may reflect a post-Temple reality of rabbinic Jews setting aside unblemished, pure, firstborn, male animals, and allowing them to pasture until they acquire the kind of permanent blemish that would render them permissible for nonsacral use.

Tractate Bekhorot

Chapter One

1:1–7 *The Firstborn Donkey*

1 One who purchases the fetus of a gentile's donkey,
or sells one to him—
even though one is not permitted to do so—
or enters a partnership with him,
or receives it from him or gives it to him on contract—
it is exempt from the law of the firstborn.
As it is said: *in Israel*—
but not among others.
Priests and Levites are exempt based on an inference of lesser and greater:
if [the donkeys of the Levites] exempted those that belonged to the Israelites in the wilderness,
logic requires that they should exempt those belonging to themselves.

2 A cow that gave birth to something like a donkey,
and a donkey that gave birth to something like a horse—

1:1 *even though one is not permitted to do so*: See *Avodah Zarah* 1:6, which prohibits the sale of animals to gentiles.

partnership: It was customary for individuals to raise cattle for their offspring; at times, they did this through joint ownership (see *Bava Metsi'a* 5:4–5).

on contract: Agreements were made to compensate laborers, who cared for the animals, with some of the offspring of the cattle with which they worked (see *Bava Metsi'a* 5:4–5).

law of the firstborn: Explained below, 1:4.

in Israel: Numbers 3:13. *In Israel* is used to draw a distinction between firstborns owned entirely by Jews (subject to the law of the firstborn) and those that are owned, either fully or partially, by a gentile (exempt, because the animal is not found entirely *in Israel*).

lesser and greater: Heb. *qal va-homer*.

Levites are exempt: See Numbers 3:41, 45. In the biblical passage, the Levites and their cattle redeem the firstborn humans and cattle of the Israelites. The reasoning is: if the status of Levites (as "the Lord's") exempted the cattle of regular Israelites from the law of the firstborn, all the more so must their status exempt their own cattle from this law.

1:2 *firstborn donkey, firstborn donkey*: Exodus 13:13; 34:20.

something like an impure animal—it may be eaten: "It" refers to the offspring, not the mother, as is explained in the summary just below.

they are exempt from the law of the firstborn.
As it is said: *firstborn donkey, firstborn donkey*, two times:
only when the one that gives birth is a donkey and the offspring is a donkey.
And what are they with respect to eating?
A pure animal that has given birth to something like an impure animal—
it may be eaten;
and an impure one that has given birth to something like a pure animal—
it may not be eaten,
for that which comes out of the impure is impure,
and that which comes out of the pure is pure.
An impure fish that has swallowed a pure fish—
it may be eaten;
and a pure one that has swallowed an impure fish—
it may not be eaten,
because it is not its growth.
3 A donkey that has never given birth and gave birth to:
two males—
one gives one lamb to the priest;
a male and a female—
one separates one lamb for oneself.
If two donkeys that have never given birth gave birth to:
two males—
one gives two lambs to the priest;
a male and a female,
or two males and a female—
one gives one lamb to the priest.
Two females and a male, or two males and two females—
there is nothing here for the priest.
4 One that has previously given birth, and one that has never given birth—
if they gave birth to two males,

pure fish—it may be eaten: "It" refers to the swallowed fish, not the one that swallowed the other one.

its growth: The Hebrew word usually refers to agricultural "produce" (cf. e.g. *Nedarim* 7:6, *Pe'ah* 1.4). In this context, the word is ambiguous: does it mean grown in it (incubated)? Or grown from it ("bred from [it]," Danby), sharing genetic material with the mother?

1:3 *one lamb for oneself*: Because one does not know whether the male or female was the firstborn, and only a male firstborn requires redemption, the case is one in which the requirement for redemption is in doubt. One designates a lamb to fulfill the first half of the commandment (substituting a lamb for the firstborn donkey), but one does not have to give that lamb to the priest because "the one who would take from his fellow bears the burden of proof" (see below, 2:6 and *Bava Metsi'a* 3:11). In order to take possession of the lamb, the priest would have to prove that the male donkey was the firstborn. Such proof is not available, so the lamb stays in the possession of its owner who may make use of the animal.

two donkeys: And the offspring became intermingled.

one lamb to the priest: In both cases one male is certainly a firstborn. In the case of two male offspring and one female, the status of a second male is in doubt, since it may also have been the sibling of a firstborn male or female.

one gives one lamb to the priest;
a male and a female—
one separates one lamb for oneself.
As it is said: *The firstborn of a donkey you shall redeem with one of the flock*—
from among the sheep or the goats,
male or female,
large or small,
unblemished or blemished.
And he may redeem with it many times.
It enters into the fold to be tithed.
And if it dies, one may derive benefit from it.

5 One may not redeem with a calf,
nor with a wild animal,
nor with a slaughtered animal,
nor with a *terefah*,
nor with a prohibited mixture,
nor with a *koy*.
R. Eleazar permits with a prohibited mixture,
because it is *flock*,
but he prohibits with a *koy*,
because it is indeterminate.
If one gave [the donkey] to the priest,
the priest is not permitted to keep it until he separates a lamb in its place.

1:4 *The firstborn of a donkey*: Exodus 34:20. This verse provides the biblical basis for this entire chapter of the Mishnah; that it is not placed at the beginning but rather midway through the chapter is typical of mishnaic style.

from among the sheep or the goats: The Mishnah is here is glossing the biblical word *seh*, normally translated "lamb," but clearly meaning either sheep *or* goats. The closest word to approximate the rabbis' understanding of *seh* would be the subfamily *Caprinae*.

may redeem with it many times: The same lamb can be used to redeem any number of donkeys. Although this passage has stated the expectation that the animal will be given to the priest, the redemption does not automatically make it the property of the priest, nor does it transfer the sanctity of the donkey, hence this rule and those that follow.

enters into the fold to be tithed: The lamb used to redeem the donkey is still considered the property of the owner, hence liable to the tithe on animals, and not of the priest. See below, 9:4.

And if it dies, one may derive benefit from it: This seems to permit the owner of the separated animal to derive benefit from it after its death. The Babylonian Talmud counterintuitively reads this passage as meaning that only the priests may derive benefit from it.

1:5 *prohibited mixture* between a goat and a lamb. See *Temurah* 2:3.

koy: An otherwise unidentified animal possessing some characteristics of the wild and some characteristics of the domesticated. See *Bikkurim* 3:8 and *Hullin* 6:1.

flock: Lit. "it is a lamb." See 1:4 above.

If one gave: The priest is not permitted to make use of the unredeemed donkey until he himself has redeemed it.

6 One who separates [a lamb for] the redemption of the firstborn donkey, and it dies—
R. Eliezer says:
One is liable to make restitution for it,
like the five *sela* for a firstborn son;
but the Sages say:
One is not liable to make restitution for it,
like the redemption of the second tithe.
R. Joshua and R. Zadok[1] testified regarding the redemption of the firstborn donkey that died,
that there is nothing here for the priest.
If the firstborn donkey dies—
R. Eliezer says:
It must be buried,
and one is permitted to derive benefit from the lamb;
but the Sages say:
One does not have to bury it,
and the lamb belongs to the priest.
7 If he did not want to redeem it—
he breaks its neck from behind with a hatchet and buries it.
The commandment of redemption has priority over the commandment of breaking its neck,
as it is said: *If you do not redeem it, you must break its neck.*
The commandment of betrothal has priority over the commandment of redemption,
as it is said: *Has not designated her, she shall be redeemed.*

[1] **P**: "R. Joshua son of R. Zadok" (one person); the verb is in the singular.

1:6 Parallel to *Eduyot* 7:1.

it dies: The lamb.

like the five sela for a firstborn son: See below, 8:7–8. Five *sela* are the redemption price for a firstborn son. If they were lost before they were given to the priest, the father is still required to make payment.

like the redemption of the second tithe: Deuteronomy 14:22–26 and *Ma'aser Sheni*, introduction. Someone who lost the money used to redeem the second tithe does not need to replace the lost money.

permitted to derive benefit from the lamb: Apparently, where the donkey died after a lamb was set aside but before it was given to the priest. According to R. Eliezer, the lamb reverts back to its regular status, and the firstborn donkey is buried (as it is dedicated to God) rather than used. The argument here relates to the question of when the redemption is fully effective. According to R. Eliezer, redemption takes place when the redemption animal is given to the priest (hence, his position earlier in which the owner of the animal is responsible for the replacement value to the priest of the redemption animal). The Sages, however, believe that the redemption is effective as soon as the redemption animal is designated, even before it reaches the hands of the priest.

1:7 *If you do not . . . neck*: Exodus 13:13.

The commandment of betrothal: The following statements are not relevant to the topic of redemption of firstborns.

Has not designated her, she shall be redeemed: Exodus 21:8. The Mishnah here reads the first Hebrew word *lo* as "not" following the biblical text as it is written (*ketiv*): the master *has not designated* or betrothed the girl (his primary obligation), and therefore (secondarily) she should be redeemed. The text as read (*qeri*) denotes the homophone "to him." Even following this reading, however, the meaning remains the same: only when the girl sold into slavery is displeasing for betrothal is she redeemed; betrothal takes priority.

The commandment of levirate marriage has priority over the commandment of *halitsah*.
[This was so] originally, when people's intentions were for the sake of fulfilling a commandment.
But now, when people's intentions are not for the sake of fulfilling a commandment, [the Sages] have said:
The commandment of *halitsah* has priority over the commandment of levirate marriage.
The commandment of redemption [from the Temple] pertains to the original owner.
He has priority over all others,
as it is said: *If it is not redeemed, it shall be sold at its assessment.*

Chapter Two

2:1 *Firstborn Pure Animals: Ambiguous Cases of the Firstborn Cow*

2 One who purchases the fetus of a gentile's cow,
or sells one to him—
even though one is not permitted to do so—
or enters a partnership with him,
or receives it from him or gives it to him on contract—
he is exempt from the law of the firstborn.
As it is said: *in Israel*—
but not among others.
Priests and Levites are obligated.
They are not exempt from the law of the firstborn for pure animals;
rather they are exempt only from redemption of the son and the donkey.

levirate marriage... halitsah: See *Yevamot* 1 and Deuteronomy 25:5–10.

now... not for the sake of fulfilling a commandment: The practice of levirate marriage is an exception to biblical laws of incest as specified in Leviticus 18:16; it is perhaps because of this that some rabbis preferred that *halitsah* be performed rather than allow a man to satisfy "incestuous" urges.

redemption: If property dedicated to the Temple is not redeemed by its original owner, only then may it be sold to someone else. Note a shift in terminology for redemption here from *padah* to *ga'al*, reflecting the language of the verse cited.

If it is not redeemed: Leviticus 27:27.

2:1 Corresponds closely to 1:1.

redemption of the son and the donkey: See below 8:1 and above, 1:1, for exemption from the law of the firstborn donkey.

2:2–3 *Firstborn Pure Animals: Consecrated Animals with Blemishes*

2 All sacred offerings whose permanent blemish preceded their consecration,
and they were redeemed,
they are liable to the law of the firstborn and the gifts;
and they become nonsacral animals that may be shorn and worked;
and their offspring and their milk are permitted after their redemption;
and one who slaughters them outside the Temple Court is exempt;
and they do not effect substitution;
and if they died, they may be redeemed,
except for the firstborn and the tithe.

3 All sacred offerings whose consecration preceded their blemish,
or whose temporary blemish preceded their consecration,
and afterward they developed a permanent blemish,
and they were redeemed,
they are exempt from the law of the firstborn and the gifts;
and they do not become nonsacral animals such that they may be shorn and worked;
and their offspring and their milk are forbidden after their redemption;
and one who slaughters them outside the Temple Court is culpable;
and they effect substitution;
and if they died, they must be buried.

2:2 Parallel to *Hullin* 10:2. These two paragraphs explicate the status of animals that are redeemed once they are blemished. The legal outcome differs depending on whether the animal was permanently blemished before it was consecrated or only afterward.

sacred offerings: Animals consecrated as sacrifices cannot be offered if blemished and must be redeemed for another animal. The question in this passage and the next pertains to the status of the original animal after its redemption. In 2:2, the animal was disqualified from being a sacrifice before it was designated. As a result, it never attained true sacrificial status and when redeemed becomes entirely nonsacral (*hullin*). In 2:3, the animal did attain sacrificial status, and therefore can never lose it.

the gifts: The shoulder, the two cheeks, and the abomasum, which must be given to the priest (see *Hullin* 10:1; Deuteronomy 18:3).

do not effect substitution: A consecrated animal cannot be substituted or exchanged; if one attempts to do so, one has violated a prohibition, and both the original animal and the substitute are considered consecrated. See Leviticus 27:10; *Temurah* introduction; and 1:2. *Do not effect substitution* means that the prohibition does not apply, and the second animal does not become consecrated if one attempts a substitution.

died, they may be redeemed: If the blemished animal died before it was redeemed, it may be redeemed and the owners may make use of the carcass (unlike the firstborn and the tithe, which must be buried).

the tithe: The animal tithe (Leviticus 27:32; see *Hullin* 1:7; 2:10).

2:3 Parallel to *Hullin* 10:2. See 2:2.

2:4–9 *Firstborn Pure Animals: Ambiguous Cases of Firstborn Sheep*

4 One who receives “iron sheep” from a gentile—
the offspring are exempt [from the law of the firstborn];
and the offspring of the offspring are liable.
If one designates the offspring [as collateral] against their mother,
the offspring of the offspring are exempt,
and the offspring of the offspring of the offspring are liable.[2]
Rabban Simeon b. Gamaliel says:
Even up to ten generations they are exempt, because the gentile has the lien.
5 A ewe that has given birth to something like a goat,
or a goat that has given birth to something like a ewe—
they are exempt from the law of the firstborn.
But if it has some signs,
it is liable.
6 If a ewe that has not previously given birth gave birth to:
two males,
and both heads emerged simultaneously—
R. Yose the Galilean says:
Both belong to the priest;
as it is said: *Males shall be the Lord's*;
but the Sages say:
It is not possible!
Rather, one belongs to him and one belongs to the priest.

[2] **K, P**: “the offspring are exempt, and the offspring of the offspring are liable.”

2:4 *“iron sheep”*: See *Bava Metsi'a* 5:6, *Yevamot* 7:1–2. A fixed value is assigned to the animals for which the contractor assumes liability, and pays the owner a fixed price per head.

offspring are exempt, as contracted animals in which one of the parties is a gentile. They are animals bought through a contract in which a gentile still has partial ownership. See 1:1 and 2:1.

2:5–9 These passages follow the organization of 1:2–4, now addressing the offspring of a pure (that is “kosher,” suitable to be eaten or sacrificed) animal.

2:5 *something like a goat*: See 1:2.

they are exempt: The Bavli quotes Numbers 18:17 to explain this exemption, which it reads as necessitating that both the mother and the offspring must be the same species, and cannot be crossbred.

some signs: Markers of the mother's species.

2:6 *has not previously given birth*: See 1:3.

Males shall be the Lord's: Exodus 13:12. This interpretation emphasizes the plural “males,” implying that the verse allows for more than one firstborn.

It is not possible for both offspring to have emerged at precisely the same moment, and therefore one has to be the firstborn. As such, one deals with the animals as one would with any case of two males in which the firstborn status is indeterminate.

R. Tarfon says:
The priest chooses the better one for himself.
R. Aqiva says:
They make an assessment between themselves;
and the second one pastures until it becomes defiled;
and it is liable to the law of the gifts;
but R. Yose exempts it.
If one of them dies—
R. Tarfon says:
They divide it.
R. Aqiva says:
The one who would take from his fellow bears the burden of proof.
Male and a female—
there is nothing here for the priest.

7 Two ewes that have not previously given birth gave birth to:
two males—
both are given to the priest.
A male and a female—
the male belongs to the priest.
Two males and a female—
one belongs to him, and one belongs to the priest.
R. Tarfon says:
The priest chooses the better one for himself.
R. Aqiva says:
They make an assessment between themselves;
and the second one pastures until it becomes defiled;
and it is liable to the gifts;
but R. Yose exempts it.
If one dies—
R. Tarfon says:

They make an assessment between themselves: It is entirely unclear from the mishnah how the owner and priest make this assessment, and it seems likely that R. Aqiva did not care what settlement was reached, so long as each party was satisfied with what they received. The Bavli seeks to harmonize R. Aqiva's statement here with an apparently contradictory one in which R. Aqiva assigns "the weaker one" to the priest.

defiled: Until it acquires a blemish that renders it unfit for an offering. At this point, it may be consumed by the owner.

R. Yose exempts it: See below, 2:8, for the reasoning behind R. Yose's statement.

They divide it: They assess the value of the living animal and divide it accordingly.

The one who would take: The priest is given nothing, because he cannot prove that the living animal is the firstborn.

Male and a female: Neither animal can be presumed to be a firstborn male offspring.

2:7 *Two... that have not previously given birth*: As in 1:3, the offspring have been mingled and it is not clear which is the firstborn of which.

R. Yose exempts: See below, 2:8, for the reasoning behind R. Yose's statement.

They divide it.
R. Aqiva says:
The one who would take from his fellow bears the burden of proof.
Two females and a male,
or two males and two females—
there is nothing here for the priest.

8 One that has previously given birth and one that has not previously given birth gave birth to two males—
one is kept and one belongs to the priest.
R. Tarfon says:
The priest chooses the better one for himself.
R. Aqiva says:
They make an assessment between themselves;
and the second one pastures until it becomes defiled;
and it is liable to the gifts;
but R. Yose exempts it;
as R. Yose used to say:
Any animal for which the priest holds an item in exchange[3] is exempt from the gifts.
R. Meir deems it liable.
If one of them dies—
R. Tarfon says:
They divide it.
R. Aqiva says:
The one who would take from his fellow bears the burden of proof.
Male and a female—
there is nothing here for the priest.

9 A caesarean birth,
and the one that comes afterward—
R. Tarfon says:
Both of them pasture until they become defiled,

[3] Lit. "the exchange of which is in the hands of the priest."

one who would take: See above, 2:6.

Two females and a male, etc.: Again, none of the animals can be presumed to be the firstborn male offspring of one of the ewes.

2:8 *One that has previously given birth*: See 1:4; again the offspring have been intermingled.

an item in exchange, as in a case of barter. Here, the priest has whichever lamb the parties agreed that he would take, in exchange for the one that the owner has.

one who would take: See above, 2:6.

2:9 *the one that comes afterward*: Via a natural birth.

Both of them pasture... and they can be eaten by the owners: Since neither can be called a firstborn, both are treated as indeterminate with regard to their firstborn status. See 2:6. Contrast, *R. Aqiva* who excludes them from the status of firstborn altogether.

and they can be eaten by the owners once they have blemishes.
R. Aqiva says:
Neither one is a firstborn:
the first, because it did not open the womb,
and the second, because another came first.

Chapter Three

3:1–2 *Ambiguity Surrounding Previous Births*

3 One who purchases a domestic animal from a gentile,
and it is not known whether the animal had previously given birth
or had not previously given birth:
R. Ishmael says:
A she-goat that is one year old or less—
with certainty to the priest;
beyond that, it is indeterminate;
a ewe that is two years old or less—
with certainty to the priest;
beyond that, it is indeterminate;
a cow or donkey that is three years old or less—
with certainty to the priest;
beyond that, it is indeterminate.
R. Aqiva said to him:
If it were only through offspring that an animal were exempted,
it would be according to your words.
However, they have said:
The sign of offspring for sheep and goats is muddy discharge;
for cattle, afterbirth;
for women, the amniotic sac and afterbirth.
This is the general rule:
Any animal that is known to have previously given birth—

3:1 *R. Ishmael* argues from the age at which animals might be expected to have had a live birth.

with certainty to the priest: If the animal is less than the specified age, its offspring is treated as definitely a firstborn.

R. Aqiva argues that there are other *signs* of nonviable birth that, apparently, are possible in younger animals.

muddy discharge: As it is considered evidence of a miscarriage or stillbirth, it apparently indicates some kind of dark-colored, vaginal discharge.

afterbirth: See *Hullin* 4:7 for parallel laws.

amniotic sac and afterbirth: See *Niddah* 3:3 and *Keritot* 1:5 for further details on human miscarriages.

nothing here belongs to the priest;
and any that has not previously given birth—
it belongs to the priest;
in an indeterminate case—
it is eaten with its blemish by the owners.
R. Eliezer b. Jacob says:
If a cow[4] discharges a large clot[5] of blood—
[the clot] must be buried;
and [the cow] is exempt from the law of the firstborn.

2 R. Simeon b. Gamaliel says:
One who purchases from a gentile an animal that is giving suck
need not be concerned that its offspring belong to a different animal.
If he entered his fold and sees animals that had previously given birth giving suck,
and those that had not previously given birth giving suck,
he need not be concerned that the offspring of this one may have come near to that,
or the offspring of that one may have come near to this.

3:3–4 *Fleece of Firstborn Animals*

3 R. Yose b. Meshullam says:
One who slaughters a firstborn—
he makes a place with the hatchet[6] on either side or plucks out hairs,
provided that he does not move them from their place.
And so too one who plucks out hairs to examine the place of a blemish.

[4] Lit. "large female cattle." [5] Lit. "cake." [6] **K, P**: "for the hatchet."

it belongs to the priest: The firstborn offspring.

it is eaten with its blemish: The indeterminate offspring may be eaten after it is no longer eligible for the altar. See 2:6.

must be buried: The Talmud comments that the clot is not actually considered a firstborn, but it is treated as such in order to make the miscarriage publicly known so that the next offspring will not be treated as a firstborn.

exempt from the law of the firstborn: The mother is no longer subject to the law; the next offspring will not be considered a firstborn.

3:2 *that its offspring belong to a different animal*: We can assume that it gave birth to the offspring it is suckling and that it is no longer liable to the law of the firstborn.

not be concerned that the offspring of this one: We can presume that the offspring of the animals that have not previously given birth are in fact firstborn, and not the offspring of the other mothers.

3:3 *or plucks out hairs*: Shearing a firstborn is explicitly forbidden in Deuteronomy 15:19. The Mishnah therefore considers how one can make sure to slaughter the animal in the appropriate place: by moving hairs to the side with an instrument (but see n. 6) or plucking by hand, neither of which constitute shearing. The Babylonian Talmud specifies that the plucking out of hairs must be done by hand, because using an instrument is forbidden.

does not move them: Leaves the plucked hairs on or in the fleece of the animal.

4 Hair that fell out of a blemished firstborn, and he put it in a wall niche,
and subsequently he slaughtered it—
Aqaviah b. Mahalalel permits it,
but the Sages prohibit it—
the words of R. Judah.
R. Yose says:
This is not what Aqaviah permitted.
Rather: hair of a blemished firstborn fell out, and one put it in a wall niche,
and it subsequently died—
this is what Aqaviah b. Mahalalel permitted, and the Sages prohibited.
Matted wool in a firstborn—
if it appears to be part of the fleece,[7]
it is permitted;
if it does not appear to be part of the fleece,[8]
it is prohibited.

Chapter Four

4:1–2 *Time Restrictions for Firstborns*

4 For how long is an Israelite obligated to tend to the firstborn?
For sheep and goats, as long as thirty days;

[7] Lit. "from the shearing." **P** reads "with the shearing." [8] Lit. "the shearing."

3:4 Cf. *Eduyot* 5:6.

put it in a wall niche: Or "window." The question here relates to whether or not the wool that fell off the blemished firstborn while it was still alive, and from which no benefit can be derived by a nonpriest, can be used after the animal's death. After a blemished firstborn is slaughtered, the wool may be used. Here, the owner put the fallen hair somewhere out of the way for safekeeping.

Aqaviah b. Mahalalel permits the hair to be used, retroactively, after the slaughter.

not what Aqaviah permitted: According to R. Judah, the disagreement between Aqaviah and the Sages concerns an animal that was slaughtered. But according to R. Yose, the disagreement is actually about a case in which the blemished animal died. R. Yose believes that once the animal has been slaughtered, everyone would permit the use of the wool, even retroactively. In the case of death, however, the wool that is on the animal may not be used, according to the Sages. But, according to R. Yose, Aqaviah permits the wool that has previously fallen out to be used after the death of the animal, although it was not slaughtered.

appears to be part of the fleece: According to everyone, after the animal is slaughtered, its fleece can be shorn and used. The question arises (as above) whether fleece that fell out prior to the slaughtering of the animal may be used. Matted wool would have fallen out prior to the slaughter and the shearing. According to Aqaviah, it would surely be permitted. However, the Sages, who prohibited wool to be used retroactively (in the view of R. Judah), might also therefore prohibit matted wool. The Mishnah therefore states that if the matted wool appears to be part of the shearing (lit. it is "seen with/from the shearing"; see nn. 7 and 9), i.e. it does not fall away as a separate clump when the wool is sheared, it is permitted. Conversely, if the matted wool does fall away separately, it would not be permitted.

4:1 *to tend to the firstborn*, before giving it to the priest.

For cattle, fifty days.
R. Yose says:
For sheep and goats, three months.
If the priest said to him during that time: "Give it to me,"
he may not give it to him.
If it had a blemish—
he said to him: "Give it to me so that I can eat it,"
it is permitted.
During the time of the Temple,
if it was unblemished—
and he said to him: "Give it to me so that I can sacrifice it,"
it is permitted.
The firstborn must be eaten within its first year,
whether unblemished or blemished,
as it is said: *In the presence of the Lord your God you shall eat it year by year.*
2 If it develops a blemish within its first year,[9]
he is permitted to keep it for the full twelve months;
after its first year,
he is not allowed keep it beyond thirty days.

4:3–6 *Examination of Blemishes, Conflicts of Interest*

3 One who slaughters a firstborn and has the blemish examined,[10]
R. Judah permits.
R. Meir says:
Since its slaughter was not at the word of an expert,[11]
it is prohibited.
4 One who is not an expert, and he examined a firstborn,
and it is slaughtered at his word—
in this case, it must be buried,

[9] Lit. "its year." [10] Lit. "shows the blemish." [11] Lit. "one who was designated"

he may not give it to him: The Bavli explains that one does not give it to the priest because the priest cannot work with the animals or on the harvests that he will be given as priestly dues, because it appears as though he is working for his own income.

whether unblemished: This refers to the time of the Temple, when it was eaten as an offering. In post-Temple times, the unblemished firstborn could not be eaten—it had to be kept by the priest until it died or developed a blemish.

In the presence: Deuteronomy 15:20.

4:2 *he is is permitted to keep it*: This mishnah sets a limit on how long a priest may hold on to the animal before slaughtering it, once it has developed a blemish.

4:3 *an expert*: Even if a blemish is apparent after slaughter, an expert examination was needed before the slaughter in order to confirm that the blemish was present.

4:4 *it must be buried*: As in 4:3, one who does not show the animal to a designated expert before slaughter is penalized. See also 5:5.

and he must pay compensation out of his own funds.
If he renders judgment—
exonerated the liable,
or held liable the exempt;
declared the pure impure,
or declared the impure pure—
what he has done is done,
and he must pay compensation out of his own funds.
If he was designated by the court,
he is exempt from paying compensation.
It once happened that there was a cow whose uterus had been removed,
and R. Tarfon fed it to the dogs.
And the incident came before the Sages,
and they permitted it.
Todos[12] the physician said:
There is no cow or pig that is exported from Alexandria unless its uterus has been excised,
in order that it not give birth.
R. Tarfon said:
There goes your donkey, Tarfon!
R. Aqiva said to him:
R. Tarfon, you are exempt, for you are authorized by the court,
and all who are authorized by the court are exempt from paying compensation.

5 If one makes his living examining firstborns,
one may not slaughter based on his assessment,

[12] **K**: "Teodros"; **P**: "Todros."

renders judgment: Someone who is not designated by the court as an expert in that subject matter. Unlike the case of the firstborn, this passage allows the verdict to stand (*what he has done is done*). The Mishnah imagines courts for monetary matters as panels of three (e.g. *Sanhedrin* 1:1); for the problem of judging alone, cf. *Avot* 4:8.

R. Tarfon fed it to the dogs: R. Tarfon deemed it torn (*terefah*) and therefore prohibited to be eaten. A *terefah* is a pure animal that has been properly slaughtered but is prohibited to be eaten because it suffers from a preexisting fatal disease or injury. See *Hullin* 3:1, 2.

and they permitted it: They declared that the cow was not torn, and permitted to be eaten.

Todos: An abbreviation of Theodoros (see n. 12). This figure appears in several places in tannaitic literature, particularly the Tosefta. His testimony is that animals can survive without a uterus.

unless its uterus has been excised, in order that it not give birth: It is likely that this was done to protect the proprietary nature of the breed.

There goes your donkey, Tarfon! R. Tarfon believed that because his judgment was in error, he would have to compensate the cow's owner from his own funds, and therefore would need to sell his donkey.

4:5 *If one makes his living examining firstborns*: The Mishnah may be concerned about overt corruption as well as unconscious biases that can occur when there is monetary incentive attached to the outcome of a decision. It seems too probable that the examiner will be inclined to declare firstborns blemished (so that the owners can keep them), which may draw a higher price or "tip" from the owners. Perhaps also if examiners are known for their leniency in declaring blemishes, they would be able to attract more customers.

unless he was an expert like Ila'i in Yavneh,
whom the rabbis permitted to accept four *issar* for sheep and goats and six for cattle,
whether unblemished or blemished.

6 One who makes his living by judging, his judgments are nullified;
by witnessing, his testimony is nullified;
by sprinkling and consecrating,
his waters are cave waters, and his ashes are wood ashes.
If he was a priest,
and he was made impure and thus prevented from eating his *terumah*,[13]
one feeds him, and gives him drink, and anoints him.
And if he was old, one has him ride on his donkey.
And one gives him the wages of a laborer.[14]

4:7–10 *Presumptions of Reliability or Unreliability*

7 One who is suspect regarding firstborns,
one may not purchase from him deer meat or untreated hides.
R. Eliezer says:
One may purchase from him female hides.

[13] Lit. "became impure from his *terumah*."
[14] **P**: "idle laborer."

Ila'i in Yavneh: An expert examiner of blemishes in Yavneh; see below 6:8. Because he was well-known, he likely had many customers—many of them priests—and so would not need to build his clientele with lenient rulings.

four issar: Despite the fact that Ila'i was deemed trustworthy, the Sages still seem to have regulated his payments.

whether unblemished or blemished: Payments could not vary according to desired or undesired outcomes.

4:6 *sprinkling and consecrating*: Both of these acts are part of the redheifer ritual. "Living water" (water from a flowing spring; see *Nega'im* 14:1) is mixed with the ashes in order to consecrate the purification waters; see *Temurah* 1:5.

cave waters: As opposed to "living waters"; the water would be precluded from the purification rite. *Wood ashes*: Merely ashes collected from a wood-burning fire rather than the ashes of the red heifer. See *Parah* 9:7.

If he the judge *was a priest*: The Mishnah turns to forms of compensation the judge is permitted. Here, the activities necessitated by judging caused the priestly judge to become *impure*.

terumah: A priestly gift. The priest must be in a state of ritual purity to eat the *terumah*; if he is impure, he must buy unconsecrated food.

one gives him the wages of a laborer: See n. 14 and *Bava Metsi'a* 2:9, 5:4. It is unclear whether he is paid as a day laborer or as a skilled laborer; both opinions are reflected in the Babylonian Talmud.

4:7 *deer meat*: Even though the law of the firstborn does not apply to deer, our concern is that the owner might pass off the meat of a firstborn domestic animal as deer meat.

untreated hides: The seller may be trying to unload the hides quickly so as not to be caught with illicit material.

female hides: Not subject to the law of the firstborn.

One may not purchase from him bleached or soiled wool,
but one may purchase spun wool and garments.

8 If someone is suspect regarding the Seventh Year,
one may not purchase flax from him,
even if it is combed;
but one may purchase spun flax or woven textiles.

9 One who is suspected of selling *terumah* under the designation of nonsacral food,
one may not purchase anything from him—even water or salt—
the words of R. Judah.
R. Simeon says:
Anything that is subject to[15] *terumah* or tithes—
one may not purchase from him.

10 One who is suspect regarding the Seventh Year
is[16] not suspect regarding tithes.
One who is suspect regarding tithes
is[17] not suspect regarding the Seventh Year.
One who is suspect regarding either this one or that one
is suspect regarding purities.
And there is one who is suspect regarding purities
but is not suspect regarding either this one or that one.

[15] Lit. "Everything that has the obligation upon it of *terumah* or tithes."
[16] **P**: "and who is"; the difference is a single letter. [17] **P**: "and who is," as above.

bleached or soiled wool: Again, (mostly) unprocessed material that the owner may be trying to unload quickly.

spun wool and garments: If the owner feared discovery, he would not hold on to the wool of a firstborn long enough to process into textiles or garments, or might be reluctant to invest time or resources into processing the hides and risk losing that investment.

4:8 *spun flax or woven textiles*: The reasoning appears to be the same as in 4:7.

4:9 *water or salt*: That is, any foodstuffs at all, even if they are not subject to the laws of *terumah* and tithes. This prohibition seems to be imposed as a sanction because selling *terumah* under the designation of unconsecrated food is considered a grave offense.

subject to terumah or tithes: Water and salt, in this view, would be permitted.

4:10 *One who is suspect*: See nn. 16 and 17. Reading with **P**, the Mishnah may be interpreted quite differently: one who is suspect regarding the Seventh Year, but not regarding tithes; *or* one who is suspect regarding tithes, but not the Seventh Year—in either case, is suspect regarding purities.

regarding the Seventh Year... tithes: Suspect of engaging in prohibited agriculture during the Seventh Year or of not properly separating tithes. See introductions to *Shevi'it* and *Ma'aserot*. Here, the concern is not necessarily deceit (passing off prohibited goods as permitted) but trustworthiness with regard to ritual matters more generally.

regarding purities: Eating food in an impure state was considered a less consequential transgression than eating tithes or Seventh-Year produce. The reasoning is that if one is not concerned about either of the latter two, one certainly would not be that concerned about purities.

This is the rule:
All who are suspect regarding something
may not render judgment nor testify about it.

Chapter Five

5:1–2 *Disqualified Consecrated Animals*

5 All disqualified consecrated animals are sold in the marketplace,
and slaughtered in the marketplace,[18]
and weighed by the pound,
except for the firstborn and the tithe,
because their benefits belong to the owners.
The benefits of disqualified consecrated animals belong to the Temple.[19]
With a firstborn, one may weigh one hundred against one hundred.

[18] The medieval versions disagree on the text of these phrases. See annotations.
[19] Some medieval witnesses insert a note to this effect in the first line of 5:1. See annotations.

This is the rule: This rule does not precisely fit the context, since it addresses the question of issuing judgements, which was not at issue in the specific cases just listed. The same general rule is repeated below in 5:4; it is likely it was appended here because it follows the theme of teachings about someone who is suspect regarding a certain matter.

5:1 The first three lines of this paragraph are consistent in the manuscript tradition, but in the print versions of the Talmud the phrase "their benefits belong to the Temple" is attested in the first line; and/or the second line is missing; and/or the third line is missing. Modern print versions of the Mishnah have "their benefits belong to the Temple" inserted in line 1 in brackets, and put line two ("and slaughtered in the marketplace") in brackets.

disqualified: Consecrated animals that develop blemishes are rendered unfit for the altar. Once they are redeemed, they may be slaughtered and eaten.

sold in the marketplace: See *Temurah* 3:5.

benefits belong to their owners... belong to the Temple: It is unseemly for holy things like consecrated animals—even if unfit—to be weighed and measured in the marketplace. Nevertheless, the Mishnah permits it when the proceeds go to the Temple, so that the Temple is not shortchanged by inaccurate measurements.

the firstborn and the tithe: Any benefit from these animals (including the sale price) belongs to the owner (the priest for the firstborn and the Israelite for the animal tithe). Consequently, the meat may not be weighed and measured in the marketplace.

one hundred against one hundred: While the meat must not be weighed and measured directly, one can estimate the value by comparing it with a piece of ordinary meat, the weight of which is already known.

2 The House of Shammai say:
An Israelite may not be counted with the priest to share in eating[20] the firstborn.
The House of Hillel permit it,
and even a gentile.

5:2 cont.–4 *Blemishes Inflicted on Firstborns*

A firstborn that is overcome with blood:
even if it is dying—
one is not permitted to let blood—
the words of R. Judah;
but the Sages say:
One may let blood,
provided that one does not give the animal a blemish.
And if one gave the animal a blemish, it cannot be slaughtered on account of it.
R. Simeon says:
One may let blood,
even if one gives the animal a blemish.
3 One who splits the ear of a firstborn,
In this case, it may never be slaughtered—
the words of R. Eliezer.
But the Sages say:
When it develops another blemish,
it may be slaughtered on account of it.
It once happened that there was an old firstborn whose hairs were hanging loose.
A Roman official saw it and said: What good is this?
They said to him: It is a firstborn, and it cannot be slaughtered unless it develops a blemish.

[20] Lit. "on account of the firstborn."

5:2 *counted with the priest*: The firstborn animal is for the priest's use. When the animal is slaughtered, nonpriests are not to be included explicitly among those who will share in it.

overcome with blood: A reference to the ancient science of balancing bodily fluids. If too much blood in the system overbalances other fluids, draining some of the excess blood (bloodletting) would be required.

not permitted to let blood: One is not permitted to deliberately cause a blemish on a firstborn animal.

even if one gives the animal a blemish: R. Simeon here permits causing a blemish in order to heal the animal. According to the Talmud and most commentators, R. Simeon would also allow the animal to be slaughtered on account of this blemish, even though the blemish was caused by the owner. What is at issue here seems to be the owner's intention; because the blemish was not caused intentionally, but was a side effect of the bloodletting, R. Simeon permits it. 5:3–4 continues discussion of intention in the creation of blemishes.

5:3 *Roman official*: Heb. *qasdor*, probably from Latin *quaestor*. The initial damage in this case was intentional, but not with the intention or consent of the owner.

He took a dagger and split its ear.
The case came before the Sages, and they permitted it.
He saw that they permitted it, and he went and split the ears of other firstborns;
and the Sages prohibited them.
Once, children were playing in a field,
and they tied the tails of two lambs together;
the tail of one of them detached,
and it turned out it was a firstborn.
The case came before the Sages, and they permitted it.
They saw that they permitted it,
and they went and tied the tails of other firstborns,
and the Sages prohibited them.
This is the general rule:
Everything [done] with foreknowledge is prohibited,
and everything without foreknowledge is permitted.

4 If a firstborn was chasing him,
and he kicked it and created a blemish—
in this case, it may be slaughtered on account of it.
Any blemishes that are plausibly caused by a human being—
shepherds who are Israelites are trusted,
but shepherds who are priests are not trusted.
Rabban Simeon b. Gamaliel says:
He is trusted regarding his fellow's [firstborn],
but not regarding his own.
R. Meir says:
All who are suspect regarding something may not render judgment nor testify about it.

children: In this case, the initial damage was not intended to change the status of the animal, but that was an accidental outcome.

foreknowledge: Or "intention," " knowledge," "consent." While the rendering "intent" is tempting, it is clear that in the first story, the blemish is created—by a gentile—with intent (both in terms of creating the blemish, and knowledge of the law). In any case, the general rule generated from both stories is open to interpretation, and it may not fully fit the specific circumstances of either story.

5:4 *are trusted*: To report that a blemish was accidental rather than intentional. The Israelite has nothing to gain, because the blemished firstborn belongs to the priest.

All who are suspect regarding something: The statement appears above, 4:10, as a general rule. Here, too, it does not quite fit its context, which is not about people who are suspect about observance, but rather people with a conflict of interests. The tradition is brought here as a rebuttal to Rabban Simeon b. Gamaliel's assertion that priests could testify on behalf of their fellow priests. R. Meir refutes that statement with this rule that if one is generally not trusted in a specific matter, one cannot testify regarding it (e.g. on behalf of one's friends).

5:5–6 *Assessment of Blemishes in Firstborns*

5 A priest is trusted if he says:
"I had the firstborn examined, and it had a blemish."
Everyone is trusted regarding the blemishes of the tithe.
A firstborn that has a blind eye,
or a severed foreleg,
or a broken hindleg—
is slaughtered on the assessment of three members of the congregation.
R. Yose says:
Even if it were a court of twenty-three,
it can only be slaughtered on the assessment of an expert.
6 One who slaughters a firstborn and sells it,[21]
and it becomes known that he did not have it examined:
what was eaten, was eaten,
and [the seller] must return the money to them;
and what was not eaten must be buried,
and he must return the money to them.
And so too one who slaughters a cow and sells it,

[21] "And sells" it absent in some witnesses.

5:5 *A priest is trusted*: The blemishes discussed here are difficult to distinguish from those above (blemishes that look like they might have been deliberately caused) and those below (blemishes that are obvious to lay people). The priest seems to be trusted here, even though above he is suspected of deliberately causing a blemish in order to acquire the animal. According to most medieval and modern commentaries, a priest would not be suspected of slaughtering an unblemished animal outside the Temple, which is a grave sin; however, he might not be trusted not to cause a blemish himself, which is a lesser sin. It is also possible that a priest is trusted if he testifies that the animal was examined since that claim is verifiable by asking the local blemish examiners, while the claim that the blemish was caused accidentally can never be verified independently.

Everyone is trusted: The mishnah does not say explicitly here (as above) that they are trusted to say that they had the blemish *examined*; many medieval and modern commentaries assume that examination by an expert is not implied. The owner's testimony that the animals were blemished and that the blemish was not caused deliberately is perhaps sufficient.

three members of the congregation: These blemishes were understood to be obvious enough that even laymen could assess them.

court of twenty-three: A "small sanhedrin" that could try death-penalty cases (see *Sanhedrin* 1:4, 6). For R. Yose, the issue was not the authority of the court but rather that the decisionmaker be an expert in examining blemishes.

5:6 Compare 4:3, above. The circumstances are a bit unclear: we expect the person who should have had the animal examined to be the original owner, and the one who slaughtered the animal to be a priest or some-one who acquired the animal from a priest. However, here, the slaughterer/seller and the one who should have shown the animal to a priest are the same person. It is possible that the scenario here is a priest who is also a shepherd and the original owner of the sheep (see 5:4, above).

and sells it: According to the reading that lacks these words, the circumstances are still less clear, but might refer to a case in which a priest inappropriately slaughtered a firstborn animal, and now owes compensation to the animal's owner.

and it becomes known that it was a *terefah*:
what was eaten, was eaten,
but he must return the money to them.
and what was not eaten—
they must return the meat to the seller,[22]
and the money must be refunded.
If [the buyers] sold it to gentiles or set it out for dogs—
they must pay him the price of a *terefah*.

Chapter Six

6:1–12 *Blemishes in Firsborn Animals*

6 On account of these blemishes one may slaughter a firstborn:
damage to the ear into[23] the cartilage—
but not if it is just on the skin—
a split ear—
even if there is no loss—
a hole in the ear the size of a bitter vetch, or desiccated.
What is desiccated?
Anything that when pierced does not release even one drop of blood.
R. Yose b. Meshullam says:
Desiccated, so that it crumbles.
2 An eyelid that was pierced, or damaged, or split;
in his eyes were: a cataract, a mixture, a snail, snake, or grape.
What is a mixture?

[22] Lit. "to him." [23] Lit. "from."

money must be refunded: All the money for a firstborn must be refunded by the seller. The Mishnah accounts for the refund in two parts: the seller must refund the money for what was eaten, as well as for what must be buried. The commentaries view the requirement to compensate for meat already eaten as a penalty for having caused the consumption of prohibited meat.

If [the buyers]...terefah: Selling to gentiles or feeding to dogs were typical uses for the meat from a *terefah*. The sellers must pay back, or deduct from the refund, the amount of money or benefit that they accrued for that portion of the meat, valued as *terefah* rather than normal (kosher) meat.

6:1 *damage*: Given that the next part adds, "even if there is no loss," here damage implies loss of some of the ear—not just the skin, but the cartilage.

bitter vetch: See *Ma'aser Sheni* 2:2, 4; *Shabbat* 1:5.

6:2 *cataract...mixture*: The Hebrew terms derive from Leviticus 21:20.

snail...grape: Growths on or adjacent to the eye.

What is a mixture? The Mishnah itself may be puzzled by the meaning of the Hebrew term. According to this explanation, the pupil, iris, and sclera do not have clearly defined borders and are thus thought to be mingled.

The white of the eye parts the ring and enters into the pupil.
From the pupil and enters into the white—
that is not a blemish,
for there are no blemishes in the white.

3 A white spot or water that is permanent.
What is a permanent white spot?
Any that has remained for eighty days.
R. Hanina b. Antigonus says:
One checks it three times over eighty days.
And what is permanent water?
If it ate wet and dry [grasses of fields] watered by rain.
Wet and dry from irrigated [fields]:
if it ate the dry and afterwards the wet—
it is not a blemish,
until it eats the dry after the wet.

4 Its nose, that has been pierced, or damaged, or split;
its lip that has been pierced, or damaged, or split;
its front teeth that have been damaged, or worn down;
or back teeth that have been uprooted.
R. Hanina b. Antigonus says:
One does not check the teeth behind the premolars,
and not even the premolars.

5 The sheath has been damaged, or female genitals in consecrated animals,
or the tail has been damaged in the bone—
but not in the joint—
or a forked tailbone;
or flesh the size of a finger between the vertebrae.

6 Having no testicles,
or having only one testicle.

6:3 *A white spot or water*: Apparently, eye ailments.

One checks it three times: If the white spots disappear and reappear over the course of eighty days, it is not considered permanent.

wet and dry [grasses]: The Babylonian Talmud understands these grasses as medicinal: if the animal consumes them in the right order, but there is still "water on the eye," the blemish is considered permanent. It is also possible that the Mishnah imagined that overconsumption of wet grasses produced watery eyes, hence the requirement to feed the animals dry grasses.

6:4 *behind the premolars, and not even the premolars*: These teeth would not routinely be visible in herbivores such as goats, sheep, or cattle.

6:5 *sheath*: That covers the penis.

in consecrated animals: Because the status of firstborn falls only on males.

the joint: That connects the tailbone to the tail.

the vertebrae: In the tail. The reference is presumably to a displacement of the vertebrae that can be seen without surgery.

R. Ishmael says:
If it has two testicular sacs, it has two testicles;
if it has only one testicular sac, it has only one testicle.
R. Aqiva says:
One turns it over on its backside and palpates:
if there is a testicle there, it will ultimately come forward.
It once happened that someone palpated and it didn't come forward;[24]
the animal was slaughtered and [the testicle] was found stuck to its loins.
R. Aqiva permitted,
but R. Yohanan b. Nuri prohibited.
7 It has five feet, or has only three;
or its feet are uncloven like a donkey's;
or a slipped one, or a thickened one.
What is a slipped one?
Its hip is dislocated.
What is a thickened one?
One of its hips is higher.
8 A broken bone in the foreleg, or the hindleg—
even if it cannot be discerned.
Ila'i designated these blemishes at Yavneh,
and the Sages agreed with him.
He added three more,
and they said to him:
We have heard only these![25]
One whose eye is round like a human's;
its mouth resembles a pig's;
one that had the majority of the tongue removed.
A court that came after said:
These are blemishes.

[24] Lit. "go out." [25] **K**:"We not heard of these. Rather . . ."

6:6 *two testicular sacs*: Probably, two chambers in the scrotal sac.

will ultimately come forward: Therefore, if one does not detect the testicle, one can assume it is missing.

R. Aqiva permitted: Even though the testicle was present, the fact that it was stuck to the loins was sufficient for R. Aqiva to consider it a blemish that renders the animal unfit for the altar.

6:7 *uncloven*: The term derives from Leviticus 22:23. In the biblical context, the term refers to a short or stunted limb; in rabbinic usage it designates an animal with uncloven hooves.

slipped . . . thickened one: Again, terms that the Mishnah considers obscure and provides definitions.

6:8 *hindleg*: The word used here is the same word used for "foot" in the previous passage. Here, the sense seems to be "hindleg" rather than "leg" or "foot," as it is contrasted with "hand," which likely means foreleg.

Ila'i: The expert in blemishes mentioned above, 4:5.

the majority of the tongue: Lit. "of the speaking part of the tongue," the body, and not the root that is attached to the throat.

9 It once happened that [an animal had] a lower jaw larger than the upper jaw,
and R. Simeon b. Gamaliel sent for[26] the Sages.
They said:
It is indeed a blemish.
The ear of a kid that was doubled—
the Sages say:
When there is one lobe,[27]
it is a blemish;
and when there is not one lobe,
it is not a blemish.
R. Hanina b. Gamaliel says:
The tail of a kid that resembles a pig's,
and that does not have at least three vertebrae—
in this case, it is a blemish.
10 R. Hanina b. Antigonus says:
One that has a wart in its eye,
or a damaged bone in its foreleg or in its hindleg,[28]
or the bone in its mouth is split;
one of its eyes is large and one is small;
one of its ears is large and one is small—
by appearance, not by measurement.
R. Judah says:
One testicle is twice as large as the other;
but the Sages did not agree.
11 The tail of a calf that does not reach the leg joint—
the Sages say:
The whole time calves are growing it is so;
as they grow, their tails grow longer.[29]
To which leg joint are they referring?
R. Hanina b. Antigonus says:
To the leg joint that is in the middle of the thigh.

[26] Or "to"; **K**, **P**: "asked." [27] Lit. "bone"
[28] **K**, **P**: *nifqam* "pierced," here and in the next clause. [29] Lit. "stretch out."

6:9 *When there is … is not one lobe*: These phrases are obscure, largely because the word rendered "lobe" literally means "bone," which ears lack. It is also unclear how exactly the ear would be *doubled*, or why with one "lobe" (which seems normal) it is a blemish. Some medieval jurists reversed the two positions.

6:10 *bone in its mouth*: The mandible (commentaries).

large … small: One eye or ear is larger than normal and the other is smaller than normal, or that they are each large or small relative to the other.

by appearance, not by measurement: If the difference in size is only discernible by measurement, but the eyes and ears appear to be the same size, it is not considered a blemish.

6:11 *leg joint*: Normally, the knee or inner knee. Because the mishnah attempts below to clarify which joint, we translate ambiguously.

leg joint that is in the middle of the thigh: Again, this likely refers to the knee.

On account of these blemishes firstborns may be slaughtered;
and disqualified consecrated animals may be redeemed on account of them.

12 One cannot slaughter on account of the following,
neither in the Temple Court nor in the provinces:
white spots or water that are not permanent;
damaged back teeth that are not uprooted;[30]
having a scab, a wart, or a skin rash;
or old, or sick, or fetid;
or one that has had a transgression committed with it;
or one that has killed a human being—
on the testimony of one witness or according to the testimony of the owners[31]—
or a *tumtum* or *androgynos*—
neither in the Temple Court, nor in the provinces.
R. Ishmael says:
There is no greater blemish than this;
and the Sages say:
It is not a firstborn, and it can be shorn and worked.

[30] **K**: "or that are worn down"; **P**: "or that are uprooted."

[31] **K, P** lack this clause.

firstborns may be slaughtered, and eaten by the priest.

disqualified consecrated animals may be redeemed, and afterwards slaughtered and eaten as ordinary animals.

6:12 *the following*: Imperfections or ailments that might appear to be blemishes, but do not disqualify. The passage is the complement to 6:1.

a scab, a wart, or a skin rash: Two of the three terms appear in Leviticus 22:22 as disqualifying. The Babylonian Talmud explains this perplexing divergence from Scripture by differentiating between the types of scabs, warts, and rashes implied by the biblical text and those suggested by the Mishnah.

skin rash: Lit. "lichen." A skin rash (such as lichen planus) named after lichen because it resembles it, not because it is caused by it.

transgression committed with it: See *Zevahim* 8:1.

testimony of one witness... of the owners: An ox that kills a human is subject to death by stoning (Exodus 21:28–32; *Bava Qamma* 2:4), but only, according to the Mishnah, if there are two valid witnesses to testify against it. (See n. 31.)

tumtum: An animal that the rabbis deem to possess neither male nor female genitalia. *Androgynos* has both male and female genitalia. The categories apply to humans as well. See *Bikkurim* 4.

There is no blemish greater than this: This refers back to the *androgynos*. According to *R. Ishmael*, the *androgynos* is a male that is *blemished* by female genitalia.

It is not a firstborn: An animal that is an *androgynos* would not be considered male, and therefore the rules of the firstborn do not apply to it.

Chapter Seven

7:1–7 *Priestly Blemishes*

1 These blemishes, whether permanent or temporary, render humans unfit.
In addition to these, in the case of humans, are:
one with a protruding forehead;
one with a mallet-shaped head,
one with a turnip-shaped head,
or one with a sunken[32] head;
and occipital flattening.
Those who have spinal curvature—
R. Judah deems them fit,
and the Sages deem them unfit.
2 A bald man is unfit.
Who is a bald man?
Whoever does not have a line of hair growing from ear to ear.
If he does have it,
in this case, he is fit.
If he does not have eyebrows,
or if he has one eyebrow—
indeed, he is the *gibben* mentioned in the Torah.
R. Dosa says:
Anyone whose eyebrows slope down.
R. Hanina b. Antigonus says:

[32] **K**, **P**: *shaqut*; printed editions: *shaku'a*.

7:1 The Mishnah now turns to blemishes among humans that would disqualify priests from performing the sacrificial service. The requirement for ministering priests to be free of blemishes is delineated in Leviticus 21:17–23. Although the Talmud and commentaries provide interpretations for all these blemishes, their precise translations are frequently uncertain.

These blemishes: Those listed in chapter 6.

protruding forehead: Heb. *kilon*; cf. Latin *cilo*.

mallet-shaped: The forehead and the back of the head protrude.

turnip-shaped: The head is narrow at the top.

occipital flattening: Meaning of the term uncertain.

spinal curvature: Hunchback. See also 7:2, for the discussion of *gibben*.

7:2 *in this case, he is fit*: A man with typical male pattern baldness.

gibben mentioned in the Torah: See Leviticus 21:20. Modern translators understand *gibben* as one with spinal curvature or hunchback. Here, the Mishnah offers three interpretations of the biblical term. The first two read it as having to do with brows (usually paired with *eye*, as in Leviticus 14:9).

Anyone who has two backs and two spines.

3 One who is *flat-nosed* is disqualified.
Who is the flat-nosed?
Someone who can paint both eyes at once.
Both eyes are turned up
or both eyes are turned down;
one eye is turned up and one eye is turned down[33]—
he sees the house and the upper story at once;
eyes that squint, or are unmatched, or watering.
One whose eyelashes fell out
is unfit, for appearance's sake.

4 His eyes are big like a calf's,
or small like a goose's;
his torso is large relative to his limbs,
or small relative to his limbs;
having a large nose relative to his limbs,
or small relative to his limbs;
the one who is pressed together,
or the one who is grown over.
Who is one who is grown over?
His ears are small.

[33] Lit. "both eyes are above, or both eyes are below; one eye is above and one eye is below."

two backs: The third interpretation fits the generally understood sense *gibben* in Leviticus 21:20.

7:3 *flat-nosed*: Leviticus 21:18.

paint both eyes at once: His hand would not be interrupted by the bridge of the nose jutting out.

turned up...turned down: The Hebrew leaves some ambiguity about whether the eyes are turned up or down or whether their placement on the face is above or below where they should be. The translation follows the more likely reading, especially given the Mishnah's gloss on the last phrase, *seeing the house and the upper story at once*. Compare, however, the Babylonian Talmud, which takes this last clause as an independent example, not a clause.

eyes that squint: Meaning obscure. It is possible that it refers to extreme photosensitivity.

unmatched: Eyes of different colors, heterochromia (commentaries).

watering: A condition called epiphora.

for appearance's sake: A rabbinic phrase used to refer to circumstances that should technically be permissible, but they are instead forbidden because they too closely resemble other circumstances that are forbidden. In this case, there is nothing technically disqualifying about eyelashes that have fallen out, but because it looks too similar to other disqualifying eye conditions, it renders the priest unfit for service.

7:4 *pressed together*: Again, the Mishnah uses a term the meaning of which was apparently uncertain and needed to be glossed. The Hebrew root seems to mean "press together," hence the rendering in the translation.

grown over: Meaning unknown.

ears are small: This may refer to a condition in which there is virtually no outer ear, or pinna, known as microtia. However, this condition is quite severe, so it is possible the mishnah simply refers to unusually small ears. It is unclear how these conditions are connected to the meanings of the terms "grown over" and "pressed together."

Who is one who is pressed together?
His ears resemble a sponge.
5 His upper lip is larger than the lower,
or his lower lip is larger than the upper—
in this case, it is a blemish.
One with teeth removed—
he is unfit, for appearance's sake.
His breasts rest on his body like a woman's;
his belly is distended;
his navel protrudes.
He has seizures, even once in many days,
or shortness of breath comes upon him,
or who has large testicles,[34]
or he has a large penis;
he is lacking testicles,[35]
or has only one testicle—
this is the one with *crushed testicles* mentioned in the Torah.
R. Ishmael says:
Anyone whose testicles are crushed.
R. Aqiva says:
Anyone whose testicles are distended.
R. Hanina b. Antigonus says:
Anyone whose skin is dark.
6 His ankles knock together,
or his knees;
he has skin growths;
or is curved.
Who is one that is curved?

[34] Heb. *me'ushkan*; **K**, **P**: *meshu'aban;* printed editions of the Babylonian Talmud: *me'ushban.*
[35] Lacking in **K**.

ears resemble a sponge: Meaning uncertain.

7:5 *lip larger than*: Lit. "remaining, left over." Perhaps projecting over or under the other lip.

for appearance's sake: Possibly because teeth that fall out of their own accord are truly considered a blemish (6:4).

his belly is distended: Possibly, a pot belly, or possibly the result of various disorders.

shortness of breath: Presumably asthmatic episodes. The Hebrew term can also mean "spirit," and so the phrase could plausibly refer to depression, but a more physical disorder would fit the context better.

large testicles: See n. 34. Meaning uncertain.

crushed testicles: Leviticus 21:20. Meaning uncertain.

distended: Having "wind," *in the testicles*, i.e. "blown up" or swollen.

skin is dark: Presumably referring to the scrotum alone. R. Hanina b. Antigonus repunctuates the two Hebrew words.

Anyone who puts his feet together and his knees do not touch each other.
A skin growth protrudes from his thumb,
his heel protruding backwards,
or his feet are wide feet[36] like a goose's.
Fingers that ride on top of one another,
or are webbed:
up to the knuckle—
he is fit;
below the knuckle and he cut it—
he is fit.
An extra digit that was cut off—
if there is a bone, he is unfit;
and if not, he is fit.
An extra digit on his hands and feet—
six and six, twenty-four—
R. Judah deems him fit,
and the Sages deem him unfit.
He has dexterity in both hands—
Rabbi deems him unfit,
and the Sages deem him fit.
He is dark-skinned,[37] red-skinned, or white-skinned;
a giant or a dwarf;
deaf-mute, cognitively impaired, or drunk;
those who have ritually pure skin afflictions—
these are unfit in the case of humans,
but in the case of animals they are fit.
Rabban Gamaliel says:
Cognitive impairment in an animal is not among the choicest.

[36] Sing. in **K**; pl. in **P**.

[37] Lit., "Cushite."

7:6 *knees do not touch each other*: i.e. bow-legged.

below the knuckle: Lit. "above," viewing the hand from the opposite perspective.

six and six, twenty-four: 2 Samuel 21:20.

white-skinned: The Hebrew term derives from Greek *leukos*, "white."

giant: It is also possible that the Mishnah here refers to Marfan syndrome, a genetic disorder characterized by, among other things, a very tall and slender build.

cognitively impaired: Heb. *shoteh*. Generally, this translation uses "legally incompetent" to render this term, which is used variably to describe people with intellectual disabilities, mental illness, or cognitive impairment due to brain injury or dementia, who as a consequence have impaired legal personhood or limited expression of will. Here, the translation is altered to reflect that a *shoteh* animal is mentioned below.

drunk: See Leviticus 10:9. In the biblical verse, a priest may not perform the sacred rituals while intoxicated, though it is unclear whether the Mishnah refers to someone who is temporarily intoxicated (as described in the Torah) or an alcoholic.

choicest: See Deuteronomy 12:11, which describes the various offerings brought to the Temple as "choice gifts." Rabban Gamaliel does not believe that cognitive impairment in an animal is enough to render it unfit for the altar in and of itself, but it may not reach the standard of "the choicest."

R. Eliezer[38] says:
Even skin tags—
are unfit in the case of humans,
but fit in the case of animals.

7 These are fit in the case of humans,
but unfit in the case of animals:
it and its offspring;
the *terefah*;
caesarean birth;
those by whom a transgression was committed;
one who has killed a human being.[39]
One who marries women illicitly is unfit,
until he undertakes a vow not to gain benefit [from her].
One who contracts corpse impurity is unfit,
until he undertakes not to contract corpse impurity.

Chapter Eight

8:1–6 *Ambiguous Cases of Human Firstborns*

8 There is a firstborn with respect to inheritance who is not a firstborn with respect to the priest;
a firstborn with respect to the priest who is not a firstborn with respect to inheritance;
a firstborn with respect to inheritance and to the priest;
and there is a firstborn who is neither a firstborn with respect to inheritance nor to the priest.

[38] R. Eleazar b. Azariah [39] "those by whom … killed a human being" lacking in **K**, **P**.

7:7 *it and its offspring*: Leviticus 22:28, which prohibits killing an animal and its offspring on the same day. An animal and its offspring cannot be offered on the same day (they are *unfit* for the altar because of it), but a priest and his son can indeed serve together on the same day.

caesarean birth … killed a human being: See *Zevahim* 8:1 for a parallel list.

caesarean birth: See Leviticus 22:27, in which "is born" is interpreted as indicating that only naturally born animals are fit for the altar.

One who: Specifically, a priest.

marries women illicitly: Leviticus 21:7 prohibits a priest from marrying a divorcee, "prostitute," or "defiled" woman.

undertakes a vow: The vow assures that the priest will have no familiar interactions with the wife. See *Nedarim*, introduction, and for a similar vow, see *Arakhin* 6:1.

contracts corpse impurity: See Leviticus 21:11, which prohibits a priest from becoming impure through contact with a corpse, even upon his own parents' death. Here, the issue is a priest's failure to habitually avoid impurity.

8:1 The tractate now returns to the topic of firstborns with a discussion of human firstborns. Compare 1:2–4, 2:4–9.

There is a firstborn … nor to the priest: Beginning a subject by delineating a complete list of permutations, even if some are hypothetical in the extreme, is characteristic of the Mishnah.

Which is the firstborn with respect to inheritance who is not a firstborn with respect to the priest?
He who comes after a discharged fetus that was alive when the head emerged;
or after a full-term birth,[40] in which the fetus was dead when the head emerged;
or one who discharges something like a domesticated animal, wild animal, or bird—the words of R. Meir.
And the Sages say:
Not unless it has a human-like form.
If one discharges a sandal;
or an afterbirth,
or an amniotic sac with an articulated fetus;
or one that emerges cut into pieces—
the one that comes after these is a firstborn with respect to inheritance,
but is not a firstborn with respect to the priest.
One who had no sons, and married a woman who had previously given birth—
even if she had been a slave woman[41] and was then freed,
or a gentile and converted—
who gave birth after coming to an Israelite—
the offspring is a firstborn with respect to inheritance,
but is not a firstborn with respect to the priest.
R. Yose the Galilean says:
He is a firstborn with respect to inheritance and to the priest,

[40] Lit. "child of nine months." [41] **K, P** add "when she gave birth."

with respect to inheritance: The double share in his father's estate, Deuteronomy 21:17. Here, firstborn status follows the father (see Deuteronomy 21:17: *the first issue of his virility*).

with respect to the priest: The child is ostensibly the property of the priest, to be redeemed with five *sela* (Numbers 18:16). Firstborn status for redemption follows the mother (Numbers 18:17: *opened the womb*). For the Torah's *sheqel*, the Mishnah assigns a *sela*—see annotations to *Bava Qamma* 4:5.

alive when the head emerged: It is possible that the scenario referred to here is one in which the head emerges and is then retracted, a scenario recounted (in animals) in *Hullin* 4:1. The Talmud is silent on this passage, and medieval commentators differ over its premises. The simplest explanation is that the infant died during birth, although it was still alive as the head emerged. In that case, the birth would be considered a stillbirth, and the next son born after a stillbirth is disqualified from firstborn status with regard to the priest, but is still considered a firstborn with regard to inheritance. See Tosefta *Bekhorot*.

discharges something like: Paralleled at *Keritot* 1:3, regarding the obligation of a woman to bring an offering after childbirth.

Not unless it has a human-like form: In order to disqualify a subsequent live birth from firstborn status, the miscarried fetus has to have been recognizably human.

sandal...afterbirth: See also *Niddah* 3:4. Since the afterbirth is a specific biological product of the birthing process (the placenta), it is possible that *sandal* refers to one as well. Alternatively, as above, it describes the form of the fetus.

cut into pieces: Likely in order to facilitate delivery of the stillborn fetus.

with respect to inheritance, but not...to the priest: The miscarried fetus or stillbirth is considered to have "opened the womb" and exempts the next son from the law of the firstborn. And so too, if the mother *had previously given birth*, but the father had *no sons*, the first child of the union, if male, would be a firstborn *with respect to the inheritance, but not with respect to the priest.*

as it is said: *Whatever is the first to open the womb in Israel*—
when they open the womb among[42] Israelites.
One who had sons and married:
a woman who had not yet given birth;
or who converted while pregnant;
or who was freed while pregnant;
or she gave birth alongside a priest's wife, or a Levite's wife,
or a woman who had previously given birth;
and so too whoever did not wait three months after her first marriage[43]
and married and gave birth,
and it is not known whether the offspring is a child of nine months from the first,
or a child of seven from the second—
it is a firstborn with respect to the priest,
but not a firstborn with respect to the inheritance.
Which is a firstborn with respect to both the inheritance and the priest?
A discharged amniotic sac filled with blood, filled with water, or filled with variegated pieces;
one who discharges something like a fish, locusts, insects, or vermin;
one who discharges the fetus on the fortieth day—
the one that comes afterward is a firstborn with respect both to the inheritance
and with respect to the priest.

2 One born by caesarean section and the one that comes afterward—
both are not firstborns with respect to the inheritance
nor with respect to the priest.
R. Simeon says:
The first—
with respect to the inheritance,

[42] Lit. "from." [43] Lit. "her husband."

Whatever is the first: Exodus 13:2.

One who had sons: Relevant to the question of firstborn for inheritance: there can be only one for a father (Deuteronomy 21:15–17).

converted while pregnant: The Mishnah may assume that the father in each case is also the husband. Even so, from the point of view of inheritance, the status of each of these offspring is impaired, since the conception took place when the woman was not fully an Israelite (see e.g. *Yevamot* 11:42, *Ketubbot* 4:3).

she gave birth alongside: And the infants were confused so it is not certain whose is whose.

a priest's wife, or a Levite's wife: Their offspring are exempt from the law of the firstborn; see above, 2:1.

did not wait three months: After her first husband's death, or after her divorce, to avoid questions of paternity. See *Yevamot* 4:10.

not... with respect to the inheritance: If there is indeterminacy regarding who the boy's father is or the boy's status as having a father is impaired, the law of inheritance does not apply.

on the fortieth day: Or before. Up to this point the embryo is not considered a fetus, and miscarriage is not considered a birth until after forty days of pregnancy. See *Niddah* 3:7.

8:2 *caesarean section and the one that comes afterward*: See 2:9.

The first... inheritance: Because for inheritance the son need not "open the womb." See 8:1.

and the second—
with respect to the five[44] *sela*.

3 A woman who has not previously given birth:
and gave birth to two males—
[the father] gives five *sela*[45] to the priest.
If one of them dies within thirty days,
the father is exempt.
If the father dies but the sons survive—
R. Meir says:
If they gave it before they divided [the inheritance]—
what they have given is binding;[46]
but if not—
they are exempt.
R. Judah says:
There is a lien on the property.[47]
A male and a female—
there is nothing here for the priest.

4 Two women who have not previously given birth:
and gave birth to two males—
[the father] gives ten *sela* to the priest.
If one died within thirty days—
if he gave it to one priest,
he must refund five *sela*;
if he gave it to two priests,
he cannot take it out of their hands.
A male and a female, or two males and a female—
he gives five *sela* to the priest.

[44] **K**: "fifty," but it seems to be in error. [45] **K**: "fifty," but it seems to be in error.
[46] Lit. "they have given." [47] Lit. "the property is obligated/liable."

the second…sela: This child "opened the womb."

8:3 *two males*, but it is unclear which is the firstborn.

the father is exempt: Because it cannot be proven that the one that is still living is the firstborn. Only first-borns that live to the age of one month are liable for redemption—see Numbers 18:16. See further, 8:6.

they have given: What is done is done, and the money ought not to be returned, since the father was obligated to pay the five *sela* for the firstborn.

they are exempt: Since neither son knows whether or not he is actually the firstborn.

There is a lien: See n. 47. The obligation remains on the father's property even after the father has died; thus, the priest is owed five *sela* out of the father's property. According to *R. Judah*, even though neither son knows with certainty that he is the firstborn, the five *sela* were owed by the father to the priest and the obligation was divided equally with the property.

A male and a female: And, again, it is unclear who was born first.

8:4 *to two priests, he cannot take it out of their hands*: Since the father cannot specify which priest was paid for which son, it is unclear which priest is required to offer the refund.

Two females and a male,
or two males and two females—
there is nothing here for the priest.
If one had previously given birth, and one had not previously given birth,
and they gave birth to two males—
the father gives five *sela* to the priest.
If one of them died within thirty days,
the father is exempt.
If the father dies but the sons survive:
R. Meir says:
If they gave it to the priest before they divided [the inheritance],
it is given;
but if not, they are exempt.
R. Judah says:
There is a lien on the property.[48]
A male and a female—
there is nothing here for the priest.

5 Two women who have not previously given birth:
married to two men,
and they give birth to two males—
this one gives five *sela* to the priest and that one gives five *sela* to the priest.
If one of them died within thirty days—
if they gave the money to one priest, he must refund five *sela*;
if they gave it to two different priests, it cannot be taken out of their hands.
A male and a female—
the fathers are exempt, but the son is obligated to redeem himself.
Two females and a male, or two males and two females—
there is nothing here for the priest.

6 One had previously given birth, and one had not previously given birth:
and they gave birth to two males—
the one whose wife had not yet given birth gives five *sela* to the priest.
A son and a daughter—
there is nothing here for the priest.

[48] Lit. "the property is obligated/liable."

nothing here for the priest: See above, 2:7.

8:5 *give birth to two males*: And it is unclear whose is whose.

he must refund five sela: As above, 8:4. Presumably, the two men would divide the refund.

obligated to redeem himself: Because it is unclear which is the father of the son, neither is obligated to pay the redemption price. The son, however, knows that he is a firstborn, so the obligation falls upon him.

8:6 cont. *The First Thirty Days*

If the son died within thirty days,
even if they already gave it to the priest—
he returns five *sela* to him.
After thirty days—
even if they had not yet given,
they must give.
On the thirtieth day—
it is like the day before.
R. Aqiva says:
If he already gave,
he does not take it back;
if he did not give,
he does not give.
If the father died within thirty days—
he has the status of not having been redeemed,
unless he brings proof that he was redeemed;
after thirty days—
he has the status of having been redeemed,
unless he brings proof[49] that he was not redeemed.
He has yet to be redeemed, and his son has yet to be redeemed,
he takes priority over his son.
R. Judah says:
His son takes priority over his own,
as the obligation for himself is his father's,
and the obligation for his son's is his.

[49] **K, P**: "they say to him" for "he brings proof."

8:6 *two males*: And it is unclear which woman gave birth to which infant.

If the son died: The topic shifts to the general issues involving a firstborn in the first thirty days. Here, the firstborn dies within thirty days.

does not give: Because the son died on the thirtieth day, and it is unresolved whether redemption is required or not.

unless he brings proof: See n. 49. The better text is "unless they say to him"; that is, unless people know that he was not redeemed.

He has yet to be redeemed: The father is a firstborn who was never redeemed.

he takes priority: If the father does not have ten *sela* at hand to redeem both himself and his son, he comes first.

the obligation... is his father's: The obligation to redeem himself only falls to him secondarily; redeeming his son is a primary obligation.

8:7–8 *Methods of Payment for Redemptions*

7 The five *sela* for the son are according to the Tyrian *maneh*.
The thirty for the slave,
the fifty for the rapist or seducer,
and the one hundred for the slanderer—
all are reckoned in the *sheqel* of the sanctuary,
according to the Tyrian *maneh*.
All are redeemed with silver, or the equivalent of silver,
aside from the *sheqel* tax.[50]

8 One does not redeem a firstborn son with slaves, contracts, land, or consecrated items.
If he wrote to a priest that he owes him five *sela*—
he is obligated to give it to him,
and his son is still not redeemed.
Therefore, if the priest wants to give him a gift,
it is permissible.
If one separated five *sela* for the redemption of the firstborn son,
and it was lost,

[50] Lit. "except for the *sheqalim*"

8:7 *Tyrian maneh*: Tyrian silver coins, minted until 65–66 CE, were purer than (especially later) Roman coinage. One Tyrian *sheqel* (corresponding to the mishnaic *sela*, or two mishnaic *sheqel*), was approximately fourteen grams of silver. At least in theory it corresponded to four roman *denarii*, the *dinar* or *zuz* of the Mishnah. According to *Ketubbot* 5:9, the Mishnah thought that Judah used a coin standard that was twice the weight of the Galilee. This fits with the convention that the biblical and Jerusalem *sheqel* are on the Tyrian standard and are valued at twice the conventional coinage of the same name.

the slave: If an ox gores a slave, the fine paid to the owner is thirty *sheqel*, Exodus 21:32.

rapist or seducer: The fine paid to the father of the young woman who was violated, Exodus 22:16–17 and Deuteronomy 22:28–29.

slanderer: The fine paid to the father in the case of the slandered bride; see Deuteronomy 22:19.

aside from the sheqel tax: The yearly half-*sheqel* Temple tax (a whole *sheqel* in the Mishnah's conventional denominations, see above) due annually from every adult Israelite man; see Exodus 30:12–16. The exception here is that the Temple duty cannot be paid in the equivalent of silver, but rather must exclusively be paid in silver coins.

8:8 *slaves, contracts, land, or consecrated items*: Transactions involving these are considered different from transactions involving currency or movable goods (*Bava Metsi'a* 4:9, and annotations). The mishnah here also lists "consecrated items," but it is clear that "consecrated items," which belong to the Temple, cannot be used to redeem firstborns. The inclusion is likely due to the erroneous carryover of an item from a standard list (cf. *Bava Metsi'a* 4:9, *Shevu'ot* 6:5). The Babylonian Talmud reads the expression as teaching that consecrated items also cannot be redeemed with slaves, contracts, or land.

he is obligated to give it to him: The father must pay the priests the five *sela* he promised, in addition to the five *sela* for the redemption of the firstborn son.

Therefore, if the priest…permissible: Since the priest was paid twice.

he is accountable for them;
as it is said: *it shall be yours* and *you shall surely redeem.*

8:9–10 *Inheritance*

9 The firstborn son receives a double share of his father's property,
but does not receive a double share of his mother's property.
He does not receive a double share of the appreciation,
nor of what is expected to be inherited, as he does of what was held [by his father].[51]
Nor does a wife in her marriage settlement,
nor daughters for their maintenance,
nor the levir—
none of them may receive the appreciation,
nor what is expected to be inherited as they do of what was held [by the deceased].
10 These are not returned in the Jubilee year:
the inheritance of the firstborn;
one who inherits from his wife;
one who performs levirate marriage with his brother's wife;
and the gift—

[51] Here and below, Heb. "of what is eligible as of what is held (or certain)."

it shall be yours, you shall surely redeem: Numbers 18:15, apparently reading these phrases as signifying that as long as "it" (the payment), is not "yours" (has not come into the priest's possession), the father is still obligated.

8:9 *double share*: As specified in Deuteronomy 21:17.

but does not… of his mother's property: See *Bava Batra* 8:4.

appreciation: From the time the father dies until they divide up the inheritance.

of what is expected: See n. 51. Expected inheritance, such as that held by a still-living grandfather, as opposed to what the father actually holds at the time of death. See the parallel passage in *Ketubbot* 10:3.

a wife in her marriage settlement: The money a woman is owed in the case of divorce or the husband's predecease cannot be claimed from appreciation to the estate. Nor is there a claim on any funds due to be inherited. The point is important in cases where the funds at the time of death were not sufficient to pay her obligation.

daughters for their maintenance: See *Ketubbot* 13:3.

the levir: The brother who marries his brother's widow in order to fulfill the commandment of levirate marriage inherits the brother's property. See *Yevamot* 4:7, introduction.

None of them may receive: This statement appears to summarize the content of the mishnah.

8:10 *not returned in the Jubilee year*: The year of release, Leviticus 25. Sale of real property was to be temporary and return to the original owner in the Jubilee year (Leviticus 25:8). The Mishnah here specifies property transfers that are not considered akin to a sale. See further *Arakhin* chapters 7–9.

one who inherits from his wife: See *Bava Batra* 8:1. Here the Mishnah assumes that the husband returns the actual property to her family, but receives payment in return.

A gift is like a sale: And thus must return to the owner.

the words of R. Meir.
But the Sages say:
A gift is like a sale.
R. Eliezer says:
All of these must be returned in the Jubilee year.
R. Yohanan b. Beroqa says:
One who inherits from his wife must return the property to the members of her family, but he may deduct from its value.[52]

Chapter Nine

9:1–6 *Animal Tithe: Who and What are Obligated*

9 The animal tithe applies in the Land and outside the Land;
in the time of the Temple and not in the time of the Temple;
to nonsacral animals but not to sacral animals.
It applies to cattle and the flock,
and one may not be tithed for the other.
On sheep and goats,
and they are tithed one for the other;
on new animals and old—
they are not tithed one in place of the other.
For logic might dictate:
if the young and the old, which do not constitute a prohibited mixture with one another, cannot be tithed one for the other;
sheep and goats, which do constitute a prohibited mixture with one another—
does logic not require that they not be tithed one for the other?

[52] **K**, **P**: "may deduct its value from them."

may deduct from its value: Perhaps for the benefit of having had use of it (Albeck).

9:1 *animal tithe*: Leviticus 27:32. For this introduction compare *Hullin* 6:1, 7:1, 11:1, 12:1.

not in the time of the Temple: Although the animal tithe could not be offered on the altar, it was considered consecrated and had to be left to pasture until it developed a blemish.

the flock or "small cattle" (see above, 1:4); this can refer to both sheep and goats, which were often kept as part of one flock. The Mishnah further explicates this term below.

for the other: One cannot use cattle to serve as the tithe for sheep and goats, or vice versa. Each group must be tithed on its own.

new…old: Those born after or before the cut-off date for the present tithing year. See below, 9:5–6.

logic might dictate: The Mishnah derives a prohibition of using sheep and goats as tithes for the other as a necessary logical conclusion from the rules delineated above.

Scripture teaches: *one of the flock*—
all that are denoted by flock are one.

2 Animals combine for the tithe as far as cattle roam to pasture.[53]
How far is the distance that cattle roam to pasture?
Sixteen miles.
If there were thirty-two miles between these and those,
they are not combined.
If he had some in between,
he brings them and tithes them [with those that are] in between.
R. Meir says:
The Jordan is a boundary for the animal tithe.

3 One that has been purchased or given to him as a gift is exempt from the animal tithe.
Brothers who are partners—
when they are liable for the *qolbon*, they are exempt from the animal tithe;
and when they are liable for the animal tithe, they are exempt from the *qolbon*.

[53] Lit. "the full foot of an animal grazing."

Scripture teaches: A directive from Scripture was required to override the logical conclusion just reached.

one of the flock: Leviticus 27:32. Scripture uses the word *flock*, according to the Mishnah, rather than different words for sheep and goats, suggesting that all that are called *flock* are considered as one.

9:2 *combine*: They are grouped together as one herd or flock. If they are spread out farther apart than a typical herd or flock would, they may not be considered a herd or flock for the purposes of the animal tithe; if there are fewer than ten animals in each group, they are exempt from the animal tithe.

How far: What may have been common knowledge for shepherds at some point in the tradition is here quantified by the Mishnah into a precise measurement.

miles: The Babylonian Talmud puts a mile at two thousand cubits (*amot*; approx. 1 km, or 0.62 miles). Alternatively, reference is to the Roman mile (*mille passuum*, or one thousand paces), which is somewhat shorter than our current mile (some 0.9 miles or 1.5 km).

thirty-two miles: Each animal has a radius of sixteen miles in any direction that they are able to roam and still be considered part of the same herd or flock, so the animals would have to be a full thirty-two miles apart to be considered separate herds or flocks.

The Jordan is a boundary: Even if the animals are closer together than thirty-two miles, if they are pasturing on either side of the Jordan river, they cannot be considered one herd or flock.

9:3 *purchased or given…as a gift*: The animal must be born into one's herd or flock to be liable for the animal tithe. The Babylonian Talmud attempts to locate the scriptural basis for this rule.

Brothers who are partners…exempt from the qolbon: Paralleled in *Sheqalim* 1:7 and *Hullin* 1:7.

qolbon: An extra charge imposed on the half-*sheqel* Temple tax. (For its characterization as a *sheqel* see above, 8:7, and *Sheqalim*, introduction.) According to *Sheqalim* 1:7, anyone who pays the Temple tax on behalf of another is not liable for the surcharge on that payment. If the partnership consists of the unseparated estate, the brothers are exempt from the *qolbon* because it is as if their father is paying on their behalf. In such a circumstance the brothers are liable to pay the tithe on the animals held in common. If the brothers have formed a partnership after separating their father's estate, they are liable for the *qolbon*. In this case, the animals are exempt from tithing, since animals held in partnership are exempt.

If they acquired [animals] from the property of the household—
they are liable;
and if not—
they are exempt.
If they divided it, and then went back and formed a partnership—
they are liable for the *qolbon*[54] and exempt from the animal tithe.

4 All enter the fold to be tithed, except:
a prohibited mixture,
a *terefah*,
one born by caesarean section,
one that is too young,[55]
and an orphan.
Which is an orphan?
Any animal whose mother has died or has been slaughtered.
R. Joshua says:
Even if the mother was slaughtered—
if the hide is intact, it is not an orphan.

5 There are three ingatherings[56] for the animal tithe:
before the Passover,

[54] **P** has "and if not" here, but it seems to be in error.
[55] Lit. "lacking time."
[56] Lit. "threshing floors."

acquired . . . from the property of the household: This appears to gloss the preceding. If the brothers in partnership acquired the animals from an undivided estate they are liable for the animal tithe, as it is still considered the father's property.

exempt from the animal tithe: The Babylonian Talmud reads *shall be yours* [sing.], Numbers 18:15, as indicating that the animals cannot be held in partnership.

if not: If the brothers acquired the herd in a manner different from inheritance, e.g. if they purchased it jointly.

went back and formed a partnership: This is considered like any other partnership, and the brothers are exempt from the animal tithe.

9:4 *prohibited mixture*: A cross between a goat and a sheep. See above, 1:5.

too young: An animal that is still less than eight days old, Leviticus 22:17.

has died or has been slaughtered: While the wording of the Mishnah is ambiguous, it seems to refer to a case in which the mother died or was slaughtered immediately before, during, or shortly after the birth. The animal would not qualify for an offering because it did not remain for *seven days with its mother*, Leviticus 22:27.

hide is intact: The Babylonian Talmud refers to a practice of wrapping the newborn animal in the hide of the mother for warmth and comfort. Also, the animal might thus qualify as having technically been "with" or, rendered literally, "under its mother," as per Leviticus 22:27.

9:5 *There are three ingatherings*: See the parallel at *Sheqalim* 3:1. Once produce reaches the threshing floor, the processing is considered complete and it becomes liable for tithes. See *Ma'aserot* 1:5.

before: The word may derive from the Semitic root meaning "half," leading some commentators to suggest that it means the half-month before the festival days. More likely, it is related to the Greek preposition "before" or "near."

before the Festival of Weeks,[57]
and before the Festival—
the words of R. Aqiva.
Ben Azzai says:
On the twenty-ninth of Adar,
on the first of Sivan,
and on the twenty-ninth of Av.
R. Eliezer[58] and R. Simeon say:
On the first of Nisan,
on the first of Sivan,
and on the twenty-ninth of Elul.
Why did they say: On the twenty-ninth of Elul
and they did not say: On the first of Tishre?
Because it is a festival day, and tithing is prohibited on a festival day;
therefore, they moved it back to the twenty-ninth of Elul.
R. Meir says:
The first of Elul is the new year for the animal tithe.
Ben Azzai says:
Animals born in Elul are tithed among themselves.

6 All those born from the first of Tishre to the twenty-ninth of Elul combine.
Five born before the first of the year and five born after the first of the year do not combine.
Five born before the ingathering and five born after the ingathering—
in this case, these can be combined.
If so, why is it said,
There are three ingatherings for the animal tithe?
Because as long as the time of the ingathering has not arrived,
it is permissible to sell and to slaughter;
once the time of the ingathering has arrived,
he may not slaughter.
But if he did slaughter,
he is exempt.

[57] Heb. *atseret*. [58] **K**: "Eleazar."

the Festival: Sukkot, or the feast of Tabernacles.

On the first of Tishre: R. Eleazar (see n. 58) and R. Simeon date the year for the animal tithe to this date (*Rosh Hashanah* 1:1). By contrast, *R. Meir* holds that *the first of Elul is the new year* for this purpose.

Animals born in Elul are tithed among themselves: Because of this disagreement, there is indeterminacy about whether animals born in Elul belong to the old year or the new year, and animals born in different years cannot be tithed together (above, 9:1).

9:6 *From the first of Tishre to the twenty-ninth of Elul*: Following the opinion of R. Eliezer and R. Simeon (9:5).

combine: As one herd or flock, for the purposes of the tithe. See above 9:1.

permissible... to slaughter: Before the "harvest" date the animals are not yet subject to the tithe, and one may slaughter them. Once the date has passed, the animals born up to that date need to be tithed before they can be slaughtered.

9:7–8 *Method of Separating the Animal Tithe*

7 How does he tithe them?
He gathers them into the fold
and creates a small opening so that two are not able to exit at once;
and he counts with a staff:
one, two, three, four, five, six, seven, eight, nine;
and the one that exits tenth—
he marks it with red dye
and says: "Here is the tithe."
If he does not mark it with red dye
or did not count them with a staff;
or if he counted them as they are lying down, or standing—
in this case, they are still tithed.
If he had one hundred, and took ten;
or ten and took one—
this is not a tithe.
R. Yose b. Judah says:
In this case, this is a tithe.
If one that was already counted jumped back in amongst them—
in this case, they are exempt;
if one of the tithed ones jumped back in amongst them,
all of them must pasture until they become unfit,
and they may be eaten by the owners with their blemishes.
8 If two exited at once—
he counts them two by two.
If he counted them as one,
the ninth and the tenth are spoiled.
If the ninth and the tenth exit at once,
the ninth and the tenth are spoiled.
If one calls the ninth, the tenth;
and the tenth, the ninth;
and the eleventh, the tenth—
all three are consecrated:

9:7 *he counts with a staff*: In fulfillment of Leviticus 27:32.

took ten: Without counting them one by one.

they are exempt: Each one might be the one that was already counted and cleared. As the status of each is possibly cleared, they are all exempt.

all of them must pasture until they become unfit: Each one might be the one that was consecrated as the animal tithe. As the status of each is possibly tithed, they are all treated as consecrated.

9:8 *spoiled*: Neither is certainly the tithe, and neither is certainly not the tithe, so both must be treated as consecrated but not given to the priest, and presumably eaten once they develop blemishes. The strange word "spoiled" used here may refer to the count, rather than the animals themselves or the tithe.

all three are consecrated: The "tenth" is consecrated, so by calling the ninth and the eleventh "tenth," the owner inadvertently consecrates them. And even though he calls the actual tenth "ninth," it is consecrated because of its actual status as the tenth of the flock or herd.

the ninth is eaten with its blemish;
the tenth is the tithe;
and the eleventh is offered as an offering of well-being,
and it effects substitution—
the words of R. Meir.
R. Judah says:
Can a substitute effect substitution?
They said in the name of R. Meir:
If it were a substitute, it would not be offered.
If one called the ninth, the tenth;
and the tenth, the tenth;
and the eleventh, the tenth—
the eleventh is not consecrated.
This is the general rule:
As long as the name of the tenth is not removed from it,
the eleventh is not consecrated.

offering of well-being: A sacrifice that may be eaten by those who bring it.

effects substitution: Since the animal becomes a sacrifice, if one attempts to substitute another animal for it, both animals are consecrated. Leviticus 27:10; *Temurah* introduction and 1:2; and above, 2:2.

Can a substitute effect substitution? R. Judah suggests that the eleventh is actually a "substitute" for the tenth, and that is why it is consecrated. Thus, if substituted for, the eleventh should not convey consecrated status on the substitute. See *Temurah* 2:3.

it would not be offered: If the eleventh were in fact considered a substitute for the tithe, then it would not be offered on the altar, as tithe substitutes are considered consecrated but they are not offered on the altar.

the name of the tenth is not removed from it: As long as the actual tenth animal is called "ten" and made the tithe, the eleventh is not consecrated. This is in contrast to the case disputed by R. Judah and R. Meir above, in which the actual tenth animal was called "ninth."

Tractate Arakhin

Jonah Steinberg

Introduction

Overview

Arakhin or "sacral valuations" refers to a form of dedication in which the dedicator pledges to the Temple the value of a person (Leviticus 27:1–8). This topic takes up a substantial portion of the tractate (chapters 1–6); however, chapter 6 also addresses other forms of dedication, as well as the redemption of consecrated property.

Structure and Organization of the Tractate

The first six chapters address sacral valuation, although with considerable digressions. Chapter 1 and the beginning of chapter 2 delineate sacral valuations. Chapter 4, which returns to the topic of sacral valuations, distinguishes these valuations (*arakhin*), which follow a schedule of payments based on Leviticus 27:1–8, from vows (*nedarim*) of a person's value, which are governed by market value. The beginning of chapter 5 deals with various ways a person can dedicate the value of things or people and their implications.

The end of chapter 5 and chapter 6 turn to the question of payment and the ability of the Temple to seize collateral in order to ensure fulfillment. As part of the discussion of seizure of collateral, chapter 6 considers what responsibility the Temple has to ensure the dedicator's livelihood, as well as the impact of collection on members of his household.

The digressions embedded in these chapters include, for instance, a listing of maximal and minimal limits for certain obligations (2:1–3), leading in turn to rules about Temple practices and especially musical performance and performers (2:4–6), and a discussion of cases of flat obligations which may result in more or less advantageous outcomes depending on circumstances (3:1–5).

Much of chapters 7–9 revolve around the implications of the Jubilee cycle, with chapter 7 addressing the redemption of ancestral holdings dedicated to the Temple that return to their respective ancestral owners at the Jubilee. Chapter 8 considers the problem of redemption of property when the Jubilee is not practiced, and particularly auctions of property consecrated to the Temple, the proceeds of which are donated in lieu of the property itself. The end of the chapter turns to the special form of dedication called "devotion" (*herem*), which involves irrevocably devoting items or their value.

Continuing the discussion begun in chapter 8, the ninth chapter begins with the sale and redemption of property when the Jubilee is not practiced. Finally, the chapter turns to the cities of the Levites and the special rights of Levites with regard to redeeming their ancestral homes.

Main Ideas

A number of areas of special concern are evident in the tractate. One is protecting the interests of the sacred treasury against those of donors redeeming their property (e.g. 7:1; 8:1–3). A second has to do with the Mishnah's representation of historical practice. Chapters 8 and 9 assume that the Temple is still standing but that the practice of Jubilees has lapsed. The Mishnah thus has to consider a system of dedications to and redemptions from the Temple treasury without the pricing and redemption mechanisms tied to the Jubilee. According to 8:1–3, the Temple auctions off dedicated lands (it does not use these properties as an ongoing source of revenue), and the original donor is forced to bid on what he donated. These two issues intersect in 8:3 when the dedicator must apparently exceed bids that are within the "fifth" (which the Rabbis assess in practice as twenty-five percent) that he is required to add to his redemption fee.

Relationship to Scripture

Many of the legal issues discussed draw on Leviticus 25 and 27. Sacral valuation itself derives from the interpretation of Leviticus 27:1–8. These verses lay out a schedule of payments based on sex and age. Scripture also provides the terminology and organizing principles for other topics discussed in the tractate. The dedication of fields as distinct from other forms of property, their valuation relative to the Jubilee, and their redemption draw on Leviticus 27:14–25. "Devotion" is tied to Leviticus 27:28–29. The Jubilee rules relating to the alienation of property and its redemption draw on Leviticus 25:13–17 and 25–31, and those for the property of Levites from 25:32–34.

Tractate Arakhin

Chapter One

1:1–2:1 *Sacral Valuations*

1 All may make a sacral valuation and be valuated sacrally,
may vow and be the subject of a vow—
priests, Levites, and Israelites,[1] women and slaves.
A *tumtum* and an *androgynos* may vow and be the subject of a vow,
and may make a sacral valuation,
but may not be valuated sacrally,
for none may be valuated sacrally
save undeniable males and undeniable females.
A deaf-mute, one legally incompetent, or a minor

[1] Singular in **K**, **P**.

1:1 *make a sacral valuation and be valuated sacrally*: Leviticus 27:3–7 sets out a schedule of rates based on sex and age for pledges of a person's "value" (*erekh*, here rendered "sacral valuation"). If one declares, "The *sacral valuation* of so-and-so is upon me" (see e.g. 4:2 below), one owes to the Temple the sacral value of that person, to be calculated in accordance with those verses. Correspondingly, anyone may be named as the referent in such a pledge, the sex and age of the person named establishing the amount owed to the Temple. The Mishnah, in 1:2 and onward, will proceed to specify exceptions to these general rules.

may vow and be the subject of a vow: For vows see *Nedarim* introduction. Here the specific concern is a vow to the Temple of a person's market value, if that person were to be sold as a slave in the marketplace. "Vow" is thus distinguished from "sacral valuation," the latter requiring the rates specified in Leviticus 27:3–7, the former not. However, when a pledge of sacral valuation is clearly the subject at hand, the Mishnah will sometimes refer to one who makes such a pledge as "the one who vows" (e.g. in 4:1 and 5:4, below), with the term "vow" used in a generic sense to distinguish the one making the pledge from the referent in the pledge, "the subject of the vow."

tumtum: One without sexual characteristics. *Androgynos*: A person with both male and female sexual characteristics. Leviticus 27:3–7 specifies values for males and females; according to the Mishnah, this biblical schedule cannot be applied to persons who do not clearly fall into one of these categories. Therefore, pledges of sacral valuation naming such people are invalid.

A deaf-mute, and one legally incompetent, or a minor: These persons may *be the subject of a vow*, and the person who makes the pledge is obligated to pay the estimated slave price of someone of this status or with this disability. Since the sacral valuations of Leviticus 27:3–7 are standardized by age and sex only, these persons *may be valuated sacrally*, and the pledger is obligated to pay the standard amount corresponding to that person's age and sex. However, as they lack understanding and thus legal competence, such persons' pledges are not valid.

may be the subject of a vow and valuated sacrally,
but may not vow and may not make a sacral valuation,
for they have no understanding.
One less than a month old may be the subject of a vow, but not valuated sacrally.

2 The gentile—
R. Meir says:
He may be valuated sacrally but may not make a sacral valuation;
R. Judah says:
He may make a sacral valuation but not be valuated sacrally.
The one and the other concede that they may vow and be the subject of a vow.

3 The dying person and the one bound for execution
may not be the subject of a vow and may not be valuated sacrally;
R. Hanina b. Aqaviah says:
He may be valuated sacrally, for his monetary value [for that purpose] is fixed;
but may not be the subject of a vow,
for his monetary value [for that purpose] is not fixed.
R. Yose says:
He may vow, and make a sacral valuation, and consecrate,
and if he caused damage, he is liable for repayment.

4 The woman bound for execution:
one does not wait for her until she gives birth.
If she has sat upon the birthing seat,
one waits for her until she has given birth.
The woman who has been put to death:

1:2 *The gentile*: Leviticus 27:2 addresses the laws of sacral valuation to the Israelite people, but then also uses the generic term "man" or "person," and refers to the schedule of valuations to be used in such pledges in the second person, i.e. as belonging or pertaining to the Israelites. This formulation likely occasions the dispute between R. Meir and R. Judah as to whether a gentile may undertake pledges of sacral valuation or be their referent.

1:3 *The dying person and the one bound for execution*: According to the first view, persons whose demise is imminent have no monetary value and therefore are not to be used as referents in either *vows* of market worth or pledges of sacral valuation.

R. Hanina b. Aqaviah holds that amounts for sacral valuations are *fixed* in Leviticus 27:3–7 according to age and sex only, without reference to any other considerations at all. Therefore the sacral valuation of an individual about to die is the same as that for any other person of the same sex and age. However, the market value of such a one is indeterminate or about to vanish, and thus is not fixed, and should not be vowed.

R. Yose clarifies that, notwithstanding one's own imminent demise, one may *vow* another's market value, or *make a sacral valuation* of another person, or may *consecrate* property to the Temple. These pledges are binding upon the estate of the dedicant after his death.

caused damage: Those about to die incur liability toward any they injure, the damages to be claimed from their estate. It is hard to determine whether this rule continues R. Yose's ruling or stands on its own.

1:4 This mishnah continues the theme of execution (1:3), and digresses from the topic of sacral valuations.

one may benefit from her hair.
The animal that has been put to death is forbidden with respect to benefit.

Chapter Two

1 In the matter of sacral valuation
there is nothing less than a *sela*
and nothing greater than fifty *sela*.
How?
If he gave a *sela*, and then became wealthy, he gives nothing;
Less than a *sela*, and then became wealthy, he gives fifty *sela*.
If he was in possession of five *sela*—
R. Meir says:
He gives only one.
And the Sages say:
He gives all.

2:1 cont.–6 *Rules With Minimum and Maximum Limits*

In the matter of sacral valuation
there is nothing less than a *sela*
and nothing greater than fifty *sela*.
In the matter of a mistaken woman,

one may benefit from her hair: According to the Talmud, false hair (a wig) is meant, and this limited use distinguishes the corpse of a woman put to death from the case of an animal that follows.

animal that has been put to death: Whether executed in consequence of repeated fatal goring or of sexual violation, all benefit from the carcass of the animal is prohibited.

2:1 *nothing less than a sela*: Leviticus 27:8 allows the priests to reduce the rate prescribed in verses 3–7 when a person who has undertaken a pledge of sacral valuation is poor, but, according to the Mishnah here, the reduced obligation can never be less than a *sela*.

gave a sela, and then became wealthy: The person paid when poor, discharging the liability properly and finally, albeit at a legally reduced rate.

Less than a sela, and then became wealthy: When capacity to remit at full value was attained, proper statutory payment had not been made, so the obligation remains and the dedicant must now pay at the full rate.

In the matter of sacral valuation: This item heads a list of several similarly formulated rulings on different matters.

mistaken woman: At issue is a woman uncertain whether a blood flow was menstrual or extended beyond her normal menstrual period and qualifies as non-menstrual (see *Niddah*, *Zavim* introductions). The inception of the seven-day period of "menstrual" flow is termed that period's *opening*. Those seven days are followed by eleven during which any bleeding observed is considered non-menstrual. According to the rabbinic laws pertaining to menstruation and non-menstrual or *zov* bleeding, a new period of expected menstruation will never be reckoned as opening at *less than seven days or more than seventeen days* after any vaginal flow of blood.

there is no "opening" fewer than seven,
nor greater than seventeen.
In the matter of afflictions,
there is none less than a week,
and none greater than three weeks.

2 In the matter of a year,
there must be no fewer than four months with intercalations,[2]
and more than eight never appears.
The two loaves eaten: not fewer than two [days],
and not more than three.
The showbread eaten: not fewer than nine,
and not more than eleven.
An infant circumcised: not fewer than eight[3]
and not more than twelve.

3 One does not have fewer than twenty-one trumpet blasts[4] in the Temple,
and one does not increase them beyond forty-eight.
One does not have fewer than two harps,

[2] Lit. "pregnant." [3] **P**: "No infant is circumcised at fewer than eight…" [4] Singular in **P**.

afflictions: See *Nega'im* 3:3–8. As prescribed in Leviticus 13:21–23 and in 26–28, respectively, for skin lesions and afflicted houses, no period of quarantine for a possible outbreak ("affliction") of *tsara'at* lasts fewer than seven days or more than three weeks.

2:2 *a year*: See *Rosh Hashanah* introduction.

no fewer than four months: A year will have at least four "embolismic" months to which a thirtieth day has been added.

more than eight never appears: When the calendar was intercalated by actual sighting of the new moon there never would have been a year with more than eight "pregnant" months. Correspondingly, no more than eight months are lengthened when the calendar is set by calculation.

The two loaves of the year's new grain, offered on the Festival of Weeks and eaten by the priests (Leviticus 23:17).

not fewer than two: Baked on the day preceding the festival and eaten on the festival itself, the loaves will be eaten by the priests on the day after they are baked. See *Menahot* 11:9.

not more than three: If the festival is preceded by a Sabbath, on which baking is prohibited, they are eaten two days after they are baked.

The showbread eaten: See *Menahot* 11:9. The showbread is baked on the eve of the Sabbath, placed atop the Temple's table on the Sabbath, and eaten on the following Sabbath. The showbread is thus consumed, at the earliest, on its *ninth* day of existence. At the latest, it is eaten on the *eleventh* day if two days of Rosh Hashanah (a two-day festival even in the Land of Israel) are observed before a Sabbath; the loaves must then be prepared three days before they can be set out.

An infant circumcised: See *Shabbat* 19:5. Circumcision is not valid before the boy's *eighth* day (Genesis 17:12). If the boy is born at twilight on the eve of the Sabbath and the subsequent Sabbath is followed by two days of Rosh Hashanah, circumcision takes place on the *twelfth* day, since Sabbath and festival prohibitions are not overridden for circumcision if the day of birth is uncertain.

2:3 *not…fewer than twenty-one blasts…not…beyond forty-eight*: See *Sukkah* 5:5.

and one does not increase them beyond six.
One does not have fewer than two flutes,
and one does not increase them beyond twelve.
And on twelve days of the year the flute strikes up[5] before the altar:
(1) at the slaughtering of the first Passover;
(2) and at the slaughtering of the second Passover;
(3) and on the first[6] festival day of Passover;
(4) and on the festival day of the Festival of Weeks.
(5–12) and on the eight days of the Festival.
And he would not strike on a pipe of bronze, but on a pipe of reed,
because its sound is pleasant;
And he did not slide[7] except upon a single pipe, because it slides well.

4 And they were the slaves of the priests—
the words of R. Meir;
R. Yose says:
They were of the families of Bet Hapegarim and Bet Tzipraya, and from Emmaus, marriageable into the priesthood;
R. Hanina b. Antigonus says:
They were Levites.

5 One does not have fewer than six inspected lambs in the Chamber of Lambs,
sufficient for the Sabbath and for two festival days of the New Year,
and one may increase them infinitely.
One does not have fewer[8] than two trumpets,
and one may increase them infinitely.
One does not have fewer than[9] nine lyres,
and one may increase them infinitely.
And the cymbal by itself.

[5] Lit. "strikes." [6] **P** lacks "first."
[7] *Mahliq* "slide"; **K**, **P**: *mehaleq*, "separate." See annotation. [8] Absent in **K**.
[9] Absent in **K**.

the Festival: i.e. Sukkot, the Festival of Booths. See *Sukkah* 5:1.

strike… slide: *Strike* may be used like the English "strike up." The musical terms are not entirely clear. *Slide* (*mahliq*) suggests descending tone, cadence, or diminuendo. The manuscript vocalization *mehaleq* may suggest solo playing, 'separating' from the ensemble.

2:4 *they*: The flute players.

marriageable into the priesthood: Of good family, suitable for marriage to daughters of the priesthood. *Qiddushin* 4:1–7.

2:5 *six inspected lambs*: See *Tamid* 3:3.

trumpets: See Numbers 10:1–10, *Tamid* 7:3.

lyres: See *Sukkah* 5:4. The Talmud notes that nine lyres, two trumpets, and one cymbal amount to twelve, the minimum number of Levites on the platform.

the cymbal by itself: i.e. one cymbal was played. Psalm 150:5 suggests multiple cymbals, but the Talmud observes that cymbals played in a pair by one person may be considered one instrument.

6 One does not have fewer than twelve Levites standing upon the platform,
and one may increase them infinitely.
A minor[10] must not enter the Temple Court for the service,
except when the Levites stand in their song.
And they did not intone[11] with harp and lyre but by mouth,
so as to give[12] savor to the melody.
R. Eliezer b. Jacob says:
They are not counted in the quorum,
and they do not stand upon the platform;
rather they stood upon the ground with their heads between the legs of the Levites;
and they were known as "the troublers of the Levites."

Chapter Three

3:1–5 *Lenient or Stringent*

3 In connection with sacral valuation
there are circumstances for leniency and for stringency;
with an ancestral field, for leniency and for stringency;
with the ox presumed harmful that has killed a slave,
for leniency and for stringency;
with the rapist and the seducer and the slanderer,

[10] **P**: "An Aramaean" (*Aram*), possibly an error for "A man (*adam*) must not enter…"
[11] Lit. "speak." [12] **K** lacks "So as to give."

2:6 *twelve Levites*: Singing psalms with instrumental accompaniment. See *Middot* 2:6.

A minor must not enter the Temple Court: Apparently an underage Levite. Speaking of the Levites, 1 Chronicles 25:8 indicates that *young and old alike, teacher as well as student, cast lots for their duties.*

they did not intone: The Levite children who joined in the Temple psalmody did not play instruments but only sang along.

not counted in the quorum: The children do not contribute to the minimum number of twelve Levites taking part in the music.

troublers of the Levites: So Talmud, commentaries, though the explanations of this strange epithet are fanciful. An alternative vocalization yields "the young Levites."

3:1 This chapter gives a list of areas where the Torah imposes a standardized payment, so that, compared to a related rule in which the actual value rather than a mandated standard is paid, the outcome may be lenient or stringent.

sacral valuation: See above, chapter 1.

ancestral field: A field inherited as part of the ancestral inheritance, Leviticus 27:15. At issue is the consequence of consecration.

ox presumed harmful: Exodus 21:28–32. See *Bava Qamma* 4:3.

rapist: See Deuteronomy 22:28–29. *Seducer*: Exodus 22:15–16. *Slanderer*: Deuteronomy 22:13–21.

circumstances for leniency and for stringency.
In connection with sacral valuation
there are circumstances for leniency and for stringency—how?
One who made a sacral valuation of the fairest of Israelites,
or the ugliest of Israelites, pays fifty *sela*.
And if he said: "I hereby owe his value," he must pay his worth.

2 With an ancestral field, for leniency and for stringency—how?
Whether he consecrated in the sands of Mahoz or in the orchards of Sebaste,
he pays for the *area required to sow a homer of barley fifty sheqel of silver*.
And in the case of the purchased field, he pays its actual worth.
R. Eliezer says:
A single law applies to both the ancestral field and the purchased field.
And what distinguishes between the ancestral field and the purchased field?
Only that in the case of the ancestral field he pays the added fifth;
but in the case of the purchased field he does not pay the fifth.

3 With the ox presumed harmful that has killed a slave,
for leniency and for stringency—how?
Whether it killed the fairest of slaves or the ugliest of slaves,
he must pay thirty *sela*.
If it killed a free person, he must pay his actual worth.
If it caused damage to the one or the other, he pays full damages.

4 With the rapist and the seducer,[13] circumstances for leniency
and for stringency—how?

[13] **P** includes "slanderer"; cf. 3:5.

the fairest... ugliest of Israelites: Payment of a pledge of sacral valuation is according to a standard rate, *fifty sela* (see above 2:1) in the case of a male from twenty to sixty years old.

"I hereby owe his value": This formulation indicates a vow of actual worth, assessed as though for sale in the slave market (1:1n.). Compared to this case, that of sacral valuation might yield a considerably higher (stringent) or lower (lenient) payment, depending on whether the referent was "fair" or "ugly."

3:2 *ancestral field*: See 3:1.

sands of Mahoz: A place characterized by sand not supporting agriculture. See also *Makhshirin* 3:4. Alternatively, a sandy region, or the sand at the shore.

area required to sow: Leviticus 27:16 (almost a verbatim quotation), specifying a standard payment per area, based on the amount of seed required.

purchased field: Leviticus 17:22. Consecration of a plot of land purchased rather than inherited.

pays the added fifth: See *Bava Metsi'a* 4:8. For ancestral land, the redeemer pays an additional fifth of the redemption value (understood by the Mishnah to be a fifth of the total, one quarter of the redemption value); see Leviticus 27:13.

3:3 *ox*: See 3:1.

fairest of slaves or the ugliest: See 3:1. Exodus 21:32 imposes a standard compensation of thirty *sheqel*, valued at a *sela* (see 2:1). In the case of a *free person* the owner of the ox may pay more or less.

caused damage to the one or to the other: In the case of nonfatal injury the ox's owner must make good the difference between the hypothetical price the victim would have fetched if sold as a slave before the injury and the estimated price after, whether the victim was slave or free.

One who raped or seduced the greatest woman of the priesthood
or the least among Israel:
he must pay fifty *sela*.
As to shame and blemish,
it is all according to the one who disgraced and the one who was disgraced.
5 With the slanderer, circumstances for leniency and stringency—how?
One who slandered the greatest woman of the priesthood
or the least among Israel:
he must pay one hundred *sela*.
We find that the one who speaks with his mouth
exceeds the one who does a deed—
for so we have found that the verdict against our ancestors in the wilderness
was sealed only on account of wicked speech,
as it is said: *Yet they tried me these ten times, and did not hearken to my voice.*

Chapter Four

4:1–4 *Pledging and Being Pledged*

4 Sufficiency of means applies to the one who vows;
and years to the one who is the object of the vow;
and sacral valuations to the one so valuated;
and sacral value [is determined at] the time of the sacral valuation.

3:4 *raped or seduced*: See 3:1.

shame and blemish: See *Ketubbot* 3:7 and *Bava Qamma* 8:1.

blemish: Permanent devaluation caused by physical injury, which would result in a lower bride price.

3:5 *the slanderer*: See 3:1.

one hundred sela: Deuteronomy 22:13–19; see *Ketubbot* 3:7.

the one who speaks with his mouth exceeds the one who does a deed in liability: the slanderer pays more than the rapist or seducer.

Yet they tried me: Numbers 14:22. The context is the episode of the ten spies who slandered the Land. Later interpreters emphasize the demonstrative "these" suggesting a sin of speech.

4:1 This list of specifications is further developed in what follows.

vows: Here apparently referring to sacral valuation. Cf. 1:1.

Sufficiency of means: See Leviticus 27:8. The Mishnah specifies that the rule about one too poor to fulfill the vow refers to the means of the dedicant, not the one whose value is pledged.

years: By contrast, the valuation according to age refers to the person referenced in the pledge.

sacral valuations: The specified rate to be paid is determined according to the age and sex of the person referenced in the pledge.

Sufficiency of means applies to the one who vows—how?
A poor man who made a sacral valuation of a wealthy man
pays a poor man's sacral valuation,
but a wealthy man who made a sacral valuation of a poor man
pays a wealthy man's sacral valuation.

2 However, with offerings it is not so.
Indeed one who said: "The offering of this person with *tsara'at* is upon me":
if the person with *tsara'at* was poor, he brings the offering of a poor person;
a wealthy person, he brings[14] the offering of a wealthy person.
Rabbi says:
I say, even in pledges of sacral valuation it is so.
Why indeed is it that a poor man who made a sacral valuation of a wealthy man pays a poor man's sacral valuation?
It is because the wealthy man does not owe anything.
But the wealthy man who said:
"The sacral valuation of myself is upon me,"
and a poor man heard and said:
"I owe what that one said,"

[14] **P**: "and a wealthy person brings..."

sacral value: The age criterion refers to *the time* the pledge was made, not when payment is eventually made.

A poor man... a poor man's sacral valuation: The rate to be paid is adjusted if the person who made the pledge of sacral valuation is poor (Leviticus 27:8), and the reduced obligation is here termed a "poor man's sacral valuation."

a wealthy man... a wealthy man's sacral valuation: The standard rate, corresponding to the age and sex of the referent in a pledge of sacral valuation, is paid without reduction by the person who can afford to do so, and is here termed a "wealthy man's sacral valuation."

wealthy man's sacral valuation and *poor man's sacral valuation* thus refer here to the wealth or poverty of the person making the pledge, not of the person named as referent in the pledge of sacral valuation.

4:2 *However, with offerings it is not so*: With vows of sacrifice things are different: obligations are fulfilled according to the wealth or poverty of the one who is obligated, not that of the person making the pledge on that person's behalf.

"*The offering of this person with tsara'at*": Leviticus 14:10–31.

the offering of a poor person: Leviticus 14:21–22.

the offering of a wealthy person: Leviticus 14:10–20.

a poor man who made a sacral valuation of a wealthy man: A poor man who named a wealthy man in a pledge of sacral valuation pays an amount corresponding to the age and sex of the individual named, reduced according to the capacity of the poor person to pay, as in 4:1.

the wealthy man does not himself *owe anything*: This is specified by way of contrast to the hypothetical case that follows, in which a poor man has invoked the self-referential pledge of a wealthy person.

the wealthy man who said: In this case a wealthy person pledges his own sacral valuation, and a poor man, overhearing this, pledges the same, with reference to that specific person. Here the Mishnah decides that the poor man is obliged to pay the exact amount due from the person who made the original pledge, i.e. *a wealthy man's sacral valuation*, rather than merely having incurred the same species of obligation as applied to himself.

he must pay a wealthy man's sacral valuation.
If he was poor and became wealthy, or wealthy and became poor,
he must pay a wealthy man's sacral valuation.
R. Judah says:
Even if he was poor and became wealthy and again became poor,
he must pay a wealthy man's sacral valuation.

3 However, with offerings it is not so.
Even if his father died and left him ten thousand,
or his ship was at sea with myriad thousands forthcoming,[15]
the sacred treasury has no claim on these.

4 Years to the one who is the object of the vow—how so?
A child who made a sacral valuation of an elder
pays the sacral valuation of an elder;
and an elder who made a sacral valuation of a child
pays the sacral valuation of a child.
And sacral valuations to the one so valuated—how?
A man who made a sacral valuation of a woman
pays the sacral valuation of a woman;
and a woman who made a sacral valuation of a man
pays the sacral valuation of a man.
And sacral value [is determined at] the time of sacral valuation—how?

[15] **P**: "forthcoming *to him*."

Even if he was poor and became wealthy or wealthy and became poor: The full rate is owed, as the person who made the pledge either, in the first case, did not invoke his poverty while poor, or, in the second case, made the pledge at a time of capacity to fulfill it in full. In both of these cases it may be deduced that fulfillment at the standard rate was intended.

R. Judah says: Beyond the previous holding, R. Judah's opinion renders moot a possible argument that non-fulfillment while wealthy of a pledge of sacral valuation made when poor may indicate an original intention to incur obligation only at a poor person's rate. In R. Judah's view, regardless of intentions and circumstances at any time, a pledge of sacral valuation must be fulfilled at the standard rate, if ever the pledge outstanding has coincided with capacity to pay it in full.

4:3 *However, with offerings it is not so*: The Mishnah here holds that, if one, when poor, has incurred obligation to an offering, as distinct from a pledge of sacral valuation, one owes only the poor person's offering regardless of subsequent circumstances, and regardless of anticipations at the time of incurring the obligation.

if his father…left him ten thousand, or his ship was at sea: These are cases in which sufficient means for a standard offering are not currently in hand but may be anticipated.

the sacred treasury has no claim on these: In contrast to the holdings in 4:2, the donor, even if now wealthy, and notwithstanding what may have been anticipated at the time the obligation was incurred, is not deemed obligated to the standard offering, but fulfills the outstanding obligation with the pauper's reduced offering.

4:4 *Years to the one who is the object of the vow*: See 4:1. According to commentators, *child* is used here with respect to the age categories in Leviticus 27, i.e. someone who has attained majority (at puberty, cf. *Niddah* chapter 5), but is younger than twenty years of age.

And sacral valuations: See 4:1.

And sacral value…time of sacral valuation: See 4:1.

If he made a sacral valuation of him when [he was] less than five years old,
and he became more than five years old,
or at less than twenty years old,
and he became twenty years old—
he pays according to the time of the sacral valuation.
The thirtieth day is as those below it;
the fifth year and the twentieth year, as those below them,
as it is said: *And if he be from sixty years and upward, if a male.*
Thus we learn with regard to all of them from the sixtieth year.
Just as the sixtieth year is as those below it,
so too the fifth year and the twentieth year are as those below them.
Is this so?
If [Scripture] made the sixtieth year as those below for stringency,
shall we make the fifth and the twentieth years as those below for leniency?
Scripture teaches, *year*, *year* for an inference from shared language.
Just as *year* stated in the case of the sixtieth year
is to be considered as those below it,
so too, *year* stated in the case of the fifth year and the twentieth year
is to be considered as those below it,
whether for leniency or for stringency.
R. Eleazar says:
Until they exceed the years by one month and one day.

The thirtieth day is as those below it: The standard rates of sacral valuation in Leviticus 27:3–7 commence at one month of age and specify changes at five, twenty, and sixty years of age. A child in the thirtieth day of life is here considered as less than thirty days—i.e. less than one month—old. Thus, if an infant in the thirtieth day of life is named in a pledge of sacral valuation nothing at all is owed.

the fifth year and the twentieth year, as those below them: On the same principle as for the thirtieth day, for a pledge naming a boy in his *fifth year* one owes five *sheqel*, not twenty, and so on.

And if he be: Leviticus 27:7.

If... for stringency...... for leniency? Might a better deduction not be drawn from the higher resulting assessment rather than the younger reckoned age? That is, if Leviticus 27:7 is to be read as excluding the sixtieth year itself from the older age category, yielding a *higher* rate of assessment for a sixty-year-old, is it not actually inconsistent to assign the fifth and twentieth years also to the respective age categories younger than them, since doing so yields a *lower* assessment?

year, year for an inference from shared language: The hermeneutical principle is that one may infer the sense of a word in one place from its sense in another. In this case, the inference is from *year* in Leviticus 27:7 to 27:8.

one month and one day: i.e. five or twenty or sixty years plus one month and one day.

Chapter Five

5:1–6 *Various Dedications of Value*

5 One who says: "My weight is upon me," must pay his weight:
if in silver, silver;
if in gold, gold.
It once happened with the mother of Yirmatiah that she said,
The weight of my daughter is upon me,
and she went up to Jerusalem, and they weighed her,
and she paid her weight in gold.
"The weight of my hand is upon me"—
R. Judah says:
He fills a barrel with water,
and puts his hand in up to the wrist,
and then puts in donkey meat with its sinews and bones until the barrel is full again.
Said R. Yose:
How is it possible to precisely match flesh to flesh and bone to bone?
Rather they estimate how much the hand is likely to weigh.
2 "The monetary value of my hand is upon me"—
they estimate how much he is worth with his hand
and how much he is worth without his hand.
This is the greater stringency of vows than of sacral valuations.
And the greater stringency[16] of sacral valuations than of vows, how?
One who says: "My sacral valuation is upon me," and dies:
the heirs pay;

[16] Lacking in **K**.

5:1 *"My weight is upon me"*: A vow to donate the monetary value of one's weight.

if in silver... in gold, depending on the specification in the vow.

fills a barrel of water, etc.: Following R. Judah, the displaced water yields the volume of the hand; and a corresponding volume of animal flesh containing a similar proportion of bone and sinew provides the weight to be paid to the Temple in gold or silver.

How is it possible...? Since the proportion of bones, sinews, and flesh from a donkey will not precisely match that of the human hand, the weight will also be different.

5:2 *"monetary value of my hand"*: A vow rather than a pledge of sacral valuation. See 1:1n.

This is the greater stringency of vows than of sacral valuations: Each can result in a payment when the other would not, and is thus more stringent. See also 3:1.

the heirs pay: The sacral valuation creates a specific debt, and that debt passes to the heirs who must pay from the estate of the deceased.

"My monetary value is upon me," and dies:
the heirs do not pay,
for the dead have no monetary value.
"The sacral valuation of my hand,"
or "The sacral valuation of my foot is upon me"—
he has not said anything.
"The sacral valuation of my head,"
or "The sacral valuation of my liver is upon me"—
he must pay the sacral value of his whole self.
This is the rule:
Something upon which life[17] depends:
he must pay the sacral value of his whole self.

3 "Half my sacral valuation is upon me"—
he must pay half his sacral valuation;
"The sacral value of half of myself is upon me"—
he must pay the sacral valuation of his whole self.
"Half my monetary value is upon me"—
he must pay half his monetary value;
"The monetary value of half of myself is upon me"—
he must pay the price of his whole self.
This is the rule:
Something upon which life depends:
he must pay the sacral value[18] of his whole self.

4 One who says,
"The sacral valuation of so-and-so is upon me"—
if the one who vows and the subject of the vow die, the heirs pay.

[17] Lit. "breath." [18] **K**: "price."

for the dead have no monetary value: After death, one's hypothetical worth on the slave market is nil, so the debt becomes void.

"*The sacral valuation of my hand... of my foot*": Leviticus 27:3–7 refers only to entire human beings; consequently the Mishnah here rules that pledges of sacral valuation for less than the entirety of a person are void.

"*The sacral valuation of my head... of my liver*": Since one cannot live without these parts, invoking head or liver is considered a reference to one's entire self.

5:3 "*Half my sacral valuation is upon me*": Undertaking half of an amount specified in Leviticus 27:3–7 creates a specific and determinate debt, and is therefore valid and binding.

"*the sacral valuation of half myself*": Following the examples in 5:2, a pledge of half of one's self is ruled as specifying a physical part without which the whole cannot live, and is therefore considered as pledging one's entire self.

"*Half my monetary value... the monetary value of half of myself*": Vows worded this way do not invoke sacral valuation, they are ruled as promising determinable amounts, and yield binding debts.

This is the rule: According to the reading of **K**—"*the* price *of his whole self*"—this ruling, like the immediately previous one, refers to vows and does not merely repeat the rule in 5:2 regarding sacral valuations.

"The price of so-and-so is upon me"—
if the one who vowed dies, the heirs pay;
if the subject of the vow dies, the heirs shall not pay,
for the dead have no price.

5 "This ox as a whole burnt offering,"
or "This house as a sacrifice"—
if the ox died or the house fell down, he is not obligated to pay.
"The price of this ox is upon me,"
or "The price of this house is upon me"—
if the ox died or the house fell down, he is obligated to pay.

6 Those obligated to sacral valuation, one exacts a pledge from them.
Those obligated to purgation offerings and guilt offerings,
one does not exact a pledge from them.
Those obligated to whole burnt offerings and offerings of well-being,
one exacts a pledge from them.
Even though atonement is not effected for him
until he offers of his own volition,
as it is said: *At his will*,
they compel him until he says: "I will it."
And so too regarding writs of divorce for women—
they compel him until he says: "I will it."

5:4 *for the dead have no price*: See 5:2.

5:5 *"This ox as a whole burnt offering" or "This house as a sacrifice"*: If one made these statements by way of pledge to the Temple treasury.

if the ox died or the house fell down: If one pledged the actual item, the debt does not survive the item's demise.

"The price of this ox" or "The price of this house": Since one has pledged the monetary equivalent of the item, the debt survives the item's demise.

5:6 *exact a pledge*: The Temple may claim property to be held as surety for payment.

does not exact a pledge: One liable to a purgation or guilt offering is presumed to be eager to achieve the atonement effected by the sacrifice; any other inducement to payment is superfluous.

At his will: Leviticus 1:3.

until he says: "I will it": For example, by seizing collateral as surety for payment.

so too regarding divorce documents: In general a writ of divorce must be given willingly in order to be valid. However, where a court has deemed that a writ should be given, but the husband stubbornly withholds it, the court may compel the man to declare himself willing.

Chapter Six

6:1–2 *Dedication of Property and Other Financial Obligations*

6 The assessment of orphans, thirty days;
and the assessment of consecrated property, sixty days.
And they proclaim in the morning and in the evening.
One who consecrates his property and owes a woman's *ketubbah*—
R. Eliezer says:
If he divorces her, he must renounce benefit by vow.
R. Joshua says:
He need not.
Similarly, Rabban Simeon b. Gamaliel said:
Even[19] a guarantor for a woman for her *ketubbah*,
and her husband divorces her,
[the husband] must renounce benefit by vow,[20]
lest he conspire against the other one's property
and take his wife back.
2 One who consecrates his property, and owes a woman's *ketubbah*
or has a creditor—
the woman may not claim her *ketubbah* from the consecrated property,
nor the creditor the debt owed him;
rather, one who redeems must redeem on condition that

[19] "Even" absent in **P**. [20] **P**: "he must prohibit her from benefit by vow."

6:1 *assessment of orphans*: Formal valuation of orphans' property that is to be sold to allow collection of parental debt. The sale is delayed *thirty days* to allow for its advertisement, to increase the income generated.

consecrated property is to be sold at best market prices and the proceeds donated to the Temple treasury. In this case, sale is delayed for *sixty days* to achieve the highest prices.

they proclaim the goods to be sold at times of high traffic in the marketplace, to attract the largest number of bidders.

and owes a woman's ketubbah: The marital settlement, which generally has legal priority over other liens on property. See *Ketubbot* introduction. Here, the dedicant's property was entailed in a marital contract before the consecration of property was made.

he must renounce benefit by vow: Since the *ketubbah* takes precedence over the consecration to the Temple, the husband must forswear any personal gain from pledged property claimed by his divorced wife in fulfillment of his *ketubbah* obligations. A concern about collusion is specified at the end of the mishnah.

guarantor: See *Bava Batra* 10:7. Someone other than the husband guarantees payment of the *ketubbah*.

6:2 *One who consecrates his property*: See 6:1.

must redeem on condition that he give... her ketubbah and... the debt owed him: According to the commentary Tosafot, the property necessary to pay the *ketubbah* or a debt does not transfer to the Temple (see 6:1), since creditors have a lien against this property. However, to avoid the appearance that the wife or creditor is pilfering consecrated property, the woman or creditor may not claim their debt directly, and the redeemer must redeem the balance in cash before repaying the *ketubbah* or the debt.

he give to the woman her *ketubbah* and
to the creditor the debt owed him.
If he had consecrated ninety *maneh*, and his debt was one hundred *maneh*,
he adds one *dinar* and with it[21] redeems the said property,
on condition that he will pay to the woman her *ketubbah,*
and to the creditor the debt owed him.

6:3–5 *Exacting Pledges against Obligations to the Temple*

3 Even though they have said:
Those owing sacral valuation, one exacts a pledge from them—
they give him thirty days' sustenance and twelve months' clothing,
and a properly made bed, and shoes, and *tefillin*;
him, but not his wife and not his children.
If he was an artisan,
they give him two tools of the trade of each and every kind:
a carpenter, two axes and two saws.
R. Eliezer says:
If he was a farmer, they give him his yoke;
an ass driver, they give him his donkey.
4 If one kind was numerous, and another few—
one does not tell him to sell from the numerous
and purchase for himself from the few;
rather one gives him two of the kinds that are numerous,
and all that he has of the kinds that are few.
One who consecrates his property, they entail his *tefillin.*

[21] "With it" absent in **K**.

he adds one dinar: As in the interpretation of Tosafot above, even though the debtor owes more to the creditor than he has consecrated, he borrows one more dinar from the same creditor and uses that *dinar* to give the appearance of "redeeming" any difference between his debts and his consecration before paying the *ketubbah* or his debt, thereby avoiding any appearance of pilfering consecrated property.

6:3 *Even though they have said*: See 5:6.

twelve months' clothing, and a properly made bed: Cf. Exodus 22:27.

tefillin: Phylacteries are here considered personal essentials on par with clothing, shoes, and home.

not his wife…children: Leviticus 27:8 reads *But if* he *be poorer than your estimation*. Although he remains responsible for their upkeep, *he*, and not his dependents, is provided for by these dispensations as a matter of the sacral valuation.

6:4 *numerous…few*: The tools in the possession of the artisan of 6:3.

of the kinds that are few: As the artisan himself has not previously sold some of his more plentiful tools to acquire more of the ones of which he has few, need for more of the latter is not now to be presumed.

they entail, lit. "lift up," his *tefillin*. The Temple treasury lays claim even to the value of his *tefillin*, which he must redeem by payment to the Temple.

5 Both the one who consecrates his property
and the one who pledges his sacral valuation:
he[22] has no claim to his wife's clothing,
nor to the clothing of his children,
nor to the dyed cloth that he dyed for them,
nor to new shoes that he acquired for them.
Even though they said:
Slaves are sold with their clothing, for increased value—
for if a garment is acquired for him at thirty *dinar*,
it increases his value by a *maneh*,
and likewise, a cow, if one delays its sale until market day
it increases in value,
and likewise a pearl, if one takes it up to the city,
it increases in profit—
the sacred treasury can claim[23] only its present place and time.

Chapter Seven

7:1–5 *Consecration of Property and the Jubilee*

7 One does not consecrate less than two years before the Jubilee,
and one does not redeem less than one year after the Jubilee.

[22] Or "it." See annotations. [23] Lit. "has."

6:5 *he* or it: If the subject is 'he," the person is the Temple official who has come to collect the pledge; if the subject is "it," the institution is the Temple treasury itself. The listed items cannot be seized for the pledge because they are no longer the property of the one who vowed.

increases his value by a maneh: By contrast, see the end of *Bava Metsi'a* 4:12, which prohibits adorning slaves for sale in this way.

up to the city: From a seaside town, where pearls may be plentiful.

can claim only its present place and time: The amount owed to the Temple is only the value of the property specified, as assessed in its place and condition at the moment of consecration. No customary marketplace enhancements are entailed or required.

7:1 For consecration and the Jubilee cycle see Leviticus 27:16–24 and 3:1, 2 above. The value of the dedicated property is prorated according to the number of years remaining before the Jubilee. Ancestral fields that are not redeemed by the dedicator become the possession of the priests (Leviticus 27:20–21, but see 7:4 below); fields purchased and dedicated revert to the seller.

less than two years before the Jubilee... less than one year after the Jubilee: According to the Talmud, deduction for "years" (Leviticus 27:18) of the Jubilee cycle can apply only when multiple years may be reckoned. One who consecrates a field when less than two years remain in the cycle, or redeems before the start of the second year of a new cycle, is assessed the full amount with no deduction.

One does not reckon months for the sacred treasury,
but the sacred treasury reckons months.
One who consecrates his field in the time of the Jubilee must pay
fifty sheqel of silver for every homer's *sowing of barley.*
If there were rifts ten handbreadths deep,
or boulders ten handbreadths high,
these are not measured along with the field;
lesser than this, these are measured along with the field.
If he consecrated it two or three years before the Jubilee,
he gives a *sela* and a *pondion* per year;
if he said: "I shall hereby give what pertains to each year yearly,"
one does not heed him;
rather, he must pay all of it at once.

2 The rule is the same for owners and for any person.
What [difference] is there between the owners and any person?
That the owners pay the fifth, and any person does not pay the fifth.

3 If he consecrated it and redeemed it—
it does not go out of his possession in the Jubilee;
if his son redeemed it—
it goes out to his father in the Jubilee;[24]

[24] "If his son . . . Jubilee" absent in **K**.

reckon months: When consecrating immovable property one does not calculate an equivalent monetary value based on the number of months remaining in the year. However, the *sacred treasury* does include partial years in assessing the redemption price.

in the time of the Jubilee: The commentaries read this as meaning "when the Jubilee laws are in force," in contrast to 8:1 and 9:1 below. Talmudic tradition deems consecration in the Jubilee year itself as generally invalid.

fifty sheqel of silver: Leviticus 27:16; see 3:2 above.

rifts ten handbreadths deep, or boulders ten handbreadths high: These are considered as separate domains from the field itself, and are deducted from the area of the field.

a sela and a pondion per year: The Mishnah reckons that fifty *sheqel* (Leviticus 27:16, corresponding to the Mishnah's *sela*: above 2:1n.), divided over forty-nine years yields one *sela* per year, plus a remainder of one *sela* or forty-eight *pondion* (see "Money, Weights, and Measures"). In addition, there is a moneychangers' premium of one *pondion* (see *Sheqalim* 1:7). The annual amount is thus one *sela* plus one *pondion*.

if he said . . . "yearly": To redeem the property by annual payments.

7:2 *The rule is the same*: The same rate of valuation applies whether it is the hereditary owners or others who seek to redeem a consecrated field.

the fifth: Leviticus 27:19, calculated as one quarter of the principal; see 3:2 above. Others, not the original owners, need not add this fifth in redeeming the field from the Temple.

7:3 *If he*, the original owner, *consecrated it and* himself *redeemed it—it does not go out of his possession* to the priests. By contrast if someone else had redeemed it, it would go to the priests in the Jubilee year (Leviticus 27:21).

if his son redeemed it: The son is not considered "any person" for these purposes, unlike other relations (as in the next passage).

if another redeemed it,
or one of the relatives,[25]
and he redeemed it from them—
it does not go out of his possession in the Jubilee;[26]
if one of the priests redeemed it,
and it is in his possession—
he may not say:
"Since it goes to the priests in the Jubilee year,
and it is in my possession,
it thereby is mine";
rather, it goes out to all his brethren the priests.

4 If the Jubilee arrived and it had not been redeemed—
the priests enter into it and pay its monetary value—
the words of R. Judah;
R. Simeon says:
They enter into it but do not pay.
R. Eliezer says:
They neither enter nor pay,[27]
but it is called an abandoned field until the second Jubilee;
if the second Jubilee arrived[28] and it had not been redeemed,
it is called an abandonment of abandonments[29] until the third Jubilee;
the priests never enter into it[30] until another has redeemed it.

5 One who purchases a field from his father—
if his father died,
and afterward he consecrated it,
it is in such a case like an ancestral field;

[25] **P**: "If his brother or another of the relatives redeemed it."
[26] **P**: "it goes out to the priests in the Jubilee."
[27] "R. Eliezer ... pay" absent in **K**.
[28] **K** lacks "if [it had] had arrived."
[29] **P**: "an abandoned field of abandonment."
[30] "Enter into it" absent in **K**.

if another ... and he redeemed it from them: If the dedicator had not redeemed it from the redeemer, it would have reverted to the priests.

he may not say ... rather, it goes out to all his brethren the priests: A priest who redeemed property as an individual may not retain the property at the Jubilee on the grounds that it now should become priestly property, and he, a priest, is already in possession. Rather, the field becomes the property of the entire priestly class in equal distribution (Leviticus 27:21: *it shall be the priests'*, in the plural).

7:4 *the priests enter into it, and pay*: The priestly families on duty on the Day of Atonement at the year of the Jubilee take possession of the actual field but they pay its full value, as specified in Leviticus 27:16.

but do not pay: According to R. Simeon, the priests do not owe the sacred treasury any compensation.

abandonment of abandonments: That is, twice abandoned.

until another has redeemed it: R. Eliezer interprets Leviticus 27:20–21 to mean that the field becomes priestly property only if the hereditary owner will not redeem the field and it is redeemed from the Temple by someone else.

7:5 *like an ancestral field*: The son purchased the field from his father, but the son was his father's heir and only vowed the consecration after his father's death, so the field is regarded as an ancestral possession.

if he consecrated it,
and afterward his father died,
in such a case it is as a purchased field—
the words of R. Meir.
And R. Judah[31] and R. Simeon say:
It is like an ancestral field,
as it is said: *And if a man consecrate to the Lord a field of his acquisition, which be not of his inherited fields*—
a field not fit to become an ancestral field,
excluding this one, which is fit to become an ancestral field.
A purchased field does not go out to the priests in the Jubilee year,
for a person may not consecrate that which is not his.
Priests and Levites may consecrate always and redeem always,
whether before the Jubilee or after the Jubilee.

Chapter Eight

8:1–3 *Consecration of Property When the Jubilee Is Not Practiced*

8 One who consecrates his field not in the time of the Jubilee—
they say to him: "You open first,"
for the owners pay the fifth, and any [other] person does not pay the fifth.

[31] R. Judah omitted and inserted by a second hand in **P**.

as a purchased field: Here, both the purchase and the consecration by the son took place within the father's lifetime when the field was not the son's property, so it is regarded as purchased rather than inherited. The son is exempt from the added fifth (7:2), and the field does not revert to the priests (see below).

And if a man consecrate: Leviticus 27:22.

fit to become an ancestral field: According to R. Judah and R. Simeon, Leviticus 27:22 excludes a field that would eventually fall by way of inheritance to the person now consecrating it.

A purchased field does not go out to the priests: Rather, it reverts to the original owners; see Leviticus 27:22–25.

A person may not consecrate that which is not his: A purchaser cannot irrevocably transfer to the Temple land that is not his ancestral possession, but that will revert as ancestral property to its original owners in the Jubilee year.

Priests and Levites may consecrate always and redeem always: According to the Talmud, priests and Levites are not restricted by the rule of 7:1; see 9:8.

8:1 *not in the time of the Jubilee*: When the laws of Jubilee are not in force, even while the Temple stands; cf. 7:1. The redemption price is determined by what redeemers are willing to bid.

"*You open first*": The owner who consecrated the field is offered the opportunity (or, in view of the following, is required) to bid first. Since *the owners pay* an additional *fifth* (7:2), this ensures that the Temple will receive no less than five-fourths of the field's value, as reckoned by the owner.

It happened that one consecrated his field on account of its poor quality:
They said to him: You open first!
He said: Let it be mine for an *issar*.
R. Yose said:
He rather said: For [the price of] an egg—
for consecrated property may be redeemed with money or that which is worth money—
he said[32] to him: It has come to you!
Thus he loses an *issar,* and his field is [still] before him.

2 If one said: "Let it be mine for ten *sela*,"
and one said: "For twenty,"
and one said: "For thirty,"
and one said: "For forty,"
and one said: "For fifty"—
if the one for fifty retracted,
one exacts a pledge from his property for up to ten;
if the one for forty retracted,
one exacts a pledge from his property for up to ten;
if the one who bid thirty retracted,
one exacts a pledge from his property up for to ten;[33]
if the one for twenty retracted,
one exacts a pledge from his property for up to ten;
if the one who bid ten retracted,
they sell it at its worth and collect the remainder from the one for ten.
If the owners say: "For twenty,"
and any [other] person says: "For twenty,"
the owners take precedence,
for they must add the fifth.

[32] **K**: "They say." [33] Missing in **K**.

on account of its poor quality: The owner sought to be rid of the cost of maintaining the property by consecrating it to the Temple.

an issar: One twenty-fourth of a *dinar*. See "Money, Weights, and Measures."

R. Yose said: An *egg* is worth less than an *issar*, and its "fifth" would be worth less than the smallest coin (a *perutah*). The view that R. Yose opposes would then hold that the minimum redemption price must be four coins of the smallest denomination.

It has come to you! The auctioneer, receiving no higher bids, proclaimed the original owner the winner of the auction. Thus, despite attempting to be rid of a burdensome field, *he loses an issar* for redemption, and his field still belongs to him. For the idiom, see Song of Songs 8:12.

8:2 *ten…twenty* etc.: Five bids to redeem consecrated property (see 8:1).

one exacts a pledge from his property for up to ten: This guarantees payment of the difference between the retracted bid and the next highest bid. The field goes to the next highest bidder at forty, and so forth for the ensuing examples. Thus, the Temple suffers no loss.

and collect the remainder: If it sells at less than ten.

the owners say: "For twenty": This hypothetical case is continued in 8:3.

for they must add the fifth: See 7:2, 8:1. Consequently the owners' bid is favored.

3 If someone said: "It is hereby mine for twenty-one," the owners pay twenty-six;
"For twenty-two," the owners pay twenty-seven;
"For twenty-three," the owners pay twenty-eight;
"For twenty-four," the owners pay twenty-nine;
"For twenty-five," the owners pay thirty—
for they do not add a fifth upon the increase offered by the other.
If one said: "It is hereby mine for twenty-six"—
if the owners are willing to pay thirty-one and one *dinar*,
the owners take precedence;
and if not, they say:
"It has come to you."

8:4–7 *Devotion (Herem) of Property*

4 A person may devote some of his flock or his cattle,
of his Canaanite male slaves and female slaves,
and of his ancestral fields;
but if he devoted them all, they are not devoted—
the words of R. Eleazar.[34]
R. Eleazar b. Azariah said:
Just as a person may not devote all his possessions to the One on High,
how much the more so is it evident
that a person must have a care for his possessions.
5 One who devotes his son or his daughter,
his Hebrew male or female slave, or his purchased field—

[34] **K:** "Eliezer."

8:3 *"mine for twenty-one," the owners pay twenty six*: Nonowners bid against a bid of twenty (plus a "fifth," totaling twenty-five) by the original owner (8:2). The original owner must be prepared to match any increase by a bidder, so long as that bidder does not raise the going price beyond twenty-five *sela* (see below).

they do not add a fifth upon the increase: The owner is not required to pay an additional fifth on the difference between the owner's base bid (twenty *sela*) and the outside bid.

"*twenty-six*": Exceeding the original owner's effective offer of twenty-five.

if the owners are willing to pay their original effective bid of twenty-five, plus the amount added by the higher bid (six *sela*), plus a "fifth" on the amount by which bidder exceeded the original (one sela, for a "fifth" of one *dinar*, see "Money, Weights, and Measures"), add an extra *dinar* to five-fourths of their own last bid of twenty *sela*, plus the rival's increase of six *sela*, for a total of *thirty-one sela and one dinar*, and this is considered to outbid the outside offer. Alternatively, the owner last bid twenty-one *sela*, thereby indicating willingness to pay twenty-six *sela* and one *dinar* (Talmud).

they say, "It has come to you": If the owner does not match this increase, the Temple treasurers assign the property to the rival bidder.

8:4 *but if he devoted them all*: Leviticus 27:28 says *"from all"* that the consecrator has, indicating that one may devote a portion, but not the entirety, of what one owns.

a person must have a care for his possessions and not squander them.

they are not devoted,
for a person may not devote that which does not belong to him.
Priests and Levites may not devote—
the words of R. Judah.
R. Simeon says:
The priests may not devote,
for devoted property belongs to them;
the Levites may devote,
for devoted property does not belong to them.
Rabbi says:
The words of R. Judah have my approval for immovable properties,
as it is said: *for it is their perpetual possession*;
and the words of R. Simeon have my approval for movable property,
for devoted property does not belong to them.

6 That which is devoted to the priests is not subject to redemption.[35]
R. Judah b. Betera says:
Devoted property without specification falls to the Temple upkeep,
as it is said: *every devoted thing is holy of holies to the Lord*;
and the Sages say:
That which is devoted without specification falls to the priests,
as it is said: *as a field devoted, the possession of it shall be the priest's.*
If so, why is it said: *every devoted thing is holy of holies to the Lord?*—
that it applies to offerings of the highest sanctity and to offerings of lesser sanctity.

7 A person may devote his holy things,
whether offerings of the highest sanctity or offerings of lesser sanctity.

[35] Some versions add "but is given to the priests like *terumah*."

8:5 *may not devote that which does not belong to him*: The indicated persons or property will all be released from the householder's possession. Valid devotion requires the power to transfer in perpetuity.

for it is their perpetual possession: Leviticus 25:34, regarding the Levite cities and their fields. Devoting these holdings to the priesthood would contravene their assignment to the Levites.

for devoted property does not belong to them, but becomes property of the priesthood. Consequently, devotion by Levites is valid.

8:6 *is not subject to redemption*: Leviticus 27:28, *Every devoted thing…shall not be sold and shall not be redeemed.*

every devoted thing: Leviticus 27:28.

The Temple upkeep: Funds that go to the general maintenance of the Temple (as opposed to sacrifices).

as a field devoted: Leviticus 27:21.

to offerings of the highest sanctity: The expression is the same as for "holy of holies" (Leviticus 27:21).

or offerings of lesser sanctity: See 8:7 for exposition of how this works.

8:7 If a person who does not owe a sacrifice pledges to offer one, this is called a "vow" (*ndr*). In a normal case the donor then designates an animal and brings it to the Temple. If the animal dies or is stolen, the donor remains under the obligation of his vow; he must therefore choose another animal and discharge that obligation. If the donor designates a particular animal for sacrifice without having previously uttered a vow,

If it be a vow,
he pays its price;
if it be a voluntary offering,
he pays what it benefits him.[36]
"This ox is a whole burnt offering!"—
one estimates how much a man would be willing to pay
to offer this ox as a whole burnt offering
for which he was not obligated.
One can devote a firstling,
whether unblemished or blemished.
How does one redeem it?
One estimates how much a person would pay
to give this firstling to the son of his daughter
or to the son of his sister.
R. Ishmael says:
One verse says: *you shall consecrate* and another says: *do not consecrate.*
It is impossible to say *consecrate*, for *do not consecrate* is already said;
and it is impossible to say *do not consecrate*, for *consecrate* is already said.

[36] **P**: "the debt of it."

that animal must similarly be brought to Jerusalem and sacrificed. In this case, however, if the animal dies or is stolen the donor is under no further obligation, since his pledge was always limited to the particular beast in question. Such a pledge is here called a "voluntary offering" (*ndv*; see Leviticus 22:23, also *Qinnim* 1:1 and *Nedarim*, introduction).

If it be a vow: The dedicator would be obliged to replace the devoted animal if necessary, so it is still accounted as his property until sacrificed. He must sacrifice as he vowed and also *pay its price* to the Temple as a devotion.

what it benefits him: Unlike the case of a vow, the animal is no longer "his"; it belongs now to the Temple, and if it is lost or stolen the donor is not liable to replace it. Having subsequently devoted this offering he does not owe the animal's full value, but only the value, now lost, of the opportunity to sacrifice it. An example now follows.

"This ox is a whole burnt offering": Exemplifies estimation of benefit in the case of a voluntary offering.

how much a man would be willing to pay: The devotion equals the amount the donor would be willing to pay to offer this ox as a whole burnt offering. This is presumably less than the market value of the ox.

not obligated: Lit. "not permitted," but rendered following traditional interpretation.

a firstling, whether unblemished or blemished: The owner is obligated to donate firstborn animals to the priests. See *Bekhorot* introduction. But here the owner devoted it, and firstlings are subject to devotion.

How does one redeem it? As in the preceding, the value of his devotion is an estimation of benefit. How is this determined?

to the son of his daughter or to the son of his sister, who are priests. The amount a nonpriestly donor would be willing to pay to give such an animal to his priestly relations.

you shall consecrate: Deuteronomy 15:19. *Do not consecrate*: Leviticus 27:26. Both scriptures refer to firstlings.

Say therefore: You may consecrate it as a consecration of value,[37]
but you may not consecrate it as consecrated for the altar.[38]

Chapter Nine

9:1–8 *Sale and Redemption of Property in the Time of the Jubilee*

9 One who sells his field in the time of the Jubilee
may not redeem it in less than two years,
as it is said: *According to the number of years of the harvest shall he sell it to you.*
If it were a year of blight, or of yellowing, or a Seventh Year,
it is not reckoned in the number.
If he plowed it or let it lie fallow,[39]
it is reckoned in the number.
R. Eliezer says:
If he sold it before New Year and it was full of fruit,
in that case the buyer[40] eats three harvests in two years.

[37] Lit. "consecrated property of cost [or elevation]."
[38] **P**: "If you consecrate it... you do not consecrate it as consecrated for the altar."
[39] **P**: "or leased it out." [40] Heb. "he."

may consecrate it: A firstling may be consecrated by pledging *a consecration* equal to the *value* of giving a similar animal to one's priestly family members, as above. However, one may *not consecrate it* to be offered on *the altar* as a sacrifice. To designate a firstling as a sacrifice is to misappropriate it since it belongs to the priests.

9:1–8 The passages in this chapter deal with sale of property in the context of the laws governing the Jubilee year (Leviticus 25:25–34). Ancestral fields revert to the sellers at the Jubilee, and both sale and redemption price are prorated to the number of years remaining to the Jubilee. Houses in walled cities may be redeemed within a year, or else become the perpetual property of the purchaser. Houses in unwalled towns are treated like fields and revert to the sellers at the Jubilee. Houses in cities assigned by the Torah to Levites may always be redeemed, and revert to the Levites in the Jubilee year.

9:1 *in the time of the Jubilee*: When the laws of Jubilee are in force; see 7:1 and 8:1.

According to the number of years: Leviticus 25:15. The plural *years* is read as requiring at least two years in the purchaser's possession.

yellowing: A symptom of crop disease.

is not reckoned in the number: Such years do not count as "years of the harvest."

plowed it or let it lie fallow: Since it was fit to bear a harvest had he not left it unsown, the year *is reckoned in the number.*

If he sold it before New Year: Two years and more before the Jubilee year. The buyer gains the right to the fruits in the field at the time of purchase. However, the purchase price is estimated based on two years to the Jubilee.

2 If he sold it to the first one for a *maneh*,
and the first one sold it to the second for two hundred,
he reckons only with the first,
as it is said: *to the man to whom he sold it.*
If he sold it to the first for two hundred,
and the first one sold it to the second for a *maneh*,
he reckons only with the second,
as it is said: *to the man*—to the man who is in it.
He may not sell of that which is distant and redeem of that which is close by;
of that which is poor and redeem that which is good.
He may not borrow to redeem, and he may not redeem by halves.
But with consecrated offerings, he is permitted to do all of these.
This is the greater stringency with ordinary property than with sacred property.

3 One who sells a house among houses in walled cities—
this one may redeem immediately,
and may redeem within twelve months.
This is akin to usury but it is not usury.
If the seller has died,
his son may redeem.
If the purchaser has died,
he may redeem from his son.
He counts a year for him only from the moment he sold it to him,

9:2 *a maneh*: One hundred *dinar*.

reckons only with the first: The original owner redeems by paying the original price, prorated to the remaining harvests in the Jubilee cycle.

to the man to whom he sold it: Leviticus 25:27.

reckons only with the second: The original owner redeems according to the lower price, prorated to the number of remaining years.

to the man who is in it: Leviticus 25:27. The apparent superfluity of "to the man" is taken to designate whichever purchase offer would be advantageous to the original owner.

may not sell…redeem by halves: May not sell less attractive ancestral property to redeem more advantageous property, nor borrow to redeem ancestral property.

But with consecrated offerings: He may sell ancestral property or borrow to redeem ancestral property that has been consecrated.

greater stringency: The seller is more limited in how he redeems sold property than consecrated.

9:3 *houses in walled cities*: Echoes Leviticus 25:29.

may redeem immediately, without waiting for two years as with a field, *and may redeem within twelve months*, an interval when fields may not be redeemed (see 9:1 above).

This is akin to usury but it is not usury: There is no proration on the redemption price, but the buyer benefits from the house until it is redeemed. The benefit has the appearance of interest on a loan (cf. *Bava Metsi'a* 5:2).

If the seller has died, the seller's heir may redeem it. Similarly, *if the purchaser has died*, the seller may reacquire the field from the heir of the purchaser.

counts a year…only from the moment he sold it: When the original purchaser sold it, not from when any subsequent holder bought it.

as it is said: *Until the completion of a year*;
and when it says *full*, this includes the intercalated month.
Rabbi says:
He must grant him a year and its intercalation.

4 If the day of twelve months has arrived and it was not redeemed,
it becomes his outright.
The rule is the same for a buyer and for the one to whom it was given as a gift,
as it is said, *in perpetuity.*
In former times the purchaser[41] would hide on the day of twelve months,
so that it would become his outright;
Hillel the Elder ordained that the seller[42] might deposit his money in the chamber and break down the door and enter;
whenever the other desires he may come and take his money.

5 Anything that is within the wall is thereby like houses within walled cities,
except for fields.
R. Meir says:
Even fields.
A house built into the wall:
R. Judah says:
It is not like houses within walled cities.
R. Simeon says:
The outer wall is its wall.

6 A city whose roofs are its wall
or that has not been surrounded by a wall
since the days of Joshua son of Nun,
is not like houses within walled cities.

[41] Heb. "he." [42] Heb. "he."

Until the completion: Leviticus 25:30, understood as a referring to a twelvemonth from the date of sale.

full: Leviticus 25:30. *The intercalated month*: In a leap year of thirteen lunar months, he may redeem the house during the thirteenth month as well.

a year and its intercalation: Rabbi reads the "full" in the biblical year as referring to a 365-day solar year.

its intercalation: Lit. "its pregnancy." Here, the term refers to the difference between a solar year and the 354-day lunar year (Talmud).

9:4 *it becomes his outright . . . in perpetuity*: Leviticus 25:30.

the purchaser would hide on the day of twelve months, to avoid its being redeemed.

The seller might deposit his money in the chamber of the court, *and break down the door and enter* the house thus redeemed.

9:5 *Anything that is within the wall*: Not only houses, but any property *except fields*—thus including movables—*is thereby like houses within walled cities*, to which Leviticus 25:29–30 applies.

It is not like houses: In this view it may be reckoned as not having all its walls entirely within the city.

The outer wall is its wall: And it has the status of a house within the walls.

9:6 *A city whose roofs* are joined one to the other to form an enclosure.

not like houses within walled cities: Such a town is not considered to have a proper wall, and is not subject to the rules for walled cities.

And these are they that are houses within walled cities:
three courtyards of two houses,
surrounded by a wall since the days of Joshua son of Nun,
such as: the old fortress of Sepphoris, the citadel of Gush Halav,
old Yodfat, and Gamla, and Gedod, and Hadid, and Ono, and Jerusalem,
and so too any like these.

7 Houses of unwalled cities—
one grants them the advantages of houses of walled cities;
and the advantages of fields:
they may be redeemed immediately,
and may be redeemed within a twelvemonth—like houses;
and they go out in the Jubilee, and with reduction of price—like fields.
And these are houses in unwalled cities:[43]
two courtyards of two houses,[44]
even though they have been surrounded by a wall
since the days of Joshua son of Nun;
in this case, these are like houses of unwalled cities.

8 An Israelite who inherited from his mother's father, a Levite,
does not redeem according to this order;
and so too, a Levite who inherited from his mother's father, an Israelite,
he does not redeem according to this order,

[43] **K** (in error): "And these are they that are houses of walled cities."
[44] **P** repeats "two," meaning "two houses each."

three courtyards of two houses: A walled enclosure containing within it at least three courtyards to each of which open at least two dwellings.

old fortress of Sepphoris: A walled stronghold within the city.

9:7 *Houses of unwalled cities*: Leviticus 25:31.

may be redeemed immediately: Above, 9:3.

they go out in the Jubilee: They revert to their original owners.

and with reduction of price—like fields: When redeemed before the Jubilee, the price of redemption is prorated according to the years remaining in the Jubilee cycle, like fields of possession sold and redeemed.

these are houses in unwalled cities: Even if ringed by outer walls.

two courtyards of two houses, or fewer.

9:8 *Israelite who inherited from . . . a Levite*: An inheritor of Levitical property who himself is not a Levite, but has inherited through his mother. The heir then sold the property.

according to this order: Note the shift in subject: this mishnah assumes that we are now talking about Leviticus 25:32–34, which allows the Levite to redeem alienated property at any time.

this order: The rules specified for Levites do not apply here because the heir who sold and wishes to redeem the property is not a Levite.

Levite who inherited non-Levitical ancestral property through his mother, sold it, and now wishes to redeem it. Since the property is not Levitical, the statutes of Levite redemption do not apply.

as it is said: *for the houses of the cities of the Levites*,
only when he is a Levite and the property is in the cities of the Levites.
These are the words of Rabbi.
And the Sages say:
These words are said only with regard to the cities of the Levites.
One may not make a field into open land,
and not open land into a field,
and not open land into city,
and not city into open land.
R. Eliezer said:
When does this apply?
To the cities of the Levites;
but with Israelite cities:
one may make a field into a pasture,
but not a pasture into a field;
a pasture into a town,
but not a town into open land—
so that they not destroy Israelite cities.
The priests and the Levites may sell always and may redeem always,
as it is said: *Redemption in perpetuity shall there be for the Levites.*

for the houses of the cities of the Levites: Leviticus 25:33. According to Rabbi, Leviticus 25:32–34 applies only *when* the holder of the property *is a Levite*, and *the property* itself is in a Levitical city.

And the Sages say: The laws for redeeming Levitical property do not depend upon the inheritor who sells and redeems such property being a Levite.

One may not make a field into open land: Leviticus 25:34 prohibits the sale of pasture land surrounding Levitical cities. Hereditary properties in the identified categories may not be converted one into the other.

R. Eliezer... To the cities of the Levites: The houses, fields, and pastures of Levitical cities. Leviticus 25:31–34 establishes these types of holdings as permanent, and prohibits conversions. See *Ma'aser Sheni* 5:14; *Sotah* 5:3.

so that they not destroy Israelite cities: R. Eliezer permits the conversion of open land into agricultural fields and fields into built-up space. The reverse are degradations that are tantamount to destroying the hereditary cities.

may sell: See 7:5. The time limits laid down in 7:1 above do not apply to priests or Levites.

Redemption in perpetuity: Leviticus 25:32.

Tractate Temurah

Tzvi Novick

Introduction

Overview

Leviticus 27:1–8 lays out the rules that apply if one dedicates to God the value of a human being. The obligated amount depends on the age and gender of the human whose value was pledged. These rules are the subject of tractate *Arakhin*. Tractate *Temurah* ("exchange" or "substitute") considers the rules laid out in the next verses of Leviticus (27:9–13). If one dedicates an animal to God but the animal is ineligible for the altar, a priest evaluates the animal and establishes the redemption price to be paid by a third party or (with a surcharge of one-fifth) by the original donor (Leviticus 27:11–13). But if the animal is eligible for the altar, substitution is not permitted (Leviticus 27:10). The prohibition of substitution recurs later in the chapter with reference to the animal tithe. Every tenth animal that passes under the shepherd's staff belongs to the priest; no substitutions are permitted (Leviticus 27:33). If one ignores the prohibition and attempts to substitute one sacrificial animal for another, both become sanctified; this is the main topic of tractate *Temurah*.

Structure and Organization of the Tractate

The main body of chapter 1 (1:1–3, 6) is concerned chiefly with exegesis of Leviticus 27:10. Only here does the tractate quote the biblical law of substitution, and only here does the tractate hew closely to the Sifra, the rabbinic midrash on Leviticus. In 1:4–5, the tractate moves by association from substitution to other cases of extension of status. Chapter 2 concerns differences between offerings of an individual and offerings of a congregation (most saliently, the latter are not subject to the law of substitution), and between the original animal and the animal that becomes sanctified under the law of substitution. In chapter 3 the Mishnah examines the sacrificial status of substitutes and offspring. The last category of sacrifice in this survey is the purgation offering, which serves as the topic of chapter 4. Chapter 5 introduces a different, permissible instance of "substitution": anticipating sanctification of the firstborn animal one consecrates it for a different purpose while it is still in the womb. The end of chapter 5 (5:5–6) addresses the formulas through which one achieves substitution, redemption, and consecration. The topic of chapter 6 is again extension of status, in this case not of sanctified things but of prohibited things. The beginning of chapter 7 (7:1–3) takes up the differences between things consecrated to the altar and things consecrated to Temple maintenance, not only because one of the differences concerns substitution but also because Leviticus 27:9–13, in the eyes of rabbinic interpreters, addresses precisely this distinction. The law of disposal of animals with ritual status, which arises incidentally in 7:3, becomes the topic of the last part of the chapter (7:4–6).

Relationship to Scripture

The central topic of tractate *Temurah* is the biblical prohibition of substitution. If an animal dedicated to the altar becomes blemished, and if its redemption price has been established by a priest, the donor may redeem it, per Leviticus 27:11–13, even by replacing it in kind with another animal. But the donor may not on his own initiative substitute another animal for the original, whether the latter remains whole or even if it has become blemished. If the donor does so, he has violated the prohibition, and both the original animal and the substitute count as sanctified.

The Babylonian Talmud appears to conceive of the sanctified status of both animals as the consequence of a penalty. Either the substitution is effective (so that the second animal becomes sanctified in place of the first), but to punish the wrongdoer, the original animal is deemed to retain its sanctity, or the substitution is ineffective (so that the original animal retains its sanctity) but as punishment, the second animal is nevertheless considered sanctified. The Mishnah does not take an explicit position on the mechanism of the law but appears implicitly to imagine the sanctity of the original animal extending out, in a kind of contagion, to the second. Hence the tractate includes other cases in which sanctity (among other kinds of status) extends beyond its point of origin. The most important of these cases involves the offspring of a sanctified animal.

Tractate Temurah

Chapter One

1:1–3 *When Is Substitution Valid?*

1 All substitute, both men and women—
not that one may substitute,
but that if one did substitute, it is deemed substituted,
and one absorbs the forty.
Priests substitute what belongs to them,
and Israelites substitute what belongs to them.
Priests do not substitute for a purgation offering, nor for a guilt offering, nor for a firstborn.
Said R. Yohanan b. Nuri:
And why do they not substitute for a firstborn?
Said R. Aqiva:
The purgation offering and the guilt offering are gifts to the priest,
and the firstborn is a gift to the priest.
Just as the purgation offering or the guilt offering are not subject to substitution,
so the firstborn is not subject to substitution.
Said to him R. Yohanan b. Nuri:

1:1 *All substitute*: A nonsacral animal for a sanctified animal.

not that one may substitute: Leviticus 27:10.

it is deemed substituted: The "substitute" animal becomes sanctified. The original animal also retains its sanctity.

absorbs the forty: The forty lashes (Deuteronomy 25:3) incurred for violation of a Torah prohibition, in this case, Leviticus 27:10.

Priests substitute what belongs to them: They substitute for sanctified animals that belong to them. The subtleties of this principle are taken up in the continuation.

And why do they not substitute for a firstborn? The firstborn is transferred, alive, by the owner to the priest, who offers it (if unblemished) as his own sacrifice (see *Bekhorot*).

R. Aqiva draws an analogy between purgation offerings and guilt offerings, which are also *gifts to the priest*.

R. Yohanan b. Nuri objects that the purgation offering and the guilt offering are offered on the owner's behalf and belong to the priest only insofar as he consumes a portion of the carcass, unlike the firstborn.

What is it to me[1] that he does not substitute for the purgation offering or the guilt offering?
For they have no right in them while they are yet alive.
Will you say so for the firstborn, where they do have a right in them while they are yet alive?
Said to him R. Aqiva:
But is it not said: *it and its substitute will be holy*?
Where does sanctity take effect upon it?
In the owner's home.
So the substitute, in the owner's home.

2 They substitute[2] from cattle upon the flock, and from the flock upon cattle,
from sheep upon goats and from goats upon sheep,
from males upon females and from females upon males,
from unblemished animals upon blemished animals
and from blemished animals upon unblemished animals,
as it is said: *One may not exchange it or substitute for it, good for bad or bad for good.*
What is *good for bad*?
Blemished animals whose consecration preceded their blemish.
They substitute one for two, and two for one,
One for one hundred, and one hundred for one.
R. Simeon says:
They only substitute one for one,
as it is said: *it and its substitute.*
As it is singular, so its substitute is singular.

3 One does not substitute limbs for fetuses, or fetuses for limbs,
or fetuses or limbs for entire animals, or entire animals for them.
R. Yose says:

[1] **K, P, L**, *Sifra*: "What pertains to it?" [2] **L**: "They do not substitute."

it and its substitute: Leviticus 27:10. The original animal (*it*) and the second (*its substitute*) are taken to be similar with respect to their sanctification.

So the substitute, in the owner's house: Since the firstborn's sanctity originates in the owner's home, at its birth, the sanctity of the substitute must also originate in the owner's home. Hence, once the animal passes to the priest, substitution for it is not effective to sanctify the second animal.

1:2 *One may not exchange it*: Leviticus 27:10.

whose consecration preceded their blemish: Only such animals, if substituted for, sanctify the substitute. But if one consecrates an already blemished animal, one is deemed to have pledged only its monetary value, and this monetary sanctity cannot sanctify a substitute. See *Hullin* 10:2.

it and its substitute: Leviticus 27:10.

so its substitute is singular: The Babylonian Talmud discusses whether R. Simeon's limitation applies only to simultaneous substitution of two for one or even to successive one-for-one substitutions.

1:3 *limbs*: Although it is possible to consecrate a limb, with the result that the entire animal becomes sanctified (see 2:3 and R. Yose below), what is true of direct consecration is not true of substitution: a limb can neither acquire nor cause sanctity via substitution.

fetuses: A fetus, too, can neither acquire nor cause sanctity via substitution, even though it can itself be consecrated.

R. Yose reasons that since sanctifying a limb renders the entire animal sanctified, attempting to substitute a nonsacral limb for a whole sanctified animal causes the sanctification of the whole nonsacral animal, but the reverse is not true.

They substitute limbs for entire animals, but not entire animals for limbs.[3]
Said R. Yose:
Is it not true that in the case of consecrated animals,
if one says:[4] "The leg of this one is a whole burnt offering,"
then all of it is a whole burnt offering?
So if one says: "The leg of this one in place of this one,"
it should in its entirety be a substitute in its place.

1:4–5 *Second Generation Extensions*

4 *Terumah* mixture conveys the status of *terumah* mixture only by proportion.
Dough leavened [by *terumah*] leavens only by proportion.
Drawn water renders the immersion pool invalid only by proportion.

[3] **K, P, L**: "but not entire animals for them." The reviser of **K** left the phrase unvocalized.
[4] **K, P, L**: "One says."

1:4 Parallel in *Terumot* 5:6.

Terumah mixture: A mixture composed of *terumah* wheat and less than one hundred times its volume in nonsacral wheat.

conveys the status of terumah mixture: To a second batch of nonsacral wheat with which part of the original mixture is mingled.

only by proportion: The original mixture is deemed thoroughly mingled, so that the proportion of *terumah* in the wheat from the original mixture that falls into the second batch is the same as the proportion of *terumah* in the original mixture as a whole. Only if the amount of *terumah* in the wheat from the original mixture, so computed, exceeds one percent by volume of the second batch, does the second batch acquire *terumah* status.

Dough leavened [by terumah]: Dough composed of nonsacral wheat that was leavened with already fermented *terumah*. Such dough is subject to the status of *terumah* mixture, no matter how small the amount of *terumah* sourdough, because of its visible effect on the whole.

leavens: Is deemed to convey status as *terumah* mixture to a second batch of dough with which part of the original dough is mingled.

only by proportion: The original dough is deemed thoroughly mingled, so that the proportion of fermented *terumah* in the part of the original dough that enters into the second batch of dough is the same as the proportion of fermented *terumah* in the original dough as a whole. Only if the amount of fermented *terumah* in the dough from the original mixture, so computed, is sufficient to leaven the second batch of dough, does the second batch acquire *terumah* status.

Drawn water: If three *log* of drawn water enter a pool of rainwater before the latter reaches a volume of forty *se'ah*, the pool may not serve as an immersion pool (*miqveh*). Following Albeck, the scenario envisioned here is one in which drawn water, before entering the immersion pool, has become mingled with water that does not invalidate the pool.

renders the immersion pool invalid: Into which some portion of the mixture of drawn water and valid water has been mingled.

only by proportion: The proportion of drawn water in the portion of the mixture that enters into the pool is deemed to be the same as the proportion of drawn water in the mixture as a whole. Only if the amount of drawn water in the portion of the mixture that enters into the pool, so calculated, is three *log*, is the pool rendered invalid.

5 Waters of purgation become waters of purgation
only with the introduction of the ashes.
A plowed-up burial does not make a plowed-up burial,
and there is no *terumah* after *terumah*,
and a substitute does not make a substitute,
and an offspring does not make a substitute.[5]
R. Judah says:
An offspring makes a substitute.
They said to him:
What is consecrated makes a substitute;
the offspring and the substitute do not make a substitute.

1:6 *Other Restrictions on the Law of Substitution*

6 Birds and grain offerings do not make a substitute,
for it says only: *for a beast.*[6]
The community and partners do not make a substitute,
for it says: *One may not substitute it*;
the individual makes a substitute,
but the community and partners do not make a substitute.
Offerings for Temple upkeep do not make a substitute.

[5] **K** lacks "and an offspring does not make a substitute," likely due to homeoteleuton.
[6] **K**, **P**, **L**: "for it says only, *A beast*."

1:5 *Waters of purgation*: The mixture of red-heifer ashes and water that effects purification from impurity arising from contact with the dead. See Numbers 19.

the introduction of the ashes: The ashes must be poured into the water. In light of the other cases in 1:4–5, this rule presumably means to exclude the possibility of adding water to the waters of purgation so as to increase their volume. In other words, waters of purgation cannot make more waters of purgation.

plowed-up burial: Heb. *bet peras*, "area containing a *peras*." If a corpse in a field is plowed over, an area one hundred cubits square around the corpse, the *bet peras*, falls under suspicion of containing bone shards, so that its soil conveys impurity through contact and carrying.

does not make a plowed-up burial: If one plows up the *peras* area, there is no concern that bone shards spread beyond the original *peras* area. See *Oholot* 17:1–2.

terumah after terumah: If one has already separated *terumah* from the harvest, separating another portion as *terumah* does not convey the status of *terumah* on it.

does not make a substitute: Though a nonsacral animal substituted for a sanctified animal becomes sanctified, if one attempts to substitute a third animal for the second, the third animal remains nonsacral.

An offspring: The offspring of a consecrated animal.

1:6 *for a beast*: Leviticus 27:10.

The community and partners: Animals offered on behalf of the community, or on behalf of multiple owners.

One may not substitute it: Leviticus 27:10. The rule is stated in the singular.

Offerings for Temple upkeep: Objects (in this case animals) donated to the Temple to fund its operation and repair, rather than dedicated as sacrifices.

Said R. Simeon:
And was not the [animal] tithe included within the general rule?
And why was it specified?
To compare to it.
As the tithe is the offering of an individual,
offerings of the community are excluded.
As the tithe is an offering for the altar,
offerings for Temple upkeep are excluded.

Chapter Two

2:1–2 *Offerings of an Individual and Offerings of the Community*

2 There are rules that pertain to offerings of an individual
that do not pertain to offerings of the community,
and rules pertain to offerings of the community
that do not pertain to offerings of an individual.
For offerings of an individual make a substitute,
but offerings of the community do not make a substitute.
Offerings of an individual apply to male and female animals,
but offerings of the community apply only to males.
Offerings of an individual,
one is accountable for them and for their libations,
but offerings of the community,
one is not accountable for them or for their libations,

Said R. Simeon: His exegesis provides an explanation for the restriction of substitution to sacrificial animals, as well as an alternative explanation (at variance with the earlier one furnished by the anonymous view) for the restriction of substitution to the offering of an individual.

the [animal] tithe: Leviticus 27:32–33.

included…why was it specified? The animal tithe might have been understood as part of the general rule of substitution in Leviticus 27:9–10. Why is substitution stated again specifically for the animal tithe (Leviticus 27:32–33)?

excluded: An exception to the law of substitution.

2:1 *male and female*: The animal sacrificed for certain individual offerings of well-being may be male or female.

accountable: If the time prescribed for making the offering has passed, the owner must make the offering afterward (Rashi).

libations: The meal and wine offerings that accompany the sacrifice.

not accountable: Once the offering's prescribed time has passed, it need not (indeed cannot) be made.

but one is accountable for their libations once the sacrifice has been made.
There are rules that pertain to offerings of the community
that do not pertain to offerings of an individual.[7]
For offerings of the community override the Sabbath and impurity,
but offerings of an individual do not override the Sabbath or impurity.
Said R. Meir:
Are not the cakes of the high priest and the bull of the Day of Atonement
the offering of an individual,
yet they override the Sabbath and impurity?
However, their time is fixed.

2 The purgation offering of an individual
whose owners have [otherwise] made atonement—
dies.
That of the community does not die.
R. Judah says:
It must die.
Said R. Simeon:
Just as we find for the offspring of a purgation offering,
and the substitute of a purgation offering,
and a purgation offering whose owners have died,
that the rule is said for an individual but not for the community;
so too one whose owners have [otherwise] made atonement,

[7] **K** lacks "that . . . an individual."

override the Sabbath: They are offered even on the Sabbath, although they involve labor prohibited on the Sabbath.

and impurity: By an impure priest, if no ritually pure priest is available.

the cakes of the high priest: The high priest's grain offering, made twice each day (Leviticus 6:13–14).

the bull of the Day of Atonement: The high priest's purgation offering (Leviticus 16:3, 6).

However, their time is fixed: In fact, the criterion for overriding Sabbath and impurity is not that the offering be of the community, but that it be designated for a specific time.

2:2 *whose owners have [otherwise] made atonement*: The purgation offering went missing, and the owners fulfilled their obligation with a different animal. Subsequently, the original animal was found.

dies: The original purgation offering must be left to die, because the transgression for which it was to atone has already been atoned. The purgation offering of an individual whose owners have atoned is one of five kinds of purgation offerings that are left to die. The others are mentioned in the continuation. See also 4:1.

does not die: It is instead allowed to graze until it develops a blemish, at which point it may be redeemed.

Said R. Simeon: Defending the first, anonymous view in the Mishnah, against R. Judah's position.

the offspring of a purgation offering: An offspring conceived after the animal was consecrated as a purgation offering.

whose owners have died: Before the offering was made.

for an individual but not for the community: A community purgation offering cannot make a substitute (2:1), nor, because it is necessarily male (2:1), can it have offspring, nor can its "owners" die.

and one whose year has passed,[8]
the rule is said for an individual but not for the community.

2:3 *Consecrated Things and Substitutes*

3 The rule is stricter for consecrated things than for the substitute,
and for the substitute than for consecrated things.
For consecrated things make a substitute,
but a substitute does not make a substitute.
The community and partners consecrate,
but they do not substitute.
And they consecrate limbs and fetuses,
but they do not substitute.
The rule is stricter for a substitute:
for sanctity falls on a permanently blemished animal,
and it does not become nonsacral such that it may be sheared and worked.
R. Yose b. R. Judah says:
The law made the unintentional equivalent to the intentional
in the case of the substitute,
but it did not make the unintentional equivalent to the intentional
in the case of consecrated things.
R. Eleazar says:
The prohibited mixture, the *terefah*, the caesarean birth, a *tumtum*, and an *androgynos*
neither are sanctified nor do they consecrate.

[8] **K, P, L**: "that which has surpassed its year."

whose year has passed: Goats and sheep may be sacrificed as purgation offerings only if they are younger than one year old. If a goat or sheep in its first year is consecrated as a purgation offering, but not sacrificed before it turns one, then it must be left to die.

2:3 *but a substitute does not make a substitute*: See 1:5.

The community and partners... do not substitute: See 1:6.

they consecrate limbs and fetuses, but they do not substitute: See 1:3.

For sanctity falls... sheared and worked: If one consecrates a permanently blemished animal, the animal acquires only "monetary sanctity": its owner must redeem it from the Temple, but once he does so, the animal may be sheared and worked. But if that animal acquires sanctity as a substitute, it may not be sheared or worked even after it is redeemed. Cf. 1:2.

unintentional is not treated as intentional in the case of consecrated things: See *Nazir* 5:1.

prohibited mixture: e.g. the offspring of a goat and a ewe.

terefah: Lit. "torn animal," an animal that will die imminently from illness or injury. See *Hullin*.

tumtum: An animal with no visible sex markers.

androgynos: An animal with visible markers of both sexes.

neither are sanctified: One cannot effectively consecrate such an animal, nor is substitution of such an animal for a consecrated animal effective.

nor do they consecrate: If such an animal had acquired sanctity, the substitution of another animal for it is ineffective to consecrate the substitute.

Chapter Three

3:1–4:1 *Sacrificial Status of Substitutes and Offspring*

3 These are the consecrated things whose offspring and substitutes are like them:
the offspring of an offering of well-being and its substitute,
their offspring, and their offspring's offspring to the end of the world,
these are as an offering of well-being,
and require leaning and libations and waving, and the breast and thigh.[9]
R. Eliezer says:
The offspring of an offering of well-being is not offered
as an offering of well-being.
But the Sages say:
It is offered.
Said R. Simeon:
They did not disagree about the offspring of the offspring
of an offering of well-being,
nor about the offspring of the offspring of a substitute,
that it is not offered.
And about what did they disagree?
About the offspring.
For R. Eliezer says:
It is not offered.
And the Sages say:
It is offered.
R. Joshua and R. Papias testified that the offspring of an offering of well-being
is offered as an offering of well-being.
Said R. Papias:
I testify that we had a cow designated to be an offering of well-being sacrifice,

[9] **K**, **P**, **L**: "waving of the breast and thigh."

3:1 *and its substitute*: The substitute of an offering of well-being.

their offspring: The offspring of the offspring or of the substitute.

and waving, and the breast and thigh: i.e. waving of the breast and thigh. See *Zevahim* 10:2.

is not offered as an offering of well-being: Rather, it is left to die (Rashi). According to one view in the Babylonian Talmud, R. Eliezer so rules out of concern that the owner of the offspring would delay offering the offspring, and instead mate it to produce whole herds of offerings of well-being, from whose flesh the owner is entitled to eat.

that it is not offered: The Sages concede to R. Eliezer in this situation, where the owner's intent is evidently to multiply his stock of offerings of well-being, that such an offering may not be offered.

About the offspring: The original offspring of the offering of well-being or of the substitute.

testified: See *Eduyot* 7:6.

and we ate it on Passover,
and we ate its offspring as an offering of well-being on the Festival.

2 The offspring of a thanksgiving offering and its substitute,
their offspring, and their offspring's offspring to the end of the world—
these are as a thanksgiving offering,
but do not require bread.
The substitute of a whole burnt offering
and the offspring of the substitute,
their offspring, and their offspring's offspring to the end of the world—
these are as a whole burnt offering,
and require flaying, cutting up, and utter consumption in the flames.

3 One who separates a female for a whole burnt offering,
and it bears a male,
it must graze until it becomes defiled,
and it is sold,
and one brings a whole burnt offering with its proceeds.
R. Eleazar[10] says:
It itself is offered as a whole burnt offering.
One who separates a female for a guilt offering,
it must graze until it becomes defiled,
and it is sold,
and one brings a guilt offering with its proceeds.
If his guilt offering was offered,

[10] K: "Eliezer."

on the Festival: The festival of Sukkot (Tabernacles).

3:2 *and its substitute*: The substitute of a thanksgiving offering.

their offspring: The offspring of the offspring or of the substitute.

bread: The leavened loaves that ordinarily accompany the thanksgiving offering. See Leviticus 7:12 and *Menahot* 7:4.

The substitute of a whole burnt offering: There is no reference to the offspring of a whole burnt offering because whole burnt offerings are exclusively male. But see 3:3.

flaying, cutting up, and utter consumption in the flames: Of the altar. See Leviticus 1:6, 8.

3:3 *a female for a whole burnt offering*: Because whole burnt offerings must be male, the sanctified female must be allowed to graze until it develops a blemish, at which point it is sold, and a (male) whole burnt offering purchased with the proceeds. The question debated here is whether the male offspring of such a female has the status of a whole burnt offering.

becomes defiled: Lit. "filthy," such that it would be disqualified for the altar.

It itself is offered as a whole burnt offering: Its mother, in R. Eleazar's view, is technically a whole burnt offering, despite her sex, and communicates this status to her offspring.

a female for a guilt offering: Guilt offerings must also be male.

If his guilt offering was offered: Another animal, male, was offered in satisfaction of the guilt-offering obligation, so that there is no need to purchase another.

its proceeds fall to a voluntary offering.
R. Simeon says:
It is sold without a blemish.
The substitute of a guilt offering,
the offspring of its substitute,
and their offspring and their offspring's offspring until the end of the world—
they graze until they become defiled,
and are sold,
and their proceeds fall to a voluntary offering.
R. Eliezer says:
They must die.
But R. Eleazar says:
One brings whole burnt offerings with their proceeds.
A guilt offering whose owners have died,
or whose owners have [otherwise] made atonement,
it grazes until it becomes defiled,
and it is sold,
and its proceeds fall to a voluntary offering.
R. Eliezer says:
It must die.
R. Eleazar says:
One brings a whole burnt offering with its proceeds.

4 And is not the voluntary offering also a whole burnt offering?
What, then, is the difference between the words of R. Eleazar and the words of the Sages?
But when it comes as an obligation,
he leans on it, and brings libations with it,

its proceeds: The proceeds from the sale of the female animal, conducted after the animal contracts a blemish.

fall to a voluntary offering: To the Temple fund designated for purchase of voluntary offerings, a species of whole burnt offering. See *Sheqalim* 2:5, 6:5. Such offerings are made when the altar is unoccupied.

without a blemish: Its female sex is itself a blemish.

their proceeds fall to a voluntary offering: They cannot be offered as guilt offerings, because the transgression was atoned for by the original guilt offering itself.

They must die: Like the offspring and substitute of the purgation offering. See 2:2; 4:1.

whose owners have died: Before the offering was made.

whose owners have [otherwise] made atonement: With a different animal. See above 2:2.

3:4 *the voluntary offering*: Mentioned by the anonymous view in the last two debates in 3:3. This view is identified as that of *the Sages* below.

also a whole burnt offering: The assumption is that the voluntary offering brought from the proceeds will be a voluntary whole burnt offering.

the words of R. Eleazar: In the last two debates in 3:3, which call for proceeds from the sale of the offering in question to be used to purchase a whole burnt offering.

as an obligation: As according to R. Eleazar.

he leans on it: Before the animal is slaughtered.

and the libations are from his own;
and if he is a priest,
its service and its hide are his own.
And when it comes as a voluntary offering,
he does not lean on it, and he does not bring libations with it,
and the libations are from the community;
even though he is a priest,
its service and its hide are of the men of the watch.

5 The substitute of the firstborn and the [animal] tithe, and their offspring,
and their offspring's offspring until the end of the world—
these are as the firstborn and the tithe,
and may, due to their blemish, be consumed by their owners.
What is the difference between the [blemished] firstborn and tithe,
and all of the other sacred offerings [when blemished]?
All of the offerings are sold in the market,
and slaughtered in the market,
and sold by weight,
except for the firstborn and the tithe.
And they are subject to redemption,

from his own: The obligated individual must pay for the libations.

its service and its hide are his own: Even if the priest does not belong to the priestly watch on duty that week, he is entitled to make the offering himself, and take possession of the hide.

as a voluntary offering: As according to the Sages.

from the community: The libations are purchased from communal funds.

3:5 *the firstborn*: The firstborn animal of the herd or flock belongs to the priest, who offers it on the altar and is then entitled to its flesh.

the [animal] tithe: Every tenth animal of the herd and flock must be offered on the altar, and consumed by its owner in Jerusalem.

as the firstborn and the tithe: While, unlike the firstborn and the animal tithe, they are not sacrificed (*Bekhorot* 9:8), they nevertheless have sanctity, with the consequences that the text proceeds to identify.

consumed: After nonsacral slaughter.

by their owners: The priest, in the case of the firstborn, and the owner, in the case of the tithe.

What is the difference: When the consecrated animal has contracted a blemish. The opening of the passage states that the offspring and substitute, when blemished, have the same status as the blemished firstborn or tithe itself. The text now explains what distinguishes the blemished firstborn or tithe from other blemished consecrated animals.

all of the other sacred offerings: After contracting a blemish and being redeemed from the Temple by their owners. See *Bekhorot* 5:1.

sold in the market…by weight: Lit. by the *litra*, "pound." They are treated in the marketplace like the carcasses of nonsacral animals. This arrangement works to the benefit of the Temple: because the owner can sell the blemished animal at its full market value, he must, to redeem it, pay the Temple its full market value. By contrast, the blemished *firsborn and tithe* remain sanctified, and the law insists that they be treated with special respect, even at the owner's expense. See *Bekhorot* 5:1.

and their substitutes are subject to redemption,
except for the firstborn and the tithe.
And they come from outside the Land,
except for the firstborn and the tithe.
If they come unblemished,
they are offered,
and if blemished,
they may, due to their blemish, be consumed by their owners.
Said R. Simeon:
What is the reason?
For the firstborn and the tithe have their sustenance in their place,
while the other offerings, even if a blemish arises in them,
persist in their sanctity.

Chapter Four

4 The offspring of a purgation offering
and the substitute of a purgation offering
and a purgation offering whose owners have died—
they must die.
One whose year has passed,[11]
and which was lost, and then found blemished[12]—

[11] **K, P, L**: "that which has surpassed its year."
[12] **K, P** have "and" between "found" and "blemished." See the annotations.

subject to redemption . . . except for the firstborn and the tithe: When the firstborn and the tithe become blemished, they are not redeemed. They may be slaughtered nonsacrally but retain their status as firstborn and tithe.

The Land: Of Israel.

If they come: If a firstborn or animal tithe from outside Israel is nevertheless brought as an offering.

the reason: That the firstborn and the tithe do not come from outside Israel.

have their sustenance in their place: It is possible to consume them without having any recourse to the Temple: one simply waits for them to contract a blemish, then slaughters them profanely.

persist in their sanctity: They must be redeemed, and the proceeds devoted to the purchase of an unblemished animal to be offered as a sacrifice. Hence, one way or another, recourse must be had to the Temple.

4:1 Parallel in *Me'ilah* 3:1.

they must die: See 2:2.

One whose year has passed: See 2:2n.

lost, and then found blemished: Like the other purgation offerings detailed to this point, such an offering is allowed to die. The case of the animal that is lost then found presents a number of complications detailed in 4:2–3.

if the owners have [otherwise] made atonement,
it must die
and does not make a substitute.
One may not benefit from them,
and they are not subject to sacrilege.
If before the owners have made atonement,
it grazes until it becomes defiled,
and is sold,
and one brings another with its proceeds,
and it makes a substitute,
and it is subject to sacrilege.

4:2–4 *Lost and Blemished Purgation Offerings*

2 One who separates his purgation offering
and it is lost,
and he offers another in its stead,
and afterward the first is found—
it must die.
One who separates money for his purgation offering
and it is lost,
and he sacrificed a purgation offering in its stead,
and afterward the money is found—
it must go to the Dead Sea.
3 One who separates money for his purgation offering
and it is lost,
and he separated other money in its stead—
if he did not manage to purchase a purgation offering with it

if the owners have [otherwise] made atonement: Offered a different animal as a purgation offering. Rashi reads: *If the owners made atonement*, i.e. after the original animal was found. Rashi's reading may "correct" 4:1 in light of 4:2, 3, where, once the second animal has been offered, the first, even if unblemished, must be left to die.

One may not benefit: One may not make use of the animal.

and they are not subject to sacrilege: If one does make use of the animal, one is not liable to make a guilt offering for trespassing on the sacred.

it grazes until it becomes defiled: The reference is specifically to the purgation offering whose year has passed. The purgation offering that was lost and found blemished is already *defiled*, and may be sold immediately.

4:2 *it must die*: The original animal must be left to die.

to the Dead Sea: i.e. the money must be discarded in an irretrievable manner, cf. *Nazir* 4:4, 6; *Avodah Zarah* 3:3, 9.

4:3 *If he did not manage to purchase a purgation offering with it before the original money was found*: If he did manage to do so, the purgation offering would be made, but the fate of the money is subject to the debate between Rabbi and the Sages that is introduced, in connection with a different scenario, at the end of the paragraph. The current scenario, and all of the others until the last, are carefully constructed to avoid this debate.

before the original money was found,
he may bring a purgation offering from this [money] or from that,
and the remainder falls to a voluntary offering.
One who separates money for his purgation offering
and it is lost,
and he separated a purgation offering in its stead;
if he did not manage to offer it before the money was found,
and the purgation offering is blemished—
it must be sold,
and he may bring a purgation offering from this or from that,
and the remainder falls to a voluntary offering.
One who separates his purgation offering
and it was lost,
and he separated money in its stead;
if he did not manage to purchase a purgation offering with it
before his purgation offering was found,
and the purgation offering is blemished—
it must be sold,
and he may bring a purgation offering from this or from that,
and the remainder falls to a voluntary offering.
One who separates his purgation offering
and it was lost,
and he separated another in its stead;
if he did not manage to offer it before the first was found,
and in this case both are blemished—
they must be sold,
and he may bring a purgation offering from this or from that,
and the remainder falls to a voluntary offering.
One who separates his purgation offering
and it is lost,
and he separates another in its stead;
if he did not manage to offer it before the first was found,
and in this case both are whole—
one of them is offered as a purgation offering,
and the second must die—
the words of Rabbi.[13]
And the Sages say:
A purgation offering does not die
unless it is found after the owners have [otherwise] made atonement,
and money does not go to the Dead Sea
unless it is found after the owners [otherwise] made atonement.

[13] **P**: "R. Meir."

and in this case both are whole: This scenario, unlike all of the previous ones, involves two unblemished purgation offerings.

unless it is found after the owners [otherwise] made atonement: So that in the case under debate, the second animal grazes until it contracts a blemish, and is then sold, and the proceeds fall to a voluntary offering.

4 One who separates his purgation offering
and it turns out to be blemished,
he sells it,
and must bring another with its proceeds.
R. Eleazar b. R. Simeon says:
If the second was sacrificed before the first has been slaughtered,
it must die,
because the owners have [otherwise] made atonement.

Chapter Five

5:1–4 *Double Consecration*

5 How does one deceive concerning the firstborn?
If an animal is pregnant with its firstborn, he says:
"What is in this one's womb,
if it is a male, it is a whole burnt offering"—
if she bears a male,
it must be offered as a whole burnt offering.
"And if it is a female, it is an offering of well-being"—
if she bears a female,
it must be offered as an offering of well-being.
"If it is male, it is a whole burnt offering,
if it is a female, it is an offering of well-being"—

4:4 *slaughtered*: By the purchaser.

it must die: That original animal must be left to die and may not be slaughtered.

because the owners have [otherwise] made atonement: It counts as a purgation offering whose owners have made atonement (2:2, 4:1), even though it was redeemed and sold. The first animal's nonsacral status is, as it were, a temporary window that closes when the replacement purgation offering is made.

5:1 *deceive*: So that the firstborn animal, instead of becoming the possession of a priest, can instead be used to satisfy a sacrificial obligation owed by the owner of the pregnant animal.

he: Its owner.

"*it is a whole burnt offering*": He designates it as the animal that will satisfy his obligation, arising from elsewhere, to offer a whole burnt offering.

"*it must be offered as a whole burnt offering*": The designation made while the newborn was in the womb trumps firstborn status, because the latter takes effect only when the newborn *opens the womb* (Exodus 13:2).

"*if it is a female*": The female is introduced to complete the scenario and to anticipate the scenarios that follow, because, given the fact that only a male can be a firstborn, sanctification of a female in the womb is obviously for a different sacrificial purpose. The Babylonian Talmud makes this clause speak to the case of a pregnant animal that has been consecrated as e.g. a purgation offering.

if it bears a male and a female,
the male must be offered as a whole burnt offering;
and the female must be offered as an offering of well-being.
2 If she bore two males,
one is offered as a whole burnt offering,
and the second is sold to those obligated to a whole burnt offering,
and its proceeds are nonsacral.
If she bears two females,
one is offered as an offering of well-being,
and the second is sold to those obligated to an offering of well-being,
and its proceeds are nonsacral.
If it bears a *tumtum* or an *androgynos*,
Rabban Simeon b. Gamaliel says:
Sanctity does not fall upon them.
3 One who says:
"This one's offspring is a whole burnt offering
and it itself is an offering of well-being"—
his words stand.
"It is an offering of well-being
and its offspring is a whole burnt offering"—
in this case, this is the offspring of an offering of well-being—
the words of R. Meir.
Said R. Yose:
If he intended this from the beginning,
then since it is not possible[14] to declare two statuses at once,
his words stand.
But if after he said:
"This one is hereby an offering of well-being,"
he reconsidered and said:
"Its offspring is a whole burnt offering"—
then this one is the offspring of an offering of well-being.

[14] **K**, **P**, **L**: "even though it is not possible." In **K**, "not" is supralinear.

offering of well-being: Whole burnt offerings are made with male animals (3:2).

5:2 *does not fall upon them*: Because they are neither male nor female.

5:3 *One who says*: Concerning a pregnant animal.

and it itself: The mother.

this: The offspring.

is the offspring of an offering of well-being: Because the owner consecrated the mother first, the subsequent consecration of the offspring as a whole burnt offering is ineffective, and the offspring instead has the status of the offspring of an offering of well-being, on which see 3:1.

intended this: To consecrate the offspring separately.

4[15] "This one is hereby the substitute for a whole burnt offering
and the substitute for an offering of well-being"—
in this case this is a substitute for the whole burnt offering—
the words of R. Meir.
Said R. Yose:
If he intended this from the beginning,
then since it is not possible[16] to declare two statuses at once,
his words stand.
But if after he said:
"The substitute for a whole burnt offering,"
he reconsidered and said,
"The substitute for an offering of well-being"—
in this case it is a substitute for the whole burnt offering.

5:5–6 *Formulas for Substitution, Redemption, and Consecration*

5 [If he said] "This one is hereby:
in this one's stead;
a substitute for this one;
an exchange for this one"—
this is a substitute.
"This one is desacralized through this one"—
it is not a substitute.
And if the animal dedicated to the Temple was blemished,

[15] Mishnah lacking in **K**. **L** includes twice.
[16] **P**, **L**: "even though it is not possible." In **L**, "not" is absent.

5:4 *"This one...and the substitute for an offering of well-being"*: The owner attempts to substitute a single animal for two consecrated animals of two types.

this is a substitute for the whole burnt offering: Once he declares it a substitute for the whole burnt offering, the animal is sanctified, and no longer subject to further sanctification.

his words stand: The animal must therefore be left to graze until it becomes blemished, whereupon it is sold, and half the proceeds go toward the purchase of a whole burnt offering, and half to that of an offering of well-being.

5:5 *"This one is"*: The formulas are legally effective alternatives.

"exchange": Cf. Leviticus 27:10.

this is a substitute: Any of the three formulas is effective: the second animal becomes sanctified, the first animal remains sanctified, and the owner receives lashes. See 1:1.

it is not a substitute: Because the declaration uses the language of redemption, not substitution. If the original animal is unblemished, it is not subject to redemption, and the declaration has no effect.

if the animal dedicated to the Temple: The one that had already been dedicated.

was blemished: So that the declaration does effect redemption.

it is reduced to nonsacral status,
and one must calculate its value.[17]

6 "This one is hereby in a purgation offering's stead,
or in a whole burnt offering's stead"—
he has said nothing.
"In this purgation offering's stead,
or in this whole burnt offering's stead,
[or] instead of the purgation offering or the whole burnt offering
that I have in the house"—
if he has,
his words stand.
If he said concerning an impure animal or a blemished animal:
"These are hereby a whole burnt offering"—
he has said nothing.
"These are hereby for a whole burnt offering"—
they are to be sold,
and he must bring a whole burnt offering[18] with their proceeds.

Chapter Six

6:1–5 *Extension of Prohibited Status*

6 All that are forbidden upon the altar
forbid in any amount:

[17] **K, P**: "it must be made monetary value." [18] **K**: "whole burnt offerings."

it: The first animal.

one must calculate its value: If the second animal is less costly than the first, one must pay the difference to the Temple.

5:6 *he has said nothing*: The animal does not become a substitute, because he has not specified the consecrated animal for which he wishes to substitute it.

"*In this purgation offering's stead*": He specifies the consecrated animal he means to substitute for.

if he has: If he indeed possesses an animal so designated in his house.

his words stand: So that the substitute becomes sanctified.

an impure animal: An animal of a species that may not be offered on the altar.

"*for a whole burnt offering*": The word "for" signifies that he does not mean to make these animals whole burnt offerings, but to use them for the purchase of whole burnt offerings.

6:1 *All that are forbidden* to be brought *upon the altar*.

in any amount: If an ineligible animal mingles with a herd of eligible animals, of whatever size, all the animals become ineligible. The list that follows also occurs in *Zevahim* 8:1, 9:3, 14:2. See also above 2:3.

one penetrating or penetrated in bestiality,
or set aside,
or worshiped,
or used as hire,
or used as payment,
or was a forbidden mixture,
or a *terefah*,
or one born of a caesarean section.
What is "one set aside"?
The one set aside for idolatry.
It is forbidden, but what is upon it is permitted.
What is "worshiped"?
Anything that they worship.
It and what is upon it are prohibited.
And this one and that one are permitted to be eaten.

2 What is *hire*?
One who says to a prostitute,
"Here is this lamb as your hire."[19]
Even one hundred, all are forbidden.
And likewise[20] one who says to his friend:
"Here is this lamb,
and let your maidservant lie with my slave."[21]
Rabbi says:
It is not *hire*.

[19] **K** lacks "this lamb"; **P**, **L** lack only "lamb." [20] So **K**, **P**, **L**. Some witnesses delete.
[21] **K**: "and give me your maidservant to be with my slave."

set aside: For the service of a foreign god. See below.

worshiped: As a god. See below

hire...payment: Deuteronomy 23:19, glossed in 6:2, 3.

forbidden mixture: e.g. the offspring of a goat and a ewe.

terefah: Lit. "torn animal." The Babylonian Talmud attempts to explain why such an animal, which, unlike the other animals in the list, bears the mark of its disqualification on its body, could not easily be distinguished from the herd.

forbidden: Upon the altar.

what is upon it is permitted: Accoutrements on the animal that was designated for idolatry may be utilized in the cult.

this one and that one: The "designated" and the "worshiped" animals.

eaten: After nonsacral slaughter. The prohibition concerns only cultic use.

6:2 *Even one hundred*: Though he only contracted to furnish one lamb, he gave her one hundred (Babylonian Talmud). Alternatively, this line introduces a different scenario: if no price was stipulated, then all the animals that he gives her count as *hire*. On the latter interpretation, animals given in excess of a stipulated price would arguably not count as *hire*.

It is not "hire": The lamb is eligible for the altar. The permissive view is that only sexual encounters specified as "nakedness" in Leviticus 18 count as illicit intercourse, to the exclusion of intercourse between slaves (Tosefta).

But the Sages say:
It is *hire*.
3 What is *payment for a dog*?
One who says to his friend:
"Here is this lamb in this dog's stead."
And likewise two partners who divided:
one took ten, and one took nine and a dog.
Those exchanged for[22] the dog are prohibited,
those with the dog are permissible.
A dog's hire and the payment of a prostitute,
in this case they are permissible,
as it is said: *Two*,[23] and not four.
Their offspring are permissible,
as it is said: *Them*, and not their offspring.
4 If he gave her money,
in this case it is permissible.
Wines, oils, and fine flours,
and anything whose kind is offered upon the altar,
it is prohibited.
If he gave her previously consecrated things,
these are permissible.
Birds,
these are forbidden.

[22] Lit. "opposite." [23] **K**, **P**: "the two of."

6:3 "*in this dog's stead*": A lamb exchanged for a dog is ineligible for the altar as *payment for a dog*.

exchanged for: The ten lambs on the other side of the ledger.

prohibited: As *payment for a dog*. It is unclear why all ten are prohibited, rather than only one, corresponding to the dog.

with the dog: The nine lambs on the same side of the ledger.

dog's hire: A lamb transferred to the dog's owner in exchange for the dog's sexual services (Rashi), or for the purpose of mating the dog with one's own dog (Albeck).

payment of a prostitute. A lamb exchanged for sexual services.

Two: Deuteronomy 23:19.

6:4 *her*: The prostitute. As the end of the paragraph makes explicit, all of the rules in the section apply not only to the law of *prostitute's hire* but also to that of *payment for a dog*.

money: Rather than a lamb or other animal.

it is permissible: An animal purchased with such money may be sacrificed.

consecrated things: Animals that he had already consecrated for the altar.

permissible: Since they already belong to the Temple, they are not his to give.

Birds: Nonsacral birds otherwise eligible for the altar, furnished to the prostitute as her hire.

For logic might have dictated:
if consecrated things, which a blemish may invalidate,
neither the status of *hire* nor the status of *payment* fall on them,
birds, which blemishes do not invalidate,
does not reason dictate that neither *hire* nor *payment* should fall upon them?
Scripture teaches: *For any vow*, to include the bird.

5 All that are forbidden upon the altar,
their offspring are permissible.
The offspring of a *terefah*:
R. Eliezer[24] says:
It is not offered upon the altar.
But the Sages say:
It is offered.[25]
R. Hanina b. Antigonus says:
A valid animal that nurses from a *terefah*
is invalidated from [being offered] upon the altar.
All consecrated offerings that became *terefah*,
one does not redeem them,
for one does not redeem consecrated things to feed them to the dogs.

[24] **P**: "Eleazar." [25] **K, P, L** lack "But... offered."

logic might have dictated: The Mishnah explains why one might have excluded birds from the category of *hire* by analogy.

which a blemish may invalidate: A consecrated animal becomes ineligible for the altar if it contracts a blemish.

blemishes do not invalidate: By contrast, birds are eligible for the altar even if blemished. See Leviticus 22:19. Since the rules governing birds are less strict, surely they too should not become *hire* or *payment*?

For any vow: Deuteronomy 23:19. The word *any* is taken to expand the scope of the prohibitions of *hire* and *payment* given in the verse *to include the bird.*

6:5 *not offered upon the altar*: The debate about the validity of the offspring applies to all of the animals forbidden upon the altar, not only the torn animal. The Babylonian Talmud offers various rationales for R. Eliezer's position.

invalidated from [being offered] upon the altar: Because its substance derives from a torn animal, it is like its offspring, and hence, in accordance with R. Eliezer's view, disqualified.

to feed them to the dogs: Exodus 22:30 prohibits eating a torn animal, but allows one to throw it to the dogs. If a consecrated animal becomes torn, it may not be redeemed and turned into dog food; rather it is left to die.

Chapter Seven

7:1–3 *Offerings for the Altar and Offerings for Temple Upkeep*

7 There are rules that pertain to offerings for the altar
that do not pertain to offerings for Temple upkeep,
and there are rules that pertain to offerings for Temple upkeep
that do not pertain to offerings for the altar:
For offerings for the altar make a substitute;
and one may be liable on their account for *piggul*, remnant, and one who is impure;
their offspring and their milk are prohibited after redemption;
and one who slaughters them outside is culpable;
and one may not give from them to craftsmen as wages;
which is not case with offerings for Temple upkeep.[26]

2 There are rules that pertain to offerings for Temple upkeep
that do not pertain to offerings for the altar.[27]
For unspecified consecrations go to Temple upkeep;
consecration to Temple upkeep falls upon anything,
and one commits sacrilege through [misuse of] what grows from them;
and priests have no right of benefit from them.

[26] The last line is missing in **K**, **P**, **L**.

[27] **K**, **L** lack "that do not pertain...to the altar."

7:1 *to offerings for the altar*: For a similar list of characteristic features of sanctified things see *Hullin* 10:2.

piggul: "An offensive thing" (Leviticus 19:7). The flesh of a sacrifice whose slaughterer intended to perform a ritual act upon it after its statutory time.

remnant: Sacrificial meat left over beyond its permitted time. In both cases, the penalty is *karet*, or "extirpation," a divine punishment. See *Zevahim* introduction.

one who is impure: An impure person who eats sacrificial meat is similarly liable to *karet*.

their offspring...after redemption: Its milk, and offspring conceived while the animal was still sanctified, may not be consumed even if it gave birth after redemption.

outside: Outside the Temple courtyard.

culpable: Incurs the penalty of *karet*.

wages: For work done for the Temple.

7:2 *unspecified consecrations go to Temple upkeep*: The animal is sold to an individual who wishes to offer it as a sacrifice, and the proceeds from the sale go to Temple upkeep. See *Sheqalim* 4:7–8.

anything: Not merely animals or produce for sacrifice.

one commits sacrilege through [misuse of] what grows from them: For instance, use of the milk of an ass dedicated to Temple upkeep. The transgressor must compensate the Temple and make a guilt offering. Such use of altar offerings is prohibited but is not punishable as *sacrilege*. See *Me'ilah* 3:5.

no right of benefit: Whereas the priest who officiates over a sacrifice generally acquires some part of the carcass.

3 The law is one and the same
for offerings for the altar and offerings for Temple upkeep:
one may not change them from sanctity to sanctity,
and one consecrates them as a consecration of their value,
and one devotes them.
And if they die, they are buried.
R. Simeon says:
Offerings for Temple upkeep—
if they die, they are to be redeemed.

7:4–6 *Disposal of Animals of Consecrated Status*

4 And these are the ones that are to be buried:
Consecrated animals that have miscarried—they are to be buried.
If it miscarried an afterbirth, it is buried.
The ox that is to be stoned;
and the calf whose neck is broken;
and the birds of the one with *tsara'at*;

7:3 *from sanctity to sanctity*: e.g. from a whole burnt offering to an offering of well-being, in the case of offerings for the altar, or in the case of offerings for Temple upkeep, from maintenance of the sanctum to maintenance of the altar (Maimonides).

consecration of their value: One form of dedication is pledging the estimated value of a thing or person (see *Arakhin*). Here, the Mishnah permits one to consecrate the value of an offering that has already been consecrated. This is not necessarily the actual value of the animal; it might be the value that an owner derives from dedicating an animal offering or a priest derives from offering an animal on the altar. See *Arakhin* 8:7.

one devotes them: From *haram*, "ban" or "utterly dedicate" to the deity. Here, the dedicator must pay the priest the value of something already consecrated (as above).

buried... redeemed: The question is whether a carcass is eligible to be redeemed from the Temple for nonsacral use. The dispute may only arise in connection with animals offered for Temple upkeep. The anonymous view is that these are to be buried even if blemished, whereas for R. Simeon, the same rule applies to offerings for Temple upkeep as to offerings for the altar, so that the blemished animal is redeemed (Tosefta, Babylonian Talmud).

7:4 *that are to be buried*: Because one may not derive benefit from them. But one need not go so far as to burn them.

they: The fetuses.

an afterbirth: The placenta.

The ox... Temple Court: The listed offerings are also buried. The list also appears in *Qiddushin* 2:9; *Avodah Zarah* 5:9.

ox: For having killed a person, Exodus 21:28.

calf: In atonement for an unsolved murder, Deuteronomy 21:4.

birds: The two birds used in the leper's purification ritual, the first of which is slaughtered, and the second of which is dipped into the blood of the first, and set free (Leviticus 14:4–7). The prohibition against benefit arises once the first bird is slaughtered but extends to the second bird only if the latter dies before it is set free (commentators).

and the hair of the *nazir*;
and the firstborn of the ass;
and meat in milk;
and nonsacral things slaughtered in the Temple Court—
[all these are to be buried].
R. Simeon says:
Nonsacral things slaughtered in the Temple Court are to be burned,
and likewise a wild animal slaughtered in the Temple Court.

5 And these are the ones that are to be burned.
Leaven on Passover is to be burned,
and *terumah* that became impure;
and *orlah* and forbidden mixtures of the vineyard.
That which is ordinarily burned, is to be burned,
and that which is ordinarily buried, is to be buried.
And they may kindle [the fire] with the bread
and oil of [impure] *terumah*.

6 All consecrated offerings that were slaughtered
[with the intention of eating them or offering them]
beyond their time or beyond their place,
they are to be burned.
A guilt offering for uncertain sin is to be burned.

hair: A *nazir* who becomes ritually defiled before he completes the specified term must shave off his hair and begin the term again (Numbers 6:9). That hair must be buried. The hair that the *nazir* shaves off after completing his term is burned (Numbers 6:18), not buried.

firstborn of the ass: That died before being delivered (cf. Exodus 13:13). See *Bekhorot* 1:6.

slaughtered: Nonsacral slaughter, but in the Temple precincts.

are to be burned: Animals disqualified in the course of sacrifice must be burned (see 7:6). R. Simeon rules, that the same should be done with nonsacral animals that were slaughtered at the Temple, lest disqualified sacrifices be confused with them, and thus buried rather than burned.

a wild animal: Even though undomesticated animals are not eligible for the altar, so that the possibility of confusion described above does not obtain, R. Simeon nevertheless extends the same rule to them.

7:5 *orlah*: The fruit produced by a tree in the first three years, Leviticus 19:23. See *Orlah*, introduction.

forbidden mixtures of the vineyard: Deuteronomy 22:9, and see *Kilayim*, introduction.

That which... is to be buried: These two lines qualify the rule that *orlah* and forbidden mixtures of the vineyard are burned (Maimonides, Rashi). In that case, *that which is ordinarily burned* refers to solid food, and *that which is ordinarily buried* to liquids.

they may kindle... terumah: When the impure *terumah* is burned, the priest may derive benefit from its heat and light, for, unlike the other items in 7:5–6, impure *terumah* is subject only to a prohibition of consumption.

7:6 *beyond their time...place*: One intended, while slaughtering the animal, to offer its sacrificial parts outside the fixed time or place, or to eat of its meat outside the time or place fixed for consumption. Such intentions make the carcass *piggul* (see 7:1 and *Zevahim*, introduction).

A guilt offering for uncertain sin: Offered when an individual is uncertain whether he sinned in such a way as to be liable for a purgation offering.

R. Judah says:
It is to be buried.
A bird purgation offering that is occasioned by doubt is to be burned.
R. Judah says:
He casts it into the channel.
All things that are to be burned are not to be buried,
and all things that are to be buried are not to be burned.
R. Judah says:
If one wishes to be stringent upon oneself
and to burn things that are to be buried,
he is allowed.
They said to him:
One is not permitted to vary.

is to be burned: If the offerer discovered that he had not so sinned before the blood was sprinkled on the altar. See *Keritot* 6:1.

is to be buried: Like nonsacral things slaughtered in the Temple Court (7:4).

A bird purgation offering that is occasioned by doubt: Offered when e.g. a woman is uncertain whether the fetus that she miscarried qualifies as "human," and thus whether she is liable for the purgation offering that ordinarily follows upon a birth.

is to be burned: The priest may not eat of it, because it is offered in doubt.

the channel: Of water that runs through the Temple Court and out into the Kidron valley, *Middot* 3:2–3. Disposal of the bird in this manner constitutes burial.

Tractate Keritot

Moulie Vidas

Introduction

Overview

The word *keritot* (sometimes vocalized *karetot*) is the plural of *karet*, usually translated extirpation, a divinely inflicted punishment that is invoked frequently in the priestly material of the Torah for the knowing transgression of the Torah's laws, mostly prohibitions. (The rabbis understood the punishment as premature death at the hands of heaven, see annotation to 1:1.)

Structure and Organization of the Tractate

Tractate *Keritot* discusses the liability of individuals in certain circumstances to bring purgation (*hattat*) or guilt (*asham*) offerings, especially the offering for uncertain guilt (*asham talui*, lit. "suspended *asham*"). Those who intentionally commit any of the grave transgressions listed in chapter 1 of the mishnah are punished with *karet*. If they commit the transgression unintentionally, they atone for their misdeed with a purgation offering; if they are uncertain whether or not they committed the transgression, they offer an *asham* for uncertain guilt.

Chapter 2 lists other circumstances that result in liability for such offerings: male and female sexual discharges, *tsara'at* (usually translated leprosy), childbirth, and miscarriage. In other cases, such as intercourse with a slave woman who was already promised to another man, a guilt offering is required, even if the sin was committed purposely (Leviticus 19:20–22).

The rest of the tractate explores the consequences of uncertain transgression, with only occasional interest in purgation or guilt offerings not connected with such transgressions. Chapter 3 concerns the conjunction of multiple inadvertent transgressions; chapters 4 and 5 are interested in uncertainty regarding transgressions and include debates on the degree of consciousness that separates inadvertence from uncertainty, and on the uncertainty that is created when one of two individuals has committed a transgression but it is not clear which one. The final chapter addresses offerings affected by new information, for example, if it was discovered that the transgression for which an offering was brought did not in fact take place.

The tractate is enriched by occasional excurses and by blocks of material that seem to have been composed independently and incorporated in our tractate. These include a lengthy discussion of the postpartum offering in chapter 1, a series of exchanges between R. Aqiva and his teachers in chapter 3, and a unit about the consumption of blood at the start of chapter 5.

Main Ideas

An intense interest in the consciousness of the inadvertent transgressor drives some of the tractate's most striking ideas. One passage questions whether lack of intention can be established by testimony of eyewitnesses (3:1). Another discusses R. Joshua's position that even if one knew for certain that he committed a transgression, he is not liable to bring an offering unless he knows exactly the nature of that transgression (4:2–3). The last chapter details how new awareness may change the status of the offering after it was already brought to the Temple (6:1–2).

Another consistent interest is the performance of multiple acts each of which requires an offering. Multiple events which impart impurity may join together, if they happened within a certain window of time, so that only a single offering is required (1:6–7, 2:3–4). In the case of inadvertent transgressions, this interest is connected with the interest in consciousness: the transgressor may bring a single offering for multiple instances of the same transgression as long as they were done in a single spell of unawareness; but if there was awareness of the transgression before the second instance, a second offering is required (3:2–3; 4:2). The question of combining instances of transgression to reduce liability also raises the issue of how different transgressions are categorized (3:2, 6, 4:3).

Relationship to Scripture

The liability of inadvertent transgressors to bring a purgation offering is treated in the Torah (Numbers 15, Leviticus 4), but it is configured quite differently by the rabbis. Most importantly, while the biblical passages refer to transgression of the commandments in general, the rabbis read them as applying only to a specific set of transgressions. According to Numbers 15:22–31, those who transgress the commandments inadvertently may atone for their sins with an offering, while those who transgress knowingly are to be punished by God with *karet* (they are to be "cut off"). But while this passage speaks of the commandments in general, other Torah passages seem to limit the extirpation punishment to the violation of specific transgressions. Following this line of thought the rabbis chose to see this punishment as applying only in specific cases; they interpreted Numbers 15:22–31 to refer to one transgression in particular, idolatry, but they also retained that passage's distinction between the purgation offering for unintentional transgression and the extirpation punishment for intentional transgression. Leviticus 4 was now understood to refer only to transgressions that are punished with extirpation.

Throughout our tractate, the Mishnah uses the consumption of forbidden fat (*helev* in Hebrew) as the archetypal transgression, perhaps because the prohibition of eating forbidden fat is mentioned, along with the consumption of blood, immediately before the discussion of the purgation offering brought on account of inadvertent transgression (Leviticus 3:17). Our tractate is aware that not all purgation offerings are brought on account of transgression (compare especially 5:8 and 1:4). Nevertheless, the tractate is clearly more interested in purgation offerings that are connected with transgressions than in those which are not, but it does not have a rigorous terminological differentiation between the two.

Special Notes for the Reader

I have consulted Yoav Rosenthal's PhD thesis on the versions of the tractate (Hebrew University of Jerusalem, 2003).

Tractate Keritot

Chapter One

1:1–2 *The Punishment of Karet*

I Thirty-six transgressors are punished with *karet*[1] in the Torah:
(1) one who has intercourse with his mother,
or (2) with his father's wife,
or (3) with his daughter-in-law;
(4) one who has intercourse with a male
or (5) with an animal;
or (6) a woman who causes an animal to have intercourse with her;
(7) one who has intercourse with a woman and her daughter
or (8) with a married woman;

[1] Lit. "thirty-six extirpations."

1:1 *karet*: The punishment of "being cut off." Neither the Bible nor the Mishnah clarify the nature of this punishment. The rabbis understood it to be a punishment inflicted by God rather than by humans (see *Megillah* 1:5) and as entailing some kind of destruction, perhaps premature death, or the cessation of one's line or the lack of afterlife.

The list groups sexual transgressions first, then all other transgressions. Within each group, transgressions are ranked according to the court-inflicted penalty to which transgressors are liable. According to the commentators, the transgressors listed in the Mishnah are punished with *karet* if they transgress intentionally (see 1:2) and if they were not forewarned by witnesses of the penalty for their transgression; if they were forewarned by witnesses of the penalty for their transgression, the transgressors are punished corporeally, whether by the court-inflicted thirty-nine lashes (see *Makkot*) or by a court-inflicted death penalty. See the parallel lists of transgressions (and punishments) at *Sanhedrin* 7:4 and *Makkot* 3:1–2.

his mother: Leviticus 18:7.

father's wife: Leviticus 18:8.

daughter-in-law: Leviticus 18:15. The penalty for all of these is stoning, *Sanhedrin* 7:4. Leviticus 18:29 specifies *karet* for all the violations in chapter 18.

with a male: Leviticus 18:22.

an animal…and the woman who causes: Leviticus 18:23. They are to be stoned (*Sanhedrin* 7:4) but are grouped separately because they concern sexual unions not between a man and a woman.

with a woman and her daughter: Leviticus 18:17; the penalty is burning, *Sanhedrin* 9:1.

a married woman: Leviticus 20:10; the penalty is strangulation, *Sanhedrin* 11:1. Perhaps grouped with *a woman and her daughter* because each is the only sexual transgression in the list with their respective penalties. Or perhaps originally the penalty for intercourse with a married woman was burning.

(9) one who has intercourse with his sister,
or (10) with his father's sister,
or (11) with his mother's sister,
or (12) with his wife's sister,
or (13) with his brother's wife,
or (14) with his father's brother's wife,
or (15) with a menstruant;
(16) one who blasphemes,
or (17) one who worships idolatry,
or (18) one who gives of his progeny to Molekh;
or (19) one who is a necromancer;[2]
(20) one who profanes the Sabbath,
or (21) an impure person who eats consecrated food,
or (22) one who enters the Temple while impure;
(23) one who eats forbidden fat or (24) blood, (25) remnant, or (26) *piggul*;
(27) one who slaughters or (28) offers up a sacrifice outside [the Temple];
(29) one who eats leaven during Passover;

[2] Lit. "One who possesses an *ov*." **K**: "One who possesses an *ov* and *yid'oni*."

with his sister: Leviticus 18:9, 20:17.

father's sister: Leviticus 18:12.

mother's sister: Leviticus 18:13.

wife's sister: Leviticus 18:18.

brother's wife: Leviticus 18:16.

menstruant: Leviticus 18:19. The penalty for (9) through (15) is lashing, *Makkot* 3:1.

blasphemes: See Leviticus 24:16–17; cf. Numbers 15:30.

idolatry: Numbers 15:31.

Molekh: Leviticus 18:21.

necromancer: Leviticus 20:6. For "*ov* and *yid'oni*" (n. 2), see Leviticus 19:13 and *Sanhedrin* 7:4; see also *Sanhedrin* 7:7.

Sabbath: Exodus 31:14. The penalty for (16) through (20) is stoning; see *Sanhedrin* 7:4.

impure person who eats consecrated food: Leviticus 22:3. This and the remaining transgressions are punished with lashing (*Makkot* 3:2).

enters the Temple: Leviticus 12:4.

forbidden fat: Heb. *helev*. Fatty parts of the animal that are sacrificed on the altar (see Leviticus 3:1; 7:25). It is prohibited even in unconsecrated animals. Extirpation is mentioned at Leviticus 7:25.

blood: See 5:1; *karet* is specified in Leviticus 7:27.

remnant: What remains of the offering after the time specified for eating. It is to be burned; eating it is punished by *karet* (Leviticus 19:8).

piggul: Offerings that were made with the intention to eat or handle them after the prescribed time; see *Zevahim* 2:3, 5. The rabbis derive this from Leviticus 7:18. *Karet* is supported by the similarity of the formulation between the punishment for *piggul* and for remnant.

slaughters…outside [the Temple]: Leviticus 17:3–4, 8–9.

leaven during Passover: Exodus 12:15.

or (30) one who eats or (31) performs labor on the Day of Atonement;
(32) one who compounds the oil, or (33) one who compounds the incense,
or (34) one who anoints with the oil of anointment;
the (35) Passover offering and (36) circumcision are cases of positive commandments.
2 For these, one is liable to *karet* in the case of an intentional transgression;
to a purgation offering in the case of an unintentional transgression;
and to an indefinite guilt offering in the case of transgression with nonknowledge,
except for one who impurifies the Temple and its sacred offerings,
as he is liable to an offering of varying value—
the words of R. Meir.
But the Sages say:
the blasphemer too,
as it is said: *You shall have the same law for anyone who acts in error.*
Excluded is the blasphemer, who does not perform an action.

1:3–7 *The Purgation Offerings of Women after Birth or Miscarriage*

3 There are women who bring a purgation offering[3] and it is eaten,
and there are women who bring a purgation offering and it is not eaten,

[3] Here and throughout, "purgation offering" is supplied where only "bring" appears.

Day of Atonement: Leviticus 23:29–30.

compounds the oil: Exodus 30:22–31, 33.

compounds the incense: Exodus 30:34–38.

anoints: Exodus 30:33.

Passover offering: Numbers 9:13.

circumcision: Genesis 17:14.

positive commandments: In the final two transgressions, *karet* is the punishment for failing to perform an obligation; all the others are punishments for transgressing a prohibition.

1:2 *in the case of an intentional transgression*: See introduction.

purgation offering: Based on Numbers 15:27.

nonknowledge: Leviticus 5:17.

impurifies the Temple: Entering the Temple or eating consecrated food while impure (see above). The rabbis understand Leviticus 5:2–3 to refer to this violation. The biblical rule is among those for which one brings *an offering of varying value*, according to the financial ability of the person liable to bring it (Leviticus 5:7–13). For other cases of offerings of varying value, see 2:4.

the blasphemer is excepted from this liability to bring a purgation offering or an offering for indefinite guilt.

You shall have: Numbers 15:29.

does not perform an action, but rather transgresses through speech.

1:3 *women* who have given birth or miscarried bring a purgation offering that is eaten by priests (as well as a whole burnt offering, not eaten by priests); Leviticus 12:6.

and it is eaten, if there was certainly a birth or a miscarriage. *It is not eaten*, in uncertain cases. Although the offering is still required, the meat is burned (*Temurah* 6:6).

and there are women who do not bring a purgation offering.
These women bring a purgation offering and it is eaten:
one who has miscarried something that resembles
a domestic animal, a wild animal, or a bird—
the words of R. Meir;
but the Sages say:
Not unless it resembles a human form.
One who has miscarried [something that looks like] a sandal,
or a placenta, or an articulated[4] amniotic sac,
or the fetus emerges cut into pieces.
And so too a female slave who has miscarried
brings a purgation offering that is eaten.

4 These bring a purgation offering and it is not eaten:
One who has miscarried,
but what she has miscarried is not known;
and so too two women who have miscarried,
one something of an exempted kind,
and the other something of an obligated kind.
R. Yose said:
In what case? When they have gone one eastward and one westward;
but if both stand as one[5]
they bring a [single] purgation offering, and it is eaten.

5 These do not bring a purgation offering:
one who has miscarried an amniotic sac
full of water,
full of blood,
full of variegated pieces;
one who has miscarried something that resembles
fish, locusts, vermin, or creeping things;
one who has miscarried on the fortieth day;
and the one born through the side.
R. Simeon deems liable in the case of born through the side.

[4] Or "developed," "textured," "formed."

[5] **K**, **P** lack "As one."

do not bring, if it is certain that the discharge was not because of a failed pregnancy. See also *Niddah* 3:1–7.

One who has miscarried: Paralleled by *Bekhorot* 8:1.

articulated amniotic sac: Containing a fetus with discernible body parts (Tosefta *Niddah*).

1:4 *not known*, whether it is a miscarriage that requires a sacrifice (1:3) or not (1:5).

two women: Since it is not known which woman is actually obligated, both sacrifices are brought for uncertain miscarriage and neither is eaten.

if both stand as one: If they are both present, they may share an offering and stipulate between them that it should be offered for the one who had the liable miscarriage. For similar cases, see 5:4–8.

1:5 *fortieth day* of the pregnancy or before. The rabbis believed a fetus is not yet formed at this stage (*Niddah* 3:7).

through the side: Usually explained as referring to birth by caesarean section. If so, this is an unusual ancient reference to the survival of the mother after caesarean section.

6 One who has miscarried on the night preceding[6] the eighty-first day—
the House of Shammai exempt her from the offering;
the House of Hillel declare her liable.
Said the House of Hillel to the House of Shammai:
How does the night preceding the eighty-first day differ
from daytime of the eighty-first day?
If it is equivalent with respect to impurity,
should it not be the same with respect to the offering?
Said to them the House of Shammai:
No.
If you said concerning one who has miscarried during daytime of the eighty-first [that she is liable],
for indeed she has come out[7] at a time that is appropriate for bringing an offering,
shall you say the same concerning one
who has miscarried on the night preceding the eighty-first,
where she has not come out[8] at a time that is appropriate for bringing an offering?
Said to them the House of Hillel:
Let the case of one who has miscarried on the eighty-first day
that fell on a Sabbath prove it,
for she has not come out[9] at a time that is appropriate for bringing an offering,
but she is liable to an offering.

[6] Here and below, lit. "light." [7] **K**, **P**: "he [the later discharge] has come out."
[8] **K**, **P**: "he [the later discharge] has not come out."
[9] **K**, **P**: "he [the later discharge] has not come out."

1:6 For this dispute between the Houses of Shammai and Hillel see also *Eduyot* 4:10.

night preceding: Lit. "light" (see *Pesahim* 1:1). After the sunset ending the eightieth day and before sunrise on the eighty-first.

eighty-first day: The case is as follows. A woman gives birth to or miscarries a female; she is now obligated to bring an offering on or after the eighty-first day after the birth (Leviticus 12). However, on the evening of the eighty-first day she miscarries again. The question debated by the Houses is whether at this point she is required to bring two offerings or just one. Had she miscarried before the eighty-first day the two Houses agree that one offering would suffice.

How does the night... differ from daytime? Both belong to the same day, and the House of Shammai too will certainly hold her liable to bring an offering if she miscarried on the eighty-first during the day.

with respect to impurity: For fourteen days after the birth of a female, the mother is impure. From the fifteenth to the end of the eightieth day, the period of "blood of purification" (Leviticus 12:4–5), vaginal blood is not considered menstrual and she does not contract menstrual impurity. On the eighty-first day her vaginal blood does make her impure.

she has come out: She has left the period connected with her prior pregnancy. The reading of **K**, **P**, referring to the discharged fetus (see n. 7), is preferable.

Sabbath: Individual sacrifices without fixed times are not offered on the Sabbath (see *Temurah* 2:1), yet it is agreed that the woman who miscarries on an eighty-first day that falls on the Sabbath is liable for a new sacrifice.

is appropriate for a communal offering: As public offerings override the Sabbath (*Temurah* 2:1), but they are not offered at night; the analogy proposed by the House of Hillel is therefore invalid.

Said to them the House of Shammai:
No. If you said concerning one who has miscarried on the eighty-first day
that fell on a Sabbath
[that she is liable],
for even though it is not appropriate for an individual offering
it is appropriate for a communal offering,
can you say the same concerning one who miscarried on the night of the eighty-first,
for the night is not appropriate for either an individual offering or a communal offering?
The blood[10] cannot prove it,
for she who has miscarried within the period of "completion,"
her blood is impure, but she is exempt from the offering.

7 A woman who is liable for five uncertain *zivah* flows
or five uncertain births
brings one offering and [afterward] may eat from sacrifices,
and the remaining offerings are not obligatory for her.
Five definite births, or five definite *zivah* flows
brings one offering and [afterward] may eat from sacrifices,
and the remaining offerings are obligatory for her.
It once happened in Jerusalem that nests stood at golden *denarii.*
Rabban Simeon b. Gamaliel said:
By this Dwelling! I will not sleep tonight, until they will be standing at [silver] *denarii.*
He entered the court and taught:

[10] Here and below, lit. "bloods."

The blood cannot prove it: This continues the House of Shammai's response, answering specifically the argument that just as nighttime and daytime of the eighty-first are treated identically with respect to the woman's impurity (her "blood"), so they should be treated identically with respect to the offering.

within the period of "completion": The phraseology derives from Leviticus 12:3.

her blood is impure, since she begins a new cycle of impurity and purity with respect to miscarriage.

1:7 *zivah flows*: A woman who discharges blood beyond her period of menstruation must wait for the discharge to stop, then count seven days in which no blood is seen and finally bring two birds as a purgation offering and a whole burnt offering (Leviticus 15:25–30); before she brings the offering she is not allowed to eat sacrificial meats (below, 2:1). The woman in our case had five uncertain instances of such discharge: in each case she was not sure if she saw the blood for three consecutive days after her menstruation ended.

uncertain births: Discharges of the type detailed above, 1:4.

one offering: One purgation offering and one whole burnt offering, rather than five of each, are sufficient to render her purification complete.

in Jerusalem: Before the destruction of the Temple.

nests: Pairs of turtle doves or pigeons, as required for bird offerings (Leviticus 12:6, 15:25–29.). See *Qinnim* introduction. A *golden dinar* is worth twenty five regular (silver) dinar.

By this Dwelling: An oath formula. Below, 6:3.

and taught a more lenient version of the law according to which a single offering suffices even for multiple definite cases, reducing the demand for such offerings.

A woman who is liable for five definite births or five definite *zivah* flows
brings one offering and [afterward] may eat from sacrifices,
and the remaining offerings are not obligatory for her.
And on that very day, nests stood at quarters.

Chapter Two

2:1–4 *Fours and Fives*

2 There are four whose expiation is incomplete,
and four who bring an offering for an intentional transgression
as for an unintentional transgression.
The expiation of these is incomplete:
(1) the *zav*,
(2) the *zavah*,
(3) the woman who has given birth, and
(4) one with *tsara'at*.
R. Eliezer b. Jacob says:
The convert is one whose expiation is incomplete until the blood is sprinkled for him;
and a *nazir*—
with respect to his wine, his shaving, and his contracting impurity.
2 These bring an offering for an intentional transgression
as for an unintentional transgression:
(1) one who had sexual intercourse with a slave woman;
(2) a *nazir* who contracted impurity;
(3) for an oath concerning a testimony;

2:1 *four whose expiation is incomplete*: Until they bring a sacrifice, they may not eat sacrificial meat. *Hagigah* 3:3 also requires immersion. See also *Kelim* 1:5 and *Nega'im* 14:3.

zav...*zavah*: See Leviticus 15; above 1:7; and introduction to *Zavim*.

has given birth: See above, 1:3.

tsara'at: Leviticus 14:10–32. See *Nega'im*, introduction.

The convert is one whose expiation: Proselytes were required to make an offering after their conversion before they could eat sacrificial meals.

nazir: See *Nazir*, introduction.

2:2 *a slave woman*: Intercourse with a slave woman who was already promised to another; see Leviticus 19:20–22 and below, 2:4–6.

nazir who contracted impurity: See Numbers 6:9–12.

oath concerning a testimony: One swears falsely that he has no testimony to offer in a particular case, Leviticus 5:1 and *Shevu'ot* 4:2–3.

(4) and for an oath concerning a deposit.
3 There are five who bring one offering for many transgressions,
and five who bring an offering of varying value.
These bring one offering for many transgressions:
(1) one who had sexual intercourses with a slave woman on many occasions;[11]
(2) a *nazir* who contracted impurity on many occasions;
(3) one who warns his wife about committing adultery[12] with many men;
and (4) one with *tsara'at* who has been afflicted with many afflictions—
if he brought his birds and became afflicted,[13]
they are[14] not effective until he brings his purgation offering;
R. Judah says:
Until he brings his guilt offering.
4 (5) A woman who gave birth to many births—
if she miscarried a female within eighty days,
and then again miscarried a female within eighty days,
or if she miscarried twins.
R. Judah says:
She brings an offering for the first, but not for the second;
she brings an offering for the third, but not for the fourth.
These bring an offering of varying value:
(1) for *hearing the adjuration*;

[11] Lit.: "many intercourses." [12] Lit. "one who is jealous of his wife."
[13] **K, P** repeat "he brought his birds and became afflicted." [14] **K, P**: "It is."

oath concerning a deposit: One swears falsely that he does not have a deposit in his possession, *Shevu'ot* 5:1–2.

2:3 *transgressions*: Used loosely in the sense of actions that result in an obligation to bring an offering.

varying value: See annotation to 1:2.

warns his wife not to be alone with another man, making her liable to the *sotah* procedure laid out in Numbers 5:11–31 (see *Sotah*). For suspicions about multiple men the husband brings only a single offering.

birds: Required for purification, Leviticus 14:4.

are not effective: Although the priest declares that the affliction has been healed before the bird sacrifice is brought (Leviticus 14:3), the official end of the affliction is the purgation offering (Leviticus 14:19). A new outbreak before the purgation offering does not require additional offerings, and only the bird offerings at the end of the entire process will effect purification.

his guilt offering, which is brought before the purgation offering (Leviticus 14:12).

2:4 *a female within eighty days*, after the birth or miscarriage of a female. The rule would be the same had the second fetus been male. However, miscarriage of a female allows consideration of third and fourth miscarriages within eighty days. The post-partum period for a male is only forty days, so a new miscarriage within this period would be less than forty days and not require an offering at all (see 1:5).

for the third: R. Judah holds a woman liable to bring an offering for a third fetus since it is outside the eighty-day period of the first.

offering of varying value: See 1:2 and 2:3.

hearing the adjuration: See 2:2 above and Leviticus 5:1.

(2) for *uttering with the lips*;
(3) for impurifying the Temple or its sacred offerings;
(4) a woman who has given birth;
(5) and one with *tsara'at*.

2:4 cont.–6 *Sexual Transgressions*

And what is the difference between [intercourse with] a slave woman
and all the other sexual transgressions?
For she is not like them,
not with respect to punishment nor with respect to offering.
For all the other sexual transgressions require a purgation offering,
but the slave woman a guilt offering;
all the other sexual transgressions require a female offering,
but the slave woman a male;[15]
all the other sexual transgressions,
the man and the woman are equal with respect to lashing and offering,
but in the case of the slave woman,
[Scripture] did not equate the man to the woman with respect to lashing,
nor did it equate the woman to the man with respect to offering;
all the other sexual transgressions,
[Scripture] equated the penetrator with the finisher,
and one is liable for each and every act of intercourse.
This is a stringency that [Scripture] stipulated in the case of the slave woman,
that it equated the intentional with the unintentional.

[15] Absent in **K**, **P**.

uttering with the lips: Leviticus 5:4.

for impurifying the Temple: Leviticus 5:2; see above, 1:2.

given birth: Leviticus 12:8.

one with tsara'at: Leviticus 14:21–32.

a guilt offering: Leviticus 19:21.

slave woman: Leviticus 19:20–22.

equal with respect to lashing for intentional transgression, *and to* purgation *offering* if unintentional.

did not equate: Women alone are liable to lashing; men alone bring an offering.

the finisher: But a betrothed slave woman incurs liability only if the man ejaculated.

for each and every act of intercourse: However, multiple acts of intercourse by the betrothed slave woman results in liability for only a single offering, see above 2:3.

stringency: In the final distinction the case of the slave woman is more stringent.

equated the intentional: See above, 2:2.

5 What is a *slave woman*?
Anyone who is partly slave and partly free,
as it is said: *And redeemed she was not redeemed*—
the words of R. Aqiva.
R. Ishmael says:
This is a definite slave.
R. Eleazar b. Azariah says:
All sexual transgressions are stated explicitly, and what is left?[16]
The only one that we have is she that is partly slave and partly free.

6 All sexual transgressions—
if one was an adult and one was a minor—the minor is exempt;
one was awake, and the other was asleep—the one who was asleep is exempt;
one was unintentional and one was intentional—
the unintentional one [atones] with a purgation offering,
and the intentional one [atones] with *karet*.

Chapter Three

3:1 *Liability for Unintentional Transgressions*

3 If they said to him: "You have eaten forbidden fat,"
he must bring a purgation offering.
If a witness says: "He has eaten," and a witness says: "He has not eaten,"
if a woman says: "He has eaten," and a woman says: "He has not eaten,"
he must bring an offering for uncertain guilt.

[16] **K, P**: "All sexual transgressions that are stated from what remains."

2:5 *partly slave and partly free*: The Torah's law of the betrothed slave woman (Leviticus 19:20) applies only if the woman was partly slave and partly free: if she is fully a slave, her betrothal is not valid. Traditional commentators have offered various scenarios to explain how this could arise. Intercourse between a slave woman and an Israelite man is prohibited (*Qiddushin* 4:1).

And redeemed she was not redeemed: Leviticus 19:20. The midrash depends on the duplication of the verb. R. Aqiva understands the verse to be saying that the slave woman was redeemed and at the same time not redeemed.

R. Ishmael rules that the law refers to a fully enslaved woman. Parallel versions of this passage address the problem of how a slave woman can be in a legally binding betrothal.

R. Eleazar b. Azariah agrees with R. Aqiva's definition of the slave woman. The first part of his statement is difficult to parse and has several versions and interpretations. Possibly, R. Eleazar holds that the stipulation that the woman be half-freed is only learned through tradition, not explicitly from Scripture (thus Albeck). Alternatively, perhaps he is saying that all other forbidden relationships have been specified, except for one about a woman who is partially a slave, and therefore this passage must refer to that situation.

3:1 *forbidden fat*: See comment on 1:1.

an offering for uncertain guilt: It is an uncertain case of an unintentional transgression.

If a witness says: "He has eaten," but he says: "I have not eaten,"
he is exempt.
If two say: "He has eaten," and he says: "I have not eaten,"
R. Meir deems him liable.
Said R. Meir:
If two could bring him to the penalty of death, which is grave,
should they not lead him to the offering, which is light?
They said to him:
What if he should choose to say, "I transgressed intentionally"?

3:2–6 *Multiple Transgressions and Punishments*

2 If he ate forbidden fat and [again] forbidden fat in a single spell of unawareness,
he is liable to bring only one purgation offering.
If he ate forbidden fat and blood, and remnant, and *piggul*
in a single spell of unawareness,
he is liable for each and every one of them.
This stringency applies to many kinds but not to a single kind;
but the following[17] is a stringency that applies to a single kind and not to many kinds,
that if he has eaten a half-olive's bulk and then again another half-olive's bulk:
of a single kind, he is liable;
of two kinds, he is exempt.

[17] Lit. "this."

exempt from any offering. Unlike the preceding case, here, the person contradicts the allegation of a single witness.

R. Meir deems him liable for a purgation offering, but the Sages declare him exempt.

death: The testimony of two witnesses suffices to convict a person of an offense whose punishment is death.

if he should choose to say: If he should say that he transgressed intentionally, he would be exempted from the offering despite the testimony of witnesses, since an intentional consumption of *forbidden fat* is punishable by *karet*. As the court would be compelled to accept his words and exempt him in that case, there is no reason not to accept his words, absolving him of the liability to bring an offering, when he claims he has not eaten at all.

3:2 *in a single spell of unawareness*: He did not realize, or forgot, that forbidden fat is prohibited, or that what he ate was in fact forbidden fat and did so repeatedly without realizing his transgression.

only one purgation offering: Both consumptions count as a single transgression, since there was only a single inadvertence. For the same principle, see *Shabbat* 7:1.

forbidden fat and blood: That is, any combination of two or more kinds of prohibited parts.

for each and every one: Eating each kind is considered a separate transgression.

single kind: Although neither of the pieces alone was of the required minimal bulk, in this case they combine to make him liable.

two kinds do not combine to make the eater liable.

3 And how long may the eater take
[before the two half-olives are not deemed to be two halves of a single thing]?
As if he were eating them as parched grains—
the words of R. Meir;
but the Sages say:
Only if he takes from beginning to end as long as it takes to eat half a loaf.
If he ate impure foods, or drank impure liquids, or drank a quarter-log of wine
and then entered the Temple, and he took time,
[he is liable] as long as it takes to eat half a loaf.
R. Eleazar says:
If he paused, or if he put any water into it, he is exempt.
4 There is one who in a single act of eating[18] might be liable on its account
for four purgation offerings and one guilt offering:
(1) an impure person ate (2) forbidden fat,
and it was (3) a remnant of sacred offerings,
and it was (4) on the Day of Atonement.
R. Meir says:
If it was Sabbath and he transported it with his mouth,
he is liable.[19]
They said to him:
It is not of the same category.

[18] Lit. "who eats a single eating."

[19] **K, P**: "If it was Sabbath and he transported it on the Sabbath."

3:3 *How long?* What amount of time can there be between the two acts of eating, where the eater still be liable?

as parched grains: Without a real pause between them: even though each parched grain is its own unit, one consumes many grains continuously without significant pause, bit by bit. For R. Meir the pieces of prohibited food only join if they are consumed in the same manner, continuously.

half a loaf: If he takes longer, then the two pieces do not join together. "The amount of time it takes to eat half a loaf" is a standard brief amount of time; see *Nega'im* 13:9–10.

ate impure foods, prohibiting him from consuming consecrated food. See *Me'ilah* 4:5.

a quarter-log of wine: Priests are prohibited from drinking before they enter to serve; see Leviticus 9:10.

as long as it takes: In all these cases, small amounts of food or drink combine to make up the minimum amount as long as all the consumption of all the pieces took less time than it would take to eat half a loaf.

R. Eleazar refers specifically to a priest drinking wine.

3:4 *four purgation offerings*: For unintentional consumption of sacrificial meat in a state of impurity; *forbidden fat*; the consumption of *remnant*; and consumption on the Day of Atonement. The *guilt offering* is for the sacrilege of unintentionally deriving benefit from the Holy (Leviticus 5:15).

transported it: Lit. "took it out," the technical expression for removing something on the Sabbath from one domain to another (see *Shabbat* 1:1), in this case by holding it in his mouth while eating.

liable: To a fifth and sixth purgation offering for unintentionally transporting on the Sabbath (in addition to transporting on the Day of Atonement).

not of the same category: This last transgression is on account of transporting, while the first four are on account of eating. For a similar exchange, see *Makkot* 3:9.

5 There is one who has intercourse a single time
and might be liable on its account for six purgation offerings.
One who has intercourse with his daughter might be liable on account of
(1) his daughter,
(2) his sister,
(3) the wife of his brother,
(4) the wife of his father's brother,
(5) a married woman, and
(6) a menstruant.
One who has intercourse with his daughter's daughter might be liable on account of
his daughter's daughter,
his daughter-in-law,
his wife's sister,
his brother's wife,
his father's brother's wife,
a married woman,
and a menstruant.
R. Yose says:
If the old man transgressed and married her,
he is liable on account of his father's wife.
And so too the one who had intercourse with his wife's daughter
and his wife's daughter's daughter.
6 One who has intercourse with his mother-in-law might be liable on account of
his mother-in-law,

3:5–6 All these are cases of unintentional transgression. The Mishnah loves brain-teasers of this sort; cf. *Makkot* 3:9.

3:5 *his daughter*: In the case imagined here, the daughter was also the man's sister (from incestuous intercourse between him and his mother), who had married the man's paternal brother and upon being widowed became wife of the man's father's brother. The man is also liable for intercourse with the wife of another man (his father's brother) and, if she was menstruating, intercourse with a menstruant.

his daughter's daughter: In this case, the granddaughter was also the man's daughter-in-law (married to his son, her mother's brother, which is a valid union); his wife's sister (the grandfather married the daughter of his granddaughter's father from another marriage, and the granddaughter was thus also the half-sister of his wife); his brother's wife (the granddaughter married the man's brother upon being widowed from his son); and his father's brother's wife (her third and last husband). Again, the man is liable for intercourse with the wife of another man (his father's brother) and because she was menstruating. This case results in seven, rather than six, offerings.

If the old man the great-grandfather *transgressed and married her*: If the father of the man from the case just described married his great-granddaughter, the woman from the case just described; the marriage is prohibited but valid.

he is liable: The man who had intercourse with his granddaughter is now also liable to bring an offering for having intercourse with his father's wife.

so too: The same number of transgressions and sacrifices result where the daughter or granddaughter in question is not his, but his wife's.

3:6 *his mother-in-law*, who was also his daughter-in-law (married to his son from another woman), his wife's sister (sister of one of his wives), and as in the preceding cases, had been married to his brother's wife and was currently married to his father's brother's wife.

his daughter-in-law,
his wife's sister,
his brother's wife,
his father's brother's wife,
a married woman,
and a menstruant.
And so too one who had intercourse with his mother-in-law's mother
and his father-in-law's mother.
R. Yohanan b. Nuri says:
One who had intercourse with his mother-in-law might be liable on account of
his mother-in-law,
his mother-in-law's mother,
and his father-in-law's mother.
They said to him:
These three are a single category.

3:7–10 *R. Aqiva and His Teachers on Deducing the Law*

7 R. Aqiva said:
I asked Rabban Gamaliel and R. Joshua in the market of Emmaus,
for they had gone there to buy an animal
for the wedding feast of Rabban Gamaliel's[20] son:
One who had intercourse with his sister, and his father's sister, and his mother's sister,
in a single spell of unawareness—
what is the law?
Is he liable to bring one purgation offering for all of them
or one for each and every one?
They said to me:

[20] **K**, **P** lack "Rabban Gamaliel's."

R. Yohanan b. Nuri offers the case of a man who had three wives: a woman, a daughter of her sister, and a daughter of her brother. Therefore his mother-in-law is also the mother of his mother-in-law and the mother of his father-in-law.

They said to him: They are all considered part of the same prohibition (Leviticus 18:17) and therefore the person in question is only liable to bring a single offering.

3:7–10 A series of exchanges between R. Aqiva and his masters. Most deal with the question of multiple transgressions; one deals with an instance of unawareness. They also demonstrate how new laws were derived from existing traditions.

3:7 *Rabban Gamaliel's son*: According to the manuscript reading, the wedding feast might have been that of the son of R. Aqiva.

One who had intercourse: The Talmud interprets this to be about a single woman who is related to this person in all three ways.

one purgation offering: All fall under the same category, as in the Sages' view in the immediately preceding case (3:6).

We have not heard [a tradition concerning this matter],
but we have heard concerning one who,
in a single spell of unawareness,
had intercourse with his five menstruating wives,
that he is liable for each and every one;
and we deem these [two] matters to be a lesser and greater.

8 And R. Aqiva asked them further:[21]
A limb dangling from an animal—what is the law?
They said to him:
We have not heard [a tradition concerning this matter].
But we have heard concerning a limb dangling from a person,
that it is pure;
for this is what those afflicted with boils in Jerusalem used to do:
one would go to a physician on the eve of Passover,
and he would cut it and leave it [connected] by skin the size of a grain of barley,
and stick it on a thorn,
and it would be pulled away from him.
And this one would bring his Passover offering,
and the physician would bring his Passover offering;
and we deem these [two] matters to be lesser and greater.

[21] "Further" lacking in **P**. **K** is missing a page here.

lesser and greater: Heb. *qal va-homer*. If in the case of menstruating women, where the same transgression was committed with each, the law still requires a sacrifice for each and every one, it will certainly make the same requirement here, where there are three distinct, if similar, transgressions.

3:8 *A limb dangling from an animal*: A limb still attached to the animal that is no longer able to grow new flesh.

what is the law? Does a dangling limb, like a completely severed limb, impart impurity? See *Hullin* 9:7–8.

that it is pure, and does not impart corpse impurity, unlike a severed one.

in Jerusalem: Before the destruction of the Temple.

One whose affliction resulted in a dangling limb would go to a physician who could cut his limb as described. Since the limb is evidently pure while attached, the reason the afflicted person wanted it removed may have had nothing to do with impurity. Rashi posits that he wanted it severed so that he would not be repulsive to others during the festival. Alternatively, the concern might have been that the limb would separate during the offering.

stick it on a thorn: The physician's method of cutting would ensure that neither he nor the afflicted person would touch the limb after it was severed. First, the physician would further separate the limb from the body but make sure it is still attached to it; he would then impale the limb on a thorn so that the afflicted person could separate from it without touching it.

And this one . . . and the physician: Both were pure and could bring the Passover offering. Since they were able to do so even though they both had come into contact with the dangling limb, we know that such a limb does not convey impurity.

lesser and greater: If in the grave case of a human limb, which would impart corpse impurity if severed, a dangling limb is not treated as severed and does not impart impurity, then certainly in the case of an animal limb, which would impart only the lesser impurity of carrion, a dangling limb should not be treated as severed and should not impart impurity.

9 And R. Aqiva asked them further:
One who slaughters five sacrifices outside in a single spell of unawareness—
what is the law?
Is he liable to bring one purgation offering for all of them
or one for each and every one?
They said to him:
We have not heard [a tradition concerning this matter].
R. Joshua said:
I have heard concerning one who eats of a single sacrifice out of five platters
in a single spell of unawareness,
that he is liable for each and every one on account of sacrilege;
and I deem these [two] matters to be lesser and greater.
R. Simeon said:
This is not how R. Aqiva asked them,
but rather [this is what he asked]:
concerning one who eats remnant of five sacrifices[22]
in a single spell of unawareness, what is the law?
Is he liable to bring one purgation offering for all of them
or one for each and every one?
They said to him:
We have not heard [a tradition concerning this matter].
R. Joshua said:
I have heard concerning one who eats of a single sacrifice out of five platters
in a single spell of unawareness,
that he is liable for each and every one on account of sacrilege;
and I deem these [two] matters to be lesser and greater.
R. Aqiva said:
If this is a received tradition, we shall accept it;
but if it is an inference from reason, there is a rebuttal.
He said to him:
Rebut!

[22] **P** adds, "outside."

3:9 *outside* the Temple Court. See 1:1.

on account of sacrilege, since they were eaten before the blood had been sprinkled (see *Me'ilah* 1:4).

lesser and greater: If mere consumption from multiple dishes results in a liability to multiple offerings, even though a single animal is concerned, surely the actual slaughtering of multiple animals makes one liable to bring multiple offerings.

one who eats remnant: R. Simeon reports a different version, or amends the earlier version, of R. Aqiva's question. In the first, R. Aqiva asked about slaughtering sacrifices and R. Joshua responded with an inference from eating. This inference may be faulted since rules for slaughtering and eating differ. In R. Simeon's version, R. Aqiva asks about eating and R. Joshua answers with the same inference from a tradition about eating.

If this is a received tradition: Heb. *halakhah*: See *Yevamot* 8:3. Received tradition is a source of authority in itself and is not subject to contradiction from logical argument. However, inferences from tradition based on logic (*din*), may be challenged since their authority stems precisely from their function as logical extensions of tradition.

He said to him:
No. If you said this in the case of sacrilege,
where [Scripture] equates the one who eats with the one who causes to eat,
and the one who derives benefit with the one who gives benefit,
that [Scripture] has joined [small portions] over a long time to qualify for sacrilege,
will you say this in the case of remnant, which has none of those strictures?

10 R. Aqiva said:
I asked R. Eliezer:
One who performs many acts of labor of one type on many Sabbaths,
in a single spell of unawareness—what is the law?
Is he liable to bring one purgation offering for all of them,
or one for each and every one?
He said to me:
He is liable for each and every one,
by an argument from lesser and greater:
If [intercourse] with a menstruant,
which does not have many derivatives and many purgation offerings,
he is liable for each and every one,
in the case of the Sabbath,
which has many derivatives and many purgation offerings,
does not logic require that he be liable for each and every one?
I said to him:

equates: The rule in the case of sacrilege is that one is liable for every separate act of eating, even from a single sacrifice.

[Scripture] equates the one who eats…the one who gives benefit: In the case of sacrilege, one who feeds consecrated meat to someone else is liable to bring the same offerings he would be liable to bring had he consumed these holies himself; similarly, one who causes others to benefit in some way from consecrated meat is liable just as he would be had he derived benefit himself. See *Me'ilah* 5:4–5.

joined [small portions]: If the several bits consumed together make up the minimal quantity for liability, the eater is liable. In the case of sacrilege, these bits are deemed to combine even over a long period of time (*Me'ilah* 5:5), unlike the eating of prohibited parts of the animal where the time is limited (above 3:3).

has none of these strictures: Thus, as R. Aqiva demonstrates, the case of sacrilege is in some respects more strict than the consumption of prohibited parts of the animal such as remnant. One cannot assume, as R. Joshua did, that strictures that apply to sacrilege, such as liability for multiple offerings, apply in the case of remnant.

3:10 *acts of labor of one type*: i.e. from the same primary category ("father") of labor, *Shabbat* 7:1.

one purgation offering for all of them: Because the transgressions are all of the same type, and in a single spell of unawareness, he is only liable to bring one offering.

for each and every one: Because the transgressions were performed on many Sabbaths, he is liable to bring an offering for each sabbath separately.

menstruant: One who transgresses with several women in a single spell of unawareness is liable *for each and every one*; see above 3:7.

derivatives: The prohibition of intercourse with a menstruant does not have many derivative transgressions that might result in liability for multiple offerings. However, the prohibition of labor on Sabbath includes many types of derivative transgressions, which might result in liability for multiple offerings.

No. If you said this in the case of the menstruant,
where there are two distinct warnings—
for he is warned about the menstruant, and she is warned about him—
will you say this about the Sabbath,
concerning which there is only one warning?
He said to me:
One who had intercourse with minors can prove it,
for concerning them there is only one warning,
and he is liable for each and every one.
I said to him:
No. If you said
this in the case of one who had intercourse with minors,
where even though there is no [warning] for them now,
there is one for them later,
will you say this in the case of the Sabbath,
where there is no [warning] whether now or later?
He said to me:
The case of one who has intercourse with an animal can prove it.
I said to him:
The animal is like the Sabbath.

Chapter Four

4:1–3 *Uncertain Transgressions*

4 If it is uncertain whether one has eaten forbidden fat or not;
or even if [it is certain that] he has eaten,
but it is uncertain whether it constituted the statutory amount;
if forbidden fat and permitted fat were before him:

he... she is warned: The Torah's prohibition extends to both of them, Leviticus 20:18.

with minors: Who are menstruating.

only one warning: The prohibition does not apply to minors.

Even though there is no [warning] for them now: Minors will be subject to the prohibition when they are older. Future liability allows us to see the act of intercourse with each woman as a separate transgression. In contrast the prohibition of Sabbath labor never presents such double prohibition.

one who had intercourse with an animal: Certainly, an animal is never warned or faulted for having intercourse with a person. The implication is that R. Eliezer holds that a person who had had intercourse with several animals in a single spell of unawareness is liable to bring an offering for each and every one.

The animal is like the Sabbath: In both cases, it is an open question whether or not the transgressor is liable for each and every one.

4:1 *If it is uncertain*: In all the cases that follow, it is not known whether he transgressed or not.

if he ate one of them, but it is not known which one he ate;
his wife and his sister were at home with him:
if he unintentionally [had sexual relations] with one of them,
but it is not known with which one he unintentionally [had relations];
it was a Sabbath or a weekday,[23]
and he performed an act of labor on one of them
but it is not known on which of them he performed it—
he brings an offering for uncertain guilt.

2 Just as, if he ate forbidden fat and again ate forbidden fat
in a single spell of unawareness,
he is liable to bring only one purgation offering,
so too for acts of nonknowledge,
he brings only one guilt offering.
If there was knowledge between them—
just as he must bring a purgation offering for each and every one,
so too he brings an offering for uncertain guilt for each and every one.
Just as, if he ate forbidden fat and blood, remnant, and *piggul*,
in a single spell of unawareness, he is liable for each and every one,
so too for [acts of] nonknowledge,
he brings a guilt offering for uncertain guilt for each and every one.
If forbidden fat and remnant were before him:
if he ate one of them, but it is not known which one he ate;
His menstruating wife and his sister were at home with him:
if he unintentionally [had sex] with one of them,
but it is not known with which one he unintentionally [had sex];
it was a Sabbath or the Day of Atonement:

[23] Lit. "Sabbath and weekday"; **P**: "Sabbath and a festival day."

Sabbath or a weekday: If the act took place on the Sabbath, it is a transgression; if on a weekday, not. Cf. 4:2.

he brings an offering for uncertain guilt: Had there certainly been an unintentional transgression, a purgation offering would be required.

4:2 *he is liable to bring only one*: See 3:2.

acts of nonknowledge: The transgressor ate several pieces of possibly forbidden fat (see 4:1) in a single instance of not knowing whether they were prohibited.

guilt offering, for uncertain guilt.

knowledge between them: Between one possible transgression and another the transgressor had become aware of the first one.

purgation offering: For certain but unintentional transgression.

forbidden fat and blood: Eating different kinds of prohibited food in a single spell of unawareness. See above, 3:2.

forbidden fat and remnant: This series of cases inflects the last three cases of 4:1. Here, in each case there certainly was an unintentional transgression, but we do not know which of the two possible transgressions occurred.

Sabbath or the Day of Atonement: One followed the other, and it is unclear on which day the transgression occurred.

if he performed an act of labor at twilight
but it is not known in which one of them he performed it—
R. Eliezer deems him liable to a purgation offering,
and R. Joshua deems him exempt.
R. Yose said:
They did not disagree about one performing an act of labor at twilight,
that he is exempt,
for I say:
He may have performed part of the labor on one day,
and part on the next.
About what did they disagree?
About one who performs it while it is day,
but it is not known whether he performed it on the Sabbath
or performed it on the Day of Atonement;
or about one who performs it
but it is not known what type of labor he performed—
R. Eliezer deems him liable to a purgation offering,
and R. Joshua deems him exempt.
R. Judah said:
R. Joshua would exempt him even from the offering for uncertain guilt.

3 R. Simeon[24] of Shezur and R. Simeon say:
they did not disagree about a matter falling under a single category,
that he is liable.
And about what did they disagree?
About a matter falling under [one of] two categories,
in which R. Eliezer holds him liable to a purgation offering

[24] **P**: "Ishmael."

R. Eliezer deems him liable: Since either way, he has certainly transgressed.

R. Joshua requires a person to know the transgression he committed in order to bring a purgation offering, as implied by Leviticus 4:23 (cited below 4:3).

R. Yose recasts the dispute (cf.3:9). According to R. Yose, even R. Eliezer would agree in the case of the initial formulation that the person is not liable to bring a purgation offering.

part of the labor on one day: The labor was performed at twilight and may have been performed in part on the Sabbath and in part on the Day of Atonement. Since liability is only incurred for acts of labor which were begun and completed on the day they are prohibited, there is no certainty that there was any liability after all.

while it is day: Labor was certainly performed on either Sabbath or the Day of Atonement, but when the transgressor became aware that he had transgressed, he could not remember which one.

even from the offering for uncertain guilt: Since that offering is only for cases of uncertain transgressions, whereas here the transgression is certain.

4:3 *a single category*: According to these rabbis, even R. Joshua agrees that a person is liable in cases where there was certainly a transgression, even if it is not clear what transgression, as long as all transgressions that may have occurred belong to the same category (lit. "name"; see 3:4 and 3:6). For instance, picking two different kinds of fruit on the Sabbath.

and R. Joshua declares him exempt.
R. Judah said:
Even if he meant to gather figs but he gathered grapes;
grapes, but he gathered figs;
black ones, but he gathered white ones;
white ones, but he gathered black ones—
R. Eliezer holds him liable to a purgation offering,
and R. Joshua declares him exempt.
R. Judah said:[25]
But I wonder if R. Joshua would exempt in this [case].
If so, why is it said:
the sin which he committed?
To exclude someone who is preoccupied.

Chapter Five

5:1 *Liability for the Consumption of Blood*

5 Blood from the slaughter of a domestic animal,
of a wild animal, or of birds,

[25] **P** lacks "R. Judah said."

R. Judah said: Even if...: According to R. Judah, R. Joshua exempts the transgressor under the requirement that he has to know precisely which act he had committed and to have intended that precise act when he brings his offering.

R. Judah said: But I wonder...: R. Judah expresses doubt whether the dispute in fact extends to such cases, or even whether R. Joshua at all supports exemption from offering in any of the cases described so far.

the sin which he committed: Leviticus 4:23.

To exclude...preoccupied: R. Judah explains that the verse does not require that the transgressor know the exact nature of his transgression to be liable to bring an offering. Rather, the act must be performed deliberately even though the transgressor is not aware that it is a transgression. A person who intended to gather fruits on a Sabbath, thinking it was a weekday and thus not intending to transgress, is liable to bring an offering; but if he *is preoccupied* with something else and did not at all intend to do the action that constituted the transgression, he is exempt.

This alternative interpretation seems to undermine not only the version of the dispute reported by R. Judah, concerning the person who gathered grapes and instead gathered figs, etc. If Leviticus 4:23 is the basis for R. Joshua through all descriptions of the dispute, beginning with 4:2, this alternative interpretation undermines R. Joshua's alleged position in all of these versions.

These last statements in 4:3 pose an additional difficulty, since they were attributed to R. Judah and challenge the version of the dispute he has just provided. (**P** omits this attribution to R. Judah, but he is still the last speaker to be mentioned.) Some interpreters and versions resolve this by attributing these statements to R. Simeon, seeing in it a response to R. Judah. Alternatively, R. Judah first cites a teaching as he had heard it and then editorializes that he himself doubts that R. Joshua would go so far.

5:1 *animal...birds*: Leviticus 17:10–14.

whether pure or impure,
the blood of stabbing,
the blood of tearing,
the blood of bloodletting,
in which the life departs:
one is liable on its account.
The blood of the spleen,
the blood of the heart,
the blood of eggs,[26]
the blood of fish,
the blood of locusts,
the oozing blood:
one is not liable on their account.
R. Judah deems him liable in the case of the oozing blood.

5:2–3 *Uncertain Sacrilege*

2 R. Aqiva deems one liable, on account of uncertain sacrilege,
for an offering for uncertain guilt;
but the Sages deem him exempt;
but R. Aqiva concedes that one need not bring the restitution of his sacrilege
until it has become known to him,
and he must bring with it an offering for certain guilt.
R. Tarfon said:

[26] Or "testicles."

in which the life departs: With respect to all items in the list, only the consumption of "life blood," by which the animal loses its life, is to be punished with *karet*.

one is liable to *karet* for intentional consumption, or a purgation offering, or guilt offering in cases where unintentional or unaware consumption has taken place.

the oozing blood: As opposed to the "life blood," which gushes out, blood that may drain from the animal after it has already died.

One is not liable to *karet*. However, with the exception of blood from fish and locusts, all the preceding are subject to different kinds of prohibitions.

R. Judah deems one liable for *karet* even for the oozing blood.

5:2 *deems one liable*: By implication, R. Aqiva holds one liable to a sacrifice for uncertain guilt now, and one for certain guilt later if it becomes clear that the person has committed sacrilege. See the dispute with R. Tarfon below.

exempt: The Sages limit the offering for uncertain guilt to uncertain cases of the transgressions enumerated in 1:1 above; see 1:2.

sacrilege: One who has committed sacrilege is liable to bring a guilt offering and restore the consecrated property from which he benefited with an added fifth of its worth; see Leviticus 5:14–16.

R. Tarfon offers a procedure that would make it unnecessary for a person uncertain of a sacrilege case to bring two offerings.

Why should this one bring two guilt offerings?
Rather, let him bring the restitution of his sacrilege and its fifth,
and let him bring a guilt offering worth two *sela*,
and let him say:
"If it is certain that I committed sacrilege,
here is the restitution of my sacrilege
and here is my guilt offering;
and if it is uncertain that I have committed sacrilege,
let the money be a donation
and the offering be one for uncertain guilt"—
for from the kind of offering he brings for knowledge
he also brings for nonknowledge.

3 R. Aqiva said to him:
Your words seem right with respect to a case of small sacrilege;
but if one had a case of uncertain sacrilege worth one hundred *maneh*,
is it not preferable for him to bring a guilt offering worth two *sela*,
and not bring restitution for uncertain sacrilege worth one hundred *maneh*?
Thus, R. Aqiva concedes to R. Tarfon in a case of small sacrilege.
The woman who brought a bird purgation offering in an uncertain case—
if, while its neck had not been pinched,
it became known to her of a certainty that she gave birth,
let her make it a definite offering,
for from the kind of offering she brings for knowledge
she also brings for nonknowledge.

worth two sela, a coin worth four *zuz* or *denarii*, or two conventional *sheqel*. Leviticus 5:15 requires a guilt offering worth *sheqel* in the plural (thus, a minimum of two).

from the kind: What allows for the open-ended nature of the offering is that all guilt offerings mentioned in the Torah (with the exception of those for the *nazir* and the one afflicted by *tsara'at*) are rams of the same age and value (*Zevahim* 10:5).

5:3 *R. Aqiva*: R. Tarfon's procedure requires one rather than two offerings. However, it also requires monetary restitution whether or not one is certain that the sacrilege took place. Therefore, when higher sums are involved, R. Tarfon's procedure may actually be much more costly.

maneh: A *maneh* is one hundred *zuz*, so one hundred *maneh* is one hundred times one hundred *zuz*.

The woman who…an uncertain case: If there was doubt whether this was a miscarriage that requires an offering, she must bring a purgation offering but it is not eaten by the priests (see above 1:4).

its neck had not been pinched: The method of sacrificial killing for birds.

of a certainty that she gave birth: She gave birth to a child or had a miscarriage with evidence of a fetus (according to the cases enumerated above, 1:3).

a definite offering, that may be eaten by the priests.

5:4–8 *Two People, One Offering*

4 A piece of unconsecrated food and a piece of consecrated food—
if he ate one of them, and it is not known which one he ate:
he is exempt.
R. Aqiva deems him liable to an offering for uncertain guilt.
If he then ate the second he must bring an offering for definite guilt.
If one ate the first,
and another came and ate the second:
this one must bring an offering for uncertain guilt,
and that one must bring an offering for uncertain guilt—
the words of R. Aqiva.
R. Simeon says:
The two of them [together] bring one guilt offering.
R. Yose says:
Two may not bring one guilt offering.
5 A piece of unconsecrated food and a piece of forbidden fat—
if he ate one of them, and it is not known which one he ate:
he brings an offering for uncertain guilt.
If he then ate the second, he brings a purgation offering.
If one ate the first, and then another came and ate the second:
this one brings a guilt offering and that one brings a guilt offering—
the words of R. Aqiva.[27]

[27] **K, P** lack "the words of R. Aqiva."

5:4 *R. Aqiva deems him liable*: This is a case of uncertain sacrilege, as described above, 5:2.

If he then ate: Since he ate both pieces he has certainly committed sacrilege; he brings *an offering for definite guilt.*

another came and ate: There was certainly a transgression, but it is not known who transgressed.

R. Aqiva, who requires *an offering for uncertain guilt* in cases of uncertain sacrilege, deems each of them liable, since neither of them can be certain that he did not commit sacrilege.

R. Simeon: Since sacrilege certainly has been committed, there is liability for a guilt offering. However, since either of them might be responsible, R. Simeon allows them together to bring a single offering.

R. Yose: As the Mishnah says below explicitly with reference to a purgation offering (5:8), R. Yose holds that an offering may not be shared if it is brought on account of a transgression; he does otherwise allow a shared offering (see above 1:4). He thus deems each person liable to bring an offering for uncertain guilt (Tosefta).

5:5 *an offering for uncertain guilt*: Unlike the previous case, here the uncertainty is whether he committed a transgression of a prohibition punishable by *karet*.

purgation offering, since he certainly transgressed.

this one brings: Both are liable to bring an offering for uncertain guilt since neither can be certain that he did not commit a transgression.

R. Simeon says:
The two of them [together] bring one purgation offering.
R. Yose says:
Two may not bring one purgation offering.
6 A piece of forbidden fat and a piece of consecrated food—
If he ate one of them, and it not known which one he ate:
he brings an offering for uncertain guilt.
If he then ate the second:
he brings a purgation offering and a guilt offering.
If one ate the first, and then another came and ate the second:
this one brings an offering for uncertain guilt,
and that one brings an offering for uncertain guilt.
R. Simeon says:
The two of them [together] bring a purgation offering and a guilt offering.
R. Yose says:
Two may not bring one purgation offering and one guilt offering.
7 A piece of forbidden fat and a piece of consecrated forbidden fat—
if he ate one of them, and it is not known which one he ate:
he brings a purgation offering.
R. Aqiva says:
He brings an offering for uncertain guilt.
If he then ate the second,
he brings two purgation offerings and an offering for certain guilt.
If one ate the first, and then another came and ate the second:
this one brings a purgation offering and that one brings a purgation offering.
R. Aqiva says:

R. Simeon allows both parties to share the offering required of a definite transgression, even though only one of them transgressed.

5:6 *offering for uncertain guilt*: The majority opinion does not deem the transgressor liable for the possible consumption of consecrated fat. He must bring this offering for an uncertain consumption of *forbidden fat*. According to R. Aqiva, he should also bring an offering for uncertain guilt, since he either consumed *forbidden fat* or committed sacrilege.

a purgation offering and a offering: He has certainly eaten *forbidden fat* and certainly committed sacrilege.

this one brings an offering for uncertain guilt: Even though the Sages do not hold them liable for the possible sacrilege, both are nonetheless liable for the uncertain transgression of eating *forbidden fat*.

The two of them [together] bring. For one of them had certainly consumed *forbidden fat* and one of them had certainly committed sacrilege by consuming consecrated fat.

5:7 *consecrated forbidden fat*: Both pieces are forbidden because of the prohibition of forbidden fat; one piece is also forbidden because it is consecrated.

R. Aqiva... offering for uncertain guilt: For the possible sacrilege of consuming consecrated food. This is in addition to the purgation offering, mentioned in the preceding sentence.

two purgation offerings, for consumption of two pieces of forbidden fat (presumably not in the same spell of inadvertence, see 3:2), *and an offering for certain guilt* for the sacrilege in consuming the consecrated piece.

This one brings an offering for uncertain guilt,
and that one brings an offering for uncertain guilt.
R. Simeon says:
This one a purgation offering, and that one a purgation offering,
and the two of them [together] bring one guilt offering.
R. Yose says:
Two may not bring one guilt offering.
8 A piece of forbidden fat and a piece of forbidden fat from remnant—
he ate one of them, and it is not known which one he ate:
he brings a purgation offering and an offering for uncertain guilt.
If he then ate the second, he brings three purgation offerings.
If one ate the first, and then another came and ate the second:
this one brings a purgation offering and an offering for uncertain guilt,
and that one brings a purgation offering and an offering for uncertain guilt.
R. Simeon says:
This one a purgation offering and that one a purgation offering,
and the two of them [together] bring one purgation offering.
R. Yose says:
Any purgation offering that is brought for a transgression, two may not bring it.

Chapter Six

6:1–2 *Changing Awareness of Guilt*

6 One who brings an offering for uncertain guilt
and it became known to him that he had not transgressed—
if before it was slaughtered,
let it go out and pasture among the flock—

This one…and that one…and the two of them [together]: Because both certainly consumed *forbidden fat*, but only one of them consumed consecrated food.

5:8 *a purgation offering and an offering for uncertain guilt*: A purgation offering, since he had certainly eaten *forbidden fat*, and an offering for uncertain guilt, since he may also have consumed the remnant, therefore simultaneously consuming different prohibited parts, which results in multiple offerings (see 3:2 above).

three purgation offerings: Two for consuming each piece of *forbidden fat* (again, not in a single spell of unawareness) and one for consuming the remnant.

and that one brings a purgation offering and an offering for uncertain guilt: As each had certainly consumed *forbidden fat*, and each may have consumed the remnant.

and the two of them [together] bring one purgation offering: Sharing the offering that is brought for the transgression of eating the remnant, which one of them had certainly committed.

for a transgression: See comment on 5:6 above.

6:1 *let it go out*: The animal has become unconsecrated, since the basis for sacrificing it on the altar, the possible transgression, no longer obtains.

the words of R. Meir.
But the Sages say:
Let it pasture until it becomes blemished and then let it be sold,
and let its price fall to a voluntary offering.
R. Eliezer says:
Let it be sacrificed, for if it does not come for this sin,
it comes for another sin.
If it became known to him after it was slaughtered,
let the blood be poured out,
and the flesh go out to the place of burning.
If [it became known to him] after the blood had been sprinkled,
let the flesh be eaten.
R. Yose says:
Even if the blood is in the cup, let it be sprinkled and let the flesh be eaten.

2 The offering for certain guilt is not so:
if before it was slaughtered
[it became known to him that he had not transgressed],
let it go out and pasture among the flock;
if after it was slaughtered,
let it be buried;
if the blood had been sprinkled,
let the flesh go out to the place of burning.
The stoned ox is not so:
if before it was stoned
[it became known that it had not gored anyone],
let it go out and pasture among the flock;
if after it was stoned,

until it becomes blemished: Although the animal may not be offered on the altar, since there is no longer a need for a guilt offering, it is still consecrated. Once it is *blemished* and no longer fit for the altar, it is *sold* and the moneys used by the Temple for whole burnt offerings (*Sheqalim* 6:6; *Temurah* 3:3).

R. Eliezer holds that offerings for uncertain guilt may be brought even when there is no uncertainty about a specific transgression; therefore this offering is a valid one. See below, 6:3.

poured out into the base of the altar and not offered (see *Yoma* 5:6).

place of burning: Outside the Temple, as with all disqualified offerings (*Temurah* 7:6).

If... the blood had been sprinkled, and then he became certain that he had not transgressed. The blood offering is the moment that determines whether the sacrifice has been "completed."

be eaten: It is a valid offering, since while the blood was being sprinkled the person was still in a state of uncertainty, and thus the reason for the offering still present.

in the cup: The blood was ready to be sprinkled while he was still uncertain.

6:2 *let it go out*: The *offering for certain guilt* is brought for definite transgressions. If it becomes known that there was no transgression, even the Sages (6:1) would agree that the animal is treated as unconsecrated.

buried: The rule for all unconsecrated animals slaughtered in the Temple (*Temurah* 7:4).

The stoned ox, the ox who is to be stoned on account of goring a human (Exodus 21:28–32). Eating it and deriving benefit from its flesh are prohibited.

it is permitted to derive benefit from it.
The calf whose neck is broken is not so:
if before its neck was broken
[the killer became known]
let it go out and pasture among the flock;
if after its neck was broken,
it is to be buried on the spot,
for from the beginning it came for an uncertainty—
it atoned for its uncertainty and departed.

6:3–5 *Offerings and Atonement*

3 R. Eliezer says:
A person may donate an offering for uncertain guilt
on any day and at any hour he may want,
and this is called the guilt offering of the pious.
They said about Bava b. Buti that he used to donate an offering for uncertain guilt
on every day except for the day after the Day of Atonement.
He said:
By this Dwelling! If they would let me,
I would bring it.
But they tell me,
Wait until you enter a state of uncertainty.
But the Sages say:
One may bring an offering for uncertain guilt only for a transgression that
when intentional is punished with *karet*, and
when unintentional is expiated with a purgation offering.[28]

[28] Lit. "whose intentional is *karet* and whose unintentional is a purgation offering."

it is permitted to derive benefit from it, but not to eat of it since it was not ritually slaughtered.

The calf, atoning for a murder whose perpetrator is unknown (Deuteronomy 21:1–9).

buried on the spot on which it was killed, to prevent anyone from deriving benefit from it. For the requirement of burial see *Temurah* 7:4.

from the beginning: The calf's neck is broken only when the identity of the killer is not known. Since that uncertainty obtained when the neck was broken, the procedure was valid when performed.

6:3 *A person may donate*: Since the suspended guilt offering is brought on account of unknown transgression, and it is always possible one may have transgressed without knowing, one may bring this offering at any time.

the pious: Pious individuals (*hasidim*) appear elsewhere in the Mishnah as taking on obligations and legal strictures out of a heightened awareness of the danger of sin. See *Berakhot* 5:1; *Sukkah* 5:4.

By this Dwelling: An oath formula; see above 1:7.

intentional... *unintentional*: See above 1:2.

4 Those liable to purgation offerings and definite guilt offerings,
upon whom the Day of Atonement passed,
are liable to bring their offering after the Day of Atonement.
Those liable to suspended guilt offerings are exempt.
One who had an uncertainty concerning a transgression on the Day of Atonement,
even at nightfall, is exempt, for the entire day atones.

5 A woman who is liable to a bird purgation offering in a case of doubt,
and upon whom the Day of Atonement has passed,
is liable to bring her offering after the Day of Atonement,
for it qualifies her to eat from the sacrifices.
A bird purgation offering that was brought in a case of doubt—
if it became known to her after its neck was pinched,[29]
let it be buried.

6:6–8 *Offering Not in Accordance with Original Designation*

6 One who designates two *sela* for a guilt offering
and bought with them two rams for a guilt offering—
if one of them was worth two *sela*:
let it be sacrificed as his guilt offering,
and the second,
let it pasture until it becomes blemished and then be sold,
and let its price fall to a voluntary offering.
If he bought with them two rams for unconsecrated use,

[29] **P** has "before its neck was pinched" (subsequently corrected).

6:4 *the Day of Atonement passed* before they brought their offerings. Since the day does not atone for known transgressions, the offering is still required.

liable…exempt: The Day of Atonement atones for uncertain transgressions, and the uncertain guilt offering is thus unnecessary.

even at nightfall: At the end of the day, after the atonement rites have been completed.

6:5 *in a case of doubt* whether a "discharge" qualifies as birth or miscarriage, above 1:4.

qualifies her to eat: See 2:1 above and Leviticus 12:6.

if it became known that she was not liable to bring a sacrifice.

buried: The reason for the offering no longer exists. See above 6:2.

6:6 *two sela*, as required for a guilt offering (above, 5:2).

worth two sela, although bought with only one.

let it be sacrificed, despite its original cost.

the second, let it pasture…: Since it was bought with money designated for an offering, the second ram cannot be treated as unconsecrated; see *Temurah* 3:3.

voluntary offering: See above, 6:1.

for unconsecrated use: Committing sacrilege with money designated for offering.

and one was worth two *sela* and the second ten *zuz*,
let the one worth two *sela* be sacrificed as his guilt offering,
and the second for his sacrilege.
[If he bought with them]
one for a guilt offering and one for unconsecrated use—
if the one for a guilt offering was worth two *sela*,
let it be sacrificed as his guilt offering,
and the second, for his sacrilege,
and let him bring with it a *sela* and its fifth.

7 One who designates his purgation offering and dies,
his son may not bring it after him.
Nor may one bring it from one sin to another:
even for forbidden fat he ate yesterday,
let him not bring it for forbidden fat he ate today,
for it is said: *your offering…for the sin that you have committed*:
one's offering must be made with specific reference to one's sin.

8 One may bring a goat from what was consecrated for a sheep;
a sheep from what was consecrated for a goat;
turtle doves and young pigeons from what was consecrated for a goat or a lamb;
a tenth of the *ephah* from what was consecrated for turtle doves and pigeons.
How?
He designated money for a sheep or a goat—

guilt offering, for sacrilege (Leviticus 5:15).

for his sacrilege: He committed sacrilege with two *sela* (eight *zuz*). This *second* ram, worth ten *zuz*, is equal in value to the required restitution (Leviticus 5:16): the original sacrilege (eight *zuz*) plus the added fifth (one quarter of the eight *zuz*, above 5:2).

as his guilt offering: The original guilt offering for which this ram was bought.

second, for his sacrilege: The ram intended for unconsecrated use should be offered as the guilt offering for sacrilege.

a sela and its fifth, in restitution of the sacrilege. The assumption is that one *sela* has been paid for each animal, so the sacrilege is valued at one *sela*. Here, the guilt offering itself does not constitute restitution. The *sela* used for the second ram is considered a surplus from the purchase of the guilt offering, and sacrilege committed with such surplus may not be paid by an offering on the altar, since the surplus of guilt offerings must be donated (see *Sheqalim* 2:5, 6:6).

6:7 *may not bring it*: The son may not bring it as an offering for his own unintentional transgression; it must be allowed to die (*Temurah* 2:2).

your offering: Leviticus 4:28.

one's sin: The transgression for which the offering was originally designated.

6:8 *goat…sheep*: One may purchase a goat for sacrifice although the money was originally designated for a sheep, and vice versa. If there are remaining funds they are considered unconsecrated.

turtle doves and pigeons: An option available to those who are liable to offering of varying value (above 2:4) and who cannot afford a lamb or a goat (Leviticus 5:7, 12:8, 14:22).

a tenth of the ephah: A tenth of an *ephah* of flour is the least expensive of the offerings (see Leviticus 5:11).

He, liable to an offering of varying value, *designated money* for an expensive sacrifice.

if he became poorer, let him bring a bird;
if he became poorer, let him bring a tenth of an *ephah*.
He designated money for a tenth of an *ephah*—
if he became wealthier, let him bring a bird;
if he became wealthier, let him bring a sheep or a goat.
He designated a sheep or a goat, and they became blemished—
if he wishes, let him bring a bird with their price.
He designated a bird, and it became blemished—
he may not bring with its price a tenth of the *ephah*,
because there is no redemption for birds.

6:9 *First Does Not Mean Preferable*

9 R. Simeon says:
Sheep precede goats in every place;
is it possible that this is because they are preferable?
The teaching says: *If one brings a sheep as a purgation offering*,
to teach that the two of them are equal.
Turtle doves precede pigeons in every place;
is it possible that this is because they are preferable?
The teaching says: *and a pigeon or a turtle dove for a purgation offering*,
to teach that they are equal.
The father precedes the mother in every place;
is it possible that the honor of the father surpasses the honor of the mother?
The teaching says: *You shall each revere your mother and father*,
to teach that they are equal.
But the Sages have said:
The father precedes the mother in every place,

if he became poorer: He may now *bring a bird*, a less expensive offering, and the rest of the money is not consecrated.

there is no redemption for birds: *Menahot* 12:1.

6:9 *every place*: Everywhere in the Torah sheep are mentioned before goats (see e.g. Exodus 12:5, Leviticus 1:10).

The teaching says: A formula for a citation from the Torah, more common in Midrash than Mishnah.

If one brings a sheep: Leviticus 4:32.

to teach that they are equal: Sheep here are mentioned after goats (Leviticus 4:28), so the order elsewhere does not establish a hierarchy.

Turtle doves precede pigeons: e.g. Leviticus 1:14, Numbers 6:10.

and a pigeon or a turtle dove: Leviticus 12:6.

The father precedes the mother: e.g. Exodus 20:12, Leviticus 20:9.

You shall each revere: Leviticus 19:3.

since he and his mother are obligated to honor his father.
Similarly, in the study of Torah[30]—
if the son acquired [Torah] from his teacher,
the master precedes the father in every place,
since he and his father are obligated to honor his master.

[30] These last lines are missing in talmudic manuscripts.

the master precedes: Here, unlike the previous cases (except perhaps father and mother), *every place* does not mean "everywhere in the Torah"; rather it means "in any respect." See also *Bava Metsi'a* 2:11. This last passage may be an addition to the Mishnah.

Tractate Me'ilah

Sarra Lev

Introduction

Overview

Me'ilah ("sacrilege") is the abstract noun that the Mishnah uses for benefit from or misuse of sacred property. In biblical usage, the root has a wider semantic range including "to act unfaithfully." The tractate concerns items consecrated for Temple use that are then misappropriated for non-Temple use.

Structure and Organization of the Tractate

Chapter 1 deals primarily with whether sacrilege applies to offerings (of both greater and lesser sanctity) that have been otherwise disqualified. The end of chapter 1 and chapter 2 specify points in the sacrificial process at which liability for sacrilege arises or lapses. Chapter 3 deals primarily with items that are not themselves sanctified but are connected with sanctified items, such as the by-products of a sacrificial item or material contained within a sacrificial item. Chapter 4 addresses the question whether prohibited substances can combine to constitute the minimum quantity to be subject to the prohibition (rules that apply to, but are not limited to sacrilege). Chapters 5–6 define the act of sacrilege more specifically. To qualify as sacrilege one has to derive benefit; if the object is subject to degradation through use (e.g. textiles), one also has to have degraded it (5:1–2). In 5:3–5 the problem is introduced of whether sacrilege can be committed by multiple users on the same object (sacrilege "after" sacrilege) and a case where the person who benefited is not the one who took the item. This leads in 6:1–5 to a discussion of agency and related cases in which the person who committed the act did so unknowingly at the direction of another. The final passage (6:6) deals with a sanctified coin that has become mingled with others.

Main Ideas

Not all use of Temple property for non-Temple purposes comes under the category of *me'ilah*. The following are the preconditions for such use falling into that category.

(1) The item must not be permitted to be used at that moment by any (human) users. This excludes, for instance, sacrificial meat and hides that priests are permitted to use.
(2) The user must misuse the item inadvertently.
(3) The user must derive the equivalent of a *perutah* in benefit from the item. In addition, the object itself may have to have become degraded or devalued in some way.

The consequences of committing sacrilege are: full restitution plus an added "fifth" and a sacrificial offering. The biblical anchor for this law is Leviticus 5:15–16, and some of the specifications listed above are linked to these verses: inadvertent error, restitution plus one fifth, and an offering. The Mishnah has qualified the biblical requirements by detailing what is or is not subject to sacrilege and how to define the actual act of sacrilege. It also greatly expands the rules by such characteristically rabbinic topics as mixtures, the division between the taker and the one who benefits, and the consequences of agency.

In discussing the transgression of *me'ilah*, this tractate also deals with several other transgressions, including *piggul*, remnant (*notar*), and sacrifices that been eaten by an impure person; see introduction to *Zevahim* and *Menahot*. There are a fair number of overlapping traditions with *Shabbat*, *Yoma*, *Zevahim*, *Tohorot*, and *Bava Metsi'a*.

Tractate Me'ilah

Chapter One

1:1–3 *Invalid Offerings and Sacrilege*

1 The offerings of the highest sanctity
that one slaughtered in the south [of the altar]
are subject to sacrilege.[1]
If he slaughtered them in the south and collected their blood in the north;
in the north, and collected their blood in the south;
slaughtered them during the day and sprinkled[2] [the blood] at night,
at night, and sprinkled during the day;
or he slaughtered them [intending to act on them]
outside of their proper time or outside of their proper place—
these are subject to sacrilege.
R. Joshua said a general rule:
Whatever has had a period of permissibility to the priests,
is not subject to sacrilege;
and whatever has not had a period of permissibility to the priests
is subject to sacrilege.
What is "has had a period of permissibility to the priests"?

[1] Lit. "they [nevertheless] commit sacrilege on them."
[2] Lit. "thrown" against the altar.

1:1 *offerings of the highest sanctity*: Sacrifices are divided into two categories, "offerings of the highest sanctity" and "offerings of lesser sanctity," which follow different protocols (see *Zevahim* 5 and below). In the examples that follow, some element of the sacrifice has disqualified it.

the south: Offerings of the highest sanctity were to be slaughtered to the north of the altar. Slaughter in the south disqualified them. Cf. Leviticus 1:11, 6:18, 7:2 and *Zevahim* 5:1.

sprinkled…at night: This was the final of four required sacrificial acts, after which the priests were permitted to benefit from the meat. Sprinkling or slaughtering at night rendered the sacrifice improperly offered and therefore disqualified. Cf. *Zevahim* 2:2, *Megillah* 2:5.

[intending to act]: This intention renders the sacrifice *piggul* (see *Zevahim* 2:2 and Leviticus 7:18, 19:7). The Mishnah uses a laconic shorthand, but intention is implied. There is disagreement in the Babylonian Talmud whether "outside its time" refers to the eating of the sacrifice or the throwing of the blood.

a period of permissibility: After the blood is sprinkled and priests are permitted to eat the meat, the sacrifice is no longer "God's property" alone. After this *period of permissibility* they are no longer subject to sacrilege. Cf. *Zevahim* 11:2.

That which is a remnant,
and that which has become impure,
and that which has left [the Temple precincts].
What is "that has not had a period of permissibility to the priests"?
That which was slaughtered with intention to act on it
outside of its proper time,
or outside of its proper place,
or for which disqualified persons received or sprinkled its blood.

2 The meat of the offerings of the highest sanctity that left
[the Temple precincts] before the sprinkling of the blood—
R. Eliezer says:
It is subject to sacrilege,
And it does not render one liable for *piggul*, for remnant, or for impurity.
R. Aqiva says:
It is not[3] subject to sacrilege,
but it renders one liable for *piggul*, for remnant, or for impurity.
Said R. Aqiva:
In the case of one who sets apart [an animal for] a purgation offering,
and it was lost,
and he sets apart another in its place,
and later the first is found,
and, indeed, the two of them stand ready—
is it not the case that just as its blood exempts its own meat
[from susceptibility to sacrilege],
so too it exempts the meat of the other?

[3] **K** lacks "not."

remnant: Sacrifices that are permitted to be eaten must be eaten on the day or night following the sacrifice. If left until the next day, they are *notar*, remnant, and prohibited.

disqualified persons: See *Zevahim* 2:1.

1:2 *left*: Offerings of the highest sanctity must be consumed inside the *Temple precincts*. If the flesh leaves the courtyard, the sacrifice is rendered disqualified and prohibited.

before the sprinkling of the blood: The status of *piggul* actually takes effect at the moment of sprinkling the blood (see *Zevahim* 2:3).

R. Eliezer holds that the meat having been taken out means that no valid sprinkling took place, and the prohibition of *sacrilege* does apply. However, one is not liable for eating *piggul* (a sacrifice slaughtered with the intention to eat it outside of its proper time), remnant (see 1:1; and cf. *Zevahim* 5:1–5; Leviticus 7:15–18, 19:5–9), or eating the sacrifice when one is impure (*Zevahim* 13:2; Leviticus 7:19–21).

R. Aqiva holds the sprinkling to be valid, whether or not the meat left the courtyard. This exempts the meat from being subject to the laws of *sacrilege*, and makes it subject to the prohibitions involving eating the animal.

Said R. Aqiva: According to R. Aqiva, if an animal was set aside to be sacrificed, then lost and replaced by another (see *Temurah* 4:1–3 and below, 3:1), the sprinkling of the blood of one of these animals exempts both its own meat and the meat of the other animal from being subject to sacrilege. By inference, in our case, where the flesh has left the sacred precincts before the offering of the blood, the offering of the blood should also exempt the meat from being subject to sacrilege.

And if its blood exempts the meat of the other,
logic requires that it should exempt its own meat.

3 The altar portions of the offerings of lesser sanctity
that left [the Temple Court]
before the sprinkling of the blood—
R. Eliezer says:[4]
They are not subject to sacrilege and they do not render one liable
for *piggul*, for remnant, or for impurity.
R. Aqiva says:
They are subject to sacrilege, and they render one liable
for *piggul*, for remnant, or for impurity.

1:4 *Valid Offerings and Susceptibility to Sacrilege*

4 Action taken with the blood in the case of offerings of the highest sanctity
has circumstances for leniency and for stringency;
and with offerings of lesser sanctity, entirely for stringency.
How?
Offerings of the highest sanctity—
before the sprinkling of the blood:
the altar portions and the meat are subject to sacrilege;
after the sprinkling of the blood:[5]
the altar portions are subject to sacrilege,

[4] **K** reverses the contents of the two opinions.
[5] **K** lacks from the preceding "blood" to here; apparently in error.

1:3 *altar portions*: Those innards and the forbidden fat of the animal that are required to be put on the altar rather than being eaten.

offerings of lesser sanctity: See 1:1, and *Zevahim* 5:6–8.

left . . . before the sprinkling: For offerings of lesser sanctity, the moment of sprinkling the blood activates the consecration of the sacrificial parts for the altar. Thus, once the blood is thrown, the sacrificial parts of the animal are normally rendered subject to sacrilege. Here, the parts were disqualified from sacrifice prior to the throwing of the blood.

R. Eliezer: As in 1:2, no valid sprinkling of the blood occurred to effect the transition for sacrificial meat that has already left the Temple Court. Thus, the sprinkling cannot change the meat from a state of susceptibility to sacrilege to nonsusceptibility, or vice versa, nor can it effect liability for *piggul*, *remnant*, or *the impure*.

R. Aqiva again understands the sprinkling of the blood as effective in consecrating the sacrificial parts of offerings of lesser sanctity regardless of their having left the Temple Court. Thus, these parts are subject to sacrilege and the transgressor of the prohibitions of *piggul*, remnant, or impurity is liable.

1:4 *Action taken with the blood*: This refers to the sprinkling of the blood, the last of the four fundamental components of the sacrifice.

circumstances for leniency and for stringency: Once the blood of a sacrifice of the highest sanctity is sprinkled there are certain respects in which the meat is treated more leniently than it was before the throwing of the blood, and certain respects in which it is treated more strictly.

but the meat is not subject to sacrilege.
For both cases,
one is liable for *piggul*, for remnant, and for impurity.
And with offerings of lesser sanctity, entirely for stringency—how?
Offerings of lesser sanctity—
before the sprinkling of the blood:
the altar portions and the meat are not subject to sacrilege;
after the sprinkling of the blood:
the altar portions are subject to sacrilege,
but the meat is not subject to sacrilege.
For both cases,
one is liable for *piggul*, for remnant, and for impurity.
It turns out that action taken with the blood in the case of offerings of the highest sanctity
has circumstances for leniency and for stringency;
and with offerings of lesser sanctity, entirely for stringency.

Chapter Two

2:1–9 *When the Prohibition of Misuse Begins: Offerings of the Highest Sanctity*

2 A bird purgation offering
is subject to sacrilege once it has been consecrated.

The meat is not subject to sacrilege: Excluding the meat of the whole burnt offering, which is fully burnt. See below, 2:2.

offerings of the highest sanctity: Sprinkling the blood makes it permissible to the priests, thereby removing the meat from susceptibility to sacrilege. The stringency is that, once the blood has been sprinkled, one becomes liable for *piggul*, remnant, and impurity.

offerings of lesser sanctity: The sacrificial parts are subject to the laws of sacrilege after the sprinkling of the blood, since no one has permission to eat them, which is a stringency, and the three transgressions also take effect after the sprinkling.

2:1–9 There are three relevant stages in offerings of the highest sanctity: (1) consecration; (2) the point at which the sacrifice becomes susceptible to disqualification (for animals, through slaughter); and (3) the sprinkling of the blood (again, for animals). Disqualification can occur through (a) contact with a *tevul yom* (one who awaits nightfall after immersing for purification); (b) contact with *one lacking atonement* (who had yet to bring an offering at the end of a period of impurity); or (c) *remaining overnight* (leaving the sacrifice beyond the proper time for consumption, or sprinkling the blood past its proper time). Each individual mishnah ends by noting when the ritual has been completed (and in some cases, when the item is permitted for consumption) and the offering ceases to be subject to sacrilege. The list of sacrifices in 2:1–5 corresponds to *Zevahim* 5:1–5.

2:1 *A bird purgation offering*: A bird is brought as a purgation offering under certain conditions including when a person cannot afford to bring a beast to sacrifice. See Leviticus 5:7–10, 12:6–8, 14:22–23, 15:14–15, 29–30; Numbers 6:10–11; *Zevahim* 6:4.

Once [its neck] has been pinched—
it has become capable of being invalidated by a *tevul yom*,
by one lacking atonement, and by remaining overnight.
Once its blood has been sprinkled—
one is liable on its account for *piggul*, for remnant, or for impurity,
and it is not subject to sacrilege.

2 A bird whole burnt offering
is subject to sacrilege once it has been consecrated.
Once [its neck] has been pinched—
it has become capable of being invalidated by a *tevul yom*,
by one lacking atonement, and by remaining overnight.
Once its blood has been wrung out—
it renders one liable for *piggul*, for remnant, or for impurity.
And is subject to sacrilege until it goes out to the ash heap.

3 Bulls that are burnt and goats that are burnt
are subject to sacrilege once they have been consecrated.
Once they have been slaughtered—
they have become capable of being invalidated by a *tevul yom*,
by one lacking atonement, and by remaining overnight.
Once their blood has been sprinkled—
they render one liable for *piggul*, for remnant, or for impurity.
And are subject to sacrilege in the ash heap until the meat is charred.

Once [its neck] has been pinched: This is the first of three stages of the bird purgation offering, in which the priest pinches the neck of the bird.

2:2 *A bird whole burnt offering*: The bird is brought as a whole burnt offering under certain conditions such as conversion or the purification of one suffering genital flux. Whole burnt offerings are consumed entirely on the altar, and never become available for human consumption. This renders them subject to sacrilege as of the moment of consecration, and does not remove them from this status until it reaches the ash heap (see below). See Leviticus 1:14–17; *Zevahim* 6:5. Cf. the verses noted above, 2:1.

subject to sacrilege... consecrated: See above, 1:4.

Once [its neck] has been pinched: See above, 2:1.

Once its blood has been wrung out: The blood service of the bird whole burnt offering requires the blood to be wrung out of the newly killed bird, rather than sprinkled.

ash heap: The final act of the whole burnt offering was to carry the ashes to a place outside of Jerusalem. Once this was completed, the offering, or its remainder, was no longer subject to sacrilege. See Leviticus 6:4. Cf. *Tamid* 2:1–2.

2:3 *Bulls... goats that are burnt*: A reference to five types of purgation offerings that, unlike the usual practice, are burned on the ash heap. No parts are consumed by the priests. See Leviticus 4:1–21 and 16; Numbers 15:24. Cf. *Horayot* 1, 2; *Zevahim* 4:4; 5:1–2.

until the meat is charred: Unlike the previous case, in which the meat is burned on the altar and the ashes carried out to the ash heap, in this case, the meat itself is burned on the ash heap. Until the meat is fully burned, the sacrifice is both incomplete and not permitted for consumption, and thus remains subject to sacrilege.

4 The whole burnt offering
is subject to sacrilege after it has been consecrated.
Once it has been slaughtered—
it has become capable of being invalidated by a *tevul yom*,
by one lacking atonement, and by remaining overnight.
Once its blood has been sprinkled—
one is liable on its account for *piggul*, for remnant, or for impurity.
And its hide is not subject to sacrilege,
but its meat is subject to sacrilege until it goes out to the ash heap.

5 A purgation offering
and a guilt offering
and offerings of well-being of the congregation
are subject to sacrilege once they have been consecrated.
Once they have been slaughtered—
they are capable of being invalidated by a *tevul yom*,
by one lacking atonement, and by remaining overnight.
Once their blood has been sprinkled—
one is liable on their account for *piggul*, for remnant, or for impurity.
The meat is not subject to sacrilege,
but the altar portions are subject to sacrilege until they go out to the ash heap.

6 The two loaves of bread
are subject to sacrilege once they have been consecrated.
Once they have crusted in the oven—
they have become capable of being invalidated by a *tevul yom*

2:4 *hide...meat*: Although the meat, bones, and innards of the whole burnt offering is offered up on the altar, the priests are permitted to use the hide (see Leviticus 7:8). However, until the sacrifice has been completed, even the hide is subject to sacrilege. Cf. *Zevahim* 12:2 and above 2:2.

2:5 *A purgation offering*: Usually brought by an individual as atonement for a specific sin or as part of certain purification rites.

a guilt offering: There are six categories of the guilt offering, also brought as atonement for specific sins or for purification of specific conditions. For details, see *Zevahim* 5:5.

offerings of well-being of the congregation: The only offering of well-being (*qorban shelamim*) that falls into the category of offerings of the highest sanctity. This offering of two lambs and two loaves of bread is brought on the holiday of Shavu'ot (Weeks, Pentecost) (see 2:6). Cf. Leviticus 23:15–21; *Zevahim* 5:5.

meat...altar portions: After the sprinkling of the blood, the meat becomes permitted to the priests, and is not subject to sacrilege. The sacrificial parts (see 1:3), however, remain the property of the altar, and are not released from their susceptibility to sacrilege until the final stage when the ashes are removed from the altar and taken to the ash heap. Cf. *Zevahim* 5:5.

2:6 *The two loaves*: The offering of well-being brought on the festival of Shavu'ot included two loaves of bread, along with the animals. See above, 2:5; cf. Leviticus 23:15–21; *Menahot* 5:1, 6; 11:4.

Once they have crusted: Grain offerings did not have a blood service that accompanied them and other markers were used to determine the stages of the ritual. In this case, the crusting of the two loaves is the second stage, at which they are capable of being disqualified.

have become capable of being invalidated: Notably missing here is the third disqualification: remaining overnight. The bread is baked before the holiday so by necessity must wait overnight; see *Menahot* 11:9.

and by one lacking atonement,
and to permit the slaughter of the offering that accompanies them.[6]
Once the blood has been sprinkled—
one is liable on their account for *piggul*, remnant, or for impurity,
but they are not subject to sacrilege.

7 The showbread
is subject to sacrilege after it has been consecrated.
Once it has crusted in the oven—
it has become capable of being invalidated by a *tevul yom*
and by one lacking atonement,
and to be arranged on the table.
Once the vessels [of frankincense] have been offered—
one is liable on its account for *piggul*, for remnant, or for impurity,
and it is not subject to sacrilege.

8 The grain offerings
are subject to sacrilege once they have been consecrated.
Once they have been consecrated in the vessel—
they have become capable of being invalidated by a *tevul yom*,
by one lacking atonement, and by remaining overnight.
Once the handful has been offered—

[6] Lit. "to slaughter on them the sacrifice."

permit the slaughter of the offering: The two loaves are attached to the sacrifice of the two goats of the offering of well-being of the congregation. Thus, the crusting of the bread not only marks the change in their own status, but also in the status of the accompanying animal sacrifices: the two goats may not be slaughtered until the loaves have crusted. See Leviticus 23:15–20. Cf. *Menahot* 4:3.

Once the blood has been sprinkled: Again, because of the connection between the two loaves and the accompanying two goats, the status of the now-crusted loaves is dependent on the sprinkling of the blood of the goats.

2:7 *The showbread*: Twelve loaves brought each Sabbath accompanied by two bowls of frankincense. These are removed the following Sabbath and eaten by the priests. See Leviticus 24:5–9, *Menahot* 11:5–9.

capable of being invalidated: Remaining overnight is again omitted from the list of disqualifications, since these loaves remain in the sanctuary for a week (see annotation to 2:6).

to be arranged: The crusting in the oven also changes the status of the showbread. It is then holy enough to be placed on the Table inside the sanctuary.

the vessels: The frankincense that accompanied the loaves each week was removed with them at the end of the week and burned on the altar. The loaves became permissible to the priests and no longer subject to sacrilege.

2:8 *The grain offerings*: Heb. *menahot*. Those offerings that consist of various types of flour or of bread. This mishnah refers to flour offerings. See Leviticus 2:1–16, and *Menahot*, introduction.

consecrated in the vessel: The priest scoops a handful of the flour offered, puts it in a sacred vessel, and burns it on the altar. The rest of the offering is eaten by the priests. This stage corresponds to the ritual slaughtering of the animal sacrifice. See 2:1–5.

Once the handful has been offered on the altar. As with the sprinkling of the blood in most animal sacrifices, the offering of the handful of flour releases the rest of the sacrifice to be eaten by the priests.

one is liable on their account for *piggul*, for remnant, or for impurity,
and the remainder is not subject to sacrilege,
but the handful is subject to sacrilege until it goes out to the ash heap.

9 The handful, and the frankincense,
and the incense,
and the grain offering of the priests,
and the grain offering of the anointed priest,
and the grain offering of the libations
are subject to sacrilege once they have been consecrated.
Once they have been consecrated in the vessel—
they have become capable of being invalidated by a *tevul yom*,
by one lacking atonement, and by remaining overnight,
and one is liable on their account for remnant, and for impurity,
but there is no *piggul* for them.
This is the general rule:
Whatever has elements that permit it,
one is not liable on their account for *piggul*, for remnant, or for impurity,
until they offer its elements that permit it.
And whatever does not have elements that permit it,
once it has been consecrated in the vessel,

the handful... until it goes out to the ash heap: Since the handful is never permissible to the priests, it remains subject to sacrilege until it is brought out to the ash heap (see above, 2:2).

2:9 This passage introduces the notion, spelled out in the *general rule* at the end, that some sacrifices have *elements that permit* them to be consumed or to be offered on the altar. These must be completed in order for the offering to be released to this next stage. Cf. *Zevahim* 2:3, 4:3–4. In the case of most meal offerings, the "permitter" is *the handful* of flour with *frankincense*, and the scooping of that handful renders the offering permissible. See 2:8.

the frankincense: Placed on the altar with the handful. The frankincense itself has no permitter.

the incense: Offered twice daily on the golden altar. The incense has no permitter. See Exodus 30:7–8.

the grain offering of the priests: Brought by the priests. These are not eaten by the priests, but burned entirely, and have no permitter. Leviticus 12–16. Cf. *Menahot* 6:2.

of the anointed priest: Brought daily by the high priest, and on the day of a priest's anointing. It is burned entirely, and has no permitter. Cf. *Menahot* 6:2.

of the libations: A grain offering brought along with whole burnt offerings and offerings of well-being, and accompanied by libations of wine. It is burned entirely on the altar and has no permitter. See Numbers 15:1–12. Cf. *Menahot* 6:2.

Once they have been consecrated in the vessel: Generally, the element that permits must be offered before the offering becomes liable for remnant, and impurity. However, because none of these have permitters, there is no stage beyond that of being put into the vessel, and it is the act of consecration in the vessel that marks the beginning of liability.

but there is no piggul for them: See below.

Whatever has elements that permit: e.g. the animal purgation offering, for which the sprinkling of the blood permits the offering to be consumed by the priests.

one is liable on its account for remnant and impurity,
but there is no *piggul* for it.

Chapter Three

3:1–4 *Sacrificial Items Not Subject to Laws of Sacrilege*

3 The offspring of a purgation offering,
and the substitute of a purgation offering,
and a purgation offering whose owners have died—
they must die.
One whose year has passed,[7]
and that which was lost, and then found to be blemished,[8]
if the owners have performed atonement—
it must die,
and does not make a substitute,
and one may not benefit from it,

[7] **K, P** add "that has surpassed its year" [8] **K, P**: "and was found and was blemished."

no piggul for it: Since these have no elements that permit them, they do not become subject to liability for *piggul*. See annotations to 1:1, 2; *Zevahim* 2:3, 4:3–4.

3:1 Parallel to *Temurah* 4:1. This mishnah discusses consecrated purgation offerings that for some reason may not be offered, and so must be allowed to die.

The offspring of a purgation offering: The dam gave birth after being consecrated. The offspring of sacred property is sacred (see 3:6); however, since the offspring was not consecrated for a specific purpose, it also cannot be offered as a purgation offering.

substitute: Heb. *temurah*. Generally, if someone attempts to substitute a nonsacral animal for one that has been designated as a sacrifice, both animals are considered consecrated. See *Temurah*, introduction. However, the substitute cannot be offered as a purgation offering.

whose owners have died: After consecrating the animal; the offering may not be brought.

must die: They are penned and starved, because neither Temple nor lay person may use them.

whose year has passed: Purgation offerings must be less than one year old. Here, the dedicator did not sacrifice in time.

found to be blemished: See n. 8. A blemished animal may not be offered.

performed atonement: Fulfilled their obligation with another animal. In the sequel if the owners have not brought a sacrifice, the animal retains its prior sanctity and restrictions.

does not make a substitute: The animal that was substituted for one that must die does not become sanctified, as in the general case of *temurah*.

and it is not subject to sacrilege.
If before the owners have performed atonement—
it grazes until it becomes defiled,
and is sold,
and one brings another with its proceeds,
and it makes a substitute,
and it is subject to sacrilege.

2 One who sets apart money for his *nazir* offering—
one may not benefit from it,
but it is not subject to sacrilege,
since it is all suitable to be used for an offering of well-being.
If he died:
if it was not specified—
it falls to the voluntary offering fund;
if it was specified—
money for the purgation offering—
should go to the Dead Sea;
one may not benefit from it,
but it is not subject to sacrilege;
money for the whole burnt offering—
he brings a whole burnt offering;[9]
money for the offerings of well-being—
they should bring offerings of well-being,

[9] **K**, **P** add: "and they are susceptible to sacrilege."

not subject to sacrilege: Although *benefiting* from the animal is prohibited, one is not liable for the particular transgression of sacrilege.

grazes until it becomes defiled: The purgation offering whose year has passed grazes until it is no longer suitable for sacrifice, and is then sold and the money is used to buy a voluntary sacrifice. The blemished animal may be sold immediately.

makes a substitute: Before it is blemished and sold.

3:2 A *nazir* ends the term of nazirite status with three offerings: a purgation offering, a whole burnt offering, and an offering of well-being (see Numbers 6:14). The first two are offerings of the highest sanctity, and subject to sacrilege from the moment they are consecrated. The offering of well-being is an offering of lesser sanctity, and is not subject to sacrilege until the sprinkling of the blood is complete. (See 1:4.)

one may not benefit: Since the money has been designated for an offering.

not subject to sacrilege, since… offering of well-being: If the *nazir* did not designate which coins were set aside for which offering, the *nazir* could potentially use any of the coins for the offering of well-being. Since the offering of well-being is an offering of lesser sanctity, it is not subject to sacrilege.

if the money *was not specified*: Divided up and designated for the three specific sacrifices.

Dead Sea: If the *nazir* has since died. Since the money was designated for a purgation offering, which requires a specific purpose, it can neither be used nor redeemed, and must be permanently disposed of.

brings a whole burnt offering: Anyone may bring whole burnt offering with this money.

and they are to be consumed over one day
and do not require bread.

3 R. Ishmael[10] says:
The rule for blood is lenient at its beginning and stringent at its end;
and the rule for libations is stringent at its beginning and lenient at its end.
The blood:
at its beginning—
it is not subject to sacrilege;
once it has gone out to the Kidron stream—
it is subject to sacrilege.
The libations:
at the beginning—
they are subject to sacrilege;
once they have gone out to the foundations[11]—
they are not subject to sacrilege.

4 The ashes of the inner altar and the lampstand—
one may not benefit from them,
but they are not subject to sacrilege.
One who consecrates the ashes initially—
they are subject to sacrilege.
Regarding turtle doves that have not reached the proper age,
and pigeons[12] that have passed[13] the proper age—

[10] **K, P**: "R. Simeon." [11] **K, P**: "went down to the foundation."
[12] "And pigeons" absent in **K**, in error. [13] **P, K** (as corrected by a later hand): "surpassed."

to be consumed over one day: A nazirite offering of well-being is unlike most offerings of well-being, which are eaten over two days and a night.

do not require bread: A nazirite offering of well-being is brought with bread. See Numbers 6:15. In this respect the sacrifice reverts to a normal offering of well-being.

3:3 This mishnah veers from the topic of borderline items and returns briefly to the issue of timing.

blood... libations: The offerings of blood for all sacrifices, and the libations brought with whole burnt offerings, the offerings of well-being, and the offerings of one with *tsara'at*. See *Menahot* 9:6.

its beginning: From the time that it is consecrated.

Kidron stream: The valley to the east of the Temple Mount. The blood was carried by drains, *Middot* 3:2; *Yoma* 5:6.

the foundations: There were two pits by the altar, used to drain the water and the wine libations. *Middot* 3:3.

3:4 Several aspects of this mishnah remain unclear.

ashes: Both the wicks from the *lampstand* and the ashes of the incense offered on the *inner altar* (see e.g. *Pesahim* 5:5) were placed with the ashes of the outer altar. Unlike the ashes of the outer altar, however, these were not subject to sacrilege once they were placed by the outer altar.

lampstand: The candelabrum that sat by the inner altar (see Exodus 25:31–40).

initially: Precise meaning is unclear.

have not reached... have passed the proper age: Turtle doves may not be offered before they have reached a certain stage of development while pigeons may not be offered after a certain stage. See *Hullin* 1:5.

one may not benefit from them, but they are not subject to sacrilege.
R. Simeon says:
Turtle doves that have not reached the proper age—
are[14] subject to sacrilege;
and pigeons that have passed[15] the proper age—
one may not benefit from them, but they are not subject to sacrilege.

3:5–8 *Consecrated, Nonsacrificial Items Not Subject to Laws of Sacrilege*

5 The milk of consecrated animals and the eggs of turtle doves—
one may not benefit from them,
but they are not subject to sacrilege.
When does this apply?
With regard to offerings for the altar;
but with regard to offerings for Temple upkeep:
if he consecrated a hen—
she and her eggs are subject to sacrilege;
an ass—
she and her milk are subject to sacrilege.
6 Anything that is appropriate for the altar and not for Temple upkeep,
or for Temple upkeep and not for the altar,
or for neither the altar nor Temple upkeep—
is subject to sacrilege.
How?
He consecrated a pit filled with water,
or a dungheap filled with manure,

[14] **K** adds "not." [15] **K**, **P**: "surpassed."

may not benefit: Since they have been set aside for a sacrifice.

not subject to sacrilege: Since they may not be sacrificed.

R. Simeon is more stringent regarding turtle doves, since they can eventually be sacrificed, in contrast with the pigeons that have passed the age of sacrifice.

3:5 *With regard to offerings for the altar*: These items cannot be offered on the altar, even though they have been consecrated, so *sacrilege* does not apply (commentaries).

offerings for Temple upkeep: Nonsacrificial donations that would be used for maintenance.

3:6 *for neither the altar nor Temple upkeep*: But is sold, and the money used for Temple upkeep or offerings.

How? Although exemplifying the three categories mentioned above, this section also introduces a further principle, that if one consecrates an item that presently contains another item, the consecration falls on the contents as well.

water: Appropriate for the Temple upkeep, but not for the altar.

manure: Appropriate for neither the altar nor the upkeep.

or a dovecote filled with doves
or a tree filled with fruit,
or a field filled with grasses—
they and their contents are subject to sacrilege.
But if he consecrated:
a pit, and it was later filled with water;
or a dungheap, and it was later filled with manure:
or a dovecote, and it was later filled with doves;
or a tree, and it was later filled with fruit;
or a field, and it was later filled with grasses—
they are subject to sacrilege, but their contents are not subject to sacrilege—[16]
the words of R. Judah;[17]
R. Simeon[18] says:
One who consecrates a field or a tree—
they and their produce are subject to sacrilege
because it is the produce of consecrated property.
The offspring of a tithed animal may not nurse from a tithed animal,
but others are donated thus.
The offspring of a consecrated animal may not nurse from a consecrated animal,
but others are donated thus.
The laborers may not eat from consecrated dried figs,
and likewise a cow may not eat from consecrated vetches.

7 The roots of a tree belonging to a lay person
that spread into consecrated [property],
or belonging to consecrated property
that spread into [property] belonging to lay persons—

[16] For this clause **K** (in error) has "their contents are susceptible to sacrilege."
[17] In **K**, **P** this is anonymous. [18] **K**, **P**: "Yose."

doves: Appropriate for the altar.

fruit: Olives and grapes are appropriate for the altar; others for neither upkeep nor the altar.

grasses: Appropriate for neither.

R. Simeon: The cases of a tree and a field differ from the rest, presumably because their contents are produced directly from them.

The offspring of a tithed animal: Three times each year a tithe of ten percent of the new animals born during that period was required by the Temple. The animals were sacrificed and eaten by their owners, rather than by the priests. See Leviticus 27:32, *Bekhorot* 9:5–7; *Temurah* 3:5.

but others are donated thus: Or "others may donate." The dedicated offspring may not nurse from the dedicated mother, but others may donate milk or nursing animals for this purpose.

The offspring of a consecrated animal: See *Temurah* 3:1.

laborers... a cow may not eat: A reference to the usual permission of both to eat from produce while they are laboring. Cf. Deuteronomy 23:25; 25:4; *Bava Metsi'a* 7:2–5.

3:7 *The roots*: In both cases, part of the tree is growing in sacral land and part in nonsacral land. The tree may not be used, but it is also not subject to sacrilege.

one may not benefit from it,
but it is not subject to sacrilege.
A spring that flows from a field that belongs to consecrated property—
one may not benefit from it,
but it is not subject to sacrilege;
if it flowed outside of the field,
one may benefit from it.
The water that is in the golden jar—
one may not benefit from it,
but it is not subject to sacrilege;
if it were put into the dish—
it is subject to sacrilege.
The willow branch—
one may not benefit from it,
but it is not subject to sacrilege;
R. Eleazar b. R. Zadok says:
The elders used to put [branches] from it in their palm fronds.

8 If a nest sits at the top of a tree that belongs to consecrated property—
one may not benefit,
but it is not subject to sacrilege.
If it is in an *asherah*—
one may cast it down with a reed.
If one consecrates a grove of trees—
all of it is subject to sacrilege.
Temple treasurers who purchased the trees—
the trees are subject to sacrilege;
but the shavings and foliage are not subject to sacrilege.

spring: Analogous with the preceding. The spring itself is not consecrated but the field is; as long as it flows in the field, its use is prohibited, although sacrilege does not apply.

golden jar: Used for keeping the water libations of Sukkot (the Festival of Tabernacles) overnight on the Sabbath, so as not to draw water on the Sabbath (*Sukkah* 4:1, 9–10). It was not yet consecrated, although use for any other purpose was prohibited.

the dish: Pouring the water into the dish used for the libations consecrated the water, *Sukkah* 4:9–10.

The willow branch: Used in the Temple to decorate the altar during the seven days of Sukkot, *Sukkah* 4:4–5.

elders: Or "old men." According to R. Eleazar b. Zadok, the elders would make ritual use of cuttings from the willow branch.

palm fronds: A combination of palm frond, willows, and myrtle used in the ritual of Sukkot, Leviticus 23:40; *Sukkah* 3:4, 4:4.

3:8 *asherah*: A tree used for pagan worship, from which one is forbidden to benefit. See *Avodah Zarah* 3:7–9.

one may cast it down: One may derive benefit from a nest that is on an *asherah*. This rule is more lenient than for trees belonging to the Temple.

Temple treasurers who purchased the trees: Or "the wood." Presumably, the wood is to be used as lumber in the Temple, and the intention was not to purchase its by-products.

Chapter Four

4:1–6 *Substances That Combine to Constitute a Prohibited Amount*

4 Offerings for the altar
combine with one another with respect to sacrilege
and to render one liable for *piggul*, for remnant, or for impurity.
Offerings for the Temple upkeep—
combine with one another.
Offerings for the altar and offerings for the Temple upkeep—
combine with one another with respect to sacrilege.[19]

2 Five elements of a whole burnt offering combine with one another—
(1) the meat, and (2) the fat, and (3) the fine flour, and (4) the wine, and (5) the oil;
and six of a thank offering—
(1) the meat, and (2) the fat, and (3) the fine flour, and (4) the wine, and (5) the oil, and (6) the bread.
Terumah, and *terumah* from the tithe, and *terumah* from the tithe from *demai*,

[19] **K** lacks "with respect to sacrilege."

4:1–6 Impurity or liability for transgression with regard to some material may depend on whether the substance was of a sufficient amount. This chapter explores which items can be combined to constitute the minimum amounts.

4:1 *combine with one another*: If, taken together, the benefit obtained from all items consecrated for the altar adds up to a *perutah*, there is liability for sacrilege. Cf. *Zevahim* 3:4.

piggul... remnant... impurity: For these, the minimum amount for liability or impurity is an olive's bulk.

Offerings for the Temple upkeep: In this case, only *sacrilege* applies, if the combined benefit is a *perutah*-worth.

4:2 *Five elements... combine*: Any combination of two or more of these items that equal an olive's bulk or a *perutah*-worth are considered to add up when calculating whether a transgression has taken place with regard to the items. A *whole burnt offering* is entirely burnt on the altar, and forbidden for any personal benefit. See Numbers 15:1–6.

fat: Heb. *helev*. Abdominal fat which is prohibited for use by anyone, and is offered on the altar. See Leviticus 3:17.

fine flour... wine... oil: These accompany most sacrifices (see *Menahot*, introduction).

thank offering: See Leviticus 7:11–15, 22:29–30; *Zevahim* 5:6. This differed from other offerings of well-being in that forty loaves of bread were brought with it. See *Menahot* 7:1.

Terumah, etc.: Donations of produce to the priests. Priests and their families may eat them in a state of purity. Lay people may not derive benefit from these portions, and may not derive benefit from their crops or dough until the priestly portion has been separated. Deuteronomy 18:4–5. Cf. Leviticus 22:10–16; *Terumot*, introduction.

terumah from the tithe: Given by Levites from the tithes they receive. Numbers 18:25–32 *Ma'aserot*, introduction.

terumah from the tithe from demai: *Demai* is produce about which there is a suspicion that the proper tithes have not been removed. See *Demai*, introduction. One who acquired *demai* had to separate the tithes, and separate the priestly portion from the tithe.

and dough offering, and firstfruits, combine with one another—
with respect to prohibition,
and to render one liable for an added fifth.

3 All *piggul* combine with one another.
All remnants combine with one another.
All pieces of carcass meat[20] combine with one another.
All vermin combine with one another.
The blood of vermin and its flesh combine with one another.[21]
R. Joshua said a general rule:
All whose impurity and prohibited statutory amounts are equal
combine with one another.
Its impurity [was equal], but not its prohibited statutory amount,
its prohibited statutory amount, but not its impurity,
neither its prohibited statutory amount, nor its impurity—
they do not combine with one another.

4 *Piggul* and remnant do not combine with one another
because they are of two categories.[22]
Vermin and carcass,
and so too carcass and the flesh of a corpse,
do not combine with one another[23] to render an item or person impure,
even according to the less stringent of the two.

[20] Lit. "carcasses." [21] **K**, **P** add "in the measure of a lentil." [22] Lit. "names."
[23] **K**: "combine with one another."

dough offering: A portion removed from the dough and donated to the priests. Numbers 15:17–21; *Hallah* 1:9 and introduction.

firstfruits: Brought on pilgrimage to the Temple and donated to the priests. Deuteronomy 26:1–4; *Bikkurim* 1:3, 3:1, and introduction.

with respect to prohibition: These combine to constitute the amount that, if mixed with other food, renders it all prohibited to lay people. The minimal amount is disputed. See *Orlah* 2:4–7.

added fifth: A nonpriest who mistakenly eats an olive's worth of any of these is required to repay the equivalent of the consumed produce plus an added fifth. See Leviticus 22:14; *Bava Metsi'a* 4:8; *Terumot* 6:1.

4:3 *All piggul* from any source that together constituted a olive's bulk. See above, 1:2.

All remnants: Above, 1:2.

carcass: Heb. *nevelah*, meat that was not properly slaughtered.

vermin: Heb. *sherets*, "creeping thing" such as insects, rodents, or lizards. Consuming these is forbidden and they transmit impurity. See Deuteronomy 14:21; Leviticus 11:24–31, 39–43.

All whose impurity and prohibited statutory amounts are equal: Items that convey impurity by the same means and/or for the same length of time (although whether both are meant is disputed) and that require the same minimum amount for prohibition or impurity to apply.

4:4 *two categories*: Although equivalent both in impurity and in statutory amount, *piggul* and remnant are considered two different legal categories, and do not combine.

even according to the less stringent of the two: The Mishnah adds to the rule of 4:3 that although one might have thought that a combination of impure substances of more and less stringent types should be sufficient to convey impurity at least at the less stringent level, even if it could not at the more stringent, such substances cannot in fact combine. See *Eduyot* 2:1 and annotations there for more on sources of impurity.

Food[24] that has been rendered impure by a primary impurity
and food that has been rendered impure by a reduced-degree impurity[25]
combine with one another to transmit impurity
according to the less stringent of the two.
5 All foods combine with one another—
to disqualify the body with the half of a half-loaf-sized bulk,
with two meals' worth of food with respect to *eruv*;
with an egg-sized bulk to render impure with food impurity;
with a dried-fig-sized bulk with respect to prohibited transporting on the Sabbath;
with a date-sized bulk with respect to the Day of Atonement;
All liquids combine with one another—
to disqualify the body with a quarter-*log*,
and with a mouthful with respect to the Day of Atonement.
6 *Orlah* and prohibited mixtures of the vineyard combine with one another.
R. Simeon[26] says:
They do not combine with one another.
Cloth and sacking, sacking and hide, hide and matting, combine with one another.

[24] **K**: "Food that has been rendered impure; all that has been rendered impure."
[25] Lit. "offspring of the impurity." [26] **K**: "Joshua."

rendered impure by a primary impurity…reduced-degree impurity: Parallel with explication at *Tohorot* 1:5–6; see also *Tohorot*, introduction. A source of primary impurity may convey lesser-degree impurity to persons or objects including foodstuffs. See *Kelim* 1 and *Eduyot* 2:1, annotations. These may in turn convey impurity in the third and fourth degree to foodstuffs of special sanctity (*terumah* or sacrificial meat).

combine…according to the less stringent of the two: A bit of second-degree foodstuff and of third-degree foodstuff combine to make a single egg-sized bulk of foodstuff that is impure in the third degree.

4:5 For the volumes specified here see *Kelim* 17:4–12.

to disqualify the body: Under rabbinic law, one who eats a half of a half-loaf-sized bulk (Heb. *peras*) of impure food is prohibited from eating the *terumah*. See *Eruvin* 8:2; *Miqva'ot* 10:7; *Tohorot* 1:3.

eruv: See *Eruvin* 8:1–2, and introduction. Rabbis understood people's travel on the Sabbath to be limited to two thousand cubits in any direction from their Sabbath residence. Depositing two meals' worth of food at a location up to two thousand cubits outside one's actual residence establishes that place as the Sabbath residence, permitting one to travel two thousand cubits beyond that location in any direction.

egg-sized bulk: See *Kelim* 17:6 and above, 4:4.

dried-fig-sized bulk: See *Kelim* 17:7; parallel in *Shabbat* 7:4.

date-sized bulk: See parallel in *Yoma* 8:2. Cf. *Kelim* 17:12. The reference is to the minimum amount for liability for eating on the fast day.

quarter-log: Drinking this amount of impure liquid renders one prohibited from eating *terumah*.

a mouthful: See *Kelim* 17:11.

4:6 *Orlah*: See Leviticus 19:23; *Orlah* 2:1 and introduction.

prohibited mixtures of the vineyard: See Deuteronomy 22:9 and *Kilayim*, introduction.

Cloth and sacking, sacking and hide, hide and matting, combine: These materials differ in terms of how they become impure, and the minimum quantity for susceptibility for impurity. See *Kelim* 27:1–3. According to *Kelim*, the amount required to make the material susceptible to impurity, and the proportion of each material in the combined fabric determine whether they in fact combine.

R. Simeon says:[27]
Because they are capable of being rendered impure by sitting.

Chapter Five

5:1–2 *Sacrilege Requires Benefit and Degradation*

5 One who benefited by a *perutah*-worth from consecrated offerings,
even if he did not degrade [the value]—
has committed sacrilege—
the words of R. Aqiva;
but the Sages say:
Anything that is subject to degradation [in value],
he has not committed sacrilege until he has degraded it;
and anything that is not subject to degradation [in value],
once he has benefited from it, he has committed sacrilege.
How?
If she put a necklace on her neck, a ring on her hand; drank from a golden goblet—
once she has benefited, she has committed sacrilege.
If he wore a tunic, or covered himself with a cloak, or chopped with an ax—
he has not committed sacrilege until he has degraded it.
If he plucked wool from a purgation offering while it was still alive—
he has not committed sacrilege until he has degraded it;
once it had died—
once he has benefited from it, he has committed sacrilege.

[27] **K** adds "what is the reason for this?"

capable of being rendered impure by sitting: Since they can all become impure if a person with a seminal discharge sits on them, they can be combined for the purpose of impurity. This contrasts with R. Simeon's view above in connection with *orlah* and prohibited mixtures of the vineyard.

5:1 *One who benefited*: See introduction. *R. Aqiva* does not require degradation of the property.

subject to degradation [in value]: If the property is of such a type that wear and tear are inevitable. The Mishnah provides examples below.

until he has degraded it: In a case where the property is subject to wear and tear, the Sages disagree and deem someone accountable for sacrilege only if that person has done something to devalue the sacred object while benefiting from it.

necklace…ring…golden goblet: These objects do not normally deteriorate through use.

tunic…cloak…ax: These objects do deteriorate through use.

plucked wool: The theory is that a live animal would be devalued if one used it, whereas a dead one would not. This is enigmatic and is unsatisfactorily explained in the Babylonian Talmud.

2 If he benefited by half a *perutah*-worth and degraded by half a *perutah*-worth
or if he benefited by the equivalent of a *perutah*-worth from one item
and degraded another item by the equivalent of a *perutah*-worth—
in this case he has not committed sacrilege
until he has benefited by a *perutah*-worth and degraded by a *perutah*-worth
from a single item.

5:3–5 *Sacrilege Split between Two or More People*

3 There is no committer of sacrilege following a committer of sacrilege
for consecrated property,
except for animals and sacred vessels
How?
If he rode on an animal,
and his fellow came and rode,
and his fellow came and rode;[28]
he drank from a golden cup,
and his fellow came and drank,
and his fellow came and drank;
he plucked wool from a purgation offering
and his fellow came and plucked,
and his fellow came and plucked—
they have all committed sacrilege.
Rabbi says:
Anything to which redemption does not apply,
there is a committer of sacrilege following a committer of sacrilege.

[28] **K** lacks this line, but retains it in the parallel cases below.

5:2 *And degraded by half a perutah-worth.* The partial damage and the partial benefit do not combine to a single *perutah*-worth.

until he has benefited…from a single item: In all cases involving objects that degrade through use, both the benefit and the deterioration must be worth a *perutah*, and must be done to a single object in order to be considered sacrilege.

5:3 *committer of sacrilege following a committer of sacrilege*: Subsequent acts of sacrilege on the same property.

except for animals and sacred vessels: These cannot be redeemed (see below), and are therefore permanently consecrated. Each time one commits sacrilege then, it is another act on a holy object. In other cases, the property ceases to be sacred and thus no longer subject to sacrilege (Rashi).

they have all committed sacrilege: Each of these cases involves a consecrated animal or sacred vessel. Thus, each actor is separately responsible for the sacrilege committed, and must bring the sacrifice and the added fifth required.

Anything for which redemption does not apply: Rabbi provides the principle that governs the above rules.

4 If one took a rock or a beam belonging to the consecrated offerings—
in this case, this one has not committed sacrilege;
if he gave it to another—
[the giver] has committed sacrilege,
and his fellow has not committed sacrilege.
If he built it into his house—
in this case, this person has not committed sacrilege,
unless he dwells under it, [benefiting] by the equivalent of a *perutah*-worth.
If he took a *perutah* belonging to the consecrated offerings—
in this case, this one has not committed sacrilege;
if he gave it to his fellow—
[the giver] has committed sacrilege
and his fellow has not committed sacrilege.
If he gave it to the bathhouse attendant—
even if he did not bathe,
[the giver] has committed sacrilege,
for [the attendant] says to him: "The bathhouse is open, come in and bathe."

5 His eating and the eating of his fellow;
his benefit and the benefit of his fellow;
his eating and the benefit of his fellow;
his benefit and the eating of his fellow—
combine with one another,
even after a long time.

5:4 *If one took a rock or a beam*: The reasoning behind this passage is mysterious. The Babylonian Talmud and later commentaries explain it as referring to a Temple treasurer who gives the object to someone unrelated to the Temple, thereby removing it from the Temple premises. Alternatively, the giving of the sacred property to one's fellow confers on the giver the benefit of the receiver's gratitude and possible willingness to return the favor at some later point.

his fellow has not committed sacrilege: Presumably, this would be sacrilege following sacrilege, as in 5:3.

If one took a perutah . . . has not committed sacrilege: There is no benefit from the taking itself.

gave it to the bathhouse attendant: The giver derives the benefit of access to the bathhouse, even without actually bathing.

5:5 *His eating and the eating of his fellow*: The first user benefited by only half a *perutah*-worth, only did half of the act of sacrilege, and gave the consecrated property to another person who similarly only benefited by half the amount. This is accounted as if the first person has received a *perutah*-worth of benefit, and has committed sacrilege.

even after a long time: Later commentaries agree the long time must still constitute a single period during which the sacrilege has not yet come to the attention of the users of the property.

Chapter Six

6:1–5 *Sacrilege Carried Out by an Agent or Other Third Party*

6 If an agent has carried out his charge—
the householder has committed sacrilege;
if he did not carry out his charge—
the agent has committed sacrilege.
How?
If he said to him:
"Give meat to the guests," and he gave them liver;
"Liver,"[29] and he gave them meat—
the agent has committed sacrilege.
If he said to him:
"Give it to them one piece at a time,"
and he said to them: "Take two at a time,"
and they took three at a time—
they have all committed sacrilege.
If he said to him:
"Bring [an item] from the wall niche[30] or from a box,"
and he brought it to him—
even if the householder said: "I meant specifically from that one,"[31]
and he brought it from the other—
the householder has committed sacrilege.
But if he said to him:

[29] Lacking in **K**. [30] Here and below, for "niche," *halon*, **K** has *hullin/m*, "nonsacral goods."
[31] Lit. "I had in my heart only from this."

6:1 *The agent* was charged to perform an act that, unknown to either the agent or the householder, constituted sacrilege. If the agent *carried out his charge* the responsibility for sacrilege falls on *the householder* on the principle that the agent is considered an extension of the householder. Cf. *Berakhot* 5:5.

if he did not ... the agent has committed sacrilege: The agent's act represents his own will, and the responsibility is his own.

they have all committed sacrilege: The householder's will that each receive one piece is both fulfilled and added to by the agent who is culpable for the second piece, and the agent's will is both fulfilled and added to by the guests who are culpable for the third.

"*Bring [an item] from the wall niche*": The householder did not specify the exact location, and thus the agent did not know the householder's intent, so the agent is considered to have carried out the will of the householder.

even if the householder said: Subsequently, the householder specified which location he meant, and the agent had chosen the other location".

"Bring me from the niche,"
and he brought it from a box;
or "From the box,"
and he brought it from the niche—
the agent has committed sacrilege.

2 If he sent it with a deaf-mute person, one legally incompetent, or a minor:
if they completed their charge—
the householder has committed sacrilege;
if they did not complete their charge—
the shopkeeper[32] has committed sacrilege;
if he sent it with one legally competent,
and he remembered before the agent arrived at the shopkeeper—
the shopkeeper has committed sacrilege when he spends it.
What should he do?
He should take a *perutah* or a utensil and say:
"The *perutah* of the offerings of the Temple, wherever it is, is deconsecrated by this,"
for a consecrated offering is redeemed by money or the equivalent value of money.

3 If he gave him a *perutah*, and said to him:
"Bring me lamps with half of it, and wicks with half of it,"
and he went and brought him lamps with all of it, or wicks with all of it;
or if he said to him:
"Bring me lamps with all of it";
or "Wicks with all of it,"
and he went and brought him lamps with half of it and wicks with half of it—

[32] **P** adds "the messenger"; **C** has "the messenger"; both are likely errors.

"from the niche," and he brought it from the box: The agent has made a change to the orders of the householder, thus the act reflects his own will.

6:2 *deaf-mute . . . minor*: A trio of individuals who do not have legally effective will; the householder remains liable. This is slightly puzzling since in principle we might expect these persons not to be able to become extensions of the householder. The cases assume that the householder has sent someone with money to a shopkeeper to purchase something.

the householder has committed sacrilege: Since the agents cannot be liable.

the shopkeeper has committed sacrilege: Since no sacrilege has occurred before the money arrived in the shopkeeper's hands, it has also not been deconsecrated (see above, 5:3). If the shopkeeper then spends it (as below), the shopkeeper will have committed sacrilege.

he remembered: Sacrilege occurs only unwittingly. Since the householder is now knowingly gaining benefit from sacred money, he is not liable for sacrilege. However, *the shopkeeper*, who does not know that the money is consecrated, does *commit sacrilege when he spends* the money. See Leviticus 5:15. Cf. *Qiddushin* 2:8.

What should he do? How should the householder prevent the shopkeeper from committing sacrilege? Alternatively, what should the shopkeeper do once he learns that the *perutah* is consecrated, but has been mixed in with other coins?

"*The perutah . . . is deconsecrated by this*": The householder (or shopkeeper) transfers the sanctity onto a new coin or object, thus rendering the money in the hands of the shopkeeper unconsecrated.

is redeemed by money: *Arakhin* 8:1.

neither of them has committed sacrilege.
But if he said to him:
"Bring me lamps with half of it from such-and-such place
and wicks with half of it from such-and-such place,"
and he went and brought him lamps from a place for wicks
and wicks from a place for lamps[33]—
the agent has committed sacrilege.

4 If he gave him two *perutah* and said to him:
"Bring me a citron,"
and he went and brought him a citron with one *perutah*
and a pomegranate with one *perutah*—
they have both committed sacrilege.
R. Judah says:
The householder has not committed sacrilege,
for he could say to him:
"I wanted a large citron,
and you have brought me a small and bad one."
If he gave him a golden *dinar*, and said to him:
"Bring me a shirt,"
and he went and brought him a shirt for three [*sela*] and a cloak for three—
they have both committed sacrilege.
R. Judah says:
The householder has not committed sacrilege,
for he could say to him:
"I wanted a large shirt and you have brought me a small bad one."

5 One who deposits coins with a moneychanger:
if they are bound—
he may not make use of them,
therefore, if he spent them he has committed sacrilege.
Loose—
he may make use of them,

[33] "Place for" lamps, wicks, lit. "house of."

6:3 *neither of them has committed sacrilege*: Neither has carried out the act with a full *perutah*-worth of consecrated property.

the agent has committed sacrilege: The agent has used the entire *perutah* according to his own will.

6:4 *they have both committed sacrilege*: One *perutah* was spent on the *etrog* (citron) fulfilling the charge of the householder, and another on the pomegranate, according to the agent's will.

R. Judah... has not committed sacrilege: The householder can claim that his charge was not fulfilled at all.

a golden dinar: Six *sela*, or twenty-four silver *dinar*.

"*Bring me a shirt*": This illustrates the same principle as above.

6:5 Parallel to *Bava Metsi'a* 3:11, stated in terms of liability for the deposit.

he has committed sacrilege: Since he has spent the bound coins according to his own will.

therefore, if he spent them he has not committed sacrilege.
With a householder:
in either case, he may not use them,
therefore, if he spent them he has committed sacrilege.
The shopkeeper is like the householder—
the words of R. Meir;
R. Judah says:
Like the moneychanger.

6:6 *Ambiguity in the Committing of Sacrilege*

6 A *perutah* of consecrated offerings that fell into a purse,
or if one said: "A *perutah* in this purse is consecrated"—
once he has spent the first he has committed sacrilege—
the words of R. Aqiva;
and the Sages say:
Not until he has spent the entire purse.
R. Aqiva concedes that in the case of the one who says:
"A *perutah* from this purse is consecrated,"
he may continue to spend until spending the entire purse.

he has not committed sacrilege: The fact that the moneychanger was permitted to use loose coins means that the moneychanger is still complying with the owner's will (Rashi). The commentaries debate whether the owner of the money is liable.

in either case, he may not use them: A householder who holds money belonging to another may never use the coins and *if* the householder *spent them he has committed sacrilege.*

like the householder... Like the moneychanger: The dispute between R. Meir and R. Judah revolves around whether the shopkeeper is assumed to be permitted to use loose money deposited with him.

6:6 *Once he has spent the first*: According to *R. Aqiva*, since it is unknown which *perutah* is the consecrated one, even the first which is removed from the purse is considered to be potentially consecrated. See *Keritot* 5:2–3.

until he has spent the entire purse: Only then is it certain that the consecrated coin has been spent.

"*A perutah from this purse is consecrated*": The dedicator dedicates an unspecified coin in a purse. *R. Aqiva concedes* that since no *perutah* was specified, the dedicator could claim that any individual coin was not the consecrated one, as long as all of the coins have not been spent.

Tractate Tamid

Naftali S. Cohn

Introduction

Overview

Tamid ("perpetual," "continual," or "daily") refers to the *qorban tamid*, the twice-daily sacrifice of a year-old lamb, and to additional associated daily rituals described in the Bible and performed in the Jerusalem Temple.

Structure and Organization of the Tractate

The tractate is in the form of a ritual narrative, a chronologically unfolding account of how the daily ritual was done. The account begins with the priests guarding the Temple (1:1), continues with the arrival of the "one in charge" and general preparations (1:2–4), and goes on to describe the acts that make up the larger ritual:

1:4–2:5 Preparing the main altar;
3:1–5 Drawing lots and preparing for the sacrifice;
3:6–9 Clearing the inner incense altar and the lampstand and relighting the lamps;
4:1–3 Slaughtering and butchering the lamb and doling out its parts;
5:1 Taking a break for prayer;
5:2–6 Drawing lots again and preparing to offer the incense;
6:1 Completing the clearing of the inner altar and lampstand and relighting of the lamps;
6:2–3 Offering the incense;
7:1 The high priest and the performing priests bowing and exiting the Sanctum;
7:2 The priests reciting the priestly blessing;
7:3 Placing the animal parts on the altar to be burnt
7:3 Pouring the wine libation
7:3 The sounding of cymbals, the Levites singing the daily psalm, and repeated soundings of trumpets and prostrations.

The tractate focuses almost exclusively on the morning ritual. The precise differences between morning and afternoon are not fully spelled out anywhere. Some details about the afternoon offering appear in 4:1 and 6:1, and more appear in tractate *Yoma*.

While the narration in the tractate is largely focused on the components of the larger set of rituals associated with the continual offering, it also gives attention to the flow of the daily schedule in the Temple and to the choreography of the daily schedule (and the daily offering) within the Temple's spaces. Frequent mention is made of the opening of gates and movement within a space or from one space to another. With this, *Tamid* overlaps to a degree with *Middot*.

The narrative style found here is not unique to *Tamid*, and can be found in many passages in the Mishnah related to the Temple, often connected with annual rituals (e.g. *Yoma* chapters 1–7, *Bikkurim* 3:2–8, *Pesahim* 5:5–10, and *Menahot* 10:3–5). Comparison with earlier accounts of similar rituals suggests that the rabbinic authors of the Mishnah have shaped these accounts, in part guided by what they understood to be the correct law, though also influenced by their own self-understanding as a group. The tractate, moreover, appears to be envisioned as a guide for the future. This can be seen in the dramatic concluding words of the main description of the ritual: "This is the order of the continual offering for the worship in the house of our God. May it be [God's] will that it be rebuilt speedily in our days" (7:3).

Main Ideas

Tamid gives details of how precisely the continual offering and the attendant daily rituals must be performed. These could only be done when there was a Temple in Jerusalem, and so what is described was not done in practice in the time of the Mishnah, when there was no Temple. The Mishnah's authors, however, did consider these rules legally binding, and believed that the rituals would (or ought to) be performed as described when the Temple would be rebuilt (7:3).

There are various technical terms used in the tractate:

Altar There were two different altars in the Temple, both of which feature prominently in the tractate. There is the larger altar outside the Sanctum, at the border between the Israelites' Court and Priests' Court, where animal sacrifices are made. And there is the smaller altar, inside the Sanctum (in the "Holy"), where the incense was offered. In the Bible, the larger altar is called either the "copper altar" or the "altar of the burnt offering." In the Mishnah, it is almost always simply called the altar (as in this tractate), but sometimes called the "outer altar" or rarely even the biblical "copper altar" and "altar of the burnt offering." The smaller altar in the Bible is "the incense altar" and "the golden altar." In the Mishnah it is usually the "inner altar" as in this tractate, or occasionally the biblical "golden altar." More descriptive details about both altars and about other Temple objects and spaces also mentioned in *Tamid* can be found in tractate *Middot*.

One in charge (memuneh) The rituals described in *Tamid* frequently include the one in charge as an important character who functions as the ritual actor with ultimate authority in overseeing and running the ritual. He appears in 1:2, 3:1–3, 5:1, 6:3, and 7:1. Similarly, he appears in the parallel passages in *Yoma* 2:1 and 3:1. Outside of these passages, the character is quite rare in the Mishnah. *Sheqalim* 5:1 and 5:4 use the term in what appears to be a slightly different way, and the term is used for a ritual role in non-Temple contexts in *Bikkurim* 3:2 and *Sanhedrin* 2:1.

Continual offering (Tamid) As noted above and below, this terminology refers especially to the twice-daily animal sacrifice mandated in the Bible, and also sometimes to the related daily rituals. Occasional references to this sacrifice appear elsewhere in the Mishnah.

Relationship to Scripture

Both Exodus 29:38–42 and Numbers 28:3–8 refer to the *tamid* ("continual") burnt offering: a year-old lamb sacrificed together with a baked grain offering and wine libation, offered every morning and afternoon. References to this offering are numerous throughout the Hebrew Bible, found repeatedly in Numbers 28–29, and in Ezekiel 46:14–15, Daniel 11:31 and 12:1, Ezra 3:5, Nehemiah 10:34, 1 Chronicles 16:40 and 23:31, and 2 Chronicles 2:3 and 24:14. See also Leviticus 6:13, Numbers 4:16, and Psalms 50:8.

In addition to the *tamid* animal sacrifice and attendant grain and wine offerings, there are further elements of the regular cult named in the Torah and elsewhere in the Bible as "continual": a "continual" incense offering (Exodus 30:8, 2 Chronicles 2:3, and possibly Numbers 4:16), a "continual" altar fire (Leviticus 6:6), "continual" lighting of the Menorah lights (Exodus 27:20 and 30:8, and Leviticus 24:2–4), "continual" showbread on the sacred table (Exodus 25:30, Leviticus 24:5–9, Numbers 4:7, and Nehemiah 10:34), and "continual" trumpet blasts (1 Chronicles 16:6). The implication in most of these examples is that the rituals are done not continuously but continually, presumably daily.

Although each of these "continual" ritual components is mentioned only briefly in the Bible, tractate *Tamid* takes them all up (with the exception of the showbread, only barely mentioned here but discussed more fully in *Menahot*), providing considerable detail about their precise choreography.

Tractate Tamid

Chapter One

1:1 *The Priests Guard the Temple at Night*

I The priests stand guard in the Temple in three places:
(1) the Place of Avtinas, (2) the Place of the Spark, and (3) the Place of the Hearth.
The Place of Avtinas and the Place of the Spark were upper chambers,
and the young men[1] stand guard there.
The Place of the Hearth was vaulted,
and it was a large room,[2] surrounded by stone landings.
And the elders of the paternal house sleep there,
and the keys to the Temple Court are in their hand.
And the young priests[3] are there as well, each with his mattress[4] on the ground.
They would not sleep in the sacred garments,
but would strip, fold them up, and place them under their heads.
And they would cover themselves with their own personal garment.
If one of them had a seminal emission,

[1] Meaning uncertain. Some interpret: "archers." [2] Or, "building."
[3] Lit. "blossoms of the priesthood." [4] **K** (as vocalized): "his garment."

1:1 *priests stand guard*: See also *Middot* 1:1, which includes Levites guarding outside of the Temple.

(1) The Place of Avtinas, (2) the Place of the Spark, and (3) the Place of the Hearth: "*Bet*," lit. "house of," or "place of," is used to designate various chambers within the Temple. *Avtinas* is the name of the priestly family associated with the incense; see *Sheqalim* 5:1; for the Place of Avtinas see also *Middot* 1:1, *Yoma* 1:5 and 3:11. The function of the the Place of the Spark is unclear; see further *Middot* 1:5 and parallel in *Middot* 1:1. On "Place of the Hearth," see *Shabbat* 1:11; see also references in 1:3 and 3:3 below; *Middot* 1:1, 5–9.

upper chambers: Located on the upper story, built atop a gate (as in *Middot* 1:5) or above the roofed colonnade surrounding the Temple or the Temple Court.

vaulted: It had a vaulted ceiling. See a slightly different version of the description of this room in *Middot* 1:6–9.

paternal house: A formal division of priests, a subset of the priestly watch. See *Ta'anit* 2:6–7. On the chief of the paternal house, see *Yoma* 3:9–4:1.

seminal emission rendered the priest impure and necessitated *immersion* (see *Miqva'ot* 8:2; and see *Kelim* 1:5 on the consequences in relation to the sacred). Cf. the version in *Middot* 1:9.

he would exit and leave by the winding passageway that goes under the structure,[5]
where lamps were burning on either side,
[continuing] until he reaches the Place of Immersion.
And there was an open fire there,
and the place of the throne[6] of honor.
And this was its honor:
if a person found it locked,
he would know there was someone inside.
And if he found it open,
he would know there was no one inside.
He went down, immersed himself, came up, dried off,
and warmed himself against the fire.
He came and sat with his brothers the priests until the gates were opened.
He would exit and go on his way.

1:2–2:2 *The Morning Continual Offering*

2 Whoever wanted to clear the ashes from the altar would arise early
and immerse himself before the one in charge arrived.
And at what time did the one in charge arrive?
The times were not always the same:
sometimes he would arrive at cockcrow,

[5] See annotations. [6] Or "chair."

winding passageway: Distinct from the passageway with the same name leading to the roof of the Temple at *Middot* 4:5 (and 4:3, 4:7, 5:3).

the structure: Some interpret this as referring to the Temple.

throne of honor: A euphemism for the toilet, located in the Place of Immersion. The expression is also used for God's "Throne of Glory" (Jeremiah 14:21 and 17:12). Here, the expression hints at the way the procedure allowed for dignity in using the toilet. On the relevance of the toilet for the purification of the one with a seminal emission, see *Miqva'ot* 8:4.

He went down, immersed himself, came up, dried off: These are standard elements of an immersion; see *Yoma* 3:4, 3:6, 7:3–4; *Parah* 3:8. The priest who has now immersed is not allowed to enter the Temple Court because he is in the state of *tevul yom*, having immersed but not yet waited until sunset (*Kelim* 1:8). This suggests that there was a direct exit out of the Temple from the Place of the Hearth (see *Middot* 1:9).

1:2 *clear the ashes*: Alternatively, "to perform the clearing ritual for the altar"; see Leviticus 6:3. The procedure is described in the subsequent paragraphs here, especially in 1:4–2:2. See also *Yoma* 1:8–2:2.

immerse himself: See also *Yoma* 3:3. Though the priests were already pure, additional immersion was necessary before entering the Temple Court. Similarly, if they had used the toilet, they would have had to immerse (*Yoma* 3:2).

one in charge: Lit. "appointed one." This expression indicates a special role in running the performance of various rituals; see also below, 3:1–3, 5:1, 6:3, 7:1; *Yoma* 2:1; 3:1; *Sheqalim* 5:1, 4; *Bikkurim* 3:2; *Sanhedrin* 2:1. *Sheqalim* 5:4 suggests that certain individuals were appointed over particular tasks, and there, the one in charge of drawing lots (see below) is Matitiah b. Samuel. In *Tamid* and *Yoma*, however, the one in charge appears to oversee the entire ritual of the daily offering.

sometimes near it, either before or after it.
The one in charge would come and knock for them,
and they opened the [gate] for him.
He would say to them:
"Whoever has immersed may come and draw lots!"
They drew lots,
and whoever won, won.

3 He took the key and opened the wicket and entered
from the Place of the Hearth into the Temple Court,
and they entered after him, and there were two torches of fire in their hands.
And they divided themselves into two groups.
One would go into the recessed hallway[7] going eastward,
and the other would go into the recessed hallway going westward.
They would make an inspection as they walked,
until they arrived at the Place of the Cake Makers.[8]
When both [groups] arrived, they said:

[7] See annotations. [8] **K, P**: alternatively, "cake making."

knock…opened: It is unclear where the one in charge knocked. According to *Middot* 1:7, the Place of the Hearth had a gate leading into the Temple Court and one leading out to the ledge. The one in charge could thus have come from inside or outside the Temple, though 1:3 seems to assume that after he enters, the gate to the Temple Court is still locked. He may also have come up the winding passageway mentioned in 1:1 (assuming this had a door).

lots: See *Yoma* 2:1–2 for the explanation that originally priests would race to the top of the altar to determine who would perform the ritual, but because this procedure turned out to be dangerous, it was changed to lots. See also further detail on the lots in 3:1 below.

1:3 *He took*: The one in charge took the keys from the elders who kept them overnight. Alternatively, the one who had won the right to clear the ashes took them.

wicket: A small gate next to the main gate; see *Middot* 1:7.

two groups…until they arrived: All the priests on duty would split up; one group would go one way through the hallway surrounding the Temple Court, the other the other way, and they would meet up outside of the place where the cakes were made. This was an inspection to ensure all was in order (See *Middot* 1:7). This paragraph thus describes preparatory steps before the clearing of the ashes. The actual clearing begins in 1:4.

recessed hallway: This Greek architectural term (*exedra*) can refer to a niche, a smaller room, or another inset structure that runs the full length of the larger space to which it is adjacent. In context it refers to a hallway running along the sides of the Temple Court. Some priests go eastward into the hallway; some go westward, eventually meeting up at a different point in the hallway. Thus this hallway leads all the way around the Temple Court. Elsewhere a different term, derived from the Greek *stoa*, is used for what appears to be a colonnade that runs along the Temple courtyard and has an open roof available for the performance of certain rituals (see *Pesahim* 1:5, *Sheqalim* 8:4, *Sukkah* 4:4). It is unclear whether these two terms designate the same structure and whether they even refer to the same parts of the Temple. The former term may refer to the space surrounding the Israelite and Priestly Courts, the latter surrounding the Women's Court.

Cake Makers: This refers to the cakes offered by the high priest; see *Menahot* 4:5 and Leviticus 6:13–14. For this location, see also *Middot* 1:4 (which calls it the "chamber of" the cake makers). Here and throughout the tractate, the English "cake" is used in the general sense of a baked bread substance.

"Peace, all is well!"[9]
They set up those who make cakes[10] to make cakes.

4 The one who had won the right to clear the ashes from the altar
would be the one to clear the ashes from the altar,
and they would say to him:
"Be careful not to touch the vessel
until you wash[11] your hands and feet using the laver."
And the coal pan was there in the corner,[12]
between the ramp and the altar at the western side of the ramp.
No one entered with him, and he did not have a lamp in his hand.
Rather, he would walk by the light of the altar fire.
They would not be able to see him or hear his voice,[13]
until they heard the sound of the wood that Ben Qatin had made
as a mechanism for the laver.
And they would say:
"The time has arrived!"[14]
He washed his hands and feet using the laver.
He took the silver coal pan and went up to the top of the altar,
and he moved the coals aside this way and that.

[9] Lit. "Peace, all is peace!" [10] **K**: "They set up the cake-making place."
[11] Lit. "sanctify," and so throughout. [12] See annotations.
[13] Alt. "or hear his sound." **K**: "but only hear his voice"; or "his sound."
[14] **K, P**: "He has arrived!"

They set up: Those from the group with the task of making these cakes would remain in this room.

1:4 *clear the ashes*: See 1:2n. The actual clearing begins here. In the Mishnah there are three stages: (1) removing hot coals (1:4); (2) moving ashes from the altar fire to the ash pile (2:1–2); and (3) removing the ashes from the altar (implied in 2:2).

the vessel: i.e. the coal pan used to remove the coals.

And the coal pan: Alternatively, this phrase is also part of what the other priests say: "The coal pan is there, in the corner, between the ramp and the altar at the western side of the ramp."

the altar fire: Lit. "woodpile"; see 2:3–5.

until they heard: The priest would use the mechanism, and this would indicate that he had arrived at the laver.

mechanism: Such a mechanism frequently included a wheel or gear for lifting weight. According to *Yoma* 3:10 the mechanism allowed for the water to be covered at night, thus protecting it from becoming disqualified for sacred use. The Talmud and commentaries suggest the mechanism lowered and raised the laver from a basin in which it was submerged. Here in the morning, the mechanism would be making the laver fully operational by lifting it out of the basin.

"The time has arrived!" See n. 14. This reading is difficult: the ritual itself was already underway, and its proper time (dawn) had already arrived (see *Yoma* 1:8 and see 1:2 above). According to the manuscript reading ("He has arrived!"), the other priests get their first indication that all is proceeding smoothly when they hear him operating the mechanism to raise the laver.

he moved: He moved the newer coals to the side so he could access the older (glowing) coals in the middle of the pile, which he removed. Most commentators suggest that the inner coals were the most fully consumed by the fire. See the same procedure for the incense in 5:5 below.

He removed the innermost, thoroughly consumed, coals,
and he went down.
When he reached the floor, he turned to face north;
he went approximately ten cubits along the east side of the ramp;
and he piled up the coals on the stone floor,
three handbreadths from the ramp,
in the place where they put crops of birds
and the cleared-out ashes of the inner altar and the lampstand.

Chapter Two

2 When his brothers saw that he had descended,
they ran and came and quickly washed their hands and feet using the laver.
They took the shovels and the hooks[15]
and ascended to the top of the altar.
The animal parts and fats from the previous evening,
that had not been fully consumed,
they would press into the sides of the altar.
If the sides do not hold them,
they arrange them on the surrounding walkway, on the ramp.

[15] Others: "spits" or "rakes."

on the stone floor: This would fulfill the biblical prescription that the ashes be placed "near the altar" (Leviticus 6:3). The ramp itself was thirty-two cubits (approximately forty-eight feet or fifteen meters) long (*Middot* 3:3), and thus the pile would still be placed some distance from the altar (twenty-two cubits, or roughly thirty-three feet, or ten meters away), though quite close to the altar ramp (three handbreadths).

bird crops: Also placed "near the altar" (and "in the place of the ashes"), specifically on "the eastern side" (Leviticus 1:16).

inner altar and the lampstand: See 3:6–9 and 6:1.

2:1 *brothers*: i.e. the other priests.

ran and came: i.e. to the laver.

animal parts: The parts of the previous day's sacrifice, which had burned through the night. See the process of creating and offering the parts in 3:5, 4:1–3, 5:2 below; see also 2:5.

fats: See 4:2–3 (and 2:5).

press . . . into the sides of the altar: Pressed together to fit as much as possible on the top of the altar, out of the way. The animal parts not fully consumed are moved aside and placed on the outer parts of the top of the altar and, if necessary, on the surrounding walkway and ramp (see next annotation) so that the ashes underneath can be removed. The parts are subsequently returned to the (new) fire in 2:5 below.

on the surrounding walkway, on the ramp: According to *Middot* 3:1 (with *Zevahim* 5:3 and 6:5), the *walkway*, or "Surround," is a one-cubit wide (1.5 feet; 0.5 meter) walkway that encircles the entire altar near the top, and is accessible from the ramp leading up to the altar. It is distinct from the ramp, so the intention must be either that both spaces are used (thus "and on the ramp"); that one or the other is used (thus "or on the ramp"), or that the parts are placed near the nexus of the two (thus "near the ramp" or "near the surrounding walkway").

2 They began to lift up the ashes onto the ash pile.[16]
And the ash pile was in the middle of the altar.
At times it held as much as three hundred *kor*.[17]
And on the pilgrimage festivals they would not clear away its ashes,
for it beautified the altar.
In all his days,[18] the priest was not lazy in removing the ashes.

2:3–5 *Arranging and Lighting the Altar Fire*

3 They began to bring up pieces of wood to arrange the altar fire.
Were all types of wood fit for the altar fire?
Yes,[19] all types of wood were fit for the altar fire,
except that of olive [trees] and grapevines.
But they typically used the following:
the branches of fig trees, nut trees, and oil trees.
4 He arranged the large altar fire to the east.[20]

[16] Lit. "apple" or "pile." [17] Or "heaps," a measure of dry volume.
[18] Perhaps "its days," referring to the altar. [19] Lacking in **K**.
[20] Alt. "He made the altar fire large; it was to the east."

2:2 *the ash pile*: A pile of ashes was kept in the middle of the altar. A volume of three hundred *kor* is very large (one hundred gallons; roughly 360 liters). In the Talmud this is considered an exaggeration.

on the pilgrimage festivals: The Mishnah never says explicitly that the ash pile was cleared from the altar, but only implies this by saying it was not cleared on the festival days. While the ash pile must have been cleared, 2:4 implies that some of it remained on the altar. Perhaps he now moved the ashes to the same spot on the floor where the thoroughly consumed coals (and inner altar and lampstand ashes) were placed in 1:4, and then disposed of them together.

beautified by giving evidence of extensive use.

In all his days…not lazy: Priests acted diligently in performing their duty to remove the ash pile. This sentence appears to deny the previous one and to argue that the ashes were not in fact left in place on the festivals. Normally, however, such a contradictory view would be attributed to a particular rabbi and would not be stated anonymously. The commentaries understand this as a clarification: the build-up on the festivals was indeed for the sake of beauty and not priestly laziness.

2:3 *bring up* to the top of the altar.

altar fire: The term means literally a pile of wood or pyre, but comes to mean the fire as well (as can be seen in *Avot* 5:5). Here they are arranging the wood before igniting it.

Were all…? This type of rhetorical question is infrequent but does occur throughout the Mishnah.

olive…grapevines: These woods do not burn well.

oil trees: Also a biblical term (appearing together with olive trees in Nehemiah 8:15). Perhaps a particular variety of olive tree that is indeed good for kindling, or the tree of some other fruit that produces oil. Some translate "pine."

2:4 *He arranged*: The switch to the singular suggests that these actions were done by the one who had won the right to clear the ashes.

large altar fire: See 2:5, which mentions a second altar fire, and *Yoma* 4:6, which suggests there may have been more. Here, "altar fire" refers to the wood that is being arranged. The location of this pyre is to the eastern side of the altar.

And the points of the pile to the east.
And the ends of the innermost pieces of wood were touching the ash pile.
And there was space between the pieces of wood
where they would ignite the kindling wood.

5 They selected from there nice fig wood[21]
in order to arrange the second altar fire for the incense,
which was located at the southwestern corner of the altar,
four cubits away from the corner in the northern direction,
making approximately five *se'ah* of coals,
and on the Sabbath making approximately eight *se'ah* of coals,
for they would place the two dishes for the frankincense of the showbread there.
The animal parts and fats from the previous evening,
that had not been fully consumed,
they would return to the altar fire.
They lit the two altar fires,
and they descended,
and they came to the Chamber of Hewn Stones.

[21] Or "fig-tree wood."

the points: Lit. "rough side." The pile of wood was arranged in such a way that the narrower end of the wood pieces largely pointed in the eastward direction. According to most traditional interpreters, however, this refers not to the points of the wood but to a window-like opening on the eastern side of the pile for aeration or reaching in to ignite the wood.

ends of the innermost pieces: The pieces on the inside of the woodpile were longer and reached to the center of the altar, touching the ash pile (see 2:2 for the location of the ash pile).

2:5 *Selected from there*: From the place where the wood was stored or piled up for this purpose.

second altar fire: The first, "large," altar fire was for burning the animal pieces and fats (as in this paragraph), the second smaller one for burning the incense.

from the corner: This fire was thus on the eastern side of the altar, four cubits from the southeastern corner.

making: They selected an appropriate amount of wood to make the amount of coals specified.

of the showbread: See *Menahot* 11:7–8. The incense for the showbread was burned on the Sabbath, hence the need for more coals on that day.

would return the animal parts and the fats: After setting up the wood, they would recollect the partially burned animal parts and fats that had been pressed to the side or placed on the walkway or the ramp (2:1) and place them on the new pile of wood to continue burning.

Chamber of Hewn Stones, where they would recite the *Shema* passage (below, 4:3–5:1), as required every morning and evening (see *Berakhot* 1:1–4). In *Middot* 5:4 and *Sanhedrin* 11:2, this chamber is where the "Great Sanhedrin of Israel," or, "the Great Court" sat; there is no indication of this institution here.

Chapter Three

3:1–4 *Lots*

3 The one in charge said to them:
"Come and draw lots:
Who will slaughter? Who will sprinkle?
Who will clear the ashes from the inner altar?
Who will clear the ashes from the lampstand?
Who will bring up the animal parts to the ramp—
the head and the hindleg; the two forelegs; the rump and the hindleg; the breast and the neck; the two flanks; the innards;
and the fine flour, and the cakes, and the wine?"
They drew lots, and whoever won, won.
2 The one in charge[22] said to them:
"Go out and see if the time for slaughtering has arrived."
If it had arrived, the one who sees it says:
"Shining!"[23]
Matia b. Samuel says:

[22] **K, L** lack "The one in charge." [23] Alt. "Rays [of light]!"

3:1 *one in charge*: See annotation to 1:2.

"*Who will slaughter*," etc.: The entire paragraph from this point is paralleled in *Yoma* 2:3 (with a few additions).

"*sprinkle*": The blood on the altar.

"*inner altar*": The golden incense altar, located in the Sanctum (in the Holy).

"*bring up the animal parts*": The list of "animal parts" includes *the fine flour, and the cakes, and the wine* as well. These aspects of ritual are elaborated in what follows. On the cakes, see also 1:3 above.

"*fine flour*": Here and in 4:3 below, the grain offering specified in the biblical verses (see introduction) is merely mentioned.

whoever won, won: The import is that a different priest won the right to perform each task.

3:2 Parallel in *Yoma* 3:1 (and see *Yoma* 3:2).

"*time for slaughtering*": Likely some stage of the dawn subsequent to its first rising (already mentioned in 1:2). "*Shining*" may indicate a small amount of light, like the flash of lightning (this is the understanding in the Talmud), or perhaps the shining or rays of the sun. The illumination of the east until Hebron is similarly ambiguous, whether a stage in the dawn or else the sunrise.

Matia b. Samuel says: According to *Sheqalim* 5:1, Matitiah b. Samuel was the one in charge over the lots (for the continual offering), presumably at a particular point in history (though some interpretations suggest that all "ones in charge" would have that name). Assuming that Matia is simply a variant of Matitiah, the one in charge thus makes a second statement, and the ritual involves a ritualized back-and-forth about seeing the light in the sky. Alternatively, according to multiple commentaries, Matia b. Samuel offers a different opinion, namely that they waited until more of the sky had lightened. In this interpretation, Matia would appear to be a contemporary of the rabbis, many of whom cut into the descriptions of Temple rituals with differing opinions.

"Has the entire face of the east until Hebron been illuminated?"
And he responds:
"Yes!"[24]

3 He said to them:
"Go out and bring a lamb from the Chamber of Lambs."
And the Chamber of Lambs[25] was in the northwestern corner.
And there were four chambers there:
one was the Chamber of Lambs;
one was the Chamber of Seals;
one was the Chamber of the Place of the Hearth;
and one was the chamber in which they made the showbread.

4 They entered the Chamber of Vessels
from which they took out ninety-three silver and gold vessels.
They washed[26] the continual offering using a gold cup.
Even though it was examined the night before,
they examine it by the light of torches.

3:5 *Those Performing the Animal Sacrifice Set Out to the Butchering Location*

5 The one who won the right to the continual offering leads it
and goes to the Butchering Place,

[24] **K**: "Yes! Yes!"
[25] **K** lacks "And the Chamber of Lambs," perhaps a scribal error or evidence of scribal intervention; **P**: "Was not the Chamber of Lambs."
[26] Lit. "watered."

"*Yes!*" See similar affirmative ritualized answers in *Menahot* 10:3 and *Parah* 3:10.

3:3 *northwestern corner…four chambers there*: Cf. *Middot* 1:6, which appears partially contradictory. *Middot* lists four chambers specifically within the Place of the Hearth and only two of the four are described identically. Commentators harmonize the two passages by suggesting the *Place of the Hearth* in *Middot* and the one that went down to the Place of Immersion here are the same, that the chamber holding the defiled altar stones from Hasmonean times in *Middot* and the Chamber of Seals here are the same, and that these four here are within the Place of the Hearth. There is a further contradiction in that the *Chamber of Lambs* is in the southeastern not in the northwestern corner of the Place of the Hearth according to *Middot* 1:6. The Talmud points out these contradictions. The simplest interpretation is that the phrase *northwestern corner* means it was in the northwestern direction from where they were.

"*Chamber of Lambs*": See also *Arakhin* 2:5.

Chamber of Seals: See *Sheqalim* 5:3–4.

3:4 *Chamber of Vessels*: See a chamber of the same name in *Sheqalim* 5:6, where it seems to have a slightly different function.

they examine it: Again now, just before slaughtering.

3:5 *the right to the continual offering*: The right to slaughter it.

and those who won the right to [handle] the animal parts follow him.
The Butchering Place was to the north of the altar,
and it contained eight short columns topped by cedar blocks.
And there were iron hooks set into them, three rows for each,
on which they would hang and flay.
On[27] marble tables between the pillars.

3:6–8 *Opening the Gates of the Sanctum*

6 Those who had won the right to clear the ashes
from the inner altar and the lampstand would go first,
and they had four vessels in their hands:
The basket, the *kuz*, and two keys.
The basket is similar to a large golden two-*qav* vessel;
it holds two and one half *qav*.
And the *kuz* is similar to a large golden pitcher.
And the two keys—
one goes down into the "arm of the armpit,"
while the other opens straight.[28]
7 He came to the northern wicket.

[27] **K, P**: "And there were..."

[28] Or "straightaway."

short columns...hang and flay: See also *Pesahim* 5:9 and *Middot* 3:5. The carcasses of slaughtered animals would be hung up on the hooks and flayed.

cedar blocks: The precise arrangement is unclear. The wood may have connected the columns, forming horizontal beams across their tops, or it may have been paneling that covered the columns or part of the columns. The hooks may have been set in the wood or the stone.

On marble tables: See n. 27. This reading does not make sense. It is clear in *Pesahim* 5:9 that the animals are flayed while hanging on the hooks, not on the tables. The manuscript reading ("And there were marble tables between the pillars") therefore seems preferable. For the use of the tables, see 4:2 below.

3:6 *basket*: This is the receptacle into which the ashes are cleared (see 3:9).

kuz: A vessel either for clearing the ashes from the lampstand or for holding new oil for the lampstand.

two-qav vessel: Most commentaries, perhaps interpreting 5:4 below, understand that it is a vessel actually holding three-*qav* volumes (or a three-*qav* measure). The *kuz* is what holds 2.5-*qav* volumes.

pitcher: Alternatively, "jug," "ladle," or "drinking vessel."

"arm of the armpit": Obscure. The expression may indicate: that the lock or receptacle into which the key is placed is this shape; that the one opening the lock must insert his arm up to the armpit; or, interpreting the words slightly differently, that the priest must bend a distance of a cubit (an arm's length).

opens straight: The precise interpretation of this phrase depends on how the "arm of the armpit" is interpreted. Perhaps it opens without sticking in the arm or without much bending necessary. Or perhaps it simply opens more easily and quickly.

And the Great Gate had two wickets,
one on the northern side and one on the southern side.
The one on the southern side was never entered by anyone,
and this is stated explicitly by Ezekiel:
The Lord said to me, "This gate will be shut, it will not be opened,
and no man will enter through it, for the Lord God of Israel has entered through it,
and it shall remain shut."
He took the key and opened the wicket,
he entered the compartment, and from the compartment entered the Sanctum,
until he reached the Great Gate.
When he reached the Great Gate, he removed the bolt and the lock, and opened it.
The one slaughtering would not slaughter
until he heard the sound of the Great Gate being opened.

8 From Jericho they used to hear the sound of the Great Gate being opened.
From Jericho they used to hear the sound of the shovel.[29]
From Jericho they used to hear the sound of the wood
that Ben Qatin made as a mechanism for the laver.
From Jericho they used to hear the sound[30] of Gevini the crier.
From Jericho they used to hear the sound of the flute.
From Jericho they used to hear the sound of the cymbal.
From Jericho they used to hear the sound of the singing.

[29] Some commentaries: the name of a musical instrument. [30] Or "voice."

3:7 *The Great Gate*: The priest enters the Sanctum through a small gate ("wicket") and opens the great Temple gate from the inside.

And the Great Gate... the Sanctum: This portion of the Mishnah parallels *Middot* 4:2 (which adds a divergent opinion). Because the inner altar and lampstand are inside the Sanctum, in order to clear them (see 3:9) a priest must now open this gate.

stated explicitly by Ezekiel: Ezekiel 44:2. The verse does not mention any wickets, nor is it clear that it refers to the Sanctum. The Mishnah fits the verse into its own map of the Temple.

He took the key: The preceding paragraph refers to two keys; the second likely opened the doors of the great gate from inside the Sanctum. See the doors in *Middot* 4:1 .

he entered the compartment: The priest opened the wicket, entered the compartment inside the wicket, passed through into the Sanctum, and opened its main gate from the inside. Cf. R. Judah in *Middot* 4:2.

The one slaughtering: The detailed description begins in 4:1.

3:8 *From Jericho*: Jericho is roughly fifteen miles (twenty-five kilometers) from Jerusalem. This poetic list of sounds that could be heard at such a great distance obviously exaggerates.

shovel: See 5:6 below (with annotation) and 2:1 above.

Ben Qatin made: See 1:4 above.

Gevini the crier: See *Sheqalim* 5:1.

flute: See *Arakhin* 2:3.

cymbal: See 7:3 below.

singing: The Levites' singing. See 5:6 and 7:3–4 below; *Bikkurim* 3:4, *Sukkah* 5:4, *Rosh Hashanah* 4:4, *Arakhin* 2:6, *Middot* 2:5, and perhaps *Pesahim* 5:7.

From Jericho they used to hear the sound of the ram's horn.
And some say:
Even the sound[31] of the high priest
when he mentioned the divine name on the Day of Atonement.
From Jericho they used to smell the smell of the compounding[32] of the incense.
R. Eliezer b. Daglai said:
My father's house had goats in Mount Mikhvar,
and they used to sneeze at the smell of the compounding of the incense.

3:9 *Clearing the Ashes*

9 The one who had won the right to clear the ashes from the inner altar entered,
took the basket,
put it down in front of him,
and took handfuls and placed them in it.
And at the end, he swept up what remained into it, put it down, and exited.
The one who had won the right to clear the ashes from the lampstand entered,
and if he found the two easternmost lamps burning,
he would clear out the rest and leave these in place, burning.
If he found them extinguished,
he would clear out their ashes and light them from those still burning,
and subsequently clear the ashes from the rest.
And there was a stone that stood before the lampstand, which had three steps in it,
and the priest would stand on it and prepare the lamps.
And he left the *kuz* on the second step, and exited.

[31] Or "voice." [32] Or "ingredients."

ram's horn: Or *shofar*. See *Rosh Hashanah* 4:1 for its use in the Temple.

when he mentioned the divine name: See *Yoma* 3:8, 4:2, and 6:2.

3:9 *basket*: See 3:6. It is possible that the basket was also used for the clearing the ashes from the lampstand (and the *kuz*, in this case, held the new oil). However, according to 6:1, the basket was at that point still at the inner altar, where it had been left according to the first sentence here, and it is only removed then, by the one who cleared the inner altar, before the other lights are cleared. If the basket was, therefore, not used for the lampstand, the *kuz* may have been a receptacle for ash from the lampstand.

handfuls...swept up what remained: The priest would repeatedly scoop up the ashes and place them in the basket with his hands, and then finally sweep up with his hand into the basket the little bits that remained.

the two easternmost lamps: The two lamps at the end of the lampstand to his left. At times these two lamps would still be burning, and he would leave these. Presumably he would extinguish the other lamps if they were still burning, clear the other lamps out (the only action actually mentioned), refill them, and relight them. If these two (or one of them?) had gone out, they were cleaned out, refilled, and relit first, and then the others would be extinguished, processed, and relit. See the completion of these ash-clearing procedures in 6:1.

prepare the lamps: This is the language of Exodus 30:7.

Chapter Four

4:1–3 *Butchering the Sacrifice, Laying its Parts on the Altar Ramp*

4 They would not tie up the four feet of the lamb,
but bound it foreleg to hindleg.
Those who had won the right to [handle] the animal parts took hold of it.
And the manner in which it was bound was thus:
its head to the south and its face to the west.
The one slaughtering it would stand to the east, with his face to the west.
The [offering] of the morning was slaughtered at the northwestern corner,
on the second ring.
That of the afternoon was slaughtered at the northeastern corner,
on the second ring.
The one slaughtering slaughtered
and the one receiving [the blood] received.
He came to the northeastern corner
and applied [the blood] to the east and to the north;
[he came] to the southwestern corner,
and applied it to the west and to the south.
He would pour what remained of the blood
onto the southern side of the altar base.[33]
2 He would not break its hindleg,
but would pierce it in the knee, and use this to hang it up.
He would flay downward, until he reached the breast.
When he reached the breast, he cut off the head

[33] Lit. "the southern base."

4:1 *animal parts*: See 3:1 and 4:2–3.

second ring: The rings are described in *Middot* 3:5. There are twenty-four rings located at the northern side of the altar. Determining the precise choreography here is complicated by ambiguity over the precise arrangement of the rows of rings and over the placement of this slaughtering within these rows. The procedure differs for the *morning* and *afternoon* offering, one using the second ring toward one end (the western end) of a row and the other toward the other (eastern) end. *Corner* refers to corners of the altar.

received…applied [the blood]: One priest would receive the blood into a vessel and ritually apply it a total of four times onto the altar. Standing at one corner of the altar, he applied the blood on the adjacent two sides (to his left and right). Then, standing at the corner diagonally opposite, he applied the blood on the remaining two sides. Thus he applied blood to all four sides.

pour…altar base: The protruding base of the altar contained a drain for the blood that was poured there (*Middot* 3:1, 2). *Zevahim* 6:2 locates the pouring at the southwestern corner (where *Middot* 3:2 places the drain rather than the pouring).

4:2 *hang it up*: To flay it and cut it up; see 3:5 above. The carcass may have been hung up by both hindlegs, or perhaps only by the left one (the right is cut off first here).

and gave it to the one who had won the right to it.
He cut off the lower legs and gave them to those who had won the right to them.
He finished the flaying.
He tore open the heart and removed its blood.
He cut off the forelegs and gave them to the one who had won the right to them.
He moved up to the right hindleg, cut it off,
and gave it to the one who had won the right to it, and it included the two testicles.
He tore the animal[34] open, and it was all visible before him.
He took out the fat and put it above the place where the head had been slaughtered.
He took out the innards
and gave them to the one who had won the right to them to wash them.
And the stomach was washed as much as necessary in the Place of[35] Rinsing.
And the innards were washed at least three times
upon the marble tables that were between the pillars.

3 He took the knife and separated the lungs from the liver,
and the lobe of the liver from the liver,
but he did not move it from its place.
He perforated the breast
and gave it to the one who had won the right to it.
He moved up to the right flank,
and would cut downward until the spinal column—
he did not touch the spinal column—
until he reached the two soft ribs.
He cut it off and gave it to the one who had won the right to it,
and the liver was attached to it.
He came to the neck,
and he left two ribs attached to it to one side
and two ribs to the other side.
He cut it off, and gave it to the one who had won the right to it,
and the windpipe, heart, and lungs were attached to it.

[34] Heb. "it." [35] **K**, **P**, as vocalized: "internally." See annotations.

lower legs: Below the knees; not listed among the parts in 3:1.

right hindleg: The animal continues to hang by the left hindleg until the entire carcass is butchered.

tore the animal: The trunk of the animal, revealing the organs.

fat…above…the head: He placed the fat on the severed head, which was held with the cut facing upwards and the fat above it. See 4:3.

stomach…Place of Rinsing: This place in the Temple is described in *Middot* 5:3. The vocalization in **K** and **P** suggests an alternative translation: the stomach was washed internally, and it was washed as much as necessary.

upon the marble tables: See 3:5 above.

4:3 *did not move it*: This refers to the lobe of the liver (gallbladder), which is left to be distributed with the rump. Similarly, the lungs and liver were left in place at this point, the former to be distributed with the neck and the latter with the right flank.

did not touch the spinal column: He left the spine in the left flank, see below.

He came to the left flank,
he left two soft ribs to the top and two soft ribs to the bottom—
and he left the same on its counterpart;
thus in total between the two flanks he left two sets of two at the top
and two sets of two at the bottom.
He cut it off and he gave it to the one who had won the right to it,
and the spinal column was with it, and the spleen was attached to it.
And this was the larger of the two flanks,
but they called the right one the bigger
because the liver was attached to it.
He came to the rump.
He cut it off and gave it to the one who had won the right to it,
and the fat-tail, the lobe of the liver, and the two kidneys were with it.
He took the left hindleg and gave it to the one who had won the right to it.
Thus, they would all stand in a row, with the animal parts in their hands:
The first with the head and the hindleg, the head in his right hand, with the nose facing his arm, the horns between his fingers, the place it was slaughtered facing up, and the fat upon it, and in his left hand, the right hindleg, its hide side facing outward;
the second with the two forelegs, the right one in his right hand and the left one in his left hand, and their hide sides facing outward;
the third with the rump and the hind leg, the rump in his right hand, with the fat-tail hanging down between his fingers, and the lobe of the liver and the two kidneys with it, and in his left hand, the left hindleg, with its hide side facing outward;

two soft ribs: One possible explanation is that this refers to the two ribs left attached to the neck. Since the animal was hanging by its (left) hindleg, this means the priest cut downward along the spine (leaving the spine to the left flank) toward the neck, making sure to leave two soft ribs attached to the neck as he finally severed the right flank from the neck section. Alternatively, this means that he made sure to include two soft ribs with the right flank (see further below).

neck... two ribs: Having already severed the right flank from the neck, the priest now cuts the neck off from the left flank. The neck portion has two ribs from the left side and two from the right side of the animal attached to it. These are either the two soft ribs mentioned elsewhere in this paragraph or two ribs distinct from the soft ribs left attached to the flanks.

he left... on its counterpart: Lit. "its fellow." The language implies that two sets of two pairs of soft ribs were left in a similar way *on* both flanks, two pairs at the neck side and two at the rump side. However, this does not explain what happened to the rest of the ribs. Thus the intention must be that the two pairs of ribs were left *off* the flanks, two pairs attached to the neck and two attached to the rump (though the butchering of the latter is not described explicitly as is that of the former).

rump: At this point only the rump and the left hindleg remained attached to the hook. When the rump was cut off, only the left hindleg remained, and it was simply removed from the hook.

Thus they would all stand: On the number of priests, see also *Yoma* 2:5.

The first... the place it was slaughtered... and the fat upon it: The fat that was placed at the site of slaughtering to cover it (in 4:2) remained there.

hide side facing outward: The legs and flanks were held with the animal's outer side—or the side that was not cut up—facing outward; the carcass had already been flayed and the hide itself was not present.

the fourth with the breast and the neck, the breast in his right hand, and the neck in his left hand, with the ribs between his fingers;
the fifth with the two flanks, the right one in his right hand and the left one in his left, with their hide sides facing outward;
the sixth with the innards, which were placed in a dish, and with the lower legs placed on top of them;
the seventh with the fine flour;
the eighth with the cakes;
and the ninth with the wine.
They went and placed them on the lower half of the ramp,[36] on the western side,
and salted them.
And they descended and came to the Chamber of Hewn Stones to recite the *Shema*.

Chapter Five

5:1 *Break for Prayer*

5 The one in charge said to them:
"Recite a single blessing,"
and they recited the blessing.
They recited the ten commandments,
Shema, *And it shall be if you obey*, and *And he said.*

[36] Lit. "halfway up the ramp and downward."

a dish: See annotations to 5:4.

on the lower half of the ramp: See the continuation of what was done with the parts in 5:2 (and 7:3), and see *Sheqalim* 8:8.

Chamber of Hewn Stones: See annotations to 2:5.

recite the Shema: Described in 5:1.

5:1 *"single blessing"*: A "blessing" is a prayer unit that begins and/or concludes with the formulaic words, "blessed are you, Lord, our God, king of the universe" (sometimes only until "Lord") and then a more specific phrasing particular to the blessing. According to *Berakhot* 1:4, there are two blessings to be said before reciting the *Shema* passage; this suggests only one was recited in the Temple. Cf. the identical language of "a single blessing" for the priestly blessing recited below, 7:2.

ten commandments: Exodus 20:2–14 or Deuteronomy 5:6–18. This seems to be part of the larger *Shema* prayer here.

Shema: Deuteronomy 6:4–9. *And it shall be*: Deuteronomy 11:13–21. *And he said*: Numbers 15:37–41. These are the three paragraphs of the *Shema* prayer; the opening word or words provide a title for each paragraph. See *Berakhot* 2:2.

They blessed the people with three blessings:
"True and firm," the Temple service, and the priestly blessing.
And on the Sabbath they added a blessing for the priestly watch that was exiting.

5:2–3 *Return to Sacrificial Ritual; Lots to Assign New Tasks*

2 He said to them:
"Those who are new to the incense, come and draw lots!"
They drew lots, and whoever won, won.
"Those who are new and those who are not,[37] come and draw lots:
who will bring up the animal parts from the ramp to the altar!"
R. Eliezer b. Jacob says:
Those who bring up the animal parts to the ramp bring them up onto the altar.

[37] Lit. "those who are old" (not normally of persons).

blessed...with three blessings: This echoes the language of 7:2 below, where "three blessings" refers to the priestly blessing (Numbers 6:24–26), when recited outside of the Temple. Here, however, the phrase refers to the three blessings, or prayer units, using the blessing formula specified: "True and firm," Temple service, and priestly blessing.

blessed the people likely means "blessed with the people," namely, recited the prayer units that use the blessing formula together with the people. The entire paragraph (5:1) is quoted in the Babylonian Talmud, where some manuscripts omit this particular phrase.

"True and firm": The blessing recited after the *Shema* prayer. See *Berakhot* 2:2 (and 1:4).

the Temple service: One of the blessings that also concludes the standard prayer (i.e. what is called today the *shemoneh esrei* [eighteen blessings] or the *amidah* [standing prayer]); see *Rosh Hashanah* 4:5 and cf. *Yoma* 7:1 and *Sotah* 7:7.

priestly blessing: This, too, is a blessing in the standard prayer (*Rosh Hashanah* 4:5; cf. *Yoma* 7:1 and *Sotah* 7:7; and see also *Sotah* 7:2). The blessing presumably incorporates the priests' reciting the blessing of Numbers 6:24–26 (see *Sotah* 7:6), as in traditional practice. Cf. 7:2 below, however, where a priestly recitation of Numbers 6:24–26 stands apart from a prayer context.

The various bits of prayer mentioned here form a condensation of the morning prayer service, described elsewhere in the Mishnah (especially in *Berakhot* 4:3, 5:2, and in the other sources mentioned here).

5:2 *"new to the incense"*, who have never won the right to perform the ritual. This lot to perform the incense ritual seems to include multiple roles within the ritual, as narrated below in 5:4–5 and 6:2–3, and so presumably multiple priests won these rights at this point.

whoever won, won: The singular language seems to refer to the one performing the incense. In 5:4–5 and 6:2–3, however, there are other priests involved in more minor roles in the incense procedure, whose roles must have been assigned now. The singular language (mirroring 1:2 and 3:1) could perhaps be taken as referring to multiple roles.

bring up the animal parts: They were left on the ramp at the end of 4:3; R. Eliezer holds that the same priests as before continue to deal with the parts. The narration of the bringing up the parts (specifically when the high priest participates) and the continuation of the ritual appears below in 7:3.

3 He handed them over to the superintendents,
who would strip them of their clothes,
leaving only their underpants.
And there were niches there,
with the use of each garment[38] written upon them.

5:4–6 *Preparing to Offer the Incense*

4 The one who had won the right to the incense would take the scoop.
And the scoop was similar to a large golden two-*qav* vessel, holding three *qav*,
and there was a dish inside of it,
full and overflowing with incense.
And it had a cover, which had a kind of pad on its top.
5 The one who had won the right to the coal pan
took the silver coal pan,

[38] Alt. "vessel."

5:3 *strip them of their clothes*: The text seems to imply that those who perform the subsequent rituals do so only in their underpants. To avoid this implication, the commentaries take the passage to mean that with all the lots now completed, those who did not win at all, and so would not be performing any of the ritual, now removed the sacred garments. They removed the underpants after they put on their own clothes. Alternatively, this paragraph may be describing how those who continued to perform the ritual got dressed in the appropriate garments. Perhaps the priests who continue to perform changed into new garments or perhaps those who have only now won the right to perform donned the appropriate clothing.

underpants: This is one of the priestly garments. See *Yoma* 7:5 and see Exodus 28:42, 39:28, Leviticus 6:3, 16:4, and Ezekiel 44:18.

niches: The name of each type of garment would be written on each niche, which functioned as a locker or storage receptacle, and so the garments would be sorted appropriately. The import here is either that the clothes they removed are stored in the niches or that new garments they will now put on are taken from the niches. Alternatively (see n. 38), it may be vessels that were stored, and these are now taken out and used in the subsequent paragraphs.

5:4 *scoop*: This was a large vessel into which the smaller *dish* was placed. The *dish, bazekh*, here holds incense, but it was also used for blood, according to *Pesahim* 5:5, and for animal parts in 4:3 above. For the *two-qav vessel*, see 3:6 above. Here, this expression may mean that a two-*qav* vessel normally holds three-*qav* volumes or it may mean that this scoop, which resembles a two-*qav* vessel, held three-*qav* volumes.

it had a cover: According to 7:2, it is the scoop that has a cover. The pad would have been made of cloth.

5:5 *the right to the coal pan*: Not mentioned explicitly in the lots of 5:2, but presumably drawn by lot at that time as well, included under the rubric of the lot for the incense.

ascended to the top of the altar,
moved the coals aside this way and that,
and removed coals.[39]
He descended and poured them into the golden vessel.
Approximately a *qav* of coals was scattered from it,
and he swept them into the water drainage channel.
And on the Sabbath, he would turn over a *pesakhter*[40] onto them.
And the *pesakhter*[41] was a large vessel holding a *letekh*.
And it had two chains on it,
one on which he pulled to lower it,
and the other onto which he held from above to ensure it did not roll.
And it was used for three different things:
They would turn it over onto the coals and onto vermin on the Sabbath,
and they would use it to remove the ashes from on top of the altar.

6 When they reached the area between the Porch and the altar,
One of them took the shovel and threw it down between the Porch and the altar.
A person would not be able to hear someone else talking in Jerusalem
over the sound of the shovel.
And it was used for three things:
A priest who heard its sound knew that his brothers the priests were entering

[39] **K**, **P**: "he took from the innermost (**P**: and from the) thoroughly burnt coals."
[40] **K**: "*pesaqter*." [41] **K**, **P**: "*pesaqter*."

moved the coals: This language mirrors that of 1:4 (even more so in the manuscripts; see n. 39). Here, the coals are taken to burn the incense. Presumably these are the coals of the second altar fire (see 2:5 above).

golden vessel: The type of vessel is not specified, perhaps a golden coal pan.

was scattered: A certain amount regularly spilled, and this was swept into the drain (or covered with the *pesakhter* vessel on the Sabbath; see the following note).

pesakhter: See nn. 39 and 40. Cf. Greek *psykter*, a vessel for cooling wine; however, the *pesakhter* is much larger than a typical wine cooler. On the Sabbath, instead of sweeping the coals, they would cover them with the overturned vessel.

letekh: Ninety *qav*, approximately 115 liters. See "Coins, Weights, and Measures."

onto vermin: These could not be removed on the Sabbath. To contain the impurity they would be covered.

to remove the ashes from on top of the altar: Which of the two altars is not specified. Use of this vessel is not mentioned when describing the clearing of the ashes (2:2, 3:6, and 3:9 above).

5:6 *Porch*: Entrance hall to the Sanctum. See annotations to 3:7 above (on the Great Gate) and see *Middot* 3:6–3:7.

the area between the Porch and the altar is considered to have its own level of sanctity (*Kelim* 1:9).

the shovel: A term used in 2:1 and 3:8. Many commentaries understand this to be a gong that was struck with something that looks like a shovel. This, however, seems unlikely, because the priests were using an actual shovel to scoop up ashes. The shovel was thrown from the top of the altar down onto the stone Temple floor, to the side of the altar that faced the Sanctum. The loud noise this made (exaggerated here) served as a signal, as specified.

in order to bow, and he would run and come [to them];
a Levite who heard its sound knew that his brothers the Levites were entering
in order to sing, and he would run and come [to them];
and the head of the *ma'amad* would set up those who were impure at the eastern gate.[42]

Chapter Six

6:1 *Clearing of the Inner Altar and Lampstand*

6 They began to ascend the steps of the Porch.
Those who had won the right to clear the ashes from the inner altar
and from the lampstand went ahead of them.
The one who had won the right to clear the ashes from the inner altar entered,

[42] **K, P**: "gates."

to bow: See 7:1 below (and perhaps 6:1–3 as well).

to sing: See 7:3–4 below, and see annotation to 3:8 above.

head of the ma'amad: A *ma'amad*, best translated as an "attending group," contains, according to *Ta'anit* 4:2, priests, Levites, and Israelites who attend on the continual sacrifice performed by a given priestly watch on their designated shift. In *Bikkurim* 3:2, the *ma'amad* also corresponds to a district within the Land of Israel.

eastern gate: This term may refer to one of three gates: (1) The eastern gate of the whole Temple complex (within the larger Temple Mount). (2) The gate within the Temple complex that separates the Court of Israelites (and the more sacred half of the Temple complex) from the Court of Women (the eastern half of the Temple)—thus the eastern gate of the more sacred half of the Temple, often called the Temple Court. (3) The gate on the eastern side of the Temple Mount.

In a number of passages, "eastern gate" (or "gates," see n. 42), also called "[the gate of the Temple Court] that is to the east," is identical to the Gate of Nicanor. See especially *Sotah* 1:5, and see *Sheqalim* 6:3, *Middot* 1:4 (with annotations), and *Middot* 2:6. In *Middot* 2:6, this is definitely the gate to the east of the more sacred half of the Temple (possibility (2) here; and see *Yoma* 1:3, which is suggestive of this possibility as well). However, in *Sukkah* 5:4, this gate is called "the Upper Gate" (but cf. this same term in *Middot* 2:6), while "the gate that exits to the east" refers to the eastern gate of the entire Temple complex (possibility (1) here). In *Middot* 1:3, a very similar term refers to the eastern gate of the Temple Mount, suggesting the third possibility. The term "eastern gate" also appears in *Berakhot* 9:5, *Orlah* 2:12, and *Ta'anit* 2:5. "the Gate of Nicanor" also appears in *Middot* 2:3 and *Nega'im* 14:8. In *Nega'im* 14:8, the one with *tsara'at* stands at this gate for the purification ritual.

6:1 *They began to ascend*: The two priests performing the incense ritual and taking the coals with the coal pan (5:4–5).

Porch: The entrance hall leading directly into the Sanctum. See 5:6.

went ahead of them: The two who are going to finish *clearing the ashes* go ahead of those taking the coals and performing the incense ritual.

entered: Past the Porch, into the Sanctum, where the inner altar and lampstand were located.

took the basket, bowed, and exited.
The one who had won the right to clear the ashes from the lampstand entered.
If he found the two easternmost lights burning,
he would clear the ashes from the easternmost one
and leave the western one burning,
for he would use this to light the lampstand in the afternoon.
If he found that it was extinguished,
he would clear its ashes and light it from the altar of the burnt offering.
He took the *kuz* from the second step, bowed, and exited.

6:2–3 *Offering the Incense*

2 The one who had won the right to the coal pan
piled up the coals onto the altar,
spread them out with the bottom of the coal pan,
bowed, and exited.
3 The one who had won the right to the incense
would take the dish from inside the scoop

took the basket: The receptacle for the ashes from the altar, apparently left near the lampstand when it was used earlier; see 3:6 and 3:9 above. Now that the ritual task is fully completed, the priest bows before exiting.

the lampstand: Cf. the earlier stage of the procedure in 3:9 above. Sometimes, the two easternmost lights would not have been cleaned out in the earlier stage. Now, the easternmost one of these two (the one at the end) is extinguished, cleaned out, refilled, and relit.

western one: The second from the easternmost light.

If… it was extinguished: If the western of the two special lights was already out, the priest would now clean it out, prepare it, and relight it as well. The implication seems to be that this light is relit from the altar fire even if others of the lampstand lights are still lit (Maimonides), though it is possible that the altar fire was only used if all were out. If some of the other lights were no longer lit at this point, presumably they would be relit as well.

to light the lampstand in the afternoon: Later, when the afternoon *tamid* is offered and the entire procedure presumably repeated, the lamp second from the eastern end of the lampstand branches (the "western" of the two) would be used to light all of the other lights (all of which would presumably again be cleaned out, refilled, and relit). In 3:9, both of the two easternmost lamps seem to have been used to light the others; perhaps the intention is that the eastern of the two is used in the morning and the western of the two used in the afternoon, east symbolizing the morning sun and west the evening sun.

altar of the burnt offering: The main, sacrificial altar. Presumably this would also be used if all the lights were out in the earlier stage of the ritual (see 3:9).

from the second step of the three-step stone stepladder, where it was left earlier (3:9). Presumably he used the *kuz* now as well; perhaps he left it on the step while he cleared into it.

6:2 *onto the altar*: Onto the inner altar, the incense altar. He took the coals from the sacrificial altar in 5:5 and now he spreads the coals evenly over the surface of the inner altar. Shortly, the one with the dish will spread the incense onto the coals.

6:3 *take the dish*: On these vessels, see 5:4 above.

and give it to his friend or relative.
It was scattered from the dish into the scoop.[43]
He would place it into his hands,
and they instruct him:
"Be careful not to begin immediately in front of yourself
so that you will not get burnt!"[44]
He began to spread[45] it out and he exits.
The one offering the incense would not offer the incense
until the one in charge says to him,
"Offer the incense!"
If it was the high priest, the one in charge says,
"Sir,[46] high priest, offer the incense!"
The people withdrew.
And he offered the incense, bowed, and exited.

[43] Lit. "From within it, into it."
[44] **K**: "extinguish," probably an error ("burnt" and "extinguished" are near homophones).
[45] **P**: "measure." [46] Or "My lord."

give it: Most likely the dish, but perhaps the scoop.

friend or relative: One of the other priests, perhaps from among those already participating, or another. This may have been a separate task won by lot, or perhaps a non-lot task (implied by the possibility of it being a relative).

from the dish into the scoop. He would place it into his hands: See n. 43. The expression is ambiguous, but seems to mean that the priest performing the incense ritual would spill the incense from the dish into the scoop, and then the friend or relative would take the scoop and pour from the scoop into the priest's hands. This draws on the biblical phrasing of Leviticus 16:12, in which the priest has his hands full of incense. Since he uses both hands, he must have poured only from his hands onto the coals. It is unclear why the dish and the scattering into the scoop are necessary. It is also unclear whether the priest takes only a small amount or the entire amount of incense into his hands, and how much he pours on the coals.

"*so that you will not get burnt*": If he begins nearest to himself, as he adds incense further away from himself and leans over the altar, he may get burnt.

He began to spread it out and he exits: This sentence, too, is ambiguous. Some commentaries understand that this refers back to the one who had won the right to the coal pan and reiterates his spreading the coals and exiting (without mentioning the bowing; see 6:2); this would highlight that the incense was spread out upon his departure. According to others, the one offering the incense would spread out the incense over the coals and exit; in this case, the narrative then goes back to describe this process more fully (*The one offering*...). Both interpretations involve unexplained redundancy. Another alternative is that the friend/relative exits at this point (though the lack of a clear subject for the verb is inexplicable). The reading in **P** ("measures out") obviates some of the redundancy, but does not explain who exits and why.

the high priest: If he was the one offering the incense. See *Yoma* 1:2 and see 7:3 below.

The people withdrew: This could refer to the friend/relative, the one in charge, and/or other priests (the plural "they" who "instruct him"). The commentaries take it to mean that all priests withdraw from the space between the altar and the Porch.

Chapter Seven

7:1–2 *The High Priest and the Priestly Blessing*

7 When the high priest entered to bow,
three people would hold onto him—
one onto his right hand, one onto his left hand,[47] and one onto the precious stones.
And as soon as the one in charge heard the sound of the high priest's footsteps,
that he was exiting,
he lifted up the curtain for him, entered,[48] bowed, and exited.
And his brothers the priests entered, bowed, and exited.
2 They came and stood on the steps of the Porch.
The first ones stood to the south of their priestly brothers,
with five vessels in their hands:
(1) the basket in the hands of one,
(2) the *kuz* in the hands of one,
(3) the coal pan in the hands of one,
(4) the dish in the hands of one,
and (5) the scoop and its cover in the hands of one.
And they blessed the people with a single blessing,

[47] Or "to his right... to his left." [48] **K, P** lack "entered."

7:1 *When the high priest entered to bow*: All the priests engaged in the morning's ritual would enter into the Sanctum and bow. Here, as well as in 6:3 and 7:2–3, the text refers to the occasional instances in which the high priest would participate in the daily ritual, and he would bow first.

precious stones: On the breastplate or on his shoulders. See Exodus 28:9–30.

lifted up the curtain: The curtain covering the entrance to the Sanctum (at the Porch). The *one in charge* lifts it up for the high priest to exit, and enters and bows himself. Alternatively (omitting "entered," see n. 48), the subject changes and it is the high priest who bows and exits. Another possibility is that the one in charge hears the high priest exiting from his chambers, and lifts the veil for him to enter and bow.

brothers the priests: Presumably all those involved in the rituals described above.

7:2 *Porch*: See annotation to 5:6 above.

first ones: This refers to the priests involved in clearing the ashes from the inner altar and the lampstand and in performing the incense ritual. These individuals and the *five vessels* they hold (five in total, among them) are mentioned in 3:6, 5:2, and 5:4–6:3. Perhaps they are called "first" because they line up first on the steps of the porch, having just completed their tasks. *Their priestly brothers* may refer to those involved in the earlier stages of the continual offering, including those who cleared the altar, those who have dealt with the slaughtering and the animal parts, and those who will only complete their tasks in 7:3. The phrase may also refer to other priests from the priestly watch on duty who did not win the right to perform any tasks.

south: The steps face out eastward, so the south is stage right.

except that outside the Temple[49] one recites it as three blessings,
but in the Temple as a single blessing.
In the Temple they used to say the divine name as written,
and outside the Temple with his[50] substitute name.
Outside the Temple the priests lift up their hands opposite their shoulders,
but in the Temple above their heads—
except for the high priest,
who does not lift his hands higher than the diadem.
R. Judah says:
Even the high priest lifts his hands above the diadem, as it says:
And Aaron lifted up his hands toward the people and blessed them.

7:3 *Placing the Parts on the Altar; The Libation; Additional Rituals*

3 When the high priest wishes to make the offering smoke,
he would ascend the ramp of the altar, with the Temple prefect to his right.

[49] Lit. "in the province," here and below.

[50] Or "its."

outside the Temple: From here to the end of the paragraph is identical to *Sotah* 7:6, where it is made clear that the topic is "the blessing [**K**, **P**: 'blessings'] of the priests." The priestly blessing is the recitation of Numbers 6:24–26. In the Temple the three verses were recited as a single blessing (perhaps with the people responding "amen" only at the end), whereas outside of the Temple it was recited as three distinct blessings. The priestly blessing came to be understood as a part of the regular daily prayer service. This may be what is implied above in 5:1 (and see annotation). *Outside the Temple* may thus refer to a regular prayer service, perhaps in synagogues, during which priests uttered these verses directed at *the people*. Here, however, the priests appear to make these utterances as a ritual distinct from the prayer service.

as written: The tetragrammaton (YHWH).

substitute name: Outside the Temple one does not utter the divine name as written. In current practice, the substitute is *adonay*, "my Lord." It is unclear what the substitute was in the time of the Mishnah or in the time of the Temple (if the Mishnah—a post-destruction text—is accurate in its claim that a substitute was indeed used in Temple times). Perhaps for the Mishnah it is *hashem* ("the name"), as the wording of *Yoma* 3:8, 4:2, and 6:2 may imply.

diadem: Exodus 28:36–38; 39:30–31; Leviticus 8:9.

And Aaron lifted up: Leviticus 9:22, taken to imply: above the diadem. Though not a strong prooftext for R. Judah's position, the verse does establish in general that the hands are lifted up for the priestly blessing.

7:3 *When the high priest wishes*: When he wishes to be the one to perform the ritual. According to *Yoma* 1:2, the high priest would offer the head and hindleg on the altar (in addition to offering the incense, preparing the lampstand lamps, and sprinkling the blood) during the week prior to the Day of Atonement, and also whenever he wished. Here, he begins by throwing the head and hindleg onto the altar fire, but he also offers all of the other parts and pours the libation (neither of which is mentioned in *Yoma*). Note that the regular instance in which the priests themselves throw the animal parts onto the altar fire and pour the libation is not narrated, and so this discussion about the high priest's involvement constitutes the continuation of the tractate's larger narrative.

to make the offering smoke refers to placing the parts on the altar fire so that they burn.

When he reached the midpoint of the ramp,
the Temple prefect took hold of his right hand and helped him up.[51]
The first one[52] passed him the head and the hindleg;
he placed his hands upon them and threw them [onto the altar fire].
The second one passed the first one the two forelegs.
He gave them to the high priest, and he placed his hands upon them and threw them [onto the altar fire].
The second one slipped away and went on his way.
And in this manner they would pass the rest of the animal parts to him,
and he would place his hands upon them and throw them [onto the altar fire].
And whenever he wished, he would place his hands and others would throw [onto the altar fire].
He came to circle the altar.
From what point does he start?
From the southeastern corner, to the northeastern,
to the northwestern, to the southwestern.
They gave him the wine for the libation.
The Temple prefect would stand on the corner,
with scarves in his hand.
And two priests would stand on the table of the fat parts,
with two silver trumpets in their hands.
They blew a *teqi'a* blast, a *teru'ah* blast, and a *teqi'a* blast.

[51] Or "lifted him up." [52] i.e. the first priest.

The first one... head and hindleg... rest of the animal parts: Normally, the priests who had won the right to the various parts (see 5:2, as well as 3:1 and 4:1–3 above) took them up and threw them onto the altar fire. Now, when the high priest performs this part of the ritual, he takes the parts from those priests and throws them onto the altar fire. The enumeration of *first* and *second* priests follows that of 4:3. Regarding 5:2, there is a difference of opinion whether these are new priests or the same ones who dealt with the parts in 4:1–3.

placed his hands upon them: This is a ritual associated with various sacrifices. See *Yoma* 3:8; 4:2; 6:2; *Betsah* 2:4; *Hagigah* 2:2–3; *Menahot* 9:7–9; *Temurah* 3:4.

circle the altar: Circling the top of the altar is also described in *Zevahim* 6:3. The priest would go up the ramp on the right side, turn to the right and walk around the top of the altar in a counterclockwise direction, until finally reaching the southwestern corner, the place where the wine libation was poured. According to *Zevahim* 6:2–3, this was the proper choreography for walking on the altar, but normally it would not be followed for the water and wine libations (see also *Sukkah* 4:9); for those, the priest would turn to his left, perform the libation at the southwestern corner, and then turn around and go down the way he came up. The Talmud suggests that making the full trip around the top of the altar would risk spilling, and so it was avoided for libations. Here in *Tamid*, when the high priest is the one to perform the libation, he does not carry the wine himself but rather someone hands it to him, and so he can follow the normal protocol for ascending and walking on the top of the altar.

corner: Or, "horn," the shape of the corners of the altar. He stood on top of the altar, at the corner.

Temple prefect: Just below the high priest in status (see *Sotah* 7:7–8).

table of fats: Likely one of the marble tables described in 3:5 and 4:2 above. These two priests stood either on or near the table.

teqi'a... teru'a: The precise nature of these blasts is unclear. The trumpet blasts begin the ritually dense and multisensory conclusion to the continual offering service, which includes the blasts, the libation, scarves waving, the cymbal sounding, the Levites singing, and repeated prostrations.

They came and stood near Ben Arza,
one to his right and one to his left.
He bent down to pour the libation,
and the Temple prefect waved the scarves,
Ben Arza played the cymbal,
and the Levites sang.
When they reached the end of a section,
they blew a *teqi'a* blast
and the people bowed.
At the end of each section there was a *teqi'a* blast
and at each *teqi'a* blast a bowing.
This is the order of the continual offering[53] for the worship in the house of our God.
May it be [his] will that it be rebuilt speedily in our days, amen.[54]

7:4 *List of the Levites' Songs*

4 The song that the Levites used to say in the Temple:
On Sunday[55] they used to say:
The earth is the Lord's and all that it holds, the world and its inhabitants.

[53] Alt. "the continual (i.e. daily) order." [54] "Amen" lacking in **K**, **P**.
[55] Lit. "first day." The translation replaces the original numerical designation of all the days of the week.

Ben Arza: See also *Sheqalim* 5:1. Some take this to be the name of one priest, perhaps one who lived at the end of the Second Temple period; others understand it as the name always taken on by the priest in charge of the cymbal.

scarves: Waved as a signal that each stage of the ritual is completed. Similar signal scarves are used ritually in *Yoma* 6:8 and *Sanhedrin* 6:1.

cymbal: Heb. *tsiltel*, an onomatopoetic name for a percussive instrument that rings or chimes.

Levites sang: Presumably they sang the psalms indicated in 7:4 below. On the location of the Levites' singing, see *Sukkah* 5:4 and *Middot* 2:5 and cf. *Arakhin* 2:6. See further in annotation to 3:8.

At the end of each section: At the end of each section (possibly each verse) of the psalm/song, the priests trumpeted and the people bowed.

order of the continual offering: "Order" may refer to the ritual procedure, which must be done in a particular order.

May it be... amen: "May it be [God's] will" is a prayer formulation, as in *Berakhot* 9:3 (and see *Avot* 5:20). Here and in *Ta'anit* 4:8, this brief prayer for the rebuilding of the Temple serves as a liturgical conclusion to the entire tractate (*Tamid* 7:4 can be taken as an appendix). The presence of this liturgical conclusion may indicate that the Mishnah tractate was read liturgically. The absence in the manuscripts of the word "*amen*," a liturgical concluding word, however, suggests that this word is a later addition (and perhaps that the liturgical use was later as well).

7:4 *On Sunday they used to say*: The Levites would recite the entire chapter of Psalms indicated by the opening verse on each day.

The earth is the Lord's: Psalm 24.

On Monday they used to say:
The Lord is great and much acclaimed in the city of our God, His holy mountain.
On Tuesday they used to say:
God stands in the divine assembly, among the divine beings he pronounces judgment.
On Wednesday they used to say:
O Lord, God of retribution; O God of retribution reveal yourself.
On Thursday they used to say:
Sing joyously to God, our strength, raise a shout for the God of Jacob.
On Friday they used to say:
The Lord is king, He is robed in grandeur.
On the Sabbath they used to say:
A psalm, a song for the Sabbath day—
a psalm, a song for the future, for a day that is all Sabbath and rest for eternal life.

The Lord is great: Psalm 48.

God stands: Psalm 82.

O Lord, God of retribution: Psalm 94.

Sing joyously: Psalm 81.

The Lord is king: Psalm 93.

A psalm, a song for the Sabbath: Psalm 92.

Tractate Middot

Naftali S. Cohn

Introduction

Overview

The name *Middot*, or "measurements," highlights the tractate's primary focus on the dimensions of the Temple's spaces. The word itself never appears within the tractate. The tractate presents an architectural tour of the Second Temple in Jerusalem, describing in detail its structures and areas, and at times pausing to tell what would happen at particular places. The interior of the Temple Mount (more or less identical with the platform accessible today) is organized in roughly concentric spaces. Within this is the Temple, a term that refers to a complex of Courts, open spaces, buildings, and installations. The Sanctum is the building housing the group of structures consisting of the Porch, the Holy, and the Holy of Holies. The terminology is further described below.

Structure and Organization of the Tractate

The tractate begins with a description and narration of the guarding of the Temple and Temple Mount (1:1–2). The guarded portals are the starting points for the tractate's spatial trajectory as the description proceeds inward to the Temple's outermost boundary, the gates of the Temple Mount (1:3), then to the gates of the Temple Court and some of the structures of the Temple Court (1:4–9).

Chapter 2 begins the trajectory again, focusing more on dimensions and chambers, beginning with the Temple Mount (2:1–2) and moving generally inward and in the direction of increasing sacredness, toward the Holy of Holies (4:5). The stages in this movement relate loosely to the "levels of sanctity" listed in *Kelim* 1:8–9. The description moves through: the partition and ledge surrounding the Temple, and the steps leading up to the Temple level (2:3); the Court of Women and its chambers (2:4–5); the Court of Israelites and the steps leading up to it (2:5–6); the Court of Priests (2:6); the space before the Porch, including the altar and adjacent slaughtering and butchering areas (3:1–6); the Porch (3:7–8); the Sanctum, and finally, the Holy of Holies (4:1–5).

The last part of the tractate, 4:6–5:4, in part repeats and partly extends the preceding material. *Middot* 4:6–7 provide an accounting of the dimensions of the Sanctum. In 5:1–2 we get east–west and north–south cross sections of the Temple Court as a whole (excluding the Court of Women). At this point (5:3–4), the tractate concludes by describing six chambers located in the Temple Court. The culmination of the entire description of the Temple in the tractate, the final place mentioned, is the Chamber of Hewn Stone, the meeting place of the great Sanhedrin, the group whom the rabbis consider their predecessors.

Main Ideas

The tractate focuses primarily on the gates, doors, stairs, passageways, chambers, compartments, roofs, and other architectural elements of the various structures in the Temple. The only furnishings that figure into its description are the altar (and surrounding appurtenances for the slaughtering and butchering of offerings), treated in detail in chapter 3, and the laver, mentioned also in chapter 3. Additional Temple furniture is mentioned in *Tamid* in relation to daily rituals performed with them, and sporadically throughout the Mishnah's descriptions of Temple ritual.

There are various technical terms used in the tractate:

Temple Mount Heb. *har habayit*. The large artificial enclosure built by Herod the Great. Today's Western Wall is the western retaining wall of this enclosure. The Temple structure is within the Temple Mount.

Temple Court: There are three courts whose names occur throughout the Mishnah: the Court of Women, of Israelites, and of Priests. In theory, women are limited to the Court of Women and the Court of Priests to priests, but this was not always the case. In *Middot*, the term Temple Court, *azarah*, refers to the enclosed space to the west of and excluding the Court of Women. This therefore includes the Court of Israelites and the Court of Priests, the altar and slaughtering areas, the Sanctum, and the space around and behind the Sanctum. Elsewhere in the Mishnah, it is likely that this term occasionally refers generically to the Court of Women alone or includes the Court of Women.

Chamber, *Place*, and *Compartment*: *Middot* describes a variety of closed spaces. *Lishkah*, is translated here as "Chamber;" *bet* (lit. "house of") is translated as "Place [of]"; *ta'im*, which occurs only in *Middot* 4:2–3 and 4:7 (and *Tamid* 3:7) is rendered "compartments."

Biblical *Hekhal* is represented here by *Sanctum*. It may mean the entire structure encompassing the Porch (*ulam*), the Holy (*qodesh*), the Holy of Holies (*qodesh qodashim*), and all surrounding walls and structures. It can also more narrowly refer to the Holy and Holy of Holies and their surrounding walls and structures, or to the Holy alone, particularly its inside space.

Relationship to Scripture

Many details in the Mishnah's description of the Temple stem from biblical passages pertaining to the Tabernacle, the first Temple, and the second Temple. More than the details, though, it is the general style of presenting an architectural description, with many specific measurements, that is built on the biblical model. Both generally and in specifics, the tractate draws heavily on Ezekiel's vision of the Temple in Ezekiel 40–44. This visionary Temple is sometimes taken in the Mishnah to refer to a temple yet to be built, but elsewhere these passages are quoted as prooftexts for individual features. To a much lesser degree, *Middot* is also similar to the descriptions of the building of Solomon's Temple in 1 Kings 6–7 (and see 2 Chronicles 3–4), quoted once, and of the Tabernacle in Exodus 25–27.

Tractate Middot

Chapter One

1:1–2 *Guarding the Temple and Temple Mount*

1 The priests stand guard in the Temple in three locations:
(1) the Place of Avtinas, (2) the Place of the Spark, and (3) the Place of the Hearth.
And the Levites in twenty-one locations:
(1–5) five on the five gates[1] of the Temple Mount;
(6–9) four on its four corners, from the inside;
(10–14) five on the five gates[2] of the Temple Court;
(15–18) four on its four corners, from the outside;
(19) one in the Chamber of the Offering;
(20) one in the Chamber of the Curtain;

[1] **K** (second hand), **P**: "on five of the gates of."

[2] **K** (second hand), **P**: "on five of the gates of."

1:1 *The Place of the Spark... the Place of the Hearth*: Described in more detail in 1:5–9. See also the similar passage in *Tamid* 1:1, and annotations there.

Levites: They guard as well. The commentaries connect the Levitical role here to that of 1 Chronicles 26 (and see, perhaps, Numbers 1:53), though the precise details differ.

Temple Mount: The large enclosure (corresponding to the platform known today by this name, or by Muslims as "the noble sanctuary") that surrounds the Temple complex itself (see 2:1–4).

from the inside: Each standing on a landing inside of the Temple Mount wall, at the top of the wall, above a corner of the walls.

the five gates of the Temple Court: Cf. 1:4, which lists seven, and 2:6, where Abba Yose b. Hanan states that there were thirteen. The reading in **K**, **P** (see n. 2) may mean that only five "of" the gates were guarded, implying that there were in fact more. Alternatively, this may be a different opinion about how many gates there were. According to 1:5, at the Gate of the Spark the Levites are at ground level.

From the outside: Likely also at ground level, outside the corners of the Temple walls, either on the ledge, or below it, on the Temple Mount platform.

Chamber of the Offering: Within the Place of the Hearth; see 1:6.

Chamber of the Curtain: The curtain mentioned could be that of the entrance to the Porch, which may have had a curtain covering the doorway (see 2:3 and see *Tamid* 7:1) or to the Holy of Holies (see *Yoma* 5:1–4). The chamber may have stored spares, or as one commentary suggests, may have been a place for weaving new curtains.

and (21) one behind the place of the *kapporet*.

2 The man[3] of the Temple Mount used to go around
to each and every watch,
with lit torches in front of him.
And to any watch that was not standing,[4]
the man of the Temple Mount would say: "Peace unto you!"[5]
If it is discernible that he is sleeping, he strikes him with his staff.
And he had permission to burn his garment.
And they would say: "What is that sound in the Temple Court?"
"The sound of a Levite being lashed and his clothes being burned,
for he fell asleep on his watch."
R. Eliezer b. Jacob says:
They once found my mother's brother sleeping and they burned his garment.

1:3–5 *Gates of the Temple Mount and Temple Court*

3 There were five gates on the Temple Mount:
(1–2) Two Hulda Gates from the south, which served for entry and exit;
(3) Kiponos from the west, which served for entry and exit;
(4) Tadi from the north, which did not have any function;
And (5) the Eastern Gate,
on which an image of Shushan the Fortress was engraved,[6]
out of which the high priest[7] who burned the red heifer,
and the red heifer, and all its attendants would go out to the Mount of Olives.

[3] Or "officer." [4] Alt. "that did not stand [when he approached]."
[5] **K, P**: "And if any watch did not stand and say to him, 'Man of the Temple Mount, Peace unto you,' it would be discernible that he (or 'it' = the watch) was sleeping. He strikes him with his staff..."
[6] Or "painted." [7] **K, P** read only "priest."

behind the place of the kapporet: Between the western end of the Sanctum, where the Ark was (but cf. *Yoma* 5:2), and the inside of the wall at the western edge of the Temple Court.

kapporet, the "mercy seat" or "cover" of the Ark, in the Holy of Holies. In the Herodian Temple there was no Ark; the Holy of Holies was an empty chamber.

1:2 *man of the Temple Mount*: An official position.

"*Peace unto you*": See n. 5. Although it is unclear who says the greeting, and whether the guards stand at all times or only at the official's approach, what is clear is that the interaction is designed to find out if the watch is alert or if they are sleeping.

"*sound of a Levite*": This likely also applies to sleeping priests on watch, who are technically from the tribe of Levi as well (commentaries).

1:3 *Hulda*: Perhaps named after the biblical female prophet (2 Kings 22:14–20 and 2 Chronicles 34:22–28).

Kiponos... Tadi: Male names, perhaps notables or wealthy donors.

Shushan the Fortress: A reference to the acropolis of Shushan (Susa) in the book of Esther. See also *Kelim* 17:9. It is unclear why this should appear on the Temple gate. *Birah*, "fortress," is translated "structure" in 1:9.

burned the red heifer: *Parah* 3:6.

4 There were seven gates in the Temple Court:
three on the northern side;
three on the southern side;
and one on the eastern side.
On the southern side:
(1) the Gate of Fuel;
(2) second to it: the Gate of the Firstborn;[8]
(3) third to it: the Water Gate.
The one on the eastern side: the Gate of Nicanor.
And it had two chambers, one to its right and one to its left—
one was the Chamber of Phineas the Dresser;
and one was the Chamber of the Cake Makers.
5 On the northern side:
(1) the Gate of the Spark.
And it was in the shape of a recessed room,
with an upper story built above it,
where the priests would stand watch up above,
and the Levites down below.
And it had a doorway to the ledge surrounding the Temple.
(2) Second to it: the Offering Gate.
(3) Third to it: the Place of the Hearth

[8] **K, P** "the Gate of Offering."

1:4 *seven gates*: This number seems to contradict the reading in 1:1 (five gates; see comment there), and 2:6 (thirteen gates). It is possible these are different (unattributed) opinions. The diagram of the Temple (Figure 2) follows the description here.

on the southern side: Based on 2:6, these seem to be listed west to east (though the reverse is also possible). See also *Sukkah* 4:9: one can walk directly from the Water Gate up the altar ramp.

the Gate of Nicanor: The gate on the eastern side of the more sacred half of the Temple, leading from the Court of Women in to the Court of Israelites. Alternatively, it could possibly be taken as the gate on the eastern side of the entire Temple, leading from the Temple Mount in to the Court of Women. See further 2:6 and *Tamid* 5:6 and cf. the gate name in *Sukkah* 5:4.

Phineas the dresser: In charge of dressing the priests; see *Sheqalim* 5:1.

Chamber of the Cake Makers: See *Tamid* 1:3.

1:5 *Gate of the Spark…Second…Third*: As above, 1:4, linear order, listed west to east (or perhaps the reverse). Cf. 2:6, which has different gate names for all the southern gates, except for *Offering Gate*. *Tamid* 1:1 has "Place of the Spark."

recessed room: Referring to a niche, a smaller room, or another inset structure that runs the full length of the larger space to which it is adjacent. Compare *Tamid* 1:3 (see annotations).

doorway to the ledge: Since all the gates would have opened to the ledge (see 2:3), this likely means that the upper story had a doorway to the ledge.

Place of the Hearth: Not a gate, but a large structure with two gates (1:7); 1:6–9 describes this structure.

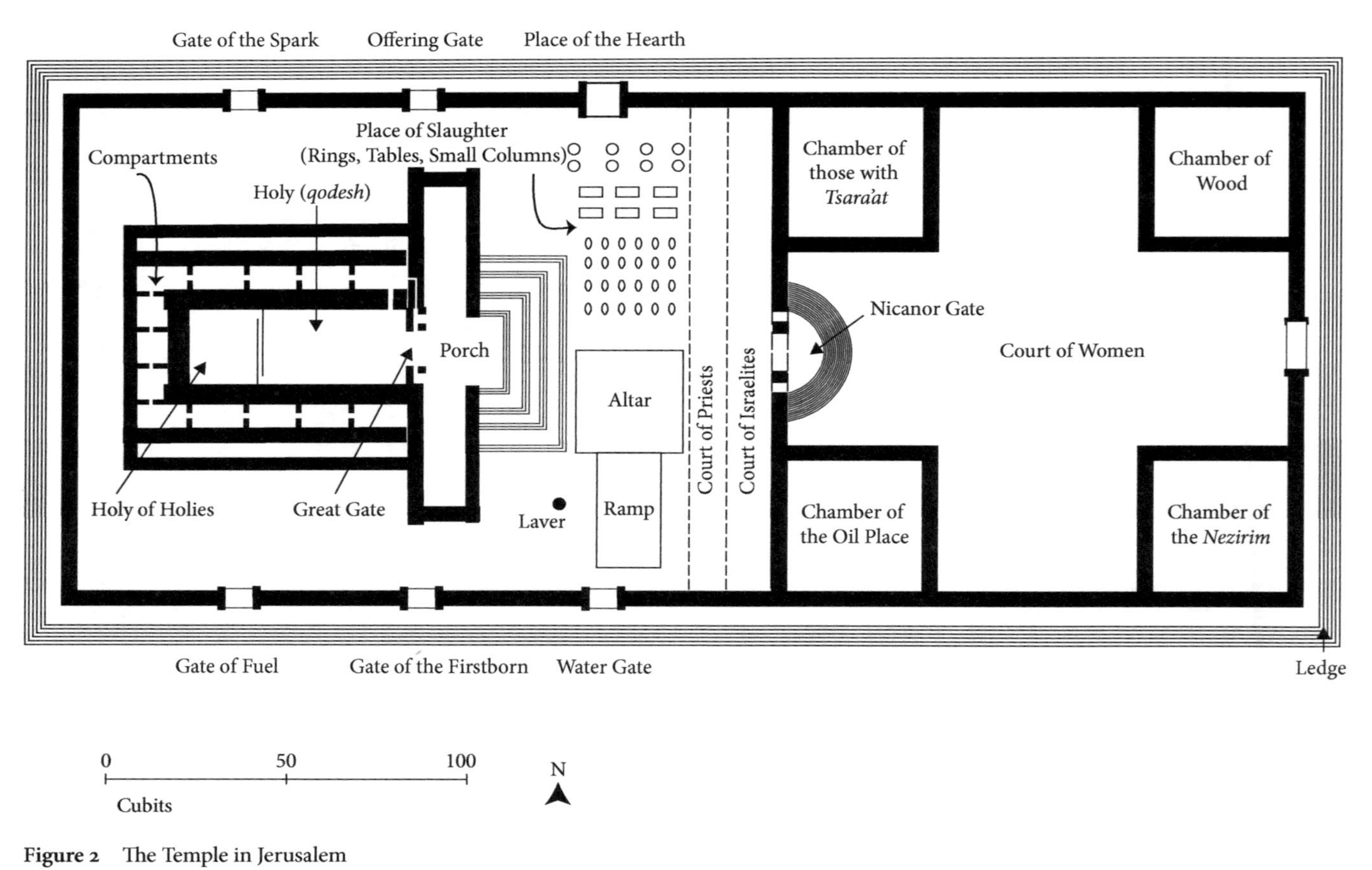

Figure 2 The Temple in Jerusalem
(Source: Author's own.)

1:6–9 *The Place of the Hearth*

6 And there were four chambers in the Place of the Hearth, like rooms opening up to a hall:
two in the sacred space and two in the nonsacred space,
with the tops of stone pavements dividing between the sacred and the nonsacred.
And what function did they serve?
The southwestern: it was the Chamber of Sacrificial Lambs.
The southeastern: it was the Chamber of the Showbread Makers.
The northeastern: in it the Hasmoneans hid away the stones of the altar
that had been defiled by the Greek kings.
The northwestern: in it they would go down to the Place of Immersion.
7 The Place of the Hearth had two gates:
one opening to the ledge surrounding the Temple, and one opening to the Temple Court.
R. Judah said:
The one that opened to the Temple Court had a small wicket
through which they would enter to inspect the Temple Court.
8 The Place of the Hearth was vaulted,
and it was a large room,[9] surrounded by stone landings.
And the elders of the paternal house sleep there,
and the keys to the Temple Court are in their hand.
And the young priests[10] are there as well, each with his mattress on the ground.
9 And there was a place there, one cubit by one cubit,
which had a marble tablet and a ring affixed to it,
and a chain from which the keys would be hanging.
When the time for locking arrived,

[9] Or "building." [10] Lit. "blossoms of the priesthood."

1:6 *rooms…hall*: Both terms derive from Greek for domestic architecture: "bed chamber" and "dining room". Four smaller rooms open up to a larger room.

sacred…nonsacred space: The chamber extended onto the ledge surrounding the Temple, so part of it was outside the sacred area.

tops of stone pavements: Lit. "heads of pebbles," so perhaps a mosaic of some sort on the floor. See similar stone pavements as boundary markers in 2:6 and 4:5 below.

Hasmoneans: Cf. 1 Maccabees 4:44–46.

go down…Place of Immersion: Perhaps a reference to seminal emission (1:9) or perhaps to other regular immersion.

1:7 *two gates*: One led into the Temple, one out of the Temple.

wicket: A small gate next to the main gate; *Tamid* 1:3 and annotations there.

1:8 Parallel to *Tamid* 1:1.

1:9 *ring…chain*: The ring was on the top, for lifting; the chain with the key was on the underside, and thus hidden.

time for locking: The gates to the Temple were locked at a certain time and the night watch began at this point.

the priest used the ring to lift up the tablet,
took the keys from the chain,
and locked it from inside.
And a Levite slept on the outside.
When he finished locking it,
he returned the keys to the chain
and the tablet to its place.
He placed his mattress on top of it and slept.
If one of them had a seminal emission,
he would exit and leave by the winding passageway
that goes under the structure,
where lamps were burning on either side,
[continuing] until he reaches the Place of Immersion.
R. Eliezer b. Jacob says:
He would go via the winding passageway
that goes under the ledge surrounding the Temple,
and go on his way through Tadi Gate.

Chapter Two

2:1–4 *The Temple Mount*

2 The Temple Mount was five hundred cubits by five hundred cubits,
the majority of which was on the south,
the second largest amount of which was on the east,
the third largest amount of which was on the north,
and the minority of which was on the west.
The place with the greatest measure also had the greatest use.

locked it: The outer gate of the Place of the Hearth, and presumably the other gates too. (For more on keys and locks in the Temple, see *Tamid* 1:3; 3:6–7.)

If one of them… Tadi Gate: Parallel to *Tamid* 1:1, with a different ending.

winding passageway: This is distinct from the passageway at 4:5.

under the structure: The precise referent of the Hebrew *birah* is unclear (cf. 1:3). For the priest's actions, compare *Tamid* 1:1.

He would go: Continues the description of the journey through the passageways out of the Temple, perhaps in disagreement with *Tamid* 1:1. Alternatively, *R. Eliezer b. Jacob* may hold a differing opinion of the path of the priest, that he leaves right away, perhaps through a hidden exit from the Temple.

2:1 *five hundred cubits*: See Ezekiel 42:15–20.

majority, etc.: The Temple was a rectangular complex (see 2:6 and 5:1 below) situated on the western and northern sides of the Temple Mount, with its length on the east–west axis. *Amount* refers to the empty space on the Temple Mount, which was free for the people's *use*. The majority was on the southern side.

2 All those who entered the Temple Mount would enter on the right,
and would circle around and exit on the left,
except for the one to whom something had happened,
who would circle to the left.
"What is your situation, circler to the left?"
"That I am a mourner."
"May the One who dwells in this house comfort you."
"That I am under a ban."
"May the One who dwells in this house
put it in their hearts to bring you close again."
These are the words of R. Meir.
R. Yose said to him:
You have made it as if they have transgressed the law on his account.
Rather, "May the One who dwells in this house
put it in your heart to listen to your colleagues
and they will bring you close again."

3 Inside of it was a partition[11] ten handbreadths high.
And there were thirteen breaches there, breached by the Greek kings.
They refenced them and decreed thirteen prostrations to correspond to them.
Inside of that was the ten-cubit ledge.

[11] Alt. "lattice."

The description of the Temple's dimensions begins here with the outer Temple Mount and moves inward to the Holy of Holies in 4:5. For a similar progression, focused on levels of holiness, see *Kelim* 1:8–9.

2:2 *enter on the right*...*exit on left*: If entering by the Gates of Hulda (1:3), the person would enter the right gate and eventually exit through the left gate (on the right from the perspective of the one exiting). Circulation is thus generally in the counterclockwise direction (cf. similar circling in *Zevahim* 6:3).

circle to the left: Presumably enter the left gate and circle against traffic in the clockwise direction. Thus the mourner or one who is ostracized would be walking toward all others, who would greet them, as indicated, and offer appropriate words of comfort. *To the left* suggests turning the body to the left when entering the gate, in order to circulate in the clockwise direction.

"*under a ban*": Alternatively, "excommunicated," "ostracized." This is a second possible response of one circling to the left.

transgressed the law: According to R. Yose, R. Meir's view places the onus of reconciliation on those who place the ban, and thus seems to blame them or question their action.

2:3 *Inside of it was a partition*: The account begins to move inward. The Hebrew word *soreg* ("lattice") may be the name of the partition or describe its appearance. It was *inside* the Temple Mount gates near the Temple structure. The partition marked off the raised ledge of the Temple. Josephus describes a stone partition with pillars at regular distances with inscriptions warning gentiles not to enter on pain of death (two of these inscriptions have been found). On the restriction of gentiles from the ledge surrounding the Temple, see *Kelim* 1:8.

Greek kings: The Seleucids. This may correspond, very loosely, to 1 Maccabees 9:54–55, where it is the inner Temple wall that was partially torn down.

thirteen prostrations: Cf. the explanation in 2:6.

ledge: According to this, the ledge surrounding the Temple was ten cubits, roughly fifteen feet (five meters) wide, and elevated (above the Temple Mount) by six cubits, or nine feet (three meters), with twelve stairs leading down to the Temple Mount.

And there were twelve steps there.
The rise of each step was half a cubit,
and its tread was half a cubit.
All the steps that were there had a rise of
half a cubit and tread of half a cubit,
except those of the Porch.
All the doorways and gates that were there
were twenty cubits high and ten cubits wide,
except that of the Porch.
All the doorways that were there had doors, except that of the Porch.
All the gates that were there were arched, except for Tadi Gate,
which had two stones leaning against each other.
All the gates that were there were altered to be made of gold,
except the Gate of Nicanor, because there was a miracle with [its doors].
Some say: Because its bronze would shine like gold.

4 All the walls that were there were high, except for the eastern wall,
for the priest who burnt the red heifer would stand at the top of the Mount of Olives,
and would intentionally look at the doorway of the Sanctum
at the moment of the sprinkling of the blood.

2:5–6 *The Temple Courts*

5 The Court of Women was 135 cubits long by 135 cubits wide.
And there were four chambers in its four corners,
each forty by forty cubits,
and they were not roofed.
And this is how they will be in the future,
as it says: *He took me out to the outer Court and led me to the four corners of the Court*

All the steps: All other stairs in the Temple; this includes the steps leading from the Court of Women to the Court of Israelites (2:5), but it is not clear which others.

that were there: Repeatedly in 2:3, 4, the rule is given for the entire Temple, with the exception noted.

two stones leaning: The top of the Tadi Gate was formed by two stones meeting in a triangular point.

miracle: See *Yoma* 3:10.

2:4 *All the walls*: Of the Temple Mount.

priest who burnt the red heifer: Cf. *Parah* 3:7–11.

2.5–6 The Mishnah envisions three courts for the entire Temple structure: The Court of Women, the Court of Israelites, and the Court of Priests.

2:5 *Court of Women*: The main open area of the Temple, on a few occasions in the Mishnah called simply "the Temple Court" (see introduction). Josephus claims that women were restricted to this area on the eastern side of the Temple (or to a space within this area), and presumably this was the source of the name. In the Mishnah, there are hints that women could in fact go beyond these boundaries. Thus ritual "waving" of offerings is at times done by women (*Qiddushin* 1:8), and this is done in the Court of Priests (*Kelim* 1:8).

He took me out: Ezekiel 46:21–22, read here as a prophecy about the future Temple yet to be built.

and in each corner of the Court there were enclosures that were qeturot,
and *qeturot* means that they are not roofed.
And what function did they serve?
The southeastern one was the Chamber of the *Nezirim*,
where the *nezirim* would cook their well-being sacrifices
and would cut their hair and throw it under the boiling pot.
The northeastern one was the Chamber of Wood,
where the priests with physical blemishes would sort out the worm-eaten wood.
And any wood in which a worm was found would be invalid for use on the altar.
The northwestern one was the Chamber of Those with *Tsara'at*.
The southwestern one—
R. Eliezer b. Jacob said:
I forgot what function it served.
Abba Saul said:
They used to put wine and oil there;
it was called the Chamber of the Oil Place.
And it was flat[12] at first.
But they surrounded it with a balcony,
where the women would see from above,
and the men from below, so that they would not be mixed.
And there were fifteen steps going up fróm it to the Court of Israelites—
corresponding to the fifteen ascents in Psalms—upon which the Levites would sing.
These were not straight, but were curved, like half of a round threshing floor.[13]

6 And there were chambers under the Court of Israelites—
which opened into to the Court of Women—
where the Levites put the lyres, harps, cymbals, and all musical instruments.

[12] Lit. "smooth." [13] Also, "granary."

southeastern one: The chamber in the southeastern corner of the Court of Women (similarly for the other corners).

Nezirim: See *Nazir* 6:6–9.

Those with Tsara'at: For this skin disease, see *Nega'im*, introduction. For the use of this chamber during the ritual, see *Nega'im* 14:8 (and 14:1–10 on the larger ritual procedure).

it was flat: The Court of Women lacked the extra built structure of the balcony.

balcony: According to Tosefta *Sukkah* 4:1, this balcony for sex segregation was specifically for the festival of the water-drawing place on the holiday of Sukkot.

fifteen steps: See also *Sukkah* 5:4.

from it: From the Court of Women to the Court of the Israelites. The dimensions of the steps are not given.

ascents in Psalms: Psalms 120–134, which all begin "A song of [or for] ascents."

half of a round threshing floor: See also *Sanhedrin* 4:3. The reason for using a metaphor to describe a semicircle is unclear. Perhaps here it highlights the link between agriculture in the land and Temple worship.

2:6 *chambers*: The Court of Israelites was to the west of the Court of Women, at the top of the fifteen steps. The chambers built under the Court of the Israelites were thus at the same level as the Court of Women, into which they opened (presumably to the side of the stairs).

The Court of Israelites was 135 cubits long by eleven wide.
And so too the Court of Priests was 135 cubits long by eleven wide.
And the tops of stone pavements divided between the Court of Israelites and the Court of Priests.
R. Eliezer b. Jacob says:
It was a step up, one cubit high,
and the platform was located on it,
and it had three steps, of one-half cubit each.
In sum,[14] the Court of Priests was two and one-half cubits higher than the Court of Israelites.
The entire Temple Court was 187 cubits long by 135 cubits wide.
And thirteen prostrations were performed there [in the Temple Court].
Abba Yose b. Hanan says:
These correspond to the thirteen gates.
The southern gates are near to the west:
(1) the Upper Gate, (2) the Fuel Gate, (3) the Firstborn Gate, and (4) the Water Gate.
And why was it called the Water Gate?
For they would bring the flask of water for the water libation through it on the Festival.
R. Eliezer b. Jacob says:
And water will gush from it and issue from below the Temple platform in the future.

[14] Lit. the Court "is found to be..."

Court of Priests: Israelites would not normally enter this space, except to perform rituals for offerings: placing the hands, slaughtering, and waving (*Kelim* 1:8). Note that women do not appear to be excluded from either the Court of Israelites or Court of Priests (*Kelim* 1:8; *Zevahim* 3:1; and see annotation to 2:5).

stone pavements: See 1:6 (and annotations); the expression also appears at 4:5. According to this view, the Court of the Priests was the continuation of that of the Israelites. According to *R. Eliezer b. Jacob*, the former was higher.

platform, or elevated step, from Greek, *bema*. In *Arakhin* 2:6, the platform is where the Levites stand to sing; cf. 2:5 above and *Sukkah* 5:4, where they stand on the steps leading from the Court of Women to the Court of Israelites. Perhaps they stood at different locations at different times. Alternatively, the platform, just at the top of these steps, could be considered an extension of the steps.

three steps: This continues R. Eliezer b. Jacob's view. It is unclear whether in his view these steps are part of the platform and thus the platform covers the majority of the Court of Priests or whether the platform is the initial element of the Court of Priests, and the three steps lead up to the rest of the Court.

In sum: This further continues the opinion of R. Eliezer b. Jacob. The initial step up of one cubit plus the three smaller steps of half cubit adds up to two and a half cubits.

entire Temple Court: This phrase appears in 5:1 below, where the 187 is elaborated. According to 5:1, this length spans from the Court of Israelites to the space behind the Sanctum, excluding the Court of Women.

thirteen prostrations: These prostrations could be in addition to those mentioned at 2:3 or refer to the same prostrations, looking from different directions. Both cases could allow that the prostrations took place in only one location, either inside *the Temple Court* or outside, but if so, the language does not make it clear which.

thirteen gates: Cf. 1:4 above where there were seven gates (and 1:1 with annotations, five gates). The diagram of the Temple in Figure 2 is based on 1:4.

water libation: See *Sukkah* 4:9.

water will gush: Ezekiel 47:1–12.

And opposite them on the north, near the to the west:
(5) Jeconiah Gate, (6) the Sacrifice Gate, (7) the Women's Gate, and (8) the Song Gate.
And why was it called Jeconiah Gate?
Because Jeconiah exited through it into his exile.
That of the eastern side: (9) the Gate of Nicanor.
And it had two wickets, (10) one to its right and (11) one to its left.
And two (12, 13) on the western side had no names.[15]

Chapter Three

3:1–5 *The Altar and the Areas for Slaughtering and Butchering*

3 The altar was thirty-two by thirty-two.
It went up a cubit and inward a cubit—
this was the altar base,
leaving[16] thirty by thirty.
It went up five and inward a cubit—
this was the Surround,
leaving twenty-eight by twenty-eight.
The place of the horns[17]
was one cubit in this direction and one cubit in that direction,

[15] **K, P**: "And there were two on the west."
[16] Lit. "It is found to be," here and below. Cf. 2:6.
[17] Alt. "corners."

Jeconiah ... exile: Also called Jehoiachin. 2 Kings 24:8–16; Jeremiah 27:20, 28:4, and 29:2; and Esther 2:6.

Gate of Nicanor: Above, 1:4 and 2:3; also *Yoma* 3:10, *Sheqalim* 6:3, *Sotah* 1:5, and *Nega'im* 14:8. None of these other passages conclusively show that the gate is to the east of the Court of Israelites, rather than that of Women. Only 2:6, taken together with 5:1, seems to imply this. If the great gate of Corinthian bronze described by Josephus (*Jewish War* 5.201–206 and see 2:3 above) is identical with our *Gate of Nicanor*, then Josephus does explicitly locate this gate at the eastern side of the Court of Israelites.

3:1 *thirty-two*: All measurements in this chapter are in cubits.

up ... inward: The Mishnah charts the sections of the altar, starting from the bottom and widest point and moving upward and inward, and marking the length and width at each stage. The commentaries point out that the height is not given and assume that it was ten cubits high, as in 2 Chronicles 4:1 and Ezekiel 43:13–15.

base: Where the blood of offerings is poured; see especially 3:2 below and throughout *Zevahim*. The one cubit *up* and *inward* denote a protrusion of one cubit outward from the main body of the altar that is one cubit high. This protruding base surrounds the lower part of the altar.

the Surround: Heb. *sovev*, lit. "encircling." This refers to the ledge roughly halfway up the altar that likely served as a walkway (see *Zevahim* 5:3, 6:5).

horns: The corners of the altar protruded upward, like horns. They were each 1 × 1 cubits in area. Their height is not specified. They did not span the entire outer edge of the altar.

leaving twenty-six by twenty-six.
The place where the priests' feet would tread
was one cubit in this direction and one cubit in that direction,
leaving twenty-four by twenty-four as a place for the altar fire.[18]
R. Yose said:
Originally it was only twenty-eight by twenty-eight,
and it went up and inward with the same measurements,
so that it left the place for the altar fire of twenty by twenty.
And when the exiles returned,[19]
they added four cubits on the southern side
and four cubits on the western side,
in the shape of a gamma,
As it says,
And the hearth is twelve in length by twelve in width, square.
It is possible that this means: it is only twelve by twelve,
but when it says: *to its four sides,*
this teaches that it is measuring from the middle,
twelve cubits in each direction.
And a thread of red paint wrapped around it like a belt in the middle,
to separate between the upper blood and the lower blood.
And the base went along the entire northern side
and the entire western side
and it took away[20] one cubit on the southern side
and one cubit on the eastern side.

[18] Lit. "woodpile." [19] Lit. "went up." [20] Lit. "ate."

where the priests' feet would tread: A one-cubit-wide track all the way around the outer edge of the top of the altar (in addition to the cubit-wide area at the very outer edge, between the horns).

altar fire: The stacked wood (lit. "arrangement") that was lit to constitute the altar fire. See *Tamid* 2:3–4. In other tractates this word is translated "woodpile."

Originally: These dimensions follow 2 Chronicles 4:1 regarding Solomon's Temple, taking 20 × 20 to be the dimensions of the altar fire, rather than the entire altar.

gamma: The Greek letter Γ.

And the hearth: Ezekiel 43:16, where the hearth (Heb. *ariel*), i.e. the altar fire, itself is taken to be 24 × 24 cubits. Compare 2:5 and 2:6 above, where Ezekiel's vision is taken as a prophecy for future times.

to its four sides: The end of Ezekiel 43:16. Twelve cubits from the center of the square altar to (the middle of) each side is a total of 24 × 24.

thread of red paint: This continues the description of the altar.

upper… lower blood: The blood of some types of sacrifices would be sprinkled above the line, and that of others below. See *Zevahim* 2:1 (annotations) and *Yoma* 5:3–5.

took away: Lit. "ate" in Hebrew. Alternatively, "took up." Thus, either the base only extended a small amount on the southern and eastern sides or it extended the full length of both sides, minus a *cubit* in each direction. Either way, the extension into the southern and eastern sides is fully part of the 32 × 32 calculation.

2 And in the southwestern corner there were two holes
in the shape of two thin nostrils,
because the blood that is put[21] on the western base and the southern base
goes[22] down in them and mixes in the pipe and goes out to the Kidron Valley.
3 Beneath the stone floor at that same corner
there was a place, one cubit by one cubit,
which had a marble tablet and a ring affixed to it
through which they could go down into the pit below the altar and clean it.
And there was a ramp on the southern side of the altar,
thirty-two by sixteen in width.
And there was a pile[23] on the western side [of the ramp]
into which they would place invalidated bird purgation offerings.
4 Both the stones of the ramp and the stones of the altar
were from the Valley of Bet Kerem.
And they would dig beneath the virgin ground,
and they would bring from that place whole stones
upon which no iron tool had been wielded.
For iron invalidates by touching and by blemishing for any purpose.
If one of them became blemished, it is invalidated but the rest are fit for use.
And they whiten them twice a year—
once on Passover and once on the Festival;

[21] **K**, **P**: "the blood is put." [22] **K**, **P**: "and goes." [23] Or "cavity."

3:2 *two holes…blood…put*: See also *Zevahim* 5:1–2 and *Tamid* 4:1. The language implies that the priest would pour excess blood onto the lip of the base that protrudes from the altar (most likely very close to the corner), from where it would flow down into these drainage holes on the corner of the base. Less likely, the holes were in the horn of the altar, with pipes leading down the side of the altar toward the base and then under and out the Temple.

Kidron Valley, separating the Temple Mount from the Mount of Olives to the East.

3:3 *same corner*: The southwestern (as in 3:2).

ring affixed: To lift up the marble tablet; cf. 1:9 above. The ring would have protruded above the floor.

ramp: 5:2 implies a different length; see annotations.

pit below the altar: An open space beneath the altar into which the blood descends (as in *Me'ilah* 3:3).

pile: Meaning of the Hebrew is uncertain. Elsewhere (Tosefta), this is described as a one by one opening in the side of the ramp where the parts would be placed to decompose, after which they could be removed and burnt.

3:4 *whole stones…no iron tool*: This takes up the language of Deuteronomy 27:5–6; see also Exodus 20:22.

blemishing: The implication (explicit in the manuscript readings) is that a cut by any substance invalidates the stones.

whiten…twice a year: This refers to the plastering mentioned later in the passage, which makes the stones of the altar white—though the word *whiten* can also mean simply to clean. In *Rabbi*'s view, more frequent plastering (perhaps just touching up) is needed to cover the bloodstains on the altar. Presumably the altar was cleaned daily but repainted with plaster either weekly or bi-annually.

the Festival: Sukkot (Tabernacles).

and the Sanctum—
once on Passover.
Rabbi says:
Every eve of the Sabbath they would whiten it with a cloth,
because of the blood.
They did not plaster it with an iron trowel,
lest it touch and invalidate,
for iron was created to shorten the days of humans
and the altar was created to lengthen the days of humans,
and it is not appropriate for that which shortens to be wielded over that which lengthens.

5 And there were rings to the north of the altar, six rows of four—
and some say: Four rows of six—
upon which they slaughter the sacrifices.
The Butchering Place was to the north of the altar,
and it contained eight short columns topped by cedar blocks.
And there were iron hooks set into them, three rows for each,
on which they would hang and flay.
On[24] marble tables between the columns.

3:6 *The Sanctum: Between the Altar and Porch*

6 The Laver was between the Porch and the altar,
more toward the southern side.

[24] **K, P**: "And there were..."

Rabbi: Judah the Patriarch.

iron was created to shorten: Iron is used to make the implements of war and murder.

not appropriate: This language could be indicating a technical, legal, or logical derivation, along the lines of "logic dictates that (it is not)..."

3:5 *rings*: See a description of their use in *Tamid* 4:1. Some commentators see these as places to tether and immobilize the animal, though this does not fit with the preposition *upon*. Other commentators see these as devices with a mechanism to hold down the animal by its neck—perhaps by inserting the neck in the ring and pushing the ring into the ground.

The Butchering Place... between the columns: Parallel to *Tamid* 3:5.

short columns... hang and flay: See also *Pesahim* 5:9. The carcasses of slaughtered animals would be hung up on the hooks and flayed.

On marble tables: The reading "And there were marble tables between the pillars" (see n. 24) seems preferable. See *Tamid* 3:5, annotations.

3:6 This mishnah continues the calculations of cross-sectional dimensions that began in 2:5–6 (and 3:1) above. This calculation will be taken up again in 4:6–7.

Porch: Heb. *ulam*. The entrance hall to the inner sancta. For ritual activity in the Porch, see *Menahot* 11:7.

Laver: For its regular use, see *Tamid* 1:4 and 2:1. See also *Yoma* 4:5, *Sukkah* 4:10, and *Sotah* 2:2. And see *Yoma* 3:10 and *Tamid* 3:8 on Ben Qatin's technological innovations for the Laver.

Between the Porch and the altar was twenty-two cubits.
And there were twelve stairs there.
The rise of each stair was half a cubit, and its tread was a cubit.
A cubit, a cubit, and a landing of three;
and a cubit, a cubit, and a landing of three;
and the uppermost—
a cubit, a cubit, and a landing of four.
R. Judah says:
The uppermost—
a cubit, a cubit, and a landing of five.

3:7–8 *The Porch or Entrance Hall of the Sanctum*

7 The doorway to the Porch was a height of forty cubits
and a width of twenty cubits.
And on top of it there were five ash-wood ceiling beams.
The lowest one extended beyond the doorway a cubit on each side.
The one above it extended beyond it a cubit on each side.
In sum:[25] the uppermost one was thirty cubits long.
And there was a row of stones between each one.
8 And there were cedar beams fixed into the wall,
going from the wall of the Sanctum to the wall of the Porch,
so that it would not sway.[26]
And there were golden chains fixed into the ceiling of the Porch,
on which the young priests[27] would go up and look at the crowns,[28]
as it is written: *And the crowns shall be in the Sanctum of the Lord*
as a memorial for Helem, Tobiah, Jedaiah, and Hen son of Zephaniah.

[25] Lit. it is "found to be." [26] Or "bulge"; "buckle"; "lean."
[27] Lit. "blossoms of the priesthood." [28] **K, P** add "in the windows/niches."

A cubit, a cubit, and a landing: Every third step was a longer landing. The *uppermost*, i.e. the very top step, was even longer. Note that we are only given the tread of the steps and landings not the width or construction design of the steps themselves. The steps seem to have come very close to the altar.

3:7 *doorway... cubits*: For the dimensions of the Porch itself, see 4:7.

beams: These decorative beams (Heb. *malteraʾot*, from the Greek) were stacked on top of each other in increasing size above the open Porch doorway, serving as a lintel. The first beam was two cubits wider than the doorway, the subsequent ones two cubits wider than the beam below it.

3:8 *beams*: Heb. *kelonasot*, perhaps from Greek, "wooden."

sway: Supports were necessary because both the Porch and Sanctum front walls were so tall (commentaries). The height of the latter is given as one hundred cubits (4:6). It is also possible that the Porch structure was not fully integrated into the Sanctum structure.

And the crowns: Zechariah 6:14. Here, the future-oriented biblical prophecy—including the instruction to leave the crowns in the Temple—is taken as having been fulfilled in the Second Temple. The crowns would have been stored in niches or windows (see n. 28) high up in the wall of the Porch.

A golden grapevine stood upon the doorway to the Sanctum,
hanging[29] over the beams.
Whoever donated a leaf, a single grape, or a cluster,
would bring it and hang it onto it.
R. Eleazar b. Zadok said:
It once happened that they called on three hundred priests because of it.

Chapter Four

4:1–5 *The Structure of the Sanctum and Various Surrounding Parts*

4 The doorway to the Sanctum was a height of twenty cubits and a width of ten cubits.
And it had four doors, two inside and two outside,
as it says: *There were two doors for the Sanctum, and for the Holy.*
The outer ones opened up into the doorway,
to cover the thickness of the wall,
and the inner ones opened up into the House,

[29] Or "trained," as in viticulture.

golden grapevine: The exact positioning is unclear. Josephus, *Jewish Antiquities*, 15.395 places this vine above the doors and lintel of the Temple itself, or the larger Sanctum—*naos* in Greek. Here, the golden vines are imagined to have hung, in the manner of grapevines, over the support beams.

donated: Golden items to be attached to the golden grapevine. Because nonpriests could not enter here, presumably the donors handed the items to a priest, who actually attached the donated items (or the items made with money given for this purpose).

three hundred priests: The commentaries, based on the expansion of this story in the Babylonian Talmud, understand that many priests were needed to hold and move the golden vine at a certain point because it was so weighted with donated ornaments.

4:1 *Sanctum*: Heb. *hekhal*. Lit. "palace," or "great hall." The term may refer to the chamber inward of the Porch, also referred to as the *qodesh*, or "Holy," which in turn opens into the Holy of Holies. Alternatively, it may refer to the whole structure including the Holy and the Holy of Holies, and in some cases, even the Porch.

four doors: Two sets of doors, one set facing out to the Porch, the other facing inward to the Holy. Because the Sanctum wall itself was six cubits thick (4:7), when the doors were closed, there was a space between the two sets of doors.

There were two doors: Ezekiel 41:23, possibly describing two distinct structures, each with a set of doors, but totaling four doors, as in the Mishnah.

outer ones: In this first opinion, both sets of doors opened inward, one into the doorway, covering the wall inside the doorway, and the other into the Sanctum, ending up flat against the inner wall, covering the ungilded back side of the door.

House: The complex of the Holy and Holy of Holies, normally termed Sanctum.

to cover behind the doors.
For the entire House was covered with gold except for behind the doors.
R. Judah said:
They were standing inside the doorway,
and, in the shape of pivots, they folded back,
these were two and a half cubits, and these were two and a half cubits,
half a cubit for the doorpost at one side, and half a cubit for the doorpost at the other side,
as it says: *A double door for the doors, with swinging doors,*
two for one door and two doors for the other.

2 And the Great Gate had two wickets,
one on the northern side and the other on the southern side.
No one entered the one on the southern side, ever,
and this is stated explicitly by Ezekiel:
The Lord said to me: This gate will be shut, it will not be opened,
and no man will enter through it,
for the Lord God of Israel has entered through it,
and it shall remain shut.
He took the key and opened the wicket,
he entered the compartment,
and from the compartment entered the Sanctum.
R. Judah says:
He would walk inside the thickness of the wall until he was standing between the two gates.
He opened the outer ones from the inside and the inner ones from the outside.

R. Judah holds that both sets of doors opened into the doorway, each door folding in half. The doorway was ten cubits wide, so each panel of the folding doors was *two and a half cubits*. The *doorposts* on the inner and outer sides of the doorway were each *half a cubit*. Together the doors and doorposts fully covered the six-cubit thickness (4:7) of the Sanctum wall.

pivots: The manuscripts have wide variation for this word and its meaning is uncertain. The translation interprets the term as *strophomata*, "pivots" in Greek. In context it is clear that the doors themselves are folding doors.

A double door: Ezekiel 41:24, continuing the verse above. Each door, according to the verse, has two folding (*swinging*) door panels.

4:2 *And the Great Gate…Sanctum*: Parallel to *Tamid* 3:7, where the passage fits the context better. See annotations there. The *Great Gate* was the gate to the Sanctum (4:1).

stated explicitly by Ezekiel: Ezekiel does not mention any wickets, nor is it clear that the verse quoted refers to the Sanctum.

The Lord said: Ezekiel 44:2.

He the priest opening the gates of the Sanctum *took the key*.

R. Judah holds that the priest would be able to pass from the wicket into the wall, and from there to the space between the two sets of closed doors (4:1).

the outer ones…from the outside: From within the space between the two sets of doors, but *outside* the Sanctum proper, the priest would pull both sets of folding doors toward himself (according to R. Judah's view of the doors; 4:1).

3 And there were thirty-eight compartments there,
fifteen on the northern side, fifteen on the southern side, and eight on the western side.
Those on the northern and southern sides were five on top of five and five on top of those.
And those on the western side were three on top of three and two on top of those.
And there were three doorways to each,
one leading into the compartment from the right, one leading into the compartment from the left,
and one leading into the compartment that was on top of it.
And in the northeastern corner there were five doorways,
one leading into the compartment from the right,
one leading into the compartment on top of it,
one leading into the winding passageway,
one leading into the wicket,
and one leading into the Sanctum.

4 The lower [level] was five [cubits]; with a stone landing[30]—six.
The middle was six, with a stone landing[31]—seven.

[30] Or "stone pavement." [31] Or "stone pavement."

4:3 *compartments*: 4:3–4 describe three stories of chambers within the southern, western, and northern outer walls of the Sanctum, surrounding the *qodesh* (Holy) and the Holy of Holies. The structure is based loosely on 1 Kings 6:5–10 and Ezekiel 41:5–7 (the former quoted in 4:4). The Mishnah does not fully describe these compartments, but conveys a picture of an extensive labyrinth of interconnected chambers surrounding the walls of the Holy and Holy of Holies from the ground to the roof, accessible only via the wicket to the right of the Great Gate and from a single opening in the Holy (and also from the roof, via the winding passageway). Maimonides has a very different reading of the architecture, envisioning a nested set of rectangles, with the chambers all open to the air, rather than the chambers stacked on top of each other.

one leading to the compartment that was on top of it: This is the case for the lower-level compartments; the middle level would have an opening up and down, and the upper level an opening to the compartment below (in addition to the ones to the adjacent compartments to the sides). Similarly, all end compartments but the lowest northeastern one would have only one sideways opening. Each compartment had a passageway to all adjacent compartments, whether up, down, or to the side.

the northeastern corner etc.: This suggests that only one of the thirty-eight compartments—the one at the northeastern corner—opened into the Sanctum, into the wicket (according to 4:2, the wicket opened into the Sanctum through the compartment), and into the winding passageway (see 4:5), and so had more doorways than the other compartments. The southern wicket was not used and so presumably did not connect to the compartment on that side.

4:4 *[level]* refers to the story of compartments (4:3). The numbers of cubits given are the depth of the space in the compartments on that level, measured between the wall facing the Sanctum and the outer wall (4:7).

stone landing, or, pavement. Compartments on the lower two levels were covered on top by a stone pavement that served as roof and also as floor for the next level up. Above the third story was the roof that covered the entire Sanctum. Each lower-level compartment had a slightly thicker wall, and thus less compartment space. The projecting additional wall would support the stone that served as the roof of that level and the floor of the level above it. The rationale for this system, according to 1 Kings 6:5–10 (quoted here), is that the stone pavement would be fully supported by the walls below it and no drilling would be required to support the floor/roof. For additional complications see 4:7 and annotations.

The upper was seven.
As it says: *The lowest story was five cubits wide;*
the middle was six cubits wide;
and the third, was seven cubits wide.

5 And a winding passageway ascended from the northeastern corner
to the northwestern corner,
through which they used to ascend to the roofs of the compartments.
He would ascend the winding passageway facing west,
walk the entire length of the northern side until he reached the western side.
When he reached the western side, he would turn and face south,
and walk the entire length of the western side until he reached the southern side.
When he reached the southern side, he would turn and face east.
He would walk the entire length of the southern side
until he reached the doorway to the upper story,
for the doorway to the upper story opened to the southern side.
And at the doorway to the upper story there were two cedar beams
upon which they would go up to the roof of the upper story.
And the tops of stone pavements on the upper story
divided between the Holy and the Holy of Holies.
And small passageways[32] opened from the upper story into the place of the Holy of Holies,
through which they would lower down artisans in boxes,
so that their eyes not feast on the place of the Holy of Holies.

[32] Or "openings;" "trap doors;" "stairwells."

The lowest story: 1 Kings 6:6.

4:5 *winding passageway*: This describes a single circuit *from the northeastern corner* (to the right of the Great Gate), along the northern wall, then along the western wall, then along the southern wall, perhaps as far as the southeastern corner (to the left of the Great Gate). This passageway led ultimately up three stories, presumably with stairs, to the upper chamber above the roof of the Sanctum (see 4:6), which was accessed via a doorway somewhere along the southern side. When the passageway went along the western side, it either went into the thickness of the outer wall or through the compartments on that side, since there is no space allotted in 4:7 for the passageway along the western wall. On the southern wall it could have gone above the place for bringing down water (4:7). The statement that the *winding passageway ascended from the northeastern corner to the northwestern corner* must refer to the cross section on the first story only, because the passageway continued along the western and southern walls according to the continuation of the passage.

upper story: The entire Sanctum—excluding only the Porch—had an upper story that brought its height to one hundred cubits (4:6). Presumably it was recessed somewhat from walls of the Sanctum, creating a landing from which there was a door into the upper story. Alternatively, there could have been a trapdoor at the top of the steps or a small chamber separating the winding passage and the upper story.

cedar beams: A ladder of sorts from the landing at the door to the upper story up to its roof.

tops of stone pavements: On the floor of the upper story, marking the differing levels of sacredness below. See such markers in 1:6 (see annotations) and 2:6 above.

artisans would enter to fix something there. The boxes must have had some sort of opening for them to do their work.

4:6–7 *Dimensions of the Sanctum*

6 And the Sanctum was one hundred by one hundred, by a height of one hundred.
The foundation was six cubits
and its height was forty cubits,
one cubit of paneling work,
two cubits for the place of drippings,[33]
one cubit of ceiling pavement,
one cubit of plastering;
the height of the upper story was forty cubits,
one cubit of paneling work,
two cubits for the place of drippings,[34]
one cubit of ceiling pavement,
one cubit of plastering,
three cubits roof railing,
and one cubit, crow deterrent.
R. Judah says:
The crow deterrent was not included in the measurement,
but rather the roof railing was four cubits.
7 From the eastern side to the western side was one hundred cubits:
the wall of the Porch was five,
the Porch was eleven,

[33] Alt. "ceiling beams" attaching and supporting ceiling and walls. [34] Alt. "ceiling beams."

4:6–7 In these passages, 4:6 accounts for the one hundred cubits in height of the Sanctum (including Porch); 4:7 for the length and width. See also 3:7–4:1, which provide the doorway dimensions.

4:6 *one hundred*: Cubits, as above.

The foundation: This begins the tally of the total height. The foundation, presumably of stone, was also the height of the stairs leading to the Porch (the entryway to the Sanctum; see the stairs in 3:6). The entire Sanctum structure was elevated upon this "foundation" above the Court of Israelites and Court of Priests and above the areas to the sides and behind the Sanctum.

paneling: Which would be visible from inside.

place of drippings: A space to catch and drain the drips of water from the roof (Maimonides). Alternatively, according to most commentaries, these are ceiling beams that support the roof and connect it to the walls.

plastering: Forming the floor of the upper story and the top of the upper roof. Plaster waterproofs these surfaces.

crow deterrent: Sharp edge or points to deter birds.

4:7 *From the eastern side*: This cross section goes from the Porch on the east, toward the Holy of Holies and to the space behind the Holy of Holies. In contrast to the architectural tally of the Temple Court in 5:1–2, the thickness of the walls of the Sanctum and its subdivisions are included in the count. On the dimensions in general, cf. Ezekiel 40–41.

Porch: See this structure in 2:3 and 3:6–8.

the wall of the Sanctum six,
its inside forty cubits,
one cubit for the partition,
twenty cubits for the place of the Holy of Holies,
the wall of the Sanctum six,
the compartment six,
and the wall of the compartment five.
From the northern side to the southern side was seventy cubits:
The wall of the winding passageway was five,
the winding passageway three,
the wall of the compartment five,
the compartment six,
the wall of the Sanctum six,
its inside twenty cubits,
the wall of the Sanctum six,
the compartment six,
the wall of the compartment five,
the place for bringing down water three cubits,
and the wall five cubits.
The Porch extended beyond it fifteen cubits to the northern side
and fifteen cubits to the southern side.
And it was called the Place of the Slaughtering Knives,
for they would hide[35] the knives there.
And the Sanctum was narrow from behind and wide from the front,
and resembled a lion,

[35] Or "store."

Sanctum: Unlike the start of 4:6, here the *Sanctum* is distinct from the *Porch*. The term, as noted, has some fluidity, referring to the entire structure, the entire structure minus the Porch, or the Holy alone.

partition: In *Yoma* 5:1, this is formed by two curtains one cubit apart.

compartment: See 4:3–5. In 4:4, five cubits was the depth of the lower level of the three stories of compartments; here floor level appears to have had a depth of six. The most likely explanation is that the lowest of the three stories was within the foundation of the Sanctum and that the middle level was the floor level. The six cubits indicated here is therefore the measure of the ground level. Alternatively, six could refer to the space of the lower level plus the "stone landing" that surrounded it and supported the floor of the middle story.

From the northern side: On the winding passageway, see 4:5. The winding passageway and its wall are not included in the tally of the western or southern sides because it went above the compartments on those sides or into the space designated for the outer wall.

bringing down water: Draining rainwater to protect the roof, and sending the rainwater into cisterns below for use in the Temple (and see 5:4).

Porch extended: The "entrance hall" was wider on both sides, forming the "wide" front of the Sanctum, the figurative head of the lion.

the Place of the Slaughtering Knives was in either one or both of the sides that jutted out, within the Porch, or in a chamber below the Porch, entered from the outside.

Slaughtering Knives: The Hebrew term is rare, and the precise meaning is ambiguous. In context it is a type of knife. They *hide* them away presumably when they are no longer usable.

as it says: *Lo, Ariel, Ariel, city where David camped*:
just as a lion is narrow from behind and wide from the front,
so too the Sanctum is narrow from behind and wide from the front.

Chapter Five

5:1–2 *Dimensions of the Temple Court*

5 The entire Temple Court was a length of 187 by a width of 135:
from the eastern side to the western side was 187.
The place the Israelites would tread was eleven cubits,
the place the priests would tread was eleven cubits,
the altar was thirty-two,
between the Porch and the altar was twenty-two cubits,
the Sanctum was one hundred cubits,
and there were eleven cubits behind the place of the *kapporet*.
2 From the northern side to the southern side was 135:
the ramp and the altar were sixty-two,
from the altar to the rings was eight cubits,
the place of the rings was twenty-four,
from the rings to the tables was four,
from the tables to the short columns was four,
from the short columns to the Court wall was eight cubits,

Lo, Ariel: Isaiah 29:1, where "Ariel," literally, "Lion of God" refers to Jerusalem or perhaps the Temple. In Ezekiel 43:15–16, the term refers to the altar fire (or the altar); on which, see above 3:1.

5:1–2 Mishnah 5:1 tallies the components of the Temple Court (excluding the Court of Women) in the east–west dimension; 5:2 in the north–south dimension.

5:1 *entire Temple Court*: As can be seen in the continuation, this excludes the Court of Women. See also 2:5–6 and annotation to 2:5.

Israelites...priests would tread: The Court of Israelites and the Court of Priests. See 2:6 above.

behind the place of the kapporet: See above 1:1.

5:2 *ramp and altar*: Combining the figures in 3:1 and 3:3, each should have a length of thirty-two, making sixty-four. To resolve this contradiction Maimonides interprets 3:3 as referring to the length of the surface of the ramp, and calculating a base length of approximately thirty.

rings...tables...short columns: See 3:5. This passage is surprisingly vague, not providing precise measurements or spacing for the columns and tables, or numbers of tables. Here it would seem that the tables were in a separate space from the (eight) columns; however in 3:5, the tables are located "between" the pillars.

remainder: A surprisingly imprecise statement; the remainder is twenty-five cubits. Note that the marble tables would also have taken up space not accounted here.

and the remainder was between the ramp and the wall,
and the place of the short columns.

5:3–4 *Chambers of the Temple Court*

3 There were six chambers in the Temple Court,
three on the northern side and three on the southern side.
Those on the northern side:
(1) the Salt Chamber, (2) the *Parvah* Chamber, (3) the Rinsing Chamber.
The Salt Chamber was where they would put the salt for offerings.
The *Parvah* Chamber was where they would salt the skins of the sacrifices;
and on its roof was the place of immersion for the high priest on the Day of Atonement.
The Rinsing Chamber was where they would rinse the innards of sacrifices
and where a winding passageway went up to the roof of the *Parvah* Place.
4 Those on the southern side:
(4) the Wood Chamber, (5) the Chamber of the Exile,[36] (6) and the Chamber of Hewn Stone.
The Wood Chamber—
R. Eliezer said:
I forgot what its use was.
Abba Saul said:
It was the Chamber of the High Priest,
and it was behind the other two, and the roof of the three was equal [in height].

[36] Alt. “cup”; “circle”; “rolling.”

between the ramp: Unlike the other cross-sectional measurements given in this and the previous chapter, the measurement is not linear, but starts with the ramp and altar and moves north, and then returns to the give the *remainder* made up of the area to the south of the altar, and of the space taken up by the short columns (and presumably the tables) themselves toward the north.

5:3–4 The tractate concludes with a description of the chambers in the Temple Court.

5:3 *Temple Court*: As earlier in the tractate, this refers to the Courts of Israelites and Priests and the area north of that, surrounding the Sanctum, but not the Court of Women (the chambers of which are described in 2:5–6 above).

northern…southern: The exact location of these chambers is unclear. It is also unclear if they were free-standing or built into the Temple Court walls or gates.

Parvah Chamber: At the end of 5:3 it is called the Parvah “Place” (cf. *Yoma* 3:3, 6).

Rinsing Chamber: Cf. *Tamid* 4:2 for similar washing.

winding passageway: A stairwell. Distinct from the other winding passageways mentioned in the tractate. This passageway led from the Rinsing Chamber to the immersion place for the Day of Atonement above the adjacent (*Parvah*) chamber.

5:4 *Wood Chamber*: A name and location distinct from the Chamber of Wood in 2:5 above.

Chamber of the High Priest: Perhaps the same as mentioned in *Yoma* 1:1.

The Chamber of the Exile was where there was a cistern set in,[37]
with a wheel placed on it,
and where they provided water for the entire Temple Court.
The Chamber of Hewn Stone was where the great Sanhedrin of Israel would sit
and adjudicate regarding the priesthood.
And a priest in whom a disqualification was found
would wear black and wrap his head in black and exit and go on his way.
And one in whom a disqualification was not found
would wear white and wrap his head in white and enter and serve with his brothers the priests.
And they would make a festival day,
because a disqualification had not been found in the progeny of Aaron the priest.
And they used to say: "Blessed is the Omnipresent, blessed is He,
because a disqualification has not been found in the progeny of Aaron.
And blessed is He who chose Aaron and his sons to stand and serve before the Lord
in the place of the Holy of Holies."[38]

[37] For "set in," **K, P** have "of the Exile," or "a cup,"
[38] "And blessed be he . . . Holies": absent in **K, P** (and other manuscripts).

behind the other two: Behind the Chamber of the Exile and the Chamber of Hewn Stone. It is unclear what "behind" means, perhaps closer to the wall or to the western side.

roof . . . was equal: Alternatively, a shared roof.

Chamber of the Exile: Heb. *golah*, also "diaspora." Perhaps this chamber is named for the returnees from exile (in the book of Ezra-Nehemiah) who rebuilt the Temple. Alternatively, the name may reflect the function of the room, referring to the wheel (*galgal*) or perhaps the large cup (*gulah*, as in Zechariah 4:2) that was used to draw water.

wheel placed on it: A pulley to draw water from the cistern.

great Sanhedrin of Israel: See tractate *Sanhedrin*.

"*the Omnipresent*": An epithet for God; this is a blessing formula.

"*place of the Holy of Holies*": Perhaps referring to the Temple as a whole, which housed the Holy of Holies, since even regular priests are being judged, and they could not serve in the Holy of Holies. Alternatively, this is simply an additional general doxology in praise of the high priesthood (Aaron and his line). Note that the final sentence is not found in the manuscripts and is likely a later addition.

Tractate Qinnim

Dalia Marx

Introduction

Overview

Tractate *Qinnim* (literally "nests"; in the singular a *qen* is a pair of birds in a nest) discusses bird offerings, sacrifices consisting of pairs of young pigeons or turtle doves. In fact, the tractate examines only a small number of issues related to bird offerings, namely cases of mixtures and mistakes. One may describe the tractate as an appendix to the discussion of bird offerings in tractate *Zevahim* (chapters 6–7). The bulk of the discussion is the determination of the maximal number of birds that can be offered when a mixture of birds occurs.

Structure and Organization of the Tractate

Tractate *Qinnim* has three chapters. The first begins with general terms and explanations of the proper offering procedure. Then it deals with cases of mixture. The discussion evolves from simple cases to more complicated ones: mixtures of purgation and whole burnt offerings (1:2); purgation or whole burnt offerings mixed with obligatory offerings (1:2); two groups that have the same number of birds dedicated as obligatory offerings (1:3); and finally, groups that contain different numbers of birds brought as obligatory offerings (1:4).

The second chapter deals with all possible cases of partial mixtures, namely a single bird flying from one group to another. It begins with the general law (2:1), then specifies the cases of two groups of the same number of birds designated as obligatory offerings (2:2); groups of obligatory offerings of different sizes (2:3); cases of mixtures of purgation and whole burnt offerings in obligatory offerings (2:4) and finally, cases of obligatory offerings in which the purgation and whole burnt offerings are not mixed (2:5).

The third and last chapter specifies a new and rather obscure term "a priest who consults," who is compared to "a priest who does not consult," probably indicating that the previous discussions in the first two chapters refer to the former. And indeed, 3:1–5 deal with matters that were already discussed in the previous chapters: 3:1–2 are parallel to 1:3 and 3:3–5 are parallel to 1:2. It has been suggested that the tractate has different layers and contains additional sections that include elaborations and further discussion of some matters that appear in the first two chapters. The sixth and last mishnah of the chapter concludes the tractate as well as the order of *Qodashim*. This passage contains a long discussion of the replacement birds a woman who made a vow must bring, and concludes with two aggadic passages; the first celebrates the superior nature of the offered animal to that of the living one, and the second speaks in favor of the "elders of Torah."

Relationship to Scripture

Leviticus 1:14 deals with personal voluntary whole burnt offerings that can be brought from turtle doves or pigeons. The Torah also deals with obligatory bird offerings brought by the following persons: a woman who has given birth and cannot afford a lamb (Leviticus 12:8), a person who was purified from *tsara'at* and cannot afford three lambs (Leviticus 14:21–23), a man or woman rendered impure because of an abnormal genital discharge (Leviticus 15), and a *nazir* who was defiled by a corpse (Numbers 6:9–11). In all these cases, one of the birds is a purgation offering while the other is a whole burnt offering.

Special Notes for the Reader

Despite the fact that men and women alike were required to bring bird offerings, almost all of the examples in the tractate feature women and feminine language. For example, "one [nest] belongs to one woman and one to another" (1:3). One explanation of this phenomenon is that probably most people who brought bird offerings were women who had given birth, but there may have been something essential about the bird offering that was deemed feminine. Perhaps the ritual killing of the two young birds may have been perceived as a protective device for the baby.

Many of the discussions in the tractate are theoretical. It contains complex mathematical calculations of situations that are not likely to occur (for example, a woman who is required to bring a hundred nests), and therefore it is sometimes called "the mathematical tractate." Moreover, even within the rabbis' vision of Temple reality, the ruling of Rabban Simeon b. Gamaliel, that a woman after multiple births needs to bring only one pair of birds for the post partum offering (*Keritot* 1:7), would seem to obviate the likelihood that one would ever need the complicated calculations of this tractate. See too *Sheqalim* 6:5, the establishment of multiple buckets for donations to the Temple, including one specifically for the price of sacrificial birds' nests. Within rabbinic tradition tractate *Qinnim* is remembered as the quintessence of rabbinic law (*Avot* 3:18).

Tractate Qinnim

Chapter One

1:1 *Introductory Principles*

I The bird purgation offering is performed below [on the altar],
and that of the beast purgation offering, above.
The bird whole burnt offering is performed above
and that of the beast, below.
If one made changes to either, it is disqualified.
The procedure for bird offerings is thus:
in the case of obligatory offerings, one bird is a purgation offering
and one is a whole burnt offering;
in the case of vows and voluntary offerings, all are whole burnt offerings.
What is a vow offering?
When one says: "I am hereby obligated to bring a whole burnt offering."
And what is a voluntary offering?
When one says: "This is hereby a whole burnt offering."
What is the difference between vows and voluntary offerings?
Only that vows, if they died or were stolen,
one is accountable for them.
Free-will offerings, if they died or were stolen,
one is not accountable for them.

1:1 *below...above*: This refers to a red line that divided the upper from the lower part of the altar (*Middot* 3:1). In the case of a *purgation offering* of a bird, the sprinkling of the blood should be performed below the line. For *whole burnt offerings* the bird's blood was to be sprinkled above the red line (*Zevahim* 6:5). In the case of the sacrifice of cattle, by contrast, the blood of the *purgation offering* is offered *above* the red line and that of *whole burnt offering below* it.

bird offerings: Heb. *qinnim*, literally "nests."

obligatory offerings: Brought in fulfillment of a biblical commandment, as for purification after abnormal genital discharge or childbirth. The obligatory offering is comprised of two birds that are set apart as a "nest" (*qen*), one as a purgation offering and the other as whole burnt offering.

vows and voluntary offerings: Offerings in which the donor has undertaken to bring a bird sacrifice. See *Nedarim*, introduction. In these cases both birds are sacrificed as whole burnt offerings.

is... is not accountable for them: When one vows "I am obligated to bring" a bird offering, the donor remains obligated to bring a sacrifice even if the original animal *died or was stolen*. If the dedication was of a specific pair of birds, their death or theft exempts the donor from making up the sacrifice.

1:2–4 *Mingled Sacrifices*

2 A purgation offering that became mingled with a whole burnt offering,
or a whole burnt offering with a purgation offering,
even if it was but one in ten thousand—
they must all die.
A purgation offering that became mingled with obligatory offerings—
only as many birds as correspond to the number of purgation offerings
among the obligatory offerings are valid.
And so too, a whole burnt offering that became mingled with obligatory offerings—
only those that correspond in number to the whole burnt offerings
among the obligatory offerings are valid,
whether the obligatory offerings are many and the free-will offerings few,
or the free-will offerings many and the obligatory offerings few,
whether they are both equal in number.
3 To what do these things refer?
To obligatory offerings mingled with voluntary offerings.
However, in the case [of pairs] of obligatory offerings that became mingled with one another:
one belongs to one [woman] and one to another;[1]
or two belong to one and two to another;
or three belong to one and three to another—
half are valid and half are disqualified.
If one pair belongs to one woman
and two to another,

[1] Lit. "one to this one and one to this one."

1:2 *A purgation offering... mingled with a whole burnt offering*: The acts that validate the one (e.g. sprinkling blood above or below) disqualify the other (1:1), and any one bird presented for slaughter might be either a purgation offering or a whole burnt offering. The birds should therefore *die*.

A purgation offering... mingled with obligatory offerings: In a pair of birds for an obligatory offering, one was a whole burnt offering and one a purgation offering. One cannot offer a whole burnt offering from the mixture discussed here, since it might be the bird already designated a purgation offering. However, up to the number of birds that *correspond to the number of purgation offerings among the obligatory offerings* can be offered as purgation offerings. Each of these is either already a purgation offering, or may be offered as the purgation offering of a pair of obligatory sacrifices. Beyond that number, one risks offering a whole burnt offering as a purgation offering.

And so too, a whole burnt offering: The same logic applies when the mingled sacrifice is a whole burnt offering.

whether the obligatory offerings are many: One does not evaluate the mixture on the basis of what the majority of the animals are. Obligatory offerings require two kinds of sacrifices; voluntary ones require whole burnt offerings alone.

1:3 *obligatory offerings that became mingled with one another*: Any bird might be from one woman or the other. If the number of the two groups of animals was equal, *half are valid*. In this way one can be sure that one is not offering extra sacrifices of the same kind (e.g. purgation offerings) from the birds belonging to one of the women.

three belong to another,
ten to another,
and a hundred to another,
the number corresponding to the fewest sets of birds is valid,[2]
whether the pairs are from one designation or from two designations,
whether from one woman or two women.

4 How "from one designation"?
One for a birth and the other for a birth;
one for a genital discharge and the other for a genital discharge—
"from one designation."
"From two designations"?
One for a birth and the other for a genital discharge.
How "two women"?
This one is obligated for a birth and the other for a birth;
this one for a genital discharge and the other for a genital discharge—
"from one designation."
"From two designations"?
This one is obligated due to a birth and the other due to genital discharge.
R. Yose says:
Two women who brought their nests in partnership,
or gave the price of their nests to the priest,
he may offer whichever he chooses as a purgation offering
and whichever he chooses as a whole burnt offering,
whether they are "from one designation" or "from two designations."

[2] Lit. "the lesser/fewer is valid."

the number corresponding to the fewest... is valid: Again, this avoids offering extra offerings of the same type from birds belonging to one of the women.

designation... women: See 1:4.

1:4 This mishnah explains 1:3, which said that the procedure for handling mingled sacrifices applies even if they fulfill different purposes or were brought by different women.

"*designation*": The specific ritual purpose (lit. "name") that the "nest" fulfills.

birth... genital discharge: See introduction.

two women, bringing sacrifices under *one designation* or *two designations*: In all these cases the fewest sets of birds can be valid (as in 1:3).

Two women who brought their nests in partnership: According to R. Yose's minority opinion, such nests are to be treated as unassigned nests (2:1).

Chapter Two

2:1–5 *Birds That Fly from One Sacrificial Group to Another*

2 An unassigned nest from which a fledgling flew into the air,
or one flew among the birds that are to die,
or one of them dies,
one must take a mate for the second one.
If it flew among those to be offered—
it is disqualified,
and it disqualifies another as its counterpart,
for the flying fledgling becomes disqualified
and it disqualifies another one as its counterpart.
2 How?
Two women, this one has two nests and this one has two nests—
if [a bird] flew from this one to that one,
it disqualifies one bird on its departure.
If it returned—
it disqualifies one on its return.
If it flew away and returned, flew away and returned—
one did not lose anything,
since even when mixed, there are never fewer than two [valid pairs].
3 If a woman has one [nest],
another has two,
another three,
another four,
another five,

2:1 *unassigned nest*: A nest whose donor has not designated which bird would be offered as purgation and which as whole burnt offering, but leaves the decision to the priest. A bird that flies from an unassigned nest is replaced with another. In contrast an *assigned nest* (see 2:4 below) is a nest where the donor designated which bird would be offered as purgation and which as whole burnt offering. Therefore, a bird that flies from an assigned nest to another nest is disqualified and it disqualifies a bird from the other nest.

2:2 *disqualifies one bird on its departure*: The bird itself is invalid, and in addition it invalidates a second bird from the group it left, as in 1:1. That woman can only offer one pair. The other woman, who now has five birds, can only offer two pairs.

If it returned: Not necessarily the original bird, but any bird in the second group.

disqualifies one on its return: Now, both groups have four birds, but only one pair from each can be offered.

flew away and returned, flew away and returned: i.e. repeatedly. Once they are further mixed, one can still offer a total of two pairs of birds, following 1:3.

did not lose anything, beyond what was already lost.

another six,
another seven:
if one flew from the first,
to the second,
to the third,
to the fourth,
to the fifth,
to the sixth,
to the seventh,
and then returned—
it disqualifies one on its departure and one on its return.
The first and the second [women] have none,
the third has one,
the fourth has two,
the fifth has three,
the sixth has four,
the seventh has six.
If it flew and returned—
it disqualifies one on its departure and one on its return:
the third and the fourth [women] have none,
the fifth has one.
the sixth has two,
the seventh has five.
If it flew and returned—
it disqualifies one by flying away,
and one by flying back:
the fifth and the sixth [women] have none,
the seventh has four.
And some say:
The seventh has lost nothing.
But if one flew from among those that are to die,
then they all must die.

2:3 *if one flew from the first... and then returned*: The mishnah applies what was said in 2:2 to a case of various donors, each with different numbers of nests. If a bird went from one woman's nest to another's and then returned, stopping again at a group of birds, each move disqualifies a nest. Each group of birds except the first and the last has had two arrivals and two departures. Although each woman has the number of birds she began with, each but the first and the last has had two pairs disqualified; the only nest of the first was disqualified, and the last has had one pair disqualified. The reasoning is not explicit in the Mishnah and the commentaries explain this at length.

If it flew and returned: A second and third time, among the groups belonging to women who still had valid birds. The same logic applies.

But if one flew from among those that are to die: All birds must die because it is not clear which is the bird that is to die (2:1).

4 An unassigned nest and an assigned nest:
if one [bird] flew from the unassigned to the assigned,
one takes a mate for the second one.
If it returned,
or if, in the first place, it flew from the assigned nest,
then they must all die.

5 A purgation offering on one side,
and a whole burnt offering on the other side,
and an unassigned [nest] in the center—
if it[3] flew from the center to the sides,
one to this side and one to that side,
one has lost nothing.
But he says:
The one that went to the purgation offerings is to be a purgation offering,
and the one that went to the whole burnt offerings is to be a whole burnt offering.
If it returned to the center,
those in the center must die;
these may be offered as purgation offerings;
and those may be offered as whole burnt offerings.
If it returned,
or flew from the center to the sides:
in that case, they must all die.
One cannot bring turtle doves [to pair] with young pigeons,
nor young pigeons with turtle doves.
How?
A woman brought a young pigeon as her purgation offering,
and her whole burnt offering is a turtle dove:
she must repeat and bring a turtle dove as her whole burnt offering.
If her whole burnt offering is a turtle dove,
and her purgation offering is a young pigeon:

[3] Here and below, "it" means "a bird."

2:4 Continues 2:1, dealing with the ramifications of mixtures between birds from *an unassigned nest* and *an assigned nest*. See annotation there. A bird which flew out of an assigned nest to an unassigned one creates a situation where the two nests *must all die*, since it is now unknown which is the purgation and which is the whole burnt offering in both.

2:5 *A purgation offering on one side...in the center*: The situation involves three groups of birds: those assigned to be offered as purgation, as whole burnt offering, and in the middle an unassigned nest. Here again a bird flying from an unassigned nest to an assigned group is valid but not the other way around, since there is a chance that an assigned bird would be offered in an inappropriate way.

they must all die: In case a bird flies back to the unassigned nest or flies again, since it is possible that purgation and whole burnt offerings would be mixed.

turtle doves...young pigeons: The species of the birds cannot be mixed, and that of the purgation offering determines that of the whole burnt offerings. Ben Azzai disagrees and gives priority to the type of the bird that was offered first.

she must repeat and bring a young pigeon as a whole burnt offering.
Ben Azzai says: One follows the first [to be slaughtered].
A woman who brought her purgation offering and died—
the heirs must bring her whole burnt offering;
her whole burnt offering and died—
the heirs need not bring her purgation offering.

Chapter Three

3:1–5 *Mingled Offerings Revisited, When the Priest Offered Them without Consultation*

3 To what do these things refer?
To a priest who consults,
But in a case of a priest who does not consult—
one [pair] belongs to one woman and one to another;
or two belong to one and two to another;
or three belong to one and three to another—
if he offered all of them above,
half are valid and half are invalid;
all of them below,
half are valid and half are invalid.
half of them above and half of them below:
those [offered] above,
half are valid and half are invalid;
those below,
half are valid and half are invalid.
2 If one [nest] belongs to one woman
and two to another,

A woman who brought her purgation offering and died: Here again the purgation offering determines the act of offering and must be complemented by the heirs of the deceased woman with a whole burnt offering but not vice versa. If a woman offered a whole burnt offering and then dies, her heirs are not obliged to bring a purgation offering.

3:1 *To what do these things refer?* The tractate has dealt so far with *A priest who consults*. It is not said with whom the priest consults; some commentators suggested that he consults with "an expert," although the simple understanding of the text is that he is to consult with the donors, who are, as the Mishnah indicates, typically women. The following deals with *a priest who does not consult*.

one pair belongs to one woman and one to another: The Mishnah deals with the maximal number of valid nests in different cases of mixtures between groups of nests of the same size (see 1:2, 1:3).

3:2 *If one nest belongs to one woman and two to another*: The Mishnah specifies the maximal number of valid nests in different cases of mixtures between groups of nests of different size (see 1:3).

and three to another,
and ten to another,
and one hundred to another—
if he offered all of them above,
half are valid and half are invalid;
all of them below,
half are valid and half are invalid;
half of them above and half of them below,
the greater part are valid.
This is the rule:
Whenever[4] you can divide the nests
so that they do not [all] belong to one woman,
whether above or below
half are valid and half are invalid;
whenever you cannot divide the nests,
so that they all belong to one woman,
whether above or below
the greater part is valid.

3 If one [woman] has a purgation offering
and another has a whole burnt offering—
if he offered both of them above,
half are valid and half are invalid;
all of them below,
half are valid and half are invalid;
half of them above and half of them below,
both are invalid.
For I say:
The purgation offering was offered above and the whole burnt offering below.

4 A purgation offering and a whole burnt offering,
an unassigned nest and an assigned nest—
If he offered all of them above,
half are valid and half are invalid;
all of them below
half are valid and half are invalid;

[4] From here to the end of 3:2 paraphrased rather than translated.

This is the rule: When all the nests are offered above or below the red line in a case in which the nests can be identified as belonging to one woman, *half are valid.* But if the nests can only be divided into two parts in such a way that some belong to one woman, then *the greater part are valid.*

3:3 Mixtures of whole burnt and purgation offerings were dealt in 1:2, where it says that they all must die. This mishnah rules differently. Since it deals with a priest who does not consult (3:1), it specifies the maximal number of birds that can be offered.

half are valid, if all the birds were offered above or below the red line.

Both are invalid, if some were offered above and some below (in a case of an assigned nest), since one cannot determine whether any of the birds was offered according to the donor's instructions.

half of them above and half of them below,
none is valid, except the unassigned nest,
and it must be divided between them.

5 A purgation offering that was mingled with obligatory offerings—
only as many birds as correspond to
the number of purgation offerings among the obligatory offerings
are valid.
If the obligatory offerings are twice as many as the purgation offerings,
half are valid and half are invalid.
If the purgation offerings are twice as many as the obligatory offerings,
the number of the obligatory offerings is valid.
And so too, a whole burnt offering that became mingled with obligatory offerings,
only those that correspond in number to the whole burnt offerings
among the obligatory offerings are valid.
If the obligatory offerings are twice as many as the whole burnt offerings,
half are valid and half are invalid.
If the whole burnt offerings are twice as many as the obligatory offerings.
the number[5] among the obligatory offerings is valid.

3:6 *Consequences of Priestly Error*

6 A woman who said:
"I am hereby obliged to offer a nest if I give birth to a male child,"
if she gave birth to a male—
she brings two nests,
one for her vow and one for her obligation.
If she gave them to the priest,

[5] "The number" refers to purgation offerings.

3:4 *none is valid, except the unassigned nest*: This mishnah repeats the discussion in 3:3 and adds the case of an unassigned nest, which is valid only when offered half above and half below the red line.

and it must be divided between them, the women who purchased the nests together.

3:5 *A purgation offering that was mingled with obligatory offerings*: The Mishnah repeats the ruling in 1:2 regarding the maximum of valid birds in cases of mixtures.

If the obligatory offerings are twice as many as the purgation offerings: Half is valid, since the obligatory birds are not assigned and thus can be offered either way. However, *if the purgation offerings are twice as many as the obligatory offerings*, only the number of the obligatory offerings is valid because there is a chance that all the birds that were assigned to be offered as purgation offerings were inappropriately offered. The same rulings apply to *a whole burnt offering that became mingled with obligatory offerings*.

3:6 *A woman who said*: The Mishnah deals with replacement birds that a woman who vowed to bring a bird offering had to bring in the case of mixtures. The more specific the vow, the higher is the risk for its inappropriate offering or the potential need for the replacement she may have to bring. This passage reviews some of the matters discussed above—the penalty for a bird offered in the wrong place, the species of the birds, and whether they are assigned.

and the priest must offer three birds above and one below [the red line].
If he did not do so,
but rather offered two above and two below the red line,
and he has not consulted,
she must bring one more bird,
and he offers it above—
[if they were] of one species.
If they were of two species,
she must bring two [more].
If she had assigned her vow,
she must bring three more birds—
if they were of one species.
If they were of two species,
she must bring four more.
If she had determined her vow,
she must bring five more birds—
if they were of one species.
If they were of two species,
she must bring six.
If she gave them to the priest,
and it is not known what she gave,
and the priest performed [the sacrifice]
and it is not known what he performed,
she must bring four more birds for her vow,
and two more for her obligation,
and one purgation offering.
Ben Azzai says:
Two purgation offerings.

3:6 cont. *Aggadic Conclusions*

R. Joshua said:
This is what they said:
While it[6] is alive it has one voice,
and when it is dead it has seven voices.
How is its voice seven?
Its two horns: two trumpets,
its two thigh bones: two flutes,
its hide: a drum,
its large intestine: for lyres,
its small intestine: for harps.
Some say:
Also its wool: for *tekhelet*.

[6] "It" refers to a lamb.

While it is alive: This aggadic passage speaks of the superior nature of the offered lamb (the first-priority offering of a woman who gave birth, see introduction) to that of the living lamb.

R. Simeon b. Aqashiah says:
The older uneducated elders become,
the more they lose their intellect,
as it is written:
He removes the speech of men of trust and takes away the sense of the elders.
But the elders of Torah are not so,
rather the older they become, the more their mind becomes composed,
as it is said:
With the aged there is wisdom and in length of days understanding.

uneducated: Heb. *amme ha'arets*. See *Demai*, introduction.

He removes the speech: Job 12:20.

Elders of Torah: Learned sages.

With aged men there is wisdom: Job 12:12.

R. Simeon b. Aqashiah's midrash alludes to the name of our tractate: *the older they become,* in the original *mazqinin,* clearly a play on *Qinnim* (in some sources spelled *Qinnin*). It has also been suggested that the phrase *with the aged there is wisdom* (Job 12:12) alludes to the Order of *Qodashim,* which is sometimes called "wisdom."

ORDER OF TOHOROT

Tractate Kelim

Michael Chernick

Introduction

Overview

Kelim ("vessels" or "utensils") with thirty chapters is the largest tractate in *Tohorot*, indeed, in the entire Mishnah; some early Mishnah manuscripts divide the tractate into three units of ten chapters each. It is possible that the tractate's basic structure existed prior to the compilation of the Mishnah; the tractate ends with R. Yose's exclamation "Happy are you, O *Kelim*; you entered with impurity and departed with purity." (Most of *Kelim* deals with ritual impurity while its last chapter speaks of objects insusceptible to impurity.) Insofar as R. Yose seems to know how *Kelim* begins and ends, its basic structure must have been set no later than R. Yose's time, at least one generation before the compilation of the Mishnah as a whole.

Main Ideas

The tractate discusses objects made of materials as diverse as metal, wood, cloth, leather, and glass. These items are utensils of all sorts; even musical instruments and their parts find their way into this tractate. In cases where a particular object is not likely to be familiar to the reader, the notes will describe the object and its function.

The tractate also considers various types and grades of ritual impurity. The main sources of impurity are (1) the impurity of a corpse, the most serious type, (2) the impurity of dead vermin, (3) the impurity of one who has an abnormal genital discharge (Heb. *zav*, fem. *zavah*), (4) the impurity of a man who has had a seminal emission, or (5) the impurity of a menstruant. The Mishnah discusses other sources of impurity in other tractates. These sources of impurity convey their impurity in different ways. Corpse impurity conveys impurity in enclosed spaces, and via overhangs ("Tent"), and if touched or carried. Whatever it makes impure can convey further impurity, though at a lower level. Dead vermin convey impurity to people and vessels by contact; in addition, they convey impurity to an earthenware vessel if their corpses have fallen inside the container. The *zav*, the *zavah*, and the menstruant convey impurity by putting pressure on items like seats, sleeping mats, and saddles. These pressure-generated impurities are called in Hebrew *midras* (treading), *mishkav* (lying), and *moshav* (sitting). *Midras* impurity occupies a great deal of this tractate's concern.

A vessel's susceptibility to impurity is determined by its material, shape, and intended use. One who manufactures a vessel that is usually insusceptible to impurity with the intention of using it as a susceptible vessel or tool thereby makes it susceptible. The opposite is also true: if one manufactures an item that is usually susceptible to impurity for a use that prevents susceptibility, that item usually is insusceptible.

Similarly, if one renders a vessel or utensil incapable of functioning in its normal fashion, whether intentionally or not, he thereby renders it insusceptible to impurity. If it was impure, his act purifies it until it is repaired for its original use, in which case it sometimes is impure at a lower level of impurity. Changing the function of an item will remove its impurity. Thus, intention at manufacture or a significant change made in an item can affect its status as susceptible or insusceptible to impurity.

Relationship to Scripture

Kelim chiefly relies on the following scriptural passages: Leviticus 11 deals with the susceptibility to impurity of earthenware, wood, cloth, leather, and sack material made of goat's hair; Leviticus 15 deals with various genital discharges and the forms of impurity they cause; Numbers 19 deals with corpse impurity, what protects an item from it, and removal of the impurity by sprinkling with purgation water, and Numbers 31, which introduces metal as a material that is susceptible to impurity.

Special Notes for the Reader

Several early Mishnah manuscripts contain significant departures from the printed text in common use. I have cited these manuscripts when they significantly change the meaning of the text. They are manuscripts **K** for manuscript Kaufmann and **P** for manuscript Parma 3173 (de Rossi 138), both of which cover the complete Mishnah and are frequently cited throughout this translation; and I cite $\mathbf{P}_2$ for manuscript Parma 2596 a different Parma manuscript that covers only the Order of Purities (*Tohorot*).

Kelim is highly technical, but it gives the reader a great deal of information about the clothing, tools, vessels, and the like that made up the realia of the mishnaic period. The following commentaries and other works are invaluable guides to these matters:

Perush ha-Geonim le Seder Tohorot with Introduction (Heb.), ed. Jacob Nahum Epstein, (Berlin: Meqitzei Nirdamim, 1921–1924; reprinted Jerusalem: Magnes Press, 2001).

Tiferet Yisrael, a classical commentary to the Mishnah by R. Yisrael Lipschitz (Germany, 1782–1860), first published in 1843, frequently reprinted in standard editions of the Mishnah.

Daniel Sperber, *Material Culture in Eretz Yisrael in the Talmudic Period* (Heb.) (Jerusalem and Ramat Gan: Yad Yitzhaq Ben-Zvi and Bar-Ilan University, 2005).

Tractate Kelim

Chapter One

1:1–4 *The Main Categories and Gradations of Impurity*

1 The primary impurities are—
vermin,
and semen,
and one who is impure with corpse impurity,[1]
and one with a *tsara'at* during his counting period,
and purgation water too little in quantity to be sprinkled.
These convey impurity to people and utensils by contact
and to earthenware utensils through [their] interior space;
but they do not convey impurity by carrying.
2 Above these—
carrion
or purgation water sufficient in quantity to be sprinkled.

[1] K: "and the impurity of one who is ritually impure with corpse impurity." See annotations.

1:1 *vermin*: Any of eight "creeping things" mentioned in Leviticus 11:29–30. See *Shabbat* 14:1.

corpse impurity: The variant in the manuscript suggests that the impurity being discussed is not corpse impurity, but rather the impurity conveyed by one who has contracted corpse impurity.

one with tsara'at during his counting period: See Leviticus 14:8. One with *tsara'at* undertakes a seven-day count from the time his symptoms are declared gone until he is ready for the ablutions and sacrifices that comprise his purification rites. On *tsara'at* (often mistranslated "leprosy") see tractate *Nega'im*.

and purgation water: See Numbers 19:1–9; *Parah*. The ashes of a red heifer were mixed with water and other ingredients to serve as the agent of purification for those who contracted corpse impurity.

too little in quantity to be sprinkled: The one who sprinkled the purification water used a hyssop stalk to do so. The amount of water that the hyssop stalk could hold was the amount required for the ritual. Less than that constituted "too little in quantity to be sprinkled."

and to earthenware vessels through [their] interior space: See Leviticus 11:33. Earthenware items contract impurity from vermin when dead vermin fall into their interior space. If the source of impurity touches the vessel's exterior it remains pure.

1:2 *Above these*: In the ability to convey impurity.

Carrion: Either an animal that died of wounds or disease or an animal whose ritual slaughter was flawed.

For these convey impurity to a person by carriage
so that he conveys impurity to garments by contact.[2]
But the garments do not become impure by contact [alone].

3 Above these—
one who has sexual intercourse with a menstruant,
for he conveys impurity to the lowest level of bedding as to the uppermost.
Above these:
the *zav* flow of a *zav*, his saliva, his semen, or his urine,
and the blood of a menstruant,
for they convey impurity by contact and by carrying.
Above these—
an object used for riding [by a *zav*];
for it conveys impurity [even when it lies] beneath a heavy stone.
Above [a *zav*'s] object used for riding—
[his] bedding,
since touching and carrying [it][3] are equivalent.
Above bedding—
the *zav* [himself],
for the *zav* conveys impurity to[4] bedding,
but [his] bedding does not convey bedding impurity.

4 Above the *zav*—
the *zavah*,
for she conveys impurity to one who has sexual intercourse with her.

[2] **K** and **P** lack "by contact." See annotations.
[3] Lit. "its touching and its carrying."
[4] Lit. "makes," here and in the next line.

these convey impurity to a person by carriage: Even if the person does not come in direct contact with the source of impurity, carrying it renders him impure. The similar case in 1:1 requires that the person come in direct contact with the source of impurity.

But the garments do not become impure by contact [alone]: i.e. the garments touching the ritually impure individual only become impure when he is actually carrying the source of impurity.

1:3 *for he conveys impurity to the lowest level of bedding as to the uppermost*: See Leviticus 15:19–24. "Bedding" is anything on which one puts pressure while lying down. See *Niddah* 4:1.

Above these: These convey impurity to human beings who touch or carry them. Unlike the previous cases, the impure party can then convey impurity to others without direct contact with the original impurity.

zav: Fem. *zavah*. Both males and females who suffer abnormal genital discharges are in this category. See Leviticus 15:1–12 and *Zavim*.

an object used for riding: e.g. a saddle. See below, 23:2.

a heavy stone: A stone does not contract or convey impurity. Nevertheless, even if one places a stone as a weight on riding equipment, if a *zav* puts any pressure on the stone it becomes impure and conveys impurity. See Leviticus 15:10.

since touching and carrying [it] are equivalent: Simply touching ritually impure bedding conveys impurity to human beings so they can convey impurity to clothing. See Leviticus 15:5.

but his bedding does not convey bedding impurity: If a *zav*'s bedding should touch utensils, they will not become impure with bedding impurity, which is one of the higher levels of impurity.

1:4 *she conveys impurity to one who has sexual intercourse with her*: i.e. he is impure for a week.

Above the *zavah*—
one with *tsara'at*,
for he renders [a house and all its contents] impure by entering.
Above the one with *tsara'at*:
a [human] bone the size of a grain of barley,
for it conveys seven-day impurity.
More stringent than all these—
a corpse,
for it conveys impurity by Tent,
which is not a way all the others convey impurity.

1:5 *Ten Types of Impurity That Emerge from the Human Body*

5 Ten [degrees of] impurity emerge from human beings:
(1) one whose expiation is incomplete may not [eat of] sacred offerings
but is permitted *terumah* and [second] tithe;
(2) if he went on to become a *tevul yom*,
he is forbidden sacred offerings and *terumah*,
but is permitted [second] tithe;
(3) if he went on to become one who had a seminal emission,
he is forbidden all three;
(4) if he went on to become one who had sexual intercourse with a menstruant,
he conveys impurity to the lowest level of bedding as to the uppermost;

a [human] bone: From a corpse.

for it conveys impurity by Tent: "Tent" means an enclosed space or an overhang. Anyone who shares such a location with a corpse becomes ritually impure. Tent impurity defiles human beings and vessels for one week. They become pure by sprinkling purgation water on them. See Numbers 19.

1:5 *One whose expiation is incomplete*: See Leviticus 16:16. The reference is to an impure individual whose purification rites have begun but whose final sacrificial rites have not been completed.

terumah: Food that must be given to members of the priestly caste. It is impermissible to eat produce from which *terumah* was not set aside. See tractate *Terumot*. *Terumah* can only be eaten in a state of purity. A person whose expiation is incomplete is pure enough to eat *terumah*, even though he is not pure enough to eat of sacrificial offerings.

[second] tithe: See Deuteronomy 14:23–26. In certain years a householder takes second tithe from produce after first tithe has been separated and given to a Levite. See tractates *Ma'aserot and Ma'aser Sheni*. Second tithe must be eaten in Jerusalem in a state of purity.

tevul yom: A person whose impurity ends completely at sunset once he has immersed. Between the time of his immersion and the setting of the sun his impurity is conveyed to sacrificial offerings and *terumah*, but not second tithe. See *Tevul Yom*.

(5) if he went on to become a *zav* who saw two emissions,
he conveys impurity where he lies and where he sits.
He requires immersion in a flowing spring[5]
but he is exempt from the [*zav*'s] offering;
(6) if he saw three [emissions] he must bring the offering;
(7) if he went on to become a quarantined [suspected case of] one with *tsara'at*,
he conveys impurity [to a house] by entering it,
but he is exempt from growing out his hair and from tearing his clothes and from shaving and from the bird offerings,
(8) but if he went on to become confirmed [with *tsara'at*],
he is liable to them all;
(9) if a limb is severed from him
and it does not have on it a suitable amount of flesh,
it conveys impurity by contact and carrying,
but it does not convey impurity by Tent;
(10) but if it has on it a suitable amount of flesh,
it conveys impurity by contact and carrying and also by Tent.
The measure of a "suitable amount of flesh":
enough to heal:
R. Judah says:
If there is one place [on the limb]
where there is enough [flesh] to surround the limb
with [the thickness of] a weaving thread,
that is the amount capable of healing.

1:6–9 *The Ten Degrees of Holiness in the Land of Israel*

6 There are ten [degrees of] holiness:
(1) the Land of Israel is holier than all [other] lands.
And what is [the mark of] its sanctity?
That one brings the *omer* and firstfruits and the two loaves from it,
which one does not bring from any other land.

[5] Lit. "coming into living waters."

two emissions...three [emissions]: One becomes a *zav* after two abnormal emissions, but is obligated to bring a sacrifice only after he has experienced a third.

quarantined: An individual with various types of skin symptoms is quarantined by a priest who will determine whether it is indeed a case of *tsara'at*. See Leviticus 13.

R. Judah: If one were to cut the flesh into strips the width of the thread that goes across a loom and that length of thread could surround the limb, then the limb has enough flesh to heal.

1:6 *ten [degrees of] holiness*: As the translation indicates, the mishnah seems to list eleven degrees; commentators differ as to which ought to be combined.

omer: A sacrifice of a sheaf of barley that inaugurated the use of the new harvest and the counting of the weeks until the Festival of Weeks (*Shavu'ot*). See Leviticus 23:10–14 and *Menahot* chapter 10.

firstfruits: Brought as an offering to the Temple. See Deuteronomy 26:1–10 and tractate *Bikkurim*.

two loaves: These were presented on the Festival of Weeks seven weeks after offering the *omer*. See Leviticus 23:17 and *Menahot* 11:1–2.

7 (2) The walled cities [of the Land of Israel] are more holy
because one must send people with *tsara'at* out of them.
One may carry around a corpse within them as much one wishes,
but once it has gone out, one may not bring it back.
8 (3) Within the walls [of Jerusalem] is still more holy,
for there one may eat offerings of lesser sanctity and second tithe.
(4) The Temple Mount is more holy,
for *zavim*, *zavot*, menstruants, and women after childbirth may not enter there.
(5) The Rampart is still more holy,
for non-Jews and one with corpse impurity may not enter there.
(6) The Court of Women is still more holy,
for a *tevul yom* may not enter there;
but one [who did so] does not owe a purgation offering.
(7) The Court of Israelites is still more holy,
for one whose expiation is incomplete may not enter there,
and one [who did so] owes a purgation offering.
(8) The Court of Priests is still more holy,
for Israelites may not enter there
except at the time of their need
for laying on of hands, slaughtering, and waving.
9 (9) Between the Porch and the Altar is still more holy,
for [priests] who have a blemish or whose hair is growing wild may not enter there.
(10) The Holy is still more holy,
for none may enter there with unwashed hands and feet.[6]
(11) The Holy of Holies is still more holy,
for none may enter there except the high priest
on the Day of Atonement at the time of the service.

[6] **K**: "for only those with washed hands and feet may enter," a smoother reading.

1:7 *The walled cities [of the Land of Israel]*: This category was limited to those which were said to have possessed walls from the time of Joshua. See *Arakhin* 9:6.

send people with tsara'at out of them: This rule is based on Leviticus 13:46.

carry around a corpse: A funeral procession could be held within the city walls in order to honor the dead in a proper manner.

1:8 *offerings of lesser sanctity*: All offerings in which the owner has a share of the sacrificial meat or flour.

Rampart: Within the outer walls of the Temple Mount was a rectangular fence that surrounded the essential part of the Temple itself. Ten cubits between this fence and the Temple comprised the Ramparts.

Court of Women: Women could be present there together with men.

purgation offering: People entering the Temple inadvertently without having completed all their purification rites violated the sanctity of the Temple and would have to bring a purgation offering (sometimes translated "sin offering") in expiation.

laying on of hands: See Leviticus 3:2.

waving: See Leviticus 7:30.

1:9 *whose hair is growing wild*: Who has not had a haircut in thirty days or more.

R. Yose said:
In five ways the space between the Porch and the Altar is equivalent to the Holy:
(1) those [priests] who have a blemish,
(2) and those whose hair is growing wild
(3) and those who have drunk wine,
(4) and those with unwashed hands and feet may not enter there,
(5) and [the priests] must exit the area between the Porch and the Altar
at the time of burning the incense.

Chapter Two

2:1–4:4 *Earthenware*

2 Utensils of wood, utensils of leather, utensils of bone, or utensils of glass:
their flat surfaces[7] are insusceptible to impurity,
but their receptacles[8] are susceptible to impurity.
If they are broken,
they have become pure.
If one remade them into utensils,[9]
they can contract impurity from then forward.[10]
Earthenware vessels and vessels of nitrum are alike regarding impurity:
they contract impurity and convey impurity through their interior space,
they convey impurity from their outsides,[11]
but they do not become impure from their exteriors,
and breaking is their means of purification.

2 The smallest [unbroken] earthenware vessels or their [broken] bottoms or sides that can stand without support:

[7] Or "the flat ones." [8] Or "the ones with receptacles."
[9] Lit. "if one went back and made..." [10] Cf. 11:1 and 15:1 below. [11] Or "bottoms."

and [the priests] must exit the area between the Porch and the Altar: See Leviticus 16:17. Though the Torah states this rule only with regard to the high priest on the Day of Atonement, rabbinic tradition applies it to any priest offering incense in the Sanctuary.

2:1 *their flat surfaces*: i.e. utensils lacking an area that can contain something. By contrast, *their receptacles are susceptible.*

nitrum: Potassium nitrate. Its common name is saltpeter.

they contract impurity and convey impurity through their interior space: See Leviticus 11:33. An impure thing must fall into the vessel for the vessel to become ritually impure. Once the interior of the vessel is impure, it conveys impurity to food and liquid that enter into it.

breaking is their means of purification: See Leviticus 11:31–33.

2:2 *or their [broken] bottoms*: Here and in R. Aqiva's opinion below, some commentators lack the "or"; in that case the reference to "smallest...earthenware vessels" is an introductory phrase and not a separate item.

that can stand without support: It is still functional, and functionality is one criterion for susceptibility to impurity.

their measure is [enough oil] to anoint a child,[12] up to a *log*.
[If an unbroken vessel can hold] from one *log* to one *se'ah*,
[it is susceptible to impurity if its shards can still hold] a quarter[-*log*].
From one to two *se'ah*, [the measure is] a half-*log*.
From two to three or up to five *se'ah*, [the measure is] one *log*—
the words of R. Ishmael.
R. Aqiva says:
I do not prescribe any [such] measure.
Rather, [with respect to] the smallest earthenware vessels,
their [broken] bottoms and sides that can stand without support:
their measure is [oil] enough to anoint a child.
[This measure applies to the remnants of vessels] up to [the size of] thin pots.
[For the remnants of vessels of a size] from thin pots to Lydda containers:
a quarter[-*log*].
From Lydda [containers] to Bethlehem [containers]:
a half-*log*.
From Bethlehem [containers] to large amphorae:
a *log*.
R. Yohanan b. Zakkai says:
The measure for large amphorae is two *log*.
The measure for the bottoms of Galilean cruses and of little containers is any amount,
but their sides are insusceptible to impurity.[13]

3 Earthenware utensils that are not susceptible to impurity:[14]
a tray without a rim,
an open-ended coal shovel,
a tube for roasting grain,[15]
gutters—

[12] Lit. "a little one," here and below. See annotations. [13] Lit. "they do not have sides."
[14] Lit. "that are [perpetually] pure." [15] Lit. "a grain-roasters' tube."

their measure: In each case, a vessel or fragment with the indicated capacity is susceptible to impurity.

a child: As noted, the text literally means "a small one." Commentators vary as to whether this means a child (as in the present translation), or any person's smallest limb (presumably a fingertip), or the smallest limb of a child.

se'ah: Twenty-four *log*; a *log* is approximately 0.7 of a US pint or 0.3 liter.

R. Ishmael uses liquid measures to determine the susceptibility of a vessel's fragmentary remnants.

R. Aqiva: Unlike R. Ishmael, R. Aqiva uses the typical size of various types of vessel plus liquid measures to determine the susceptibility of the vessels' fragmentary remnants.

Lydda…Bethlehem [containers]: These were earthenware storage containers produced in various towns, each with a known characteristic size.

but their sides are insusceptible: Their small size leaves them without a space that can contain anything.

2:3 *not susceptible to impurity*: Because they lack a receptacle.

a tube for roasting grain: The tube's apertures allow the fire to roast grain or nuts thoroughly but prevent the device from serving as a container.

even if they are bent,
even if they can contain,
a vessel that is used [for] a breadbasket,
a container used for grapes,
a swimmers' barrel,
a barrel[-shaped attachment to a] ladle,
a bed,
a stool,[16]
a bench,
a table,
a ship,
an earthenware lamp:
these are insusceptible to impurity.
This is the general rule:
Any earthenware vessel that has no inside
cannot [become impure from] its outside walls.[17]

4 A lantern that has a container for oil is susceptible to impurity.
If it does not have one, it is insusceptible to impurity.
A potter's wheel on which he begins [to shape the clay] is insusceptible to impurity,
but the one on which he finishes [a vessel] is susceptible to impurity.
A householder's funnel is insusceptible to impurity,
but a peddler's is susceptible to impurity,
because it [serves as a] measure—

[16] Or "chair." [17] Lit. "has no outside wall."

even if they are bent: A bent gutter can contain water, but that is not its intended purpose.

even if they can contain: Pebbles or plant waste sometimes build up and block these gutters, but they are not intended to hold contents. They are built to relieve the weight of water on a roof.

a vessel… used [for] a breadbasket, etc.: The remaining items in the list are insusceptible because they are not used as containers. In this case the vessel has capacity to hold something but is being used as a cover for the basket.

a swimmers' barrel: A float.

ladle: A cup-like protrusion that serves as a handle for a ceramic ladle can hold fluid but that is not its intended purpose.

a ship: Though a ship with an earthenware part is a container, and made with the intention of being a container, rabbinic interpretation compared the ship to the sea itself. Just as the sea is insusceptible, so is the ship.

outside walls: Just as such vessels "have no sides" (2:2) they "have no outside walls."

2:4 *If it does not have one*: One places an oil lamp inside the lantern, rather than the lantern having an internal fuel reservoir.

it is insusceptible: Even if the lantern has walls so that it could function as a container, since they exist to protect the flame from wind and not to contain the lantern's fuel they do not render the lantern susceptible.

but the one on which he finishes [a vessel] is susceptible: Those wheels have walls that keep the almost completed product from falling off. Hence, they constitute a sort of container.

the words of R. Judah b. Betera;
but R. Aqiva says:
Because he lays it on its side to allow the buyer to smell.

5 The covers of wine jars and oil jars and Nayyarot jars are insusceptible to impurity,
but if they were adapted for use [as a container] they are susceptible to impurity.
The cover of a stewpot:
if there is a hole in it or it has a point,
it is insusceptible to impurity.
If there is no hole in it or it does not have a point,
it is susceptible to impurity,
because [a woman] drains vegetables in it.
R. Eliezer[18] b. Zadok says:
Because she turns out the [stewpot's] contents into it.

6 If a *gistera* was found in the [potter's] furnace:
before its manufacture was completed,
it is insusceptible to impurity.
From the time its manufacture was completed,
it is susceptible to impurity.
A *titros*:
R. Eliezer[19] b. Zadok deems [it] insusceptible to impurity,

[18] **K, P**: "Eleazar." [19] **K, P**: "Eleazar."

R. Judah b. Betera: According to him, a peddler's funnel serves double purposes. One is the typical function of a funnel, but the peddler often stops up the funnel with his finger and uses it to measure a beverage or liquid he is selling. Since it can serve as a container, it is susceptible.

R. Aqiva holds that a peddler's funnel is susceptible because it acts as a container in a different fashion: one who sells fragrant liquids pours a small amount of his product into the funnel and lays it on its side so the customer can assess the fragrance's freshness.

2:5 *Nayyarot jars*: *Nayyarot* seems to be a place name. Alternatives: papyrus (or paper) covers or covers of papyrus (or paper) containers.

are insusceptible: Covers are generally insusceptible; even though they may be capable of containing items, but containing items is not the cover's main purpose.

If…it has a point, it is insusceptible: That is, if the top of the cover is pointed and as a result cannot stand, it cannot function as a container at all.

[a woman] drains vegetables in it: That is, the housewife puts vegetables with their liquid into one of these covers so that the liquid separates out.

R. Eliezer b. Zadok holds that the woman empties fully drained or uncooked vegetables into the cover. There is no practical difference between the mishnah's anonymous view and that of R. Eliezer b. Zadok. Each provides a common example of these covers' uses.

2:6 *gistera*: A damaged or unfinished earthenware jar.

before its manufacture was completed: Before one fires a clay container in the kiln it cannot function properly as a container and is not a "vessel."

titros: Related to the English word titration, this "vessel" is a dropper. Placing one's finger on one end of the *titros* created a vacuum that held or released the liquid in it. A contemporary equivalent would be an eyedropper or dropper for children's medicine. Today a rubber bulb creates the vacuum that either holds or releases liquid.

R. Eliezer b. Zadok: Since the dropper is actually open on both sides, R. Eliezer (or Eleazar) b. Zadok holds that it is not a container.

but R. Yose deems [it] susceptible to impurity
because it only lets out *perutot.*[20]

7 That which is susceptible to impurity among earthenware vessels:
a tray with a rim,
an unbroken coal shovel,
and a tray full of [several] dishes.
If one of [the dishes] was rendered impure by [dead] vermin,
they are not all rendered impure.
If [the tray] has a rim higher [than the rims of the dishes],
then if one dish was rendered impure,
all become impure.
This is also so for an earthenware spice container
or a double inkwell.
And if one [section] of a wooden spice container is rendered impure by a liquid,
the other is not rendered impure.
R. Yohanan b. Nuri says:
One divides the thickness of the partition [separating the two sections]:
that which serves the impure part is accounted impure,
and that which serves the pure part is accounted pure.
But if it has a rim higher [than the openings to the sections],
if one part becomes impure,
the other part also becomes impure.

8 A torch is susceptible to impurity,
and the reservoir of a lamp receives impurity through its interior space.
The "comb" of a water jug:
R. Eliezer declares insusceptible to impurity,
but the Sages declare it susceptible to impurity.

[20] Meaning uncertain; the translation follows **K** and $\mathbf{P}_2$.

R. Yose holds that since no liquid can escape the *titros* when there is a vacuum, it constitutes a susceptible container. Further, even if liquid escapes from the *titros* it does so in such small amounts (*perutot*) that one might still view the container as effective.

2:7 *they are not all rendered impure*: Though they are connected to the tray, each dish remains a separate entity unless they are all surrounded by the tray's rim. If that is the case, the tray is viewed as a single vessel with sections and it all becomes defiled.

earthenware spice container…double inkwell: The spice container has separate sections for different spices. The inkwell has separate sections for different types of ink and pens. Since each section is separate they do not defile each other.

R. Yohanan b. Nuri claims that the wall of each section of the spice container is half-pure and half-impure.

2:8 *torch*: This item has a receptacle that holds a wick and fuel.

"comb" of a water jug: Surrounding the mouth of some earthenware jugs there was a filter attached by clips.

R. Eliezer declares the vessel insusceptible if something impure gets caught in the clips because the clips are neither "vessels" themselves nor inherently part of the jug.

the Sages declare the "comb" susceptible because the clips attach to the inner part of the jug and are therefore considered part of its inner container.

Chapter Three

3 The measure of an earthenware vessel [for it to become or remain] pure:
if it is made for food,
its measure is in olives.
If it is made for liquids,
its measure is in liquids.
If it is made for either,
one applies the more stringent rule:
olives.

2 The measure of a container is in dried figs—
the words of R. Simeon.
R. Judah says:
In nuts.
R. Meir says:
In olives.
A stewpot or cooking pot:
their measure is in olives.
A cruse or pail:
In oil.
A water jug:
its measure is in water.
R. Simeon says:
For all three of them the measure is in seeds.
A lamp:
its measure is in oil.
R. Eliezer says:
A small coin.
A lamp that has lost its wick holder

3:1 *The measure of an earthenware vessel*: If an impure vessel has a hole in it, it can no longer serve its purpose and is therefore pure. A pure vessel with such a hole is immune to impurity. This mishnah provides minimum sizes for such holes in various utensils.

its measure is in olives: If there is an opening in a vessel used for foods that would let an olive through, that vessel is not deemed a container.

its measure is in liquids: Is the hole large enough that liquids will pass through?

the more stringent rule: A hole that admits olives is larger than one that allows fluids to pass through.

3:2 *For all three of them*: That is, the cruse, the pail, and the water jug.

A small coin: Oil lamps sometimes served as containers for small coins called *perutot* (in plural; *perutah* in singular; see 2:6 above). This coin was wider than a stream of oil. As long as the lamp is still useful for storing, it is still a useful vessel and therefore is still susceptible to impurity.

is insusceptible to impurity,
and [a lamp of] unbaked clay whose wick holder was burnt by the wick
is insusceptible to impurity.

3 If a container was pierced through
and one repaired it with pitch
and it broke—
if at the place of the pitch it can hold a quarter-*log*,
it is susceptible to impurity because it has not lost the status of "vessel."[21]
If a shard was pierced through and one repaired it with pitch,
even though it can hold a quarter-*log*—
it is insusceptible to impurity
because it has lost the status of "vessel."

4 If a container was cracked and one plastered it with cattle dung:
even if the shards fall when he removes the dung—
it is susceptible to impurity,
since it has not lost the status of "vessel."
If it was broken and one stuck its shards together,
or if he brought shards from elsewhere and plastered them over with dung—
even though if he removes the dung the shards remain,
it is not susceptible to impurity,
because it has lost the status of "vessel."
If it contained a shard that can hold a quarter-*log*—
it all [can] become impure by contact,
and the area opposite [the shard] [can] become impure through its interior space.

5 One who plasters over a sound earthenware vessel—
R. Meir and R. Simeon deem [the plaster] susceptible to impurity.
But the Sages say:
If one plasters over what was sound,

[21] Lit. "the name 'vessel' has not been voided from it," here and below.

[a lamp of] unbaked clay: The container for the wick has been fired by the wick's heat, but this does not make the entire lamp a completed earthenware vessel. Only firing of the entire lamp can do so. Since it is not a completed vessel, it is not susceptible to impurity.

3:3 *if at the place of the pitch*: If the shard can hold a quarter-*log* even though pierced, it is susceptible.

a shard was pierced through: A shard from a smashed earthenware vessel ceases to be considered a vessel and can never become ritually impure again, even if repaired.

3:4 *If it contained a shard*: Every shard is viewed as a support for the one shard that is big enough to constitute a vessel, namely, the one that can hold a quarter-*log*. However, "supports" can only be rendered impure by direct contact since they have no receptacle.

the area opposite [the shard]: The shard that can hold a quarter-*log* constitutes an earthenware vessel. Dead vermin can render such a vessel impure even without contact by being inside the vessel.

3:5 *R. Meir and R. Simeon deem [the plaster] susceptible*: Because the plaster is connected to the vessel, it becomes part of it. Consequently, if the vessel becomes impure the plaster becomes impure.

the Sages say: Their view is that because the vessel can function without the plaster it is unconnected to the "vessel." Hence, it remains pure even if the "vessel" contracts impurity.

[the plastering] is not susceptible to impurity.
[Over] what was cracked,
[the plastering] is susceptible to impurity.
And so too for the hoop [around] a gourd shell.
6 The grass with which one smears a *pitos*—
whatever touches it[22] is impure.
The plug of a container does not [constitute] a connective.
One who touches the [reinforcing] plaster of an oven is impure.
7 A kettle that one plastered with mortar and[23] clay—
what touches the mortar is impure,
the clay, is pure.
A cauldron that was punctured and one repaired it with pitch—
R. Yose deems it insusceptible to impurity
since it cannot hold hot water as it does cold.[24]
And he used to say thus of [all] pitched vessels:
pitched copper vessels are insusceptible to impurity.
But if they are for wine,
they are susceptible to impurity.
8 If a container was punctured and one mended it with more pitch than it needed—
what touches the pitch that was needed is impure;
that which was not needed is pure.
If pitch dripped onto a container, what touches the pitch remains pure.

[22] Perhaps "the one who touches it" here and below. [23] Or "or."
[24] Lit. "it cannot receive hot as cold."

a gourd shell: i.e. a dried gourd used to draw water. Sometimes a hoop was put around it to strengthen it. The dispute between R. Meir and R. Simeon and the Sages applies in this case as well.

3:6 *pitos*: Greek word for an extremely large storage container (*pithos*). See *Rosh Hashanah* 3:7. Wet grass was regularly smeared onto the vessel to prevent leakage.

whatever touches it: The grass smeared on the *pitos* is considered connected to the *pitos*.

The plug of a container: Since it is an independent object that is often removed and replaced, it is not considered to be connected to the container.

plaster of an oven: It is considered connected sufficiently to the oven to convey impurity as the oven does.

3:7 *mortar and clay*: Since mortar is thick and sticks to the vessel when fired, it is connected to the vessel. Thin clay, however, which does not stick well to the vessel when fired, is not deemed to be connected.

since it cannot hold hot water as it does cold: The hot water will melt the pitch. Because it does not qualify as a vessel that can hold all the liquids that a regular cauldron can, it is insusceptible.

pitched copper vessels are insusceptible: If a copper vessel, which is usually meant to be used with hot liquid, has a pitched area, both it and the pitch are insusceptible since it cannot hold hot liquid.

if they are for wine: Since the vessel was made to hold a cold liquid, the pitch will remain connected to the vessel. The vessel and the pitch will always be in the same state of (im)purity.

3:8 *that which was not needed is pure*: Since it is excess it is not part of the vessel.

If pitch dripped onto a container: By accident. The pitch has nothing to do with the container's functionality.

If a wooden or earthenware funnel was stopped with pitch—
R. Eleazar b. Azariah deems it susceptible to impurity.
R. Aqiva deems it susceptible to impurity if it was wooden
but insusceptible to impurity if it was of earthenware.
R. Yose deems both insusceptible to impurity.

Chapter Four

4 A shard that cannot stand because of its handle,
or that had a point
and the point causes it to lean over,
is insusceptible to impurity.[25]
If the handle came off or the point broke—
it is insusceptible to impurity.
R. Judah deems it [still] susceptible to impurity.
A container that broke
but could still hold something in its sides,
or was divided like two dough troughs—
R. Judah[26] deems it insusceptible to impurity,
but the Sages deem it susceptible to impurity.
2 A container that was cracked
and cannot be moved with half a *qav* of dried figs
is insusceptible to impurity.

[25] **K**: "A shard that cannot stand because of its handle, or it had a point and the point causes it to lean, *or* the handle came off, or the point was broken off, is insusceptible to impurity."
[26] **K**: "R. Yose."

R. Eleazar b. Azariah: It is susceptible because it now can hold liquid, so it has a "receptacle."

R. Aqiva: Pitch adheres to wood and becomes connected, but pitch does not adhere well to earthenware and is therefore unconnected.

R. Yose: Since people are likely to want to use the funnel in its usual way, they will remove the pitch seal. Since the seal is not intended to be a permanent part of the funnel, it is unconnected.

4:1 *because of its handle*: The weight of the handle tips it over.

R. Judah holds that a purified shard can return to susceptibility if it can function as a vessel.

in its sides: If they are laid flat.

R. Judah holds that for a broken earthenware container to be considered susceptible it must stand on its base as it normally would. A vessel whose base is broken or which was divided into two cannot stand on its base.

the Sages disagree because containers are created to be turned on their sides in order to pour out their contents. Hence, even when they are not standing on their bases they function as vessels.

4:2 *half a* qav: About a liter.

A *gistera* that was cracked and cannot hold liquid—[27]
even if it can hold food,
is insusceptible to impurity
since there are no "remnants of remnants."

3 What is [considered] a *gistera*?
Any [vessel] that has lost its handles.[28]
If it has points that extend out of it—[29]
any [part] that can contain olives becomes impure through contact
or via the interior space opposite [the point];
any [part] that cannot contain olives becomes impure only by contact,
but the interior space opposite [the point] is insusceptible to impurity.
If it leans on its side like a kind of throne—
any [part] that can contain olives becomes impure by contact
or via the interior space opposite;
any [part] that cannot contain olives becomes impure only by contact,
but the opposite interior space is insusceptible to impurity.
The bottoms of Qorfian [jugs] and the bottoms of Sidonian bowls,
even though they cannot stand unsupported,
are susceptible to impurity
because they were made [for this purpose] from the outset.

4 If an earthenware vessel has three rims
and the innermost exceeds [the others in height]—

[27] **P**: "If a container was so cracked that it could not be moved with even half a *qav* of dried figs in it, it is not susceptible to impurity. *Similarly,* if a partly broken earthenware vessel became cracked and could not hold liquid…"

[28] Lit. "ears."

[29] **K**: "Any whose handles have been removed *and* has points sticking out…"

remnants of remnants: Shards broken off a vessel might still retain their status as vessels. However, this law applies only to remnants of whole vessels. Shards that are damaged again are categorized as "remnants of remnants" and are always insusceptible.

4:3 *gistera*: A broken earthenware vessel as in 2:6 above.

Any [vessel] that has lost its handles: Because it is difficult to carry from place to place as one would a regular vessel.

has points that extend out of it: When the vessel broke, points formed around its rim. If these teeth-like points are close enough to each other to hold olives between them, they are considered connected and that part of the vessel is still whole enough to become impure.

any [part] that cannot contain olives: If the points are so widely spread apart as to be unable to hold olives, that part of the vessel is no longer a container, but they are still physically connected to the vessel and so are susceptible by contact.

like a kind of throne: The vessel broke vertically into two pieces, each with a piece of the base intact, so that it would look somewhat like a chair with a seat and a back.

Qorfian: From Corfu.

because they were made [for this purpose]: The intention to manufacture these items with a need for support allows them to be viewed as "vessels" subject to the purity laws.

4:4 *If an earthenware vessel has three rims*, etc.: See above, 2:7. In each case an impure thing enters the vessel or a space between two rims.

everything [outside this rim] is insusceptible to impurity.
If the outermost exceeds—
everything is susceptible to impurity;
If the middle exceeds—
from it and inward is susceptible to impurity,
from it outward is insusceptible to impurity.
If they [all] were equal—
R. Judah says:
One divides the middle one.
But the Sages say:
Everything is insusceptible to impurity.
When do earthenware vessels become susceptible to impurity?
From when they are fired in the kiln,
and that is the completion of their manufacture.

Chapter Five

5:1–7:6 *Laws Regarding Ovens and Stoves*

5 An oven
[is susceptible to impurity if its] original [height] is four [handbreadths],
and [it remains impure when broken if] its remains are four handbreadths [high]—
the words of R. Meir.
But the Sages say:
When does this apply?
To a large [oven],
but a small one
[is susceptible to impurity] in its original state of any [size],
and [it remains susceptible to impurity] if most of it remains.[30]
[An oven is susceptible to impurity] after its manufacture is complete.
What constitutes the completion of its manufacture?
When one heats it sufficiently to bake spongy cakes.

[30] **K, P**: "... [if it has] its remains plus a majority [of the oven] ..."

If the outermost exceeds, etc.: Whatever area is contained within the highest rim is susceptible.

R. Judah says: One divides the middle one: From the middle of the second rim inward is susceptible, and from the middle of that rim outward is not.

the Sages say: According to the Sages each rim can be considered as if it were the outer edge of the actual vessel, and any impurity that is further inside is prevented from affecting the more outward rims.

When do earthenware vessels become susceptible: Throughout this tractate a vessel becomes susceptible to impurity the moment that it becomes functional. This principle is articulated just below, in 5:1.

5:1 *[is susceptible] in its original state of any [size[*: A vessel does not lose its status if most of it remains and it still can function.

When one heats it: An oven is made of raw clay, which is then fired through use.

R. Judah says:
When one has heated the new oven sufficiently to bake spongy cakes
in an old oven.

2 A stove[31]
[is susceptible to impurity if its] original [height] is three [handbreadths],
and its remains [are susceptible if they] are three handbreadths [high].
[This rule applies] after its manufacture is complete.
What constitutes the completion of its manufacture?
When it has been heated sufficiently to cook the lightest egg,
beaten and put in a pan.
A small stove—
if one made it for baking,
its measure is like an oven's;
if one made it for cooking,
its measure is like a [large] stove's.
A stone that projects one handbreadth from an oven
or three fingerbreadths from a stove
serves as a connective.
One that projects from a small stove—
[if] one made it for baking,
the prescribed measure is like an oven's;
[if] one made it for cooking,
the prescribed measure is like a stove's.
R. Judah said:
They said "handbreadth" only [concerning the space] between the oven and the wall.
If there were two ovens side by side,
one grants a handbreadth to this one and a handbreadth to the other one
and the remainder [of the intervening stone is always] insusceptible to impurity.

[31] **P**, **P**$_2$: "A stove that was divided into two..."

R. Judah: An old oven needs less heat for baking than a new one. In R. Judah's view the oven becomes susceptible at an earlier point than in the Sages'.

5:2 *A stove*: An ordinary stove has a place for fire in its lower section and places for several cooking pots on its top.

its remains: If the stove is broken up, any pieces three handbreadths high remain susceptible. If already impure, they remain in that state.

small stove: With space for only one pot.

made it for baking...for cooking...its measure: Its measure for susceptibility is three handbreadths in height. Intended function determines the required measurement for a stove's susceptibility.

serves as a connective: The stone supports the oven or stove and is therefore considered part of it. If the stone becomes impure, the oven or stove becomes impure and vice versa. But this applies only to the portion of the stone adjacent to the stove or oven, up to the specified distance.

R. Judah: According to R. Judah, when a stone is placed between an oven and a wall only one handbreadth of stone is used in order to bring the oven close to the wall. Therefore, just one handbreadth and no more functions as a connective to the oven.

one grants a handbreadth: No matter how large the stone between the two ovens, only one handbreadth attached to each oven is susceptible. This follows the opinion of R. Judah, as given in the previous clause.

3 The "crown" of a stove is insusceptible to impurity.
The "tower" of an oven—
when it is four handbreadths[32] high
it is susceptible to impurity by contact
and through its interior space.
Less than this
it is insusceptible to impurity.
If one joined it to [the oven],
even on three [unconnected] stones—
it is susceptible to impurity.
The places on a stove for the oil cruse, spice pot, and lamp
can contract impurity by contact
but cannot contract impurity from the interior space—
the words of R. Meir.
R. Ishmael[33] deems them insusceptible to impurity.
4 An oven that was heated from its outer wall
or heated unwittingly
or heated while in the craftsman's house,
is susceptible to impurity.
It once happened
that fire once broke out among the ovens at Kefar Signah
and the case was brought to Yavneh
and Rabban Gamaliel deemed them susceptible to impurity.

[32] **K** has "ten handbreadths," but this is most likely an error based on the Mishnah's frequent use of "ten handbreadths" as a measurement.

[33] Most witnesses have "R. Simeon."

5:3 *The "crown" of a stove*: A removable frame surrounding a stove to preserve its heat. Since it is removed after the stove's use it is not deemed to be connected to the stove.

The "tower" of an oven: A wall-like structure surrounding an oven that provides a place to put freshly baked bread.

Less than this it is insusceptible: If the "tower" is as high as the stove, then it and the stove work in conjunction in baking bread and one is functionally part of the other. This is not so if the "tower" is lower than the oven.

even on three [unconnected] stones: Though the connection is flimsy it is sufficient to generate susceptibility.

The places on a stove for the oil cruse, spice pot, and lamp: According to Torah law these places are not true connectives because they neither support the stove nor aid in cooking.

R. Meir holds that the rabbis enacted that the above places on a stove should be considered connectives because they are physically attached to it. In order to distinguish their enactment from Torah law they said that impurity occurred only by contact and not via the vessel's interior space. In R. Ishmael's opinion (or R. Simeon's: see n. 33), they are not true connectives and therefore not susceptible to impurity at all.

5:4 *An oven that was heated from its outer wall*, etc.: These are not the usual methods for firing up an oven, but any manner of doing so is deemed to complete its manufacture.

in the craftsman's house: Even if its manufacture was not yet finished.

5 An addition to a householder's oven
is insusceptible to impurity,
but that of a baker
is susceptible to impurity
because he rests the roasting spit on it.
R. Yohanan ha-Sandlar says:
Because he bakes with it when he is pressed for time.
So, too,
an addition to olive seethers' vats
is susceptible to impurity,
but that of dyers
is insusceptible to impurity.

6 If an oven was filled halfway with earth:
from the earth downward, it is susceptible to impurity through contact,
from the earth upward, it is susceptible to impurity [even] through its interior space.
If one put it over the mouth of a cistern or the mouth of a cellar,
and laid a stone there—
R. Judah says:
If one heats it from below and it becomes heated above,
it is susceptible to impurity.
But the Sages say:
Since in any case it has been heated,
it is susceptible to impurity.

5:5 *An addition*: Additional clay that is placed around the smoke hole of an oven.

householder's: Such clay on a private oven serves no additional purpose.

but that of a baker: Bakers often sold both bread and cooked meat. Thus the addition to the oven is a useful part of the oven and a connective.

R. Yohanan ha-sandlar: His view is that additions to the oven must serve the same purpose as the oven itself. Cooking meat is not the basic function of a baker's oven.

an addition to olive seethers' vats: Olive seethers used the rim to keep heated water in the vat throughout the entire seething process. It is considered a connective because it enhances the function of the vat.

that of dyers: Dyers use the rim only to prevent boiling water from overflowing. Once they put in the dye they remove the rim since overheated water can ruin the dyeing process. Since the rim is used only temporarily it is not a connective.

5:6 *from the earth downward*: The earthen filling deprives the earthenware vessel of part of its interior space. Impurity inside the dirt must therefore actually touch the side of the oven to convey impurity to the oven.

from the earth upward: Where there is interior space, impurity is conveyed even without direct contact.

cistern…cellar: A stone has been placed alongside the oven and the cistern walls to hold the oven in place.

R. Judah: According to R. Judah an oven is susceptible only if it is attached to the ground. If the cistern's or cellar's heat raises the oven's temperature sufficiently for it to be fired, this proves it is attached.

the Sages hold that an oven need not be attached to the ground to become susceptible, and if it is heated to any degree it is sufficiently fired to be susceptible.

7 If an oven becomes impure, how does one purify it?
One divides it into three parts [vertically]
and scrapes off the plaster until he reaches the base.[34]
R. Meir says:
He need not scrape off the plastering
nor does [the scraping] have to reach the base.
Rather, he reduces it from within to [less than] four handbreadths [in height].
R. Simeon says:
And he needs to move it.
If he divided it into two parts,
one large and the other small:
the larger is impure and the smaller has been rendered pure.
If he divided it into three parts,
one as large as the other two together—
the large part is impure and the two small parts have been rendered pure.

8 If he cut it horizontally into rings
of less than four handbreadths [in height]—
it is pure.
If he smeared it with clay—
it contracts impurity after it has been heated enough to bake spongy cakes.
If he distanced the coating from it

[34] Lit. "until he (or it) is in the earth."

5:7 *One divides it into three parts [vertically]*: If each remnant is smaller than the size of half the oven, it has lost its function and therefore becomes insusceptible.

scrapes off the plaster: The plaster holds the oven together and is a connective.

R. Meir holds that one should remove the oven's rim from within and thereby reduce its height to less than four handbreadths. One should start the rim's removal from the oven's inner side to ensure that it is completely removed.

[less than] four handbreadths [height]: The minimum height of an oven. See R. Meir's position above in 5:1.

R. Simeon: The oven's destruction is not complete until all its pieces are separated from each other.

If he divided it the oven *into two parts*, etc.: If half the oven or more remains intact it still retains its status as an oven.

If he divided it into three parts, etc.: As in the previous case, half or more of the oven remains intact; the largest part is big enough to retain the status of an oven.

5:8 *he cut it*: i.e. an oven.

rings: Ovens were made out of rings of clay piled on one another. The final product was covered with clay or mud and fired. If the oven is reduced to its original rings it is considered destroyed and purified.

after it has been heated enough: It has been turned back into an oven.

he distanced the coating: If one places sand or gravel between a plaster wall and an oven, they will support the oven sufficiently for one to bake in it. In actuality, however, the oven remains unrepaired. Consequently, it remains insusceptible, and *a menstruant and a pure woman may bake in it and it is* still *pure.*

and put sand or gravel between them:
regarding this they said:
A menstruant and a pure woman may bake in it,
and it is pure.

9 If an oven came in pieces from the craftsman's house,
and one made hoops for it
and placed them on it
while it was pure:
if it became impure
and he removed the hoops—
it is pure.
If he replaced them,
it is [still] pure.
If he smeared it with clay,
it contracts impurity,
and he need not fire it since it has been fired already.

10 If he cut it into rings and put sand between each ring—
R. Eliezer deems it insusceptible to impurity,
but the Sages deem it susceptible to impurity.
This is the oven of Akhnai.
[Regarding] the cauldrons of the Arabs,
which he digs in the ground and plasters with clay—
if the plastering can stand by itself
it is susceptible to impurity.
If it cannot,
it is insusceptible to impurity.
This is the oven of Ben Dinai.

11 An oven of stone or metal is insusceptible to impurity,
but [the latter] is susceptible to impurity as a metal vessel.
If it was pierced, damaged, [or] split,

5:9 *one made hoops*: The purchaser attached the parts of the oven with hoops.

he removed the hoops: Since it will fall apart, it no longer has the status of an oven.

If he smeared it with clay: Since the clay holds the pieces together, the oven becomes susceptible.

fired already: Before it was dismembered.

5:10 *R. Eliezer*: Even if the oven was covered, R. Eliezer considers it broken since the essential pieces of the oven are only connected by sand.

the Sages hold that once it is covered with clay, it has the status of an oven.

Akhnai...Ben Dinai: Persons known either for making or using such ovens.

cauldrons of the Arabs: Used by Arabs for baking bread.

5:11 *An oven of stone or of metal is insusceptible*: These types of oven are insusceptible according to the rules governing earthenware ovens. Stone is always insusceptible, but metal is susceptible from its exterior only.

[and] one made it a patch or an addition of clay,
it is susceptible to impurity [as an earthenware vessel].
How large must the hole be?
Enough so that a flame comes through.
So too for a stove.
A stove of stone or metal is insusceptible to impurity,
but [the latter] is susceptible to impurity as a metal vessel.
It was pierced, damaged, [or] split,
and one made [clay] props for it—
it is susceptible to impurity [as an earthenware vessel].
If he smeared it with clay,
whether on its inside or outside—
it is insusceptible to impurity.
R. Judah says:
On its inside,
it is susceptible to impurity,
but on its outside,
it is insusceptible to impurity.

Chapter Six

6 If one who makes three clay props in the ground
has joined them together with clay
so that he could set a cooking pot on them—
it is susceptible to impurity.
If he fixed three nails in the ground
so that he could set a pot on them,
even if he fashioned their ends to make a place for the cooking pot to rest—
it is insusceptible to impurity.

one made it a patch of earth *or an addition of clay*: Since the oven has been restored to functionality with earth, it is viewed as an earthenware oven and is susceptible to impurity via its interior space.

props: Here, too, because one makes the stove functional by adding earthenware props, the stove becomes susceptible according to the rules of earthenware vessels.

smeared it with clay: Since the stove functioned perfectly without the clay, the clay can be disregarded.

R. Judah holds that once one adds clay to the inner part of a stove, that becomes the surface that cooks. As the effective means of cooking, it becomes susceptible, and being earthenware it becomes susceptible via its interior space.

6:1 *one who makes three clay props in the ground*: Since the tripod is the item that makes cooking possible, and the parts have been joined into a whole, the whole is considered a "vessel."

If he fixed three nails: Since this tripod cannot stand without support it does not constitute a "vessel." Even if it is supported and becomes equivalent to a stove, it is deemed a metal stove.

If one who uses two stones as a stove
has joined them together with clay—
it is susceptible to impurity.
R. Judah deems it insusceptible to impurity
until one adds[35] a third stone
or until one leans it against a wall.
If one [stone was joined to the ground] with clay and one without clay—
it is insusceptible to impurity.
2 The stone on which one would place [a pot]—
if on it and on an oven,
on it and on a stove,
on it and on a small stove—
it is susceptible to impurity.
On it and on [another] stone,
on it and on bedrock,
on it and on a wall—
it is insusceptible to impurity.
This was the *nezirim* stove that was [used] in Jerusalem, set against bedrock.
A butcher's stove—
if[36] he places one stone next to another
and one of them becomes impure,
they all have not become impure.
3 If one made three stones into two stoves,
if one of the outer stones became impure,

[35] Lit., "uses...." [36] Lit. "when."

one who uses two stones as a stove: One puts two stones side by side and rests a pot on them in a space with fire between them. Since he *joined them together with clay*, the anonymous mishnah considers the entire device a susceptible earthenware stove.

R. Judah holds that a stove made of props or stones must form a tripod to be susceptible. If one places the stone against a wall, the wall is equivalent to a third stone.

and one without clay: This arrangement does not form a tripod, so R. Judah deems it insusceptible.

6:2 *The stone*: Attached to the ground with clay.

if on it: If the pot is supported by both the stone and the oven or stove.

is susceptible: Because the stone is considered a part of the oven or stove and it is attached with clay, similar to the case in the previous mishnah of the two stones attached with clay.

On it and on [another] stone: The second stone is not attached with clay.

it is insusceptible: A stove formed in this way is a stone stove. See *Kelim* 5:11.

nezirim: The offering of a *nazir* (Numbers 6:18–19) had to be kept ritually pure, so a *nazir* would use an insusceptible stove made of rock or stone.

butcher's stove: Butchers' stoves had stones set side by side. The space between the stones allowed fire to keep food warm but not to cook it. Since the stones are not connected to one another they cannot transmit impurity to each other.

6:3 *two stoves*: The middle stone is connected to each of them. Depending on the status of the outside stones, it can be half-pure and half-impure.

the [part of the] middle stone that supports[37] the impure stone is impure;
[the part] that supports the pure stone remains pure.
If the pure one was removed,
the middle one is altogether impure.
If the impure one was taken away,
the middle is altogether pure.
If the two outer stones became impure
and the middle stone was large,
he gives one[38] [of the outer stones] the measure that is necessary to support a cooking pot from one side,[39]
and to the other the measure necessary to support another cooking pot on the other side,
and the remainder is pure.
But if it was small,
all of it is impure.
If the middle one was removed,
and he can support a large cauldron on it—
it is impure.
If he replaced it—
it is pure.
If he plastered it with clay—
it becomes susceptible to impurity
after it has been heated enough to cook an egg.

4 If one made two stones into a stove
and they became impure—
if he placed one stone next to this one[40] from one direction[41]
and one stone next to that one from the other direction:
half of this is impure and half of it is pure
and half of that[42] is impure and half of it is pure.
If the pure [stones] were removed—
these return to their impurity.

[37] Lit. "serves."
[38] Lit. "to this…and [below] to this."
[39] Lit. "from here…and [below] from here."
[40] Lit. "this," here and in the next line.
[41] Lit. "from here," here and in the next line.
[42] Lit. "this."

if it was small: All of the middle stone is needed to support the two pots.

support a large cauldron: If the remaining stones can hold a cauldron without the middle stone, they are considered a stove and remain susceptible.

he replaced it: The stove is considered to be a new entity and becomes pure.

plastered it with clay: This "new" stove can now become impure according to the general rule of earthenware stoves; see *Kelim* 5:2. It must, however, be fired in order to complete its construction.

6:4 *one…next to…one*: Four stones are placed parallel to one another, the original two impure ones in the middle and two new pure ones to the left and right of them.

half of this is impure: The two middle stones work together in cooking, but they also cook in conjunction with the pure stones. Therefore, the middle stones become half-pure and remain half-impure.

If the pure [stones] were removed: If the two external pure stones are removed, the two original impure ones return to a state of full impurity because now they alone form a stove.

Chapter Seven

7 If a householder's warming stove was diminished [at its bottom]
by less than three handbreadths—
it is susceptible to impurity,
because he heats from below and the pot above will boil.
More than this—
it is insusceptible to impurity.
If he put in a stone or gravel,
it is insusceptible to impurity.
If he plastered over [the filling] with clay—
it is susceptible thereafter.
This was the answer of R. Judah
about the oven that one set over the mouth of a cistern or cellar.
2 If a shelf has a container to hold cooking pots—
it is not susceptible to impurity as a stove,
but it is susceptible to impurity as a container.
What touches its sides does not become impure as with a stove.
[Regarding] its width—
R. Meir deems it insusceptible to impurity,
but R. Judah deems it susceptible to impurity.

7:1 *was diminished*: The ground under the stove has been removed, so that the fire in the stove is lower down that it used to be, by less than three handbreadths.

warming stove: A small stove with thick sides and bottom. One can fill it with coals and then place a dish on top for warming.

will boil: If the fire has not been distanced from the pot by more than three handbreadths, the stove will continue to fulfill its cooking function and thereby remain a vessel.

More than this: If the warming stove's interior is made deeper than three handbreadths it no longer functions as a stove since the fire is too far away from the pot to heat it.

stone or gravel: If the stone or gravel raises the diminished floor of the warming stove to within three handbreadths of the pot.

insusceptible: Since the stone or gravel is not an intrinsic part of the warming stove.

susceptible thereafter: The stone or gravel is now part of the warming stove since the clay is firmly attached to it.

This was the answer of R. Judah: See 5:6.

7:2 *shelf*: Or ash chest, or hob. A projection from the side of the stove that can hold pots.

not susceptible... as a stove: It is not a part of the stove.

susceptible... as a container: All items having a container are susceptible.

R. Meir: The flat top of the shelf, i.e. the *width*, is insusceptible because the shelf is not attached to the stove.

R. Judah: The shelf is susceptible because it aids in the stove's function.

So too for the one who inverts a basket
and makes a stove on it.

3 A stove that was divided lengthwise
is insusceptible to impurity.
Breadthwise—
it is susceptible to impurity.
A small stove that was divided in two,
whether lengthwise or breadthwise—
is insusceptible to impurity.
If the fireguard[43] around a stove
is three fingerbreadths high—
it contracts impurity by contact and through its interior space.
Less than this—
it contracts impurity by contact
but does not contract impurity through its interior space.
How does one measure it?
R. Ishmael says:
One places a spit from the top downward:
Whatever is opposite becomes impure through its interior space.
R. Eliezer b. Jacob says:
If the stove became impure the fireguard becomes impure;
if the fireguard became impure, the stove does not [necessarily] become impure.

4 If it was separate from the stove—
when it is three fingerbreadths high,

[43] Lit. "courtyard."

So too the one who inverts a basket: The same rules apply when one uses the part of the basket that extends beyond the stove as a shelf.

7:3 *stove*: That can hold multiple pots.

lengthwise: That is, along its longer axis (left to right). Now the stove cannot hold pots and is therefore no longer usable.

Breadthwise: That is, along its shorter axis (front to back). This leaves undamaged the areas where pots rest, and the double stove still can function as two single stoves.

small stove: Since a small stove holds only one pot, any division makes it nonfunctional.

fireguard: A earthenware slab with walls to which a stove is connected. Pots were put on it for warmth or cooking.

three fingerbreadths high: See 5:2.

from the top downward: He leans a spit or other rod diagonally from the top of the stove to the top of the fireguard.

Whatever is opposite becomes impure: Anything beneath the diagonal rod, even if it is above the rim of the fireguard, is considered within the interior space of the stove–fireguard combination.

R. Eliezer b. Jacob: The fireguard is an adjunct to the stove, but the stove is not an adjunct to the fireguard.

7:4 *separate from the stove*: Despite the lack of attachment, the fireguard becomes impure according to the same rules as above.

it is becomes impure by contact and through its interior space.
Less than this, or if it was smooth—
it is insusceptible to impurity.
The props of a stove—
three of three fingerbreadths' [length]
become impure by contact and through their interior space.
Less than this—
they are all the more susceptible to impurity,
even if there were four [props].

5 If one of them was taken away—
they contract impurity by contact
but not through their interior space—
the words of R. Meir.
But R. Simeon deems them insusceptible to impurity.
If one made two [props],
one opposite the other—
they contract impurity by contact and through their interior space—[44]
the words of R. Meir.
But R. Simeon deems them insusceptible to impurity.
If they were more than three fingerbreadths high—
from three [fingerbreadths high] and downward
they contract impurity by contact and through the interior space;
from three and upward
they contract impurity by contact but not through their interior space—
the words of R. Meir.

[44] Maimonides' version apparently read "they are susceptible to impurity by contact but not through their interior space."

props: Attached to the stove to hold the cooking pot in place. Since they serve the stove's purpose of cooking, they are equivalent to it. The shorter the props, the closer they bring the pot to the fire and the more they are like the stove itself.

four: Though the fourth prop is not absolutely necessary to support the pot, it is still susceptible since it provides some support.

7:5 *one of them*: The props mentioned in the previous mishnah.

they contract impurity: That is, the remaining props.

R. Meir: If one of the three props is missing, the stove is no longer fully usable; therefore the remaining props are susceptible only by rabbinic decree. The rabbis distinguished their decree from Torah law by declaring the two earthenware props susceptible only by contact.

R. Simeon denies that the rabbis enacted any susceptibility at all.

If one made two…R. Meir: If the stove was made at the outset with two props capable of supporting a pot, the two props support the stove just as three would and are susceptible.

R. Simeon: Two props are insusceptible, perhaps because fewer than three props cannot be fully functional.

If they were more than three fingerbreadths high…R. Meir: From three fingerbreadths and lower, the props are part of the stove and are governed by its impurity rules. Props that rise three handbreadths above the stove's cooking area are susceptible only by rabbinic decree.

But R. Simeon deems them insusceptible to impurity.
If they were extended away from the [stove's] rim—
within three fingerbreadths
they contract impurity by contact and through their interior space.
Beyond three fingerbreadths
they contract impurity by contact but not through their interior space—
the words of R. Meir.
But R. Simeon deems them insusceptible to impurity.
6 How does one measure them?
Rabban Simeon b. Gamaliel says:
He places a straight edge between them:
from the straight edge outward is insusceptible to impurity;
from the straight edge inward,
including the place of the straight edge,
is susceptible to impurity.

Chapter Eight

8:1–9:3 *Impurities in Interior Spaces*

8 If one divided an oven with boards or curtains—
if vermin was found in one part,
the whole is impure.
If a broken-down beehive was patched with straw and was hung in the interior space of the oven—
if it had vermin in it,
the oven is impure.

R. Simeon deems them: The part that is above three fingerbreadths. Anything higher than three fingerbreadths from the stove's top is not part of the stove and is insusceptible.

If they were extended away from the [stove's] rim: Analogous to the preceding case, but the props extend outward rather than upward.

7:6 *How does one measure them*: That is, the interior space of the inner three fingerbreadths of the props in the last mishnah. One marks the three props where they are three handbreadths from the lip of the pot, then one laces a ruler between the props. This forms a triangle. Whatever is inside the triangle is susceptible to impurity; whatever lies outside is not.

8:1 *divided...with boards or curtains*: Nonearthenware entities do not count as dividers in an earthenware vessel. Therefore the entire vessel is still considered one entity.

a broken-down beehive: A hive is an earthenware enclosure that holds the beehive and honeycombs. A broken one sealed with straw is not considered a "vessel" until one patches it with clay or earth. Therefore it cannot protect itself or another earthenware vessel from impurity. For the law about an intact beehive, see the next mishnah.

If vermin was in the oven,
food in it is impure.
R. Eliezer deems it pure.
R. Eliezer said:
If [the hive] protects in the graver matter of corpse impurity,
should it not also protect in the lighter matter of [impurity in] an earthenware vessel?
They said to him:
If it protects in the graver matter of corpse impurity,
where one divides Tents,
will it afford protection in the lighter matter of [impurity from] an earthenware vessel
where one does not divide earthenware vessels?[45]

2 If [the hive] was undamaged—
and so too for a basket and so too for a water flask—
if the vermin is in it, the oven is pure.
If the vermin is in the oven, food in it is pure.[46]
If they became perforated—
that which was made for food,
their measure is for olives.
That which was made for liquids,
their measure is for liquids.
That which was made for either—
one applies the more stringent condition,
for liquids to enter.

[45] **K**: "They answered him: If it protects in the graver matter of corpse impurity for one does not partition earthenware." There is an obvious lacuna, no doubt the product of a scribal error arising from the similarity of language in the first and second sections of the Sages' argument.

[46] **K**: "If the [hive] was undamaged—and the same applies to a basket or a water-flask—vermin **that** is in it [i.e. the hive]: the oven remains pure. Vermin **that** is in the oven: food in the hive remains pure."

food in it: In the beehive. That is, impurity in the interior space of the oven is transmitted to the contents of the hive.

R. Eliezer deems it pure: R. Eliezer considers a broken hive repaired with straw sufficiently whole to count as a vessel.

If it protects in the graver matter of corpse impurity: Corpse impurity is the highest form of impurity. If a sealed hive protects against corpse impurity in a house or tent, should it not do so as well in an earthenware vessel that is susceptible only to a lower form of impurity?

They said to him: The Sages argue that the impurity of Tents is not consistently more severe than the impurity of earthenware vessels. Partitions in Tents prevent the spread of impurity, but the beginning of this mishnah establishes that this is not the case for earthenware containers.

8:2 *If [the hive] was undamaged*: The oven remains pure because earthenware becomes impure only via its interior space, but not via "an interior space within an interior space." This principle protects food and liquids in the hive, basket, or water flask from impurity.

food in it: In the hive, basket, or water flask.

their measure is for olives: If the new perforation is large enough to allow olives to slip through, the protection just described is lost. In a vessel made to hold liquids, even a smaller hole has the same effect. See also above, 3:1.

3 If a sifter[47] without handles[48] was put over the mouth of the oven
and it sank into it—
if vermin is in it,
the oven is impure.
If vermin is in the oven,
food in it is impure,
since only vessels afford protection from earthenware vessels.
If a container that is full of pure liquid
is placed beneath the bottom of the oven,
[and] vermin is in the oven—
the container and the liquid are pure.
If it was placed upside down with its mouth within the interior space of the oven,
[and] vermin is in the oven—
liquid at the bottom of the container sufficient to wet one's hand is pure.
4 A pot that was put into an oven—
if vermin is in the oven:
the cooking pot is pure,
because an earthenware vessel does not convey impurity to [other] vessels.
If [the pot] contained liquid sufficient to wet one's hands—
[the moisture] is made impure and it renders impure.
Thus [the pot] says:
What renders you impure does not render me impure,
but you have rendered me impure.
5 If a rooster swallowed vermin and fell into the interior space of an oven,
it is pure.

[47] Alt. "kneading board." [48] Alt. "rims."

8:3 *without handles*: If a closed vessel enters an impure vessel it does not contract impurity. However, the sifter lacks handles and so is not a proper utensil. Therefore, it does not protect an oven that it enters or food that it holds from impurity. The alternative translation "rims" comes to the same thing: the item cannot hold foods or liquids and so is not a proper utensil.

food in it: The sifter.

beneath the bottom of the oven: Since the container and the liquid are beneath the interior space of the oven and not inside it, they remain pure.

liquid at the bottom...is pure: If the bottom of the upside-down container is above the interior space of the oven, residual liquid that adheres to the bottom and does not enter the oven's interior space is pure.

8:4 *A pot that was put into an oven*: Empty.

an earthenware vessel does not convey impurity to [other] vessels: It can only convey impurity to food or liquids. See Leviticus 11:33–34.

[the moisture] is made impure: The oven renders the liquid in the pot impure if the pot is open and completely within the oven's interior space.

it renders the pot *impure*.

[the pot] says: The liquid, but not the pot, contracts impurity because it is in the oven's interior space. The pot then contracts impurity from the impure liquid. Cf. *Parah* 8:2–7.

8:5 *it is pure*: The oven is pure.

If it dies, [the oven] is impure.
If vermin was found in an oven—
the bread that is in it [is impure] to the second degree
because the oven [is impure] to the first degree.

6 If a container of leaven, enclosed by a tightly sealed cover, was put inside an oven
and leaven and vermin were inside
but separated by a partition—
the oven is impure,
but the leaven is pure.
And if there was an olive's bulk of corpse matter
[in the container, separated from the leaven by a partition],
the oven and the house are impure,
but the leaven is pure.
If there is an opening one handbreadth square,
everything is impure.

7 If vermin was found in the vent[49] of an oven , the vent of a stove,
[or] the vent of a small stove—
from the inner rim [of the vent] and outward—
it is pure.
And if it was in the open air—
even if an olive's bulk of corpse matter [was in its vent],
it is pure.

[49] Lit. "eye."

If it dies: A living animal cannot convey impurity. Once the animal is dead, the vermin in its body renders the oven impure unless it has been fully digested. The dead bird itself would not render the oven impure.

to the second degree...to the first degree: See the introduction to *Kelim*. The bread is impure because of contact with the impure oven, not because of contact with the interior space of the oven.

8:6 *tightly sealed cover*: See Numbers 19:15.

separated by a partition: The partition extends from the sealed vessel's bottom to its cover. Thus, the vessel can be seen as two different sealed vessels.

the oven is impure but the leaven is pure: Tightly sealed covers protect pure items from impurity, but they do not prevent impure items from conveying their impurity. The oven becomes impure because the tightly sealed vessel contains vermin. The leaven remains pure because it is protected by the sealed vessel.

an olive's bulk of corpse matter: A piece at least the size of an olive of a dead human body. See *Oholot* 2:1.

the oven and the house are impure: The oven becomes impure as above. The house becomes impure because it constitutes a Tent containing an olive-sized piece of a corpse.

one handbreadth square: In the partition; see *Oholot* 3:6.

8:7 *vent*: A hole in the lower part of an oven's or stove's side that lets out smoke, lets in air, and is used to pour out ash.

from the inner rim...it is pure: As long as the vermin is found in the inner rim of the vent or below it. The vent is not considered to extend into the oven or stove and so does not convey impurity.

in the open air: Outside. Corpse matter conveys impurity through Tent only in a covered space or beneath an overhang.

If there is an opening one handbreadth square [in the vent],
everything is impure.

8 If it was found in the opening where the wood is put in—
R. Judah says:
[If it was found] from the outer rim [of the aperture] inward,
it is impure.
But the Sages say:
From the inner rim outward,
it is pure.
R. Yose says:
From where the cooking pot is set and inward,
it is impure;
from where the cooking pot is set and outward
it is pure.
If it was found where the bathkeeper sits,
or where the dyer sits,
or where the olive seethers sit—
it is pure.
It is impure only [if vermin was found] from the [oven's] closed space and inward.

9 If a furnace[50] has a place on which to set a pot—
it is susceptible to impurity.
A glassmakers' [crucible],
if it has a place on which to set a pot,
is susceptible to impurity.
A lime-burners' furnace, or a glassblowers', or a potters'
is insusceptible to impurity.

[50] **K, P, P_2**: "furnace." The Vilna edition has "cistern." See annotations.

one handbreadth square: An opening this large permits the corpse impurity to travel into the interior space of the oven or stove.

8:8 *R. Judah* considers the oven's wall and the opening in it as part of the oven.

the Sages say: The inner rim of the fuel aperture that does not actually enter into the oven's receptacle but lies even with its wall is insusceptible because it is not part of the oven.

R. Yose: A typical stove had one or more holes in its upper surface where pots were placed to cook. These holes define the functional boundary of the stove's interior. According to R. Yose, only the part of the stove directly beneath the cooking pots is the interior of the stove.

where the bathkeeper sits: These seats are physically connected to a bath's heating stoves, but outside of them; they are not used for the purpose of heating but for the convenience of the operator.

closed space: The heating pot blocks the hole on which it rests and defines the border of the stove's interior space.

8:9 *furnace*: Or "cistern" in the Vilna edition. In Hebrew the words differ by a single letter.

glassmakers'…glassblowers': The first prepares the unshaped glass out of sand and other ingredients; the second forms the glass into usable objects.

lime-burners' furnace: These are never used for cooking or baking.

A baking oven,
if it has a rim,
is susceptible to impurity.
R. Judah says:
If it is roofed.
Rabban Gamaliel says:
If it has borders.
10 If one who touched a person with corpse impurity
had food or liquids in his mouth,
and he put his head into the interior space of an oven that was pure—
they have rendered it impure.
And if a pure person who had food or liquids in his mouth
put his head into the air space of an impure oven—
they have become impure.
If he was eating fig cakes with unwashed[51] hands,
and he put his hand into his mouth to take out a stone—
R. Meir deems it impure;
R. Judah deems it pure.
R. Yose says:
If he turned it over [in his mouth],
it is impure.
If he did not turn it over,
it is pure.
If he had a *pondion* in his mouth:

[51] "Sullied" or "defiled."

A baking oven: One bakes bread in this oven by placing dough on the oven's floor through a door in its side. Since the baking is done on the ground, the oven as such is not a utensil. Alternatively, without a border it would have no proper interior space and so not qualify. If it has a border for pots, neither of these considerations applies.

if it has a rim: The rim gives the oven an interior space.

If it is roofed: Roofing creates an interior space.

8:10 *touched*: One who contacts a person with corpse impurity becomes impure in the first degree (one degree reduced from the person with corpse impurity, who has primary impurity).

food or liquids in his mouth: The liquids (though not the solid food) become impure and render the oven impure via its interior space. Although a first-degree impurity does not normally render vessels impure, first-degree impure liquids do so by rabbinic decree.

a pure person who had food or liquids in his mouth…they the food *has become impure*: See above, 8:5.

unwashed hands: By rabbinic decree, though not by Torah law, unwashed hands are presumed to be impure.

R. Meir…R. Judah…R. Yose: According to R. Meir, saliva in the mouth conveys impurity. R. Judah holds that saliva conveys impurity only when it has left a person's mouth. R. Yose holds that saliva that has moved from its place of origin in one's mouth conveys impurity. The process of turning over the fig cake in his mouth will displace saliva from its original place.

pondion: A *pondion* is a coin. Placed in the mouth it can bring forth thirst-quenching salivation. R. Yose holds that this is saliva that moved from its original place.

R. Yose says:
If for his thirst,
it is impure.

11 If a woman's breast dripped milk into the interior space of an oven—
it is impure,
since liquid conveys impurity whether willingly or not.
If she was cleaning the oven out
and a thorn pricked her
and she bled[52]
or she burnt herself
and put her finger in her mouth:
it is impure.

Chapter Nine

9 If a needle or a ring were found [embedded] in the bottom of an oven,
visible but not projecting:
if one bakes the dough and it touches them,
it is impure.
About what kind of dough did they speak?
About a middling dough.
If they were found in the plastering of an oven with a tightly sealed cover:
if in an impure [oven],

[52] **P**: "and a quarter-*log* of blood came forth…" "A quarter-*log* of blood" is a common phrase used in reference to corpse impurity, but this is not such a case.

8:11 *a woman's breast*: While she was impure.

milk…it is impure: The impure milk has conveyed impurity to the oven through its interior space.

willingly or not: It does not matter that the woman had no desire for her milk to drip into the oven and has gained no benefit from the occurrence.

bled…burnt…it is impure: The blood from her wound and the saliva on her fingers are both impure liquids that now convey impurity to the oven.

9:1 *a needle or a ring*: According to rabbinic enactment all metal objects of unknown origin are considered impure with corpse impurity. If they do not project into an oven's interior space, the oven remains pure.

it touches them, it is impure: If the dough touches the needle or ring it becomes impure, and because it reaches into the oven's interior space, it conveys impurity to the oven.

middling dough: The texture of the dough is neither very soft nor very hard. If the dough is too soft, it will flow into cracks in the oven and encounter the ring or needle. If it is too hard it may not sink deeply enough into the oven's bottom to touch the needle or ring at all.

tightly sealed cover: The oven has a tightly sealed cover. Thus impurity cannot enter or leave the oven; see Numbers 19:15. Thus even in a Tent containing a corpse, the needle or ring remain pure if the interior of the oven itself is pure.

they are impure.
If in a pure [oven],
they are pure.
If they were found in a container's seal:
on its sides,
they are impure;
opposite its mouth,
they are pure.
If they were visible within it
but not [projecting] into its interior space—
they are pure.
If they are sunk into it
but beneath them there is still [clay] as thin as garlic peel—
they are pure.

2 If a container full of pure liquids with a siphon inside it
is tightly sealed and placed in a corpse Tent:
the House of Shammai say:
The container and the liquids are pure but the siphon is impure.
And the House of Hillel say:
Even the siphon is pure.
The House of Hillel retracted
and taught according to the words of the House of Shammai.

3 If vermin was found beneath the base of an oven,
[the oven] is pure,
for I [may] say:
"It was alive when it fell

on its sides, they are impure: Since clay seals on a container's side do not cover its opening, they do not form "tightly sealed vessels," so the container, the ring, and the needle are not protected from Tent impurity.

opposite its mouth, they are pure: If the needle and ring are in clay that covers the opening of the container, they together with the clay constitute a "tightly sealed cover," protecting the needle, ring, and container from Tent impurity.

visible within it: i.e. the needle or ring are visible in the seal of the container.

not [projecting]: As long as the needle or ring do not enter the tightly sealed container's interior space, even if the separation between them and the interior is negligible, they remain pure.

9:2 *siphon*: Made of metal.

The container and the liquids are pure but the siphon is impure: According to the House of Shammai a "tightly sealed cover" protects only earthenware and liquids, but not metal.

Even the siphon is pure: Originally the House of Hillel held that a "tightly sealed cover" protected earthenware and everything in it from corpse impurity. Commentators differ as to the reason for the Hillelites' retraction.

9:3 *beneath the base of an oven*: Vermin could fall into an oven and crawl through the small space between the oven and its base to the area beneath the base. To do so it must be alive and therefore incapable of rendering the oven impure.

and it died now."
If a needle or a ring were found beneath the bottom of an oven
[the oven] is pure,
for I [may] say:
"They were there before the oven came."
If they were found in the ashes—
[the oven] is impure,
since there is nothing to depend on.

9:4–6 *Liquids As Conveyors of Impurity*

4 If a sponge soaked up impure liquids
and its outer surface became dry
and it fell into the interior space of an oven,
it is impure,
since the liquid will ultimately emerge.
So, too, [with] a piece of turnip or reed grass.
R. Simeon deems these two pure.
5 If shards that were used for impure liquids
fell into an oven's interior space
and the oven was heated,
it is impure,
since the liquid will ultimately emerge.
So too with fresh olive waste,
but with old [olive waste],
it is pure.
But if it is known that liquid is [still] emerging—
even after three years—
it has been rendered impure.
6 If olive waste or grape waste had been prepared in [conditions of] purity,
and impure persons walked on them

a needle or a ring: Being immobile they must be supposed to have been in place before the oven's base. Hence, they would never have been in the oven's interior space.

there is nothing to depend on: If the needle or ring was found in the oven's ashes one could never know whether they fell into the ashes before or after they were removed from the oven. Therefore there is no presumption of purity.

9:4 *it is impure*: The oven.

R. Simeon holds that the turnip or reed grass will not necessarily discharge the liquid.

9:5 *olive waste*: The solid olive residue that is a by-product of pressing olives.

Old [waste]: Presumably the absorbed liquids have all dried out.

9:6 *[conditions of] purity*: Pure persons prepared oil or grape juice in pure vessels leaving ritually pure waste.

impure persons walked on them: Since the impure individuals had no intention of extracting liquid from the waste when they walked on it, any liquid emerging from it remains pure. The waste itself does

and afterward liquid emerged from them—
they are pure,
since they were prepared in [conditions of] purity at the outset.
If a spindle hook sank into the spindle,[53]
or a nail into the ox goad,
or a ring into the clay brick,
while they were pure,
and they were brought[54] into a corpse Tent,
they have been rendered impure.
If a *zav* moved them,
they have been rendered impure.
If [after becoming impure in a corpse Tent] they fell into a pure oven's interior space,
they have rendered it impure.
If [after becoming impure in a corpse Tent] a loaf of *terumah* touched them,
it is pure.

9:7–8 *Holes in Vessels and the Purity Laws*

7 If a sifter was put over the mouth of an oven,
[so that it forms] a tightly sealed cover:
if [the seal] between the oven and the sifter cracked,
its measure is the size of the tip of an ox goad
[even if it] cannot enter [the split].

[53] Lit. "A spindle that swallowed the hook," and so in the following cases as well.
[54] Lit. "entered."

not contract impurity, being neither food nor vessel, and liquid only contracts impurity when it is extracted deliberately.

spindle hook…nail…ring: The first two items have wooden handles into which the hook or nails can sink. The ring was used to mark bricks before they were hardened and could easily sink into the brick's clay. Both wooden handles and clay bricks are themselves insusceptible to impurity.

they have been rendered impure: They become impure with corpse impurity since they are metal items, even though they are surrounded by wood or clay. The items into which they sank are not considered "vessels" that could form a protective "tightly sealed cover."

zav: See *Kelim* 1:3. If a *zav* moves an article it becomes impure even if protected by a "tightly sealed cover," which these are not.

oven's interior space…impure: Since impurity can be imparted to an earthenware vessel without actually touching the vessel, these impure items, though covered by wood or clay, render impure the oven into which they fall.

a loaf of terumah touched the spindle hook, etc.…*pure*: *Terumah* becomes defiled only by actual contact with something impure. Here, the impure items (the spindle, etc.) are embedded in something else.

9:7 *sifter*: A flat piece of clay with holes in it. The translation is uncertain; see above, 8:3n.

the tip of an ox goad: A split a third of a handbreadth wide. If there is a split this size, even if the tip of an ox goad cannot enter it, the oven is not tightly sealed.

R. Judah says:
[The seal remains valid unless] it can enter the split.
If the sifter [itself] was cracked[55]—
its measure
is the size of the tip of an ox goad that can enter [the split].
R. Judah says:
[Even if] it cannot enter.
If it was round and
one does not see it as straight[56]—
its measure is the size of the tip of an ox goad that can enter.
8 If a hole was made in an oven vent,
its measure is a spindle staff
that enters and exits while burning.
R. Judah says:
[Even if] it is not burning.
If a hole is made in the side,
its measure is a spindle staff
that enters and exits when not burning.
R. Judah says:
[Even if] it is not burning.[57]
R. Simeon says:
If [the hole was] in the middle,
[the measure is it must] enter.
If at the side,
it [need not] enter.
So, too, he used to say of the plug of a container that was pierced:

[55] This line through R. Judah's second opinion is missing in **K**.
[56] Lit. "long." [57] **P** lacks the latter opinion of R. Judah.

R. Judah requires a more significant split in the clay in order to invalidate the sieve as a "tightly sealed cover." If, however, the sieve itself is split, R. Judah requires a smaller crack to invalidate the seal.

If it was round: A curved split is not viewed as if it were straight and therefore large enough to have an ox goad tip enter it. Only if an ox goad tip can actually enter it at some point along the curve is it susceptible.

9:8 *oven vent*: See above, 8:7. If there is a hole in the seal of the vent, the vent no longer serves this purpose. The anonymous mishnah holds that this is so only in the case of a relatively large perforation. R. Judah holds that even a smaller hole signifies that the oven is no longer sealed.

enters and exits while burning: i.e. the spindle staff enters not burning but exits the oven on fire.

the side: Commentators differ as to whether the side of the vent is meant here or the side of the oven itself. The dispute between the first opinion and R. Judah is as in 9:7 above.

R. Simeon: Again, commentators differ as to whether R. Simeon's distinction pertains to the plug or the oven itself.

its measure is the thickness of the second knot in an oat stalk.
If [the hole was] in the middle,
it [should be able to] enter.
If at the side,
it [need] not enter.
So, too, he used to say of large amphorae that were pierced:
their measure is the thickness of the second knot in a reed.
If [the hole was] in the middle,
it [should be able to] enter.
If at the side,
it [need] not enter.
When does this apply?
If they were made [to store] wine,
but if they were made for other liquids,
however small the hole,
[the contents] are susceptible to impurity.
When does this apply?
When [the holes] were not manmade.
But if they were manmade,
however small the hole,
[the contents] are susceptible to impurity.
If the vessels were pierced—
[in the case of] vessels used for produce,
their measure is olives.
If they were made for liquids,
their measure is liquids.
If they were made for either,
one applies the more stringent rule
regarding the tightly sealed cover:
that a liquid can enter.

second knot: An oat stalk grows in three sections. The second section is thicker than the uppermost section and smaller than the lowest one.

the second knot in a reed: This measure is larger than that of an oat stalk.

wine...other liquids: Owners of wine do not want holes in the wine containers lest the wine lose its bouquet. Regarding other liquids, the owners may want the aeration. A hole of any size can accomplish that. Other commentators differ: wine containers are often furnished with bungholes, and the hole here in question must be larger than the usual to break the "tight seal."

not manmade...manmade: A person who intentionally pierces an earthenware vessel intends to keep it from being completely sealed. When there is no human intentionality, only the holes' size reflect whether they are generally perceived as efficient or inefficient covers.

Chapter Ten

10:1–6 *Corpse Impurity and Tightly Sealed Vessels*

10 These vessels protect when they have a tightly sealed cover:
vessels of dung, stone, clay, earthenware, or alum crystal,
fishbones or fishskin,
the bones of an animal that lives in the sea or its skin,
and wooden vessels that are insusceptible to impurity.
They afford protection whether from their mouth or their side,
whether they stand on their bottom or lean on their sides.
If they are turned upside down,
they afford protection to all that is beneath them
to the furthest depth.[58]
R. Eliezer deems [such] susceptible to impurity.
They afford protection to everything
except [for] an earthenware vessel,
which protects only foods, liquids, and [other] earthenware vessels.

2 With what may one seal?
With lime or gypsum,
pitch or wax,
mud or excrement,
crude clay or potter's clay,
or anything used for plastering.
One may not seal with tin or lead,
because they serve as a covering but do not seal tightly.
One may not seal [a vessel] with a fat fig cake
or with dough kneaded with fruit juice,

[58] Lit. "to the abyss."

10:1 *protect*: From corpse impurity.

dung, etc.: Items in these vessels, once they are tightly sealed, are protected from impurity.

wooden vessels that are insusceptible: See below, 15:1.

from their mouth or their side: It does not matter whether the vessel is open at the top or the side, so long as the opening is tightly sealed.

R. Eliezer holds that since Numbers 19:15 declares insusceptible a vessel with "a tightly sealed cover upon it" the requirement is that the sealed cover be "upon it" literally, i.e. on its uppermost surface. Sticking the mouth of the vessel into the ground does not create a tight seal.

except [for] an earthenware vessel: Earthenware vessels protect only items that cannot be purified by immersion.

10:2 *With what may one seal?* That is, what materials may be used to form a "tightly sealed cover"?

a fat fig cake…dough kneaded with fruit juice: These items may not be used as a "tightly sealed cover" because they are susceptible to impurity once liquid is on them or mixed into them (Leviticus 11:38). An impure item cannot protect against impurity. Alternatively, they are too likely to dry up and crumble, thereby breaking the "tight seal."

lest they lead it to disqualification.
But if a vessel was sealed with it,
it does afford protection.

3 A container plug that wobbles but does not fall out:
R. Judah says:
It protects.
But the Sages say:
It does not protect.
If its finger hold was sunk into [the container]:
[if there was] vermin in [the finger hold],
the container is impure.
If vermin was in the container,
food within [the finger hold] is impure.

4 If one placed a ball or coil of reed grass over the mouth of the container:
if he plastered the sides, it does not protect,
until he plasters it above and[59] below.[60]
And so too with a patch of cloth.
If [the cover was] of paper or leather,
and he bound it with a cord:
If he plastered it at the sides,
it protects [from corpse impurity].[61]

5 A container whose [external] clay peeled off
but whose [internal] pitch remained,
and so too clay jars of fish brine

[59] Or "or." [60] **P**, $\mathbf{P}_2$: "from top to bottom."
[61] **K** adds "if he plastered the sides it does not afford protection until he plasters it at the sides." **K** then continues "it does not afford protection until he plasters it above and below."

But if a vessel was sealed with it: After the fact, if the fig cake or dough remain pure and intact, they are "tightly sealed covers" and do prevent impurity.

10:3 *wobbles*: R. Judah requires only covering the mouth of the vessel; the Sages require tight covering of the vessel.

finger hold: This is a slight depression in a container's plug or cork that helps one to pull it out. In this case it extends into the interior space of the container, disqualifying it as a "tightly sealed cover."

food within [the finger hold] is impure: Just as vermin in the container affect the protruding plug, so too vermin in the finger hold affect the container.

10:4 *a ball or coil of reed grass*: Since these are not solid and contain holes they do not form a "tightly sealed cover." If the owner plasters them only at their sides, holes remain in their top and bottom. Therefore, he must plaster their entire surface.

paper or leather: Since these form a continuous cover, one need not plaster their tops and bottoms as long as they are tightly bound to the vessel. However, to make certain they form a tight seal their sides require plastering.

10:5 *A container whose [external] clay peeled off*: A clay container would remain tightly sealed by pitch on the inside of the cask, even though part of its external wall had been broken. The same would be true of a brine container that had been sealed inside with pitch.

that one covered with pitch level with its rim—
R. Judah says:[62]
They do not protect [from corpse impurity].
But the Sages say:
They protect.

6 If a [tightly sealed] container had a hole in it
and wine lees sealed it up—
they protect it [from corpse impurity].
If one stopped it up with a vine shoot—
[it protects] if he plasters it at the sides.
If there were two [vine shoots],
[they do not protect] until he plasters at the sides
and between one vine shoot and the other.
If a board is placed on an oven—
if he plastered [it] at the sides,
it protects.
If there were two—
[they do not protect from corpse impurity] until he plasters the sides
and between one board and the other.
If he places bush or cork chips[63] between them,
he need not plaster between them.

10:7–8 *Vessels within Vessels*

7 If an old oven was within a new [oven]
and a sifter[64] lay over the mouth of the old,[65]
[and] if one removes the old [oven],

[62] **P**: "R. Yose."
[63] See annotation for an alternative interpretation.
[64] See 8:3 above.
[65] Var. "new." See annotations.

R. Judah…the Sages: R. Judah bases his ruling on Numbers 19:15, which says "a tight sealed cover upon it." His interpretation of this was "'upon it,' but not "from within it." The Sages require just a tight seal of any kind.

10:6 *at the sides*: That is, around the shoot that has been placed in the hole.

a board: A flat board is insusceptible and can therefore be used to make a "tightly sealed cover," but only if it is sealed around the edges.

bush or cork chips: These materials close the gap between two boards as well as plaster. An alternative interpretation sees here a reference to a mortise-and-tenon connection between the boards.

10:7 *If an old oven was within a new [oven]*: A new (not yet fired) oven is not yet a utensil but can serve as a Tent if it is "tightly sealed." A new oven is insusceptible to corpse impurity but its contents are not protected unless the oven is sealed, but not necessarily "tightly." An old (previously heated) oven has become susceptible itself, but it can protect its contents if it is "tightly sealed."

if one removes the old [oven]: Since the sifter is actually resting on the old oven, only a "tightly sealed cover" would provide protection, and the sifter does not so provide. The variant (see footnote on "old") has the sifter resting on the outer new oven that does not require a "tight seal," but even so if it requires the old oven for stability it cannot serve to protect the contents.

the sifter will fall—
everything is susceptible to impurity.
If not, everything is insusceptible to impurity.
If a new [oven] was within an old,
and a sifter lay over the mouth of the old,
if the space between the new oven and the sifter
was less than one handbreadth—
whatever is in the new oven is insusceptible to impurity.
8 If [earthenware] frying pans lie one within another
and their rims are at the same level:
if vermin is in the upper one or in the lower one,
[only] that one [containing the vermin] is impure,
and all [the others] are pure.
If [there was a hole] that lets in liquid:
if vermin is in the upper one,
all of them are impure.
If [vermin] was in the lowest one,
it is impure and all [the others] are pure.
If vermin was in the uppermost [frying pan]
and [the mouth of] the lower was higher,
it and the lower one are impure.
[If vermin was] in the uppermost

If not, everything is insusceptible: If the sifter was resting on the inner old oven, we must presume that the mouth of that oven was higher than the mouth of the outer new one, so that the sifter would simply settle on the new oven mouth if the old one were removed. According to the variant, if removing the old oven leaves the cover in place, the outer new oven continues to serve as a "Tent" and the contents are all protected.

less than one handbreadth: A handbreadth's or larger opening allows the passage of corpse impurity.

whatever is in the new oven is insusceptible: The old oven's contents are, however, impure with corpse impurity because it cannot be a "Tent" and there is no "tightly sealed cover."

10:8 *[only] that one [containing the vermin]*: A "container within a container" is insusceptible to impurity. All the pans stacked one within the other are "containers within containers" except the innermost and outermost ones.

[a hole] that lets in liquid: A vessel with such a small hole is considered broken regarding liquids but still usable regarding food. See 8:2 above.

If vermin is in the upper one: Because of the holes in the vessels they are no longer "containers within containers" and so the impurity travels throughout.

If [vermin] was in the lowest one: If the upper vessels are considered whole, the bottommost vessel cannot render them impure because they are "containers within containers." If they are considered broken, they cannot be made impure at all.

[the mouth of] the lower was higher: If the rim of the lower pan rises above the rim of the upper, both enclose the vermin in their own way, and both become impure.

[and the mouth of] the lower was higher,
all that have liquid sufficient to wet one's hand are impure.

Chapter Eleven

11:1–14 *Metalware*

11 Metal utensils—
their flat surfaces and receptacles are susceptible to impurity.
If they are broken,
they have become insusceptible to impurity.
If one remade them into utensils,
they return to their original state of impurity.
Rabban Simeon b. Gamaliel says:
This does not [apply] to every [form of] impurity
but only to corpse impurity.
2 Any metal article that has an independent designation
is susceptible to impurity,
except a door, door bolt, lock, hinge socket, hinge, knocker, or [threshold] groove,
since these are made [to be joined] to the ground.
3 One who makes vessels from a piece of iron [ore],
or from a lump [of iron],

[the mouth of] the lower was higher: Further discussing the same case.

all that have liquid sufficient to wet one's hand are impure: That is, the pans in the middle of the pile, if they are wet. The innermost and outermost pans convey impurity to the liquid, because it is in their interior space with the vermin, and the liquid conveys impurity to the pans.

11:1 *flat surfaces and receptacles*: Unlike some other materials (see above, 2:1), metal utensils receive and convey impurity whether or not they have a receptacle. Numbers 31:23 implies that any item that can withstand fire is susceptible under all conditions.

If they are broken: They no longer serve their function and are insusceptible. If they are repaired the pieces return to their previous state of susceptibility or actual impurity.

Rabban Simeon b. Gamaliel: According to this position, the ability of metal to return to its previous state when made into a new utensil is unique to corpse impurity.

11:2 *independent designation*: A name that shows it is not a subsidiary part of another vessel.

door, door bolt, etc.: These items either connect to a door or help connect a door to the ground. Anything metal attached to the ground, or even attached to an item attached to the ground, is insusceptible.

11:3 *vessels from a piece of iron [ore]*, etc.: Since none of these metal items constitute vessels or utensils, they are insusceptible. Therefore, when one makes a vessel out of these materials, one does not have to be concerned that it will return to a previous state of impurity.

lump: After the iron was smelted it was made into round "cakes" that were later formed into vessels or tools.

or from the hoop of a wheel,
or from sheet metal,
or from plating,
or from bases of vessels or rims of vessels or handles of vessels,
or from metal chips or filings:
they are pure.
R. Yohanan b. Nuri says:
Also [vessels made] from that which has been cut up.[66]
[If they were made from] the fragments of vessels,
from refuse,
or from nails known to have been made from other vessels,
they are impure.
If from nails [of unknown origin]—
the House of Shammai deem them impure,
but the House of Hillel deem them pure.

4 Impure iron that one mixed together with pure iron:
if the majority was from the impure,
it is impure.
If the majority was from the pure,
it is pure.
Half and half,
it is impure.
So, too, [for vessels] of cement and dung.
A door bolt is susceptible to impurity,
but if it was [only] plated,
it is insusceptible to impurity.
Teeth [of a key] or of a skeleton key are susceptible to impurity.

[66] Or "cut off."

that which has been cut up: The reference may be to utensils that have been intentionally destroyed, or to chunks of metal that were cut off articles in the course of manufacture.

the fragments of vessels: The articles in question may originally have come from impure vessels and remaking them has returned them to their original state of impurity.

nails: One does not know whether the nails were fashioned from ore or from a vessel. The House of Shammai assume that they may have been made from the fragments of impure vessels. The House School of Hillel do not make this assumption.

11:4 *Impure iron…pure iron*: The rules governing mixtures are: the greater part of a mixture nullifies the lesser part; the most stringent rules apply to an even mixture.

[vessels] of cement and dung: Cement vessels are susceptible as a form of earthenware vessels, while dung vessels are not susceptible. Combinations between the materials follow the rule above: The greater part nullifies the lesser part and even mixtures are treated stringently.

door bolt: Made of wood. Though it lacks a receptacle, a door bolt has a small button-like protuberance on it that locks the door. One can use this "button" as a pestle.

plated: This follows the rule that an object's status is judged by its essential element. The wood, and not the metal plating, is this element.

Teeth: Other interpreters apply these terms to various parts of a lock.

[As for] the door bolt:
R. Joshua says:
One may take it off one door and hang it on another
on the Sabbath.
R. Tarfon says:
It is like all other vessels for him
and may be moved within the courtyard.

5 The "scorpion" of a bridle is susceptible to impurity,
but the cheekpieces are insusceptible to impurity.
R. Eliezer deems the cheekpieces susceptible to impurity,
but the Sages say:
The "scorpion" alone is susceptible to impurity,
but when they are joined together
the whole is susceptible to impurity.

6 A metal spindle knob:
R. Aqiva deems it susceptible to impurity,
but the Sages deem it insusceptible to impurity.
If it is plated,
it is insusceptible to impurity.
If a spindle, distaff, rod, double flute, or pipe are made of metal,
they are susceptible to impurity.
If they are plated,
they are insusceptible to impurity.
If the double flute has a receptacle for the "wings,"
it is in either case susceptible to impurity.

7 A curved horn is susceptible to impurity,
and a straight one is insusceptible to impurity.

R. Joshua . . . R. Tarfon: Only the mention of a door bolt connects these rules to this mishnah. Otherwise, this is purely Sabbath law. Compare the discussion at *Eruvin* 10:10.

11:5 *"scorpion"*: Bridle bits were made in the shape of a scorpion.

R. Eliezer holds that the cheekpieces constitute together a single device for guiding a horse whether they are connected or not.

the Sages hold that each part of the reins is independent unless they are actually attached to each other.

11:6 *spindle knob*: A round piece of metal placed toward the middle or top of a spindle so that wool wraps around it more easily.

R. Aqiva . . . the Sages . . .: These differ over whether the metal spindle knob has its own name. If it is made of wood and only plated with metal, R. Aqiva agrees that it is not susceptible.

distaff: The rod holding unspun fibers. Spun fibers are collected on the spindle.

"wings": Flute players would put movable round stops in the holes of their flutes. The stops had small wing-like handles on each side of the stop to facilitate changing the scale of the flute.

it is . . . susceptible: Since the groove acts as a receptacle for the "wings" it is susceptible.

11:7 *A curved horn*: A curved horn is susceptible to impurity because it can be a receptacle.

If its narrow end is of metal, it is susceptible to impurity.
[Regarding] its wide end:
R. Tarfon deems it susceptible to impurity,
but the Sages deem it insusceptible to impurity.
And when they are joined together the whole is susceptible to impurity.
So, too, the branches of a candlestick are insusceptible to impurity,
but the cups and the base are susceptible to impurity.
And when they are joined together everything is susceptible to impurity.
8 A helmet is susceptible to impurity,
but the cheekpieces are insusceptible to impurity.
If they have a container that will hold water,
they are susceptible to impurity.
All weapons of war are susceptible to impurity:
the javelin, spear head, and the shinguards and breastplate are susceptible to impurity.
All women's adornments are susceptible to impurity:
the "golden city," necklace, earrings, rings—
rings with a seal or without a seal—
and noserings.
If a necklace has metal beads on a thread of flax or wool
and the thread breaks,
the beads are susceptible to impurity,
since each one is a distinct article.
If it has a thread of metal,
with beads of precious stones, pearls, or glass,
and the beads broke and the thread alone remains—
it is susceptible to impurity.
The remnants of a [metal] necklace [remain susceptible to impurity]
if they encompass a little girl's neck—

If its narrow end is of metal it is susceptible: Like all flat metal articles. The narrow end is the mouthpiece of the horn.

wide end: If made of metal.

the branches of a candlestick are insusceptible to impurity, but the cups and the base are: Despite the principle that a metal object cannot be susceptible unless it has a distinctive name (11:2), the cups and the base of a candlestick, which have no such name, are susceptible because they serve as receptacles.

when they are joined together: The assembled article is now called "a lamp."

11:8 *helmet... cheekpieces*: Helmets are susceptible because they have independent designation. The cheekpieces are subsidiary to the helmet and are insusceptible. If the cheekpieces can be used to drink from, they are susceptible "vessels."

weapons of war... women's adornments: They are made of metal and have independent designations.

the "golden city": A crown-like ornament shaped like Jerusalem.

beads... thread...: If they are metal, they are susceptible.

a little girl's neck: A necklace that fits around a little girl's neck is the smallest measure that would be considered jewelry.

R. Eliezer says:
Even if only a single link [remains, it is susceptible to impurity]
because [one can] hang [even one link] on the neck.

9 If an earring is made with a pot-shaped bottom and a lentil-shaped top
and the pieces come apart—
The pot-shaped piece is susceptible to impurity
because it is an article with a receptacle.
The lentil-shaped piece is independently susceptible to impurity.
The hook [of the earring] is insusceptible to impurity.
If [an earring] made in the shape of a grape cluster falls apart,
it is insusceptible to impurity.

Chapter Twelve

12 A ring worn by people is susceptible to impurity,
but a ring for cattle or for utensils and all other rings are insusceptible to impurity.
The beam of arrows is susceptible to impurity,
but that of prisoners is insusceptible to impurity.
A neck iron is susceptible to impurity.
A chain that has a lock is susceptible to impurity,
but if it is used for tying, it is insusceptible to impurity.
The chain of merchants is susceptible to impurity,
but that of householders is insusceptible to impurity.

11:9 *The lentil-shaped piece is independently susceptible*: It can still be worn as an ornament by itself.

The hook [of the earring] is insusceptible: It does not have independent designation; it is called "the hook of an earring" and not just "a hook."

they are insusceptible: The earring is designed to have the look of a grape cluster. Once the cluster falls apart the individual pieces no longer serve as ornaments.

12:1 *but a ring for cattle or for utensils and all other rings are insusceptible*: "Vessels" are defined by their utility to human beings.

beam of arrows: The metal rod that holds a target in place.

but that of prisoners: A prisoner's foot cuff does not serve a productive function but merely inhibits his movement.

A neck iron is susceptible: The neck iron was put on slaves and prisoners to force them to move. It serves the needs of the masters or wardens.

A chain that has a lock is susceptible: It is clearly a metal article with independent designation and multiple uses, e.g. chaining a door. On the other hand, a lock used *for tying* down an animal was seen as meeting the animal's needs rather than its owner's.

The chain of merchants: A merchant's chain is used to lock his weights and measures to his cart. Since the chain is always attached to these measures it takes on their characteristic as a "vessel."

that of householders: Householders' chains are usually fastened to a wall. As such they are considered "attached to the ground," i.e. immovable, and insusceptible.

R. Yose said:
When?
When it has one link.[67]
But if there were two
or if it had a snail piece tied on its end—
it is susceptible to impurity.

2 The beam of the wool combers' scale is susceptible to impurity
because of the hooks.
That of householders
is susceptible to impurity
if it has hooks.
A porters' hook is insusceptible to impurity,
but peddlers' are susceptible to impurity.
R. Judah says:
A peddlers' front [hook] is susceptible to impurity;
his behind [hook] is insusceptible to impurity.
The hook of a small leather bed[68] is susceptible to impurity,
but that on bed poles is insusceptible to impurity.
That of a box is susceptible to impurity,
but that of a fishtrap is insusceptible to impurity.
That of a table is susceptible to impurity,

[67] Alt. "key." See annotations.

[68] Or "bedframe" or "footstool."

one link: Once there is a second link, the chain can no longer be seen as entirely attached to the wall. The translation "key" (that is, lock) means something similar: once the chain can be detached at either end it is no longer merely adjunct to the wall.

snail piece: An attached hook in the shape of a snail. With such an attachment the chain can simply be lifted off the wall and so cannot be seen as part of the house.

12:2 *wool comber's scale*: The wool comber's scale is made of a plain wooden bar with hooks on the end to weigh the wool. These metal hooks are susceptible to impurity, and they and the bar form a single implement.

householders: Most nonprofessionals' scales do not have hooks. Rather, objects and weights are simply tied to the ends of a rod to be weighed.

porters: The main functional part of a porters' yoke is the wooden bar that allows the porter to carry things.

peddlers: Peddlers are sellers of spices, cosmetics, and the like, and keep their merchandise in small weighing pans that hang from hooks on the peddler's yoke.

R. Judah: The front hook and pan hold the peddler's products. Therefore, the front hook and receptacle serve the basic purpose the peddler has in mind. The rear hook merely provides balance.

small leather bed: Translations vary, as indicated in the footnotes. The Mishnah seems to envision a hammock hanging by hooks from two poles. Since the hooks cause the bed to hang they are a functional part of the bed. The poles of larger beds may have such hooks as well, but they serve only for hangings and the like.

box: i.e. the hook that locks a box. Since the box is susceptible to impurity as a container, so is the hook.

fishtrap: A fishtrap is a box-like trap made of reeds. The netting is held in place by hooks. The trap is not a receptacle because it is not meant to hold the fish permanently.

table: A table is obviously a "utensil" since it serves the needs of human beings. Whatever hooks or hinges hold the table together are susceptible as part of the table.

but that of a wooden lampstand is insusceptible to impurity.
This is the general rule:
Whatever is attached to what is susceptible to impurity is susceptible to impurity, and whatever is attached to what is insusceptible to impurity is insusceptible to impurity.
And they are all insusceptible to impurity by themselves.

3 The metal covering of a householders' basket—
Rabban Gamaliel deems it susceptible to impurity,
and the Sages deem it insusceptible to impurity.
And physicians' [basket covers] are susceptible to impurity.
The door of a householder's cabinet[69] is insusceptible to impurity,
but that of physicians is susceptible to impurity.
Smelters' tongs are susceptible to impurity,
but tongs attached to a vessel are insusceptible to impurity.
The "scorpion" of an olive press is susceptible to impurity,
but a hook in the walls is not susceptible to impurity.

4 The bloodletter's lancet[70] is susceptible to impurity,
but that of a sundial is insusceptible to impurity.
R. Zadok deems it susceptible to impurity.
A weaver's pin is susceptible to impurity,
and [regarding] the ground-bean seller's chest—
R. Zadok deems it susceptible to impurity,

[69] Or "cupboard," lit. "tower" from its shape.

[70] Lit. "nail," here and in "weaver's pin" below.

wooden lampstand: Wooden lampstands were plain wooden staves on which oil lamps were set; they had no receptacle and so were insusceptible to impurity. The hooks may have held the oil lamp's handle.

they are all insusceptible: Hooks unattached to any utensil are never susceptible because they serve no independent function.

12:3 *Rabban Gamaliel*: The metal cover is susceptible because it has a receptacle into which one places metal scrap.

the Sages: The cover is not normally used as a container and also lacks a distinctive name.

physicians: The metal cover of a physician's basket is susceptible because physicians use the cover to make medicated bandages or to display medicines.

cabinet: Since the metal door is subsidiary to the cabinet, itself insusceptible, it too is insusceptible.

Smelters' tongs: These are removable and serve as utensils in their own right. Tongs attached to a vessel or to the wall share the (in)susceptibility of their base.

"scorpion": A scorpion-shaped hook embedded in the olive press that serves to hang parts of the press.

12:4 *lancet…sundial*: A lancet is a freestanding metal tool and therefore susceptible. The point of a sundial is inserted into a stone that is fixed to the ground.

R. Zadok deems it susceptible: Because the point of the sundial is removed from time to time and is the essential part of the sundial. It is therefore a "vessel."

A weaver's pin: This is a piece of metal used to smooth or take knots out of material during the weaving process.

R. Zadok: It has a receptacle that holds the ground beans.

but the Sages deem it insusceptible to impurity.
If its wagon was made of metal,
it is susceptible to impurity.

5 If one fashioned a nail
so that he can open or lock with it—
it is susceptible to impurity.
If it was [only] made as a safeguard—
it is not susceptible to impurity.
If he fashioned a nail
so that he can open a container with it—
R. Aqiva deems it susceptible to impurity,
but the Sages deem it insusceptible to impurity
until it he retempers[71] it.
The nail of a moneychanger is insusceptible to impurity,
but R. Zadok deems it susceptible to impurity.
R. Zadok declared three things susceptible to impurity,
and the Sages declared them insusceptible to impurity:
(1) the nail of a moneychanger,
(2) a ground-bean seller's chest,
(3) and the point of a sundial.
R. Zadok deems them susceptible to impurity,
and the Sages deem them insusceptible to impurity.[72]

6 Rabban Gamaliel deemed four things susceptible to impurity,
and the Sages deemed them insusceptible to impurity:
the metal basket cover of householders,

[71] Or "reforges." [72] Also found in *Eduyot* 3:8.

the Sages: The chest and the wagon it rests on work together. When the chest is not attached to its wagon, it is incomplete and therefore insusceptible.

If its wagon was made of metal: The wagon is clearly a metal utensil.

12:5 *open or lock*: If the nail was fashioned at the outset to function as a key, then it is an article designated to serve a useful purpose and is a "utensil."

a safeguard: One might place a nail on the threshold at a house's doorway so that strangers cannot enter without moving it. (Alternatively, such a nail might simply hold a door shut against wild animals.) Since the nail was not originally fashioned for this purpose it remains insusceptible.

R. Aqiva: If the nail was fashioned to open a container, it is a utensil created to serve a specific purpose and is susceptible.

the Sages: Nails used to open containers had to be stronger than plain nails and required reheating to strengthen them.

nail of a moneychanger: i.e. the nail on which the moneychanger hangs his store's shutters. The nail is insusceptible because it is fixed into an object attached to the ground.

three things: The Sages and R. Zadok differ over articles that are mostly grounded but sometimes moved.

12:6 *the metal basket cover of householders*: See above, 12:3. Rabban Gamaliel held that since it has a receptacle it is a vessel. The Sages hold that because it is a cover and thus subsidiary to the main vessel, it is not a vessel.

the hanger of a massage comb,
unfinished metal vessels,
and an [earthenware] plate broken into two [equal] pieces.
But the Sages agree with Rabban Gamaliel
that if the plate was broken into two pieces,
one large and the other small,
the large one is susceptible to impurity
and the small one is insusceptible to impurity.[73]

7 If a *dinar* became invalid
and one fashioned it to hang around a young girl's neck,
it is susceptible to impurity.
And so, too, if a *sela* became invalid
and one fashioned it for use as a weight,
it is susceptible to impurity.
How defective [can a *sela*] be and one still be allowed to keep it?
So long as [it is still worth] two *dinar*.
Less than this,
he should cut it up.

8 A penknife and a reed for writing and a plummet
and weights and pressing plates and a straight edge and a measuring table

[73] Also found in *Eduyot* 3:9.

the hanger of a massage comb: Rabban Gamaliel considers the chain by which a massage comb hangs a "vessel." The Sages hold that since it is subsidiary to the main vessel, it is not one.

unfinished metal vessels: These are vessels that are complete regarding their basic function but still require polishing or smoothing. Rabban Gamaliel considers such vessel complete since they function as intended. The Sages hold that until all finishing processes are complete they do not qualify as susceptible "vessels."

an [earthenware] plate broken into two [equal] pieces: Rabban Gamaliel still considers this a utensil because a serving plate (*tabla*) still retains its functionality if halved. The Sages hold that since most people consider evenly broken dishes unusable, they are insusceptible. The item in question is made of earthenware and has a rim, unlike other vessels in this part of the tractate.

But the Sages agree with Rabban Gamaliel: If the plate breaks into two clearly uneven pieces, the large piece is susceptible even according to the Sages since it still can function as a serving implement.

12:7 *invalid*: Whether by government decree or worn down by ordinary handling.

to hang around a young girl's neck: In such a case the *dinar* coin becomes jewelry and its status changes to "vessel."

How defective [can a sela] be and one be allowed to keep it? This rule has no bearing on the impurity laws. The rabbis did not permit individuals to keep invalid or defective coins lest they use them to cheat merchants or moneychangers. Cf. *Bava Metsi'a* 4:5.

two dinar: Half of its original value. Even if the *sela* has been modified for use as a weight, it should be destroyed if it is worth less than two *dinar*.

12:8 *pressing plates*: Iron plates placed on beaten olives. A beam is placed on top of this to squeeze out the oil.

straight edge…measuring table: The first is an implement used to draw lines on paper or parchment. The second is the table on which one places the paper or parchment. Certain commentators reverse these translations.

are susceptible to impurity.
And all unfinished wooden utensils are susceptible to impurity
except for those of boxwood.
R. Judah says:
Also an olive branch is insusceptible to impurity
unless it is has been heated.

Chapter Thirteen

13 The sword, knife, dagger, spear, hand sickle, harvest sickle, razor, and barbers' scissors that were divided
are susceptible to impurity.
R. Yose says:
[The part] near the handle is susceptible to impurity,
but that near the point[74] is insusceptible to impurity.
Shears that were divided in two:
R. Judah deems them susceptible to impurity,
but the Sages deem them insusceptible to impurity.
2 If a shovel fork lost its shovel end,
it is susceptible to impurity
because of its pointed end.
If it lost its pointed end,
it is susceptible to impurity
because of its shovel end.
If a kohl stick lost its spoon,

[74] Lit. "head."

unfinished wooden utensils: When wooden utensils have a receptacle, they are susceptible even though more is needed to complete them.

boxwood: Boxwood's bark is very thick. Utensils made from it are never considered complete until the bark is removed.

olive branch: That is, items manufactured from olive wood.

unless it has been heated: The heating was designed to drive out moisture.

13:1 *that were divided are susceptible*: Even half a pair of scissors can be used as a knife.

R. Yose says: One can use the article from the area of its handle. One cannot do this from the implement's sharp end lest he hurt himself.

R. Judah: Since the single part of the shears can still cut, it is a "utensil" susceptible to impurity.

the Sages: The broken shears are insusceptible because they function only with great difficulty.

13:2 *shovel fork*: This tool contained a shovel on one end to remove ashes and a fork on the other to grasp meat or bread from the oven.

kohl stick: This implement had a pointed tip for applying mascara. It also had a spoon-shaped part with which to clean one's ears.

it is susceptible to impurity
because of its point.
If it lost its point,
it is susceptible to impurity
because of its spoon.
If a stylus lost its writing point,
it is susceptible to impurity
because of its eraser.
If it lost its eraser,
it is susceptible to impurity
because of its writing point.
If a soup ladle lost its spoon,
it is susceptible to impurity
because of its fork.
If it lost its fork,
it is susceptible to impurity
because of its spoon.
So too for the prong of a mattock.
The measure of all:
[they must be] sufficient to carry out their function.

3 A plow blade that is damaged
is susceptible to impurity
until it has lost its greater part.
If its socket is broken,
it is insusceptible to impurity.
If a hatchet lost its sharp edge,
it is susceptible to impurity
because of its splitting edge.
If it lost its splitting edge,
it is susceptible to impurity
because of its sharp edge.

writing point…eraser: The point incises letters in wax. The eraser, which was thick and smooth, could tamp down the wax, erasing the letters written in it.

soup ladle…fork: This soup ladle was used for meat soups. The spoon was used to ladle out the soup. The fork was used to grasp the meat.

mattock: A tool for digging. One side is like an ax blade that opens the soil. The prongs on the other side reduce the soil to clods of earth.

The measure of all: How much must be left to remain susceptible to impurity?

13:3 *plow blade…lost its greater part*: Once most of the blade is broken it becomes nonfunctional and is no longer a susceptible "vessel."

If its socket is broken it is insusceptible: A plow blade attaches to the plow by means of a hole cut into it. If this socket is broken, the blade can no longer function. The same can be said of a hatchet head, immediately below.

sharp edge…splitting edge: A hatchet has a sharp cutting edge on one side of its head and an oval hammer head on its other side.

If its socket is broken,
it is insusceptible to impurity.
4 If an ash shovel has lost its blade,
it is susceptible to impurity
because it is like a hammer—
the words of R. Meir.
But the Sages deem it insusceptible to impurity.
A saw that has lost one tooth out of every two
is insusceptible to impurity.
If there remains a full *sit*'s measure in one place,
it is susceptible to impurity.
If an adze, scalpel, plane, or drill is damaged,
it is susceptible to impurity.
If it has lost its cutting edge,
it is insusceptible to impurity.
And if any of them was split in two,
it is susceptible to impurity,
except the drill.
But the [wooden handle of a] plane by itself
is not susceptible to impurity.
5 If a needle has lost its eye or its point,
it is insusceptible to impurity.
If one fashioned it into a stretching pin,[75]
it is susceptible to impurity.
A sackmakers' [needle] whose eye is lost
is susceptible to impurity
because he [can] write with it.
If it loses its point,
it is insusceptible to impurity.

[75] **K, P**: "shuttle." **P**$_2$: "stretching pin" in the body of the text but a marginal emendation to "shuttle."

13:4 *it is like a hammer*: An ash shovel has a metal handle.

R. Meir: One can use this as a hammer. Therefore it is a "vessel."

the Sages: The intended original function defines the character of the "vessel." Since the ash shovel's handle no longer functions as it was originally intended, it is insusceptible.

one tooth out of every two: The loss of this many teeth in a saw makes it unusable.

sit: About two inches. If the saw has a *sit*'s length of contiguous teeth, it remains usable.

If an adze, scalpel, plane, or drill is damaged: All these sharp instruments can still be used if they become dull or the blade is chipped.

except the drill: A split drill cannot make a hole.

The [wooden handle of a] plane: The handle alone is not useful without the blade.

13:5 *stretching pin*: Weavers use stretching pins to prevent woven cloth from wrinkling. A stretching pin only needs to be straight in order to function. It needs neither an eye nor a point.

write with it: A sackmaker's pin is thick enough to make a noticeable mark in wax.

A stretching pin in either case is susceptible to impurity.
If a needle became rusty:
if this hinders sewing,
it is insusceptible to impurity,
if not, it is susceptible to impurity.
If a hook was straightened,
it is insusceptible to impurity;
if one bent it back,
it is susceptible to impurity again.

6 Wood that serves [as a part of] a metal utensil
is susceptible to impurity,
but metal that serves [as a part of] a wooden utensil
is insusceptible to impurity.
How?
A wooden key whose teeth are metal,
even if [there is] only one,
is susceptible to impurity.
A metal key whose teeth are wood
is insusceptible to impurity.
A metal ring whose seal is coral
is susceptible to impurity.
A coral ring whose seal is metal
is insusceptible to impurity.
The tooth in a lock's frame or in a lock or in a key
is susceptible to impurity by itself.

7 Ashkelon grappling irons that have broken
but their hooks remain
are susceptible to impurity.
A pitchfork, a winnowing rake, or [a plain] rake,
and similarly a head comb

13:6 *Wood that serves*: Under normal circumstances flat wood is insusceptible. When used as part of a metal utensil, it becomes intrinsic to that tool and is subject to its rules. The reverse is also true, so wood tools with metal parts are not susceptible to impurity.

teeth: The part of a key that opens a lock is the tooth. As such, it is considered the basic tool. Its handle, whether wood or metal, is subsidiary to it and is susceptible or insusceptible accordingly.

A metal ring: The part of the ring that holds the finger is primary even though the seal has a function.

coral: Like all stone it is insusceptible.

susceptible…by itself: The tooth may be used independently as an immovable bolt or as part of a skeleton key.

13:7 *Ashkelon grappling irons*: This tool with hooks inserted into a wooden handle was used for retrieving items that fell into a well or cistern. The hooks remain susceptible even if part of the handle breaks because they perform the major function of the tool.

A pitch-fork, etc.: All these tools are normally wooden and without space for containing anything, and they are therefore insusceptible. The addition of a functional metal prong makes them a combined wooden and metal tool, and the Sages deem these susceptible.

that lost one of its teeth, and one repaired them using metal:
these are susceptible to impurity.
Concerning all these, R. Joshua said:
The Scribes have invented a new thing,
and I cannot explain it.[76]

8 A flax comb that has lost its teeth
but two are left
is susceptible to impurity.
And if one [remains],
it is insusceptible to impurity.
Each one [of the teeth] by itself is susceptible to impurity.
A wool [comb] that has lost one of every two teeth
is insusceptible to impurity.
If three remain in a single place,
it is susceptible to impurity.
If one of them was the outermost [tooth],
it is not susceptible to impurity.
If two teeth were missing,
and one made them into tweezers,
they are susceptible to impurity.
If one [was missing] and he made it for a lamp
or as a stretching pin,
it is susceptible to impurity.

Chapter Fourteen

14 What is the measure of metal vessels?
A bucket: sufficient to draw water.

[76] Lit. "I do not have anything to respond."

The Scribes: R. Joshua could not understand why repairing a wooden tool with a single metal tooth should make it susceptible. The tool was basically wood without a receptacle. Why would a single metal tooth have changed that status?

13:8 *flax comb*: Such a comb is still functional with two teeth, although not with one.

Each one [of the teeth] by itself is susceptible: Because it can be used as a writing implement on a waxed surface.

wool [comb]: A wool comb is susceptible or insusceptible according to its ability to comb wool properly.

If one of them was the outermost: The last tooth on the comb is broad and cannot comb wool. Hence, even if there are two functional teeth in addition to the end tooth the comb is nonfunctional.

tweezers ... lamp ... stretching pin, it is susceptible: These are all items with a function and are therefore "utensils." The single tooth can be used to extract used wicks from a lamp.

14:1 *measure of metal vessels*: If a metal vessel is broken, what size must the pieces be to remain susceptible to impurity?

A small kettle: sufficient to heat [liquid] in it.
A large kettle: sufficient to hold *sela'im*.
A cauldron: sufficient to hold jugs.
Jugs: sufficient to hold *perutot*.
Wine measures [large enough to measure] wine;
and oil measures [large enough to measure] oil.
R. Eliezer says:
All of them [must be able to hold] *perutot*.[77]
R. Aqiva says:
Any vessel that lacks covering[78]
is susceptible to impurity,
but that which lacks [its final] polishing is insusceptible to impurity.

2 If one made a staff with a chestnut-shaped nail on its top,
it is susceptible to impurity.
If he studded it with nails,
it is susceptible to impurity.
R. Simeon says:
Only if he puts in it three rows.
And any of them that he makes for decorative purposes
are insusceptible to impurity.
If he put a tube on its end—
and similarly in the case of a door—
it is insusceptible to impurity.
But if it was [already used as] a utensil

[77] Lit. "All of them in *perutot*." [78] Or "sealing"; see annotations.

hold sela'im: The hole must be too small for a coin the size of a *sela* to slip through. A similar criterion governs the rest of this list.

R. Aqiva: A container capable of fulfilling its basic function but lacking only its cover is susceptible. Alternatively, the vessel lacks only a final trimming but is already usable.

polishing: The final polishing required the hand of a skilled craftsman, and the vessel was unfinished and therefore unusable before this was done.

14:2 *chestnut-shaped nail*: This type of nail was placed at the end of a wooden staff so that the blow it delivered would be harder than usual. This would also be the purpose of studding the rod with nails (immediately below).

it is susceptible: i.e. the whole assembly, including the staff, which would normally not be susceptible because it is a wooden article without a receptacle.

three rows: R. Simeon holds that a staff cannot deliver a significant blow without being studded with three rows of nails.

decorative purposes: The decorative nails, though metal, are not intended to enhance the rod's effect and may be considered subsidiary to the wooden rod. Since this rod is primarily a wooden article without a receptacle, it remains insusceptible.

tube: The function of the tube was to protect the rod or the bottom of the door from wear. The metal items do not directly affect the function of the rod or the door and as above are subsidiary to them.

[already used as] a utensil: e.g. as a siphon. Attaching the tube to a rod or door is insufficient to change its established status as a "vessel."

and was fastened to it,
it is susceptible to impurity.
When does it become insusceptible to impurity?
The House of Shammai say:
When he damages it.
And the House of Hillel say:
When he fastens it.

3 A builder's crowbar and a carpenter's drill[79] are susceptible to impurity.
Tent pegs and surveyors' pegs are susceptible to impurity.
A surveyor's chain is susceptible to impurity;
one made for logs is insusceptible to impurity.
A large bucket's chain [is susceptible to impurity up to] four handbreadths [from the bucket];
that of a small one up to ten handbreadths.
A blacksmith's "donkey" is susceptible to impurity.
A saw in which one inserted the teeth in their socket is susceptible to impurity,
but if they were inserted upside down, it is insusceptible to impurity.
All covers are insusceptible to impurity except that of a [large] kettle.

4 The [parts] in a wagon susceptible to impurity:
the metal yoke,
and the crossbar,[80]
and the side pieces[81] that receive the straps,
and the iron that is under the neck of the livestock,
the connecting pin,
and the girth,
and the trays,
the bell clapper,
and the hook,
and a nail that holds any of these together.

[79] Or "pick." [80] Or "pin." [81] Lit. "wings," here and in 14:5.

When does it become insusceptible: In what circumstance would a former utensil become insusceptible when attached to a rod or door?

House of Shammai...of Hillel: The former require that the tube be actively made unusable for its previous function. The latter hold that the mere act of attaching it to the rod or door achieves this purpose.

14:3 *made for logs*: That is, for tying logs into bundles.

bucket's chain: Chains longer than the indicated sizes are too unwieldy to serve their function properly.

A blacksmith's "donkey": Commentators vary; perhaps a metal seat connected to an anvil.

saw: The Mishnah presumes that the teeth were made separately and then installed in sockets, properly in the first case but improperly in the second because the saw cannot now be used.

covers: All covers share the name of the utensil they cover, e.g. pot cover, so lack independent designation. Kettle covers are also used independently as trays and are therefore susceptible.

14:4 *[parts]...susceptible*: The listed parts of an ox cart connect either the ox to the cart or parts of the cart to one another. The shared character of all the items is that they are made of metal. Commentators differ as to the precise identity of the some of the items in this list.

5 The [parts] in a wagon insusceptible to impurity:
the plated yoke,
side pieces made as decoration,
and tubes that produce sound,
and the lead [pieces] by the side of the neck of the livestock,
the rim of the wheel,
the sheets and the plating,
and any other nails—
these are insusceptible to impurity.
The metal shoes of livestock are susceptible to impurity,
but those made of cork[82] are insusceptible to impurity.
When is a sword susceptible to impurity?
As soon as one polishes it.
And a knife?
As soon as one sharpens it.
6 If one made a mirror from a metal basket cover:
R. Judah deems it insusceptible to impurity,
but the Sages deem it susceptible to impurity.
If a mirror is broken
and does not reflect the greater part of the face,
it is insusceptible to impurity.
7 Metal utensils can be rendered impure and pure [even] when broken—
the words of R. Eliezer.

[82] Or "bark."

14:5 *insusceptible*: All the items in this list are decorative. Decoration is insusceptible since it is subsidiary to the decorated item.

lead…sheets and the plating: Sheet metal or plating that is installed for decoration.

metal shoes: In emergency situations soldiers used these "shoes" as drinking vessels, so they are susceptible. If they only served animal needs, they would be insusceptible.

cork: Metal cattle shoes could be cleaned sufficiently to be used as drinking vessels, but cork ones could not. Therefore, they served only the needs of animals.

polishes…sharpens: These steps constitute the completion of the items' manufacture.

14:6 *a metal basket cover*: See above, 12:6. The issue is whether a previously insusceptible article can become susceptible when it is remade into another article.

R. Judah: Even if he polished a metal cover till it could reflect, it can still serve as a cover, and covers are insusceptible.

the Sages: The intention to make the basket cover into a mirror changes it from being a "cover" and makes it a "mirror."

If a mirror is broken: If the broken mirror does not reflect the greater part of one's face, it no longer functions as a mirror.

14:7 *can be rendered impure and pure [even] when broken*: According to Torah law, a vessel that breaks becomes pure and cannot become impure again. The context here is corpse impurity.

But R. Joshua says:
They can be made pure only [when] whole.
How so?
If one sprinkled on them
and they were broken the same day
and he repaired them
and sprinkled on them a second time on the same day,
they are pure—
the words of R. Eliezer.
But R. Joshua says:
There is no sprinkling before the third day and the seventh day.

8 If a knee-shaped key is broken at its knee,
it is insusceptible to impurity.
R. Judah deems it susceptible to impurity
since one can still open [the door] from within.
If a *gamma*-shaped [key] was broken off at its bend,
it is insusceptible to impurity.
If [it] had teeth and gaps,
it is susceptible to impurity.
If it lost its teeth,
it is susceptible to impurity
because of the gaps.
If the gaps were blocked up,
it is susceptible to impurity
because of the teeth.
If the teeth were lost
and the gaps were blocked up or
they broke through into one another,
it is insusceptible to impurity.

can be made pure only [when] whole: If broken when impure, the pieces can only be purified when reassembled.

How so? What follows is an unrelated dispute, and certain commentators have deleted this question.

R. Eliezer: A rabbinic enactment requires repeating the purification rites for corpse impurity for a repaired broken vessel, but since the law is of rabbinic origin the repetition need not take the usual seven days (see Numbers 19). The rabbis made this rule in order to remind people to carry out these rites for truly impure vessels.

R. Joshua: The rules here are rabbinic ones, but he demands full reenactment of the purification rites for corpse impurity just the same.

third day...seventh day: See Numbers 19:12, 19.

14:8 Throughout this mishnah the question concerns both susceptibility and the possible purification of an impure implement. Once rendered useless, an impure metal object is restored to purity.

R. Judah: The broken key can work from the inner side of the door, where it can reach that part of the lock's mechanism that opens the door.

If a gamma-shaped [key] was broken off at its bend: This key is in the shape of the Greek letter Γ. If it is broken where it bends, the tooth cannot unlock the lock.

teeth and gaps: Such a key, even if broken, has all the necessary elements to be functional. Even with only teeth or gaps it can be used, though not if it loses both.

A mustard strainer in which three holes merged into one another[83] in its underside
is insusceptible to impurity.
A metal funnel is susceptible to impurity.

Chapter Fifteen

15:1–16:3 *Wood*

15 Utensils of wood, utensils of leather, utensils of bone, or utensils of glass:
their flat surfaces are insusceptible to impurity,
but their receptacles are susceptible to impurity.[84]
If they are broken they have become pure.
If one remade them into utensils,
they [can] become impure from then on.[85]
A chest, and a box, and a cabinet, and a straw basket, and a reed basket, and the tank of an Alexandrian ship
that have bottoms
and that hold forty *se'ah* of liquid,
which is equivalent to two *kor* of dry goods,
are not susceptible to impurity.
All other vessels,
whether they hold [that much] or not,
are susceptible to impurity—
the words of R. Meir.
But R. Judah says:
The tub of a wagon, and kings' provision chests, and a tanner's trough,
and the tank of a small ship, and a coffin,[86]

[83] **P**$_2$: "three holes merged side by side." [84] See 2:1.
[85] The beginning of this paragraph is repeated from 2:1 above. [86] Or "chest."

strainer: A mustard-seed strainer's function is to separate extremely fine foreign material from the tiny mustard seeds. If several holes in the strainer become one large hole, the mustard seeds will fall through and the strainer becomes nonfunctional.

funnel: The funnel's purpose is to allow grain to flow through it into the mill. The hole is necessary for its function, and therefore it is susceptible, even though it has no receptacle.

15:1 *chest...Alexandrian ship*: All the items in this list are made of wood. Although they function as containers, they are so large that whether empty or full they cannot be moved. Portability is required for an item to be considered a "vessel."

forty se'ah: Recent traditional scholars have put this amount between 87 and 151 gallons. Academic scholars have estimated a slightly lower amount: 7.3 liters per *se'ah*, or about 77 gallons for forty.

two kor: About seven bushels.

R. Meir: Vessels other than those listed are made to be moved even if it takes many people to do so. The ones listed are meant to remain in their places.

even if they hold [forty *se'ah*],
are susceptible to impurity
since they are made to be moved with their contents.
All other vessels that hold [forty *se'ah*]
are insusceptible to impurity,
and those that do not hold [that amount]
are susceptible to impurity.
There is no difference between the words of R. Meir and R. Judah
except [regarding] the householder's baking trough.

2 Bakers' baking boards[87] are susceptible to impurity,
but those of householders are insusceptible to impurity.
If one colored them red or saffron,
they are susceptible to impurity.
A baker's shelf that is fixed to the wall:
R. Eliezer deems [it] insusceptible to impurity,
but the Sages deem [it] susceptible to impurity.
The baker's stand[88] is susceptible to impurity,
but that of householders is insusceptible to impurity.
If it is shut in [by a frame] on all four sides,
it is susceptible to impurity,
but if one side is open,
it is insusceptible to impurity.
R. Simeon says:
If one arranged it so that he could cut on it,
it is susceptible to impurity.
So, too, a rolling pin[89] is susceptible to impurity.

[87] Translation reflects the manuscripts; the printed text is uncertain. See also *Eduyot* 7:7.
[88] Or "frame." [89] Or "counter."

There is no difference: R. Meir lists all the wooden vessels he considers insusceptible. We may infer that all others are susceptible including a householder's trough. R. Judah lists those wooden vessels he considers susceptible, implying that all others are insusceptible including a householder's trough.

15:2 *Bakers' baking boards*: These are flat wooden boards on which the baker places loaves for baking. Since professional bakers use them as tools of their trade, they are considered "vessels" even though they do not have receptacles.

householders: Nonprofessional bakers use these boards only occasionally and sometimes for other purposes than baking. If, however, they have been painted it is a sign that they have been set aside as utensils.

baker's shelf: This shelf is made of metal. If it were made of wood it would be insusceptible. See above, 11:2 and below, 20:4.

baker's stand: For a professional baker this functions as a table and is therefore susceptible.

If it is shut in [by a frame]: The stand now offers a receptacle created by the frame. If one side remains open it is insusceptible because the receptacle is incomplete.

R. Simeon: If the nonprofessional baker consciously designated a stand as a cutting board then he has declared it a utensil and made it susceptible.

rolling pin: This was also used as a handle to place the rolled dough into the oven, so it is a "receptacle" of sorts.

3 The large bowl[90] of flour sellers
is susceptible to impurity,
but that of householders
is insusceptible to impurity.
R. Judah says:
Also that of hairdressers
is susceptible to seat impurity
since girls sit in it to have their hair dressed.

4 All hangers are susceptible to impurity
except for the hanger of a householder's sieve or sifter—
the words of R. Meir.
But the Sages say:
All of them are insusceptible to impurity
except the hanger for flour dealers' sieves,
and the hanger of a threshing floor sifter,
and the hanger of a hand sickle,
and the hanger of the tax collector's staff,
since they are helpful at worktime.
This is the general rule:
That made to be useful at worktime
is susceptible to impurity,
but that made [only] as a hanger,
is insusceptible to impurity.

5 The shovel of grist dealers is susceptible to impurity,
but that of storehouses is insusceptible to impurity.
That of winepresses is susceptible to impurity,
but that of threshing floors is insusceptible to impurity.
This is the general rule:
That made to hold anything is susceptible to impurity,
but [that made] for gathering is insusceptible to impurity.

[90] Lit. "sea."

15:3 *The large bowl*: These bowls collect fine flour that falls into them from the sieve. The flour seller collects the flour, so the entire bowl is a "utensil."

householders: Householders generally do not bother to collect the coarse flour they produce except from the bowl's flat floor.

seat impurity: *Zavim* and *zavot* render impure objects that they have used as seats (see Leviticus 15:4). A hairdresser's customers would sit in large bowl-like seats in order that their hair should not get all over the floor. Since one can never be sure which of these customers is impure, these bowls are susceptible to seat impurity. Commentators differ as to whether these bowl seats resemble the bowls of flour merchants; such bowls possibly served a double purpose.

15:4 *hangers*: These are not modern clothes hangers but loops or handles attached to various instruments so they can be hung up when not in use. The question here is whether they facilitate use of the instrument in some other way besides hanging.

15:5 Certain of the implements listed here are used to carry produce from place to place (e.g. into the mill). Others serve only to push material into smaller piles and are not considered "receptacles" at all.

6 The harps used for [nonsacred] singing are susceptible to impurity,
but the Levites' harps are insusceptible to impurity.
All liquids are susceptible to impurity,
but the liquid in the [Temple's] slaughterhouse is insusceptible to impurity.
All [scriptural] scrolls render the hands impure
except the scroll used in the Temple Court.
The *markof* is insusceptible to impurity.
The lute, the *niqtimon*, and the drum are susceptible to impurity.
R. Judah says:
The drum is susceptible to impurity to seat impurity
since a wailing woman sits thereon.
A weasel trap is susceptible to impurity,
but a mousetrap is insusceptible to impurity.

Chapter Sixteen

16 Any utensil of wood is pure
after it is broken into two pieces,
except a folding table,
a partitioned dish,
and a householder's footstool.
R. Judah says:
Also a large bowl and a Babylonian tray are like those.
When do utensils of wood become susceptible to impurity?
A bed and a cot after one has rubbed them with fishskin.

15:6 *harps*: Secular singers' instruments were like the contemporary *oud*. The musician used the rounded part behind the strings to collect and hold money given for the entertainment. Thus, the instrument was used as a receptacle. The Levites did not collect money for their work; alternatively, Temple implements were exempted from susceptibility to impurity.

liquids: Tradition alone made water and blood in the Temple's slaughterhouse insusceptible; see *Eduyot* 8.4.

scrolls: Rabbinic law enacted that handling sacred scrolls renders one's hands impure; see *Yadayim* 3:5. The Temple Court's scroll was exempted from this law.

markof: A wooden horse used by clowns; alternatively a musical instrument that had no interior. The instruments listed as susceptible either had receptacles or (in the case of the drum) might be used as seats.

niqtimon: Apparently a kind of drum, but see *Shabbat* 6:8, where a similar word refers to a prosthetic limb.

A weasel trap: Weasels were trapped for their skins. The traps were either cages or baskets that had a receptacle to hold them. The purpose of a mouse trap was to kill the mouse. Only a flat piece of wood and a killing mechanism was required for it to function.

16:1 *Any utensil of wood is pure*: That is, if pure it becomes insusceptible, and if impure it becomes pure. This rule applies to all broken articles that cannot fulfill their functions.

except a folding table, etc.: The listed articles are meant to be taken apart and put back together.

rubbed them with fishskin: Dried fish skin served as a form of sandpaper for removing splinters and making the wood usable.

If he decided not to rub them,
they are susceptible to impurity.
R. Meir says:
A bed after one has woven three rows.

2 Wooden baskets [become susceptible to impurity] after one closes and trims,
but palm-branch [baskets],
even if he has not trimmed on the inside,
are susceptible to impurity,
because one keeps them thus.
A basket[91] [is susceptible to impurity when] one has closed and trimmed
and finished its hanger.
A case for flasks or for cups,
even if one has not trimmed on the inside,
is susceptible to impurity
because one keeps them thus.

3 Small food baskets[92] and vase-shaped baskets [become susceptible to impurity]
after one closes and trims [them].
Large food baskets and large hampers—
after one makes two rows along their width.
The interior[93] of a sifter or sieve and the cup of a scale—
after one makes one row along their width.
A willow basket—
after one makes two circles around its width,
and a rush basket—
after one makes one circle [around its width].

[91] The word here is different from the one above. See annotations.

[92] The precise identity of many items in this mishnah and the next is uncertain. Commentators differ widely.

[93] Lit. "sea."

If he decided: An intentional decision to use the bed without sanding it is as good as completing it.

R. Meir says: Commentators vary. According to some, R. Meir holds that even if the bed or cot frame has been smoothed down, it is not complete until ropes that support the mattress are installed. Others claim that in R. Meir's view the installation of support ropes is sufficient to make the bed usable, even if the maker intends to smooth down the frame but has not done so yet.

16:2 *Wooden baskets...palm-branch [baskets]*: Wooden baskets lacking smoothing inside cannot be handled without leaving splinters. Palm-branch baskets can and are used without trimming.

A basket...hanger: As indicated in the n. 91, a different word for *basket* is used here, and commentators differ as to what the difference indicates. Certain baskets typically had a reed rope attached in order to hang them, and so were only complete when the hanger was added.

16:3 *closes and trims*: The rims.

two rows: When baskets are woven, reeds are placed vertically in the base and other reeds are woven through them in a circle. When two such rows have been completed, the basket has a receptacle.

one row: One row woven on to these articles' foundations creates a receptacle.

16:4–8 *Leather*

4 When do leather articles become susceptible to impurity?
A shepherd's bag—
after one closes and trims and makes its folds.
R. Judah says:
After one makes its handles.
An apron—
when one closes and trims and makes its fringe.
R. Judah says:
After one makes its rings.
A mat—
after one closes and trims.
R. Judah says:
After one makes its folds.
A leather cushion or mattress—
after one closes and trims.
R. Judah says:
After one sews them up and leaves less than five handbreadths.
5 A fig basket is susceptible to impurity,
but a storage basket is insusceptible to impurity.
Baskets made of leaves are insusceptible to impurity,
but those made of twigs are susceptible to impurity.
Wrapping into which one can put [an item]
or from which he can take out
is susceptible to impurity.
If he cannot [do this] without tearing it or unbinding it,
it is insusceptible to impurity.

16:4 *folds*: These are small folds with holes. A thong is placed in the holes to form a drawstring, so that when one pulls it the bag closes.

handles: Lit. "ears." These are flaps on two side of the bag. R. Judah considers the bag finished once it has flaps that can loosely close the bag or easily open it.

fringe: The strings by which the apron can be tied.

rings: The rings were sewn on the apron's edge and the apron strings were tied through them, closing the apron around the tanner's body.

sews them up: This step normally preceded the "closing and trimming" of the final product.

16:5 *a storage basket is insusceptible*: It is too heavy to move.

Baskets made of leaves: Susceptibility depends on permanence. Baskets made of leaves are impermanent.

Wrapping: The wrapping protected one's hands from becoming soiled by sticky fruit. The permanency or lack thereof of the wrapping determines susceptibility.

6 The glove of winnowers, travelers, or flax workers is susceptible to impurity,
but that of dyers or blacksmiths is insusceptible to impurity.
R. Yose says:
Also ground-bean dealers' gloves are of this kind.
This is the general rule:
What is made to contain is susceptible to impurity,
because of perspiration is insusceptible to impurity.

7 The bag of a bullock and its muzzle, a bees' shelf, and a fan
are insusceptible to impurity.
The cover of a box is susceptible to impurity.
The cover of a clothes chest is insusceptible to impurity.
The cover of a chest, the cover of a basket, and a carpenter's vise,
and the cushion under a chest and its arched cover,
and a book stand, a bolt socket, a lock socket, and a *mezuzah* case,
and a harp case and a lyre case,
and a turbanmaker's form, and a singer's *markof*, and a wailing women's clapper,
and a poor man's parasol, and bed struts, and a phylactery mold,
and a clothesmaker's form—
[all] these are insusceptible to impurity.
R. Yose stated this general rule:
Anything subsidiary to items that serve a person,

16:6 *The glove of winnowers*, etc.: All these gloves, made of leather, help the wearer to grasp something more effectively.

that of dyers or blacksmiths: Their function is to protect their hands or the product they are handling from sweat. Since their only function is protection or absorption, they are not considered "vessels."

R. Yose: Ground-bean dealers' gloves only protect the ground beans from the dealer's sweat and so are insusceptible.

16:7 *bag of a bullock*: A bag tied to a field animal to catch its dung. The first three items on this list are insusceptible because they serve animals rather than human beings.

bees' shelf: A board on which one sets a fire in order to chase bees away from their hive when harvesting honeycombs.

The cover of a box: The cover of a jewelry box is susceptible because women remove jewelry from the main box and place it in the box cover. It is therefore a receptacle. The cover of a clothes chest cannot serve this function.

The cover of a chest, etc.: In general the items in this long list are insusceptible because they are not directly usable but serve to enhance or facilitate the use of something else.

the cushion under a chest, etc.: The leather cushion protects the chest from wetness beneath.

markof: See above, 15:6. In this case, a base for an instrument.

parasol: An inverted parasol might serve as a receptacle, but this unlikely possibility is disregarded.

phylactery mold: The form used to shape the leather boxes or *tefillin*, usually called phylacteries, that are tied to the arm and head. Each box contains four scriptural passages written on parchment. See Exodus 13:9, 13:16, Deuteronomy 6:8, 11:19.

R. Yose stated this general rule: This rule relates to all wooden or leather items used in a subsidiary way with other articles.

whether during his work or not during his work,
is susceptible to impurity.
Anything [that serves] a person only during his work
is insusceptible to impurity.

8 The case[94] of a sword, or of a knife, or of a dagger,
the case of a bent blade, or scissors, or a razor,
or the case of a kohl stick, or a packet of kohl, or the case of a stylus,
or a multipartitioned box,[95] a case for a table and for a mat,
a quiver, and a javelin holder—
[all] these are susceptible to impurity.
[Regarding] a double flute's case—
when one puts it in from above, it is susceptible to impurity.
from its side, it is insusceptible to impurity.
A pipes' case—
R. Judah deems it insusceptible to impurity,
since one puts it in from the side.
The cover of a club, a bow, or a spear—
these are insusceptible to impurity.
This is the general rule:
What is made as a case is susceptible to impurity,
as a cover is insusceptible to impurity.

Chapter Seventeen

17:1–4 *The Measure of Damage Required for Insusceptibility*

17 All householders' vessels—
their measure is in pomegranates.

[94] That is "sheath."

[95] Or "[the case of a] compass," or "[…of a] writing fork."

16:8 *The case of a sword*, etc.: The listed items serve as receptacles.

table: That is, an astrological/astronomical table.

mat: This was the meaning of the word in 16:4. Alternatively, the word here designates wooden tables while the previous word designates metal tables.

puts it in: That is, the flute or (in the next case) the pipes.

When one puts it in from above, etc.: If one puts the instrument into the case from above, it indicates that the case's interior receptacle is being used. If one puts the instrument into the side of the case, then the case is being used as a cover.

17:1 *their measure is in pomegranates*: The vessel remains susceptible or impure as long as the hole is too small for a pomegranate to fall through. Householders deem usable "vessels" that are slightly broken. Therefore, the measurements for them to become insusceptible must be substantial.

R. Eliezer says:
[Their measure depends] on what they are.
Gardeners' baskets—
their measure is in bundles of vegetables.
Householders' baskets—
in straw.
Bathkeepers' baskets—
in shavings.
R. Joshua says:
All of them in pomegranates.

2 A waterskin—
its measure is coils of warp thread.
If it cannot hold warp thread,
but[96] it can hold woof thread,
it is susceptible to impurity.
A dish holder that cannot hold dishes
but can hold trays
is susceptible to impurity.
A chamber pot that cannot hold liquids
but can hold excrement
is susceptible to impurity.
Rabban Gamaliel deems [these] insusceptible to impurity,
since one does not keep it.

3 Breadbaskets—
their measure is bread loaves.
A papyrus lattice
for which one wove in reeds from bottom to top to strengthen it

[96] Lit. "even though" here and in the next two instances. See annotations.

R. Eliezer: The measure of damage for insusceptibility in all cases depends on the item's ordinary use. The text provides three examples.

shavings: Bathhouse keepers used wood shavings, twigs, and leaves, as starter for heating the bathhouse. These were brought to the bathhouse in baskets.

R. Joshua: It is not clear whether his view simply repeats the first, anonymous view or whether he deems vessels of every kind to become insusceptible only when their damage is the measure of a pomegranate.

17:2 *warp thread…woof thread*: In weaving, the warp consists of threads arranged vertically on the loom. The woof is passed through the warp horizontally to form the woven work. Warp thread is thinner than woof thread.

But it can hold: Here and in the next clauses the text as it stands is incoherent. The translation reflects the most widespread commentators' interpretation.

Rabban Gamaliel: People generally dispose of such articles, and the intention not to use them is sufficient to make them insusceptible.

17:3 *papyrus lattice*: For hanging vines, etc. Papyrus is so weak that it will tear when used even when strengthened with other materials.

is insusceptible to impurity.
If he made any frames[97] at all for it,
it is susceptible to impurity.
R. Simeon says:
If it cannot be moved by its frames,
it is insusceptible to impurity.
4 The pomegranates of which they spoke
are three connected to one another.
Rabban Simeon b. Gamaliel says:
A sifter or sieve—
enough that one takes it and walks [and holds pomegranates].
A large basket—
enough that one throws it behind his back [and holds pomegranates].
All other vessels that cannot hold pomegranates,
such as the quarter-*qav* and the eighth-*qav* and small baskets,
their measure is the majority [of the vessel]—
the words of R. Meir.
R. Simeon says:
In olives.
If they crack,
their measure is in olives.
If they are chipped,
their measure is the smallest amount.

17:5–12 *Measurements Frequently Used in Halakhic Discourse*

5 The pomegranate of which they have spoken
is neither big nor little,
but of middle size.
And why were the pomegranates of Baddan mentioned?
In order that they consecrate in any amount—

[97] Alt. "handles."

frames: If one creates even light frames for its sides and bottom that will allow it to hold some article, then it becomes a susceptible receptacle.

R. Simeon: If the structure is still too fragile to be moved, it remains insusceptible.

17:4 *three connected one to another*: Commentators differ. The simplest explanation is that the hole must be sufficiently large to allow a pomegranate to fall through even though it is still connected to two others.

Rabban Simeon b. Gamaliel: Even though a pomegranate might not fall through the sieve or basket at rest, if it does so when jostled by movement the vessel is insusceptible.

17:5 *pomegranates of Baddan*: Baddan was a town in Samaria.

consecrate in any amount: One may not benefit from the first three years' growth (*orlah*) of fruit from certain trees (Leviticus 12:23; see tractate *Orlah* in general and *Orlah* 3:7 with particular connection to the mishnah here). In R. Meir's view, if *orlah* fruit is mixed with other fruits and Baddan pomegranates are in the mix, the entire quantity is forbidden ("consecrated"); the proportion of *orlah* fruit with the others is of no consequence.

the words of R. Meir.
R. Yohanan b. Nuri says:
To measure [breaches in] vessels with them.
R. Aqiva says:
They were mentioned for both reasons:
to measure vessels
and to consecrate in any amount.
R. Yose said:
Pomegranates of Baddan and leeks of Geva were mentioned
only [to teach] that they require certain tithing everywhere.
6 The measure of an egg of which they have spoken
is neither big nor little,
but of middle size.
R. Judah says:
One brings the biggest of the big and the littlest of the little
and puts them in water
and divides the water.
R. Yose said:
But who can inform me which is the biggest and which the littlest?
Rather, everything is according to the judgment of the observer.
7 The measure of a dried fig of which they have spoken
is neither big nor little,
but of middle size.
R. Judah says:
The biggest[98] in the Land of Israel
is of middle size in [other] lands.
8 The measure of an olive of which they have spoken
is neither big nor little,
but of middle size.
This is an *egori* [olive].
The measure of a barley kernel of which they have spoken

[98] Alt. "smallest." See annotations.

R. Yose: Those who buy these agricultural products must tithe them because those who sell them never do. The obligation to tithe is certain. The Mishnah discusses doubtful or uncertain obligation to tithe in tractate *Demai*.

17:6 *The measure of an egg*: The size of an egg is often used as a halakhic measure of volume.

divides the water: One takes half the combined displacement measure of a big and a little egg and considers that to be the displacement of a middle-sized egg.

R. Yose: Big and little are subjective measures.

17:7 *biggest*: It is not clear whether R. Judah's comment is meant to have halakhic consequence. The alternative reading "littlest" is not supported in the manuscripts but has been proposed by numerous later commentators because it appears to make more sense.

17:8 *egori*: Commentators differ: this may be a place name, or it may refer to some feature of a particular kind of olive.

is neither big nor little,
but of middle size.
This is desert barley.
The measure of a lentil of which they have spoken
is neither big nor little,
but of middle size.
This is an Egyptian [lentil].
All movables transmit impurity
via an ox goad's thickness—
neither big nor little,
but of middle size.
Which is middle-sized?
Any whose circumference is a handbreadth.

9 The cubit of which they have spoken
is a middle-sized cubit.
There were two cubits in Shushan the Capital,
one at the northeastern corner
and one at the southeastern corner.
The one at the northeastern corner was longer than that of Moses
by half a fingerbreadth.
The one at the southeastern corner was longer than it
by half a fingerbreadth:
thus it was longer than that of Moses
by one fingerbreadth.
And why did they say "one large and one small"?
Only that the craftsmen take according to the small one
and return according to the large one,
in order that they not come to sacrilege.

10 R. Meir says:
All the cubit measures were middle-sized

desert barley: That is, wild barley.

All movables convey impurity: Tent impurity.

an ox goad's thickness: If a movable object is as thick as an ox goad, and part of it is above a corpse, then everything else underneath it becomes impure.

17:9 *Shushan the Capital*: See *Middot* 1:3.

that of Moses: The cubit Moses used in his time for the building of the desert Tabernacle. According to tradition its measure was six handbreadths.

according to the small one…according to the large one: Workers detailed to the Temple's maintenance were supplied with material according to the small cubit measure. When they returned their finished product, they measured it according to the larger cubit measure. The point was to avoid suspicion of *sacrilege* by profiting from Temple property.

17:10 *All the cubit measures*: In the Temple. The indicated exceptions were built to a smaller cubit of five handbreadths.

except those of the Golden Altar, the [Altar's] horn, the Circuit, and the [Sacrificial Altar's] Base.
R. Judah says:
The cubit used for the [Temple] building was six handbreadths
and that for the utensils five.

11 And there are [times when] they spoke of a small measure—
liquid and dry measures follow the Italian [measure],
which is the desert [measure].
And there are [other contexts] 'in which' they say
everything is according to the person as he is—
one who grasps a handful of the grain offering,
and one who takes a handful of incense,
and one who drinks a cheekful of liquid on the Day of Atonement,
and [one who sets aside] food for two meals for an *eruv*.
[This means] his food for weekdays and not for the Sabbath—
the words of R. Meir.
R. Judah says:
For the Sabbath and not for weekdays.
Both intend to be lenient.
R. Simeon says:
[Two meals consist] of two-thirds of a loaf
[when] three [loaves are made from] a *qav*.
R. Yohanan b. Beroqa says:
One loaf worth a *pondion*
[when wheat costs] one *sela* for four *se'ah.*

12 And there are [times when] they have spoken of a large measure—
a ladleful of decayed corpse is according to the size of a physician's large ladle,
and the split bean of *tsara'at* is according to the Cilician bean.
One who eats on the Day of Atonement [is culpable for eating] a large date's bulk, its meat[99] and its pit;

[99] Lit. "by itself".

[Altar's] *horn*: At each corner of the Sacrificial Altar there was a protrusion (see Exodus 27:2, *Middot* 3:1.)

Circuit: This was a walkway around the Sacrificial Altar.

17:11 *desert [measure]*: The measure used by Moses in the wilderness.

one who grasps a handful of the grain offering, etc.: All these activities are measured according to the size of the one who performs the act.

eruv: See *Eruvin* 8:2.

Both intend to be lenient: R. Meir held that since one ate smaller meals on weekdays, it was lenient to require two weekday meals for an *eruv*. R. Judah held that on the Sabbath people would eat less at each meal knowing there were three Sabbath meals to be eaten.

qav: Each loaf would be about one pound if they were equal in size.

one loaf worth a pondion: Somewhat less than R. Simeon's "two weekday meals."

17:12 *a ladleful of decayed corpse*: This is the amount that causes corpse impurity (*Oholot* 2:1).

tsara'at: The minimum size for a spot on the skin to be impure as *tsara'at*. See *Nega'im* 1:5; 6:1.

One who eats on the Day of Atonement: See *Yoma* 8:2.

wine and oil flasks are measured according to their large stopper.
A window not made by human hands
is measured by the size of a large fist;
that is the fist of Ben Batiah.
R. Yose said:
That is the size of a large person's head.
[And if it was] made by human hands,
it is measured according to the size of [a hole made by] the large drill
of a Temple chamber,
which is the size of an Italian *pondion* or a Neronian *sela*,
or like the size of a hole in a yoke.

17:13–14 *Susceptibility of Items from the Sea or Land*

13 Everything in the sea is insusceptible to impurity
except the sea dog,
since it seeks refuge on dry land—
the words of R. Aqiva.
If one makes utensils from what grows in the sea
and has attached to them that which grows on land—
even a thread,
even a cord,
something that contracts impurity,
[the resulting item] is susceptible to impurity.
14 And there is susceptibility in what was created on the First Day.
There is no susceptibility in [what was created on] the Second Day.
There is susceptibility in [what was created on] the Third Day.
There is no susceptibility in [what was created] on the Fourth and on the Fifth Day

window not made by human hands: For example, a hole that water or animals formed in a wall connecting two rooms. If this hole meets the minimum size, then it connects two rooms for Tent impurity.

fist of Ben Batiah: If the hole described above is the size of a huge fist like that of the giant Ben Batiah, it will transfer corpse impurity from one space to another.

made by human hands: Human acts are intentional. Hence, if one intentionally created a window smaller than a fist, it was made that way on purpose and transfers corpse impurity from one domain to another.

the large drill of a Temple chamber: See *Oholot* 2:3.

Italian pondion…Neronian sela: Two types of Roman coin.

17:13 *except the sea dog*: That is, something made from this creature's bones or skin would be susceptible.

17:14 *on the First Day*: Land was created on the first day, and earthenware vessels are susceptible.

Second Day: The sky.

Third Day: Plants. Wooden vessels are susceptible.

Fourth Day: Sun, moon, stars.

Fifth Day: Fish and birds.

except the wing of the vulture[100] and the plated egg of an ostrich.
R. Yohanan b. Nuri said:
How does the wing of the vulture differ from all other wings?
And everything that was created on the Sixth Day is susceptible to impurity.

17:15–17 *Receptacles and Susceptibility*

15 If one makes a receptacle of any sort,
it is susceptible to impurity.
If one made any sort of [article usable for] lying or sitting,
it is susceptible to impurity.
If one made a purse of untanned hide or of paper,
it is susceptible to impurity.
A pomegranate, acorn, or nut
that children hollowed out
to measure dust,
or which they made into a scale,
is susceptible to impurity,
for they have [the legal ability to] act,[101]
but not intention.
16 A beam of a scale or a level
that has a receptacle for metal,
or a carrying yoke
that has in it a receptacle for money,
or a poor man's cane
that has a receptacle for water,
or a stick
that has a receptacle for a *mezuzah* or for pearls—
these are susceptible to impurity.
And of all these Rabban Yohanan b. Zakkai said:
Woe is me if I speak,
and woe is me if I do not speak.

[100] The precise species is uncertain.

[101] Lit. "they have action."

the wing of the vulture: Vultures' feathers are thick and look like bone. To prevent people from thinking that bone is insusceptible, the rabbis declared vulture wings susceptible.

and the plated egg of an ostrich: Though eggshell is insusceptible, a plated ostrich egg looks like a metal vessel.

R. Yohanan b. Nuri: In his view there is no significant difference between one kind of bird feather and another.

Sixth Day: Animals. Leather and bone vessels are susceptible.

17:15 *for they have [the legal ability to] act*: Since they have no legal capacity, they cannot form an intention that generates susceptibility, but their actions can. This principle also appears at *Tohorot* 8:6 and *Makhshirin* 3:8. See also below, 25:9.

17:16 *A beam of a scale*, etc.: All these receptacles are concealed and are used in order to defraud. For example, a scale's secret compartment has metal in it and gives unfair weight. A cane with pearls in it helps in smuggling.

And of all these Rabban Yohanan b. Zakkai said: If I speak of these cases, those inclined to deceive will learn how to do so. If I fail to speak of them, the tricksters will assume that the Sages are naive and will do worse.

17 The base of a goldsmith's anvil is susceptible to impurity,
but that of a blacksmith is insusceptible to impurity.
A whetstone that has a receptacle for oil
is susceptible to impurity;
if it does not,
it is insusceptible to impurity.
A writing tablet that has a receptacle for wax
is susceptible to impurity;
if it does not,
it is insusceptible to impurity.
A mat of straw or a tube of straw—
R. Aqiva deems [them] susceptible to impurity.
R. Yohanan b. Nuri deems [them] insusceptible to impurity.
R. Simeon says:
And so too for similar items made of gourd.
Matting of reed or of rushes is insusceptible to impurity.
A reed tube that one cut in order to hold anything
is insusceptible to impurity until he takes out all the pith.

Chapter Eighteen

18.1–2 *Determining the Proper Measurement for Susceptibility*

18 A chest:
the House of Shammai say:
It is measured from inside.
And the House of Hillel say:
It is measured from outside.
They agree that the thickness of the legs and the thickness of the trimming
is not measured.

17:17 *The base of a goldsmith's anvil*: Such an anvil has a receptacle in its base for catching excess pieces of precious metal. This is not so with a blacksmith's anvil.

R. Aqiva…R. Yohanan b. Nuri: R. Aqiva holds these mats are durable, even if only for a short time. R. Yohanan b. Nuri holds their durability is so short that they cannot be considered "vessels."

Matting of reed or of rushes is insusceptible: If used for purposes other than a place to sit or lie.

all the pith: If one intends to use the reed as a receptacle, all of its interior fiber must be removed.

18:1 *A chest*: A chest that can contain forty *se'ah* of liquid is insusceptible (see 15:1 above).

The House of Shammai: The House of Hillel include the wall's thickness in the measurement. This allows for smaller chests to be insusceptible.

R. Yose says:
They agree that the thickness of the legs and of the trimming
is measured,
but the space between them
is not measured.
R. Simeon of Shezur says:
If the legs were a handbreadth high
the space between them is not measured;
but if not
the space between them is measured.

2 If its carriage[102] can be removed,
it is not a connective,
nor is it measured with it,
nor does it afford protection with it in a corpse's Tent,
and one may not pull it on the Sabbath if there is money in it.
But if it cannot be removed,
it is a connective,
and it is measured with it,
and it affords protection with it in a corpse's Tent,
and one may pull it on the Sabbath even if there is money in it.
If its arched cover is affixed,
it is a connective
and it is measured with it.
If it is not affixed,
it is not a connective
and it is not measured with it.

[102] Lit. "mechanism."

R. Yose: The dispute between the Houses is over whether the space between the chest's legs counts in the measure. According to *R. Simeon Shezur*, legs shorter than a handbreadth are treated as extending the chest down to the ground, so that *the space between* the legs is included in the measure.

18:2 *carriage*: Either the wheels or the base on which the chest rests.

connective: A separable carriage does not share impurity with the chest because it is viewed as an independent "vessel."

nor is it measured with it: When measuring the chest to determine whether it contains forty *se'ah*, the carriage does not count in the measurement.

afford protection: Even if the chest is a "tightly sealed vessel" that protects from corpse impurity in a Tent, a removable carriage cannot similarly protect.

money in it: Since the carriage is separable from the chest it is considered the money's sole container. Money cannot be handled on the Sabbath.

But if it cannot be removed: If the carriage is an intrinsic part of the chest, then it and the chest are a single entity.

even if there is money in it: Since the carriage and chest form a unit, the money in the carriage is viewed as being mixed together with objects in the chest that may be transported on the Sabbath and may be transported.

How is it measured?
[In] oxhead [fashion].
R. Judah says:
If it cannot stand by itself,
it is insusceptible to impurity.

18:3–9 *Dismantled and Repaired Items*

3 A chest, a box, or a cabinet that has lost one of its legs,[103]
even if it can still contain [items],
is insusceptible to impurity
since it cannot contain in its usual fashion.
R. Yose deems it susceptible to impurity.
Bed poles, the bed base,[104] and [the bed's] decoration
are insusceptible to impurity.
Only the bed [itself] and the frame
are susceptible to impurity.
But frames [used by] the Levites
are insusceptible to impurity.
4 If a bedframe is set up on props,
R. Meir and R. Judah deem it susceptible to impurity,
but R. Yose and R. Simeon deem it insusceptible to impurity.
R. Yose said:
How does this differ from frames [used by] the Levites,
for the Levites' frames are insusceptible to impurity?

[103] Lit. "from which one of its legs was removed."

[104] Lit. "donkey."

oxhead [fashion]: An isosceles triangle is superimposed on the arch. Whatever falls within the triangle's walls is considered part of the chest. If sufficient it can bring the chest's volume to forty *se'ah*.

R. Judah: A chest less than forty *se'ah* that would normally be susceptible becomes insusceptible if it is non-functional.

18:3 *R. Yose*: As long as an item can contain anything, it is susceptible.

Bed poles, etc.: None of these constitutes a "vessel" since none of them has a receptacle.

the frame... [used by] the Levites: The Levites traveled frequently to Jerusalem. In order to travel lightly, they use only the bedframe or mattress support to sleep on. Mattress supports are rectangular boards inserted into a frame to hold the mattress.

18:4 *a bedframe is set up on props*: Not built into a bed but resting on freestanding legs.

R. Meir and R. Judah: The assembly serves as a bed so the frame is susceptible, since beds are always susceptible to impurity.

R. Yose and R. Simeon: The bedframe is merely resting on props and is not truly a bed, as is true for the Levites.

5 If a bed was *midras* impure
[and one of its] short [sides] and two legs were removed,
it is impure.
[If one of the] long [sides] and two legs [were removed],
it is pure.
R. Nehemiah deems it impure.
If one cut off two props on the diagonal,
[or] cut off two legs on the diagonal
(one handbreadth by one handbreadth),
or reduced it to less than a handbreadth [off the ground],
it is pure.

6 If a bed was *midras* impure
[and one of its] long boards was broken
and then he mended it,
it is [still] *midras* impure.
If the second side was broken
and he mended it,
it is purified of *midras* impurity,
but it is impure from contact with *midras*.
If he did not mend[105] the first before the second was broken,
it is pure.

7 If a [bed] leg was impure with *midras* impurity
and one joined it to the bed,
the whole is *midras* impure.
If it was separated,
it is *midras* impure,
and the bed [is impure with] *midras* contact.

[105] Lit. "have enough [time] to mend."

18:5 *midras impure*: This is the impurity of an object on which a *zav* or *zavah* has sat or ridden or lain (see *Zavim* 2:4).

short [sides] and two legs: i.e. one of the boards running the width of the bed at its head or foot plus one set of legs.

it is impure: Because people can still lie on it.

long [sides] and two legs: i.e. one board running the bed's length was removed with one leg at each end of the board. The bed is pure because it tips to one side and is nonfunctional.

R. Nehemiah: The bed remains impure for the present and future since it can still be used if propped against a wall or some other support.

If one cut off two props on the diagonal, etc.: In all these situations the bed is rendered nonfunctional and pure.

one handbreadth by one handbreadth: Commentators differ as to where the removal is made. Some give the phrase the unusual meaning of one handbreadth from each corner. Still others remove the phrase entirely since it is so obscure and seems unnecessary.

18:6 *If the second side was broken*: The full breakage of the bed frees it of *midras* impurity. Since, however, the wood of the repaired bed had touched the bed when it was *midras* impure, it retains a lesser form of impurity that can affect foods and liquids. In the last clause, the entire bed has been replaced at once and it is considered a new entity.

If it was impure with seven-day impurity
and one joined it to a bed,
the whole is impure with seven-day impurity.
If it was separated,
it is impure with seven-day impurity,
and the bed is impure with evening impurity.
If it was impure with evening impurity
and one joined it to a bed,
the whole is impure with evening impurity.
If it was separated,
it is impure with evening impurity,
and the bed is pure.
So, too, with the prong[106] of a mattock.

8 A phylactery [consists of] four [separate] "vessels."
If one unloosed the first section and then mended it,
the phylactery is corpse impure,
and so too [if he unloosed] the second
and so too [for] the third.
If he unloosed the fourth [section],
it is free of corpse impurity,
but it is impure with corpse-impurity contact.
If he returned to the first [section],
unloosed it and mended it,
it is impure with contact impurity,
and so too for the second [section].
If he unloosed the third [section],
it is pure,
since the fourth is impure because of contact,
and contact impurity cannot create contact impurity.

[106] Lit. "tooth."

18:7 *seven-day impurity*: Corpse impurity.

the bed is impure with evening impurity: If an article that is impure with corpse impurity touches another article such as clothing, that article becomes impure only until the evening of the day it is immersed. See Numbers 19:22.

So, too, with the prong of a mattock: Whatever level of impurity affects the prong defiles the entire mattock when it is a single unit. If the prong comes off, it remains at the same level of impurity as before, but the mattock from which it separates either becomes pure or is impure at a lower level.

18:8 *A phylactery*: See note on 16:7. The phylactery has contracted impurity from a corpse.

unloosed the first section…mended it: The intact majority of the phylactery retains its corpse impurity. Therefore the new section becomes corpse impure when it again becomes an integral part of the phylactery.

the fourth [section], etc.: Once the last section of the head phylactery is removed, the phylacteries are non-functional and therefore pure. Since some sections of the phylactery touched corpse impurity during dismantling, they are impure with corpse-contact impurity for one day rather than seven.

contact impurity cannot create contact impurity: Original corpse impurity is transmitted by contact, albeit to a lower degree. Such a lower degree of impurity cannot be transmitted by further contact.

9 If half [an impure] bed was stolen,
or if half was lost,
or if brothers or partners divided it,
it is pure.
If it was restored,
it is susceptible to impurity from then forward.
A bed contracts impurity when bound together
and is rendered pure when bound together—
the words of R. Eliezer.
But the Sages say:
It contracts impurity in parts[107]
and is rendered pure in parts.

Chapter Nineteen

19:1–6 *Bed Ropes and Binders*

19 If one dismantles a bed in order to immerse it
and[108] he touches the [support] ropes,
he is pure.
When does the rope count as a connective with the bed?
After he has woven in it three "houses."
One who touches the rope from the knot inward [on an impure bed]
is impure;
from the knot outward,

[107] Lit. "limbs." [108] Alt. "or one who touches."

18:9 *it is pure*: Since it is unlikely that the halves will be brought back together, the bed is considered broken.

from then forward: Once the bed is restored, it regains the potential for becoming impure.

R. Eliezer: The bed must have all its parts together in order to become impure or to be purified because only complete "vessels" can be made impure or purified by immersion.

the Sages: If enough of the bed is present to be used, it can contract impurity, and any item, in whatever condition, that is impure and immersed is purified.

19:1 *he is pure*: Once he dismantles the bed the rope that holds the mattress or bedding becomes pure and cannot transmit impurity, because it is no longer part of a vessel.

"houses": The ropes are woven through one another to form large squares called "houses."

the knot inward: From the bedframe toward the "houses" is considered inward. One who touches this area is touching part of the bed.

from the knot outward: The knot of the rope that is tied to the bedframe but not yet woven into the bed's support ropes. In this state the rope is not yet a useful part of the bed.

he is pure.
[Regarding] the strands of the knot—
one who touches those that are needed for it
is impure.
How much is needed for it?
R. Judah says:
Three fingerbreadths.

2 If a rope extends beyond the bed:
up to five handbreadths—
it is insusceptible to impurity.
From five to ten—
it is susceptible to impurity.
From ten handbreadths outward—
it is insusceptible to impurity,
for with this [length]
one ties Passover offerings
and lowers beds.

3 A binder that extends beyond the bed
[is susceptible to impurity] in any amount—
the words of R. Meir.
R. Yose says:
Up to ten handbreadths.
The remnants of a binder [are susceptible to impurity]
if they are seven handbreadths [long],
enough to use as donkey's binder.[109]

[109] Alt. "cover."

needed for it: The *strands of the knot* are the part of the knot where the rope protrudes. Some length is *needed* to prevent a knot from untying.

Three fingerbreadths: Beyond this measure, the rope is pure, as is the person who touches it.

19:2 *a rope extends beyond the bed*: If such a short piece dangles from the "houses" after the bed is finished it is insusceptible, since this length of rope does not serve any useful function.

From five to ten: This amount of rope is susceptible because one can use it (see below). As such it is a connected "handle."

ties Passover offerings: The custom was to choose the Passover lamb in advance and tie it to one's bed until the festival. A rope that was five to ten handbreadths long would be used for this purpose, or (in the next clause) to lower a bed from an upper story if that had to be done.

19:3 *A binder*: A woolen belt that encircles a bed's frame in order to strengthen it. If the binder is attached with some hanging off the bed, the excess is considered susceptible to impurity since it is connected.

R. Yose: Only the first ten handbreadths of binder hanging off the bedframe are considered "connected."

donkey's binder: A belt that attaches the saddle to the donkey's back. Others interpret the word here as referring to a cover or blanket for the donkey.

4 If a *zav* was carried on a bed and on a binder,
this renders impure at two removes
and renders invalid at one [more] remove—
the words of R. Meir.
R. Yose says:
If a *zav* was carried on a bed and on a binder—
ten handbreadths renders impure at two removes
and renders invalid at one [more] remove.
From ten [handbreadths] outward it renders impure at one remove
and renders invalid at one [more] remove.
If he was carried on the binder—
from ten [handbreadths] inward,
it is impure;
from ten [handbreadths] outward,
it is pure.

5 If a bed had contracted *midras* impurity
and one wrapped a binder around it,
the entirety is impure [on account of] *midras*.
If it was removed,
[the bed] is *midras* impure
and the binder [is impure on account of] *midras* contact.
If it had contracted seven-day impurity
and one wrapped a binder around it,
the entirety is impure with seven-day impurity.
If it was removed,
[the bed] is seven-day impure,
and the binder is impure with evening impurity.
If it had contracted evening impurity
and one wrapped a binder around it,
the entirety is impure with evening impurity.
If it was removed,

19:4 *a zav was carried on a bed*: A *zav* renders impure anything on which he lies, sits, or puts pressure.

renders impure at two removes: The bed and binder can cause foods and liquids to become impure. These items can then render something else impure once more. These last items can then invalidate *terumah*, requiring its destruction, but do not transmit further impurity.

R. Yose: Ten handbreadths of a bed binder qualify as a connective with the bed's impurity. Beyond ten handbreadths constitutes a separate section rendered impure by the bed but not connected to it. That section can only render food or liquid impure once, and that impure food or liquid can invalidate *terumah*.

carried on the binder: If the *zav* was carried on the part of the binder protruding from the bed, but not on the bed itself.

from ten [handbreadths] inward: If the *zav* was carried on the part of the binder near the bed.

from ten [handbreadths] outward: If the *zav* was carried on the part of the binder farther away from the bed.

it is impure…pure: Commentators differ as to whether the bed or the binder is meant.

19:5 On this entire mishnah see above, 18:7.

[the bed] is impure with evening impurity,
but the binder is pure.

6 If a binder was wrapped around a bed
and a corpse touched them,
they are impure with seven-day impurity.
If they are separated,
they are impure with seven-day impurity.
If vermin touched them,
they are impure with evening impurity;
if they are separated,
they are impure with evening impurity.
If the two longer sides of a bed were removed
and one made new ones for it
but did not change the sockets—
if the new ones become broken,
it is impure.
If the old,
it is pure,
since everything follows the old ones.

19:7–8 *Items with Separate Parts*

7 A box whose opening is at the top is susceptible to corpse impurity.
If its top was damaged,
it is susceptible to corpse impurity.
If it was damaged from below,
it is pure.
The drawers[110] within it are susceptible to impurity
and they are not a connective with it.

[110] Or "compartments."

19:6 *if they are separated*: Since the bed and binder are independent utensils, and they both became corpse-impure directly, they retain their original impurity.

longer sides of a bed: The bed is impure. The owner wishes to purify the bed by making it unusable and then reconstruct it from new materials.

if the new ones become broken: As long as the old sockets remain and the old bedframe boards are whole, the bed can be returned to its original impure state.

19:7 *A box whose opening is at the top*: Corpse impurity is given as an example; since the box has a receptacle, it is a "vessel" and can become impure. The exception is *midras* impurity, since it cannot serve as a seat.

top was damaged: Since one can still use its interior, it remains susceptible.

damaged from below: Since it no longer can serve as a box, it is now insusceptible.

The drawers within it: That is, if they are whole, they can still function as containers.

not a connective: Each drawer is a separate "vessel," as is the chest itself; each can contain items independently, so if one becomes impure the others do not necessarily follow.

8 If a bag was damaged,
its inner pocket is impure,
but it is not a connective with it.
A water flask whose testicular sacs receive with it—
if they were damaged,
they are pure,
because they no longer receive in their usual fashion.

19:9–20:1 *Primary and Secondary Purposes*

9 A box whose opening is at the side
is susceptible to *midras* impurity and to corpse impurity.
R. Yose said:
When is this so?
When it is not ten handbreadths high
or[111] does not have a rim of one handbreadth.
If it was damaged from above
it is susceptible to corpse impurity.
If it was damaged from below,
R. Meir deems it susceptible to impurity.
The Sages deem it insusceptible to impurity,
since [if] the primary [purpose] is annulled,
the secondary is annulled.

[111] Alt. "and."

19:8 *bag*: This item holds small pockets within a larger pouch. If the large pouch is damaged it becomes insusceptible (or pure if already impure). The pockets, however, remain susceptible (or impure), because each is a separate container and therefore not a connective with the pouch. The same is true for the water-skin in the following rule.

it is not a connective with it: The inner bag is not a connective with the outer.

testicular sacs: A person making a pouch could cut a circle from the animal's hind legs until somewhat above its testicles.

if they were damaged: If a testicular sac tears but can still hold some water if held with from the aperture, it nevertheless becomes insusceptible since it no longer functions normally.

19:9 *midras impurity…corpse impurity*: It is susceptible to *midras* impurity because one can sit on it without impeding its regular use as a container. Hence, it serves as both a seat and a box. As a box it is susceptible to corpse impurity.

R. Yose: If the box is ten handbreadths high or has a large rim, it is too uncomfortable to function as a seat and is insusceptible to *midras* impurity.

R. Meir: As long as the box can function as a seat, it is susceptible to impurity.

primary [purpose]: As a box.

secondary purpose, as a seat.

10 If a dung basket was so damaged
that it will not hold pomegranates:
R. Meir deems it susceptible to impurity.
The Sages deem it insusceptible to impurity,
since [if] the primary [purpose] is annulled,
the secondary is annulled.

Chapter Twenty

20 Mattresses, cushions, sacks, and packing bags that have been damaged
are susceptible to *midras* impurity.
A four-*qav* fodder bag, a five-*qav* bag, a one-*se'ah* small canteen,[112]
a seven-*qav* waterskin—
R. Judah says:
Also a spice bag and a food bag of any size—
are susceptible to *midras* impurity.
And if any of them are damaged,
they are insusceptible to impurity
since if the primary [purpose] is annulled,
the secondary is annulled.

20:2 *Miscellaneous Rules*

2 Bagpipes are not susceptible to *midras* impurity.
A mortar trough—
the House of Shammai say:
[It is susceptible to] *midras* [impurity],

[112] Or "traveling bag."

19:10 *dung basket*: A mesh basket for transporting dung.

so damaged that it will not hold pomegranates: See above, 17:1.

R. Meir: Though it cannot serve as a basket anymore, it can still be used as a seat.

20:1 *Mattresses*, etc.: Though these items can no longer function as receptacles, they remain useful as seats and mats.

fodder bag, etc.: These leather items are made primarily as receptacles but can function as seats or mats if of the indicated size. As above, however, if they cannot function as receptacles their secondary use is annulled. One *se'ah* is six *qav*.

20:2 *Bagpipes*: Though one can sit on the bags, they were not manufactured for that purpose.

House of Shammai…Hillel: According to the House of Shammai one can use a trough for a seat. The House of Hillel holds that the trough was never made to serve as a seat. It is however susceptible *to corpse impurity* and all other impurities.

but the House of Hillel say:
[It is susceptible to] corpse impurity.
If a trough [that holds] from two *log* to nine *qav* is split,
it is susceptible to *midras* impurity.
If it was left in the rain and it swelled,
it is susceptible to corpse impurity.
[If it was left] during the east [wind] and it split,
it suffers[113] *midras* impurity.
This is the greater stringency for the remnants of wooden vessels
than for their beginning
and the greater stringency for the remnants of wicker vessels
than for their beginning,
since at first they do not suffer impurity
until they are edged.
Once edged,
even if their rims fall off
[leaving only] the smallest amount,
they are susceptible to impurity.

20:3–7 *Use and Usability*

3 A staff that one made into a hatchet handle
is a connective for impurity at the time of use.
A yarn winder
is a connective for impurity at the time of use.
If one attached it to a post,
it is susceptible to impurity,
but [the post] is not a connective to it.

[113] Lit. "it receives."

two log to nine qav: A trough is usually used for kneading. If it splits it can only function as a seat, so it remains susceptible to *midras* impurity. If the trough holds less than two *log*, it is considered a plate and is insusceptible to *midras* impurity. If it is larger than nine *qav* it is too large to act as a comfortable seat.

swelled: If the trough swelled the crack in it will close. It will then become usable again as a trough, but not a seat. Since it has a receptacle, it is susceptible to corpse impurity.

east [wind]: Which dries it and restores the split that had swelled and closed.

This is the greater stringency, etc.: When the trough is whole it is insusceptible to *midras* impurity, but when it is cracked, it is susceptible. The same applies to wicker baskets once their upper edge has been completed.

20:3 *A staff*: A plain piece of wood that is insusceptible. However, while it serves as a hatchet handle, it is considered connected to the hatchet because one cannot use the hatchet without its handle.

yarn winder: This tool is made up of a wooden rod with metal pegs at its top and bottom. Yarn is wrapped around the pegs to make skeins. The rod and pegs are connectives; impurity of one causes impurity of the other.

If one attached: The post by itself is a wooden article lacking a receptacle.

If he made the post into a yarn winder,
only the necessary part is susceptible to impurity.
If a chair was fixed to the post,
it is susceptible to impurity,
but [the post] is not a connective to it.
If he made the post into a chair,
only the place [where one sits] is susceptible to impurity.
If he attached [the chair] to the pressing beam of an olive press,
it is susceptible to impurity,
but it is not a connective to it.
If one made a chair out of the end [of the beam],
it is insusceptible to impurity,
because people say to him
"Get up and let us do our work!"

4 If a large kneading trough was damaged
so it could not contain pomegranates
and one prepared it as a seat:
R. Aqiva deems it susceptible to impurity.
The Sages deem it insusceptible to impurity
unless he smoothes it.
If he made it a feeding trough for cattle,
even if he fastened it to the wall,
it is susceptible to impurity.

5 If one attached a wooden seat into a layer [of bricks on a wall]—
if he attached it but did not build on it,
or built on it but did not attach it,
it is susceptible to impurity.

If he made the post into a yarn winder: For example, if he attached the yarn winder onto a post in such a way as the winder could rotate on it, or perhaps attached pegs directly to the ends of the post itself.

the necessary part: The part between the two pegs that can serve as a yarn winder.

but [the post] is not a connective to it: The seat and the post continue to be considered separate items, and the post is a plain wooden item that is always insusceptible.

"Get up and let us do our work!": The beam's function is to press olives and not to act as a seat. Therefore, the entire beam is insusceptible.

20:4 *R. Aqiva*: All that R. Aqiva requires for susceptibility is that one can sit on the trough.

The Sages: If the trough has a rough surface people will not sit on it.

feeding trough: Though the trough does not hold pomegranates, it can hold fodder for cattle.

fastened it to the wall: Articles fastened to a wall are considered attached to the ground since both are immovable and are usually insusceptible (see above, 11:2). Here, however, attaching the trough to a wall has no effect on its function.

20:5 *wooden seat*: A large block of wood built into a row of bricks as a wall is constructed.

it is susceptible: Unless the block is absorbed into the structure being built, it is considered an independent item subject to *midras* impurity even though attached to the ground. If it is doubly fixed (attached and built upon) it loses its susceptibility. The same rule applies to matting laid upon a roof.

If he attached it and built on it,
it is insusceptible to impurity.
If one placed matting over roof beams—
if he attached it but did not lay plaster over it,
or laid plaster over it but did not attach it,
it is susceptible to impurity.
If he attached it and laid plaster over it,
it is insusceptible to impurity.
If one attached a dish to a chest, box, or cabinet
according to its usual way of containing,
it is susceptible to impurity;
not according to its usual way of containing,
it is insusceptible to impurity.

6 If one made a sheet
that was susceptible to *midras* impurity into a curtain,
it is insusceptible to *midras* impurity,
but it is susceptible to corpse impurity.
When does it cease to be susceptible to impurity?
The House of Shammai say:
After it has loops.[114]
And the House of Hillel say:
After it has been tied.
R. Aqiva says:
After it has been attached.

7 A mat on which one placed reeds lengthwise
is insusceptible to impurity.
The Sages say:
[It is susceptible] until he places them in the form of *chi*.

[114] Alt. "has been sewn." Translation uncertain; see annotations.

cabinet: A tower-shaped chest for holding spices or bathhouse supplies.

usual way of containing: The dish is attached right side up to the floor of the chest, box, or tower so that it can hold articles as it usually does.

not according to its usual way of containing: The dish is attached to the walls or top of the chest, box, or tower so that it can only hold items when these containers are turned in odd positions.

20:6 *insusceptible to midras impurity*: Fabric of this sort was often used as a form of sleepwear or bed linen, but once it has been made into a curtain, it is no longer meant for sitting or lying on.

The House of Shammai…Hillel: The translations of the Houses' respective requirements are speculative; commentators differ as to what is demanded in each case.

R. Aqiva holds that the sheet is transformed into a curtain only when it is hung.

20:7 *lengthwise*: Reeds placed across a mat's width created spaces in which people might sit or lie comfortably. This is not so when reeds are woven in widthwise. Widthwise reeds were used for reinforcement, and were themselves too hard for comfort.

in the form of chi: A Greek letter that resembles the English *X*. Arranging the reeds thus would make the mat nonfunctional because it would be impossible to sit or lie on it in any direction.

If he placed them along the width
but there are not four handbreadths between each reed and its counterpart,
it is insusceptible to impurity.
If it was divided along its width,
R. Judah deems it insusceptible to impurity.
So, too, if one unties the end knots, it is insusceptible to impurity.
If it was divided along its length,
but three end knots remained within six handbreadths,
it is susceptible to impurity.
When does a mat become susceptible to impurity?
After it has been trimmed,
and that is the completion of its manufacture.

Chapter Twenty-One

21:1–3 *Conveying Impurity by Touch*

21 1 One who touches the upper beam or the lower beam,
or the heddles,
or the reed,
or the thread that is drawn over fine purple,
or a shuttle that is not to be returned
is pure.
[But if one touched] the woof thread,
or the standing warp,
or the double [thread] that is drawn over fine purple,
or a shuttle that is to be returned,
he is impure.
One who touches the wool that is on the distaff or on the spool
is pure.

four handbreadths: Less than four handbreadths between reed and reed, even if placed widthwise, make the mat too uncomfortable for use.

R. Judah holds that because the mat will inevitably unravel, it ceases to be a "vessel."

If it was divided along its length: If it was divided along its length, it is still wide enough for comfort. If it has enough knots, it will not unravel.

21:1 The items in the first two lists are all connected with the process of weaving; they are parts of either the loom or the fabric under production. Those in the first list are not considered connectives with the fabric, and therefore do not transmit impurity if the fabric itself becomes impure. Those in the second list are considered connectives; therefore anyone who touches them while an impure textile is being woven becomes impure.

is pure: Unwoven wool is insusceptible since its manufacture is incomplete. Alternatively, the wool is not considered a connective with the spinning wheel.

One who touches the spindle head
before it is laid bare
is impure.
After it is laid bare,
he is pure.

2 One who touches the yoke, the bar, the blanket, or the ropes,
even at the time of their use,
is pure.
[If one touches] the plow handle, the plow "knee," or the plow base,
he is impure.
[If one touches] the metal ring, or the moldboard, or the blade,
he is impure.
R. Judah deems pure in the case of the moldboard
since it is used only to gather in the soil.

3 One who touches a saw handle
from either end
is impure.
The saw's string, cord, crosspiece, or struts, or a carpenter's press, or the bow handle of a drill—
he is pure.
R. Judah says:
Also, if he touched the frame of a large saw,
he is pure.
One who touches bow strings or a bow,
even when it was stretched,
is pure.
A mole trap is insusceptible to impurity.
R. Judah says:
As long as it is set
it is a connective.

spindle head: A metal button with a hole in it attached to the top of the spindle used for spinning wool. When the wool is attached to it, it is considered a connective "handle" holding the wool. Once the wool is detached, the spindle head is no longer considered a "handle."

21:2 All the items in these lists are associated with the process of plowing; they belong either to the plow itself or to the yoke that connects the plow and the animals that will pull it. Commentators vary widely as to the identity and function of each, but the overall distinction here is between parts that are essential to the act of plowing and therefore conduct impurity if the plow itself is impure and those that are not. R. Judah differs with respect to a single item.

21:3 The questions that underlie these rules are the same as above (21:1). Certain items are deemed not connective either because they are not essential for the proper operation of the tool or because they are assembled only temporarily.

frame of a large saw: This type of saw is used to cut large beams. A huge handle ("frame") was placed on two sides for two men to use. R. Judah holds that one who touched this frame was pure because sometimes it was removed if the saw was used on thinner pieces of wood.

A mole trap: The wooden parts of a trap are insusceptible because they have no receptacle. The spring is not a connective to the wooden parts because one removes it to dispose of the dead mole.

R. Judah: Since no one will remove the spring when it is set, it is a connective.

Chapter Twenty-Two

22:1–8 Damage and Susceptibility

22 If a table or a serving table[115] were damaged
or one overlaid it with marble
and left room to set down cups,
it is [still] susceptible to impurity.
R. Judah says:
Room to set down pieces [of food].
2 A [three-legged] table that has had one leg removed
is insusceptible to impurity.
If a second was removed,
it is insusceptible to impurity.
If a third was removed,
it is susceptible to impurity
if one intends [to use] it.
R. Yose says:
Intention is not necessary.
And so too for a serving table.
3 A bench that has had one of its end legs removed
is insusceptible to impurity.
If the second was removed,
it is insusceptible to impurity,
but if it is one handbreadth high,
it is susceptible to impurity.
A footstool that has had one of its legs removed
is susceptible to impurity;
and so too for the stool in front of a throne.

[115] Lit. "Delphic-style," and so too in 22:2.

22:1 *table*: Although lacking a receptacle, tables are susceptible when they serve human needs and support vessels.

marble: An insusceptible material.

22:2 *third*: The last of three legs.

if one intends [to use] it: The table is a flat surface resting on a tripod. If the tripod is disassembled one is left with a flat wooden surface, which is insusceptible. However, intention to use the surface for some purpose makes it susceptible; see 25.9 below.

22:3 *bench*: With two legs at each end, each made from a board.

but if it was still one handbreadth high: If the thickness of the legless bench seat is one handbreadth higher than ground level it still can function as a seat.

footstool...susceptible: Because one can still rest one's feet on it.

4 A bride's chair whose seat coverings have been removed:
the House of Shammai deem it susceptible to impurity
and the House of Hillel deem it insusceptible to impurity.
Shammai says:
Even the frame of a chair
is susceptible to impurity.
If one attached a chair to a baking trough:
the House of Shammai deem it susceptible to impurity
and the House of Hillel deem it insusceptible to impurity.
Shammai says:
Even one that was made inside it.[116]

5 If the seat boards of a chair did not protrude
and they were removed,
it is susceptible to impurity
since it is usual to turn it on its side
and sit on it.

6 A chair from which the center seat board was removed
but the outer ones remain
is susceptible to impurity.
If the outer ones were removed
but the center one remains,
it is susceptible to impurity.
R. Simeon says:
If it was a handbreadth wide.

7 A chair that had two seat boards removed,
one next to the other:
R. Aqiva deems it susceptible to impurity,
but the Sages deem it insusceptible to impurity.
R. Judah said:
Even a bride's chair whose seat coverings were removed

[116] Also found in *Eduyot* 1:11.

22:4 *seat coverings*: The seat, armrests, and decorations.

House of Shammai: If one can sit on an object that was made to function as a seat, the object is susceptible.

House of Hillel: If a seat no longer functions as it was meant to, or does not function solely as a seat, it is insusceptible, as if it were broken.

made inside it: The seat was built into the trough from the very beginning and not a freestanding chair simply attached at a later time.

22:5 *chair*: Some chairs consisted of a seat, legs, and boards connecting the legs. If the chair's seat did not extend over its legs, one could turn the chair on its side without it wobbling and sit on it. If the seat boards did extend, no one would consider it designed to be used in this way.

22:6 *the center seat board was removed*: One can still sit on a chair even if some seat boards are removed.

R. Simeon: A board that is a handbreadth wide provides enough room for sitting.

22:7 *R. Aqiva*: A chair in this condition still can act as a container.

R. Judah: See above, 19:9.

but a receptacle remained on it
is insusceptible to impurity,
since if the primary [purpose] is annulled
the secondary is annulled.

8 A chest whose top was removed
is susceptible to impurity
because of its bottom.
If its bottom was removed,
it is susceptible to impurity
because of its top.
If the top and the bottom were removed:
R. Judah deems it susceptible to impurity
because of its sides;
but the Sages deem it insusceptible to impurity.
A stonecutter's seat is susceptible to *midras* impurity.

22:9–10 *Midras Impurity and Seat Impurity*

9 If one painted a wooden block red or saffron
or polished it,
R. Aqiva deems it susceptible to impurity,
but the Sages deem it insusceptible to impurity
unless he hollows it out.
If one filled a small or large basket with straw or soft fabric,
and he made them into a seat,
they are insusceptible to impurity.
If he laced them around with reeds or cords,
they are susceptible to impurity.

10 A privy stool is susceptible to *midras* impurity and corpse impurity.
If it came apart,
the leather is susceptible to *midras* impurity,
and the iron form is susceptible to corpse impurity.

22:8 *If the top and the bottom were removed*: R. Judah holds that the chest's sides can still function as a receptacle. The Sages hold that since the chest no longer functions as it originally did it is insusceptible.

A stonecutter's seat: The temporary seat the stonecutter makes on one end of a board as he cuts stone on its other end.

22:9 *R. Aqiva…the Sages*, etc.: R. Aqiva considers staining and polishing preparation for making the wooden block into a seat. The Sages demand that a specific spot for sitting have been carved into the wood.

straw or soft fabric: The seat is insusceptible in the first case because the filling of the seat can be pushed out of the basket; it is therefore not yet a permanent seat. Once the filling cannot be pushed out, the seat's manufacture is complete.

22:10 *privy stool*: Made of leather stretched over a metal frame.

the iron…corpse impurity: Since the frame no longer functions as a seat it is insusceptible to *midras* impurity but still susceptible to other impurities. However, the *leather* can still function as a seat.

A table[117] whose coverings are leather
is susceptible to *midras* impurity and to corpse impurity.
If it came apart,
the leather is susceptible to *midras* impurity,
and the table is not susceptible to anything.
A bathhouse bench that has two wooden legs
is susceptible to impurity.
If one is of wood and the other of stone,
it is insusceptible to impurity.
If one joined the boards in a bathhouse together:
R. Aqiva deems them susceptible to impurity,
and the Sages deem them insusceptible to impurity
since they are used only for the water to flow away beneath them.
A fumigation cage in which there is a receptacle for garments
is susceptible to impurity,
but if it is made like a beehive
it is insusceptible to impurity.

Chapter Twenty-Three

23:1–5 *Midras, Riding Impurity and Seat Impurity*

23 If a ball, craftsman's form, amulet, or phylactery became torn,
the one who touches them is impure;

[117] Alt., "folding chair."

A table whose coverings are leather: A leather cover makes the table comfortable enough to lie on.

not susceptible to anything: Since it is a flat wooden surface with no receptacle, it is completely insusceptible.

bathhouse bench: Susceptibility or insusceptibility in the case of a bathhouse bench depends on the material that is essential for the bench to function. If the material is wood, the bench is susceptible like wood. If it is stone, the bench is insusceptible like stone.

R. Aqiva: If boards in a bathhouse were joined to make a bench, R. Aqiva considers them susceptible because people sit on them.

the Sages hold that the primary purpose of the bathhouse boards is not sitting but preventing clients from being dirtied by used bath water.

fumigation cage…like a beehive: The cage is used for delousing clothes placed in it by smoking the lice out. A fumigation cage built like a beehive has an open top and bottom but no interior receptacle. Clothes are laid on top.

23:1 *If a ball…became torn*, etc.: Each of these objects consists of an exterior covering filled with some material. If they became torn in a state of corpse impurity but still retain their contents, they remain impure and convey impurity to humans and clothing.

craftsman's form: A shoemaker's last or tailor's form or the like.

[if he touched] what was in them,
he is pure.
If a saddle was torn open,
the one who touches what is in it
is impure,
since the stitching joins it together.

2 These are susceptible to impurity as things used for riding:
an Ashkelon girth, a Median mortar, a camel's pack saddle, and a horsecloth.
R. Yose says:
A horsecloth is also susceptible to seat impurity
since people stand upon it in the arena.
But the female camel's saddle
is susceptible to impurity.

3 What is the difference between riding and sitting?
Riding [impurity] differentiates between touching and carrying,
but sitting [impurity] does not differentiate between touching and carrying.
A donkey's cover
on which a person may sit
is insusceptible to impurity.
If he changed its spaces
or broke them into one another
it is susceptible to impurity.

[if he touched] what was in them, he is pure: The filling of these objects is not a connective because it is not actually sewn to its containers.

stitching joins it together: In the case of a saddle, the contents are connected to the seat.

23:2 *Ashkelon girth*: A belt for tying a saddle to a donkey.

Median mortar: A type of saddle that has an indentation like a mortar cut into it.

since people stand upon it in the arena: Commentators differ: either riders stand on these blankets when they perform feats on their horses' backs or spectators use them for support. With respect to *midras* impurity, standing on something is the equivalent of sitting on it.

female camel's saddle: Commentators differ as to whether this rule continues R. Yose's teaching or resumes the rabbinic consensus; in the former case the "but" seems awkward. It is also not clear whether the impurity in question is seat impurity or saddle impurity. In the latter case such a saddle would remain pure if used only as a seat.

23:3 *riding and sitting*: A *zav* or *zavah* can transmit *midras* impurity by either riding or sitting on various objects, but the two modes of transmittal work slightly differently. See 1:3 above.

touching and carrying: One who touches a saddle on which a *zav* or *zavah* has ridden does not convey impurity to clothing and vessels. If he lifted or carried it, however, he does.

does not differentiate: Whether one touches or lifts an object used as a seat, he conveys impurity to clothing and vessels.

donkey's cover: Commentators differ: either a ladder-like wooden contraption on which the donkey's burden is placed or a cover like the horse's cover in 23:2. It is not normally used either as a saddle or a seat.

changed its spaces: If one widens the spaces in the frame so one can sit comfortably or extends the slats so that he had a seat next to the donkey's burden, the pack frame becomes susceptible. If the cover is more like a blanket, one must imagine similar alterations.

4 The bier, mattress, and pillow of a corpse:
these are susceptible to *midras* impurity.
A bride's seat, a birthing stool, and a launderer's stool
on which he folds[118] the clothes:
R. Yose said:
They are not in the category of seat.

5 A fishnet is susceptible to impurity
because of its woven bag.
Nets, snares, bird traps, spring traps, and fishermen's snares
are susceptible to impurity.
A round fishnet, a bird lasso, and a bird cage
are insusceptible to impurity.

Chapter Twenty-Four

24:1–17 *Midras Impurity, Corpse Impurity, and Insusceptibility*

24 There are three [kinds of] shield—[119]
(1) the bent shield
is susceptible to *midras* impurity;
(2) that with which they play in the arena
is susceptible to corpse impurity;
(3) and the toy of the Arabs
is totally insusceptible to impurity.

[118] Alt. "piles" or "presses."

[119] Lit. "three shields," and so throughout the chapter.

23:4 *The bier, mattress, and pillow of a corpse*: While people do not generally sit on these, women who mourn their dead do. This makes them susceptible to *midras* impurity.

not in the category of seat: These seats are either used only once, e.g. the bride's chair, or are not used as seats at all despite their shape.

23:5 *A fishnet*, etc.: All these items are susceptible because they have the ability to contain the animals they catch.

A round fishnet, etc.: None of these has a receptacle.

24:1 This chapter follows a tripartite pattern: things susceptible to *midras* impurity; related things susceptible to corpse impurity; related things that are insusceptible to impurity.

the bent shield: A shield that protects the soldier from three sides. On campaign he sleeps in it.

play in the arena: Since it is metal, if it touches a corpse or is housed in a Tent, it contracts corpse impurity. But it cannot be used as a bed or seat, so it is immune to *midras* impurity.

toy of the Arabs: It does not actually function as a shield at all, and so is insusceptible.

2 There are three [kinds of] wagon—
(1) one made like a throne
is susceptible to *midras* impurity;
(2) [one made] like a bed
is susceptible to corpse impurity;
(3) and [one made] for stones
is totally insusceptible to impurity.

3 There are three [kinds of] baking trough—
(1) a baking trough from two *log* to nine *qav*
that was split
is susceptible to *midras* [impurity];
(2) when whole,
it is susceptible to corpse impurity;
(3) and one of [full] size
is totally insusceptible to impurity.

4 There are three [kinds of] chest—
(1) that with its door at the side
is susceptible to *midras* impurity;
(2) [with its door] on top
is susceptible to corpse impurity;
(3) and one of [full] size
is totally insusceptible to impurity.

5 There are three [kinds of] leather box[120]—
(1) that of barbers
is susceptible to *midras* impurity;

[120] See annotations.

24:2 *like a throne*: It is enclosed on three sides like a throne and is meant as a seat. Since it is meant for people to sit on it, it is susceptible to *midras* impurity.

like a bed: A long wagon or cart for carrying merchandise but not meant for people to lie in. Since it is not meant for people to sit or lie on, it is not susceptible to *midras* impurity, but is susceptible to other impurity.

for stones: For transport of large stones. This cart contains large openings in its floor. These openings make it insusceptible; see 17:1 above.

24:3 *from two log to nine qav*: See above, 20:2.

when whole: It has a receptacle and is not meant for sitting; see above, 20:3.

[full] size: Forty *se'ah*: see above, 15:1.

24:4 *susceptible to midras impurity*: Since its door is on its side it can be used even if someone is sitting on it.

susceptible to corpse impurity: If the chest's door is on the top, those who need the chest will tell the one sitting on it to get up. This indicates that the chest is primarily a receptacle and not a seat.

[full] size: As in 24:3 above.

24:5 *leather box*: The word has been variously translated as dresser top, or leather sheet, or leather-covered block. The barber's box is a seat for the client. A leather table and anything else that serves human needs is susceptible to corpse impurity. A surface for spreading olives is neither functional as a seat or table nor is it usable as a receptacle. It is not considered a "vessel."

(2) that on which one eats
is susceptible to corpse impurity;
(3) and that for olives
is totally insusceptible to impurity.

6 There are three kinds of base[121]—
(1) that which is before a bed
or before scribes
is susceptible to *midras* impurity;
(2) that of a serving table[122]
is susceptible to corpse impurity;
(3) and that of a cupboard[123]
is totally insusceptible to impurity.

7 There are three [kinds of] writing surface—
(1) that of papyrus
is susceptible to *midras* impurity;
(2) that which has a receptacle for wax
is susceptible to corpse impurity;
(3) and a smooth [surface]
is totally insusceptible to impurity.

8 There are three [kinds of] bed—
(1) that used for lying upon
is susceptible to *midras* impurity;
(2) that of glassmakers
is susceptible to corpse impurity;
(3) and that of netmakers[124]
is totally insusceptible to impurity.

9 There are three [kinds of] baskets—
(1) that for compost
is susceptible to *midras* impurity;

[121] Alt. "foundation" or "pedestal." [122] Lit. "Delphic-style," see 22:1 above.
[123] Lit. "tower." [124] See annotations.

24:6 *base*: The first type is a footrest for one sitting on a bed or at a desk. Since this serves as part of a bed or seat it is susceptible to *midras* impurity. The second is used to put food or items on, but not people. The third type is subsidiary to some other item and is not a "vessel" in its own right at all.

24:7 *papyrus*: Sheets of papyrus could be so large that a scribe might sit on one while working.

receptacle for wax: A pad might have an indented container to hold the wax on which the scribe wrote.

smooth [surface]: A parchment surface for writing.

24:8 *used for lying upon*: This is obvious, but the point is to distinguish an ordinary bed from other objects called beds that have distinctly different purposes. The rule in 24:10 has a similar explanation.

glassmakers: Glassmakers placed their finished work inside a bed-like display case.

netmakers: The netmakers laid their work on a bed-like structure, but it had no receptacle, nor did it directly serve human needs. Others translate "harnessmakers" or "chariotmakers," but the point is the same.

24:9 *for compost*: When one tired of fertilizing a field, one might sit or lean against the basket.

(2) that for straw
is susceptible to corpse impurity;
(3) and a camel's bale
is totally insusceptible to impurity.

10 There are three [kinds of] mat—
(1) that made for sitting
is susceptible to *midras* impurity;
(2) that of dyers
is susceptible to corpse impurity;
(3) and that used in winepresses
is totally insusceptible to impurity.

11 There are three [kinds of] water flask
and three kinds of shepherd's bag—
(1) those holding the prescribed quantity
are susceptible to *midras* impurity;
(2) those that do not hold the prescribed quantity
are susceptible to corpse impurity;
(3) and those made of fishskin
are totally insusceptible to impurity.

12 There are three [kinds of] hide—
(1) that made as a rug
is susceptible to *midras* impurity;
(2) as a wrapper for utensils
is susceptible to corpse impurity;
(3) and for straps and sandals
is totally insusceptible to impurity.

13 There are three [kinds of] sheet—
(1) that made for lying upon
is susceptible to *midras* impurity;

for straw: This basket has an opening on the top for collecting straw. If someone sits on it he will be told to get up to allow collection to continue. Hence, this basket is not a seat. It is, however, susceptible to corpse and other types of non-*midras* impurity.

camel's bale: A net-like basket made out of thick rope used to hold a camel's load in place. The holes in it are too large to contain even straw.

24:10 *mat*: Made out of wood fibers, reed, or similar material. It has no receptacle.

that of dyers: A mat into which dyers wrap their finished product. Wrapping produces a receptacle.

that used in winepresses: The mats are used to cover grapes. Covers, if they have no receptacle and cannot be used as seats, are always insusceptible.

24:11 *holding the prescribed quantity*: To be big enough to sit on, seven *qav* for a water flask or five *qav* for a shepherd's bag. See above, 20:1.

fishskin: Articles made from sea creatures are not susceptible. See above, 10:1; 17:13.

24:12 *rug*: To sit on.

straps and sandals: They possess no receptacle and are not used for sitting or lying.

(2) as a curtain
is susceptible to corpse impurity;
(3) with patterns
is totally insusceptible to impurity.

14 There are three [kinds of] napkin[125]—
(1) that for the hands
is susceptible to *midras* impurity;
(2) for book coverings
is susceptible to corpse impurity;
(3) for a shroud and for the Levites' harps
is totally insusceptible to impurity.[126]

15 There are three [kinds of leather] glove[127]—
(1) that of those who hunt wild animals and birds
is susceptible to *midras* impurity;
(2) that of [those who hunt] locusts
is susceptible to corpse impurity;
(3) and that of fruit pickers[128]
is totally insusceptible to impurity.

16 There are three [kinds of] hairnet—
(1) that of a young girl
is susceptible to *midras* impurity;
(2) that of an old woman

[125] See annotations. [126] **P** and **P**$_2$: "as a wrapper for the Levites' harps."
[127] Or "headband" or "legging." [128] **K**, **P**$_2$: "for thorns."

24:13 *a curtain*: A curtain that hangs in a doorway. In cold weather one who guards the door may wrap himself in it. Since it sometimes serves as clothing, it is susceptible to corpse impurity though not *midras* impurity.

patterns: Painted or dyed to guide stitching a design. Such an item would simply be hung as decoration.

24:14 *napkin*: Alt. "kerchief," that is, any kind of flat cloth.

that for the hands: A napkin used to dry one's hands might be placed on the pillow used as support during the meal. See *Berakhot* 8:3.

book coverings: Since they contain the book, they have a receptacle, and they are susceptible to corpse impurity.

shroud…Levites' harps: Once the shrouds have been used for the dead no other benefit may be had from them. Since the harps are sacred, associated equipment is not permitted for human use. In either case, the fact that the article is forbidden for human use makes it insusceptible.

24:15 *susceptible to midras impurity*: Hunters sometimes lean on their gloves.

[those who hunt] locusts: This glove has a receptacle for storing locusts.

fruit pickers: More specifically, fig pickers (or driers). Even with the variant "for thorns," the gloves function only as protection, not as tools, and are therefore not "vessels."

24:16 *susceptible to midras impurity*: A young girl may place her hairnet on her pillow or wear it when she falls asleep.

is susceptible to corpse impurity;[129]
(3) that of [a woman] who goes outside[130]
is totally insusceptible to impurity.
17 There are three [kinds of] basket—
(1) if a worn out basket is patched on to one that is sound,
one follows the sound one;
(2) a small one on to a large one:
one follows the large one;
(3) if they are equal,
one follows the inner one.
R. Simeon says:
If the [impure] pan of a scale is patched on to the bottom of a [pure] cauldron—
on the inside,
it is impure;
on the outside,
it is pure.
Onto the side,
whether inside or outside,
it is pure.

Chapter Twenty-Five

25:1–9 *Interior and Exterior Parts of a Vessel*

25 All vessels have an exterior and interior.
For example:

[129] See annotations here and in 28:9 below. [130] Possibly a euphemism for "prostitute."

susceptible to corpse impurity: An old woman would put the net aside for safekeeping when sleeping or lying down, so the net is insusceptible to *midras* impurity. Since, however, it has a container for her hair it is susceptible to corpse impurity. A parallel text reverses the cases of the hairnet of the young girl and the old woman. This variant is consistent with 28:9 below, which contradicts the rule as given here.

insusceptible: Because it is too small.

24:17 *follows the sound one*: The purity status of the sound basket determines that of the unsound one, because it renders the latter usable. In the next case, the larger basket represents the majority of the combined "vessel."

the inner one: The inner one has the receptacle.

on the inside...on the outside: If the scale pan is on the inside, the cauldron is susceptible, following the intact scale pan. If the scale pan is on the outside, the cauldron is insusceptible, since the "inner one" is the broken cauldron.

onto the side: Following the previous rule, if the balance is patched onto any of the cauldron's sides, neither item is "innermost."

25:1 *exterior and interior*: By definition a vessel has a discernible interior and exterior. If impure liquid touches a vessel's interior, its exterior becomes impure as well; if it touches the exterior, it only affects the exterior.

mattresses, pillows, sacks, and packing bags—
the words of R. Judah.
R. Meir says:
Anything that has loops
has an exterior and interior.
But anything that does not have loops
does not have an exterior and interior.
A table or serving table has an exterior and interior—
the words of R. Judah.
R. Meir says:
They do not have an exterior,
and so too for a rimless tray.

2 An ox goad has an exterior and interior,
seven [handbreadths] from the blade
and four [handbreadths] from the goad—
the words of R. Judah.
R. Meir says:
They do not have.
Four and seven were mentioned only regarding the remnants.

3 Wine and oil measures, a fork ladle, a mustard strainer, and a wine strainer
have an exterior and interior—
the words of R. Meir.
R. Judah says:
They do not have.
R. Simeon says:

R. Meir: Once the object has loops that can hold a string or belt, the loops provide a border between the inner and outer part of the item.

R. Judah: The top of the table is its "interior" because that is the part that enables the table's function. All other parts are its "exterior."

R. Meir: A table can be inverted and still be usable, so neither top nor bottom is "exterior" with respect to the other.

25:2 *ox goad*: An ox goad consists of a rod with a blade at one end to remove roots as the plowing proceeds and a sharp point at the other to guide the ox. R. Judah considers its "interior" anything within seven handbreadths of the plow blade or four handbreadths of the prod because those areas carry out the goad's function.

R. Meir: An ox goad consists of a single undifferentiated "exterior." The tradition of seven handbreadths and four handbreadths refers to the susceptibility of an ox goad's remnants if it falls apart.

25:3 *ladle*: A fork ladle has a spoon on one end and a fork at the other.

R. Meir: Even though these items are always submerged entire, nevertheless they have an "exterior" and "interior" that defile in different ways since one can distinguish between their inner and outer sections.

R. Judah: Since both interior and exterior parts are necessarily used together, if one section becomes impure the whole item becomes impure.

R. Simeon agrees with R. Meir that the contents remain pure. Nevertheless, the vessel as a unit is now impure and so must be immersed, in accordance with R. Judah.

They do have:
if they become impure from their exterior
the interior contents are pure,
but it must be immersed.

4 The Quarter and Half-Quarter [measure]—
If the Quarter becomes impure,
the Half-Quarter does not become impure.
If the Half-Quarter becomes impure,
the Quarter does not become impure.
They said before R. Aqiva:
Since the Half-Quarter is the exterior of the Quarter,
then if the interior section of the vessel becomes impure
does not the outer part become impure?
He said to them:
Which measure has precedence?[131]
Perhaps the Quarter is the exterior of the Half-Quarter:
if the exterior of the vessel becomes impure
its interior does not become impure!

5 If the Quarter's interior became impure,
the Quarter and its exterior are impure,
but the Half-Quarter and its exterior are pure.
If the Half-Quarter's interior became impure,
the Half-Quarter and its exterior are impure,
but the Quarter and its exterior remain pure.
If the Quarter's exterior became impure,
the Half-Quarter's exterior is pure—
the words of R. Meir.
But the Sages say:
One does not divide exteriors.
And when he immerses it, he immerses all of it.

6 Bases, rims, handle sockets, or handles of vessels that have a receptacle
upon which [impure] liquids fell—

[131] A very difficult phrase. See annotations.

25:4 *The Quarter and Half-Quarter [measure]*: A single measuring cup that measures both a quarter-*log* (= half-liter) and an eighth-*log*. The cups are separated by a partition.

Which measure has precedence? Is this a situation in which either half of the utensil can be considered the exterior of the other? An alternative translation would be "that question was already asked at an earlier time." Numerous manuscripts reflect a variant that might refer to the measure named in 1 Kings 7:26, 38 and Ezekiel 45:11, but such a reading yields a text that is no less obscure. Other later commentators reflect still different variants in the text.

25:5 *R. Meir*: The Quarter and Half-Quarter measures are separated by a wall, so neither defiles the other.

the Sages: The wall separating the measures is actually an "exterior" to each measure. Hence, if one vessel's exterior becomes impure, so does the other's exterior and the entire vessel requires immersion.

25:6 *handle sockets*: Vessels made with a round depression or extension into which one inserts a handle.

one dries them, and they are pure.
[Regarding] other vessels lacking an exterior and interior:[132]
if liquids fall on part of it,
all of it is impure.
A vessel whose exterior was rendered impure by liquid—
its exterior is impure.
its interior, rims, handle sockets, and handles [remain] pure.
But if its inner part becomes impure
the whole is impure.

7 "All vessels have an exterior and interior,"
and they have an area by which they are held.
R. Tarfon says: [This applies only] to a large wooden baking trough.
R. Aqiva says: To cups.
R. Meir says: To impure and pure hands.
R. Yose said: What they have said applies only to pure hands.

8 How so?
If one's hands were pure
and the cup's exterior was impure—
if one held it by its holding area,
he need not be concerned
whether his hands became impure through the cup's exterior.
If one was drinking from a cup
whose exterior was impure,

[132] Certain editions add "that cannot hold pomegranates" (see 17:4).

he dries them and they are pure: Only impurity in a vessel's "interior" can convey impurity to its entirety. The rule that the outside of vessels can become impure is a rabbinic ordinance, and it was not extended to the listed auxiliary parts of the vessel.

lacking an exterior and interior: The entire vessel is impure because all its parts are used together. The reference to pomegranates provides an alternative description of a vessel that cannot hold anything, but most commentators remove the phrase.

25:7 *All vessels have an exterior and interior*: Quoted from 25:1 above.

an area by which they are held: i.e. an indentation near the top of the vessel. This area is considered distinct; it can neither convey impurity to other parts of a vessel nor have impurity conveyed to it by the vessel itself.

R. Tarfon: Because of its size a large baking trough must be lifted by its holding area, which is not the case with smaller vessels. The Sages enacted a special rule for troughs in order to reduce cases of impurity that would make the trough unusable.

R. Aqiva: Cups can become impure more frequently than other vessels because they are mainly used with liquids. Therefore, the Sages enacted a special rule that protects cups from impurity that would make them unusable.

R. Meir holds that a cup's holding area does not let liquid in or out. One with impure hands will not render the cup impure if there is liquid on its exterior. Conversely, impure liquid on the holding area will not render the hands of the holder impure.

R. Yose: Unlike R. Meir, R. Yose holds that someone with pure hands holding a cup's holding area can neither receive impurity or convey it to or from the cup. This is not the case when one has impure hands.

25:8 *How so?* How does the distinction between the exterior and the holding area work in practice?

drinking from a cup…kettle boils over: It is unlikely that impure liquid that has left a vessel will return to it and defile it.

he need not be concerned
whether the liquid in his mouth became impure through the cup's exterior
and then conveyed impurity to the cup.
If a kettle boils over,
one need not be concerned
whether liquid came out of it
and touched its exterior
and returned again into its interior.

9 Sacred vessels do not have an exterior and an interior,
and they do not have [rules regarding] the part by which they are held.
And one may not immerse
vessels that are used for Sacred Things
while one is inside the other.
All articles become susceptible to impurity[133] through intention,
but they cannot be rendered insusceptible to impurity[134]
except through change in use.
For [a change in] use can annul both use and intention,
but intention cannot annul use or intention.

Chapter Twenty-Six

26:1–3 *Laced Items and Gloves*

26 An Imki sandal or a laced-up bag—
R. Judah says:

[133] Lit. "descend into impurity." [134] Lit. "ascend from impurity."

25:9 *Sacred vessels*, etc.: Vessels used in the Temple for sacrifices are always treated stringently. If any part of a vessel becomes impure the entire vessel is impure, and the previous distinctions do not apply.

Sacred Things: Sacrifices.

while one is inside the other: The purifying immersion water may not fully reach all the parts of both vessels. This stringency only applies to vessels used for Sacred Things.

intention: For example, a necklace for an animal is insusceptible because it serves no human need, but if one designates it for human use it becomes susceptible even before it has been used. On the other hand the same necklace, once susceptible, cannot lose its susceptibility unless it is changed in such a way that it could no longer be used for a human.

intention cannot annul: Once a thing has been made or even designated for human use, intention without rendering the item unfit for that use will never be sufficient to render the item insusceptible. A physical act must change its usefulness.

26:1 Most of the items in this and the following paragraphs are made of leather.

Imki: A site northeast of Acre. Alternatively, the phrase means a "valley sandal."

Imki sandal: A simple piece of leather that covers the sole of one's foot. It is insusceptible because it is flat but becomes susceptible when one adds straps that can fold it into a receptacle. Removing the straps makes the leather insusceptible again.

laced-up bag: When the drawstring is not present the bag is insusceptible because one cannot close it.

Also an Egyptian basket;
Rabban Simeon b. Gamaliel says:
The same applies also to a Laodicean sandal—
become susceptible to impurity or insusceptible to impurity
without [the aid of] a craftsman.
R. Yose said:
Do not all articles become susceptible to impurity or insusceptible to impurity
without [the aid of] a craftsman?
But these,
though they are unlaced,
are susceptible to impurity
since a common person can restore them.
They spoke only of an Egyptian basket,
which even the craftsman cannot restore.

2 If a laced-up bag has its laces removed,
it is susceptible to impurity.
If it is flattened,
it is insusceptible to impurity.
If one patched it from below,
it is susceptible to impurity.
If a bag is within a bag
and one of them is made impure by liquid,
the other does not become impure.
A packet of pearls is susceptible to impurity.
A packet of coins:
R. Eliezer deems it susceptible to impurity,
but the Sages deem it insusceptible to impurity.

Egyptian basket: A basket woven out of palm-leaf strips, which are initially insusceptible. When made into a basket they become susceptible. If the strip that holds the basket together is removed, the basket's material becomes insusceptible again.

without [the aid of] a craftsman: No special skill is needed to make or unmake these items.

R. Yose: Most items are susceptible even when they are disassembled because they are easily reassembled. The Egyptian basket is an exception because if it becomes undone even a craftsmen cannot reassemble it, so the Egyptian basket is insusceptible once disassembled.

26:2 *laced-up bag*: Because it can easily be repaired even by a nonexpert, as noted in 26:1.

flattened: It becomes a flat piece of leather without a receptacle.

If one patched it from below: If a separate patch had been sewn into the middle of the bag it might form a receptacle.

the other does not become impure: The two bags are not connectives.

A packet of pearls is susceptible to impurity: Because pearls are stored in it for long periods, after a while the leather will form a pouch.

R. Eliezer makes no distinction between packets of money and packets of pearls.

the Sages: A pearl pouch is not opened and closed frequently, thereby allowing the pearls to shape the leather. A money pouch is in constant use and there is no guarantee that it will take on the shape of a pouch.

3 The glove of a thorn collector is not susceptible to impurity.
A girdle and leg guards are susceptible to impurity.
Sleeves are susceptible to impurity,
but gloves[135] are not susceptible to impurity.
All finger gloves are insusceptible to impurity
except that of fruit pickers,
since it is used to contain sumac berries.
If it was torn
and cannot hold the greater part of a sumac berry,
it is insusceptible to impurity.

26:4–9 *Leather Items and Midras Impurity*

4 A sandal, one of whose loops[136] had been torn off,
and one mended it
is susceptible to *midras* impurity.
If a second [loop] was torn off
and he mended it,
it is pure regarding *midras* impurity
but is susceptible to *midras*-contact impurity.
If he did not have enough time to repair the first loop
before the second one tore off,
it is pure.
If the heel was torn off or if the toe piece was removed,
or if it was torn in two,
it is pure.
A slipper without heels
that is torn anywhere

[135] Or "headbands" or "leggings." See 24:15 above.

[136] Lit. "ears."

26:3 *The glove of a thorn collector*: The "glove" is actually a flat piece of leather tied to the hand to protect a thorn collector's palm when he clears thorny weeds from a field.

girdle... leg guards... Sleeves: All these leather clothes are "containers" for the body or limb.

gloves: These are flat pieces of leather tied around the head or some other part of the body (see n. 135) for protection.

All finger gloves are insusceptible: Since finger gloves do not cover the entire hand they are not considered receptacles. The fruit pickers' finger gloves, however, are receptacles because the pickers put small berries into them.

26:4 *A sandal, one of whose loops had been torn off*: A sandal has two loops on each side through which the main straps pass. The sandal remains usable if one loop tears off, so it remains subject to *midras* impurity.

If a second [loop] was torn off: The sandal is still functional but is considered new on account of the two new loops. If it was impure it remains so, but to a lesser degree.

If he did not have enough time to repair the first loop: If both loops are missing at the same time the sandal becomes unusable and insusceptible to impurity.

is pure.
A shoe that was damaged,
if it cannot contain the greater part of one's foot,
it is pure.
A shoe that is still on the shoe form:
R. Eliezer deems it insusceptible to impurity,
but the Sages deem it susceptible to impurity.
All water flasks that have been tied up
are insusceptible to impurity
except those of Arabs.
R. Meir says:
With an impermanent knot,
they are insusceptible to impurity;
with a permanent knot,
they are susceptible to impurity.
R. Yose says:
All tied-up water flasks
are insusceptible to impurity.

5 These hides are susceptible to *midras* impurity—
a hide that one intended for a rug,
the hide of an apron,
a hide [used as] a bedcover,
the hide of an ass driver or flax worker or porter or physician,
a hide [used for] a cradle,
a hide for a child's heart,
the hide of a pillow,
the hide of a blanket;
[all these are susceptible to] *midras* impurity.
A hide for combed wool[137]

[137] Var.: "a hide for flax combers."

R. Eliezer: Since the shoe has not been removed from the shoe form, the work on the shoe is incomplete.

the Sages: Placing the leather on the form gives the shoe its shape and thereby completes its manufacture.

water flasks that have been tied up: To repair a hole.

those of Arabs: All knots other than Arabian knots are easily undone. A water flask tied with a regular knot is a temporary insusceptible "vessel." A water flask tied with an Arabian knot is a real vessel.

R. Meir: There are permanent knots other than Arabian knots. Permanent knots repair a flask and render it susceptible.

R. Yose: All knots, including Arabian knots, fix a water flask temporarily. Only sewing it up completely repairs the flask.

26:5 *ass driver*: Ass drivers and flax workers used leather coverings to protect their clothing from dust and flax chaff. Porters wear a piece of leather to protect their shoulders. Physicians' aprons protected them from the blood of open wounds.

a hide for a child's heart: Perhaps a bib to protect the child's clothing, perhaps protection from animals.

[all these are susceptible to] midras impurity: They are used for sitting or lying.

and the hide of a wool comber:
R. Eliezer says: *Midras* impurity,
but the Sages say: Corpse impurity.

6 A bag or wrapper for garments
[is susceptible to] *midras* impurity.
A bag or wrapper for purple wool:
the House of Shammai say:
[Susceptible to] *midras* impurity;
and the House of Hillel say:
[Susceptible to] corpse impurity.
A hide that one made into a covering for utensils
is insusceptible to impurity.
[But if it is used] for weights,
it is susceptible to impurity;
R. Yose deems it insusceptible to impurity
in his father's name.

7 [In] any situation in which no labor is lacking,
intention makes it susceptible to impurity.
And [in] any situation where labor is lacking,
intention does not make it susceptible to impurity,
except for a skin.

8 Hides of a householder are made susceptible to impurity by intention,
but those of a tanner[138] are not made susceptible to impurity by intention.

[138] Or "leatherworker."

R. Eliezer: R. Eliezer holds that these objects are occasionally used for sitting. The Sages hold that this is unlikely. In any case these articles can function as clothing and are susceptible to corpse impurity.

26:6 *A bag or wrapper for garments*: All items in this mishnah are made of leather. The House of Shammai hold that anything that can potentially be used for sitting or lying, even occasionally, is susceptible to *midras* impurity. The House of Hillel's view is that the owners of these items are concerned about their being clean and do not use them as seats or mats. Nevertheless, as leather containers they are susceptible to corpse impurity.

A hide that one made into a covering for utensils: See above, 16:8.

[But if it is used for weights], it is susceptible to impurity: The leather cover will take on the shape of the weights, forming a receptacle.

R. Yose: In this view leather that covers weights only prevents the weights from becoming diminished due to use. The leather covers are secondary to the weights and are considered null.

26:7 *except for a skin*: Normally an unfinished item must actually be used before it becomes susceptible, but an unfinished skin can serve many purposes.

26:8 *Hides of a householder*: A householder who is unlikely to do any further work on the hides views them as finished. Intention to use them makes them susceptible.

those of a tanner: A tanner will not make use of his tanned hides so as not to spoil them before their sale. The hides are therefore insusceptible.

Those of a thief are made susceptible to impurity by intention,
but of a robber are not made susceptible to impurity by intention.
R. Simeon says:
The opposite:
those of a robber are made susceptible to impurity by intention;
those of a thief are not made susceptible to impurity by intention,
since the owners have not given up hope.

9 Leather that is impure with *midras* impurity
and one intended to use it for straps and sandals,
as soon as he puts the knife into it,
it is pure—
the words of R. Judah.
But the Sages say:
Until he has reduced it to less than five handbreadths.
R. Eliezer b. R. Zadok says:
Even one who makes an apron[139] from the hide,
it is impure.
From a cushion,
it is pure.

[139] Alt. "kerchief."

thief: Thieves steal surreptitiously so that their identity is unknown. Therefore, the hides' owners give up hope of retrieving them. Their loss of hope makes the object the thief's property, and so his plan to use them as they are renders them susceptible.

robber: A robber does not hide his identity when he steals, so his identity is known. Since the owner knows who the robber is, he does not give up hope of recovering his property. He retains ownership and the robber's intentions are void.

R. Simeon: A robber's temerity shows him to be a violent person from whom the hides' retrieval is unlikely. Therefore, the hides' original owners give up hope of getting them back and they become the robber's and his intentions are now significant. The thief, however, is timid and if caught can easily be sued for the hides' return. Therefore, the owner does not give up hope of retrieving them, and they remain legally his.

given up hope: Of retrieving their property. When owners despair of retrieval they are deemed to have renounced their ownership.

26:9 *R. Judah*: Hide for straps and sandals is insusceptible (above, 24:12). Once one designates them for this purpose and acts on that intention, they are insusceptible.

the Sages: See below, 27:2.

R. Eliezer b. R. Zadok: Since the new object can serve as a mat, the original *midras* impurity persists.

cushion: The change in function is so marked that the object is essentially a new utensil.

Chapter Twenty-Seven

27:1–28:10 *Cloth and Sack Material*

27 Cloth becomes impure because of [items of] five categories,[140]
sack material because of four,
leather because of three,
wood because of two,
and earthenware vessels because of one.
(1) An earthenware vessel becomes impure as a container.
Any earthenware vessel
that has no interior has no exterior.
(2) Wood exceeds it
in that it becomes impure [also] as a seat.
Thus a serving table[141] that has no rim
is susceptible to impurity if it is wooden
but insusceptible to impurity if it is earthenware.
(3) Leather exceeds it
in that it becomes impure [also] by Tent.
(4) Sack material exceeds it
in that it becomes impure [also] on account of being woven.
(5) Cloth exceeds it
in that it becomes impure [also] if it is three by three [fingerbreadths].

2 Cloth becomes impure with *midras* on account of being three by three [handbreadths]
and on account of being three by three [fingerbreadths] to corpse impurity.

140 Lit. "names." 141 Or "plank, board."

27:1 *sack material*: Made of woven animal (usually goat) hair.

serving table that has no rim: Such a table has no receptacle, and therefore is not susceptible if made of earthenware. But it can serve as a seat, and therefore is susceptible if made of wood.

Tent: Leather can become impure as a receptacle, as a seat, and as an enclosure over a corpse. Wood can become impure as a result of serving as a Tent only if it not attached to the ground.

on account of being woven: Weaving animal hair makes it susceptible even if it is not made into a sack. Sack material is susceptible as a receptacle, as a seat, by means of Tent, and by weaving. (Sheep hair becomes wool, and is therefore considered ordinary cloth.)

three by three [fingerbreadths]: Any cloth of this size is susceptible in addition to the ways listed above, even if it is not otherwise a "vessel".

27:2 *midras…corpse impurity*: Three by three handbreadths of cloth is subject to *midras* impurity because one can sit on it. A three by three fingerbreadths' measure is sufficient for corpse impurity because that amount of cloth can be used for patching or for the clothing of the poor.

Sack material: four by four [handbreadths],
leather: five by five [handbreadths],
matting: six by six [handbreadths];
they are equal regarding *midras* impurity and corpse impurity.
R. Meir says:
Sack material
when its remnants are four [by four handbreadths],
but at the outset when it is complete.

3 If one combines[142] two [handbreadths] of cloth and one of sack material,
three of sack material and one of leather,
four of leather and one of matting,
it is insusceptible to impurity.
Five of matting and one of leather,
four of leather and one of sack material,
three of sack material and one of cloth,
it is susceptible to impurity.
This is the general rule:
If one connects one material
to one which is stricter,
it is susceptible to impurity.
[To] one which is more lenient,
it is insusceptible to impurity.

4 If one cuts a handbreadth by a handbreadth
from any of them—
it is susceptible to impurity;
a handbreadth by a handbreadth
from a basket's bottom—
it is susceptible to impurity.

[142] Lit. "makes."

Sack material, etc.: The different measurements for sack material, leather, and matting refer to the smallest amounts of these materials that people usually use.

They are equal: Sack, leather, and matting have only one measurement, for both *midras* and corpse impurity.

R. Meir holds that when sack material is first made it is insusceptible even beyond four by four handbreadths until one has completed its manufacture. Once completed, if the material is torn into four by four handbreadths pieces, it remains susceptible.

27:3 *it is insusceptible*: Though the criterion of the proper measure for susceptibility for one ingredient is met, these mixed products are insusceptible. In the first case the measure of the cloth is completed by a product with more demanding purity rules, namely sack material, and there is not enough altogether to render the sack material impure.

it is susceptible: If a product's measure for susceptibility is met by adding a more highly susceptible material, e.g. leather completed by using sacking material, it is susceptible. Thus adding one handbreadth of leather to five of sack material produces six by six, which is enough to render either material impure.

27:4 *a handbreadth by a handbreadth…it is susceptible*: One cuts one of the four materials from 27:2 specifically for use as a seat. The previous paragraphs speak of cases in which this specific intention was not present.

From the basket's sides—
R. Simeon deems it insusceptible to impurity,
but the Sages say:
If one cuts one handbreadth by one handbreadth from anywhere,
it is susceptible to impurity.

5 If one prepared
worn-out pieces of a sifter or sieve
for use as a seat,
R. Aqiva deems them susceptible to impurity,
but the Sages deem them insusceptible to impurity
unless he trims their rough ends.
A child's chair that has legs,
even if it is less than a handbreadth high,
is susceptible to impurity.
[Regarding] a child's shirt:
R. Eliezer says:
Even the smallest measure [is susceptible to impurity];
but the Sages say:
Only if it is of the prescribed size;
and it should be measured double.

6 These are measured double—
clogs, breeches, pants, a hat, and the pocket of a hollow belt.
A patch that one attached to a rim—
if it is not doubled it is measured plainly.[143]
And if it is doubled it is measured double.

[143] Lit. "If it is stretched out it is measured stretched out."

R. Simeon: The basket's sides are curved and not fit for use as a seat.

the Sages: If one intends to use a part of a basket for a seat, no matter what its shape, the intention makes it a seat.

27:5 *R. Aqiva*: Any change in the utensil's pieces that will allow someone to use them as a seat is sufficient to generate susceptibility.

the Sages: The pieces must be refashioned into a proper seat.

even if it is less than a handbreadth high: An adult's chair has to be at least one handbreadth high in order to be functional. A child's chair serves the child's needs even if it is lower.

R. Eliezer: As long as the shirt is functional, any amount of it is susceptible.

the Sages: The shirt remains a cloth item and must be the stipulated size (see 27:3) to be susceptible.

measured double: There should be three handbreadths of cloth in the shirt's front and back, as well as its width.

27:6 *These are measured double*: They must have the requisite size in both front and back.

clogs: Shoes or socks of some kind.

breeches: Pants that reach from the waist to the thighs, or perhaps a kind of loincloth.

hollow belt: A belt folded to create a hollow space that functions as a pocket, or perhaps a sling.

If it is not doubled: A straight patch will have to be three by three handbreadths only on one side. If it has been folded over the rim, it will have to be three by three handbreadths on back and front.

7 If one wove a cloth of three by three [handbreadths]
and it contracted *midras* impurity,
and he finished the whole piece of cloth
and afterward removed one thread from the first part,
it is free of *midras* impurity
but impure with *midras*-contact impurity.
If he removed one thread from the first part
and afterward he finished the whole piece of cloth,
it is impure with *midras*-contact impurity.

8 So, too, if one wove a cloth three by three [fingerbreadths]
and it contracted corpse impurity
and he finished the whole piece of cloth
and afterward removed one thread from the first part,
it is free of corpse impurity,
but impure from contact with corpse impurity.
If he removed one thread from the first part
and afterward finished the whole piece of cloth,
it is pure,
for they have said:
If a piece three by three [fingerbreadths] is lessened,
it is pure.
But if [a piece] three by three [handbreadths] is lessened,
though it is insusceptible to *midras* impurity,
it is susceptible to all [other] impurities.

9 If a sheet contracted *midras* impurity
and one made it into a curtain,
it is pure regarding *midras* impurity
but is impure with *midras*-contact impurity.

27:7 *one thread from the first part*: He reduced the original cloth from the requisite measure for impurity, thus rendering it free of *midras* impurity.

impure with midras-contact impurity: Even though the reduction of the cloth's size removes *midras* impurity, the remaining cloth still had been in contact with cloth that was *midras* impure and can render food impure.

and afterward he finished: Removing the thread made the initial cloth pure of *midras*. When later expanded, the larger cloth will nevertheless have *midras*-contact impurity, the highest level of impurity it will reach from the initial *midras* impurity.

impure with midras-contact impurity: Even after he reduced the original cloth to less than three handbreadths, so it lost its *midras* impurity, it was still big enough to contract and maintain other forms of impurity, which only requires three fingerbreadths (see above, 27:2 and below, 27:8).

27:8 *three by three [fingerbreadths]*: The measurement for corpse impurity is considerably smaller than that for *midras* impurity because corpse impurity only requires that cloth be usable as a part of a garment, while *midras* impurity requires that it be usable as a seat.

it is pure: It becomes entirely pure since it is useless as a part of a garment.

27:9 *pure regarding midras impurity but is impure with midras-contact impurity*: The curtain is no longer available as a seat, so the change removes *midras* impurity. Nevertheless, the curtain remains impure with *midras*-contact impurity.

R. Yose said:
What *midras* impurity has this touched?
But if a *zav* touched it,
it would be impure with *zav*-contact impurity.
10 [If a piece of cloth] three by three handbreadths [that had contracted *midras* impurity] was divided,
it is pure regarding *midras* impurity,
but impure with *midras*-contact impurity.
R. Yose said:
What *midras* impurity has it touched?
But if a *zav* touched it,
it would be impure with *zav*-touch impurity.
11 [Cloth] three by three [handbreadths]
on a garbage heap—
[is susceptible to impurity] if it is sturdy[144] and able to hold salt.
In the house—
if it is either sturdy
or able to hold salt.
How much salt must it hold?
A quarter[-*qav*].
R. Judah says:
Fine [salt].
But the Sages say:
Coarse.
Both intend to be lenient.
R. Simeon says:
Three by three [handbreadths] on a garbage heap
is equal
to three by three [fingerbreadths] in the house.
12 If [cloth] three by three [handbreadths] was torn
and one put it on a chair

[144] Lit. "healthy."

R. Yose holds that the radical change from a seat or sheet into a curtain completely purifies the cloth.

impure with zav-contact impurity: Whatever a *zav* touches becomes impure until the evening of that day.

27:10 *was divided*: Now lacking the requisite measure for *midras* impurity, it is completely free of *midras* impurity, but because of contact with *midras* impurity it is impure with *midras*-contact impurity.

27:11 *Both intend to be lenient*: R. Judah is lenient in that fine salt puts more pressure on the cloth because it is densely packed. The Sages also seek to be lenient in that coarse salt's rough edges will tear most regular cloth.

In the house: cloth that is useful can become impure when smaller than three handbreadths.

R. Simeon: In the house a fragment that is only three fingerbreadths square is not subject to *midras* impurity at all; according to R. Simeon the same holds for cloth of any size that has been thrown onto the trash heap. No one would wish to sit on it.

27:12 *[cloth] three by three [handbreadths] was torn*: If one's skin touches the seat at the tear it is a sign that the cloth no longer possesses the proper measure for susceptibility to *midras* impurity.

and his flesh touches the seat,
it is insusceptible to impurity;
if not, it is susceptible to impurity.
[Cloth] three by three [fingerbreadths]
from which a thread was worn away,
or in which a knot was found,
or two threads running alongside each other,
is insusceptible to impurity.
[Cloth of] three by three [fingerbreadths]
that one threw on a garbage heap
is insusceptible to impurity.
If he retrieved it,
it is susceptible to impurity.
Its disposal always renders it insusceptible to impurity,
and its retrieval renders it susceptible to impurity,
except for purple or fine crimson.
R. Eliezer says:
The same applies also to a patch of new cloth.
R. Simeon says:
They are all insusceptible to impurity.
These were mentioned
only concerning the return of lost property.

Chapter Twenty-Eight

28 [Cloth] three by three [fingerbreadths]
that one put into a ball
or made into a ball by itself

thread was worn away: Three fingerbreadths by three fingerbreadths are susceptible to corpse impurity. The slightest diminution of this measure renders cloth insusceptible. Similarly with the knot and the parallel threads, these are not normal weaving, so do not count as cloth.

Its disposal... its retrieval: Disposal indicates intention to end functionality by making the material garbage. Retrieval reinstates the product's usability.

purple or fine crimson: The value of these dyed materials is such that someone might use them even if they were discarded by someone else.

R. Eliezer holds that fresh new cloth similarly is useful to someone even if someone else has discarded it.

R. Simeon: No one will use material from a garbage heap since it is ruined there, and therefore it is insusceptible. However, materials like purple and crimson found there are so valuable that they are considered lost, and one is required to return them to their original owners.

28:1 *put into a ball*: As stuffing.

is insusceptible to impurity.
But [cloth] three by three [handbreadths]
that he put into a ball
is susceptible to impurity.
If he made it into a ball by itself
it is insusceptible to impurity,
because the stitching reduces its size.

2 [Cloth] less than three by three handbreadths
that one prepared to stop up a bath,
to stir a pot,
to wipe a mill,
whether ready [for that use] or not ready,
is susceptible to impurity—
the words of R. Eliezer.
R. Joshua says:
Whether ready [for that use] or not ready,
it is insusceptible to impurity.
R. Aqiva says:
If ready [for that use]
it is susceptible to impurity;
if not ready
it is insusceptible to impurity.

3 If one makes a plaster[145] of cloth or leather,
it is insusceptible to impurity.
R. Yose says:
[If] of leather it is insusceptible to impurity.[146]
If one made a poultice[147]

[145] That is, a bandage soaked in ointment.
[146] R. Yose's comment does not appear in **K**, **P**, and $\mathbf{P}_2$. It is apparently a transfer from 28:6 below.
[147] That is, a bandage covered with flour and other ingredients.

insusceptible: If three by three fingerbreadths of cloth is used for anything other than patching it is pure on account of its insignificant size.

three by three [handbreadths]: Cloth of this size is not insignificant; even when stuffed into a ball it can be seen as placed there for storage and still potentially useful. But if made into a ball by itself, the sewing thread will pull it into a smaller, insufficient size.

28:2 *prepared to stop up a bath*, etc.: Since one can use it, it is a susceptible "vessel."

stir a pot: One prepared to use the cloth to protect the hands from the hot pot.

ready…not ready: That is, not stored away but available for immediate use. The cloth is insusceptible to *midras* impurity, and the dispute concerns other sorts of impurity and various kinds of "readiness." Commentators differ as to the precise opinion of each named teacher.

28:3 *a plaster of cloth or leather…is insusceptible*: Covering these materials with ointment degrades them so that they are unusable for anything else.

poultice: If it is made of cloth, the cloth becomes degraded and unusable, as above. If it is made with leather, the mixture of flour, medicine, and fat can be scraped off once it dries with little damage to the leather. *Rabban Simeon b. Gamaliel* holds the same regarding cloth.

of cloth,
it is insusceptible to impurity;
of leather,
it is susceptible to impurity.
Rabban Simeon b. Gamaliel says:
Even one of cloth
is susceptible to impurity,
since it [can] be shaken.

4 Wrappers for scrolls,
whether embroidered or not embroidered,
are susceptible to impurity
according to the words of the House of Shammai.
The House of Hillel say:
Embroidered,
they are insusceptible to impurity.
Those that are not embroidered
are susceptible to impurity.
Rabban Gamaliel says:
These and these
are insusceptible to impurity.

5 If a head covering that had contracted *midras* impurity
was placed on a scroll,
it is free of *midras* impurity
but susceptible to corpse impurity.
If a waterskin was used as a rug,
or a rug was used as a waterskin,
it is pure.
If a waterskin was used as a shepherd's wallet,
or a shepherd's wallet was used as a waterskin,
or a mattress was used as a sheet,
or a sheet as a mattress,
or a cushion was used as a napkin,
or a napkin as a cushion,
it is susceptible to impurity.

28:4 *House of Shammai*: These wrappers serve not only the scroll but the people who read it. Items must serve human needs for susceptibility.

House of Hillel: The embroidered wrappers were clearly dedicated to beautifying the Torah scroll and not to serve human needs. Unembroidered wrappers, however, could be put to many uses, including ones that served human needs.

Rabban Gamaliel: Once the wrapper had been used on a sacred scroll, it could be used for no other purpose.

28:5 *midras impurity…corpse impurity*: Once the head wrap was dedicated as a scroll wrapper it became forbidden to sit or lie on it because of its sanctity. Therefore it could no longer contract *midras* impurity.

a waterskin…rug…pure: If an item is impure with *midras* impurity, then changing its use is viewed as breaking and then repairing it for a new purpose. For example, a waterskin is susceptible as a receptacle, but a rug is susceptible as a seat.

general rule: The new item must be completely different to lose its impurity.

This is the general rule:
If one changed it into a use of the same category,
it is susceptible to impurity,
but if into a use of different category,
it is pure.

6 If one patched [an impure] patch onto a basket,
[the basket] renders impure at one [remove]
and renders invalid at one [further remove].
If he removed it from the basket,
the basket renders impure at one [remove]
and renders invalid at one [further remove];
but the patch is pure.
If it is patched onto cloth,
it renders impure at two [removes]
and renders invalid at one [further] remove.
If one removed it from the cloth,
the cloth renders impure at one [remove]
and renders invalid at one [further remove].
The patch renders impure at two [removes]
and renders invalid at one [further remove].
So, too, one who patches onto sacking or leather—
the words of R. Meir.
R. Simeon deems [these] insusceptible to impurity.
R. Yose says:
If on leather,

28:6 *patch onto a basket*: If the patch has *midras* impurity it defiles the basket with *midras*-contact impurity. This level of impurity, one step away from the original *midras* impurity, can convey impurity to food. The impure food, two steps away from the *midras* impurity, can "invalidate" *terumah*, making it prohibited for eating.

the basket renders impure: The removal of the cloth patch from the basket does not remove *midras*-contact impurity from the basket. Therefore, all the rules applicable in the first case are applicable here as well.

but the patch is pure: When the patch was attached it became an integral part of the basket and lost its previous function. Even the patch now suffers only *midras*-contact impurity as part of the basket and loses that status as well when it is removed.

patched onto cloth: Since the patch and the cloth are both fabric, the combined whole takes the status of the patch, and the whole has the *midras* impurity that the patch started with.

it renders impure at two [removes]: Because of the patch's addition, the cloth becomes *midras* impure and can convey *midras*-contact impurity to foods and liquids. The impure foods and liquids then disqualify *termuah* from being eaten.

patch renders impure at two [removes]: The patch did not lose its identity, because it was attached to a similar fabric.

R. Meir: Since leather and sack material are used to make clothing, they are like fabric here and are susceptible.

R. Simeon: Sack material and leather are clearly not of the same category as fabric. Putting a cloth patch on them changes the patch's regular use to what is irregular and purifies it.

R. Yose differs with R. Simeon in the case of patching together of cloth and sacking material. Both are woven, so both are considered "fabric."

it is pure.
If onto sacking
it is impure,
since this is woven stuff.

7 The three by three [fingerbreadths] of which they spoke
does not include the hem—
the words of R. Simeon,
but the Sages say:
Three by three [fingerbreadths] exactly.
If one patched in onto cloth
by one of its [the patch's] edges,
this is not a connective.
By two opposite edges,
it is a connective.
If he [sewed] it *gamma*-wise:
R. Aqiva deems it impure,
but the Sages deem it pure.
R. Judah said:
When does this apply?
In the case of a cloak.
But in the case of a shirt,
[a patch] from above is a connective;
but from below
is not a connective.

8 The garments of the poor,
even though they are not three by three [fingerbreadths in size]
are susceptible to *midras* impurity.
If one began to tear a cloak,

28:7 *not a connective*: A patch attached on only one edge is not secure. If the patch is impure, the larger cloth is not affected; if the larger cloth is impure, the patch is not affected.

opposite sides: If the patch has been sewn on both ends or both edges, it is secure.

gamma-wise: If the patch was sewn on two adjacent sides forming a right angle.

R. Aqiva: The patch is sufficiently attached not to fall off. Therefore, it is a connective.

the Sages: Since two edges of the patch are loose they form a flap. If the flap opens, the tear in the clothing is visible. Hence, the patch does not serve its purpose and cannot be considered a connective.

When does this apply? When is a patch sewn on one edge not a connective?

cloak…shirt: A "cloak" is a plain rectangle of cloth that can be wound or draped around the body; it has no top or bottom, no outside or inside. A "shirt" has a top and a bottom as well as an outside and an inside. A patch sewn onto a "cloak" by one edge can never cover the hole, because the garment can be worn upside down and the patch will hang loose. In the case of a shirt, it all depends on which edge is sewn.

above…below: Commentators differ; "from above" may refer to the top of the garment or the top of the hole being patched. In either case the point is that the patch sewn above will hang over the hole and cover it, while a patch sewn below will hang loose and the hole will remain visible.

28:8 *garments of the poor*: Clothing made of cloth scraps none of which are three by three fingerbreadths is susceptible to *midras* impurity if they are sewn together.

as soon as the greater part is torn
[the fragments] are not connectives.
Very thick or very thin [cloth]
is not subject to the [rule of] three by three [fingerbreadths].

9 A porter's pad is susceptible to *midras* impurity.
A wine filter is not subject to seat impurity.
An old woman's hairnet is susceptible to impurity because one can sit on it.
A harlot's shift made like a net is insusceptible to impurity.
If one makes a garment out of a fishnet,
it is insusceptible to impurity.
But out of the net's bottom,
it is susceptible to impurity.
R. Eliezer b. Jacob says:
Also if one makes a garment from fishnet
and doubles it,
it is susceptible to impurity.

10 If one began [to make] a hairnet from its mouth,
it is insusceptible to impurity until he completes its skull.
If he began with its skull,
it is insusceptible to impurity until he finishes its mouth.
Its headband is independently susceptible to impurity.
Its strings are susceptible to impurity because they are connectives.

as soon as the greater part is torn: Once the cloak's greater part is torn, it is nonfunctional and pure. If one part becomes impure it cannot affect the other because they are no longer deemed connected.

Very thick or very thin cloth: Neither one is useful to patch clothing. The first is too hard to sew on. The second is not durable. Such material is susceptible to impurity only if it meets the larger minimum size of three by three handbreadths.

28:9 *A porter's pad*: Since it is pillow-like, the porter may sometimes sit on it. Hence, it is susceptible to *midras* impurity.

wine filter: This is a long leather sieve for removing lees from wine. No one sits on it because of its dirt and stickiness.

An old woman's hairnet: At first glance this rule contradicts that in 24:16 above, but see the variant tradition cited there.

A harlot's shift...fishnet: These items are so open that they do not thoroughly cover one's body like proper clothing and so are insusceptible.

net's bottom: The net's bottom is a solid weave. Clothing made from it covers one's body thoroughly.

R. Eliezer b. Jacob: By doubling the fishnet one makes it thick enough to cover one's body thoroughly, so it becomes susceptible.

28:10 *mouth...skull*: The "mouth" is the part of the net that goes around the forehead. The "skull" is the part that covers the greater part of the head.

headband: Since one can easily remove an ornamental headband that holds the hairnet in place and put it on another hairnet, it is susceptible independent of the hairnet.

strings: i.e. the strings with which one ties the hairnet on.

If a hairnet is torn,
if it cannot contain the greater part of the hair,
it is insusceptible to impurity.

Chapter Twenty-Nine

29:1–8 *Connectives*

29 The fringes of a sheet, scarf, hat, or kerchief
[are connectives up to] six fingerbreadths.
Those of an undershirt
[up to] ten [fingerbreadths].
The fringes of a thick wool coat, a veil, a shirt, or cloak
[up to] three fingerbreadths.
The fringes of an old woman's cap, an Arab's face protector,
a Cilician goat-hair cloth, a money belt, a turban, or a curtain—
their fringes [are connectives] whatever their length.

2 Three woolen cushions, six linen cushions, three sheets, twelve napkins, two arm protectors, one shirt, one cloak, one thick woolen cloak
are connectives for impurity and for sprinkling.
More than this,
they are connectives for impurity
but not for sprinkling.
R. Yose says:
Not even for impurity.

3 The cord of a plumb line
[is a connective up to] twelve [handbreadths];

If a hairnet is torn: It is insusceptible because it no longer carries out its function.

29:1 *fringes*: Decorative fringes left by a weaver on woven goods.

six…ten…three fingerbreadths…whatever their length: These measurements are dependent on the article and what is typical in terms of its decorative fringe.

29:2 *Three woolen cushions*, etc.: These items are either sewn or woven together.

arm protectors: Sleeves one uses to protect one's arms during work.

for sprinkling: For purification from corpse impurity. They can be treated as a single object for purification.

More than this: If the number of items exceeds the number given above, both susceptibility and sprinkling are handled stringently. All become susceptible as one, but each component requires sprinkling.

R. Yose rejects the need for stringency in the case of impurity. Once the connections are so attenuated, the items cannot be considered connected. Therefore, they cannot convey impurity to one another.

29:3 *twelve [handbreadths]…eighteen…fifty cubits*: After the first, the *plumb lines* mentioned suit the needs of artisans.

that of a carpenter's,
[up to] eighteen;
that of a builder,
[up to] fifty cubits.
More than that,
[even] if one wanted to maintain it,
it is insusceptible to impurity.
Those of plasterers or artists
[are susceptible to impurity] whatever their length.

4 The cord of a goldsmith's or a fine purple dealer's scale
[is a connective up to a length of] three fingerbreadths.
An ax handle behind him
[up to] three fingerbreadths.
R. Yose says:
[If there is] one handbreadth [behind him] it is insusceptible to impurity.

5 The cord of shopkeepers' or householders' scales
[is a connective up to] one handbreadth.
An ax handle in front of him
[up to] one handbreadth.
The remnant of a compass handle:
one handbreadth.
The shaft of a stonemason's chisel:
one handbreadth.

More than that: Even though a particular individual feels that he needs a longer plumb line than his profession typically demands, general practice renders his intention null.

plasterers or artists: Since these artisans' work must look right; they need to know that no part of the wall where they are working juts out and ruins their product.

29:4 The lists from here to the end of the chapter are arranged by increasing amounts of length that form connectives.

three fingerbreadths: Due to the high value of gold and fine purple wool their weight has to be exact. The short string guarantees that the scale will be accurate.

An ax handle behind him: Since a cutter holds an ax handle toward its middle, some of it extends behind his hand. The amount that typically sticks out is three fingerbreadths. Therefore, that much of the ax handle is a connective.

R. Yose: If the area behind the cutter's hand is a handbreadth in length, the ax is unwieldy and unusable; the entire handle is insusceptible.

29:5 *one handbreadth*: All these implements are held in one hand or are functional only if one handbreadth extends beyond one's grip.

remnant of a compass handle: Architects use this compass for drawing circles, and it is quite large. Even if the handle breaks, as long as there is a handbreadth left the architect can still use the compass. Other commentators see here a maximum as is usual in this chapter: only the first handbreadth of the remnant is a connective. This reading also is more compatible with the following rule about a mason's chisel.

6 The cord of wool dealers' and glass weighers' scales
[is a connective up to] two handbreadths.
The handle of a millstone drill:
two handbreadths.
The handle of a legionaries' battle-ax:
two handbreadths.
The handle of a goldsmith's hammer:
two handbreadths.
Of a blacksmith's:
three handbreadths.
7 The remnants at the upper part of an ox prod
[are a connective up to] four [handbreadths].
The handle of an irrigation spade:
four [handbreadths].
The handle of a weeding spade:
five [handbreadths].
The handle of a small hammer:
five [handbreadths]
and of a regular hammer:
six [handbreadths].
The handle of an ax for splitting wood or hoeing:
six [handbreadths],
and the handle of a stone trimmer's chisel:
six [handbreadths].
8 The remnants at the lower part of [the shaft inserted into] a plow blade
[are a connective up to] seven [handbreadths].
The handle of a householder's oven shovel:
the House of Shammai say:
Seven [handbreadths],
the House of Hillel say:
Eight [handbreadths].
That of a plasterer:
the House of Shammai say:
Nine [handbreadths],
the House of Hillel say:
Ten [handbreadths].
More than that,

29:6 *two handbreadths*: All the items in this list are held with two hands; a blacksmith's hands takes an extra handbreadth to avoid the heat.

29:7 *at the upper part*: The end near the blade.

four [handbreadths]: The various utensils mentioned must have handles of four, five, or six handbreadths in order to be usable and therefore susceptible.

29:8 *the lower part of [the shaft inserted into] a plow blade*: This is a pole inserted into the blade that digs into the ground. If the pole breaks and seven handbreadths remain, it still can be used for plowing.

oven shovel: Used to clear ashes from the oven.

if one wanted to maintain it,
it is susceptible to impurity.
The handle of fire implements
[is a connective] whatever its length.

Chapter Thirty

30:1–4 *Glassware*

30 Glass utensils:
flat ones are insusceptible to impurity,
those with a receptacle are susceptible to impurity.
If they are broken,
they become pure.
If one remade them into utensils,
they are susceptible to impurity from then on.
A glass tray and plate
are insusceptible to impurity.
If they have a rim,
they are susceptible to impurity.
If the [concave] bottoms of a glass tray or plate
were prepared for use,
they are insusceptible to impurity.
If they were scraped or filed,
they are susceptible to impurity.
2 A mirror is insusceptible to impurity.
A tray made into a mirror
is susceptible to impurity,

if one wanted to maintain it: Unlike the plumb lines in 29:3 above, handles are essential for the proper function of the vessels to which they are attached. If one wishes to use the entire handle, for that person it is a susceptible "vessel" and a connective to the rest of the tool.

whatever its length: Since everyone wishes to maintain distance from a fire.

30:1 *Glass utensils*: See 15:1 above.

If they have a rim: The rim forms the object into a receptacle.

the bottoms of a glass tray or plate: After the object broke, one found a use for the remnants, but his intention is insufficient to make these items susceptible because their damaged edges are dangerous.

scraped or filed: The sharp edges of the glass, making the bottom usable.

30:2 *A mirror is insusceptible*: Since it has no receptacle.

A tray made into a mirror: Since the tray's shape, which has a receptacle, has not changed; such a mirror remains susceptible.

but if at the outset it was made as a mirror,
it is insusceptible to impurity.
A spoon[148] placed on the table:
if it can contain any amount,
it is susceptible to impurity.
If not:
R. Aqiva deems it susceptible to impurity,
R. Yohanan b. Nuri deems it insusceptible to impurity.
3 If the greater part of a cup is broken off,
it is insusceptible to impurity.
If it was broken in three [places] over its majority,[149]
it is insusceptible to impurity.
R. Simeon says:
If it lets the greater part of the water leak out,
it is insusceptible to impurity.
If there was a hole in it
and it was mended with tin or pitch,
it is insusceptible to impurity.
R. Yose says:
If with tin,
it is susceptible to impurity;
if with pitch,
it is insusceptible to impurity.
4 A small flask that lost its mouth
is susceptible to impurity.

[148] Alt. "scoop" or "ladle."
[149] **P**$_2$: "If it was damaged in one third of its majority."

if at the outset: If from the very beginning one made a tray-shaped vessel to be used as a mirror, one's intention determines that the vessel is a mirror.

spoon: Made of glass.

If not: The spoon is so unstable when lying on the table that it will spill its contents.

R. Aqiva declares such a spoon susceptible because when one uses it by hand it contains its contents without difficulty. Since one typically uses a spoon with one's hand it is a "vessel."

R. Yohanan b. Nuri considers the unstable spoon insusceptible because its ability to contain anything is momentary rather than long term. As such it cannot be said to have a functioning container.

30:3 *If the greater part of a cup is broken off*: The cup's remnants are broken pieces of a "vessel" and are insusceptible.

in three [places] over its majority: That is, in three places that cover most of its surface. People usually throw away cups that are damaged to this degree. Garbage is insusceptible.

tin or pitch: Since these do not adhere well to glass, it continues to leak and no longer possesses a receptacle.

R. Yose: Tin adheres well enough to glass to allow for the cup to receive cold and hot liquid, thereby making it a functional "vessel." Pitch melts when a hot liquid touches it, leaving the cup without a receptacle.

30:4 *small flask…susceptible, large [flask]…insusceptible*: One can hold a small glass flask broken at its neck with one hand and pour from it without scratching oneself, because one is only touching it below the break. One would find it difficult to avoid scratches when using two hands to lift a large broken flask and pour from it.

A large [flask] that lost its mouth
is insusceptible to impurity.
One for spikenard oil that lost its mouth
is insusceptible to impurity
because it scratches the hand.
Large jugs that have lost their mouths
are susceptible to impurity
because one can repair them for pickles.
A glass funnel is pure.
R. Yose said:
Happy are you, O [tractate] *Kelim*,
for you entered in impurity, but have departed in purity!

mouth: The neck that leads to the opening of the flask.

because it scratches the hand: Putting one's finger into the spikenard oil flask to apply the oil may result in a cut.

pickles: Even though the flask is chipped, one can use it as a pickle container. The mouth is generally wide enough for one to remove the pickled products without scratching one's hand and most people use tongs to remove the product.

funnel: Since the funnel is designed to let its contents escape, it has no true receptacle and is insusceptible.

for you entered in impurity, but have departed in purity: The tractate began with a list of things that cause impurity, and ends describing an article that is always pure.

Tractate Oholot

Yehudah Cohn

Introduction

Overview

The title *Oholot*, meaning "Tents," is presumably derived from Numbers 19:14, where a tent in which someone has died is said to impart impurity lasting seven days to people entering it as well as anything inside it. The tractate is largely concerned with the halakhic variants of this kind of corpse impurity (or animal-carcass impurity), which can be viewed as radiating within a bounded area from an impure source. Alternative means of contracting impurity—by direct physical contact with an impure source (cf. Numbers 19:11 and 19:16, Leviticus 11:39), or its carriage without direct contact (cf. Leviticus 11:40)—are also addressed. Once transmitted to an object or person, impurity can then be further retransmitted, with limitations that are discussed in the opening mishnayot 1:1–5.

Main Ideas

Minimum size limits are required of different sources in order for these to convey impurity, and such qualifying limits are discussed. The classic example of a size limit, frequently encountered, is an amount from a corpse equal in volume to an olive. Usually the idea of a limit is implied rather than explicitly mentioned—so that the "olive" actually refers to an amount equal to an olive *or larger*. The minimum size of the halakhic "Tent" itself is a cube that measures 1 × 1 × 1 handbreadths, as mentioned in 3:7, and such notional Tents are best imagined by the reader as hollow spaces rather than as freestanding objects. Importantly, such Tents can even be formed by people, including passers by. The formation of "Tents," and conditions under which they are not formed, are frequent topics of the tractate.

While halakhic Tents convey impurity, they also contain its spread by barring further transmission, so that (for example) objects on the roof of a Tent do not become impure. When, on the other hand, the dimensions of the Tent are less than 1 × 1 × 1 handbreadths there is nothing to bar impurity, which is then contained in a different way. In such a case the impurity does not spread to the sides of the impure source but rather in an infinite vertical line directly above and below the impure source itself, and is accordingly said to "break through and up, and break through and down."

In addition to the biblical verses mentioned above, the halakhah of the "tight closure," in 8:6 and 12:2 below, is derived by the rabbis from Numbers 19:15, which is the verse following the biblical discussion of impurity in a Tent.

Throughout, the tractate refers to objects or people "being" pure or impure, and this generally refers to them remaining pure or becoming impure, respectively. Impurity contracted can be further transmitted, as mentioned above, and the context determines whether the text is referring to the initial contraction of impurity, or its transmission.

Special Notes for the Reader

An invaluable resource for the study of the text of *Oholot* is A. Goldberg's edition (Jerusalem: Magnes Press, 1955, in Hebrew). This critical edition of the tractate, based on manuscripts, early printed editions, and witnesses to the text in the writings of medieval rabbis, has been consulted throughout.

The sigla used herein for the Kaufmann and Parma Biblioteca Palatina 3173 manuscripts (the latter also known as DeRossi 138) are **K** and **P** respectively. I have also made reference, in 2:1 below, to a variant found in the Parma Biblioteca Palatina 2596 manuscript (also known as DeRossi 497), for which the siglum $\mathbf{P}_2$ has been used.

Tractate Oholot

Chapter One

1:1–5 *Degrees of Impurity*

1 When two contract impurity from a corpse—
one [of them] contracts seven-day impurity and the other evening impurity.
When three contract impurity from a corpse—
two contract seven-day impurity and one evening impurity.
When four contract impurity from a corpse—
three contract seven-day impurity and one evening impurity.
Two—how so?
A person who touches a corpse contracts seven-day impurity,
and someone touching him contracts evening impurity.
2 Three—how so?
When objects touch a corpse, and [those] objects [touch other] objects,
they [all] contract seven-day impurity.
The third, whether a person or objects, contracts evening impurity.
3 Four—how so?
When objects touch a corpse, and a person [touches] those objects,

1:1 *When two contract impurity from a corpse*: This sentence and the following two are expressed as riddles, which will be solved at the end of this mishnah and in 1:2 and 1:3.

Two—how so? Referring to the first sentence in the mishnah.

A person who touches a corpse contracts seven-day impurity: i.e. is impure for seven days. Cf. Numbers 19:11, 16.

someone touching him: i.e. someone touching a person who contracted seven-day impurity by touching a corpse.

contracts evening impurity: That is, becomes impure until the evening of the day on which the event causing impurity took place. This rule is based on the rabbinic understanding of Numbers 19:22. Someone with evening impurity does not transmit it further.

1:2 *Three—how so?* Referring to the second sentence of 1:1.

objects: The word rendered here as "objects" generally refers to usable manmade objects. *Kelim*, the preceding tractate, deals with purity regulations governing a vast range of such objects.

The third: If somebody (or something) touched an object that had touched another object—which had in turn touched a corpse—then the furthest in the chain merely *contracts evening impurity* (see 1:1).

1:3 *Four—how so?* Referring to the third sentence of 1:1.

and objects [touch] that person,
they [all] contract seven-day impurity.
The fourth, whether a person or objects, contracts evening impurity.
R. Aqiva said:
I have a fifth—
a pole stuck in a tent.
The tent, the pole, and someone who touches the pole, and objects [that touch] that person—
they [all] contract seven-day impurity.
The fifth,
whether a person or objects,
contracts evening impurity.
They said to him:
The tent does not count.

4 People and objects [both] become impure from a corpse,
[but] there is an aspect of severity toward a person relative to objects,
as well as toward objects relative to a person—
as objects are three, but people are two.
"There is an aspect of severity toward a person"—
as whenever one is in the middle there are four,
but if there is none in the middle there are three.

5 A person and clothing [both] become impure from a *zav*,
[but] there is an aspect of severity toward a person relative to clothing,

The fourth: If somebody (or something) touched an object that had touched a person who had touched another object—which had in turn touched a corpse—then the furthest in the chain merely *contracts evening impurity* (see 1:1).

R. Aqiva said: I have a fifth: A case in which the status of seven-day impurity persists as far as four degrees of contact away from a corpse, with the fifth degree of contact merely contracting evening impurity.

They i.e. anonymous interlocutors *said to him: The Tent does not count* as a distinct degree of contact from the pole, as the latter's impurity is directly due to the corpse itself, and not to the Tent.

1:4 *there is an aspect of severity…relative to objects…relative to a person*: The law treats people more severely than objects in some respects, but less severely in others.

objects are three, whereas people are two: An object that contracts impurity by touching a corpse can transmit impurity to other objects, which can transmit it in turn to a third party (whether an object or a person—see notes to 1:2). For people, on the other hand, transmission ends after only the second degree of contact with the corpse (see notes to 1:1), so that the law treats objects more severely than people.

whenever one i.e. a person *is in the middle there are four* that contract impurity; as described in the notes to 1:3, the fourth degree of contact becomes impure in a situation where the first and third are objects, and the second ("in the middle" of the two objects) is a person. Here the law is more severe when a person is the second degree of contact than it would be if an object were the second degree of contact; as *if there is none in the middle there are* only *three* that contract impurity—if both the first and second degrees of contact are objects, then transmission stops after the third degree of contact (as in 1:2).

1:5 *zav*: A man suffering from a genital discharge, as discussed in Leviticus 15:1–15 and tractate *Zavim*.

there is an aspect of severity…relative to clothing…relative to a person: Again, the law treats people more severely than clothing in some respects, but not in others.

as well as toward clothing relative to a person.
For a person who touches a *zav* transmits impurity to clothing,
but clothes touching a *zav* do not transmit impurity to [other] clothes.
"There is an aspect of severity . . . toward clothing"—
as clothing bearing a *zav* transmits impurity to a person,
but a person bearing a *zav* does not transmit impurity to [another] person.

1:6 *Departure of the Soul as a Precondition*

6 A person does not transmit impurity until his soul departs,
and even if he were cut up, or even at death's door,
he can still oblige levirate marriage and exempt from levirate marriage,
still permit *terumah* to be eaten and disqualify [the eating of] *terumah*.
And so too for domestic and wild animals—
they cannot transmit impurity until their souls depart.
If their heads are cut off,
then even though they twitch—like a lizard's tail, which twitches—
they are impure.[1]

[1] The last three words have been moved for clarity from their place in the text before the preceding phrase.

a person who touches a zav transmits impurity to clothing: Leviticus 15:7. The law treats people more severely than clothing in that *clothes touching a zav do not transmit impurity to [other] clothes*. Clothing that has been in contact with a *zav*— while itself becoming impure—does not transmit impurity when it comes into contact with other clothes.

clothing bearing a zav transmits impurity to a person: Leviticus 15:5. In this way the law treats clothing more severely than people: *a person bearing a zav does not transmit impurity to [another] person*. A person carrying a *zav* becomes impure thereby, but does not transmit impurity when coming into contact with others.

1:6 *A person does not transmit impurity* as a corpse.

cut up: Dismembered, or possibly a reference to severed veins.

oblige levirate marriage: His sister-in-law, if otherwise obliged to undergo a levirate marriage to him, is not permitted to marry another. See Deuteronomy 25:5–10 and tractate *Yevamot*.

exempt from levirate marriage: As surviving issue of his father he would exempt his widowed mother from a levirate marriage obligation, even though he is barely hanging on to life.

still permit terumah to be eaten: See tractate *Terumot*. His mother continues to be allowed to eat *terumah* (presuming that he is a priest), even if otherwise disqualified from doing so after her son's death.

disqualify [the eating of] terumah: Cf. Leviticus 22:13. Even though barely hanging on to life he would disqualify his mother, if she herself were the daughter of a priest, from resuming eating *terumah* after the death of her nonpriestly husband.

domestic and wild animals . . . cannot transmit impurity as carrion.

even though they twitch, which might suggest that their souls have not yet departed, they are nevertheless impure.

like a lizard's tail, which twitches even after being cut off.

1:7–8 *Complete Body Parts and Their Transmission of Impurity*

7 There is no qualifying limit for [complete] body parts.
Even less than the size of an olive—[if] from a corpse,
or less than the size of an olive—[if] from an animal carcass,
or less than the size of a lentil—[if] from vermin,
can transmit impurity,
each in its own way.

8 Man has 248 body parts:
Thirty in the foot—[namely] six for each toe;
ten at the ankle, two at the lower leg, five at the knee, one at the thigh, three at the hip, and eleven ribs.
Thirty in the hand—[namely] six for each finger;
two at the forearm, two at the elbow, one at the upper arm, and four at the shoulder.
101 on each side.
And the eighteen links of the spine, [and] nine at the head, eight at the neck, six at the chest, and five around the body's orifices.
Each one can transmit impurity through contact, and through carriage, and in a Tent.
When is this?
Whenever they have proper flesh on them.
But if they do not have proper flesh on them,
then they can transmit impurity through contact and through carriage, but do not transmit impurity in a Tent.

1:7 *[complete] body parts*: The olive and lentil sizes mentioned are indeed qualifying limits, but only for incomplete body parts.

can transmit impurity, each in its own way: There are differing criteria for each with regard to transmission of impurity; see *Kelim* 1:1, 1:2, and 1:4.

1:8 *Man has 248 body parts*: The word rendered here and elsewhere as "body part" seems here to refer to bones, together with the flesh/tendons attached to them.

in the foot…in the hand: Lit. "in the sole of the foot" and "in the palm of the hand."

at the chest: Lit. "at the key to the heart."

Each one can transmit impurity through contact, and through carriage, and in a Tent: See the introduction to this tractate.

proper flesh: The term is not defined here. See *Kelim* 1:5, where it seems to be the minimum amount of flesh required for the limb concerned to heal, were it still attached to a live person.

But if they do not: Cf. 2:3.

Chapter Two

2:1–3 *Qualifying Limits for Transmission of Impurity*

2 These transmit impurity in a Tent:
a corpse, [a piece] the size of an olive from a corpse,[2] [an amount] of exudate that is the size of an olive, a ladleful of mold, a spine, a skull,[3]
a body part from a corpse or body part from a live person, provided there is proper flesh on them,
a quarter[-*qav*] of bones from the larger part of the skeletal frame, or from a numerical majority,
and the larger part of the corpse's skeletal frame, or numerical majority of the corpse, [which] are impure even when less than a quarter[-*qav*].
How much is a numerical majority? 125.

2 A quarter[-*log*] of blood, or a quarter[-*log*] of *tevusah* blood, provided from a single corpse.
R. Aqiva says:
From two corpses.

[2] According to $\mathbf{P}_2$, the beginning of this mishnah reads: "These do transmit impurity in the tent of a corpse: [a piece] the size of an olive from a corpse..."
[3] The list up to this point is also found at *Nazir* 7:2.

2:1 *These transmit impurity in a Tent*: It hardly seems necessary to mention that a corpse transmits impurity in a Tent when a small piece of a corpse, the size of an olive, is equally said to do so. Commentaries address the issue, although it is noteworthy that according to one important manuscript (see n. 2) the mishnah is not asserting that a corpse transmits impurity, which would be unnecessary, but simply referring to any Tent, in which small remains of a body are known to be present, as "the Tent of a corpse."

[an amount] of exudate that is the size of an olive, a ladleful of mold: From a corpse, in both cases.

body part from a live person: A body part severed from a live person.

provided there is proper flesh on them: See notes to 1:8.

a quarter[-qav]: The *qav* is a standard dry measure in the Mishnah, equivalent perhaps to about three-quarters of a U.S. pint.

from the larger part of the skeletal frame: Perhaps referring to the torso. The word rendered here as "skeletal frame" literally means structure.

or from a numerical majority of body parts in the human anatomy.

are impure: i.e. they transmit impurity.

How much is a numerical majority? 125 body parts. This being just over half the total number of 248 body parts enumerated in 1:8.

2:2 This mishnah continues the list of qualifications for transmission of impurity.

A quarter[-log]: The *log* is a standard fluid measure in the Mishnah, with around the same capacity as the *qav* mentioned above.

tevusah blood: Mishnah 3:5 will elaborate on the meaning of *tevusah* blood.

R. Aqiva says: Even when the minimal quantity is combined *from two corpses*. It is not clear whether he is referring to both ordinary blood and *tevusah* blood, or only to the latter.

From an infant who had all bled out—
R. Aqiva says:
Any amount,
but the Sages say:
A quarter[-*log*].
Maggots [amounting to] the size of an olive, whether alive or dead—
R. Eliezer deems impure, like [the corpse's] flesh,
but the Sages deem them pure.
Ash of people who were cremated—
R. Eliezer says:
Its measure is a quarter[-*qav*],
but the Sages deem it pure.
More than a ladleful of earth from graves is impure,[4]
but R. Simeon deems it pure.
A ladleful of mold, though mixed with water, is not joined together for impurity.

3 These transmit impurity through contact or carriage,
but do not transmit impurity in a Tent:
Bone the size of a barley grain, earth of the nations, and a grave area;
a body part from a corpse or body part from a live person that do not have proper flesh on them,
and a spine or skull that were deficient.
What is "deficiency" for a spine?
The House of Shammai say:
Two vertebrae,

[4] In **K** the rest of this mishnah reads as follows: "R. Simeon deems pure a ladleful of mold, though mixed with water, as it is not joined together for impurity."

From an infant who had all bled out: While the normal qualifying minimum for transmission of impurity is a quarter-*log* of blood, there is no such minimum for an infant whose entire blood volume amounts to less than a quarter-*log*. The Sages proceed to disagree with this position.

Maggots [amounting to] the size of an olive: The reference is to maggots from a corpse, and the rabbis here may be regarding a group of maggots as a single organism.

R. Eliezer deems impure, like [the corpse's] flesh: The maggots transmit impurity, just as if they were the flesh of the corpse.

A ladleful of mold from a corpse, *though mixed with water, is not joined together for impurity*: It had been asserted in 2:1 that a ladleful of mold from a corpse does transmit impurity in a Tent. This last sentence appears to be a comment on that earlier clause, pointing out that such a ladleful would in fact not transmit impurity through contact, as none of the individual pieces of mold would be large enough. Nor would it change matters in this regard were the entire amount to be mixed together in water. The notion of "joining together" will be discussed in the notes to 3:4.

2:3 *These transmit impurity*: See the introduction to this tractate.

earth of the nations: Earth from outside the Land of Israel.

a grave area: Discussed at length in chapters 17 and 18.

a body part from a corpse...and a spine or skull that were deficient: It is implicit from 2:1 that these would fail the qualification requirements for transmission of impurity in a Tent, but here we are told that they nevertheless meet the requirement for transmission of impurity through contact or carriage.

What is considered "deficiency" for a spine...a skull, and thereby disqualifies its transmission of impurity in a Tent?

but the House of Hillel say:
Even one vertebra.
And for a skull?
The House of Shammai say:
The size of a drill bit,
but the House of Hillel say:
[An amount] such that were it taken from a live person, he would die.
Of which kind of drill bit did they speak?
Of the small [type] belonging to physicians.
[These are] the words of R. Meir,
but the Sages say:
Of the large one from the [Temple] Chamber.

2:4 *Transmission of Impurity by Stones Associated with Graves*

4 The grave cover and its support stone transmit impurity through contact or in a Tent,
but do not transmit impurity through carriage.
R. Eliezer says:
They do transmit impurity through carriage.
R. Joshua says:
When there is earth from graves [stuck] beneath them
they transmit impurity through carriage,
but otherwise they do not transmit impurity through carriage.
Which is the support stone?
The one on which the grave cover leans.
However, a support stone for support stones remains pure.

The size of a drill bit: A hole the size of a drill bit.

Of which kind of drill bit did they say speak? "They" refers to the House of Shammai, who specified the size of a drill bit as the governing amount for determining whether a skull is "deficient" or not.

the small [type] belonging to physicians: Presumably used for trepanning.

the Sages say: Of the large one: The Sages disagree with R. Meir about the House of Shammai's statement, saying that the latter spoke of the large drill bit *from the [Temple] Chamber* where a drill was known to have been kept (cf. *Kelim* 17:12 and below, 13:1).

2:4 *The grave cover*: Typically a stone rolled over the mouth of a grave to seal it, discussed more generally in 15:8–9.

earth from graves: Previously mentioned in 2:2.

The one on which the grave cover leans: As a practical matter graves in Palestine were often in the form of niches in the wall of a cave, requiring an additional stone to buttress the grave cover and keep it from falling.

However, a support stone for support stones remains pure: Should the stone buttressing the grave cover require another stone in turn, to keep it in place, then the latter does not become impure and accordingly does not transmit impurity of any kind.

2:5–7 *Qualifying Limits for Transmission of Impurity, Resumed*

5 The following, if they were deficient, are pure:
[a piece] the size of an olive from a corpse,
[an amount] the size of an olive of exudate,
a ladleful of mold,
a quarter[-*log*] of blood,
bone the size of a barley grain,
and a body part from a live person, when some of its bone was missing.[5]
6 A spine or skull from two corpses,
a quarter[-*log*] of blood from two corpses,
a quarter[-*qav*] of bones from two corpses,
a body part from two corpses,
and a body part from two live men—
R. Aqiva deems [these] impure,
but the Sages deem [them] pure.
7 Bone the size of a barley grain that was split in two—
R. Aqiva deems it impure,
but R. Yohanan b. Nuri deems it pure.
Said R. Yohanan b. Nuri:
They did not say "bones the size of a barley grain,"

[5] The last clause might also be rendered "when its bone was missing."

2:5 *The following, if they were deficient, are pure*: Qualifying limits, for the items on the ensuing list to transmit impurity in various ways, were covered in 2:1–3. Here it is made explicit that when these limits are not met, the items do not become impure, and accordingly do not transmit impurity of any kind.

[a piece] the size of an olive from a corpse, [an amount] the size of an olive of exudate, a ladleful of mold: Cf. 2:1.

a quarter[-log] of blood, bone the size of a barley grain: Cf. 2:2 and 2:3 respectively.

and a body part from a live person, when some of its bone was missing: The bone from a body part severed from a live person has not previously been discussed, but such body parts having some amount of flesh on them (implicitly on the bone) were mentioned in 2:1 and 2:3.

2:6 *A spine or skull* combined *from two corpses*: Cf. 2:1, which had specified that either of these transmits impurity in a Tent, presumably when from a single corpse.

a quarter[-log] of blood combined *from two corpses*: Cf. 2:2, which had specified that this amount of blood transmits impurity in a Tent, presumably when from a single corpse.

a quarter[-qav] of bones combined *from two corpses, a body part* combined *from two corpses, and a body part* combined *from two live men*: "Men" is likely a figure of speech, and there is no suggestion that the issue is actually gendered in any way. Cf. 2:1, which had specified the conditions under which these transmit impurity in a Tent, when from a single corpse or live person.

R. Aqiva deems [these] impure: There had been no earlier hint of his opinion, except with regard to the quarter-measure of blood, mentioned in 2:2.

but the Sages deem [them] pure: Their view is presumably limited to the failure of these items to transmit impurity in a Tent, and does not address impurity through contact or carriage—cf. 2:3, where bone is said to transmit impurity through contact or carriage even when no bigger than a barley grain.

2:7 *They did not say: "bones the size of a barley grain," but rather "bone the size of a barley grain"*: Since 2:3 refers to bone the size of a barley grain as transmitting impurity through touch or carriage, this

but rather "bone the size of a barley grain."
A quarter[-*qav*] of bones that were ground up,
and in which is there no single piece the size of a barley grain—
R. Simeon deems it pure,
but the Sages deem it impure.
A body part from a live person is pure when split in two.
R. Yose deems it impure,
but concedes it to be pure when severed in pieces.

Chapter Three

3:1–5 *Qualification for Impurity by Combining Elements That on Their Own Would Not Qualify, and Disqualification of Those That Would Normally Qualify*

3 All things that transmit impurity in a Tent,
if split up and then brought inside—
R. Dosa b. Harqinas deems them pure,
but the Sages deem them impure.
How so?
If someone touches two [pieces] of the size of half an olive from an animal carcass, or carries them;
or, with a corpse, touches [a piece] the size of half an olive

implies (according to R. Yohanan b. Nuri) that a piece of this size would not transmit such impurity when split in two.

A quarter[-qav] of bones that were ground up: See the previous clause, as well as the mention of a quarter-*qav* of bones as transmitting impurity in a Tent under specific conditions, in 2:1.

A body part from a live person: Cf. previous mentions of a body part severed from a live person, in 2:1, 2:3, 2:5, and 2:6.

3:1 This mishnah also appears as *Eduyot* 3:1.

All things that transmit impurity in a Tent: The qualification is obscure, as the first example—a piece of an animal carcass—does not transmit impurity in a Tent (see *Kelim* 1:2, 1:4); this is why the mishnah proceeds to restrict the first ruling to touching or carrying. A piece the size of an olive from a corpse does, however, transmit impurity in a Tent—see 2:1.

if first *split up and* only *then brought inside*: Here too the qualification "brought inside" (literally "brought them into the house") does not seem apposite for the cases that follow.

with a corpse: i.e. in the case of a corpse.

touches [a piece] the size of half an olive and himself *"forms a Tent over"* another piece *the size of half of an olive*: e.g. touches a piece the size of half an olive with one hand, and places his other hand over another piece the size of half an olive.

and "forms a Tent" over [a piece] the size of half of an olive;
or touches [a piece] the size of half an olive
and [a piece] the size of half of an olive "forms a Tent" over him;
or "forms a Tent" over two [pieces] the size of half an olive;
or "forms a Tent" over [a piece] the size of half an olive
and [a piece] the size of half an olive "forms a Tent" over him—
R. Dosa b. Harqinas deems these pure,
but the Sages deeem them impure.
However, when someone touches [a piece] the size of half an olive
and something else "forms a Tent" over him and over [a piece] the size of half an olive;
or [when someone] "forms a Tent" over [a piece] the size of half of an olive
and something else "forms a Tent" over him and over [a piece] the size of half of an olive—
then he remains pure.
R. Meir said:
Even then R. Dosa b. Harqinas deems it pure,
but the Sages deem it impure.
All become impure,
excepting contact when together with carriage and carriage when together with a Tent.
This is the general principle:
Any case involving a single category is impure,
but [a case involving] two categories is pure.

2 When a ladleful of mold is dispersed inside a house,
that house is impure;
but R. Simeon deems it pure.
When a quarter-[*log*] of blood is absorbed in a house,

[a piece] the size of half of an olive "forms a Tent" over him: The circumstances are unspecified, but presumably entail a person being under a structure of some kind, which incorporates such a piece.

However…then he remains pure: Not only according to R. Dosa b. Harqinas, but also in the view of the Sages. The last sentence in this mishnah casts light on this view—apparently the Sages see these two cases as involving "two categories," namely a combination of touch impurity and Tent impurity, and in such a case two below-limit qualifying amounts are not combined so as to qualify for impurity. (Earlier cases in this mishnah that also seemed to involve these two categories did not, however, do so, as under certain circumstances impurity that results from a "Tent" is actually deemed to be caused by contact impurity, rather than Tent impurity. Engagement with these complexities can be found in the Talmud and traditional Mishnah commentaries.)

All become impure, excepting a case of *contact* impurity *when together with* a case of *carriage* impurity *and* a case of *carriage* impurity *when together with a* case of *Tent* impurity: This is apparently the principle underlying R. Meir's statement—the Sages' "two categories" exception does not (in his view) cover a case of contact impurity together with Tent impurity.

the general principle is that in every case where there would be a ruling of impurity were only one category involved, there cannot be impurity if two categories are involved. Here the principle underlying the opposing view to R. Meir's is elucidated.

3:2 *a ladleful of mold* from a corpse. Cf. 2:1, 2:2, and 2:5.

a quarter[-log] of blood: Cf. 2:2 and 2:5.

is absorbed in a house: e.g. in the floor of the house.

that house remains pure.
When absorbed in a garment—
if upon laundering a quarter[-*log*] of blood comes out then it has become impure, but if not it remains pure.
For anything absorbed that cannot come out is pure.

3 When spilled outdoors and a Tent formed over part of it—
if its place was on a slope then it[6] remains pure;
if it was in a puddle, or congealed, then it is impure.
When spilled on a threshold and the house "forms a Tent" over it—
if it was a slope, whether inward or outward, then it remains pure;
if it was in a puddle, or congealed, then it is impure.
Every part of a corpse is impure other than the teeth, hair, and nails.
When connected, all are impure.

4 How so?
When the corpse is outside and its hair stretches inside
then the house is impure.
A bone on which there is flesh the size of an olive—
if someone placed part of it inside,
so that the house "forms a Tent" over it,
then it is impure.

[6] Or "he." These rules apply to both people and objects, and so throughout.

3:3 *When* a quarter[-*qav*] of blood *spilled outdoors and a Tent formed over part of it*: This mishnah is a continuation of 3:2. The "Tent" can be a person or any suitable object.

if its place: i.e. where the blood was spilled.

then it: Anything or anyone beneath the "Tent."

if it was in a puddle, or congealed, then anything or anyone beneath the "Tent" *is impure*: Even though the "Tent" only covered part of the blood.

and the house: Adjacent to the threshold.

if it was a slope, whether inward or outward, then it remains pure: If the threshold sloped, the house and its contents remain pure.

if it was in a puddle, or congealed, then it is impure: If the blood puddled or congealed, then the house and its contents become impure.

When connected, all are impure: Even teeth etc. are impure while still part of the corpse.

3:4 *How so?* A continuation of 3:3.

When the corpse is outside and its hair stretches inside then the house is impure: Since the hair is connected to the corpse, the house and its contents become impure. This illustrates the last ruling in 3:3.

if someone placed part of it inside, so that the house "forms a Tent" over it, then it is impure: i.e. the house and its contents become impure. The part of the bone covered over by the house is presumed to have no flesh on it, and bone on its own does not engender Tent impurity (see 2:1). Nevertheless, in this case it does so by virtue of being joined to the other part of the bone with the qualifying olive-sized piece of flesh on it (even though that part of the bone is not covered over by the house). The halakhic notion of "joining together" (see also 2:2) can be exemplified by this mishnah.

Two bones on which there are two pieces of flesh [each] the size of half an olive—
if someone placed parts of them inside,
so that the house "forms a Tent" over them,
then it is impure.
If they were artificially inserted then it remains pure,
for manmade joining together does not count as joining together.

5 What is "*tevusah* blood"?
When an eighth[-*log*] had bled out of a corpse while he was alive,
and an eighth[-*log*] after death—
the words of R. Aqiva.
R. Ishmael says:
A quarter[-*log*] while he was alive,
and a quarter[-*log*] after death,
[with] a quarter[-*log*] [then] taken from this and that.
R. Eleazar b. Judah says:
"This and that" are like water!
What then is "*tevusah* blood"?
When the blood of a crucified person is flowing,
and a quarter[-*log*] of blood is found under him—
it is impure.
However, when a corpse is dripping blood,
and a quarter[-*log*] of blood is found under him—
then it is pure.
R. Judah says:
Not so;
rather, the flowing [blood] is pure,
and the dripping [blood] is impure.

Two bones on which there are two pieces of flesh [each] the size of half an olive: Cf. 3:1.

If they were artificially inserted: If bones were stuck into flesh artificially, but had not previously been attached to that flesh.

3:5 *What is "tevusah blood"?* This relates to the opening of 2:2, which provided "a quarter[-*log*] of *tevusah*-blood" as one of the qualifying limits for transmission of impurity in a Tent.

When an eighth-[log] had bled out of a corpse while he was alive, and an eighth-[log] after death: This would combine to a quarter-*log*, and the mixture concerned is known as *tevusah* blood.

[with] a quarter[-log] [then] taken from this and that: A quarter-*log* of the blend created from one quarter-*log* each of predemise and postdemise blood.

"This and that" are like water! The blend is merely like water—i.e. it does not transmit impurity. Thus R. Eleazar b. Judah disagrees with the views of R. Aqiva and R. Ishmael.

What then, in R. Eleazar's view, *is "tevusah blood"?*

When the blood of a crucified person is flowing, and a quarter-[log] of blood is found under him after his death.

it is impure: And would then transmit impurity in a Tent.

3:6–4:3 *Egress of Impurity*

6 [In the case of a piece] the size of an olive from a corpse
an exit must be handbreadth-size,
in order to save [other] exits from impurity,
or the size of four handbreadths
in the case of a corpse.
However, for the purpose of giving passage to impurity,
a handbreadth-sized opening [is enough].
[Any piece] larger than the size of an olive is like a corpse.
R. Yose says:
The spine and skull are like a corpse.
7 A [space] that is a handbreadth by a handbreadth by a handbreadth high
is enough to transmit impurity
and to bar impurity.
How so?
A vaulted pipe under a house,
which has a handbreadth-sized space inside it
and a handbreadth-sized space at its outlet—
when there is impurity inside it, the house is pure,

3:6 This mishnah presupposes the ideas, which will be elaborated in 7:3, that

(a) when there is corpse impurity inside a house, even the doorways opening beyond the house become "Tents" for the purpose of transmitting impurity, but

(b) intent to remove a corpse via a particular exit diverts impurity from other exits and limits it to the intended one.

[In the case of a piece] the size of an olive from a corpse an exit must be handbreadth-size,... or the size of four handbreadths in the case of a corpse: i.e. in order to divert impurity as mentioned in 7:3, the intended exit for a piece of a corpse (which only engenders impurity when it is at least the size of an olive) is required to be handbreadth-size or larger. The corresponding size requirement for an entire corpse is 4 × 4 handbreadths.

for the purpose of giving passage to impurity: In order to spread impurity from the space where the corpse is located to another, via an opening between them.

[Any piece] larger than the size of an olive is like a corpse: And requires an exit the size of 4 × 4 handbreadths in order to divert impurity from other exits.

The spine and skull are like a corpse: These require an exit the size of 4 × 4 handbreadths in order to divert impurity, but nothing else would—short of an entire corpse. (This seems the simplest explanation for R. Yose's view.)

3:7 *is enough to transmit impurity* when, for example, there is a piece of a corpse the size of an olive that is inside *and to bar impurity*: The one-handbreadth cube is the minimum dimension for the halakhic "Tent" (see introduction).

How so? How does it serve to bar impurity?

A vaulted pipe: The pipe or drain is closed off at its point of entry to the house.

a handbreadth-sized space at its outlet: Where the pipe would discharge, into a shared courtyard or a street, there is a handbreadth-sized outlet.

when there is impurity inside it the house is pure, and equally *when there is impurity in the house, whatever is inside* the pipe *is pure*: Impurity is barred from transmission between the two distinct spaces.

and when there is impurity in the house, whatever is inside it is pure.
For it is the manner of impurity to depart, but not to enter.[7]
If there is a handbreadth-sized space inside it
but not at its outlet—
when there is impurity inside it, the house is impure,
but when there is impurity in the house, whatever is inside it is pure.
For it is the manner of impurity to depart, but not to enter.
If it does not have a handbreadth-sized space inside it,
nor a handbreadth-sized space at its outlet—
when there is impurity inside it, the house is impure,
and when there is impurity in the house, whatever is inside it is impure.
[The above applies] whether a hole was made by water, or by vermin, or by salt eating away at it,
and so too for a row of stones or a pile of beams.
R. Judah says:
Any Tent that is not manmade is not [deemed to be] a Tent,
but he concedes in [the cases of] holes and [crevices in] rocks.

Chapter Four

4 A turret[-shaped chest] standing outdoors—
when there is impurity inside it, objects in its thickness are pure,
when there is impurity in its thickness, objects inside it are pure.

[7] This sentence is missing in **K** and **P**, here and below.

For it is the manner of impurity to depart: Impurity has a way of passing from small spaces to larger ones, but not vice versa. As mentioned in the textual note to the translation (n. 7), important manuscripts do not include this sentence, and its relevance here is questionable.

when there is impurity inside it the house is impure: In such a case the aperture at the outlet is not large enough to enable the impurity to leave, and it breaks through from the pipe into the house.

but when there is impurity in the house, whatever is inside the pipe *is pure.*

For it is the manner of impurity to depart: As before, important manuscripts do not include this sentence, and its relevance here is questionable.

when there is impurity in the house, whatever is inside the pipe *is impure*: Because impurity is not barred from transmission between the two spaces.

[The above applies] whether a hole was made by water, or by vermin, or by salt eating away at it, and so too for a row of stones, or a pile of beams: In all such cases, if a space was somehow enclosed adjacent to a house, then similar rulings apply regarding the passage of impurity from the house to the space, and vice versa.

R. Judah says: Any Tent that is not manmade is not [deemed to be] a Tent: The "Tent" here is a one-handbreadth cube. See first note to this mishnah. R. Judah thus disagrees with the previous opinion.

concedes: R. Judah agrees that such natural formations do indeed constitute "Tents."

4:1 *in its thickness*: Inside niches/holes in its side panels.

R. Yose says:
Half and half.
If [it is] standing inside a house—
when there is impurity inside it, the house is impure,
but when there is impurity in the house, whatever is inside it is pure.
For it is the manner of impurity to depart, but not to enter.
Objects between it and the ground,
between it and the walls,
between it and the beams—
if there is a handbreadth-sized space there they are impure,
but otherwise they are pure.
When there is impurity there, the house is impure.

2 A drawer within the turret[-shaped chest],
with a handbreadth-sized space inside it,
but without a handbreadth-sized space at its aperture—
when there is impurity inside it, the house is impure,
but when there is impurity in the house, whatever is inside it is pure.
For it is the manner of impurity to depart, but not to enter.
R. Yose deems it pure,
because one could take it out in halves, or burn it in its place.

3 If [the chest is] standing in an entranceway and opens outward—
when there is impurity inside it, the house is pure,
but when there is impurity in the house, whatever is inside it is impure.

Half and half: According to R. Yose, the inner half of any side panel is deemed to be entirely inside the chest for purity purposes, and thus excluded from the special rulings mentioned earlier in this mishnah. Objects or impurity in the outer half would, however, have the separate status mentioned.

For it is the manner of impurity to depart: Cf. 3:7. Impurity can pass from the chest into the house, but cannot penetrate the chest from the house.

Objects…if there is a handbreadth-sized space there i.e. between the chest and the house *they are impure* presuming the presence of impurity somewhere else in the house *but otherwise they are pure*: Impurity cannot enter the space unless it meets the qualifying requirement.

when there is impurity there: In the space itself, between the chest and the house.

4:2 *A drawer within the turret[-shaped chest], with a* cubic *handbreadth-sized space inside it, but without a* square *handbreadth-sized space at its aperture…*

For it is the manner of impurity to depart, but not to enter: Impurity can pass from the drawer into the house, but cannot penetrate into the drawer, as its aperture does not meet the qualifying requirement.

R. Yose deems it pure: Even when there is impurity in the drawer the house remains pure.

because one could take it out in halves, or burn it in its place: The intact source of impurity will not inevitably be moved out of the drawer into the house. Thus an olive-sized piece from a corpse might first be split into two halves (neither of which meets the qualifying size requirement for transmission of impurity) before being moved, or perhaps be burned inside the box. R. Yose views these possibilities as negating the capacity of the impure item in the drawer to render the house impure.

4:3 *If [the chest is] standing in an entranceway and opens outward*: The chest is at the entrance to a house, and its door opens away from the house.

inside it…inside it: Inside the chest.

For it is the manner of impurity to depart, but not to enter.
If its device extended three fingers back from it
and there is impurity there, across from the beams,
then the house is pure.
Concerning what are [these] things said?
As long as there is a handbreadth-sized space there,
and it does not leave,
and the turret[-shaped chest] comes to [the right] size.

Chapter Five

5:1 *A Curved Oven Flue*

5 When there is an oven standing inside a house,
with its flue curved to the outside,
and people burying a corpse "formed a Tent" over it—
The House of Shammai say:
Everything is impure.
And the House of Hillel say:
The oven is impure, but the house is pure.
R. Aqiva says:
Even the oven is pure.

For it is the manner of impurity: Here the repeated maxim means that impurity can move from a house to a chest at its entrance, but not from such a chest into the house, as the impurity is somehow discharged instead via the chest's door, which leads outside.

device: Either wheels or a trailer at the base of the chest, or perhaps the base itself—see *Kelim* 18:2.

extended three fingers back from it: The device extends from the entranceway into the house itself, but by less than a handbreadth. Under such circumstances the device becomes assimilated to the chest and is deemed to be inside it, and even though an item capable of transmitting Tent impurity is lying inside the device, directly below the ceiling of the house, the latter nevertheless remains pure.

there is a handbreadth-sized space there: The device encloses a space of a cubic handbreadth.

it does not leave: The device is permanently attached to the chest.

comes to [the right] size: See 8:1 below, which will discuss the capacity requirement that a turret-shaped chest must meet in order to bar impurity.

5:1 Rules specific to the purity of ovens are discussed in tractate *Kelim*, esp. chapters 5–7.

flue curved to the outside: Precise translation is difficult, but the oven is indoors and the flue open to the outdoors.

people burying a corpse "formed a Tent" over it: Passing by, they created a halakhic "Tent" (see introduction) over the opening of the flue.

Everything is impure: Both house and oven.

5:2–5 *A Covered Hatch to an Upper Room*

2 When there is a hatch between the house and its upper room,
and a pot is placed over it,
perforated [so as to allow] the ingress of liquid—
the House of Shammai say:
Everything is impure.
And the House of Hillel say:
The pot is impure, but the upper room remains pure.
R. Aqiva says:
Even the pot is pure.
3 Were it intact—
the House of Hillel say:
It protects everything.
The House of Shammai say:
It only protects food, drink, and earthenware containers.
The House of Hillel reversed themselves,
teaching in accordance with the opinion of the House of Shammai.
4 A jug full of pure liquid—
the jug [itself] contracts seven-day impurity,
but the liquid remains pure.

5:2 *When there is a hatch between the* main, lower part of the *house and its upper room…*

a pot…perforated [so as to allow] the ingress of liquid: Via another hole than its normal aperture. The pot, in this mishnah and the following one, is presumed by commentators to be a tightly closed earthenware pot—cf. 8:6, 12:2, and *Kelim* 10:1. Its normal aperture is sealed, and does not allow in impurity, and in general earthenware vessels are not susceptible to contracting impurity via their exterior surfaces.

Everything is impure: Presuming the presence of a corpse in the main part of the house (which is thus indubitably impure), both the upper room and the pot also become impure.

The three views expressed in this mishnah—of the House of Shammai, the House of Hillel, and R. Aqiva—closely parallel the views in the name of these authorities in 5:1.

5:3 This mishnah continues the discussion in 5:2 about a house and its upper room, with a tightly closed earthenware pot covering the hatch between them, and a corpse below.

Were it the pot *intact*: Unlike the situation described in 5:2, where the pot was perforated.

It protects everything: Everything in the upper room remains pure, because the pot does not contract impurity via its exterior surfaces, and is both sealed and nonperforated.

The House of Shammai say: The earthenware pot over the hatch protects food, drink, and other earthenware containers in the upper room from becoming impure (in the presence of a corpse in the house below), but does not protect anything else. The former items are not susceptible to purification by ritual immersion, leading to some lenience in their halakhic treatment for purity purposes.

The House of Hillel reversed themselves: *Eduyot* 1:12–14 explains how they were persuaded to do so.

5:4 This mishnah continues the discussion in 5:3.

A jug full of pure liquid in the upper room: Not an earthenware jug, but one susceptible to purification by ritual immersion.

contracts seven-day impurity: Becomes impure for seven days, and then requires ritual immersion to regain a state of purity.

However, if removed to another container it becomes impure.
A woman kneading [dough] in a trough—
the woman and the trough contract seven-day impurity,
but the dough is pure.
However, if she removed it to another container it becomes impure.
The House of Hillel reversed themselves,
teaching in accordance with the opinion of the House of Shammai.

5 Were the vessels [made] of animal dung, stone, or earth,
[then] everything is pure.
Were [it] a vessel [kept] pure for sacred duty, or for the purification ritual,
[then] everything is pure,
for all are considered reliable with respect to the purification ritual.
Because the vessels are pure
and the earthenware vessels are pure,
and they protect together with panels in Tents.[8]

[8] **K, P** lack a single Hebrew letter found in the printed edition, and their text of the last sentence is to be rendered as follows: "Because the vessels are pure, and pure earthenware vessels protect together with panels in Tents."

if removed to another container: If the liquid were poured into another container (which had already become impure in the upper room) then the liquid itself would become impure.

A woman kneading [dough] in a trough: In the upper room. The issue is gendered insofar as someone kneading dough was imagined to be a woman.

The House of Hillel reversed themselves: This sentence is an apparent non sequitur here, as there is no disagreement articulated in 5:4, and the reversal has already been mentioned in 5:3 with regard to the disagreement there. The duplication has attracted commentarial attention, but there is no known witness for deletion, in neither manuscript nor early printed editions.

5:5 *Were the vessels* i.e. the one(s) covering the hatch *made of animal dung, stone, or* unfired *earth, then everything is pure*: According to 5:3, only items not susceptible to purification by ritual immersion are protected from impurity when in an upper room, with its hatch covered by an intact, tightly closed pot, with a corpse below. Mishnah 5:5 (see also *Kelim* 10:1) removes the limitation when the pot is made from animal dung, stone, or unfired earth—which are not susceptible to contracting impurity at all—in which case everything above the hatch remains pure. (In 5:3 the pot concerned is of ordinary fired earthenware, which does contract impurity, albeit not via its exterior surface.)

Were [it] a vessel [kept] pure for sacred duty, or for the purification ritual: Had the owner of an earthenware vessel on top of the hatch declared that it was fit to be used for Temple service, or for carrying the ashes of the red heifer (see Numbers 19 and *Parah*).

all are considered reliable: Whoever the owner, the above-mentioned declaration is believed. This in turn broadens the leniency mentioned in the notes to 5:3. Thus whereas in 5:3 only the listed items remain pure when above the hatch, in 5:5—subject to the owner's declaration—everything above the hatch remains pure, without limitation.

with respect to the purification ritual and presumably for that matter with respect to the fitness for sacred duty mentioned in the previous clause.

the vessels are pure: The ones that cannot become impure under any circumstances, as listed at the beginning of the mishnah.

and the earthenware vessels are pure: The ones that, although susceptible to contracting impurity, are indubitably pure, since they were declared by their owners to be pure for sacred duty, or for the purification ritual (see earlier clause).

and they protect: Vessels of this kind protect everything in the upper room from contracting impurity when *together with panels in Tents*. In the case(s) under consideration here, this refers to the ceiling between the

5:6–7 *Protection from Impurity by Panels in Tents*

6 How so?
A pit or cellar inside a house, with a large basket on top, is pure.
But a sheer well or a beehive that is missing a piece,[9]
with a large basket on top,
is impure.
(If there were a smooth plank, or sifter without rims, then it would be pure.)
For vessels cannot "protect together with panels in Tents,"
unless these actually have panels.
And how [large] should the panel be?
A handbreadth.
Were it to have half a handbreadth on each side?
It is not a "panel,"
unless it has a handbreadth from one place.

[9] **K, P** have "open" where the printed edition has "missing a piece"; in Hebrew the difference arises from the reversal of two letters.

ground floor and upper room, which is regarded as joining the vessels covering the hatch to make a single protective barrier.

5:6 This mishnah is a follow-on to the end of 5:5.

How so? What are other examples of indubitably pure containers protecting a space from impurity in conjunction with the panels in halakhic "Tents"? (See introduction.)

A pit or cellar inside a house, with a large basket on top, is pure: A basket of this kind is not susceptible to contracting impurity (cf. 18:1); when there is a corpse in the house above it, it protects the contents of the pit or cellar from impurity.

But a sheer well or a beehive that is missing a piece, with a large basket on top, is impure when there is a corpse in the house above it. The significant difference between a sheer well—a well whose opening is level with the floor—and the pit or cellar mentioned earlier, is the absence of a ledge jutting out around it. In the absence of such a ledge there is no halakhic "Tent panel," as needed to protect the contents of the well from impurity by joining together with the indubitably pure basket. Similarly the incomplete/open beehive (see n. 9) does not combine with the basket so as to protect its contents from impurity.

If there were a smooth plank: The sentence is a parenthetical insertion, as the following one refers to the previous sentence. Its force is that, when covering over open spaces—even sheer wells or incomplete/open beehives (see previous note)—the smooth plank and simple sifter would protect their contents from contracting impurity. Unlike the large basket, which meets the requirements for a halakhic "vessel"—in this context by being a crafted object—the plank and sifter are too simple to be considered such, and do not even need to combine with halakhic "Tent panels" in order for the contents of the space below them to be protected from impurity. (The translation of the word rendered here as sifter is uncertain—it has also been translated as "kneading board.")

"protect together with panels in Tents": The closing words of 5:5.

And how [large] should the panel be? So as to protect the contents of the Tent beneath it from impurity, in conjunction with the right kind of object above (such as a large basket).

It is not considered *a "panel" unless it has a handbreadth from one place*: Thus the pit or cellar, mentioned at the beginning of the mishnah, would need to have a ledge jutting out above it, at least one handbreadth in size, for it to join together with a large basket in protecting the contents of the pit/cellar from impurity.

7 Just as they protect from indoors, they also protect from outdoors.
How so?
When a large basket is placed on pegs outdoors,
and there is impurity beneath it,
objects in the basket are pure.
If it was a courtyard wall or garden wall [then] it does not protect.
A beam placed from wall to wall,
with a pot suspended from it—
when there is impurity beneath it,
R. Aqiva deems [objects in the pot] pure,
and the Sages deem [them] impure.

Chapter Six

6:1–2 *People and Objects Transmitting/Barring Impurity*

6 People and objects can form "Tents" for transmitting impurity,
but not for securing purity.
How so?
Four people carrying a large broad stone[10]—

[10] **K, P** have "a box carried on poles."

5:7 This mishnah continues the discussion in 5:6.

Just as they protect from indoors, they also protect from outdoors: Just as containers/panels protect from inside a house (as described in 5:5 and 5:6), they also protect outdoors.

When a large basket is placed on pegs outdoors adjacent to the wall of a house *and there is impurity beneath it, objects in the basket are pure*: The large basket is not susceptible to contracting impurity (cf. 5:6), and combines with the wall of the house (the halakhic "panel" in this case) to protect objects in the basket from contracting impurity.

If it was a courtyard wall or garden wall rather than the wall of a house *[then] it does not protect*: Such walls are not part of a halakhic "Tent."

A beam placed from wall to wall: Outdoors, between two houses.

beneath it: Beneath the beam.

R. Aqiva deems [objects in the pot] pure, and the Sages deem [them] impure: Commentaries follow a parallel passage that specifies that there is less than a handbreadth between the mouth of the pot and the beam (although they are not touching). According to R. Aqiva, the absence of a handbreadth's height from pot to beam protects the contents of the pot.

6:1 *People and objects can "form Tents"*: See introduction.

not for securing purity: They do not "form Tents" that act as a barrier that bars impurity.

when there is impurity beneath it, objects on top of it are impure;
when there is impurity on top of it, objects beneath it are impure.
R. Eliezer deems them pure.
When placed on four objects,
even if objects [made] of animal dung, stone, or earth—
when there is impurity beneath it, objects on top of it are impure;
when there is impurity on top of it, objects beneath it are impure.
When placed on four stones, or a living thing—
when there is impurity beneath it, objects on top of it are pure;
when there is impurity on top of it, objects beneath it are pure.
2 If those burying the dead passed through a portico,
and one of them shut the door
and held it in place with a key—
if the door would stay closed on its own it is pure,
but if not it is impure.
So too [for] a barrel of dried figs, or box of straw, placed in a window.
If the dried figs or straw would stay in place on their own they are pure,
but if not they are impure.
A house partitioned with jars plastered over with mud—
if the mud would stay in place on its own it is pure,
but if not it is impure.

When there is impurity beneath it, objects on top of it are impure. When there is impurity on top of it, objects beneath it are impure: The people and large broad stone serve as a "Tent," which transmits impurity rather than acting as a barrier to it.

objects made of animal dung, stone, or unfired *earth*: These are not susceptible to contracting impurity (cf. 5:5), but nevertheless do not bar it. Accordingly, similarly to the first case in the mishnah *when there is impurity beneath* the large broad stone *objects on top of it are impure. When there is impurity on top of it, objects beneath it are impure.*

When placed on four stones, or a living thing: i.e. an animal. The stones/living thing are not considered halakhic "objects," since they are not manmade and together with the large broad stone they form a Tent that bars impurity. Accordingly *When there is impurity beneath* the large broad stone *objects on top of it are pure. When there is impurity on top of it, objects beneath it are pure.*

6:2 *a portico*: In front of a house.

shut the door: To the house before the corpse passed under the portico.

on its own: Without the key.

it is pure: The house remains pure, because the door serves as a barrier, which prevents the passage of impurity when the corpse passes under the portico.

If the dried figs or straw would stay in place on their own they are pure: If the figs or straw would stay in place on their own, without the barrel or box, then they bar any impurity on one side of the window from passing through to the other.

If the mud would stay in place on its own it is pure: If the mud would stay in place without the jars, then it bars any impurity on one side of the partition from passing through to the other.

6:3–7 *Impurity in Various Elements of a House*

3 A wall that serves a house should be judged as "half and half."
How so?
When an exterior wall has impurity inside it—
if [it is] between the halfway point and the inside, then the house is impure,
but someone[11] standing above is pure;
if [it is] between the halfway point and the outside, then the house is pure,
but someone standing above is impure;
if exactly halfway, then the house is impure.
As for someone standing above—
R. Meir deems him[12] pure,
but the Sages deem him impure.
R. Judah says:
The entire wall is part of the house.
4 A wall between two houses, with impurity inside it—
the house closer to the impurity is impure,
and the one closer to purity is pure.
If exactly halfway, both are impure.
When there is impurity in one of them
and there are objects inside the wall—
if [the objects are located] over halfway toward impurity, they are impure,
if over halfway toward purity, they are pure.
If exactly halfway, then they are impure.
Plasterwork between a house and its upper room, with impurity inside it—
if it is over halfway down, the house is impure and the upper room is pure,

[11] Or "something," and so in the remainder of the mishnah.
[12] Or "it," and so in the next clause as well.

6:3 *has impurity inside it*: e.g. a piece of a corpse.

if [it is] between the halfway point and the inside: If the impurity is within the inner half of the wall, it renders the house impure. Someone (or something) on top of the wall remains pure, just as if on top of the roof.

if [it is] between the halfway point and the outside...someone standing above is impure: As the exterior wall in such a case is not considered part of the house—which remains pure—the impurity is not deemed to be contained by a "Tent" (see introduction), and rises uninterrupted.

As for someone standing above: In a case where the impurity is exactly halfway between the inside of the wall and the outside.

The entire wall is part of the house: R. Judah disagrees with the idea of a 50/50 split mentioned at the beginning of the mishnah.

6:4 Cf. 6:3.

closer to purity: Close to the half of the wall that is free of impurity.

If exactly halfway: If the impurity is exactly halfway between the two houses.

When there is impurity in one of them: That is, in one of the houses.

toward impurity: i.e. toward the impure house; *toward purity*: i.e. towards the pure house.

Plasterwork between the lower part of *a house...with impurity inside it*: See the notes to the previous case of "a wall between two houses, with impurity inside it," to which this one is conceptually a parallel.

if it is over halfway up, the upper room is impure and the house is pure.
If it is exactly halfway, both are impure.
When there is impurity in one of them and there are objects inside the plasterwork—
if [the objects are located] over halfway toward impurity, they are impure,
if over halfway toward purity, they are pure.
If exactly halfway, then they are impure.
R. Judah says:
All the plasterwork is part of the upper room.

5 When there is impurity between the beams,
with [plaster] like garlic peel beneath it—
if there is a handbreadth-sized space there, everything is impure;
if the space there is not handbreadth-size, then the impurity is considered to be a plug.
If it is visible from within the house,
in either case the house is impure.

6 When a house serves a wall, the garlic-peel rule applies.
How so?
When there is a wall between two burial niches
or between two caves—
if there is impurity in the chambers and objects in the wall,

if it is over halfway down: If the impurity is located over halfway down the plasterwork, i.e. toward the lower part of the house, then the lower part of *the house is impure* and similarly *if it is over halfway up.*

All the plasterwork is part of the upper room, so that wherever the impurity is found, the house remains pure but the upper room becomes impure. (Presumably too objects inside the plasterwork do not become impure unless the upper room is impure.)

6:5 *between the beams*: Ceiling beams separating a lower and upper story. Plaster covers the ceiling/floor, but there may remain open spaces between the beams.

[plaster] like garlic peel: Even though no thicker than garlic peel, so that there is, in effect, nothing but an optical barrier between it and the lower part of the house.

a handbreadth-sized space there: The impurity is located in an empty space of at least one cubic handbreadth.

everything is impure: Whether in the lower or upper part of the house.

the impurity is considered to be a plug: Commentators are not in agreement as to the explanation of the phrase. It possibly means that the impurity separates the two parts of the house, with the upper room alone becoming impure. Some commentaries have suggested that the principle at work here might entail the impurity being restricted to the spaces in a vertical line above and below the "plug," evoking the ruling mentioned at the end of 6:6.

Were the source of impurity *visible from within* the lower part of *the house*, with no plaster beneath it at all, *in either case* (i.e. whether or not there is a space next to the impurity of at least $1 \times 1 \times 1$ handbreadth) the lower part of *the house is impure.*

6:6 *When a house serves a wall*: This is in contrast to the beginning of 6:3. In 6:6 the houses were apparently created by excavating between what became its walls, as in manmade caves.

the garlic-peel rule applies: As will now be explained. Cf. the garlic peel in 6:5.

and [a partition] like garlic peel above them,
they are pure;
if there is impurity in the wall and objects in the chambers,
and [a partition] like garlic peel above them,
they are pure.
When there is impurity beneath a pillar,
the impurity breaks through and up
and breaks through and down.

7 Objects beneath the capital[13] [of a pillar] are pure.
R. Yohanan b. Nuri deems them impure.
When there are impurity and objects beneath the capital—
if there is a handbreadth-sized space there, they are impure,
but otherwise they are pure.
Two wall closets next to each other, or above each other—
if one of them was opened,
both it and the house are impure,
but the other is pure.
And the wall closet is considered to be a plug.
It is judged [by the rule of] half and half
for bringing impurity into the house.

[13] Lit. "flower."

and [a partition] like garlic peel: Even though no thicker than garlic peel, and thus the flimsiest partition imaginable.

above them: Above such objects.

they are pure: The objects concerned remain pure provided there is any partition whatsoever, no matter how flimsy.

if there is impurity in the wall and objects in the chambers, and [a partition] like garlic peel above them: Some commentaries have interpreted this to refer to a partition above the impurity, rather than above the objects.

they i.e. the objects concerned *are pure*: Cf. previous case.

When there is impurity beneath a pillar: This seems to refer to a pillar inside any kind of house, and not specifically to the type of house mentioned at the beginning of this mishnah.

breaks through and up, and breaks through and down: Anything immediately above or below the impurity becomes impure, but the impurity is also contained, in that the area around the pillar remains pure. See introduction.

6:7 *Objects beneath the capital [of a pillar]*: When there is impurity under the pillar.

if there is a handbreadth-sized space there: Most simply understood to mean that the capital protrudes from the pillar by at least a handbreadth.

they are impure: The objects become impure.

if one of them, having a source of impurity inside it, *was opened*.

but the other closet, if closed, remains pure.

the wall closet is considered to be a plug: As if filled in and part of the wall, rather than hollow. Cf. the usage of "considered to be a plug" in 6:5.

It is judged [by the rule of] half and half for bringing impurity into the house: Cf. 6:3 and 6:4. For the purpose of determining the 50/50 split mentioned there, the hollow closet is considered to be solid wall.

Chapter Seven

7:1–3 *Some Special Rules for "Tents"*

7 When there is impurity in a wall,
and the space around it is one handbreadth by one handbreadth by one handbreadth high—
all upper rooms above it,
even if there are ten of them,
are impure.
If a single upper room straddled two houses, it is impure,
but all upper rooms above it are pure.
[If there is] a second[14] wall,
the impurity breaks through and up, and breaks through and down.
Someone touching the sides of a solid grave monument is pure,
because the impurity breaks through and up, and breaks through and down.
If the place of the impurity were a space
one handbreadth by one handbreadth by one handbreadth high—
someone touching it anywhere would be impure,
for it is like a closed-up grave.
If booths were placed next to it, they are impure;
R. Judah deems them pure.

[14] The text is uncertain—see annotations.

7:1 *the* hollow *space around it is one handbreadth by one handbreadth by one handbreadth high*: Cf. 6:3–4. The rulings there were made for a situation in which, unlike 7:1, there is no qualifying hollow space around the impurity that would constitute a halakhic "Tent."

all upper rooms above the impurity, *even if there are ten of them*: In this first case the mishnah seems to be imagining upper rooms on top of each other, all built out from the wall.

If a single upper room straddled two houses and there was a source of impurity in the wall between the two, then *it* i.e. the upper room *is impure.*

[If there is] a second wall: The reading is uncertain, and the translation provided is the simplest one for the word as it appears in the standard printed edition. (The meaning of the variant reading is obscure.) The case is understood by Maimonides to involve a source of impurity between two walls.

breaks through and up, and breaks through and down: The impurity does not, however, spread sideways—cf. 6:6.

Someone touching the sides…because the impurity breaks through and up, and breaks through and down: It is only transmitted in the vertical plane, and not to the sides of the grave monument.

If the place of the impurity were a space such that, in contradistinction to the mishnah's previous sentence, the grave monument contained a hollow *one handbreadth by one handbreadth by one handbreadth high* at a minimum.

for it is then treated *like a closed-up grave*, which transmits impurity to all sides.

If booths were placed next to it they are impure: This is a practical consequence of the previous ruling. Booths might be built next to grave monuments to protect visitors from the sun.

R. Judah deems them pure: The monument only transmits impurity to someone touching it, but not to an adjacent structure.

2 All the sloping parts of tents are like Tents.
When a tent slopes down, ending at one finger—
if there is impurity in the Tent, objects under the sloping part are impure.
If there is impurity under the sloping part, objects in the tent are impure.
When the impurity is inside it,
someone touching it on the inside contracts seven-day impurity,
and [someone touching it] on the outside contracts evening impurity.
When the impurity is on its outside surface,
someone touching it on the outside contracts seven-day impurity,
and [someone touching it] on the inside contracts evening impurity.
When there is [impurity] the size of half an olive on the inside,
and the size of half an olive on the outside,
someone touching it,
whether on the inside or the outside,
contracts evening impurity.
If part of it was flat on the ground,
impurity under it or on top of it breaks through and up, and breaks through and down.
When a Tent is pitched in an upper room,
with part of it flattened over a hatch between the house and the upper room—
R. Yose says:
This protects.
R. Simeon says:
It cannot protect unless pitched, like a Tent.

7:2 *All the sloping parts of Tents are like Tents*: A Tent has vertical walls and a flat roof (see introduction). Sloping parts are nonetheless treated as parts of the Tent.

ending at one finger: Even if at the top of the Tent the sloped parts almost meet, so that there is no flat roof to speak of. Alternatively, even if the sloping section almost reaches the ground.

If there is impurity in the Tent: When there is a source of impurity under the flat part of the Tent.

objects in the Tent i.e. under the flat roof of the Tent *are impure.*

When the impurity is inside it: Anywhere inside the Tent.

touching it on the inside…on the outside: Touching the inside/outside surface of the Tent.

seven-day impurity…evening-impurity: See 1:1.

the size of half an olive: A piece from a corpse that is the size of half an olive, i.e. half the qualifying amount for transmission of impurity.

touching the surface of the Tent, *whether on the inside or the outside.*

If part of the Tent *was flat on the ground*: The mishnah seems to have in mind a real tent, rather than a house that is considered a halakhic "Tent" (see introduction), as in most of the tractate. Here the surplus material from an actual tent is flat on the ground.

This protects from impurity. The flattened piece of the tent prevents the passage of impurity from one part of the house to the other part.

It cannot protect unless pitched, like a Tent: i.e. it does not block the passage of impurity when flat.

3 When there is a corpse in a house with many doorways,
they are all impure.
If one of these is opened, it is impure
and all [the others] are pure.
If someone had intent to remove it through one of them,
or through a window that is four handbreadths by four handbreadths in size,
he has protected all the doorways [from impurity].
The House of Shammai say:
One must be thinking [that] before the death of the corpse.
The House of Hillel say:
Even after death.
If it was blocked up
and someone decided to open it—
the House of Shammai say:
Once he opens up four handbreadths.
And the House of Hillel say:
Once he begins.
But they concede that someone making an opening for the first time
must open up four handbreadths.

7:4–6 *Considerations of Purity and Lifesaving in Childbirth*

4 When a woman is in difficult labor
and they took her out from one house to another,
then the first is impure by virtue of doubt, and the second for certain.

7:3 Cf. 3:6.

When there is a corpse in a house with many closed *doorways, they are all impure*: When there is impurity from a corpse inside a house, then even the closed doorways extending beyond the house become halakhic "Tents" for the purpose of transmitting impurity.

had intent to remove it through one of them: To remove the corpse via one of the doorways.

he has protected all the doorways [from impurity]: Other than the one from which he intended to remove it.

One must be thinking [that] before the death of the corpse: Intent to remove the corpse by one way or another, unless it occurred prior to its demise, is irrelevant to the purity of such exits.

If it was blocked up: If the doorway by which one intended to remove the corpse was blocked up (e.g. with stones).

Once he opens up four handbreadths: Immunization of the others from impurity is not accomplished until the blocked doorway is partially cleared to yield a space of 4 × 4 handbreadths.

Once he begins opening it.

But they concede that someone making an opening for the first time must open up four handbreadths: In the case of a new doorway, they concede that immunization of the others from impurity is not accomplished until the doorway has been partially cleared, to yield a space of 4 × 4 handbreadths.

7:4 The presumption underlying this mishnah is that a stillborn baby transmits impurity once the womb is open.

and they took her out from one house to another: And ultimately the baby was found stillborn in the second house, *then the first* house *is impure by virtue of doubt*: Perhaps the womb was already open in the first house, even though no one realized that at the time.

and the second house is impure *for certain.*

Said R. Judah:
When [is that]?
When she is carried by her arms,
but if she was walking, the first house is pure.
For once the grave is opened there is no possibility to walk.
Stillborns are not deemed to open the grave
until their heads are rounded like the spindle's knob.[15]

5 When the first came out dead and the second alive it is pure.
If the first was alive and the second dead it is impure.
R. Meir says:
If both were in one [amniotic] sac it is impure;
if in two [amniotic] sacs it is pure.

6 When a woman is in difficult labor,
one may cut up the fetus in her stomach
and take it out limb by limb,
for her life takes precedence over its life.
Once most of it has come out one may not touch it,
for one may not push aside one soul for another.

[15] **K** has "*in* the spindle's knob" in place of "*like* the spindle's knob." The prepositional prefixes are almost identical.

When she is carried by her arms from one house to another, *but if she was walking* freely on her own *the first house is pure.*

For once the grave is opened there is no possibility to walk: The grave here refers to the woman's womb. The mishnah asserts that a woman would not be able to walk freely once the womb has opened, so that if she were indeed walking freely between the two houses her womb could not possibly have been open in the first house.

Stillborns are not deemed to open the grave and thus begin to transmit impurity *until their heads are rounded like the spindle's knob*: Until the top of the baby's head has grown to the size of a spindle's knob. If the head is smaller than that, the baby is not deemed to transmit impurity until it emerges.

7:5 See introductory note to 7:4.

When the first of twins *came out dead and the second alive it is pure*: Presuming the first was removed from the house before the second emerged, the second baby did not contract impurity.

it is impure: The first baby contracted impurity as soon as the womb opened (presuming that the second was already dead).

if in two [amniotic] sacs it is pure: In such a case the live first baby does not become impure from the stillborn second one.

7:6 This mishnah is unrelated to rules of purity, but does relate to 7:4–5.

one may cut up the fetus in her stomach and take it out limb by limb: To save the mother's life.

Once most of it has come out: If risk to the mother's life, due to her difficulty in giving birth, occurred after most of the baby had come out.

one may not touch it: At that stage one does nothing that might prejudice the life of the baby (cf. the mishnah's first clause).

for one may not push aside one soul for another: At that point the baby is deemed a living creature, and there is no longer any ground to privilege the mother's life.

Chapter Eight

8:1–5 *Things That Convey and/or Block Impurity*

8 There are things that convey impurity and block [it],
that convey impurity but do not block [it],
that block [it] but do not convey [it],
and that neither block [it] nor convey [it].
The following convey [it] and block [it]:
a chest, a box, and a turret-shaped chest, a straw beehive, a reed beehive, and the hold of an Alexandrian ship—
when they have a base
and can hold forty *se'ah* of liquid,
which is two *kor* in dry measure.
And a curtain, a leather apron, a leather mat, a sheet, matting, and a mat;
when these are made into Tents.
And a herd of domestic animals, impure or pure,[16] a pack of wild animals, and of birds,[17] and a resting bird, and one who makes a place for her child[18] in the sheaves.
Iris, ivy, squirting cucumber, Greek gourds, and pure foods.
R. Yohanan b. Nuri did not agree about "pure foods,"
other than cakes made of dried figs.

2 Wall projections, balconies, dovecotes, rock crevices, rocks, holes in rocks, spiky rocks,
and *sekhakhot* and *pera'ot* that can take light plasterwork—

[16] i.e. of prohibited ("nonkosher") or permissible ("kosher") species.
[17] "And of birds" is missing in **K**.
[18] The Hebrew words meaning "for her child" and "of brick" have the identical consonantal spelling, and **P** may have the latter reading.

8:1 Cf. 3:7, *Kelim* 15:1, 16:4.

that convey impurity: By serving as a "Tent" (see introduction).

and can also *block [it]*: By acting as a barrier against its transmission.

turret-shaped chest: Cf. chapter 4.

matting, and a mat: The matting might be made from papyrus. Many of the terms in this mishnah are obscure.

one who makes a place for her child in the sheaves: Presumably this actually refers to the covered place itself (not the person making it).

pure foods: i.e. dry foods, which according to halakhah are impervious to impurity (only after becoming wet would foodstuffs be susceptible to contracting impurity).

8:2 The mishnah is a continuation of 8:1, in listing those things that convey impurity and also block it.

sekhakhot and pera'ot. etc: According to R. Meir these convey and block impurity when the branches of the tree, or projections off a fence, are so close together that if a light layer of plasterwork were applied to them, it would hold. According to the Sages, however, they would need to hold a medium layer of plasterwork in order to belong on this list.

the words of R. Meir.
And the Sages say:
Medium plasterwork.
What are *sekhakhot*?
A tree that shades the ground beneath.
And *pera'ot*?
[Projections] coming off a fence.

3 The following convey [it] but do not block [it]:
a chest, a box, and a turret-shaped chest, a straw beehive, a reed beehive, and the hold of an Alexandrian ship—
when they do not have a base,[19]
or cannot hold forty *se'ah* of liquid,
which is two *kor* in dry measure.
And a curtain, a leather apron, a leather mat, a sheet, matting, and a mat,
when these are not made into Tents.
And domestic or wild animals that have died,
and foods susceptible to impurity;
add to these—millstones operated by hand.

4 The following block [it] but do not convey [it]:
a spread-out weave, bed ropes, wastebaskets and window screens.

5 The following neither convey [it] nor block [it]:
seeds, and plants connected to the soil,
except for the plants listed [above],
and hailstones, and snow, and frost, and ice and salt;
and someone skipping from place to place,
and someone jumping from place to place;
and a flying bird, and a flapping cloak, and a boat sailing over the water.
If someone tied the boat to something that could hold it in place,
or put a stone over the cloak,
then it conveys impurity.

[19] **K**: "when these do have a base but cannot hold forty *se'ah* of liquid."

8:3 Cf. 8:1.

add to these: Something that is not in contradistinction to 8:1, unlike the previous items in this mishnah, namely *millstones operated by hand*. Lit. "millstones of a human"; as opposed to millstones operated by animals, these are presumably portable.

8:4 Cf. 8:1.

A spread-out weave: Probably a loom, with only the warp threads laid out on it.

8:5 Cf. 8:1.

except for the plants listed [above]: Presumably the "iris, ivy, squirting cucumber, Greek gourds" mentioned in 8:1.

and someone: This could equally mean "and something," and might refer to an animal.

If someone tied the boat to something that could hold it in place, or put a stone over the cloak: Thus preventing them from moving about freely.

R. Yose says:
The cabin of a boat does not convey impurity.

8:6 *Tight Closure*

6 Two jars, each with a piece the size of half an olive inside,
[each] with a tight closure around and placed in a house—
they are pure, and the house is impure.
If one of them is opened—
it and the house are impure, and the other is pure.
So too for two rooms that open into a house.

Chapter Nine

9:1–4 *Beehives Extending out of a House*

9 When there is a beehive in a doorway, with its opening to the outside—
if a piece from a corpse, the size of an olive, is placed beneath it, or on top of it outside,
[then] anything opposite the [piece the size of an] olive, beneath it or on top of it, is impure;
and anything not opposite the [piece the size of an] olive, [as well as] its inside and the house [itself], is pure.

The cabin of a boat does not convey impurity: It does not qualify as a halakhic "Tent" (see introduction).

8:6 *a piece the size of half an olive*: From a corpse; each piece on its own is too small to cause impurity.

a tight closure: Cf. notes to 5:2. The halakhah of the tightly closed container is derived from Numbers 19:14–15.

they are pure: i.e. the jars.

the house is impure: The tight closure does not block impurity from leaving the containers (although it does block the entry of impurity), and the two pieces combine to render the house impure (cf. 3:1).

So too for two rooms that open into a house: Understood by commentators to refer to a situation where each room contains a piece, half the size of an olive, from a corpse. With their doors closed, each room would remain pure, but the rest of the house would be impure. This is conceptually similar to the halakhah of the two jars.

9:1 *with its opening* i.e. the entrance to the hive *to the outside* of the house to which the doorway connects.

on top of it outside: On top of any part of the hive that is outside the house.

anything opposite the [piece the size of an] olive, beneath it or on top of it: Anything directly below it, or directly above it.

If in the house, nothing is impure other than the house.
If inside [the hive], everything is impure.
2 If it was a handbreadth above the ground,
[with] impurity beneath it, or in the house, or on top of it,
[then] all is impure, other than its inside.
If inside [the hive], everything is impure.
3 When does this apply?
When it is an object that is loose.
If it was missing a piece and stopped up with straw,
or tight—
what is tight?
whatever does not have a handbreadth on any side—
[then] if a piece from a corpse, the size of an olive, is placed beneath it,
anything directly below that is impure, until the depths;
if on top of it, anything directly above that is impure, until the sky.
If in the house, nothing is impure other than the house.
If inside [the hive], nothing is impure other than its inside.

its inside: The inside of the hive.

If the piece is *in the house*...

nothing is impure other than the house: i.e. the hive is not.

everything is impure: Both the hive and the house.

9:2 *If* the hive, as described in the first line of 9:1, i.e. in a doorway, with its opening outside the house.

impurity refers to a piece from a corpse, the size of an olive.

[then] all is impure, other than its inside: The house and the outer surface of the hive become impure, but inside the hive remains pure.

If the impurity was *inside* the hive.

everything is impure: The entire hive, as well as the house.

9:3 *When does this apply?* When do the matters discussed in 9:1 and 9:2 apply?

When it is an object: i.e. when the hive is intact and therefore a usable "utensil." This is the meaning of this phrase throughout.

loose...tight: An alternative translation understands "loose" to mean that the hive has holes in its sides through which the bees come and go, and "tight" to mean that these holes are plugged.

If it was missing a piece and thus not a true "object" *and stopped up with straw* to replace the missing piece.

whatever does not have a handbreadth on any side: The hive is considered tight when the gap between it and the doorway does not, at any point on its surface, amount to a handbreadth.

anything directly below that becomes impure, until the depths: Objects directly below the piece become impure, including any objects in the ground.

if the piece is *on top of it...until the sky*: Objects in the air directly above the piece become impure, all the way up to the sky.

If the piece is *in the house* and the hive is missing a piece or tight (as earlier defined), then *nothing is impure other than the house* itself, but the hive and around it remain pure.

If the piece *is inside* inside the hive and the hive is missing a piece or tight (as earlier defined), then *nothing is impure other than its inside*, but the area below and above it remain pure, as does the house.

4 If it was a handbreadth above the ground,
[with] impurity beneath it, or in the house,
[then] beneath it, and the house [itself], are impure,
[but] its inside, and above it, are pure.
If inside [the hive], then nothing is impure other than its inside.
If on top of it, anything directly above that becomes impure, until the sky.

9:5–8 *Beehives Extending into a House*

5 When does this apply?
When its opening is to the outside.
When its opening is to the inside—
if a piece from a corpse, the size of an olive, is placed beneath it, or on top of it outside,
[then] anything opposite the [piece the size of an] olive, beneath it or on top of it, and inside it[20] is impure;
and anything not opposite the [piece the size of an] olive, [as well as] its inside and the house [itself], is pure.
If inside it or in the house, then everything is impure.
6 If it was a handbreadth above the ground,
[with] impurity beneath it, or in the house, or inside it, or on top of it,
[then] everything is impure.
7 When does this apply?
When it is an object that is loose.
If it was missing a piece and stopped up with straw,
or tight—
what is tight?
whatever does not have a handbreadth on any side—
[then] if a piece from a corpse, the size of an olive, is placed beneath it,
anything directly below that is impure, until the depths;
if on top of it, anything directly above that is impure, until the sky.
If inside it or in the house, then its inside and the house are impure.

[20] **K**, **P** lack "and inside it."

9:4 This mishnah continues the discussion in 9:3 of the incomplete or tight hive. *It/its* refer to such a hive throughout, and *impurity* refers to a piece from a corpse, the size of an olive.

If the impurity was *inside it*... *If* the impurity was *on top of it*.

9:5 See notes to 9:1, which this mishnah parallels. In 9:5 the entrance to the beehive is inside the house, as opposed to outside it, as specified in 9:1.

and inside it: See n. 20. The version in the printed editions is quite likely a late insertion.

9:6 See notes to 9:2, which this mishnah parallels. In 9:6 the entrance to the beehive is inside the house, as opposed to outside it, as in 9:2.

9:7 See notes to 9:3, which this mishnah parallels. In 9:7 the entrance to the beehive is inside the house, as opposed to outside it, as in 9:3.

8 If it was a handbreadth above the ground,
[with] impurity beneath it, or in the house, or inside it,
[then] everything is impure, except on top of it.
If on top of it, anything directly above that becomes impure, until the sky.

9:9 *Beehives inside a House*

9 If it filled the entire house,
with not a handbreadth's space between it and the beams,
[then] when there is impurity inside it, the house is impure,
[but] when there is impurity in the house,
[then] anything inside it is pure.
For it is the manner of impurity to depart, but not to enter.
[This is] whether it is upright or turned on its side, whether one or two.
10 If it was standing in the doorway,
with not a handbreadth's space between it and the lintel,
[then] when there is impurity inside it, the house is pure,
[but] when there is impurity in the house,
[then] anything inside it is impure.
For it is the manner of impurity to depart, but not to enter.

9:11–14 *Beehives Outdoors*

11 If it was turned on its side outdoors,
and a piece from a corpse, the size of an olive, is placed beneath it, or on top of it,
[then] anything opposite the [piece the size of an] olive, beneath it or on top of it, is impure;

9:8 See notes to 9:4, which this mishnah parallels. In 9:8 the entrance to the beehive is inside the house, as opposed to outside it, as in 9:4. This mishnah continues the discussion in 9:7 of the incomplete or tight hive. "It" refers to such a hive throughout.

9:9 *It* refers to a beehive throughout.

when there is impurity: e.g. a piece from a corpse, the size of an olive.

For it is the manner of impurity to depart, but not to enter: Cf. 3:7, 4:1.

one hive or *two* hives, one on top of the other.

9:10 Cf. 9:9 and the first part of 4:3. *It* in 9:10 refers to a beehive throughout.

9:11 Cf. 9:1.

If it: i.e. a beehive.

anything opposite the [piece the size of an] olive, beneath it or on top of it: Anything directly below it, or directly above it.

and anything not opposite the [piece the size of an] olive, [as well as] its inside is pure.
If inside it, everything is impure.

12 If it was a handbreadth above the ground
[with] impurity beneath it, or on top of it,
[then] everything is impure, except inside it.
If inside it, [then] everything is impure.
When does this apply?
When it is an object.
If it was missing a piece and stopped up with straw,
or able to hold forty *se'ah*, according to the Sages—
[then] if a piece from a corpse, the size of an olive, is placed beneath it,
anything directly below that is impure, until the depths;
if on top of it, anything directly above that is impure, until the sky.
If inside it, then nothing is impure other than its inside.
If it was a handbreadth above the ground [with] impurity beneath it, [then] beneath it is impure;
if inside it, [then] its inside is impure;
if on top of it, [then] anything directly above that is impure, until the sky.

13 If it was resting on its base, and it was a container,
[with] impurity beneath it, inside it, or on top of it—
the impurity breaks through and up, and breaks through and down.
If it was a handbreadth above the ground,
or covered over, or turned upside down on its opening,

its inside: The inside of the hive.

If the piece is *inside* the hive.

9:12 A continuation of 9:11. *It* again refers to a beehive throughout.

everything is impure, except inside it: Everything beneath it and above it becomes impure.

If the source of impurity is *inside it, then everything* beneath it and above it, as well as objects inside it, *is impure.*

When it is an object: i.e. when the hive is intact.

or able to hold forty se'ah, according to the Sages: According to 8:1, straw and reed beehives that can hold forty *se'ah* act as barriers to the transmission of impurity. There is, however, no indication there that this is a matter of dispute between the Sages and others, and commentaries disagree as to the import of their mention here.

if the source of impurity is *on top of it.*

If the source of impurity is *inside it.*

If it was a handbreadth above the ground: This continues the discussion of a beehive that is not an intact container, in contradistinction to the first part of the mishnah.

9:13 A continuation of 9:12. *It* again refers to a beehive throughout.

it was a container: The intent of this qualification here is a matter of dispute among commentaries; in 9:12 the word had referred to an intact container, and was contrasted with one that was missing a piece and stopped up with straw.

the impurity breaks through and up, and breaks through and down: So that anything directly in line with its source becomes impure. The impurity does not, however, spread sideways: cf. 6:6.

[with] impurity beneath it, inside it, or on top of it—
[then] everything is impure.

14 When does this apply?
When it is an object.
If it was missing a piece and stopped up with straw,
or able to hold forty *se'ah*, according to the Sages—
[when] impurity is beneath it, inside it, or on top of it,
the impurity breaks through and up, and breaks through and down.
R. Eleazar and R. Simeon say:
Impurity does not arise from it, nor descend from it.
If it was a handbreadth above the ground [with] impurity beneath it, [then] beneath it is impure.
If inside it or on top of it,
[then] anything directly above that is impure, until the sky.

9:15 *A Casket*

15 A casket that is wide beneath and narrow above, with a corpse inside it—
someone touching the lower part is pure, and [someone touching] the higher part is impure.
If wide above and narrow beneath,
[then] someone touching any part of it is impure.
If it was uniform,
[then] someone touching any part of it is impure—
the words of R. Eliezer.
R. Joshua says:
From a handbreadth on down, he is pure,
[and] from a handbreadth on up, he is impure.
If made like a clothes chest,
[then] someone touching any part of it is impure;
if like a *glusqom*,
[then] someone touching any part of it, other than its opening, is impure.

[then] everything is impure: Beneath, inside, and above the hive.

9:14 Cf. notes to 9:12 and 9:13. *It* again refers to a beehive throughout.

Impurity does not arise from it, nor descend from it: In diametric opposition to the previous opinion.

If the source of impurity is *inside it*.

9:15 *casket*: Most commentators explain this as referring to a tomb hewn out of rock, but some see it as an ossuary.

wide beneath and narrow above: Wider at its base than at the top.

If it was of *uniform* width.

From a handbreadth on down…up: An obscure phrase, perhaps referring to touching the casket less/more than a handbreadth from the top of the grave within.

If made like a clothes chest: If the casket/tomb were constructed like a clothes chest, understood by commentaries to mean that its cover is above its sides.

like a glusqom: Apparently with its lid blocking the aperture only, but not extending to its sides.

9:16 *A Barrel*

16 A barrel that is resting on its base outdoors,
with a piece the size of an olive, from a corpse, placed beneath it or inside it—
if directly opposite its floor,[21]
[then] impurity breaks through and up, and breaks through and down,
and the barrel [itself] is impure.
If beneath its side wall and outside,
[then] impurity breaks through and up, and breaks through and down,
and the barrel [itself] is pure.
If inside it and beneath its side wall,
[then] if there is a handbreadth-sized space in the side walls everything is impure,
but directly in line with its mouth remains pure.
But if not, [then] impurity breaks through and up, and breaks through and down.
When does this apply?
When it is pure.
But if it was impure or a handbreadth above the ground
or covered over or turned upside down on its opening,
[with] impurity beneath it, inside it, or on top of it—
[then] everything is impure.

Chapter Ten

10:1–5 *Hatches*

10 When there is a hatch inside a house,
with a handbreadth-sized opening—

[21] K: "placed beneath it or inside it or opposite its floor, [then] impurity..."

9:16 Cf. 9:13 and notes, for a similar discussion regarding a hive. 9:16 refers to a convex barrel, so that a source of impurity can be both *beneath its side wall and outside* the barrel.

if the source of impurity is *directly opposite its floor*: i.e. in the same vertical plane as a point on the floor of the barrel, but not in line with the curved sides.

If inside it and beneath its side wall: Inside the barrel and within the convex space of the side walls, but not directly above the floor of the barrel.

a handbreadth-sized space 1 × 1 × 1 handbreadth.

everything is impure: Beneath the barrel, inside it, and in a direct line above any part of it.

But if not: If the space within the convex sidewalls is not 1 × 1 × 1 handbreadth.

When it is pure: When the barrel was pure before the piece of the corpse was placed there.

10:1 *a*[n open] *hatch.*

if there is impurity in the house, beneath the hatch is pure;
[however,] if the impurity is beneath the hatch [then] the house is pure.
Whether the impurity is in the house or beneath the hatch—
if someone put his foot above he has bridged over the impurity.
If part of the impurity is in the house and part beneath the hatch—
the house is impure, and directly in line with the impurity is impure.

2 If the hatch does not have a handbreadth-sized opening—
if there is impurity in the house, beneath the hatch is pure;
[however,] if the impurity is beneath the hatch [then] the house is pure.
If the impurity is in the house,
and someone put his foot above, [then] he is pure.
If the impurity is beneath the hatch,
[and] someone put his foot above it,
R. Meir deems him pure;
and the Sages say:
If the impurity preceded his foot he is impure,
[but] if his foot preceded the impurity he is pure.
R. Simeon says:
When two feet on top of one other preceded the impurity—

if there is impurity in the house beneath the cover of the ceiling.

anything in a direct line *beneath the hatch is pure* but anything beneath the covered part of the ceiling becomes impure.

[then] the entire *house is pure.*

Whether the impurity is elsewhere *in the house or beneath the hatch.*

put his foot above the hatch *he has bridged over the impurity*: The consequence of putting his foot over the skylight, so that there is no longer a square handbreadth of opening, is that he has completed a halakhic Tent (see introduction) that was previously incomplete. Anything in the house now becomes impure, whether beneath the hatch or not, and the person himself becomes impure.

If part of the impurity is in the house and part beneath the hatch: The Mishnah has gone back to the earlier scenario, where the hatch was unobstructed by a human foot.

the house is impure beneath the ceiling, *and* anything *directly in line with the impurity is* also *impure* if beneath the hatch, but presumably objects beneath the hatch, when not directly in line with the source of impurity (i.e. not in its vertical plane), do not become impure.

10:2 Cf. notes to 10:1, of which this mishnah is a continuation.

If the hatch does not have a handbreadth-sized opening: In the first two cases the size of the hatch is in fact immaterial, as 10:1 and 10:2 have identical rules.

If the impurity is in the house, and someone put his foot above, [then] he is pure: The impurity cannot pass from the house, because the hatch is too small (unlike the rule for the analogous case in 10:1).

If the impurity preceded his foot: If the impurity was in the house before he put his foot over the hatch then it does pass through the aperture and make him impure.

[but] if his foot preceded the impurity he is pure: In such a case the Sages agree with the view of R. Meir.

R. Simeon says: When two feet on top of one other over the small hatch mentioned here *preceded the impurity*: i.e. were in place before the impurity was present.

if the first withdrew his foot and the foot of the second is still there, [then] he is pure,
since the foot of the first had preceded the impurity.

3 If part of the impurity is in the house and part beneath the hatch—
the house is impure, and directly in line with the impurity is impure—
the words of R. Meir.
R. Judah says:
The house is impure, [but] directly in line with the impurity is pure.
R. Yose says:
If there is enough impurity to be split up and render the house impure
and render impure that which is directly in line with the impurity,
[then] it is impure.[22]
But if not, the house is impure [but] directly in line with the impurity is pure.

4 When hatches with a handbreadth-sized opening are on top of one another—
if there is impurity in the house, beneath the hatches is pure;
if the impurity is beneath the hatches, the house is pure.
Whether the impurity is in the house or beneath the hatches,

[22] **K, P**: "[then] that which is directly in line with the impurity is impure," instead of "[then] it is impure."

if the first withdrew his foot and the foot of the second (the higher foot) *is still there, then he* i.e. the second person *is pure*: Even though at that point the source of impurity is in place, and "preceded the foot" of the second person, so that the Sages might declare him impure, he nevertheless remains pure according to R. Simeon, *since the foot of the first had preceded the impurity.* In R. Simeon's view that fact is dispositive, even though the first foot has since been withdrawn.

10:3 *If part of the impurity is in the house and part beneath the hatch*: This seems to refer to the scenario in 10:2, where the hatch is less than handbreadth-size. (A similar case was previously discussed in 10:1, where the hatch is handbreadth-size. See notes to 10:1, where the ruling on the matter was identical to R. Meir's view here.)

[but] anything beneath the hatch *directly in line with the impurity is pure*: Although the Mishnah does not address anything beneath the hatch that is not in line with the impurity, it can be presumed that such objects or people would also be pure.

If there is enough impurity to be split up and render the house impure, and also *render impure that which is directly in line with the impurity*: e.g. there is a piece half the size of an olive from a corpse beneath the hatch, and a similar piece the size of an olive and a half inside the house, but not beneath the hatch. The two sources of impurity could be split up differently than is actually the case, to leave the size of an olive in each location.

[then] it is impure: i.e. anything directly in line with the impurity becomes impure. The manuscript readings are more explicit.

10:4 Cf. 10:1.

are on top of one another: e.g. in a two-story house there is a hatch in the ceiling over the ground floor, and another hatch (i.e. a skylight) over the floor above, with the two openings directly above one another.

if there is impurity in the house beneath the cover of the ceiling.

anything *beneath the hatches is pure* but anything beneath the covered part of the ceiling is impure; however, *if the impurity is beneath the hatches, the* entire *house is pure.*

Whether the impurity is elsewhere *in the house or beneath the hatches.*

if someone placed something susceptible to impurity above or below,
[then] everything is impure.
And anything not susceptible to impurity—
below it is impure, [but] above it is pure.

5 When the hatches do not have a handbreadth-sized opening—
if there is impurity in the house, beneath the hatches is pure;
if the impurity is beneath the hatches, the house is pure.
When the impurity is in the house—
if someone placed something above or below,
whether susceptible to impurity or not,
only the lower part is impure.
When the impurity is beneath the hatches—
if someone placed something susceptible to impurity above or below,
all is impure.
But if that thing is not susceptible to impurity—
whether above or below,
only the lower part is impure.

10:6–7 *A Pot beneath a Hatch or Lintel*

6 When there is a hatch in a house,
with a pot beneath it,

susceptible to impurity: Even where the object closed the lower hatch. Unlike the insusceptible object (below), the susceptible object does not prevent purity from traveling.

above or below: Covering the top hatch or the bottom one.

[then] everything is impure: Anything in the house now becomes impure, whether directly in line with the hatches or not, and the object covering the hatch becomes impure.

below it is impure: Anything in the house, below the object covering the hatch, whether directly beneath the hatch or not.

[but] above it: Anything in the house, above the object covering the hatch, whether directly above the hatch or not, *is pure.*

10:5 This mishnah follows on from 10:4 in discussing hatches on top of one another.

However, *when* (unlike the scenario in 10:4) *the hatches do not have a handbreadth-sized opening—if there is impurity in the house,* beneath the cover of the ceiling, anything *beneath the hatches* in a direct line *is pure.*

then *the* entire *house is pure.*

When the impurity is in the house beneath the cover of the ceiling.

above or below: Covering the top hatch or the bottom one.

the lower part of the house, beneath the lower of the hatches.

all is impure: i.e. the entire house.

whether placed *above or below*: Covering the top hatch or the bottom one.

10:6 *When there is a hatch in a house, with a pot beneath it* on the ground

such that if it were raised its rim would not touch the hatch—
if there is impurity beneath it, inside it, or on top of it,
the impurity breaks through and up, and breaks through and down.
If it was a handbreadth above the ground
with impurity beneath it, or in the house—
beneath it, as well as the house, are impure,
[but] inside it, as well as its exterior surface, are pure.
If inside it or on top of it [then] all are impure.

7 When placed on the side of the threshold,
such that if it were raised a handbreadth-sized area would touch the lintel—
if there is impurity beneath it, inside it, or on top of it,
the impurity breaks through and up, and breaks through and down.
If it was a handbreadth above the ground
[with] impurity beneath it, or in the house,
then beneath it, as well as the house, is impure,
[but] inside it, as well as its exterior surface, are pure.
If inside it or on top of it, then all are impure.
[However, when placed on the side of the threshold,]
such that if it were raised a handbreadth-sized area would not touch the lintel,
or if it is stuck to the lintel—
if there is impurity beneath it,
nothing is impure, other than [what is] beneath it.

such that if it were raised its rim would not touch the hatch: i.e. if raised straight up, to the level of the hatch, its rim could pass through unimpeded, without touching the frame of the hatch.

beneath it, inside it, or on top of it: Here and for the balance of this mishnah and the next "it" refers to the pot.

the impurity breaks through and up, and breaks through and down: So that anything directly in line with its source becomes impure.

If it was a handbreadth or more *above the ground.*

or elsewhere *in the house.*

as well as the rest of *the house.*

all are impure: Inside it as well as its exterior surface, beneath it, and the house itself.

10:7 This mishnah follows on from 10:6.

When the pot is *placed on the* ground on the *side of the threshold*: i.e. just outside the door to the house.

such that if it were raised, a handbreadth-sized area would touch the lintel: i.e. if raised straight up, to the level of the lintel, then an area on the surface of the pot, of at least 1 × 1 handbreadth, would be in contact with the lintel.

the impurity breaks through and up, and breaks through and down: So that anything directly in line with its source becomes impure.

or elsewhere *in the house.*

then all are impure: Inside the pot, on top of it, beneath it, and the house itself.

[However, when placed on the side of the threshold,] such that if it were raised a handbreadth-sized area would not touch the lintel: This is to be contrasted with the first case in the mishnah.

or if it is stuck to the lintel: The pot is not on the ground beneath the lintel but is attached to the latter, with less than 1 × 1 handbreadth, on the surface of the pot, in contact with the lintel.

Chapter Eleven

11:1–3 *Cracked Roofs*

11 **1** When a house has cracked apart—
if there is impurity in the outer part, objects in the inner part are pure.
If there is impurity in the inner part, then as for the objects in the outer part—
the House of Shammai say:
The fissure needs to be four handbreadths.
The House of Hillel say:
Any amount.
R. Yose says,
in the name of the House of Hillel:
A handbreadth-sized opening.
2 When a portico has cracked apart—
if there is impurity in one side, objects in the other side are pure.
If he placed his foot or a reed above it, then he has bridged over the impurity.
If he placed the reed on the ground it does not convey impurity;
only when it is raised by a handbreadth over the ground.
3 A thick wool coat, and a thick piece of wood,
only convey impurity when raised a handbreadth above the ground.

11:1 *When a house has cracked apart*: The roof is cracked open.

the outer part: Between the crack and the entrance.

The fissure needs to be four handbreadths or more, otherwise the objects in the outer part become impure.

the House of Hillel say: Any amount: i.e. any size fissure maintains the purity of the objects in the outer part. *R. Yose*, however, has an alternative tradition about the House of Hillel's ruling, and he *says, in the name of the House of Hillel: A handbreadth-sized opening* (i.e. fissure) is needed to maintain the purity of the objects in the outer part.

11:2 *a portico*: Being open, it has different rules from those that govern the house in 11:1.

above it: Across the crack.

bridged over the impurity: i.e. joined the two parts of the portico, so that the impurity is now in both of them (cf. 10:1).

on the ground: Directly beneath the crack.

it does not convey impurity: So its presence is immaterial.

only when it is raised by a handbreadth over the ground: When a reed or stick beneath the crack is a handbreadth above the ground, it does convey impurity. This enables the impurity to pass from one part of the portico to the other and reside in both parts.

11:3 The first two sentences of this mishnah are repeated in 15:1. The remainder of the mishnah is paralleled in *Eduyot* 4:12.

A thick wool coat, and a thick piece of wood, only convey impurity from one side of a crack to another when placed beneath a crack in a roof…Cf. 11:1 and 11:2. Their thickness is relevant because the lower part of the object would need to be *a handbreadth above the ground.*

Folded over,
they only convey impurity when the uppermost fold is raised a handbreadth above the ground.
If a human was placed there—
the House of Shammai say:
He does not convey impurity.
But the House of Hillel say:
A human is hollow,
and the upper part conveys impurity.

11:4–6 *Humans Serving as "Tents"*

4 If someone was looking out of a window
and formed a "Tent" over those burying a corpse—
the House of Shammai say:
He does not convey impurity.
And the House of Hillel say:
He does convey impurity.
And they agree that if he were dressed in his clothes,
or there were two—one on top of the other—
that they do convey impurity.

Folded over: Referring to the coat.

when the underside of the *uppermost fold is raised a handbreadth above the ground.*

If a human was placed there lying under the crack.

a human is considered *hollow, and the upper part of the body conveys impurity*: According to the House of Hillel, the upper part of the body is viewed as a separate entity, sufficiently elevated to convey impurity by bridging the crack. (Since it is considered "hollow," a body lying on the ground is not comparable to a stick lying on the ground—see 11:2.) In the view of the House of Shammai, however, the human body is not considered hollow, and—when lying on the ground—does not have the handbreadth of space underneath that would result in the conveyance of impurity.

11:4 Cf. 11:3 for the underlying disagreement between the House of Hillel and the House of Shammai regarding the "hollow" nature of the human body.

If someone was looking out of a window: i.e. leaning outside it.

and formed a "Tent": See introduction.

He does not convey impurity...*He does convey impurity* into the house in which he is standing.

he were dressed in his clothes: The person leaning out of the window is dressed.

there were two people looking through the window.

they: The clothes, or the uppermost person, both of which are more than a handbreadth over the ground (cf. 11:2 and 11:3) *do convey impurity.*

5 If someone was lying on a threshold,
and people burying a corpse formed a "Tent" over him—
the House of Shammai say:
He does not convey impurity.
And the House of Hillel say:
He does convey impurity.
6 If the impurity is in the house
and pure people formed a "Tent" over him—
the House of Shammai deem [them] pure,
and the House of Hillel deem [them] impure.

11:7 *A Dog That Ate Flesh from a Corpse*

7 If a dog ate flesh from a corpse,
and the dog died and was lying on a threshold—
R. Meir says:
If there is a handbreadth-sized space in its neck,
it conveys impurity,
but if not
it does not convey impurity.
R. Yose says:
They investigate the impurity.
From directly beneath the lintel and further inward, the house is impure;
from directly beneath the lintel and further outward, the house is pure.

11:5 Cf. 11:3 for the underlying disagreement between the House of Hillel and the House of Shammai regarding the "hollow" nature of the human body.

If someone was lying on a threshold partly inside and partly outside a house.

people burying a corpse passed by outside the house and *formed a "Tent"*: See introduction.

He does not convey impurity…He does convey impurity to the house.

11:6 This mishnah follows on from 11:5.

If the impurity is in the house where someone was lying on the threshold, partly inside and partly outside (see 11:5), *and pure people* passed by outside the house and *formed a "Tent"* (see introduction).

deems the passersby *pure*: The dispute between the Houses with respect to this case apparently reflects their underlying dispute in 11:3, as to whether a human is considered hollow.

11:7 *lying on a threshold* partly inside and partly outside a house; cf. 11:5.

it conveys impurity…it does not convey impurity to the house.

They investigate the impurity to determine its precise location in the dog's body.

From directly beneath the lintel and further inward…from directly beneath the lintel and further outward: The ruling depends on whether the vertical plane, in which the impurity is found, lies inward or outward from the lintel of the house.

R. Eleazar says:
If its mouth faces inward, the house is pure;
if its mouth faces outward, the house is impure,
for the impurity exits from its haunches.
R. Judah b. Betera says:
In either case the house is impure.
How long will it stay in its intestines?
Three full days.
For fowl and fish?
As long as it would take to burn up, if it fell in a fire.
[These are] the words of R. Simeon.
R. Judah b. Betera says:
For fowl and fish—one full day.

11:8–9 *A Lamp in a Cellar*

8 If there is a cellar inside a house
with a lamp inside it,
and its receptacle extends out,
and a large basket is placed over it
that would stay over the rim of the cellar if the lamp were taken away—
the House of Shammai say:
The cellar is pure, but the lamp is impure;
the House of Hillel say:
Even the lamp is pure.
And they agree that if the basket were to fall when the lamp is taken away,
everything is impure.

If its mouth faces inward…faces outward: It is the position of its body with respect to the house that governs the ruling, not the position of the impurity itself.

How long will it stay in its intestines? The question might be rephrased as follows: If a dog ate flesh from a corpse, at what point (prior to its own death), would that flesh be considered fully digested, and no longer a cause of impurity?

For fowl and fish? How long would it take such animals to digest what they have eaten?

11:8 The mishnah presumes impurity inside a house with a cellar.

with its receptacle: Lit. "its flower," i.e. a receptacle for oil, or a candle.

extends out of the cellar into the house above.

a large basket: See 5:6–7 for previous discussion of a large basket not susceptible to impurity in a cellar.

that would stay over the rim of the cellar if the lamp were taken away: i.e. the lamp is not holding the basket in place.

everything is impure: Both the cellar and the lamp.

9 Objects between the rim of the basket and the rim of the cellar
are pure, even to the depths.
When there is impurity there, the house is impure.
When there is impurity in the house,
[then as for] objects inside the cellar walls—
if there is space where they are, a handbreadth by a handbreadth by a handbreadth high,
they are pure,
but otherwise they are impure.
If the walls of the cellar were broader than those of the house,
they are pure in either case.

Chapter Twelve

12:1–3 *Covered Ovens*

12 When a board is placed over the mouth of a new oven,
with a handbreadth of excess space on all sides—
if there is impurity beneath it,
the objects on top of it are pure;
if there is impurity on top of it,
the objects beneath it are pure.
But with a used one it is impure,
R. Yohanan b. Nuri deems [it] pure.
When placed over the mouths of two ovens—

11:9 This is a continuation of 11:8.

even to the depths: Even objects beneath the cellar floor remain pure, provided the basket is not supported by the lamp.

When there is impurity there: Inside the cellar.

objects inside the cellar walls: In niches in the walls.

in either case: Even if the niches concerned are smaller than 1 × 1 × 1 handbreadths.

12:1 *a new oven* is not susceptible to impurity, whereas a used one is susceptible (*Kelim* 5:1).

with a handbreadth of excess space: i.e. the part of the board not covering the oven measures a handbreadth *on all sides.*

beneath it…on top of it: Beneath or on top of the "excess."

But with a used one it is impure: However, a used oven becomes impure under such circumstances, as do the vessels beneath and on top of the "excess."

When a board is *placed over the mouths of two ovens*: Here no explicit distinction is made between new and used ovens, and commentaries differ on the implicit meaning.

if there is impurity between them,
they are impure.
R. Yohanan b. Nuri deems [them] pure.
2 When a sifter is placed over the mouth of an oven
with a tight closure around it—
if there is impurity beneath it, or on top of it,
everything is impure,
[but] directly above the interior space of the oven is pure.
When the impurity is directly in line with the interior space of the oven,
anything directly above it is impure, until the sky.
3 When a board is placed over the mouth of a used oven,
extending a handbreadth at both ends,
but not to the sides—
if there is impurity on one side,
objects on the other side are pure.
R. Yose deems [them] impure.
A[n outside] window sill does not convey impurity.
If there were a projection above it—
R. Eliezer says:
That does not convey impurity.
R. Joshua says:
We consider the outside window sill as though it were not there,
and the upper projection does convey impurity.

between them: Between the ovens.

12:2 *When a sifter is placed over the mouth of an oven*: The oven is presumably used and therefore susceptible to impurity (see 12:1). This mishnah seems to be a continuation to 12:1 in similarly presuming a situation where there is a handbreadth of "excess" space on all sides of the sifter, not covering the oven.

with a tight closure around it: In 12:2 the rules of the "tight closure" apply (cf. notes to 8:6). The ruling that *if there is impurity beneath it, or on top of it, everything* beneath it or on top of it *is impure* only applies to the "excess" space on the sifter, *[but]* anything *directly above the interior space of the oven is pure*, in view of the tight closure.

12:3 *extending a handbreadth at both ends, but not to the sides*: In contradistinction to 12:1, the board does not have sufficient excess space in all directions.

on one side of the board.

A[n outside] window sill (following Maimonides' explanation for the obscure Hebrew word) *does not convey impurity*: A house does not become impure when there is a source of impurity beneath a window sill attached to it, projecting outward.

If there were a projection above it: A projection above the window sill, also facing out, which would normally (in the absence of another projection beneath it) convey impurity from beneath it into the house.

R. Eliezer says: That does not convey impurity into the house, in view of the intervening window sill (which, as previously mentioned, "does not convey impurity").

R. Joshua says: In such a case *We consider the outside window sill as though it were not there.*

12:4 *The Shoe of a Cradle, in an Attic*

4 When the hole for the shoe of a cradle reaches into the house [below]—
if there is a handbreadth-sized space in it,
everything is impure.
And if not,
then it is reckoned in the same way as a corpse.

12:5–7 *Impurity beneath Beams and Pillars*

5 Beams of a house and an attic
that have no plasterwork on them—
if they are aligned,
and there is impurity under one of them,
beneath that is impure;
if [it is] between a lower and an upper [beam],
between those is impure;
if [it is] on top of an upper [beam],
anything directly above that becomes impure, until the sky.
If the upper [beams] seem to be between the lower ones,

12:4 *When the hole for the shoe of a cradle reaches into the house [below]*: The "shoe" seems to have been an attachment placed at the base of a cradle leg. The mishnah refers to a situation where there is a hole, inside which such a shoe rests, beneath a cradle in an attic, and this hole reaches through the ceiling below and into the main part of a house.

if there is a handbreadth-sized space in it: i.e. in the hole.

everything is impure: Presuming a corpse in the house below, everything in the attic above becomes impure.

And if not i.e. if the hole is smaller than that, *then it* i.e. the shoe *is reckoned in the same way as a corpse*: Understood by commentators to refer to 1:2—"When objects touch a corpse, and [those] objects [touch other] objects, they [all] contract seven-day impurity. The third, whether a person or objects, contracts evening impurity." The mishnah accordingly implies that in such a case the shoe is deemed to be touching the corpse, and the cradle itself also contracts seven-day impurity, whereas an infant in the cradle merely contracts evening impurity, and anything else found in the attic remains pure.

12:5 *Beams of a house and an attic that have no plasterwork on them—if they are aligned*: When the ceiling beams, for the lower part of a house, are in line with the floor beams for the attic above it, and there is no plasterwork between them.

there is impurity (e.g. a piece from a corpse, the size of an olive) *under one of them*: Under one of the ceiling beams.

beneath that is impure: The space beneath the beam, but not above it, becomes impure.

if the source of impurity *is between a lower and an upper [beam], between those is impure*: But anything above the upper beam, and below the lower one, remains pure.

if the source of impurity *is on top of an upper [beam]*: i.e. on top of one of the attic-floor beams, *anything directly above that becomes impure*: But nowhere else.

If the upper [beams] seem to be between the lower ones: The upper beams are not aligned with the lower ones, but are rather above the spaces between the latter.

and there is impurity under one of them,
[the space] beneath all of them is impure;
if [it is] on top of them,
anything directly above it is impure, until the sky.

6 When a beam stretching from wall to wall has impurity under it—
if [the beam is] one handbreadth wide
it conveys the impurity under all of it;
but if not,
the impurity breaks through and up, and breaks through and down.
How much is it all around if its width is a handbreadth?
When circular it is three handbreadths all around;
when square it is four,
since a square exceeds a circle by a third.

7 A [circular] pillar placed on the ground outdoors—
if it measures twenty-four handbreadths all around,
it conveys impurity beneath its entire side.
And if not,
the impurity breaks through and up, and breaks through and down.

then *[the space] beneath all of them is impure*: As though the two sets of beams formed a single ceiling.

if the source of impurity *is on top of them*, then *anything directly above it is impure*: But nowhere else.

12:6 *it conveys the impurity under all of it*: i.e. the area under the entire beam becomes impure.

impurity breaks through and up, and breaks through and down: Anything directly in line with it becomes impure, but the rest of the space under and above the beam remains pure.

When circular it is three handbreadths all around: The rabbis understood pi to have a value of three (see 1 Kings 7:23), and thus a circular beam one handbreadth wide would have a circumference of three handbreadths.

since a square exceeds a circle by a third: If pi is three, then the ratio of the combined length of the sides of the square to the circumference of the circle is 4:3 (as is the ratio of the area of a square to a circle inscribed within it).

12:7 *if it measures* at least *twenty-four handbreadths all around*: The mishnah presumes a circular pillar with a circumference of twenty-four handbreadths lying on its side on the ground, with a source of impurity resting below it. Within the space created by the underside of such a pillar there could be room for a cube, of one handbreadth, which is the minimum volume required for the halakhic "Tent" (see introduction), which then conveys the effect of the impurity to the entire space between the ground and the curved sides of the pillar.

The rabbinic mathematics can be reconstructed as follows: the diameter of such a pillar is 24/3 = 8 handbreadths (see 12:6). The diagonal of a square, built around the vertical cross section of the pillar, would be approximately 11 handbreadths (based on Pythagoras' theorem; the rabbis might have arrived at this number by trial and error), and the part of the diagonal that extends beyond the surface of the underside of the pillar would be approximately 1.5 handbreadths (half of 11 – 8). Accordingly there is room for a one-handbreadth cube in the space created by the underside of the pillar, as the faces of such a cube would have a diagonal equal to the square root of 2, which is close to 1.5.

And if not, the impurity breaks through and up, and breaks through and down: Anything directly in line with its source becomes impure, whether above or below it, but—unlike the case of the larger pillar—the remainder of the area beneath the pillar remains pure.

12:8 *Impurity around a Threshold or Lintel*

8 When a piece from a corpse, the size of an olive, is stuck to a threshold—
R. Eliezer deems the house impure;
R. Joshua deems [it] pure.
If placed beneath the threshold then it should be judged as "half and half."
When the piece is stuck to the lintel the house is impure;
R. Yose deems [it] pure.
If the piece is placed inside the house
someone touching the lintel becomes impure.
As for someone touching the threshold—
R. Eliezer deems [him] impure;
R. Joshua says:
From a handbreadth on down he is pure,
from a handbreadth on up he is impure.

Chapter Thirteen

13:1–4 *Holes through Walls and Doors*

13 When one makes a light hole for the first time,
its [minimum] measure is the size of the large drill bit from the Chamber.
[For] traces of a light hole,
[it is] two fingers high by the width of a thumb.
What are "traces of a light hole"?
A window that someone closed up,

12:8 *R. Eliezer declares the house impure*: Even if the impurity is technically outside the house.

should be judged as "half and half": Cf. 6:3, where this expression is defined. In the case here the implication is that if the source of impurity is beneath the part of the threshold that is beyond the house, then the house itself remains pure, but otherwise it becomes impure.

From a handbreadth on down he is pure, and from a handbreadth on up he is impure: If touching the threshold less than a handbreadth from the ground, he remains pure, but if touching it more than a handbreadth away he becomes impure. Cf. 9:15 and notes, for a somewhat similar dispute.

13:1 *a light hole*: A hole in a wall, made to bring light into a house.

its [minimum] measure: The smallest size hole that can convey impurity from one side of the hole to the other.

the hole made by the *large drill bit from the Chamber*: The reference is to a chamber in the Temple, where a drill was known to have been kept or used (see 2:3 above).

two fingers high: Presumably meaning that its height is the width of two fingers.

A window that someone closed up, but did not manage to do it completely: In such a case impurity would pass from one side of the remaining aperture to the other, provided its size was the width of two fingers by the width of a thumb.

but did not manage to do so completely.
When the hole was made by water, or by vermin, or by salt eating away at it,
its [minimum] measure is the size of a fist.
If one had thought to put it to use
its [minimum] measure is a handbreadth-sized opening.
[If one had thought to use it] as a light hole,
its [minimum] measure is the size of a drill bit.
Window netting and window bars join together as though the size of a drill bit,
in the words of the House of Shammai.
The House of Hillel say:
Not until there is the size of a drill bit in one place.
[The above is] both for bringing impurity in and for letting impurity out.
R. Simeon says:
It is only for bringing impurity in,
but for letting impurity out a handbreadth-sized opening [is required].
2 A window facing outdoors
has a [minimum] measure the size of a drill bit,
[but] if one built a house outside it,
then its [minimum] measure is a handbreadth-sized opening.

When the hole was made by water: Cf. 3:7. If at least fist-size, such a hole conveys impurity even if the owner of the structure concerned had no particular plans to use it at all.

If one had thought to put it to use: If one had thought to use such a naturally occurring hole for purposes other than bringing in light, then it introduces impurity even if only 1 × 1 handbreadth in size (apparently understood as less than the size of a fist).

[If one had thought to use it] as a light hole: As in the case at the beginning of this mishnah, where someone purposefully creates a light hole.

Window netting and window bars join together as though the size of a drill bit: When the accumulated size of the holes in the netting, or gaps between the bars, amounts to the size of the aforementioned drill bit, then these can convey impurity from one side of the holes/gaps to the other. (Commentators differ as to the precise meaning of the words rendered here as *Window netting and window bars*.)

Not until there is the size of a drill bit in one place: Only when a single hole or gap meets the size requirement can impurity be conveyed from one side to the other.

[The above is]: Referring to the drill-bit rules taken as a whole.

for bringing impurity in and for letting impurity out: Of a house.

a handbreadth-sized opening is required: Cf. 3:6.

13:2 *A window facing outdoors has a [minimum] measure the size of a drill bit*: Such a window can convey impurity from one side to another, provided only that it is at least the size of a drill bit. See the first clause of 13:1 and the comments there.

[but] if one built a house outside it: Immediately outside the window, so that it no longer opens to the outdoors.

If one placed the ceiling at the middle of the window,
then for the lower part it would be a handbreadth-sized opening,
and for the upper part it would be the size of a drill bit.

3 A hole in a door
has a [minimum] measure the size of a fist—
the words of R. Aqiva.
R. Tarfon says:
A handbreadth-sized opening.
If a craftsman had left a gap in it
at the bottom or the top,
or someone closed it but did not shut it tightly,
or the wind blew it open—
its [minimum] measure is the size of a fist.

4 If someone makes a space for a rod or a weaver's stave or a lamp—
its measure is any size,
in the words of the House of Shammai.
The House of Hillel say:
A handbreadth-sized opening.
[If made] to feast one's eyes or speak to one's fellow or [any other] use,
a handbreadth-sized opening.

If one placed the ceiling of the adjacent house *at the middle of the window*, so that the lower part of the window opens into that house, while the upper part faces outdoors.

13:3 This mishnah is a continuation of the previous one, and thus of 13:1, which provided the size of a fist as the minimum needed to convey impurity from one side of a hole to the other (in the case of a naturally occurring hole).

R. Tarfon says: A handbreadth-sized opening: As specified in 13:1, for a case where one had thought to put a naturally occurring hole to use.

If a craftsman had left a gap in it at the bottom or the top: Not having completed building it (or perhaps because the boards used were too short).

or someone closed it but did not shut it tightly, or the wind blew it open: Thereby creating a "hole" of sorts.

In the cases mentioned in the last sentence of the mishnah, R. Tarfon agrees with R. Aqiva.

13:4 *If someone makes a space for a rod or a weaver's stave or a lamp—its measure is any size*: No minimum size is called for in order to convey impurity from one side of a hole to another, when the hole is made for the purposes listed here. (Cf. 13:1–3, and notes.)

The House of Hillel say: A handbreadth-sized opening is needed in order to convey impurity from one side of a hole to the other, when the hole is made for the purposes listed here.

[If the hole is *made] to feast one's eyes* (i.e. gaze outside) *or speak to one's fellow or [any other] use, a handbreadth-sized opening*: Cf. the clause in 13:1: "If one had thought to put it to use its [minimum] measure is a handbreadth-sized opening."

13:5–6 *Items That Reduce the Size of an Opening*

5 These reduce the handbreadth:
a piece of flesh, [if] less than the size of an olive,
reduces in a place of[23] a quarter[-*qav*] of bones;
and bone, [if] less than the size of a barley grain,
reduces in a place of a piece of flesh the size of an olive.
A piece of flesh from a corpse, [if] less than the size of an olive;
a piece of flesh from an animal carcass, [if] less than the size of an olive;
a piece of vermin, [if] less than the size of a lentil;
foodstuffs, [if] less than the size of an egg;
produce in a window;
a spider web, with anything of substance to it;
the carcass of a bird, provided one had not designated it,

[23] Here and subsequently in 13:5 and 6, lit. "at the hand of" or "adjacent to."

13:5 *These reduce the handbreadth*: A precisely handbreadth-sized hole or opening, in a wall or door of a house, can be sufficient to convey impurity in certain cases or according to certain opinions (see 13:1–4). It can, however, be rendered too small to do so if items are found inside it, as these are deemed to reduce the opening to less than the minimum size. (In consequence, the opening would have to be correspondingly larger than handbreadth-size in order to convey impurity.) The list in this mishnah is of items that, perhaps surprisingly, block impurity (just as a stone would, undoubtedly). In the first two cases the source of impurity that is being occluded also plays a role, if only to provide an example. In the first six cases the small quantity concerned blocks impurity from passing through the opening, whereas a larger amount, somewhat paradoxically, would not. The reason is that the larger items, which are themselves sources of impurity, do not block the passage of impurity. Similar reasoning is at play in the final case.

a piece of flesh, [if] less than the size of an olive, reduces in a place of a quarter[-qav] of bones: Even a piece of flesh from a corpse, if it is less than the size of an olive, blocks the passage of impurity when found in a handbreadth-sized opening, in a situation where there is a quarter-*qav* of bones inside the house concerned. 2:1 above had mentioned a quarter-measure of bones as constituting a source of impurity in a "Tent" (and by extension a house), and a handbreadth-sized opening would allow the passage of such impurity outwards, to another structure. 13:5 specifies, however, that even flesh from a corpse would block the passage of this impurity when placed in the opening, provided the amount of such flesh was less than the size of an olive.

and even *bone, [if] less than the size of a barley grain, reduces in a place of a piece of flesh the size of an olive*: A piece of bone, if it is less than the size of a barley grain, blocks the passage of impurity when found in a handbreadth-sized opening, in a situation where there is a piece of flesh from a corpse, the size of an olive, inside the house concerned. According to 2:3 bone is a source of impurity, provided it is the size of a barley grain (although it does not actually transmit impurity "in a Tent").

even a *piece of flesh from a corpse, [if] less than the size of an olive*: This is implicit from the first clause of the mishnah, where it was adduced with reference to a particular example.

even *foodstuffs, [if] less than the size of an egg*: Foodstuffs can transmit impurity (in the rabbinic conception of biblical law), provided the amount of food concerned has the volume of an egg.

produce in: Growing into the space of *a window*.

even *a spider web*: The Hebrew is obscure, but this rendering—suggested by commentators—seems to fit the context.

even *the carcass of a* permissible, kosher *bird*.

even *the carcass of an impure bird*, i.e. of a prohibited species, *when one had designated it, provided one had not made it susceptible, or had made it susceptible, provided one had not designated it*: The rules applying to

and the carcass of an impure bird when one had designated it, provided one had not made it susceptible,
or had made it susceptible, provided one had not designated it.

6 These do not reduce:
bone does not reduce in a place of bone,
nor flesh in a place of flesh;
nor does a piece from a corpse that is the size of an olive,
nor a piece from an animal carcass that is the size of an olive,
nor a piece from vermin that is the size of a lentil,
nor foodstuffs the size of an egg,
nor produce in windows,[24]
nor a spider's web with no substance to it,
nor the carcass of a pure bird
when one had designated it,
nor the carcass of an impure bird
when one had designated it and made it susceptible,
nor warp and woof [threads] that are rendered impure by a blight,
nor a brick from a grave area—
the words of R. Meir.
But the Sages say:
A brick does reduce,
as its dust is pure.

[24] **K** lacks "nor produce in windows."

bird carcasses are found in tractate *Tohorot*. In order for a kosher bird's carcass to transmit impurity one must have designated its meat for human consumption, and in the case of a nonkosher bird one must additionally have wet it, as it is otherwise not susceptible to impurity.

13:6 See 13:5 and notes.

These do not reduce the handbreadth. All cases on the list that follows, excluding the final two, are in contradistinction to cases in 13:5.

Bone does not reduce in a place of bone, nor flesh in a place of flesh: This illuminates the first two clauses in 13:5, which specified not only the size of the object that "reduces," but also a distinct type of impurity in the opening, as opposed to the impurity in the house. The implication here is that a piece of flesh from a corpse, even if less than the size of an olive, would not "reduce" if there were a similar but olive-sized piece in the house concerned, and that bone, even if less than the size of a barley grain, would not "reduce" if there were a quarter-*qav* of bone in the house.

nor produce growing *in windows*: This appears to contradict 13:5 (and is omitted in **K**), but makes sense if the words *with no substance to it* modify the *produce in windows* as well as the *spider's web*.

pure bird, impure bird: As in 13:5, birds of permissible ("kosher") or nonpermissible ("nonkosher") species.

nor warp and woof [threads] that are rendered impure by blight: See *Nega'im* 11:8.

a grave area: A field where a grave was plowed up, discussed at length in chapters 17 and 18.

But the Sages say: A brick from a grave area *does reduce, as its dust is pure*: The dust from which the brick is made is deemed pure, even though it comes from a grave area.

This is the general rule:
The pure reduces and the impure does not reduce.[25]

Chapter Fourteen

14:1–7 *Wall Projections*

14 A wall projection of any size conveys impurity,
the *gizrah* and *givlit* if handbreadth-size.
Which is the wall projection?
The one that faces down.
And the *gizrah*?
The one that faces up.
And with regard to which situation did they say:
"A wall projection of any size conveys impurity"?
When the wall projection is [up to] three courses [of stones] above the doorway,
equaling twelve handbreadths.
If more than that,
then it conveys impurity only if handbreadth-size.
Cornices and carvings convey impurity if handbreadth-size.
2 A wall projection over a doorway conveys impurity if handbreadth-size;
if over a window two fingers high,
[or] above [a hole that is] the size of a drill bit—

[25] K, in an apparent scribal error, is missing "as its dust is pure. This is the general rule—the pure reduces."

This is the general rule: the pure reduces and the impure does not reduce: This principle largely explains the distinctions between 13:5 and 13:6 where—at first sight counterintuitively—smaller items "reduce" the size of an opening whereas larger ones do not, and an item as substantial as a bird's carcass might similarly not "reduce."

14:1 *A wall projection of any size conveys impurity*: The slightest projection above a house doorway, with impurity beneath it, conveys impurity to the house.

the gizrah and givlit: From the next clause it seems as though the *gizrah* is a wall projection that differs from the above-mentioned one only in shape; no explanation is provided for *givlit*.

if handbreadth-size: Otherwise they do not convey impurity.

Which is the aforementioned *wall projection?* i.e. what shape overhang is denoted by the term?

The one that faces down: Convex, when viewed from below.

The one that faces up: Similar to the "wall projection," but concave rather than convex.

14:2 Cf. 14:1 and notes.

A wall projection over a doorway conveys impurity if handbreadth-size: This rule seems to contradict the first clause of 14:1, and commentators have naturally tried to explain otherwise. One plausible interpretation asserts that 14:2 refers to a sealed door, and this explanation has been followed throughout.

if over a window two fingers high, [or] above [a hole that is] the size of a drill bit: See 13:1 (and notes), which discusses the introduction of impurity via a hole "the size of the large drill bit from the Chamber," and a window "two fingers high by the width of a thumb."

any size at all;
R. Yose says:
Its full size.

3 A rod of any size over a doorway
conveys impurity even if one hundred cubits high—
these are the words of R. Joshua.
R. Yohanan b. Nuri says:
Let this be no more severe than a wall projection.

4 If a wall projection around an entire house
takes up three fingers of the doorway—
when there is impurity inside the house,
objects underneath it are impure.[26]
If there is impurity beneath it,
R. Eliezer deems the house impure,
and R. Joshua deems it pure.
So too for a courtyard enclosed by a colonnade.

5 If two wall projections are on top of one another,
with each being handbreadth-size,
and with a handbreadth of space between them—
when there is impurity beneath them,
beneath them is impure;
when [there is impurity] between them,

[26] **P** originally had "pure" instead of "impure," but this was subsequently corrected.

any size at all: A wall projection of any size, with impurity beneath it, can convey impurity via the two aforementioned apertures.

R. Yose says: Its full size: In contradistinction to the previous clause, R. Yose asserts that a minimum size of wall projection is required in order to introduce impurity via these two apertures, and this minimum size corresponds to the size of the opening concerned.

14:3 Cf. 14:1.

Let this be no more severe than a wall projection: In the view expressed here by R. Joshua, the law pertaining to such a rod would be more severe than the law pertaining to an ordinary wall projection (as provided by 14:1), which needs to be no more than twelve handbreadths above a doorway if it is to convey impurity. R. Yohanan b. Nuri disagrees.

14:4 *takes up three fingers of the doorway*: The language here is obscure—literally "eats up three fingers in the doorway." Here, it seems, the wall projection is imagined as extending into this doorway, but being less than a handbreadth wide (the handbreadth consisting of four fingers), or perhaps as extending outward from the doorway by less than a handbreadth.

So too for a courtyard enclosed by a colonnade: Presumably a covered colonnade, whose roof extends into (or over) the doorways of the houses in the courtyard, although by less than the width of three fingers. Impurity in another part of the colonnade would affect the house, and vice versa, in the same way as ruled in the first part of the mishnah—with a similar disagreement between R. Eliezer and R. Joshua.

14:5 Cf. 12:5.

when there is impurity beneath them: Beneath the lower of the two.

anything *beneath them* (i.e. beneath the lower of the two) *is impure.*

between them is impure;
when [there is impurity] on top of them,
anything directly above that is impure, until the sky.
[However,] if the upper protrudes beyond the lower by a handbreadth—
whether there is impurity beneath them or between them,
beneath them and between them is impure;
when [there is impurity] on top of them,
anything directly above that is impure, until the sky.
If the upper protrudes beyond the lower, by less than a handbreadth—
when there is impurity beneath them,[27]
beneath them as well as between them is impure;
when [there is impurity] between them, or beneath the excess—
R. Eliezer says:
Beneath them and between them is impure;
R. Joshua says:
Between them and beneath the excess is impure,
but beneath them is pure.

6 If they are handbreadth-size,
but with less than a handbreadth of space between them—
when there is impurity beneath them,
beneath them is impure;
when [there is impurity] between them or on top of them,
anything directly above that is impure, until the sky.[28]

7 If they are less than handbreadth-size,
whether there is a handbreadth of space between them or not—
when there is impurity beneath them, between them, or on top of them—

[27] **K**: "beneath them or between them."

[28] **P:** "If they are handbreadth-size, but with less than a handbreadth of space between them—when there is impurity beneath them or between them, beneath them and between them is impure; when [there is impurity] on top of them, anything directly above that is impure, until the sky."

anything *between them is impure.*

when [there is impurity] on top of them: On top of the higher of the two.

beneath them and between them is impure: i.e. anything beneath the upper of the two.

beneath the excess: e.g. on the ground, beneath the part of the upper projection that protrudes beyond the lower one.

but beneath them is pure: Anything directly beneath the lower of the two remains pure.

14:6 Continuation of 14:5.

If they i.e. the wall projections.

anything *beneath them* i.e. beneath the lower of the two *is impure.*

14:7 Continuation of 14:6.

If they i.e. the wall projections.

the impurity breaks through and up, and breaks through and down.
So too for two curtains that are raised a handbreadth above the ground.

Chapter Fifteen

15:1–2 *Objects That Are a Handbreadth above the Ground*

15 A thick wool coat, and a thick piece of wood,
only convey impurity when raised a handbreadth above the ground.
Folded over,
they only convey impurity when the uppermost fold is raised a handbreadth above the ground.
Blocks of wood [stacked] on top of one another
do not convey impurity
unless the upper one is a handbreadth above the ground;
but as for marble ones—
impurity breaks through and up, and breaks through and down.
2 When wooden blocks are touching at their corners
and are a handbreadth above the ground—
if there is impurity under one of them,
[even] someone touching the other one contracts seven-day impurity.
Objects under the first one are impure,
but those under the second one are pure.

breaks through and up, and breaks through and down: See introduction. This is in contradistinction to 14:5 and 14:6, where impurity does not travel downward in any of the cases mentioned.

So too for two curtains that are raised a handbreadth above the ground: Under the same conditions as the wall projections described in 14:5–7, two curtains parallel to the ground, and at least a handbreadth above it, would be subject to similar rules.

15:1 *A thick wool coat, and a thick piece of wood*: The first two sentences repeat those of 11:3. See annotation there. Here the immediate context is the very end of chapter 14, *So too for two curtains that are raised a handbreadth above the ground.* 15:1 deals with impurity becoming transmitted to objects anywhere under the coat/wood/blocks, by virtue of a source of impurity in that area.

but as for marble ones stacked on top of one another, even with the upper one only one handbreadth above the ground.

impurity breaks through and up, and breaks through and down: See introduction.

15:2 *someone touching the other one contracts seven-day impurity*: Cf. 1:1–3 for previous discussion of seven-day impurity.

the first one…the second one: The "first" block is the one with a source of impurity under it. The "second" block conveys impurity via touch, as just mentioned, but even though a handbreadth above the ground it is not deemed to be a "Tent" (see introduction), and accordingly does not convey impurity to objects beneath it.

A table does not convey impurity
unless it contains a square of one handbreadth by one handbreadth.

15:3 *Several Barrels Together*

3 When barrels are outdoors,
resting on their bases or leaning on their sides,
and their area of contact is handbreadth–size—
if there is impurity beneath one of them,
the impurity breaks through and up, and breaks through and down.
When does this apply?
With pure ones.
However, if they were they impure,
or a handbreadth above the ground—
if there is impurity beneath one of them,
[everything] underneath any of them is impure.

15:4–5 *Partitions*

4 When a house is partitioned
with boards or curtains,
from the sides or the beams—
if there is impurity in the house,
objects in the partitioned-off section are pure;
if there is impurity in the partitioned-off section,
objects in the house are impure,
[as for] objects in the partitioned-off section—
if there is a handbreadth-sized [volume of] space there they are impure,
but otherwise are pure.

A table does not convey impurity at its base to objects elsewhere beneath it *unless it contains a square of one handbreadth by one handbreadth*: i.e. unless the base is at least one handbreadth by one handbreadth in size.

15:3 Cf. 9:16.

their area of contact is handbreadth–size: The barrels are stacked next to each other, such that a handbreadth-sized area of one barrel is in contact with another.

impurity breaks through and up, and breaks through and down: See introduction.

pure ones: The insides of the barrels had been pure prior to their encounter with the impurity beneath them.

However, if they were they impure from beforehand, *or a handbreadth above the ground* even if "pure ones."

15:4 *from the sides or the beams*: i.e. whether the partition is in a vertical or horizontal plane.

if there is impurity in the main part of *the house.*

objects in the main part of *the house.*

if there is a handbreadth-sized [volume of] space there: If the partitioned-off area contains enough space to form a halakhic "Tent" then objects inside it become impure, but otherwise they remain pure even as the contents of the main part of the house become impure.

5 When one partitioned it at ground level—
if there is impurity in the partitioned-off section,
objects in the house are impure;
if there is impurity in the house—
[as for] objects in the partitioned-off section,
if where they are placed there is a [hollow] space one handbreadth by one handbreadth by one handbreadth high,
they are pure;
but otherwise they are impure,
for the ground of a house is considered part of it, until the depths.

15:6–7 *Buildings That Have Been Filled Up*

6 When a house is full of straw,
with less than a handbreadth between it and the beams—
if there is impurity on the inside,
objects opposite the exit are impure.
If there is impurity on the outside—
[as for] objects on the inside,
if where they are placed there is a [hollow] space one handbreadth by one handbreadth by one handbreadth high,
they are pure;
but otherwise they are impure.
If there is a handbreadth between the straw and the beams,
they are impure in either event.

15:5 This mishnah is a continuation of 15:4.

When one partitioned it at ground level: The boards or curtains partitioning off the house are on the ground, although with a source of impurity/objects beneath them.

objects in the partitioned-off section beneath the partition.

a [hollow] space one handbreadth by one handbreadth by one handbreadth high: Another way of describing the "handbreadth-sized [volume of] space" mentioned in the previous mishnah.

but otherwise they are impure, for the ground of a house is considered part of it, until the depths: Just as the house is impure, anything at its ground level (or for that matter below it) becomes impure, even if partitioned off—unless the space beneath the partition forms a halakhic "Tent."

15:6 Cf. 15:4–5.

on the inside: Inside the straw.

objects opposite the exit in the space between the straw and the door.

If there is impurity on the outside between the straw and the door.

If there is at least *a handbreadth between the straw and the beams*: In contradistinction to the beginning of the mishnah.

in either event: Even if they are in a hollow space that is one handbreadth by one handbreadth by one handbreadth high inside the straw. (The empty space over the straw has turned the entire house into a halakhic "Tent"—see introduction.)

7 When a house filled with earth or gravel is abandoned—
or so too for a heap of produce or a pile of gravel,
even if similar to Akhan's pile—
even if impurity is [there], right next to objects,
the impurity [merely] breaks through and up, and breaks through and down.

15:8–9 *Impurity around Graves*

8 Someone standing in the courtyard of a grave is pure
provided there are four cubits within it,
according to the words of the House of Shammai.
The House of Hillel say:
Four handbreadths.
If a beam was made into a grave cover—
whether upright or on its side—
only the part opposite the opening is impure.
If its top is made into a grave cover,
up to four handbreadths only is impure.
And when he plans to cut it

15:7 *is abandoned*: Once abandoned it is no longer considered a halakhic "Tent" (see introduction).

or so too for a heap of produce or a pile of gravel: The ruling in the next clause applies to these, as it does to earth or gravel in an abandoned house.

even if similar to Akhan's pile: A rhetorical flourish—Akhan's pile of stones is mentioned in Joshua 7:26.

impurity is [there], right next to objects: There is impurity inside the house or the piles, adjacent to (but not touching) objects.

the impurity [merely] breaks through and up, and breaks through and down: But does not render the adjacent objects impure, since no halakhic "Tent" has been formed.

15:8 *the courtyard of a grave*: Commentaries interpret this as referring to a common area giving access to multiple graves.

provided there are four cubits within it: If the courtyard is at least four cubits square then someone standing in it remains pure, but otherwise becomes impure.

If a beam was made into a grave cover—whether upright or on its side: The beam is vertical or horizontal, and part of it covers the mouth of a grave. See 2:4, where the grave cover and its support stone "transmit impurity through contact or in a Tent."

only the part opposite the opening is impure: The part of the beam that actually seals off the grave becomes impure, but the rest of the beam does not.

If its top is made into a grave cover, up to four handbreadths only is impure: If the end of the beam were being used as the cover then not only would the part immediately covering the grave become impure, but up to four handbreadths away from it, along the beam, would also become impure.

And when he plans to cut it: He plans to lop off the part of the beam that is not covering the grave, but has not yet done so.

R. Judah says:
It is all [deemed] connected.

9 If a barrel full of pure liquid,
with a tight closure around it,
was used as a grave cover—
anyone touching it contracts seven-day impurity,
but the barrel and the liquid are pure.
If an animal was used as a grave cover,
anyone touching it contracts seven-day impurity.
R. Meir says:
Anything alive does not transmit impurity as a grave cover.

15:10 *Combinations*

10 If someone touches a corpse and touches some objects,
or forms a Tent over a corpse and touches some objects,
they are impure.
If someone forms a Tent over a corpse and forms a Tent over some objects,
or touches a corpse and forms a Tent over some objects,
they are pure;
[but] if his hands[29] cover a [square] handbreadth,
they are impure.
When two houses each contain pieces from a corpse,
half an olive in size,
and someone stretched his two hands into them—

[29] Some printed editions have "hand."

it is all [deemed] connected: The entire beam, even the part to be removed, is deemed to be one piece and is therefore impure.

15:9 *pure liquid*: Prior to being placed over the grave, the liquid in the barrel was ritually pure.

with a tight closure around it: See notes to 5:2 and 8:6.

seven-day impurity: See introduction and 1:1.

If an animal was used as a grave cover: Cf. *Eruvin* 1:7.

15:10 See introduction and 1:1–4.

If someone touches a corpse and touches some objects...they i.e. the objects *are impure*: Commentaries differ as to whether the ruling is limited to simultaneously touching both a corpse and objects, or whether it would also include someone who touched objects after having touched a corpse. (The difference extends to the following case of someone who *forms a Tent over a corpse and touches some objects.*)

they i.e. the objects *are pure.*

[but] if his hands cover a [square] handbreadth and he had one hand each over the corpse and over the objects *they* i.e. the objects *are impure*: By definition the palm of a hand would seem to cover a square handbreadth, so the rabbis here seem to have a known size of "handbreadth" in mind.

someone stretched his two hands into them: With one hand in each.

if his hands cover a square handbreadth, he conveys the impurity,
but otherwise he does not convey the impurity.

Chapter Sixteen

16:1–2 *Thin Objects and Mounds*

16 All movable objects convey impurity via the thickness of a cattle prod.
R. Tarfon said:
May I be bereft of children if this is not a bereft *halakhah*,
for the hearer heard it and was mistaken.
For a farmer was walking along
with a cattle prod on his shoulder,
and one side of it formed a Tent over a grave,
and they declared it[30] impure
because of objects that form a Tent over a grave.
Said R. Aqiva:
I will correct it,
so that the words of the Sages are upheld—
all movable objects convey impurity to a person carrying them
via the thickness of a cattle prod,

[30] Or "him."

he conveys the impurity: From one house to the other, so that the two pieces are considered as being combined to an olive-sized piece in each of the two houses. See 2:1 for the requirement that a piece from a corpse needs to be olive-sized in order to transmit impurity "in a Tent."

16:1 *All movable objects convey impurity via the thickness of a cattle prod*: In order to be able to convey impurity from one entity to another, movable objects need to be at least as thick as a cattle prod. This sentence is also found in *Kelim* 17:8, where the text continues "not large or small, but a medium one. What is considered medium? Any encompassing a handbreadth." In other words, provided the circumference of a movable object exceeds one handbreadth, then if part of it is above a grave, and another part is carried by a person, it conveys impurity from the corpse to the person by forming a "Tent" over the latter. The mishnah's rule, in this formulation, will now be modified.

May I be bereft of children: An oath, expressing his view that this law, as expressed here, is incorrect.

for the hearer heard it and was mistaken: Someone heard a case, and mistakenly concluded that the rule was as expressed in the mishnah's first clause.

A farmer was walking along: R. Tarfon proceeds to recount a case that occurred that had led to the misapprehension.

and they declared it impure because of objects that form a Tent over a grave and not because it was thick enough to convey impurity.

I will correct it, so that the words of the Sages are upheld: The rule at the beginning of the mishnah is correct though expressed incompletely.

but [become impure] themselves if any size at all,
and [convey impurity] to other people or objects if the size of a handbreadth.

2 How so?
If a spindle is stuck into a wall,
with a piece half the size of an olive below it
and a piece half the size of an olive above it—
even if these are not in line—it is impure.
Thus it conveys impurity to itself if any size at all.
If a potter is walking along with a yoke[31] on his shoulder,
and one end of it formed a Tent over a grave,
objects at the other end are pure.
If the yoke is handbreadth-size, they are impure.
Mounds, if close to a town or to a road—
both newly made and old ones are impure;
[as for] remote ones—
new ones are pure, but old ones are impure.
What constitutes "near"? Fifty cubits;
and "old"? Sixty years—
the words of R. Meir.
R. Judah says:
"Near"? When none are nearer than it.
And "old"? That no one remembers it.

[31] The standard printed edition has basket, but **K** and **P** have a rare word differing by one Hebrew letter, which commentators have understood to mean yoke.

and [convey impurity] to other people or objects if the size of a handbreadth: A movable object that simultaneously "forms a Tent" over a grave, as well as over another person or object, only conveys the impurity from the grave if the movable object that "forms the Tent" is at least the size of a handbreadth.

16:2 *a piece half the size of an olive* from a corpse.

Thus it conveys impurity to itself if any size at all: The spindle is less than a square handbreadth in size, but would nevertheless become impure by virtue of the two pieces of the corpse "combining" for this purpose. The case presumably arose as an example of the principle of combination, and not in the context in which it appears in this mishnah, where it seems more complex than necessary for demonstrating the point under consideration.

If a potter is walking along with a yoke on his shoulder: Potters would carry their wares on a yoke.

If the yoke is handbreadth-size, they are impure: This is an example of R. Aqiva's statement in the previous mishnah. In practice a yoke would be far more than a handbreadth long, so that the distinction is whether it is a handbreadth wide, or not.

Mounds, if close to a town or to a road…are presumed *impure*: Commentaries understand the impurity to arise from women burying stillborn or aborted babies in such mounds. (This section on mounds seems to bear no relation to the earlier part of the mishnah; if anything it looks connected to the following one.)

remote ones—new one are pure: They are presumed not to have been used as burial places.

but old ones are presumed *impure*: Perhaps they were, at some point, close to a settlement or road that no longer exists and were used at the time for burials.

That no one remembers it: No one remembers when the mound was made.

16:3–5 *Checking for a Graveyard*

3 One who initially encounters a [single] corpse
put to rest in the usual way
may remove it,
together with whatever is mixed together with it.
If one found two,
one may remove them,
together with whatever is mixed together with them.
If one found three—
if there are between four and eight cubits between them,
which is the space for the bier and those burying it—
then it is a graveyard.
Then one checks twenty cubits beyond.
If one found another within twenty cubits,
one checks a further twenty cubits beyond,
as there is a basis for the matter.
But if one initially encountered it,
one may remove it,
together with whatever is mixed together with it.
4 The one inspecting checks one cubit by one cubit,
then leaves a cubit [unchecked],
[and] until he reaches rock or virgin soil.
One removing earth from a place of impurity may eat *terumah*.

16:3 This mishnah is also found in *Nazir* 9:3.

initially: That is, without any previous sign that a body would be found there.

put to rest in the usual way: Understood by commentators to mean that it can be identified as buried in the Jewish manner.

may remove it for reburial.

together with whatever is mixed together with it: Cf. 3:5. Here the text seems to refer to the earth around the corpse, into which the body may have bled.

then it is a graveyard: Removal is prohibited and the field concerned may not be plowed over.

Then one checks twenty cubits beyond: This is done in an attempt to mark out the area of the graveyard.

as there is a basis for the matter: For suspecting the presence of a graveyard.

But if one initially encountered it: Essentially a repetition of the first clause of this mishnah.

16:4 *The one inspecting checks…until he reaches rock or virgin soil*: The check mentioned in the previous mishnah requires every other square cubit to be checked, until twenty cubits has been reached. In addition, the depth of the check is specified: "until rock or virgin soil"—presumably the latter is soil that has not been turned over. (A similar depth is mentioned in *Niddah* 9:5.)

One removing earth from a place of impurity: As part of the checking process described above.

may eat terumah: As long as the status of the area is merely suspect, a priest working there is presumed pure, and may accordingly eat *terumah* (see *Terumot*). The Hebrew word used here is actually not the word *terumah* and might refer only to *terumah* that has become mixed up with ordinary food. In that case regular *terumah* would by implication be forbidden to a priest.

One clearing a heap of stones may not eat *terumah.*

5 If while checking he arrived at a brook, or pool of water, or public thoroughfare, he may stop checking.
In a field where people have been killed
he collects bones one by one,
and all is [then] pure.
Someone clearing a grave belonging to him from his field
collects bones one by one,
and all is [then] pure.
In a cistern in which aborted babies or slain people are thrown,
one collects bones one by one,
and all is [then] pure.
R. Simeon says:
If he designated it as a grave from the outset
then its contents are considered to be mixed together.

Chapter Seventeen

17:1–18:6 Creating and Purifying "Grave Areas"

17 One who plows over a grave creates a "grave area."
How far does it extend?
A full furrow,
which is one hundred cubits

One clearing a heap of stones: A priest clearing a heap of stones that had fallen on someone and perhaps killed him.

16:5 *If while checking* as specified in 16:3.

he may stop checking: One may presume that the ground is not a graveyard beyond this point.

In a field where people have been killed he collects bones one by one, and all is [then] pure: Understood by commentators to mean that there is no requirement to check twenty cubits, nor is the ground around the bones considered to have impurity mixed up with it (cf. 16:3).

Someone clearing a grave belonging to him from his field: Similarly, if someone is moving the contents of a grave that belongs to him from his own field, there is no requirement to check twenty cubits (cf. 16:3).

In a cistern: The bodies are presumably not losing blood when cast into the cistern (cf. 16:3).

If he designated it as a grave from the outset then even though it was ultimately used for aborted babies or people who had been killed *its contents are considered to be mixed together*: The ground of such a pit is considered akin to the ground of any other grave.

17:1 *One who plows over a grave creates a "grave area"*: The grave area is the subject of much of the remainder of the tractate. It is the area around a grave in a plowed field designated impure because a piece of bone may have been moved by the plow to some distance from the grave.

A full furrow, which is one hundred cubits: Most simply explained as an area around a grave, 100 × 100 cubits in size, notionally "created" when someone plowed over a grave and proceeded to plow the entire field around it.

and room for four *se'ah*.
R. Yose says:
Room for five.
[However,] on a downward slope, and on an upward slope,
one places a quarter-measure of vetch [seed] at the knee of the plow,
[and] the grave area extends up to where three vetches still grow next to one another.
R. Yose says:
On a downward slope, but not on an upward slope.

2 If while plowing he struck a rock, or fence,
or if he shook off the plow,
he creates a grave area only until there.
R. Eliezer says:
One grave area can create another grave area.
R. Joshua says:
Sometimes it creates [one], sometimes it does not.
How so?
If he plowed half a furrow, and then returned and plowed another half,
and so too [if he plowed] to the sides,
he does create a grave area.
If he plowed an entire furrow,
and then returned and plowed from within it to beyond it,
he does not create a grave area.

3 When one plows away from a pit full of bones,
or away from a pile of bones,

room for four se'ah: It would take four *se'ah* (encountered in 8:1 as a liquid measure) to sow a field one hundred cubits square.

Room for five: R. Yose may be asserting that the grave area created holds 25% more grain than the four *se'ah* expressed in the earlier opinion, and is thus 12,500 square cubits as opposed to 10,000. (It is also possible that he simply disagrees as to the amount of grain that can be sown in a 10,000 square-cubit area.)

one places a quarter-measure of vetch [seed] at the knee of the plow, and the grave area extends up to where three vetches still grow next to one another: Once the crop in a sloping field grows, there is a point in the field at which three vetches will no longer be found growing next to one another, because almost all the seed had already dropped from the plow by the time it reached there. That part of the field is said to lie beyond the grave area. Presumably this is done after the fact—i.e. having plowed over the field, he then returns to determine the extent of the grave area created when he did so. (On the "knee" of the plow see *Kelim* 21:2.)

but not on an upward slope: According to R. Yose, no grave area is created in a field sloping upward from a grave at its edge, presumably because in his view any bone picked up by the plow falls off at the grave, as soon as it is plowed.

17:2 *he creates a grave-area only until there*: But not beyond, as bone initially left on the plow would have been shaken off, and no longer moved around by the plowing action.

R. Eliezer says…R. Joshua says: It is not clear whether R. Joshua disagrees with R. Eliezer, or is merely clarifying the latter's statement.

and so too [if he plowed] to the sides after plowing half a furrow he plowed at right angles to it.

17:3 The list of cases in this mishnah suggests that the impurity of a grave area was legislated largely in order to discourage careless plowing over known graves. One might in fact have moved bones around even in

or from a field in which a grave has been lost,
or in which a grave was [subsequently] found,
or one plows [a field] that is not his—
and so too when a gentile plowed—
he does not turn it into a grave area,
for there is no grave area for Samaritans.[32]

4 If a grave-area field was above a pure one
and rains flooded down from the grave area to the pure one,
even if it had been red and they turned it white,
or white and they turned it red,
they do not make it into a grave area.

5 When someone built a house and attic
in a field in which a grave had been lost;
if the doorway to the attic was directly above the doorway to the house,
the attic is pure,
and if not, the attic is impure.
Soil from a grave area or soil from outside the Land that had adhered to vegetables—
these combine if equivalent to the seal on sacks of produce—
the words of R. Eliezer.

[32] **K**: "and so too when a gentile plowed he does not turn it into a grave area for Samaritans." **P**: "and so too when a gentile plowed—they do not turn it into a grave area, nor is there a grave area for Samaritans."

situations like these, but legislating in such cases would not have addressed the concern about careless plowing over known graves, and was therefore unnecessary.

from a field in which a grave has been lost: A grave is known to have been there but its precise location is now unknown, and one plows from that field into an adjacent one.

one plows [a field] that is not his: As legislation would only affect the owner, who did nothing wrong, rather than the plowman.

and so too when a gentile plowed…for there is no grave area for Samaritans: When a Samaritan plows over a grave he does not create a *halakhic* grave area. The same ruling must *a fortiori* apply to gentiles, who are presumed to be even more removed from normative Jewish practice than Samaritans.

The words *he does not turn it into a grave area* apply to all the previously mentioned cases in this mishnah.

17:4 *If a grave-area field was above a pure one*: On a terrace or incline.

even if it had been red and they turned it white: Even if the flooding changed the color of the lower field, so that one can be sure that soil from the upper field had been swept into it, the laws of the grave area are not invoked for the lower field. This is an instance in which one grave area does not create another grave area (cf. 17:2).

17:5 *in which a grave had been lost*: A grave is known to have been there but its precise location is now unknown.

the attic is pure: Although the house itself becomes impure, for fear that the grave is underneath it.

soil from outside the Land: From beyond the Land of Israel. Such soil is deemed impure. Cf. "earth of the nations" in 2:3.

these combine if equivalent to the seal on sacks of produce: If the total amount of such earth adhering to a clump of vegetables is at least equal in size to one of these seals, then it is deemed impure. Such seals were apparently made of clay and were of a standard size.

The Sages say:
Only if there is an amount equivalent to the seal on sacks of produce, all in one place.
Said R. Judah:
It once happened that letters came from across the seas to the sons of high priests,
with about one *se'ah* or two *se'ah* of seals on them,
yet the Sages were not concerned about their impurity.

Chapter Eighteen

18 How do they harvest the grapes in a grave area?
They sprinkle the people and the vessels
and then repeat,
and then harvest the grapes
and remove them from the grave area.
And others receive [the grapes] from them
and take them to the winepress.
If they touched one another,
they are impure,
according to the words of the House of Hillel.
The House of Shammai say:
One holds the sickle in palm fiber,
or harvests the grapes with a flint,
and puts [them] in a large basket
and takes them to the winepress.

all in one place: In the view of the Sages the pieces of earth do not combine, as R. Eliezer said. Rather, in order for impurity to be conveyed, a single piece of earth of the size mentioned would be required.

It once happened that letters…yet the Sages were not concerned about their impurity: R. Judah's story is designed to back up the view of the Sages, expressed above, that the combined amount of soil is irrelevant. The individual clay letter seals from across the seas were small, and undersize for conveying impurity as "soil from outside the Land," even though there were so many of them that there would, in total, have been a large amount of such soil in the batch of letters. The story has particular force because it concerns the sons of high priests, who would have been affected by impurity.

18:1 *How do they harvest the grapes in a grave area?* Without compromising the purity of the wine produced from them.

They sprinkle the people and the utensils and then repeat: Cf. Numbers 19:19.

others receive [the grapes] from them: Although sprinkling the people and utensils saves the grapes from impurity, the harvesters themselves are presumably impure. Accordingly another group of uncontaminated people is required to take the grapes to the press.

If they touched one another they are impure: If the harvesters came into physical contact with people from the second group then the latter become impure, and so do the grapes that they are taking to the winepress.

One holds the sickle in palm fiber…and takes them to the winepress: The entire operation is handled by one group of people using utensils that cannot convey impurity, and this keeps the grapes pure. The large basket was mentioned in 5:6 above, and is of a sort not susceptible to impurity.

Said R. Yose:
When does this apply?
In [the case] of a vineyard that became a grave area,
but if someone plants in a grave area,
it should be sold to the market.

2 There are three kinds of grave area.
If one plows over a grave it may be planted with any kind of plant,
but may not be sown with any seed
other than of produce that gets cut.
And if one uprooted it,
then one heaps up the threshing floor within it
and sieves it with two sieves—
the words of R. Meir.
And the Sages say:
Grain with two sieves,
but pulses with three sieves.
And one burns the stubble and stalks.
And it transmits impurity through contact and carriage,
but does not convey impurity in a Tent.

3 A field in which a grave has been lost
may be sown with any seed,
but may not be planted with any kind of plant,

a vineyard that became a grave area: A grave within it was plowed over, and after the fact the vineyard became a grave area.

but if someone plants in a grave area the produce *should be sold to the market*: It must not be made into wine but instead is sold as grapes, which can be kept insusceptible to impurity. This penalizes the owner.

18:2 *There are three kinds of grave area*: These will be individually discussed in this and subsequent mishnayot.

If one plows over a grave: This is the first kind of grave area.

but may not be sown…other than of produce that gets cut: If instead of planting trees the owner prefers to sow the field, then the only permissible produce is a type that can be cut, rather than plucked. A crop that called for plucking would be problematic, as a small piece of bone from the grave might be gathered with the harvest.

And if one uprooted it: If produce that might have been cut was plucked instead.

then one heaps up the threshing floor within it: That is, within the field itself, rather than taking the harvest to a threshing floor away from the field, as would have been common practice.

and sieves it with two sieves: i.e. sieves it twice.

And one burns the stubble and stalk left over from the harvest.

It transmits impurity through contact and carriage, but does not convey impurity in a Tent: The earth from such a grave area transmits impurity in the same way as the pieces of bone it is suspected of containing—cf. 2:3.

18:3 *A field in which a grave has been lost*: A grave is known to have been in the field concerned, but its precise location is now unknown. This is the second of three types of grave area to which the previous mishnah referred.

and nor may one maintain any tree there—
other than a *seraq* tree that bears no fruit.
And it transmits impurity through contact and carriage and in a Tent.

4 A wailers' field[33] may neither be planted nor sown,
but its soil remains pure,
and one may use it to make ovens for sacred purposes.
And the House of Shammai and the House of Hillel agree that one checks for a Passover offering,
but not for *terumah*.
As for a *nazir*,
the House of Shammai say:
One checks;
and the House of Hillel say:
One does not check.
How does one check?
One takes soil that can easily be shifted
and places it in a sieve with small holes,
and crumbles it.
If a piece of bone the size of a barley grain is found there,
he is [deemed] impure.

5 How do they make a grave area pure?
They remove three handbreadths from it,

[33] K: "field of burial niches." This differs from the more widespread text by only one Hebrew letter.

and nor may one maintain any tree there: If trees are found growing there they need to be uprooted.

And it transmits impurity through contact and carriage and in a Tent: The earth from a field in which a grave has been lost does transmit impurity in a Tent—cf. the previous mishnah and see introduction.

18:4 *A wailers' field*: There is no grave in the field, but corpses lie there before burial, during eulogies. This is the third of three types of grave area to which 18:2 refers.

ovens for sacred purposes: Used for baking for Temple service.

one checks for a Passover offering: One checks the field for sources of impurity if someone who had been in it wishes to bring the Passover offering, and would therefore need to be in a state of ritual purity. The discussion of checking fields presumably applies to all three types of grave area mentioned in 18:2–4.

but not for terumah: One does not, however, check the field if a priest who had been in it wishes to eat *terumah* (see tractate *Terumot*), which similarly calls for his being in a state of ritual purity. It is unclear whether the reason for not checking is that no check is considered sufficient, or whether a check is deemed unnecessary.

nazir: See Numbers 6, and tractate *Nazir*. The ambiguity mentioned in the previous annotation persists here for the view expressed in the name of the House of Hillel. In general, however, the House of Hillel are more lenient in their rulings, suggesting that they would deem a check unnecessary.

he is [deemed] impure: The person wishing to offer the Passover offering, etc.

18:5 *How do they make a grave area pure?* Thereby turning it back again into being a regular field.

They remove three handbreadths from it, or add three handbreadths on top of it: Commentaries explain this as being the depth of a plow. Removing or adding such an amount in depth would take away any concern that someone plowing in future might unearth a fragment of bone. The new soil would need to be from a field that is not a grave area.

or add three handbreadths on top of it.
If one removed three handbreadths from one half,
and added three handbreadths on top of the other half,
it is [similarly] pure.
R. Simeon says:
Even if one removed one and a half handbreadths from it, and added one and a half handbreadths from another place on top,
it is pure.
If someone paves over a grave area,
with stones that he cannot easily shift,
it is pure.
R. Simeon says:
So too if one digs up a grave area it is pure.

6 Someone moving around a grave area
over stones that he cannot easily shift,
or borne by a strong person or animal,
is pure;
if over stones that he can easily shift,
or borne by a weak person or animal,
he is impure.
Someone traveling around the lands of the nations
in the hills or over rocks,
is impure;
if by the sea or on the *shunit*
he is pure.
And what is [considered] the *shunit*?
Any place where the sea rises in a storm.

18:7–10 *Impurity Associated with Gentiles*

7 When someone buys a field in Syria
adjacent to the Land of Israel—
if he is able to enter it in purity, it is pure,

So too if one digs up a grave area and discovers no bones *it is pure.*

18:6 *Someone moving around a grave area*: If one manages to traverse the grave area entirely on stones that cannot be easily shifted then one can be presumed pure. So too if borne above the ground by a strong person or animal.

if walking *over stones that he can easily shift, or borne by a weak person or animal*: Because he is likely to move soil around himself, even though seemingly supported above it.

the lands of the nations: The ground outside the Land of Israel (cf. 2:3 and 17:5) is generally deemed impure.

Any place where the sea rises in a storm: The *shunit* is defined as the furthest point to which the sea rises.

18:7 *if he is able to enter it in purity*: If the land is contiguous with the Land of Israel then it can be entered in a state of purity (cf. note on "the lands of the nations" in 18:6).

and requires tithing and observance of the Seventh Year.
And if he is unable to enter it in purity it is impure,
and requires tithing and observance of the Seventh Year.
Gentile residences are impure.
After how long living there does it need to be checked?
Forty days,
even if there is no woman with him;
and if a slave or woman was watching it,
[then] it does not need to be checked.

8 What do they check?
Deep sewers and smelly water.
The House of Shammai say:
Even dung heaps and soft earth.
And the House of Hillel say:[34]
Wherever a pig or weasel can reach
does not need checking.

9 Colonnades are not considered to contain "gentile residences."
Rabban Simeon b. Gamaliel says:
A destroyed gentile city is not considered to contain "gentile residences."
East Caesarea and West Caesarea[35] [contain] graves.

[34] **K, P** lack "The House of Hillel say."

[35] **K, P**: "Qeserion." Perhaps understanding "East Caesarea" and "West Caesarea" as two distinct, similarly named, places rather than two parts of the same city.

tithing: See Numbers 18:21–24 and tractate *Ma'aserot*.

observance of the Seventh Year: For observance of the Seventh Year as it pertains to agriculture see Exodus 23:10–11, Leviticus 25:3–7, and tractate *Shevi'it*.

if he is unable to enter it in purity it is impure, and nevertheless *requires tithing, and observance of the Seventh Year.*

Gentile residences are impure: Gentiles are suspected of burying or discarding stillborn or aborted fetuses in their homes, and therefore such residences are impure even in the Land of Israel.

After how long living there does it need to be checked? Forty days: If a gentile has been living in a house for forty days, a Jew intending to go there is obliged to check it for the presence of a fetus.

even if there is no woman with him: As she might have left after the fetus was buried or discarded.

and if a slave or woman was watching it: If a Jew's slave or a Jewish woman was watching the house, and would know if there had been a fetus there.

18:8 *What do they check?* When the check mentioned in the previous mishnah is conducted.

Deep sewers and smelly water…Even dung heaps and soft earth: Places where a fetus might be buried or discarded.

Wherever a pig or weasel can reach does not need checking: Presumably they would have eaten the fetus or removed it.

18:9 *considered to contain "gentile residences"*: For the purposes of the discussion in the latter part of 18:7.

East Caesarea and West Caesarea [contain] graves: And the areas are accordingly impure. This may refer to two places—Caesarea Maritima on the sea, and Caesarea Philippi near the sources of the Jordan (see n. 35).

And East Acre was in doubt,
but the Sages deemed it pure.
Rabbi and his court voted on *Qeini* and declared it pure.

10 Ten places are not considered to be "gentile residences":
the tents of Arabs, and field huts, and simple tents, and guard posts, and summer huts, and a gatehouse, and the open space in a courtyard, and a bathhouse, and an armory, and the legions' camp.

East Acre was in doubt as to its purity.

Rabbi: R. Judah the Prince.

voted on the purity of a place by the name of *Qeini*.

18:10 *Ten places are not considered to be "gentile residences"*: For the purposes of the discussion in the latter part of 18:7.

Tractate Nega'im

Mira Balberg

Introduction

Overview

Tractate *Nega'im* (literally, "afflictions") addresses the topic of visible abnormalities in persons, clothes, and houses. It provides elaborate guidelines for the diagnosis of these abnormalities as potential causes of ritual impurity and for the procedures required for the purification of persons and objects rendered impure on account of such abnormalities.

The term *nega*, here translated as "affliction," refers to any kind of abnormal patch in the skin or hair of persons, in clothes, or in houses, which must be inspected in order to discern its status of purity. If the affliction meets certain criteria of color, size, and location, the person/clothing/house in question must be inspected again after one week, so as to see whether certain "signs of impurity" have appeared in the affliction. If they have appeared, the person/clothing/house is rendered impure and certain procedures must be followed; if signs of impurity did not appear, then usually after one or two additional inspections at one-week intervals the person/clothing/house is declared pure. The tractate presents a systematic treatment of the various kinds of afflictions, the criteria that warrant their inspection, and the exact nature of the signs of impurity that are pertinent to each kind of affliction.

Relationship to Scripture

Tractate *Nega'im* relies heavily on Leviticus 13–14, and closely follows it both in terminology and in order. While the tractate does not include many biblical quotations (except for 12:5–7, in essence a verse-by-verse *midrash* on Leviticus 14:35–45), it is immediately discernible that the organizing principle of the different mishnaic units are the biblical verses. Thus, for instance, the first chapter of the tractate, which is concerned with distinctions between different kinds of skin abnormalities, corresponds with Leviticus 13:2, which elaborates those different kinds; then the second chapter of the tractate, which describes the visual conditions and impediments of the inspection procedure, corresponds with Leviticus 13:3, *and the priest shall inspect the afflictions*, etc.

Structure and Organization of the Tractate

Faithful to the order in which the different subtopics of afflictions unfold in the biblical text, the tractate is structured as follows: chapters 1–7 are concerned with discolorations in one's skin in which appear any of the three "signs of impurity," and with their inspection procedure (= Leviticus 13:2–11); chapter 8 is concerned with the rather peculiar principle that a person who has already been rendered impure is rendered pure if the affliction spread throughout the body (= Leviticus 13:12–16); chapter 9 is concerned with scabs and boils (= Leviticus 13:17–28); chapter 10 is concerned with afflictions of the head and the beard (= Leviticus 13:29–44); and chapter 11 is concerned with afflictions in clothes (= Leviticus 13:47–59). Only the last two topics are discussed in the Mishnah in reverse order to the biblical text: chapters 12 and 13 are concerned with afflictions in houses (= Leviticus 14:33–57), whereas chapter 14 is concerned with the purification of the person with scale-disease (= Leviticus 14:1–32). This deviation from the biblical order probably derives from an attempt to end the tractate on a positive note, as is often the case in the Mishnah.

Main Ideas

To a great extent, then, tractate *Nega'im* can be seen as a systematic development and elaboration of Leviticus 13–14, and it offers very few practices, concepts, or ideas that are uniquely rabbinic. Nevertheless, it is important to note that in some places the mishnaic tractate is colored with cultural and social concerns that seem particularly relevant to the world of the rabbis and have no trace in the Bible. One of the most notable examples of this is the Mishnah's marginalization of the priest's role in the inspection procedure to the bare minimum, allowing laypersons to perform the inspection as well (3:1). This ruling echoes a recurrent theme in rabbinic literature in which authority is transferred from the priests to the Sages, who are "experts" in the various fields of law. These and other aspects of power, supervision, and authority underlie the tractate and attest to the questions and themes with which its creators were preoccupied.

Special Notes for the Reader

The tractate is replete with technical terminology, almost all of it biblical in origin; I have attempted to explain the technical terms in the annotations as they appear. In my translation of the technical terms I have usually followed the Jewish Publication Society Bible version, except in several cases, of which I will mention the two most notable:

1. One of the more difficult terms to translate, both in the biblical and the mishnaic text, is the word *metsora,* which refers to a person who has been certified as impure on account of his or her affliction. The Septuagint famously translated this word as *lepros,* and many English translations, including JPS, accordingly chose the term "leper." However, as has long been noted, there is probably little if any connection between the biblical *tsara'at* and the disease now identified as leprosy, and more recent Bible translators and commentators have preferred to use the more neutral term "scale-disease." The editors have chosen to retain the untranslated term *tsara'at*; for one afflicted we use "one with *tsara'at*."
2. The first week after the initial inspection, in which the priest is waiting to see whether signs of impurity have appeared in the affliction, is referred to as a week of *hesger*—literally "shutting in," because in this week the person or clothing is put away and no contact with them is allowed (houses are quite literally "shut down" and forbidden for entrance during this week). I chose here to translate the term

hesger as "quarantine," a word which efficiently connotes the procedure of seclusion until further inspection (more so than "isolation" chosen by JPS). While "quarantine" suits the case of persons and clothing quite well, it is not ideal for the case of houses, which are not put away as much as they are sealed for access. Nonetheless, for the sake of unity of translation I used the same term throughout the tractate.

In the preparation of the translation, I referred to the three complete manuscripts of the Mishnah—Kaufmann (**K**), Parma 3173 (**P**), and Cambridge-Lowe (**CL**)—as well as MS Parma 2596 to Order *Tohorot* ($\mathbf{P}_2$). I made extensive use of the classical commentaries of Maimonides, Obadiah of Bertinoro, and Samson of Sens, as well as the modern work of Albeck and Kehati.

Tractate Nega'im

Chapter One

1:1–4 *Primary and Secondary Appearances of Skin Afflictions*

1 The appearances of skin afflictions are two, which are four:
(1) a "discoloration" is as white as snow,
(2) and the one secondary to it is as white as the lime of the Temple.
(3) a "swelling" is as white as an egg membrane,
(4) and the one secondary to it is as white as white wool—
the words of R. Meir.
But the Sages say:
A "swelling" is as white as white wool,
and the one secondary to it is as white as egg membrane.
2 The red hue in [a discoloration] as white as snow—
like wine mixed with snow.
The red hue in [a discoloration] as white as lime—
like blood mixed with milk—
the words of R. Ishmael.
R. Aqiva says:
The reddish in both this one and that one appears like wine mixed with water,
but the one as white as snow is bright,
and the one as white as lime is duller than it.

1:1 *The appearances of skin afflictions*: The first part of the tractate concerns the identification of afflictions on the skin, which are diagnosed as pure or impure according to two criteria: first, a particular spot on one's skin must appear to be white, and second, this spot must have a certain "sign of impurity" in it, as will be discussed below. This passage addresses the first criterion.

two, which are four: Leviticus 13:2–8 mentions three kinds of skin abnormalities that appear as white spots on the skin and could potentially be further diagnosed as a scaly affliction: *baheret* (discoloration), *se'et* (swelling), and *sapakhat*, which is often translated as "rash" but has the semantic connotations of adding or appending. The rabbis interpret the verse to mean that "discoloration" and "swelling" are two primary forms of whiteness, and that each one of those primary forms of whiteness also has a *sapakhat* or secondary manifestation. There are therefore two major kinds of skin abnormalities (discoloration and swelling), but four varieties of whiteness in which those abnormalities can appear. For this formulation cf. *Shabbat* 1:1, *Shevu'ot* 1:1.

1:2 *The red hue*: Leviticus 13:19 mentions that a discoloration can also appear as "white-reddish." This passage concerns the ways in which this red streak appears in the primary and secondary forms of discoloration mentioned above.

3 These four appearances[1] can join together one with another
to dismiss, to certify, and to quarantine:
to quarantine the one who remains unchanged at the end of the first week,
to dismiss the one who remains unchanged at the end of the second week,
to certify the one in whom "living flesh" or "white hair" appeared—
[either] at the beginning, at the end of the first week, at the end of the second week, [or] after dismissal.
To certify the one in whom the affliction spread—
[either] at the end of the first week, at the end of the second week, [or] after dismissal.
To certify the one who turned entirely white after dismissal.
To dismiss the one who turned entirely white either after certification or quarantine.
These are the appearances of skin afflictions on which depend all afflictions.

4 R. Hanina the Prefect of the Priests says:
The appearances of skin afflictions are sixteen.[2]
R. Dosa b. Harqinas says:
The appearances of skin afflictions are thirty-six.
Aqaviah b. Mahalalel says:
Seventy-two.

1:4 cont.–6 *Inspection of Skin Afflictions in One-Week Intervals*

R. Hanina[3] the Prefect of the Priests says:
One may not inspect skin afflictions for the first time
on the first day after the Sabbath,
for the day of inspection after the first week will then take place on the Sabbath.

[1] All manuscripts: "*from* these four appearances" (i.e. each one of those four appearances).
[2] Hanina's statement is missing in all the manuscripts.
[3] All manuscripts: "Hanania."

1:3 *can join together with one another*: The rabbis define a minimum size for a skin affliction (see 4:5–11, 6:1), and assert that any smaller skin affliction is to be disregarded. Here the Mishnah states that if there are two afflictions on one's skin, each of which is smaller than the minimum but which when taken together amount to the minimum size, the two afflictions are "joined together" and are considered as one affliction that requires further inspection.

to dismiss, to certify, and to quarantine: After a skin affliction is initially identified on one's skin, this person is to be quarantined for seven days and then inspected again. If the affliction then contains "signs of impurity" (white hair, living flesh, or spreading), this person is certified as impure; otherwise he is quarantined for another week, at the end of which he is either certified as impure (if there are "signs of impurity") or dismissed and declared pure.

1:4 *sixteen... thirty-six... Seventy-two*: Several interpretations have been suggested as to how those Sages reached those numbers: by suggesting different combinations of the various "appearances," or by adding other kinds of afflictions not mentioned thus far.

One may not inspect skin afflictions: A skin affliction is inspected three times: initially, after one week of quarantine, and after an additional week of quarantine (thus there are thirteen days between the initial inspection and the final inspection; see 3:3, 3:5, 3:7). According to R. Hanina, an initial inspection cannot be held on either Sunday or Monday, because then the seventh or thirteenth day, respectively, will be the Sabbath.

and not on the second day after the Sabbath,
for the day of inspection after the second week will then take place on the Sabbath.
And for houses, not on the third day after the Sabbath,[4]
for the day of inspection after the third week will then take place on the Sabbath.
R. Aqiva says:
One may [make the initial] inspection of skin afflictions at any time;
if [a subsequent inspection, as a result, is scheduled] to take place during the Sabbath,
one postpones it until after the Sabbath.
And this [ruling of R. Aqiva] has aspects that are both lenient and stringent.[5]

5 How is it lenient?
If [the skin affliction] had white hair in it,
and the white hair disappeared [by the time of the inspection];
if the hairs were white,
and they turned black;
if one was white and one was black,
and they both turned black;
if they were long,
and then became short;
if one was long and one was short,
and they both became short;
if a boil was adjoined to both of them,
or to one of them;
if a boil encompassed both of them,
or one of them,
or divided them.
[The same law applies for] a boil, and living flesh of a boil, and a scald, and living flesh of a scald, and for a bright spot.
If [the skin affliction] had living flesh in it,
and the living flesh disappeared;
if the living flesh was quadrangle,
and it became round or elongated;
if it was in the center,
and it came to be on the margins;
if it was concentrated,
and it became dispersed;
if a boil appeared inside it,

[4] **CL** lacks "And not on the second day after the Sabbath, for the day of inspection after the second week will then take place on the Sabbath."

[5] Lit. "And there is in this to be lenient and to be stringent."

R. Aqiva says: According to R. Aqiva, the initial inspection may take place any day of the week, but the second and third inspections must be postponed if in the regular schedule (the seventh/thirteenth day) they would have occurred on the Sabbath. This postponement might be the occasion for a more lenient outcome (1:5) or a more stringent outcome (1:6) than that resulting from the original schedule.

1:5 *How is it lenient?* In all of the following cases, the postponement of the inspection prescribed by R. Aqiva allows for a change in the affliction that yields a verdict of purity (1:5) or impurity (1:6).

if a boil appeared inside it: As in the case of white hairs, if the area of living flesh is divided by a boil, a scald, or a bright spot, it is no longer seen as one affliction and therefore the living flesh is not a sign of impurity.

and it was encompassed, divided, or diminished by a boil
or by living flesh of a boil, or by a scald, or by living flesh of a scald, or by a bright spot;
if [the skin affliction] spread,
and the spreading disappeared;
or if the original skin affliction[6] disappeared,
or was diminished
so that in both this one and that one together
there is less than the size of a split bean;
if a boil, or living flesh of a boil, or a scald, or living flesh of a scald, or a bright spot
constitute a division between the original skin affliction and the spreading.
All of these, then, are cases of leniency.

6 How is it stringent?
If [the skin affliction] had no white hair in it,
and white hair appeared [by the time of the inspection];
if the hairs were black,
and they turned white;
if one was black and one was white,
and they both turned white;
if they were short,
and then became long;
if one was short and one was long,
and they both became long;
if a boil was adjoined to both of them,
or to one of them,
or if a boil encompassed both of them,
or one of them,
or divided them—
[the same law applies for] a boil, and living flesh of a boil, and a scald, and living flesh
of a scald, and for a bright spot—
and [by the time of the inspection] it disappeared;
if [the skin affliction] had no living flesh in it,
and living flesh appeared in it;[7]
if the living flesh was round or elongated,
and it became four-sided;
if it was on the margins,
and it came to be in the center;
if it was dispersed,
and it became concentrated;
if a boil appeared inside it,
and it was encompassed, divided, or diminished by a boil—

[6] Lit. "the mother."
[7] Lit. "living flesh was born in it," and so frequently throughout the tractate.

if the original skin affliction disappeared: If the original affliction no longer exists at the time of the second or third inspection, and only the spreading remains, the affliction is considered pure.

in both this one and that one together: In the original affliction and in the spreading.

or by living flesh of a boil, or by a scald, or by living flesh of a scald, or by a bright spot—
and [by the time of the inspection] it disappeared;
if the skin affliction did not spread, and [by the time of the inspection] a spreading appeared in it;
or if a boil, or a living flesh of boil, or a scald, or living flesh of a scald, or a bright spot constituted a division between the original skin affliction and the spreading,
and [by the time of the inspection] it disappeared.
All of these, then, are cases of stringency.

Chapter Two

2:1–3 *The Brightness of the Discoloration and the Priest's Examination*

2 A bright discoloration appears in a German as dark,
and a dark discoloration appears in an Ethiopian as bright.
R. Ishmael says:
The children of Israel,[8] may I be their atonement![9]
They are like boxwood,
not black and not white,
but intermediate.
R. Aqiva says:
Painters have colors with which they paint black, white, and intermediate figures;
one brings an intermediate color and encompasses [the affliction] from the outside,
so it will be seen as if on [a person of] intermediate [complexion].
R. Judah says:
The appearances of skin afflictions are to be considered leniently and not stringently:
let the German be inspected leniently according to his own flesh,
and let the Ethiopian be inspected leniently according to an intermediate [complexion].[10]
But the Sages say:
Let both be inspected according to an intermediate [complexion].

[8] In all manuscripts: "the House of Israel." [9] **P**$_2$: "we are their atonement."
[10] **K** lacks "And let the Ethiopian ... according to an intermediate."

2:1 *A bright discoloration appears in a German as dark*: The passage discusses cases in which one has to examine a person whose skin tone is extremely light (like the inhabitants of *Germania*) or extremely dark (like the inhabitants of *Kush* in Africa). In a person with extremely light skin, a bright (i.e. potentially impure) discoloration will appear to be darker than it is, whereas in a person with extremely dark skin, a dark (i.e. pure) discoloration will appear to be brighter than it is.

may I be their atonement: An idiomatic expression of affection and endearment.

Let the German ... and the Ethiopian be inspected leniently: The affliction that appears as dark in the German's skin will be considered as though it is indeed dark and will be dismissed as pure, whereas the affliction that appears as bright in the Ethiopian's skin will be assessed against the skin of someone with an intermediate skin tone, in which it will appear as dark and also be dismissed as pure.

2 One may not inspect skin afflictions at dawn and at dusk,
and not inside a house,
and not on a cloudy day,
for then the dark discoloration seems bright,
and not at noon,
for then the bright discoloration seems dark.
When may one inspect it?
At three, at four, at five and at seven, at eight, and at nine—
the words of R. Meir.
R. Judah says:
At four, at five, at eight, and at nine.

3 A priest who is blind in one of his eyes
or whose eyes[11] grew dim
may not inspect skin afflictions,
for it is said:
in accord with the vision of the eyes of the priest.
A dark house—
one need not open up windows in it to see its affliction.

2:4–5 *The Inspection Procedure for Skin Afflictions*

4 The inspection of a skin affliction—
how [is it done]?
A man is inspected as though hoeing, or harvesting olives.
A woman is inspected as though rolling out [bread], nursing her child, or weaving at an upright loom,
[the latter] for [the inspection of] the armpit of her right arm.[12]

[11] Lit. "the light of whose eyes." [12] Lit. "hand."

2:2 *At three, at four,* etc.: The Mishnah is referring here not to fixed hours of the day, but to the number of hours (= sunlight time divided into twelve units) that have passed since sunrise. Thus, for instance, if the sun rises at 6 a.m. and sets at 6 p.m., then "three" refers to 9 a.m., "four" to 10 a.m., "seven" to 1 p.m., etc.

2:3 *A priest who is blind...A dark house*: The rabbis deduced from the verse *in accord with the vision of the eyes of the priest* (Leviticus 13:12) that the priest must be able-sighted in both his eyes in order to inspect skin afflictions, as well as that whatever the priest cannot immediately see is not inspected further.

2:4 *The inspection of a skin affliction*: In accordance with the notion that whatever the priest cannot immediately see need not be inspected further, only areas in the body that are normally visible need to be inspected for skin afflictions (see also 6:8). This passage concerns bodily areas (the genitals, the armpits, and under the breasts for women) that are usually hidden, but are occasionally partially exposed, particularly when performing certain labors. During the inspection procedure men and women must assume positions in which those partially hidden areas would be exposed.

hoeing, or harvesting olives: When one hoes, he spreads his legs in such a way that his genital area is partially exposed. When one picks olives from a tree, he lifts up his arms in such a way that his armpits are exposed.

rolling out...nursing her child: When a woman rolls dough, she is assumed to be sitting on the ground with her legs somewhat spread, in such a way that her genital area is partially exposed. When she nurses a child, the area under her breast is partially exposed.

R. Judah says:
Also as though spinning flax—
for [the inspection] of her left [arm].
As he is inspected for his affliction,
so is he inspected for his shaving.

5 A person may inspect all skin afflictions,
except for his own skin afflictions.
R. Meir says:
Also not the skin afflictions of his relatives.
A person may release all vows,
except for his own vows.
R. Judah says:
Also not the vows of his wife
that are between her and others.
A person may inspect all firstborn [animals],
except for his own firstborns.

Chapter Three

3:1–2 *Who Is Subject to Inspection and Who May Perform the Inspection?*

3 All become impure by skin afflictions,
except for gentiles and the resident alien.
All are fit to inspect skin afflictions,
but the [declaration of] impurity and purity are in the hands of a priest.[13]
They tell him: Say: "impure"
and he says: "impure."[14]

[13] **K**: "from the mouth of a priest." [14] **CL** lacks "and he says 'impure.'"

he is inspected for his shaving: As in the case of the inspection, only bodily areas that are visible or occasionally visible must be shaved as part of the purification ritual, whereas bodily areas that are always hidden need not be shaved.

2:5 These three rulings are structured in the same pattern: "A person may [perform an action in respect to] all…except for…" Only the first ruling pertains to skin afflictions, and the two other rulings were juxtaposed with it because of the shared pattern.

A person may release all vows: See *Nedarim* 9.

all firstborn [animals]: Every male of the flock or herd that was the first to come out of its mother's womb is consecrated to God. It is brought to the sanctuary and consumed there by the priests. However, if there are certain kinds of blemishes in the animal, it is given to a priest and may be consumed or used by him in an ordinary fashion. See Exodus 13:12, Numbers 18:15, and tractate *Bekhorot*.

3:1 *resident alien*: A gentile who resides in the Land of Israel and has taken upon himself certain commandments. See also *Zavim* 2:1.

Say: "pure," and he says: "pure."
One may not inspect two skin afflictions at once,
whether in one man or in two men.
Rather, he inspects one
and quarantines it, or certifies it, or dismisses it,
and returns to the other.
One may not quarantine someone who has [already] been quarantined,
nor may one certify someone who has [already] been certified,
one may not quarantine someone who has already been certified,
nor may one certify the quarantined.
However, at the beginning,
or at the end of the week—
the one who quarantines may quarantine,
and the one who certifies may certify,
or may quarantine [the one] and exempt [the other],
or may certify [the one] and exempt [the other].[15]

2 A bridegroom in whom a skin affliction was seen—
one gives him the seven days of the feast:
him, his house, and his garment.
And likewise during a festival—
one gives him all the days of the festival.

3:3–8 *The Different Types of Skin Afflictions*

3 The skin of the flesh is [declared] impure within two weeks,
and by three signs:

[15] **K**, **P**: "quarantines and quarantines, certifies and certifies."

he inspects one: Any one of the afflictions in one person who has several afflictions, or one person out of multiple people who each have an affliction.

One may not quarantine . . . nor may one certify: If someone was already quarantined on account of one affliction, and during the time of quarantine another affliction appears that requires quarantine, the second affliction may not be addressed until the status of the first affliction is clarified. The same is the case even if the second affliction could be immediately certified as impure—the priest does not address the second affliction until the first one has been adjudicated.

the one who quarantines may quarantine: The priest who quarantines the first affliction in the inspection process can then also examine and quarantine the second affliction, or quarantine one and exempt the other.

3:2 *in whom a skin affliction was seen*: This passage concerns cases in which a person has a visible affliction (in his body, garments, or house), but the official inspection of the affliction by a priest is delayed so as not to compromise the celebration of a public or private joyous occasion.

The festival: One of the three pilgrimage festivals: Sukkot (Booths), Passover, and the Festival of Weeks; the first two last seven days. Cf. *Mo'ed Qatan* 1:5.

3:3 The next several paragraphs, through 3:8, present a systematic list of the different afflictions mentioned in Leviticus, their signs of impurity, and the procedures of their quarantine and certification.

by white hair, by living flesh, or by spreading.
By white hair and by living flesh—
at the beginning,
or at the end of the first week,
or at the end of the second week,
[or] after dismissal;
and by spreading—
at the end of the first week,
or at the end of the second week,
[or] after dismissal.
And it becomes impure within two weeks,
which are thirteen days.

4 The boil and the scald are [declared] impure within one week,
and by two signs:
by white hair and by spreading.
By white hair—
at the beginning,
at the end of the week,
[or] after dismissal;
And by spreading—
at the end of the week,
[or] after dismissal.
And they become impure within one week,
which is seven days.

5 Scalls are [declared] impure within two weeks,
and by two signs:
by thin yellow hair and by spreading.[16]
By thin yellow hair—
at the beginning,
at the end of the first week,
at the end of the second week,
[or] after dismissal;
and by spreading—
at the end of the first week,
at the end of the second week,
[or] after dismissal.
And they become impure within two weeks,
which are thirteen days.

6 A bald head and a bald forehead are [declared] impure at the end of two weeks,
and by two signs:
by living flesh and by spreading.
By living flesh—

[16] **CL** lacks "by spreading."

thirteen days: The seventh day of the first quarantine is also the first day of the second quarantine; see note on 1:4.

3:5 *Scalls*: Bald patches that appear in one's head or beard; see Leviticus 13:37.

at the beginning,
at the end of the first week,
at the end of the second week,
[or] after dismissal;
and by spreading—
at the end of the first week,
at the end of the second week,
[or] after dismissal.
And they become impure within two weeks,
which are thirteen days.

7 Garments are [declared] impure within two weeks,
and by three signs:
by green, by red, and by spreading.
By green and by red—
at the beginning,
at the end of the first week,
at the end of the second week,
[or] after dismissal;
and by spreading—
at the end of the first week,
at the end of the second week,
[or] after dismissal.[17]
And they become impure within two weeks,
which are thirteen days.

8 Houses are [declared] impure at the end of three weeks,
and by three signs:
by green, by red, and by spreading.[18]
By green and by red—
at the beginning,
at the end of the first week,
at the end of the second week,
at the end of the third week,
[or] after dismissal.
And by spreading—
at the end of the first week,
at the end of the second week,
at the end of the third week,
and after dismissal.[19]
And they become impure within three weeks,
which are nineteen days.
There is not less than one week in afflictions,
and not more than three weeks.

[17] "And by spreading... after dismissal" appears twice in **CL**.
[18] **K** lacks "by green, by red, and by spreading."
[19] **K** lacks "and by spreading... after dismissal."

3:7 *green... red*: See Leviticus 13:49.

3:8 *not less than one week in afflictions, and not more than three weeks*: That is, no quarantine is shorter than one week or longer than three. Cf. *Arakhin* 2:1.

Chapter Four

4:1–4 *Comparing the Signs of Impurity in Skin Afflictions*

4 White hair has features that spreading does not have,
and spreading has features that white hair does not have.[20]
For white hair renders one impure at the beginning,
and renders one impure in any appearance of whiteness,
and does not have a sign of purity.
Spreading has its distinctive features,
in that it renders one impure in any amount,
and renders one impure in all afflictions,
outside the affliction [itself],
which is not the case for white hair.
2 Living flesh has features that spreading does not have,
and spreading has features that living flesh does not have.
For living flesh renders one impure at the beginning,
and renders one impure in any appearance,
and does not have a sign of purity.
Spreading has its distinctive features,
in that it renders one impure in any amount,
and it renders one impure in all afflictions,
outside the affliction [itself],
which is not the case for living flesh.
3 White hair has features that living flesh does not have,
and living flesh has features that white hair does not have.
For white hair renders one impure in a boil and a scald,

[20] **CL** lacks "and spreading has features."

4:1 *at the beginning*: In the initial inspection, as opposed to spreading (which is only considered a sign of impurity after a week of quarantine).

in any appearance of whiteness: The shade of whiteness of the hair makes no difference, as opposed to the whiteness of the spreading, which has to be one of the four shades mentioned in 1:1 in order to constitute a sign of impurity.

and does not have a sign of purity: If the affliction spread throughout the entire body, this is a "sign of purity" that undoes the impurity (Leviticus 13:12). In contrast, white hair can never have this effect.

renders one impure in any amount: There is no statutory minimum, whereas at least two hairs are required for white hair to be considered a sign of impurity.

all afflictions: Of the skin, garment, and house.

outside the affliction: As opposed to white hair, which has to appear inside the affliction to be considered a sign of impurity.

4:2 *in any appearance*: Living flesh constitutes a sign of impurity whatever its color, while spreading has to be one of the four shades of whiteness mentioned in 1:1.

when concentrated and when dispersed,
when encompassed and when not encompassed.
Living flesh has [its distinctive features],
in that living flesh renders one impure in the bald head and in the bald forehead,
turned or unturned,
and it prevents [the purification of] the one who turns entirely white,
and it renders one impure in any appearance,
which is not the case for white hair.

4 Two hairs:
if their roots are black
and their tips are white—
he is pure.[21]
If their roots are white
and their tips are black—
he is impure.
How long[22] should the white part be?
R. Meir says:
Any length.
R. Simeon says:
Enough to clip with scissors.
If [a hair] was one at the root,[23]
and it was split at the tip
so that it looks like two—
he is pure.
If there is a discoloration in which there is white hair or black hair—[24]
he is impure.
One need not suspect that the place of the black hair diminished the discoloration,
because it is not substantial.

[21] **K** lacks "pure." [22] Lit. "How much?" [23] Lit. "If it was one at the bottom."
[24] Var.: "white hair and black hair."

4:3 *when concentrated and when dispersed*: White hair constitutes a sign of impurity whether the two hairs are concentrated in one place or each of the hairs is located in a different part of the affliction, as opposed to living flesh that has be concentrated in one spot of the affliction.

when encompassed and when not encompassed: White hair constitutes a sign of impurity whether the two hairs are located at the middle of the affliction or on its side, as opposed to living flesh that has to be situated in the middle of the affliction so that the affliction encompasses it.

turned or unturned: Whether the affliction preceded the living flesh (that is, some of the affliction "turned" into living flesh in the course of time) or the patch of living flesh existed first and the affliction later appeared around it—in both these cases living flesh constitutes as sign of impurity. In contrast, white hair constitutes a sign of impurity only if the affliction preceded the white hair ("turned").

and it prevents [the purification] of the one who turns entirely white: A patch of living flesh in the skin of one who turned entirely white does not allow him to be declared pure.

in any appearance: Whereas white hair has to be white (albeit any shade of white), living flesh can be in any color.

4:4 *Two hairs, if their root*, etc.: Cf. *Parah* 2:5.

If there is a discoloration in which there is white hair or black hair: In this context, it should be understood that the discoloration in question is exactly the minimal size required to constitute an affliction (the size of a split bean, see 6:1). The question is whether any hair that appears in the discoloration—whether black or white—should be seen as reducing the size of the discoloration itself to less than the required minimum.

4:5–11 *Discolorations with Various Signs of Impurity*

5 If a discoloration is the size of a split bean and a streak extends from it—
if [the streak] is as broad as two hairs,
it subjects it to being rendered impure by white hair and spreading,
but not by living flesh.
If there are two discolorations and a streak extends from one to the other—
if it is as broad as two hairs, it conjoins them;
and if it is not, it does not conjoin them.[25]
6 If a discoloration was the size of a split bean,
and inside it there was living flesh the size of a lentil,
and there was white hair inside the living flesh—
if the living flesh disappeared,
it is impure on account of the white hair;[26]
if the white hair disappeared,
it is impure on account of the living flesh.
R. Simeon deems it pure,
because the discoloration did not turn it [white].[27]
If a discoloration and its living flesh were the size of a split bean,
and there is white hair inside the discoloration—
if the living flesh disappeared,

[25] P_2: "If it is as broad as two hairs they join together, and if not, they do not join together."
[26] CL: "because it is white hair."
[27] CL: "because a discoloration the size of a split bean did not turn it."

4:5 *and a streak extends from it*: A thin stripe, as white as the discoloration, extends from the discoloration to the skin around it.

it subjects it to being rendered impure by white hair and spreading: That is, the streak subjects the discoloration to the possibility of being declared impure. If white hair appears inside the streak, or if the streak itself spreads, the entire discoloration is rendered impure on account of the streak.

but not by living flesh: Since living flesh has to be encompassed by the discoloration on all sides, if living flesh appears in the thin streak it cannot constitute a sign of impurity.

it conjoins them: Since the streak that connects the two discolorations turns them into one, if signs of impurity appear in one discoloration, they render the other impure as well.

4:6 *if the living flesh disappeared*: If the area that was once living flesh became part of the discoloration, the white hair is now seen as if it is inside the discoloration, and it constitutes a sign of impurity.

R. Simeon deems it pure, because the discoloration did not turn it [white]: R. Simeon maintains that the white hair constitutes a sign of impurity only if it appears in a discoloration that already exists, and in this case the white hair did not first appear in an existing discoloration but rather in a patch of living flesh.

If a discoloration and its living flesh were the size of a split bean: The area of the discoloration itself is less than the minimal required size of a split bean, but when taken together with the area of living flesh inside it, the combined area of the discoloration and the living flesh meets that requirement.

and there is white hair inside the discoloration: Not in the area of the living flesh (as in the former case), but somewhere else in the discoloration.

if the living flesh disappeared: The place of the living flesh became white as the rest of the discoloration, in such a way that now the discoloration itself is the size of a split bean.

it is impure on account of the white hair;
if the white hair disappeared,
it is impure on account of the living flesh.
R. Simeon deems it pure,
because a discoloration the size of a split bean did not turn it [white].
And he concedes that if the place of white hair
was the size of a split bean
it is impure.

7 If there was a discoloration in which there were living flesh and spreading—
if the living flesh disappeared,
it is impure on account of the spreading;
if the spreading disappeared,
it is impure on account of the living flesh.
And likewise with white hair and spreading.[28]
If [the skin affliction] disappeared and reappeared at the end of the week—
it is as it was.
After dismissal,
it should be inspected anew.
If it was bright and became dark,
dark and became bright—
it is as it was,
provided that it is not diminished from the four appearances.
If it shrank and then spread,
or spread and then shrank[29]—
R. Aqiva deems it impure,
but the Sages deem it pure.

[28] **K** and **P** lack "and spreading."

[29] **K**: "shrank or spread and shrank."

R. Simeon deems it pure, because a discoloration the size of a split bean did not turn it [white]: When the white hair first appeared, the discoloration itself was less than the required size of a split bean.

if the place of white hair was the size of a split bean: If there is both white hair and living flesh in a discoloration that is already the size of a split bean, and the white hair is located not inside the living flesh but somewhere else in the affliction, even R. Simeon concedes that if the living flesh disappears the white hair will constitute a sign of impurity.

4:7 *disappeared and reappeared at the end of the week—it is as it was*: If a quarantined discoloration (i.e. a discoloration without any signs of impurity in it) disappeared during the time of the quarantine and then reappeared by the time of the inspection, the disappearance and reappearance do not affect the status of the affliction.

After dismissal, it should be inspected anew: If the discoloration has already been dismissed as pure, and then it disappears and reappears, it needs to be inspected as if it is new.

not diminished from the four appearances: As long as the discoloration remains in the range of whiteness of the four shades mentioned in 1:1.

If it shrank and then spread: During the days of quarantine the discoloration shrank and its size was diminished to less than the minimum size, and by the day of the inspection it grew again to the minimal required size.

8 If a discoloration was the size of a split bean,
and it spread as much as another half of a split bean,
and then half the size of a split bean disappeared from the original [skin affliction]—
R. Aqiva says:
It should be inspected anew;
but the Sages deem it pure.

9 If a discoloration was the size of a split bean,
and it spread as much as a half of a split bean and more,
and then half the size of a split bean disappeared from the original [skin affliction]—
R. Aqiva deems it impure,
but the Sages deem it pure.
If a discoloration was the size of a split bean,
and it spread as much as a split bean and more,
and then the original [skin affliction] disappeared—
R. Aqiva deems it impure,
but the Sages say:
It should be inspected anew.

10 If a discoloration was the size of a split bean,
and it spread as much as a split bean,
and living flesh or white hair appeared in the spreading,
and the original [skin affliction] disappeared—
R. Aqiva deems it impure,
but the Sages say:
It should be inspected anew.
If a discoloration was the size of half a split bean
and there was nothing in it,
and [another] discoloration the size of half a split bean appeared
with one hair in it—
in this case it is to be quarantined.[30]

[30] **K** lacks this clause.

4:8 *R. Aqiva says: It should be inspected anew*: R. Aqiva sees the two afflictions (the half split bean that remained from the original one and the half split bean of the spreading) as constituting a new affliction that requires inspection, whereas for the Sages, since the original affliction no longer meets the requirements of minimal size, it is pure.

4:9 *and it spread as much as a half of a split bean and more*: The half split bean that remained from the original discoloration, together with the spreading that is *more* than half of a split bean, constitute a discoloration that is all in all *larger* than the original discoloration. The question, then, is whether this is considered to be a case of "spreading" or not.

R. Aqiva deems it impure, but the Sages say: It should be inspected anew: Even though the original discoloration no longer exists, for R. Aqiva the discoloration that spread from it is impure. For the Sages, since the original discoloration no longer exists, the discoloration that spread from it is seen as an entirely new affliction and requires new inspection.

4:10 *If a discoloration was the size of half a split bean... and [another] discoloration the size of half a split bean appeared*: In all the following three cases, the original discoloration is not of significant enough size to require quarantine until another discoloration of the same size appears and combines with it into the size of one split bean.

If a discoloration was the size of half a split bean with one hair in it,
and [another] discoloration the size of half a split bean appeared
with one hair in it—
in this case it is to be quarantined.
If a discoloration was the size of half a split bean
with two hairs in it,
and another discoloration the size of half a split bean appeared
with one hair in it—
in this case, it is to be quarantined.

11 If a discoloration was the size of half a split bean
and there was nothing in it,
and another discoloration the size of half a split bean appeared
with two hairs in it—
in this case, it is to be certified [as impure].[31]
For they said:
If the discoloration preceded the white hair—
it is impure;[32]
and if the white hair preceded the discoloration—
it is pure,
and if it is doubtful,
it is impure.
And R. Joshua protested.[33]

Chapter Five

5:1 *Doubtful Impurity: The Rule and the Exceptions to the Rule*

5 All doubtful [cases of] skin afflictions are pure,
except for [the above-mentioned] one and another one.

[31] CL: "If a discoloration was the size of half a split bean with two hairs in it, in this case, it is to be certified."
[32] CL adds "and if it is doubtful, it is impure."
[33] An obscure word. The manuscripts offer different spellings and the commentaries offer different interpretations.

half a split bean with one hair in it, and [another] discoloration the size of half a split bean appeared with one hair in it: Even though the combined discoloration (which consists of the two smaller discolorations) does have two hairs in it, since the hair in the first discoloration appeared before the second discoloration existed, the two hairs do not meet the requirement of being preceded by the discoloration in respect to which they are examined.

4:11 *protested*: See n. 33; this word is not found elsewhere in the Mishnah. Some commentators connect the term to an idiom meaning "set the teeth on edge," familiar from the Passover *Haggada*, where it denotes sharp rebuke; a similar usage appears in 1 Samuel 3:13. Others interpret the verb as "declared pure" or as denoting uncertainty and ambivalence.

5:1 *All doubtful [cases of] skin afflictions are pure*: In any case in which it not certain whether an affliction is pure or impure, the default is to render it pure. Cf. *Nazir* 9:4, *Tohorot* 4:12.

except for [the above-mentioned] one: That is, uncertainty as to whether the white hair preceded or came after the discoloration.

And what case is that?
One in whom there was a discoloration the size of a split bean
and it was quarantined;
at the end of the week it was the size of a *sela*,
and it is doubtful whether it is the same one or another that came instead of it—
it is impure.

5:2–3 *Changes in the Skin Affliction*

2 If [the priest] certified him [as impure] by reason of white hair,
and the white hair disappeared,
and then the white hair reappeared
(and likewise for living flesh and spreading)—
at the beginning
or at the end of the first week,
at the end of the second week,
and after dismissal—
it is as it was.
If he certified him by reason of living flesh,
and the living flesh disappeared,
and then the living flesh reappeared
(and likewise for white hair and spreading)—
at the beginning
or at the end of the first week,
at the end of the second week,
and after dismissal—
it is as it was.
If he certified him by reason of spreading,
and the spreading disappeared,
and then the spreading reappeared
(and likewise for white hair)—
at the end of the first week
and at the end of the second week,
and after dismissal—
it is as it was.

at the end of the week it was the size of a sela: That is, much larger than a split bean. Within the week of quarantine the discoloration has changed so radically that one cannot be sure whether it is in fact the same discoloration, which has spread to several times its original size, or a different discoloration altogether. If the latter, it must be quarantined as a new appearance.

5:2 *by reason of white hair*: That is, because of white hair inside the discoloration.

likewise: That is, even if the white hair disappears but living flesh or spreading develops in its place.

it is as it was: The affliction remains certified as impure.

and likewise for white hair: It is most likely that the words "and for living flesh" should have been added here, as is found in several medieval anthologies and commentaries.

3 Sentinel hair[34]—
Aqaviah b. Mahalalel deems it impure,
but the Sages deem it pure.
What is sentinel hair?
If someone had in him a discoloration with white hair in it,
and the discoloration disappeared
but left the white hair in its place,
and then it reappeared—
Aqaviah b. Mahalalel deems it impure,
but the Sages deem it pure.
R. Aqiva said:
I concede regarding that one,
that he is pure.
[But] what is sentinel hair?
If one had in him a discoloration
the size of a split bean
with two [white] hairs in it,
and half a size of a split bean of it disappeared
but white hair was left in the place of the discoloration,
and then it reappeared.
They said to him:
Just as they rejected the words of Aqaviah,[35]
so too your words are not established.

5:4–5 *Doubtful Impurity before and after Certification*

4 All doubtful cases of skin afflictions—
at first each is [considered] pure,

[34] Lit. "hair of absence" or "deposited hair." Cf. *Eduyot* 5:6.
[35] **K, CL**: "the words of Aqiva," probably a mistake.

5:3 *Sentinel hair*: Hair that appears in a discoloration and remains in its place like a "sentinel" of the spot after the discoloration itself disappears. See also *Eduyot* 5:6.

Aqaviah b. Mahalalel deems it impure: Once the second discoloration appears, it is immediately declared impure on account of the white hair. For Aqaviah b. Mahalalel, even though technically in this case the white hair preceded the (second) discoloration, the white hair is seen as a "residue" of the first discoloration and thus it connects the two discolorations and turns them into one. For the Sages, however, they are separate.

I concede regarding that one: R. Aqiva accepts the opinion of the Sages on the case just described, but he has another notion of what "sentinel hair" means, as he continues to elaborate.

Just as they rejected the words of Aqaviah: See *Eduyot* 5:6 regarding Aqaviah b. Mahalalel's ostracism.

5:4 *All doubtful cases of skin afflictions*: This passage modifies the rule of 5:1, according to which in nearly every case of doubt regarding afflictions the default is purity; here the rule is that in such a case a person remains in the same status of purity or impurity that existed before.

for as long as it is not associated with impurity.
Once it is associated with impurity,
a doubtful case is [considered] impure.
How?
If two people came to the priest,
on this one there was a discoloration the size of a split bean
and on this one there was a discoloration the size of a *sela*;
at the end of the week,
there was in this one and in that one the size of a *sela*,
and it is not known on which of them it spread:
whether in one person or in two people,[36]
it is pure.
R. Aqiva says:
In one person it is impure,
and in two people it is pure.[37]

5 Once associated with impurity, a doubtful case is [considered] impure.
How?
If two people came to the priest,
on this one there was a discoloration the size of a split bean
and on this one there was a discoloration the size of a *sela*;
at the end of the week
there was on this one a discoloration the size of a *sela* and more
and on this one the size of a *sela* and more—
both of them are impure.
Even if they become again the size of a *sela*,
both of them are impure,
until they return to the size of a split bean.
This is that which they said:
Once associated with impurity,
a doubtful case is [considered] impure.

[36] "Person . . . people": lit. "man . . . men," and so immediately below.
[37] **CL** lacks R. Aqiva's statement.

associated with impurity: That is, already declared impure for some other reason.

If two people came to the priest: This case demonstrates the first principle mentioned above, namely that if one was not yet declared impure, then in a case of doubt they will be declared pure.

and it is not known on which of them it spread: It is not certain which of the two people had the smaller affliction and which had the bigger affliction.

whether in one person or in two people: The same applies whether there were two different people, each with one discoloration, or one person in whom there were two different discolorations.

5:5 *both of them are impure*: Even though it cannot be said with certainty which of the two people originally had which affliction, it is known for a fact that in both of them the affliction spread and is larger than it was before.

Chapter Six

6:1–6 *Size Definitions and Measures in Skin Afflictions*

6 The minimum size[38] of a discoloration is [that] of a Cilician split bean squared.
The size[39] of a split bean is [that] of nine lentils.
The size of a lentil is [that] of four hairs.
Thus, thirty-six hairs.
2 If a discoloration was the size of a split bean,
and inside was living flesh the size of a lentil—
if the discoloration expanded,
it is impure;
if it diminished,
it is pure.
If the living flesh expanded,
it is impure;[40]
if it diminished,
it is pure.
3 If a discoloration was the size of a split bean,
and inside it there was living flesh of less than the size of a lentil—
if the discoloration expanded,
it is impure;
if it diminished,
it is pure.
If the living flesh expanded,

[38] Lit. "body." [39] Lit. "the place," here and in the next line.
[40] **P_2, CL**: "pure." See annotations.

6:1 *The minimum size of a discoloration*: See n. 33. The smallest size that would be subject to inspection for signs of impurity.

Cilician: Native to Cilicia in Asia Minor (cf. *Ma'aserot* 5:8). See also *Kelim* 17:12.

Thus, thirty-six hairs: The discoloration must measure at least this much on all its sides, or it is exempt from inspection.

6:2 *living flesh the size of a lentil*: The minimal size of living flesh that constitutes a sign of impurity is that of a lentil.

If the living flesh expanded, it is impure: According to several manuscripts and commentaries, this line should read: "if the living flesh expanded, it is pure." The logic behind the latter version is that if the living flesh is larger than the size of a lentil but the discoloration remains in the size of a split bean, the discoloration might no longer encompass the living flesh from all its sides, and therefore the living flesh does not constitute a sign of impurity.

6:3 *If the discoloration expanded, it is impure*: Not because of the living flesh, which is not large enough to render the discoloration impure, but because the affliction spread outward, which is a sign of impurity.

it is impure;
if it diminished:
R. Meir deems it impure,
but the Sages deem it pure,
because a skin affliction does not spread inward.

4 If a discoloration was more than the size of a split bean,
and inside it there was living flesh of more than the size of a lentil—
if either of them expanded or diminished,
they are impure,
provided that they do not diminish below the [minimum] size.

5 If a discoloration was the size of a split bean
and it was encompassed by living flesh the size of a lentil,
and outside the living flesh there was [another] discoloration:
the inner one is to be quarantined,
and the outer one is to be certified.
R. Yose said:
The living flesh is not a sign of impurity for the outer one,
because it has a discoloration inside it.
If [the living flesh] diminished or disappeared:
Rabban Gamaliel says:
If it fades away from within,
it is a sign of spreading for the inner one,
and the outer one is pure;
and if from without,
the outer one is pure,
and the inner one is to be quarantined.[41]
R. Aqiva says:
In either case it is pure.

[41] All manuscripts lack "and the inner one is to be quarantined."

R. Meir deems it impure... because a skin affliction does not spread inward: R. Meir sees the diminishing of the living flesh (i.e. the replacement of the living flesh with a discoloration) as an indication that the affliction spread inward, and thus sees it as a sign of impurity. Conversely, *the Sages* maintain that an affliction spreads only outward.

6:5 This passage discusses a case in which there are two discolorations, one inside the other, with a rim of living flesh between them.

the inner one is to be quarantined, and the outer one is to be certified: The inner one is seen as a discoloration without any sign of impurity in it, which needs to be examined further, whereas the outer one is certified as impure because it has an area of living flesh inside it.

If it fades away from within: If the inner perimeter of the rim of living flesh started to disappear first, it is seen as though the inner discoloration spread outward, and thus it is rendered impure. In contrast, since the outer discoloration no longer has living flesh inside it, it is rendered pure.

and if from without: If the outer perimeter of the rim of living flesh started to disappear first, it is seen as though the outer discoloration spread inward. As the Sages ruled in the previous passage, spreading inward is not considered to be a sign of impurity.

6 R. Simeon said:
When [does R. Aqiva's ruling apply]?
When it is exactly the size of a lentil.
If it was more than the size of a lentil,
the excess is a sign of spreading for the inner one,
and the outer one is impure.
If there was a bright spot less than the size of a lentil—
it is a sign of spreading for the inner one,
and it is not a sign of spreading for the outer one.

6:7–8 *Bodily Areas That Cannot Be Made Impure by Skin Afflictions*

7 [There are] twenty-four extremities in a person
that do not[42] become impure by living flesh:
the tips of the fingers and the toes,
and the tips of the ears,
and the tip of the nose,
and the tip of the penis,[43]
and the tips of the nipples in a woman.
R. Judah says:
Also in a man.
R. Eliezer[44] says:
Also, warts and dangling flesh do not become impure by living flesh.

[42] **K, P, CL**: "The twenty-four extremities in a person are not rendered impure."
[43] Lit. "the tip of the body." [44] **K, P**: "R. Eleazar."

6:6 *When?* R. Simeon interprets R. Aqiva's ruling in the preceding passage, according to which if the living flesh is diminished, the outer discoloration is pure whether it was diminished from within or without.

When it is exactly the size of a lentil: The diminishing of the living flesh allows the outer discoloration to be rendered pure only if the living flesh was exactly the size of a lentil, and so when it diminished, there remains less than the minimal size of a lentil.

If it was more than the size of a lentil: Initially the living flesh was more than the size of a lentil, and although it diminished an area the size of a lentil remains.

the excess is a sign of spreading for the inner one: Whatever amount of living flesh was diminished (as long as living flesh in the minimal size of a lentil remained) is seen as a spreading of the inner discoloration. In this case, the inner discoloration will be rendered impure on account of spreading, and the outer discoloration will be rendered impure on account of the living flesh the size of a lentil that remained in it.

If there was a bright spot less than the size of a lentil: This clause presents a variation of the previous case: instead of living flesh between the inner and outer discoloration, there is a bright spot (that is, a patch of skin darker than the four shades of white, which does not constitute a sign of impurity).

6:7 *twenty-four*: This list counts the two earlobes as one and the two nipples as one.

do not become impure by living flesh: Because of the pointed shape of bodily extremities (fingertips, etc.), the priest cannot see the affliction with the living flesh on it in one glance, and the condition of "according to the sight of the priest" is not met. Therefore, if there is an affliction in one of the "extremities" mentioned in this passage, living flesh does not constitute a sign of impurity for it.

8 The following places on a person do not become impure by a discoloration:
the inside of the eye, the inside of the ear, the inside of the nose, the inside of the mouth;
wrinkles, and the wrinkles of the neck, under the breast,[45] and the armpits,
the sole of the foot,
the nails,
the head and the beard,
the festering boil, scald, or puncture.[46]
These do not become impure by skin afflictions
and do not combine with other skin afflictions,
a skin affliction does not spread into them,
they do not become impure on account of living flesh,
and they do not prevent the [purification of] one who becomes entirely white.
If the head and the beard afterward become bald,
or if the boil, scald, or puncture [afterward] become a scab,
they become impure by skin afflictions,
and they do not combine with other skin afflictions,
and a skin affliction does not spread into them,
and they do not become impure by living flesh,
but they do prevent the [purification of] one who becomes entirely white.
The head and the beard before they [ever] grew hair
and dangling flesh in the head and the beard
are considered like any other skin of the body.[47]

[45] **K**: "The inside of the wrinkles... the inside of the breast."
[46] **CL**: "and the festering," as a separate item.
[47] Lit. "like the skin of the flesh."

6:8 *The following places on a person do not become impure by a discoloration*: This passage lists various bodily areas that need not be inspected for discolorations at all, either because these areas are not immediately visible (see chapter 2), or because they cannot be considered "skin." If an affliction does happen to appear in one of these bodily areas, it is ignored altogether.

the sole of the foot: According to some commentators, the sole of the foot is not susceptible to the impurity of discolorations because it is invisible; other commentators maintain that since its skin is very rigid and often without sensation, it is not seen as "the skin of the flesh."

and do not combine with other skin afflictions: If there is an affliction in one of these areas and an affliction in another bodily area, they are not added together to constitute together the minimal size of a split bean.

a skin affliction does not spread into them: If a discoloration that was adjacent to one of the listed bodily areas spread so that it now covers one of the listed areas, this is not considered to be a case of "spreading" for this discoloration.

and they do not prevent [the purification of] one who turns entirely white: If a person was certified as impure and then his entire skin turned white *except* for one of the listed areas, he is still seen as "entirely white" (see Leviticus 13:12 and chapter 8 below).

afterward become bald... become a scab: The bald patch or the partially healed lesion ("scabs") *can* become impure (9:2), but with limitations on how these combine with other afflictions.

Chapter Seven

7:1–3 *Changes in the Person and Natural Changes in the Body*

7 The following discolorations are pure:
those that were in one before the giving of the Torah,
in the gentile who [then] converted,
in an infant who was born,
in a wrinkle [whose hidden part] was revealed,
in the head and the beard [that later became bald],
in a festering boil, scald, or puncture [that were later healed].
If the head and the beard became bald,
if the boil, scald, or puncture became a scab—
they are pure.
If there were discolorations in] the head and the beard before they grew hair,
[and then] they grew hair,
and [then] they became bald again,
[or in] a boil, scald, or puncture before they became a scab,
[and then] they became a scab,
and [then] they healed—
R. Eliezer b. Jacob deems them impure,
because their beginning and their end is impure,
but the Sages declare them pure.
2 If the appearances [of any of these discolorations] changed,
whether to the side of leniency, whether to the side of stringency[48]—
(How to the side of leniency?
It was [white] as snow,
and it became as the lime of the Temple,

[48] Lit. "Whether to be lenient, whether to be stringent."

7:1 *The following discolorations are pure*: This list mentions six cases in which a discoloration is initially not susceptible to impurity, and later on either the person or the bodily area changes in such a way that they are now susceptible to impurity. Nonetheless, if the discoloration preceded the change, this discoloration remains inconsequential even afterward.

those that were in one before the giving of the Torah: Before the people of Israel received the Torah, they were not subject to the laws of purity and impurity; therefore, any discoloration that appeared in the skin of an Israelite prior to the giving of the Torah was seen as nonexistent.

in the gentile who [then] converted: Gentiles are not rendered impure by discolorations (see 3:1). If a gentile converts to Judaism and becomes subject to the laws of purity and impurity, any discolorations that appeared prior to conversion remain inconsequential.

[or in] a boil, scald, or puncture before they became a scab: That is, first a discoloration appeared in an area of the skin, and then a boil, scald, or puncture appeared in this area.

7:2 *whether to the side of leniency, whether to the side of stringency*: Whether the appearance of the discoloration changed in such a way that it is now more likely to be declared pure (since it is darker than it was), or changed in such a way that it is now more likely to be declared impure (since it is brighter than it was), as explained below.

as white wool,
and [it became] as egg membrane,
[or] it became secondary to a swelling,
or secondary to a bright spot.
How to the side of stringency?
It was [white] as egg membrane,
and it became as white wool,
as the lime of the Temple,
and [became] as snow.)
R. Eleazar b. Azariah deems [such cases] pure.
R. Eleazar Hisma says:
To the side of leniency,
it is pure,
and to the side of stringency,
let it be inspected anew.
R. Aqiva says:
Whether to the side of leniency or to the side of stringency,
let it be inspected anew.[49]

3 If there is a discoloration with nothing in it—
At the beginning
[or] at the end of the first week,
[the priest] shall quarantine it.
At the end of the second week
[or] after dismissal,
he shall dismiss it.
If while he was quarantining or dismissing it
signs of impurity appeared in it,
he shall certify it.
If a discoloration contains signs of impurity,
he shall certify it.
If while he was certifying it
the signs of impurity disappeared, at the beginning,
[or] at the end of the first week,
he shall quarantine it.
At the end of the second week,
[or] after the dismissal,
he shall dismiss it.

[49] **K** lacks R. Aqiva's statement.

it became secondary to a swelling, or secondary to a bright spot: This sentence is best read as a comment on the previous statement: an affliction in one of the primary shades of whiteness (snow or wool) became darker such that it is now in one of the secondary shades (lime or egg membrane). The discoloration thus became "secondary to the swelling" (from wool to egg membrane) or "secondary to the bright one" (from snow to lime).

7:3 *with nothing in it*: As in 4:10, with no signs of impurity in it.

If while he was quarantining: The text seems to be describing an improbable situation where the discoloration suddenly changes its character just as the priest is examining it. The point seems to be that the priest must base his pronouncement on what he actually sees, any previous intention notwithstanding.

7:4–5 *Intentional Changes in Discolorations*

4 One who plucks out signs of impurity
and one who cauterizes the living flesh
transgresses a negative commandment.
And regarding purity,
[if he did this] before he came to the priest,
he is pure.
After his certification,
he is impure.
Said R. Aqiva:
I asked Rabban Gamaliel and R. Joshua as they were walking to Gadvad:[50]
[If he did this] during the time of his quarantine, what is [the rule]?
They told me:
We have not heard,
but we have heard
"before he came to the priest he is pure, after his certification he is impure."
I started bringing forth proofs for them.
Whether he is standing before the priest
or he is in his quarantine,
he is pure, until the priest declares him impure.
As of when may he be purified?
R. Eliezer says:
As of when another skin affliction appears in him
and he is purified from it.
But the Sages say:
Until [the original skin affliction] spreads all over his body,
or until his discoloration is diminished to less than the size of a split bean.
5 If one had a discoloration and it was cut off,
he is pure.[51]
If he cut it off intentionally,

[50] This name of this place is variously spelled in the manuscripts.
[51] Lit. "it (the discoloration) is pure."

7:4 *plucks out signs of impurity*: One who intentionally plucks out the white hair in his affliction.

transgresses a negative commandment: See Deuteronomy 24:8.

before he came to the priest…after his certification: In accordance with the rule mentioned in 5:4.

We have not heard: We have not received a tradition from our masters. Cf. *Keritot* 3:7–10.

I started bringing forth proofs for them: The Mishnah does not preserve R. Aqiva's proofs, only his conclusion.

As of when may he be purified? If a person who has already been certified as impure removed his own signs of impurity, then their disappearance cannot change his status. What allows him ever to become pure again?

7:5 *If one had a discoloration and it was cut off*: Accidentally.

If he cut it off intentionally: The assumption here is that if one cut off his own skin intentionally to get rid of the discoloration, he is immediately declared impure, no matter whether he has already been certified as impure or not.

R. Eliezer says:
[He may become pure] when another skin affliction appears in him
and he is purified from it.
But the Sages say:
Until it spreads all over his body.
If [the discoloration] was at the tip of the foreskin[52]
he may be circumcised.

Chapter Eight

8:1–4 *Turning White from a State of Impurity and from a State of Purity*

8 One whose [entire body] breaks out [with a skin eruption] while he is impure
is pure.
If the extremities return [to normal]
he is impure
until his discoloration should diminish in size to less than a split bean.
[One whose entire body breaks out with a skin eruption] while he is pure
is impure.
If the extremities return [to normal]
he is impure,
until his discoloration should return to be as it was.
2 If a discoloration is the size of a split bean
and inside it is living flesh the size of a lentil,
and it broke out all over him,
and then the living flesh disappeared;
or the living flesh disappeared
and then it broke out all over him,

[52] CL: "if it was the foreskin."

If [the discoloration] was at the tip of the foreskin he may be circumcised: Even though one is not allowed to cut off the afflicted area, if the affliction was in the foreskin, circumcision may be performed, and the foreskin removed. See also *Nedarim* 3:11.

8:1 *One whose [entire body] breaks out*: The mishnaic word "breaks out" derives from Leviticus 13:12–13; if a person who has *already* been certified as impure on account of an affliction becomes entirely white (i.e. if the discoloration spreads and covers his entire skin), that person becomes pure.

If the extremities return: If after a person became entirely white parts of his skin return to a normal color again, even if these body parts are only his fingertips or the like (see 6:7), he is no longer considered as "entirely white" and is declared impure again.

as it was: To the size in which it was before it spread all over his body.

he is pure.
If living flesh appeared in him,
he is impure.
If white hair appeared in him,
R. Joshua deems it impure,
but the Sages deem it pure.

3 If a discoloration that had white hair in it
broke out all over him,
even though the white hair is [still] in its place,
he is pure.
If a discoloration had a spreading in it
and it broke out all over him,
he is pure.
And in all these cases
if the extremities returned [to normal],
they are impure.
If it broke out in some of him,
he is impure.
If it broke out all over him,
he is pure.

4 Every breaking out of the extremities
that in their breaking out rendered the impure pure:
when they return [to normal],
they are impure.
Every reappearance of the extremities
that in their return [to normal] rendered the pure impure:
if they were covered,
he is pure,
and if they were revealed,
he is impure,
even a hundred times.

8:2 *R. Joshua deems it impure*: R. Joshua sees this case like any other case of skin affliction: if there is a discoloration that manifests signs of impurity—whether white hair or living flesh—this discoloration is to be declared impure, and the fact that in this case the discoloration covers the entire body does not matter. In contrast, the Sages consider it a unique case and follow Leviticus 13:14; only living flesh is a sign of impurity for one who turns entirely white.

8:3 *in some of him*: Even if the affliction is rapidly spreading, it does not render one pure until it covers his entire body.

8:4 *Every breaking out of the extremities*: This passage states the general rule that the extremities have the power to transform the purity status of a person repeatedly. Whenever the extremities break out and complete the body's turning white, the person is declared pure; when the extremities return to normal, even if the rest of the body is still white, the person is declared impure (see 8:1).

if they were covered: Turned white again.

and if they were revealed: Returned to normal.

8:5–6 *Hindrances to "Turning Entirely White"*

5 Whatever [part of the body] is capable of becoming impure by the skin affliction of discoloration
prevents "breaking out."
Whatever is not capable of becoming impure by a skin affliction of discoloration
does not prevent "breaking out."
How?
If it broke out all over him,
but not in the head or in the beard,
or in the festering boil or scald or puncture,[53]
and then the head and the beard became bald,
or the boil, scald, or puncture became a scab,
they are pure.
If it broke out all over him,
but not in [an area of skin the size of] half a lentil
that is adjacent to the head and to the beard,
or to the boil, scald, or puncture,
and then the head and the beard became bald,
or the boil, scald, or puncture became a scab—
even though the place of living flesh became a discoloration—
he is impure,
[and he remains impure] until it breaks out all over him.
6 If there were two discolorations,
one impure and one pure,
and one broke out into the other,
and then broke out all over him,

[53] CL: "and in the festering."

8:5 *Whatever... is capable of becoming impure by the skin affliction of discoloration*: This is to exclude the list in 6:8 of bodily areas that are not susceptible to the impurity of discolorations.

If it broke out all over him... became a scab: The case described here is of a person who became entirely white except in an area not susceptible to impurity, and then this bodily area was revealed in such way that it is now susceptible to impurity. The rule is that as long as the person became entirely white before the change, these areas do not impede his purity even if they have not turned entirely white.

but not in... half a lentil that is adjacent: The second case described here is of a person who became entirely white except in one of the areas not susceptible to impurity, and also except in a small spot adjacent to one of these areas that *is* susceptible to impurity. Such a person cannot be declared pure, because of the spot that did not become white.

even though the place of living flesh became a discoloration: Even if the small spot that hindered the person's purity has in the meantime turned white too, not all of his body was white when the newly revealed areas were still insusceptible, so these areas cannot be excluded from the requirement for overall whiteness.

8:6 *and one broke out into the other, and then broke out all over him*: Whether the pure discoloration (the one with no signs of impurity in it) spread into the impure one or vice versa, once they are conjoined, they are seen as one impure discoloration that subsequently *broke out all over him*, and consequently the person is pure (8:8).

he is pure.
In his upper lip, in his lower lip, in two of his fingers, in two of his eyelids—
even though they cleave together and they seem as one,[54]
he is pure.
If it broke out all over him,
but not in a bright spot,
he is impure.
If the extremities returned to an appearance like that of a bright spot,
he is pure.
If the extremities returned with less than the size of a lentil,
R. Meir deems him impure,
but the Sages say:
A bright spot [or] less than the size of a lentil
is a sign[55] of impurity at the beginning,
but it is not a sign of impurity in the end.

8:7–9 *One Who Is Entirely White at His Initial Inspection*

7 If one comes [before the priest] entirely white,
he should quarantine him.
If white hair appeared in him,
he should certify him.

[54] **K, P**: "even though he cleaves them together and they seem as one."
[55] **P** lacked from "R. Meir" to "a sign," but the words were restored in the margin.

In his upper lip, in his lower lip: If there was one discoloration in his upper lip and one in his lower lip, so that they seem as one only when he closes his mouth.

even though they cleave together and they seem as one: This sentence is grammatically problematic, and is best understood in its context in the following way: "even so, since when they cleave together they seem as one, he is pure." That is, even though the affliction in the two lips or fingers or eyelashes actually consists of two separate afflictions, since they seem like one affliction when the two cleave together, when this seemingly one affliction spreads throughout the entire body, the person can be declared pure.

not in a bright spot: If there is a spot of abnormal skin tone that is darker than the four shades of whiteness mentioned in 1:1, and this spot does not turn white with the rest of the body, this person cannot be declared pure.

A bright spot [and] less than a size of a lentil: The text lacks "and," but lays down the same rule for two different situations, namely a bright spot or a discoloration that is less than the size of a lentil.

a sign of impurity in the beginning, but... not a sign of impurity in the end: If the entire body initially turned white except for a bright spot or except for one less than the size of a lentil, this does not allow the person to be declared pure. However, if the person had already turned entirely white and was declared pure, and then a bright spot or living flesh the size of less than a lentil appeared in him, this does not undo his purity.

8:7 *If one comes... entirely white*: This and the two following passages pertain to a case in which one was already entirely white when he came to be initially inspected, rather than after an affliction had been identified in him.

If both of [the hairs] became black,
or one of them;
if both of them became shorter,
or one of them;[56]
if a boil was adjoined to both of them,
or to one of them;
if the boil encompassed both of them,
or one of them,
or divided them
(the boil, and the living flesh of the boil, and the scald, and the living flesh of the scald, and the bright spot);
if living flesh appeared in him,
or white hair,
he is impure.
If neither living flesh nor white hair appeared in him,
he is pure.
And in all of these,
if their extremities returned [to normal],
they are as they were.
If it broke out in some of him,
he is impure;
if it broke out all over him,
then he is pure.

8 If it broke out all over him at once:
[if] from [a state of] purity,
he is impure;
and [if] from [a state of] impurity,
he is pure.
One who becomes pure out of quarantine
is exempt from disheveling and from rending and from shaving and from the birds;
out of [a state of] certification,
he is required to do all of those.

[56] P_2 lacks "If both of them became shorter, or one of them."

If both [the hairs] became black…the bright-spot: See above 1:5. Here the text neglects to add "he is pure."

they are as they were: If there are no signs of impurity in the person who came entirely white, he remains pure even after his extremities turn normal again; if there are signs of impurity in him, he remains impure even after his extremities turn normal again.

8:8 *If it broke out all over him at once…he is pure*: Repeats the rule in 8:1.

One who becomes pure out of quarantine: This clause introduces a new subject.

from disheveling and from rending: See Leviticus 13:45.

and from shaving: Leviticus 14:9 and below 14:2–3.

from the birds: Leviticus 14:2–7 and below 14:1–2.

And both this one and that one render a space impure
by entering it.[57]

9 If one comes [before the priest] entirely white,
and in him there is living flesh the size of a lentil,
and it broke out all over him
and then the extremities returned [to normal],
R. Ishmael says:
It is like the return [to normal] of the extremities in a large discoloration.
R. Eleazar b. Azariah says:
It is like the return of the extremities in a small discoloration.

8:10 *The Importance of Timing in the Inspection Procedure*

10 There is one who shows his skin affliction to the priest to his benefit,[58]
and there is one who shows his skin affliction to the priest to his detriment.[59]
How?
If one was certified,
and the signs of impurity went away,
and he did not have time to show it to the priest
before it broke out all over him,
he is pure,
for if he had [immediately] shown to the priest [that the signs of impurity had gone away],
he would have been impure.

[57] Lit. "render impure by entering."

[58] Lit. "and benefits."

[59] Lit. "and loses."

And both this one and that one render a space impure by entering it: Both the one who is quarantined and the one who has already been certified as impure render every space into which they enter impure; see below 13:7–12 and *Kelim* 1:4.

8:9 *If one comes [before the priest] entirely white...then the extremities returned*: The case described here consists of three stages: (1) the person is entirely white with one area of living flesh and is declared impure on account of the living flesh; (2) the living flesh turns white too, and the person is declared pure; (3) the extremities return to a normal color.

It is like the return [to normal] of the extremities in a large discoloration: The person is like the one mentioned in 8:7, who remains pure after even after the extremities return to normal. "A large discoloration" means here a discoloration that covers the entire body during the initial inspection.

It is like the return of the extremities in a small discoloration: The person is like the one mentioned in 8:1, who becomes impure after his extremities return to normal. "A small discoloration" means here an ordinary discoloration that renders one pure if it spreads throughout the entire body.

8:10 *one who shows his affliction to the priest to his benefit...to his detriment*: Sometimes hurrying to have the affliction inspected by a priest sooner rather than later is advantageous for the examinee, and sometimes it is disadvantageous.

for if he had [immediately] shown it to the priest...he would have been impure: In this case, immediately showing the affliction to the priest would have been disadvantageous. If he had shown the priest that his signs of impurity had disappeared, the priest would have declared him pure, and when the affliction had spread all over him, he would have become impure again; but since the priest does not know that this person had a phase of purity before he turned entirely white, he declares him pure.

If there was a discoloration with nothing in it,
and he did not have time to show it to the priest
before it broke out all over him,
he is impure;
for if he had [immediately] shown it to the priest,
he would have been pure.

Chapter Nine

9:1–3 *The Boil and the Scald*

9 A boil and a scald are declared impure
at the end of one week,
and by two signs:
by white hair and by spreading.
Which is a boil?
If he was injured by wood, or by stone, or by olive waste, or by the water of Tiberias,
anything that is not on account of fire—
this is a boil.
Which is a scald?
If he was scalded by coals or by an ember,
anything that is on account of fire—
this is a scald.
2 The boil and the scald do not join together with one another,
and they do not spread from one to the other,

If there was a discoloration with nothing in it... he is impure: This is a case in which immediately showing the affliction to the priest would have been advantageous. If he had shown the discoloration to the priest before it spread all over his body, the priest would have quarantined him and then, when he had turned entirely white, would have declared him pure; but since he did not show his discoloration when it was still small, he is now subject to quarantine like one who is initially entirely white (see 8:7).

9:1 *A boil and a scald*: Boils and scalds that are still festering are not susceptible to any impurity (see 6:8), while boils and scalds that have somewhat healed and became "scabs" are susceptible to impurity if an affliction appears in them; see Leviticus 13:18–28, and above 3:4.

by olive waste: The waste that is left from olives after they were pressed, which can irritate the skin or scald it.

the water of Tiberias: Hot springs, which can scald the skin.

9:2 *do not join together with one another*: If there was less than a size of a split bean of a boil and less than the size of a split bean of a scald on one person, the boil and the scald do not together constitute one whole affliction the size of a split bean.

they do not spread from one to the other: If the boil and the scald were adjacent to each other, and one of them spread into the other, it is not considered to be the kind of spreading that constitutes a sign of impurity.

and they do not spread into the skin of the flesh,
and the skin of the flesh does not spread into them.
If they were festering,
they are pure.
If they have formed a crust as thick as a peel of garlic,
this is the "scab of the boil" mentioned in the Torah.
If they subsequently healed,
even if there is a scar in their place,
they are treated like the [ordinary] skin of the flesh.

3 They asked R. Eliezer:
[What is the rule for] one in whose hand appeared[60] a discoloration the size of a *sela*,
and its place is that of the scab of a boil?
He said to them:
[The priest] should quarantine it.
They said to him:
Why?
To grow white hair—
it is not capable;
as for spreading—
it cannot spread,
and by living flesh—
it is not rendered impure!
He said to them:
Lest it shrink and then spread.

[60] Lit. "one into whose hand a discoloration went up."

and they do not spread into the skin of the flesh: Afflictions that appear inside the scabs of boils or scalds are only considered impure if they spread further inside the scab itself; if they spread further into the skin of the flesh outside the scab, this is not considered to be a sign of impurity.

If they were festering, they are pure: While festering they are not susceptible to impurity at all (see 6:8).

formed a crust...mentioned in the Torah: The intermediate phase between festering and complete healing is the one mentioned in Leviticus 13:23 and 13:28, to which the rules in 9:1 and 9:2 pertain.

9:3 *one in whose hand appeared a discoloration the size of a sela, and its place is that of the scab of a boil*: What is the rule when one has a scab of a boil on his hand, and a discoloration appears on his hand that entirely covers the scab?

Why? As the disciples continue to point out, there is no scenario in which a sign of impurity might appear in the affliction in this situation, and therefore there is no point in quarantining it to see what happens.

To grow white hair—it is not capable: Since hair does not grow on one's hand, no white hair will appear in the affliction.

it cannot spread: Since the discoloration already covers the scab, it cannot spread further into the scab itself, and afflictions in scabs can only spread into the scab and not to the skin of the flesh (9:2).

and by living flesh—it is not rendered impure! Since living flesh does not constitute a sign of impurity for boils and scalds.

Lest it shrink and then spread: The discoloration should be quarantined in case during the week of quarantine it shrinks so that it becomes smaller than the scab, and then spreads further into the scab and covers it again—in which case the spreading will be considered a sign of impurity.

They said to him:
But what if its place is the size of a split bean?[61]
He said to them:
I have not heard.
R. Judah b. Betera said to him:
Shall I reason[62] regarding this?
[R. Eliezer] said to him:
If to uphold the words of the Sages, yes!
[R. Judah] said to him:
Lest another boil appear in him outside of it,
and spread into it.
[R. Eliezer] said to him:
You are a great Sage,
for you have upheld the words of the Sages.

Chapter Ten

10:1–4 *Yellow Hair as a Sign of Impurity in Scalls*

10 Scalls are declared impure at the end of two weeks,
and by two signs:
by thin yellow hair and by spreading.
By thin yellow hair
when it is lacking and short—
the words of R. Aqiva.
R. Yohanan b. Nuri says:
Even when it is long.
Said R. Yohanan b. Nuri:
What is the expression that they use:[63]
"This stick is thin, this reed is thin":
either that it is lacking and short,
or that it is lacking and long.[64]

[61] Lit. "Is not its place the size..." [62] Lit. "learn."
[63] Lit. "what is the language that they say." **P**, **P**$_2$: "what does language say."
[64] **P**: "lacking and short, and not lacking and long."

But what if its place is the size of a split bean? Here the disciples introduce a new consideration: the scab itself is only the size of a split bean. Therefore, if the discoloration shrinks and becomes smaller than the scab, it will actually be smaller than the minimal size of afflictions that requires quarantine.

I have not heard: A tradition from my masters; cf. 11:7.

Lest another boil appear in him outside of it, and spread into it: The affliction should be quarantined in case another boil appears in the person's hand during the week of quarantine, and the affliction spreads into the new boil, in which case the spreading will be considered a sign of impurity.

10:1 *Scalls*: Bald patches that appear in one's head or beard; see Leviticus 13:29–37 and above 3:5.

Said to him R. Aqiva:
If we have come to learn from the reed,
let us learn from the hair:
"So-and-so's hair is thin":
thin so that it is lacking and short,
not thin so that it is lacking and long.

2 Thin yellow hair renders [one] impure[65]
[whether] concentrated or dispersed,
encompassed or not encompassed,
turned or unturned—
the words of R. Judah.
R. Simeon says:
It renders one impure only if it is turned.
R. Simeon said:
Logic requires this:
if it is the case that white hair,
from which another hair cannot save,
cannot render one impure unless it is turned,
does not logic require that thin yellow hair,
from which another hair can save,
will not render one impure unless it is turned?
R. Judah says:
Wherever it was necessary so say "turned,"
it said "turned,"
but the scall,
about which it was said *and there was no yellow hair in it*,
renders one impure both turned and unturned.

3 [Black hair] that grows [inside a scall] saves [it] from yellow hair and from spreading,
[whether it is] concentrated or dispersed,

[65] CL adds: "in a boil and in a scald."

lacking and short: The yellow hair is both thinner and shorter than the rest of one's hair.

What is the expression that they use: In common use the word "thin" denotes only thickness, not length.

10:2 *[whether] concentrated or dispersed*: Whether the two yellow hairs (which is the minimum for impurity) are adjacent to one another or not. Cf. 4:3.

encompassed or not encompassed. Whether the two hairs are at the center of the scall or on the side. Cf. 4:3.

turned or unturned: Whether the scall preceded the hair (i.e. the hair "turned yellow" when the scall already existed), or the hair preceded the scall. Cf. 4:3.

from which another hair cannot save: Yellow hair is no longer a sign of impurity in a scall if black hair appears in the scall (Leviticus 13:37); in contrast, in a regular discoloration that has white hair in it, the appearance of black hair makes no difference.

and there was no yellow hair in it: Leviticus 13:32. According to Scripture the only thing that matters is the presence of yellow hair in the scall; it does not discuss whether the hair turned yellow only after the scall appeared. It can therefore be deduced that the time in which the yellow hair appeared is of no consequence.

10:3 *saves [it] from yellow hair and from spreading*: If black (i.e. normal) hair grows in a scall, the scall cannot be rendered impure even if yellow hair appears in it or if it spreads.

encompassed or not encompassed.
And remaining [previous hair] saves [it] from yellow hair and from spreading,
[whether] concentrated, dispersed,[66] or encompassed.
And it does not save[67] from the side,
unless there is a distance of two hairs between it and the surrounding hair.
If one [hair] was yellow and one was black,
or if one was yellow and one was white, they do not save.

4 Yellow hair that preceded the scall
is pure;
R. Judah deems it impure.
R. Eliezer b. Jacob says:
It neither renders it impure,
nor does it save it.
R. Simeon says:
Whatever is not a sign of impurity in a scall
is thereby a sign of purity in the scall.

10:5–7 *Spreading as a Sign of Impurity in Scalls*

5 How does one shave a scall?
He shaves outside it
and leaves two hairs adjacent to it,
so that it would be recognizable if it spread.
If [the priest] certified it on account of yellow hair,
and the yellow hair disappeared,
and then the yellow hair returned,
and likewise for the spreading:
at the beginning,
at the end of the first week,
at the end of the second week,
after dismissal,
it is as it was.
If he certified it on account of spreading,

[66] K lacks "dispersed."
[67] K lacks "and it does not save."

remaining [previous hair]: Black hair that remained in the scall after most of its original hair was lost.

And it does not save from the side: If the remaining black hair is at the edge of the scall, it does not constitute a sign of purity.

the surrounding hair: The hair outside the scall.

10:4 *Yellow hair that preceded the scall*: Repeats the controversy in 10:2 above.

10:5 *How does one shave the scall?* See Leviticus 13:32–33.

If [the priest] certified it on account of yellow hair... it is as it was: In any case in which the scall was certified as impure, and the sign of impurity disappeared and then returned (or a different sign of impurity appeared), the scall remains impure as it was in the beginning.

and the spreading disappeared,
and then the spreading returned,
and likewise for yellow hair:
at the end of the first week,[68]
at the end of the second week,
after dismissal,
it is as it was.

6 If two scalls are next to one another,
and a line of [normal] hair separates them:
if [the line of hair] was breached in one place,
he is impure;
in two places,
he is pure.
How [large] should the breach be?
The [size of] the place of two hairs.
If it was breached in one place
[and the breach was] the size of a split bean,
he is impure.

7 If two scalls are one within the other,
and a line of hair parts between them:
if [the line of hair] was breached in one place,
he is impure,
in two places,
he is pure.
How [large] should the breach be?
The [size of] the place of two hairs.
If it was breached in one place
[and the breach was] the size of a split bean,
he is pure.

[68] **P** adds "at the beginning," but this is an error: "spreading" cannot be detected on first inspection.

10:6 *If [the line of hair] was breached in one place, he is impure*: Since the scall spread into the line of hair, and spreading is a sign of impurity.

in two places, he is pure: If one scall spread into the line of hair in two places, the two scalls now seem like one scall with several black hairs inside it, and black hair inside a scall is a sign of purity.

How [large] should the breach be? So that the two scalls be seen as one.

If it was breached in one place [and the breach was] the size of a split bean: Even if the breach is as large as a split bean, as long as there is a single breach the two scalls are not seen as one and the person remains impure.

10:7 *two scalls one within the other*: One scall is surrounded by a line of hair on all its sides, and this line of hair is surrounded by another scall.

the size of a split bean, he is pure: Since in this case the two scalls are one within the other, a significantly large breach in the partition turns the two scalls into one scall with hair inside it and renders it pure.

10:8–9 *Signs of Purity in Scalls*

8 One in whom there was a scall with yellow hair in it
is impure.
If black hair appeared in it,
he is pure.
Even though the black hair [later] disappeared,
he [remains] pure.[69]
R. Simeon b. Judah says in the name of R. Simeon:[70]
Every scall that has become pure for one hour
never again has impurity.
R. Simeon says:
Every yellow hair that has become pure for one hour
never again has impurity.
9 One in whom there was a scall the size of a split bean,
and then his entire head was scalled,[71]
is pure.
The head and the beard do not impede one another—
the words of R. Judah.
R. Simeon says:
They do impede one another.
Said R. Simeon:
Logic requires this.
If it is the case that the skin of the face and the skin of the flesh,
which something else separates,
impede each other,
Does not logic require that the head and the beard,
which something else does not separate,
would impede each other?
The head and the beard do not join together with each other,
and do not spread from one to the other.

[69] **P_2** lacks "even though... pure." [70] **K** lacks "in the name of R. Simeon."
[71] **K, P**: "and all his hair was removed."

10:8 *Every scall that has become pure for one hour never again has impurity*: A scall that has been rendered pure on account of black hair at any point can never become impure again, even if new yellow hair appears in it or if it spreads.

Every yellow hair that has become pure for one hour never again has impurity: According to this view, black hair only serves to undo the impurity of yellow hair, but if the scall spread after black hair appeared in it, it is rendered impure once again.

10:9 *his entire head was scalled*: See Leviticus 13:40–41. The rabbis apply here the principle of "one who turns entirely white" as in 8:1 above.

The head and the beard do not impede each other: If the entire head was scalled but the beard was not entirely scalled, or vice versa, this person can still be declared pure.

which something else separates: The hair of the head and the beard constitutes a partition between the face and the body, and nonetheless the skin of the face and the skin of the body are seen as one unit in terms of

Which is the beard?
From the joint of the jaw to the bone of the windpipe.

10:10 *Afflictions of the Bald Head and the Bald Forehead*

10 The bald head and the bald forehead become impure at the end of two weeks, and by two signs:
by living flesh and by spreading.
What is a bald head?
If one ate *neshem* or applied *neshem*,
or a wound that is not capable of growing hair.
Which is the bald head?
From the crown of the head sloping backward down to the bone of the neck.
Which is the bald forehead?
From the crown of the head sloping forward up to the hair above.
The bald head and the bald forehead do not join together with each other,
and do not spread from one to the other.
R. Judah says:
If there is hair between them
they do not join together,
but if there is not,
then they do join together.

Chapter Eleven

11:1–3 *The Susceptibility of Different Garment Materials to Affliction Impurity*

11 All garments become impure by afflictions,
except for those owned by gentiles.
If one buys garments from gentiles,

impurity. It thus makes sense, according to R. Simeon, that the head and the beard, which are clearly one continuous unit, should impede each other if one was entirely scalled and the other was not. R. Judah, in contrast, considers the head and the beard to be two separate units, possibly following Leviticus 13:40, which mentions the loss of the entire hair of the head as sufficient condition for purity without mentioning the beard.

10:10 *What is a bald head?* The assumption here is that baldness is caused by some external factor.

neshem: A substance that causes the loss of hair.

up to the hair above: Up to where the front hair of the head starts to grow.

11:1 *All garments*: Made of either wool, linen, or leather; see Leviticus 13:47–48.

they should be inspected anew.
Hides from the sea do not become impure by afflictions.
If one attached to them anything that grows on land,
even a string, even a thread,
anything that is capable of contracting impurity,
[the garment] can become impure.

2 If one blended together the wool of camels with the wool of sheep:
if the majority is from camels,
they do not become impure by afflictions;
if the majority is from sheep,
they become impure by afflictions.
Half and half,
they become impure by afflictions.
And likewise for flax and hemp that one blended together.

3 Colored hides and garments do not become impure by afflictions.
Houses, whether colored or uncolored, become impure by afflictions—
the words of R. Meir.
R. Judah says:
Hides are like houses.
R. Simeon says:
Those colored naturally[72] can become impure,
but those colored artificially[73] cannot become impure.[74]

11:4–7 *Inspection and Purification of Garments*

4 If the warp of a garment is colored and its woof is white,
or its woof is colored and its warp is white,
it is all decided[75] according to what is visible.
Garments become impure by the greenest of the greens and by the reddest of the reds.
If it was green and it spread red,

[72] Lit. "by heaven." [73] Lit. "by man."
[74] **K** lacks "those colored naturally cannot become impure." [75] Lit. "everything follows."

Hides from the sea: Garments and other articles made of skins of animals (fish, crocodiles, etc.) that live in the sea.

11:2 *If one blended together*: Cf. *Kilayim* 9:1.

the majority is from camels: Unlike wool of sheep, wool of camels is not susceptible to impurity, since it is not what people usually have in mind when referring to wool.

flax and hemp: Garments made of hemp are not susceptible to impurity, whereas garments made of flax are.

11:4 *it is all decided according to what is visible*: If the garment looks white, it can become impure by afflictions, and if it looks as though it is colored, it cannot become impure by afflictions.

by the greenest of the greens and by the reddest of the reds: Afflictions in garments, which are considered impure when their color is either green or red (Leviticus 13:49, and see above 3:7), must be in a bright shade of green or a bright shade of red to be seen as impure.

red and it spread green,
it is impure.
Whether it changed and spread
or changed and did not spread,
it is as if it did not change.
R. Judah says:
It should be inspected anew.

5 If it remains unchanged at [the end of the] first [week of quarantine],
he should wash it and quarantine it.
If it remains unchanged at the [end of the] second [week of quarantine],
it should be incinerated.
If it spreads during either [week],
it should be incinerated.
If it is dark at the beginning:
R. Ishmael says:
He should wash it and quarantine it;
and the Sages say:
He does not need [to quarantine] it.
If it is dark at the [end of the] first [week of quarantine],
he should wash it and quarantine it.
If it is dark at the [end of the] second [week of quarantine],
he should rend it and incinerate what he has rent,
and it needs a patch;
R. Nehemiah says:
It does not need a patch.

6 If the affliction returned to the garment,
he may save the patch.
If it returned to the patch,
he must incinerate the garment.
If one sews a patch from a quarantined [garment] onto a pure [garment]:

Whether it changed and spread: If the original affliction changed its color from red to green or vice versa, this does not make any difference in the procedure of inspection.

11:5 *If it is dark at the beginning*: The affliction is in a dull (rather than bright) shade of red or green—a shade that does not constitute a sign of impurity—already at the initial inspection, before it is first quarantined.

rend it: Tear out the afflicted piece from the garment.

it needs a patch: After the afflicted piece is removed from the garment, it is necessary to sew a patch in the place of the torn piece, to see whether an affliction will reappear in the same place.

11:6 *If the affliction returned to the garment*: If an affliction reappears in a garment after the afflicted piece was torn from it, the entire garment must be incinerated, but the patch may be saved.

If one sews a patch from a quarantined [garment] on a pure [garment]: One takes a piece of fabric from a garment that was quarantined on account of an affliction and uses it as a patch for a garment that is not afflicted.

if the affliction returned to the [quarantined] garment,
he should incinerate the patch;
if it returned to the patch,
the first garment should be incinerated,
and the patch shall be used for signs in the second garment.

7 If a robe[76] has white and colored stripes in it,
[afflictions] spread from one [stripe] to the other.
They asked R. Eliezer:
But what if there is a single [white] stripe?
He said to them:
I have not heard.
R. Judah b. Betera said to him:
Shall I reason regarding this?
He said to him:
If to uphold the words of the Sages, yes!
He said to him:
Lest it remain unchanged in it for two weeks,
and that which remains unchanged in garments for two weeks is impure.[77]
He said to him:
You are a great Sage,
for you have upheld the words of the Sages.
An adjacent spreading may be of any size;
a distant one,
the size of a split bean;
and a returning one,
the size of a split bean.

[76] Or "curtain." [77] **K** lacks "and that which remains ... is impure."

the patch shall be used for signs in the second garment: The second garment should be quarantined, and its status will be decided based on the state of the affliction in the patch sewn on it: if it spreads or does not disappear within two weeks, the entire second garment will be incinerated, and if no further signs of impurity appear in the patch, the garment can be declared pure but the patch must be incinerated.

11:7 *[afflications] spread from one [stripe] to the other*: Even though colored garments do not contract the impurity of afflictions, if the affliction spread from the white stripe to the colored stripe or vice versa it is considered to be a sign of impurity.

But what if there is a single [white] stripe? And the rest of the garment is colored. Presumably, in this case the affliction in the white stripe has nowhere to spread and therefore there is no reason to quarantine it.

I have not heard: A tradition from my masters; cf. 9:3.

An adjacent spreading may be of any size: If the affliction spread to an area in the garment that is adjacent to the original affliction, the spreading renders the garment impure no matter what its size.

A distant one: If the affliction spread to an area in the garment that is *not* adjacent to the original affliction, it has to be at least the size of a split bean to constitute a sign of impurity.

a returning one: An affliction that returns to the garment after the second week of quarantine, and after the afflicted piece was removed from the garment.

11:8–10 *Afflictions in the Warp and the Woof*

8 The warp and the woof become impure by afflictions immediately.
R. Judah says:
The warp—after it is boiled,[78]
and the woof—immediately,
and bundles of flax—after they are bleached.
How much should there be in a coil so that it would become impure by afflictions?
Enough to weave three by three [fingers] of warp and woof from it,
even if all of it is warp,
or all of it is woof.
If it was of broken strings,
it cannot become impure by afflictions.
R. Judah says:
Even if it was one broken string and he tied it,[79]
it cannot become impure.
9 If one winds [a string] from one coil to the other,
from one reel to the other,
from the upper beam to the lower beam,
(and likewise with two sides of a robe)
and an affliction was seen in one of them—

[78] Var.: "after it has been drawn out (of the boiling water)."
[79] **K**: "even if it was one tied broken string."

11:8 *The warp and the woof*: Strings designated to be used as warp or woof in linen and wool; threads for the woof were usually thicker than those for the warp.

immediately: Once these strings have been woven.

boiled: Put in boiling water so as to smoothen and whiten it, which is considered to be the last stage in the preparation of the warp.

How much should there be in a coil: What quantity of string should there be in a coil so as to render it susceptible to impurity?

Enough to weave three by three: There should be enough string in the coil to weave a patch the size of three fingers of warp on three fingers of woof.

even if all of it is warp, or all of it is woof: Even if the coil consists only of strings of warp or strings of woof.

Even if it was one broken string and he tied it: Even if the entire coil was one long string that was broken in one place and was then tied again.

11:9 *If one winds [a string] from one coil to the other*: If one transfers a string from one coil to another, so that the two coils are connected by this single string. The question here is whether the string that connects the two coils can also transfer impurity from one to the other.

reel: A rod around which strings are wound.

from the upper beam to the lower beam: Looms have two wooden beams, upper and lower, and warp strings are stretched out between them.

and likewise with two sides of a robe: The robe referred to here consists of two separate pieces of fabric that are tied together with a string.

the second one is pure.
[If there is an affliction] in the shedded weft or in the upright warp,
those become impure by afflictions immediately.
R. Simeon says:
If the warp was closely woven,
it can become impure.
10 If it was seen in the upright warp,
the fabric is pure;
if it was seen in the fabric,
the upright warp is pure.
If it was seen in a sheet,
he should incinerate the fringes;
if it was seen in the fringes,
the sheet is pure.
If an affliction was seen in a robe,
he may save its hems,
even if they are of purple wool.

11:11 *Types of Objects That Are Susceptible to Affliction Impurity*

11 Anything susceptible to corpse impurity,
even though it is not susceptible to pressure impurity,
can become impure by afflictions,
such as the sail of a boat, and a curtain,
and the band of a hairnet, and wrappings of scrolls, and a girdle,
and straps of shoes and sandals that are as wide as a split bean—
all of these can become impure by afflictions.

The second one: In all of these cases, a pure object remains so even if it is connected through a single string to an afflicted object.

the shedded weft: The woof strings that are intertwined with warp strings to form the basis of the garment.

the upright warp: The warp strings that stretch from the upper beam to the lower beam.

those become impure by afflictions immediately: All of the strings that are woven together are affected by an affliction in one of them.

11:10 *the fabric*: The part of the garment that has already been woven.

fringes: Threads that extend beyond the sheet.

he may save its hems: The hems of garments, which are made for decoration only, can be removed from an afflicted garment and they need not be incinerated with it.

even if they are of purple wool: Even though purple wool is susceptible to impurity, hems made of it can be removed from the garment.

11:11 *corpse...pressure impurity*: Pressure (*midras*) impurity is conveyed by persons with genital discharges to everything on which they lie, sit, tread, or lean. This impurity can only be conveyed to objects that are designated for lying, sitting, etc., or that can at least be used for this purpose. In contrast, sharing a space with a corpse or touching a corpse can make any object impure, as long as it is usable and made of certain materials (see *Kelim*). This passage makes the point that every garment item that is considered usable enough to become impure by a corpse contracts the impurity of skin afflictions, even if it cannot be used for lying, sitting, etc.

A woolen mantle in which an affliction was seen:
R. Eliezer b. Jacob says:
[It is not impure] unless [the affliction] was seen in the fabric and in the soft bits.
A waterskin and a satchel are inspected as they are,
and [the affliction] can spread from the inside out,
and from the outside in.

11:12 *Quarantined vs. Certified Garments*

12 If a quarantined garment was mixed with others,
they are all pure.
If he shredded it and turned it into tatters,
it is pure,
and he is allowed to derive benefit from it.
If a certified garment was mixed with others,
they are all impure.
If he shredded it and turned it into tatters,
it is impure,
and he is prohibited from deriving benefit from it.

Chapter Twelve

12:1–4 *The Susceptibility of Houses to Affliction Impurity*

12 All houses can become impure by afflictions,
except for those of gentiles.
If one buys houses from gentiles,
they should be inspected anew.
A round house, a triangular house, a house built on a ship or a raft, or on four beams

A woolen mantle: A mantle consists of a fabric (the main surface) and "soft bits"; these are either its external "hairier" surface or shreds and tatters used as lining to soften it.

as they are: There is no need to untie and lay out the waterskin or the satchel in order to inspect them for afflictions, even though not all of their surface is immediately visible.

from the inside out: If an affliction was seen in the inside of the waterskin or the satchel and then it spread to the outside, or vice versa, this is considered to be a sign of impurity.

11:12 *mixed with others*: It is no longer known which of them is the quarantined garment.

he is allowed to derive benefit from it: If one shredded a quarantined garment into tatters, he may sell the tatters, use them to stuff pillows, or in any other way gain something from them. The rule is stricter for a *certified garment*.

12:1 *A round house, a triangular house*: The plural "walls" appears twice in Leviticus 14:37–39; this is taken to mean that the house must have four walls to be susceptible.

on four beams: Houses have to be connected to the ground to be rendered impure, so a house built on beams that extend from another structure is not susceptible to impurity.

cannot become impure by afflictions.
But if it was quadrangular,
[or] even on four pillars,
it can become impure.

2 If one of the sides of a house is covered with marble,
[or] one with rock, or one with bricks, or one with dirt,
it is not susceptible to impurity.[80]
If there were no stones and timber and dirt in a house
and an affliction was seen in it,
and later on they brought stones and timber and dirt,[81]
it is not susceptible to impurity.
And so too a garment in which one had not yet woven [a breadth of] three by three [fingers],
and an affliction was seen in it,
and afterward he wove three by three,
it is not susceptible to impurity.
A house does not become impure by afflictions
unless it contains stones and timber and dirt.

3 And how many stones should there be in it?
R. Ishmael says:
Four.
R. Aqiva says:
Eight.
For R. Ishmael used to say:
[A house becomes impure] only if [an affliction] the size of two split beans is seen
on two stones or on one stone.
R. Aqiva says:
Only if [an affliction] the size of two split beans is seen on two stones,

[80] Lit. "is pure," and so too throughout the paragraph.
[81] **CL** lacks "and an affliction was seen in it and later on they brought stones and timber and dirt."

on four pillars: That are connected to the ground.

12:2 *a house... and one with dirt*: Since Leviticus 14:45 explicitly mentions timber, stones, and dirt (earth or mud) when discussing afflictions in houses, the rabbinic rule is that a house must contain all those components to contract impurity (as mentioned in the end of the passage).

three by three: If one started weaving a garment, and before the garment was the size of three fingerbreadths square an affliction appeared, this garment is not considered consequential enough to become impure; cf. *Kelim* 27:2.

12:3 *how many stones should there be in it?* What is the minimum number of stones required to make a house susceptible to impurity?

Four: One stone for each side of the house, as explained below.

Eight.: Two stones for each side of the house, as explained below.

only if [an affliction] the size of two split beans is seen on two stones or on one stone: An affliction in a house does not render it impure unless there are two afflictions, each the size of a split bean, or one affliction the size of two split beans, and the affliction(s) appear(s) either on one stone or on two stones. Therefore, at least four stones are required, so that the affliction will be able to appear in any of the walls of the house.

but not if seen on one stone.[82]
R. Eleazar b. R. Simeon says:
Only if [an affliction] the size of two split beans is seen on two stones,
on two walls at the corner;
its length [must be] two split beans,
and its width one split bean.
4 [How much] timber [must there be in a house]?
Enough to set under the lintel.
R. Judah says:
To make a support[83] for the back of the lintel.
[How much] dirt [should there be in a house]?
Enough to apply between one beam and another.
The walls of a manger and the walls of a partition cannot become impure by afflictions.
Jerusalem and [places] outside of the Land cannot become impure by afflictions.

12:5–7 *The Inspection of Afflicted Houses*

5 How is a house inspected?
Then he who owns the house shall come
and tell the priest,
something like an affliction has appeared in my house.
Even [if he is] a disciple of a Sage[84]
and knows that it is a definite affliction,
he should not rule and say:
"An affliction was seen in my house,"
but rather "Something like an affliction was seen in my house."
Then the priest shall command
that they empty the house
(before the priest goes to examine the affliction,
lest all that is in the house be declared impure,
and afterward the priest shall go in to see the house):[85]

[82] **CL** lacks "or on two stones, R. Aqiva says: Until it is seen as two split beans, on two stones."
[83] Lit. "sandal." [84] **K**, $\mathbf{P}_2$: "a disciple of the Sages."
[85] The completion of the verse, here enclosed in parentheses, is missing in many witnesses.

on two stones but not... on one stone: Therefore, eight stones are required.

on two walls at the corner: There have to be two afflictions the size of a split bean on two adjacent stones in the corner of a house, so that one stone belongs to one wall and the other stone belongs to another wall.

12:4 *a partition*: A wall made to divide one room into two.

Jerusalem and [places] outside of the Land: Since Leviticus 14:34 explicitly refers to "the land you possess" when discussing afflictions in houses, neither houses in places outside the Land of Israel nor houses in Jerusalem (which is not possessed by any of the tribes of Israel but belongs to all of them) can become impure by afflictions.

12:5 *Then he who owns*: Leviticus 14:35.

Then the priest shall command: Leviticus 14:36.

even bundles of wood, even bundles of reeds—
the words of R. Judah.
R. Simeon says:
It is a task to empty [the house].[86]
Said R. Meir:
What of his might become impure?
If you say his wooden utensils, his garments, and his metalware,
he can immerse them and they shall become pure!
Rather, what is it that the Torah spares?
His clay utensils,
and his pitcher and ewer.
If the Torah thus spares his negligible property,
all the more so his precious property;
if for his property thus,
all the more so for the lives of his sons and daughters;
if for the property of the wicked thus,
all the more so for that of the righteous.

6 [The priest] may not go into his own house and quarantine [the afflicted house],
nor into the house in which the affliction is and quarantine it,
but rather he stands at the door of the house in which the affliction is and quarantines it,
as it is said:
Then the priest shall go out of the house to the door of the house and shut up the house seven days.
Then he comes at the end of the week

[86] Translation uncertain.

even bundles of wood, even bundles of reeds: Normally bundles of wood and bundles of reeds are not susceptible to impurity, but here, according to R. Judah, even those are susceptible to the impurity caused by the affliction of the house.

It is a task to empty [the house]: According to R. Simeon, the bundles of wood and reeds will not contract impurity even if they remain in the house, but one should take them out of the house anyway.

What of his might become impure? What are the possessions that might become impure in the afflicted house, in order to save which one is required to empty the house of all there is in it.

what is it the Torah spares? As in the preceding annotation, by mandating their removal in order to save them.

His clay utensils, and his pitcher and ewer: Unlike articles of metal, wood, leather, or cloth, which can be purified through ritual immersion in water, articles made of clay cannot be purified in water and must be broken if they have become impure; see Leviticus 11:33.

if for the property of the wicked thus: Although neither the Bible nor the Mishnah says so explicitly, there is an established notion according to which afflictions come about as a punishment for sin (e.g. Numbers 12, 2 Kings 25:27, 2 Chronicles 26:16–23). Therefore the one whose house is afflicted is identified here and in the following passage as "wicked."

12:6 *[The priest] may not go into his own house and quarantine*: The priest may not go back to his own house and give the ruling that the house is quarantined through an emissary or messenger.

Then the priest shall go: Leviticus 14:38.

and sees whether it has spread. [If so,]
Then the priest shall command that they take out the stones in which the affliction is and throw them into an impure place outside the city...
Then they shall take other stones and put them in the place of those stones, and he shall take other dirt and plaster the house.
He may not take stones from one side
and bring them to the other side,
nor may he bring dirt from one side to the other side,
nor lime from anywhere.
He may not bring one [stone] in the place of two,
nor two in the place of one,
but rather he brings two in the place of two,
in the place of three,
or in the place of four.
On the basis of this [verse] they said:
Woe to the wicked and woe to his neighbor.
They both remove [the stones],
they both scrape off the plaster,
they both bring the [new] stones,
but [the owner of the afflicted house] alone brings the dirt,
for it was said:
he shall take other dirt and plaster the house:
his fellow does not attend to the plastering with him.

7 [The priest] then comes at the end of the week
and sees whether [the affliction] returned,
And he shall destroy the house, its stones and timber and all the plaster of the house, and he shall carry them out of the city to an impure place.
An adjacent spreading [can be] of any size,
and a distant one [must be] the size of a split bean,
and one that returns in houses [must be] the size of two split beans.

Then the priest shall command: Leviticus 14:40.

Then they shall take: Leviticus 14:42.

He may not take stones from one side and bring them to the other side: The new stones or dirt that one uses to replace the afflicted ones may not be taken from another wall in the same house, but only from a different place altogether.

nor lime from anywhere: Lime cannot be used for plaster instead of dirt (mud).

He may not bring one [stone] in place of two: If two stones were taken out of the wall, the priest may not use one large stone instead of the two; but he may bring two large stones instead of three or four.

Woe to the wicked and woe to his neighbor: Since Leviticus 14:42 uses the plural form (*Then* they *shall take other stones and put them in the place of those stones*), it is understood that the owner of the neighboring house must help the owner of the afflicted house in the removal and reinsertion of stones. Thus the neighbor is also affected by the afflictions that came upon the house of the "wicked."

They both remove [the stones]: The owner of the afflicted house and his neighbor.

12:7 *And he shall destroy*: Leviticus 14:45.

An adjacent spreading [can be] of any size: See above, 11:7.

Chapter Thirteen

13:1–3 *The Purification of Afflicted Houses*

13 There are ten [possible scenarios for] houses:
(1) [if the affliction is] dark at [the end of] the first [week],
(2) or if it disappeared [by the end of the first week]—
he may peel [the afflicted area] off,
and [the house] is pure.
(3) [If the affliction is] dark at [the end of] the second [week],
(4) or if it disappeared [by the end of the second week]—
he may peel it off,
but it requires birds.
[If the affliction] spreads during the first week,
he removes [the afflicted stones] and scrapes and plasters and gives it a week:
(5) if [the affliction] returns,
[the house] should be broken down,
(6) if it does not return,
it requires birds.
If it remained unchanged at [the end of] the first [week]
but spread during the second [week]—
he removes [the stones] and scrapes and plasters and gives it a week:
(7) if it returns,
[the house] should be broken down,
(8) if it does not return, it requires birds.
If it remained unchanged in both this one and that one,
he removes [the stones] and scrapes and plasters and gives it a week:
(9) if it returned,
it should be broken down,
(10) if it did not return,
it requires birds.
If before he purified it with birds an affliction was seen in it,
it should be broken down,
and if after he purified it with birds an affliction was seen in it,[87]
it should be inspected anew.

2 The stone at the corner:
when he removes it,
he should remove all of it;

[87] **CL** lacks "it should be broken down, and if after he purified it with birds an affliction was seen in it."

13:1 *it requires birds*: The purification rite described in Leviticus 14:49–53; see below 14:1–2.

13:2 *The stone at the corner*: The large stone at the corner of a house, which is part of both the wall of the afflicted house and the wall of the neighboring house.

when he removes it: If the corner stone was afflicted and needs to be removed, all of it should be removed even though this damages the wall of the neighbor as well.

but when he breaks down [the house],
he should break down his and leave his fellow's.
Thus there is a stringency in the removal
that does not apply to the breaking down.
R. Eleazar[88] says:
[In the case of] a house built of head stones and small stones,[89]
if [an affliction] was seen in a head stone,
he takes all of it;
if it was seen in a small stone,
he takes his
and leaves his fellow's.

3 If there was an upper chamber on top of a house in which an affliction was seen,
he gives the beams to the upper chamber.
If it was seen in the upper chamber,
he gives the beams to the house.
If there was no upper chamber on top of it,
its stones and timber and dirt are broken down with it,
but he may save the frames and the window lattices.
R. Judah says:
A frame that is built on top of it is to be broken down with it.
Its stones and its timber and its dust convey impurity in the volume of an olive;
R. Eleazar Hisma says:
In any amount.

13:4–5 *The Quarantined House*

4 A quarantined house conveys impurity from within,
but a certified one both from within and from without.[90]

[88] **K, P_2**: "Eliezer." [89] Or "a main beam and crossbeams." [90] Lit. "from its back."

[In the case of] a house built of head stones and small stones: The shared wall between the two houses is built in such way that some of its stones are large and protrude into both houses ("head stones"), and some of the stones are small and do not protrude from the wall. Even though the entire wall is shared, only the head stones are effectively part of both houses.

13:3 *he gives the beams to the upper chamber*: In a house of two stories, the beams of the ceiling of the house are the beams of the floor of the upper chamber (cf. *Bava Metsi'a* 10:1–2). If the house was afflicted and needs to be broken down, the beams of the ceiling of the house are seen as part of the upper chamber and do not need be broken down with the rest of the house. If the upper story can be preserved by supporting it with pillars, it can be preserved.

its stones and timber and dirt are broken down with it: Everything that belongs to the house that is made of stones, timber, or dirt is broken down with it.

Its stones and its timber and its dust convey impurity in the volume of an olive: Whoever touches any of the timber, stones, or dust that used to be part of an afflicted house becomes impure, as long as the amount with which one had contact is in the volume of an olive or more.

In any amount: Even less than an olive volume.

13:4 *from within…from without*: One becomes impure by touching one of the inner walls of a quarantined house, but not one of the outer walls. The case is different with a certified house.

and both convey impurity though entrance.
5 If one [takes stones] from a quarantined [house],
and builds them into a pure [house],[91]
and an affliction returns to the [quarantined] house,
he must remove the stones [from the pure house].
If it returns to the stones,
the first house should be broken down,
and the stones will serve the second house as signs.

13:6–12 *Affliction Impurity Conveyed through Entrance*

6 If a house overshadows an afflicted house,
and likewise, if a tree overshadows an afflicted house,
one who enters the outer area is pure—
the words of R. Eleazar b. Azariah.
R. Eleazar said:
If one stone of it conveys impurity through entrance,
will [the house] itself not convey impurity through entrance?
7 [If][92] an impure person stands under a tree
and a pure person passes by,
he [becomes] impure.
If a pure person stands under a tree

[91] Lit. "If one builds from the quarantined into the pure."

[92] **CL** begins "How?"

and both convey impurity though entrance: If one enters either a quarantined or a certified house, one becomes impure even without directly touching the walls.

13:5 *If it returns to the stones*: The actual stones that were integrated into the pure house.

will serve the second house as signs: The second house should be quarantined, and its purity status will be decided based on the state of the affliction in the stones: if it spreads or does not disappear within three weeks, the entire second house is to be broken down, and if it disappears or becomes darker, the house is to be rendered pure. The original afflicted stones, however, must be removed and broken. Cf. 11:6.

13:6 *If a house overshadows an afflicted house*: The roof of a pure house extends over an afflicted house in such a way that the afflicted house stands in the shadow of the pure house.

one who enters the outer area is pure: If one enters the pure house, or stands under the tree, even though the house and the tree overshadow the afflicted house, this person remains pure.

one stone of it conveys impurity through entrance: If a single stone from an afflicted house is placed in another house, this stone conveys impurity to anyone who enters the house.

will [the house] itself will not convey impurity through entrance? For R. Eleazar, anything that creates a roof for the afflicted house is seen as part of it, and therefore anyone who enters the overshadowing house or stands under the overshadowing tree is seen as though he entered the impure house itself.

13:7 *If an impure person stands under a tree*: So that the tree overshadows him. Here "impure" necessarily means impure on account of *tsara'at* (scale-disease).

he [becomes] impure: The rule here is that every roof shared with a person with *tsara'at* renders everyone and everything under this roof impure. In this case, the branches of the tree function like a roof and render the pure person impure.

and an impure person passes by,
he [remains] pure;
if [the impure person] stood,
[the pure person becomes] impure.
And likewise with an afflicted stone—
he [remains] pure;
but if [the one carrying the stone] put it down,
[the other] is impure.

8 A pure person who brings his head and most of his body into an impure house becomes impure,
and an impure person who brings his head and most of his body into a pure house has made it impure.
A pure cloak of which one brings [a piece the size of] three by three [fingers] into an impure house
has become impure,
and an impure [cloak] of which one let a piece
even the volume of an olive into a pure house
has made [the house] impure.

9 If one enters an afflicted house with his garments on his shoulder
and his sandals and rings in his hands,
he and they are impure immediately.
If he was wearing his garments
and his sandals were on his feet
and his rings were on his hands,
he is impure immediately,
but they are pure until he stays there long enough to eat half a loaf of bread.
(Wheat bread and not barley bread,
reclining,
and eating with a condiment.)

if [the impure person] stood: Under the tree for a while, rather than just passing under it.

And likewise with an afflicted stone: If someone was passing under a tree while carrying a stone from an afflicted house, a pure person standing under the tree remains pure, but if the stone was put down under the tree, the pure person is rendered impure.

13:8 This passage presents the two-sided principle of entrance impurity: an impure person or object that enters a pure house renders the house impure, and a pure person or object that enters an impure house is rendered impure.

A pure cloak: A piece the size of three by three fingers of a cloak that was in the space of the afflicted house is enough to make the entire cloak impure.

13:9 *with his garments on his shoulder*: This passage makes a distinction between garments and articles that one carries, which are rendered impure immediately upon entrance to an afflicted house, and garments and articles that one wears, which are "saved" from impurity for a certain duration of time.

long enough to eat half a loaf of bread: Cf. *Keritot* 3:3.

Wheat bread and not barley, reclining, and eating with a condiment: This sentence serves to provide a more accurate definition of the time required to eat half a loaf of bread. It is assumed that a loaf of wheat is eaten more quickly than a loaf of barley, one eats while reclining more quickly than one eats sitting or standing, and bread is eaten more quickly with a condiment than without it.

10 If one was standing inside
and stretched his hand to the outside
with his rings on his hands—
if he stayed [inside] long enough to eat half a loaf,
they are impure.
If he was standing outside
and stretched his hand to the inside
with his rings on his hands,
R. Judah deems them to be impure immediately,
but the Sages say:
Until he stays there long enough to eat half a loaf.
They said to R. Judah:
If, when all of his body is impure, he does not convey impurity to what is on him
unless he stays there long enough to eat half a loaf,
when all of his body is not impure,
does not logic require[93] that he will not convey impurity to what is on him
unless he stays there long enough to eat half a loaf?
11 If one with *tsara'at* entered a house,
all the utensils in there are impure,
even all the way to the beams.
R. Simeon says:
Up to a height of four cubits.
Utensils become impure immediately.
R. Judah[94] says:
[Only] if he stayed there long enough to light a lamp.

[93] The words "does not logic require" are missing from all the manuscripts. P_2 reads "even when all his body is not."
[94] P_2: "R. Simeon."

13:10 *If one was standing inside*: A pure person standing inside an afflicted house.

and stretched his hand to the outside: Presumably, the person stretched his hands out of the house before the time required to eat half a loaf of bread has passed, and therefore the articles he is wearing did not become impure.

If he stayed... they are impure. Even though the rings themselves are not inside the house.

R. Judah deems them to be impure immediately: The rings become impure as soon as the hand enters the space of the afflicted house.

does not logic require: If the rings on one's hands remain pure even when the person himself is standing inside an afflicted house, it seems logical that the rings on one's hand will remain pure if only one's hands are inside the house, but not the rest of the body.

13:11 *one with tsara'at*: One who has been certified as impure on account of one of the afflictions discussed in chapters 1–10.

all the way to the beams: Even utensils placed next to the beams of the ceiling are rendered impure.

Up to a height of four cubits: Only utensils that are placed within a distance of four cubits from the floor (which is the estimated height of the afflicted person) are rendered impure, but whatever is higher remains pure.

12 If he enters a synagogue,
they make a partition for him,
ten handbreadths high and four cubits wide.
He enters first, and he exits last.
Whatever [vessel] saves [from impurity] through a tight seal in the Tent of the dead
saves through a tight seal in an afflicted house,
and whatever saves when it is covered in the Tent of the dead
saves when it is covered in an afflicted house—
the words of R. Meir.
R. Yose says:
Whatever saves through a tight seal in the Tent of the dead
saves when it is covered in an afflicted house,
and whatever [vessel] saves [from impurity] when it is covered in the Tent of the dead
even when it is uncovered in the afflicted house,
is pure.

Chapter Fourteen

14:1–14 *The Rite of Purification*

14 How do they purify one with *tsara'at*?
[The priest] would bring a new clay vial,
and put a quarter-*log*[95] of living water in it,
and bring two free birds.
He slaughtered one of them over the clay vessel and the living water,
dug a hole, and buried it
in front of [one with *tsara'at*].
He took cedar wood and hyssop and scarlet wool

[95] **K**: "half a *log*."

13:12 *Whatever [vessel] saves [from impurity] through a tight seal in the Tent of the dead*: See Numbers 19:15 and *Kelim* 10:1.

and whatever saves when it is covered in the Tent of the dead: There are certain vessels that "save" their contents from impurity even if they are merely covered and not sealed with a tight seal; see *Oholot* 5:6.

R. Meir…R. Yose: Whereas R. Meir considers corpse impurity and affliction impurity to be completely analogous to one another, R. Yose considers the latter to be less severe than the former and subject to less stringent rules.

14:1 *living water*: Water from a flowing spring.

two free birds: Birds that do not live in captivity.

He slaughtered: It is occasionally unclear throughout this description which acts were performed by the priest and which might be performed by anyone.

and tied them together with the remainder of the strip [of wool]
and encompassed them with the tips of the wings and the tip of the tail of the second [bird].
He dipped, and sprinkled seven times on the back of the hand of one with *tsara'at*,
and some say:
On his forehead.
And in the same way he would sprinkle on the lintel of a house from the outside.

2 He then came to set free the living bird.
He did not turn his face to the sea,
nor to the city,
nor to the desert,
for it is said:
And he shall set the living bird free out of the city into the open country.
He then came to shave one with *tsara'at*.
He passed a razor over all of his flesh,
and washed his garments,
and immersed.
He was then [sufficiently] pure so as not to convey impurity though entrance [into a house],
but still conveyed impurity like vermin;
he might enter within the walls [of a city],
but he was banned from his house for seven days,
and he was prohibited from having sexual intercourse.

3 On the seventh day he shaves for the second time,
in the same manner as in the first shaving,
he washed his garments and immersed;

the remainder of the strip [of wool]: This strip was long enough to be included in the bundle and then wound around it.

encompassed: That is, held them together but without tying them into the bundle.

dipped, and sprinkled: The priest should dip the bundle of cedar, hyssop, and scarlet wool, together with the living bird, in the mixture of water and blood in the cup, and then use the bundle to sprinkle the mixture on the person with *tsara'at*.

And in the same way he would sprinkle on the lintel of a house: In case the priest is purifying an afflicted house.

14:2 *And he shall set*: Leviticus 14:53.

like vermin: After the bird rite, the shaving, and the washing and immersion, the person with *tsara'at* is still mildly impure until he brings his sacrifices to the Temple. This mild impurity is compared to the impurity of vermin (lit. a creeping-crawling creature), which conveys impurity to everything it directly touches for one day only.

he might enter within the walls: Following Leviticus 14:8, which allows one who went through the purification rite to go back into the camp of Israel; in the rabbinic interpretation "the camp" is the area within the walls of a city.

14:3 *a tevul yom*: A person who has performed all the necessary actions for purification and is now waiting for the sun to set so as to complete his purification process. Such a person does not convey impurity to anyone or anything; the only restriction is that he is not allowed to partake in *terumah* and holy foods. See *Kelim* 1:5 and tractate *Tevul Yom*.

he was [sufficiently] pure so as not to convey impurity like vermin,
and he is like a *tevul yom*,
and may partake in tithes.
Once the sun has set,
he may partake of *terumah*.
Once he has brought his atoning offerings,
he may partake of holy foods.
Thus there are three levels of purification for one with *tsara'at*
and three for the parturient.

4 There are three who shave, and shaving is a commandment for them:
(1) the *nazir*,
and (2) one with *tsara'at*,
and (3) the Levites.
And all of them,
if they shaved not with a razor,
or if they left two hairs,
have done nothing.

5 It is a commandment that the two birds be equal in appearance,
and in height,
and in value,
and that they be bought together,
but even if they are not equal,
they are fit [for the ritual].
If he bought one on one day
and one on the next day,
they are fit.[96]
If he slaughtered one of them
and it was found not to be a free bird,
he should buy a companion for the second one,
and the first one may be eaten.
If he slaughtered it and it was found to be *terefah*,
he should take a fellow for the second one,

[96] **K** lacks "If he bought one on one day . . . they are fit."

three levels of purification for one with tsara'at and three for the parturient: There are three stages in the purification process of the person with scale-disease: immersion, sunset, and sacrifices. The same three stages apply to a woman who has given birth before she can partake in the holy foods.

14:4 *The nazir*: See Numbers 6:1–21 and tractate *Nazir*.

the Levites: Before first serving in the Tabernacle; see Numbers 8:7.

have done nothing: They did not perform the commandment of shaving.

14:5 *equal in appearance*: Cf. *Yoma* 6:1.

terefah: A bird or an animal that is likely to have died a natural death on account of a disease or injury within a year of the time in which it was slaughtered. Such birds or animals are not fit for sacrifice and cannot be eaten.

and benefit may be derived[97] from the first one.
If the blood was spilled,
the one who was to be set free must die;
if the one who was to be set free died,
the blood must be spilled.

6 It is a commandment that the cedar wood be one cubit long,
and as wide as a quarter of the leg of a bed:
one into two, and two into four.
It is a commandment that the hyssop not be Greek hyssop,
nor blue hyssop,
nor Roman hyssop,
nor wild hyssop,
nor any other hyssop that has an additional name.

7 On the eighth day [one with *tsara'at*] brings three animals:
purgation offering
and guilt offering
and a whole burnt offering.
And a poor person would bring a bird purgation offering and a bird burnt offering.

8 He approached the guilt offering
and laid both his hands on it
and [someone] slaughtered it
and two priests collected its blood:
one in a vessel and one in his hand.
The one who collected it in a vessel came
and threw it on the wall of the altar,
and the one who collected it in his hand
approached the one with *tsara'at*.
And the one with *tsara'at* had immersed
in the chamber of those with *tsara'at*;

[97] Lit. "and the first one is permitted for benefit."

benefit may be derived from the first one: He may sell the remains of the slaughtered bird to a gentile, feed it to a dog, or otherwise gain something from it—even though he may not consume it himself.

If the blood was spilled, the one who was to be set free must die: If the blood of the first bird, which was slaughtered over the cup, was spilled before the sprinkling, the second bird cannot be used for the ritual and must be left to die, and the ritual must be performed from the beginning with another pair of birds.

14:6 *one into two, and two into four*: The width of the quarter of the leg of the bed is discerned by taking one leg and dividing it into two parts, and then taking those two parts and further dividing each of them into two parts.

not be Greek hyssop: Cf. *Parah* 11:7.

14:7 *And the poor one would bring a bird purgation offering and a bird burnt offering*: All three sacrifices should be of sheep (Leviticus 14:10). However, if one cannot afford three sheep, he may bring two doves for the purgation and whole burnt offerings, and a sheep for the guilt offering (Leviticus 14:21–22).

14:8 *He approached the guilt offering and laid both his hands on it and [someone] slaughtered it*: The actual slaughter might be performed by a priest, the person undergoing purification, or anyone else.

he [now] came and stood at the Gate of Nicanor.
R. Judah says:
He did not need to immerse.

9 He inserted his head
and [the priest] put [the blood] on the lobe of his ear;
his hand,
and [the priest] put [the blood] on the thumb of his hand;
his foot,
and [the priest] put [the blood] on the toe of his foot.
R. Judah says:
He would insert all three of them in at the same time.
If he has no right thumb or toe or ear
he cannot ever be purified.
R. Eliezer says:
[The priest] may put [the blood] on their place.
R. Simeon says:
If he put it on the left ones
he fulfilled his obligation.

10 [The priest then] took from the *log* of oil
and poured into his fellow's palm;
and if he poured into his own palm, he fulfilled his obligation.
He dipped [his finger] and sprinkled seven times
in the direction of the Holy of Holies,
a dip for every sprinkling.
He then approached the one with *tsara'at*.
In the same place that he puts the blood,
there he puts the oil,
as it is said:
In the place where the blood of the guilt offering was put...
And the rest of the oil that is in the priest's hand he shall put on the head of him who is to be purified,
to make atonement.

he [now] came and stood at the Gate of Nicanor: Since the person with *tsara'at* is still impure, he may not actually go into the Temple Court itself; rather, the final purification ritual takes place as he stands at the gate of the court known as the Gate of Nicanor (see *Sheqalim* 6:3, *Middot* 2:3). The priest stands inside the Court and the person with *tsara'at* stands outside, and the contact between them takes place through the gate, as is explained in the next passage.

14:10 *the log of oil*: See Leviticus 14:10.

his fellow's palm: That is, the palm of another priest.

He dipped... and sprinkled seven times in the direction of the Holy of Holies: One priest would dip his right finger in the oil that is in the other priest's palm.

a dip for every sprinkling: Every time he is about to sprinkle, he dips his finger in the oil; cf. *Parah* 3:9.

In the place: Leviticus 14:28–29.

If he put it,
he atoned,
and if he did not put it,
he did not atone—
the words of R. Aqiva.[98]
R. Yohanan b. Nuri says:
These are the remains of the commandment;
whether he put it or not, he atoned,
but it is accounted to him as though he did not atone.
If the *log* was lacking before he poured it,
he may fill it up;
after he poured it out,
he must bring another one [and start] anew—
the words of R. Aqiva.
R. Simeon says:
If the *log* was lacking before he put it,
he may fill it up;
after he put it,
he must bring another one [and start] anew.

11 If one with *tsara'at* brought his offering while poor and [then] became wealthy,
or while wealthy
and [then] became poor,
it is all determined by the purgation offering—
the words of R. Simeon.
R. Judah says:
By the guilt offering.

[98] **P**, **P**$_2$, **CL**: "R. Jacob."

If he put it he atoned: Only if the oil that remained at the end of the purification process was put on the person's head (see Leviticus 14:18) has full atonement been attained.

These are the remains of the commandment: Putting the remaining oil on the head is not an actual part of the purification process, but simply a way of making use of the remainder of the oil that was used to fulfill the commandment.

But it is accounted to him as though he did not atone: The purification ritual was effective, but the priest is not seen to have performed the commandment properly.

If the log was lacking before he poured it: If there was less than a quantity of a *log* in the pitcher before the priest poured it into the other priest's hand, the amount in the pitcher can be complemented with additional oil.

If the log was lacking before he put it: On the earlobe, finger, and toe of the person with *tsara'at*.

14:11 *and... became wealthy... and... became poor*: There are different sacrificial requirements for poor and for wealthy people (see Leviticus 14:21–22 and above 14:7).

it is all determined by the purgation offering: If the person was still wealthy at the time that he brought his purgation offering, his other offerings should also be those of a wealthy person (even if he became poor in the meantime); if he was poor at the time that he brought his purgation offering, his other offerings may also be the offerings of a poor person.

12 A poor person with *tsara'at*
who brought the offering of a wealthy person
fulfilled his obligation;
but a wealthy one who brought the offering of a poor one
did not fulfill his obligation.
One may bring an offering of the poor
for his son, for his daughter, for his slave and female slave,
and enable them to eat sacrificial meat.
R. Judah says:
He may also bring an offering of the wealthy for his wife,
as is the case with every offering she is obligated to bring.

13 If the offerings of two people with *tsara'at* were mixed,
and the offering of one of them was offered,
and [then] one of the [people] died:
[regarding] this the people of Alexandria asked R. Joshua.
He said to them:
He should write over his property to another person
and bring an offering of the poor.

14:12 *One may bring an offering of the poor*: A rich person may provide the offering of the poor for another person who is under his guardianship and cannot afford to bring a sacrifice of their own.

and enable them to eat sacrificial meat: The offering brought for the aforementioned people by their guardians allows them to consume holy food.

he may also bring an offering of the wealthy for his wife: A person's wife is considered like himself; therefore, if he is wealthy he must provide her with an offering of the wealthy.

14:13 *One of the [people] died*: If one of the two persons with *tsara'at* died, the remaining sacrifice cannot be offered, since it is prohibited to sacrifice for a dead man, and it is not known for sure whether the remaining sacrifice was brought by the living person or by the dead person. There thus arises the question what shall be done in order to purify the person with *tsara'at* who is still alive.

He should write over his property to another person and bring an offering of the poor: The living person must bring a whole new set of sacrifices, but in order not to make him bring the three expensive sacrifices after he has already given them, he may temporarily turn himself into a poor person by transferring all his property to another, and then he can bring a sacrifice of the poor. (Presumably, after he has sacrificed he can recover his property.)

Tractate Parah

Marcus Mordecai Schwartz

Introduction

Name of the Tractate

The evocative name of our tractate, *Parah*—literally "A Cow" (though here translated as "heifer" in deference to the King James Version of the Bible, published in 1611)—refers to the purification ritual of Numbers 19. The ash of the heifer, mixed with water is sprinkled on a person as a necessary step in the removal of corpse impurity.

Structure and Organization of Tractate

After some preliminaries dealing with sacrificial rules (chapter 1) the tractate addresses possible disqualifiers of the heifer, notably the presence of nonblack hair, horns, or hooves, but also actions that might be construed as "work" with the animal (chapter 2). Chapter 3 lays out the procedure of sacrifice, starting with the segregation of the priest in anticipation of the slaughter and ending with the pounding of the ashes, with a discussion of the extraordinary protection of the purity of the water leading up to mixing in 3:2–3. Chapter 4 follows with the consequences of defects in the slaughter or immolation. Beginning in Chapter 5, the tractate returns to the collection of the water and its combination with the ash, focusing on the vessel itself (chapter 5) and possible acts that can disqualify the mixture (6:1–9:9). A digression organized around a set of expressions used in 8:2 and repeated in what follows extends to 8:7.

Chapter 10 outlines the special purity rules connected with the consecrated waters, followed by a discussion of purity rules (11:1–6) only partly connected to the rite of the red heifer or the waters (especially 11:1–2). The end of the tractate concerns the hyssop used to sprinkle the waters and other rules having to do with the sprinkling itself (11:7–12:11), including a section analyzing connections between parts of things that have been sprinkled by the mixture (12:9–10).

Main Ideas

Numbers 19 calls this sacrifice a purgation offering, as does the Mishnah throughout. However, it differs from the typical purgation offering as presented in Leviticus 4 in a number of key ways: it decontaminates rather than atoning for sin, it is never offered on the altar, and its blood is sprinkled toward the sanctuary from outside rather than being sprinkled or spilled out within. Further compounding this puzzlement, readers of the Mishnah will see the term "purgation offering" used seemingly inconsistently to refer to the ash, the water, or the combined solution, in addition to the actual sacrifice.

The Mishnah extends the biblical prohibition on working the heifer to the consecrated water, and invalidates the water if the owner does any unrelated work with it from the time it is drawn until the purification procedure is completed. The tractate also lays great emphasis upon the purity of the performers of the ritual. The priest is quarantined before he oversees the sacrifice to ensure his purity. And all those involved must be purified with the proper intention, namely that they will be the ones to carry out the ritual.

Ironically, at the end of chapter 3, rabbis of the Mishnah imagine that their Temple-era predecessors would intentionally contaminate the priest on the day of the ritual. The Sages maintained that he remained valid to perform the purgation offering, and in practice required this defilement to counter the view of the Sadducees who invalidated such a person.

Relationship to Scripture

As noted, the subject matter derives from a rite described in Number 19. The main scriptural features are:

1. Priests slaughter a red (really reddish-brown) heifer, lacking any invalidating imperfections, and its owner must not have yoked it for work (Numbers 19:2).
2. After slaughter, the priests were to burn the heifer outside of the camp (Numbers 19:3–6), adding cedar wood, hyssop, and scarlet wool to the fire, reducing it to ash.
3. Ash is to be combined with "living water" in a vessel (Numbers 19:17), creating so-called "water of purgation."
4. A priest is to sprinkle the solution on impure people and objects using a hyssop branch (Numbers 19:18) on the third and seventh days after contamination (Numbers 19:19).
5. Performance of the purification ritual decontaminates the contaminated, but nonetheless contaminates those performing the decontamination: the priest, the collector of the ash, and the sprinkler (Numbers 19:21), or indeed anyone who touches the Water of Purgation (Numbers 19:22).

Each of these features is extensively reworked in the tractate.

Special Notes for the Reader

The Mishnah calls the act of placing of the ash on the water *qiddush*. While this term is most often translated "sanctification," I have translated it as "consecration" throughout. This is for two reasons: first, unlike other acts of sanctification in the Mishnah, it is not an act of human will or declaration that affects the change in status, but rather the combination—or perhaps the reaction—of two physical substances that does so. This makes it different from other acts of sanctification in the Mishnah, and requires that we use another term in translation. Second, the "con-" prefix implies the combination of two or more things to create holiness, exactly the procedure followed.

Tractate Parah

Chapter One

1:1–4 *The Proper Ages for the Sacrificial Offerings*

I R. Eliezer says:
"A calf" is one year old,
and "a heifer" is two years old.
But the Sages say:
"A calf" is two years old,
and "a heifer" is three years old, or four.
R. Meir says:
Even five years old.
An older heifer is valid,
but they do not wait lest it blacken,
so that it does not become invalid.
R. Joshua said:
I have only heard "a thirdling."
They said to him:
What does "thirdling" signify?
He said to them:
Thus I have heard without explanation.
Ben Azzai said:
I will explain it:
When they say "third," it means its number in relation to the others;
but when they say "thirdling," it means something three years old.
In like manner they said: "A fourthling vineyard."
They said to him:

1:1 *A calf* whose neck they will break in accordance with the ritual of atonement for murder by persons unknown. See Deuteronomy 21:1–8 and *Sotah* 9:1–8. These ages are upper limits.

A heifer whose ash will be used in the purification ritual that is the main topic of this tractate. See Numbers 19:1–22.

Lest it blacken: Black hairs make the heifer unfit for use in the ritual. See below 2:5.

A thirdling: Heb. *sheloshit*. An unusual term.

I have heard the tradition transmitted with this confounding term.

What does "fourthling" signify?
He said to them:
Thus I have heard without explanation.
Ben Azzai said:
I will explain it:
When they say "fourth," it means its number in relation to the others;
but when they say "fourthling," it means something four years old.
In like manner they said:
If he eats in an afflicted house—
a half-loaf, from a batch of three loaves to the *qav*.
They said to him:
Say eighteen to the *se'ah*.
He said to them:
Thus I have heard without explanation.
Ben Azzai said:
I will explain it:
If you say "three to the *qav*,"
it means that it was not liable for the dough offering.
But when you say "eighteen to the *se'ah*,"
it means that the dough offering has reduced the remainder.

2 R. Yose the Galilean says:
Bulls must be not more than two years old, for it is written:
...and bull two from the herd take for a purgation offering.

fourthling: Heb. *revai'i*. A term as confounding as *sheloshit*.

A fourthling vineyard: Leviticus 19:23–25 forbids a tree's fruit in its first three years. In year four the fruit is holy, but one may redeem it. See *Peah* 7:6 and *Shevi'it* 5.4. Beginning in year five the fruit may be eaten normally.

an afflicted house that a priest has declared to have *tsara'at*. See Leviticus 14:34–53 and *Nega'im* 12:5–7, 13:9.

a half-loaf: This is a measurement of time. The afflicted house contaminates him if he stays inside it long enough to eat a half-loaf. The disputed tradition claims that the imagined half-loaf is the size of one taken from a batch of three loaves formed from a *qav* of flour.

qav: A measurement equivalent to the volume of approximately two dozen eggs.

se'ah: A measurement equivalent to the volume of six *qav*. It appears to be the more common measurement of volume. A loaf made from a batch of three loaves to the *qav* appears, in the first analysis, to be the same size as one from a batch of eighteen loaves to the *se'ah*, since three loaves multiplied by the six *qav* in a *se'ah* is eighteen loaves ($3 \times 6 = 18$). *Ben Azzai* points out a difference.

liable for the dough offering: See Numbers 15:17–21. According to *Hallah* 1:4, dough is only liable if it is made from at least 1.25 *qav*. See also *Eduyot* 1:2. Therefore, while they would not have removed a dough offering from the *qav* batch, they would indeed have removed a dough offering from the *se'ah* batch.

the dough offering has reduced the remainder: Since the loaves in the *se'ah* batch are missing the amount that was removed for the dough offering, they are necessarily smaller and take less time to eat. A *qav* batch, from which the dough offering has not been removed, has larger loaves that take longer to eat.

1:2 *Bulls* for sacrifice.

...and bull two: Numbers 8:8. If "two" merely means a second bull, it seems superfluous to R. Yose the Galilean. He takes "two" to refer to the age.

But the Sages say:
They may even be three years old.
R. Meir says:
Even if they are four years old or five they are valid;
but they do not offer them that old out of respect.

3 Lambs—one year old,
and rams—two years old;
all of them to the day.
A thirteen-month-old is not valid as a ram or as a lamb.
R. Tarfon calls it a *pallax*.
Ben Azzai calls it a *noqed*.
R. Ishmael calls it a *parakharagma*.
If a man offered it with the libations of a ram upon it,
it does not count for him as a proper sacrifice.
If it was thirteen months and a day—
now that is a ram.

4 The purgation offering of the community and their whole burnt offerings,
the purgation offerings of an individual,
the guilt offering of a *nazir*, and the guilt offering of one with *tsara'at*
are valid from the time that they are thirty days old and up,
and even on the thirtieth day.
But if he offered them from the eighth day they are valid.
Vow offerings and voluntary offerings,
the firstborn and the tithe and the Passover offering
are valid from the eighth day onward,
and even on the eighth day.

out of respect for the altar.

1:3 *all of them to the day*: A full year; from a date in year one until the same date in year two.

pallax: Likely Greek for "youth."

noqed: Heb. "herdsman." See 2 Kings 3:4 and Amos 1:1.

parakharagma: Perhaps the Greek term for a counterfeit coin.

1:4 *the purgation offering of the community*: Leviticus 4:14.

whole burnt offerings that are completely consumed by fire on the altar. This sacrifice is mentioned 289 times in the Bible. In its communal form either a lamb or a he-goat could be called for.

the guilt offering of a nazir: Numbers 6:14.

the guilt offering of one with tsara'at: Leviticus 14:12.

the eighth day: Leviticus 22:27.

the firstborn: Exodus 22:30.

the tithe of cattle. Leviticus 17:32.

Chapter Two

2:1–5 *Things That Disqualify the Heifer*

2 R. Eliezer says:
If the heifer for the purgation offering was pregnant, it is [still] valid.
But the Sages deem it not valid.
R. Eliezer says:
It may not be purchased from gentiles.
But the Sages deem it valid.
And not only that,
but they may bring all public or private offerings from within the Land of Israel or from without,
from new grain or from old,
except for the *omer* and the two loaves,
which they may bring only from new grain from within the Land of Israel.
2 If a heifer's horns or hooves are black, he should lop them off.
Its eye socket, or teeth, or tongue can make a heifer not valid.
A miniature animal is valid.
If there was a wart on it, and he cut it off,
R. Judah deems it not valid.
R. Simeon says:
Any place it was removed—if that place did not sprout new red hair—it is not valid.
3 If it was born by caesarean section, or was the hire [of a prostitute], or the price [of a dog], it is not valid.
R. Eliezer deems it valid,
for it is written:
You shall not bring the hire of a harlot or the price of a dog to the house of the Lord your God,
and it will not go into the Temple.
All blemishes that make sacrifices not valid make the heifer not valid.
If he rode on it,
or leaned on it,

2:1 *from new grain or from old*: Leviticus 23:14

the omer and the two loaves: Leviticus 23:15–17.

Its eye socket, or teeth, or tongue: Blemishes in these locations. See Leviticus 22:17–25.

2:3 *hire…price*: If it was purchased with funds earned by prostitution, or was gotten in trade for sexual favors.

You shall not bring: Deuteronomy 23:18.

If he rode on it: All of the cases in this list are derived from the words of Numbers 19:2, *on which no yoke has been laid.* The Heifer may carry nothing on its back, or perform any other work.

or something had been hung from its tail,
or if he crossed the river with its help,
or folded up its reins on its back,
or put his cloak on it,
it is not valid.
But if he tied its reins,
or made shoes for so it would not slip,
or spread his cloak over it because of flies,
it is valid.
This is the rule:
Anything done for its needs—it is valid.
For the needs of another—it is not valid.

4 If a bird landed on it, it is valid.
If a male mounted it, it is not valid.
R. Judah says:
If he made it mount, it is not valid.
But if it did it on its own, it is valid.

5 If it had two black or white hairs in a single dimple, it is not valid.
R. Judah says:
Or even from within a single hollow.
If they grew from within two hollows,
and each is evidence against the other, it is not valid.
R. Aqiva says:
Even four or even five, but they are scattered, he may pluck them.
R. Eliezer says:
Even fifty.
R. Joshua b. Betera says:
Even if there is one on its head and one on its tail, it is not valid.
If there were two hairs—
their roots blackening but their tips reddening,
or their roots reddening but their tips blackening—
it all goes by what can be seen—
the words of R. Meir.
But the Sages say:
Follow the root.

2:5 *a single hollow* somewhere on its body. It is unclear if the issue is merely one of vocabulary—and the dimple and the hollow are two words for the same thing—or if there is an actual substantive difference in size or location at stake.

each is evidence against the other: Their proximity is such that they can be seen at the same time.

Even fifty: This is not really a quantitative upper limit. It is a very large round number selected to indicate that he may pluck an indefinite number of nonred hairs.

Follow the root: This evocative statement may be a double entendre, hinting at a larger unrelated moral message: it is the unseen root that ultimately matters, not the appearance of the thing before deeper investigation.

Chapter Three

3:1–11 *The Ritual Sacrifice and Burning of the Red Heifer*

3 Seven days before the burning of the heifer,
they would remove the priest who burns the heifer from his household
to a chamber that faced the compound, in the northeast.
And it was called the Stone House.
And all seven days they would sprinkle him,
from all the purgation offerings that were there.
R. Yose says:
They sprinkled him on the third and seventh day only.
R. Hanina the Chief of the Priests says:
They would sprinkle the priest who burns the heifer all seven days,
but it was the one for the Day of Atonement
that they would sprinkle only on the third and seventh days.
2 There were courtyards in Jerusalem built over the rock,
and under them was a hollow,
lest there be a grave in the abyss.
And they would bring pregnant women and they would give birth there,
and they would raise their sons there,
and they would bring oxen with doors on their backs,
and the children would sit on them.
and they had stone cups in their hands.
When they reached the Siloam,

3:1 *remove the…priest*: They would quarantine him inside the Temple compound to protect him from sources of ritual impurity.

the compound: The Temple. See *Zevahim* 12:5 and *Tamid* 1:1.

all seven days: This period of time recapitulates the purification period from corpse impurity and *tsara'at*. See Numbers 19:11–13 and Leviticus 14:8–9.

the one for the Day of Atonement: They would also quarantine the priest due to perform the Day of Atonement rituals. See *Yoma* 1:1.

3:2 *lest there be a grave in the abyss*: The impurity of a grave below the ground is considered to rise to the heavens. A hollow space of at least one cubic handbreadth acts as a barrier. See *Oholot* 3:7.

they would give birth there to prevent their sons from ever becoming impure.

their sons: The word in Hebrew could be construed to refer to either sons or children of both sexes, although "sons" is more likely.

with doors on their backs: To act as a barrier against impurity.

the Siloam: Just as Numbers 19:2 invalidates an animal that has been worked, the water used for the ritual must also have not been previously used for work, so it is drawn from this natural source near Jerusalem. See 4:4 below.

stone cups: Stone was considered impervious to impurity. See *Oholot* 5:5.

they would dismount and fill them,
and mount and sit on their backs.
R. Yose says:
He would fill it from his place, dangling it and filling it.
3 They came to the Temple Mount,
and they dismounted for the Temple Mount and the Courts.
and under them was a hollow,
lest there be a grave in the abyss.
At the entrance of the Courtyard,
a vessel of the ash of purgation was fixed.
And they would bring a male from among the sheep,
and tie a rope between its horns,
and bind a wand all around with the other end of the rope,
and throw it into the vessel.
And he would strike the sheep,
startling it backward, [spilling the ashes],
and he would take and mix enough to be seen on the water.
R. Yose says:
Don't give the Sadducees a chance to snivel!
Rather, *he* would take and mix them.
4 They would not prepare a purgation offering as a stand-in for an earlier purgation offering,
or another child as stand-in for his fellow.
The children would need to be sprinkled—
the words of R. Yose the Galilean.
R. Aqiva says:
They would not need to be sprinkled.
5 If they did not find [the ashes] from the seven purgation offerings,
they would make it from six,
or from five,
or from four,

from his place on the ox.

3:3 *a male from among the sheep*: This elaborate procedure is to prevent the child from touching the remaining ashes in the vessel, possibly contaminating them. Some commentators claim that this procedure was followed only once, when the exiles returned from Babylonia, and all were ritually impure.

Rather, he would take and mix them: The pronoun is italicized to indicate the unusual Hebrew syntax; the subject precedes the verb, emphasizing it. The child takes the ashes himself, without resort to any overcomplicated exercise.

3:4 *as a stand-in*: The entire procedure must be performed for only one heifer. If something went awry partway through, they could not substitute another, as opposed to the standard practice with regular purification offerings. See *Temurah* 4.2–5.

sprinkled with the waters of lustration, as if they had somehow contracted impurity. Leviticus 19:19.

3:5 *the seven purgation offerings*: The author seems to imagine that the ash of each of these offerings had its own separate vessel. A bit of ash from each of those that remain is used in the present version of the ritual. See above 3:1.

or from three,
or from two,
or from one.
Who made them?
The first? Moses made it.
And the second? Ezra made it.
And the other five? After Ezra and beyond—
the words of R. Meir.
But the Sages say:
There were seven after Ezra and beyond.
And who made them?
Simon the Just and Yohanan the High Priest made two each.
Elihoenai ben ha-qof, Hanamel the Egyptian, and Ishmael b. Piabi made one each.

6 They would make a ramp from the Temple Mount to the Mount of Olives,
arch upon arch,
each arch directly above each pier,
lest there be a grave in the abyss.
For the priest who burns the heifer was there,
and the heifer and all its attendants would go out to the Mount of Olives.

7 If the heifer did not want to go out,
they would not bring a black heifer out with it,
lest they say: "They slaughtered a black heifer!"
and not a red one,
lest they say: "They slaughtered two!"
R. Yose says:
It was not because of that!
Rather, because it is written: *and he shall bring it out*—by itself.
And the Elders of Israel would go in advance of them on foot to the Mount of Olives.
There was a house of immersion there.
And they made the priest who burns the heifer ritually impure,
because of the Sadducees.
So they would not say,
"Only by those on whom the sun has set may it be done."

8 They laid their hands upon him and said,
"O high priest sir, immerse once."
He went down and immersed himself,
and he came up and dried himself.
Wood was arrayed there:
Cedar wood, and pine, and spruce, and logs of smooth fig-tree wood.

Elihoenai ben ha-qof: These three unfamiliar names are not mentioned elsewhere in the Mishnah. *Ishmael b. Piabi* appears in a late passage added at the end of *Sotah*.

3:7 *and he shall bring it out*: Numbers 19:3.

ritually impure: Not by corpse impurity, which would cling to him for a week, but by a swarming thing, which only costs him a day. After immersion he is in an intermediate state of impurity, and will only be completely purified when the sun sets. See Leviticus 22:5–7 and *Kelim* 1:5. The Sadducees deem him too impure to perform the ritual, but the Sages maintain that his contamination is slight enough for him to proceed and insisted on this impurity to make this point.

And they stacked it like a tower and opened windows in it,
with its rough edge to the west.

9 They bound it with a bast rope;
they placed it on the wood stack,
its head to the south and its face to the west.
The priest stood to the east, his face to the west.
He slaughtered it with his right hand,
and collected the blood with his left.
R. Judah says:
He would collect with his right hand,
place it in his left hand,
and sprinkle with his right.
He dipped and sprinkled the blood seven times,
opposite the Holy of Holies,
dipping for each sprinkling.
When he finished sprinkling,
he wiped his hands on the heifer's body.
He came down and kindled the fire with twigs of fig wood.
R. Aqiva says:
With branches of date palm.

10 When the heifer ruptured,
he stood beside its firepit.
He took cedar wood, and hyssop, and scarlet wool.
And he said to them:
Is this cedar wood?
Is this cedar wood?
Is this hyssop?
Is this hyssop?
Is this scarlet wool?
Is this scarlet wool?
Three times for each item.
And they would say to him:
Yes! Yes! Yes!
Three times.

11 He wrapped them up with the edge of the wool strip,
and threw them in the fire.
When it was incinerated,
they beat it with rods
and sifted the remains through sieves.
R. Ishmael says:
It was done with stone mallets and stone sieves.
Pieces of charcoal with ash—they would crush up.
Without—they would leave.

3:9 *A bast rope* considered impervious to impurity.

3:10 *Is this cedar wood?* See *Menahot* 10:3. This antiphonal repetition has an incantatory effect, heightening the ritual's significance in the minds of the participants.

A bone—either way they would crush it up.
They divided it into three parts:
One part was placed within the pavement,
one placed on the Mount of Olives,
and one was divided among the priestly courses.

Chapter Four

4:1–4 *Defects in the Ritual*

4 If the heifer for the purgation offering was slaughtered without its proper designation,
if he collected its blood or sprinkled it without its proper designation,
or with its proper designation and without its proper designation,
or without its proper designation and with its proper designation—
it is not valid.
But R. Eliezer deems it valid.
If [offered] by the unwashed of hands or feet, it is not valid.
But R. Eliezer deems it valid.
If not by the high priest, it is not valid.
But R. Judah deems it valid.
Or if by one lacking the proper garments, it is not valid.
And it was done in a white garment.
2 If he burned it outside its firepit,
or in two firepits,
or if he burned two in the same firepit, it is not valid.
If he sprinkled but did not aim for the Entrance, it is not valid.

3:11 *the pavement*: Or: "Palisade" or "Rampart." It was placed in the space between the Temple's protective outer wall and the interior wall surrounding the courtyards. See *Middot* 1:4, 1:6–7.

the priestly courses: As established in 1 Chronicles 24:1–19.

4:1 *without its proper designation*: When he slaughters it, his intention is not for it to serve as the Red Heifer, but that it be another type of sacrifice. See *Zevahim* 1:1.

with its proper designation and without its proper designation: His intention is that it serve as two types of sacrifice at the same time; primarily the Red Heifer, but another as well.

without its proper designation and with its proper designation: His intention is that it serve primarily as some other type of sacrifice, but the Red Heifer as well. See *Zevahim* 1:4.

4:2 *It is not valid*: This translation adopts the neuter pronoun once the heifer is reduced to ash. No such change occurs in the Hebrew, as the language lacks a neuter pronoun.

the Entrance to the Sanctuary's antechamber. See *Middot* 3:7.

If he sprinkled from the sixth a seventh,
and went back and sprinkled a seventh, it is not valid.
From the seventh an eighth, it is valid.

3 If he burnt it without wood,
or with any wood,
even with straw,
even with stubble,
it is valid.
If he flayed and butchered it, it is valid.
If he slaughtered it in order to eat of its meat or to drink its blood, it is valid.
R. Eleazar says:
Intentions do not disqualify as regards the heifer.

4 All that deal with the heifer—
from start to finish—
make garments impure.
And they disqualify it by working it.
If a defect occurred in its slaughter,
it does not make garments impure.
If a defect occurred in the sprinkling,
anyone who dealt with it before the defect communicates impurity to garments.
After the defect,
he does not make garments impure.
It turns out that a stringency is a leniency.
At all times:
one may commit sacrilege,
and one may add wood,
and its rituals belong to the daytime,
[done] by a priest.
And work disqualifies it until it is reduced to ash.
And work disqualifies the water until they put the ash into it.

from the sixth a seventh: He dipped his finger in the blood before the sixth sprinkle, and sprinkled twice without pausing to dip again before the seventh time. See above, 3:9.

an eighth, it is valid: Since he has already performed the seven required sprinklings properly, further sprinklings create no defect.

4:4 *make garments impure*: See Numbers 19:7–11.

they disqualify it by working it: See above 2:3 and Numbers 19:2.

It turns out that a stringency is a leniency: Because it is the defect, and the resulting loss of the heifer's purifying ashes, that caused the later participants in the sacrifice to avoid ritual impurity.

one may commit sacrilege: The danger of misusing the heifer and thereby committing sacrilege is always present.

the water: See 3:2 above.

Chapter Five

5:1–9 *The Fitness of the Vessel in Which the Water Is Consecrated*

5 If he brings a ceramic vessel for the purgation offering—
he immerses and spends the night at the kiln.
R. Judah says:
He may even bring it from the house,
and it will still be valid—
for everyone is trustworthy as regard the purgation offering.
For *terumah*,
he may open the kiln and take [a vessel].
R. Simeon says:
From the second stack.
R. Yose says:
From the third stack.

2 If he immerses a vessel for the purgation offering in water that was not valid to consecrate,
he must dry it.
In water that was valid to consecrate,
he need not dry it.
If it was to gather consecrated water in it,
either way he must dry it.

5:1 *spends the night*: So that he knows that no one has contaminated it. Vessels cannot contract impurity until the last stage of their production is complete.

everyone is trustworthy: See *Oholot* 5:5.

For terumah: Because of its lower standard of purity, he need not wait by the kiln.

the second stack: Lest some contaminated person unintentionally touched a vessel directly behind the kiln door when he removed his vessel, R. Simeon requires one who eats *terumah* to take his vessel from behind the first stack.

the third stack: R. Yose is even more concerned about possible contamination and obliges him to go three stacks back from the door of the kiln when acquiring his vessel.

5:2 *water that was not valid*: It must be "living water" in accordance with Numbers 19:17. For a listing of valid and invalid waters, see below 8:8–11.

to consecrate: This is the first time the tractate uses this technical term, which will be used very frequently from this point on. It means the act of mixing the ash of the heifer with the waters drawn from the Siloam. This mixture results in the creation of purgation water. This consecrated water will decontaminate those who have contracted corpse impurity in accordance with Numbers 19.

he must dry it: Lest some of the invalid water remaining on the vessel mix with the valid water.

either way he must dry it: Even living water invalidates already consecrated water. See below, 6:2.

3 If they immersed a gourd shell in water that was not valid to consecrate,
they may consecrate with it,
until it is made impure.
If it was made impure,
they may not consecrate with it.
R. Joshua says:
If he may consecrate with it at first,
he may also consecrate with it later.
If he may not consecrate with it later,
he also may not consecrate with it at first.
Either way,
he may not gather consecrated water in it.

4 A reed flask that he cut for the purgation offering—
R. Eliezer says:
He should immerse it immediately.
R. Joshua says:
If it becomes impure,
then he should immerse it.
All are valid to consecrate it,
except a deaf-mute,
one legally incompetent,
and a minor.
R. Judah deems a minor valid,
but disqualifies a woman and an *androgynos*.

5 One may consecrate with any vessel,
even with vessels of dung,
with vessels of earth,
with vessels of stone.
And as for a ship, one may consecrate with it.
But one may not consecrate with fragments of vessels,
or a scuttle's bails,

5:3 *a gourd shell*: The hollowed-out shell is dried and retained as a vessel. However, it still absorbs water. Since the immersion water is absorbed, it does not mix with the water for consecration and invalidate it.

until it is made impure: At this point, the concern is that impure liquid in the walls of the gourd *will* mix with the water for consecration. *R. Joshua* rejects the distinction between these two situations.

5:4 *A reed flask*: See *Kelim* 17:17.

immediately: Out of concern for its greater holiness. See *Hagigah* 3:2. *R. Joshua* requires the vessel to be made impure first and then immersed (cf. 3:7).

androgynos. A hermaphrodite. This person is treated as being of doubtful sex. See below 12:10.

5:5 *with any vessel*: *Yadayim* 1:2.

vessels of earth: Unfired clay, for instance.

a ship: Making use of the ship's cavity as the actual mixing vessel. See *Shabbat* 9:2, *Kelim* 2:3, and below 9:6.

fragments of vessels: These are no longer considered vessels. See *Kelim* 4:1. Numbers 19:17 requires that a vessel must be used.

a scuttle's bails: The bails of this bucket-like container are not the hoop of the modern pail. Rather, they are open at the top, closed at the bottom, and worked into the scuttle's sides for ease of carrying. If one were

or in the bung of a cask,
or with his cupped hands.
For one may only pour,
or consecrate,
or sprinkle the purgation water with a vessel.
Only vessels can rescue by means of a fastened cover,
for only a vessel can rescue from [the impurity] of ceramic vessels.

6 The potters' egg is valid.
But R. Yose deems it not valid.
A hen's egg—
R. Judah and R. Meir deem valid.
But the Sages deem it not valid.

7 A trough carved into the rock—
one may not pour into it,
or consecrate in it,
or sprinkle from it,
and it does not need a fastened cover,
and it does not validate an immersion pool.
If it was a [separate] vessel,
and it had been attached to the ground with plaster—
one may pour into it,
or consecrate in it,
or sprinkle from it.
And it needs a fastened cover,
and it invalidates an immersion pool.
If he had pierced it on the bottom
and stopped it up with a rag,
the water in it is not valid,
since it is not contained by a vessel.
From the side
and he stopped it up with a rag,
the water in it is valid,
since it is contained by a vessel.

broken off, it could hold a small amount of water in its own right. Nonetheless, it is not considered a vessel. See *Tohorot* 10:7.

the bung of a cask: Both the cask and its bung were ceramic. The bung was hollow, having been thrown on the wheel during production. Nonetheless, it is not considered a vessel.

Only vessels, and not nonvessels, protect their contents from impurity by means of *a fastened cover*. See Numbers 19:15 and *Kelim* 10:1.

rescue...from a ceramic vessel: Leviticus 11:33 decrees that anything inside an impure ceramic vessel also becomes impure. However, a second vessel resting inside that impure vessel shelters its contents from impurity if it is properly closed.

5:6 *The potters' egg*: This is most likely the "egg of clay" mentioned in *Shabbat* 2:4. There it is used as a reservoir for a larger amount of fuel than an oil lamp can hold.

R. Yose: He seems not to deem it a vessel in its own right, since it is of no use when separated from the oil lamp.

5:7 *A trough*: Since it is hewn from the living stone, it is not considered a vessel. See *Miqva'ot* 4:5.

contained by a vessel: Since the hole is not on the bottom, we can consider the container to be a vessel.

If they made it a crown of clay—
and the water gathered there,
it is not valid.
But if the crown was secure,
so that the vessel could be carried by it,
it is valid.

8 Two troughs carved out of the same stone—
if he consecrated one of them,
the water in the second is not consecrated.
If they were pierced from one to the other,
the size of the spout of a waterskin,
or if the water overflowed on them,
even if only by the thickness of a garlic peel—
if he consecrated one of them,
the water in the second is consecrated.

9 Two stones that he drew near each other,
and he made them a trough,
or also with two kneading tubs,
or with a trough that was divided—
the water between them is not consecrated.
But if he sealed them with plaster or gypsum,
and they could be carried as one—
the water between them is not consecrated.

Chapter Six

6:1–5 *Things That Disqualify the Water*

6 If he was consecrating,
and the consecrated ash fell on his hand or off to the side,
but afterward fell into the trough,

a crown of clay: A decorative brim. If it is purely cosmetic it is not considered part of the trough, and it certainly is not a vessel in its own right. The water that collects on or around such a brim is invalid.

5:8 *Two troughs*: Though conjoined, they have been detached from the earth.

the spout of a waterskin: Roughly large enough to insert two fingers.

5:9 *that he drew near each other*: This is not an accidental occurrence. The same verb is used in *Betsah* 4:5 in a manner that demonstrates intent.

two kneading tubs: Clearly, the tubs are attached, but they must be slightly separated so that the water cannot flow freely from one to the other.

the water between them: Any water that collects in crevices, gaps, or cracks between the two basins.

it is not valid.
If it fell from the flask onto the trough,
it is not valid.
If he took the ash from the flask and covered it,
or if he closed the door,
the consecrated ash is valid,
but the water is not valid.
If he positioned it on the ground,
it is not valid.
If he gripped it in his hand,
it is valid,
because it is impossible to do anything else.

2 If consecrated ash was floating on the surface of the water,
R. Meir and R. Simeon say:
He may take some and consecrate it [again].
But the Sages say:
One may not consecrate with anything that touched water.
If he emptied out the water and consecrated ash was found at the bottom,
R. Meir and R. Simeon say:
He may dry it out and consecrate it [again].
But the Sages say:
One may not consecrate anything that touched water.

3 If a man was consecrating in a trough and a ewer was in it,
even if its mouth was as narrow as can be,
the water inside it is consecrated.
If there was a sponge,
the water in it is not valid.
What should he do?
Empty it out until he gets to the sponge.

6:1 *it is not valid*: The consecrator must physically place the ash directly on the water, without it taking an intermediate path, even accidentally.

the flask: It contains the ash. See above, 5:4.

covered it: If he replaced the flask's lid before he placed the ash on the water.

if he closed the door: After he withdrew the ash, but before he placed it on the water. Since he did some amount of unrelated work (covering a flask, closing a door) at the time reserved for placing the ash, he has invalidated the water. The ash remains valid, as work does not affect its status. See above 4:4.

If he positioned it on the ground: There is a disagreement among the commentators whether this refers to the flask or the ash. The grammar points to the flask as the more likely interpretation. The Mishnah considers positioning the flask on the ground an invalidating act of work.

6:2 *floating on the surface of the water*: Some ash visibly remains on the surface of the water following consecration. Can it be reused for another consecration?

6:3 *as narrow as can be*: Even though it lacks the size of the spout of a waterskin, the water in the submerged ewer is considered one with the surrounding water. See 5:8 above.

a sponge: It is not considered a vessel, therefore any water it contains is invalid. See below 6:5.

until he gets to the sponge: It is reasonable to assume the sponge only absorbed the water near it.

If he touches the sponge,
even if the water gathered on it was as small as can be,
it is not valid.

4 If he put out his hand,
or his foot,
or leaves of vegetables
to direct water into the cask,
it is not valid.
Leaves of reed
and leaves of nut—
it is valid.
This is the rule:
Anything that is susceptible to impurity is not valid,
but anything that is not susceptible to impurity is valid.

5 If he redirected a spring into a wine vat,
or into a cistern—
it is not valid for those with *zav* flow,
or those with *tsara'at*,
or to consecrate purgation water
since it was not gathered in a vessel.

Chapter Seven

7:1–12 *What Sort of Work Invalidates the Water*

7 If five people filled five casks to make five consecrations,
but they reconsidered and made a single consecration;
or if to make one consecration,
but they reconsidered and made five consecrations—
in such a case all of them are valid.
If one person filled five casks to make five consecrations,
but reconsidered and made a single consecration,
only the last is valid.

If he touches the sponge: Touching a saturated sponge causes it to emit some water. In our case, that means that the invalid water has mixed with the valid water.

6:4 *to direct water into the cask*: He channels the flow of the water into the cask prior to consecration.

Leaves of reed: Neither sort of leaf is considered food. As a result it is not susceptible to impurity. See *Eduyot* 7:4.

6:5 *it is not valid*: In all three of these cases Scripture requires "living water." See Leviticus 15:13, 14:5, and Numbers 19:17. He invalidates the water by stopping its flow.

7:1 *only the last is valid*: Work at the time of the consecration invalidates the water. See above 6:1. In our case, since he originally intended to do five separate acts of ash placing after he had poured all the water,

If to make one consecration,
but he reconsidered and made five consecrations,
only the one he consecrated first is valid.
If he said to one person:
"Consecrate these for your benefit,"
only the first is valid.
"Consecrate these for my benefit,"
they are all valid.

2 If he was pouring with one of his hands,
but doing work with his other hand,
or was pouring for his benefit and that of another,
or was pouring for two at once,
both are not valid,
for work invalidates the pouring,
whether it was for his benefit or for that of another.

3 If he was consecrating with one of his hands,
but did work with his other hand—
if it was for his benefit,
it is not valid.
But if it was for that of another,
it is valid.
If he was consecrating for his benefit and that of another,
his is not valid but the other's is valid.
If he consecrates for two at once, both are valid.

4 "Consecrate for my benefit and I will consecrate for yours"—
the first one is valid.

each time he pours the water it is now considered a new act of work and each pouring of water invalidates the previous one. Only in the final pouring does he do no new work before placing the ash.

the one he consecrated first is valid: Placing the ash is also considered an act of work. Since he originally intended only a single act of ash placing after pouring all the water, the placement of ash upon the water of each previous cask invalidates the four subsequent acts of pouring. Only in the first consecration does he accomplish both the pouring and the placement of ash without his work for the other casks intervening.

Consecrate these for your benefit: The speaker filled the casks intending one act of consecration. However, the listener views each as a separate act. Functionally this is the same as the one who intended to make one consecration, but made five instead. The final four acts of pouring are invalidated by the placement of the ash on the water of the previous cask.

Consecrate these for my benefit: Unlike the rule governing the act of pouring, unrelated work that one performs while placing the ash on the water for another's benefit does not invalidate the consecration. See below 7:3. Consequently, the listener does not invalidate the consecration he performs for the speaker's benefit by working.

7:2 *whether it was for his benefit or that of another*: This is true of the pouring, but not for the placement of ash. He does not invalidate the ash if he does work. See 7:3.

7:3 *If he consecrates for two at once, both are valid*: Since they are both for the benefits of others.

7:4 *the first one is valid*: Since the owner of the second cask invalidated his own water by placing the ash on the first cask for his fellow—an invalidating act of work—before the owner of the first cask placed the ash on the second cask.

"Pour for me and I will pour for you"—
the last one is valid.
"Consecrate for my benefit and I will pour for yours"—
both are valid.
"Pour for my benefit and I will consecrate for yours"—
both are invalid.

5 One who fills [a vessel] for himself and for the purgation offering—
he pours his own first and ties it to the yoke,
and afterward pours for the purgation offering.
But if he poured for the purgation offering first,
and afterward poured his own,
it is not valid.
He puts his own in the rear,
and the one for the purgation offering in the front.
But if he placed the one for the purgation offering in the rear,
it is not valid.
If they were both for the purgation offering,
and he placed one in the front and one in the rear,
they are valid because it is impossible to do anything else.

6 If he was delivering the rope by hand,
provided it was on his way,
it is valid.
But if it was not on his way,
it is not valid.
This [question] went to Yavneh three festivals running,
and on the third festival,

the last one is valid: Since the owner of the first cask invalidated his own water by filling the second cask for his fellow—an invalidating act of work—before the owner of the second cask placed the ash on the first cask.

both are valid: Since work does not invalidate the ash. See 7:2.

Both are invalid: Since work invalidates the water under all circumstances. See 7:3.

7:5 *for himself*: For his mundane needs: drinking, cooking, washing, and the like.

the yoke: A pole that he carries on one of his shoulders to which one container is attached in front of him, and another behind. This simple machine uses his shoulder as a fulcrum, counterbalancing the weight of the containers, easing the burden.

and afterward poured his own: He invalidates the water for the offering with this act of work.

the one for the purgation offering in the front: Numbers 19:9 requires the ash of the heifer be "kept" for the community of Israel. Rabbinic interpretation extends this to the waters: he must keep the water under his watch until he consecrates it.

because it is impossible to do anything else: Absent the mechanical advantage afforded by the counterbalancing yoke, he would not be able to carry both containers.

7:6 *delivering the rope*: If he returns a rope he borrowed to draw the water on his way to consecrate it.

if it was not on his way: If he alters his route, it is considered an invalidating act of work.

they validated it,
as a stopgap directive.[1]

7 If he wound the rope around his hand,
it is valid.
But if he wound it up at the end,
it is not valid.
R. Yose says:
It was this that they validated as a stopgap directive!

8 If he put the cask away so that it wouldn't break,
or flipped it on its mouth to dry—
intending to fill it,
it is valid;
intending to carry the consecrated water in it,
it is not valid.
If he removed potsherds from the trough—
intending that it would hold more water,
it is valid;
but if it was so that they would not hinder him
in emptying out the water later,
it is not valid.

9 One who whose water was riding on his shoulders—
if he rendered a ruling,
or showed others the way to go,
or killed a snake or a scorpion,
or picked up food and stored it,
it is not valid.

[1] Lit. "a ruling for the hour," here and below.

a stopgap directive: They set the law aside for a short period of time in order to ensure that they would be able to make full use of the ash remaining after the destruction of the Temple.

7:7 *If he wound the rope*: As he was drawing the water. This is considered to be part of the act of drawing and not an unrelated act of work.

if he wound it up at the end: This is work that is unrelated to the act of drawing, since it is only an attempt to care for the rope, and invalidates the water.

It was this that they validated as a stopgap directive! He disagrees with the account in 7:6.

7:8 *intending to fill it*: This is an act of work related to the needs of consecration.

to carry the consecrated water: Once he completes the consecration, no act of work for the resulting waters is considered related to the needs of consecration.

intending that it would hold more water: This would benefit the act of consecration.

later: After the consecration.

7:9 *water was riding on his shoulders*: In containers attached to a yoke. See 7:5.

rendered a ruling, etc.: These acts are unrelated to the consecration.

If the food was to eat,
it is valid.
If the snake or the scorpion obstructed him,
it is valid.
R. Judah says:
This is the rule:
If something was for the sake of work,
whether he stopped,
or whether he did not stop,
it is not valid.
But if something was not for the sake of work,
if he stopped,
it is not valid.
But if he did not stop,
it is valid.

10 If he deposited his water with an impure man,
it is not valid.
But with a pure man,
it is valid.
R. Eliezer says:
Even with an impure man,
it is valid,
so long as the owners did no work.

11 If two were pouring water for the purgation offering,
and they each raised it up for the benefit of the other,
or if one pulled out the other's thorn,
if it was for one consecration,
it is valid.
But if it was for two consecrations,
it is not valid.
R. Yose says:
Even if it was for two consecrations
it is valid,
provided they had made terms together.

If the food was to eat... the scorpion obstructed him: These are acts he performs to speed his arrival at the place of consecration and are considered valid related acts.

7:10 *an impure man*: Even if he does not touch the water it is invalid, for how can he keep watch over the purity of the waters if he himself is impure?

Even with an impure man: Even though he is impure, he is still able to guard the water to prevent contamination.

7:11 *one consecration*: In that case all the work was related to the single act of consecration and is valid.

two consecrations: Since one did work for the other before completing his own consecration, it is considered to have been unrelated work and invalidates his water.

made terms together: If they agreed to share the work in advance, all the work is considered related to the consecrations. If one of them does do unrelated work, the other's presence spares the water from invalidity. See below 8:1.

12 If he broke through with the intention to fence it back up,
it is valid.
But if he fenced it,
it is not valid.
If he ate intending to store the figs,
it is valid.
But if stored them, it is not valid.
If he was eating and left food over,
and threw what was in his hand underneath the fig tree,
or into the storage pile
so that it wouldn't go to waste,
it is not valid.

Chapter Eight

8:1–2 *The Purity of the Purgation Water*

8 Two people were keeping watch over the trough:
if one contracted impurity,
it is valid,
since it was in the possession of the second one.
If he became pure,
and then the second one became impure,
it is valid,
since it was in the possession of the first one.
If they both contracted impurity at the same time,
it is not valid.
If one of them did work,
it is valid,
since it was in the possession of the second one.
If he stopped and the second one did work,
it is valid,
since it was in the possession of the first one.
If they both did it at the same time,
it is not valid.

7:12 *If he broke through* a fence on the way to the place of consecration. Since he is speeding his arrival to the place of consecration, this is considered valid related work.

the intention to fence it back up: His intent is to do this later, after he completes the consecration.

But if he fenced it before his consecration was complete. This conception also applies to the cases below involving figs: if he made a mental commitment to do work later, it is valid; if he actually did the work, it is invalid.

8:1 *the possession of the second one*: See 7:11 above.

2 If he was consecrating the purgation water,
he should not put on his sandals,
for if liquid falls on his sandal,
it contracts impurity,
and communicates impurity to him.
Now, he could say:
"What communicates impurity to you doesn't make me impure.
But you have made me impure!"
If liquid fell on his flesh,
he is pure.
If it fell on his clothes,
it contracts impurity,
and communicates impurity to him.
Now, he could say:
"What communicates impurity to you doesn't make me impure.
But you have made me impure!"

8:3–7 *A Collection of Purity Topics Organized With a Common Phrase*

3 If he burns the heifer,
or the bulls,
or the sends off the scapegoat,
he makes garments impure.
The heifer,
and the bulls,
and the scapegoat,

8:2 This mishnah introduces a series of legal paradoxes that continues through 8:7 below.

If he was consecrating: Presumably, this would be true if he was sprinkling it as well. This passage seems to use only the case of consecration for simplicity's sake, but it probably does not mean to limit this rule to that case exclusively.

it contracts impurity: The sandal is susceptible to impurity from the water.

communicates impurity to him: Paradoxically, he is immune to impurity from direct contact with the water, but he is susceptible to impurity from the sandals if he is wearing them. Thus, the sandals serve as a sort of ironic vector for impurity from which he would otherwise be safe.

Now, he could say to the sandals.

What communicates impurity to you doesn't make me impure: The water will contaminate the sandals with direct contact, but it will not contaminate him if it directly contacts his skin.

But you have made me impure: The impure sandals have transferred the impurity to him.

If it fell on his clothes: This is conceptually identical to the case of the sandals. See also *Kelim* 8:4 and *Tohorot* 8:7.

8:3 *the bulls*: Leviticus 4:3–21.

the scapegoat: Leviticus 16:20–26.

do not themselves make garments impure.
Now, he could say:
"What communicates impurity to you doesn't make me impure.
But you have made me impure!"

4 If he eats from the carrion of a pure bird,
and it was in his throat,
he makes garments impure.
Carrion itself does not itself make garments impure.
Now, he could say:
"What communicates impurity to you doesn't make me impure.
But you have made me impure!"

5 All reduced-degree impurities can only make liquids impure,
not vessels.
If a liquid is made impure, it does communicate impurity to them.
Now, it could say:
"What communicates impurity to you doesn't make me impure.
But you have made me impure!"

6 A ceramic vessel can only make liquids impure,
not its companion.
If a liquid is made impure, it can communicate impurity to it.
Now, it could say:
"What communicates impurity to you doesn't make me impure.
But you have made me impure!"

7 Anything that invalidates *terumah* communicates impurity to liquids,
so that they become first-degree impurities
that communicate impurity to one [degree of contact]
and invalidate one [more],

Do not themselves make garments impure: Although the people engaged in the ritual are impure and convey impurity to garments, the sacrifices themselves do not.

8:4 *carrion*: It died without proper kosher slaughter. See *Hullin* 2:4.

it was in his throat: See *Zevahim* 7.3, 5–6; *Tohorot* 1:1–3; *Zavim* 5:9.

Carrion itself: Although eating carrion makes the eater impure and conveys impurity to clothing, the actual carrion itself does not.

8:5 *reduced-degree impurities*: See *Tohorot* 1:5 and *Yadayim* 3:1.

it does communicate impurity to them: The vessels, even though they are not susceptible to direct contamination from the reduced-degree impurities.

8:6 *not its companion*: One ceramic vessel cannot directly contaminate another.

it can communicate impurity to it: The companion ceramic vessel.

Now, it could say: That is, the companion vessel could say this to the liquid.

8:7 *Anything that invalidates terumah*: See *Zavim* 5:12.

that communicate impurity: They contaminate nonsacral food and drink, which can then pass on contamination, albeit at a reduced degree.

and invalidate one [more]: They can invalidate *terumah*, but the now impure *terumah* would not pass on further impurity. This is the difference between "communicate impurity" on the one hand, and "invalidate"

except for the *tevul yom*.
Now, it could say:
"What communicates impurity to you doesn't make me impure.
But you have made me impure!"

8:8–11 *Which Sources of Water Are Valid?*

8 All seas are like an immersion pool,
as Scripture states:
And the pool of waters He called Seas—
the words of R. Meir.
R. Judah says:
The Great Sea is like an immersion pool.
Seas was said only [of the Great Sea, which] contains many types of sea.
R. Yose says:
All seas purify with flowing water.
But they are not valid for those with *zav* flow,
or those with *tsara'at*,
or to consecrate purgation water.
9 Stricken water is not valid.
Which are stricken?
The salty or warm.
Failing water is not valid.
Which are failing?
If they fail once in a week of years.
Failing water in wartime,
or years of drought,

on the other: anything to which impurity has been communicated can still pass on impurity; anything which is invalidated is impure, but does not pass on its impurity.

tevul yom: See Leviticus 22:5–7 and *Kelim* 1:5.

Now, it could say: That is, the nonsacral food and drink to the contaminating liquid.

What communicates impurity to you doesn't make me impure: Since nonsacral food and drink cannot drop below second-degree impurity, things that invalidate *terumah* would not affect them. However, as we have seen, if those things contaminate liquids, the liquids can then contaminate nonsacral food and drink.

8:8 *All seas*: *Miqva'ot* 5:4

an immersion pool: While valid for immersion for decontamination from impurity, it is not valid for those with *zav* flow or those with *tsara'at*, or to consecrate purgation water since it is not considered "living water." See above, 6:5, and Leviticus 15:13, 14:5, and Numbers 19:17.

And the pool of waters He called Seas: Genesis 1:10.

The Great Sea: The Mediterranean. But not lakes, no matter how large.

8:9 *Stricken water is not valid*: See Exodus 7:14–24.

The salty or warm: They are not considered to be "living water," and are not valid for those with *zav* flow, those with *tsara'at*, or to consecrate purgation water. See above 6:5 and 8:8.

Failing water: The water stops running at times, so that it cannot be relied upon. See Isaiah 58:11.

is valid.
R. Judah deems it not valid.
10 The water of the Karmion and water of the Pugah are not valid,
since they are bog water.
The water of the Jordan and water of the Yarmuk are not valid,
for they have mixed waters.
Which are mixed waters?
One was valid and one not valid, and they became mixed.
Two valid waters that became mixed are valid.
R. Judah deems them not valid.
11 Ahab's Well and the Banias Cave are valid.
Water that changed [in appearance] and the change is due to itself is valid.
A channel of water that came from a distance is valid,
so long as he keeps watch so that no one will stop it.
R. Judah says:
In this case there is a presumption that it is permitted.
If potsherds or earth fell into a well,
he should wait until it clears up—
the words of R. Ishmael.
R. Aqiva says:
There is no need to wait.

Chapter Nine

9:1–9 *Foreign Contaminants in the Water or the Ash*

9 A flask into which some water fell—
R. Eliezer says:

8:10 *the Karmion*: Maybe the Kishon. See Judges 4–5.

the Pugah: Likely Nahal Na'aman. The source of this river, which empties into the bay of Haifa north of the Kishon, is the springs of Ein Afek.

bog water: The Ein Afek nature reserve is today the last remnant of this once large wetland. The Israeli suburb of Kiryat Bialik now rests on most of its drained lands. It is the proximity of the two rivers to this primeval bog that make their identification plausible.

the Yarmuk: This river is the largest of three main tributaries that flow into the Jordan between the Sea of Galilee and the Dead Sea.

mixed waters: Both the Jordan and the Yarmuk are fed by tributaries that frequently fail, making them invalid.

8:11 *Ahab's Well*: A natural spring, as seen by the manner in which Mishnah juxtaposes it with the better known natural spring of the Banias Cave. At times it has been identified with the Harod spring (Ain Jalut) because of its location. It may also be the spring listed as proximate to Afek in 1 Samuel 29:1.

due to itself: And not to tributaries or foreign materials.

9:1 *A flask*: From this point on the tractate will use this word to indicate a container holding consecrated water.

Let him sprinkle twice.
But the Sages deem it not valid.
If dew condensed into it,
R. Eliezer says:
Let him lay it in the sun and the dew will evaporate.
But the Sages deem it not valid.
If liquid or fruit juice fell into it,
he should pour it out,
and he must dry it.
Ink,
gum,
or sulfate of iron,
or anything that leaves an imprint—
he should pour it out,
but he does not need to dry it.

2 If insects or crawling things fell into it—
and they burst,
or if it changed in appearance,
it is not valid.
A scarab invalidates it in any case,
because it is like a reed tube.
R. Simeon and R. Eliezer b. Jacob say:
As for the maggot and the weevil that infest grain—
it is valid,
as they hold no moisture.

3 If cattle or game drank of it,
it is not valid.
All birds invalidate it,
except for the dove,
for she suctions it up.
Of all vermin,
only the weasel invalidates it,
since she laps at it.
Rabban Gamaliel says:
Also the snake,
because it disgorges.
R. Eliezer says:
Also a mouse.

sprinkle twice: Ensuring that some of the water that landed on him was consecrated. R. Eliezer does not consider the mixing of the waters to have invalidated the consecrated parts of the total solution.

he must dry it: See above 5:2.

he does not need to dry it: Since any remaining foreign substance would be visible.

9:2 *A scarab*: Because of its notable size and the large amount of moisture in its flesh, it is considered to hold the same volume of liquid as a reed tube and to mix with the water in the flask.

9:3 *she suctions it up*: The dove is thought not to lose any water in drinking. Therefore, no invalid spittle falls back into the consecrated water.

4 If he was planning to drink the water of purgation—
R. Eliezer says:
He has invalidated it.
R. Joshua says:
When he inclines it.
R. Yose says:
When does this ruling apply?
If the water was not consecrated.
But with consecrated water,
R. Eliezer says:
Once he inclines it.
R. Joshua says:
Once he drinks.
But if he gulped it, it is valid.

5 He should not knead plaster with water of purgation that became invalid,
so that he not make it an impediment to others.
R. Judah says:
It has been annulled!
The flesh of a cow that drank the water of purgation is impure for twenty-four hours.
R. Judah says:
It has been annulled in its gut!

6 He should not carry the water of purgation,
or the ash of purgation,
over a river,
or on a boat,
nor may he float them over the water's surface.
And he may not stand on one bank,
and throw them over to the other bank.
But he may ford the water up to his neck.
One purified to make the purgation offering may cross over,
an empty vessel purified to make the purgation offering in his hand,
or with unconsecrated water.

7 Valid ash that mixed with roasting ash,
one follows the majority for becoming impure.

9:4 *If he was planning*: And he declared this intention. See *Zevahim* 1:4, 2:4–5.

When he inclines it: To drink. In R. Joshua's opinion a mere declaration is insufficient to invalidate the water.

if he gulped it: So that no water washed back from his mouth.

9:5 *an impediment to others*: Since it would communicate impurity to them, presumably without their knowledge.

It has been annulled! In R. Judah's opinion, the water once invalidated can no longer render impure.

9:6 *He should not carry*: The concern cannot be potentially mixing the water, since he is allowed to ford. According to the Talmud the issue is potential corpse contamination, if there is a body aboard ship. This seems equally unlikely, since he is forbidden to float the vessel on the river water itself. The reason for these prohibitions remains obscure.

9:7 *for becoming impure*: Whether or not it communicates impurity.

But one does not consecrate with it.
R. Eliezer says:
One consecrates with all of it.
8 Water of purgation that became invalid
invalidates a person purified for *terumah*
by touching his hands
or his body.
But a person purified to make the purgation offering:
neither by touching his hands,
nor his body.
If it became impure,
it communicates impurity to a person purified for *terumah*,
by touching his hands,
or his body.
But a person purified to make the purgation offering—
by touching his hands,
but not his body.
9 Valid ash that they placed on the top of water unfit to consecrate,
makes a person purified for *terumah* impure,
by touching his hands
or his body.
But a person purified to make the purgation offering:
neither by touching his hands,
nor his body.

Chapter Ten

10:1–6 *The Higher Standard of Purity for the Water and the Vessels*

10 Anything susceptible to *midras* impurity
is *madaf* impure for the purgation offering,

9:8 *by touching his hands*: Invalid, but pure, purgation water invalidates (but does not communicate impurity to) those prepared to eat *terumah* if it contacts their hands or their body. See above 8:7. Such water does not affect those prepared to make the purgation offering.

10:1 *Anything susceptible to midras impurity*: Lit. "a place of treading." The term refers to impurity communicated by a new mother, one afflicted with *zav* impurity, or the menstruant when they sit, lie, ride, or lean on an object. Objects used for sitting, lying upon, or riding upon, and which are durable enough to withstand this usage, are susceptible to *midras* impurity. See *Zavim* 4:4.

madaf impure: "Wind-driven impurity." See Leviticus 26:36. The term refers to lesser impurity communicated by one afflicted with *zav* impurity, or the menstruant, to foodstuffs, or to liquids, even without direct contact. It is limited to impurity of the second degree, and is considered to derive from the authority of the Scribes, rather than that of the Torah. The upshot of this, in our case, is that one cannot carry or rest the

whether it is impure or pure.
And a person is treated the same way.
Anything susceptible to corpse impurity,
whether it is impure or pure:
R. Eliezer says:
It is not *madaf* impure.
R. Joshua says:
It is *madaf* impure.
And the Sages say:
If it is impure, it is *madaf* impure;
but if it is pure, it is not *madaf* impure.

2 One purified for the purgation offering
who touched a *madaf* impurity
is impure.
A bottle for the water of purgation
that touched a *madaf* impurity
is impure.
One purified for the purgation offering,
who touched food or drink—
with his hands,
he is impure;
with his foot,
he is pure.
If he jostled them with his hand,
R. Joshua deems him impure,
but the Sages deem him pure.

3 A pitcher for the purgation offering
that touched vermin
is pure.
If he put [the jar] on top of [the vermin],
R. Eliezer deems it pure,
but the Sages deem it impure.
If it touched food or drinks,
or Holy Scripture,
it is pure.
If he put [the jar] on top of these,

water, or the ash, or the consecrated water over things susceptible to *midras* impurity, even if they are still technically pure. See *Zavim* 4:6 and *Tohorot* 8:2.

a person is treated the same way: Practically, this means that all persons not purified for the purgation offering are assumed to be *zav* impure.

10:2 *If he jostled them with his hand*: Without direct contact.

10:3 *A pitcher*: It is made of ceramic. Ceramic vessels only contract impurity when an impure thing enters their inner chamber.

the Sages deem it impure: See *Eduyot* 7:5.

Holy Scripture: It invalidates *terumah*. See *Zavim* 5:12.

R. Yose deems it pure,
but the Sages deem it impure.
4 One purified for the purgation offering
who touched an oven
with his hands
is impure.
With his foot,
he is pure.
If he was standing atop an oven,
and he reached his hand out past the oven,
while holding a bottle—
or a yoke likewise resting on top of an oven,
with two pitchers attached to it,
one on its end,
and the other on its opposite end—
R. Aqiva deems it pure,
but the Sages deem it impure.
5 If he was standing away from the oven,
and he reached his hand to the window,
and took the pitcher,
and passed it over the oven,
R. Aqiva deems it impure,
but the Sages deem it pure.
However,
one purified for the purgation offering
may stand over an oven,
holding in his hand an empty vessel
purified for the purgation offering,
or holding unconsecrated water.
6 A bottle for the water of purgation,
which touched [a container] for sacral food
or for *terumah*—
that of the water of purgation
is impure,

10:4 *an oven*: Since it is a ceramic vessel, an oven can only contaminate liquids and food. See 8:6 above. Accordingly is not susceptible to *madaf* impurity. However, it is still susceptible to *midras* impurity.

he was standing atop an oven: The bottle is not over the oven, but one may construe it as connected to his body. This is the source of the disagreement.

R. Aqiva deems it pure: Since it is not susceptible to *madaf* impurity, and the containers of water are not in direct contact with the oven.

but the Sages deem it impure: Since it is susceptible to *midras* impurity, and they consider the containers to be atop the oven, through the vector of his body or the yoke.

10:5 *R. Aqiva deems it impure*: Unlike the previous case, the bottle passes directly over the oven. R. Aqiva considers it as if it had been resting atop it. Since it is susceptible to *midras* impurity, he deems it impure.

10:6 *that of the water of purgation is impure*: Since it contacted a vessel not purified for the purgation offering. See below 11:3.

but those for sacral food
or for *terumah*
are pure.
If the two of them
were in each of his hands,
both of them are impure.
If the two of them
were both in papyrus,
they are both pure.
If that of the water of purgation was in papyrus,
but that of *terumah* was in his hand,
they are both impure.
If that of *terumah* was in papyrus,
but that of the water of purgation was in his hand,
both of them are pure.
R. Joshua says:
That of the water of purgation is impure.
If they were resting on the earth,
and he touched them,
that of the water of purgation is impure,
but those for sacral food
or for *terumah*
are pure.
If he jostled them,
R. Joshua deems them impure,
but the Sages deem them pure.

Chapter Eleven

11:1–2 *Cases of Doubtful Purity*

11 If he left a flask open
and came back and found it closed,

both of them are impure: A complex chain of ritual contamination: first, the contact with the sacral vessel invalidates him from the purgation offering. Then he contaminates the vessel for the purgation offering, since he is no longer valid to perform the ritual. However, the purgation water itself is contaminating, and now communicates impurity to him, which finally flows into the sacral vessel, contaminating it.

both in papyrus: This wrapping blocks the impurity.

that of terumah was in his hand: The contact with the *terumah* invalidates him from the purgation offering, and he contaminates the vessel for the purgation offering, merely by lifting it. See below 11:6.

that of terumah was in papyrus: Blocking its invalidating effect.

but those for sacral food: They are pure because he never picked up the vessel for the purgation offering, which does not contaminate through contact alone.

it is not valid.
If he left it closed,
and came back and found it open,
if a weasel could have drunk from it,
or a snake
according to Rabban Gamaliel,
or if dew condensed into it over the night,
it is not valid.
The water of purgation is not preserved by a fastened cover.
But unconsecrated water is preserved by a fastened cover.

2 Anything that would be of doubtful purity if it were *terumah*
is pure in the case of the water of purgation.
Anything that would be of suspended status if it were *terumah*
is spilt out in the case of the water of purgation.
If they made pure foods on the basis of such,
they are of suspended status.
Lattices are pure for sacral food,
for *terumah*,
and for the water of purgation.
R. Eliezer says:
Fretwork lattices are impure for the water of purgation

11:3–6 *Immersion*

3 If a *terumah* cake of figs fell into the water of purgation,
and he took it and ate it.
If it was egg-sized,
whether it was impure or pure,
the waters are impure,

11:1 *or a snake*: See above 9:3.

dew: See 9:1 above.

preserved by a fastened cover: From corpse impurity; see Numbers 19:15.

11:2 *doubtful purity*: See the example in *Tohorot* 4:2.

suspended status: Cases in which the *terumah* may neither be eaten nor incinerated. See *Tohorot* 4.5–6.

on the basis of such: If they purified him with water or ashes of suspended status, and he then made pure food.

Lattices: The lattice window was formed of intertwining meshwork, and could be quite ornate. It often featured hinges, which allowed it to be shut for privacy while maintaining ventilation. It helped in lowering the temperature as well, by compressing air through its perforations. When air passed through these openings, its velocity would increase, cooling the air by convection. The Mishnah considers it to be axiomatically pure, since it is not a vessel in its own right.

R. Eliezer: He considers fretwork lattices to be significant enough to be a vessel in their right. According to commentaries, this lattice might be used as a seat.

11:3 *egg-sized*: The minimum measurement to become impure. See below 12:6 and *Tohorot* 2:1.

and its eater is deserving of death.
If it was not egg-sized,
the waters are pure,
but its eater is deserving of death.
R. Yose says:
If it is pure,
the water is pure.
If there was one purified for the waters of purgation
who immersed his head and most of himself into waters of purgation,
he became impure.

4 Anyone obliged to immerse in water
on the authority of the Torah
communicates impurity to sacral food,
terumah,
nonsacral food,
and tithes,
and is forbidden to go into the Temple.
After immersing,
he communicates impurity to sacral food,
and invalidates *terumah*—
the words of R. Meir.
But the Sages say:
He invalidates sacral food,
but is permitted nonsacral food and tithes.
And if he went into the Temple,
either before his immersion
or after his immersion,
he is liable.

5 Anyone obliged to immerse in water
on the authority of the Scribes
communicates impurity to sacral food,
and invalidates *terumah*,
and is permitted nonsacral food and tithes—
the words of R. Meir.
But the Sages forbid tithes.
After immersing,
he is permitted all of them,
and if he went into the Temple,
either before his immersion
or after his immersion,
he is exempt.

deserving of death at God's hands. See Leviticus 22:9–15.

his head and most of himself: See *Zavim* 5:12.

11:4 *obliged to immerse in water*: If he contracted impurity from a primary impurity. See *Kelim* 1:1–4.

After immersing: Before the sun sets. See above 3:7 and 8:7.

11:5 *on the authority of the Scribes*: See *Zavim* 5:12 and *Shabbat* 1:3.

6 Anyone obliged to immerse in water,
either on the authority of the Torah
or on the authority of the Scribes,
communicates impurity to the waters of purgation,
and the ash of purgation,
and the one who sprinkles the waters of purgation
by touching or carrying.
And the hyssop that has been made susceptible,
and unconsecrated water,
and an empty purgation-purified vessel—
by touching or carrying—
the words of R. Meir.
But the Sages say:
By touching,
but not by carrying.

11:7–12:1 *The Fitness of the Hyssop*

7 Any hyssop species
that has a modifying adjective in its name
is not valid.
"This is hyssop"
is valid.
Miniature hyssop,
blue hyssop,
Roman hyssop,
and desert hyssop,
is not valid.
[Hyssop that is] from impure *terumah* is not valid.
And with [hyssop from *terumah* that is] pure
he should not sprinkle,
but if he did sprinkle,
it is valid.
One does not sprinkle with embryonic shoots,
and not with budding branches.
He not culpable for the embryonic shoots
when going in the Temple.
R. Eliezer says:

11:6 *been made susceptible*: If one of seven liquids falls on it, it becomes susceptible to impurity. See *Makhshirin* 6:4 and Leviticus 11:34–38.

11:7 *"This is hyssop"*: See 3:10 above.

That of impure terumah: Hyssop that is *terumah* but has become impure.

when going in the Temple: He may enter the Temple without culpability, since he is pure, even though the sprinkling was done with embryonic shoots.

Not even for buds!
Which are embryonic shoots?
Stalks that have not hardened.

8 Hyssop that he used for sprinkling
is valid for use in purifying one with *tsara'at*.
If he picked it for wood,
and liquid fell on it,
he should dry it,
and it is valid.
If he picked it as food,
and liquid fell on it,
even if he dried it,
it is not valid.
If he picked it for the purgation offering,
it is treated as if it was picked for food—
the words of R. Meir.
R. Judah and R. Yose and R. Simeon say:
As if it was picked for wood.

9 The requirement[2] of the hyssop:
Three stems with three stalks.
R. Judah says:
Three each.
A hyssop that has three stems,
he should separate them,
and bind them together.
If he separated but did not bind,
bound but did not separate,
neither bound nor separated,
it is valid.
R. Yose says:
The requirement of the hyssop:
three stems containing three stalks,
and two should remain,
and a small amount of remnant.

[2] Lit. "commandment," here and below.

11:8 *one with tsara'at*: See *Nega'im* 14:1.

If he picked it for wood: Wood is not susceptible to impurity, but food is.

11:9 *Three each*: Three stalks on each stem, for a total of nine.

and two should remain: He may drop no more than one during the sprinkling.

and a small amount of remnant: If the hyssop disintegrates during the sprinkling, a small amount must remain in his hand for the sprinkling to be valid.

Chapter Twelve

12 He should attach a string
or a reed
to a stunted hyssop,
dip
and raise it,
hold the hyssop,
and sprinkle with it.
R. Judah and R. Simeon say:
Just as the sprinkling is with the hyssop,
so too
the dipping is with the hyssop.

12:2–6 *The Validity of the Sprinkling*

2 If doubt exists
whether he may have sprinkled
from the string,
or from the reed,
or from the stalk,
his sprinkling is not valid.
If doubt exists
whether he sprinkled
on two vessels,
or whether it dripped from one to the other,
his sprinkling is not valid.
If a needle was resting on ceramic,
and a doubt exists
if he sprinkled on it,
or whether it dripped from the ceramic,
his sprinkling is not valid.
He should dip and raise
from a narrow-mouthed flask
in his customary way.
R. Judah says:
For the first sprinkling.

12:1 *a stunted hyssop*: Or one made too short by breaking from overuse. He cannot hold it in his hand during the dipping without making physical contact with the water, invalidating it.

the dipping is with the hyssop alone. An intermediary handle is prohibited.

12:2 *from the string*: If the water of the sprinkling originated from anything but the hyssop, it is invalid.

For the first sprinkling: Drawing the hyssop out of the flask will not cause water to drip out, but reinserting it very well may. After the first sprinkling, he must take care of this.

If the waters of purgation dwindled,
he may dip even the tips of the stalks
and sprinkle,
provided he does not wipe.
If he intended to sprinkle to the front,
but he sprinkled rearward;
rearward,
but he sprinkled to the front,
his sprinkling is not valid.
To the front,
and he sprinkled
to the sides in front of him,
his sprinkling is valid.
One sprinkles people
with their consent,
or without their consent.
One sprinkles on people and on vessels,
even a hundred of them.

3 If he intended to sprinkle on something
that is susceptible to impurity,
but he sprinkled on something
that is not susceptible to impurity,
and some is still on the hyssop,
he need not repeat.
On something
that is not susceptible to impurity,
but he sprinkled on something
that is susceptible to impurity,
and some is still on the hyssop,
he should repeat.
On a person,
but he sprinkled on an animal,
and some is still on the hyssop,
he need not repeat.
On an animal,
but he sprinkled on a person,
and some is still on the hyssop,
he should repeat.
Water that drips
is valid.

provided he does not wipe: If the hyssop rubs against the side of the flask, it will have been moistened without being "dipped," and the correct procedure will have been violated.

without their consent: Volition is not required: the impure are purified merely through the physical act.

12:3 *he need not repeat* the dipping. No valid ritual has been performed yet, so the water may still be used, provided that a sufficient amount of water remains on the hyssop.

he should repeat: The ritual was effective, and the water remaining on the hyssop has become ineffective.

Therefore,
it still communicates impurity
as water of purgation.
4 If he sprinkles from a public window,
and he goes into the Temple,
but the waters are found to have been not valid,
he is exempt.
If he sprinkles from a private window,
and he goes into the Temple,
but the waters are found to have been not valid,
he is liable.
But with a high priest,
whether it was from a private window
or from a public window,
he is exempt,
since a high priest is never liable for going into the Temple.
They were wont to stagger
before the public window,
and would not refrain from trampling there.
For they said:
Water of purgation that performed its proper purpose
does not render impure.
5 One who is pure
can grasp an impure adze
in his hem and sprinkle onto it.
Even if it has a proper amount of water on it for sprinkling,
he is pure.
And how much water must there be to make a proper amount for sprinkling?
Enough that he can dip the tips of the stalks and sprinkle.
R. Judah says:
One pretends they are on a hyssop of copper.
6 If one sprinkles with impure hyssop:
if it was the size of an egg,

12:4 *If he sprinkles… and he goes*: These are two different people; the one entering the Temple has received the sprinkled water from the first.

from a public window: Doubtful purity in a public place is presumed pure. The opposite is true of a private place. See *Tohorot* 6:10.

exempt… liable: For a purgation sacrifice on account of having entered the Temple while impure.

would not refrain: The presence of used purgation water did not induce them to avoid the area for fear of becoming impure, since such water that had *performed its proper purpose* no longer rendered impure. See *Eduyot* 5:3.

12:5 *proper amount of water*: This is the amount that renders one who carries it impure.

copper: Metal does not absorb water. While the buds may have absorbed water, only the visible, unabsorbed water is accounted.

12:6 *the size of an egg*: The minimum measurement to become impure. See above 11:3 and *Tohorot* 2:1.

the waters are not valid,
and his sprinkling is not valid.
If it was not the size of an egg,
the waters are valid,
and his sprinkling is not valid.
It communicates impurity to its companion,
and its companion communicates impurity to its companion,
even if there are a hundred of them.

12:7–11 *Sprinkling Component Objects; Who May Sprinkle; When May They Sprinkle*

7 One purified for the purgation offering
whose hands became impure,
his body becomes impure.
He communicates impurity to his companion,
and his companion communicates impurity to his companion,
even if there are a hundred of them.
8 A bottle of water of purgation
whose outer surface became impure,
its insides become impure,
and it communicates impurity to its companion,
and its companion communicates impurity to its companion,
even if there are a hundred of them.
The bell and the ball are a connective.
He should not sprinkle a distaff for rough material on the rod,
or on the whorl.
But if he sprinkled,
he sprinkled.
For flax, they are a connective.
Leather of a cradle that is attached to its fasteners is a connective.
A frame is a connective for impurity or purity.
All drilled-out handles of vessels are connectives.
R. Yohanan b. Nuri says:
Even the wedged in.

It communicates impurity to its companion: Hyssop with the bulk of an egg will transmit impurity to other hyssop, thus disqualifying it from use for sprinkling. This phrase recurs in 12:7 and 8.

12:8 *its insides becomes impure*: See *Kelim* 25:9.

The bell and the ball are a connective: The ball is the sounding clapper in the bell. The two parts of these vessels listed in these passages are considered to be shared components of a single whole. They both become pure or impure when the appropriate contact occurs on either part. See *Kelim* 11:5, 11:7.

a distaff for rough material: Or perhaps, with the Tosefta, of Arbel near Tiberias. At issue is whether the rod and the whorl are deemed "connected" to the distaff.

But if he sprinkled, he sprinkled: It is effective, nonetheless.

9 Saddle bags,
a threshing sledge,
the corner of a bier,
a traveler's canteens,
a keychain,
the launderer's stitch,
and a garment stitched with Mixed Species
are connectives for impurity,
but not connectives for sprinkling.
10 The cover of a water heater that is connected to a chain—
the House of Shammai say:
It is a connective for impurity,
but not for sprinkling.
The House of Hillel say:
If he sprinkled onto the water heater,
he has sprinkled on the cover;
but if he sprinkled on the cover,
he has not sprinkled on the water heater.
All are valid to sprinkle,
except for a *tumtum*,
an *androgynos*,
a woman,
and a child that does not possess understanding.
A woman may assist him and sprinkle,
and she can grasp the water for him
while he dips and sprinkles.
If she grasped his hand,
even at the moment of sprinkling,
it is not valid.
11 If he dipped the hyssop by day,
and sprinkled by day,
it is valid.
By day and sprinkled by night;
by night and sprinkled by day,
it is not valid.
But he can immerse himself at night,
and sprinkle by day,
for one does not sprinkle until the sunrise.
But anything they did after dawn is valid.

12:9 *Saddle bags*, etc.: These components are designed to be detachable, as part of regular use. So, while joined they can contract impurity as a unit, but they must be sprinkled separately.

a garment stitched with Mixed Species: See Leviticus 19:19. The forbidden elements must be removed, dismembering the garment. Conceptually, this makes it detachable like the other things on this list.

12:10 *a tumtum*: A person with indeterminate genitalia. This person is treated as being of doubtful sex.

androgynos: A hermaphrodite. See above 5:4.

a woman: Numbers 19:18 describes a man performing the ritual. The Mishnah understands this as prescriptive.

Tractate Tohorot

Yair Furstenberg

Introduction

Overview

The term "purities" in the Mishnah denotes foods that must be treated in a state of purity. The laws governing such pure food constitute the major subject matter of this tractate "Purities." *Tohorot*, along with *Makhshirin*, *Tevul Yom*, and *Uqtsin* deals with the range of impurity diffusion among foods, and the possibility of restricting its effect.

Relationship to Scripture

Significantly, in marked contrast to the various "impurities," the field of "purities" is only weakly founded on any scriptural basis. All we learn from the Priestly Code is that an earthenware dish is defiled if a crawling thing falls directly into it (Leviticus 11:33), that food is protected from corpse impurity if placed in closed vessels (Numbers 19:15), and that impure persons are warned not to render holy foods impure (Leviticus 22:3–7). Nonetheless, as a result of this Levitical warning, the treatment of pure food became a major expression of religious piety during the Second Temple period. Subsequently, in rabbinic halakhah this practice was further shaped into an extremely complex system of degrees of impurity.

Main Ideas

The field of "purities" addresses two major issues pertaining to the spread of impurity among foods:

(a) *Susceptibility*: Under what conditions food can contract impurity from a carrier of impurity. In most cases (following Leviticus 11:38) food is rendered susceptible to impurity only after being moistened with liquids. Therefore, foods were left dry as long as possible to allow impure people to handle them.

(b) *Spread of impurity among foods*: Impurity travels from food to food through three basic modes of diffusion. Any attempt to restrict the spread of impurity is based on a careful knowledge of these principles. (1) *Connection of foods*: Occasionally, what seem to be different foods merge into one unit. (2) *Liquid connectivity*: The power of liquids to convey impurity is such that it preserves the level of impurity it conveys from food to food. Consequently, in some conditions liquids are considered as connecting separate foods into one unit (1:9; 8:8–9; 9:8). (3) *Contact*: In cases where separate articles of food are merely touching, the level of impurity decreases with the spread from one item to another. The scope of dissemination depends on the sanctity of the foods through which the impurity travels.

Another recurring issue concerning the diffusion of impurity from food to food is the minimal size required for the food to impart impurity. Whereas liquids convey impurity even through the smallest quantity, solid foods impart impurity only through a minimal volume of an egg's bulk (see especially 3:1–4).

Structure and Organization of the Tractate

Tohorot mentions in passing a large variety of foods and dishes, but it relates above all to the basic Mediterranean triad known also from the Torah (Deuteronomy 11:14): bread (chapters 1, 8), oil (chapter 9), and wine (10:3–8). The first chapters also offer a general survey of the basic rules concerning contact of separate foods and the system of impurity grades.

The purity of foods defines the basic structure of the tractate and its major concerns. At the same time, the practical attempt to maintain purity in a daily context entails one major problem: How does one cope with uncertainty, a key feature of daily conduct? The tractate refers to doubts with respect to the purity of foods (such as in 3:4–8), but this issue clearly exceeds the limited considerations of food purity. Consequently, two large units on the determination of doubts in general were added, and these now comprise a significant portion of the tractate as a whole.

The first unit includes chapters 4–6, which surveys what can be considered as the basic principles for determining cases of doubt. First, a case of doubt is a defined event of uncertain contact. Thus, if the impure object has no defined place, we cannot take the doubt into consideration. The second principle concerns the awareness of the person involved (chapter 5). The basic case of doubt arises when there is a factual foundation for the uncertainty, and the person is aware of two possibilities, for example if there are two loaves, one pure and one impure, and the person is unsure which one he ate (5:6). The last part of this subtractate (chapter 6) addresses whether a case took place in the public domain (if so, it is pure) or in the private domain (it is impure). The definition of these domains differs from the definition for Sabbath law (see *Shabbat*).

The second unit examines the relationship with the impure *am ha'arets*, one who is not careful in matters of purity (7:1–8.5; see also 10:1–3). The Mishnah describes a social reality in which the presence of the impure *am ha'arets* is unavoidable. As we learn, the *am ha'arets* does not necessarily have bad intentions, but he lacks the knowledge, care, and awareness required for maintaining purity. Since seclusion is presumably not an option, the pure associate can manage such a hazardous social reality only through constant supervision.

Special Notes for the Reader

Manuscript key:

K = Kaufmann A50; **P** = Parma, Palatina 3173 (de Rossi 138, 139); **C** = Cambridge (Lowe edition); **EP**: *editio princeps*; $\mathbf{P_2}$ = Parma, Palatina 2596 (de Rossi 497); **M** = Munich; **A** = Antonine 262

Tractate Tohorot

Chapter One

1:1–4 *Connection of Carcass Body Parts*

1 Thirteen things apply to the carcass of a pure bird:
it requires deliberation
but does not require liquids
in order to be rendered susceptible;
it conveys food impurity through an egg's bulk
and through an olive's bulk when in the throat;
one who eats it is obliged to wait past sundown;

1:1–4 The following mishnayot amalgamate laws mostly concerning carcass impurity of pure and impure birds and of animals. However, the major issue that strings these mishnayot together and sets the grounds for the following unit (1:5–9) is the issue of connectivity: what parts defile together with the carcass flesh? The Mishnah distinguishes the parts that convey carcass impurity from those parts that (like any other food) may contract impurity from external sources but do not convey carcass impurity. This latter kind of impurity is considered "food impurity" and is the subject matter of the tractate as a whole. Here we learn that food impurity is lighter than carcass impurity, but its spread is wider and thus its threat is greater.

1:1 *Thirteen*: The commentaries disagree as to which details in this mishnah should be counted toward the thirteen and which constitute a single item.

pure bird: In this context the distinction between pure and impure refers to species; "pure" birds are those that one may eat if properly slaughtered, while "impure" birds come from forbidden species. The distinction does not concern Levitical purity.

It requires deliberation but does not require liquids in order to be rendered susceptible: Impurity is conveyed only by foods prepared for consumption. The nature of the preparation varies, depending on the substance. A carcass that is not regularly consumed because it is forbidden in Scripture is considered as food only if one deliberately decides to eat it (see below 8:6). However, on account of its inherent impurity, the carcass of a pure bird does not have to be moistened in order to render it susceptible to impurity. This requirement applies only when substances contract impurity from external sources.

egg's bulk: The minimal quantity for any substance to be considered as food, so that it may render other foods coming in contact with it impure.

olive's bulk: The minimal quantity of carcass flesh that renders a person impure. According to rabbinic interpretation of Leviticus 17:15, animal carcass defiles through touch or carrying (Leviticus 11:39), but bird carcass defiles only through ingestion ("when in the throat").

wait past sundown: Following Leviticus 17:15 quoted above.

those eating it are culpable for entering[1] the Temple,
and *terumah* is burnt on its account;
one who eats a limb from a living [pure bird]
receives forty lashes;
slaughtering and pinching the nape of the neck purifies it,
if it is found to be a *terefah*—
the words of R. Meir.
R. Judah says:
They do not purify.
R. Yose says:
Slaughtering does purify it, but not pinching the nape of the neck.

2 The wings and the feathers contract and convey impurity
but do not join [with the meat to reach the minimum quantity].
R. Ishmael says:
The feathers do join.
The beak and claws contract and convey impurity
and join [with the meat].
R. Yose says:
Also the ends of the wings and the end of the tail join,
since they are left on fattened birds.

[1] **K**: "defiling."

culpable for entering the Temple: As in all biblically sanctioned impurities, people defiled by carcass impurity are banished from the Temple precincts.

and terumah is burnt on its account: According to Leviticus 22:5–6, a priest who is defiled by such impurities is warned not to touch holy foods, and the Sages interpret this warning as specifically referring to *terumah*.

one who eats a limb from a living pure bird: This is not a case of a carcass, but of a living bird. However, it is mentioned here as another one of the distinctions between pure and impure birds. The Torah prohibits eating living flesh that was not slaughtered beforehand (Deuteronomy 12:23), and this prohibition applies only to pure animals and birds.

slaughtering and pinching the nape of the neck purifies it: The bird that was slaughtered or had its neck pinched (a sacrificial form of killing birds) is not considered a carcass, and does not carry such impurity, even if it was found unfit for consumption due to fatal diseases found in it (*terefah*). A fuller version of this dispute appears in *Zevahim* 7:6.

1:2 *The wings and the feathers* are considered separate parts of the pure bird. At the same time, they may be rendered impure. Therefore, they impart impurity from and to the flesh, but they do not join with the meat to the minimal quantity required to cause impurity: less than an olive's bulk of pure bird flesh does not join with the wings to convey carcass impurity to one who eats it, and less than an egg's bulk does not join with the wings to convey food impurity to other foods. However, an olive's bulk of carcass impurity spreads from the meat to the wings, which in turn defile the person eating them. In addition, an egg's bulk of impure flesh conveys food impurity to the wings, and they spread the impurity to other foods.

The beak and claws are considered part of the meat and therefore join with it to the minimal bulk to convey carcass impurity.

since they are left on fattened birds: Presumably to improve their taste when being cooked.

3 The carcass of an impure bird
requires deliberation
and must be rendered susceptible.
It conveys food impurity through an egg's bulk,
and it renders the body unfit through half a half-loaf;
it does not convey impurity through an olive's bulk
when in the throat.
One who eats it is not obliged
to wait past sundown;
those eating it are not culpable
for entering the Temple,
but *terumah* is burnt due to it;
one who eats a limb
from a living [impure bird]
does not receive forty lashes,
and slaughtering it does not purify it.
The wings and the feathers contract and convey impurity
and join [with the meat].
The beak and claws contract and convey impurity
and join [with the meat].
4 Concerning an animal:
the hide, the broth, the sediment, the flayed-off meat, the bones, the sinews, the horns, and hooves
join [with the meat] to impart food impurity,
but not carcass impurity.

1:3 *The carcass of an impure bird*: Since Leviticus 17:13–15 refers to the carcass of that which may be eaten, a dead forbidden ("impure") bird does not convey severe carcass impurity, but only the lighter food impurity (the impurity of foods will be discussed in the latter part of the chapter). Almost all the differences between the carcass of an impure bird and that of a pure bird stem from this point.

must be rendered susceptible: Since the impure bird carries no inherent carcass impurity, it must be made susceptible to external sources of impurity by being moistened. See tractate *Makhshirin*.

renders the body unfit through half a half-loaf: That is, one who has consumed this quantity may not partake of *terumah* until the impurity has been removed. This measure is regularly employed to define the size of a meal. A loaf is taken to have a volume of eight eggs; thus, half a half-loaf is equal to about two eggs. In contrast to the carcass of a pure bird, which defiles through an egg's bulk, defiled foods render a person impure only if one has eaten a substantial portion. The eater then carries only light impurity (see below 2:2) that renders *terumah* impure but is removed through immersion alone and does not require waiting past sundown as in biblically sanctioned impurities.

those eating it are not culpable: Since the light impurity brought upon one by eating impure foods is considered a rabbinic decree, one is not culpable for entering the Temple while bearing this impurity.

slaughtering it does not purify it: Since carcass impurity does not apply to impure birds, slaughtering such a bird has no effect on its halakhic status. The impure bird should not be consumed, but it does not convey carcass impurity.

The wings and the feathers: In the case of impure birds, these parts join together with respect to food impurity only. Thus any part of it that can be consumed is considered food: Flesh, wings, feather, beaks, and claws.

1:4 *Concerning an animal*: Parallel to *Hullin* 9:8. The wider range of food impurity, in comparison to carcass impurity, is reflected with regard to animal carcasses as well. The carcass parts mentioned here are considered as foods and therefore convey food impurity, whereas carcass impurity is limited to the animal's meat.

Likewise,
one who slaughters an impure animal
for a gentile
and it is still convulsing—
it imparts food impurity,
but does not impart carcass impurity
until it dies,
or until one chops off its head.
[Scripture] extended the range of food impurity
beyond that of carcass impurity.

1:5–9 *Connection of Dough and Bread*

5 Food made impure by a primary impurity
and food made impure by reduced-degree impurity
join together to make impure as the lighter of the two.
How so?
Half an egg's bulk of first-degree food
mixed together with half an egg's bulk of second-degree food
is second.
Half an egg's bulk of second-degree food
mixed together with half an egg's bulk of third-degree food
is third.
An egg's bulk of first-degree food
mixed together with an egg's bulk of second-degree food
is first.
If he divided them,
each is second.[2]
If each of the parts[3]

[2] Lit. "this is second and this is second," and so too below.
[3] Lit. "this by itself and this by itself," and so too below.

Likewise: Even before the impure animal dies, parts of it are fit for consumption and therefore convey food impurity in contrast to carcass impurity.

1:5–6 These two mishnayot address various cases of mixtures of foods with different degrees of impurity (the basic system of grades of impurities is presented in the next chapter). The minimal quantity of food to convey impurity is an egg's bulk, and therefore all the rulings are based on one fundamental distinction. If each of the two foods is smaller than an egg's bulk, the mixture retains only the lighter impurity of the two. If, however, each is larger than an egg's bulk, the food at the higher degree of impurity extends its impurity to the rest of the mixture. Although at the outset the Mishnah sets a principle fitting only the first group of cases ("join together to defile as the lighter of the two"), the examples are of both kinds. It must be borne in mind that a lower degree of impurity is the more severe, since the number denotes the distance from the source of impurity.

1:5 *If he divided them*: Even after being joined together the two eggs in the mixture retain their original grades of impurity. Thus, when the mixture is divided each portion contains half of each egg, and the lighter impurity is maintained.

If each of the parts fell separately on a loaf of terumah: Food of the second degree does not defile everyday unconsecrated food, but it renders *terumah* unfit for consumption (see below, 2:3–5). Therefore, an egg's

fell separately on[4] a loaf of *terumah*,
they rendered it unfit.
If they both fell at once,
they rendered it second.

6 An egg's bulk of second-degree food
mixed together with an egg's bulk of third-degree food
is second.
If he divided them,
each of the two parts is third.
If each of the parts
fell separately on a loaf of *terumah*,
they did not render it unfit.
If they both fell at once,
they rendered it third.
An egg's bulk of first-degree food
mixed together with an egg's bulk of third-degree food
is second.
If he divided them,
each of the two parts
is second,
since even if a food of the third degree touches the first
it becomes second.
Two eggs' bulk of first-degree food
mixed together with two eggs' bulk of second-degree food
are first.
If he divided them,
each of the two parts is first;
into three or four parts,
they are second.
Two eggs' bulk of second-degree food
mixed together with two eggs' bulk of third-degree food
are second.
If he divided them,
each of the two parts
is second;
into three or four parts,
they are third.

[4] So **P**, **C**, **M**; **K**, **P**$_2$, **A**, and Genizah fragments: "into." See also below 1:6.

bulk comprising of a half an egg's bulk of first degree and a half an egg's bulk of second degree is considered of the second degree, and can only render the *terumah* to be of the third degree. If, however, the two eggs fall simultaneously, the combined egg's bulk of the first degree renders the *terumah* (as well as any other food) second degree.

1:6 These basic principles also apply to the cases in 1:6, which introduces two variations: (1) The mixture of egg's bulks of the first and third degree render the mixture to be second, following the principle that the severer impurity, of the first degree, defiles the other piece. (2) In the case where two foods of two eggs' bulk were mixed, the higher degree of impurity is maintained also after they are divided.

7 Pieces of dough attached together
and loaves attached to each other:
if one of them has been made impure by vermin,
all are first;
if they are separated,
all are first.
[Made impure] by liquids,
all are second;
if they are separated,
all are second.
[Made impure] by the hands,
all are third;
if they are separated,
all are third.

8 A piece of dough of the first degree,
which he adjoined to others:
all pieces are first;
if they were[5] separated,
it is first,
and the rest are second.
If it was second
and he adjoined others to it,
all pieces are second;
if they were separated,
it is second,
and the rest are third.
If it was third

[5] P_2, **K**, **P**, **C**, **A**, **M**: "it was." And again further below in the mishnah.

1:7–1:9 The Mishnah moves from mixtures to the spread of impurity through the connection of separate foods. It first deals with dough and loaves baked together, which may be considered at times as one extended food, and it then discusses the possibility of connecting completely separate loaves, through the properties of liquids.

1:7 *Pieces of dough attached together*: Each of them larger than an egg's bulk. As in the previous mishnayot, as long as the dough is left in one piece the degree of impurity is uniform, and is determined according the most severe impurity. However, in contrast to the above, if all pieces are defiled at once they remain at the same degree of impurity even after their separation.

vermin: A primary source of impurity, which therefore renders the dough to be of the first degree (Leviticus 11:32–38).

liquids serve as a powerful impurity conductor and are therefore considered to be in the first degree of impurity, rendering anything which comes in contact with them as second.

hands are decreed by the Sages to be of the second degree. They render *terumah* unfit, and can defile unconsecrated foods only through the facilitation of liquids (see 2:1 below).

1:8 This mishnah, in contrast to the previous one, deals with dough attached to other pieces only after having contracted impurity. Therefore, as in 1:5–6 above, the degree of impurity is maintained only when all pieces are attached. After being separated again the other pieces are considered to be one degree removed, as in any other case in which a defiled food touches other foods (see below 2:3–5).

and he adjoined others to it,
it is third,
and all are pure,
whether separated or not.

9 Holy bread loaves
with consecrated liquids in their indentations:[6]
If one of them was made impure by vermin,
all are impure.
In a case of *terumah*,
[the vermin] renders two grades impure and disqualifies one.
If there was running liquid between them,
even in a case of *terumah*,
all is impure.

Chapter Two

2:1 *Transmission of Impurity through Liquids*

2 If a woman was preserving vegetables in a pot
and she touched a leaf

[6] **P$_2$**, **P**, **C**: "and in their indentations"; **M**: "inside their holes"; **K**, **A**: "inside their indentations the liquids are consecrated."

whether separated or not: In this last case, the piece is of the third degree (for example, when impure hands touch *terumah* they render it third). This degree of impurity makes *terumah* unfit, but it does not have any defiling force (see 2:4 below). This degree of impurity cannot spread from the first piece to the others, and they remain pure.

1:9 The ability of impurity to spread among entirely separate loaves is quite limited and depends on the nature and degree of their sanctity and the presence of liquids.

Holy bread loaves impart impurity also when they are of the third degree (below, 2:6). Therefore, if vermin touches a row of loaves with liquids on them, the first is of the first degree (and so are the liquids on it), the second of the second degree (and the liquids are of the first). The third loaf, which is initially of the third degree, defiles the liquids on it, and renders them to be of the first degree (1:7 above). These liquids defile the loaf back again and render it impure in the second degree, so it in turn defiles the next loaf in the row to be of the third degree, which renders the liquids impure, and so on endlessly. Therefore, in the case of wet holy bread loaves the vermin impurity is spread without limit.

In a case of terumah: The third loaf is only rendered unfit and does not impart impurity. Thus, it cannot defile the water on it, and the impurity does not spread through the liquids. Although the second loaf defiles the liquids, they cannot in turn redefile the loaf, which remains of the second degree.

If there was running liquid: Once the liquids are rendered impure, they convey impurity to all loaves they touch.

2:1 *a woman* whose hands are impure (compare *Makhshirin* 5:11). Hands of second-degree impurity (1:7 above) defile liquids and render *terumah* unfit.

and she touched a leaf: At a dry spot, she renders that leaf unfit if it is *terumah*. However, this leaf does not spread the impurity to the rest of the pot.

outside the pot
or[7] at a dry spot,
even though it holds an egg's bulk,
[the leaf] is impure,
and the rest is pure.
If she touched a wet spot:
if it holds an egg's bulk,
all is impure.
If it does not hold an egg's bulk,
[the leaf] is impure,
and the rest is pure.
If it returned to the pot,
all is impure.
If she had come in contact with a carrier of corpse impurity
and she touched,
whether a wet or a dry spot,
if it holds an egg's bulk,
all is impure.
If it does not hold an egg's bulk,
[the leaf] is impure,
and the rest is pure.
If a *tevul yom* woman shook the pot
with unclean hands,
and she saw liquids on her hands,
and it is uncertain
whether they splashed from the pot
or whether the stalk touched her hand
the vegetable is disqualified,
and the pot is pure.

[7] **P_2**, **C**, **EP**; "or" absent in **K**, **P**, **A**; **M**: "if."

If she touched a wet spot: She renders the liquids impure in the first degree, and they in turn defile the leaf. The impurity is conveyed from the leaf to the rest of the pot only when bigger than an egg's bulk.

If it returned to the pot, all is impure: On account of the impure liquids on the leaf.

If she had come in contact with a carrier of corpse impurity: In this part of the mishnah the woman is in a more severe state of impurity, and she spreads impurity even without the actions of liquids. If she has come in direct contact with a primary source of impurity she is considered to carry first-degree impurity. In such a case, she defiles the leaf, in the second degree, and it in turn defiles the liquids in the dish.

If a tevul yom woman: This separate section refers to *Tevul Yom* 2:2, and not to the previous material here. The concept of *tevul yom* is elaborated in that tractate. Both impure hands and *tevul yom* are of second-degree impurity. However, the impurity of hands is a rabbinic decree, whereas the status of the *tevul yom* is biblically sanctioned. This holds implications in the case of a doubt. Doubts with regard to biblical laws are resolved stringently, whereas doubts with regard to rabbinic decrees are resolved leniently.

the vegetable is disqualified, and the pot is pure: Such a *terumah* vegetable is rendered unfit for consumption because it may have come in contact with the *tevul yom*. The rest of the pot can be defiled only by her hands, but it is doubtful whether her hands did in fact contact the liquids, and this kind of doubt is resolved leniently.

2:2–8 *The Degrees of Impurity*

2 R. Eliezer says:
One who eats food of first-degree impurity
is [rendered] first;
second degree—
second;
third degree—
third.
R. Joshua says:
One who eats food of first-degree
or[8] of second-degree impurity
is second;
third[-degree]—
second with respect to holy foods,
but not second with respect to *terumah*
(which was prepared at the purity level of holy foods).[9]
3 Nonsacral food of the first degree
[becomes] impure and renders impure;
the second [degree] is unfit [for consumption]
but does not render impure;
and the third
is eaten in a stew
containing *terumah*.

[8] Lit. "and."
[9] So $\mathbf{P_2}$; **K, C, P, A, D**: "purity level of *terumah*"; **M**: "in the case of unconsecrated food prepared according to the level of *terumah*."

2:2 According to rabbinic decree, eating defiled foods renders the person impure (see *Zavim* 5:12, compare Mark 7:15). The two rabbis here agree that eating food of the second degree renders one second and thus disqualified from eating *terumah*, but they dispute all other cases.

R. Eliezer holds that one is identified with the food he ingested, and he is considered to be on the same degree of impurity.

R. Joshua assumes that the food defiles by means of liquids. One's inner liquids, of the first degree, defile the person in the second degree.

third[-degree]—second with respect to holy foods: A food of the third degree is considered defiling only with respect to holy foods (see 2:5 below). Thus one who eats foods of the third degree can convey impurity through his inner liquids only to holy foods. He does not defile *terumah*, and the mishnah adds in closing that this is the case even if this *terumah* was prepared at a higher degree of purity (see below 2:6).

2:3–7 The system of grades of impurity is presented most comprehensively in these mishnayot. The capacity of impurity to spread through separate foods depends on their degree of sanctity. The holier the food is the more sensitive it is to impurity.

2:3 *Nonsacral food* is defiled both by a primary source of impurity, such as carcass or vermin, and by a secondary source of impurity. For example, a pot defiled by vermin conveys impurity to unconsecrated food. A loaf defiled by vermin renders another unconsecrated loaf impure in turn.

unfit foods cannot convey impurity to other foods through contact, but they remain at their degree of impurity within a mixture (see above 1:5).

eaten in a stew containing terumah: In this case there is no trace of impurity, and it does not render impure even when mixed with other foods.

4 *Terumah* of the first and of the second degree
[becomes] impure and renders impure.
The third [degree] is unfit
but does not render impure;
and the fourth
is eaten in a stew containing holy foods.

5 Holy food of the first, second, and third degree [becomes] impure and renders impure;
the fourth [degree] is unfit
but does not render impure,
and the fifth
is eaten in a stew containing holy foods.

6 Unconsecrated food of the second degree
renders unconsecrated liquids impure
and renders *terumah* foods unfit.
Terumah of the third degree
renders holy liquids impure
and renders holy foods unfit,
if it was prepared at the purity level of holy foods.
But if it was prepared at the purity level of *terumah*
it renders two grades impure,
and disqualifies one
in the case of holy foods.

7 R. Eleazar says:
All three are equal.
Holy foods, *terumah*, and unconsecrated foods of the first degree
render two [grades] impure
and disqualify one
with respect to holy foods;
they render one impure
and disqualify one
with respect to *terumah*,
and they disqualify unconsecrated food.
The second degree of all kinds
renders one [grade] impure
and disqualifies one
with respect to holy foods;
it renders unconsecrated liquids impure,

2:6 What happens if foods in different degrees of sanctity come in contact?

if it was prepared: This phrase refers back to the *terumah* at the head of the sentence. The mishnah comments that *terumah* not prepared according to a higher degree of purity is considered completely impure with respect to holy foods, as though it came in direct contact with a source of impurity (compare *Hagigah* 2:7).

2:7 *R. Eleazer* suggests a slightly different and more simplified system than that presented in 2:3–6.

All three: Unconsecrated food, *terumah*, and holy food. A practical difference between the systems arises in the case of unconsecrated food in the third degree in relation to holy foods. According to 2:3–6, this food has no defiling force, whereas R. Eleazar holds that it renders holy foods and liquids impure. This case is also addressed in the next mishnah.

and it disqualifies *terumah* foods.
The third degree of all kinds
renders holy liquids impure
and disqualifies holy foods.

8 One who eats food of second-degree [impurity]
may not work in the olive press.
And unconsecrated food prepared with holy food
follows the rules[10] of unconsecrated food.
R. Eliezer b. Zadok says:
It is follows the rules of *terumah*,
which renders two grades impure
and disqualifies one.

Chapter Three

3:1–4 *Transmission of Impurity through Liquids or Solids*

3 Broth, split beans, and milk:
As long as they are [in a state of] running liquid,
they are [considered] of first-degree impurity;
if they congeal,
they are [considered] second.
If they liquefy again:[11]
if they are exactly an egg's bulk,
they are pure;
more than an egg's bulk,
they are impure.
For once the first drop has been extracted
an egg's bulk renders it impure.

[10] Lit. "is like," here and in the next sentence.

[11] Lit. "return to being liquid."

2:8 *One who eats*: See above, 2:2. All rabbis agree that in this case the person is rendered impure in the second degree and may defile liquids. Therefore he is distanced from the olive press.

unconsecrated food prepared with holy food: The rabbis dispute the sensitivity to impurity of unconsecrated food that is intended for consumption together with holy food (for example, bread eaten in a sacrificial meal).

3:1 *split beans*: The assumption is that they make up wet mass.

running liquid: Wet enough to moisten anything it touches.

first-degree impurity: If they become impure, their impurity is of the first degree.

if they congeal: As they congeal, the liquids of the first degree render the solid parts second degree.

If they liquefy again: A drop of liquid is enough to convey impurity to the solidifying foods, but food conveys impurity to the extracted liquids only when it is the size of an egg's bulk. Therefore, food exactly the size of an egg's bulk cannot defile the liquids, for once they are extracted the volume of the food is too small to impart impurity.

2 R. Meir says:
Oil at all times
is [considered of] first[-degree impurity],
and the Sages say:
Honey as well.
R. Simeon of Shezur says:
Wine as well.
And a lump of olives that fell into an oven
that was [later] heated:
if it is exactly an egg's bulk,
it is pure;
more than an egg's bulk
is impure.
For once the first drop is extracted
the egg's bulk is defiled.
If they were separated[12]—
even a *se'ah* of them—
it is pure.
3 If one with corpse impurity pressed olives and grapes:
If [he pressed] exactly an egg's bulk
it is pure,
as long as he did not touch the moistened spot;
more than an egg's bulk is impure,
for once the first drop is extracted
the egg's bulk is defiled.
If he was a *zav* or a *zavah*
even a single fruit is impure,
for once the first drop is extracted
it is defiled though carrying.
If a *zav* milked a goat
the milk is impure,

[12] **P, EP**: "crumbs." The words are distinguished only by two very similar letters.

3:2 In contrast to the cases specified in 3:1, oil, honey, and wine are considered liquids, regardless of their physical state.

a lump of olives: In contrast to impure liquids, impure foods do not render the oven impure (see Leviticus 11:34). If a lump of impure olives fell into an oven, it is not rendered impure as long as they are in their solid form. As in the previous mishnah, these olives can render the extracted liquids impure, and they in turn render impure the oven, only if they amount to more than an egg's bulk.

If they were separated: Each of the impure olives does not render the liquids impure, and therefore the oven remains pure.

3:3 *one with corpse impurity* is a primary source of impurity, but he transmits impurity only through direct contact. In this case the person brought the olives and grapes to press, but made an effort not to touch the liquids.

If he was a zav or zavah: Suffering from a genital discharge. These persons convey impurity also indirectly, through "carrying" (see *Zavim* chapters 2–3), and so affect the liquids extracted from the fruits.

for once the first drop is extracted
it is defiled through carrying.
4 An egg's bulk of [impure] food
that was left in the sun and shriveled—
and so too an olives bulk of a corpse,
and an olive's bulk of a carcass,
and a lentil's bulk of [dead] creeping things,
an olive's bulk of *piggul*,
and an olive's bulk of leftover sacrificial meat,
and an egg's bulk of prohibited fat—
these are pure,
and one is not culpable on their account
for [violating] the rule of *piggul*, leftover sacrificial meat, and impure food.
If he left them in the rain and they swelled up,
they are impure
and one is culpable on their account
for [violating] the rule of *piggul*, leftover sacrificial meat, and impure food.

3:5–8 *Impurity Found around the House*

5 All impurities [are deemed]
according to the time they were found:
if impure—impure,
and if pure—pure.
If covered—covered,
and if exposed—exposed.
A needle found full of rust or broken
is pure,
for all impurities [are deemed]
according to the time they were found.

3:4 The mishnah addresses the possible change in the volume of an impure object due to weather conditions. To the question of impurity the mishnah adds other considerations that entail punishment only when a minimal quantity is consumed.

piggul: Sacrificial meat disqualified by the intention to bring it to the altar or consume it after its appropriate time. The consumption of this meat results in *karet* punishment (see *Zevahim* 2.2).

leftover sacrificial meat: See Leviticus 7:17–18.

prohibited fat: Leviticus 7:23–25.

3.5 *covered*: Corpse impurity spreads in the house ("tent") except for closed containers, which are saved from impurity (Numbers 19:15). If objects are now in such a container, we need not be concerned lest they were previously removed and became impure. If objects are now exposed, we cannot presume they were covered while the corpse was present.

A needle: Since only functioning utensils are susceptible to impurity, a broken or rusty needle is made pure. Thus, if we find such a needle we need not be concerned lest it was previously impure and possibly defiled other things around it.

6 If a deaf person, a legally incompetent person, or a minor
is found in an alleyway with impurity therein,
they are presumed to be in a state of purity.
All the intellectually sound are presumed to be in a state of impurity.
If anyone is not capable of being asked,
any doubtful case concerning him
is [deemed] pure.

7 If a child is found standing by a cemetery[13]
with lilies in his hand,
and the lilies come only from an impure place,
he is [deemed] pure,
since I [can] say
that someone else picked them
and handed [them] to him.
Similarly, if a donkey is found among graves,
his equipment is [deemed] pure.

8 If a child is found standing[14] by dough
and a piece of dough is in his hand,
R. Meir deems it pure,
and the Sages deem it impure,
since the child is accustomed[15] to slap it.
If a piece of dough with hen peckings
and impure liquids is in the house—
if there is enough space
between the liquids and the loaves
for them to wipe their beaks on the ground,

[13] In most manuscripts the term is "among graves"; **P**, **C**, **M**: "in a cemetery," which differs in only one letter.
[14] **K**, **P**, **C**, **M**, **EP** lack "standing." [15] Lit. "it is a child's way."

3:6 Only doubts that are associated with accountable persons may be deemed impure (see below chapter 5). One who is not aware of the situation is not in a state of doubt, and others cannot externally impose their judgment on the situation. Thus, paradoxically, mentally impaired persons, who are most prone to contract impurity on account of their lack of awareness, are not considered impure in the case of a doubt.

An *alleyway* is a private domain, and cases of doubt occurring there are considered impure (see chapter 6).

3:7 *a child is found standing by a cemetery*: Although the child most probably entered the cemetery to pick the lilies, he is deemed pure in this case of doubt since he is unaccountable. To justify the lenient ruling, the mishnah offers an alternative reconstruction of the occurrence.

Similarly, if a donkey: It is unknown whether the equipment overshadowed the graves, and the donkey cannot be asked.

3:8 A child who cannot mind himself is impure, and since it is probable that he has slapped the dough, the Sages deem it impure. Interestingly, since the child is unaccountable for his actions, the mishnah assesses his actions similarly to those of domestic animals (compare below 10:2).

a piece of dough with hen peckings: The hen is pure, but we fear that it has transferred the impure liquids to the dough. The question therefore is whether the liquids had dried out on the way to the dough, and the mishnah distinguishes in this respect between hens, cows, and dogs, and all other animals.

[the dough] is pure.
In the case of a cow or a dog,
if there is enough space
for them to lick their tongue.
In the case of other animals,
enough for the liquids to dry.
R. Eliezer b. Jacob deems the dough pure
in the case of a dog,
since he is clever
and does not regularly[16] abandon food to go for water.

Chapter Four

4:1–4 *Principles of Resolving Doubts: the Place of Impurity*

4 One who throws an impure object from place to place—
a loaf amidst keys
or a key amidst loaves,
it is [deemed] pure.
R. Judah says:
A loaf amidst keys is impure,
and a key amidst loaves is pure.
2 If [dead] vermin is in the mouth of a weasel
walking on loaves of *terumah*:
if there is a doubt
whether it touched the loaves or not,
this doubt is [deemed] pure.
3 If vermin was in the mouth of a weasel
or a carcass in a mouth of a dog,
and they walked by pure people,
or pure people walked by them—
this[17] doubt is [deemed] pure,
since the impurity has no resting place.

[16] Lit. "it is not his way."   [17] Lit. "their."

4:1 *One who throws impurity*: In the first case he threw a loaf amidst impure keys, and in the second, he threw an impure key amidst pure loaves, and it is uncertain whether one of the loaves came in contact with the impure key.

it is [deemed] pure: An impurity that has no definite place does not spur uncertainty. This principle is perhaps related to the need for full awareness when the doubt occurs, made explicit at the end of 4:3.

4:2 *this doubt is [deemed] pure*: The vermin has no resting place but travels with the animal. This rule applies with regard to both pure food (4:2) and pure people (4:3).

If they were pecking at them on the ground,
and someone said:
"I walked in that place, but I don't know whether I touched it or not"—
this doubt is deemed impure,
since the impurity has a resting place.

4 If an olive's bulk of a corpse is in the mouth of a raven,
and there is a doubt
whether it overshadowed
a person or artifacts
in a private domain—
the doubt [with regard to] the person is [deemed] impure;
the doubt [with regard to] the artifacts is [deemed] pure.
If one fills ten buckets
and vermin is found in one of them—
this bucket is impure
and the rest are pure.
If one pours from one vessel to another
and vermin is found in the bottom one—
the upper one is pure.

4:5–6 *Cases of Doubt for Which Terumah Is Burnt*

5 On account of six cases of doubt
one burns *terumah*:
(1) doubt regarding a grave area;
(2) soil coming from gentile land;

4:3 *If they were pecking at them on the ground*: The animal was not carrying the impurity, but pushing it around on the ground. Even though the vermin or carcass wasn't strictly stationary, it was on the ground in a small area; this is enough to "have a resting place."

4:4 *an olive's bulk of a corpse*: Corpse impurity is unique in that it defiles by overshadowing, and is thus considered to have a resting place even when in the air. A human being is capable of asking whether he was defiled or not; therefore he is deemed impure (see above, 3:6). The artifact cannot be asked, so it is deemed pure.

the rest are pure: We assume the vermin was in the bucket from the start, and did not originate in the shared cistern.

the upper one is pure: Here again we assume that from the start the vermin was in the bottom vessel.

4:5 *On account of six cases of doubt one burns terumah*: In contrast to standard cases of doubt that involve a one-time incident of possible contact with a source of impurity, these substances are a regular part of one's environment and require a fixed policy. Therefore, they are considered definitively impure. It is prohibited to burn *terumah* unless it is impure, so in most cases the *terumah* is "suspended" (neither consumed nor burned), but here the impurity is considered certain.

grave-area: Heb. *bet ha-peras*. A plowed field where a grave was lost. We do not know for sure where the crushed bones are, but it is assumed they have spread all over the field (*Oholot* 17:1).

soil coming from gentile land is considered impure, for the gentiles are believed to bury their dead everywhere and not in designated burial areas (*Oholot* 18:5–10).

(3) doubt regarding the clothes of *am ha'arets*;
(4) doubt regarding found artifacts;
(5) doubt regarding found spittle;
(6) doubt regarding human urine found alongside animal urine.
If one touches these things for certain,
[when] their impurity is uncertain,
one burns *terumah*.
R. Yose says:
[Such is the rule] even if the touch is uncertain,
[but it occurred] in a private domain.
But the Sages say:
In a private domain,
one leaves the *terumah* in suspense,
and in the public domain,
it is pure.

6 Two [deposits of] spittle,[18]
one impure and the other pure:
one leaves the *terumah* in suspense
if they were touched, carried, or[19] shifted in the private domain.
In the public domain [it is left in suspense]—
if it is moist when being touched,
and whether moist or dry when being carried.
If there was only one [deposit]

[18] Lit. "two spittles."
[19] So **C**; in the rest of the manuscripts "and," but the meaning is presumably the same.

clothes of an am ha'arets: An *am ha'arets* is not trustworthy in matters of purity (see chapter 7), and his clothes are considered a primary source of impurity; they defile people by contact (*Hagigah* 2:7).

found artifacts from an unknown source are considered impure.

spittle: The spit of gentiles and those suffering genital discharge is a primary source of impurity. Those careful in matters of purity are cautious to dispose of their spit, but it is quite common for people (specifically gentiles, see below 5:8) to spit in public and leave it exposed.

human urine: As in the case of spittle, urine of an impure person is defiling source of impurity. If the human urine is distinguishable from that of an animal, such as in cases of gathered urine in separate vessels, it is considered to come from an impure source.

R. Yose: The Sages and R. Yose dispute whether the *terumah* is burnt when the doubt is double and the contact itself with these substances is uncertain.

4:6 *Two [deposits of] spittle*: One deposit is known to come from a pure person, and the other from an unknown source (see previous mishnah), but it is uncertain which of them was touched.

if they were touched: That is, either of the two.

in the private domain: The doubt is resolved towards stringency. In this case the *terumah* cannot be burnt since its impurity is uncertain, so it is suspended and may not be used.

In the public domain: Doubts occurring in the public domain are normally ruled to be pure, though if the doubt takes place on the person's body it is treated as though it happened in a private domain.

If there one only one [deposit]: The mishnah repeats the ruling in the previous mishnah concerning spittle found in the public domain.

and someone touched it, carried it, or shifted it
in the public domain—
one burns *terumah* on its account.
Needless to say,
[also] in the private domain.

4:7–13 *Cases of Doubt Deemed Pure by the Sages*

7 These cases of doubt were deemed pure by the Sages:
doubt concerning drawn water for the immersion pool,
doubt concerning impurity floating on the water,
doubt concerning liquids
(if [the doubt is whether] they have contracted impurity,
it is deemed impure;
if it is [whether] they have conveyed impurity,
it is deemed pure),
doubt concerning hands—
[whether] they have contracted impurity, conveyed it, or been purified—
is deemed pure,
doubt occurring in the public domain,
doubt with regard to words of the Scribes,
doubt in the case of unconsecrated foods,
doubt concerning vermin [impurity],
doubt concerning [skin] afflictions,
doubt concerning *nezirut*,

4:7 *These cases of doubt were deemed pure*: Even in the private domain. Most of the cases specified in this mishnah are further elaborated in the following mishnayot.

drawn water for the immersion pool: Three *log* of drawn water invalidate an immersion pool, but in a case of uncertainty it is deemed pure (see *Miqva'ot* 2:3–4).

impurity floating on the water is deemed pure, similarly to cases of impurity without a resting place (above 4:1–3).

liquids: The susceptibility of liquids to impurity is scripturally based, and therefore in the case of a doubt it is impure, but its power to convey impurity is understood to be a rabbinic decree. Therefore a doubt concerning the spread of purity through liquids is deemed pure.

hands: Hand impurity is a rabbinic decree (*Yadayim* 3:2), and therefore the ruling is lenient in any case of doubt.

words of the scribes: These cases are specified below, 4:11.

doubt in the case of unconsecrated foods: That is, any doubt that occurs to those eating their daily food in purity, such as the Pharisees (see below 4:12) and the *haverim*.

doubt concerning vermin [impurity]: Following 3:6 and 9:9, if vermin is found burnt on some food we only take into consideration its current state and the food is deemed pure.

[skin] afflictions: See below, 4:12, for the following items.

doubt concerning nezirut: If someone made a *nazir* vow, on the condition that some event take place, and it is uncertain whether it actually happened, the vow does not apply.

doubt concerning firstborn,
doubt concerning sacrifices.

8 "Doubt concerning impurity floating on the water,"
whether in vessels or on the ground.[20]
R. Simeon says:
In vessels it is impure,
and on the ground it is pure.
R. Judah says:
If the doubt arises while descending,
he is impure;
if while ascending,
he is deemed pure.[21]
R. Yose says:
Even if there was space therein
only for a person and the impurity,
he is pure.

9 "A doubt concerning liquids—
whether they contracted impurity—
is deemed impure":
How so?
An impure person
who stretched his leg
amidst pure liquids,
and there is a doubt
whether he came in contact
or did not come in contact with them—
this doubt is deemed impure.
If he was holding an impure loaf
and he threw[22] it amidst pure liquids,
and there is a doubt whether it came
or did not come in contact with them—
it is deemed impure.

[20] In **K**, **P**, **C**, **A** in plural. [21] In **K** in plural: "they are impure... they are pure."
[22] So in $\mathbf{P}_2$; **K**, **P**, **L**, **A**, **M**: "he stretched his arm."

firstborn: In cases it is uncertain whether an animal or person is a firstborn, or whether the mother suffered a previous miscarriage.

sacrifices: See below 4:13.

4:8 *R. Simeon* claims that the floating impurity has no resting place and any case of doubt concerning it is deemed pure, but if the water is in a vessel it assumes its place.

R. Judah says the person immersing in the water *is impure*. When one descends into the water it is likely that the impurity has been drawn near the person and has conveyed its impurity. In contrast, when a person ascends from the water, things in the water tend to move away.

4:9 In the first two cases, concerning both people and foods, the question is whether the water contracted impurity from the impure source. In the last case the question is whether the impure liquids on the stick imparted impurity to the loaves.

"Whether the liquids conveyed impurity—
is deemed pure."
How so?
If one held a stick covered with impure liquids,
and he threw it amidst pure loaves,
and there is a doubt whether it touched them
or did not touch them,
this doubt is deemed pure.

10 R. Yose says:
[Concerning] a doubt concerning liquids:
with regard to foods it is deemed impure,
and with regard to utensils it is deemed pure.
How so?
Two jars,
one impure and one pure,
and someone prepared dough
with one of them,
and there is a doubt whether he prepared it
from the impure jar
or from the pure jar—
this is
"[concerning] a doubt concerning liquids:
with regard to foods it is deemed impure,
and with regard to utensils is deemed pure."

11 "Doubt concerning hands—
[whether] they have contracted impurity, conveyed it, or been purified"—
is deemed pure;
"doubt occurring in the public domain"—
is deemed pure;
"doubt with regard to words of the Scribes."
If one ate impure foods,
drank impure liquids,
immersed his head and most of his body in drawn water,
or if three *log* of drawn water
fell on his head

4:10 *R. Yose* holds that the power of liquids to impart impurity to other foods is scripturally based, and in such cases the doubt is deemed impure, whereas the power of liquids to impart impurity to vessels is a rabbinic decree, and therefore in the case of a doubt the vessel is deemed pure.

Two jars: Containing water. In such a case, the dough prepared with this water is deemed pure, but the jars containing it are impure.

4:11 *If one ate impure foods*: Explicates *doubt with regard to words of the Scribes* in the preceding line. The Sages decreed that specific actions (listed in *Zavim* 5:12) render people impure, but any doubt concerning these actions is deemed pure. These decrees seem to reject nonrabbinic purity practices, by preventing the practitioner from eating *terumah*.

But if he ate a primary source of impurity…is deemed impure: In contrast to the former decrees, which created new modes of impurity, the expansion of biblical modes of defilement is not included in this category of doubts that are deemed pure.

and on most of his body—
doubt with regard to this person
is deemed pure.
But if he ate
a primary source of impurity
according to the words of the Scribes—
a doubt with regard to this person
is deemed impure.

12 "A doubt in the case of unconsecrated foods":
this refers to purity of the Pharisees.
"A doubt concerning vermin [impurity]"
is deemed according to the state in which they are found.
"A doubt concerning [skin] afflictions"
in the beginning is pure,
for as long as he was not declared impure.
After he was declared impure,
he is impure in a case of doubt.
"A doubt concerning the *nazir*,"
is deemed permitted.
"A doubt concerning firstborn":
either human firstborn or animal firstborn,
whether pure or impure,
since anyone claiming [property] from his fellow
has the burden of proof.

13 "A doubt concerning sacrifices":
a woman who suffered five uncertain miscarriages,
or five uncertain abnormal discharges,
brings only one sacrifice,
and may eat animal offerings;
the rest are not an obligation upon her.

4:12 *purity of the Pharisees*: Lit. "purity of abstinence," referring to the practice of the Pharisees and of the *haverim* or "associates" to eat their ordinary food in purity (see *Hagigah* 2:7; *Demai* 2:3).

"A doubt concerning [skin] afflictions": In the case of two afflictions, and it is uncertain which of them expanded and is defiling (see *Nega'im* 5:4–5).

in the beginning is pure: The priest cannot pronounce the affliction to be impure if he is not certain which of them expanded. However, once the affliction was declared impure by the priest, it remains so even in cases of doubt.

anyone claiming [property]: The priest demanding a firstborn animal or redemption money for a firstborn human for himself must prove he is in fact entitled to it.

4:13 This last case does not actually belong to this list of doubts. The uncertain miscarriages or discharges do not exempt the woman completely from bringing the sacrifice, but only restrict her obligation to the minimum. According to *Keritot* 1:7 this law was decreed by Rabban Simeon b. Gamaliel, in order to lower the prices of bird sacrifices.

Chapter Five

5:1–6 *Contact with Pairs of Pure and Impure*

5 Vermin and a frog in the public domain,
and so too an olive's bulk of a corpse and an olive's bulk of a carcass, and a bone of a corpse and a bone of a carcass,
and a piece of soil from a pure land and a piece of soil from gentile land,[23]
two paths, one impure and one pure:
if someone walked on one and it is unknown in which of them,
or overshadowed one and it is unknown over which of them,
or shifted one and it is unknown which of them—
R. Aqiva[24] deems him impure,
and the Sages deem him pure.

2 One who says
"I have touched this,
but I do not know whether it is impure or it is pure,"
[or] "I have touched, but I don't know which of the two I touched":
R. Aqiva deems him impure,
and the Sages deem him pure.
R. Yose deems all these cases impure,
but deems pure the case of a path,
since people regularly[25] walk
but do not touch.

[23] **K**, **P**, **C**, **A**, **M** add "a piece of soil from a grave area and a piece of soil from a pure land."
[24] **K**: "Joshua."
[25] Lit. "it is the way of people... but it is not their way..."

5:1 *Vermin and a frog*: Only the former is impure.

A *corpse* defiles through overshadow.

A *carcass* defiles only through contact or carrying.

The *bone of a carcass* does not defile, whereas a human bone does (see *Yadayim* 4:6).

soil from gentile land: See above, 4:5.

if someone walked: This sentence refers only to the three latter cases, and not to the first case of frog and vermin that contaminates through touch.

R. Aqiva holds that cases of uncertainty resulting from active human involvement are deemed impure. According to the Sages these cases are no different from any other case of doubt in the public domain.

5:2 The mishnah repeats the views of R. Aqiva and the Sages, but adds R. Yose's mediating opinion. In general, he follows R. Aqiva his teacher, but he does not consider walking to be an active involvement since it is a semiautomatic motion and in this case it was not exercised directly towards the possible source of impurity.

3 Two paths, one impure and one pure:
if someone walked on one of them,
prepared pure food,
and it was eaten,
he was sprinkled once and twice,
immersed
and became pure,
and walked on the second path
and prepared pure food—
these [foods] are pure.
If the first food remains,
both are left in suspense.
If he has not immersed meanwhile,
the first are left in suspense,
and the second are to be burnt.

4 Vermin and a frog in the public domain:
if someone touched one of them,
prepared pure food,
and it was eaten,
he immersed,
touched the other
and prepared pure food—
these [foods] are pure.
If the first food remains,
both foods are left in suspense.
If he has not immersed meanwhile,
the first are left in suspense,
and the second are to be burnt.

5:3–4 In this pair of mishnayot, a person comes into contact with two uncertain sources of impurity consecutively, inevitably causing defilement.

5:3 *if someone walked on one of them*: In the public domain and subsequently prepares food. As in 5:1–2, according to the predominant opinion such a case of doubt is deemed pure.

sprinkled once and twice: In the case of the paths the presumed impurity is from a buried corpse, and so the full regimen of purification from corpse impurity (Numbers 19) is necessary. In the second case, the only concern is possible contact with impure vermin.

walked on the second path: The person has certainly encountered impurity at one point or another, but he underwent purification in between so each of the situations is examined separately and thus is deemed pure, as in any case of doubt in the public domain.

If the first food remains: One of the foods is certainly impure; we cannot determine which of them is to be burnt, so both are left in suspense.

5:4 In the case of *vermin*, only immersion is required, not a full regimen of purification.

If he has not immersed: The second food has certainly become impure and is to be burnt.

5 Two paths, one pure and one impure:
if someone walked on one of them
and prepared pure food,
and his fellow came
and walked on the second
and prepared pure food—
R. Judah says:
If they inquired of each by himself
they are both pure,
but if they inquired both together,
they are impure.
R. Yose says:
In either case the food is impure.

6 Two loaves, one pure and the other impure:
if someone ate one of them
and prepared pure food,
and his fellow came
and ate the second
and prepared pure food,
R. Judah says:
If they inquired of each by himself
they are both pure,
but if they inquired both together,
they are impure.
R. Yose says:
In either case they are impure.

5:7–8 *Uncertain Contact with Impure People*

7 One who sat in the public domain
and another person came
and stepped on his clothes,
or if one spat
and [the other] touched his spit—
on account of the spit,

5:5–6 In this pair of mishnayot two separate people simultaneously come in contact with objects of uncertain impurity.

5:5 *R. Judah says: If they inquired of each by himself*: With regard to each of them we apply the basic rule that cases of uncertainty in the public domain are deemed pure. However, if they come together their impurity cannot be ignored and they must undergo purification.

5:6 *if someone ate one of them and prepared pure food* he renders *terumah* impure (compare 2:2; 2:7).

5:7 *One who sat*: In the case of touch in the public sphere with an unknown person, the mishnah assumes the other person conveys *zav* impurity. Therefore he renders clothes he steps on impure, and his spittle does the same to other people. As in 4:5 above, spittle found on the street is regularly deemed impure.

terumah is burnt;
with respect to the clothes,
one follows the majority.
If one slept in the public domain and woke up—
his garments carry *midras* impurity—
the words of R. Meir,
but the Sages deem it pure.
If he touched someone during the night,
and it is unknown
whether that person was alive or dead,
and in the morning he woke up and found him dead—
R. Meir deems him pure,
but the Sages deem him impure,
since all impurities [are deemed]
according to the time they are found.

8 If there is one legally incompetent woman,
or a gentile woman,
or a Samaritan woman
in a town,
all spits in the town are impure.
If a woman stepped on one's clothes
or sat with him in a boat:
if she knows that he eats *terumah*,
his garments are pure;
otherwise, he must ask her.

with respect to the clothes, one follows the majority: According to rabbinic ruling gentiles convey *zav* impurity. Therefore, if the majority of the residents are gentiles, the clothes—like the clothes of the *zav* himself—impart severe *midras* impurity.

If one slept: According to R. Meir, the clothes carry *midras* impurity even if only a minority of the people there are gentiles or carry *zav* impurity, since the person cannot know how many people crossed him during his sleep.

since all impurities: Above, 3:4–5.

5:8 *legally incompetent woman*: The mishnah assumes that any Jewish woman, even the wife of an *am ha'arets* who is not generally careful in matters of purity, will follow the rabbinic ordinances concerning menstrual impurity (see *Niddah* 4:1–2) and dispose of her spit when she is impure. The only exception is a legally incompetent, intellectually impaired woman, who is not properly attentive to her body.

gentile woman: Although they are not subject to impurity according to Scripture, the Sages decreed that gentile women are impure to the same degree as menstruants. See *Niddah* 4:3.

Samaritan woman: The Samaritans have a different system from that of the Sages for calculating their impure days and they do not distinguish different kinds of menstruation blood, therefore they are considered perpetually impure. See *Niddah* 4:1.

if she knows that he eats terumah: Both here and in 8:2, the nonrabbis, whether this woman sitting in the boat or the *am ha'arets* in the mishnah below, are considered competent in matters of purity, and are trusted to mind their impurity with respect to the priestly *terumah*.

5:9 *A Doubt Raised by Others*

9 If a witness says: "You have become impure,"
and he says: "I have not become impure,"
he is pure.
If two say: "You have become impure,"
and he says: "I have not become impure,"
R. Meir deems [him] impure,
and the Sages say:
He is trustworthy with regard to himself.
If a witness says: "He has become impure,"
and two say: "He has not become impure"—
whether in a private or in a public domain—
he is pure.
If two witnesses say: "He has become impure,"
and one says: "He has not become impure"—
whether in a private or in a public domain—
he is impure.
If a witness says: "He has become impure,"
and a witness says: "He has not become impure";
a woman says: "He has become impure,"
and a woman says: "He has not become impure"—
in the case of a private domain he is impure,
and in the case of a public domain he is pure.

Chapter Six

6:1–3 *Movement from Domain to Domain*

6 If a place that was a private domain
became a public domain

5:9 *a witness*: A sole witness is not more trustworthy than the person himself.

two say: According to the Sages one's self-perception is held in higher esteem than two witnesses. Although witnesses are considered to supply the ultimate kind of evidence, in the sphere of purity there is no substitute for self-awareness, which is indispensable to the maintenance of purity.

two say: "He has not become impure": Although one witness is deemed trustworthy in such matters, his testimony is worthless in face of the contradictory testimony of the two witnesses.

a witness...and a witness: In these last cases there is equal evidence for both sides of the doubt, so the basic distinction between the public and private domains, to be discussed in detail in the next chapter, is applied.

6:1 The distinction between private and public domains with regard to cases of doubt is never justified in the mishnah. With regard to Sabbath, the prohibition to carry in and out of the house and carry in the market is rooted in Scripture, and subsequently the Sages or their forerunners divided all space into private and public domains. With respect to doubts in cases of impurity, the assumption is that private and hidden

and again became a private domain—
while a private domain,
doubts occurring in it[26] are [deemed] impure;
while a public domain,
doubts occurring in it are [deemed] pure.
If a dying person[27] was in the private domain,
and they removed him to the public domain
and brought him back to the private domain—
when he is in the private domain,
the doubt concerning him is [deemed] impure;
when he is in the public domain,
the doubt concerning him is [deemed] pure.
R. Simeon says:
The public domain interrupts.

2 There are four doubts that R. Joshua deems impure,
and the Sages deem pure.
How so?
(1) When the impure person is standing
and the pure person passes by;
(2) when the pure person is standing
and the impure person passes by;
(3) when the impurity is in the private domain
and the purity is in the public domain;
(4) when the purity is in the private domain
and the impurity is in the public domain.
In all these cases,
if it is uncertain whether he touched,
or whether he overshadowed it,
or whether he shifted it—
R. Joshua deems it impure,
and the Sages deem it pure.

[26] Lit. "its doubt is," and so throughout.

[27] Lit. "one in danger."

areas are more liable to impurity, and this determines the nature of the domains. Other texts tie this distinction to the case of *sotah*, the woman who is suspected of impurity on account of her intimate actions in the private domain.

a dying person: The case concerns a person who is found to have died but the time and location of his death are unknown. If he is found in a private domain then anything with him, even items from his previous stay in the private domain, is deemed impure; if he is found in the public domain, even those items that were with him in a private domain are deemed pure.

R. Simeon says: The public domain interrupts: Since we assume the person may have been alive while in the public domain and all that came in contact with him is pure, we must inevitably assume that he was still alive beforehand in the private domain.

6:2 In all four cases disputed by R. Joshua and the Sages, the pure and impure do not share the same space when the uncertain contact between them takes place. In the first two cases, one of them is in motion, and thus not fixed to that domain. In the latter two cases, each of them is present in a separate domain. According to the Sages, cases of doubt occurring in the private domain are deemed impure only if both partners belong equally to that space. This mishnah also appears at *Eduyot* 3:7.

3 If a tree is standing in a public domain
and there is an impurity in it:
if someone climbs it,
and it is uncertain whether he touched
or did not touch,
his doubt is deemed impure.
If someone stretched his hand into a hole with impurity in it,
and it is uncertain whether he touched
or did not touch,
his doubt is deemed impure.
If an impure shop is open to the public domain,
and it is uncertain whether he entered it
or did not enter,
his doubt is deemed pure.[28]
Two stores, one impure and the other pure:
if one entered one of them,
and it is uncertain whether he entered the impure
or the pure one,
his doubt is deemed impure.

6:4–6 *The Contrast between the Two Domains*

4 However much you can multiply doubts
and doubts of doubts,
in the private domain
the case is deemed impure,
and in the public domain,
pure.
How so?
If someone entered an alley

[28] **P** adds "if it is uncertain whether he touched or did not touch, his doubt is deemed pure."

6:3 *a tree*: Although the tree is standing in the public domain, it is a place to itself. Thus if one reaches into the tree, and it is unsure whether he touched an impure object, he is deemed impure as if in a private domain.

If someone stretched his hand: As he is standing in the public domain.

a hole is considered a private domain.

an impure shop: A private domain. If he is uncertain whether he entered the place, his doubt belongs to the public domain. If, however, he knows he entered, but is unsure where, the doubt belongs to the private domain and is deemed impure.

6:4 *How so?* Although the opening clause refers to doubts in both the private and the public domain, the complex example relates only to such cases in the private domain. Despite the uncertainty of so many of the details and the chance that the person was not defiled, we follow the basic rule, which deems doubts in the private domain impure.

alley: A private domain. The movement is within the private domain. Whereas previous mishnayot refer to possible transition between public and private domains, this mishnah addresses the difficulty of reconstructing one's motion within the complex urban space.

and there was an impurity in a courtyard,
and there is a doubt whether he entered
or did not enter;
[or] if there was impurity in a house,
and there is a doubt whether he entered
or did not enter;
and even if he did enter,
there is a doubt whether the impurity was present
or was not present;
and even if it was present,
there is doubt whether it was the necessary quantity
or was not the necessary quantity;
and even if it was the necessary quantity,
there is doubt whether it was pure
or impure;
and even if it was impure,
there is doubt whether he touched [it]
or did not touch [it]—
his doubt is deemed impure.
R. Eleazar says:
A doubt concerning his entry
is deemed pure,
a doubt concerning
his touch is deemed impure.

5 If someone entered a valley
during the rainy season
and there was an impurity
in one specific field,
and he said:
"I walked to that place,
but I don't know whether I entered that field
or I did not enter,"
R. Eleazar[29] deems [him] pure,
and the Sages deem [him] impure.

6 A doubt occurring in a private domain is impure,
unless he says: "I have not touched,"

[29] In a Genizah fragment: "Aqiva."

R. Eleazar applies in this case the principle appearing in 6:3 with regard to the movement from public to private domain. If one is uncertain whether he entered an area, even within the private domain, the doubt is deemed pure.

6:5 *a valley* with fields *during the rainy season* is considered a private domain (see below 6:7). The movement from the valley to a private field corresponds to the previous case of walking from an alley into the courtyard. In this case too, R. Eleazar applies the principle in 6:3: a doubt concerning uncertain entry to an area is deemed pure.

6:6 *A doubt occurring*: This is a reformulation of the statement in 6:4. Any level of uncertainty is deemed pure in the public domain, even if the person was most likely defiled, and any uncertainty is deemed impure in the private domain, even if he most likely did not come in contact with impurity.

and a doubt occurring in the public domain is pure,
unless he says: "I have touched."

6:6 cont.–9 *Domains with regard to Sabbath and Impurity*

What is [considered] a private domain?
The paths of Bet Gilgul and the like
are a private domain with regard to Sabbath
and a public domain with regard to impurity.
Said R. Eleazar,
The paths of Bet Gilgul were mentioned
as being a private domain with regard to both.
Paths that are open to wells, ditches, and winepresses
are a private domain with regard to Sabbath
and a public domain with regard to impurity.
7 A valley in the sunny season
is a private domain with regard to Sabbath
and a public domain with regard to impurity.
In the rainy season,
it is a private domain with regard to both.
8 A basilica is a private domain with regard to Sabbath
and a public domain with regard to impurity.
R. Judah says:
If while standing in this entrance
he can see those coming in and out of the other entrance,
it is a private domain with regard to both.
Otherwise, it is a private domain with regard to Sabbath
and a public domain with regard to impurity.

paths of Bet Gilgul: Unknown place, but the paths there were apparently very narrow and winding or extremely steep, so that people could walk but not carry loads.

R. Eleazar disputes the exact formulation of the early mishnah concerning Bet Gilgul.

Paths that are open to wells, etc.: Such paths are publicly used, but they end in a closed area and are considered as an extension of that area and so a private domain with respect to Sabbath.

6:7 *valley*: With respect to Sabbath the prohibition of carrying in the public domain specifically relates to settled areas, since it is associated with bringing goods to the market, and Nehemiah 10:31 and 13:15–22 explicitly refers to Jerusalem. With respect to impurity, the only consideration is the size of the crowd. Many people come to cultivate their fields during the summer and therefore the whole area is considered a public domain.

6:8 The mishnah turns from agricultural nonurban environs to a conspicuously Roman urban context.

basilica: An open public building characteristically located by the forum in Roman cities (see below 6:9). It serves the public, but on account of its closed structure it is considered a private domain with regard to Sabbath.

R. Judah: If one can see all the people from one side of the basilica to the other, it presumably does not serve a large crowd, and is closer to being a private domain.

9 A forum is a private domain with regard to Sabbath
and a public domain with regard to impurity,
and so are the sides.
R. Meir says:
The sides are a private domain with regard to both.
A stoa is a private domain with regard to Sabbath
and a public domain with regard to impurity.
A courtyard
that the public enters on one side
and exits on the other
is a private domain with regard to Sabbath
and a public domain with regard to impurity.

Chapter Seven

7:1–6 *Am Ha'arets in the House of a Haver*

7 If a potter put down his pots
and descended to drink,
the inner [pots] are pure
and the outer are impure.
Said R. Yose:
When does this apply?
With untied pots,
but if they are tied together,
all is pure.
If someone hands his key to *am ha'arets*,
the house is pure,
since he only handed him the keeping of the key.

6:9 *forum*: The Roman public square, surrounded by the *stoa* mentioned below, a covered walkway lined with columns. Some editions start a new mishnah (6:10) with *a stoa*.

7:1 Before turning to the main subject of the chapter, concerning an *am ha'arets* who is not scrupulous in matters of purity, the mishnah addresses one last case of uncertain impurities in the public domain.

If a potter put down his pots in the middle of the road: the pots have been left unguarded in a place where impure people may have touched or otherwise affected them.

the outer are impure: For we fear that a carrier of severe *zav* impurity (such as a gentile, or a menstruating woman) shifted these pots as he walked by (compare above, 5:7).

if they are tied together: It is impossible to unintentionally shift individual pots, and all the stack is pure.

If someone hands his key: It is assumed that the houseowner is a *haver* ("associate"). The *am ha'arets* has access to the *haver* 's house, but even though he holds the key to the house we assume he would not enter without permission. In the following cases, however, the *am ha'arets* was left inside the house.

2 One who leaves an *am ha'arets* inside his house:
if he left him awake and finds him awake,
awake and finds him asleep,
asleep and he finds him asleep—
the house is pure;
asleep and he finds him awake—
the house is impure—
the words of R. Meir.
But the Sages say:
Only the places that he can reach out and touch are impure.
3 If someone leaves artisans inside his house,
the house is impure—
the words of R. Meir.
But the Sages say:
Only the places that they can reach out and touch are impure.
4 If the wife of a *haver*
left the wife of an *am ha'arets*
grinding inside her house:
if the millstone stopped,
the house is impure.
If the millstone did not stop,
only the places that she can reach out and touch are impure.
If there were two of them,
the house is impure in either case,
for one [can] grind and the other handle [household effects]—
the words of R. Meir,
but the Sages say:
Only the places that they can reach out and touch are impure.

7:2 This and the following mishnayot assume that the only way to manage the impurity of an *am ha'arets* is through direct supervision. If he is left alone, he will allow himself to touch the house indiscriminately and defile its contents.

if he left him awake: Since he is in the *haver*'s house and supervised by him, the *am ha'arets* fears touching the house even if the associate has temporarily left the house.

asleep and he finds him asleep: We can assume that he has not woken up in the meanwhile and returned to sleep, but has slept continuously.

asleep and he finds him awake: In this case the *am ha'arets* is unaware of the *haver*'s supervision and therefore allows himself to touch items in the house.

the house is impure: R. Meir and the Sages dispute the degree of freedom the *am ha'arets* allows himself, whether he will feel free to wander about the house or only touch his immediate surroundings.

7:3–4 The dispute between R. Meir and the Sages in the previous mishnah is presented again with respect to two familiar situations: artisans working in one's house, and women sitting together to grind flour. The women can work together since at this stage the flour is not yet susceptible to impurity (see *Shevi'it* 5:9), but surrounding objects are in danger of becoming impure.

7:4 *if the millstone stopped*: As long as the mill can be heard, the impure woman is presumably busy at work; if it has stopped, she may be walking around.

5 If someone leaves an *am ha'arets* in his house to guard it:
if [the owner] can see the people entering and exiting,
foods, liquids, and open earthenware are impure,
but beddings, seats, and sealed earthenware are pure.
If he cannot see either the people entering or the people exiting,
even if [the *am ha'arets*] is carried or[30] bound hand and foot,
all is impure.

6 If tax collectors entered a house
the house is impure.
If there was a gentile with them,
they are trusted to say:
"We did not enter,"
but they are not trusted to say:
"We entered but we did not touch."[31]
If thieves entered a house,
only the place of the thieves' feet is [deemed] impure.
And what do they render impure?
Foods, liquids, and open earthenware,
but beddings, seats, and sealed earthenware are pure.
If there was a woman or a gentile with them,
all is impure.

[30] Or "and."

[31] So **M, EP; K, P, C, P_2, A**: "Tax collectors who entered a house: If there was a gentile with them—they are trusted in saying: 'We entered but we did not touch.'" According to this version, the gentile supervisor restrains the collectors (compare Bab. Talmud Hagiga 26a).

7:5 In this mishnah the *am ha'arets* takes charge over the house, inevitably resulting in greater exposure to impurity. If the owner can see whether others have entered or left the house, it is considered to have been defiled only through the light impurity of the *am ha'arets* himself; his direct touch defiles foods and also open clay vessels he may have touched from inside. If, however, this is not the case, we fear that bearers of more severe impurity, such as gentiles and menstruating women, may have entered as well (see 7:6). In that case, these people may have imparted severe *midras* impurity to the beds and mattresses, and may have shifted even sealed clay vessels.

even if [the am ha'arets] is carried: The mishnah emphasizes that the *am ha'arets* is not the suspected source of impurity, but others with more severe impurity who may have entered the house.

7:6 *tax collectors*: Violent intrusion exposes the house to impurity. In this section the mishnah does not address the degree of impurity, as in the surrounding sections, but the question is whether the tax collectors are reliable to say they have not touched the objects in the house (compare *Hagigah* 3:6).

If there was a gentile with them: The gentile is presumably a government official who is supervising the local collectors. The text is uncertain, and therefore it is not clear whether the intruders would be more or less credible in the gentile's presence.

a woman or a gentile: See the annotation to 7:5.

7:7–9 *The Consequences of Unawareness*

7 If someone leaves his clothes in the bathhouse cubbyhole—
R. Eleazar b. Azariah deems it pure,
and the Sages say:
Only if he hands him the key or a seal,
or if he makes some mark.
If someone leaves his tools[32] from one vintage to the following one—
his tools are pure,
But if he was a nonpriest,[33]
only if he says:
"I intended to guard them."
8 If someone was pure
but[34] his mind was distracted from eating,
R. Judah deems [him][35] pure,
for it is the way of impure people to separate from him,
but the Sages deem [him] impure.
If his hands were pure
and his mind was distracted from eating,
even if he says:
"I know my hands were not defiled,"
his hands are impure,
since hands are busy.

[32] Or "clothing." See annotations. [33] Lit. "Israelite." [34] Lit. "and."
[35] See annotations.

7:7 *R. Eleazer b. Azariah* holds that the clothes in the closed cubbyhole are safe, and no one, including impure gentiles, is suspected of having touched them. The Sages, however, demand to secure the cubbyhole by locking or marking it.

If someone leaves his tools: The first part of this rule presumably refers to a priest, who is in the habit of guarding his possessions from impurity. The mishnah contrasts the priest and the nonpriest with respect to their level of attention to purity and care in guarding their belongings. The nonpriest (lit. "Israelite") is required to complement his low standard of maintenance through a higher level of awareness. He must declare that he has left the tools in a safe manner.

tools: Although the same word (*kelim*) appears in both section of the mishnah, the context determines its different meanings: clothing in the case of the bathhouse, and tools in the case of the winepress. Both meanings are well attested for this word.

7:8 *his mind was distracted from eating*: Self-awareness is a prerequisite for maintaining a pure body. Since purity is associated with eating, one is especially careful about one's purity in connection with his meal. The mishnah, however, distinguishes between two levels of awareness. If one has immersed and his body is pure, his purity is mainly threatened by other impure people. Since these people are careful not to come in direct contact with others, R. Judah maintains that his status is not solely dependent on his own attentiveness. In contrast, hands are easily defiled even by impure foods and vessels. Therefore, a short failure of awareness is enough to render one's hands impure. The mishnah rules that in such a case retrospective assurance is not enough, but only incessant awareness.

9 If a woman entered [the house]
in order to bring out bread for a poor person,
and came out and found him standing by loaves of *terumah*;
likewise, if a woman came out
and saw her friend raking coals under a pot of *terumah*—
R. Aqiva deems [it] impure,
and the Sages deem [it] pure.
Said R. Eleazar b. Pila:
Why does R. Aqiva deem [it] impure since the Sages deem it pure?
Since women are gluttonous,
and she is suspected of uncovering her friend's pot
to know what she is cooking.

Chapter Eight

8:1–2 *In the Domain of an Am Ha'arets*

8 If one lives with an *am ha'arets* in the courtyard,
and forgot utensils in the courtyard,
even sealed jars or a sealed oven—
in such a case they are [considered] impure.
R. Judah deems the oven pure,
as long as it is sealed.
R. Yose says:
Even the oven is impure,
unless he builds for it a partition ten handbreadths tall.
2 If one deposits utensils with an *am ha'arets*—
they [are deemed to be] impure with corpse impurity and *midras* impurity.

7:9 The commentators assume that both the poor person and the woman who surprisingly entered the front yard without authorization are *amme ha'arets*. Alternatively, following the previous mishnah, they may have defiled the exposed *terumah* with their impure hands.

8:1 *even sealed jars*: Since clay vessels contract impurity only from within, they are regularly sealed to save them from most sources of impurity, including corpse impurity (Numbers 19:15). However, a menstruating woman and those suffering *zav* impurity convey impurity through moving things, even if the vessel is closed (see above, 7:5–6). Since these people are present in the domain of an *am ha'arets*, the vessels have possibly been shifted by them.

R. Judah: Since the oven is too big to be shifted.

R. Yose: Only the separation of domains ensures purity.

8:2 *they [are deemed] . . . corpse impurity*: In case someone died in the house and the *am ha'arets* was not careful to remove the objects from the house. At the same time, it is assumed that the *am ha'arets*, if he wills, is capable of preventing contamination by corpse impurity. He will do so if he apprehends its importance for the depositor, who is a priest who eats *terumah*.

If he knows him to be an eater of *terumah*—
they are pure of corpse impurity
but impure with *midras* impurity.
R. Yose says:
If he gave him a chest full of clothes:
if it is packed—
the clothes [are deemed] impure with *midras* impurity.
If it is not packed—
they impart *madaf* impurity,
even if the owner holds the key.

8:3–5 *Unattended Items*

3 If one lost [something] during the day
and found it that day—
it is pure.
If he lost it during the day
and found it at night,
during the night
and found it at day,
during the day
and found it the following day—
it is impure.
This is the general rule:
Whenever the night or part of it has passed,
it is impure.
If one spreads garments:
if in the public domain—
they are pure.
If in the private domain—

midras impurity: Clothes and other objects used for sitting or lying contract severe impurity in case a menstruating woman pressed on them as she sat or leaned on them. It is extremely difficult to prevent the spread of such impurity, even if the *am ha'arets* is careful about the artifacts deposited with him.

If he knows: See above, 5:8.

R. Yose demonstrates the severity of *midras* impurity. Even if the clothes were locked in a closed chest, the menstruant has possibly indirectly pressed on the clothes when sitting on it and defiled them. But even if there are only few clothes inside and they are not pressed by sitting on the chest, her mere presence above the clothes entails a light impurity, which affects only foods and clay vessels and not people (*madaf* or "shelf" impurity: see *Zavim* 5:2).

a chest full of clothes: A menstruant may have sat or pressed on the chest.

8:3 *Whenever the night or part of it has passed, it is impure*: An impure person may have stepped upon it accidentally during the night (compare 5:7).

If one spreads garments to dry. These are presumably not left on the ground, where people may step on them and make them dirty, so *midras* impurity is not in question. Still, an impure person may have touched them.

they are impure.
If he was watching them—
they are pure.
If they fell
and he went to bring them—
they are impure.
If his bucket fell into the well of an *am ha'arets*
and he went to bring something to draw it up—
it is impure,
for it was left in the domain of an *am ha'arets*
[even] for a short while.

4 If one leaves his house open and finds it open,
locked and finds it locked,
open and finds it locked—
it is pure;
locked and finds it open—
R. Meir deems it impure,
and the Sages deem it pure,
since [we maintain that] thieves came,
changed their mind and left.

5 If the wife of an *am ha'arets*
entered the house of a *haver*
to take his son[36] or animal—
the house is pure,
since she entered without permission.

8:6–9 *An Early Collection Concerning Food Impurity*

6 A rule has been said[37] concerning food purity:
Anything designated for human food[38] is impure[39]

[36] **C, M, D** add "or daughter." [37] Lit. "They said a rule."
[38] In most manuscripts "for humans," and not "for human food" (as in $\mathbf{P}_2$).
[39] That is, susceptible to impurity.

If they fell: He failed to supervise the clothes ceaselessly, and someone may have stepped on them.

well of an am ha'arets: The previous paragraph ruled that anything brought into the domain of an *am ha'arets* is impure. Here the mishnah adds that even if the item brought into his domain is beyond reach it is impure.

8:4 In 7:6 above we know the identity of the thieves and deem the house impure accordingly, but here we can only suspect a housebreak.

8:5 In 7:3–4 above, the *am ha'arets* was knowingly left in the house, with the *haver*'s consent. Therefore, we fear that the *am ha'arets* allowed himself to walk around and handle the household effects. Here the wife of *am ha'arets* entered without permission, therefore she carried out her mission and quickly left without picking anything up.

8:6 *Anything designated for human food*: Only things that may properly be considered as food, including foods forbidden to observant Jews, are susceptible to impurity. The criteria for this determination are laid out in *Uqtzin* 3.

until it is unfit for dog food,
and anything not designated for human foods is pure
until someone designates it for humans.
How so?
A chick that fell into a winepress
and someone intended to draw it out:
if for a gentile—
it is impure;
if for a dog—
it is pure.
R. Yohanan b. Nuri deems it impure.
If a deaf person,
one who is not legally competent,
or a minor
had intentions with respect to it,
[the bird] is pure;
if they drew it out,
it is impure,
for they possess the [legal] ability to act
but not to intend.

7 If the exterior of a dish was made impure by liquids—
R. Eliezer says:
It renders liquids impure
but does not disqualify foods.
R. Joshua says:
It renders liquids impure
and disqualifies foods.

A chick: Within a Jewish context (such as described in this case) a carcass of a pure bird is considered unfit for consumption. Therefore, the chick is rendered susceptible to impurity only through expressed intention to eat it (compare above 1:1).

fell into a winepress: The purity of the wine in the press depends on the status of the floating carcass, and whether it is considered food or garbage, and this depends on the intention of the person who lifts it out.

R. Yohanan b. Nuri deems it impure: Since the pure bird was available for consumption while alive.

If a deaf person, etc.: Compare *Makhshirin* 6:1.

for they possess: On account of their intellectual impairment they are able to define the status of a food only through their actions, but not by their presumably inconsequential intentions.

8:7 *If the exterior of a dish*: With regard to many utensils, including dishes, the Sages separate their internal, main part from its surrounding secondary surfaces. Liquids defile the whole utensil only if they come in contact with its interior; otherwise they defile only the part they directly touched (see *Kelim* 25). In the present case the exterior of the dish is now a carrier of liquid impurity and can therefore spread the defilement further through the mediation of liquids. In turn, these liquids (of first-degree impurity) defile all foods. The question is whether the back of the dish can defile foods directly.

R. Eliezer holds that impurity spreads beyond its source only through the mediation of liquids.

R. Joshua: In analogy to the system of degrees of impurity among foods, R. Joshua infers that whatever defiles liquids (such as food of the second-degree impurity) also disqualifies *terumah* (see above 2:6).

Simeon the brother of Azariah says:
Not thus and not thus.
Rather, liquids that have been made impure through the exterior of a dish
render one impure and disqualify one.
In such a case [the food] says [to the liquids]:
"The source of your impurity has not made me impure,
but you have made me impure."

8 If a slanted kneading trough
[has impure] dough above
and dripping liquids below the dough,
three pieces do not join together to an egg's bulk,
but two pieces do join.[40]
R. Yose says:
Even two pieces do not join together,
unless they press [upon] the liquids.
But in the case of standing liquid,
even if the dough was like mustard seed,
they join together.
R. Dosa says:
Crumbled foods do not join together.

9 If a stick is full of impure liquids,
as soon as it comes into contact with an immersion pool,
it becomes pure—
the words of R. Joshua.[41]

[40] **K, C, M, EP** lack "but two pieces do join." [41] **K**: "Simeon."

Simeon the brother of Azariah basically agrees with R. Eliezer, but formulates the tradition somewhat differently. His formulation assumes that only liquids may be rendered impure by the exterior of the dish, and he clarifies their subsequent defiling force.

render one impure and disqualify one: This is a standard definition for the defiling force of liquids. Liquids are impure in the first degree. They render the food they contact second (= *render one impure*), and that food, in turn, can disqualify *terumah* (= *and disqualify one*, see 2:4).

[the food] says [to the liquids]: Liquid impurity is paradoxical, as it seems to amplify the force of impurity it carries. The dish cannot directly render foods impure, but the liquids defiled by the dish, although they are farther removed from the source of impurity, do spread impurity to foods (for a list of such paradoxes see *Parah* 8:2–7).

8:8 *A slanted kneading trough*: If the liquids are running down a slope, they can serve as a connective only if all the pieces of dough touch one another. This will not happen with three, since one will separate the other two. Therefore only two pieces can be joined to an egg's bulk the minimum to convey impurity (see chapter 1 above). In standing liquids, however, even if the pieces are very small (*like mustard seed*) they are joined into one dish.

press [upon] the liquids: In R. Yose's view the pieces never combine unless they are so close that the liquid seems compressed between them.

R. Dosa: Compare *Eduyot* 3:1–2.

8:9 *If a stick is full of impure liquids*: Impure liquids are regularly purified through attachment to a source of pure water (in an immersion pool or a large stone vessel, see *Betsah* 2:3). R. Joshua and the Sages dispute whether dripping liquids on a stick are sufficient to form a connection to the pool below.

But the Sages say:
Only when it is immersed completely.
A steady stream, a flow of water, and dripping liquids
are not [considered] a connection,
neither for impurity nor for purity.
A [standing] pool is [considered] a connection
for impurity and for purity.

Chapter Nine

9:1–7 *Maintaining Purity during the Production of Olive Oil*

9 From when are olives susceptible to impurity?
After they sweat in the vat,
but not in the basket,
according to the words of the House of Shammai.
R. Simeon says:
The period of sweat is three days.
The House of Hillel say:
After three [olives] connect together.
Rabban Gamaliel says:
After their preparation is completed,
and the Sages accept his view.[42]

[42] Lit. "say according to his words."

A steady stream: These are all forms of steady downward stream, and none is considered to form a connection to that which is above. Therefore, if there is a source of impurity in the lower part of the stream it does not defile the upper part of the stream (the impure water does not move upward). At *Yadayim* 4:7 the Sadducees criticize this rule.

9:1 *olives*: On their way to the press olives are regularly stored in vats for a few days, until they become moist and soft before being pressed. Other processes that ensure a higher quality of oil are specified below (9:5–7). As all other fruits, olives are susceptible to impurity only when prepared for consumption. The rabbis dispute at what stage the olives are ready to be processed into oil.

the House of Shammai hold the most stringent position, and deem the olives susceptible to impurity if they sweat at any time after being moved from the collection basket to the vat.

R. Simeon requires a waiting period of three days even after the olives have been moved.

The House of Hillel wait until the soft olives begin to stick together.

Rabban Gamaliel introduces a new consideration, unmentioned by the Houses, which enhances the role of human intention in determining the moment of susceptibility. The owner determines susceptibility by deciding to press the olives and collect the oil.

2 If one completed the harvest
but still plans to buy [olives],
[or] if he finished buying [olives]
but still plans to borrow [more];
[or] if mourning, a feast or an unavoidable interference befell him,
even if *zavim* or *zavot*[43] step on [the olives],
they are pure.
If impure liquids fell upon them,
only the place of contact is impure,
and the sap that exudes from them is pure.
3 After their preparation has been completed,
the olives are susceptible.
If liquids fell upon them,
they are impure.[44]
[As for] the sap that exudes from them,
R. Eliezer deems it pure,
and the Sages deem it impure.
Said R. Simeon:
Their dispute did not concern sap exuding [directly] from the olives,
which is pure;
on what did they dispute?
[On] sap exuding in the pit,
which R. Eliezer deems pure,
and the Sages deem impure.
4 If one completes [the preparation of] his olives in the vat,
and leaves one basketful,
he must place it in the priest's sight[45]—
the words of R. Meir.

[43] **K** adds "and menstruating woman."
[44] Alt. "if impure liquids fell upon them," with the sentence remaining incomplete.
[45] **EP**: "give it to a poor priest," which differs by only a single letter.

9:2 *If one completed*: The mishnah further develops the position of Rabban Gamaliel accepted above: even if external circumstances delay the final gathering of the olives into storage, the olives are not rendered susceptible to impurity and remain pure even if impure people step on them.

If impure liquids fell upon them: Since the olives and the liquids extracted from them at this stage are not susceptible to impurity, the impurity is confined to the area directly moistened by the liquids.

the sap that exudes from them: The sap is detrimental to the olives and the oil, and must be removed during the production process. The rabbis dispute whether it is considered a liquid susceptible to impurity.

9:3 *R. Simeon* distinguished between the stages of production. The preliminary preparation is intended to soften the olives and to remove the harmful sap. This sap is clearly unwanted and therefore not susceptible to impurity. Only the sap extracted with the oil in the press, almost inseparable from it, is considered a susceptible liquid.

9:4 *If one completes*: The produce is now susceptible to impurity. The owner, an *am ha'arets*, is not careful in matters of purity but he wishes to separate *terumah* in a state of purity. He leaves one basket that he does not add to the vats, and hands it to a supervising priest, so as to prepare it for *terumah* in purity.

R. Judah says:
He must bring him the key immediately.
R. Simeon says:
By the next day.

5 One who leaves olives in a damping basket:
if in order to moisten them
so they are easily pressed,
[the olives] are susceptible to impurity;
if in order to moisten them
so they may be salted,
the House of Shammai say:
The olives are susceptible,
and the House of Hillel say:
They are not susceptible.
If one crushes olives with impure hands,
they are impure.

6 If one leaves olives on the roof
in order to manually select from them—
even if they are a cubit high—
the [olives] have not been rendered susceptible.
If he placed them in the house until they soften,[46]
and he plans to move them up to the roof,
or if he placed them on the roof to soften
or so he can open them,[47]

[46] Lit. "rot," here and in the next clause.

[47] **K**, **P**: "so he can salt them and open them."

R. Judah suggests a different solution. Instead of separating one basket to be handled by the priest in purity, he suggests locking the storage place and handing the key immediately to the priest, who will take charge over the place until the *terumah* is removed.

R. Simeon agrees with R Judah's solution, but allows twenty-four hours for delivery of the key.

9:5 *moisten them, so they may be salted*: This is a longer process, required in cases of harder olives being prepared for the press. Therefore, the House of Hillel hold that the olives are not yet ready to produce oil and are not susceptible to impurity.

If one crushes: The olive oil renders the olives susceptible to impurity, and his hands immediately defile them.

9:6 *If one leaves olives on the roof*: This mishnah describes a high-quality production of olive oil. Instead of processing the olives in the vat, as described above, the olives are softened in the sun and only the very best are manually chosen and brought to the press (compare *Menahot* 8.4). In this case, only after picking out the olives are they rendered susceptible, while the rest of the pile is not yet ready for the press.

in order to manually select from them: According to some commentators, the olives were left on the roof to fully ripen. Others understand that they are being dried out on the roof. My interpretation accords with the standard meaning of the verb, as evident in *Menahot* 8.4.

even if they are a cubit high: In such a thick stack the upper layers will press down on the lower and squeeze liquid out of them. However, that liquid is not desired and therefore does not render the olives susceptible to impurity.

If he placed them in the house until they soften: In this case, the preparation of the olives takes place in the house, and they are brought to the roof only at the final stage.

they have been rendered susceptible.
If he placed them in the house
until his roof is safe,
or to carry them to another place,
they have not have been rendered susceptible.

7 If one has decided to take away
only one pressload or two pressloads—
the House of Shammai say:
He may chop the olives out in a state of impurity,
but he must cover them in purity.
The House of Hillel say:
He may also cover in a state of impurity.
R. Yose says:
He may dig with metal hatchets
and bring them to the press in a state of impurity.

9:8–9 *Transmission of Impurity in the Olive Press*

8 If vermin is found in the millstones,
only the place touched by it is impure.
If the liquid was flowing,
all is impure.
If [the vermin] was found on the leaves,
the workers are asked whether they [can] say: "We have not touched it."

If he placed the olives *in the house until his roof is safe*: The roof must be prepared to receive the olives, and the house only serves as a preliminary storage place; preparation of the olives will not advance while they are inside. Therefore, even if the olives have softened while in the house they are not rendered susceptible to impurity.

9:7 *one... or two pressloads of olives*: From the piles that have not yet been rendered susceptible to impurity.

the House of Shammai contend that the pile from which the olives are removed is not yet susceptible to impurity and he may therefore use impure people or tools for the task. However, once the olives are being transported to the press their preparation for pressing is complete, and they must therefore be covered for protection. They will be rendered susceptible by any liquid that exudes from them and must be handled in a state of purity.

The House of Hillel allow handling the olives in a state of impurity because the bulk of the pile has been left unfinished.

R. Yose: According to the commentaries, R. Yose permits removal of the entire mass, even with metal implements that are themselves susceptible to impurity. The olives themselves will remain unsusceptible until they arrive at the press. It is unclear what R. Yose adds to the position of the House of Hillel.

9:8 *If vermin is found in the millstones*: At this stage the olives are already susceptible to impurity.

only the place touched by it is impure: Since the olives are smaller than an egg's bulk they do not spread impurity to their surroundings. Only the extracted liquids convey impurity. However, at this stage of the process the millstones are still rather dry. The situation is different if *the liquid was flowing* because sufficient oil had already been extracted.

found on the leaves that cover the block of olives and protect them from contracting impurity.

the workers are asked whether they came in contact with the vermin so that it defiled them and therefore the olives.

If it touched the mass of olives,
even by a hair,[48]
it is impure.

9 If [the vermin] was found upon broken-off [olives][49]
and it was touching an egg's bulk,
[all] is impure.
If there were broken-off [olives] on top of broken-off [olives], even if it touched an egg's bulk,
only the place touched by it is impure.
If it was found between the wall and the olives,
[the mass is] pure.
If it was found on the roof,
the vat is pure.
If it was found in the vat,
the roof is impure.
If it was found burnt upon the olives,
and so too a worn cloth,
it is pure,
for all impurities [are deemed] according to the time they are found.

Chapter Ten

10:1–3 *Supervising Am Ha'arets Workers*

10 If one locks his workers in the olive press,
and there were utensils therein with *midras* impurity—

[48] **K, P, C, M**: "barleycorn"; **P_2, A, EP** as here. The two versions differ by a single letter.
[49] **P, M, EP**: "crumbs"; **K, C, A, P_2** as here. The two differ by a single letter.

If it touched the mass of olives: If the olives have stuck together through the process of softening, the whole mass is considered one unit larger than an egg's bulk and it conveys impurities to other foods.

9:9 *broken-off [olives] on top of broken-off [olives]*: Unlike the preceding case, here there is more than one "layer" between the vermin and the mass of olives. The separate pieces are not regarded as joined.

If it was found: In the last cases it is uncertain whether in fact the vermin has come in contact with the olives.

If it was found on the roof… If it was found in the vat: These cases refer to the process described in 9:6 above. The olives were brought from the vat to the roof, and it is uncertain whether the vermin has already from the start fallen into the vat. If it was found in the vat, but only then, all olives including those removed to the roof are deemed impure (compare 4:4).

If it was found burnt: See above 3:4–5.

10:1 *If one locks his workers* who are *am ha'arets*. They are not careful in matters of purity and require ongoing supervision.

and there were utensils therein with midras impurity: These impart impurity indirectly if one causes them to shift in location. The rabbis dispute whether the workers can be trusted to keep away from these

R. Meir says:
The olive press is impure;
R. Judah says:
The olive press is pure.
R. Simeon says:
If the workers consider [these utensils] pure
the olive press is impure,
and if they consider them impure,
the olive press is pure.
Said R. Yose:
But for what reason are they [considered] impure?
Rather, they are not proficient in matters of indirect shift.

2 If olive-press workers were walking in and out
and there were impure liquids inside the olive press,
if there was enough space between the liquids and the olives
for them to wipe their feet off on the ground,
[the olives] are pure.
If an impurity was found in front of olive-press workers and grape harvesters,
they are trusted to say: "We have not touched it,"
and so too for the children among them.
They may go outside the door of the olive press
and relieve themselves behind the fence,
and they are [considered] pure.
How far may they go
and still be considered pure?
As far as he can see them.

3 Olive-press workers and grape harvesters—
it is enough for [the owner] to bring them into the cave—
the words of R. Meir.

artifacts. The arguments of R. Simeon and R. Yose reveal some of the characteristics of an *am ha'arets* in the eyes of the rabbis. Both assume that an *am ha'arets* tries to maintain some level of purity but has not mastered the details and complexities of the rabbinic system. According to R. Simeon, only if the workers *consider* the utensils *impure*—for example, if they saw a menstruant touching them directly—would they be careful to stay away from them and maintain the purity of the olive press. According to R. Yose, on the other hand, even if they acknowledge the artifacts to be impure, they are not aware of the level of care that is required to prevent the spread of their impurity. Therefore he agrees with R. Meir that the olive press is impure.

10:2 *if there was enough space*: If the workers can dry their feet, they will not track impure fluids onto the olives (compare 3:8).

If an impurity was found: Compare above, 9:8. Even an *am ha'arets* will be careful not to touch a source of impurity such as vermin (in contrast to defiled implements, such as in the previous mishnah, or impure liquids).

They may go outside: The workers, as well as children, require constant supervision. Compare chapter 7 above.

10:3 *and grape harvesters*: The inclusion of grape harvesters in this rule forms a transition to the rest of the chapter.

into the cave: Immersion pools were regularly built in caves adjacent to agricultural installations.

R. Yose says:
He must stand over them
until they immerse.
R. Simeon says:
If they consider themselves to be pure,
he must stand over them
until they immerse,
if they consider themselves impure,
he need not stand over them
until they immerse.

10:4–8 *Maintaining Purity during the Production of Wine*

4 If one is taking [grapes] from the baskets [for the treading basin]
or from the spread-out area on the ground—
the House of Shammai say:
He [must] place them with pure hands,
and if he placed them with impure hands,
he has made them impure.
The House of Hillel say:
He [may] place with impure hands,
but [he must] separate the *terumah*[50] in purity.
[If they are taken] from the grape basket
or from a spread-out area of leaves,
all agree that he must place them with pure hands,
and if he placed them with impure hands,
he has made them impure.
5 If one eats [grapes directly] from the baskets
or from the spread-out area on the ground,
even if they are split open

[50] **K**, **C**, **A**, **M**, **EP** add "from it/them."

until they immerse: Either themselves or their implements.

R. Yose... R. Simeon...: The dispute here is consistent with their positions in 10:1.

10:4 In contrast to olives, grapes are susceptible to impurity from their harvest, and must be handled in a state of purity from the start. Impure persons are therefore barred from the entire process (compare 9:2). However, impure hands defile the grapes only through the mediation of liquids. The Houses discuss the cases where one must take into consideration the possible presence of liquids on the grapes even before they are placed in the treading basin, and refrain from handling the grapes with impure hands.

spread-out area: Where the grapes are left before transportation.

The House of Hillel distinguishes the dry grapes placed in baskets or on a soil surface from those placed in large designated grape baskets or on a leaf surface in order to preserve the liquids.

separate the terumah in purity: Since *terumah* requires a higher level of purity, it contracts impurity directly from the impure hands even when they are dry (*Zavim* 5:12).

10:5 *If one eats [grapes]* and his hands are impure, as in the previous mishnah. In the first case his hands do not defile the grapes taken from the basket or soil surface. Consequently, the liquids in the treading basin remain pure.

and dripping into the treading basin,
the treading basin is pure.
[If he takes them] from the grape basket
or from the leaf surface
and one fruit fell:
if it has a seal,
[the fruit] is pure.
If it does not have a seal,
[the fruit] is impure.
If some of the grapes[51] fell
and he trod them in an empty area,
an exact egg's bulk is pure,
more than an egg's bulk is impure;
for once the first drop emerges,
[the pile] is rendered impure
by the egg's bulk.

6 If one was standing and talking
at the edge of the [wine] cistern
and spittle was sprayed from his mouth,[52]
and there is a doubt
whether it reached the cistern or not—
this doubt is [considered] pure.

7 If one empties out a cistern [into barrels]
and vermin was found in the first one,
all of them are impure.
[If it was found] in the last one,
it is impure
and the rest are pure.
When?

[51] **P**: "impure grapes."

[52] **P_2** adds "on his clothes" (compare *Tevul Yom* 3:6).

from the grape basket or from the leaf surface: In this case his hands defile the grapes. However, the impure grape, smaller than an egg's bulk, does not impart impurity, and only the impure liquids can defile the treading basin. Thus, if the grape falling into the basin was not sealed, the liquids emerging from it are rendered impure by one's hands, and these liquids in turn can impart impurity to the basin.

has a seal: If the stalk of the grape is in place and prevents the emergence of any liquid.

If some of the grapes fell: The impure grapes impart impurity to the liquids only through an egg's bulk. Therefore the total volume of the grapes, including the liquids contracting impurity from them, must be larger than an egg's bulk (compare 3:2).

10:6 The production of the wine includes a period of a few days of fermentation in an open cistern. During this time some impurity might fall in, whether from an impure person (10:6) or vermin (10:7).

If one was standing at the edge of the cistern: If the person is an *am ha'arets*, his spittle may be considered to be an impure liquid, which conveys impurity to other liquid and foods. Even if he suffers a more severe impurity the rule is the same.

10:7 *If one empties out a cistern*: In the first case the vermin is assumed to have been in the cistern from the start, and all of the wine is impure. But if it was found in the last jar, it may have fallen into the wine later on, and the first jars are still pure (compare above 4:4).

If he poured directly into each [of the jars],
but if he poured it with a ladle
and vermin was found in one of them
only [that jar] is impure.
When?
If he checked but did not cover,
or covered but did not check,
but if he checked and covered,
and the vermin was found—
everything is impure;
in the cistern,
everything is impure;
in the ladle,
everything is impure.

8 [The space] between the pressing beams and the grapeskins
is a public domain.
The vineyard in front of the harvesters
is a private domain,
and behind them
is a public domain.
When?
If the public enters on one [side] and exits on the other.[53]
The equipment of the olive press and the winepress and the pressing basket:
if they are made of wood,
he dries them
and they are pure.
If they are made of reeds,
he lets them age for twelve months
or blanches them in boiling water.
R. Yose says:
If he put them into the river stream,
that is sufficient for him.

[53] Lit. "on this . . . on this."

if he poured it with a ladle: i.e. a jug used for pouring the wine from the cistern to the jars. The vermin may have originated in the ladle and not in the wine in the cistern, and in that case none of the other jars would be implicated.

but if he checked and covered each of the jars before filling them; inevitably the vermin originated in the cistern and rendered the whole produce impure.

10:8 Within the complex of the winepress, between the treading basin and the cistern, stood a wooden press into which broken grapes were loaded from the treading basin for a secondary extraction. People were not allowed to walk freely in the winepress, in order to maintain the purity and quality of the wine, except for the area around the wooden press, where the workers were busy loading the grapeskins. This confined area is considered a public domain with respect to cases of doubt (chapter 6).

The vineyard in front of the harvesters is a private domain: Due to purity regulations required during the grape harvest, the vineyard was a restricted area, and was thus considered a private domain. On the other hand the area behind them was open to the public since the grapes had already been removed.

The equipment: These are rules for purifying the equipment and preparing it for the following crop in case some of the wine was impure and had been absorbed into the various tools.

Tractate Miqva'ot

Yonatan Adler

Introduction

Overview

Miqva'ot (or *Mikvot* in some of the manuscripts) is the plural of *miqveh*, the biblical term for various kinds of pools or gatherings of water (Genesis 1:10, Exodus 7:19, and Leviticus 11:36). In the Mishnah, here as well as in other tractates, the term becomes a legal one, used only when the issue at stake is the status of the pool vis-à-vis its purity and/or its ability to purify humans, utensils, and other water immersed therein. Note that the word "pool" always refers to the pooled water itself rather than the cavity or installation that holds the water, which in our tractate is referred to as a "pit" (2:7–9, 3:2–3) or "cave" (4:4, 6:1, 7:7).

Relationship to Scripture

The Torah repeatedly mandates "washing" in water for the ritual purification of humans and "laundering" to purify impure clothing (see especially Leviticus 11–15 and Numbers 19). Certain kinds of impure utensils are to be purified by being *brought into water* (Leviticus 11:32) or *rinsed in water* (Leviticus 15:12; see also Numbers 31:23). The type of water to be used for all of these purifications is never specified, aside from the case of the *zav*—who is instructed to wash in *living water* (Leviticus 15:13). Although the Torah notes that *a spring and a pit of pooled water shall be pure* even if vermin were to fall into them (Leviticus 11:36), nothing is said of the ability of such waters to purify impure persons or objects.

Late Second Temple period sources indicate that contemporary practice involved immersion in water as the specific method whereby purificatory washings were performed. Archaeological evidence of hundreds of stepped immersion installations unearthed throughout the Land of Israel points to the widespread character of the practice at this time.

For the rabbis of the Mishnah, purification in water is possible only if the entire body or object to be purified is immersed in water, either pooled or in a flowing spring, with nothing interposing between the water and that which is immersed. For a pool to purify, it must contain a minimum volume of forty *se'ah* (about 480 liters). A pool containing less than this measure is rendered permanently invalid by the addition of three *log* (around one and a half liters) of "drawn water," i.e. water intentionally collected in a utensil. Once a pool contains the forty *se'ah* minimum of valid water, it can no longer be invalided by the addition of drawn water. Additionally, pooled water must be standing still (i.e. not flowing) in order to purify. None of these restrictions apply to immersion in spring water, which purifies when flowing, regardless of volume or the addition of any amount of drawn water.

Nowhere in the Mishnah is any rationale provided for these rules, all of which entail substantive legal expansions upon the simple biblical instruction to purify through washing. Elsewhere the forty-*se'ah* minimum is explained as the minimum amount of water necessary to completely cover an immersed human body.

Structure and Organization of the Tractate

The first chapter of *Miqva'ot* is something of an introduction, dedicated to a classification of "pools" into six grades, listed in ascending order according to the relative advantages of each with regard to the laws of purity. The first two grades, discussed at some length (1:1–6), are types of puddles that are invalid for purification as they contain less than forty *se'ah*—and are discussed only insofar as they might be rendered impure themselves. It is only the later four grades of "pools"—which actually include both pools and springs—that do in fact purify, and it is these kinds of water upon which the remainder of the tractate focuses.

Following a brief discussion on cases of doubt regarding immersions in pools (2:1–3), the Mishnah proceeds to discuss at length how three *log* of drawn water invalidate a pool (2:4–4:5). This is followed by a chapter dedicated to purification in springs and various kinds of flowing water (5:1–6). The next chapter (6:1–11) explores cases where adjoining collections of water are deemed to be as one ("mingled") pool for the purpose of determining the forty-*se'ah* minimum or of purifying an invalid pool. The next section (7:1–5) discusses substances other than water that fill a pool and/or invalidate it. Following a brief discussion on immersion in a pool that contains the bare minimum volume of forty *se'ah* and is diminished through use (7:6–7), and after delineating differences between pools in the Land of Israel and abroad (8:1), the Mishnah examines details relating to the immersion of men and women who have experienced seminal discharges (8:2–4).

The final section, standing on its own, takes up the question of interpositions during immersions, where foreign elements come in the way of pool water covering the entirety of the human body (8:5–9:4) or utensils (9:5–10:8).

Special Notes for the Reader

In addition to manuscripts **K** and **P**, which were consulted throughout this edition, the notes on this tractate will also reference manuscript Munich, Bayerische Staatsbibliothek—Cod. hebr. 95 (= **M**).

Tractate Miqva'ot

Chapter One

1:1–5 *Purity Rules Relating to Puddles*

I There are six grades[1] of pools,
one superior to the other.[2]
(1) Puddles:
if an impure person drank [from a puddle]
and [subsequently] a pure person drank from it,
[the latter is rendered] impure.[3]
If an impure person drank [from a puddle]
and [afterward one] drew from it into a pure utensil,
[the utensil is rendered] impure.
If an impure person drank [from a puddle]
and [afterward] a loaf of *terumah* bread[4] fell into it,

[1] Or "advantages." [2] Lit. "this one above this one and this one above this one."
[3] **M** adds "and invalidates *terumah*" (see annotation). [4] **K**: "a purse of *terumah*."

1:1 *grades*: Or perhaps "advantages"; there are six different types of pooled water, each having certain advantages over the preceding with regard to the laws of purity.

pools: gatherings of water, whether naturally occurring or in artificially constructed installations. Cf. Genesis 1:10; Leviticus 11:36.

one superior to the other: The six types of pools are listed in ascending order according to the relative advantages of each with regard to the laws of purity. Mishnah 1:1–5 is devoted to the first type of pool: puddles.

Puddles: The term used elsewhere refers to water gathered in cavities in the ground (cf. Isaiah 30:14; *Parah* 6:5). Below (1:4), the Mishnah lists different types of pools that are equivalent to puddles; from both this mishnah and from 1:7 we may infer that the reference here is to small puddles measuring less than forty *se'ah* in volume. This amount (around 480 liters) is the smallest that is considered a valid pool for immersion.

[the latter is rendered] impure: The impure person rendered the puddle impure through contact when he drank from it, and as a result, a pure person who subsequently drinks from this water is rendered impure (see *Zavim* 5:12: one who drinks impure liquids becomes impure to the degree that he disqualifies *terumah* through contact).

and [afterward one] drew from it: Presumably the subject is someone other than the impure person.

[the utensil is rendered] impure: As in the previous case, a pure vessel is similarly rendered impure through contact with the impure water in the puddle (again, see *Zavim* 5:12: utensils that come into contact with impure liquids become impure to the degree that they disqualify *terumah* through contact).

terumah bread: i.e. bread baked from grain separated as *terumah*, priests' due (see *Terumot*).

if [the person who retrieved the bread] rinsed,
it is impure,
but if he did not rinse,
it is pure.

2 If one drew [water from a puddle] into an impure utensil
and [subsequently] a pure person drank [from the puddle],
[the latter is rendered] impure.
If one drew [water from a puddle] into an impure utensil
and [then] drew [from the puddle] into a pure utensil,
[the second utensil is rendered] impure.[5]
If one drew [water from a puddle] into an impure utensil
and [subsequently] a loaf of *terumah* bread fell [into the puddle],
if [the person who retrieved the bread] rinsed,
it is impure,
but if he did not rinse,
it is pure.

3 If impure water fell [into a puddle]
and [subsequently] a pure person drank [from the puddle],
he is [rendered] impure.
If impure water fell [into a puddle]
and [subsequently] one drew [water from the puddle] into a pure utensil,
[the utensil is rendered] impure.[6]
If impure water fell [into a puddle]
and subsequently a loaf of *terumah* bread fell [into the puddle],
if [the person who retrieved the bread] rinsed,
it is impure,
but if he did not rinse,
it is pure.
R. Simeon says:

[5] **M** lacks this case. [6] **M** lacks this case.

if [the person who retrieved the bread] rinsed, it is impure: The exact meaning of the Mishnah is unclear: does the rinsing pertain to the hand of the person who retrieves the loaf of bread from the puddle, or to the loaf of bread? In either case the question may relate to the issue of intention; an impure puddle is capable of conveying impurity only if human intent to make use of the water for some purpose has been shown. In the first two cases, such intent is shown when the pure person drinks from the puddle or draws water from it into a pure vessel, but in the last case, the *terumah* bread fell into the puddle unintentionally. In such a case, the impure puddle conveys impurity to the bread only if the person who retrieves it from the puddle makes intentional use of the water by the act of rinsing. See also the same phrase in 1:2.

1:2 In this mishnah the impurity arises through contact with an impure utensil rather than an impure person. An impure vessel used to draw water from a puddle renders the puddle impure through contact.

1:3 Now the impurity results from contact with impure water.

if [the person who retrieved the bread] rinsed, it is impure: See above on 1:1.

R. Simeon rules that the bread is rendered impure whether or not the person who retrieves it from the puddle has rinsed it or his hand in the puddle. Possibly, the ruling attributed to R. Simeon refers not only to the

Whether he rinsed or did not rinse,
[the bread is rendered] impure.

4 If a corpse fell into [a puddle],
or if an impure person waded through it,
and [subsequently] a pure person drank from it,
[the latter remains] pure.
[The above rules apply equally to] puddles,
water in pits,[7]
water in ditches,
water in caves,
seep water that has stopped [flowing],
and pools that do not contain forty *se'ah*.
When it rains,
all is pure.[8]
Once the rain has stopped,
those [pools lying] close to the city or to the road are impure,
while those distant [from the city or the road] are pure,
unless numerous people pass by.[9]

[7] Or "cisterns." [8] **M** adds "the reason being that [the rain] caused [the pools] to overflow."
[9] Lit. "will walk." **P**: "will walk upon them." **M**: "will walk in them."

case found in our mishnah, but also to the cases mentioned in the previous two mishnayot. If that is the case, it is possible that R. Simeon disagrees with the premise that intention is required for the conveyance of impurity.

1:4 The first part of the mishnah continues the discussion of the previous mishnayot (1:1–3) regarding when a puddle conveys impurity.

corpse: A human corpse can transmit impurity through contact (Numbers 19:11–22).

pure: Unlike in the cases found in the previous mishnayot (1:1–3), a puddle is not rendered impure if a corpse falls into it or if an impure person wades through it. Possibly the reason is related to the issue of intention: a puddle is susceptible to impurity only if at the time when it came into contact with the source of impurity there was present human intent to utilize the water for some purpose. Since the corpse undoubtedly fell into the puddle unintentionally and the impure person who waded through the puddle also presumably had no intention to reap benefit from the water, the puddle remains pure. It is unclear, however, why these two cases differ from the case in the previous mishnah (1:3) where impure water fell into a puddle, unless we are to assume that the impure water "fell" intentionally. Possibly, water falling into a puddle is presumed to be a positive occurrence, and satisfaction is perhaps equivalent to intention.

seep water: Groundwater that has been absorbed into the ground and has now oozed to the surface.

that has stopped [flowing]: If the water has stopped flowing, that which oozed previously has the same rule as a puddle or as water in a pit or a ditch. The rule concerning seep water that has not stopped flowing is discussed below (1:6).

When it rains: Rainwater nullifies impure water gathered in the above-listed pools (cf. *Makhshirin* 2:3). Below (1:5), various opinions are cited regarding the quantity of rain required to accomplish this.

close to the city or to the road: Since pools of water of the type under discussion are rendered impure when an impure person drinks from them, any pool located near a city or a road is considered impure as we may assume that an impure person drank from it.

5 When are [these pools] purified?[10]
The House of Shammai say:
When [the rainwater] has become the majority
and caused [the pool] to overflow.
The House of Hillel say:
When [the rainwater] has become the majority,
even though it has not caused [the pool] to overflow.
R. Simeon says:
When [the rainwater] has caused [the pool] to overflow,[11]
even though it has not become the majority.
[After becoming pure again, all of these waters] are valid
for [preparing] *hallah*
and for the washing of hands.

1:6–8 *The Other Grades of Purifying Water*

6 (2) Superior to these:
seep water that has not stopped [flowing]:
if an impure person drank [from such water]
and [subsequently] a pure person drank from it,
[the latter remains] pure.
If an impure person drank [from it]
and [afterward one] drew from it into a pure utensil,
[the utensil remains] pure.
If an impure person drank [from it]
and [afterward] a loaf of *terumah* bread[12] fell [into the water],
even if [the person who retrieved the bread] rinsed,
it is pure.
If one drew [from it] into an impure utensil
and [subsequently] a pure person drank [from the water],[13]
[the latter remains] pure.
If one drew [from it] into an impure utensil

[10] Lit. "From when is their purity?"
[11] **K** lacks: "R. Simeon says: When [the rainwater] has caused [the pool] to overflow," probably a scribal mistake.
[12] **K**: "a purse of *terumah*."
[13] **K, P**: "and subsequently one drank with a pure vessel."

1:5 The previous mishnah ruled that rainwater nullifies the impure water in puddles (and similar small pools), and our mishnah addresses the question of how much rainwater is necessary to produce this effect.

valid for [preparing] hallah: The dough offering given to a priest (Numbers 15:17–21), who may eat it only if it remains pure (see introduction to tractate *Hallah*).

washing of hands: i.e. for the purification of hands through ritual washing (see tractate *Yadayim*).

1:6 This mishnah continues the enumeration of the six types of pools begun in 1:1, listing the second grade of pool: oozing seep water (see annotation above, 1:4). The cases described here repeat the cases found in 1:1–3 regarding puddles. In all of these cases, the oozing seep water remains pure.

and [then] drew [again from it] into a pure utensil,
[the latter utensil remains] pure.
If one drew [from it] into an impure utensil
and [subsequently] a loaf of *terumah* bread fell [into the seep water],
even if [the person who retrieved the bread] rinsed,
it is pure.
If impure water fell [into seep water]
and [subsequently] a pure person drank [from it],
he [remains] pure.
If impure water fell [into it]
and [subsequently] one drew [from it] into a pure utensil,
[the utensil remains] pure.
If impure water fell [into it]
and [subsequently] a loaf of *terumah* bread fell [into it],
even if [the person who retrieved the bread] rinsed,
it is pure.
[In all of these cases, the seep water is] valid[14] for [use with] *terumah* and for the washing of hands.

7 (3) Superior to these:
a pool that contains forty *se'ah* [of water],
for in it [people] may immerse
and [objects] may be immersed.[15]
(4) Superior to these:
a spring with a small flow of water,
and a greater quantity of drawn water was added to it;
it is equal to a pool [containing forty *se'ah*]
in that it purifies only when its water is standing,
and [equal] to a spring in that [objects] may be immersed[16] in it,
whatever its quantity.

8 (5) Superior to these:
impaired[17] water,
which[18] purifies [even] when it is flowing.
(6) Superior to these:

[14] **M**: "but they are not valid." [15] Lit. "one immerses and causes to be immersed."
[16] Lit. "[one may] cause to be immersed." [17] Lit. "stricken." [18] Or "since this."

valid for [use with] terumah and for the washing of hands: Whether an impure person drank from the seep water, an impure utensil was used to draw water from it, or impure water fell into it—in all of these cases the seep water remains pure and as such may be used in conjunction with pure *terumah* and for the purificatory washing of hands.

1:7 The third and the fourth of the six grades of pools mentioned in 1:1.

a pool that contains forty se'ah [of water]: But not spring water (which is discussed below).

a spring with a small flow of water: Discussed more fully below, 5:3.

1:8 The fifth and the sixth of the six grades of pools mentioned in 1:1.

impaired water: Brackish or lukewarm spring water (cf. *Parah* 8:9).

flowing: Unlike the previous two grades (described in 1:8), impaired spring water purifies even if it is flowing.

living water,
which[19] may be used
for the immersion of *zavim*
and for sprinkling upon those with *tsara'at*,
and is valid for use in the sanctification of purgation water.

Chapter Two

2:1–3 *Cases of Doubt regarding Pools*

2 If an impure person went down to immerse
[and] there is a doubt whether or not he [actually] immersed;
[or], even if he [certainly] immersed,
[but] there is a doubt whether or not there were forty *se'ah* [of water in the pool];
[or, there were] two pools,
one that had forty *se'ah* [of water] in it
and one that did not,
[and] he immersed in one of them,
but does not know in which one he immersed,
his doubtful condition [in all of these cases] is [regarded as] impure.

[19] Or "since this."

living water: Spring water that is neither mixed with a majority of drawn water (grade 4) nor impaired (grade 5).

zavim: According to Leviticus 15:13, a man with an abnormal sexual discharge (*zav*) must wash his flesh in "living water" in order to become pure; see *Zavim* 1:1.

sprinkling upon those with tsara'at: According to Leviticus 14:4–7, the procedure for the purification of one who has been cured of his scale-disease involves the use of "living water" (see also *Nega'im* 14:1).

purgation water: The mixture of "living water" together with ashes of a red heifer that is used in the purification of the corpse-impure (Numbers 19:17–19).

2:1 The preceding two mishnayot listed various types of "pools" that purify people and objects immersed in them. The next three mishnayot consider various cases of doubt regarding purificatory immersions in pools of the first type found in 1:7, i.e. pools that contain forty *se'ah* of water that is not spring water.

went down to immerse: The impure person entered the pool, but it is not known whether he actually performed a valid immersion.

a doubt whether or not there were forty se'ah: The second case of doubt listed here involves a situation in which the impure person is known to have immersed himself in the pool, but there is doubt regarding the validity of the pool itself. Immersion in a pool that holds less than forty *se'ah* of water is ineffective for effecting purification.

impure: We assume that the impure person has not performed a valid immersion in a valid pool, and as such remains impure (see the explanation given by R. Yose in 2:2 below).

2 A pool that was measured and found lacking [forty *se'ah* of water]:
all things [previously] prepared in purity[20] on the basis of [immersion in] it,[21]
whether in the private domain or in the public domain,
[are regarded as] impure.
When does this apply?
In [cases of] severe impurity.
But in [cases of] light impurity,
such as if one ate impure foods or drank impure liquids,
[or] if one's head and the majority of his body were dipped in drawn water,
or if three *log* of drawn water fell on one's head and the majority of his body,
if he [then] went down to immerse
[and] there is a doubt whether or not he [actually] immersed,
[or] even if he [certainly] immersed
[but] there is a doubt whether or not there were forty *se'ah* [of water in the pool];
[or there were] two pools,
one that had forty *se'ah* [of water] in it
and one that did not,
[and] he immersed in one of them,

[20] Lit. "pure things." [21] Lit. "made upon it."

2:2 The following mishnah discusses whether the ruling in 2:1 applies to all types of impurity or perhaps only to "severe" impurities.

found lacking: Holding less than forty *se'ah*.

things...prepared in purity on the basis of [immersion in] it: i.e. an impure person immersed in the pool, and then came into contact with pure food, liquids, or utensils on the assumption that his immersion rendered him pure. If the pool did not contain the requisite forty *se'ah* of water at the time that he immersed in it, he will have remained impure and consequently the objects with which he came into contact will have become impure.

private domain...public domain: A doubtful case regarding purity that arises in the public domain is generally considered pure (*Tohorot* 4:11 and chapters 5–6).

impure: It is assumed that the pool held less than forty *se'ah* at the time when the impure person immersed.

When does this apply? The question pertains to the rulings given above (2:1–2) on cases of doubt regarding purificatory immersions.

severe impurity: Prior to his immersion, the one who immersed in the pool contracted his impurity from a primary source of impurity (see *Kelim* 1:1). Any case of doubt regarding impurity conveyed from a primary source of impurity is impure—even if the source of impurity is only rabbinic (*Tohorot* 4:11).

light impurity: Impurity contracted from a secondary source of impurity. According to biblical law, a person contracts impurity only from primary sources of impurity; any impurity conveyed to a person from a secondary source of impurity is only of rabbinic origin.

ate impure foods or drank impure liquids: A primary source of impurity had rendered these impure, so they are secondary sources of impurity.

if one's head and the majority of his body were dipped in drawn water: Such a person invalidates *terumah* through contact; i.e. his impurity is equal to that of one who contracted impurity from a secondary source of impurity (*Zavim* 5:12). The same rule appears there with regard to the next case in our mishnah: *if three log of drawn water fell on one's head and the majority of his body.*

three log: Around one and a half liters.

but does not know in which one he immersed,
his doubtful condition [in all of these cases] is [regarded as] pure.
R. Yose deems [him] impure,
for R. Yose says:
Anything that has the presumed status of impurity
remains permanently[22] in its defective state[23]
until it becomes known [for certain] that it has been purified.
But if there is a doubt whether something has become impure
or has imparted impurity,
it is [regarded as] pure.

3 [These are cases of] doubt concerning drawn water[24]
that the Sages have deemed pure:
doubt whether or not [drawn water] fell [into a pool];
[or] even if it [certainly] fell,
[but] there is a doubt
whether or not there are [already] forty *se'ah* [of water] in [the pool];
[or in a case where there are] two pools,
one that has forty *se'ah* [of water]
and one that does not,
[and drawn water] fell into one of them,
but it is not known[25] into which of them it fell,
[in all of these cases] the doubtful condition is [regarded as] pure

[22] Lit. "forever." [23] Lit. "invalidity"; **K**, **M**: "impurity."
[24] Lit. "doubtful drawn water." [25] Lit. "he does not know."

pure: In all of these cases the doubt concerns only a "light impurity," so we assume that the impure person has performed a valid immersion in a valid pool and has been purified (cf. *Tohorot* 4:11).

R. Yose: Cf. *Yadayim* 2:4.

presumed status of impurity: This is a common legal-factual presumption: the continued existence of a once-ascertained state of affairs is presumed until the contrary is proven to be the case.

defective state: i.e. impure.

But if there is a doubt: R. Yose's presumption of impurity applies only if it is known that there was previously a state of impurity and the doubt concerns the question whether or not the impurity was removed. If, however, something was known to have been pure, and the doubt concerns the question of whether or not it has become impure, in such a case it is presumed to be pure as long as the doubtful impurity is only a "light impurity."

has become impure: For example, if there is a doubt whether or not a person has eaten impure food.

has imparted impurity: For example, if a person ate impure food and there is a doubt whether or not he has come into contact with *terumah*.

2:3 A pool containing less than forty *se'ah* is invalidated (i.e. loses its power to purify) if three *log* of drawn water fall into it (see *Eduyot* 1:3), but this is the case only if there were less than forty *se'ah* of valid water in the pool at the time the drawn water fell in. The pool now remains permanently invalid, even if valid water is later added to the pool to complete the forty-*se'ah* minimum.

that the Sages have deemed pure: See *Tohorot* 4:7.

it is not known into which of them it fell: The pool that had forty *se'ah* certainly remains valid; the question is whether the pool that did not have forty *se'ah* is invalidated.

since it has something on which to depend.[26]
If [,however,] both [of the two pools held] less than forty *se'ah* [of water],
and [drawn water] fell into one of them and it is not known into which,
the doubtful condition is [regarded as] impure,[27]
since it lacks something on which to depend.

2:4–6 *When Does Drawn Water Invalidate a Pool?*

4 R. Eliezer says:
A quarter[-*log*] of drawn water in the beginning[28] renders a pool invalid,
as do three *log* on the surface of the water.
But the Sages say:
Whether in the beginning or at the end,
the measure [that renders a pool invalid][29] is three *log*.
5 A pool that has in it three cavities containing drawn water,
each containing one *log*;[30]
if it is known that forty *se'ah* of valid water fell into [the pool]

[26] **P** lacks "since it has something on which to depend."
[27] **P**: "pure," amended in the margin to: "impure." [28] **M** lacks "in the beginning."
[29] Lit. "its measure."
[30] **K**: "filled with drawn water of snow," differing from the standard text by two letters, and apparently written over an erasure; **P**: "filled with drawn water of a wheel," corrected in the margin to the standard text.

since it has something on which to depend: In each of these cases, the possibility exists that drawn water did not fall into any pool in a way that would have disqualified it.

both [of the two pools] held less then forty se'ah . . . it lacks something on which to depend: In such a case it is certain that drawn water invalidated one of the two pools, and the doubt relates only to which of the two pools it was. Since one of the two is surely invalid, the situation is one in which a lenient ruling has nothing "on which to depend." Cf. *Kelim* 9:3.

2:4 Although a pool containing less than forty *se'ah* is invalidated only if three *log* of drawn water fall into it, the mishnah here explores whether or not a smaller volume of drawn water invalidates if this falls into a pool that is completely empty.

in the beginning: Prior to any water filling the pool. If only a quarter-*log* (around one-eighth of a liter) of drawn water falls into an empty pool, the pool is invalid even if it is subsequently filled with forty *se'ah* of valid water.

on the surface of the water: After the pool has been filled with some valid water but before it has been filled with forty *se'ah*.

Whether in the beginning or at the end: Whether the drawn water falls into the pool when it is still completely empty (*in the beginning*), or after it has already begun to be filled with valid water (*at the end*), the volume of drawn water that invalidates a pool is three *log*.

2:5 This and the following mishnah discuss various situations in which three *log* of drawn water are added in an indirect manner to a pool containing less than forty *se'ah* of valid water.

three cavities: In either the floor or the wall of the larger pit that holds the pool.

before the [water] reached the third cavity,
[the pool is] valid.
but if not,
it is invalid.
R. Simeon deems it valid,
since it is like a pool adjacent to a pool.

6 If one presses mud [in a pool] against the sides,
and three *log* [of water] drained out of it,
[the pool remains] valid;
if one removed[31] the mud [from the pool],
and three *log* [of water] drained out of it,
[the pool is] invalid.
R. Simeon deems it valid,
since he did not intend to draw [water].

[31] Lit. "detached."

before the [water] reached the third cavity: At first the pit was empty, save for the drawn water in the three cavities. Valid water then fell into the pit, and as it spread and the pool filled the pit, it mixed with the drawn water in the three cavities, one after the other. If forty *se'ah* of this valid water had entered the pit before the water spread to reach the last cavity—*[the pool is] valid*—since the third *log* of drawn water mixed with valid water already measuring forty *se'ah*, and a pool containing forty *se'ah* of valid water is not invalidated by the admixture of drawn water (see above, 2:3).

but if not: The valid water that fell into the pit measured less than forty *se'ah* at the moment that the water spread to reach the third cavity. Alternatively: if it is not known for sure that the valid water that fell into the pit measured forty *se'ah* at that moment, *it is invalid*, since the three *log* of drawn water in the cavities mixed with valid water that measured less than forty *se'ah*.

R. Simeon deems it valid: R. Simeon views the cavities as distinct receptacles, separate from the pool, and as such the three *log* of drawn water in the cavities are not considered to have mixed with the pool of valid water.

like a pool adjacent to a pool: That is, a pool with valid water adjoining a pool with invalid water. Drawn water invalidates only if it "falls into" a pool of valid water, not if it simply adjoins it.

2:6 *presses mud [in a pool] against the sides*: In order to clear part of the floor of the pool from mud that accumulated there, but without removing the mud from the pool. The pool under discussion contains less than forty *se'ah* of water.

three log [of water] drained out of it: i.e. three *log* of water were expressed from the sodden mud into the pool.

[the pool remains] valid: As the water absorbed in the mud was never lifted out of the pool, and hence never obtained the status of "drawn water."

if one removed the mud [from the pool]: If the mud is removed from the pool, however, the water absorbed in the mud becomes "drawn water," and three *log* of such water that fall back into the pool render it *invalid*.

R. Simeon deems it valid: Since the intention was only to remove the mud from the pool and not to draw water, the water absorbed in the mud is not considered "drawn water" according to R. Simeon.

2:7–9 *Is Valid Water Unintentionally Collected in Utensils Considered "Drawn"?*

7 If one leaves jars on the roof to dry,
and they became filled with water,
R. Eliezer says:
If it is the rainy season,
[and][32] if there is a little water in the pit,
he may break [the jars so that the water in them flows into the pit];
but if not,
he may not break [them].
R. Joshua says:
In either case,
he may break [the jars]
or overturn [them],
but he must not pour out [from the jars into the pit].
8 If a plasterer forgot a mixing tub in a pit,
and [the pit subsequently] became filled with water,

[32] **K, P, M**: "or."

2:7 The subject of this and the next two mishnayot is a pit, an empty cavity where water can gather and become a "pool."

became filled with water: It rained and the jars became filled with rainwater.

If it is the rainy season: During the rainy season, one who places jars on the roof should be aware that they may become filled with rainwater and must therefore be suspected of having intended to fill the jars.

a little water: The exact meaning of this phrase is unclear.

he may break [the jars so that the water in them flows into the pit]: By breaking the jars, he allows the water to flow into the pit by itself without becoming "drawn."

but if not: There was no water in the pit.

he may not break [them]: Since this occurred during the rainy season, R. Eliezer holds that the filling of the jars with rainwater cannot be considered completely unintentional, and as such the water in the jars is regarded as a kind of drawn water. A lack of any water whatsoever in the pit is an aggravating factor (cf. the opinion of R. Eliezer in 2:4), and even this quasi-drawn water invalidates any water that later falls into the pit. According to the variant reading in the manuscripts, R. Eliezer allows the jars to be broken if *either* it is the rainy season *or* there is water in the pit; both are considered ameliorating factors.

R. Joshua says: R. Joshua holds that rainwater that falls into the jars is not considered "drawn" at all.

In either case: Whether or not there was any water in the pit. According to the variant reading in the manuscripts, also whether or not it was the rainy season.

or overturn [them]: R. Joshua (apparently in dissent with R. Eliezer) holds that overturning the jars, like breaking them, does not render the water that spills out of them "drawn."

but he must not pour out [from the jars into the pit]: Even according to R. Joshua, actively pouring from the jars into the pit would render the water "drawn."

2:8 *If a plasterer forgot*: Pools, cisterns, and other water installations were regularly coated with plaster in order to prevent leakage. Here the tub used by the plasterer to mix the plaster is unintentionally left behind in the empty pit.

became filled with water: The pit, together with the mixing tub found in it, became filled with valid water. The water in the pit itself measured less than forty *se'ah*.

if any amount of water at all was covering [the tub],
he may break [the tub so that the water in it flows into the pit],
but if not,
he may not break [it]—
the words of R. Eliezer.
R. Joshua says:
In either case
he may break [the tub].

9 If one arranges jars in a pit,
and they became filled with water,
even though the pit absorbed its water,
he may break [the jars].

2:10 *Mud in a Pool*

10 A pool that contains forty *se'ah* of water and mud [together]—
R. Eliezer says:
One may immerse [objects] in the water,
but one may not immerse in the mud.
R. Joshua says:

if any amount of water at all: If water in the pit covers the rim of the tub, the water in the tub is considered one with the valid water in the pit, and hence not "drawn."

he may break [the tub] but he may not pour from the tub into the pit, as this would render the water "drawn."

but if not: If the water is too shallow to cover the tub, the water in the tub is considered separate from the valid water in the pit and would constitute "drawn water" if combined with the other.

he may not break [it]: Even though the tub was left in the pit unintentionally, the water is considered "drawn."

In either case: Whether water covers the tub or not.

he may break [the tub]: Since the tub was left unintentionally in the pit, the water that subsequently filled it is not considered "drawn." It appears that here, unlike the previous case, R. Joshua and R. Eliezer agree that where the water in the tub is not considered "drawn" it may be broken but not overturned.

2:9 *arranges jars in a pit*: Empty jars are placed in a pit filled with valid water. The commentators explain that the intention is to saturate the porous sides of the jars with water so that they will not absorb the wine that is to be put in them later.

and they became filled with water: Unintentionally, the jars became filled with water from the pit.

even though the pit absorbed its water: If the water in the pit seeped out such that the pit no longer contained forty *se'ah* aside from the water in the jars.

he may be break [the jars]: Since the water entered the jars unintentionally, it is not considered "drawn."

2:10 *water and mud [together]*: The mud is counted toward the minimum measure of forty *se'ah*.

One may immerse [objects] in the water but... not... in the mud: Even though the mud is counted toward the forty *se'ah*, R. Eliezer holds that the immersion itself must take place in actual water.

In the water and in the mud.
In what mud may one immerse?
In mud that is covered with water.
If the water was at one side,
R. Joshua agrees that one may immerse in the water
but may not immerse in the mud.
Of what kind of mud did they speak?
Mud into which a reed sinks by itself—
the words of R. Meir.
R. Judah says:
Where the measuring rod does not stand.
Abba Eleazar[33] b. Dulai says:
Where the plummet sinks.
R. Eliezer says:
[Mud] that goes down into the mouth of a jar.[34]
R. Simeon says:
[Mud] that enters the spout of a waterskin.
R. Eleazar b. Zadok[35] says:
[Mud] that is measured by the *log*.

[33] **K**, **P**: "Abba Eliezer."
[34] **K**, **P**, **M** use a rare term that apparently denotes a jar used for cleaning out sewers and pits.
[35] **M**: "R. Eliezer b. Isaac."

In the water and in the mud: Either in the water or in the mud.

In what mud may one immerse objects? According to R. Joshua.

If the water was at one side and the mud at the other.

Of what kind of mud did they speak? R. Eliezer and R. Joshua.

into which a reed sinks by itself: Mud is considered sufficiently aqueous if a reed placed on its surface sinks into it by virtue of its own weight.

Where the measuring rod does not stand: Mud is considered sufficiently liquid if a measuring rod inserted into it falls over, not being able to stand of its own, even if it does not sink.

Where the plummet sinks: Mud that is soft enough to allow a plumb bob to sink into it by virtue of its own weight.

that goes down into the mouth of a jar: Mud that, when placed on the mouth of a jar, falls into it, not being sufficiently viscous to hold itself in place.

that enters the spout of a waterskin: Mud that is sufficiently soft that it can flow through the spout of a waterskin (cf. below, 6:7).

that is measured by the log: Mud sufficiently aqueous that it is measured in units of liquid measure. Alternatively: mud that is fluid enough that it can be poured into, and out of, a utensil used to measure *log* units.

Chapter Three

3:1–3 *How a Pool Invalidated by Drawn Water Is Made Valid Again*

3 R. Yose says:
Two pools, neither of which contains forty *se'ah* [of water]:
if a *log* and a half [of drawn water] fell into each one,[36]
and [the two pools subsequently] were mingled together,
[the water is] valid,
since [the water][37] never came under the category of "invalid."
But a pool that does not contain forty *se'ah* [of water],
if three *log* [of drawn water] fell into it,
and [the pool subsequently] was divided into two,
it is invalid,
since [the pool] had [already] come under the category of "invalid";[38]
but R. Joshua deems [the pools] valid,
for R. Joshua used to say:
Any pool that does not contain forty *se'ah* [of water],
if three *log* [of drawn water] fell into it,

[36] Lit. "and a *log* and a half fell into this one and a *log* and a half fell into that one."
[37] Or "[the pools]."
[38] **P** lacks "since [the pool] had already come under the category of 'invalid.' "

3:1 The previous chapter indicated that drawn water that falls into a pool containing less than forty *se'ah* invalidates the pool even if it is later filled with forty *se'ah* of valid water (2:4), and that the amount of drawn water that invalidates is three *log* (2:5). The main topic now is how a pool that has become invalidated by such an admixture is made valid again by removing water from the pool.

and [the two pools subsequently] were mingled together: And consequentially the drawn water in both pools now amounts to three *log*. The joined volume of the two pools presumably now amounts to forty *se'ah*, but this is not clearly specified.

[the water is] valid: The new combined pool is valid.

since [the water] never came under the category of "invalid": Since the drawn water joined to measure three *log* at the same moment that the valid water joined to measure forty *se'ah*, the water never became invalidated.

divided into two such that neither pool contained three complete *log* of drawn water.

it is invalid: Even if either pool ever fills up to forty *se'ah*, it remains invalid.

since [the pool] had [already] come under the category of "invalid" at the moment the three *log* of drawn water had fallen into the original pool. According to R. Yose, a pool invalidated by three *log* of drawn water is not validated again by simply removing some of the drawn water.

R. Joshua deems [the pools] valid since neither pool now contains three complete *log* of drawn water.

three log [of drawn water] fell into it: Thereby invalidating it.

and [then] even a *qurtov* [of water] was removed,
it is valid,
since [some of the] three *log* has been removed.
But the Sages say:
It remains invalid,
until its entire volume and more
is removed from it.

2 How?
If a pit is in the courtyard,
and three *log* [of drawn water] fell into it,
[the pit] remains invalid
until its entire volume and more is removed from it,
or until one installs in the courtyard [another pool holding] forty *se'ah* [of valid water],
[such that] the upper [water] is purified by[39] the lower [water].
R. Eleazar b. Azariah deems it invalid,
unless he has stopped it up.[40]

[39] **K**: "purifies." [40] **P**: "[the water] has stopped."

a qurtov [of water]: A *qurtov* equals 1/64 of a *log*. Here (as elsewhere in the Mishnah) the term simply means a very small amount.

since [some of the] three log has been removed: Since the valid water is completely mingled with the drawn water, by removing any amount whatsoever from the pool one thereby removes some of the drawn water as well, lowering the volume of drawn water in the pool to less than three *log*.

until its entire volume and more is removed from it: i.e. a volume of water greater than the volume in the pool at the time the drawn water fell into it. This removes the full measure of the invalidating three *log*.

3:2 *How?* The Mishnah provides an example of how a pool invalidated by three *log* of drawn water may be made valid again according to the Sages.

If a pit is in the courtyard: The word "pit" refers to the empty cavity where water can gather and become a "pool" (see above, 2:7).

and three log [of drawn water] fell into it: Presumably, the pit did not contain forty *se'ah* of valid water when the three *log* of drawn water fell into it.

the upper [water] is purified by the lower [water]: A pool invalidated by drawn water may be made valid (*purified*) by being brought into contact with forty *se'ah* of valid water (cf. below, 6:8).

R. Eleazar b. Azariah deems it invalid: i.e. the invalidated water in the pit that has been brought into contact with a pool containing forty *se'ah* of valid water.

unless he has stopped it up: The referent is unclear, and the commentaries have suggested a number of explanations. It seems that according to the Sages one may channel valid water into the pit containing the invalidated water such that the pit overflows and fills the pool installed in the courtyard with forty *se'ah* of water; the water in the upper pit, in turn, is made valid by being brought into contact with the valid water in the lower pool. According to R. Eleazar b. Azariah, however, the valid water must be channeled directly into the lower pool, as water channeled via the upper pit would be mingled with invalid water; in order to insure that only valid water enters the lower pool, the outflow openings of the upper pit must be stopped up. Versions such as **P** that read "unless [the water] has stopped" are to be understood similarly: the water in the upper pit is made valid by coming into contact with the lower pool only if the flow of water from the upper pit has stopped and the valid water has been channeled directly into the lower pool.

3 If a pit is filled with drawn water,
and a channel [of valid water] leads into and out of it,
it remains invalid,
until it is calculated
that three *log* of the original water
no longer remain.

3:3 cont.–4 *Drawn Water Poured into a Pool (or onto a Person) Piecemeal*

If two people poured [drawn water] into a pool,
each [pouring] a *log* and a half;
[or] if he wrung his garment,
causing [water] to pour out from many places,
and if one poured from a strainer jug,
causing [water] to pour out from many places,
R. Aqiva deems the pool valid,
but the Sages deem it invalid.
R. Aqiva said:
They did not say:
[If] they pour,
but rather [If] one pours.
They replied:

3:3 *a channel [of valid water] leads into and out of it*: A channel carrying valid water leads into the pit, and another channel carrying run-off water from the pit leads out.

until it is calculated that three log of the original water no longer remain: The water in the pit becomes valid only when it is assessed that almost all of the drawn water has been displaced by the valid water carried in by the channel, with less than three *log* of the original water remaining.

If two people poured: This begins a new topic: whether or not drawn water invalidates a pool if the three *log* are poured in by different people or from different places.

into a pool that does not contain forty *se'ah* of water.

[or] if he wrung his garment: The water is expressed into the pool in a dispersed manner from various parts of the garment.

strainer jug: Probably a closed vessel with a strainer covering its opening (cf. *Kelim* 2:9). Here too, the water pours into the pool in a diffuse manner.

R. Aqiva deems the pool valid since the three *log* of drawn water did not fall into the pool as one.

but the Sages deem it invalid: According to the Sages, three *log* of drawn water invalidate a pool even if the water enters the pool from different places or by means of different people.

R. Aqiva said in support of his ruling.

They did not say: [If] they pour, but rather: [If] one pours: The early Sages who promulgated the original decree invalidating a pool into which three *log* of drawn water had been poured worded their dictum in the singular: "if one pours three *log* of drawn water into a pool...," rather than in the plural: "if they pour..."

They replied: The Sages to R. Aqiva.

They said neither this nor that,
but rather:
[A pool] into which
three *log* [of drawn water] fell.

4 [Three *log* that were poured into a pool] from one utensil, from two, or from three,
are counted together;
but from four [utensils],
are not counted together.
A man with a seminal discharge who was ill,
and nine *qav* of water fell on him,
and one who was pure
who had three *log* of drawn water fall
on his head and on the majority of his body,
from one utensil, from two, or from three,
[the water] is counted together;
but from four [utensils],
[the water] is not counted together.
When does this apply?
When the second [utensil] began to pour before the first stopped;
And when does this apply?
When one did not intend to increase;

They said neither this nor that: The original decree worded without naming an agent responsible for the falling of the water. *[A pool] into which three log [of drawn water] fell.* This is taken to imply that the pool is invalidated no matter how the drawn water falls into it.

3:4 *are counted together*: This is in accordance with the ruling of the Sages in the previous mishnah who ruled that drawn water invalidates even if it is not poured as one.

but from four [utensils]: The three *log* of water *are not counted together*—and the pool remains valid.

A man with a seminal discharge who was ill and thus unable to immerse in a pool. Although a man with a seminal discharge must *wash all his flesh* and await sundown to become pure again (Leviticus 15:16), one who is ill may suffice with pouring nine *qav* (thirty-six *log*) of water over his body. This washing enables the man to recite certain prayers and study Torah (see *Berakhot* 3:4–6), but does not remove his basic impurity; only immersion in a valid pool can accomplish this.

one who was pure: According to *Zavim* 5:12, a pure person who had three *log* of drawn water fall on his head and on the majority of his body is made impure, invalidating *terumah* through contact (cf. above, 2:2).

[the water] is counted together: Purifying the man with a seminal discharge, and making impure the one who was pure who had three *log* of drawn water fall on his head and on the majority of his body.

When does this apply that water poured from one, two, or three utensils is counted together to complete the measurement of three *log* or of nine *qav*?

When the second [utensil] began to pour before the first stopped: Thus associatively uniting the water poured from the two utensils.

And when does this apply that water is counted together only if one began to pour water from the second utensil before completing to pour from the first? Alternatively: that water poured from four utensils is not counted together?

When one did not intend to increase: When pouring from the first utensil, he had no intention of pouring any additional water from a second utensil.

but if one intended to increase,
even [only] a *qurtov* over the course of an entire year,
[the water] is counted together
to complete the measurement of three *log*.

Chapter Four

4:1–2 *Utensils Left under the Opening of a Duct*

4 If one put utensils under the [opening of a] duct,
whether large utensils or small utensils,
even utensils made of dung, utensils made of stone, [or] utensils made of [unfired] clay,
they render the pool invalid.
[This is true] whether one placed them [intentionally]
or forgot them,
according to the words of the House of Shammai.
But the House of Hillel deem it pure
in the case of one who forgot them.
R. Meir said:
They were counted,
and the House of Shammai outnumbered the House of Hillel;
and they agree regarding one who forgot [a utensil] in a courtyard,

but if one intended to increase: Such intention is enough to associatively unite the water poured from the various utensils.

a qurtov: Cf. above, 3:1.

over the course of an entire year: Even if only a small amount of water is poured from each utensil and at separate times.

4:1 *utensils under the [opening of a] duct*: To catch rainwater under a duct serving as a drainpipe; here valid water flowing from the duct has filled the utensils and they have spilled over into a pool.

even utensils made of dung, utensils made of stone, [or] utensils made of [unfired] clay: Although utensils made of these raw materials cannot themselves contract impurity, they nonetheless render water in them "drawn water."

render the pool invalid: If the water then pours out of the utensils into a pool containing less than forty *se'ah*.

deem it pure: i.e. valid, so that what is immersed in the pool becomes pure.

in the case of one who forgot them: Since there was no intention to fill the utensils with water, the House of Hillel do not consider the water "drawn" (cf. above, 2:6–9).

They were counted: It was decided to resolve the matter by majority opinion, and it was found that the members of the House of Shammai outnumbered the members of the House of Hillel.

and they agree: The House of Shammai.

regarding one who forgot [a utensil] in a courtyard and the utensil is subsequently filled with rainwater. Although the House of Shammai attributes some degree of intentionality to the act of leaving a utensil

that it remains pure.
R. Yose said:
The dispute remains in its place.[41]

2 If one places a board beneath the [opening of a] duct:
if [the board] has a raised rim,
it renders the pool invalid,
but if not,
it does not render the pool invalid.
If he set [the board] upright to be rinsed,
in either case it does not render the pool invalid.

4:3 *Cavities Hollowed into a Duct*

3 If one hollows out [a cavity] in a duct in order to catch pebbles,
if [the duct] is made of wood,
[a cavity that holds] any amount whatever [renders the duct a "utensil"],
but if [the duct] is made of earthenware,
[a cavity that holds] a quarter[-*log* renders the duct a "utensil"].
R. Yose says:
Even if [the duct] is made of earthenware,

[41] **P** lacks "R. Yose said: The dispute remains in its place."

under a duct, they agree that no intention is present if the utensil is forgotten in a courtyard and only by chance becomes filled with rainwater.

that it remains pure: i.e. the pool remains valid. That is, if the water then pours out into a pool containing less than forty *se'ah*, the pool remains valid.

The dispute remains in its place: Even if the utensil is forgotten in a courtyard, the House of Shammai still dispute with the House of Hillel and hold that the pool is invalid. Alternatively: R. Yose contends that no decision by majority was made to settle the dispute between the Houses, and the matter remains unsettled.

4:2 *a board*: A slab, plank, tablet, or flat tray.

beneath the [opening of a] duct and valid water flowed from the duct onto the board, and from there the water continued to flow into a pool that contained less than forty *se'ah* of water.

if [the board] has a raised rim around its edge; since it is a receptacle capable of holding something inside, it is deemed a "utensil" and renders water that falls into it "drawn."

but if not: It is not a receptacle, and as such does not come under the category of a "utensil" and does not render water that falls onto it "drawn."

If he set [the board] upright to be rinsed: Thereby indicating that he has no intention of collecting water in the receptacle.

in either case: Even if the board has a raised rim around its edge.

it does not render the pool invalid as the water that pours onto the board is not considered "drawn."

4:3 *hollows out [a cavity] in a duct in order to catch pebbles*: The cavity is meant to prevent clogging by catching pebbles that pass through the duct.

[a cavity that holds] any amount whatever [renders the duct a "utensil"];
they spoke of a quarter[-*log*] only with regard to broken earthenware utensils.
If pebbles were rolling about in[42] [the cavity],
it renders the pool invalid.
If earth fell into [the cavity] and was pressed tight,[43]
[the pool] is valid.
A pipe that is narrow at both ends
and wide in the middle
does not render [a pool] invalid,
since it was not made to hold anything.

4:4 *Drawn Water That Mingles with Valid Water Prior to Entering a Pool*

4 Drawn water and rainwater that were mingled together
in a courtyard, in a hollow, or on the steps of a cave:

[42] **K, P, M**: "into." [43] **K**: "and he dried them." The meaning of this variant is unclear.

any amount whatever: Even a cavity that can hold only very small pebbles renders the duct into a "utensil" (see above, 4:2), and water that passes through the duct is considered "drawn water."

a quarter[-log]: A duct made of earthenware is considered a "utensil" only if one hollowed into it a cavity that holds a volume of a quarter-*log*.

they spoke of a quarter[-log]: When the rabbis reckoned that the smallest capacity that makes an earthenware receptacle into a "utensil" is a quarter-*log*, this was *only with regard to broken earthenware utensils*; i.e. an earthenware vessel that has broken continues to contract impurity as a "utensil" only as long as it can still hold a minimum volume of a quarter-*log* (see *Kelim* 2:2). With regard to other matters, such as the ability to render water "drawn," an earthenware receptacle made to hold any volume whatever is considered a "utensil."

If pebbles were rolling about in [the cavity]: If the cavity in the duct was filled with pebbles, these are not considered as canceling the cavity if there is still room for them to move about.

it renders the pool invalid: Water that flows through such a duct and passes into a pool that does not contain forty *se'ah* of valid water invalidates the pool.

If earth fell into [the cavity] and was pressed tight: The blocked-up cavity is canceled and the duct is no longer considered a "utensil."

[the pool] is valid: If water flows through such a duct and passes into a pool that does not contain forty *se'ah* of valid water, the pool remains valid.

A pipe that is narrow at both ends and wide in the middle and water that flows through such a pipe collects at the point where the pipe becomes narrow again.

does not render [a pool] invalid: If water flows through such a pipe and passes into a pool that does not contain forty *se'ah* of valid water, the pool remains valid.

since it was not made to hold anything: Even though the water is hindered in its flow by the narrowing of the pipe, since the pipe was not designed to actually hold anything it is not considered a "utensil" (cf. *Kelim* 2:3).

4:4 *mingled together in a courtyard* and then proceeded to flow into a pool.

in a hollow: A small pit.

or on the steps of a cave: Steps hewn into the floor of a cave, which lead down into a pool (cf. below 6:1, 7:7).

if the majority was composed of valid [water],
it is valid;
but if the majority was composed of invalid [water],
it is invalid;
If both parts were equal,[44]
it is invalid.
When?
When [the waters] mingled together before they reached the pool.
If they flowed [separately] in the midst of[45] the water:
if it is known that forty *se'ah* of valid water fell into [the pool]
before three *log* of drawn water went down into it,
it is valid,
but if not,
it is invalid.

4:5 *When Is a Trough Considered a "Utensil"?*

5 A trough [hewn] in the bedrock:
one may not fill [purgation water] from[46] it,

[44] Lit. "half to half." [45] **K, P**: "into." [46] **K, P, M**: "in."

if the majority was composed of valid [water]: The invalid drawn water is nullified by the majority of valid water.

it is valid: The pool into which the mixture of water flowed is valid.

but if the majority was composed of invalid [water]: The invalid drawn water is not nullified by the minority of valid water, and invalidates the pool into which the mixture flows.

When? When does a majority of valid water nullify a minority of invalid water?

When [the waters] mingled together before they reached the pool: As in the cases described above (*in a courtyard*, etc.).

If they flowed: The majority of valid water as well as the smaller amount of invalid water both flowed into the pool separately, without mingling prior to entering the pool.

if it is known: If the pool contained forty *se'ah* of valid water before three *log* of drawn water flowed into it the pool remains valid, as a pool containing forty *se'ah* of valid water is not invalidated by drawn water (see above, 2:3).

but if not: If the valid water in the pool measured less than forty *se'ah* at the moment that three *log* of drawn water flowed into the pool. Alternatively: if it is not known for sure how much valid water the pool contained at the moment that three *log* of drawn water flowed into it.

4:5 The first half of this mishnah teaches that a receptacle that has been hewn into the bedrock is not considered a "utensil," whereas one that is movable and only afterward attached to the ground is considered a "utensil." This section is repeated word for word in *Parah* 5:7.

one may not fill [purgation water] from it: Purgation water is prepared by putting "living water" on ashes of a red heifer that had been placed in a utensil (Numbers 19:17). This purgation water is then sprinkled by a pure person on corpse-impure people and objects (Numbers 19:18). A trough hewn into the rock is not considered a "utensil," and therefore may not be used to collect water that is to be made into purgation water. (As the manuscripts here, *Parah* 5:7 reads "in it" instead of "from it".)

one may not sanctify [purgation water] in it,
and one may not sprinkle [purgation water] from it:
it does not need a lid fastened down,
and it does not render a pool invalid.
If [the trough] was a utensil and
one attached it [to the ground] with lime,
one may fill [purgation water] in it,
one may sanctify [purgation water] in it,
and one may sprinkle [purgation water] from it:
it needs a lid fastened down,
and it renders a pool invalid.
If one pierced a hole through its bottom
or through its side
[in such way that] it can hold no water at all,
[the trough] is valid.
How large must the hole be?
Like the spout of a waterskin.
R. Judah b. Betera said:
It once happened
that the trough of Jehu
that was in Jerusalem

one may not sanctify [purgation water] in it: By mixing red-heifer ashes with "living water" in the trough. Even if the "living water" had been drawn into a genuine utensil, if the water was then poured into a trough hewn into the bedrock, one may not sanctify it as purgation water by placing ashes into it since the rite of mixing the ashes with the water must be performed in a "utensil."

one may not sprinkle [purgation water] from it: As in the previous clause, the rite of sprinkling too must be performed from a "utensil."

it does not need a lid fastened down: According to Numbers 19:15, every open utensil found in a Tent wherein a corpse lies is impure unless it has on it a "lid fastened down" (see also *Kelim* 10:1; *Ohalot*, introduction). Since a trough hewn into the bedrock is not considered a "utensil," if such a receptacle is found in a Tent where a corpse lies anything found inside it remains pure even if the trough is covered with an unfastened lid.

it does not render a pool invalid: If the trough is filled with valid water that then flows into a pool, the pool remains valid since the trough is not considered a "utensil" and therefore does not render the water in it "drawn."

If [the trough] was a utensil: i.e. a movable receptacle, detached from the bedrock.

one may fill [purgation water] in it, etc.: Since it was once a detached receptacle, it continues to be considered a "utensil" even after it has been attached to the ground.

If one pierced a hole: Once the trough can no longer hold any water, it is rendered useless and loses its status as a "utensil."

[the trough] is valid: The water in the trough does not invalidate a pool.

Like the spout of a waterskin: Cf. below, 6:7.

R. Judah b. Betera said: He relates a story meant to show that the House of Shammai disagree, and insist that the majority of the trough must be broken off for it to lose its status as a "utensil."

the trough of Jehu that was in Jerusalem: Apparently a well-known feature in the city during the late Second Temple period.

was pierced like the spout of a waterskin,
and all of the pure things in Jerusalem
were prepared on the basis of it,[47]
and the House of Shammai sent [messengers]
and reduced its size,
for the House of Shammai say:
[It is still considered a utensil] until the majority of it is reduced.

Chapter Five

5:1–2 *Spring Water That Flows over Various Receptacles and Utensils*

5 A spring that one had made to flow over a trough
is invalid.
If one made it flow over a rim [of the trough]
[in] any amount whatever,
[any water that is] outside of [the trough] is valid,

[47] Lit. "made upon it."

pure things: Foodstuffs prepared in a manner to ensure their purity.

were prepared on the basis of it: Jerusalemites relied on immersion in a pool filled with water that passed through this trough in order to prepare food and liquids in purity.

sent [messengers] and reduced its size: The messengers broke off most of the trough so that it would no longer be considered a "utensil" and invalidate the adjacent pool.

5:1 Spring water differs from a pool in that spring water of any amount purifies (even if it does not contain forty *se'ah*), it purifies even if it is still flowing, and it may be used whenever scripture calls for "living water"—such as for the immersion of a man who experienced an abnormal sexual discharge (*zav*), for the rite of purification of those with *tsara'at*, and for the sanctification of purgation water. The bulk of this chapter clarifies the validity of spring water under various circumstances.

to flow over a trough: A trough that is a detached utensil, not hewn into the bedrock (see above 4:5). The water flows into the trough.

is invalid: Since the trough is considered a "utensil," any water that flows into it becomes "drawn water" and remains invalid even after it has overflowed out of the trough.

If one made it flow over a rim: Not all of the water flowed into the trough, but rather some of it flowed over the rim without entering the receptacle of the trough itself.

any amount whatever: Even if the water that flowed over the rim was of minimal quantity.

[any water that is] outside of [the trough]: The overflow of the trough is valid (but not the water that still remains in the trough).

as a spring purifies whatever its quantity.
If one made it flow over a basin
and then stopped its flow,
[the water in the basin][48] is like a pool;[49]
if he made it flow once again,
it is invalid for [the immersion of] *zavim*,
for [the rite of purification of] *tsara'at*,
and for the sanctification of purgation water
until it is known that the original water went out.

2 If one made [the spring water] flow over utensils or over a bench,
R. Judah says:
[The water][50] remains as it was before.
R. Yose says:
It is like a pool,
as long as one does not immerse [objects][51] above the bench.

[48] The literal antecedent is the spring, but the actual referent is the water that came from the spring.
[49] **K**: "remains as it was before." [50] See the note in the previous mishnah.
[51] Lit. "cause to be immersed." **K**, **P**: "immerse," that is, himself.

as a spring purifies whatever its quantity: Since the spring water that flowed over the rim remains valid, even a negligible quantity of it validates ("purifies") all of the "drawn water" that had entered the trough and then overflowed out of it.

flow over a basin: i.e. flow into a basin. A basin is a type of installation built into the ground (and hence not a "utensil").

stopped its flow: The water in the basin is cut off from the flow emanating from the spring.

like a pool: Since the water in the basin is no longer physically connected to the spring, it loses its quality of spring water and becomes like regular pool water, purifying only if it contains forty *se'ah* and only if it is standing still (see above 1:7), and invalid for use in cases when Scripture calls for "living water."

if he made it flow once again: The water in the basin is once again physically connected to the flow of spring water.

invalid for [the immersion of] zavim, etc.: Scripture requires "living water" for each of these rites (see above, 1:8). Once water loses its status of "living water" by becoming cut off from the spring, it cannot regain this status by simply reconnecting to an uninterrupted flow of spring water.

until it is known that the original water went out: The water in the basin is considered "living water" only after it is made to overflow such that there is nothing left of that water that was standing in the basin when it had been detached from the spring.

5:2 *flow over utensils or over a bench*: As distinct from the previous case of the trough, here the water flows over the utensils or bench, not into them.

remains as it was before: The water still has the status of spring water.

It is like a pool: Purifying only if it contains forty *se'ah* and only if it is standing still, and invalid for use in cases when Scripture calls for "living water." Even though the water has not entered into a receptacle and become "drawn water," in R. Yose's view the fact that it flowed over utensils causes the water to lose its character as "living water."

as long as one does not immerse [objects] above the bench: The actual act of immersion must take place elsewhere in the water, not directly above the bench. No explanation is offered for this limitation.

5:3 *Spring Water to Which Other Water Was Added*

3 A spring that is drawn out like a centipede:
if one added to it and extended its flow,
it remains as it was before.
If it was standing
and one added to it and extended its flow,
it is equal to a pool in that it purifies [only] when its water is standing,
and to a spring in that one may immerse [objects] in it, whatever its quantity.

5:4 *Sea Water*

4 All seas are like a pool,
as it is said:
and the pooled waters He called Seas—
the words of R. Meir.
R. Judah says:
The Great Sea is like a pool;
"Seas" was said only [with regard to] that which has in it many kinds of seas.

5:3 *drawn out like a centipede*: Its stream branching out laterally into smaller streamlets like the legs of a centipede spread out from both sides of its elongated body.

if one added to it: Additional water, presumably by pouring into it "drawn water" (see reference to 1:7 in what follows).

and extended its flow: The extra water caused the stream to spread out more than before the water was added.

it remains as it was before: The stream retains the status of spring water (see introduction to 5:1).

If it was standing and not "drawn out like a centipede."

and one added to it and extended its flow: This is apparently identical to the case described above (as the fourth of the six grades of pools): "a spring with a small flow of water, and a greater quantity of drawn water was added to it" (above, 1:7).

it purifies [only] when its water is standing: Since it spreads out only as a result of drawn water having been added to it, its flowing character is unrelated to its having emanated from a spring, and as such it is regarded as a pool that purifies only when its water is standing still.

one may immerse, whatever its quantity: Since the ability of spring water to purify no matter what its quantity is unrelated to the flowing character of a spring, this capability is not affected by the fact that the spring's flow was extended only as a result of the addition of drawn water.

5:4 This mishnah appears verbatim in *Parah* 8:8.

All seas are like a pool: All seas purify like a pool and not like a spring (see introduction to 5:1).

as it is said: Genesis 1:10.

He called Seas: That is, seas and pools are equivalent.

The Great Sea: The Mediterranean Sea.

is like a pool but other seas are like a spring.

"Seas" was said: In the plural.

that which has in it many kinds of seas: According to R. Judah, the verse that equates the sea with a pool refers to only one body of water, the Mediterranean, which is called "Seas" in the plural because it is

R. Yose says:
All seas purify [even] when they flow,
but are invalid for [the immersion of] *zavim*,
for [the rite of purification of] *tsara'at*,
and for the sanctification of purgation water.

5:5 *Spring Water That Flows and Spring Water That Drips*

5 Flowing [water] is like a spring,
[whereas] dripping [water] is like a pool.
R. Zadok testified regarding flowing [water]
that outmeasured dripping [water],
that it is valid.
And [in the case of] dripping [water]
that one made into flowing [water],
one may lean [against it] even a rod, even a reed, even a *zav* or a *zavah*
[and then] go down and immerse—
the words of R. Judah.

composed of "many kinds of seas." The upshot, in his opinion, is that no other sea is equated with a pool. Exactly why R. Judah regards the Mediterranean as having in it "many kinds of seas" is unclear.

All seas purify [even] when they flow: Like a spring.

but are invalid, etc.: Like a pool. According to the opinion of R. Yose, the rule regarding seas is equivalent to that stated with regard to "impaired water" above, 1:8.

5:5 Spring water collected in a basin that has been cut off from the flow of the spring has lost the status of spring water and is considered to be like a pool (above, 5:1). The present mishnah discusses the status of spring water that is connected to the source of the spring through a stream of dripping water.

Flowing [water]: Spring water that flows uninterruptedly from a spring.

is like a spring: For the differences between a spring and a pool, see above, 5:1.

dripping [water] is like a pool: If, however, the stream of spring water drips instead of flowing uninterruptedly, it is considered disconnected from the spring and therefore has the status of only a pool.

R. Zadok testified: This passage is repeated in *Eduyot* 7:3.

regarding flowing [water] that outmeasured dripping [water]: Spring water flowing uninterruptedly from the source of the spring that has mixed in a pool with spring water that drips, and the flowing water forms the majority of the pool.

it is valid: The water has the status of the majority, and is regarded as spring water.

dripping [water] that one made into flowing [water]: Some sort of contrivance turned a dripping stream into an uninterrupted flow.

one may lean [against it] even a rod, even a reed: One may lean a rod or a reed against the dripping stream, producing the effect that the stream flows continuously along the surface of the rod or the reed instead of dripping in the air.

even a zav or zavah: The dripping stream may even be made to flow along the body of an impure person such as a *zav* or *zavah*.

R. Yose says:
One may not use anything that is [capable of] receiving impurity to cause [water] to flow by means of it.

5:6 *Immersion in a Wave, in Various Crevices and in a Torrent of Water*

6 If a wave that broke off [from the sea]
contained forty *se'ah*
and fell on a person or on utensils,
they are pure.
Any place that contains forty *se'ah* [of water],
one may immerse
and [objects] may be immersed.
[Objects] may be immersed
in ditches, in channels, and in a donkey's hoofprint mingled [with others] in a valley.
The House of Shammai say:
[Objects] may be immersed in a torrent of water.
[But] the House of Hillel say:
[Objects] may not be [so] immersed.
But they agree
that one may dam up [the torrent with] utensils
and immerse in [the water],

anything that is [capable of] receiving impurity and certainly that which is already impure, such as a *zav* or *zavah*.

5:6 *and fell on a person or on utensils* that were impure.

they are pure: The impure person or utensils are made pure by the crashing wave as if they had been immersed in the sea itself (see above, 5:4).

Any place that contains forty se'ah [of water]: Even in irregular gatherings of water, as will be described presently.

one may immerse and [objects] may be immersed: Impure people and objects are purified through immersion in such water.

[Objects] may be immersed in ditches, in channels: The mishnah proceeds to list various unusual places where forty *se'ah* of water may gather.

in a donkey's hoofprint mingled [with others] in a valley: Donkey tracks filled with valid water and adjoining one to another such that the water that mingles together measures forty *se'ah*.

The House of Shammai say: This dispute is listed in *Eduyot* 5:2 among the leniencies of the House of Shammai and the stringencies of the House of Hillel.

in a torrent of water: In a parallel text in the Tosefta the term is explained as "rainwater flowing down an incline."

the House of Hillel say: Flowing water does not purify (unless it is spring water).

But they agree: Even the House of Hillel agrees.

one may dam up [the torrent with] utensils: Thereby causing the water to gather into a standing pool.

though those utensils used for damming
are not [deemed as having been] immersed.[52]

Chapter Six

6:1 *When Is Water Adjoining a Pool Considered "Mingled" as One with the Pool?*

6 Any [collection of water] that mingles with [water in] a pool
is like the pool [itself].
[As for] holes of a cave and fissures of a cave,
one may immerse [objects] in them as they are.
[As for] a hollow of a cave,
one may not immerse [objects] in it
unless it was pierced through [to the pool] like the spout of a waterskin.
R. Judah said:
When does this apply?
When [the hollow] stands of its own.[53]

[52] Lit. "were not immersed."
[53] **M**: "stirs itself up," here and in the next line. The meaning of this reading is unclear.

those utensils used for damming: The utensils that form the dam are not considered to have been immersed since one side of the utensils is outside the dammed-up water.

6:1 *Any [collection of water] that mingles with [water in] a pool*: Any water adjoining a pool that contains forty *se'ah* of valid water in such a way that the waters mingle with one another.

is like the pool [itself]: It is viewed as one body of water with the pool, and one may immerse in the adjoining water even if it contains less than forty *se'ah*. The Mishnah proceeds to detail when adjoining water is considered "mingled" with a pool.

holes of a cave and fissures of a cave: i.e. a cave filled with a pool containing forty *se'ah* of valid water. Holes and fissures are found in the walls of the cave containing this pool and are filled with its water.

as they are: One may immerse objects in the holes or fissures no matter how large the aperture between the hole or fissure and the pool itself, as the water in these clefts is considered to be "mingled" with the pool.

a hollow of a cave: A small pit filled with less than forty *se'ah* of water that stands beside the pool of a cave.

pierced through [to the pool] like the spout of a waterskin: The aperture that connects the hollow and the cave must be as wide as the spout of a waterskin. Unlike holes and fissures in the wall of a cave, which are clearly adjunctive elements of the cave itself, a hollow is a distinct feature of its own, and as such the water found in it is not considered "mingled" with the water in the cave unless the connection between the two is sufficiently large.

When does this apply? That the opening connecting a hollow with a cave must be the size of the spout of a waterskin?

When [the hollow] stands of its own: The walls of the hollow are strong enough to stand on their own when the hollow is filled with water, even without the counterpressure of the water in the adjoining cave. In such a case the hollow is considered an entity distinct from the cave.

But if it does not stand of its own,
one may immerse [objects] in it as it is.

6:2 *Immersion of a Bucket Filled with Utensils*

2 If a bucket is filled with utensils
and one immersed them [in a pool],
they are pure.
But if he did not immerse [the bucket],[54]
the waters [in the bucket and in the pool] are not mingled,[55]
unless they are mingled as if [through] the spout of a waterskin.

6:3 *Two Valid Pools That Mingled via a Pool of Drawn Water*

3 Three pools,
two of which contain twenty *se'ah* each [of valid water],
while the third contains twenty *se'ah* of drawn water,[56]
and the drawn [pool is situated] to the side,
if three went down
and immersed in [the pools],

[54] **M** lacks "But if he did not immerse."
[55] **K, P, M** read "in mingled water" instead of "the waters [in the bucket and in the pool] are not mingled." The meaning of this reading is unclear.
[56] Lit. "in this twenty *se'ah*, and in this twenty *se'ah*, and in this twenty *se'ah* of drawn water."

But if it does not stand of its own: Since the hollow cannot hold water without the counterpressure of the water in the cave, the two are regarded as one entity, and their waters are considered "mingled."

as it is: No matter how large the opening between the hollow and the cave.

6:2 *If a bucket is filled with utensils* and the utensils are impure.

and one immersed them [in a pool]: The bucket containing the utensils is submerged entirely in the pool.

they are pure: The utensils are purified by the pool, as the water in the submerged bucket is considered "mingled" with the water in the pool, and it is as if the utensils were immersed in the pool itself.

But if he did not immerse [the bucket] but filled it with water through a hole in the bottom of the bucket or its side and thereby immersed the utensils.

the waters [in the bucket and in the pool] are not mingled: The water inside the bucket is not considered "mingled" with the water of the pool, and the utensils therefore remain impure.

unless they are mingled as if [through] the spout of a waterskin: If the opening between the bucket and the pool is the size of the spout of a waterskin, the water in the bucket is considered "mingled" with the water in the pool, and the utensils in the bucket therefore are purified as if they were immersed in the pool itself.

6:3 *Three pools* in a row, one next to the other.

to the side: i.e. not between the two pools containing the valid water.

if three went down and immersed: Three impure people immersed themselves at the same time, one in each pool.

and [the pools] mingled together,
the pools are pure,
and those that immersed are pure.[57]
If the drawn [pool] was in the middle,
and three went down and immersed in them,
and [the pools] mingled together,
the pools remain as they were,
and those that immersed remain as they were.

6:4 *A Sponge or Bucket Holding Drawn Water That Falls into a Pool*

4 If a sponge or a bucket
that held three *log* of water
fell into a pool,
they did not render [the pool] invalid,
since they said only: Three *log* [of drawn water] that fell.

6:5–6 *Immersion in Utensils Submerged in a Pool*

5 A chest or a box[58]
that is in the sea[59]—

[57] **M** lacks: "The pools are pure . . . mingled together," possibly a scribal mistake.
[58] **M** adds "or a cupboard."
[59] **P** lacks "that is in the sea."

and [the pools] mingled together: As a result of the immersion the three pools overflowed and the displaced water connected the three pools such that they "mingled."

the pools are pure: i.e. valid. The two pools containing twenty *se'ah* of valid water each are now considered one pool containing forty *se'ah* of water; since the third pool is also "mingled" with these, it too is made valid.

and those that immersed are pure: Since all of the pools are valid, all three of those who immersed in them are made pure, even the one that had immersed in the drawn water.

If the drawn [pool] was in the middle: Between the two pools containing the valid water.

the pools remain as they were: Since the connection between the two pools containing the valid water was only through the intermediary of the drawn water situated in between, the two pools are not considered "mingled" as one pool containing forty *se'ah*.

and those that immersed remain as they were: Since none of the pools contains forty *se'ah* of valid water, the impure people who immersed in them are not purified thereby.

6:4 *If a sponge or a bucket that held three log of water* and the water is "drawn."

fell into a pool that contained less than forty *se'ah* of valid water (see above, 2:3).

since they said only: Three log [of drawn water] that fell: The wording of the original decree (see above 3:3) refers only to water, which is understood to mean that drawn water invalidates only if it falls into a pool by itself—and not when it is contained inside something else, such as a sponge or a bucket.

6:5 *A chest or a box that is in the sea*: i.e. submerged in the sea and filled with seawater.

one may not immerse [objects] in them
unless they were pierced like the spout of a waterskin.
R. Judah says:
With a large utensil,
[the hole must be] four handbreadths;
but with a small [utensil],
[the hole must equal] its greater part.
If it was a sack or a basket [that was in the sea],
one may immerse [objects] in them as they are,
since the water is mingled.
If these were placed under the [opening of a] duct,
they do not render the pool invalid;
but rather one may immerse them
and lift them [out of the pool] in their usual fashion.
6 If a potsherd is in the pool,
and one immersed [other] utensils in it,
they are purified of their impurity,

one may not immerse [objects] in them: Since they are utensils.

unless they were pierced like the spout of a waterskin: If the chest or the box was pierced with a hole the size of the spout of a waterskin, the water in these utensils is considered "mingled" with the sea (see above 6:1–2), and one may immerse objects in them.

With a large utensil: If the chest or box submerged in the sea was large.

[the hole must be] four handbreadths: The chest or box must be pierced with a hole at least four handbreadths wide in order to allow immersion inside it.

[the hole must equal] its greater part: The chest or box must be pierced with a hole more than half of one of its sides.

If it was a sack or a basket submerged in the sea and filled with seawater. Sacks and baskets are more porous than chests and boxes.

one may immerse [objects] in them as they are: Even if the sack or basket is not pierced like the spout of a waterskin.

since the water is mingled: The water in the sack or basket is considered "mingled" with the sea due to the highly permeable nature of these utensils.

If these were placed under the [opening of a] duct and valid water flowing from the duct pours through the sack or basket into a pool (cf. above 4:1).

they do not render the pool invalid: Water that pours through a porous sack or basket is not rendered "drawn water."

one may immerse them and lift them [out of the pool] in their usual fashion: According to 7:6 below, if utensils that hold water are immersed in a pool, they must be lifted out of the pool upside down in order to prevent the water retained in them from becoming "drawn"; in the present case, however, the sack or basket may be lifted out of the pool rightside up; because of their porous structure, they do not render water "drawn."

6:6 *If a potsherd is in the pool*: A broken, impure earthenware vessel was partially submerged in a pool.

and one immersed [other] utensils in it: Impure utensils were immersed in the water found in the partially submerged potsherd.

they are purified of their impurity: The original impurity of the utensils is removed through immersion in the pool.

but they are impure
due to [the impurity imparted by] an earthenware utensil.
If any amount of water at all was covering [the potsherd],
they are pure.
If a spring flows out of an oven,
and one went down and immersed in it,
he is pure,
but his hands are impure;
but if there was above the [oven a volume of water] the height of his hands,
his hands are pure as well.

6:7 *Specifications of the Measurement "Like the Spout of a Waterskin"*

7 The mingling of pools [requires an opening]
like the spout of a waterskin,
in its thickness and its aperture,[60]

[60] Lit. "space."

but they are impure due to [the impurity imparted by] an earthenware utensil: As the utensils are lifted out of the partially submerged impure potsherd, they must pass through the interior space of the portion of the potsherd protruding from the water, and this impure interior space renders the water remaining on the sides of the utensils impure—which in turn renders the utensils themselves impure (cf. *Kelim* 8:4).

If any amount of water at all was covering [the potsherd]: If, however, the potsherd was completely submerged in the pool, even if it was covered over by only the smallest amount of water.

they are pure: The utensils are completely pure, since they have not passed through the interior space of the impure potsherd.

If a spring flows out of an oven: An impure clay oven is filled with spring water.

and one went down and immersed in it: An impure person immersed himself in the spring water found in the oven.

he is pure: The body of the one who immersed is made pure through immersion in the spring, even though he entered the space of the impure oven—since an impure utensil does not render a person's entire body impure.

but his hands are impure: The hands of the person who immersed are rendered impure since they entered the space of the impure oven, and an impure utensil renders a person's hands impure (see *Yadayim* 3:1).

but if there was above the [oven a volume of water] the height of his hands: If the oven was completely covered with spring water, and the height of the water above the oven was at least the height of his hands when he stood.

his hands are pure as well: His hands were completely immersed in the spring water outside of the oven as he emerged from the water subsequent to immersing.

6:7 *The mingling of pools [requires an opening] like the spout of a waterskin*: If a pool that contains less than forty *se'ah* is connected to another pool, and the combined volume is more than forty *se'ah*, the two pools may be considered "mingled"— that is, as if both were one body of water—if the opening connecting them is "like the spout of a waterskin" (see 6:1–2, 5 above). The present mishnah describes what is meant by this measurement.

its thickness and its aperture: The diameter of the opening connecting the two pools must be as wide as the spout of a waterskin measured externally, that is including the thickness of the body of the spout itself.

[that is—if it is as large] as two fingers returning to their place.
[If there is] doubt whether or not it is like the spout of a waterskin,
[immersion in such a pool is] invalid,
since [the obligation of immersion] is mandated by the Torah.
And so too [concerning] an olive's bulk of a corpse,
or an olive's bulk of carrion,
or a lentil's bulk of a dead creeping thing.
Anything that stands in [the opening the size of] the spout of a waterskin,
diminishes it.
Rabban Simeon b. Gamaliel says:
Anything that is a creature of the water,
[if it stands in the opening, the pool] is pure.

6:8 *Purification of an Impure Pool by means of a Pure Pool*

8 One may purify pools,
an upper one from a lower one,

as two fingers returning to their place: The mishnah provides an additional measurement. While the exact meaning of *returning to their place* is unclear, the commentaries explain that the opening must be wide enough to allow two fingers to be inserted and rotated inside it.

[If there is] doubt whether or not it is like the spout of a waterskin: If one immersed in a pool connected to another, and there is doubt as to whether or not the opening between the two was the necessary size.

mandated by the Torah: Cases of doubt regarding Torah obligations are decided stringently.

And so too: Any similar cases of doubt that may arise with regard to measurements in the application of Torah law are likewise decided stringently.

an olive's bulk of a corpse, etc.: Flesh detached from a corpse conveys corpse impurity only if its volume equals at least an olive's bulk, carrion flesh imparts carrion impurity only if it measures at least an olive's bulk in volume, and a dead creeping thing conveys impurity only if its volume measures at least a lentil's bulk (see *Shabbat* 10:5, *Tohorot* 3:4). If doubt arises as to whether any of these contain the minimum volumes, we rule stringently.

Anything that stands in [the opening the size of] the spout of a waterskin: Any object that partially blocks up the opening between the pools.

diminishes it: Only the portion of the opening that remains unblocked is counted toward the measurement of "like the spout of a waterskin."

Rabban Simeon b. Gamaliel says: See *Yadayim* 2:2.

Anything that is a creature of the water: Living beings that generate out of water.

pure: Such creatures are regarded as water, and as such do not diminish the measurement of the opening between two pools. The word "pure" is somewhat out of place here, and appears to derive from the parallel in *Yadayim* 2:2.

6:8 *One may purify pools*: A pool that contains less than forty *se'ah* of valid water can become impure through contact with impurity. Our mishnah teaches how such an impure pool is made pure again.

an upper one from a lower one: An impure pool may be purified by means of a second pool situated on a lower level.

and a distant one from a near one.
How so?
One brings a pipe of earthenware or of lead,
places his hand beneath it until it is filled with water [from one pool],
and he draws it along
and brings it into contact [with water in the second pool];
even [if only by] a hair's breadth,[61]
it suffices.
If there were forty *se'ah* [of water] in the upper [pool]
and nothing at all in the lower,
one may fill [utensils with water and carry them] on the shoulder,
and pour [from these] into the upper [pool]
until forty *se'ah* [of water] flows down into the lower [pool].

6:9 *The Joining of Pools via a Crack or Breach in the Wall between the Two*

9 If a wall between two pools has cracked vertically,[62]
[one pool] joins [with the other];
but if horizontally,[63]
[one pool] does not join [with the other],
unless in there was in one place [an opening] like the spout of a waterskin.

[61] **P**: "a barley's breadth"; **M**: "a lentil's breadth."
[62] Lit. "along the warp." [63] Lit. "along the weft."

a distant one from a near one: Similarly, an impure pool may be purified by means of a second pool situated at a distance.

places his hand beneath it until it is filled with water: An angled pipe is placed in one of the pools, and after it has filled with water, a hand is placed beneath one end of the pipe, stopping up the water inside. This end of the pipe is then removed from the pool, brought into contact with the second pool, and the hand is removed—causing the water in the two pools to be connected via the pipe.

even [if only by] a hair's breadth: Even if the pipe connecting the two pools only touches the second by a negligible amount.

it suffices and the impure pool is made pure.

If there were forty se'ah [of water] in the upper [pool] and nothing at all in the lower and one wished to fill the empty pool with valid water.

one may fill [utensils with water and carry them] on the shoulder: That is, one may take drawn water.

and pour [from these] into the upper [pool]: The drawn water is poured into the full upper pool, causing it to overflow into the empty lower pool, thereby filling it. A pool filled with at least forty *se'ah* of valid water is not made invalid by drawn water (see above 2:3), and indeed drawn water that is poured into such a pool itself becomes valid.

6:9 *a wall between two pools*: Neither of which holds forty *se'ah* of water.

joins: The two pools are considered as one body of water, and if together they measure forty *se'ah* of water they form a valid pool.

R. Judah says:[64]
The opposite.
If [the pools] are breached through one to the other,
[they are considered joined if] the height is like [the thickness of] a garlic peel,
and its width is like the spout of a waterskin.

6:10–11 *The Validity of Pools in a Bathhouse*

10 The outlet that is in a bathhouse:
if it is in the middle [of the bathtub],
it renders [the water in the bathtub] invalid;
at the side,
it does not render[65] [the water in the bathtub] invalid,
since it is like a pool adjacent to a pool—
the words of R. Meir.[66]
But the Sages say:
If the bathtub holds a quarter-*log* [of water]
before it reaches the outlet,
[the water in the bathtub] is valid,
but if not,

[64] **M** lacks "R. Judah says…like the spout of a waterskin."
[65] **M**: "it renders." [66] **P** lacks "the words of R. Meir."

The opposite: A horizontal crack joins the pools, not a vertical one.

breached through one to the other: The top of the wall between the two pools is breached, and water from the pools flows over the breach and connects the two pools.

the height is like… a garlic peel: If the water in the breach connecting the two pools is as deep as the thickness of a garlic peel (that is, even the smallest amount), and its width is like the spout of a waterskin, the two pools are considered joined.

6:10 *The outlet*: A term whose exact meaning is unclear. A number of commentaries explain that it refers to a pipe with a stopper that, when opened, drains the bathtub of its water. Such a pipe is a receptacle meant to hold water, and as such the water in it is regarded as "drawn" (see above, 4:3). The outlet is presumed to hold at least three *log* of water.

that is in a bathhouse: i.e. a bathtub found in a bathhouse. The bathtub is filled with valid water.

if it is in the middle [of the bathtub]: i.e. if the pipe of the outlet lies at the floor of the bathtub.

invalid: Since the drawn water in the outlet is considered to be mixed with the pool, and three *log* of drawn water invalidates a pool that has in it less than forty *se'ah* of water (see above 2:3ff.).

at the side: i.e. if the pipe of the outlet is in the wall of the bathtub and conducts out from the side.

like a pool adjacent to a pool: See above 2:5.

If the bathtub holds a quarter-log: The outlet is high enough from the floor of the bathtub that when the bathtub is being filled with water, a quarter-*log* of water collects in the bathtub before the water level reaches the outlet.

valid: Even if the outlet is in the middle.

but if not: If the water level reaches the outlet before a quarter-*log* of water collects in the bathtub.

it is invalid.
R. Eleazar b. R. Zadok[67] says:[68]
If the outlet holds any [water] at all
it is invalid.

11 The ablution basin[69] that is in a bathhouse,
the bottom one being full of drawn [water]
and the upper one being full of valid [water],
if there are three *log* [of drawn water] opposite the hole,
[the water is] invalid.
How large must the hole be
so that there will be in it three *log* [of drawn water]?
One part to 320 parts of the basin—
the words of R. Yose.
But R. Eleazar[70] says:
Even[71] if the lower one is full of valid [water],
and the upper one is full of drawn [water],
and there are three *log* [of drawn water]
by the side of the hole,
[the bath is] valid,
since they said only: Three *log* [of drawn water] that fell.

[67] **P**: "R. Josah." [68] **M** lacks "R. Eleazar b. R. Zadok says…it is invalid." [69] Lit. "purifier."
[70] **M**: "R. Eliezer." [71] **K** lacks "Even."

it is invalid: Even if the outlet is at the side.

If the outlet holds any [water] at all: The outlet is considered a utensil, and invalidates the water in the bathtub even if the outlet is at the side, and even if the bathtub holds a quarter-*log* [of water] before the water level reaches the outlet.

6:11 *The ablution basin*: A rare word whose exact meaning is unclear. Most commentaries explain that it is some type of basin or pool found in a bathhouse; it may have been used by bathers at the end of their visit to restore their purity.

the bottom one . . . the upper one: In this bathhouse there are two adjacent ablution basins, a lower and an upper one, adjoined via a hole between the two. The lower one is filled with drawn water, while the upper is filled with less than forty *se'ah* of valid water.

opposite the hole: If the water in the lower ablution basin directly opposite the hole connecting the two installations measures three *log*.

[the water is] invalid: The water in the upper ablution basin is invalid since we consider it mingled with the three *log* of drawn water.

How large…? How does one measure the volume of water "opposite the hole" to determine if it equals three *log*?

One part to 320 parts of the basin: This is the proportion of three *log* to the minimum measure of forty *se'ah*.

Even if the lower one is full of valid [water] and all the more so if it is the upper ablution basin that is filled with the valid water, such that gravity does not cause the drawn water to flow into the valid pool.

by the side of the hole: Opposite the hole.

since they said only: Three log [of drawn water] that fell: The wording of the original decree (see above 3:3 and 6:4) refers only to water that fell into a pool, which is understood to mean that drawn water invalidates only if it actually falls into a pool—and not when it stands separately and is merely adjoined to a pool from the side.

Chapter Seven

7:1–2 *Substances Other Than Water That Serve to Fill a Pool and/or Invalidate It*

7 There are [some things] that raise a pool [to its prescribed measure of forty *se'ah*], but do not render it invalid;
[some that] render it invalid but do not raise it;
[and some that] neither raise it nor render it invalid.
These raise it but do not render it invalid:
snow, hail, frost, ice, salt, and thin mud.
R. Aqiva said:
R. Ishmael was arguing against me, saying:
Snow[72] does not raise a pool,
but the men of Medeba testified in his name,
that he had said to them:
Go and bring snow, and make [of it] a new pool.[73]
R. Yohanan b. Nuri says:
A hailstone is like water.
How so that they raise [a pool] but do not render it invalid?
A pool that holds forty *se'ah* [of valid water] less one,
and a *se'ah* of one of these fell into it,
and raised it [to forty *se'ah*]—
they are thus found to raise [a pool] but not render it invalid.

[72] **P**: "snow and hail and frost."
[73] Lit. "a pool from the beginning." **K** lacks "and make [of it] a new pool."

7:1 *There are [some things] that raise a pool*: Some substances are like water in that they are counted toward the measurement of forty *se'ah*.

but do not render it invalid: However, if three *log* of these substances fall into a pool containing less than forty *se'ah*, unlike drawn water they do not invalidate the pool.

[some that] render it invalid: As with drawn water, if three *log* of such substances fall into a pool containing less than forty *se'ah* they render the pool invalid.

but do not raise it: Unlike water, if such substances are added to a pool they are not counted toward the measurement of forty *se'ah*.

thin mud: Watery mud; cf. 2:10.

Medeba: Madaba, a city located on the central plateau of Transjordan.

a new pool: One entirely made of snow. Consequently, merely raising is certainly permitted.

A hailstone is like water: On the one hand it raises a pool to its prescribed measure of forty *se'ah*, and on the other hand it also renders a pool invalid if it is "drawn."

and a se'ah of one of these: Snow, hail, frost, ice, salt, and thin mud.

and raised it: The pool is thereby filled to the requisite forty *se'ah*.

but not render it invalid: These substances are never regarded as "drawn water."

2 These render [a pool] invalid but do not raise it:
[drawn] water,
whether pure or impure,
water in which food has been pickled
and water in which food has been cooked,
and piquette that has not yet turned sour.
How so that they render [a pool] invalid but do not raise it?
A pool that has in it forty *se'ah* [of water] less a *qurtov*,
and a *qurtov* from any of these fell into it,
it has not raised it,
[but] it invalidates it if it measures three *log*.
However, other liquids, and fruit juice, and brine, and garum, and piquette once it has soured,
sometimes raise up [a pool] but sometimes do not raise it up.
How so?
A pool that has in it forty *se'ah* less one,
if a *se'ah* from any of these fell into it,
it has not raised it up;
[however,] if it held forty [complete] *se'ah*,
if he put [into it] a *se'ah* [of one of these]
and then removed a *se'ah* [from the pool],
in such a case it is valid.

7:3–5 *Pollutants That Change the Appearance of a Pool*

3 If one rinsed baskets of olives or baskets of grapes in [a pool],
and they changed its appearance,

7:2 *These render [a pool] invalid*: If three *log* of one of these substances falls into a pool containing less than forty *se'ah* of valid water, the pool cannot purify.

water in which food has been pickled or…cooked: Such water is by definition "drawn water."

and piquette that has not yet turned sour: Piquette is a weak alcoholic beverage made from grape pomace (the skins, pulp, seeds, and stems of grapes after they have been pressed to make wine) soaked in water. Piquette that has not turned into vinegar is regarded as water, and since it is stored in utensils it has the status of "drawn water."

less a qurtov: See above, 3:1.

it has not raised it: It does not make the pool valid, as all of these have the status of "drawn water."

other liquids: The conventional rabbinic "liquids" (aside from water) are dew, wine, oil, blood, milk, and bees' honey (see *Makhshirin* 6:4).

garum: A type of fermented fish sauce popular in the ancient Greco-Roman world.

it has not raised it up: These liquids are not regarded as water.

and then removed a se'ah [from the pool]: From the admixture of pool water mixed with the other liquid.

it is valid: The pool remains valid. If the pool already contains forty *se'ah* of valid water, any of these liquids that is poured into the pool becomes nullified, and as such the entire admixture is regarded as valid water.

7:3 *they changed its appearance*: The baskets of fruit caused a change in the color of the pool.

[the pool remains] valid.
R. Yose says:
Dye liquid renders [a pool] invalid with three *log*,[74]
but it does not render it invalid by changing its appearance.
If wine fell[75] into [a pool], or olive juice,
and changed its appearance,
[it is] invalid.
What should one do [to make it valid]?
One should leave it until it rains,
and the appearance of the [water in the pool]
has once again attained the appearance of water.
If there were forty *se'ah* [of water] in [the pool],
one may fill [utensils with water and carry them] on the shoulder,
and pour [from these] into [the pool]
until the [water in the pool]
has once again attained the appearance of water.[76]
4 If wine or olive juice fell into [a pool]
and changed some of its appearance,
if there is not [in the pool] forty *se'ah*
[that have] the appearance of water,
one may not immerse in it.

[74] **P** seems to have begun adding the word "extra" and then deleted the incomplete word.
[75] **M**: "If you put wine."
[76] **M** lacks "If there were forty *se'ah* . . . the appearance of water," probably a scribal mistake.

with three log: Dye liquid is like water: three *log* of it that fall into a pool containing less than forty *se'ah* of valid water render the pool invalid.

changing its appearance: If less than three *log* of dye liquid fall into the pool, or if the pool already contains forty *se'ah*, the pool remains valid even though it has been colored by the dye liquid.

olive juice: The aqueous liquid expressed from the olive together with the oil.

invalid: Wine and olive juice are distinct substances, unlike rinse water and dye liquid, which are merely water-based solutions or mixtures.

What should one do if wine or olive juice has fallen into a pool and changed its color?

until it rains and the pool is filled with clean rainwater. The proposed solution is based on the assumption that the wine or olive juice fell into a pool that did not contain forty *se'ah* of valid water so that drawn water could not be poured into the pool to dilute it.

If there were forty se'ah: Drawn water may be poured in to dilute the water.

one may fill, etc.: Cf. above, 6:8.

7:4 *changed some of its appearance*: Only part of the water in the pool changed color.

forty se'ah [that have] the appearance of water: If the volume of water that remained clear measured less than forty *se'ah*.

one may not immerse in it: The entire pool is invalid, even the part of the pool that was not polluted.

5 Three *log* of [drawn] water,
and a *qurtov* of wine fell into them,
and their appearance, then,
was like the appearance of wine,
if they [subsequently] fell into a pool,
they have not rendered it invalid.
Three *log* of [drawn] water, less a *qurtov*,
and a *qurtov* of milk fell[77] into them,
and their appearance, then,
was [still] like the appearance of water,
if they [subsequently] fell into a pool,
they have not rendered it invalid.
R. Yohanan b. Nuri says:
Everything follows the appearance.

7:6–7 *A Pool That Contains the Bare Minimum Volume of Forty Se'ah*

6 A pool that held exactly forty *se'ah* [of water],
[and] two went down and immersed themselves,
one after the other,
the first is pure,
but the second is impure.
R. Judah says:
If the feet of the first were [still] touching the water,

[77] **P**: "and one put a *qurtov* of milk."

7:5 *a qurtov*: Cf. above, 3:1.

and their appearance, then, was like the appearance of wine: The *qurtov* of wine changed the color of the three *log* of drawn water to that of wine.

if they [subsequently] fell into a pool: The mixture of drawn water and wine fell into a pool containing less than forty *se'ah* of valid water.

they have not rendered it invalid: Since the mixture is no longer considered "water" (see above, 7:3).

and their appearance, then, was [still] like the appearance of water: The milk did not change the color of the drawn water.

if they [subsequently] fell into a pool containing less than forty *se'ah* of valid water.

they have not rendered it invalid: Since it was not a full three *log* of drawn water that fell into the pool, the milk does not count toward the measure of three *log*.

Everything follows the appearance: Since the mixture of water and milk has the appearance of water and measures three *log*, it renders the pool invalid.

7:6 *but the second is impure*: When the first person ascended from the pool, the small amount of water that remained on his body was removed from the pool, lowering the volume of water in the pool to below the minimum measure of forty *se'ah*.

If the feet of the first were [still] touching the water: Although the water remaining on the body of the first person is removed from the pool, it is still physically connected to the pool.

even the second is pure.
If one immersed a mantle in [such a pool]
and lifted it [out of the water],
if part of it [remains] touching the water,
[one who immersed in the pool is] pure.
A cushion or mattress made of leather,
once one has lifted their upper edges out of the water,
the water contained in them [becomes] "drawn."
What should one do?
One should immerse them
and lift them out by their bottoms.

7 If one immersed a bed [in such a pool],
even though its legs sink
into[78] the thick mud,
it is pure,
since the water precedes [the legs' sinking into the mud].
A pool whose water is shallow,

[78] P: "touch."

even the second is pure: The water remaining on the body of the first is counted toward the forty *se'ah* minimum.

mantle: A coarse woolen cloak or blanket capable of soaking up water.

in [such a pool]: Containing exactly forty *se'ah* of water.

if part of it [remains] touching the water: Although the water absorbed into the mantle has been removed from the pool, it is still physically connected to the pool.

[one who immersed in the pool is] pure: The pool is still valid since the water in the mantle is counted toward the forty *se'ah* minimum; this ruling is in accord with the opinion of R. Judah above.

A cushion or mattress made of leather: The bottom and sides of these objects are made of leather, allowing them to retain water if held upright.

once one has lifted their upper edges out of the water: After immersing such a cushion or mattress in a pool, one lifts it out of the pool upright, removing its upper edges from the water first.

the water contained in them [becomes] "drawn": Since the cushion or mattress can function as a utensil with a receptacle capable of holding water.

What should one do? If one wishes to immerse such an object in a pool containing exactly forty *se'ah* of water, and one wishes to avoid rendering the water retained in it from becoming "drawn water" that might fall back into the pool and invalidate it.

and lift them out by their bottoms: i.e. upside down, in such a way that no water is held in the cavity of the cushion or mattress as it is lifted out of the water; cf. above 6:5.

7:7 *If one immersed a bed*: The bed is impure and requires immersion; however, since its legs are long and the pool is shallow, it cannot be completely submerged unless its legs are pushed into the muddy floor of the pool.

even though its legs sink into the thick mud, which is too thick to be regarded as part of the pool itself (see above, 2:10).

since the water precedes: Water from the pool enters into the cavities in the mud formed by the legs of the bed as it is pushed down, and so the entire bed is considered to be immersed in the pool all at once.

A pool whose water is shallow: Even though the pool contains forty *se'ah* of water, the shallow level of the water precludes one from immersing his entire body in the pool at one time.

one pushes down [into the water]
even bundles of wood[79] or bundles of reeds
so that the water swells,
and [then] one [may] go down and immerse oneself.
A needle that was put on the steps of a cave,
and one was causing the water to move back and forth,
once a wave has passed over it,
it is pure.

Chapter Eight

8:1 *Pools in the Land of Israel and Abroad*

8 The Land of Israel is pure
and its pools are pure.
Pools of the nations[80] outside of the Land [of Israel],
are valid for those who have had a seminal discharge
even if they were filled with a well sweep.
Those in the Land of Israel

[79] **M**: "olives."

[80] **M**: "Pools of water" (differing from the standard text by one letter).

bundles of wood or bundles of reeds so that the water swells: One may submerge bundles of wood or reeds into the pool in order to displace the water and thereby raise the water level.

A needle that was impure and required immersion.

that was put on the steps of a cave: Steps hewn into the floor of a cave that led down to a pool (cf. above 4:4 and 6:1).

and one was causing the water to move back and forth: The water in the pool was agitated, causing a wave to ride up onto the step where the needle lay.

it is pure: As if the needle was immersed in the pool itself.

8:1 *The Land of Israel is pure*: Unlike "the land of the nations," which conveys impurity (*Oholot* 2:3).

and its pools are pure: Any pool found in the Land of Israel is presumed pure until known otherwise.

Pools of the nations: Belonging to gentiles.

a seminal discharge: A man with a seminal discharge must "wash all his flesh" and await sundown (Leviticus 15:16); although immersion in a valid pool is necessary to remove this basic impurity, immersion in drawn water enables him to recite certain prayers and study Torah (see *Berakhot* 3:4–6).

well sweep: A device for drawing water consisting of a long, suspended rod with a bucket at one end and a weight at the other. Pools outside the Land of Israel are presumed to be filled with drawn water, and thus suitable for purifying only those with a seminal discharge.

Those in the Land of Israel: Those belonging to gentiles. Another possibility is that all pools are meant, with this clause qualifying the initial ruling: *its pools are pure*.

that are outside the entrance,[81]
are valid even for menstruants;
inside the entrance,
they are valid for those who have had a seminal discharge
but are invalid for all [others] who are impure.
R. Eliezer[82] says:
Those near the city and the road
are impure because of the washing [of clothes],
but those far away
are pure.

8:2–4 *Seminal Discharges*

2 The following are those who have had a seminal discharge
who require immersion:
[if] he passed urine[83] that is broken or turbid,
in the beginning[84]—
[he is] pure;[85]
in the middle and at the end—
[he is] impure;
from the beginning[86] to the end—
[he is] pure.
[If it was] white and[87] continuous—
[he is] impure.
R. Yose says:
White is like turbid.

[81] According to the vowels in **K**: lit. "the key." [82] **K, P, M**: "R. Eleazar."
[83] Lit. "saw water." [84] **K, P**: "as the beginning." [85] **M** lacks "[he is] pure."
[86] **K, P**: "as the beginning." [87] **M** lacks "and"; **K**: "white that is continuous."

those outside the entrance of the town.

are valid even for menstruants: Pools found outside of a town's entrance are presumed to be filled with valid water.

inside the entrance: Pools found inside a town's entrance are presumed to be filled with drawn water.

because of the washing [of clothes]: Pools found near a city or a road are presumed to have been used for washing clothing, and hence filled with drawn water.

far away from the city and road.

8:2 *who require immersion*: See 8:1. This list includes only doubtful cases and does not trouble to include the unambiguous case of a man who has ejaculated semen.

urine that is broken into discontinuous drips or possibly into a split stream.

in the beginning: When he began to urinate.

impure: Urine that was continuous and clear at the start, but then became broken or turbid, is regarded as mixed with semen.

White is like turbid: Urine that appears white is like turbid urine, which renders impure only if clear urine was passed first.

3 One who discharges thick drops from the penis
[is] impure—
the words of R. Eleazar Hisma.
One who has [erotic] thoughts at night,
and arose and found his flesh warm,
[is] impure.
[A woman] who discharges semen on the third day [after intercourse]
[is] pure—
the words of R. Eleazar b. Azariah.
R. Ishmael says:
Sometimes they are four periods of time,
sometimes they are five,
[and] sometimes they are six.[88]
R. Aqiva says:
[They are] always five.
4 If a gentile woman discharged semen from an Israelite man,
[it is] impure;
if an Israelite woman discharged semen from a gentile,
[it is] pure.
A woman who had sexual intercourse[89]
and went down and immersed
but did not clean the vagina[90] [first]

[88] **M**: "sometimes they are five periods that are six."
[89] Lit. "served her house."
[90] Lit. "sweep the house."

8:3 *thick drops*: These are assumed to contain semen.

and found his flesh warm: Even if he did not notice any discharge, it is assumed that an emission of semen occurred.

discharges semen: From the vagina. Semen discharged from the vagina after intercourse renders the woman impure just as semen renders cloth and leather impure through contact (Leviticus 15:17).

on the third day: The impurity of semen lapses three days after ejaculation (see *Shabbat* 9:3). According to R. Eleazar b. Azariah, this occurs on the third day itself.

Sometimes they are four periods of time, etc.: A "period of time" consists of either a day or a night. R. Ishmael holds that semen becomes pure only on the fourth day after ejaculation; depending on what time of day ejaculation occurred, the amount of time when semen remains impure may amount to four periods (if ejaculation occurred at the end of the first day), five periods (if ejaculation occurred in the middle of the first day), or six periods (if ejaculation occurred at the beginning of the first day).

always five: R. Aqiva holds that semen remains impure for five periods of day and night, no matter what time of day ejaculation occurred.

8:4 *a gentile woman*: Semen is impure only if it came from a Jewish man; such is the case even if the semen is later discharged from a gentile woman with whom the Jew had sexual intercourse. Semen from a gentile man is pure even if it is later discharged from a Jewess with whom the gentile had sexual intercourse.

[it is] impure: i.e. the semen.

clean the vagina of semen.

is as if she had not immersed.
A man who had a discharge of semen
who immersed
but did not urinate[91] [first],
when he will urinate[92]—[he will be] impure.
R. Yose says:
With one who is ill or old—
impure;
with one who is young or healthy—
pure.

8:5–9:2 *Things That Interpose in Immersion*

5 A menstruant who put coins in her mouth
and went down and immersed
[is] pure from her [initial] impurity,
but she is impure due to her saliva.
If she put her hair in her mouth,
clenched her hand,
[or] pursed her lips,
[it is] as if she had not immersed.
If one holds a person
or utensils
and immerses them,
[they remain] impure,
but if he rinsed his hand in the water,

91 Lit. "discharge the water." **P**: "discharge into the water."
92 Lit. "discharge the water." **P**: "discharge into the water."

as if she had not immersed: It is assumed that semen will discharge from the vagina subsequent to the immersion, rendering her once again impure.

when he will urinate: After immersing; it is assumed that residual semen will discharge together with the urine, rendering him impure.

With one who is ill or old: Residual semen in the urine, resulting from weak ejaculation, is assumed.

with one who is young or healthy: No residual semen in the urine is assumed.

8:5 *pure from her [initial] impurity*: The coins do not interpose between her body and the pool since they touch only in a "hidden part" (see below).

but impure due to her saliva: Saliva from a menstruant renders people impure upon contact; saliva that came onto the coin prior to her immersion is not made pure through immersion, and consequently renders her impure.

If she put her hair in her mouth, etc.: Since the water of the pool is unable to reach the entire surface of her body, the immersion is invalid.

If one holds a person or utensils: His hand interposes between the water of the pool and the object being immersed, rendering the immersion invalid.

but if he rinsed his hand in the water prior to grasping the object being immersed.

[they are] pure.
R. Simeon says:
He should loosen [his hold]
so that[93] water passes into them.
Hidden parts[94] [and] wrinkled parts[95]
do not require that water pass into them.

Chapter Nine

9 These interpose with regard to humans:
cords of wool
and cords of flax,
and the ribbons that are on the heads of girls.
R. Judah says:
[Those] of wool and of hair
do not interpose,
since the water can pass into them.
2 The matted hair [over] the heart and of the beard,
and of the hidden parts[96] of a woman,
mucus outside of the eye,
and a scab outside of a wound,[97]

[93] **K**: "until." [94] Lit. "the house of hidden things." [95] Lit. "the house of wrinkles."
[96] Lit. "the house of hidden things." [97] **P**: "on the wound."

[they are] pure as the place held by the hand has come into contact with water of the pool.

so that water passes into them: i.e. so that water of the pool reaches beneath the hand to all surfaces of the object being immersed.

Hidden parts: Internal parts of the body, such as inside the mouth, inside the ear, etc.

wrinkled parts of the body, covered with folds of skin.

9:1 *interpose* between the body of the one immersing and the water of the pool. For immersion to be valid, no part of the body's surface or of the hair may be untouched by water of the pool.

cords of wool and cords of flax tied to the hair or body.

of wool and of hair: In R. Judah's view cords made of wool or of hair do not interpose since water permeates through these materials.

9:2 The list of materials that constitute interposition continues.

The matted hair [over] the heart: Tangled hair growing on the chest interposes and invalidates the immersion.

of the beard: Matted hair of the beard.

of the hidden parts of a woman: Female pubic hair that has become matted.

mucus outside of the eye: Rheum that accumulated on the skin surrounding the eye.

outside of a wound: On the skin surrounding a wound.

and the bandage upon it,
and dried sap,
and clots of excrement on one's flesh,
and dough under[98] the nail,
and crumbs [of dried sweat],
thick mud,
potters' clay,
and thick gypsiferous soil.
Which is "thick mud"?
This is mud of pits, as it is written:
He lifted me out of the miry pit, the thick mud.[99]
[Which is] potters' clay?
As it [usually] means.
R. Yose deems potters' clay pure
but deems that used for burnishing impure.
And [which is] thick gypsiferous soil?
These are road pegs.
For one may not immerse into these,
nor may these be immersed;
but any other [kind of] mud,
one may immerse [objects] into it[100] when it is wet.
One may not immerse with the dust[101] that is on one's feet.
One may not immerse a kettle with soot, unless he rubbed [it].

[98] **K, M**: "on." [99] **K** adds the next four words in the verse: "and set my feet on a rock."
[100] Or perhaps "with it"; see annotation. [101] **M**: "dirt."

and dried sap that adheres to the skin or hair.

under the nail on the hands or feet.

He lifted me out: Psalms 40:3.

As it [usually] means: Clay used by potters in the manufacture of pottery.

deems...pure: Potters' clay does not interpose, so one who immersed with potters' clay adhering to the body is pure.

that used for burnishing: Clay used as an abrasive for polishing objects.

impure: Clay used for burnishing interposes; if one immersed with such clay adhering to his body, the immersion is invalid and he remains impure.

road pegs: Mud on roads that dries in the form of peg-shaped obstacles.

may not immerse into these: aforementioned types of mud, which are too viscous to be considered water (see 2:10).

nor may these be immersed: i.e. they interpose if they adhere to the body.

one may immerse [objects] into it: All other types of mud, when wet, are regarded as water, and objects may be immersed into them. Alternatively, *one may immerse [objects] with it*, i.e. objects with such mud adhering to them may be immersed as it does not interpose.

unless he rubbed the kettle to remove any soot remaining from the charcoals.

9:3–4 *Things That Do Not Interpose during Immersions of People*

3 These do not interpose:
matted hair of the head
and of the underarm,
and of the hidden parts[102] of a man.
R. Eliezer[103] says:
Whether a man or a woman,
anything about which one is fastidious
interposes,
but that about which one is not fastidious
does not interpose.
4 Mucus that is in the eye,
and a scab that is on a wound,
and moist sap,
and dregs of excrement on one's flesh,
and excrement under the nail,
and a dangling nail,
[and] the downy hair of a child.
They are not impure[104] and they do not[105] render impure.
The membrane that is on a wound
is impure and renders impure.

[102] Lit. "the house of hidden things." [103] **K**, **P**: "Eleazar."
[104] **K**, **P**, **M**: "They do not become impure." [105] Lit. "it is not…it does not…"

9:3 *of the hidden parts of a man:* male pubic hair that has become matted.

Whether a man or a woman: With regard to matted pubic hair, no distinction should be made on the basis of gender, but rather we apply the general rule (stated in 9:7): *anything about which*…

about which one is fastidious: If the person wishing to immerse is particular about something found on his or her body, that thing interposes.

9:4 The Mishnah continues to describe things that do not interpose.

in the eye itself.

on the wound itself.

dregs of excrement that are still moist.

nail of the hands or feet.

dangling nail: A fingernail or toenail that has become partially severed from the body.

downy hair of a child: Fine hair that is shed as the child matures.

They are not impure: All of the things listed in 9:1–4, whether they interpose or not, are not an integral part of the body with regard to the conveyance of impurity. A person is not made impure if impurity comes into contact with one of these but not with the body itself. Conversely, if the person is impure, he does not convey impurity to another person or object that comes into contact with one of these.

The membrane that is on a wound is considered an integral part of the body, and therefore impurity is conveyed through it as through the body itself.

9:5–7 *Things That Interpose during Immersions of Utensils*

5 These interpose with regard to utensils:
pitch and myrrh.
On glass utensils,
whether inside or outside.
On a table, on a board, and on a footstool:
on[106] those that are clean,
they interpose;
on those that are dirty,
they do not interpose.
On beds belonging to a householder,
it interposes;
but on [those] belonging to a poor person,
it does not interpose.
On a saddle belonging to a householder,
it interposes;
but on [that] belonging to waterskin carriers,
it does not interpose.
On a packsaddle,
it interposes.
Rabban Simeon b. Gamaliel says:
[Only] until around [the size of] an Italian *issar*.
6 On clothing:
on one side,
[such a substance] does not interpose;

[106] **K**, **M**: "and on."

9:5 *These interpose with regard to utensils*: As with the immersion of people, for the immersion of utensils to be valid no part of the utensil's surface may be untouched by water of the pool.

pitch and myrrh and presumably all other similarly tenacious and viscous substances.

On glass utensils: When found on glass utensils, substances that interpose do so even if they adhere only to the outside of the utensil; by implication, such substances interpose on nonglass utensils only if found on the inside.

On a table, etc.: Tenacious substances that adhere to these utensils interpose only if the utensils are otherwise clean.

belonging to a householder: Householders are assumed to be more fastidious than poor people with regard to the cleanliness of their beds.

it interposes: Any viscous substance interposes.

On a packsaddle: All are presumed to be fastidious with regard to the cleanliness of a packsaddle.

until around [the size of] an Italian issar: Foreign substances that adhere to a packsaddle (and perhaps other utensils listed above as well) interpose only if they cover an area the size of a coin called an "Italian *issar*" (probably the Roman *as*) or greater.

9:6 *On clothing*: Viscous substances found on clothes.

on both sides,
[it] interposes.
R. Judah says in the name of R. Ishmael:
Even on [only] one side.
R. Yose says:
That of builders[107]
on one side,
but that of a pit
on both sides.

7 [On] an apron of pitch workers, of potters, and of tree trimmers,
[such substances] do not interpose.
R. Judah says:
The same applies to [the apron] of fruit pickers.
This is the general rule:
Anything about which one is fastidious
interposes,
but that about which one is not fastidious
does not interpose.

Chapter Ten

10:1–5 *Parts of Utensils That Must Come into Contact with Water of the Pool*

10 All handles of utensils
that one inserted [into the utensil] differently from their usual manner,
or [even] if one inserted them in their usual manner,
but did not finish [inserting] them,
or [even] if one finished [inserting] them,

[107] A variant in **K** has no clear meaning.

That of builders: Plaster used by builders, when adhering to clothes, interposes even if found on only one side.

that of a pit: Plaster used in coating pits (i.e. cisterns) interposes only when found on both sides of the clothing.

9:7 *do not interpose*: Viscous substances adhering to aprons of such workers do not interpose since people are not fastidious about such clothing.

about which one is fastidious: If the clothing is such that one is particular about a viscous substance adhering to it, the substance interposes.

10:1 *All handles of utensils*: A handle on a utensil that is properly attached and functioning is an intrinsic part of the utensil, but a handle affixed improperly or that has broken is regarded as an extraneous appendage that interposes between the utensil itself and the water.

but did not finish: The handle was not inserted all the way into its place.

but they have broken:
these interpose.
A utensil that one immersed via its mouth,
[it is] as if he had not immersed [it].
If one immersed it in its usual manner
without [immersing the] rim,
[it remains impure] until he tilts it on its side.
A utensil that is narrow at either end
and wide in the middle,
is not [made] pure
until one tilts it on its side.
A bottle whose mouth is downturned,
is not [made] pure
until one drills a hole in its side.[108]
An inkwell [of] ordinary [people][109]
is not [made] pure until one drills a hole in its side,
and the inkwell of Joseph the priest was drilled in its side.

2 A cushion or mattress of leather:
these require that the water [of the pool] enter inside them.
A round mattress, and a ball, and a form block, and an amulet, and a *tefillin* [case],[110]
do not require that the water [of the pool] enter inside them.
This is the general rule:

[108] **P** adds "or until one tilts it on its side."
[109] **K, P, M** lack "[of] ordinary [people]."
[110] The singular "*tefilah*" is used.

these interpose: The utensil remains impure until it is immersed without such a handle.

immersed via its mouth: i.e. upside down, in such a way that the air inside the utensil could not escape and the internal walls of the utensil remained untouched by the water of the pool.

without [immersing the] rim: The exact meaning of this word is uncertain.

narrow at either end and wide in the middle: If the vessel is immersed horizontally, an air pocket will remain inside.

tilts it on its side in order to release the trapped air, and allow the interior of the utensil to be brought into contact with the water of the pool.

A bottle whose mouth is downturned: The rim turns inward in order to prevent the escape of liquid if the bottle is overturned. With such a bottle, an air pocket will remain caught inside even if it is tilted on its side.

until one drills a hole in its side to create an opening for the air to escape.

An inkwell [of] ordinary [people]: i.e. as opposed to one used by scribes. The form of the rim on such inkwells is similar to a *bottle whose mouth is downturned*, and the same rule applies.

Joseph the priest: Presumably a well-known personage, mentioned also in *Hallah* 4:11; his identification with any known historical figure is uncertain.

10:2 *cushion or mattress of leather*: With both of these, the stuffing is regularly removed and reinserted.

round mattress: The stuffing of which is not regularly taken out and put back in.

form block: A sealed, hollow block over which products such as shoes are shaped.

amulet: A case that holds an amulet.

tefillin [case]: A leather case, worn on the arm or head, containing a parchment slip (or multiple slips) inscribed with Exodus 13:1–10, 11–16, Deuteronomy 6:4–9, 11:13–21.

Anything whose [contents are] not[111] regularly put in and taken out,
one may immerse [it] sealed up.

3 These do not require that the water [of the pool] enter inside them:
knots of a poor person and of fringes,
and the thong of a sandal,
and a *tefillin* [case] of the head when it is[112] tight,[113]
and [a *tefillin* case] of the arm when it does not move up and down,[114]
and the handles of a waterskin,
and the handles of a bag.

4 These require that the water [of the pool] enter inside them:
the knot on undershirts[115] that[116] is [tied] at the shoulder,
and the hem of a sheet
(it must be stretched out),
and a *tefillin* [case] of the head when it is not tight,
and of the arm when it moves up and down,[117]
and straps of a sandal.
And clothes that one has immersed laundered,[118]
[remain impure] until they bubble up;
if one immersed them when they are dry,
[they remain impure] until they bubble up
and [then] cease from bubbling.

[111] **M** lacks "not." [112] **P** adds "not." [113] **M** lacks "tight."
[114] **K**: "when it moves up and down." [115] **M** lacks "on undershirts." [116] **P**: "and that."
[117] **K**: "when it does not move up and down." [118] **P** lacks "laundered."

10:3 *These do not require*: All of the items listed are knots or fastenings that are not regularly opened, and so do not need to be loosened prior to immersion.

knots of a poor person: Knots tied in the ragged clothing of a poor person.

of fringes: i.e. knots tied in the fringed edge of cloth.

a tefillin [case] of the head…of the arm: A leather strap that passes through the *tefillin* case attaches the case to the wearer; a strap that fits securely into the case of head *tefillin* must be *tight*; while on arm *tefillin* it suffices if it *does not move up and down*, i.e. is not regularly opened.

handles of a waterskin…handles of a bag: Knots where the handles are tied to these receptacles are not regularly opened.

10:4 *These require*, etc.: The items listed (with the exception of *the hem of a sheet*) are knots or fastenings that are regularly opened, and as such must be loosened prior to immersion in a pool in order to allow the water to enter inside of them.

the knot on undershirts: An undergarment with a strap at the shoulder that is tied when it is worn.

the hem of a sheet must be drawn taut in order to allow water of the pool to enter into its creases. Like knots that are regularly undone, folds and creases in a sheet's hem are also frequently stretched open.

straps of a sandal that are opened whenever the sandal is removed.

laundered and still wet.

until they bubble up: When the air trapped in the wet clothing bubbles to the surface, it is a sign that the entire surface of the clothing has come into contact with the water of the pool.

bubble up and [then] cease from bubbling: If the clothing was dry prior to being immersed, one must wait until all of the air trapped in the clothing has finished bubbling to the surface.

5 Any handles of utensils that are long
and that [one intends] to shorten in the future,
one immerses them until[119] the point of the [intended future] length.
R. Judah says:
[It remains impure] until he has immersed its entirety.
The chain of a large bucket
[is reckoned like the bucket itself to a length of] four handbreadths,
and that of a small bucket,
[to a length of] ten;
one immerses them until the[120] point of the [aforementioned] measure.
R. Tarfon says:
[It remains impure] until one immerses the entire ring.
A rope that is tied to a basket
is not a connective
unless one has sewn [it on].

10:6–8 *Immersion of Utensils Filled with Liquids and Distinctions between Water and Other Liquids*

6 The House of Shammai say:
One does not immerse hot [water] in cold,
nor cold in hot,
nor fresh in foul,
nor foul in fresh.
The House of Hillel say:
One does immerse.

[119] **P**: "at." [120] **P**: "at the."

10:5 *until the point of the [intended future] length*: The part of the handle that one intends to cut off does not need to be immersed, even though at present it is still attached.

until he has immersed its entirety: Even the part that he intends to cut off later.

chain: If a chain is attached to a bucket, the part of the chain nearest the bucket is considered like the bucket itself, such that if it comes into contact with impurity, the bucket becomes impure as well (see *Kelim* 14:3).

large bucket... small bucket: Due to its excessive weight, a large bucket cannot be held by its chain beyond a distance of four handbreadths, while a small bucket may be held by its chain until a distance of ten handbreadths. Since the lengths of chain beyond these limits are extraneous to the function of the bucket, they are not reckoned as part of the bucket itself.

the entire ring: If the specified length of chain (four or ten handbreadths respectively) ends at the middle of a ring, the entire ring must nonetheless be immersed.

is not a connective: It is not reckoned like the basket itself with regard to impurity.

10:6 *immerse hot [water] in cold*: Water that has become impure is purified by immersion in a pool. According to the House of Shammai, the impure water must be of the same type as the water of the pool into which it is immersed in terms of both temperature and quality.

If a utensil is full of liquid,
and one immersed it,
[it is] as if he had not immersed [it].
[If it is] full of urine,
one regards [the urine] as if it is water.
[If it is] full of purgation water,
[it is impure] until the water [from the pool] becomes more than the purgation water.
R. Yose says:
Even if a utensil holds a *kor*,
and there is only a quarter-*log* [of purgation water] in it,
[it is] as if he had not immersed [it].

7 All foods join together to render the body unfit [to eat *terumah*]
by means of [eating] half a *peras*.
All liquids join together to render the body unfit [to eat *terumah*]
by means of [drinking] a quarter[-*log*].
This is a greater stringency for one who drinks impure liquids
than for the pool,
for with regard to him,
they have made other liquids like water.

8 If one ate impure food and drank impure liquids,
[and then] immersed and vomited them out,
[they remain] impure,
since they are not [made] pure in the body;

If a utensil is full of liquid: Liquids other than water are not purified through immersion in a pool, and consequently the immersion of an impure utensil filled with such liquids is invalid since the liquid interposes between the interior of the utensil and the water of the pool.

as if it is water: Both the urine and the utensil are made pure.

purgation water: See 1:8.

becomes more than the purgation water: The utensil must be more than half empty so that when immersed, the majority of the water in it will be from the pool.

a kor = 720 *log*, around 360 liters.

only a quarter-log: Around one-eighth of a liter. Even a small amount of purgation water in the utensil interposes.

10:7 *All foods join together*: One who eats impure food measuring the volume of half a *peras* (approximately the bulk of two eggs) is rendered unfit to eat *terumah* until he has immersed in a pool. Different kinds of impure foods are counted together when calculating this minimum volume (cf. *Me'ilah* 4:5).

All liquids join together: Similarly, one who drinks a quarter-*log* of impure liquid is rendered unfit to eat *terumah*, and different kinds of impure liquids are counted together when calculating this volume.

greater stringency: With the immersion of utensils in a pool a distinction is made between a utensil filled with water and one filled with other liquids (see above 10:6). With regard to one who drank impure liquids no such distinction is made, and water joins with other liquids to complete the minimum volume of a quarter-*log*.

10:8 *not [made] pure in the body*: Although immersion in a pool purifies the body, it does not purify impure foods or liquids ingested into the body.

[made] pure in the body: Immersion purifies both the body and the impure water imbibed into the body.

if one drank impure water,
[and then] immersed and vomited it out,
[it is] pure,
since it is [made] pure in the body.
If one swallowed a pure ring,
[and then] entered the Tent of a corpse,
[and then] sprinkled and repeated and immersed,
and [then] vomited it out,
it remains as it was before.
If one swallowed an impure ring,
he immerses and [then] eats of *terumah*;
if he vomited it out,
it is[121] impure and has rendered him impure.
An arrow that is lodged in a person[122]—
when it is visible,
it interposes;
but if it is not visible,[123]
he immerses and [then] eats of his *terumah*.

[121] **P**: "it has become impure."
[122] **P**: "base" (differs from standard version by one letter).
[123] **K** adds "it does not interpose."

the Tent of a corpse: A space, covered from above, in which a human corpse lies; people, utensils, food, and liquids that enter this space are rendered impure (see Numbers 19:14–15 and tractate *Oholot*).

sprinkled and repeated and immersed: Those rendered impure from a corpse are purified through sprinkling of purgation water on the third day subsequent to defilement and on the seventh day, followed by immersion (Numbers 19: 17–19).

it remains as it was before: The ring is pure.

eats of terumah: The ingested impure ring does not render his body impure from within.

it is impure: It was not purified through his immersion and remains impure.

has rendered him impure: Contact with the impure ring, once vomited out, renders the one who vomited it impure.

when it is visible: The arrow juts out of the flesh.

interposes: If the person with the embedded arrow immerses in a pool, the arrow interposes between his body and the water of the pool.

not visible: The arrowhead is completely buried in the flesh and none of the shaft remains projecting.

he immerses and [then] eats of his terumah: The arrow does not interpose.

Tractate Niddah

Charlotte Elisheva Fonrobert

Introduction

Overview

The word "*niddah*" applied to a woman's menstrual cycle appears in two different legal contexts in the Torah: impurity and prohibited sexual intercourse. The Mishnah primarily uses *niddah* to refer to the woman herself, to a class of women, or to the menstrual period. Although focused on menstrual impurity, the tractate has the character of a gynecological treatise, in that it includes a number of related topics including, abortions and miscarriages (chapter 3), maturation of the body (chapter 5, including 6:1 and 11), and virginal bleeding (9:11).

Structure and Organization of Tractate

The tractate opens with retroactive menstrual impurity. (Chapter 1). The end of that chapter introduces a regime of checking before sexual intercourse, which continues in 2:1–4. The unit that follows, 2:5–7, discusses the appearance of blood and its presumed purity or impurity. The section from 3:1 to 5:1a considers childbirth impurity, but also includes discussion of the presumptive purity of Israelite as opposed to Samaritan and Sadducaean women (4:1–3); and (an Israelite) woman's presumed impurity during parts of her cycle (4:7).

Following this, the tractate addresses the life cycle to adulthood in general (5:2–9), and puberty and menstrual impurity for females in particular (6:1, 11–12) interrupted by an extended anthology about asymmetrical pairs (6:2–10).

Niddah 6:13–7:2 serves as a transition to a unit on the topic of bloodstains (as opposed to blood from self-examination), in 7:3–9:7. Similarly to 4:1–2, the Mishnah considers the status of bloodstains from Reqem (thought to be that of converts) and of Samaritans (7:3). In this extended section, the Mishnah attends to characteristic questions of uncertainty: whether the blood is genital (8:1–4); or which woman a bloodstain came from (9:3–5). Diagnostic methods for distinguishing menstrual from other stains closes this section (9:6–7).

A number of relatively short units on a variety of topics concludes the tractate, which ends with a paragraph on menstrual impurity and sexual morality (10:8).

Main Ideas

In many ways, tractate *Niddah* adheres to its biblical precedents (see below). However, it displays a recognizable concern for sexual discipline beginning with the expectation and even requirement of self-examinations with wiping cloths before and after sexual intercourse, right from the beginning of the tractate (1:1, 7; 2:1–2) till its very end, where it ends with a moralizing rather than neutral legal tone (10:8). Indeed, the practical relevance of those rulings and discussions in the tractate is entirely independent of the institution of the Temple and its historical existence.

A number of innovations enter the discussion of menstrual purity. One is the notion of retroactive impurity. In the case of genital bleeding, retroactive impurity is derived midrashically from Leviticus 15:19 ("*in* her flesh"), which is read to mean that a woman can become impure while the blood is still inside her body (Niddah 5:1).

Particular anatomical understandings of the female body support these rules (2:5; 5:7). The Mishnah posits a cycle consisting of seven regular menstrual days and a subsequent timespan of eleven days (see 4:4, 6:14, and 10:8). (It is not clear whether the Mishnah envisions an eighteen-day cycle for a woman or assumes that additional days may be typical; this problem is taken up in later rabbinic literature.) For every day during the eleven that a woman experiences bleeding she has to count one day with no blood before being able to resume a state of purity. Three consecutive days' bleeding is taken to correspond to "many days" in Leviticus 15:25. A woman in this circumstance is a deemed *zavah*, with more stringent purification requirements (see *Zavim*).

The tractate differentiates between different kinds of genital bleeding and genital blood. The differentiations take into account kinds of blood and bloodstains (chapters 7–8); their origin in the body (2:5 and 5:1); the colors of the blood (2:6–7), on what kind of woman—Jewish, non-Jewish, Jews outside the rabbinic orbit (4:1–3; 7:3)—discharged the blood. All these categorizations and distinctions enable a distinct kind of rabbinic authority over women's bodies and their physiology, due to the specialized expertise required.

Relationship to Scripture

Leviticus 15 lays out the priestly rules pertaining to the ritual impurity of genital discharges, regular and irregular, of both men and women, with their processes of purification. Of primary relevance to our tractate, Leviticus 15:19–24 outlines the rules of menstrual impurity, how that impurity is transmitted, and the implication of sexual intercourse for the purity of her partner during this period. In the context of prohibited sexual relations, Leviticus 18:19 includes relations with "a woman during the *niddah* of her impurity" (18:19), as a consequence of which that person is "cut off" (in rabbinic understanding, *karet*, a severe divine punishment). The Torah does specify purification practice for the woman with either a regular or irregular flow. The explicit prescription of washing in water for men with genital discharges (15:13, 16) came to apply to women as well, and was understood to require full body immersion.

Tractate Niddah

Chapter One

1:1–2 *Introduction: Calculating a Woman's Time of Menstrual Impurity*

I Shammai says:
[For] all women it is sufficient to calculate their impurity from the time of their bloodflow.[1]
Hillel says:
From [the current] examination to [a previous] examination, and[2] even for many days [retroactively].
But[3] the Sages say:
Neither like this one's words, nor like that one's words.
Rather, [a timespan of] twenty-four [retroactive] hours reduces [the time span] from [the current] examination to [the previous] examination,
or [the time span] from [the current] examination to [the previous] examination reduces twenty-four hours.
[For] each[4] woman who has a regular menstrual period,
it is sufficient to calculate her impurity from the time of her bloodflow.[5]

[1] Lit. "their time is sufficient for them," here and repeatedly below.
[2] Or "but." Word absent from **P**. [3] **K** lacks "and/or."
[4] **K**: "And [for] each woman," making this clause potentially part of the Sages' statement.
[5] Lit. "her time is sufficient for her."

1:1 The tractate opens with a disagreement between the two Sages considered founding figures of the rabbinic movement, Hillel and Shammai (see *Avot* 1:12). It has an exact parallel in the opening paragraph of *Eduyot*. The dispute between Hillel and Shammai concerns the calculation of a woman's time of impurity once she begins to menstruate. In certain circumstances impurity can be retroactive, that is prior to the moment of its discovery, and this gives rise to the dispute here. The tractate's opening paragraph introduces the theme of the chapter with a disagreement between general, seemingly principled positions, while the rest of the chapter seeks to clarify and narrow these general positions.

Shammai says: [For] all women: A category so broad (*all* women) that it is almost immediately narrowed in the last part of this paragraph and subsequently (see 1:3ff.).

it is sufficient to calculate their impurity from the time of their bloodflow: Lit. "their hour is sufficient for them," an elliptical formulation, but explained in the following paragraph as implying that a woman's status of impurity begins only once her bloodflow becomes evident. Shammai thus rejects the principle of retroactive impurity as far as women's menstruation is concerned.

Hillel says: From [the current] examination to [a previous] examination: According to Hillel, a woman's status of impurity is effective retroactively, back to the last previous self-examination, however long ago that may

And[6] if a woman has intercourse with [her husband and uses] wiping cloths,
then this is like an examination that reduces [the time span of] twenty-four hours or [the time] from [the current] examination to [the previous] examination.

2 How "sufficient to calculate her impurity from the time of her bloodflow"?
If she were sitting on her bed,
and handling objects that need to be handled in a state of purity,
and[7] she got up and saw [blood][8]—
she is impure, but [the objects] all [remain] pure.
Even though they said:
She conveys impurity[9] twenty-four hours [retroactively],
she counts [her days of *niddah*] only from the time that she saw [blood].

[6] Or "but." **K** lacks this word. [7] **K**, **P** lack "and."
[8] **P** has "blood" as object of the verb. As an intransitive verb, "to see" itself can mean "to have a bloodflow."
[9] **K**: "she becomes impure."

have been. The procedure of the exam remains unspecified. The end of the paragraph refers to the use of wiping cloths (lit. "witnesses," see also 2:1) as a valid form of such an examination. *Niddah* 1:7 describes a vaginal check but uses a different verb.

But the Sages say: The woman is retroactively impure to the preceding inspection, if less than twenty-four hours before. Otherwise the retrospective time period is twenty-four hours.

[For] each woman who has a regular menstrual period: This statement could be read either as part of the Sages' preceding statement, especially if it includes "but" as per **K**, or as an independent statement as in **P**, which starts a new paragraph here. Either way, the intent seems to be a narrowing of Shammai's general statement; see also 10:2 below. For how a regular cycle can be established, see 9:8 below, which also has exactly the same formulation.

And if a woman has intercourse with [her husband and uses] wiping cloths: See 1:7, according to which women generally, with some exceptions, should check themselves twice a day, and see also 2:1. Note that the verb rendered as "to have intercourse" is the same as the term for serving in the Temple (e.g. *Yoma* 7:5). With reference to intercourse it can be used as an intransitive verb, as frequently in this tractate, or as a transitive verb, lit. "to serve/officiate the house(hold)" (see also *Miqva'ot* 8:4).

1:2 *How...?* This paragraph expands on the preceding one. For further discussions of the statement, see also 1:6 and 1:7.

and handling objects: This scenario connects *Niddah* to the order ("Purities") in which the tractate is situated, rather than foregrounding the aspect of sexual taboo.

saw [blood]: The meaning of the verb, here (and often) deployed as intransitive, ranges from 'seeing' to 'experiencing' the blood flow itself. Visual evidence is of course part of, but not the same as, the experience of the blood flow. See also 6:13 below and the comment there.

Even though they said: She conveys impurity twenty-four hours [retroactively]: "They" sometimes means the authorities of past generations. If this is a precise citation the source is unclear, but see 10:2 below. Otherwise this citation completes the Sages' elliptical formulation in 1:1.

she counts [her days of niddah] only from the time that she saw [blood]: The act of "counting" her status as a menstruant is therefore distinct from calculating her impurity, which may work retroactively.

1:3–5 *Four Stages of a Woman's Reproductive Cycle When Retroactive Impurity Is Suspended*

3 R. Eliezer says:
For four [types of] women it is sufficient to calculate their time of impurity from the time of their bloodflow:
(1) a virgin,
(2) a pregnant woman,[10]
(3) a nursing woman,[11]
(4) and an elder woman.
R. Joshua said:
I heard this only about a virgin.
But the *halakhah* is in accordance with R. Eliezer.
4 Who is considered a virgin?
Any [woman] who has never experienced a bloodflow in her lifetime,
even though she is married.
A pregnant woman?
From [the time] when her pregnancy is noticeable.
A nursing woman?
Till she weans her child.[12]
If she gives her child to a wet nurse, she weans him, or [the child] dies:
R. Meir says:
She conveys impurity[13] twenty-four hours [retroactively].
But the Sages say:
It is sufficient to calculate her impurity from the time of her bloodflow.
5 Who is considered an elder woman?
Any [woman] who missed three consecutive periods close to her menopause.[14]
R. Eliezer says:
For any woman who misses three [consecutive] periods,

[10] **K, P**: "*and* a pregnant woman." [11] **K**: "*and* a nursing woman." [12] Lit. "son."
[13] As in 1:2 above **K** has "she becomes impure" and **P** seems to have a masculine verb.
[14] Lit. "old age."

1:3 *R. Eliezer says: For four [types of] women*: R. Eliezer holds that at four points in a woman's life cycle the concept of retroactive impurity is suspended when she experiences a bloodflow.

But the halakhah is in accordance with R. Eliezer: This can be read either as part of R. Joshua's opinion, or as an editorial gloss.

1:4 *even though she is married*: Even if she has had sexual intercourse, and had experienced bleeding from that, with respect to menstrual impurity she is still considered a "virgin." See further 9:11 and 10:1.

Till she weans her child: According to early rabbinic tradition a mother regularly nurses her child for its first two years of life. See *Gittin* 7:6.

she weans him: Before the end of the two years.

1:5 *close to her menopause*: The Hebrew term denotes old age. In the context of a woman's reproductive cycle, this would seem to refer to her expected menopause.

R. Eliezer says: For any woman: That is, not just when she is close to her menopause.

it is sufficient to calculate her impurity from the time of her bloodflow.
R. Yose says:
For a pregnant woman or a nursing woman who misses three [consecutive] periods,
it is sufficient to calculate their time of impurity from the time of their bloodflow.

1:6–7 *Implementing the Calculation of Impurity*

6 For what [situation] did they say:
"It is sufficient to calculate her impurity from the time of her bloodflow"?
For the first appearance [of blood].[15]
But for the second [appearance of blood],
"she conveys impurity[16] for twenty-four hours [retroactively]" applies.
But if she had experienced the first [bloodflow] due to force,
"it is sufficient to calculate her impurity from the time of her bloodflow" [applies] also to the second appearance.
7 Even though they said:
"It is sufficient to calculate her impurity from the time of her bloodflow,"
she must check herself,
except for a menstruant and
a woman who is counting her days of blood purification [after birth].

[15] Or "flow of blood"; see annotations. [16] K: "she becomes impure."

R. Yose says: For a pregnant woman or a nursing woman: He disagrees with the preceding opinion (1:4) that the concept of retroactive impurity is suspended immediately upon the recognition of pregnancy or nursing.

1:6 *For what [situation] did they say "it is sufficient…"*: Referring to 1:3 and the four stages in a woman's reproductive cycle when the menstrual cycle starts or restarts after interruption.

the first appearance [of blood]: The noun like the verb (see comment on 1:2 above) connotes both seeing, that is the visual evidence, as well as the experience of the bloodflow itself. With the first flow of her menarche, the principle of retroactive impurity is suspended for a pubescent girl, while for the second bloodflow it applies in accordance with the Sages' opinion in 1:1.

due to force: If the first bloodflow can be attributed to a factor that has nothing to do with a girl's or woman's cycle, it is not considered for the calculation of her impurity.

1:7 *Even though they said*: With probable reference back to 1:1–2. The paragraph here draws a distinction between the calendar of impurity and the requirements of personal care. Suspension of the principle of retroactive impurity for the four stages in the reproductive cycle and for the woman with a regular cycle does not excuse a woman from checking herself regularly.

except for a menstruant: Lit., *niddah*. This is the first appearance of the term that has given its name to the tractate. Once established as a menstruant, a woman is in a status of impurity for seven days by biblical law (Leviticus 15:19–25), so there is no point in checking for additional flow.

a woman who is counting her days of blood purification: Any vaginal bleeding during the thirty-three days following the first week after the birth of a male child, or sixty-six days following the first two weeks after the birth of a female child, does not render the mother impure. Certain restrictions do remain in effect; see Leviticus 12:4–5.

And she should have intercourse [with her husband] using wiping cloths,[17]
except for a woman who is counting her days of purification blood [after birth]
and a virgin whose blood is pure.
And[18] twice [daily] she must check herself:
in the morning and at dusk,
and at the time when she prepares herself for marital intercourse.
Beyond these, priestly women at the time[19] when they eat *terumah*.
R. Judah says:
Also at the time after she has finished eating *terumah*.

Chapter Two

2:1–4 *Preparation for Marital Intercourse by Checks for Bleeding*

2 Each hand that checks frequently
in the case of women is praiseworthy
but in the case of men should be chopped off.
The deaf-mute [woman],
or the legally noncompetent [woman],

[17] **K**: "and [the woman] who has intercourse [by using] wiping cloths," making her one of the categories of women who need not check themselves. However, the syntax in this version is awkward.

[18] **K** lacks "and."

[19] **K**: "*and* at the time when they eat *terumah*."

using wiping cloths: See 1:1 and 2:1. Calculating the calendar of impurity is distinguished from sexual discipline. In spite of the suspension of retroactive impurity for certain women, they do have to check themselves before and after intercourse with their husbands.

a virgin whose blood is pure: If she has intercourse with her husband prior to her menarche, she is exempted from the presexual check. For an expansion on this see 10:1.

And twice [daily] she must check herself: This regular daily check is performed for the sake of food items that she handles during the day that must be kept in a state of purity.

and at the time when she prepares herself for marital intercourse: Lit. "for serving her 'house.'" The verb is also used above in this paragraph, and see 1:1. This statement implies that the presexual check is distinct from the purity checks.

priestly women at the time when they eat terumah: Consumption of *terumah* in priestly households requires extra care with respect to personal purity. See also 5:2 for the male priest.

after she has finished: This inspection protects the purity of the *terumah* should she have a bloodflow within twenty-four hours.

2:1 *in the case of women*: Women are encouraged to practice rigorous self-examinations, both for purity purposes and for the purpose of sexual practice.

but in the case of men: Regarding men, however, the worry seems to be the difficulty of differentiating between self-stimulation and self-examination.

or the blind [woman],
or the one whose mind has become confused:
if they have women of sound mind [taking care of them],
they prepare them, and they can eat *terumah.*
It is the way of the daughters of Israel to have marital intercourse [by using] two wiping cloths: one for him and one for her.
Modest women prepare for themselves a third,[20] to prepare the "house."

2 If [blood] is found on his—
they are [both] impure and need to bring an offering.
If [blood] is found on hers immediately [after intercourse]—
they are [both] impure and need to bring an offering.
If [blood] is found on hers after some time—
they are [both] doubtfully impure and exempt from [bringing] an offering.

3 What is to be considered as "after some time"?
So that she can get off the bed and rinse her "face."
And after that,
she conveys impurity[21] for twenty-four hours [retroactively]
but does not convey impurity to the one who had intercourse with her.
R. Aqiva says:
She also conveys impurity to the one who had intercourse with her.

[20] **K** has "*one* to prepare the house" with a second hand adding "*and* one."
[21] **K**: "she has become impure."

if they have women of sound mind: If these variously incapacitated women, who cannot care for themselves in terms of the purity precautions, are members of a priestly household, they would be unable to consume *terumah*, which is part of their diet, but for which they need to be in a status of purity. Thus, this ruling allows for caretakers.

It is the way of the daughters of Israel: See also 4:1 below and the note there. Here the Mishnah shifts the rhetoric to a descriptive statement, as compared to the hypothetical case scenario in 1:1 (if she has intercourse that way), and the normative in 1:7 (she should have intercourse that way).

Modest women: The term appears only here in the Mishnah.

to prepare the "house": This euphemistic locution for intercourse is different from "serving the 'house' " (see 1:7). The noun—"house"—is the same in both cases, but the verb is different. Here it serves more clearly as metaphor for her vagina, whereas in 1:7 "house" could also imply household.

2:2 *they are [both] impure*: As per Leviticus 15:24, both of them are in a status of impurity for seven days.

an offering: A purgation offering, since they inadvertently transgressed the biblical prohibition of intercourse while she menstruates.

after some time: It would not be clear whether she started bleeding during intercourse or only afterward. See next paragraph for clarification.

2:3 *and rinse her "face"*: Another euphemistic metaphor, most likely her vulva.

but does not convey impurity to the one who had intercourse with her: This first statement applies the principle of retroactive impurity only to food items requiring purity, not to sexual intercourse, as opposed to R. Aqiva in the next statement who equates the two. The *one who had intercourse with her* presumably would be her husband, but the Hebrew here is more generic than "serving her house."

And the Sages agree with R. Aqiva in [the case] of [a woman] who sees a stain,
that she conveys impurity to the one who had intercourse with her.

4 All women are in a presumptive state of purity for their husbands.
If [husbands] return from a journey,
their wives are in a presumptive state of purity for them.
The House of Shammai say:
She needs two wiping cloths for each and every act of intercourse,
or she should have intercourse by the light of a lamp.
The House of Hillel say:
Two wiping cloths for the whole night are sufficient for her.

2:5–7 *Determining Impurity of Vaginal Bleeding Based On Source or Color*

5 The Sages made a metaphor for the woman:
chamber, antechamber, and upper room.
Blood of the chamber is impure.
If it is found in the antechamber,
it is doubtfully impure,
since it is presumed[22] to originate from the "source."

6 There are five [types] of impure blood in a woman:
(1) the red,
(2) the black,
(3) and one like saffron,
(4) and one like muddy water,

[22] Lit. "its presumptive state."

[a woman] who sees a stain: Seeing a blood stain is different from finding blood as previously. A stain is stronger and more lasting evidence. See chapters 8 and 9.

2:4 *in a presumptive state of purity*: Absent a contrary indication, a husband may simply assume that his wife is in a status of purity and therefore sexually available.

for each and every act of intercourse: Every single sexual act requires checking, as opposed to requiring such a check only once for the entire night.

2:5 *The Sages made a metaphor for the woman*: For the expression, which can be found only in this tractate, see also 5:7.

chamber, antechamber, and upper room: Since blood from the chamber is impure, it would seem that the chamber is the uterus. Blood that originates in "the source" (see Leviticus 12:7 and 20:18) is only doubtfully impure, which suggests that the "source" and the "chamber" are distinct. The anatomical identification of these architectural metaphors has exercised the minds of many commentators, ancient through modern. Suggestions for the antechamber range from cervix to vulva, and for the upper room from fallopian tubes to cervix to ovaries to vagina to bladder, all depending on how the woman's body is imagined.

2:6 *There are five [types] of impure blood*: The impurity of blood can be determined by its appearance, aside from its source in the body. The first five colors are not contested. The paragraph then adds two that are.

(5) and one like mixed wine.
The House of Shammai say:
Also the one like the waters of fenugreek
and the one like the juice of roast meat.
But the House of Hillel deem [them] pure.
The yellow—
Aqaviah b. Mahalalel deems [it] impure,
but the Sages deem [it] pure.[23]
Said R. Meir:
If it does not convey impurity [in the form of] a stain,
it does convey impurity [in the form of a] liquid.
R. Yose says:
Neither [as] this nor [as] that.
7 Which is considered "the red"?
Like the blood of a wound.
Which is considered "the black"?
Like ink sediment.
Darker than that—it is impure.[24]
Lighter than that—it is pure.
And like saffron?
Like the brightest [shade] of it.
And "like muddy water"?
[Dirt] from the Valley of Beit Qerem, covered thinly with water.
And "like mixed wine"?
Two parts water, and one wine, from the wine of Sharon.

Chapter Three

3:1–7 *Miscarriages of a Variety of Uterine Material and the Associated Birth Impurity*

3 If a woman aborts[25] a piece,
if there is blood with it—

[23] **P** has the reverse: "Aqaviah b. Mahalalel deems *pure*, but the Sages deem *impure*."
[24] **P** lacks this clause. [25] Lit. "she who aborts." See annotations.

But the House of Hillel deem [them] pure: Presumably they do not consider vaginal blood of this color to have its source in the uterus.

3:1 *If a woman aborts*: Every paragraph in this chapter starts with the phrase "she who aborts." The chapter can thus be described as a kind of diagnostic manual, a catalogue of miscarriages, with the goal to determine whether the woman becomes impure on account of menstruation or birth-related impurity. Other rabbinic texts recount case stories where the Sages consulted with "doctors."

a piece: A more solid piece of uterine material.

she is impure.
but if not—she is pure.
R. Judah says:
Whether this or that—
she is impure.
2 If a woman aborts something
like a kind of peel,
like a kind of hair,[26]
like a kind of dust,
like a kind of red flies,
she should put it in water.
If it dissolves—she is impure,
but if not—she is pure.
If a woman aborts something
like a kind of fish,
locusts,
creeping and crawling creatures:
if there is blood with them—she is impure,
but if not—she is pure.
If a woman aborts something
like a kind of domestic animal,
wild animal, or
bird,
whether they are impure or pure,
if it is male—
she should count [her days of birth impurity] for [the birth of] a male,
and if a female—
she should count [her days of birth impurity] for a female.
But if it[s gender] is not recognizable—

[26] **K**, **P**: "barley," which is written with the same consonants.

she is impure: Due to the blood, which is considered menstrual. But if there is not (liquid) blood, the emission is not considered menstrual, nor does birth-related impurity apply to her.

R. Judah says: He holds that with or without the presence of blood the excretion is to be considered menstrual.

3:2 *hair*: Or "barley," as in the manuscripts. The category "[grain of] barley" is used in discussions of impurity to determine the minimal quantity of bone or flesh that can impart corpse impurity; see *Keritot* 3:8 and *Oholot* 2:3.

red flies: The etymology of the word for "flies" is unclear. It appears only here in the Mishnah and only rarely elsewhere in early rabbinic literature. The dictionaries suggest various kinds of water insects.

she is impure: If it dissolves, the material is considered coagulated menstrual blood.

if it is male: If the uterine material has the recognizable shape of an animal, it could be human and therefore fetal, in R. Meir's view. Accordingly, the woman should start to count the days of her birth impurity prescribed in Leviticus 12, based on the perceived gender of the fetal material.

But if it[s gender] is not recognizable: According to the Yerushalmi and Rashi's commentary to the Mishnah, the stringencies of both apply. She should count two weeks of birth impurity as for a female child and days of purification blood only till the fortieth day after her birth, as for a male child.

she should count [her birth impurity as] for both male and female—
the words of R. Meir.
But the Sages say:
Anything that does not have something of a human form—
is not [considered] a fetus.
3 If a woman aborts an [amniotic] sac
filled with water,
filled with blood,
filled with various matter,
she need not be concerned about it being a fetus.
But if its parts were shaped,
she counts [her birth impurity as] for both male and female.
4 [If] a [woman] aborts a "sandal" or a placenta,
she should count [her birth impurity as] for both male and female.
[If] a placenta [was miscarried] inside a house—
the house is impure.
It is not that the placenta [is considered] a fetus,
but that there is no placenta without a fetus.
R. Simeon says:
The fetus might have been dissolved, before it came out.
5 [If] a [woman] aborts a *tumtum* or an *androgynos*,[27]
she should count [her birth impurity as] for both male and female.
A *tumtum* and a male,
an *androgynos* and a male,

[27] **P** adds "and a male," probably a mistake.

it is not [considered] a fetus: The Sages hold that in order to count as a human miscarriage, the aborted material needs to exhibit some human form. Otherwise birth impurity does not apply, nor does menstrual impurity if there are no traces of blood; see in 3:1.

3:3 *she need not be concerned*: If the uterine material is merely liquid in a membranous sac, she does not need to consider it a miscarriage, and therefore need not worry about birth impurity. Note the switch to the woman's perception, instead of the "objective" diagnostic definition of the excretion.

But if its parts were shaped: The term connotes embroidering fabric; that is, if there is material in the amniotic sac that suggests the shape of an embryo.

for both male and female: As in 3:2, if the gender is not recognizable the impurity stringencies for both apply.

3:4 *a "sandal"*: The term derives from the Greek. It is not clear what the Mishnah has in mind here, but the Talmud suggests this was a kind of flatfish. This would have been a more solid piece of uterine material.

the house is impure: Because of corpse impurity, since there must have been a fetus.

The fetus might have been dissolved: R. Simeon disagrees with the previous point, since the house where this abortion took place would not have been subject to corpse impurity, as the fetus dissolved while emerging.

3:5 *a tumtum or an androgynos* fetus: A *tumtum* displays the characteristics of neither sex, an *androgynos* those of both. These two terms often appear together as mirror opposites, as for instance in *Yevamot* 8:6, or in longer lists of people not male, as for instance in *Hagigah* 1:1.

she should count [her birth impurity as] for both male and female.
A *tumtum* and a female,
an *androgynos* and a female,
she should count [her birth impurity as] for a female only.
[If the fetus] came out in pieces, or in breech position,
once most of it emerges, it is then considered born.
[If the fetus] came out its [regular] way,
[it is not considered born] until most of its head emerges.
And what is [to be considered] "most of its head"?
When its forehead emerges.[28]

6 [If] a [woman] aborts, and it is not recognizable what it is,
she should count [her birth impurity as] for both male and female.
[If] it is not recognizable whether it was a fetus or not,[29]
she should count [her birth impurity as] for both male and female, and her menstrual impurity.

7 [If] a [woman] aborts on the fortieth day,
she need not be concerned about [it being] a fetus.
On the forty-first day,
she should count [her birth impurity as] for both male and female, and her menstrual impurity.

[28] **K**'s main script has "*from when* most of its head emerges, from when its forehead emerges," and in the margins someone has scribbled the missing text as in our text here.

[29] **P** differs: "If it is known whether it is a fetus, she should count..." This seems to make little sense.

for both male and female fetus: Since the fetus in question could be either male or female, the mother should consider her birth impurity as in 3:2.

for a female fetus *only*: For the female baby the mother should consider her birth impurity accordingly; as far as the potential maleness of the other baby is considered, its required birth impurity is included in the counting for a female birth.

in pieces: Lit. "cut up."

in breech position: The Hebrew term suggests a situation out of order (the same word can describe a change in the order of words in a verse) or upside down. As a verb it denotes emasculation; as a noun it denotes a eunuch (see 5:9 below). Here it means the opposite of the baby's coming out "its [regular] way."

until most of its head emerges: **K** has *from when* instead of *until when* most of its head emerges. But since the subject is missing either way, presumably the meaning is that once the head emerges it is considered a birth.

3:6 *and her menstrual impurity*: If it is not even clear whether the uterine material was a fetus at all (though it could have been), she first of all counts her birth impurity for both a male and a female fetus, as in 3:2 above. If then she experiences bleeding during the thirty-three days of purification blood that she is counting in case she has aborted a male fetus, she has to count that bleeding as menstrual bleeding instead, since she cannot even be sure she had aborted a fetus at all.

3:7 *on the fortieth day*: Counting from presumed conception or intercourse.

she need not be concerned about [it being] a fetus: Since in rabbinic embryology the fetus is not formed before the end of the fortieth day, anything a woman aborts before that would not be considered a miscarriage, and birth impurity need not be considered.

On the forty-first day: From the forty-first day after conception and onward anything a woman aborts could be considered a miscarriage and therefore a fetus, and she would have to consider her impurity as in 3:6.

R. Ishmael says:
[On] the forty-first day, she should count [her birth impurity as] for a male[30] and her menstrual impurity.
[On] the eighty-first day, she should count [her birth impurity as] for both male and female, and her menstrual impurity,
since the male [fetus] is completed on the forty-first day,
and the female [fetus] on the eighty-first.
But the Sages say:
The creation of male and female are one and the same—
both [are completed] on the forty-first day.

Chapter Four

4:1–3 *The Status of Impurity for Different Groups of Women*

4 The daughters of the Samaritans are [to be considered as] menstruants[31] from their cradle on.
Samaritans convey impurity to the lower as much as to the upper bedding,

[30] **K**'s main script has "and for a female," but it is crossed out.
[31] In **P**, a second hand adds this word in the margin.

for a male and for her menstrual impurity: In R. Ishmael's view, a female fetus is formed later than a male fetus, perhaps mirroring the days of counting impurity plus purification after birth as in Leviticus 12, so a miscarriage on the forty-first day could only have been of a male fetus. She would account seven days to birth impurity, and any bleeding that occurred after that to menstrual impurity.

on the eighty-first day: A miscarriage on the eighty-first day could be either of a male or a female fetus so it is not clear what the gender of the aborted fetus might have been; she would have to count her impurity as in 3:6.

The creation of male and female are one and the same: The Sages disagree with R. Ishmael as to the fetal development of male and female. Both are formed fully at the same time.

4:1 *menstruants from their cradle on*: This formulation could be meant technically, with reference to 5:3, which rules that a baby girl one day old could theoretically start her menstrual calendar if she has a discharge of blood. Samaritan women, who do not count a menstrual calendar from day one as rabbinic women would do, are therefore to be considered menstruants from their cradle on in terms of impurity. It is, however, also possible that the Mishnah attributes a categorical status of menstrual impurity to Samaritan women.

to the lower as much as to the upper bedding: For this formulation see *Kelim* 1:3. Since Samaritan husbands have intercourse with women who are to be considered menstruants, they themselves attain a derivative impurity status by way of intercourse, by virtue of which they convey impurity to what they lie upon. The referent of upper and lower bedding is ambiguous. Some commentaries explain this with reference to ten mattresses that they may lie on, and the lowest would become as impure as the uppermost, a scenario the talmudic discussion considers and dismisses as obvious. Others explain the reference of the lower as that which they lie on and the upper as that which covers them.

because they have intercourse with menstruants.
And they calculate their impurity based on any blood.
But one does not become culpable because of them
for entrance into the Temple,
nor does one have to burn *terumah* because of them,
because their impurity is [only] in doubt.

2 The daughters of the Sadduceans,
if they follow the ways of their fathers,
are then considered like Samaritan women.
If they separate themselves
to walk in the ways of Israel
they are then considered like Israel.
R. Yose says:
They are always considered like Israel,
until they separate themselves
to walk in the ways of their fathers.

3 The [vaginal] blood of a non-Jewish woman
and the blood of purity of a woman with *tsara'at*:
the House of Shammai deem it pure,
but the House of Hillel say:
It is like her spittle or like her urine.

they calculate their impurity based on any blood: Not only are Samaritan women to be considered menstruants categorically, they also do not distinguish between different types of vaginal blood, as the rabbis determine (see 2:6–7), and hence do not keep a rabbinic menstrual calendar at all.

one does not become culpable because of them: Although the ruling attributes a status of categorical menstrual impurity to the Samaritan women and by derivation to their husbands, that status is only a rabbinic ordinance and therefore causes only doubtful impurity with respect to holy things. That is, their touch does not invalidate *terumah* or prevent a rabbinic Jew from entering the Temple.

4:2 *if they follow the ways of their fathers*: Sadducean women are not categorically different from rabbinic women with reference to menstrual impurity in that they can choose a "path" to follow, i.e. either their own traditional or the rabbinic way of accounting for menstrual impurity.

like Samaritan women: Note the change in terminology from "daughters of the Samaritans" to "Samaritan women" or "female Samaritans."

They are always considered like Israel: According to R. Yose's view, Sadducean women have to choose to leave the path of "Israel," rather than having to choose to join "Israel."

4:3 *the blood of purity of a woman with tsara'at*: If she is Jewish but suffers from scale-disease, her birth impurity is still counted like regular birth impurity, and any bleeding that occurs during the thirty-three days after the first week of a baby boy's birth, or during the sixty-six days after the first two weeks of a baby girl's birth, is considered birth-related and not menstrual, and is called "purification blood." See 1:7 above.

the House of Shammai deem it pure: In the case of the vaginal blood of a non-Jewish woman, they hold that the purity laws of vaginal fluids apply to Jews only (Leviticus 15:2). In the case of the woman with *tsara'at*, they hold that the laws of purification of a new mother are the same for such a woman as for anyone else. In *Eduyot* 5:1 this ruling is listed as one of the six cases where the House of Shammai are more lenient than the House of Hillel.

like her spittle or like her urine: According to *Makhshirin* 6:6, the spittle and urine of a man with an irregular emission, a *zav*, can convey impurity. See also 7:1 below where spittle of impure people is listed as a fluid that renders someone else impure only when moist.

The blood of a woman after childbirth who has not yet immersed herself:
the House of Shammai say:
It is like her spittle or like her urine.
But the House of Hillel say:
It conveys impurity whether moist or dry.
But they agree
about a woman who gives birth while a *zavah*,
that it conveys impurity whether moist or dry.

4:4–6 *Definition of Bleeding During Protracted Labor*

4 A woman in difficult labor is [considered a] menstruant.
If she was in difficult labor three days during [the] eleven days
and then had relief for twenty-four hours
and then gave birth,
she is [considered] a woman who gives birth while a *zavah*—
the words of R. Eliezer.

a woman after childbirth who has not yet immersed herself: At the end of the first seven days after the birth of a baby boy, or two weeks after the birth of a baby girl, as per Leviticus 12:2–4.

It conveys impurity whether moist or dry: The House of Hillel puts her blood in the more severe category of menstrual blood that, unlike the spittle of an impure person, conveys impurity both dry and moist. See also 7:1 below.

a woman who gives birth while a zavah: According to medieval commentaries the reference here is to a woman who has discharges during the extramenstrual days on her regular cycle calendar in proximity to her giving birth, as per the next paragraph (see note to 4:4). In that case, both houses agree about the severity of the impurity of her discharge. According to *Eduyot* 5:4 this ruling is transmitted by R. Eliezer.

4:4 *A woman in difficult labor*: Or protracted labor, since the concern here is her calendar, and her labor would be accompanied by bleeding. See the fourth chapter of *Hullin* on animals in difficult labor when giving birth.

is [considered a] menstruant: Difficult to understand. In connection with the last clause of the previous paragraph, bleeding that occurs during protracted labor falls into the category of menstrual bleeding and not *zivah* bleeding, regardless of when in her cycle calendar it occurs.

three days during [the] eleven days: Her protracted labor accompanied by bleeding occurred for at least three days during her extramenstrual days. She would have gone on calculating her regular cycle calendar during her pregnancy.

eleven days: For the specific category of "eleven days" see also 4:7. The source of these eleven days as a part of a woman's cycle is not clear. Leviticus 15 assigns (regular) seven days for menstrual bleeding (15:19) and speaks of "many days" for extramenstrual bleeding (Leviticus 15:25): each has a different regimen of purification. Vaginal bleeding for "many days" during these eleven days between her menstrual periods renders her a *zavah* in mishnaic terminology, a woman with a bloodflow who has to count seven so-called "clean" or "pure" days, i.e. days without any bleeding, once her bloodflow ceases. Medieval scholars debate whether the Mishnah's intent was for specifically eleven days between menstrual periods, or for at least eleven days.

and then had relief for twenty-four hours: From her labor before giving birth. She would then be considered a *zavah*, since the bleeding would seem to be unrelated to the actual birth.

R. Joshua says:
one night and one day,
like the night of the Sabbath and its day,
since she [may have] had relief from the pain but not from the blood.

5 How long can her difficult labor last?
R. Meir says:
Even forty or fifty days.
R. Judah says:
Her [last] month is sufficient for her.
R. Yose and R. Simeon say:
Difficult labor cannot last more than two weeks.

6 If a woman is in difficult labor
during the eighty days [after the birth] of a female baby,
any blood that she sees [then] is pure,
till the fetus emerges.
R. Eliezer deems [her] impure.
They said to R. Eliezer:
If in a case where stringency was applied with regard to "blood of relief,"

one night and one day: R. Joshua makes a qualifications with regard to R. Eliezer's opinion: she has to have had relief for a whole night and the subsequent day, rather than any twenty-four-hour period, in order for her to be considered a "woman who gives birth while a *zavah*."

since she [may have] had relief from the pain but not from the blood: This statement could either be part of R. Joshua's statement and constitute a second qualification of R. Eliezer's opinion, or it could constitute an anonymous statement, a further comment on R. Eliezer. Either way, it differentiates between relief from pain and relief from bleeding. R. Eliezer's opinion applies if she has relief from the birth-related pain only. But if she has relief from bleeding as well for the twenty-four-hour period, the bleeding afterward is considered birth-related.

4:5 *How long can her difficult labor last* in order to be considered labor and not irregular bleeding unrelated to the birth?

Even forty or fifty days: R. Meir allows for such a time period before the birth for bleeding to be considered birth-related, and not considered as other, irregular vaginal bleeding (*zivah*). R. Judah gives her only the ninth month; anything before then would be considered irregular vaginal bleeding, rendering her impure.

4:6 *If a woman is in difficult labor during the eighty days*: The reference is to a second pregnancy: if a woman after having given birth to a female baby is now counting the sixty-six days of birth purification after the initial fourteen days of birth impurity, and during those sixty-six days becomes pregnant again and goes into difficult labor, then any bleeding in conjunction with that can still be considered part of the birth purification period of the initial birth. Once the actual fetus of the second pregnancy emerges, she will have to account for birth impurity anew.

R. Eliezer deems [her] impure: He considers the bleeding to be part of the difficult labor, and therefore subject to menstrual impurity as per 3:4.

If in a case where stringency was applied: For the same reasoning see *Bava Qamma* 2:5.

with regard to "blood of relief": If she gives birth as a *zavah*, the stringency is that she needs to count seven days without bleeding for her *zivah*, after the initial week or two weeks of birth impurity (depending on the gender of the baby).

leniency was applied with the "blood of difficulty,"
does not logic require that
in a case where leniency was applied with regard to "blood of relief,"
leniency should be applied to "blood of difficulty"?
He said to them:
It is sufficient that that which is inferred by logic be equal to that from which it is inferred.
With regard to what is leniency applied to her?
With regard to the impurity of an irregular bloodflow.
But she still conveys impurity by menstruant impurity.

4:7 *Presumptive States of Purity and Impurity in a Woman's Cycle*

7 During all of the eleven days she is presumed to be pure.
If she sat down and did not examine herself,
acted inadvertently, by force, or with premeditation
and did not examine herself,
she is [still] pure.[32]
If the time of her regular menstrual period arrived
and she did not check herself,
in that case she is impure.
R. Meir says:
If she was in a hiding place

[32] K: "impure," a scribal error.

leniency was applied with the "blood of difficulty": If she has continuous bleeding associated with difficult labor, this is not considered birth as a *zavah*, but as a menstruant, as per 4:4. This is considered a leniency since she does not need to count seven clear days as after *zivah*.

a case where leniency was applied with regard to "blood of relief": During her days of birth purification, where bleeding does not render her impure.

leniency should be applied to "blood of difficulty": As in the case under consideration, namely if she has bleeding associated with difficult labor during her days of birth purification. The rabbis' reasoning is that if in the particular case of labor during birth purification from the previous birth the ruling is lenient with regard to the "blood of relief," then the ruling should certainly be lenient for "blood of difficulty" and not render her impure.

It is sufficient that that which is inferred by logic be equal to that from which it is inferred: R. Eliezer holds that the specific case of a woman's bleeding associated with difficult labor ("blood of difficulty") during her period of birth purification should be equal to that of "blood of difficulty" during labor otherwise. That is, it should be attributed to menstrual impurity. This to R. Eliezer constitutes a leniency, since the woman would not need to consider impurity of *zivah* and the protracted purification associated with that.

4:7 *she is presumed to be pure*: Lit. "presumption of purity," since she is not expected to bleed during those days. But once the time of her regular period arrives, she should check herself (see 1:7).

she is impure: Without contrary evidence she is considered to be menstruating in accordance with her calendar, so she can no longer claim "presumption of purity."

in a hiding place: Such as during a persecution, causing her fear.

and the time of her regular menstrual period arrived
and she did not check herself
in that case she is pure,
because fear holds the blood back.
But during the days of a *zav* or *zavah*
or if a woman counts day for day,
in those cases they are all presumed to be impure.

Chapter Five

5:1 *Birth Impurity in the Case of Nonvaginal Birth*

5 If [the baby] came out by way of the abdomen
one does not need to count the days of impurity and the days of purity
nor does one need to bring an offering because of it.[33]
R. Simeon says:
It is indeed considered a birth.

5:1 cont.–2 *The Difference between Male and Female Impurity*

All woman convey impurity [when blood is] in the outer house,
as it is said:
her discharge being blood in her body.
But a *zav* and an ejaculant only convey impurity
when their impurity appears outside.
2 If someone was eating *terumah*
and felt that his limbs were shaking,

[33] **P**: "because of her."

because fear holds the blood back: The teaching exhibits awareness of the effect of a woman's psychological state on a woman's cycle, such that external duress suspends a presumptive state connected with her cycle.

during the days of a zav or zavah: A woman or a man who has had irregular genital emissions and is subsequently counting seven clean days, here called the days of a *zav* or a *zavah*, cannot claim a presumptive state of purity.

5:1 *by way of the abdomen*: By caesarean section.

nor does one need to bring an offering because of it: As per Leviticus 12:1–8. This clause considers only vaginal births as subject to the biblical birth impurity rules.

It is indeed considered a birth: R. Simeon by contrast considers a caesarean like a vaginal birth.

the outer house: Another metaphor; compare 2:5.

her discharge being blood in her body: Leviticus 15:19. The rabbis read the biblical verse to emphasize the preposition: she is already impure when the blood is still "*in* her body," while for male discharge Leviticus 15:2 has "*from* his body."

he should grab the member,
and swallow the *terumah.*
And they convey impurity in any amount,
even [only] the size of a mustard seed,
or with less than that.

5:3–9 *Life Cycle from One Day through Twenty Years Old*

3 A young girl who is one day old
can become impure as a menstruant.
One who is ten days old
can become impure through *zav*-flow.[34]
A young boy who is one day old
can become impure through *zav*-flow,
and can become impure through skin disease,
and can become impure through corpse impurity,
and can bind for levirate marriage,
and can release [his mother] from levirate marriage,
and can enable consumption of *terumah*,
and can disqualify from consumption of *terumah*,

[34] K has "menstruant" here, but that must be a mistake.

5:2 *he should grab the member*: As long as his ejaculation does not exit his body, the *terumah* that the priest is consuming does not become impure and have to be burned.

they convey impurity in any amount: Plural—the reference presumably is to the various kinds of discharge: irregular flow, menstrual blood, and seminal ejaculation.

5:3 This paragraph starts a life-cycle calendar for both women and men, determining various age limits that are relevant to mishnaic law, starting with the first day of life till age twenty.

A young girl who is one day old: If the baby girl has a discharge of blood, her cycle calendar starts. Compare 4:1 with respect to the Samaritans.

One who is ten days old: If after counting the first seven days designated for her menstrual period, the baby girl has a discharge of blood for three consecutive days, she is considered a *zavah*.

A young boy who is one day old: For a baby boy also a halakhic calendar begins at day one of his life, starting with impurity laws. In contrast to the baby girl, he becomes immediately subject to a much longer set of commandments.

and can bind for levirate marriage: If his older brother dies and leaves behind a widow but no children, the baby boy "binds" his widowed sister-in-law for levirate marriage as long as his lifetime overlapped with his deceased brother's; see also *Yevamot* 2:5.

and can release [his mother] from levirate marriage: If the baby boy is his father's only son and his father died, his birth releases his mother from the levirate bond, even if he dies immediately after birth.

and can enable consumption of terumah: If his nonpriestly mother had married a priest who then died after conceiving the child with her, she retains her membership in the priestly household because of the baby.

and can disqualify from consumption of terumah: If his mother is the daughter of a priest and had married a nonpriest and her husband died, she could have returned to her father's household and been eligible to partake of *terumah* again. But the baby binds her to her deceased husband's status; see Leviticus 22:12–13 and *Yevamot* 7:4. For a similar list see *Oholot* 1:6.

and can inherit [property],
and can [bequeath] inheritance,
and one who kills him is culpable.
And to his father and his mother and to all his relatives
he is considered a "full bridegroom."

4 A girl who is three years and one day old
can be betrothed by way of intercourse,
and if her levirate brother-in-law had intercourse with her,
he has acquired her [as a levirate wife].
And one can be culpable of adulterous intercourse with her,
and she can convey impurity to the one who has intercourse with her
so that he conveys impurity to the lower as much as to the upper bedding.
If she is married to a priest,
she can eat *terumah*.
If one of the disqualified men has intercourse with her,
he has disqualified her from the priesthood.
If one of the prohibited relatives listed in the Torah has intercourse with her,
they are put to death because of her,
but she is exempt.
[Intercourse with a girl] less than this [age] is like putting a finger in the eye.

5 A boy who is nine years and a day old
and has intercourse with his levirate sister-in-law,

and can inherit [property]: If his mother died, he can inherit her property.

and can [bequeath] inheritance: If he then dies, his brothers from the same father but a different mother can inherit from him.

one who kills him is culpable: Presumably this applies to a baby girl as well.

"full bridegroom": The expression may be related to the biblical expression "bridegroom of blood" in Exodus 4:26. According to the Talmud, the intent here is that the laws of mourning apply to the baby boy.

5:4 *by way of intercourse*: One of the three ways of "acquiring" a wife; see *Qiddushin* 1:1.

he has acquired her [as a levirate wife]: The levirate bond can be sealed by sexual intercourse with such a girl.

adulterous intercourse with her: Since intercourse with her is a valid form of marital "acquisition," she can have the status of a wife, and the laws of adultery apply to her.

she can convey impurity: If she is menstruating.

to the lower as much as to the upper bedding: See 4:1.

one of the disqualified men: See *Qiddushin* 4:1.

like putting a finger in the eye: This phrase, seemingly a demeaning or at least careless image, concludes a troubling paragraph. In the best case, the point of the paragraph is that if a girl is above three years of age, intercourse with her has potential legal validity or consequences so that it would transform the girl's legal status for life, while before then her legal status would not be affected. The rule does not necessarily condone intercourse with a girl that young.

5:5 *intercourse with his levirate sister-in-law*: As above, the ruling is defining a limit. Once a boy is above nine years old, he is considered to be capable of sex that has legal force and consequences. For the age limit in the laws of levirate marriage, see further *Yevamot* 10:6–9.

acquires her [in marriage], and cannot divorce her till he has reached maturity,
and he can be rendered impure [through intercourse] with a menstruant,
so that he conveys impurity to to the lower as much as to the upper bedding,
and he can disqualify [a woman from the priesthood],
but cannot qualify her for eating *terumah*,[35]
and he can disqualify an animal from the altar,
and it can be stoned because of him,
and if he has intercourse with one of the forbidden relatives that are listed in the Torah,
they are put to death because of him,
but he is exempt.

6 A girl who is eleven years and a day old,
her vows must be examined.
A girl who is twelve years and a day old,
her vows are valid, and one examines [them] throughout the twelfth year.
A boy who is twelve years and a day old,
his vows must be examined.
A boy who is thirteen years and a day old,
his vows are valid,
And one examines [them] throughout the thirteenth year.
Before this time,
even if they said:
"We understand in whose name we made the vow,
in whose name we have made a sanctification [of something]"—
their vows are not a vow,
and their sanctification is not a sanctification.
After this time,
even if they said:
"We do not understand in whose name we made the vow,
in whose name we have made a sanctification,"
their vow is a vow,
and their sanctification is a sanctification.

[35] **P** lacks "*terumah*," probably by mistake.

cannot divorce her till he has reached maturity: Although he can have legally valid intercourse with her, he cannot divorce her to release her from the levirate bond till he has reached legal maturity.

he can disqualify [a woman from the priesthood]: If he is among the category of people who can render a woman ineligible for the priesthood; see *Qiddushin* 4:1.

cannot qualify her for eating terumah: If he is a priest, he still cannot elevate his nonpriestly levirate sister-in-law to priestly status at that age, even though intercourse with her seals the bond.

disqualify an animal from the altar: Through intercourse with it, and there is only one witness to the act. See *Zevahim 8:1*. For capital punishment two witnesses to the act are required.

it can be stoned because of him: Through intercourse with it, based on Leviticus 20:15.

but he is exempt: In parallel to the girl above age three, he is a minor with respect to the laws of capital punishment.

5:6 *her vows must be examined*: Whether she understands their import.

7 The Sages made a metaphor for a woman:
an unripe fig, a ripening fig, and a ripened fig.[36]
An unripe fig—she is still a young girl.
Ripening fig—these are the days of her youth.
During both [stages] her father has the right to what she finds, to the labor of her hands, for the dissolution of her vows.
A ripened fig—when she reaches maturity:
her father has no longer rights over her.
8 What are her signs?
R. Yose the Galilean says:
When a fold develops under her breast.
R. Aqiva says:
When her breasts start to hang.
Ben Azzai says:
When the ring around her nipple starts to darken.
R. Yose says:
So that when one puts one's hand on the nipple, it sinks in and does not come back up right away.
9 A woman who is twenty years old
who has not yet grown two [pubic] hairs
has to bring proof that she is twenty years old,[37]
and she is considered an *aylonit*:
she does not perform *halitsah*, nor is she married off as a levirate wife.

[36] **K** lacks – probably by mistake - the first-stage fruit in the list of three.
[37] **K** lacks "years."

5:7 *The Sages made a metaphor for a woman*: See 2:5 for the same phrase, which appears only in this tractate. There are no parallel metaphors for men.

an unripe fig, a ripening fig, and a ripened fig: Hebrew has distinct terms for each of the ripening stages of a fig. See also *Ma'aserot* 1:2.

the days of her youth: In connection with 5:6 this would seem to be a specific legal stage.

During both [stages] her father has the right to what she finds, etc.: See *Ketubbot* 4:4.

5:8 *What are her signs?* The referent is not clear, i.e. whether the middle stage or her maturity (thus the Talmud) is intended.

When a fold develops under her breast: A graphic visualization of her breasts that runs counter to the general rabbinic attitude of modesty when it comes to female nudity. See also *Sotah* 1:5–6 regarding imagining a woman's disrobement, there deliberately intended as degradation.

5:9 *who has not yet grown two [pubic] hairs*: Pubic hair is treated here as an indicator of fertility or biological maturity, since the immediate legal context is levirate marriage for which the only justification is production of a son for a deceased brother. If by the age of twenty a potential levirate wife does not grow a minimal amount of pubic hair, she is released from the levirate bond to her brother-in-law and does not have to do *halitsah*.

aylonit: A mishnaic neologism that is difficult to translate, since the etymology is unclear. The Talmud suggests a derivation from the Hebrew for "ram," presumably because the word suggests masculinity. She is the female equivalent of the eunuch and often listed together with him. See also *Yevamot* 8:5. The implication, in any case, is infertility.

A man who is twenty years old
who has not yet grown two [pubic] hairs
has to bring proof that he is twenty years old,
and he is considered a eunuch:
he does not perform *halitsah*, nor does he marry his levirate sister-in-law.
These are the words of the House of Hillel.[38]
The House of Shammai say:
For both they [have to be] eighteen years old.
R. Eliezer says:
The male follows the words of the House of Hillel,
but the female follows the words of the House of Shammai,
since a woman develops faster than a man.

Chapter Six

6:1 *The Relationship between Her "Lower" and "Upper" Symptoms of Puberty*

6 If the lower sign appears before the upper sign,
she may either perform *halitsah* or be married as a levirate wife.
If the upper sign appears before the lower sign,
even though that is not possible,
R. Meir says:
She can neither perform *halitsah* nor be married as a levirate wife.
But the Sages say:
She may either perform *halitsah* or be married as a levirate wife,

[38] K: "*like* the words of the House of Hillel."

eunuch: The male equivalent of the *aylonit*. As in her case, the lack of pubic hair by the age of twenty indicates infertility and he is released from the obligation to levirate marriage. See *Yevamot* 8:4–5.

since a woman develops faster than a man: In R. Eliezer's view, the man is declared infertile at the age of twenty, the House of Hillel's age limit for both, and the woman is declared infertile at the age of eighteen, which is the House of Shammai's age limit for both, because girls mature biologically faster than boys.

6:1 The first paragraph of this chapter is connected to the preceding chapter.

If the lower sign appears before the upper sign: If the pubic hair appears before her breasts start to develop.

she may either perform halitsah or be married as a levirate wife: If she was married and her husband died, and she is in a levirate situation. The two public hairs are sufficient as a sign of maturity; see 6:11.

even though that is not possible: R. Meir relies on the usual pattern of development, and since it is deemed impossible that her breast development precede the growth of pubic hair, she is potentially still a minor. Accordingly, if the girl is in a levirate situation, that bond is not yet valid.

she may either perform halitsah or be married as a levirate wife: The Sages, however, hold that since the reverse development is impossible, there must have been hairs there. Accordingly, a levirate situation would constitute a valid bond for her.

because they said:
It is possible that the lower [sign] appears before the upper one,
but it is impossible for the upper one to appear before the lower one.

6:2–10 *Anthology of Pairs of Related Items*

2 Likewise,
any clay vessel that takes in liquid also lets it out.[39]
But there is that which lets out but does not take in.
Any limb that has a nail also has a bone.
But there is that which has a bone and not a nail.

3 Anything that can become impure by *midras* can also become impure by corpse impurity.
But there is that which can become impure by corpse impurity but not by *midras*.

4 Anyone who is fit to judge capital cases is also fit to judge monetary cases.
But there are those that are fit to judge monetary cases but not capital cases.
Anyone who is eligible to judge can also serve as witness.
But there are those who are eligible to serve as witness but not to judge.

5 Anything that is subject to tithing can become impure by food impurity.
But there is that which can become impure by food impurity but is not subject to tithing.

6 Anything that is subject to gleaning is also subject to tithing.
But there is that which is subject to tithing, but not to gleaning.

7 Any animal that is subject to [the law of] "the first of the fleece" is also subject to the [law of] gifts [to the priests].
But there are those that are subject to the [law of] gifts [to the priests] but not subject to [the law of] "the first of the fleece."

[39] **K**: "all clay vessels take in and let out liquid."

6:2 Since the first paragraph establishes the relationship between the "upper" and the "lower sign" in a girl's maturation process, the Mishnah takes this as an occasion to insert a collection of similar pairings whose relationship is not symmetrical (6:2–10).

Any limb that has a nail: See *Oholot* 1:7.

6:4 *but not capital cases*: For instance a convert, or a *mamzer* (see *Sanhedrin* 4:2).

but not to judge: Someone who is not learned.

6:5 *can become impure by food impurity*: Since only food items are subject to tithing.

but is not subject to tithing: Since only that which grows from the ground is subject to tithing (cf. *Ma'aserot* 1:1)

6:6 *subject to tithing, but not to gleaning*: *Pe'ah* 1:4 lists five conditions for a crop to be subject to the law of "gleaning." If one of them does not obtain, the crop is not subject to the law of "gleaning" but may be subject to tithing. Elsewhere in early rabbinic texts we learn that figs for example are not subject to the law of "gleaning," because they are not harvested all at once, but they would still subject to tithing.

6:7 *first of the fleece*: The initial shearing must be given to the priests; see Deuteronomy 18:4 and *Hullin* 11:1.

gifts [to the priests]: The shoulder, cheeks, and maw of a slaughtered animal (Deuteronomy 18:3); see *Hullin* 10:1.

8 Any [crop] to which [the law of] Removal applies, [the law of] the Seventh Year also applies.
But there is that to which [the law of] the Seventh Year applies, but not [the law of] Removal.

9 All [fish] that have scales also have fins.
But not all [fish] that have fins have scales.
All [animals] that have horns also have hoofs.
But not all [animals] that have hoofs have horns.

10 Anything that requires a blessing afterward also requires a blessing beforehand.
But there is that which requires a blessing beforehand but does not require a blessing afterward.

6:11–12 *The Legal Force of the Two Pubic Hairs Discussed Earlier*

11 A girl who has grown two [pubic] hairs
either has to perform *halitsah* or be married as a levirate wife,
and she is subject to all the commandments listed[40] in the Torah.[41]
And likewise a boy who has grown two [pubic] hairs
is subject to all the commandments listed in the Torah,
and he is fit to be considered a stubborn and rebellious son
from the time that he grows two [pubic] hairs till the "beard" fills out—
the lower and not the upper one,
but the Sages spoke euphemistically.[42]
A girl who has grown two [pubic] hairs cannot exercise the right of refusal.
R. Judah says:
[She can] until the black has increased.

[40] Lit. "spoken," "said." [41] In **K** and **P** the order of the last two clauses is reversed.
[42] Lit. "in clean language."

6:8 *[the law of] Removal*: Removal of Seventh-Year produce from the house once it is no longer available in the fields. See *Shevi'it* 9:2–3 and *Ma'aser Sheni* 5:6.

but not [the law of] Removal: See *Shevi'it* 7:2 for examples.

6:9 *All [fish] that have scales also have fins*: Cf. *Hullin* 3:2. Therefore, if a fish has scales, it is certainly kosher.

not all [animals] that have hoofs have split *horns*: A pig.

6:10 *but does not require a blessing afterward*: Any of the commandments for which one says a blessing before performance, such as the washing of hands, the shaking of the *lulav*, laying *tefillin*, and multiple others.

6:11 This and the following paragraph continues where 6:1 left off.

she is subject to all the commandments listed in the Torah that apply to her, since she has reached maturity. Compare 5:6, which made absolute age the definition of maturity.

a stubborn and rebellious son: See *Sanhedrin* 8:1.

the right of refusal: See *Yevamot* 13:1ff. If a girl whose father had died is married off by her mother or brothers, she can repudiate the marriage only till she reaches maturity, but not afterward.

12 The two hairs spoken of in *Parah* and in *Nega'im*,
or spoken of in any other place,[43]
[must be long enough] in order to be able bend their tip to their root—
the words of R. Ishmael.
R. Eleazar says:
In order to be able to grasp them between one's fingernails.
R. Aqiva says:
In order to be cut off with scissors.

6:13–14 *Problems in Calculating the Cycle Calendar*

13 If she sees a stain,
she is thrown in disarray,[44]
and she has to worry about an [irregular] discharge—
the words of R. Meir.
But the Sages say:
Stains are not connected with [the issue of an irregular] discharge.[45]
14 If she sees [blood] on the eleventh day of her cycle at twilight,
or at the beginning or end of her period of menstruation,
at the beginning or end of her days of irregular discharge,
on the fortieth day after the birth of a baby boy,
or on the eightieth day after the birth of a baby girl—
all at twilight—
then all of these are mistaken [in their counting].

[43] **K** here has question "What should be their measurement?"
[44] Lit. "spoiled" or "ruined."
[45] **P** has "bloodstain" at the end of the line, which must be a mistake.

6:12 *The two hairs spoken of in Parah and in Nega'im*: The category of two hairs is relevant in these two other halakhic areas, namely the red heifer and the laws of skin disease as well; see *Parah* 2:5 and *Negaim* 1:5, 4:4.

in any other place: Also in other places two hairs are relevant as a limit, for instance where people are required to cut off their hair or shave, such as the *Nazir*, or one with *tsara'at*; see *Nega'im* 14:4. But the reference here is in particular to the two pubic hairs that are considered signs of biological maturity.

6:13 This is a transitional paragraph, since chapters Seven and Eight will deal with the problem of the bloodstain and how to identify the source of such a stain.

a stain: Note that here the verb is transitive, she "sees" a stain, in contrast to the intransitive use of the verb for "seeing (blood)" or "experiencing (the bloodflow)." See the comment at 1:2.

thrown in disarray: The counting of days for her cycle calendar is thrown into disarray; from a stain she will not know when on her calendar the actual bleeding occurred, and therefore how to categorize that bleeding as menstrual or irregular. Under certain circumstances she may actually be a potential *zavah*, at least in R. Meir's opinion.

6:14 *then all of these are mistaken [in their counting]*: In all these cases, it will be difficult for women to associate the bleeding with either the preceding or the following day. *Arakhin* 2:1 rules that in such a case a woman has to count seven "pure" days without bleeding, that is, has to consider herself a "potential *zavah*."

Said R. Joshua:
Before you[46] arrange [things] for women who are not legally competent,
you should arrange [things] for women who are of sound mind.

Chapter Seven

7:1 *Impurity of Bodily Fluids in Dry or Liquid State*

7 The blood of a menstruant and the flesh of a corpse
convey impurity when moist
and convey impurity when dry.
But irregular discharge,
phlegm,
spittle,
[dead] vermin,
carrion,
and semen
convey impurity when moist
but do not convey impurity when dry.
And if they can, when soaked, return to their former state,
they convey impurity when moist,
and they convey impurity when dry.
And how long must they be soaked?
For twenty-four hours, in lukewarm water.
R. Yose says:
If the flesh of a corpse is dry,
and it cannot, when soaked, return to its former state,
it is pure.

[46] "You" is plural.

for women who are not legally competent: The same term as used in 2:1, there among those who cannot properly conduct their self-examinations. Similarly, "women of sound mind" is used in 2:1 as well. It is unclear whether R. Joshua's statement refers back to 2:1, or how it is related to the immediately preceding statement. Since the accounting of the calendar is so difficult in the cases cited in this paragraph, he possibly means that the Sages should "fix" this before making sure that noncompetent women are helped in this matter.

7:1 *irregular discharge*: The discharge from a *zav*.

convey impurity when dry: See 4:3 with regard to impurity of vaginal fluids related to birth when dry or moist.

it is pure: According to *Oholot* 2:1–2, an olive's amount of flesh from a corpse or a ladleful of dust from a grave conveys impurity by overshadowing.

7:2 *Retroactive Impurity and Introduction of the Bloodstain*

2 [Dead] vermin that is found in an alleyway
conveys impurity retroactively,
till the moment that one [can] say:
"I checked this alleyway and there were no [dead] vermin in it,"
or to the last sweeping.
And likewise a bloodstain
that is found on a shirt,[47]
conveys impurity retroactively,
till the moment that one [can] say:
"I checked this shirt and there was no bloodstain on it,"
or to the last laundry,
and it conveys impurity moist or dry.
R. Simeon says:
That which is dry conveys impurity retroactively, but that which is moist conveys impurity [retroactively] only till the moment that it could still be moist.

7:3–5 *Ethnic Geography of Impurity*

3 All bloodstains coming from Reqem
are pure.
R. Judah deems them impure,
because they are converts and are mistaken.
[The bloodstains] that come
from among non-Jews
are pure.
From among Jews,[48]

[47] Or "undershirt," and so too below. [48] Lit. "Israel."

7:2 *conveys impurity retroactively*: To items that need to be handled in purity that it may have touched. This ruling harkens back to the discussion of retroactive impurity at the beginning of the tractate.

bloodstain: At 2:3 above, a woman who finds a bloodstain when checking herself after intercourse retroactively conveys impurity to her partner. Here it is the bloodstain itself on the garment that conveys impurity.

and it conveys impurity moist or dry: Applying to both the dead creeping creature and the bloodstain.

that it could still be moist: If the stain were any older it would be dry by now.

7:3 *from Reqem*: Reqem is mentioned at the beginning of *Gittin* as located at the eastern edge of the Land of Israel and has having a distinctive halakhic status in that context; see *Gittin* 1:1–2.

are pure: Presumably because the majority of inhabitants there are non-Jews. In contrast to the *blood* of a non-Jewish woman, about which there is an early dispute as to its purity, the bloodstains from non-Jews are categorically pure. See 4:3.

they are converts and are mistaken: R. Judah disagrees about the demography of Reqem: since to him the inhabitants there are mostly converts, the impurity law of the bloodstain applies to them.

from among non-Jews are pure: See above and 4:3.

or from among Samaritans:
R. Meir deems them impure
but the Sages deem them pure,
because they are not suspected [of negligence] with regard to their bloodstains.

4 All bloodstains found anywhere
are pure,
except those that are found indoors,[49]
or in the vicinity of a house of impurities.
A house of impurities of the Samaritans
conveys [corpse] impurity by overshadowing,
because they bury their miscarriages[50] there.
R. Judah says:
They did not use to bury them but threw them out, and a wild animal would drag them away.

5 They[51] are believed to say:
"We have buried miscarriages there," or
"We did not bury [miscarriages there]."
They are believed to say
that an animal bore a firstborn,
or that it did not.
They are believed in pointing out graves,
but they are not believed with respect to overhanging boughs, or protruding stones, or grave areas.
This is the general rule:
In any matter in which they are under suspicion,
they cannot be believed.

[49] Lit. "in rooms." [50] Or "abortions." [51] i.e. the Samaritans.

Samaritans: At 4:1 above the Samaritans are contrasted with "Israel" because they have a different system of counting. Here they are grouped with "Israel" with regard to bloodstains.

7:4 *anywhere*: In the Land of Israel.

indoors: If they are found indoors, the assumption is that they were deliberately kept there. If they are found outdoors, they certainly are not menstrual stains, since Jewish women can be relied upon in these matters.

house of impurities: This institution is curious. In most manuscripts the word can be rendered "house of impure women" (a difference of one vowel). The latter would suggest something like a menstrual hut, which is what Rashi's commentary to the version of the Mishnah in the Babylonian Talmud suggests. But rabbinic literature in general does not suggest the existence of such an institution. A parallel text speaks of bathhouses for women and bathhouses for Samaritans. In the version here another translation could be a "place for impurities."

A house of impurities of the Samaritans: See *Oholot* 18:7, where the residence of non-Jews in the Land of Israel is declared impure, since it is assumed that they bury their miscarriages there.

7:5 *overhanging boughs*: See *Oholot* 8:2 for a list of things that give passage to impurity by overshadowing.

grave areas: See *Oholot* 17:1 for a definition of such a grave area.

they cannot be believed: Compare the formulation of the general rule with regard to suspicion of breaking the law in *Bekhorot* 4:10.

Chapter Eight

8:1–4 *Rules concerning Bloodstains on Her Body or Clothes*

8 If she sees a bloodstain on her flesh, opposite her genitalia,
she is impure,
and if not opposite her genitalia,
she is pure.
On her heel—
or on the tip of her big toe—
she is impure;
if it is on the inner side of her thigh or of her feet,
she is impure,
[if] on the outside—
she is pure;
if on the flanks at either side—
she is pure.
If she saw it on her shirt,
from the girdle downward,
she is impure;
from the girdle upward—
she is pure.
If she saw it on a sleeve of her shirt,
if it touched the genitals,
she is impure;
and if not—
she is pure.
If she had taken it off,
or put it on at night,
regardless of where the bloodstain[52] is found,
she is impure,
since it could have been turned around.
And likewise a *pallium*.

2 She can attribute [it] to any cause to which she can attribute [it]:

[52] **P**: "blood."

8:1 *opposite her genitalia*: The Hebrew expression has a negative tone, with the verbal root of the noun indicating decay or rot.

On her heel: If she squats, the heel can touch her genitalia, as can the tip of the big toe since it is still within reach of bleeding from her genitalia.

if on the flanks at either side: The front or back of her legs.

on a sleeve of her shirt: If the sleeve is long enough to touch her genitalia.

since it could have been turned around: Since at night she could not see, she may not have put it on properly.

a pallium: Latin, a rectangular cloth worn as a cloak or mantle; see also *Kelim* 29:1.

8:2 *She can attribute* bloodstains that she finds *to any cause* other than menstrual bleeding.

if she slaughtered a wild animal, or a bird, or
if she was occupied with bloodstains, or
sat down next to those so occupied,
if she killed a louse,
she can then attribute it to these.
How large a stain may she attribute to this?
R. Hanina b. Antigonus says:
[A bloodstain] the size of a bean,
and even if she did not kill it.
She may attribute it to her son,
or to her husband.
If she had a wound
that can open again and exude blood,
then she can attribute it to that.

3 It once happened that a woman came to R. Aqiva.
She said to him:
I saw a bloodstain.
He said to her:
Perhaps there was a wound in you.
She said to him:
Yes, but it healed.
He said to her:[53]
Perhaps it could have been rubbed open and exuded blood.
She said to him:
Yes—
and R. Aqiva declared her pure.
He saw his students glancing at each other and said to them:
Why is this matter difficult in your eyes?
Because the Sages did not rule in this matter to impose a stringency,
but rather to institute a leniency,
since it is said:
When a woman has a discharge, her discharge being blood in her body...—
blood[54]—and not a bloodstain.

4 A wiping cloth that was put under a pillow,
and blood was found on it:
if round—it is pure,
if extended—it is impure—
the words of R. Eleazar b. Zadok.

[53] This line not in **P**. [54] Word absent in **K** and **P**.

How large a stain may she attribute to this? To a killed louse.

and even if she did not kill it: In R. Hanina b. Antigonus' view she does not actually have to have killed it.

8:3 *When a woman has a discharge*: Leviticus 15:19.

blood—and not a bloodstain: In biblical law, therefore, bloodstains are pure anyhow. But the rabbis in the Mishnah institute the law of bloodstains, and then differentiate between pure and impure stains, those that are clearly menstrual stains, and those that are not. As in R. Aqiva's case story, the rabbis can claim leniency in the law of bloodstains.

Chapter Nine

9:1–2 *Connection between Urination and Genital Bleeding*

9 If a woman urinates[55] and has a bloodflow,
R. Meir says:
If she is standing, she is impure,
but if she is sitting, she is pure.
R. Yose says:
In either case, she is pure.
2 If a man or a woman were urinating into a pot,
and blood was found in the urine,[56]
R. Yose deems [it] pure,
but R. Simeon deems [it] impure,
because a man does not commonly discharge blood.
Rather, the presumption is that blood is from the woman.

9:3–5 *How to Attribute a Bloodstain if Women Share Clothes or a Bed*

3 If she lent her shirt to a non-Jewish woman,
or to a menstruant,
then she can attribute [a bloodstain] to her.
If three women had worn the same[57] shirt, or
if they sat on the same bench
and blood was found on it,
they are all impure.
If they sat on a bench of stone, or

[55] Lit. "takes care of her needs," here and below. [56] Lit. "water."
[57] **K** was originally missing this word, and either a second hand or the scribe himself inserted it. This whole chapter contains a number of corrections of obvious omissions.

9:1 *if she is standing, she is impure*: The physiological thinking here is difficult to follow, but perhaps urination while standing is considered to add pressure and therefore possibly flushing out uterine blood, while urination while squatting would have the opposite effect. Any blood that is discharged with urination would not then be considered menstrual.

9:2 *the presumption is that blood is from the woman*: R. Simeon considers it more likely that the blood came from the woman, even though both R. Yose and R. Meir declared genital blood that she discharged while urinating in a sitting position pure.

9:3 *If three women had worn the same shirt*: Here presumably three Jewish women are all in a similar situation, in contrast to the first clause.

they are all impure: If none of them has any different status than the others with regard to knowing their menstrual cycles, none of them can attribute the blood to another.

a bench of stone: Stone is not susceptible to impurity.

on a colonnade projection in the bathhouse—
R. Nehemiah deems [them] pure,
since R. Nehemiah used to say:
Everything that is insusceptible to impurity, is insusceptible to [the impurity of] bloodstains.

4 If three women had been sleeping in the same bed,
and blood was found beneath one of them—
they are all impure.
If one of them examined [herself] and she was found[58] to be impure—
She is impure, but the other two are pure,[59]
for they may attribute [the blood] each to the other.
And if none of them was susceptible to have a bloodflow,
one regards them all as if they were susceptible.

5 If three women were[60] sleeping in the same bed,
and blood was found beneath the woman in the middle,
they are all impure.
If beneath the one on the inside,
the two on the inside are impure,
but the one on the outside is pure.
If beneath the one on the outside,

[58] **P**: "she found herself impure."

[59] **K**: "she found herself pure, she is pure and the other two are impure"; **P**: "she is impure and all are pure."

[60] **K** has "who" instead of "were."

colonnade projection in the bathhouse: What precisely is meant is unclear, but the projection would be connected to the pillar in a colonnade and therefore also to the ground, and as such would not be susceptible to impurity.

R. Nehemiah used to say: His rule makes the impurity of bloodstains dependent on the material on which they are found.

9:4 *for they may attribute [the blood] each to the other*: The two other women can attribute the blood to the woman who found herself to be impure.

if none of them was susceptible to have a bloodflow: That is, if they were from among the four categories of women listed in 1:3.

one regards them all as if they were susceptible: Since the blood must have come from one of them, and none of them can claim special exemption, they are all considered the same.

9:5 *If three women were sleeping in the same bed*: In the previous paragraph all three women are initially declared impure, while in this paragraph the impurity of each depends on the precise location of the stain, and only when it is found under the woman in the middle are they all impure. The two paragraphs seem to contradict each other, but R. Judah's explanation may be an attempt to reconcile them.

the one on the inside: Presumably the one closest to the wall. In that scenario the woman on the outermost side cannot possibly have shifted as far as over to her while sleeping, while the one in the middle might have.

the two on the outside are impure,
but the one on the inside is pure.
Said R. Judah:[61]
When?
When they climb into bed by way of the foot of the bed.
But if all three of them climb in over her,[62]
they are all impure.
If one them examined [herself] and was found[63] to be pure,
she is pure, and the other two are impure.
If two of them examined [themselves] and found [themselves] to be pure,
they are pure, and the third is impure.
If all three of them [examined themselves] and found [themselves] to be pure,
they are all impure.
To what can this be compared?
To an impure pile that was mixed up with two pure piles,
and they examined one of them and found it to be pure,
It is pure, and the other two are impure.
If two, and they found them to be pure
they are pure, and the third is impure.
If all three, and they found them to be pure,
they are all impure—
the words of R. Meir,
because R. Meir used to say:
Everything that is in [a status of] presumptive impurity
continues in its impurity,
till the source of the impurity becomes known to you.[64]
But the Sages say:
One should examine till one reaches rock or virgin soil.

[61] **K** lacks "said R. Judah."
[62] **P** has "upper chamber," a difference of one letter.
[63] **K**, **P**: "she found [herself]."
[64] **K**: "till its impurity becomes clear."

by way of the foot of the bed: If they get into bed without having to climb over each other, then the ruling in this paragraph applies.

if all three of them climb in over her: Note that some versions have something like "from above," lit. "by way of the upper chamber." Either way the implication is that they had to climb over the first one.

an impure pile that was mixed up with two pure piles: One of the piles was thought certainly to have a minimal amount of corpse matter mixed into it. It is unclear what the simile adds to the situation above.

because R. Meir used to say: For the same formulation, see 7:3.

till one reaches rock or virgin soil: To be understood literally as in *Oholot* 16:4, where one is enjoined to dig or sift the dirt till one finds untouched ground where definitely no corpse matter could be located. If one has not found any dead matter, all the piles can be assumed to be pure. However, this does differ from the case of the women since here there is the evidence of the blood.

9:6–7 *How to Distinguish a Bloodstain from a Mere Blot of Color*

6 Seven substances should be rubbed over a bloodstain:
tasteless spittle,
or water from grits,
or urine,
or natron,
or lye,
Cimolian earth,
or alkali.
If one soaks it,
and handles on it things requiring a status of purity,
and then rubs it with these seven substances,
and it does not disappear,
then it is [mere] color.
Anything requiring [a status of] purity remains pure,
and one need not immerse [it].
If it disappears, or grows fainter,
then this is a bloodstain,
and things requiring [a status of] purity are impure,
and one needs to immerse [it].
7 What is "tasteless spittle"?
Anything that does not have any taste.
Water from grits?
A paste [made from] the grits of beans that have been peeled.
Urine?
That has acidified.
And one must rub [the stain] three times with each of these [substances].
If one does not rub them in this order,
or if one rubs all seven at once,
then one has not done anything at all.

9:6 *Seven substances should be rubbed over a bloodstain*: In order to check whether a stain is actually blood. See *Shabbat* 9:5 for the same last five items of laundering substances.

Cimolian earth: After the name of the Aegean island Kimolos. This substance was widely known in ancient literature as a laundering and as a medical substance.

one need not immerse [it]: The object of immersion here is unclear, but presumably the fabric itself is intended. In the sequel, the stains have not disappeared. The fabric having been immersed before the seven substances were applied, now needs to be immersed again.

9:7 *A paste [made from] the grits of beans*: The verbal root of paste here is chewing, so perhaps the intention is the chewing of the bean grits till it forms a paste. It has been suggested that the spit after chewing is the "the water" of the grits.

that have been peeled: The meaning of the Hebrew is unclear. Perhaps this is the name of the kind of bean. In midrashic literature a similar phrase connotes pressure of the soul, depression, mourning. Some early medieval citations have this phrase here, suggesting that it connotes "almost swallowed."

then one has not done anything at all: Even if the stain does not then fade, it is still presumably blood.

9:8–9 *Physiological Symptoms of the Onset of a Menstrual Period*

8 [For] each woman who has a regular menstrual period,
it is sufficient to calculate her impurity from the time of her bloodflow.[65]
And these are the [symptoms of] regular menstrual periods:
she yawns,
or she sneezes,
or she has a sensation in her stomach,
or in the lower part of her abdomen,
or if she discharges,
or if a kind of feverish flush takes a hold of her,
similar [symptoms] like these.
And if any [of these] have affected her regularly three times,
this is then [a symptom of] a regular menstrual period.
9 If she used to have her bloodflow regularly at the onset of these [symptoms for] her menstrual periods,[66]
all the food items requiring a status of purity that she prepared
while her symptoms lasted
are impure.
If at the end of these [symptoms for] her menstrual periods,
all the food items requiring a status of purity that she prepared[67]
while her symptoms lasted
are pure.

[65] Lit. "her time is sufficient for her."
[66] **K**, **P**: "menstrual period," the term for the period itself rather than the plural form that connotes the symptoms.
[67] **K** has masculine verbal form here.

9:8 *[For] each woman who has a regular menstrual period*: This paragraph starts out by reiterating word for word a phrase from the beginning of the tractate; see 1:1. While in 1:1 it was simply assumed that the meaning of "regular period" was understood, the Mishnah now sets out to explain what kind of regularity is imagined. This paragraph for the first time uses the plural term, rendered here as "[the symptoms of] regular periods," since what follows is a list of physiological symptoms.

this is then [a symptom of] a regular menstrual period: The "regularity" described here is not one of regular calendar, but of the physiological symptoms, which is somewhat confusing. The talmudic discussion makes a distinction between regularity of time (intended in 1:1) and regularity of the "body," of physiological symptoms here. The easiest explanation would seem to be that if her menstrual bleeding is regularly—that is, at least three times—accompanied by one of the symptoms listed here, by yawning for instance, she can then assume regularity going forward, and every time she has a bloodflow accompanied by yawning, she need not worry about counting any impurity retroactively.

9:9 *If she used to have her bloodflow regularly at the onset of these [symptoms for] her menstrual periods*: The Mishnah here introduces another period of minimal retroactivity. If she regularly starts her menstrual bleeding with one of these symptoms (e.g. yawning), then she has to assume that it always does. And if she had not checked herself with the onset of the symptomatic yawning, all the purity-dependent food items she has handled become impure. The symptom is the starting point of her regular "period."

If at the end of these [symptoms for] her menstrual periods: If on the other hand her bleeding usually starts at the end of her symptoms, the timespan her symptoms last is not yet considered part of her period of impurity.

R. Yose says:
[Symptoms for] her regular periods can also be days and hours.
If she used to [start] having her bloodflow regularly after sunrise,
she becomes forbidden only after sunrise.[68]
R. Judah says:
The entire day is hers.

9:10 *Establishing Regular Chronology of Menstruation*

10 If she used to [start] having her bloodflow regularly on the fifteenth day,
and this changed so that she [started] having her bloodflow on the twentieth day,[69]
both [days] are forbidden.
If it changed twice to the twentieth day,
both [days] are forbidden.
If it changed three times to the twentieth day,
the fifteenth [day] becomes permitted,
and she determines the twentieth day [as her regular period],
because a woman cannot determine her regular period,
unless it has occurred three times,
nor can she consider herself pure at [the time of] her regular period,
unless she has missed it three times.

9:11 *Virginal Bleeding*

11 Women in their[70] virginity are like vines:
there are vines the wine of which is red,

[68] **P**: "till the sun rises." [69] **K**: "and it changed [to] the twentieth day." [70] **K, P** lack "their."

If she used to [start] having her bloodflow regularly after sunrise: This may or may not be part of R. Yose's statement. The manuscripts start a new paragraph here, suggesting the latter.

she becomes forbidden: The ruling here switches to the sexual prohibition linked with her menstruation. Since she regularly starts her menstrual period with sunrise, she becomes "forbidden" to her husband with sunrise, but before then she is permitted to engage in intercourse with him the entire night.

The entire day is hers: The phrasing is ambiguous, as it sounds permissive but includes a prohibition also. According to Rashi's reading of this text, R. Judah insists that the day is hers if she has not actually started her menstrual period, but during the night before that sunrise she cannot engage in intercourse. R. Judah therefore disagrees with R. Yose—if the preceding ruling is part of R. Yose's statement—about the night before.

9:10 *both [days] are forbidden*: If the regular starting day of her period is the fifteenth day of the month, she is "forbidden to her husband" on that day, as well as on the day she actually starts bleeding, e.g. on the twentieth day of the month. If this pattern repeats itself a second time, the same applies. Only at the third time is the fifteenth day released from being the expected day of her menstrual period.

9:11 *Women in their virginity*: With respect to bleeding when they have their first sexual encounter, different women's bodies behave differently. It is not clear whether the text intends this to apply to menstrual bleeding as well, as suggested in the talmudic discussion elsewhere.

like vines: See 5:7 for the comparison of the woman's body with fruit.

and there are vines the wine of which is black,
and there are vines the wine of which is plentiful,
and there are vines the wine of which is sparse.
R. Judah says:
Every vine produces wine,
but if it does not produce wine
then this is *dorkati*.

Chapter Ten

10:1 *Menstrual Blood and the Blood of Virginity*

10 A young girl whose [appropriate] time to experience a bloodflow has not yet come and was married—
the House of Shammai say:
One gives her four days.
But the House of Hillel say:
Till her wound heals.
If her [appropriate] time to experience a bloodflow has come and she was married,
the House of Shammai say:
One gives her the first night.
But the House of Hillel say:
Till the end of the Sabbath, four nights.
If she experienced a bloodflow
and she is still at her father's house,
the House of Shammai say:
One gives her [one act of] obligatory intercourse.

dorkati: The manuscripts have different spellings of this word, derived from Greek. In the later talmudic discussion this is considered a family name.

10:1 *whose [appropriate] time to experience a bloodflow has not yet come*: If she is too young to experience menarche. See also 6:11.

One gives her four days: As in 5:4, the Mishnah here exhibits a certain expectation that young girls can be married and be subjected to marital intercourse. Note that the ruling phrases this as "giving her" rather than "giving him" four days. Accordingly, the House of Shammai hold that for the first four days of her marriage, any bleeding that occurs then can be attributed to her "virginal" bleeding, rather than having to be considered menarche.

Till her wound heals: Note that the virginal intercourse is phrased as inflicting a wound.

If her [appropriate] time to experience a bloodflow has come: If on the other hand the girl has reached the appropriate age for menarche.

Till the end of the Sabbath, four nights: As a virgin she would have been married on Wednesday, see *Ketubbot* 1:1.

she is still at her father's house: If—as a final scenario—she has experienced her menarche.

obligatory intercourse: Then the married couple can have their obligatory first sexual encounter according to the House of Shammai.

But the School of Hillel say:
The entire night is hers.

10:2–3 *Impurity Calendars of a Menstruant, a Zav, and a Zavah*

2 A menstruant who examined herself on the seventh day[71] in the morning
and she found that she was pure,
and at twilight did not mark the separation,
and after [some] days examined herself and found that she was impure,
she is then [for the days in between] in the presumptive state of purity.
If she examined herself on the seventh day in the morning,
and found that she was impure,
and at twilight did not mark the separation,
and after [some] time examined herself
and found that she was pure,
she is then [for the days in between] in the presumptive state of impurity,
and conveys impurity[72] [retroactively] for twenty-four hours
and for the time between the two examinations.
But if she has a regular menstrual cycle,
it is sufficient to calculate her impurity from the time of her bloodflow.[73]
R. Judah says:
Any woman who did not mark the separation in purity after *minhah* and onward
is then in a presumptive state of impurity.

[71] **P**: "on the Sabbath." [72] **K**: "she becomes impure." [73] See 9:8 above.

The entire night is hers: For the phrasing see 9:9 and the comment there. Some medieval versions, however, have only "the entire night." The House of Hillel disagree with the House of Shammai, in that the couple can engage in intercourse the entire first night.

10:2 *on the seventh day* of her menstrual period.

at twilight did not mark the separation: The text does not say, but presumably refers to her "separation" from her impurity, in that she would check herself to confirm that the bleeding has stopped and then immerse herself.

in the presumptive state of purity: With regard to the purity-dependent food items that she had handled after finishing her period without checking herself at its end, she does not have to worry about retroactive impurity, since during the morning of the last day of her period she *had* checked herself and found that her bleeding had stopped.

in the presumptive state of impurity: By contrast, if she found herself still bleeding on the last day of her menstrual period but then at the end of the day had not checked again, it has to be assumed that the bleeding could have continued, and all the purity-dependent food items that she has handled since have retroactively to be considered impure based on the counting established in 1:1.

after minhah and onward: R. Judah disagrees: her last check at the end of her *niddah* period to establish that the bleeding has stopped has to be done at midafternoon at the latest, and not in the morning, to allow her to consider herself in a presumptive state of purity afterward.

But the Sages say:
Even if she examined herself on the second day of her menstrual period
and found that she was pure,
and at twilight did not mark the separation,
and then after some time[74] examined herself[75]
and found that she was impure,
she is then in a presumptive state of purity.

3 A *zav* and a *zavah* who examined themselves on the first day,
and found that they were pure,
on the seventh day,
and found that they were pure,
but during the rest of the days in between[76] did not examine themselves:
R. Eliezer says:
They are then in a state of presumptive purity.
R. Joshua says:
They have only the first and the seventh day.[77]
R. Aqiva says:
They have only the seventh day.

10:4–5 *Physiological Impurities at Death*

4 A *zav*, and a *zavah*, and a menstruant, and a woman who gave birth, and a person with *tsara'at* who died
convey impurity by carrying until their flesh starts decaying.

[74] **K**, **P**: "days." [75] **P** lacks the verb, an apparent error. [76] Word missing in **K**.
[77] **P** has only R. Joshua pronouncing what is here R. Aqiva's opinion. The missing text is written into the margins, perhaps by a second hand.

on the second day of her menstrual period: The Sages hold, in opposition to R. Judah, that she can check herself as early as on the second day of her menstrual period, and if no blood is found then she can still consider herself in a presumptive state of purity.

10:3 *A zav and a zavah*: They both have to count seven days without discharge, the so-called pure days or seven days in purity, and normally they have to check every day, to establish that seven-day period as part of their purification.

a state of presumptive purity: According to R. Eliezer the inbetween days can be considered presumptively pure, if she checked herself only on the first and seventh day and found herself bleeding-free on those days.

They have only the first and the seventh day: R. Joshua allows only the actual days of checking, so she would still have to count the last six days.

They have only the seventh day: And she has to count another six days without any bleeding.

10:4 *A zav, and a zavah, and a menstruant, and a woman who gave birth, and a person with tsara'at who died*: These five categories of person convey impurity when being carried when alive, while a corpse does not convey impurity by carrying, see *Kelim* 1:2. The ruling here specifies that the status of impurity of these people carries over into their death and their corpse conveys impurity when being carried. For a comparison of the impurity of the *zav* and corpse impurity, see also *Zavim* 4:6 and 5:3.

A non-Jew who died does not convey impurity by carrying.
The House of Shammai say:
All women who died [are considered like] menstruants.
But the House of Hillel say:
She is not a menstruant, unless she died as a menstruant.

5 A woman who died and a quarter-*log* of blood exuded from her body
conveys impurity because of the bloodstain,
and conveys impurity by overshadowing.
R. Judah says:
She does not convey impurity because of the bloodstain,
since it got detached after she died.
But R. Judah agrees regarding a woman sitting on a birthing chair, who died
and a quarter-*log* of blood exuded from her,
that she conveys impurity because of the bloodstain.
Said R. Yose:
Therefore she does not convey impurity by overshadowing.

10:6–7 *Special Considerations for a Woman Counting her Days of Blood Purification*

6 At first they used to say:
A woman who is counting her days of blood purification
can pour out water over the Passover offering,

A non-Jew who died does not convey impurity by carrying: Lit. "is pure from conveying impurity by carrying." That is, in life he does convey impurity when being carried and is considered like a *zav* in that regard, but in death he is no longer considered that way. Cf. 4:3 on the disagreement about the impurity of the non-Jew.

All women who died [are considered like] menstruants: With regard to impurity, any woman's corpse is to be considered like a menstruant's, and therefore would convey impurity by carrying. The House of Shammai here differ from the opening statement of the paragraph, according to which a woman's corpse does so only if she actually died while a menstruant.

10:5 *a quarter-log of blood*: The minimal quantity applies to corpse impurity, see *Oholot* 2:2.

conveys impurity by overshadowing: That is, if her corpse discharges the minimal amount of genital blood, it conveys impurity both by corpse impurity and the impurity of a bloodstain, i.e. through by touch and carrying.

R. Judah agrees regarding a woman sitting on a birthing chair: Rabbi Judah agrees in this case that the blood exuding from her corpse is connected to the birthing process, and therefore conveys impurity accordingly.

she does not convey impurity by overshadowing: R. Yose clarifies that if the blood is considered part of the birthing process it does not convey corpse purity.

10:6 *can pour out water over the Passover offering*: If a woman had given birth and had immersed herself at the end of the first week (for a baby boy) or first two weeks (for a baby girl) and is now merely counting the appropriate number of days of her birth purification, she is allowed to pour water over the offering to rinse it. Her status of impurity is such—comparable to the *tevul yom*—that she would not convey impurity to the vessel from which she pours the water on the Passover offering. But she could not touch the Passover offering directly.

but they reversed [their opinion] to say:
With regard to holy things,
she is actually like someone who touched a person who was impure by corpse impurity,
according to the words of the House of Hillel.
The House of Shammai say:
Even[78] like the one who was impure by corpse impurity.
7 But they agree that she can eat tithes,
and that she can cut off the *hallah* [from the dough],
and that she can bring [the container that contains the *hallah*] close [to the dough] and designate it [as dough offering].
And if some of her spittle or blood of purification fell on the loaf of *terumah*,
that it is pure.
The House of Shammai say:[79]
She needs immersion at the end [of the days of her purification].
But the House of Hillel say:
She does not need immersion at the end.[80]

10:8 *Concluding Paragraph on Sexual Morality*

8 A woman who had a bloodflow on the eleventh day
and immersed herself in the evening

[78] Word missing in **K**. [79] **K, P**: "because the House of Shammai says."
[80] **P** lacks the House of Hillel's opinion, but has it added in the margin.

With regard to holy things: The reversed opinion changes her impurity status with regard to sacred food, such as the Passover offering, with the result that she could convey impurity to the water and thereby indirectly to the Passover offering. In order to prevent this she is no longer allowed to pour the water.

like the one who was impure by corpse impurity: The House of Shammai consider her status of impurity such that she conveys impurity even to the vessel.

10:7 *But they agree*: i.e. both houses agree.

she can eat tithes: See *Nega'im* 14:3, which equates the impure status of the woman counting the days of blood purification after birth to the impurity of the person with *tsara'at* after he had washed and immersed himself. The latter is attributed with the status of the *tevul yom*, who can eat second-tithe food, which must be kept in a state of purity.

she can cut off the hallah [from the dough]: The *hallah* portion of the dough, which needs to be given to a priest and can only be consumed by priests, needs to be handled in a status of purity; see tractate *Hallah*. In the case under discussion, the woman may cut off the *hallah* portion and set it aside in a container, and then bring it close to the rest of the dough again in order to designate it as *hallah* of that dough. See *Tevul Yom* 4:3 for a similar procedure.

that it is pure: *Tevul Yom* 2:1 rules that liquids from people who are in the status of *tevul yom* do not convey impurity.

immersion at the end [of the days of her purification]: See 4:3 above, which suggests that a woman immerses initially after the first week (for a baby boy) or the second (for a baby girl) after birth. Here the House of Shammai hold that she has to do another immersion at the end of the forty or eighty days of counting her birth purification before she can eat *terumah* in the evening again, see *Nega'im* 14:3.

10:8 *on the eleventh day*: Of the days following the seven days assigned to her menstrual period. For the concept, see above 4:4.

and then had intercourse [with her husband]—
the House of Shammai say:
They convey impurity to what they lie or sit on,
and they are liable for the offering.
The House of Hillel say:
They are exempt from the offering.
If she immersed on the next day,
and [then] had intercourse with her husband,
and after that had a bloodflow—
the House of Shammai say:
They convey impurity to what they lie or sit on,
but are exempt from the offering.
But the House of Hillel say:
This is actually a glutton.
But they agree with respect to the woman who had a bloodflow during the eleven days
and then immersed in the evening
and had intercourse [with her husband]
that they convey impurity to what they lie or sit on,
and are liable for the offering.
If she immersed during the following day
and had intercourse [with her husband],
this is actually wicked behavior,
and [the question of impurity regarding] their touch and their sexual intercourse is left suspended.

and then had intercourse: If she immersed in the evening of the same day to have intercourse with her husband, the House of Shammai hold that they both owe a purgation offering, since she should have counted another day without bleeding against the eleventh day before immersing and resuming sexual intercourse. Her impurity status accordingly is like that of a *zavah*.

They are exempt from the offering: The House Hillel exempt them from the purgation offering, since the eleven-day period is a rabbinic and not a biblical institution.

If she immersed on the next day: In this second scenario she immerses herself during the twelfth day and not at its end.

exempt from the offering: In this case, the House of Shammai also exempt them from the purgation offering, even though they did not wait till the end of the day with the immersion and postintercourse proved to be impure again.

a glutton: The House of Hillel exempt them even from a status of impurity, but nonetheless they do not consider intercourse licit under the indicated circumstances. This introduces a moralizing tone at the end of the tractate.

and are liable for the offering: In the third scenario, where she immerses at the end of the day when she had a bloodflow *during* the eleven days following her menstrual period, the House of Hillel agree with the House of Shammai that they owe the purgation offering, since during the eleven days she must count one entire day without bleeding against every day that she bled before she can immerse and resume intercourse with her husband.

this is actually wicked behavior: Note again a moralizing tone. In this fourth and final scenario husband and wife again wait for only part of the day following the day she experienced bleeding, and she immerses herself during the day rather than waiting till the end of the day. Technically they have not (yet) transgressed, and the question of consequence—the purgation offering for transgressive sex, and conveyance of impurity to purity-dependent materials—is kept in suspense till the end of the day. It is not clear whether this is still the voice of the House of Hillel, or the general ending statement of the tractate.

Tractate Makhshirin

Hannah Harrington

Introduction

Overview

Tractate *Makhshirin* discusses the effect of liquids on other items with respect to susceptibility to or transfer of ritual impurity. *Makhshirin* literally means "those items which make fit, suitable, proper, or capable." In the context of purities, a *makhshir* is a liquid which enables an item, usually produce, to receive impurity. The guiding principle is that produce cannot receive impurity unless it is wet. The only exception to this rule occurs when the produce comes into direct contact with a principal source (a "Father") of impurity (on this concept see *Kelim* 1).

Main Ideas

Most often in this tractate, the term "impure" refers to being susceptible to impurity rather than being impure. Likewise, "pure" usually refers to being insusceptible to impurity rather than being pure. "Pure" can also refer to an animal from an edible species (6:5). A different term, meaning "clean," occurs as well (e.g. 6:7, referring to clear liquid).

Most significantly from a legal standpoint, *Makhshirin* explores the factor of human intention in determining an item's purity. If an individual did not intend for produce to become wet, then it does not become susceptible to impurity. This notion is grounded in Leviticus 11:37–38: *If such a carcass falls upon seed grain that is to be sown, it is clean; but if water is put on the seed and any part of a carcass falls upon it, it shall be unclean for you* (Jewish Publication Society). Verse 38, which is cited throughout *Makhshirin*, explains that a partial carcass transfers impurity onto produce only if it comes in contact with water. The rabbis infer from the phrase *if water is put* that a human being must intentionally moisten the produce or its seed in order for it to become susceptible to impurity. Conversely, unintentional wetting of produce, e.g. by rain, need not affect its purity status (see below).

Structure and Organization of the Tractate

Tractate *Makhshirin* begins by setting forth the divisibility of intentionality. Perhaps at the beginning of a process of wetting produce, water was not desired, but later it was. For example, a farmer may want to shake water out of his tree to dislodge something from the tree, but he did not expect or intend for water to fall on vegetables growing underneath it (1:3).

Chapter 2 begins by explaining the transfer of impurity by sweat, which becomes an issue in a bathhouse which creates its own "sweat" or steam (2:2). The Mishnah then analyzes the problem of mixtures, e.g. of pure and impure water (2:3) or the status of food in a city with both gentile and Jewish residents (2:6). The status of the mixtures is usually according to the majority of items in the mixture, or, when both parts are equal, the more stringent alternative.

Chapter 3 discusses the absorption of liquid by produce without human intervention. Rain is the primary example. But, while rain is clearly outside the realm of human intention, what if the individual was happy that the produce became wet without his effort (3:6–7)? Does this qualify as human intention, since now he is clearly satisfied with the result?

Chapter 4 explores the status of secondary water in the wetting process. For example, if the body became wet from spilling liquid while drinking, or if water splashed out of a trough, does this secondary water cause susceptibility to impurity (4:5)? Or, if someone intentionally immersed his hands in water, what is the status of that water when it splashes onto other items (4:6)?

Chapter 5 examines the process of human intervention with respect to water that fell on produce naturally. For example, if rain fell on produce in a container, it remains insusceptible to impurity, but if an individual subsequently mixed pieces of produce so that they would dry evenly and quickly, he now introduces the element of intention and susceptibility (5:3). The Mishnah also analyzes the purity status of an unbroken stream of liquid pouring from an upper vessel into a lower one (5:9–10).

Chapter 6 presents two major issues. The first concerns the status of fruits and vegetables in the marketplace where one is unsure whether the laws of purity have been observed. The second asks which liquids are like water and so are subject to the rule of "if water is put."

Special Notes for the Reader

In addition to the Kaufmann (**K**) and Parma (**P**) manuscripts of the Mishnah, two other versions have informed this translation: Cambridge Add. 470.1, as transcribed in *The Mishnah on which the Palestinian Talmud Rests*, ed. W. H. Lowe (**C**: Cambridge: Cambridge University Press, 1883), and *Ginze Mishnah* (**G**: Jerusalem: Mossad haRav Kook, 1970).

Tractate Makhshirin

Chapter One

1:1 *The Impermanence of Intentionality*

I Every liquid that was welcome at the beginning,
even though at the end it was not welcome,
or that was welcome at the end,
even though at the beginning it was not welcome,
is under "if water is put."
Impure liquids render impure,[1] welcome or unwelcome.

1:2–5 *The Intention for Water to Remain or Come Out*

2 If one shakes a tree in order to get food or impurity out of it,
they are not under "if water is put."
In order to get liquid to fall:
the House of Shammai say:
Whatever comes out and whatever [remains] in it

[1] **K**, **P**, **G**: "impure liquids render impure"; **C**: "liquids are impure and render impure."

1:1 *welcome at the beginning*: The Mishnah considers a difference in the law if at first the wetness of the crop was welcome, e.g. it needed rain, but later it was no longer welcome, e.g. the rain resulted in a flood.

welcome at the end: Perhaps the water was not welcome at first, but later it was found to be acceptable. The Mishnah decides that even if the owner's intention for the item to be wet was only temporary (i.e. only at the beginning or ending of the process), even his partial intention makes the item susceptible to impurity.

Impure liquids: If the liquid (see below, 6:4) itself is impure, it will simultaneously render items susceptible to impurity and pollute them in fact.

1:2 *impurity out of it*: A farmer might wish to get a piece of a dead insect or rodent out of his crop, but it will only pollute the produce if it has become wet. The carcass must be whole to convey impurity directly to an item without the wetness.

In order to get liquid: If the water was not intentionally put on the produce, but perhaps fell as raindrops and then, due to the shaking, onto fruit, this does cause susceptibility to impurity.

the House of Shammai say: The houses discuss the case of water that falls on a tree and is shaken out onto produce indirectly when a farmer shakes down the fruit. The farmer does not mean for the fruit to get wet

is under "if water is put."
The House of Hillel say:
Whatever comes out is under "if water is put,"
but whatever [remains] in it is not under "if water is put,"
because he intends for all of it to come out.

3 If one shakes a tree and it[2] fell on its neighbor,
or a bush,[3] and it fell on its neighbor,
and underneath them were unpicked[4] seeds and vegetables,
the House of Shammai say:
It is under "if water is put,"
but the House of Hillel say:
It is not under "if water is put."
R. Joshua said in the name of Abba Yose Holiqofri,[5] a man from Tivon:
You should be surprised
if there is any liquid in the Torah
that renders susceptible
unless he intends and puts,
as it is said: *if water is put on a seed.*

4 If one shakes a bunch of vegetables,
and [drops of water] dripped from the upper side to the lower,
the House of Shammai say:
[They are] under "if water is put."

[2] See annotations. [3] Or "branch." See annotations.
[4] Lit. "connected to the ground." [5] **K**: "Haliqufri"; **P, C**: "Holi Qofri."

but cannot help this side effect of the shaking. The House of Shammai regard both the raindrops that fall and the raindrops still in the tree and dropping on fruit later on as agents of susceptibility.

The House of Hillel say: The House of Hillel counter that only the raindrops coming out of the tree at present convey susceptibility: the farmer was expecting all the raindrops to fall down at the time he was shaking the tree. He was not considering drops that might fall later on.

1:3 *it fell*: Variant readings create uncertainty whether it was the tree (or bush) that fell or water that fell from one tree (or bush) onto another. In either case, rainwater fell onto the other tree (or bush) rather than onto the ground. This outcome was not intended by the farmer shaking the tree, who expected the water to fall to the ground, and therefore it does not cause susceptibility to impurity.

bush: At Judges 9:48 the word means "branch," but the sense here is most likely "bush."

and underneath them were unpicked seeds and vegetables: According to the House of Shammai, even though the produce was not picked, it still receives susceptibility to impurity. The House of Hillel do not agree with the House of Shammai because produce that is still connected to the ground cannot receive impurity.

Holiqofri: Holiqofri could be Abba Yose's family name or the town of his residence. Tivon is probably a village in the Galilee.

You should be surprised: Literally, the text reads "impure liquid" but in the Mishnah "impure" often means "susceptible to impurity." R. Joshua may be reading Leviticus 11:38 as "If he puts water" rather than the Masoretic "If water is put," emphasizing his point that human agency and intention are required for liquids to cause susceptibility to impurity. In fact, **P** points this phrase as "if he puts..." throughout *Makhshirin*, while **K** maintains the traditional pointing.

1:4 *the House of Shammai*: The water renders susceptible because it was welcome in the first place.

The House of Hillel say:
They are not under "if water is put."
The House of Hillel said to the House of Shammai:
If one shakes a stalk,
are we concerned lest it drip from leaf to leaf?
The House of Shammai said to them:
[The difference is] that the stalk is single and a bunch of stalks is many.
The House of Hillel said:
Look, if someone lifted a full sack of fruit
and put it on the bank of the river,
are we concerned lest it drip from the upper side to the lower?
But if someone lifted two [sacks]
and put one on top of the other,
the lower is under "if water is put."
R. Yose says:
The lower one is insusceptible.
5 If one rubs a leek,
or wrings out his hair with his garment,
R. Yose says:
That which comes out
is under "if water is put,"
and that which remains in it
is not under "if water is put,"
because he intends that it will come out from all of it.

1:6 *Miscellaneous Intentions for Wetting Produce*

6 If one blows on lentils to examine if they are good,
R. Simeon says:
They are not under "if water is put,"
But the Sages say:
[They are] under "if water is put."

The House of Hillel: If the water simply travels from leaf to leaf or from one part of the sack of fruit to another but does not actually come out (i.e. fall off the leaves or sacks), there is no susceptibility because the farmer intended for the water to come out.

The lower one is insusceptible: R. Yose claims that even the lower sack of fruit does not become susceptible to impurity (lit. "the lower one is pure") because the water has simply dripped from sack to sack; it has not gone out, as the farmer had intended.

1:5 *If one rubs a leek*: That is, to wipe off any moisture. R. Yose discusses two more examples of water loosened by intention: rubbing drops of water off a leek to dry it or squeezing water out of one's hair. In both cases, the water renders an item susceptible to impurity only after it comes loose.

1:6 *If one blows on lentils*: The issue here concerns the moisture of breath. For R. Simeon, either breath does not qualify as a liquid or its moistening effect is unintentional, so it does not convey susceptibility. The Sages disagree and regard breath as moisture intentionally blown in order to examine the lentils.

And if one eats sesame seeds with his finger
and gets liquid on his hand,[6]
R. Simeon says:
They are not under "if water is put,"
but the Sages say:
[They are] under "if water is put."
If one hides his fruit in water because of thieves,
it is not under "if water is put."
It happened once
that the people of Jerusalem hid their fig cakes in water
because of the Sicarii
and the Sages deemed them insusceptible.
If one puts his fruit on the current of a river
in order to bring it along with him,
it is not under "if water is put."

Chapter Two

2:1–2 *The Susceptibility of Sweat*

2 The sweat of houses, pits, ditches, and caves is pure.
Human sweat is pure.
If one drank impure water and sweated,
his sweat is pure.
If one entered drawn water and sweated,
his sweat is impure.
If one dried off and afterward sweated,
his sweat is pure.

[6] **K, P**: "hands."

And if one eats sesame seeds with his finger: Saliva wets the finger when he puts the seeds into the mouth. In R. Simeon's view he did not intend to get his hand wet.

Sicarii: Sicarii were zealots active before and during the siege of Jerusalem (ca. 70 CE); the word is also applied to those who took confiscated property after the defeat of Bar Kokhba (see *Gittin* 5:6).

insusceptible: The people put their fig cakes in water of necessity, not because they wished to do so. The same logic applies to the person who floats a heavy bag of fruit down the river using the current for mobility. Since the wetness was not welcome, the food remains insusceptible to impurity.

2:1 *pure . . . impure*: Throughout this series of paragraphs, "pure" and "impure" mean "render susceptible" or "do not render susceptible."

If one drank impure water: Impure water is converted within the body and so becomes a different entity that does not affect the character of perspiration.

If one entered drawn water: Drawn water is susceptible to impurity and can convey it. Because sweat has combined with drawn water, it takes on the character of the latter.

If one dried off: In this instance there is no mingling of sweat and drawn water.

2 If a bath house is impure,
its sweat is impure.
If it is pure,
it is under “if water is put.”
If a pool is in a house,
[and] the house sweats on its account:
if [the pool] is impure,
the sweat of all of the house that is on account of the pool
is impure.

2:3–4 *Variables of Distance and Quantity in a Mixture*

3 Two pools, one pure and one impure:
that which sweats near the impure one[7]
is impure;
that near the pure
is pure.
at a point halfway between,
[any sweat] is impure.
If impure iron was mixed with pure iron,
if the majority is impure,
then it is impure,
and if the majority is from the pure,
then it is pure.
Half and half,
it is impure.
[Regarding] pots into which Israelites and gentiles urinate:
if the majority [of the urine] is impure,
[all of it] is impure.[8]
If the majority is pure,
it is pure.

[7] K: “impurity.” [8] K lacks “if the majority [of the urine] is impure, [all of it] is impure.”

2:2 *its sweat is impure*: The sweat of the bathhouse is considered part of the water of the bath.

If it is pure: If the water in the bath is pure, the sweat of the bathhouse is also pure, but it will still operate according to the law, “if water is put” and make other items susceptible to impurity.

If a pool is in a house: A pool in an ordinary house resembles a pool in a bathhouse: the sweat of the house is caused by the water of the bath. The sweat of a house with no pool of water does not cause susceptibility (above, 2:1).

2:3 *That which sweats near the impure one*: That is, sweat of the wall nearer to the impure pool will combine with the water of the impure pool and become impure as well. If it lies closer to the pure pool, its sweat remains pure. If it is located halfway between the two pools, its sweat becomes impure.

If impure iron was mixed with pure iron: Similarly, if the majority of a lump of iron is impure the whole lump is impure, and vice versa. The same rule applies to a vessel made from such a lump.

[Regarding] pots: The urine of gentiles is impure, but the urine of Israelites is ritually pure (*Niddah* 4:3).

Half and half,
it is impure.
If rainwater fell on waste water,
and the majority is from the impure,
[all of it] is impure.
If the majority is from the pure,
it is pure.
Half and half,
it is impure.
When?
Whenever the waste water was there first.
But if rainwater,
no matter the amount,
precedes the waste water,
it is impure.

4 If one plasters his roof or launders his clothing
and then rain falls on them:
if the majority [of the water] is from the impure,
it is impure.
If the majority is from the pure,
it is pure.
Half and half,
it is impure.
R. Judah says:
If [the rain] continued to drip.

2:5–9 *A Town with Both Israelite and Gentile Residents*

5 A town in which Israelites and gentiles reside,
and there was a bathhouse in it
where bathing was provided[9] on the Sabbath:
if the majority are gentiles,
one washes in it[10] immediately [after the Sabbath];
if the majority are Israelites,

[9] Lit. "a bathhouse that bathed."

[10] **C**, **G**, and **P** lack "in it."

If rainwater fell on waste water: Rain, which is insusceptible to impurity, can purify waste water if it comprises the majority of the mixture. However, if the rain fell first, the assumption is that it was collected in a vessel and later waste water was poured into it. In this case, the rain becomes impure even if it represents the majority of the water, because rain that has been intentionally collected and stored in a vessel becomes susceptible to impurity and has no purifying power. The exception to this rule is rain that falls directly into a cistern without human agency and measures at least forty *se'ah* in volume (*Miqva'ot* 1:1).

2:4 *If one plasters his roof*: Plastering or smoothing the roof requires pouring water—presumably impure waste water—on the roofing material Laundry water is presumably the same. Then rain falls into this water.

R. Judah: If the rain drips at a greater rate than the impure water is poured, it will comprise the majority of the water and hence all of the water will be considered pure.

one must wait enough time to heat the water.
Half and half,
one must wait in order for them to heat the water.[11]
R. Judah says:
In the case of a small bath,
if there is a government in [the town],
one may wash in it immediately.

6 If one found in it vegetables for sale,
if the majority were gentiles
one may buy them immediately [after the Sabbath],
but if the majority were Israelite,
one must wait until he might come from a place nearby.
Half and half,
one must wait until he might come from a place nearby.[12]
And if there is a government in it
one may buy immediately.

7 If one found in it an abandoned child:
if the majority [of residents] are gentile,
[it is considered] a gentile,
and if the majority are Israelite,
an Israelite.
Half and half,
an Israelite.
R. Judah says:
One goes by the majority who abandon.

[11] **P** lacks "Half and half, one must wait in order for them to heat the water."
[12] **C** lacks "Half and half, one must wait until he might come from a place nearby."

2:5 *enough time to heat the water*: If a gentile performs work for a Jew on the Sabbath, the Jew is forbidden to enjoy the fruits of that work even after the Sabbath until enough time has passed to have done the work after the Sabbath was over. However, if the majority of residents are gentiles, a Jew can in good conscience enter the bathhouse right after the Sabbath, knowing that the water was heated on the Sabbath for gentiles.

R. Judah: In the case of a bath heated for a gentile official, the Jew may wash in it immediately after the Sabbath even if most residents are Jews, since the water was presumably not heated on the Sabbath for him, but for the gentile official.

government: That is, local gentile officials.

2:6 *vegetables for sale*: Vegetables picked by gentiles on the Sabbath for purchase by gentiles are permitted for Jews since they were not harvested wrongfully on the Sabbath on their account. The farmers would have harvested them on the Sabbath anyway for the gentiles in the town.

Half and half: If at least half of the residents in the town are Jews, the Jew must wait until vegetables that were not picked on the Sabbath might have been brought from elsewhere or until he could arrive at a nearby place where they might have been picked. One need not know whether the vegetables were actually picked after the Sabbath in such a place but must simply wait sufficient time for that to have been possible.

government: As in 2:5, if there were a minority of gentiles but a gentile official resided there, the vegetables would have been harvested and ready for his household's consumption anyway. In this case, a Jew may purchase them at once.

2:7 *the majority who abandon*: There may be an implicit assumption that gentiles are more prone to abandon unwanted babies, so R. Judah holds that the child is considered a gentile.

8 If one found a lost item in it:
if the majority are gentile,
one need not proclaim it,
if the majority are Israelite,
one must declare it.[13]
Half and half,
one must declare it.
If one found bread in it,
one goes by the majority of the bakers.
If it was bread made of pure flour,
one goes by the majority of those who eat bread made of pure flour.
R. Judah says:
If it was bread made of coarse meal,
one goes by the majority of those who eat coarse meal.
9 If one found meat in it,
one goes by the majority of the butchers.
If it was cooked,
one goes by the majority of those who eat cooked[14] meat.

2:10–11 *The Status of Doubtfully Tithed Produce*

10 One who finds produce on the road:
if the [local] majority take it into their houses,
it is exempt;
[if to] sell in the market,
it is liable.
Half and half,
it is *demai.*
[Regarding] a storage bin into which Israelites and gentiles put [produce]:
if the majority are gentile,
it is [considered] certainly [untithed];
if the majority are Israelites,

[13] **K** lacks "if the majority are Israelite, one must declare it."
[14] **K** and **G** lack the second occurrence of "cooked."

2:8 *the majority of the bakers*: If most of the bakers in the city are gentiles, the bread is prohibited. If most of them are Jews, the bread can be presumed to be kosher (see *Avodah Zarah* 2:6).

2:9 *the majority of the butchers*: If most of the butchers in the city are Jewish, raw meat found there can be presumed kosher.

those who eat cooked meat: Application of this rule actually depends on those who cook the meat. If most of the cooks are gentile, even though most of the butchers are Jewish, cooked meat found within the city cannot be presumed kosher.

2:10 *exempt…liable*: Produce that the farmer keeps at home is not liable to tithes until it has arrived from the field, whereas produce intended for sale must be tithed as soon as it is collected. If the local custom is to store, then it can be presumed that the produce was lost on the road and was not yet liable. (This rule applies only to "informal" consumption: see *Ma'aserot* 1:5.) On *demai*, see the introduction to *Demai.*

it is [considered] *demai*;
half and half, it is [considered] certainly [untithed]—
the words of R. Meir.
But the Sages say:
Even if all are gentile
and one Israelite puts into it,
it is [considered] *demai*.
11 [Regarding] produce of the second [year] that was greater than that of the third,
or of the third that was greater than that of the fourth,
or of the fourth that was greater than that of the fifth,
or of the fifth that was greater than that of the sixth,
or of the sixth that was greater than that of the seventh,
or of the seventh that was greater than that of the year following the seventh,
one goes by the majority;[15]
half and half,
stringently.

Chapter Three

3:1–3 *The Absorption of Liquid*

3 If a sack is full of produce
and one put it on the bank of the river
or over the mouth of a pit
or on the steps of a cave,

[15] C adds "to ease, alleviate," forming a parallel with "stringently."

R. Meir... But the Sages say: The gentile-owned produce has presumably not been tithed. R. Meir applies the same considerations as throughout this chapter. According to the Sages, however, even a single contribution by an Israelite renders the whole amount *demai*, "doubtfully tithed."

2:11 *[Regarding] produce... one goes by the majority*: At issue here is the confusion of produce from different years of harvest, since various years of the sabbatical cycle carry different tithing restrictions: normally, first-, second-, fourth-, and fifth-year produce is liable for first and second tithes. First tithe is given to the Levite and second tithe is eaten in Jerusalem. The produce of the third and sixth years is liable for first tithe and a tithe for the poor. According to the present rule, if produce from different years is mixed together, the tithing rules for the greater amount of the produce apply.

fourth... fifth: Since these two years follow the same tithing rules the previous consideration would not apply, and some commentators accordingly delete the clause. However, there is also a requirement that each year's produce must be tithed from that year's crop (see *Terumot* 1:5), and this rule would apply even in the present case.

half and half: If there is an equal amount of produce from different years in the same bin, the stricter rules apply. If one batch is liable to the second tithe and the other batch is liable to the poor tithe, one separates the second tithe, desanctifies and sells it (see *Ma'aser Sheni* 4), and gives the produce itself to the poor; the owner must take the money used to desanctify the tithe and spend it in Jerusalem.

and it absorbed—
anything they absorbed is under "if water is put."
R. Judah says:
Anything against the water is under "if water is put,"
but anything[16] not against the water is not under "if water is put."

2 If a barrel full of produce
is put into liquid,
or it is full of liquid
and put into produce,
and it absorbed—
anything they absorbed is under "if water is put."
About which liquids did they say [this]?
Water, wine, and vinegar.
But all the remaining liquids
are pure.
R. Nehemiah deems pulse insusceptible
because pulse does not absorb.

3 If one takes hot bread out of the oven
and puts it on the mouth of a jug of wine:
R. Meir deems[17] [the bread] susceptible to impurity,
and R. Judah deems it insusceptible to impurity.
R. Yose deems [the bread] insusceptible in the case of wheat,
and susceptible in the case of barley,
because barley absorbs.

3:4–8 *Accidental Moisture That Brings Satisfaction*

4 If one sprinkles water in one's house
and then puts wheat in it,

[16] **K, C** lack "anything."
[17] **P** lacks from here to "deems" following "R. Yose," apparently in error.

3:1 *and it absorbed*: That is, the produce absorbed water, presumably from its surroundings. The Sages regard produce that has absorbed any water to be susceptible to impurity. According to R. Judah, however, the produce must be in direct contact with the water.

3:2 *Water, wine, and vinegar*: This ruling seems contrary to the rule that seven liquids cause susceptibility (below, 6:4), but the Mishnah is making a distinction among these seven. The others do not cause susceptibility to impurity in the case of produce contained by earthenware, because those liquids are too thick to be absorbed through the container.

3:3 *If one takes hot bread out of the oven*: The concern here is that the hot bread will become damp by drawing up the vapor of the wine and so become susceptible to impurity. See also *Terumot* 10:3.

3:4 *If one sprinkles water*: One pours water on the floor to clean it or reduce the dust. If wheat in the house gets wet because of the water, it becomes susceptible to impurity because the individual intentionally sprinkled the floor with water. The issue here is secondary intentionality: the floor was intended to become wet but not the wheat.

and it becomes damp:
if on account of the water,
it is under "if water is put,"
but if on account of the [wet] rock [floor],
it is not under "if water is put."
If one launders one's clothes in a trough,
and then puts wheat in it,
and it becomes damp:
if on account of the water,
it is under "if water is put,"
but if [it becomes damp] of itself,
it is not under "if water is put."
If one dampens [wheat] in sand,
this is under "if water is put."
It once happened among the people of Makhoz
who used to dampen wheat in sand:
the Sages said to them:
If that is the way you have been doing it,
you have never kept purity in your lives.[18]

5 If one dampens [produce] with dried clay:
R. Simeon says:
If there is dripping moisture in it,
it is under "if water is put,"
but if not,
it is not under "if water is put."
One who sprinkles one's threshing floor
does not need to worry
if they put wheat in it

[18] Lit. "You have never done purity in your days."

but if on account of the [wet] rock [floor]: The rock did not become moist by human intention. If the wheat becomes moist by the wetness of the rock floor, it does not become susceptible (and see above, 2:1).

but if [it becomes damp] of itself: Commentators differ. According to some "itself" means the wheat, which has spontaneously absorbed moisture from the air. Others, supported by a variant text, understand "itself" to refer to the trough and to moisture that emerges from it. In either case, if the wheat in the trough becomes damp because of water left by the laundry it becomes susceptible to impurity, but if the wheat becomes wet by some other natural process its status does not change.

If one dampens [wheat] in sand: The reference is to putting wheat in wet sand in order to dampen it.

you have never kept purity in your lives: The "purity" referred to here is the preparation of food according to the rules of ritual purity.

3:5 *If there is dripping moisture in it*: The individual must have been aware that the wheat would get wet when he applied the dripping clay.

but if not: If the clay seems to have dried, the one who applies it to the wheat cannot be held liable for dampening it. Although the wheat is wet, it was not the man's intention to dampen it since he thought the clay was dry.

does not need to worry: The original intention was not to dampen the grains but only the floor.

lest it become damp.
If one gathers herbs to dampen wheat
and they had dew on them,
it is not under "if water is put."
If he intended thus,
it is under "if water is put."
If one takes wheat[19] to grind
and rain falls on it:
if he was happy [about it],
it is under "if water is put."
R. Judah says:
It is impossible[20] not to be happy,
but only if he stood.

6 If one's olives were put on the roof
and rain fell on them:
if he was happy,
it is under "if water is put."
R. Judah says:
It is impossible[21] not to be happy,
but only if one stopped up the drain
or if he shook them.

7 If donkey drivers were crossing the river
and their sacks fell into the water:
if they were happy,

[19] **P, C**: "his wheat." [20] **K, C**: "possible."
[21] **K, C**, and the original text of **G** read "possible."

and they had dew on them: The dew was already on the herbs, so the wheat was dampened by natural processes, not by human interference.

It is impossible not to be happy: Grain prepared for grinding must be damp, so the farmer would undoubtedly be happy that the rain has wet the grain. A variant reads "It is possible that he is not happy," meaning that it does not matter if one is happy or not in this case, because only the action is important.

but only if he stood: The wheat is rendered susceptible only if he stopped purposely so that more rain could fall on it.

3:6 *It is impossible not to be happy*: As before, rainfall is outside of the intention of the owner of the grain unless "he was happy about it." Again, a variant reads, "It is possible not to be happy." It does not matter whether the individual was happy or unhappy about it; what matters is his reaction.

if one stopped up the drain or if he shook them: If the farmer has purposely stopped up the drain in order to soak the olives or shaken them so the rainwater can penetrate the pile, his action demonstrates intention to wet the grain and so the law "if water is put" applies.

3:7 *but only if they turned [the sacks] over*: This action would make them completely wet by human intention.

if he was happy: If the owner was happy about the rinsing, the water would then be desired. If afterward it fell on produce, the latter would become susceptible to impurity. R. Judah requires intentional action to support the claim that the water was desired and so falls under the law of "if water is put."

it is under "if water is put."
R. Judah says:
It is impossible not to be happy,
but only if they turned [the sacks] over.
If one's feet were full of mud,
and so were the feet of his animal,
[and] he crossed the river:
if he was happy,
it is under "if water is put."
R. Judah says:
It is impossible not to be happy,
but only if he stopped and rinsed [the mud off].
With regard[22] to a human being or an impure animal,
[the water falling from their feet] always causes susceptibility.

8 If one takes wagon wheels and plowing tools down to the water
at the time of the east winds
so that they swell:
it is under "if water is put."
If one takes an animal down to drink,
water that comes up on its mouth
is under "if water is put,"
but that which comes up on its feet
is not under "if water is put."
If he intended for its feet to be rinsed off,
even the water on its feet
is under "if water is put."
In a time of footsoreness or threshing,
[this] always causes susceptibility.
If a deaf-mute, someone legally incompetent, or a minor took [an animal] down,
even though he intended for its feet to be rinsed off,
it is not under "if water is put,"
because they have [the legal ability to] act,
but not to intend.

[22] **C**: "[the Sages] say with regard."

With regard to a human being or an impure animal: Perhaps the point here is that it is always desirable to keep the feet of a human being or a riding animal (e.g. donkeys and horses, which are nonkosher) clean, whereas pure animals will be butchered for food. Commentators differ as to whether this proviso continues R. Judah's remarks or represents a separate consensus.

3:8 *so that they swell*: The wood will swell and seal any cracks, so the water is desired.

but that which comes up on its feet: Water that comes off the animal's legs when it is brought down to the river to drink will not cause susceptibility since it was not intended by the owner. However, if it was desired, as in the example of giving comfort to the animal's feet, then it will cause susceptibility in produce onto which it drips afterward.

because they have [the legal ability to] act: The Mishnah does not ascribe the power of intention to a deaf-mute, someone legally incompetent, or a minor. For all legal purposes, they can act but they cannot demonstrate forethought.

Chapter Four

4:1–5 *Susceptibility of Splash and Overflow*

4 If one bends down to drink,
the water that comes up on his mouth or on his mustache
is under "if water is put."
On his nose, his head, or his beard,
it is not under "if water is put."
If one draws water[23] with a jug,
the water that comes up on the outside of it
or with the rope that is wound around its neck
or with the rope that is needed for it
is under "if water is put."
How much [rope] is needed?
R. Simeon b. Eleazar says:
A handbreadth.
If he put it under a waterspout,
it is not under "if water is put."
2 If rain fell on someone,
even one with primary impurity,
it is not under "if water is put."
But if he shook [the rain] off,
it is under "if water is put."
If one stood under the waterspout to cool off or to rinse off:
in the case of an impure person,
[the water] becomes impure;
in the case of a pure person,
It is under "if water is put."

[23] Lit. "fills," that is, the jug itself.

4:1 *on his mouth or on his mustache*: Since drinking the water is desired by the man, and he cannot avoid getting water on his mouth and mustache, the law applies.

On his nose, his head, or his beard: These are not intrinsically needed to drink water.

A handbreadth: The handbreadth of rope nearest to the jug is indispensable for lowering and raising it, so water dripping from that handbreadth can render produce susceptible. Not so the remainder of the rope.

under a waterspout: If one put the jug directly under a drainpipe or waterspout, the water would not necessarily splatter on the outside of the jug and a rope would be unnecessary. Therefore, water splattered on the outside of the jug would not be desired or intentionally "put" there and would not cause susceptibility to impurity.

4:2 *But if he shook [the rain] off*: Rain does not normally cause susceptibility, but if it is shaken off, then it has been intentionally splattered by the individual, and qualifies as intentionally "put" elsewhere.

impure…pure: An impure individual will pollute the water splattering on him. The water splashing off a pure individual will render produce susceptible to impurity since the individual was pleased by its movement.

3 If one leans a dish against[24] a wall
in order for it to be rinsed,
it is under "if water is put."
If it was in order that the wall not suffer,
it is not under "if water is put."
4 If [rain] dripped into a barrel—
the House of Shammai say:
One should break [the barrel].
The House of Hillel say:
He can pour out [the water].
And they agree that if he reaches in
and takes out fruit,
it is pure.
5 If [rain] dripped into a trough,
the water that splashed out or overflowed
is not under "if water is put."
If he lifted [the trough] in order to pour out [the water]—
the House of Shammai say:
It is under "if water is put,"
[but] the House of Hillel say:
It is not under "if water is put."
If he placed it so that [rain] would drip into it,

[24] **K**, **G**, **C**: "to"; **P**: "on."

4:3 *that the wall not suffer*: Perhaps the individual placed dishes against the wall so that it would not get wet. In this case, the person clearly does not desire the water so it cannot cause susceptibility to impurity.

4:4 *One should break [the barrel]*: For the House of Shammai there is no other recourse but breaking the barrel to demonstrate the undesirability of the water. The water will drain away without having caused susceptibility, and the food can be recovered.

He can pour out [the water]: The House of Hillel suggests pouring off the water to demonstrate undesirability without having to break the container. If one pours out the produce as well as the water, the poured water will land on the produce, and this intentional action will cause susceptibility. As long as the produce remains in the jar, it is not susceptible to the water therein because the owner did not approve of rainwater in the jar in the first place.

it is pure: That is, not susceptible to impurity. The produce may be removed at any time. Even if some drops of water remain on it, the produce remains insusceptible because that water was undesired.

4:5 *water that splashed out or overflowed*: The water within the trough remains insusceptible as well since it was there without the approval of the owner.

If he lifted [the trough] in order to pour out [the water]: The House of Shammai regard the water poured out of the trough as causing susceptibility since it happened by human intention and not because of a natural overflow. For the House of Hillel, since the water is unwanted, as evident from the owner's effort to drain it, it does not cause susceptibility.

If he placed it so that [rain] would drip into it: According to the House of Shammai, the intention of the owner to place the trough in order to fill it with rainwater causes susceptibility to both the inside the trough and its overflow. According to the House of Hillel, while the water inside the trough now causes susceptibility since it has been situated by intention, water that splashes out or overflows is not approved by the owner and so is not under the law and does not cause susceptibility.

[then as to] the water that splashes out or overflows—
the House of Shammai say:
It is under "if water is put,"
[but] the House of Hillel say:
It is not under "if water is put."
If he lifted [the trough] in order to pour out [the water],
both [houses] agree that it is under "if water is put."
One who immerses his vessels
or who launders his clothes in a [pool in a] cave:
the water going up on his hands is under "if water is put."
[Water going up] on his feet is not under "if water is put."
R. Eleazar says:
If[25] it is impossible for him to go down [into the pool] without his feet becoming muddy,
the water going up on his feet is under "if water is put."

4:6–9 *Immersion of Produce, Vessels, and Hands*

6 [With respect to] a basket that is full of lupines
that was put into an immersion pool:
one may reach in and take lupines out of it,
and they are insusceptible to impurity.
If one raised them[26] out of the water,
those [lupines] that touch the basket are susceptible to impurity
but all the rest of the lupines are insusceptible.

[25] **K** lacks "if." The scribe of **G** inserts "if" by way of correction.

[26] **K** and **C** lack "them."

Both [houses] agree: Even if he now discards the water, the fact remains that he had intentionally collected it.

water going up on his feet: The person who washed vessels or clothes in a pool must necessarily get his hands wet but not his feet. Thus, the water on his hands is subject to the law "if water is put" because he wants the water for the washing process, but the water on his feet was never desired.

R. Eleazar: If an individual gets his feet muddy as an unavoidable part of the washing process, he will want to rinse them. Since this water will be desired, R. Eleazar considers it subject to the law of "if water is put."

4:6 *one may reach in*: Water from a natural pool does not cause susceptibility to impurity unless it was detached from the pool intentionally (e.g. scooped out with a vessel) because the pool is connected to the ground. In this case, drops of water on the lupines were not detached from the *miqveh* intentionally since the owner wanted only the lupines, not the water.

If one raised them: That is, the basket together with the lupines that it contains.

all the rest of the lupines are insusceptible: The water on the basket was desired in order to purify it but now it has been detached from the *miqveh*. However, the water on the lupines was not desired, so it cannot render them susceptible to impurity.

[Concerning] a radish in [a pool in a] cave:
a menstruant may rinse it
and it [remains] pure,
but if she at all raised it out of the water,
it is impure.

7 If produce fell into a water channel,
and someone with impure hands reached out and took it,
his hands are [now] pure and the produce is pure.
But if he intended for his hands to be rinsed off,
his hands become pure,
but the produce is under "if water is put."

8 If a pot that is full of water was put into an immersion pool,
and a Father of Impurity reached into it,
it is impure.
If [it was] someone who had touched impurities,
it is pure,
but any other liquids are impure,
because water cannot purify other liquids.

9 [Water] drawn with a sweep bucket renders susceptible to impurity for three days.
R. Aqiva says:
If [the water] has dried up,
the produce is considered insusceptible to impurity at once,
and if it has not dried up,
it causes susceptibility even up to thirty days.

a radish in [a pool in a] cave: While the radish is still in the pool, it is insusceptible to impurity even from a menstruant since the water of the pool cannot cause susceptibility as long as it is not detached. However, after she raises the radish out of the pool, the drops of water on her hands and on the radish are now detached from the pool with her approval since she wanted to rinse off the radish. The menstruant, herself impure, conveys impurity through the water to the radish.

4:7 *If produce fell into a water channel*: Even though the person did not intend to ritually immerse his hands, his action suffices. Other rabbinic sources disagree.

But if he intended for his hands to be rinsed off: If the person intended to clean his hands, then he has intentionally wet them, and the dripping water has rendered the produce susceptible to impurity.

4:8 *a Father of impurity*: Earthenware cannot be purified in a ritual pool. Thus, the presence of a Father of Impurity (see introduction) inside it renders the pot impure.

someone who had touched impurities: Only a Father of Impurity can pollute earthenware and this must be through its interior, not by touching its outer side. However, if someone was not a Father of Impurity but had simply touched impurities, he would be in the first degree of impurity, and so he would not cause the pot to become impure. The water inside the pot is protected by being in a ritual immersion pool. However, if any other liquid was in the pot, it would not be protected by the pool because water cannot purify other liquids.

4:9 *sweep bucket*: The term is variously explained. This is perhaps some kind of trough from which a bucket can be filled, alternatively a bucket designed to draw water from a deep well or cistern. See also *Miqva'ot* 8:1.

If [the water] has dried up: If it is known that the bucket is dry.

4:10 *Mixture of Impure Liquids and Rain on Wood*

10 If [impure] liquids fell on wood,
and then rain fell on it:
if [the rain] was greater,
[the combined liquid] is pure.
If someone took [the wood] outside
so that rain could fall on it,
even though [the rain] was greater,
it is impure.
If [the wood] absorbed impure liquid,
even though one took it outside in order that rain would fall on it,
[the rain] remains pure.
And one may not ignite [such pieces of wood]
except with pure hands only.
R. Simeon says:
If they were wet when one ignited them,
and more liquid came out of them than the liquid they had absorbed,
they are pure.

Chapter Five

5:1–2 *First and Second Water*

5 If one immersed in a river
and in front of him was another river
and he crossed it,
The second [water] purifies the first.

4:10 *[impure] liquids fell on wood*: Normally, the rain would purify the impure liquid since the rain was greater, but if the individual wanted the rain to fall on the wood, the status of the rain has changed from a purifying agent to one that causes susceptibility. It is not clear whether the term here means "impure," on account of the original exposure to impure liquids, or "renders susceptible to impurity," that is, from some other source.

absorbed…remains pure: The rain did not make contact with the impure liquid because the latter was absorbed within the wood.

except with pure hands only: If the person's hands are impure, they will cause the raindrops on the wood (which are now susceptible to impurity because they were desired) to become impure and the drops will in turn convey impurity to the oven.

5:1 *the second [water] purifies the first*: The first water is the water that is dripping off the person after coming up from the immersion. This water was desired by the person because it restored his purity, and it is now detached from the river so it can cause susceptibility to impurity. Since the person is crossing a second river and that water was not particularly desired, it mingles with and cancels the power of the detached water to cause susceptibility. Here "purifies" refers to canceling the power to convey susceptibility.

If his friend pushed him due to his drunkenness,[27]
or so too with his animal,
the second [water] purifies the first.
But if his friend was playing with him,
this is under "if water is put."
2 If one swam in the water,
the water that splashes is not under "if water is put."
But if he intended to splash his companion,
it is under "if water is put."
If one "makes a bird" in the water,
the water that splashes and [the water] inside [the "bird"]
is not under "if water is put."

5:3–5 *Human Intervention by Mixing or Measuring*

3 If water dripped onto pieces of produce
and someone mixed them so that they would dry,
R. Simeon[28] says:
It is under "if water is put,"
but the Sages say:
It is not under "if water is put.[29]
4 If one measures a cistern,
whether for its depth or for its width,
it is under "if water is put"—

[27] MSS: "to break him," a difference of one letter [28] MSS: "Rabbi."
[29] Following **G**. **K**: "Rabbi says: It is not under 'If water is put.'" **K** seems to be in accord with **G** but lacks the dictum of the Sages. **P** gives the reverse, "Rabbi says: It is under 'If water is put,' but the Sages say, 'It is not under "if water is put."' **C** lacks the entire dispute.

If his friend pushed him due to his drunkenness: Perhaps with the sense of "to sober him up." The person did not fall into the water intentionally, so the water on him does not render him susceptible to impurity. The alternative reading essentially means the same thing: and does not change the point at issue: in either case the man fell into the river against his will.

or so too with his animal: If an animal was pushed into the water without the owner's desire, water dripping from the animal would not render susceptible. If the animal pushed a person into the water, the same rule would apply.

But if his friend was playing with him: The wrestling was in fun and so intentional.

5:2 *swam* The swimmer does not intend to detach any water from its source, and water unintentionally detached does not render susceptible to impurity. The matter is different if he was intentionally splashing another.

"makes a bird": The phrase is unclear. It may refer to making bubbles or squirting water out of one's mouth or a tube, or it may refer to an inflated object or float that aids the swimmer. In any case, the water involved in accidental splashing and squirting, or water penetrating into an inflatable, is undesirable.

5:3 *and someone mixed them so that they would dry*: Someone moved around the fruit so that the water would spread more widely and dry out more quickly. This meant that some of the fruit had been intentionally moistened, but the Sages rule that the water was never intended in the first place.

the words of R. Tarfon.
R. Aqiva says:
For its depth,
it is under "if water is put";
but for its width,
it is not under "if water is put."

5 If one reached out his hand or leg or rod into a cistern to determine if water was in it,
it is not under "if water is put."
If in order to determine how much water was in it,
it is under "if water is put."
If one threw a stone into a cistern to determine if there was water in it,
the water that splashes
is not under "if water is put."
And [the water] that is on the stone does not cause susceptibility to impurity.

5:6–8 *Human Intervention by Beating or Shaking*

6 If one beats a [wet] hide outside of the water,
it is under "if water is put."
If in the water,
it is not under "if water is put."
R. Yose says:
Even if [the hide] is in the water,
it is under "if water is put"
because he intends that [the water] will go out with the dirt.

7 Water that comes up on [the hull of] a ship, in the bilge,[30] or on the oars
is not under "if water is put."
[Water] on snares, on nets, or on traps
is not under "if water is put."

[30] Or "ballast."

5:4 *R. Aqiva* refines the matter: the wetness of the measuring rod is necessary in order to measure the depth of the water in the cistern, but the width can be determined without getting any water on the rod.

5:5 *If in order to determine how much water was in it*: In the first instance, the person did not wish to draw water, but in the second instance drawing water was necessary in order to perform the desired measuring. The second clause duplicates the opinion of R. Aqiva in 5:4.

5:6 *If one beats a [wet] hide*: If the wet hide has been taken out of the water and one is beating it in order to dry it, then the water in it is being detached with approval and so causes susceptibility to impurity. If the hide is still in the water, while one is beating the dirt out of it, the water is not being detached from the hide.

the dirt: The person wants the water to flow out of the hide with the dirt in order to allow clean water to take its place, and so, according to R. Yose, the law of "if water is put" applies.

5:7 *on [the hull of] a ship*, etc.: These terms have been variously translated, but in any case they denote parts of a ship where unwanted water may accumulate.

But if one shook [them],
[they are] under "if water is put."
If one takes a ship out to the Great Sea to tighten it,
[or] takes a [glowing] nail out into the rain to temper it,
[or] puts a firebrand in the rain to extinguish it,
it is under "if water is put."
8 A covering for tables and the matting[31] for bricks
are not under "if water is put."
But if one shook [them],
[they are] under "if water is put."

5:9–10 *The Purity Status of a Stream of Liquid*

9 Any unbroken stream is pure
except Zifin honey or *Tsappakhat*.
The House of Shammai say:
Even porridge made of grits or beans,
because it shrinks backward.
10 If one pours hot [liquids] into hot [liquids],
or cold [liquids] into cold [liquids],
or hot [liquids] into cold [liquids]:
[the stream of liquid] is pure.

[31] The various manuscripts have different terms here, all of which can be translated as "shavings" or "matting" for bricks or baskets.

If one takes a ship: The purpose is to moisten the wood and thus protect the seams from opening up as the wood shrinks. In all these latter cases the water is desired.

5:8 *A covering for tables*: Rain that collected on coverings does not cause susceptibility to impurity because it was not desired.

If one shook [them]: However, if the owner shakes the covering the water is now where the owner wanted it to be and therefore does cause susceptibility.

5:9 *Any unbroken stream*: When one pours liquid from a pure vessel into an impure one it will become impure on entering the impure vessel but not before; while it is in the connecting column or stream it remains pure (see *Tohorot* 8:8–9). Similarly, liquid in the second vessel is there with approval and therefore causes susceptibility, but this will not affect the unbroken stream.

Zifin honey or Tsappakhat: The meanings of *Zifin* and *Tsappakhat* are unclear. They may refer to places or certain liquids or batters that include types of honey or types of bees. The point is that the liquid is viscous; after it stops flowing, it may ooze backward and pollute the liquid above it.

shrinks backward: Like the aforementioned honey, the porridge oozes backward after it stops flowing forward. If it has contracted impurity from the contents of the second vessel, according to the House of Shammai, it will transfer that impurity backward to the liquid above it.

5:10 *If one pours*, etc.: In all these cases the lower liquid is impure and the liquid in the upper vessel is pure. The concern is not only for the purity of the flowing stream of liquid, but also for the contents of the upper vessel to which it is connected. As long as the lower liquid is cold, it will not emit steam that can travel up into the higher vessel, so too if both liquids are hot. But see R. Simeon in the next clause.

From cold [liquids] to hot [liquids]:
[the stream of liquid] is impure.
R. Simeon says:
Even the one who pours from hot [liquids] to hot:
if the force of the lower is greater than that of the upper,
[the stream] is impure.

5:11 *Dripping Sweat and Juice*

11 If a woman whose hands were pure stirred in an impure pot,
if her hands sweated, they are impure.
If her hands were impure,[32]
and she was stirring in a pure pot,
if her hands sweated, the[33] pot is impure.
R. Yose says:
If they dripped.
If one weighs grapes in the pan of a scale,
the wine that is on the pan
does not cause susceptibility to impurity
until it is poured into a vessel.
This is similar to baskets of olives and grapes
when[34] they drip [juice].

Chapter Six

6:1–3 *Produce on the Roof and in the Marketplace*

6 If one takes his produce up to the roof because of maggots
and dew came down on it,
it is not under "if water is put."

[32] **K** lacks "if her hands were impure." [33] **K**: "into the pot." [34] **G, K, C**: "that drip."

From cold [liquids] to hot: In this case, the steam of the hot liquid in the lower vessel ascends into the liquid of the upper vessel and pollutes it. R. Simeon makes this point even when one pours pure hot liquids into impure hot liquids, if the steam of the impure lower liquids is greater than that of the upper liquids.

5:11 *if her hands sweated*: Sweat on the woman's hands, caused by the steam of the liquid in the pot, conveys the impurity of the food in the pot to the hands or the impurity of the hands to the food in the pot, as the case may be.

the pot is impure: Both the pot and the food within it become impure.

the wine that is on the pan: Juice that oozed from the grapes.

until it is poured into a vessel: The liquid in the pan of a scale does not cause impurity until someone intentionally pours it into a vessel. It was not intended to leak into the pan of the scale.

If he had intended such,
it is under "if water is put."
If a deaf-mute, one legally not competent, or minor brought them up,
even though he intended that dew would fall on them,
it is not under "if water is put,"
because they have [the power of] action,
but they do not have [the power of] intention.

2 If one takes bundles [of produce], cut figs, or garlic to the roof
so that they will keep fresh,
they are not under "if water is put."
All bundles [of produce] in the marketplace are considered impure.
R. Judah deems fresh [bundles] pure.
R. Meir said:
And why did they deem [these] impure?
Only because of the liquid from the mouth!
All [kinds of] meal and flour in the marketplace are considered impure.
Split grain, groats, and grits are considered impure everywhere.

3 All eggs are presumed to be pure
except those belonging to sellers of liquid.
And if they were selling dry produce also,
[the eggs] are considered pure.
All fish is presumed to be impure.
R. Judah says:
Slices[35] of *Iltit* fish, Egyptian fish packed in baskets, and Spanish mackerel

[35] C reads "the box," which is closely similar in Hebrew script.

6:1 *If he had intended such*: If the person intended that dew would fall on the produce, then the case falls under the law of susceptibility of liquids. If the intention was to rid the produce of maggots, the dew is considered coincidental and does not make the produce susceptible to impurity.

but they do not have [the power of] intention: Although their acts can have legal force, in this case intention is the defining criterion. See above, 3:8.

6:2 *so that they will keep fresh*: These items were not taken to the roof to be wet down by dew but in order to moisten and soften in the outside air (and cf. *Tohorot* 9:5).

All bundles [of produce] in the marketplace are considered impure: Vegetables in the public market are assumed to be impure because the merchants pour water on them and then they are handled by the public, even impure persons. They are also exposed to dead insects.

R. Judah deems fresh [bundles] pure: The recently harvested vegetables are still moist naturally and so have not been wetted down by the merchants.

the liquid from the mouth: The merchants have perhaps dripped saliva on the produce when untying the bundles with their teeth, making even fresh vegetables impure.

split grain, groats, and grits: Commentators vary as to why these three types of produce are singled out here for impurity concerns. Some suggest that it is because they are handled by everyone, both pure and impure. A better explanation is that these grains need to be soaked for ease of pounding and thus are inevitably made susceptible to impurity.

6:3 *Slices... are presumed to be pure*: These types of fish are not wetted down by the merchants.

are presumed to be pure.
All brine is presumed to be impure.
With regard to any of these, an *am ha'arets* is trusted
when he states that they have not been rendered susceptible to impurity
except that of small fish,[36]
because these are under the charge of an *am ha'arets*.
R. Eliezer b. Jacob[37] says:
If any water at all fell into pure brine,
it becomes susceptible to impurity.

6:4–8 *Liquids That Render Susceptible*

4 There are seven liquids [to which the law, "if water is put," applies]:
(1) dew,
(2) water,
(3) wine,[38]
(4) oil,
(5) blood,
(6) milk,
and (7) bees' honey.
The honey of hornets does not cause susceptibility to impurity,
and it is permitted for eating.
5 Derivatives of water:
[liquids] that come out of the eye, ear, nose, mouth, and urine,
whether of adults or children,
whether discharged consciously or unconsciously.
Derivatives of blood:
blood from the slaughtering of pure cattle, wild animals, or birds

36 **G, K, C**: "from small fish"; **P**: "from that [i.e. the brine] of small fish." 37 **C** lacks "b. Jacob."
38 **K** lacks "wine."

An am ha'arets is trusted: The clear assertion of an *am ha'arets* overrides the presumption just mentioned, except in the case of (the brine of) small fish.

because these are under the charge of an am ha'arets: Apparently fishermen deposited their catch with vendors who were *amme ha'arets*, persons not trustworthy in matters of tithes and ritual purity. Although an *am ha'arets* might be careful to separate produce in purity, he might not be meticulous regarding small fish (or, according to **P**, "the brine of small fish") that has become impure or susceptible to impurity. It is also possible that an *am ha'arets* may know that the brine or fish has become impure or susceptible to impurity, but he might not acknowledge this since he has a vested interest in selling it.

6:4 *and it is permitted for eating*: Although honey from hornets, unlike bees' honey, does not convey impurity, it is like bees' honey in that it is permitted for eating.

6:5 *Derivatives*: Lit. "offspring": liquids that render susceptible as subcategories of one of the seven main fluids.

whether of adults or children: Lit. "whether big or small." Certain commentators refer the "big" and "small" here to liquid excrement and urine respectively.

pure cattle, wild animals, or birds: That is, kosher species. Nonkosher ("impure") species are treated in 6:7 below.

and blood let out from the veins for drinking.
Whey is like milk,
and [olive] sap is like oil,
since sap is not excluded from the category of oil—
the words of R. Simeon.
R. Meir says:
Even if there is no oil in[39] it.
The blood of vermin is like its flesh:
it renders impure but does not convey susceptibility to impurity,
and we do not have anything else like it.
6 These render impure and convey susceptibility to impurity:
the flow of the *zav*,
and his saliva,
and his semen,
and his urine,
and a quarter[-*log*] of blood from a corpse,
and menstrual blood.
R. Eliezer says:
Semen does not cause susceptibility to impurity.
R. Eleazar b. Azariah says:
Menstrual blood does not cause susceptibility to impurity.
R. Simeon says:
The blood of a corpse does not cause susceptibility to impurity,
and if it fell on a gourd,
one scrapes it off,
and [the gourd] remains insusceptible to impurity.
7 These do not render impure[40] or convey susceptibility to impurity:
Sweat,
and stinking pus,
and excrement,
and blood that issues with them,
and fluid [that comes out from] an eight-month [birth].
R. Yose says:
Except for its blood.
[Also the fluid of] a person who drinks the water of Tiberias

[39] **P**: "with it." [40] **K** lacks "do not."

blood…for drinking: That is, blood given to animals to drink.

we do not have anything else like it: The singularity of the blood of the eight vermin named in Leviticus 11:29–30 is that it pollutes as part of the impure creature, but does not convey susceptibility to seedstuffs that have not yet come under "if water is put."

6:6 *one scrapes it off*: The blood is scraped off the gourd because it is forbidden to eat blood (Leviticus 17:10–12).

6:7 *a person who drinks*: The liquid in question must be fulfilling some desired purpose for the owner. If it is simply the byproduct of an action, rather than its primary intention, the discarded liquid will not convey impurity. However, R. Eliezer disagrees with this conclusion.

even though it comes out clean,
the blood of slaughtering from impure cattle, wild animals, and birds,
and blood let from the veins for healing.
R. Eliezer deems all these impure.
R. Simeon b. Eleazar says:
The milk of a male is pure.

8 A woman's milk renders susceptible to impurity whether intentionally drawn or not,[41]
but the milk of cattle renders susceptible to impurity only if it is intentionally drawn.
R. Aqiva said:
The matter is a case of lesser and greater:
if the milk of a woman,
which is intended for children only,
causes susceptibility to impurity whether it is drawn intentionally or not,
does logic not require that the milk of cattle,
which is intended for both children and adults,
should render susceptible to impurity
whether it is drawn intentionally or issues unintentionally?
They said to him:
No! If a woman's milk that issues unintentionally causes susceptibility to impurity,
since blood from her wound causes susceptibility to impurity,
should the milk of cattle that issues unintentionally cause susceptibility to impurity,
since the blood of its wound does not cause susceptibility to impurity?
He said to them:
I apply a stricter ruling to milk than to blood,
since if one draws milk from a cow for healing,
[the milk] causes susceptibility to impurity,
but if one lets blood for healing,
it does not cause susceptibility to impurity.
They said to him:
Let baskets of olives and grapes prove,
since liquids issuing from them intentionally cause susceptibility to impurity,
while those [that issue] unintentionally do not cause susceptibility to impurity.
He said to them:
No! If you say so about baskets of olives and grapes,
whose first state is food and last state is liquid,
will you say so about milk,

[41] C lacks "or not."

it comes out clean: That is, the discharge has the appearance of clear water.

The milk of a male: Fluid that emerges from the nipples of a male.

6:8 *but if one lets blood for healing*: As in 6:7 above.

blood from her wound... its wound: Such blood also flows without intention, and we should treat the discharge from humans differently.

those [that issue] unintentionally: Juice that oozes from the fruit without the farmer's manipulation or desire does not convey impurity.

whose first and last state is liquid?
The argument[42] was up to to this point.
R. Simeon said:
After that, we continued to argue before him:
Let rainwater prove the case,
because its first and last states are liquid
and it does not convey impurity except by intention.
He said to us:
No! If you say so about rainwater,
most of which is not for human beings but for soil and trees,
while most milk is intended for human beings.

[42] Lit. "response."

for human beings: Most milk is drawn intentionally for the benefit of human beings. R. Aqiva's final response is presented in abbreviated form.

Tractate Zavim

Shlomo Zuckier

Introduction

Overview

The literal meaning of the word *zov* is "flow" or "flux," and the term refers to the release of fluid from a person's genitalia. In rabbinic literature, a man experiencing the repeated irregular release of seminal fluid (*zov*) is called a *zav*, while a woman experiencing the release of a nonmenstrual flow of blood is called a *zavah*. The name of the tractate, the plural *zavim*, thus means "those experiencing irregular genital flux."

Structure and Organization of the Tractate

Zavim discusses the following matters: the extent of time that the *zav* remains impure in various scenarios; those susceptible to becoming a *zav*; rules for testing if an emission qualifies as *zov*. There is a lengthy analysis of the ways in which a *zav* (and some others) transmits impurity, primarily through a bed or chair (*midras* impurity: see below), as well as transmission of impurity though touch, carrying, and displacement. Finally, rules of transmitting impurity in other contexts are considered at the end of the tractate.

Aside from more usual forms of transmission such as touching, one particular means of transferring impurity is unique to the *zav*, *zavah*, menstruant, and parturient. The category is called *midras* (lit. "trampling"); the rule is that seats and beds of various sorts on which the *zav* leans become impure and transmit impurity as well (see, e.g. 4:1). Additionally, the spittle and other bodily fluids of a *zav* (not only the irregular emission itself) transmit impurity (see 5:7).

Relationship to Scripture

Leviticus 15 is the biblical source for these categories of impurity, offering a fairly detailed presentation of the laws that govern various genital discharges, most prominently *zov*. In the biblical account, men and women experiencing *zov* are rendered impure, as is everything they touch or sit or lie upon, as well as those who touch those items. The *zav* is purified by washing in "living [i.e. running] water" following a seven-day wait free of *zov*, and he must then bring two birds as purification and wholly burnt offerings. Those coming into contact with the *zav*/*zavah* or items they have defiled are purified by washing and waiting until nightfall.

Main Ideas

Elsewhere, an early rabbinic source distinguishes between *zov* and semen: "*zov* comes from flaccid (lit. "dead") flesh, while semen comes from erect (lit. "live") flesh; *zov* is watery like the white of a fertile egg, while semen is viscous like the white of a nonfertile egg." Such a distinction is likely presumed by tractate *Zavim* (see, e.g. 1:1), although it is not stated explicitly. This description of a man with irregular genital flux accords with gonorrhea symptoms, although this edition will transliterate rather than translate the word *zav* throughout.

Tractate *Zavim* consistently refers to the experience of *zov* emission as a *re'iyyah*, literally a "seeing," even when it refers to the experience of emission more generally. This translation will use "emission" in these cases.

The number of times that a man "sees" his emission determines his status. Having two emissions qualifies him as a *zav* for all purposes other than the requirement to bring the two bird offerings, while one who sees a third time must present those offerings as well. (See *Megillah* 1:7.) The extent of the chain of impurity, namely how many degrees of impurity can be derived from the impurity of the *zav*, *zavah*, and others, is discussed in 5:6.

Following Leviticus 15, rabbinic literature recognizes additional categories of impurity: a *ba'al qeri* (one who has a regular seminal emission), and a menstruant (*niddah*; to be distinguished from a *zavah*). The *ba'al qeri* and menstruant each have their own impurity laws and purification processes, but are not the primary topic of this tractate. (See *Miqva'ot* 8 and *Niddah* overall for further treatments of these categories.) While the *zavah* is not explicitly mentioned much in tractate *Zavim*, the laws pertaining to a *zavah* are generally identical to those of the *zav*, with the exception that she does not need running water in her purification.

Special Notes for the Reader

The translation generally follows the printed edition. Footnotes indicate significant textual variances from manuscripts Kaufmann A50 (**K**), Parma 3173 (**P**) and 2596 (**P$_2$**), and Munich 95 (**M**).

Tractate Zavim

Chapter One

1:1–6 *Calculating a Zav's Period of Impurity*

1 One who sees one emission of *zov*—
the House of Shammai say:
He is like a woman who waits a day per day,
and the House of Hillel say:
He is like one with a seminal emission[1] [and need not wait a day].
If he saw one emission [on the first day]
and on the second [day] he stopped,
and on the third [day] he saw two emissions
or one emission that was the length of two,
the House of Shammai say:
He is a complete *zav*,
and the House of Hillel say:
He defiles beds and chairs
and must immerse in running waters,

[1] **P**: "like a *ba'al qeri-zav*." It is not clear what category this would be.

1:1 *One who sees one emission of zov*: The term generally translated here as emission, or more literally as "seeing" (*re'iyah*), is the general term for an episode of seminal emission. In this case it is specified that this is an emission of *zov*, i.e. an irregular emission that can confer *zav* impurity.

like a woman who waits a day per day: A woman who sees blood for three days not during her menstrual period becomes a complete *zavah*, the female correlate to a *zav*. If she sees blood for only one day, she must wait one clean day, after which she is pure; during the interim, she is impure and defiles beds and chairs. This opinion equates a man who has one emission (where three emissions would render him a complete *zav*) to a woman who has one emission (where three days of emissions would render her a complete *zavah*).

a day per day: Although this implies that one would wait one subsequent day for one emission and two for two emissions, it appears (based on *Pesahim* 8:5) that whether a woman has emissions for one day or two, she need only wait one additional day before becoming pure.

one with a seminal emission: One who has a seminal emission not on account of a disease but as a result of sexual arousal. This impurity is less severe than that of a woman who waits a day per day, as it does not defile beds and chairs.

a complete zav: Not only does he defile what he is sitting on and require immersion in running waters, but he must offer a sacrifice after waiting seven days, as well. See Leviticus 15:14.

beds and chairs: These terms are used throughout for any objects on which a person can lie or sit.

but he is exempt from a sacrifice.
R. Eliezer b. Judah says:
The House of Shammai concede in this [case]
that he is not a complete *zav*.
Regarding what do they dispute?
Regarding one who sees two [emissions]
or one [emission] as long as two [on the first day],
and on the second [day] he stopped,
and on the third he saw one [emission],
the House of Shammai say:
He is a complete *zav*,
and the House of Hillel say:
He defiles beds and chairs
and must immerse in running waters,
but he is exempt from a sacrifice.

2 One who sees a seminal emission on the third day of his *zov* count—
the House of Shammai say:
It undoes the two preceding days,
and the House of Hillel say:
It only undoes that day itself.
R. Ishmael says:
One who sees [an emission] on the second [day]:
[it] undoes the [day] before it.
R. Aqiva says:
Both one who sees [an emission] on the second day
and one who sees on the third day,
for the House of Shammai say:
It undoes the two days preceding it,
and the House of Hillel say:
It only undoes the day itself.

he is exempt from a sacrifice: On this rendering, the dispute whether he is a complete *zav*, and therefore must bring a sacrifice, depends on whether a singular emission can "carry over" and connect to two subsequent emissions across an intervening, emission-free day.

on the third he saw one [emission]: On R. Eliezer b. Judah's rendering, the dispute whether he is a complete *zav* only applies when there is the added "momentum" of having two emissions on the first day, where one position argues that it can overcome the intervening, emission-free day and connect to the single emission on the third day.

must immerse in running waters: Most purification processes for blood and seminal emissions involve immersion either in a pool of water or running water, but the *zav* must immerse in running water. (See Leviticus 15:13.)

1:2 *his zov count*: If he sees *zov* emissions for three consecutive days, he must wait seven "clean days" as part of the purification process. (See Leviticus 15:13.) If he sees a *zov* emission during those seven days, the emission undoes his clean days and he must restart his count from the beginning. The dispute here is to what extent having a seminal, non-*zov* emission affects the count.

It undoes the two preceding days: And he must restart the count. Despite not being *zov* emissions, they still undo the clean days.

It only undoes that third *day itself*: The non-*zov* emission cannot count as a clean day, but it also fails to undo previous clean days.

They agree that if one sees on the fourth [day],
it only undoes the [fourth] day itself
if he saw a seminal emission;[2]
but if one saw a *zov* emission,
even on the seventh day,
it undoes the [day] before it.
3 If he saw one [emission] today and two [emissions] tomorrow,
[or] two [emissions] today and one [emission] tomorrow,
[or] three times over three days or three nights,
he is a complete *zav*.
4 If he saw one [emission]
and it stopped [for time] sufficient to immerse and dry off,
and afterwards he saw two [emissions]
or one [emission] as long as two,
or he saw two [emissions] or one as long as two
and it stopped [for time] sufficient to immerse and dry off,
and afterwards saw one,
he is a complete *zav*.
5 If he saw one [emission] as long as three,
which is like [the time it takes to walk] from Gad Yavan to Shiloah,
which is [the time it takes to do] two immersions and two dryings off,
he is a complete *zav*.
If he saw one [emission] as long as two,
he defiles beds and chairs
and needs to enter running waters,
but he is exempt from a sacrifice.
R. Yose said:

[2] **P_2**: "like one who saw a *qeri* emission."

if one sees on the fourth [day], it only undoes the [fourth] day itself: Since he has already seen three clean days, all agree that a seminal emission cannot affect the earlier count and only prevents rendering this a "clean" day.

if he saw a seminal emission: This gloss directly modifies the previous clause, but it accurately delimits the entire mishnah until this point. The next line turns to irregular emissions.

it undoes the [day] before it: A *zov* emission always undoes the count, and the *zav* must count a completely new set of seven clean days.

1:3 *he is a complete zav*: This is the most basic, standard account of what causes one to become a full *zav*—a total of three emissions over two or three consecutive days. Note that this is different for a *zavah*, who requires three *days* of emissions. (See Leviticus 15:25.)

1:4 *immerse*: In a ritual pool.

he is a complete zav: This mishnah presumes that a doubly long emission is to be viewed as split into two discrete emissions. This double emission, combined with a single emission, aggregates to three emissions, rendering him a complete *zav*.

1:5 *he is a complete zav*: Building upon 1:4, a triply long emission counts as three emissions, qualifying him as a full *zav*.

They only said "One [emission] as long as…" if it was as long as three.
6 If he saw one [emission] today and one at twilight,
[or] one at twilight and one the next day,[3]
if it is known that part of the emission is from today and part is from tomorrow,
he is certain regarding a sacrifice and impurity.
If it is unclear whether part of the emission was today and part of it was tomorrow,
he is certain regarding impurity and doubtful regarding a sacrifice.
If he saw [for] two days at twilight,
he is doubtful regarding impurity and sacrifice.
If he saw one day at twilight
he is doubtful regarding impurity.

Chapter Two

2:1 *Susceptibility to Become a Zav*

2 Everyone can become impure by *zav* emission:
even converts,
even slaves, whether freed or not,
a deaf-mute, one not legally competent, or a minor,
a eunuch due to human causes,
a eunuch due to the sun.
[Regarding] a *tumtum* and *androgynos*, one places upon them the stringencies of a man and the stringencies of a woman.

[3] **K**: "If he sees one [emission] today and one at twilight and one the next day."

They only said…if it was as long as three: R. Yose argues with 1:4, only accepting the splitting of triply long emissions into three, but not doubly long emission into two. It emerges that the Mishnah allows a fair degree of leeway in counting the requisite three emissions to qualify as a full *zav*. They can take place as distantly as over three days, or as closely as one extended emission split into three.

1:6 *twilight*: The Mishnah expects one to take into account all possible eventualities, for each of the events to have occurred on the earlier or later day. The scenarios yielded in the various cases of this mishnah include scenarios where one certainly or possibly had emissions on one, two, or three days, the last two cases potentially yielding partial or full *zav* status.

certain regarding a sacrifice and impurity: That is, he must surely bring a sacrifice when he is finally pure and must meanwhile consider himself confirmed as impure.

doubtful regarding a sacrifice: This mishnah does not clarify what the procedure is in such a case of doubt. One might bring an offering but not eat it in this scenario.

2:1 *even converts*: Gentiles and resident aliens are notably missing from this list.

a deaf-mute, one not legally competent, and a minor: Even those without agency can become impure.

tumtum and androgynos: A *tumtum* has hidden genitalia; an *androgynos* has both male and female genitalia. Since their status as man or woman is in doubt, their purity status must account for both possibilities, yielding a stringency.

They become impure through [menstrual] blood like a woman
and through white [emission] like a man,
and their impurity is [treated as] doubtful.

2:2–3 *Attributing Flow to Non-Zav Causes*

2 One checks a *zav* in seven ways before he qualifies as being a *zav*:
(1) concerning food and
(2) concerning drink and
(3) concerning carrying,
(4) concerning jumping,
(5) concerning sickness and
(6) concerning [sexual] sights and
(7) concerning [sexual] thoughts.
[Even] if he thought [about a woman] without seeing [her] or saw [her] without thinking [about her].
R. Judah says:
Even if he saw a domesticated or wild animal or a bird dealing [sexually] with one another,
even if he saw colored garments belonging to a woman.
R. Aqiva says:
Even if he ate any food, whether good or bad, or drank any drink.
They said to him:
[If so,] there will be no more *zavim* from here on.
He said to them:
[Preserving] *zavim* is not your responsibility.[4]
Once he qualifies as a *zav*, one does not check him.
His accidental [emission] and his uncertain case [of emission] and his semen are impure,

[4] **P**: "There is no responsibility of *zavim* from here on."

2:2 The first part of this mishnah appears verbatim at *Nazir* 9:4.

One checks: Since a *zav* is only rendered impure by irregular flow, if it is possible to attribute the flow to a specific trigger of regular flow, the man will not become a *zav*.

before he qualifies: This presumably refers to the second emission, which would render him a *zav*. See also below.

concerning food... drink, etc.: Presumably, consumption of an unusual quantity or quality of food, exertion, disease, or arousal.

[Even] if he saw a domesticated: For R. Judah, even nonhuman sexuality or the sight of human clothes can trigger a seminal emission.

Even if he ate any food: For R. Aqiva, even normal food consumption can be assigned as the trigger.

Preserving zavim: If this ruling renders the category of *zav* obsolete, that does not pose a problem.

because there is a likelihood to the matter [that his emission was one of *zov*].
If he saw the first [emission]—one checks him;
for the second—one checks him;[5]
for the third—one does not check him.
R. Eliezer says:
Even for the third [emission] one checks him
because of the sacrifice.

3 One who sees a [regular seminal] emission does not defile with *zav* impurity for twenty-four hours.
R. Yose says:
His[6] day.
A gentile[7] who saw a seminal emission and converted
can immediately be rendered impure by *zav* impurity.
A [woman] who sees [menstrual] blood
or has difficulty [in childbirth]—
twenty-four hours.
And one who hits his slave [and the slave dies within] "a day or two":
twenty-four hours.
A dog who ate flesh of a corpse
[for] seventy-two hours [the flesh] is like its original state [and conveys impurity].

[5] **K, P, P$_2$**: "If he saw the first [emission]—they check him; for the second and third—they do not check him.

[6] Or "Its."

[7] All manuscripts have "gentile" (*goy*), although the printed edition reads "foreigner," a result of censorship.

Because there is a likelihood: Attaining the *zav* status creates a presumption to view the questionable cases as *zov* emissions in doubtful cases. This fits with the broader mishnaic presumption of persistence of prior status (see, e.g. *Yevamot* 4:3).

because of the sacrifice: A third emission would oblige the cured *zav* to bring a sacrifice as part of his return to a state of purity.

2:3 *for twenty-four hours*: Lit. "from time to time." All emissions for the next twenty-four hours can be attributed to his seminal emission.

His day: That is, the day on which he saw the emission. The remainder of the twenty-four hours will not protect him from impurity.

A gentile who saw: R. Yose is cited in the Talmud as saying that conversion renders the convert as a newborn. In this case, it renders the seminal emission detached from any future flux and thus it cannot be accounted as anything other than *zov*.

A [woman] who sees [menstrual] blood: This and the following cases are mentioned by association because they also use the phrase "twenty-four hours" (lit. "from time to time"). See *Niddah* 1:1. Such a woman conveys impurity retroactively or for the duration of her labor, but not the more stringent impurity of a *zavah*.

a day or two: This ruling applies for a twenty-four-hour period from the time of striking (see Exodus 21:21). Because the twenty-four-hour period necessarily extends over two days, it is deemed to cover the "two-day" interval mentioned in the Torah.

2:4 *Transferring Impurity through a Bed*

4 A *zav* renders a bed impure in five ways to defile man in such a way that he can defile clothing:
(1) standing, (2) sitting, (3) lying down, (4) hanging, and (5) leaning.
And the bed defiles[8] a person in such a way that he can defile clothing:
(1) standing, (2) sitting, (3) lying down, (4) hanging, and (5) leaning, (6) by touch, and (7) by carrying.

Chapter Three

3:1–4:7 *Scenarios of Possible Transfer of Midras Impurity*

3 A *zav* and a pure person who sat [together]
on a boat or on a raft or who rode on an animal:
even though their clothing does not touch
it is impure through *midras* [sitting or lying].
If they sat on a plank,[9] on a bench, on a bedframe, or on a beam
when they are unstable;
if they ascended a weak tree, a weak branch on a strong tree, an Egyptian ladder that is not set with nails;
on a ramp, on a beam, or on a door
when they are not made with clay—
[the clothing] is impure.
R. Judah deems [them] pure.

2 They [a *zav* and a pure person] close or open [doors together and thus transfer impurity],

[8] **K**: "And the bed defiles (1) standing, (2) sitting..."   [9] **M**: "on a river."

2:4 *A zav renders a bed impure*: Any manner in which the *zav* places his weight on the bed renders it impure as *midras*.

standing...sitting...lying down: If the *zav* stands on the bed or sits or lies on it.

hanging: If the *zav* hangs in one side of a balance and the bed in the other, then if the two sides go up or down, the impurity of the *zav* is transferred to the other side.

And the bed defiles a person: One contracts impurity from a bed defiled by a *zav* in the five ways listed above and also in the more common forms of transferring impurity, i.e. touch and carrying.

3:1 *clothing does not touch*: That is, come in contact with the clothing of the other.

[the clothing] is impure: The consistent factor among the thirteen cases in this mishnah is that the seats are not fully stable, and thus the *zav* and pure person sharing the seat are likely shifting and displacing one another, triggering the transfer of impurity.

deems [them] pure: R. Judah apparently sees the vibration as insufficient to qualify as *midras*.

3:2 *close or open [doors together and thus transfer impurity]*: In each of the disputes in this mishnah, there is one expansive and one limiting position. Despite the gnomic nature of the Mishnah, a textual parallel and

but the Sages say:
[Impurity does not transfer] unless this one seals [the door] and that one opens [it].
They raise one another from a pit [together and thus transfer impurity].
R. Judah says:
[Impurity does not transfer] unless the pure one raises the impure one.
They stretch out ropes [together and thus transfer impurity],
but the Sages say:
[Impurity does not transfer] unless one pulls one way and one the other way.[10]
They weave whether while standing or sitting,
or mill [together and thus transmit impurity].
R. Simeon deems all pure
except for milling with hand millstones.
If they unload a donkey or load [a donkey]:
if their load is heavy, they become impure;
if their load is light, they remain pure.[11]
And all[12] [cases] are pure for the people of the congregation[13] and impure for *terumah*.

3 A *zav* and a pure person who sat on a large boat:
what is a large boat?[14]
R. Judah says
One that is not liable to topple with a person [ascending it].[15]

[10] **M**: "They raise one another from a pit [and are impure]. R. Judah says: [Impurity does not transfer] unless the impure one ties it with a rope. And the Sages say: [Impurity does not transfer] unless this one pulls this way."

[11] **M**: "A *zav* and a pure person: unloading a donkey or loading, at a time when their load is light, they are pure."

[12] Some versions lack the word "all."

[13] **P**: "before the congregation." The difference is a single letter.

[14] **P** lacks this line.

[15] **M, P, K**: "as long as a person cannot topple in it."

the consensus of traditional commentators suggest that the first position renders impure generally, with a second position limiting the scope of impurity.

unless this one seals [the door] and that one opens it: According to the Sages, the two will only lean on one another and contract impurity through *midras* if they are doing distinct actions, not if they are working in the same direction. A parallel distinction applies in the two cases to follow.

and the formerly pure *one the other way*: Given various clear scribal errors in this section of **M**, it is likely that the variant reading reflects scribal error rather than an alternative tradition.

if their load is heavy they become impure: If the weight is heavy, the *zav* and the pure man are likely supporting one another, transferring impurity through touch or *midras*.

and all [cases] are pure for the people of the congregation and impure for terumah: This appears to relate to all cases in this chapter until this point, though the variant lacking "all" suggests a more narrow application.

pure for the people of the congregation…for terumah: In one interpretation, congregation refers to non-priests who seek to eat all their meals in purity (*Hagigah* 2:7), who need not be concerned by the merely possible defilements just mentioned. Alternatively, the *congregation* is the community gathered as for prayer and the ruling here is that those deemed impure on a presumption of likely contact or *midras* need not be placed in a separate section of the synagogue as *zavim*.

impure for terumah: These doubtfully or presumptively impure people should nevertheless avoid contact with *terumah*.

If they sat on a plank, on a bench, on a bedframe, on a beam:
at a time when they are not secured;
if they ascended a strong tree, a solid branch, a Tyrian [ladder] or an Egyptian ladder that is set with a nail;
on a bridge, on a beam, or on a door
at a time when they are made with cement, even on one side—
they are pure.
If the pure one hits the impure one, [the former remains] pure
If the impure one hits the pure one, [the latter becomes] impure
[because] if the pure person would be pulled [away],
the impure person would fall.

Chapter Four

4 R. Joshua says:
A menstruant who sat with a pure woman on a bed:
[even] the hat on her head is impure by *midras.*
If [a menstruant] sat on a boat,
[even] the vessels at the head of the mast of the ship are impure by *midras.*
If she takes a basin full of garments:
if they are heavy in weight,
they are impure;
if they are light in weight,
they are pure.

3:3 *If they sat... they are pure*: This section is set up in contrast to 3:1. These structures are similar but more solid than their counterparts in 3:1, so the presumption is that there is no shifting of movement and thus no transfer of impurity.

If the pure one: There is no ground for assuming the *zav* moved under the impact and put pressure on the other, therefore there is no reason to presume that *zav* impurity has been conveyed. Ordinary impurity, which is transmitted by simple contact, presumably has been transferred.

the impure person would fall: The impure person was leaning on the pure and thereby transmitting his impurity to the other.

4:1 *A menstruant*: This chapter, like the previous one, applies to all who defile through *midras*, namely *zav*, *zavah*, menstruant, and parturient. This mishnah uses the example of a menstruant rather than the previous chapter's example of a *zav*.

[even] the hat: Some commentators note that this teaching diverges from 3:1 above; that text rules that *garments* are defiled but does not mention a hat.

[even] the vessels at the head of the mast: This may refer to the sail, or to other vessels. The logic here follows from the previous teaching; the ship's hat, like that of the woman, is impure as well.

they are impure: When the clothing is heavy, the menstruant shifts her weight and effectively leans on the clothing within the basin, transferring impurity by *midras.*

If a *zav* bumped into a balcony and a loaf of *terumah* fell,
it is pure.

2 If he bumped into a beam, a beam frame, a pipe, a board—even though it is set by ropes; an oven, a millstone flour receptacle, a lower millstone, a hand-operated millstone jack, or a large olive-grinder receptacle, [the loaf is pure].
R. Yose says:
Even [if he bumped] into a beam [seat] of the bathhouse,[16]
it is pure.

3 If he bumped into a door, a doorbolt, a lock, an oar, or a millstone flour receptacle, or a weak tree, or a weak branch on a strong tree,[17] an Egyptian ladder when it is not set with a nail, a ramp, a beam, or a door
when they are not set with clay,
they are impure.
[If he bumped] against a box, on a chest, or on a cabinet,[18]
they are impure.
R. Nehemiah and R. Simeon deem these pure.

4 A *zav* who is placed on five benches, or on five bags:
lengthwise—
they are impure.
Widthwise—
they are pure.
If he slept
[and] it was doubtful whether he turned over onto them,

[16] **M**: "beam [seat] of the utensils."
[17] **K**: "a weak hut and a strong tree." The words for *hut* and *branch* differ only in their vowels.
[18] Lit. "tower" or "turret."

it is pure: In this case, and in the mishnah to follow, the balcony or location of the bread is stable, such that the *zav* bumping into it does not count as truly moving the item and thus *midras* impurity does not arise.

4:2 These cases all deal with a loaf of *terumah* that fell, at the end of 4:1. In every case it is ruled that the loaf of *terumah* fell on account of the vibration of its perch, and not because of pressure caused by the *zav*.

even though it is set by ropes: This is a less stable arrangement than the more common practice of nailing the board to a firm surface.

beam seat: The beam on which the bathhouse attendant customarily sat.

4:3 *they are impure*: In this mishnah the subject seems to have switched to the listed items themselves rather than a loaf of bread resting on them. The *zav* bumping into one of these does count as moving the item and so *midras* impurity is conveyed.

turret: A type of storage unit.

4:4 *lengthwise*: That is, parallel with the benches. It is assumed that he will have rolled over and lain on each bench at some point in his sleep.

Widthwise: i.e. perpendicular to the benches, assuming no single bench ever bore most of the sleeper's body.

[and] it was doubtful: It is not immediately clear why this case would not follow the usual rule of following an item's status as it is found (see *Tohorot* 5:7), which would mean the benches have remained pure. Perhaps it is presumed that a person going to sleep lies down along the length of a single bench but turns and moves while sleeping.

they are impure.
If he was placed on six chairs,
his two arms on two [chairs],
his two legs on two,
his head on one,
his torso on one,
none is impure except the one under his torso,
If he stands on two chairs,
R. Simeon says:
If they are far from one another,[19]
they are pure.
5 There are ten cloaks one on top of another:
if he sleeps on the top one,
they are all impure.
[If a] *zav* is on one side of a scale and a bed or seat is opposite it,
if the *zav* descends [due to his side's greater weight],
they are pure;
if they descend [due to their greater weight],
they are impure.
R. Simeon says:
When there is one [bed on the scale],
it is impure;
but if there are multiple [beds],
it is pure
as no one [bed] is carrying most of [the *zav*].
6 [If a] *zav* is on one side of a scale
and food or liquid is on the other side,
they are impure.
But if a corpse [is on one side],
everything [on the other side] is pure
except for a person.
This is a stringency [connected to] a *zav* but not a corpse,
and there is [also] a stringency of a corpse but not a *zav*.

[19] **K**: "If they are far from this one and from that one." **M**: "If they are far from this one."

the one under his torso: Only the chair under his torso bears most of his weight.

far from one another: It is unlikely that the *zav* shifted his weight to be fully on either chair. If the chairs were closer together, given the greater likelihood of such a shift they would be impure.

4:5 *if they descend* due to their greater weight *they are impure* because they are hoisting the *zav*.

4:6 *food or liquid is on the other side*: The food is impure regardless of which side of the scale descends. Food is susceptible to impurity, even without direct contact, if a source of impurity causes it to move or it causes the impurity to move. Since both sides of the scale will be in motion, each responding to the other, the food becomes impure in any case. The food is immune to *midras* impurity because the *zav* can neither sit nor lie on it.

A *zav* makes a bed or seat underneath [impure through *midras*]
so that it defiles a person [who will then] defile clothing,
and [the *zav* defiles anything] overhead [as] *madaf* so that it defiles food and liquid,
which a corpse does not defile.
A stringency of corpse [impurity over that of a *zav*]:
That a corpse defiles in a Tent,
And it defiles [with] an impurity of seven [days],
which a *zav* does not defile.

7 If [a *zav*] was sitting on top of a bed,
and [there were] four cloaks under the four legs of the bed,
they are impure
because [the bed] cannot stand on three [legs].
R. Simeon deems it pure.
[If a *zav*] was riding on top of an animal,
and [there were] four cloaks under the four legs of the animal,
they are pure,
because it can stand on three.
If there was one cloak under two forelegs, under two hindlegs, under a foreleg and a hindleg,
it is impure.
R. Yose says:
A horse defiles with his hindlegs,
and a donkey with his forelegs
since a horse supports itself on its hindlegs,
while a donkey supports itself on its forelegs.
[If a *zav*] sat on the beam of the olive press,
utensils in the revolving container are impure.
[If he sat] on a clothing press,

a corpse: A corpse does not defile through *midras* or *displacement* unless a person carries it.

madaf: Lit. "shelf"; see 5:2. This is the inverse of the rule of *midras* taught in 4:5. If items are piled on top of the *zav*, they contract a lighter degree of impurity.

a corpse defiles: A corpse defiles with impurity of the longest duration and through being in the same covered space even without physical contact or the other means of defilement discussed in this chapter. See further Numbers 19:10, 14 and *Oholot* 2.

4:7 *four cloaks under the four legs*: In each of these cases the standard (of the anonymous position) is whether the cloaks being leaned upon are indispensable for supporting the *zav*. If they are, they become impure through *midras*; if not, they remain pure. Indispensability is determined by considering the result of removing the cloak and the adjacent leg(s).

R. Simeon deems it pure: For R. Simeon, the cloak must be not only indispensable but it must support the majority of the *zav*'s weight. This is consistent with his position in 4:5 regarding the scale.

R. Yose accepts the principle of the anonymous position but he defines the indispensability of an animal's legs differently.

the beam of an olive press: For the olive press and clothing press cases, it is necessary to determine whether or not the clothing or olive are supporting the *zav*'s weight. The olive press supports his weight and thus receives impurity through *midras*; the garments do not, and thus do not contract impurity.

clothes under him are pure;
R. Nehemiah deems them impure.

Chapter Five

5:1–5 *Modes of Transferring Impurity from a Zav*

5 One who touches a *zav*,
or a *zav* touches him,
one who causes a *zav* to move,
or a *zav* causes him to move:
[the one so affected] defiles foods and liquids and washable utensils by touch,
but not by carrying.
R. Joshua stated a rule:
Anyone who defiles clothing at the time of his touching defiles foods and liquids,
making them a first[-degree impurity]
and the hands a second,
but he does not defile a man or an earthenware vessel.
After his separation from the items that defiled him,[20]
he defiles liquids to be a first
and foods and hands to be a second,
and he does not defile clothing.
2 And they said another rule:
Anything that is carried above[21] the *zav* becomes impure

[20] **K**: "After his separation, whom does he defile?"
[21] Lit. "on the back of."

R. Nehemiah deems them impure: In his estimation, the clothing also supports the weight of the *zav* and thus they contract impurity.

5:1 *One who touches:* This mishnah provides the basic rules about when and how the *zav* transmits impurity.

One who touches… or causes him *to move*: The two effective modes of contact with the *zav* that are mentioned here are touching and causing to move. Carrying appears to be excluded.

R. Joshua stated a rule: The first scenario, described both anonymously and in a friendly reformulation by R. Joshua, is one where a person is still touching the *zav*. In such a case, that person contracts a first degree of impurity, along with his clothing, any food or liquid that he contacts, and most utensils; his hands are impure only on a secondary level of impurity. If, while touching the *zav*, the person touches a third person or earthenware vessels, these remain pure. The second scenario comes into play after he has disengaged from direct contact with the *zav*; food is downgraded to second-degree impurity and the clothes are not impure at all.

5:2 *Anything that is carried above*: The Mishnah plots out cases of impurity above the *zav* and cases of impurity below the *zav* for various items and in circumstances involving both continuing contact with the impurity and afterward.

carried above the zav: In addition to the category of *midras* for items below the *zav*, impurity is also transmitted when anything is found above the *zav*, even if separated from him.

and anything upon which the *zav* is carried is pure,
unless it is something one can lie or sit on or a person.
How so?
If the finger of a *zav* is positioned under a layer of stones
with a pure person above,
[the formerly pure person] defiles two and disqualifies one.
If he separates,
he defiles one and disqualifies one.
If the impure person is above [the layer of stones] and the pure person below,
he defiles two and disqualifies one.
If he separates,
he defiles one and disqualifies one.
If foods and liquids, a surface for lying or sitting, or a *madaf* are above [the *zav*],
they defile two[22] and disqualify one
If they separated,
they defile one and disqualify one.
And[23] if the surface for lying or sitting is below,
they defile two and disqualify one.
If they separated,
they defile two and disqualify one.
If the foods and liquids or the *madaf* are below [the *zav*],
they are pure.

3 Because they said:
Anything that carries or is carried on a bed is pure except for a person;
anything that carries or is carried on a carcass is pure except for the one who causes it to move.

[22] **K, M, P_2**: "one." **P** has "two" crossed out and replaced by "one." The reading "one" should be preferred, as it fits with the rule laid down above even though it diverges from the preceding line.

[23] This "and" is not found in all the manuscripts. It breaks the logical flow and may be a scribal error.

something one can lie or sit on: The category of *midras* is limited to things on which one can normally sit or lie, such as chairs and beds. The category of displacement, on the other hand, is not limited in this way; anything that is moved or shaken by an impure person becomes impure.

defiles two: The formerly pure person is now a "father of impurity"; anything he touches contracts first-degree impurity and can in turn convey second-degree impurity. A second-degree source can defile yet another object, but this third-degree source can longer transmit impurity still further.

If he separates: If the newly impure person breaks off contact with the stones or the *zav* removes his finger, the "father of impurity" is reduced to the first degree of derived impurity and the whole sequence of defilement by contact is adjusted accordingly.

madaf: "Shelf." The term refers to a lighter form of impurity that results from an object being on top of a zav, but not in direct contact. Here the term is used to refer to a surface not suited for sitting or lying on.

5:3 *Because they said*: It is hard to know the intended reference of these words. Some modern editors have proposed that they were mistakenly transferred from some other location.

except for a person: In a case where an object is neither touching nor causing the bed of a *zav* to move, carrying alone is insufficient to cause impurity. The only exception is a human being, who indeed becomes impure under these circumstances.

on a carcass: Both the Talmud and medieval commentators argue that R. Eliezer requires both moving *and* carrying in order to transmit impurity, although this is not clear from the text itself.

R. Eliezer says:
Also the one who carries it.
Anything that carries or is carried on a corpse is pure
except for that which is "tenting" above it
and a person while he causes it to move.

4 If part of an impure person is on a pure person,
or part of a pure person is on an impure person:
if attachments of an impure person are on a pure person,
or the attachments of a pure person are on an impure person:
he is impure.
R. Simeon says:
If part of the impure person is on the pure person,
he is impure,
but if part of the pure person is on the impure person,
he [remains] pure.

5 If an impure person is on part of a [pure] bed
or a pure person is on part of [an impure] bed,
[the formerly pure] becomes impure.
If part of an impure person is on a [pure] bed
or part of a pure person is on [an impure] bed,
[the pure] remains pure.
One thus finds that impurity enters and exits [the bed] through a [mere] part [of it].
And similarly:
if a loaf of *terumah* is placed on an [impure] bed and there is paper between them,
whether above or below,
it is pure.
And similarly for a stricken stone:
it is pure.
R. Simeon deems this case impure.

except for that which is "tenting" above it: i.e. being under the same cover (ceiling, tree, etc.) as the corpse transmits impurity to anything. See *Oholot* 2, which deals with impurity transfer through "tenting." As before, people are more susceptible to impurity than things.

5:4 Throughout this mishnah and the next, the person designated "impure" is a *zav* or *midras*-impure.

part of a pure person: Such as fingertips, hands, or feet. In contrast to the rule in 4:4 above that for *midras* the majority of the *zav* must rest on the bed, in the case of carrying no such proportion is required. Note the contrast to 5:5 below.

attachments: The nonfleshy parts of the body, such as teeth, fingernails, or hair.

5:5 Throughout this mishnah, the term translated "bed" refers to anything on which a person might lie.

[the formerly pure]: Whether the person or the bed.

[the pure] remains pure: Because a majority of the *zav* is not on the bed.

through a [mere] part [of it]: While most of the *zav* must be on the bed, it is not necessary that most of the bed be below the *zav* or the other person in order to transmit impurity.

similarly: A variant reading lacks this word. Its reference is unclear.

stricken stone: That is, a stone stricken with *tsara'at* (incorrectly, "leprosy": see Leviticus 14:33–45).

5:6–8 *Defilement by Touch, Carrying, and Displacement: Attached and Not Attached*

6 One who touches *zav* or *zavah* or menstruant or parturient or "one with *tsara'at*":
a bed or a seat defiles two [stages] and disqualifies one.
If he separates [from the defiling person or item],
he defiles one and disqualifies one,
whether he touches it or causes it to move or carries or is carried.

7 One who touches the *zov* of a *zav*
or his spittle or
his semen, his urine;
or the blood of a menstruant
defiles two [stages] and disqualifies one.
If he separates [from that source of impurity],
he defiles one and disqualifies one.
[This is the case] both [for] one who touches or causes to move;
R. Eliezer says:
Also [for] one who carries.

8 One who carries a saddle
and one who is carried by it
and one who causes it to move
defiles two and disqualifies one.
If he separates [from the saddle],
he defiles one and disqualifies one.
One who carries a carcass

5:6 *zav or zavah or menstruant or parturient or "one with tsara'at"*: This list is drawn from Leviticus 15:32–33. *Metsora*, or "one with *tsara'at*": see also 5:10 and tractate *Nega'im*.

bed: Anything on which the above individuals have lain.

defiles two: This is the standard of a "first" level of impurity noted above in 5:1–2.

defiles one: This is the standard of "secondary" impurity noted above in 5:1–2.

whether he touches it or causes it to move or carries or is carried: But not for *midras*, which has particular limitations, as above, 5:4.

5:7 *the zov of a zav or his spittle or his semen, his urine; or the blood of a menstruant*: These defile the one coming into contact with them as on a "first" level of impurity; as above. See *Kelim* 1:1, 3, 4, where these are called "fathers" of impurity. See also 5:10 below.

R. Eliezer says: Also [for] one who carries: R. Eliezer appears to be expanding the scope of modes of defilement here. See above, 5:3. Medieval commentators interpret R. Eliezer as saying that merely shifting the item is insufficient, and carrying it is necessary in order to defile.

5:8 *saddle*: One sitting on a saddle where the *zav* had sat becomes impure; see Leviticus 15:9.

defiles two: As a "primary" impurity, and similarly for the cases to follow. These rulings are laid out in principle in 5:1 below and in some detail and broader context at *Kelim* 1, esp. 1:2.

carries a carcass: See Leviticus 11:39–40: one who touches an animal carcass is impure until the evening.

or the water of purgation
that has sufficient to sprinkle
defiles two and disqualifies one.
If he separates,
he defiles one and disqualifies one.

5:9–11 *Rules for Transmitting Various Other Forms of Impurity*

9 One who eats from a carcass of a pure bird:
while it is in his throat,
he defiles two and disqualifies one.
If he enters his head into the interior space of an oven,
he is pure[24] and the oven is pure.
If he vomited or swallowed [the carcass],
he defiles one and disqualifies one.
And while it is in his mouth before he swallows it
he is pure.
10 One who touches vermin or
semen or
one impure through a corpse or
a "one with *tsara'at*" during his counting period or
purgation waters insufficient to sprinkle or
a carcass or
saddle:
he defiles one and disqualifies one.
This is the rule:
Anyone who touches one of the Fathers of Impurity in the Torah

[24] **M** lacks "he is pure." **K** adds it in a marginal note. Some commentators advise excision.

water of purgation: Part of the red heifer ritual for removing corpse impurity. See Numbers 19:21: *one who touches the waters of purgation is impure until the evening.*

sufficient to sprinkle: For definitions of what is considered "sufficient to sprinkle," see *Parah* 12:5.

5:9 *carcass of a pure bird*: i.e. of a kind permissible to eat, "kosher." See Leviticus 11:23 and 17:15. Several rules regarding this are codified at *Tohorot* 1:1.

he is pure and the oven is pure: He is pure in a case where the carcass is not yet in his throat. The oven is pure, even if the carcass has already entered his throat, because the impurity is sufficient only to defile clothing and items the eater touches, but not the oven (or room) in which he is situated. Those who do not have the text "he is pure" avoid this incongruous shift between scenarios.

5:10 *defiles one*: Each of these cases has a lower level of impurity, such that this person only defiles a single item that can then disqualify one item. The impurity remains the same whether one is attached or not. See *Kelim* 1:1–2, which presents the cases of this mishnah as lesser than those listed in 5:9 above.

"Fathers of Impurity" in the Torah: Each of these cases is a supercategory of impurity that creates "first-order" impurity. The language is somewhat overly general, as the cases in 5:9 qualify as an obvious exception, where they defile two to disqualify one while still attached.

defiles one and disqualifies one
except for [the corpse of] a person.
If he separates [from any other form of impurity],
he defiles one and disqualifies one.

11 One who had a seminal emission is like one who touches vermin.
And one who has intercourse with a menstruant is like one who becomes impure through [contact with] a corpse,
except that one who has intercourse with a menstruant is more stringent in that he defiles beds and chairs with a minor impurity,
so that they defile foods and liquids.

5:12 *Items that Disqualify Terumah*

12 The following disqualify *terumah*:
one who eats [food of] first[-degree impurity];
or eats [food of] second[-degree impurity];
or drinks impure drinks;
or immerses his head and most of his body in drawn waters;
a pure person who had three *log* of drawn waters fall on his head;

except for [the corpse of] a person: That is, human corpse impurity. In this case, one who becomes impure from a human corpse defiles two to disqualify one.

5:11 *One who had a seminal emission*: That is, not a *zav*.

one who touches vermin: This category and the preceding acquire "first-degree" impurity. The species of "crawling animal" that convey impurity are listed at Leviticus 14:29–30.

one who has intercourse with a menstruant: This impurity is decreed at Leviticus 15:24, which asserts such a man is impure for seven days. This is the status of a "father" of impurity.

one who has intercourse with a menstruant is more stringent: It was understood that only the *zav* (along with *zavah*, menstruant, and parturient) is subject to impurity through *midras*, but not one who has a regular emission, a stricken stone, one who comes into contact with a human corpse, and a corpse itself.

5:12 *disqualify terumah*: In the Mishnah's system, this is a tertiary level of impurity, as items that are a "first" level of impurity can defile an item that can then disqualify *terumah*. Since this tertiary impurity cannot defile anything further, it is called "disqualification" rather than "impurity." A quaternary level of impurity applied only to Temple sacrifices; see *Parah* 11:4, *Hagigah* 3:2.

one who eats: One who eats food of first- or second-level impurity or drinks impure liquids is not impure in any biblical account; the rabbis declared him impure for these purposes. The Talmud suggests that this rabbinic decree was meant to prevent the eating impure foods along with *terumah*, which must be kept pure.

drawn waters: As opposed to running water or a natural pool, which qualifies as a ritual bath. Drawn waters and one who immerses in them disqualify *terumah*. The Talmud suggests the rabbis decreed this impurity so that people would not think drawn waters count as a ritual pool.

three log: Around 1,650 cubic centimeters.

a [biblical] book;
and the hands;
and a *tevul yom*;
food and utensils that were defiled by liquids.

A [biblical] book: *Yadayim* 4:6 suggests that biblical books are impure "according to their belovedness," to discourage using holy things for ordinary purposes, or perhaps a reflex of a the notion of holiness as "contagious." Alternatively, the Talmud explains this impurity is meant as a safeguard so that people do not store their scripture with their *terumah*; this risks damage to the scrolls from vermin that infest the grain.

hands: The rabbis also decreed impurity of the hands, possibly because hands may touch impure things without a person noticing. Hands are generally considered impure on a second level of impurity. See *Yadayim*, esp. chapter 3.

tevul yom: Literally "immersed by day.": After the ritual bath, the impure person must wait until the evening to become pure; see Leviticus 22:7.

food and utensils that were defiled by liquids: Liquids, even if touched by a lower level of impurity, become a first level of impurity and then defile foods and utensils such that they would disqualify *terumah*. See *Parah* 8:7 and *Yadayim* 3:2.

Tractate Tevul Yom

David Levine

Introduction

Overview

Tevul yom, lit. "immersed of day," refers to an impure person who has completed the ritual acts necessary for purification before nightfall. However, the period of impurity only lapses with sunset. Consequently, the *tevul yom* is treated as an in-between category neither fully impure nor fully pure.

Structure and Organization of the Tractate

The first chapter is devoted to the ingredients of *terumah* food and the possible connectives between them. It is structured as three contrasting pairs of lists (1:1–2; 3–4, and 5 respectively). The entire chapter is brought together by a recurring formulation at the end of each list describing the *tevul yom* in relation to other types of impurity.

The second chapter opens with the issue of liquids contracting impurity (2:1–2). The next section of the chapter (2:3–5) deals with components of cooked preparations, and the effect of one component on the purity of the others. The focus then returns to a *tevul yom*'s contact with liquids, specifically when separating *terumah* from wine (2:6–7). The final mishnah (2:8) deals with other sources of impurity, more serious than a *tevul yom*.

The start of the third chapter considers when different parts of produce, or connected parts of other foods, are considered distinct for the purposes of transmitting impurity (3:1). The next section (3:2–5) deals with nonsacral food and *terumah* in one preparation and continues the treatment of this topic in the previous chapter (2:3–5). A legal detail concerning saliva as a liquid creating susceptibility to impurity introduces a basic disagreement over the very concept of *tevul yom* (3:6).

Chapter 4 is organized around separating appointed portions of foodstuffs—tithes, *terumah*, *hallah*—with some tangential exceptions. Cases of separating *terumah* and *hallah* are cited in 4:1–3, with the same refrain ending each case. *Tevul yom* 4:4 presents the possibility of suspending the onset of *terumah* status, even after the physical separation of the food. This possibility is picked up again in 4:7, where conditional separation of *terumah* is discussed. Between these, 4:5–6 brings together cases from different areas of *halakhah*, with their common denominator not readily clear. The final statement of R. Joshua seems to apply at least to the assorted cases of 4:5–6 and is especially suited for the leniencies described in the two "in the beginning" cases.

Some sequences in the tractate are earlier units that were subsequently embedded into the tractate: (1) 1:1–5 is a highly edited text dealing with preparations of *terumah* for eating, the connection of their ingredients, and the consequences of impure contact with them. A similar concluding formula appears at the end of each of six parts. (2) 4:1–3 has a thrice-repeated refrain establishing the principle that a *tevul yom* does not convey impurity to nonsacral food. (3) The sweeping statement in 4:6—"on all these R. Joshua said"—refers to a preexisting list of cases whose precise extent is not clear.

Main Ideas

Rabbinic *halakhah* identifies distinct features of *tevul yom* status: (1) When a *tevul yom* touches regular, nonsacral food, it remains pure (4:1). (2) A *tevul yom* is still prohibited from coming into contact with *terumah* (*a fortiori* sacrificial foodstuffs). However, his touch merely disqualifies the *terumah* but does not make it impure and therefore does not create third-degree impurity (*Parah* 11:4). (3) The contact of a *tevul yom* with liquids is another leniency. Contact with impurity causes any liquid to contract first-degree impurity, which can subsequently cause second-degree impurity, et cetera. By contrast, when a liquid is touched by a *tevul yom* it becomes disqualified for sacral use but does not subsequently cause impurity (2:1). (4) A *tevul yom* is less able than others of impure status to impart impurity through connected, though distinct, components of different food preparations.

The relative purity of a *tevul yom* was debated among different groups and sects of the late Second Temple period. The legal tradition of the Qumran sectarians rejected this distinction and viewed a person who had immersed but upon whom sun had not yet set as completely impure. The sectarian scrolls indicate that this was a bone of contention between themselves and their rivals. Rabbinic tradition preserves its own recollection of the issue when it presents the *tevul yom* as prominent in Sadducean–Pharisaic controversies (*Parah* 3:7–8). The Pharisaic promotion of this category may reflect a desire to expand the availability of different religious experiences to laypeople. Treating the *tevul yom* as only mildly defiled would make it easier for people to partake in meals, such as consuming the second tithe in Jerusalem or table fellowship designed to maintain ritual purity when eating nonsacral food.

Relationship to Scripture

Biblical prescriptions for the ritual purification of people and objects indicate bathing and the onset of evening as the concluding stages of the varied processes. Even though both stages are usually specified (e.g. Leviticus 11:32, 15:5–11, 22:6–7, Numbers 19:19), sometimes only one is mentioned (e.g. Leviticus 11:31, 40, 14:9, 51–53, 15:13). The presence of these two stages—bathing and nightfall—may have provided an interpretive opening, creating (or validating) the category of *tevul yom* (lit. "immersed of day"). This in-between category—not yet pure, nor still impure—is not explicit in the Torah, and is a postbiblical development.

Tractate Tevul Yom

Chapter One

1:1–2 *Baked Goods and Cooked Preparations Conveying Impurity*

1 One who collects multiple *hallah* [portions] intending for them to remain separate, but they join together—
the House of Shammai say:
This is a connective in the case of a *tevul yom.*
The House of Hillel say:
This is not a connective.
Pieces of dough that join together;
loaves that join together;
one who bakes a flat cake on top of another flat cake before their crusts formed in the oven;
the bubbling of a thin liquid;
the initial froth from [boiling] split beans;
the froth from new wine—
Rabbi Judah says:
Also [froth from boiling] rice—
the House of Shammai say:
This is a connective in the case of a *tevul yom.*
The House of Hillel say:
This is not a connective.
They agree about all other impurities,
whether of milder or more severe status.

1:1 *hallah*: *Hallah* is the dough offering that must be kept from impurity and given to priests for their consumption; see Numbers 15:17–21.

is a connective: If a *tevul yom* touched one of the dough pieces, the others are affected as well.

Pieces of dough: The preparations enumerated are *terumah*, and their purity status must be maintained.

the bubbling of a thin liquid: This contrasts with the "thick liquid" of 1:2, which has stricter status. The consonants that read as "the bubbling of a liquid" can also be read as "the bone of an offering of well-being." The bone here is described as partially hollow, i.e. without all its marrow, and contrasts with 1:2, where the bone is not hollow at all, i.e. has its marrow.

R. Judah says: A comment on the previous list.

They agree: The House of Hillel agree with the House of Shammai concerning other types of impure people and objects, that if they touch the above foods then a connective of impurity is formed rendering all parts impure. The House of Hillel regard the *tevul yom* as a special category, which has less effect on certain types of purity.

2 [However,] if a person collects multiple *hallah* [portions] without intending to separate them;
one who bakes a flat cake on top of another flat cake after their crusts formed in the oven;
the bubbling of a thick liquid;
the second froth from [boiling] split beans;
the froth from old wine;
the froth from any oil [old or new];
the froth from [boiling] lentils—
R. Judah says:
Also [froth from boiling] peas—
[all] are impure in the case of a *tevul yom*,
and needless to say in the case of other impurities.

1:3–4 *Distinct Loaves of Bread Conveying Impurity*

3 A piece [of dough] protruding outside a loaf,
a small grain of salt [on a loaf],
burnt crust that is less than a finger's width—
R. Yose says:
Any [burnt crust] that is eaten with it [the loaf]—
[the loaf is] impure in the case of a *tevul yom*,
and needless to say in the case of other impurities.

4 A pebble in a loaf [of *terumah*],
a large grain of salt, a lupine [on a loaf],
burnt crust that is more than a finger's width—
R. Yose says:
Any [burnt crust] that is not eaten with it [the loaf]—

1:2 *[However]*: This list contrasts with the one in the previous mishnah.

bubbling of a thick liquid: See the comment on the previous mishnah.

R. Judah says: An addition to the previous list.

impure in the case of a tevul yom: If a *tevul yom* touches them, they serve as a connective of impurity rendering all parts impure.

1:3 *A piece [of dough]*: The protruding piece of dough, a grain of salt, or burnt crust do not constitute a distinct component of the loaf of bread on account of their small size. Therefore, they are considered part of a whole and any impurity caused to them affects the entire loaf.

a loaf: Of *terumah*.

needless to say: If contact with a *tevul yom* causes impurity, *a fortiori* the same occurs upon contact with a more stringent type of impurity.

1:4 *A pebble in a loaf*: This list enumerates things that are recognizably distinct from the loaf of bread on which they might be found.

salt... lupine: These can serve as means of differentiation, identifying one's loaf in a larger batch being baked in a communal oven.

[the loaf remains] pure if [these are touched by] a primary impurity,
and needless to say in the case of a *tevul yom*.

1:5 *Grains and Lupines on Loaves Conveying Impurity*

5 Unpeeled barley or spelt, crowfoot root, asafetida, silphium—
R. Judah says:
Also black beans—
[the loaf remains] pure if [these are touched by] a primary impurity,
and needless to say in the case of a *tevul yom*—
the words of R. Meir.
The Sages say:
[The loaf is] pure in the case of a *tevul yom*,
and impure in the case of other impurities.
Peeled barley or spelt, wheat, whether peeled or unpeeled, nigella, sesame, pepper—
R. Judah says:
Also white beans—

primary impurity: The first chapter of *Kelim* enumerates these principal imparters of impurity.

needless to say: If contact with a principal type of impurity does not affect the whole loaf but only the pebble etc. touched, *a fortiori* neither does contact with a *tevul yom*.

1:5 This mishnah deals with types of seeds that may be found in or on a loaf of bread. However, this mishnah does not explicitly mention a loaf of bread. Therefore, there are commentators who see this mishnah as dealing more generally with the susceptibility of these grains and herbs to impurity from a *tevul yom*. The list of whole grains and herbs at the beginning of 1:5 reflects a leniency in that they remain ritually pure even if touched by a *tevul yom*.

Unpeeled barley or spelt: Types of whole grain on a loaf of *terumah* that are considered distinct from the loaf of bread. In the present context "peeled" grain is just the seed without the husk, while "unpeeled" means the whole grain.

crowfoot root, asafetida, silphium: Types of herbs used as spices or medicine that are likewise considered distinct from the loaf of bread.

R. Judah says: An addition to the preexisting list.

[The loaf remains] pure: Because the grain or herbs in or on a loaf of bread are distinct enough to constitute a separate component, their impurity is not conveyed to the rest of the loaf.

needless to say…R. Meir: Here too R. Meir sees no link in the stricter case of a primary impurity, and this extends to the more lenient case of a *tevul yom*.

The Sages say: This opinion sets out a distinction: contact with a primary impurity makes the grains and herbs listed above a connective of impurity so that the whole loaf is impure, but contact with a *tevul yom* does not create the link and the rest of the loaf remains pure.

Peeled barley or spelt on a loaf of *terumah* are considered an integral part of the loaf.

wheat, whether peeled or unpeeled: Wheat is considered an integral part of the loaf.

nigella, sesame, pepper:These herbs and spices are part of the loaf.

R. Judah says: An addition to the preexisting list.

[the loaf is] impure in the case of a *tevul yom*,
and needless to say in the case of other impurities.

Chapter Two

2:1–2 *Tevul Yom and Liquids*

2 Fluids of a *tevul yom* are similar to liquids that he touches—
neither cause impurity.
Other impure people,
whether of more mild or severe status:
fluids emitted from them
are similar to liquids they touch—
both are a first[-degree impurity],
except for liquid that is a primary impurity.
2 A pot full of liquid that was touched by a *tevul yom*—
if the liquid was *terumah*,
the liquid is disqualified and the pot is pure;
if the liquid was nonsacral food—
all is pure;

the case of a tevul yom: If a *tevul yom* touches the impure beans on a loaf, they constitute a connective of impurity and render the whole loaf impure.

needless to say: This link of impurity extends to contact with more extreme sources of impurity.

2:1 *Fluids of a tevul yom*: Bodily fluids such as spit or tears or urine. *Parah* 8:7 notes that any person or object that disqualifies *terumah* similarly imparts impurity to liquids, except for a *tevul yom* who disqualifies but does not impart impurity to nonsacral food.

neither cause impurity: The contact with the bodily fluids of a *tevul yom* disqualifies *terumah*, but no further impurity is conveyed through the *terumah* (see introduction). It is also possible to translate "neither contract impurity." This would be so because the bodily fluids are nonsacral food, and a *tevul yom* does not affect nonsacral food at all.

first[-degree impurity]: Whoever comes in contact with a primary impurity contracts impurity of a first degree; whoever comes in contact with someone or something with a first degree of impurity contracts impurity of a second degree.

liquid that is a primary impurity: See *Zavim* 5:7.

2:2 *pot full of liquid*: The pot and the liquid are deemed separate entities.

touched by a tevul yom: From the next sentences it is clear that the *tevul yom* touched the liquid contents but not the pot itself. The contents are regarded as being directly affected and the pot only indirectly.

if the liquid was terumah: A *tevul yom* disqualifies the *terumah* he touched, but that disqualified *terumah* does not impart impurity and so does not affect the pot, which would remain pure.

if the liquid was nonsacral food: A *tevul yom* does not affect the *nonsacral food*, and therefore the pot remains unaffected as well.

if his hands were defiled—
all is impure.
This is [an example of] a stringency of hands over a *tevul yom*.
A stringency of a *tevul yom* over hands:
uncertainty regarding a *tevul yom* disqualifies *terumah*,
however, uncertainty regarding hands keeps [*terumah*] pure.

2:3–5 *Are the Ingredients of Preparations Connected?*

3 Broth of *terumah* with garlic and oil of nonsacral food,
and a *tevul yom* touched some [of the garlic or oil]—
he has disqualified it all.
Broth of nonsacral food with garlic and oil of *terumah*,
and a *tevul yom* touched some [of the garlic or oil]—
he has only disqualified what he touched.
If the garlic was plentiful,
one follows the majority.
R. Judah said,
When [does one follow the majority]?
When [the garlic] was one lump in a bowl;
however, if it had been ground[1] in a mortar—

[1] Lit. "scattered."

his hands were defiled: A person's hands are regarded as being impure if they are not washed. This is a further extension of the concept of hand impurity, where mishnaic law regards a person's hands as being able to contract a low degree of impurity even when the rest of the person's body is ritually pure. A person's hands are purified by being ritually washed (see introduction to *Yadayim*).

all is impure: Impure hands cause the liquid in the pot to become first-degree impure, and the liquid imparts impurity to the pot.

stringency of hands over a tevul yom: Both liquid and pot become impure by contact with impure hands.

stringency of a tevul yom over hands: The uncertainty in question is whether the *tevul yom*, or the person with impure hands, touched *terumah* or other holy food. Each of these two categories adheres to its own rules, which yield the above distinction.

2:3 *Broth of terumah*: The broth is the main component of the preparation while the oil and garlic are condiments. If the broth is *terumah*, then the status of the condiments does not matter and any contact with a *tevul yom* disqualifies everything.

Broth of nonsacral food: If only the condiments are *terumah*, then a *tevul yom* disqualifies only the place where he touched the *terumah* ingredient.

If the garlic was plentiful: Either the garlic itself or the garlic mixed together with the oil.

one follows the majority: There are two ways of understanding this ruling: (1) If the plentiful garlic is *terumah* then a *tevul yom*'s contact with the garlic disqualifies the nonsacral broth as well. However, we do not apply this rule when the plentiful garlic is nonsacral food and the broth is *terumah*. (2) One follows the more plentiful component consistently in that second case as well.

one lump in a bowl: If the garlic is whole, then the quantity determines whether it is a connective.

ground in a mortar: If the garlic was in powder or crumb form.

it is pure because he wants it to be scattered.
[Likewise,] all things that are [usually] ground,
if he grinds them with liquid.
However,[2] things that are usually ground with liquid,
but he ground them without liquid,
and they are a lump in the dish—
these are regarded as a ring of dried figs.

4 Broth or a flat cake that are nonsacral food
with oil of *terumah* floating on them,
and a *tevul yom* touched the oil—
he has only disqualified the oil.
If he stirred [the preparation]—
wherever the oil has reached is disqualified.

5 Sacral meat on which gravy formed a crust,
if a *tevul yom* touched the [crusted] gravy,
the pieces [of meat] are permitted;
if he touched a piece [of meat],
that piece and all that lifts with it are a connective to one another.
R. Yohanan b. Nuri says:

[2] **K**, **P** lack "However."

it is pure because he wants it to be scattered: Whatever its relative quantity, it remains secondary to the rest of the broth because it is clearly a supplementary condiment.

[Likewise]: The same rule just considered regarding the garlic applies as well to foodstuffs that are usually ground and mixed with liquid (such as oil). When they are ground dry and then mixed in a preparation, they are part of the broth regardless of their quantity.

However: If they are usually ground and intended to be mixed with a liquid or in a preparation, but are ground and kept dry and lumped or piled together on a dish. Without the word *However* (see n. 2), the mishnah equates the moist and dry substances, but here the small ground parts are considered distinct and do not constitute a connective when a *tevul yom* touches one part.

a ring of dried figs: *Terumot* 2:1 states that if one fig on a ring of dried figs becomes impure, the rest of the ring is unaffected. Each part is separate and not regarded as a connective of impurity affecting the rest. The same applies with the pile of dry, ground herbs or spices on a dish: they are not considered connected and not a connective for transmitting impurity.

2:4 *floating on them*: The *terumah* and ordinary components are distinct from one another.

he has only disqualified the oil: The disqualified *terumah* oil does not impart impurity to the nonsacral preparation.

If he stirred: Then the actual and conceptual distinction between the *terumah* oil and the nonsacral preparation is blurred.

wherever the oil has reached: Whatever the mixing has affected.

2:5 *Sacral meat*: Meat from Temple sacrifices that are destined for consumption must not contract impurity.

formed a crust: Thereby distinguishing the pieces of meat from the crusted gravy.

that piece and all that lifts with it: The disqualified part is only that piece and what sticks to it when removed.

Both are a connective to one another.
The same applies to legumes
that formed a crust on slices of bread.
A stew[3] with legumes[4] [of *terumah*]:
when they are separate—
they are not a connective;
when they are a lump—
they are a connective;
if there were several lumps,
they are to be counted.
Oil that is floating on top of wine,
and a *tevul yom* touches the oil—
he has only disqualified the oil.
R. Yohanan b. Nuri says:
Both are a connective to one another.

2:6–8 *A Tevul Yom's Contact with Terumah Liquids and Perforated Jars*

6 A jar that sank into a cistern of wine,
and a *tevul yom* touched it—
[if he held the jar] from inside the rim,
it is a connective;
from outside the rim,

[3] Lit. "a pot preparation." [4] **K**, **P**: "and legumes."

Both are a connective: Even the gravy is a connective that imparts impurity to the piece of meat, and a *tevul yom* disqualifies the whole preparation by touching any part of it.

The same applies: The bread parallels the pieces of meat and the crust of the legumes parallels the crusted gravy.

with legumes: The variant "and legumes" would mean either a pot preparation or cooked legumes.

separate: When the ingredients have not yet combined.

counted: They form links for transmitting impurity, and the degree of impurity lessens with each link.

Oil... wine: Both are *terumah*.

Both are a connective: A *tevul yom* disqualifies both wine and oil by touching either.

2:6 *jar* with *terumah* wine in it.

cistern of wine that is nonsacral.

touched it wanting to pull it out.

inside the rim and had direct contact with the *terumah* wine inside the jar.

is a connective: The wine in the jar is disqualified *terumah*.

from outside the rim: Directly touching the nonsacral wine in the pit, which is unaffected by contact with a *tevul yom*.

it is not a connective.
R. Yohanan b. Nuri said,
Even if [the jar] is a person's height deep [in the pit],
and he touched opposite its opening—
it is a connective.

7 A jar that became perforated,
whether at its opening, bottom, or its side,
and a *tevul yom* touched it—
it is impure.
R. Judah says:
At its opening or bottom
it is impure;
at its sides
from either side it is pure.
If one pours from one vessel to another
and a *tevul yom* touches the stream,
if there is [enough] in it
it will be nullified by one to a hundred.

is not a connective: The wine in the jar remains pure *terumah*. A parallel text formulates a similar case of a jar submerged in a cistern, but where both the wine in the jar and wine in the cistern are *terumah*, and the disputed issue is whether defiling one space—jar or cistern—defiles the other. This might be a different interpretation of the mishnah here.

even if it is a person's height deep and there is no direct contact between the *tevul yom* and the jar or the wine in it.

it is a connective: This dissenting opinion sees the alignment with the jar's opening as creating a connective between the wine opposite the contact of the *tevul yom* and the *terumah* wine in the jar rendering it all impure.

2:7 *jar* of *terumah* liquid.

became perforated: Sprung a leak.

touched it to stop the leak.

impure: The wine directly touched is a connective and conveys its impurity to the rest of the wine.

At its opening or bottom it is impure: A connective conveying impurity to the whole jar is created only when contact is made at a bottom hole where the flow is directed; or at the top where the liquid beneath the point of contact serves as its base.

from either side it is pure: Only the immediate point of contact becomes impure, but that small quantity is nullified by the rest of the unaffected wine. One part impure *terumah* is nullified by one hundred parts pure *terumah*; the impure part may be disregarded, and the whole amount remains pure (see *Terumot* 5:4).

If one pours any liquid that is *terumah*.

the stream of liquid being poured.

if there is [enough] in it: Sufficient liquid in the vessels to nullify the impure amount at the point of contact.

nullified by one to a hundred: As noted, this is the ratio in which impure *terumah* is nullified if it is accidentally mixed with pure *terumah*.

8 A bubble in a jar that was perforated on the inside and the outside:
if the two perforations were (either at the top or bottom)[5]
opposite one another,
it is impure by [contact with] a primary impurity
and by [being in] a Tent of a corpse.
If the inside [perforation] is lower and the outside one is higher,
it is impure by [contact with] a primary impurity
and by [being in] a Tent of a corpse.
If the inside [perforation] is higher and the outside one is lower,
it is pure by [contact with] a primary impurity
but impure by [being in] a Tent of a corpse.

Chapter Three

3:1 "*Handles*"

3 All handles of edibles that are a connective for a primary impurity
are [likewise] a connective for a *tevul yom*.
Food that has been sliced but is still partially connected:

[5] **K**, **P** lack the bracketed words.

2:8 *bubble in a jar*: Clay vessels could form cavities in their sides during fabrication.

was perforated: The bubble was not contained and sealed in the vessel's wall, but had fissures in two directions, into the vessel cavity and to the outside.

opposite one another… inside [perforation] is lower and the outside one is higher: In these two situations the flow of liquid from inside the jar is hampered and impurity from the outside "spreads" and the contents of the jar contract impurity.

it is impure: The source of impurity renders the leaking liquid impure, which becomes a connective to disqualify the contents of the jar.

primary impurity: Direct contact is made between the impure source and the jar's leaking fissures.

Tent of a corpse: A corpse can impart impurity without direct contact by being under one "Tent" (any overhead cover) with other objects (see introduction to *Oholot*). The corpse's impurity spreads to nearly all objects under the same covering and here the impurity spreads through the opening into the perforated jar. Even if the mouth of the jar is tightly sealed (see Numbers 19:15), which normally protects objects beneath the seal, the impurity can enter through the perforation.

the inside [perforation] is higher and the outside one is lower: If the flow of the leak is facilitated by the inside fissure being higher, then the contraction of impurity from a principal source is abated; however, corpse impurity is considered more potent than other types and the liquid inside the jar is affected.

3:1 *handles of edibles*: Stems, stalks, edges of produce that a person might grip while eating as listed in *Uqtsin* 1:1–5.

are a connective: If the "handle" becomes impure, so does the main part of the edible.

R. Meir says:
If [a person] picks up the larger piece
and the smaller piece lifts with it,
[the latter] is likened to [the former].
R. Judah says:
If a person picks up the smaller piece
and the larger piece lifts with it,
[the latter] is likened to [the former].
R. Nehemiah says:
Only with a pure piece.
And the Sages say:
Only with an impure piece.
All other edibles—
if they are usually held by the leaf,
he holds it by the leaf;
and [if it is usually held] by the stem,
he holds it by the stem.

3:2–5 *Mixtures of Terumah and Nonsacral Food*

2 A vegetable of *terumah* with a beaten egg on top of it,
and a *tevul yom* touched the egg—
he only disqualified the stem opposite it.
R. Yose says:
All the upper layer [is disqualified].
If [the egg] was like a cap,
it is not a connective.

lifts with it and does not tear off.

R. Meir... R. Judah...: The relative mass of the pieces determines whether there is a connective. Meir's opinion regards a weaker connection, the smaller piece carried by the larger, as enough to constitute a connective; Judah's opinion requires a stronger connection, the weight of the larger piece carried by the smaller, for a connective to form.

R. Nehemiah... with a pure piece: If the untouched (pure) part were picked up and the impure piece lifted with it, regardless of their respective mass, they are deemed connected and impure.

the Sages... with an impure piece: If the piece touched by an impure person were picked up and the untouched (pure) piece lifted with it, they are deemed connected and impure.

All other edibles: The usual way of handling produce determines the link. If while holding the handle, leaf, or stem, the rest does not tear off there is a connective, but if it tears off there is no link.

3:2 *vegetable... egg* being cooked together.

a tevul yom touched the egg: The egg is nonsacral food and cannot be rendered impure by contact with a *tevul yom*.

disqualified the stem opposite it: The only vegetable affected is the one adjacent to where contact was made.

All the upper layer directly in contact with the egg on top.

like a cap: If the egg puffed up over the vegetables and contact was made only with the egg, the vegetable is pure since there was no direct contact with the *terumah* vegetable.

3 A streak of an egg that formed a crust on the side of a stew pot,
and a *tevul yom* touched it inside the rim—
it is a connective;
outside the rim—
it is not a connective.
R. Yose says:
The streak and everything that peels away with it [are connected].
The same [applies] to legumes that formed a crust on the rim of a boiling pot.
4 Dough that became mixed or leavened with *terumah* yeast
is not disqualified by a *tevul yom.*
R. Yose and R. Simeon disqualify [the dough].
Dough that had become susceptible [to impurity] by liquids
and was then kneaded with fruit juice,
and a *tevul yom* touched it—
R. Eleazar b. Judah of Bartota says in the name of R. Joshua:
He has disqualified it all;
R. Aqiva says in his name:
He has only disqualified the place he touched.
5 A nonsacral vegetable that had been cooked in oil of *terumah,*
and a *tevul yom* touched it—
R. Eleazar b. Judah of Bartota says in the name of R. Joshua:
He has disqualified it all;

3:3 *egg...stew pot...*: The egg is nonsacral food and the preparation in the pot is *terumah.*

stew pot...boiling pot...: The two utensils seem to be distinguished here by the type of food being prepared in each.

everything that peels away with it: All that peels off is impure but the rest remains pure, even if it comes from inside the pot.

3:4 *Dough that became mixed*: This mixed dough, with *terumah* and nonsacral food combined, is fit solely for consumption by priests and the issue contested here is the effect of the *tevul yom*'s contact with it.

Dough of *terumah.*

susceptible [to impurity]: Food (produce) can only contract impurity if previously dampened by liquid (see introduction to *Makhshirin*). Contact with impurity before it is dampened does not affect the food.

kneaded with fruit juice: Fruit juice is not considered one of the liquids that render food susceptible to impurity (see *Makhshirin* 6:4). In this case, initial susceptibility was caused by another liquid, but the kneading, which creates one mass of dough, was with fruit juice.

says in his name: In R. Joshua's name. R. Eleazar b. Judah and R. Aqiva each present a different report as to their master's position.

disqualified: The difference of opinion is whether to regard the dough simply as *terumah* susceptible to impurity by a *tevul yom* or to view the kneading with fruit juice as a mitigating factor because the amalgam was facilitated by an agent that does not create susceptibility.

3:5 *touched* the nonsacral vegetable.

R. Aqiva says in his name:
He has only disqualified the place he touched.

3:6 *Saliva and Susceptibility to Impurity*

6 A pure person who bit off food
that [then] fell on his clothes and on a loaf of *terumah*—
[the loaf] is pure.
If he was eating cracked olives, moist dates,
or anything whose pit he would want to suck
and it fell on his clothes or on a loaf of *terumah*—
it is impure.
If he was eating dried olives, dry dates,
or anything on whose pit he would not want to suck,
which then fell on his clothes or on a loaf of *terumah*—
it is pure.
Both a pure person and a *tevul yom* are similar [with regard to this susceptibility].
R. Meir says:
All these [instances] are impure in the case of *tevul yom*,
because liquids from an impure person create susceptibility [to impurity]
whether he desires it [the liquid] or not,
and the Sages say:
A *tevul yom* is not impure.

disqualified: The difference of opinion is whether the *terumah* oil is viewed as thoroughly integrated in the vegetable preparation, connecting all its parts, or not.

3:6 *who bit off food*: Even though the food becomes moist in a person's mouth, it does not become susceptible to impurity because the secretion of saliva must be acceptable to the person for it to cause the susceptibility (see *Makhshirin* 1:1, 6:5).

of terumah: Although framed in connection to *terumah*, the susceptibility to impurity as a result of secreting saliva is relevant to nonsacral food as well.

pure…impure: In this context the designations "pure" and "impure" indicate susceptibility to contracting impurity.

cracked olives, etc.: In these three instances a person desires the salivating to enable the sucking and therefore it creates susceptibility to impurity.

dried olives, etc.: In these instances the salivating is not wanted and it does not create the susceptibility.

R. Meir…the Sages: The issue at stake is the basic status of the *tevul yom*: is he regarded as one who has not yet concluded his purification procedure hence "impure," albeit with several leniencies, or as a person who has done all the necessary purification actions and is waiting for sunset to automatically conclude the process? R. Meir sees the *tevul yom* as impure since he disqualifies *terumah*; the Sages focus on the lessened effect of a *tevul yom* and his "liquids" (see 2:2) and do not designate him as "impure."

Chapter Four

4:1–3 *Third-Degree Contact with Impurity Does Not Affect Nonsacral Food*

4 If food from the [first] tithe had become susceptible [to impurity] by liquid and was then touched by a *tevul yom*
or by defiled hands—
one can [still] separate *terumah* of the tithe from it
in [a state of] purity,
for [the tithe] is third[-degree contact with impurity],
and third[-degree contact] is pure regarding nonsacral food.

2 A woman who is a *tevulat yom*[6] [can] knead dough,
cut off the *hallah*, and separate it.
She [must then] place [the *hallah*] in a basket of reeds[7] or on a wooden board,
and bring [the mass of dough] together,
and [only then] designate [the *hallah*] by name.
For [the dough] is third,
and third is pure regarding nonsacral food.

3 A kneading trough that is of *tevul yom* status
[can] be used to knead dough,

[6] Feminine form of *tevul yom*.
[7] Or "Egyptian basket." In either case **K**, **P** lack the word; see annotations.

4:1 *[first] tithe*: After being separated from the rest of the produce, the first tithe is [theoretically] given to a Levite (see Numbers 18:21–24). The first tithe is still in a state of unseparated food that is forbidden for consumption until one tenth of it is given to a priest (see Numbers 18:25–32); this is the "*terumah* of the tithe" mentioned below.

defiled hands: See note on 2:2.

terumah of the tithe: This portion is treated as regular *terumah*, and is to be kept pure and consumed only by priests in a state of purity.

third[-degree contact] is pure regarding nonsacral food and the first tithe is like nonsacral food regarding contraction of impurity.

4:2 *cut off the hallah, and separate it*: The woman has not yet explicitly designated the separated part as *hallah*, so it is still nonsacral food and cannot become impure by contact with a *tevul(at) yom*.

basket of reeds: Or "Egyptian basket." The basket in question may have been made of reeds in a distinctively Egyptian manner; hence the variation in published translations. The manuscripts that do not have "of reeds" may indicate a stone vessel.

basket . . . wooden board: Neither utensil can contract impurity.

bring . . . together: By her holding the dough in the utensil and the separated part next to each other, they are still thought of as one batch of dough.

[only then] designate [the hallah] by name: Because the *tevulat yom* has not directly touched designated *hallah*, its purity is intact.

4:3 *knead dough*: Maintaining purity.

and [a person can] cut off the *hallah*,
and bring [the two pieces] together,
and [only then] designate it by name.
For [the dough] is third,
and third is pure regarding nonsacral food.

4:4 *Suspended Separation of Terumah*

4 A jug that is of *tevul yom* status,
which has been filled from a jar containing a [first] tithe that still contains unseparated *terumah*:
if he said: "This will be the *terumah* of the tithe when it is dark,"
it is the *terumah* of the tithe.
If he said: "This shall be an *eruv*,"
he has said nothing.
If the jar broke [before dark]—
the jar remains unusable;
if the jar broke [before dark]—
the jar remains unusable.

4:5–6 *Miscellaneous*

5 In former times they would say
that one could exchange [the second tithe] for the produce of an *am ha'arets*.
They reconsidered and said

[a person] who is pure (not a *tevul yom*).

cut off the hallah: Physically cutting off the piece of dough but not yet designating it as *hallah*.

bring [the two pieces] together: As in the previous mishnah, by holding the dough and the small separated piece next to each other, they are thought of as one batch of dough.

[only then] designate it by name: The person doing the kneading is not impure so it is only the *tevul yom* utensil that cannot touch the separated *hallah*.

4:4 *terumah of the tithe*: The *tevul yom* jug will be completely pure at nightfall, and since the "*terumah* of the tithe" status is delayed until nightfall, there is no disqualifying contact of a *tevul yom* utensil with *terumah* foodstuff.

eruv: Setting a small amount of food that is required for permission to carry things out to a courtyard and into its adjacent houses on Sabbath, or for being permitted to walk farther than the two-thousand-cubit city limit on Sabbath. See *Eruvin*.

he has said nothing: The food of the *eruv* must be set aside and ready before nightfall, however, the liquid in the jug is still not permitted for general consumption (and therefore not for use as an *eruv*) until the "*terumah* of the tithe" separation applies at dark.

remains unusable: Both the principal entity (i.e. the whole tithe) and the separated part must be present when the separation formally takes effect; the absence of either causes the other to remain unusable.

4:5 *In former times*: This expression presents a conscious development in legal tradition by contrasting former practice with subsequent norm. Sometimes the reason or motivation is noted, though not in this occurrence.

exchange the [second tithe]: Second-tithe produce must be consumed in Jerusalem or exchanged for money that in turn is to be spent in Jerusalem (see introduction to *Ma'aser Sheni*).

[one could exchange] for the money [of the *am ha'arets*] as well.
In former times they would say
that if one were leaving in chains
and said: "Write a bill of divorce for my wife,"
they write and deliver [the bill of divorce].
They reconsidered and said
also a person setting sail or leaving in a convoy.
R. Simon Shezuri said:
Also a person who is dangerously ill.

6 Ashkelonite levers that broke but their hook is still whole—
these are impure.
A pitchfork, a winnowing fan, a rake, and also a comb,
whose missing [wooden] tooth was replaced with one made of metal—
these are impure.
On all these R. Joshua said:
This is an innovation that scribes have innovated and I have no response.

am ha'arets: The term denotes those whom mishnaic tradition regarded as lax in their observance of tithing and maintaining purity.

for the money [of the am ha'arets] as well: The *am ha'arets* is trusted to supply coins that are not second-tithe money themselves. This facilitates greater transactions between people in Jerusalem during pilgrimage holidays and other occasions.

leaving in chains: As a prisoner led away by the Roman authorities.

Write a bill of divorce: The husband's motivation is to prevent his wife from being in limbo as to her marital status. Rather than her still being married, not knowing whether her husband is alive or not, she will be divorced and legally able to remarry.

they write and deliver: Even though the person did not explicitly mention delivery, those around him are empowered to see the divorce process to its conclusion (see *Gittin* 6:5).

also a person setting sail: The reconsideration of the law broadens this dispensation of finalizing the divorce without explicit instruction to a greater range of occurrences: not only under coercion by the authorities but also when anticipating a voluntary dangerous journey are a person's partial instructions taken to include the whole process.

dangerously ill: The dispensation is expanded to include a deathbed divorce intended to prevent the widow from being subject to a levirate marriage. Conceptually, the law is broadened from the cases of a potential absentee husband to cases where the husband will remain present and the concern is the levirate requirement.

4:6 The mishnah also appears in *Kelim* 13:7.

Ashkelonite levers: Long wooden beams with hooks or pegs affixed to them for retrieving buckets or other utensils from wells or for hanging jugs of water to cool.

impure: In these cases "impure" means "susceptible to impurity" because it is a whole, functioning utensil. If a utensil breaks, its pieces are no longer susceptible to impurity. In the case of the lever, as long as the hook is whole it is not regarded as broken and its susceptibility to impurity remains.

pitchfork, etc.: All these tools are "plain wooden tools" and cannot contract impurity (however, the Talmud ascribes a rabbinically ordained status of impurity to these tools).

impure: That is, susceptible to impurity. The addition of a metal component enables them to contract impurity.

On all these R. Joshua said: This response is difficult to understand: is he grudgingly agreeing or registering his reservation, albeit without being able to back it up? The context for R. Joshua's response is not readily

4:7 *Conditional Separation of Terumah*

7 One who was separating *terumah* from a cistern and said:
"This shall be *terumah* on condition that it emerged safely":
"safely" is only with regard to breaking and spilling,
but not with regard to [contracting] impurity.
R. Simeon says:
Also with regard to [contracting] impurity.
If [the jar] broke,
it does not render the produced mixed.
To what distance can [the jar] break and not render the produce mixed?
[Close enough] for it to roll [back] to the cistern.
R. Yose says:
Even one who is capable[8] of making the stipulation [but] did not stipulate—
if it broke it does not create a mixture,
because it is a stipulation of the court.

[8] Lit. "has knowledge in him."

evident either: is it just the preceding cases of the levers and pitchforks as implied in *Kelim* 13:7, or all cited cases of permissive legal development (4:5–6), or maybe the rules at the beginning of the chapter that establish that a *tevul yom* cannot impart impurity to nonsacral food?

4:7 *separating terumah from a cistern*: Removing a jar of wine or oil from a pit and designating it as the *terumah*.

emerged safely from the cistern. Had this not been stipulated, there would be the danger of the jar, already of *terumah* status, falling back into the pit and mixing in with the rest of wine. This would render the whole quantity a mixture of *terumah* and nonsacral food, prohibited from regular consumption.

safely: The stipulation that separation be completed successfully is only with regard to physical breaking and spilling, but not intended to include the danger of contracting impurity.

[contracting] impurity: The Jerusalem Talmud sees this part of the stipulation as indicating that the person separating the *terumah* is a *tevul yom*. A *tevul yom* does not render wine in an unseparated cistern impure. It is only by direct contact with separated and legal *terumah* that the *tevul yom* can do harm. The broadening of the stipulation to include purity disqualification addresses the presence of a *tevul yom* as the person at the pit.

If [the jar] broke... mixed: The produce in the cistern is not considered a mixture of *terumah* and nonsacral food (see note to 3:4) because the "safely" stipulation was not fulfilled and the wine in the jar never became *terumah*.

it does not render the product mixed: If the separation has not yet legally occurred, the spilling and mixing of the wine does not involve *terumah* and nonsacral food, but rather still unseparated food that remains pure and can yet be separated.

To what distance: How far from the pit can the jar of wine break and still not cause the mixed status?

for it to roll [back]: The jar with the separated liquid. Within this proximity the separating process has not been completed and is canceled by the stipulation.

one who is capable: This can also be rendered "intended to stipulate, but did not."

the stipulation regarding the "safe" separation of the *terumah* from the main quantity of the liquid.

stipulation of the court: A stipulation that is automatically presumed, even if not expressly stated by a person.

Tractate Yadayim

Leib Moscovitz

Introduction

Overview

Tractate *Yadayim* ("Hands") is the next-to-last tractate of the Order of *Tohorot.* The principal theme of this tractate is the impurity of the hands and purification from such impurity. Purification is achieved by pouring water from a utensil on the hands up to the wrist, or, according to another interpretation, up to the finger joint. This hand washing was (sometimes? ordinarily?) a two-step process: water was poured once over the impure hands to purify them ("first water"), and then "second water" was poured over the first water to purify the water on the hands.

Main Ideas

According to the Talmud, hand impurity, whereby the hands become impure while the rest of the body remains pure, is of rabbinic origin. Hands are rendered impure if they touch certain types of objects that impart impurity by rabbinic decree but not by biblical law (e.g. scrolls containing biblical texts); a detailed list of such items appears in chapter 3 of our tractate. A person whose hands are impure renders certain types of food (*terumah* and sancta) that he touches impure. The Torah's only reference to the ritual purification of the hands appears in connection with the *zav* (Leviticus 15:11); why the rabbis chose in so many more cases to render only the hands impure and not the entire body is not fully clear.

The rabbis further decreed that all people who eat bread (even non-*terumah* bread), and possibly other types of foodstuffs as well, had to ritually wash or immerse their hands even if they had not come in contact with impure objects as described above. The reason for this ruling is not fully clear, and the Talmud and commentators suggest that it might stem from hygienic considerations, to ensure that people would wash their hands before they eat.

Structure and Organization of the Tractate

Yadayim contains four chapters, and the structure and organization of the tractate are relatively straightforward. Chapter 1 discusses the requisite quantities of water, the utensils that may be used, and the types of water that may be used for hand washing. Chapter 2 discusses the purity and impurity of water used to wash the hands, whether "first water" or "second water," as well as the laws that apply when it is not certain whether hand purification has been performed correctly. Chapter 3 discusses the types of objects that render the hands impure. This chapter contains a detailed discussion of hand impurity imparted by handling biblical texts, and this discussion would seem to illuminate rabbinic views about the scope of the biblical canon, since noncanonical books presumably do not render the hands impure.

Most of chapter 4 consists of digressions adduced associatively because of their similarity to other parts of the tractate. Thus, 4:1–4 cites a series of rulings issued "on that day" (i.e. on the day when R. Eleazar b. Azariah was appointed head of the rabbinic academy in Yavneh), by association with another ruling issued "on that day" and mentioned in the previous mishnah (3:5). These rulings address a variety of themes: laws of ritual purity, sacrificial laws, laws pertaining to the seventh (Sabbatical) year, and laws pertaining to Ammonite and Moabite proselytes. The tractate resumes with a brief discussion of hand impurity imparted by biblical texts, and this is followed by a second and final digression that deals with disputes between the Sadducees (or a Galilean heretic) and Pharisees; this section is an important source for rabbinic views about Sadducean *halakhah*. (This digression was adduced because the first debate here between the Sadducees and Pharisees mentions hand impurity imparted by biblical texts, the theme addressed in the previous part of the Mishnah.) These disputes between Sadducees and Pharisees treat a variety of themes: laws of ritual purity, torts, and even a debate about mentioning the names of God and a secular ruler together in a single document. The tractate concludes with a quotation from Exodus 9:27, Pharaoh's admission that *The Lord is the Righteous One*, which is not directly relevant to the previous discussion, but which was presumably included in order to end on a positive note.

Tractate Yadayim

Chapter One

1:1 *Quantities of Water for Hand Washing*

I One may pour a *revi'it* of water on the hands of one [person], even of two;
half a *log* for three or four;
a *log* for five, for ten, and for a hundred.
R. Yose says:
Provided that one does not [pour] less than a *revi'it* for the last of them.
One may add to the second [water], but one may not add to the first.

1:2 *Utensils That May Be Used for Hand Washing*

2 One may pour on the hands with all [kinds of] utensils,
even with utensils of dung, utensils of stone, and utensils of [unfired] earth.
One may not pour on the hands with the sides of utensils, or the bottom of a ladle, or the seal of a jar.

1:1 *One may pour*: For ritual hand washing; see introduction. The term "pour" (*ntn*) used here and below, in contrast to "wash" (*ntl*) found elsewhere in our tractate (e.g. 2:1–2), apparently indicates that another person (perhaps a servant) poured the water over the hands of the person being washed.

a revi'it: A quarter of a *log*, approximately an eighth of a liter.

even of two people, since multiple people may wash their hands simultaneously; cf. 2:3.

half a log: Two *revi'it*, approximately a quarter of a liter.

Provided that one does not [pour] less than a revi'it for the last of them: This requirement presumably applies not just to the last person, but to all of the people. Thus, R. Yose presumably disagrees with the opening line of the mishnah.

One may add to the second [water], but one may not add to the first: Ordinarily water must be poured on the hands twice (see introduction), once to purify the hands (the "first water"), and a second time (the "second water") to purify the water remaining on the hands. If the second water did not reach the joint (see 2:3), additional water may be added. However, if the first water did not reach the joint additional water may not be added, and one must wash again.

1:2 *even utensils of dung, utensils of stone, and utensils of [unfired] earth*, which are not susceptible to ritual impurity (see e.g. *Oholot* 5:5). Nevertheless, such objects are deemed valid utensils for washing the hands.

the sides of utensils: The parts of the utensils remaining after the utensils were broken. Such sides (and similarly the other items mentioned below) are not considered valid utensils, since they are broken and hence unfit for use.

One may not pour [water] on someone else with his cupped hands,
since one may only draw, sanctify, and sprinkle purgation water
and pour [water] on the hands
with a utensil.
And only utensils can protect [from impurity] with a sealed lid,
for[1] only utensils can protect [from impurity] in earthenware utensils.

1:3–5 *Water That May Be Used for Hand Washing*

3 Water that became unfit for animals to drink—
if in utensils, it is unfit,
but if on the ground, it is fit.
If ink, gum, or vitriol fell into [water]
and its appearance changed,
it is unfit.
If he did work with [water]
or soaked his bread in it,
it is unfit.
Simeon the Timnite says:
Even if he intended to soak in one [utensil] and it fell into another,
it is acceptable.
4 If one rinsed utensils with it or scrubbed measures with it,
it is unfit.
If one rinsed [previously] rinsed or new utensils with it,

[1] This sentence appears verbatim in *Kelim* 8:3, where the word "for" is more appropriate.

draw, sanctify, and sprinkle purgation water: *Parah* 5:5. This is the water used for purification from corpse impurity (Numbers 19:2–20). Such water must be "drawn" from a source of flowing water and "sanctified" by adding the ashes of a burnt red heifer to it (Numbers 19:17), after which it is sprinkled on the unclean person to purify him (18–20).

only utensils can protect [from impurity] with a sealed lid: Utensils located in a tent that contains a corpse protect their contents from impurity if they are closed with a sealed lid; cf. Numbers 19:15 and *Kelim* 10:1.

only utensils can protect [from impurity] in earthenware utensils: *Kelim* 8:3. If a dead reptile is found in an earthenware utensil, the utensil's contents are deemed impure (Leviticus 11:35), unless they were inside another utensil that was sealed or whose lip extends above the top of the earthenware utensil, which then protects its contents from impurity. Only objects that are defined as utensils protect their contents from impurity in this way (cf. above).

1:3 *Water... on the ground... is fit*: Immersion of the hands in nondrinkable water found in a pool on the ground is acceptable, since ritual immersion (including that of the hands) may be performed in nonpotable water; cf. *Miqva'ot* 2:10.

ink, gum, or vitriol: Types of dye (cf. e.g. *Shabbat* 1:5, *Gittin* 2:3) that change the color of the water into which they were poured.

If he did work with [water]: For example, using it to wash dishes (cf. 1:4).

Even if he intended to soak in one [utensil] and it fell into another, it is acceptable: Even if one intended to soak bread in a particular utensil (which constitutes work), if the bread fell unintentionally into another utensil, the water in the second utensil is fit for washing hands.

it is fit.
R. Yose deems it unfit [if it was used to rinse] new [utensils].
5 Water in which a baker dips loaves of fine flour is unfit.
And when he rinses his hands in it, it is fit.
All [people] are fit to pour [water] on the hands,
even a deaf-mute, one who is not legally competent, and a minor.
He may place a jar between his knees[2] and wash.
He may tilt a jar on its side and wash.
A monkey may pour [water] on the hands.
R. Yose deems these two unfit.

Chapter Two

2:1–3 *Purity and Impurity of Water Used to Wash the Hands*

2 If he washed one hand with one rinsing,
his hand is pure.
[If he washed] both hands with one rinsing,
R. Meir deems [him] impure
until he washes from a *revi'it*.
If a loaf of *terumah* fell [into the water],
it is pure.
R. Yose deems [it] impure.

[2] **P**: "his thighs."

1:4 *R. Yose deems it unfit [if it was used to rinse] new [utensils]*: R. Yose maintains that washing a new utensil is considered washing.

1:5 *when he rinses his hands in it, it is fit*: The water remaining in the utensil after the baker has rinsed his hands with it is fit, since no work was done with it.

even a deaf-mute, one who is not legally competent, and a minor, who lack understanding according to the rabbinic sources; cf. e.g. *Gittin* 2:5, *Hullin* 1:1. Generally those who lack understanding cannot perform acts with ritual validity.

R. Yose deems these two unfit: Tilting a jar on its side and washing with the water that flows from it, and having a monkey pour water over someone's hands, since in these cases the water was not actively poured by a human being.

2:1 *terumah*: A portion of the produce given to the priests; see e.g. Numbers 18:8 and tractate *Terumot, passim. Terumah* is susceptible to certain types of ritual impurity—for example, that caused by contact with impure hands—to which ordinary produce (*hullin*) is not susceptible.

if a loaf of terumah fell [into the water], it is pure: Even though the hands washed were impure, they do not render the water used to wash them impure. R. Yose, below, disagrees.

2 If he washed the first [water] on one place and the second in another place
and a loaf of *terumah* fell on the first water,
it is impure.
[If the loaf fell] on the second water,
it is pure.
If he washed [with] first [water] and second [water] on one place
and a loaf of *terumah* fell [on it],
it is impure.
If he washed [with] first [water]
and a chip of wood or a pebble was found on his hands,
his hands are impure,
for the last water purifies only water on the hand.
Rabban Simeon b. Gamaliel says:
Any creature [that lives in] water is pure.

3 The hands become impure and become pure up to the joint.
How?
If he washed [with] the first [water] up to the joint
and the second [water] outside of the joint
and it returned to the hand,
it is pure.
If he washed [with] the first and the second [water] outside of the joint
and it returned to the hand,
it is impure.

2:2 *If... a loaf of terumah fell on the first water, it is impure*, since the first water was rendered impure by the hands that touched it. This ruling may thus reflect the viewpoint of R. Yose in the previous mishnah, according to which water used for washing the hands becomes impure. Alternatively, the Mishnah might distinguish between cases where the hands were only washed once—presumably, with the requisite quantity of a *revi'it*—so no "second water" was used, and cases where second water was used (presumably, because the hands were washed the first time with less than a *revi'it*). In the former case the water does not become impure when it touches the hands, whereas in the latter case it does.

[If the loaf fell] on the second water, it is pure: Since the second water is pure, unlike the first water.

If he washed [with] first [water] and second [water] on one place, and a loaf of terumah fell [on it], it is impure: The first water is not purified by the second water, since second water only purifies first water on the hands (cf. 2:3). Hence the impure first water in the mixture renders objects that fall into it impure.

If he washed [with] first [water] and a chip of wood or a pebble was found on his hands, they are impure, for the last water only purifies water on the hand: The second water cannot purify water on a chip or pebble on the hand. Therefore, the water on the chip or pebble renders the hand impure when it falls back on the hand.

Any creature [that lives in] water: *Miqva'ot* 6:7. Something that originates in the water (e.g. a gnat) is treated like water. Therefore, if such an object was found on the hand after washing, the second water renders it pure.

2:3 *joint*: This could refer to the knuckle at the near end of the finger, the middle joint of the fingers, or the wrist.

If he washed [with] the first [water] up to the joint and the second [water] outside of the joint and it returned to the hand, it is pure: Since water cannot contract impurity outside of the joint, the second water does not become impure there. Therefore, it does not render the hand impure when it returns there.

If he washed [with] the first and the second [water] outside of the joint and it returned to the hand, it is impure: Since the second water cannot purify water outside of the joint, the first water there remains impure, and when it returns to the hand it renders the hand impure.

If he washed [with] the first [water] on one hand
and he changed his mind and he washed [with] the second [water] on both hands,
they are impure.
If he washed [with] the first [water] on both hands
and changed his mind and washed [with] the second [water] on one hand,
his hand is pure.[3]
If he washed one hand and rubbed it against the other [hand],
it is impure.
[If he rubbed it] on his head or on the wall,
it is pure.
Four and five [people] may wash next to one another or one over another,
provided that they loosen [their hands] so the water flows between them.

2:4 *Doubts Related to Hand Washing*

4 If there is a doubt whether work was done or was not done with [water];
if there is a doubt whether it had the requisite quantity or did not have the requisite quantity;
if there was a doubt whether it was impure or pure,
the doubt is pure.
For they said:
Doubts about hands becoming impure, rendering impure, or becoming pure are pure.

[3] **P**: "his hands are pure."

If he washed [with] the first [water] on one hand and he changed his mind and he washed [with] the second [water] on both hands, they are impure: The second water poured on the hand that had not been washed originally is treated like first water with regard to that hand. Therefore this water becomes impure, and when it returns to the other hand it renders that hand impure.

If he washed [with] the first [water] on both hands and changed his mind and washed [with] the second [water] on one hand, his hand is pure, since the second water purifies the hand that had already been washed with first water.

If he washed one hand and rubbed it against the other [hand], it is impure, since the hand that had not been washed renders the water on the first hand impure, and that water renders the first hand impure.

[If he rubbed it] on his head or on the wall, it is pure, since neither one's head nor the wall is impure.

Four and five [people] may wash next to one another or one over another: Cf. 1:1.

2:4 *If there is a doubt whether work was done or was not done with [water]*: Using water for work renders it unfit; cf. 1:3.

the requisite quantity: A *revi'it*; see 1:1 and 2:1.

if there was a doubt... the doubt is pure: Doubts regarding the validity of hand washing are adjudicated leniently, as is generally the case with doubts concerning laws of rabbinic origin, such as those related to hand washing (cf. *Tohorot* 4:7).

they said: Earlier, unidentified sages.

Doubts about hands becoming impure, because they might have touched something impure.

rendering impure: If impure hands had touched something pure.

or becoming pure: If the hands were washed in a manner of doubtful validity, as described above.

R. Yose says:
[A doubt about] becoming pure is impure.
How?
If his hands were pure,
and in front of him were two impure loaves,
and there is a doubt whether he touched or did not touch [one of them];
if his hands were impure,
and in front of him were two pure loaves,
and there is a doubt whether he touched or did not touch [one of them];
if one of his hands was impure and one was pure,
and in front of him were two pure loaves,
and he touched one of them,
and there is a doubt whether he touched with the impure [hand]
or he touched with the pure one;
if his hands were pure,
and in front of him were two loaves,
one impure and one pure,
and he touched one of them,
and there is a doubt whether he touched the impure one
or he touched the pure one;
if one of his hands was impure and one was pure,
and in front of him were two loaves,
one impure and one pure,
and he touched both of them,
and there is a doubt whether the impure [hand] touched the impure [loaf]
and the pure [hand] touched the pure [loaf]
or whether the pure [hand] touched the impure [loaf]
and the impure [hand] touched the pure [loaf],[4]
the hands are as they were,
and the loaves are as they were.

[4] **K**: "or whether the impure [hand] touched the pure [loaf] and the pure [hand] touched the impure [loaf]."

[A doubt about] becoming pure is impure: Since it is certain that the hands were initially impure, only conclusive evidence that the hands were washed properly can alter their initial status. Similarly, if the hands or something they touched were initially pure, only conclusive evidence to the contrary can alter their initial status, and hence they are deemed pure in cases of doubt.

How? Here the Mishnah illustrates the principle that doubts about hands becoming impure or rendering other things impure are resolved leniently.

in front of him were two impure loaves, and there is a doubt whether he touched or did not touch [one of them], rendering his hands impure.

the hands are as they were, and the loaves are as they were: The doubt is resolved leniently, so neither the pure hands nor the pure loaves become impure.

Chapter Three

3:1–2 *Things That Render the Hands Impure*

3 One who puts his hands into an afflicted house—
his hands are impure to the first degree—
the words of R. Aqiva.
And the Sages say:
His hands are impure to the second degree.
Anyone who renders clothing impure while touching [a source of impurity]
renders the hands impure to the first degree—
the words of R. Aqiva.
And the Sages say:
They are impure to the second degree.
They said to R. Aqiva:
Where do we find that hands are impure to the first degree anywhere?
He said to them:
And how is it possible for them to be impure to the first degree unless his body became impure,
except for this case?
Food and utensils that were rendered impure by liquids
render the hands impure to the second degree—
the words of R. Joshua.
And the Sages say:
What was rendered impure by primary impurity renders the hands impure;

3:1 *an afflicted house*: A "leprous house" (see Leviticus 14:34–53) renders people and objects that entered it impure. However, if only one's hands enter the house, they become impure and the person's body remains pure.

his hands are impure to the first degree, and they render food and drink that they touch impure to the second degree; see below. For further discussion of the various degrees of ritual impurity, see *Tohorot* 2:3–7.

impure to the second degree: Objects impure to the second degree can render *terumah* and sacrifices impure, but not nonsacred food (*hullin*).

Anyone who renders clothing impure: People who make physical contact with certain types of impurity render clothing that they touch impure (see e.g. Leviticus 15:5, 7, *Zavim* 5). If such people touch the hands of ritually pure people, the hands of the latter become impure.

Where do we find that hands are impure to the first degree anywhere? Hand impurity is invariably of the second degree (see further below and 3:2).

how is it possible for them to be impure to the first degree unless his body became impure, except for this case? R. Aqiva admits that the only cases where hands can contract first-degree impurity even though the rest of the person's body remains pure are those mentioned above—one who inserts his hands into a leprous house, or someone whose hands touched a person who renders clothing impure while touching a source of impurity.

Food and utensils that were rendered impure by liquids that are impure to the second degree.

primary impurity: Certain types of dead reptiles and animal corpses (see *Kelim* 1:1). Such items render objects that they touch impure to the first degree.

[what was rendered impure] by reduced-degree impurity does not render the hands impure.
Rabban Simeon b. Gamaliel[5] said:
It happened that a woman came before Father;
she said to him:
My hands entered the air of an earthen utensil.
He said to her:
My daughter,[6] what was its impurity?
And I did not hear what she said to him.
The Sages said:
The matter is clear;
What was rendered impure by primary impurity renders the hands impure;
[what was rendered impure] by reduced-degree impurity does not render the hands impure.

2 Whatever renders *terumah* unfit renders the hands impure to the second degree.
One hand renders another impure—
the words of R. Joshua.
And the Sages say:
Something of second-degree impurity cannot render something [else] of second-degree impurity.
He said to them:
But the Holy Scriptures are of second-degree impurity [and] render the hands impure!
They said to him:
One cannot infer words of Torah from the words of the Scribes,
nor words of the Scribes from words of Torah,
nor words of the Scribes from words of the Scribes.

[5] **K, P**: "Rabban Gamaliel." [6] **K** lacks "My daughter."

reduced-degree impurity: Anything not of first-degree impurity, such as the food and utensils rendered impure by liquids mentioned above. According to the Sages, such items do not render the hands impure.

3:2 *Whatever renders terumah unfit*: Objects of second-degree impurity; see *Zavim* 5:12.

renders the hands impure to the second degree: According to this view, something of second-degree impurity can render hands impure to the same degree.

One hand renders another impure: A hand that is impure to the second degree can also render a pure hand impure to the second degree.

But the Holy Scriptures are of second-degree impurity [and] render the hands impure: According to the Talmud, the reason that the rabbis decreed that biblical texts should impart ritual impurity to *terumah* (see further below, 3:3–5 and 4:6) is that people might be inclined to leave *terumah* near biblical texts, since both are sacred. Thus, mice inclined to eat the former would probably also damage the latter. To prevent this from happening, the Sages decreed ritual impurity on biblical texts generally and ruled that they render the hands impure, whereas *terumah* must be protected from impurity and so would be stored in a separate place.

One cannot infer words... words of the Scribes from words of the Scribes: Hand impurity and the impurity of certain items that render *terumah* unfit are of rabbinic provenance ("words of the Scribes"), just like the impurity imparted by books of Scripture. However, not all types of rabbinically ordained impurity are considered legally equal, and thus inferences regarding the impurity conferred by contact with impure hands may not be drawn from the laws governing impurity associated with biblical texts.

3:3–5 *Hand Impurity Caused by Contact with Biblical Texts*

3 The straps of *tefillin* with *tefillin* render the hands impure.
R. Simeon says:
The straps of *tefillin* do not render the hands impure.
4 The margin of a scroll,
above and below [the writing],
in the beginning and in the end,
renders the hands impure.
R. Judah says:
[The margin] at the end does not render impure
until one makes a roller for it.
5 A scroll that was erased,
and eighty-five letters of it were left,
as [in] the section *And when the Ark traveled*,
renders the hands impure.
A sheet in which eighty-five letters were written,
like the section *And when the Ark traveled*,
renders the hands impure.
All books of Scripture render the hands impure.[7]
The Song of Songs and Ecclesiastes render the hands impure.
R. Judah says:
The Song of Songs renders the hands impure,

[7] **P** lacks this sentence, presumably through scribal error (homeoteleuton).

3:3 *The straps of tefillin with tefillin*: If the straps were attached to *tefillin*.

tefillin: Boxes worn on the head and arms containing parchments with certain biblical texts: Exodus 13:1–16 and Deuteronomy 6:4–9; 11:13–21.

render the hands impure: Since the parchments inside the *tefillin* contain biblical texts, which render the hands impure (see 3:4–5), *tefillin* also render the hands impure. The same applies to the straps connected to *tefillin*, which are treated as an integral part of the *tefillin*.

The straps of tefillin do not render the hands impure, since they are not biblical texts.

3:4 *a scroll*: A parchment containing text from the Bible.

in the beginning and in the end of the parchment.

[The margin] at the end does not render impure until one makes a roller for it: Since one can cut off the parchment at the end if the book lacks a roller, such parchment is not considered an integral part of the scroll.

3:5 *A scroll*: A piece of parchment containing text from the Torah.

And when the Ark traveled: Numbers 10:35–36. The rabbis considered this passage a self-contained unit of text, and hence inferred that this is the minimum quantity of biblical text that can render the hands impure.

A sheet: A single sheet of parchment, perhaps waiting to be sewn together with others into a scroll.

The Song of Songs and Ecclesiastes render the hands impure: These books were mentioned because their status as sacred scripture was disputed (see below), presumably due to their contents. Thus, the Song of Songs

and Ecclesiastes is [the subject of] a dispute.
R. Yose says:
Ecclesiastes does not render the hands impure,
and the Song of Songs is [the subject of] a dispute.
R. Simeon says:
Ecclesiastes is among the leniencies of the House of Shammai and the stringencies of the House of Hillel.
R. Simeon b. Azzai said:
I received a tradition from seventy-two elders
on the day that they appointed R. Eleazar b. Azariah in the academy[8]
that the Song of Songs and Ecclesiastes render the hands impure.
R. Aqiva said:
Heaven forbid!
No Israelite ever disagreed regarding the Song of Songs
that it should not render the hands impure,
for the whole world is not worthy as the day when the Song of Songs was given to Israel,
for all the Writings are holy,
but the Song of Songs is Holy of Holies.
If they disagreed,
they only disagreed about Ecclesiastes.
R. Yohanan b. Joshua[9] the son of R. Aqiva's father-in-law said:
[It is] according to the words of Ben Azzai,
so they disagreed and so they decided.

[8] **K** lacks this phrase. [9] **K**: "Shamua."

might have been construed as secular love poetry rather than sacred Scripture, while Ecclesiastes might have been considered the nondivinely inspired personal wisdom of King Solomon.

Ecclesiastes is [the subject of] a dispute: Among earlier rabbis, not specified here by name.

Ecclesiastes is among the leniencies of the House of Shammai and the stringencies of the House of Hillel: Ecclesiastes does not render the hands impure according to the House of Shammai, although it does according to the House of Hillel. These rulings deviate from the approach generally taken by the Houses, according to which the House of Shammai usually rule strictly and the House of Hillel leniently.

on the day that they appointed R. Eleazar b. Azariah in the academy: As head of the academy in Yavneh (ca. 100 CE).

the whole world is not worthy as the day when the Song of Songs was given to Israel: R. Aqiva evidently interpreted the Song of Songs allegorically, as depicting the love between God and Israel, and therefore considered this book to be of the greatest sanctity. Hence he assumed that its status as sacred scripture was undisputed.

R. Yohanan...said: [It is] according to the words of Ben Azzai, so they disagreed: Ben Azzai himself held that both the Song of Songs and Ecclesiastes render the hands impure (see above). According to R. Yohanan, the earlier sages agreed with Ben Azzai's assumption that both books are treated equally. Nevertheless, these sages, in contrast to Ben Azzai himself, maintained that the status of both books was initially disputed (see below).

and so they decided: Later they decided that both the Song of Songs and Ecclesiastes render the hands impure.

Chapter Four

4:1–4 *Rulings Issued "On That Day"*

4 On that day
[the rabbis] voted and decided
about a footbath
that is from two *log* to nine *qav*
that was cracked—
it is susceptible to *midras* impurity.
For R. Aqiva says:
A footbath is like its name.
2 On that day they said:
All sacrifices that were offered in the name of another sacrifice[10] are fit,
although they do not count for their owners toward [their] obligation,
except for the Passover and the purgation offering—
the Passover at its time,
and the purgation offering at any time.

[10] Lit. "not in their own name."

4:1 *On that day*: When R. Eleazar b. Azariah was appointed head of the academy. The entire series of rulings that follows, which were issued "on that day," was apparently adduced here because of the stylistic similarity to the previous mishnah, which also cites a ruling issued "on that day."

from two log to nine qav: *Kelim* 20:2. Between approximately a liter and eighteen liters.

a footbath . . . that was cracked, and hence cannot retain liquids.

susceptible to midras impurity: Even though a cracked footbath cannot retain liquids and so does not qualify as a utensil, people can use it as a seat, and objects designated for sitting become impure ("*midras* impurity") if someone with a flux (*zav*) sits on them (see Leviticus 15:6).

For R. Aqiva says: A footbath is like its name: According to R. Aqiva, anything called a footbath, regardless of its size, is subject to *midras* impurity. However, the anonymous Sages cited in the beginning of the mishnah disagreed, maintaining that only a footbath of the specified sizes is subject to *midras* impurity.

4:2 *All sacrifices that were offered in the name of another sacrifice*: *Zevahim* 1:1, 3. For example, an offering of well-being sacrificed with the intention of treating it as a whole burnt offering.

are fit so one may proceed with the remaining parts of the sacrificial ritual, namely, sprinkling the blood on the altar and offering the necessary parts of the sacrifice there.

although they do not count for their owners toward [their] obligation: Someone who vowed to bring such a sacrifice has not fulfilled his obligation, so he must bring another sacrifice of the type originally specified.

except for the Passover and the purgation offering, which, if offered in the name of another sacrifice, are unacceptable.

the Passover at its time: On the fourteenth of the Hebrew month of Nisan (see e.g. Leviticus 23:5 and *Zevahim* 1:3).

R. Eliezer[11] says:
Also the guilt offering—
the Passover at its time,
and the purgation offering and the guilt offering at any time.
R.[12] Simeon b. Azzai said:
I have received [a tradition] from seventy-two elders
on the day that they appointed R. Eleazar b. Azariah in the academy
that all sacrifices that are eaten
that were offered in the name of another sacrifice are acceptable,
but they do not count toward their owners for [their] obligation,
except for the Passover and the purgation offering;
Ben Azzai only added the whole burnt offering,
and the Sages did not agree with him.

3 On that day they said:
Ammon and Moab—what are they with regard to the Seventh Year?
R. Tarfon decreed:
Poor tithe.
And R. Eleazar b. Azariah decreed:
Second tithe.
R. Ishmael said:
Eleazar b. Azariah, you must bring proof,
for you are strict,
for whoever is strict must bring proof.
R. Eleazar b. Azariah said to him:
Ishmael my brother,

[11] **K**: "Eleazar." [12] **K** lacks "R."

the guilt offering: See e.g. Leviticus 5:15–26.

they appointed R. Eleazar b. Azariah in the academy: As head of the academy in Yavneh (see 3:5).

all sacrifices that are eaten, but not whole burnt offerings, which are not eaten by the priests or by the people who brought them, but are offered up in their entirety on the altar.

Ben Azzai only added the whole burnt offering as a type of sacrifice that is unacceptable if offered in the name of another sacrifice.

4:3 *Ammon and Moab—what are they with regard to the Seventh Year?* These countries are located near the Land of Israel, the only place where agricultural precepts apply according to Torah law. No tithes are separated there according to Torah law, although their residents were required to bring various types of tithes by rabbinic decree, as were the residents of other nearby countries, Egypt and Babylonia (see below). During the Seventh Year no tithes at all are due in the Land of Israel, so these other countries cannot simply repeat as in other years what is done there.

poor tithe: Tithe given to the poor during the third and sixth years of the seven-year Sabbatical-year cycle (see Deuteronomy 26:12).

second tithe, which the owner of produce must bring to Jerusalem and consume there (see Deuteronomy 14:22–27) during the first, second, fourth, and fifth years of the seven-year cycle.

for you are strict: By requiring the residents of Ammon and Moab to give second tithe, which is holy, in contrast to poor tithe, which is not.

I did not deviate from the order of the years;
Tarfon[13] my brother deviated,
so he must bring proof.
R. Tarfon replied:
Egypt is outside the Land [of Israel] and Ammon and Moab are outside the Land.
Just as Egypt [separates] poor tithe in the Seventh Year,
so Ammon and Moab [separate] poor tithe in the Seventh Year.
R. Eleazar b. Azariah replied:
Babylonia is outside the Land, and Ammon and Moab are outside the Land.
Just as Babylonia [separates] second tithe in the Seventh Year,
so Ammon and Moab [separate] second tithe in the Seventh Year.
R. Tarfon said:
Egypt, which is[14] close—
they made it [separate] poor tithe,
so the poor of Israel would rely upon it in the Seventh Year.
Similarly we should make Ammon and Moab, which are close, [separate] poor tithe,
so the poor of Israel would rely upon them in the Seventh Year.
R. Eleazar b. Azariah said to him:
Lo, you are like one who bestows money upon them,
but you are only like one who destroys souls.
You rob the heavens,
that dew and rain should not fall, as it is written:
Will a man rob God? Yet you rob Me!
And you say, How have we robbed you? With tithe and terumah![15]
R. Joshua said:
Lo, I am like one who replies to my brother Tarfon,
but not with regard to the topic of his words:

[13] **K**: "R. Tarfon." [14] **K, P**: "because it is."
[15] **P**: "he replied to R. Tarfon." **K**: "Replied R. Tarfon," which seems a scribal error but differs from **P** only in the added one-letter prefix "to" before the words "R. Tarfon."

I did not deviate from the order of the years: Second tithe is ordinarily given the year after that when poor tithe is given. Hence, if tithe must be separated in the Seventh Year, it ought to be second tithe, since poor tithe was separated in the sixth year.

Egypt [separates] poor tithe in the Seventh Year: By rabbinic decree, to help support the poor (see below).

Babylonia [separates] second tithe in the Seventh Year: By rabbinic decree.

the poor of Israel would rely upon it: Poor residents of the Land of Israel could use poor tithe from nearby Egypt.

Lo, you are like one who bestows money upon them, but you are only like one who destroys souls: While you bestow money upon the poor by giving them poor tithe, you harm the owners of produce by not having them fulfill their obligation properly by giving second tithe. As a result rain will not fall (see below), and all will suffer. It is not clear whether the destruction of souls refers to the spiritual damage of inducing farmers to withhold the proper tithe or to the deaths that will follow from the lack of rain.

Will a man rob God?... With tithe and terumah! Malachi 3:8. The text continues (3:10): *Bring all the tithe into the public storehouse... I will surely open the floodgates of the heavens for you and pour down blessings upon you*. By implication, there will not be rain if tithes are not brought.

Lo, I am like one who replies to my brother Tarfon, but not with regard to the topic of his words: I disagree with R. Tarfon's reasoning, but not with his actual ruling (viz., that Ammon and Moab separate poor tithe).

Egypt is a new act,
and Babylon is an old act,
and the case before us is a new act.
Let a new act be inferred from a new act,
and let a new act not be inferred from an old act.
Egypt is an act of the elders
and Babylon is an act of the prophets,
and the case before us is an act of the elders.
Let an act of the elders be inferred from an act of the elders,
and let an act of the elders not be inferred from an act of the prophets.
They voted and decided:
Ammon and Moab tithe poor tithe in the Seventh Year.
And when R. Yose son of the Damascene came to R. Eliezer in Lod,
he said to him:
What new thing did you have in the house of study today?
He said to him:
They voted and decided:
Ammon and Moab tithe poor tithe in the Seventh Year.
R. Eliezer cried and said:
The Lord's secret is for those who fear Him, and He reveals to them His covenant.
Go out and tell them:
Do not be concerned about your vote;
I have a tradition from R. Yohanan b. Zakkai,
who heard from his teacher,
and his teacher from his teacher,
back to a *halakhah* from Moses at Sinai,
that Ammon and Moab tithe poor tithe in the Seventh Year.

4 On that day Judah, an Ammonite convert,
came and stood before them in the house of study.
He said to them:
May I enter the congregation?
Rabban Gamaliel said to him:
You are prohibited.
R. Joshua said to him:
You are permitted.

Egypt is a new act: Its laws were decreed more recently than Babylonia's (by the elders of Temple times; see below).

R. Eliezer cried and said: The Lord's secret is for those who fear Him, and He reveals to them His covenant: Psalm 25:14. R. Eliezer presumably cried out of emotion because the Sages reached the correct decision—apparently, through some sort of divine inspiration—even though they lacked the tradition that he had.

Do not be concerned about your vote: Do not be concerned that your ruling, which was based on logical reasoning rather than tradition, might be incorrect.

back to a halakhah from Moses at Sinai: A rule based on ancient tradition. Commentators explain that this expression should not be taken literally, since the requirement to separate tithes in Ammon and Moab is of rabbinic origin.

4:4 *May I enter the congregation?* Am I permitted to marry a Jewish woman? (Precisely what prompted this question is not clear.)

Rabban Gamaliel said to him:
The verse says:
An Ammonite and a Moabite shall not enter the congregation of the Lord, even the tenth generation.
R. Joshua said to him:
And are the Ammonites and the Moabites in their [original] place?
Sennacherib king of Assyria has already arisen
and mixed up all the nations, as it is written:
I have erased the borders of the nations and I have plundered their treasures, and I have exiled their vast populations.
Rabban Gamaliel said to him:
The verse says:
And afterwards I shall return the captivity of the children of Ammon,
and they have already returned!
R. Joshua said to him:
The verse says:
I shall return the captivity of my people Israel and Judah,
and they have not returned yet.
They permitted [him] to enter the congregation.

4:5 *Hand Impurity Caused by Contact with Biblical Texts*

5 The Aramaic[16] in Ezra and in Daniel renders the hands impure.
Aramaic that was written in Hebrew
and Hebrew that was written in Aramaic

[16] Lit. "translation," here and throughout the paragraph.

An Ammonite and a Moabite shall not enter the congregation of the Lord: Deuteronomy 23:4.

R. Joshua said to him: And are the Ammonites and the Moabites in their [original] place? Since the original Ammonites and Moabites were dispersed among the nations (see below), the people living there now are not real Ammonites, so Jews may marry them.

I have erased the borders of the nations: Isaiah 10:13. Thus, the current inhabitants are not the original inhabitants.

And afterwards I shall return the captivity of the children of Ammon, and they have already returned! Jeremiah 49:6. This verse does not state that the Ammonite exiles will return "in the end of days," as we read in connection with other exiles (e.g. those from Moab; see Jeremiah 48:47). Hence we may infer that the Ammonite exiles had already returned to their original places.

The verse says, I shall return the captivity of my people Israel and Judah, and they have not returned yet: Amos 9:14. Here the words "I shall return" clearly describe a future event, and the same presumably applies to the verse describing the return of the Ammonite exiles.

4:5 Here the Mishnah resumes the discussion in 3:3–5 about impurity conveyed by biblical texts, which had been interrupted by a series of rulings issued "on that day" (4:1–4); cf. the notes on 4:1.

The Aramaic in Ezra and in Daniel renders the hands impure: The Aramaic parts of these books: Ezra 4:8–6:18, 7:12–26 and Daniel 2:4–7:28. This material renders the hands impure even though it was not written in Hebrew, since this is the original text of Scripture.

Aramaic that was written in Hebrew and Hebrew that was written in Aramaic... do not render the hands impure, since translated material is not the original text of scripture.

and Hebrew script
do not render the hands impure.
[The Bible] does not render [the hands] impure until he writes it in square script, on parchment, and with ink.

4:6–8 *Disputes between the Sadducees and the Pharisees*

6 The Sadducees say:
We complain against you, Pharisees, for you say:
Books of Holy Scripture render the hands impure,
and books of Homer do not render the hands impure.
R. Yohanan b. Zakkai said:
Do we have only this against the Pharisees?
Lo, they say:
The bones of a donkey are pure,
and the bones of Yohanan the High Priest are impure!
They said to him:
According to their preciousness is their impurity,
so a man will not make the bones of his father and his mother into spoons.
He said to them:
Similarly, books of Scripture—
according to their preciousness is their impurity,
and books of Homer,
which are not precious,
do not render the hands impure.
7 The Sadducees say:
We complain against you, Pharisees,

Hebrew script: Paleo-Hebrew script of the sort found in ancient coins and inscriptions (e.g. the Siloam and Moabite inscriptions). Such writing is unfit for ritual use, so biblical texts written in these characters do not render the hands impure.

square script: Lit. "Assyrian." The script of the Hebrew characters in current use.

on parchment, and with ink, since only biblical texts written this way are fit for ritual use.

4:6 *R. Yohanan b. Zakkai said: Do we only have this against the Pharisees?* R. Yohanan b. Zakkai's remarks were made sarcastically (or perhaps to shock his listeners or attract their attention), since he clearly adopts the Pharisaic position, as indicated below.

The bones of a donkey are pure, and the bones of Yohanan the High Priest are impure! The bones of animal carcasses are pure (donkeys were mentioned as an example), whereas human bones are not (again, the bones of Yohanan the High Priest were mentioned as an example).

According to their preciousness is their impurity, so a man will not make the bones of his father and his mother into spoons: This answer might not reflect R. Yohanan's real reasoning (see above on 3:2), and thus might have been offered to summarily dismiss the position of his Sadducean opponents.

4:7 *The Sadducees say: We complain against you, Pharisees*: The discussion here and in the next mishnah, which presents various disputes between the Sadducees and the Pharisees, does not deal with any of the main themes of the tractate. It was apparently cited here because of its formal similarity to the dispute between the Sadducees and the Pharisees appearing in the previous mishnah.

for you declare a liquid stream pure.
The Pharisees say:
We complain against you, Sadducees,
for you declare the stream of water that comes from a cemetery pure.
The Sadducees say:
We complain against you, Pharisees, for you say:
My ox and my donkey that caused damages are liable,
and my male slave and female slave who caused damages are exempt.
Now, if my ox and my donkey,
towards whom I do not have religious obligations—
in that case I am liable for their damages,
my male slave and female slave,
towards whom I do have religious obligations—
does not logic require that I should be liable for their damages?
[The Pharisees] said to [the Sadducees]:
No; if you say [this] about my ox and my donkey,
which have no understanding,
would you say [this] about my male slave and my female slave,
who do have understanding,
for if I anger him,
he will go and set someone else's stack of grain on fire,
and I will be obligated to pay!
8 A Galilean Sadducee[17] said:
I complain against you, Pharisees,

[17] So the printed editions; the manuscripts read "A Galilean heretic" here and below.

you declare a liquid stream pure: If a stream of liquid is poured from a pure utensil into an impure utensil, the Pharisees hold that the contents of the upper, pure utensil remain pure (cf. *Tohorot* 8:9, *Makhshirin* 5:9).

you declare the stream of water that comes from a cemetery pure: Thus, the Sadducees ostensibly agree that streaming liquid is not rendered impure by contact with something impure, as they consider such water pure even though it had passed through a cemetery, which is impure. However, the Pharisees apparently distinguished between these two cases, since liquids on the ground are not susceptible to impurity, as per Leviticus 11:36, in contrast to liquid streams that are not located on the ground, as discussed in the beginning of the mishnah.

My ox and my donkey that caused damages are liable: See Exodus 21:35–36. Donkeys are not mentioned in these verses, but the Mishnah apparently assumes that all animals that caused damages should be treated identically.

my male servant and female servant who caused damages are exempt: Their owners are exempt for damages that they caused (see further below).

My male servant and female servant, towards whom I do have religious obligations, such as circumcising male servants or making sure that one's male and female servants do not work on the Sabbath.

if I anger him, he will go and set someone else's stack of grain on fire, and I will be obligated to pay! Slaves' owners were exempted by rabbinic decree from liability for damages caused by their servants. Otherwise, angry slaves might decide to take revenge on their masters by causing damages for which the latter would have to pay.

for you write the [name of the] ruler
along with Moses in a bill of divorce!
The Pharisees say:
We complain against you, Galilean Sadducee,
for you write the [name of] the ruler
with the [Divine] name on the [same] page!
And not only that,
but you write the [name of the] ruler on top
and the [Divine] name below,[18] as it is written:
And Pharaoh said, Who is the Lord that I should listen to his voice and let Israel go?
And when he was stricken, what did he say?
The Lord is the righteous One.

[18] **K**: "you write [the name of] God on top and the ruler below."

4:8 *you write the [name of the] ruler along with Moses in a bill of divorce!* Bills of divorce are dated according to the reign of the secular king ("during the *n*th year of King X"). Hence the ruler's name appears there, as does Moses', since a bill of divorce ordinarily states that it was executed "according to the law of Moses and Israel." Such mention of the secular ruler's name along with Moses' might seem demeaning to Moses.

for you write the [name of] the ruler with the [Divine] name on the [same] page of the Torah, in the biblical verse cited below (Exodus 5:2), where Pharaoh and Moses are mentioned together.

And not only that, but you write the [name of the] ruler on top and the [Divine] name below: Pharaoh's name appears before God's in the verse cited.

And when he was stricken, what did he say? The Lord is the righteous One: This statement is not an integral part of the discussion. It is presumably a later addition, included to end the tractate on a positive note ("The Lord is the righteous One"), instead of the negative note sounded in the previous sentence ("Who is the Lord that I should listen to his voice?").

Tractate Uqtsin

Richard Hidary

Introduction

Overview

The name of this tractate can be vocalized either as *uqtsin* or *oqatsin* and is the plural of *uqats* or *oqets*, meaning the stem of a fruit or vegetable. The tractate discusses various nonedible parts of foods; stems are a representative example and form the subject of mishnah 1:6. The subject of this tractate was considered obscure even in Talmudic times.

Structure and Organization of the Tractate

Mishnayot 1:1–2:8 legislate the impurity status of parts of food that are not themselves edible; examples include stems, roots, rinds, shells, pits, and bones. Mishnah 1:1 establishes the fundamental criteria for judging these items, and the subsequent mishnayot provide examples.

The rest of the tractate, 2:9–3:11, deals with whether or not various food items are susceptible to contracting food impurity. In order for something to contract impurity it must be disconnected from the ground, be recognized as edible to humans, and must have become wet. This half of the tractate includes legislation regarding plant containers (2:9–10), animal carcasses (3:1–3, 9), spices (3:4–5), and beehives (3:10–11). The tractate concludes (3:12) with homiletic teachings about reward for the righteous and the value of peace.

Main Ideas

In order for food to become impure when it touches a source of impurity such as a dead rodent or other impure food, it must first be susceptible to contracting impurity by three criteria:

(1) It must be something regularly eaten by humans. For example, the carcasses of nonkosher animals are not generally eaten even by non-Jews and therefore cannot contract impurity. If, however, someone has the specific intention to eat such a food, then it is considered human food and becomes susceptible to impurity.

A part of a food that is not itself edible would also not be susceptible to contracting impurity unless it serves either as a handle or as a protectant to the edible portion. For example, if something impure touches the stem of a pear then the flesh of the pear also becomes impure and vice versa (1:1).

Something that serves to protect the edible part of the food, such as the rind of a fruit, not only transfers impurity—just as a handle does—but also joins together with the edible part when measuring its volume (see *Tohorot* 2:1).

(2) Anything that grows must first be severed from the ground in order to be susceptible to impurity. In contrast, a vegetable that was cut or one growing inside a container that has no connection to the ground would be susceptible to impurity.

(3) Food is only susceptible to contracting impurity if it is first intentionally wet with one of seven liquids designated at *Makhshirin* 6:4: dew, water, wine, oil, blood, milk, and bees' honey.

These basic principles of food impurity already appear in other tractates, especially *Tohorot*, *Makhshirin*, and *Tevul Yom*. *Uqtsin* adds little to these principles but does lay out some of these rules with greater clarity; it also adds significant details regarding their application.

Relationship to Scripture

The main topic of this tractate—the status of stems, peels, and pits—is not raised in the Bible. However, purity law in general and some of the other laws discussed in this tractate do have a basis in the Bible. For example, the requirement for food to become wet in order to become susceptible to contracting impurity derives from Leviticus 11:34, 38, and the law that the corpses of animals impart impurity is learned from Leviticus 11:24–28, 39–40. The Sifra and the Talmud midrashically derive the laws of handles and protectants from these verses.

Special Notes for the Reader

In addition to manuscripts Kaufmann A 50 (**K**) and Parma 3173 (**P**), the notes also refer to manuscripts Parma 2596 ($\mathbf{P}_2$), Munich 95 (**M**), Cambridge Add. 470 (**C**), and Geniza fragments Cambridge T-S E1.151-153 ($\mathbf{G}_1$), Oxford MS heb. c. 17/43 and Friedberg MSS 9-001 published partially by P. Kahle in *Hebrew Union College Annual* 12–13 (1937–1938), 322–25, and fully by Y. Yevin, *Collection of Mishnaic Geniza Fragments With Babylonian Vocalization* (Hebrew) (Jerusalem: Makor, 1974) ($\mathbf{G}_2$), JTS ENA 1487.42-44 ($\mathbf{G}_3$), CUL T-S NS 330.3 ($\mathbf{G}_4$), CUK T-S NS 329.344 ($\mathbf{G}_5$), CUL T-S AS 81.101 ($\mathbf{G}_6$), CUL T-S NS 215.29 ($\mathbf{G}_7$), ENA 3057.2 ($\mathbf{G}_8$), and CUL T-S NS 215.59 ($\mathbf{G}_9$). This translation notes only major variants.

Tractate Uqtsin

Chapter One

1:1–2:4 *Handles and Protectants*

1 Anything that is a handle
but not a protectant
contracts impurity and imparts impurity
but does not join.
If it is a protectant,
even if is not a handle,
it contracts impurity and imparts impurity and joins.
If it is neither a protectant nor a handle,
it neither contracts impurity nor causes impurity.
2 The roots of garlic, onions and leeks that are moist,[1]
and their top part, whether moist or dry,
the central shoot aligned with the bulb,[2]
the roots of lettuce, the radish, and the rape—[3]
the words of R. Meir;
R. Judah says:
The large root of a radish joins,
but its fibrous roots do not join,
the roots of mint and rue, wild herbs and garden herbs

[1] C begins with "These impart impurity, contract impurity but do not join."
[2] Lit. "the edible [part]."
[3] G_1 adds "do not join." Commentators vary in translating the term here rendered "rape."

1:1 *handle*: Anything that is used to hold food but is not itself edible, such as the stem of a fruit.

protectant: Such as the nonedible rind of a fruit or anything that keeps the fruit fresh.

contracts impurity: If the edible part of the food becomes impure then so does the handle.

imparts impurity: If the handle becomes impure then so does the edible part of the food.

join: Food must have a minimum volume equivalent to an egg in order to impart impurity (*Tohorot* 2:1). A handle that does not protect does not join together with the food when measuring its volume. However, a part of the fruit that protects its edible part does join together with the edible part to make up the volume of an egg such that the combination can impart impurity to another food item.

1:2 *the central shoot aligned with the bulb*: As opposed to the smaller offshoots that grow from it.

that were uprooted in order to be replanted,
the spine of grain and its husk:
R. Eleazar[4] says:
Even the cobweb-like growth,
all these impart impurity, contract impurity, and join.[5]

3 These impart impurity and contract impurity but do not[6] join:
the roots of onions, garlic, and leeks that are dry,
the part of the shoot that is not aligned with the bulb,
and the handle of a vine[7] one handbreadth on either side,
the handle of a grape cluster any amount,
and the tail of a grape cluster that was stripped,
and the handle of the broom-shaped stems of a date palm for four handbreadths,
and the stalk of grain for three handbreadths,
and the handle of anything that is cut for three handbreadths;
but[8] for plants that are not usually cut,
their handles and their roots any amount,
and the outer husks of grain:
all these impart impurity and contract impurity
but do not[9] join.

4 These do not impart impurity nor contract impurity nor join:
the roots of cabbage heads,
and shoots of beets and turnips,
and anything that is normally chopped off but is instead uprooted.

[4] G_3: "Eliezer." [5] C: "do not join." [6] C lacks "do not." [7] G_1 inserts "and."
[8] G_3 lacks any conjunction here. [9] C lacks "do not."

uprooted in order to be replanted: Since one intends for them to be replanted, their roots are necessary for their preservation.

the spine of grain: The stem to which the grain kernels are attached to form a spike.

cobweb-like growth: This may refer to a powder-like layer that grows on the leaves of some plants.

1:3 *the handle of a vine*: The twig from which the cluster of grapes hangs is considered a handle to the grapes for the length of one handbreadth on either side of the place where the cluster attaches to the twig.

the handle of a grape cluster: The stem to which the grapes are attached serves as a handle, no matter how long it is.

the tail of a grape cluster that was stripped: If the grapes from part of the stem have been removed, that stem—no matter how long it is—serves as a handle for the part of the stem that still has grapes attached to it.

the handle…four handbreadths: The twig from which the stems of the dates grow serves as a handle to the dates for a length of four handbreadths.

the handle of anything that is cut with a sickle.

outer husks of grain: Commentators explain that this refers to the awn or hair-like bristles that grow from an ear of grain.

1:4 *cabbage*: Others identify this with kale or kohlrabi.

shoots of beets: These are normally left in the ground in order to sprout again the next year.

anything…instead uprooted: If the roots are normally chopped off and left in the ground, then even if one happens to uproot the entire plant without cutting off the roots, those roots are considered neither handles nor protectants to the vegetable.

R. Yose deems all of them to be susceptible to impurity,
but he deems pure the roots of cabbage stalks and the turnips.

5 All handles of food that were threshed on the threshing floor are not susceptible to impurity.
R. Yose deems [them] susceptible to impurity.
The sprig of a grape cluster that was stripped is not susceptible to impurity.
If one left a single grape then it is susceptible to impurity.
The sprig of a date palm that was stripped is not susceptible to impurity.
If one left a single date then it is susceptible to impurity.
And likewise regarding legumes:
a pod that was stripped is not susceptible to impurity.[10]
If one left a single bean then it is susceptible to impurity.
R. Eleazar[11] b. Azariah deems the pods of beans insusceptible to impurity
but deems pods of other legumes susceptible to impurity
because one wants to use them.

6 The stalks of figs, dried figs, acorns, and carobs,
all these impart impurity, contract impurity, and join.
R. Yose says:
Also the stalk of a gourd.
The stalks of pears, pippins, quinces, and hawthorns,
the stalk of a gourd[12] up to one handbreadth,

[10] **G**$_3$ lacks this and the previous two lines: "If one…impurity" due to homeoteleuton.
[11] **G**$_3$: "Eliezer."
[12] **G**$_3$ lacks from "The stalks" on the previous line until "gourd" due to homeoteleuton.

R. Yose opines that such roots, although normally cut off, are considered handles if left attached except for the roots of cabbages and turnips, which are not usable as handles.

1:5 *threshed*: One opinion in the Talmud says that the grain in this case is fully threshed while another opinion says it is only untied from its bundles.

not susceptible to impurity: Since the stems are crushed and loosened from the grain, they are no longer usable as handles and therefore cannot become impure as part of the food.

R. Yose opines that the stems are still usable as handles when overturning the grain with a pitchfork.

stripped: Once the edible fruit is detached from the sprig, the sprig can no longer serve as a handle and therefore is not susceptible to impurity.

R. Eleazar b. Azariah rules that the pods of beans are not susceptible to impurity even when they contain beans since the beans are large enough to be handled without the pod. The pods of smaller legumes, however, are susceptible to impurity because they do help with the handling of their contents.

1:6 *acorns*: Commentators identify this variously with a type of dried fig, a type of bean, fruit of the Judas tree, locust fruits, or *Prosopis stephaniana*.

the stalks of pears…hawthorns: Some read this line as a continuation of the words of R. Yose. The punctuation here follows others who read it as part of the next category of items that do not join. The latter reading is also indicated in **P**$_2$, which includes a pausal cantillation sign on the word "gourd."

pippins: Others identify this with crustumina.

hawthorns: Other commentators identify this with crabapples, sorb apples, or medlars.

one handbreadth: This measurement is only mentioned regarding the stalks of gourds and artichokes since the stalks of the other fruits are in any case shorter than a handbreadth.

the stalk of an artichoke up to one handbreadth—
R. Eleazar[13] b. R. Zadok says:
Two handbreadths—
all these impart impurity and contract impurity but do not join.
Stalks of all other fruits neither impart impurity nor contract impurity.

Chapter Two

2 If one pickled olives with their leaves, [the latter] are not susceptible to impurity because one only pickled them for their appearance.
The fine hair on cucumbers
and their blossoms
are not susceptible to impurity.
R. Judah says:
As long as it lies before the merchant
it is susceptible to impurity.

2 All fruit pits contract impurity and impart impurity
but do not join.
The pit of a fresh date,
even if it protrudes,
joins.
The pit of a dried date does not join.
Therefore, the membrane surrounding the pit[14] of a dried[15] date joins,
but the membrane surrounding the pit of a fresh date does not join.[16]

[13] **G_3**: "Eliezer." [14] that is, a stone; **P**, **G_2**, **G_9**: "seal." See annotations.
[15] **G_1** lacks from the previous "dried" to "dried" here due to homeoteleuton.
[16] **C** lacks from the previous "but" to here, probably due to homeoteleuton.

2:1 *fine hair…blossoms*: These do not serve as a handle nor as a protectant.

the merchant: The fine hair and blossoms keep the vegetables looking fresh and therefore more tempting to buyers. They are therefore considered protectants while in the hands of the merchant.

2:2 *fruit pits* serve as handles since it is easier to grip a fruit with a pit or stone inside without crushing it. They do not, however, serve as protectants and therefore do not combine with volume of the rest of the fruit.

fresh date: The pit helps to preserve the date's freshness by keeping in its moisture. Since it acts as a protectant, the pit also joins with the rest of the date when measuring its volume. Alternatively, the pit is itself considered food because one can suck on it.

a dried date does not require the pit to keep from spoiling and it therefore does not act as a protectant. Alternatively, the pit is not considered food because it has no juice on it, similar to pits of other fruits.

membrane surrounding the pit: Since it is the pit itself that preserves the moisture in a fresh date, the layer of skin surrounding the pit is unnecessary for it to keep its freshness. However, a dried date, which does not require the pit to keep it from spoiling, does need at least this layer of skin. Since this layer of skin is a protectant to the dried date, it joins with the rest of the date when measuring its volume.

Others read "seal" and explain that it refers to the stem, which seals in the pit. According to this reading, the seal of a dried date holds in the pit and thereby serves as a protectant. However, with a fresh date, the pit itself is edible because one can suck the juice from it and so the pit does not need the protection of the stem.

If a pit is partially protruding,
whatever is within the edible part of the fruit joins.
If a bone has meat on it,
that part of the bone covered by[17] meat[18] joins.
If there is only meat on one side of the bone,
R. Ishmael says:
One considers it as if [the meat] surrounds [the bone] in a ring.
But the Sages say:
Whatever is covered by [the meat] joins
[as with], for example, savory, hyssop, and thyme.

3 If a pomegranate or watermelon became partially rotten,
that part does not join.
If it is good[19] on both sides
but rotten in the middle,
it does not join.
The top part of a pomegranate joins.
Its blossoms do not join.
R. Eleazar[20] says:
The comb is also[21] not susceptible to impurity.

[17] Or "close to," here and below.
[18] Lit. "food," here and below.
[19] **C** erroneously adds "rotten."
[20] $\mathbf{G}_3$: "Eliezer."
[21] $\mathbf{G}_1$ lacks "also."

partially protruding: This line qualifies the previous: only the section of the pit within the date joins but not the part of the pit that protrudes. Alternatively, only in the case of a fresh date do we join the volume of the entire pit, even if it is protruding, since it can be sucked on; however, regarding other fruits, the part of the pit that protrudes does not join.

a bone is considered a protectant to the meat surrounding it. However, the part of the bone without meat on it serves only as a handle, not as a protectant.

one side of the bone: If the meat does not surround the entire circumference of the bone then, according to R. Ishmael, if the meat on one side of the bone is sufficiently thick, we consider it as if the bone is entirely encompassed by the meat.

covered by [the meat]: The Sages say that only the top layer of the bone directly under the meat joins but not the rest of the width of the bone.

savory, hyssop, and thyme: These three herbs have an edible part only on one side of their stem. Just like the meat on one side of the bone, only the part of the stem directly under the edible part serves as a protectant and joins when measuring its volume.

2:3 *partially rotten*: The rotten part does not serve as a protectant to the good part and therefore does not join when measuring its volume.

good on both sides: The two good sides do not join each other to make up the volume necessary to impart impurity.

the top part: The bulge on the blossom end of the pomegranate protects its edible part and therefore joins when measuring its volume.

blossoms: Actually blossom-like fibers growing from that bulge. These do not serve as a protectant and therefore do not join, but they do serve as a handle and are therefore susceptible to impurity.

comb: The calyx at the top of the pomegranate, whose teeth resemble that of a comb, serve as neither a handle nor a protectant and therefore would not become impure with the rest of the fruit.

4 All peels contract impurity, impart impurity, and join.
R. Judah says:
There are three [layers of] peel on an onion:
the innermost,
whether whole or perforated,
joins;
the middle joins when it is whole
but does not join when it is perforated;
and the outermost
in either case
is not susceptible to impurity.

2:5–6 *Connections between Parts of Food*

5 If one chops up food in preparation for cooking,
even if he did not sever [the pieces] completely,
they are not [considered] connected.
[In preparation for] pickling or boiling
or to put out on the table,
they are [considered] connected.
If he began to separate the pieces,
then the food with which he began is not[22] [considered] connected.
Nuts that were strung together
or onions that were piled together:
these are [considered] connected.
If he began to separate the nuts or strip the onions,
they are not [considered] connected.
[The shells of] nuts and almonds

[22] **G_3** lacks "not."

2:4 *peels*: Skins, rinds, husks, and shells of fruits, nuts, and eggs all serve as protectants.

the innermost layer is the edible portion of the onion.

the middle layer serves as a protectant if it is whole but serves only as a handle if it is perforated.

the outermost layer of skin that easily falls off does not even serve as a handle.

2:5 *for cooking*: Since one does not want the pieces to be attached and they will in any case become separated while cooking, it is considered as if they are separated; if one piece becomes impure the other pieces do not contract that impurity.

pickling, etc.: In this case one does want the pieces to remain attached to make them easier to handle. Therefore, impurity would transfer from one to the next.

began to separate: Those pieces which have been separated are obviously no longer connected, but it is impossible to tell how much he intends to separate and how much he intends to leave connected. Therefore, the commentators differ. According to some, we assume he intends to continue the process, and even the pieces that remain connected are already considered as if they were separated. According to other interpreters, only those items which he has begun to take apart are considered entirely separated; the rest remain connected.

strung together by their stems.

piled: Onions would be gathered and tied together for storage.

are [considered] connected
until they are crushed.

6 [The shell of a part-]roasted[23] egg [is considered connected]
until it is chipped.
[The shell of] a hardboiled egg [is considered connected]
until it is [completely] crushed.
A bone that has marrow[24] [is considered connected]
until it is [completely] crushed.
A pomegranate that was split is [considered] connected
until one smacks it with a stick.
Similarly,
the [loose] stitching of the launderers
and a garment that is stitched with mixed threads
[are considered connected] until one begins to undo them.

2:7–8 *Measuring Volume of Leaves*

7 The leaves of vegetables:
green [ones] join;
white ones do not join.

[23] Alt. "part-cooked." [24] **C** lacks "marrow."

crushed: Even if the shell of a nut is cracked, it is still serves as a protectant and is therefore considered connected until it becomes completely crushed.

2:6 *roasted*: Rolled in ashes until slightly cooked but still liquid inside.

chipped: People can break a hole in the shell and drink the contents of the egg. Once the shell is perforated, it no longer acts as a protectant to its contents and therefore is no longer considered attached for the purposes of transferring impurity.

hardboiled: Even a broken shell can still protect what is under it but not if the shell is completely shattered.

bone: The bone, even if it is broken, protects the marrow as long as the bone is not completely shattered.

pomegranate: The rind of a pomegranate is considered a protectant to its edible seeds and therefore connected for the purpose of transferring impurity. However, hitting the rind in order to dislodge the seeds reveals one's intention that the rind should no longer be a protectant but only a vessel to hold the seeds; therefore the rind is not connected for the purpose of transferring impurity.

launderers used to tie garments together in order that they not get lost or mixed with other people's garments. Since these ties are meant to be undone, once one begins to untie them, they are all considered as if already disconnected.

mixed threads: Deuteronomy 22:11 prohibits wearing a garment woven with threads from wool and linen. If woolen garments are woven together with linen thread, for example, they are considered connected for the purpose of transferring impurity until one begins to separate them.

2:7 *leaves of vegetables* are edible when fresh and therefore join with the rest of the vegetable when measuring its volume.

white: Once the leaves have withered they are no longer edible.

R. Eleazar[25] b. Zadok says:
White ones join in [the case of] cabbage
because they are edible,
and in [the case of] lettuce
because they[26] protect the edible part.

8 The leaves of onions and the shoots of onions:
if they have sap in them,
they are measured as they are;
if they have empty space in them,
one compresses their empty space.
Spongy bread is measured as it is.
If it has empty space in it,
one compresses its empty space.
Meat of a calf that expanded or
meat of an old animal that shrank
are measured as they are.

2:9–10 *Plant Containers*

9 A cucumber that one planted in a container
and that grew
and extended beyond the container
is not susceptible to impurity.
R. Simeon says:
What is in its character that would make it insusceptible to impurity?
Rather,
the impure part remains in its impurity
and the pure part can be eaten.

[25] G_3: "Eliezer." [26] G_2 erroneously adds "do not."

cabbage: Others identify this with kale or kohlrabi. Its leaves are edible even when withered.

2:8 This mishnah explains how to measure the volume of foods to see if they make up the bulk of an egg and are therefore able to impart impurity.

expanded: Calf meat usually expands while cooking while meat from an older animal generally shrinks while cooking.

as they are: After they are cooked.

2:9 *container*: Any vegetable that is still attached to the ground does not contract impurity. However, if it grows in a container that has no hole on its bottom, it is not connected to the ground and therefore can contract impurity.

extended: If the cucumber plant reaches beyond the container and implants itself in the ground, then it is considered connected to the ground and the entire plant becomes pure and not susceptible to impurity.

in its character: The part of the plant within the container does not change its character but rather remains potentially impure.

10 Vessels made from dung
and vessels made from earth
through which roots can emerge
do not render the seeds susceptible to impurity.
A perforated container does not render the seeds susceptible to impurity.
A nonperforated container does render the seeds susceptible to impurity.
What is the measure of the hole?
So that a small root emerges through it.
If one fills [a container] with soil up to its brim,
then it is like a board that has no rim.

Chapter Three

3:1–9 *Preparation and Intention*

3 Some [foods] require preparation but not intention,
intention and preparation,
intention but not preparation,
neither preparation nor intention.
All foods designated as edible to humans
require preparation but do not require intention.
2 One who cuts [live flesh] from a human,
or from a domesticated animal,

2:10 *earth*: Unbaked clay.

do not render the seeds: Do not allow the seeds to become susceptible to impurity if they are wet. Since the vessel can be penetrated by the roots, it is considered part of the ground and so water that falls into the pot is considered connected to the ground.

perforated container: Since soil in the container touches the ground directly, any water in the container is considered connected to the ground and therefore does not prepare the plant to receive impurity.

What is the measure…? That is, what is the minimum size of such a hole?

like a board: *Kelim* 2:3 teaches that a flat board with no rim is not considered a receptacle and therefore cannot contract impurity. A container that is completely filled with soil has the same status because it has no inner space. Therefore, water that falls into this container is considered connected to the ground.

3:1 *preparation*: Moistening that will render them susceptible to impurity.

intention: Intention to use as human food.

designated as edible: Food items that are regularly used for human consumption need not have specific intention to be eaten by humans.

3:2 Foods that require intention and preparation to become susceptible.

flesh from a live being is not generally eaten and therefore requires specific intention to be eaten by somebody. Since a live being is pure, a piece cut from it is also pure and therefore requires preparation by becoming wet in order to be susceptible to contracting impurity.

or from a wild animal,
or from live birds,
or from the carcass of an impure bird,
and the fat in villages,
and all other field vegetables
except for[27] truffles and mushrooms—
R. Judah says:
Except for[28] wild leeks, purslane, and asphodel;
R Simeon says:
Except for cardoon;
R. Yose says:
Except for acorns[29]—
all these require intention and preparation.

3 The carcass of an impure animal in all places
and the carcass of a pure bird[30] in villages
require intention but do not require preparation.[31]
The carcass of a pure[32] animal in all places
and the carcass of a pure[33] bird and fat

[27] **K, M, P, P$_2$,** and **C** lack "except for." [28] **P$_2$** erroneously omits "except."
[29] **K, P, P$_2$, C, G$_2$, G$_3$** have a slightly different spelling that may refer to the Tassel Hyacinth, a type of fig for cooking, or a type of onion.
[30] **M** and **G$_2$** add "and the fat." [31] **G$_2$** lacks "but do not require preparation."
[32] **G$_2$** reads "impure." [33] **G$_2$** reads "impure," and the continuation of the line is corrupt.

impure bird: Those listed in Leviticus 11:13–19 as prohibited. Impure birds are not sources of impurity in themselves (see *Tohorot* 1:3) and therefore require preparation. They are not generally eaten in villages where there are fewer people and therefore require intention.

fat: The forbidden fat of pure animals, which remains pure even if the animal dies on its own (*Uqtsin* 3:9).

field vegetables that grow on their own are not generally eaten by humans.

truffles and mushrooms are generally eaten by humans and therefore do not require specific intention. According to manuscripts which omit "except for," truffles and mushrooms are also not generally eaten by humans and require intention.

cardoon: Others identify this with *Gundelia tournefortii.*

3:3 Items belonging in the third and fourth categories of 3:1.

carcass: An animal that died without ritual slaughter.

The carcass of an impure animal is itself a source of impurity as per Leviticus 11:24–28 and so does not require preparation by becoming wet. Such carcasses are not generally eaten anywhere and therefore require specific intention to be eaten in order to be considered human food.

the carcass of a pure bird that was not ritually slaughtered is itself a source of impurity (see *Tohorot* 1:1). Since this is not regularly eaten in villages, it requires intention in such locations.

The carcass of a pure animal that was not ritually slaughtered is itself a source of impurity as per Leviticus 11:39–40 and therefore does not require preparation to contract impurity by becoming wet. It is also regularly eaten by non-Jews and so does not require intention.

fat: This refers to fat of a ritually slaughtered pure animal, which is prepared to receive impurity by becoming wet from its own blood at the time of slaughter.

in the marketplace
require neither intention nor preparation.
R. Simeon says:
Also the camel, the hare, the daman, and the pig.

3:4–8 *What is Considered Food?*

4 Once dill has given over its flavor into a pot,
it is no longer considered *terumah*
nor does it contract[34] food impurity.
The sprouts of the service tree and of cress and the leaves of the wild ginger
do not contract[35] food impurity
unless they are sweetened.
R. Simeon says:
Also the leaves of colocynth.

5 Costus, and amomum, and the principal spices, crowfoot and asafetida, and pepper, and lozenges of saffron
may be bought with tithe money
but do not contract[36] food impurity—
the words of R. Aqiva.
R. Yohanan b. Nuri said to him:[37]
If they may be bought with tithe money,

[34] **K**, **P**, **P_2**, **C**, **G_1**, **G_4**: "impart." [35] **K**, **P**, **P_2**, **C**, **G_1**, **G_2**, **G_4**: "impart." [36] **P_2**, **C**, **G_1**, **G_4**: "impart."
[37] **K**, **P**, and **M** lack "to him."

in the marketplace there are many more people, some of whom would normally eat a carcass of such a bird and animal fat.

camel, etc.: These impure animals are also regularly eaten and therefore do not require intention. A parallel tradition records a different version of this statement: "R. Simeon b. Yokhai says, the camel, the hare, the daman, and the pig require intention in all places."

3:4 *dill* that has been cooked until it has no flavor left in it is no longer considered food.

terumah: This flavorless dill is no longer considered food and therefore may be eaten by a nonpriest.

contract food impurity: Since it is no longer food, it does not contract (or according to the reading in the manuscripts, convey) impurity as food normally would.

service tree: Others identify this as a hawthorn or sorb tree.

cress: Others identify this as candytuft or a vegetable similar to a radish.

wild ginger: Others identify this as arum, *Scolopendrium hemionitis*, serpentaria, or a type of onion.

sweetened: These leaves are normally bitter and not edible on their own. Once they are pickled, however, they do become edible and hence susceptible to food impurity.

3:5 *tithe money*: Money that redeemed second-tithe produce that would be used to buy food in Jerusalem (see *Ma'aser Sheni*). Even though these various spices are not edible on their own, they may be bought with tithe money because they enhance the taste of food.

If they may be bought with tithe money: R. Yohanan b. Nuri challenges R. Aqiva to be consistent. Either these spices are considered food and one should therefore be able to buy them with tithe money and they should be able to contract food impurity or they are not considered food and neither of these laws should apply.

why do they not contract[38] food impurity?
And if they do not contract[39] food impurity,
they should not be bought with tithe money.

6 Unripe figs and unripe grapes:
R. Aqiva deems them susceptible to food impurity;
R. Yohanan b. Nuri says:
When they reach the season for tithes.
Hardened olives and grapes:
the House of Shammai deem [them] susceptible to impurity
and the House of Hillel deem [them] not susceptible to impurity.
Black cumin:
the House of Shammai deem [it] not susceptible to impurity
and the House of Hillel deem [it] susceptible to impurity.
And likewise for tithes.

7 Heart of palm is like wood in every respect
except that it may be bought with tithe money.
Unripe dates[40] are [considered] food,
but they are exempt from tithes.[41]

8 From when do fish contract impurity?
The House of Shammai say:
From when they are caught.
The House of Hillel say:
From when they die.
R. Aqiva says:

[38] **K, P, P_2, C, G_1, G_4**: "impart." [39] **K, P_2, C, G_1, G_4**: "impart." [40] Alt. "date blossoms."
[41] **K** and **P** place this entire mishnah after 3:8. **G_2** and **G_4** lack this mishnah entirely; **G_6** also does not record this mishnah at this point, but the fragment stops here and may have contained the text in the lost continuation.

3:6 *R Aqiva* thinks that unripe figs and grapes are still edible and therefore susceptible to food impurity.

season for tithes: Produce is liable to tithing when it begins to ripen (*Ma'aserot* 1:2).

Hardened olives that became dry and hard before they got a chance to ripen. The House of Shammai opine that they are nevertheless edible.

tithes: Any item that is not edible and not susceptible to impurity is also not obligated in tithes and may not be purchased with tithe money. Any item that is edible and susceptible to impurity will also be obligated in tithes and one may purchase them with tithe money.

3:7 *Heart of palm* is edible while soft but not edible in the winter when it hardens.

like wood: It is not considered edible and so is not susceptible to food impurity.

tithe money: Heart of palm is may be bought with tithe money even though it is not considered food.

Unripe dates are [considered] food and are therefore susceptible to food impurity and can be bought with tithe money.

tithes: Unripe dates are not subject to tithing because one must take tithes from produce only when it begins to ripen.

3:8 *caught*: Live fish cannot contract impurity. However, according the House of Shammai, once the fish is caught it is already considered dead with regard to its ability to contract impurity.

If they can survive.
A fig branch that was broken
but still attached by its bark:
R. Judah deems it insusceptible to impurity;
but the Sages say:
If it can survive.
Grain that was uprooted but still attached,
even if only by a small root,
is not susceptible to impurity.

9 The fat[42] of a pure animal does not contract[43] carcass impurity;
therefore, it requires preparation.
The fat of an impure animal does contract[44] carcass impurity;
therefore,[45] it does not require preparation.
Impure fish and impure locusts require intention in the villages.

3:10–11 *Beehives*

10 A beehive:
R. Eliezer[46] says:
It is like land,

[42] Var. "milk," an apparent error. [43] **K, P, P_2, C**: "impart." [44] **P, P_2**: "impart."
[45] **K** and **G_4** lack from the previous "therefore" until "therefore" here.
[46] **G_2**: "Eleazar."

If they can survive: As long as the fish can survive if put back in the water, it is not susceptible to impurity. Once it can no longer survive, even if not yet dead, it is susceptible to impurity.

R. Judah considers this hanging branch as still connected to the tree.

the Sages consider it still attached only if it could bear fruit if reattached to the tree.

a small root is sufficient for the grain's survival and is therefore considered connected to the ground.

3:9 See 3:1–3, above.

fat: See above, 3:3.

requires preparation: Since the fat remains pure when the animal dies, it cannot contract impurity until becoming wet.

does not require preparation: Since the fat is already impure with carcass impurity, there is no need for it to be prepared by becoming wet.

Impure fish and impure locusts: Prohibited (nonkosher). These are not generally eaten in the villages and are therefore not considered food that is susceptible to impurity unless someone intends to eat them.

3:10 This mishnah is repeated in *Shevi'it* 10:7.

like land: One acquires a beehive using the same procedures as one acquires land. These procedures are listed at *Qiddushin* 1:5.

and one may use it [as security] when writing a *prozbul*,
and it does not contract impurity [as long as it remains] in its own place,
and one who scrapes honey from it on the Sabbath is liable [to bring] a purgation offering.[47]
But the Sages say:
It is not like land,
and one may not use it [as security] when writing a *prozbul*,
and[48] it can contract impurity [even if it remains] in its own place,
and one who removes honey from it on the Sabbath is exempt.

11 From when do honeycombs contract[49] impurity as a liquid?
The House of Shammai say:
Once the bees are smoked out from it.
The House of Hillel say:
Once the honeycombs are chopped.

3:12 *Conclusion*

12 R. Joshua b. Levi said:
The Holy One, blessed be He, will bestow to each and every righteous person three hundred and ten worlds,
as it is said:
I endow those who love me with substance and I will fill their treasuries.
R. Simeon b. Halafta said:
The Holy One, blessed be He, could find[50] no vessel to contain blessing for[51] Israel except for peace,
as it is said:
May the Lord give strength to his people; may the Lord bless his people with peace.[52]

47 **K, P, P_2, C, G_1, G_2, G_5** lack "a purgation offering" 48 **G_2** adds "but."
49 **K, M, C, G_2**: "impart." 50 **K, P, P_2, G_2, G_7** replace "The Holy... find" with "There is no."
51 **K** and **P** lack "Israel." **P_2** and **G_2** instead of "Israel" have "and goodness for the world."
52 This entire mishnah is lacking in **M** and **C** and may be a later addition. **G_7** and **G_8**, which are not Mishnah manuscripts but liturgical documents, repeat this mishnah as part of a prayer service and without any connection to the tractate.

A *prozbul* is a document that allows one to extend his debts beyond the Seventh Year. In order for the *prozbul* to be valid, the debtor must own a piece of land that could be used as security against the loan.

removes honey: Since the beehive is considered to be connected to the ground, removing honey from it is equivalent to plucking a vegetable from the ground, which is prohibited on the Sabbath.

3:11 *liquid*: A honeycomb itself is considered a solid while honey is considered a liquid (*Makhshirin* 6:4). Since the laws of impurity for liquids are more stringent than those for solids, the Mishnah inquires about exactly when the honey acquires the status of a liquid.

smoked out: Others interpret the House of Shammai to rule that the honeycomb is considered liquid once it is heated in order to melt the honey.

3:12 *I endow*: Proverbs 8:21.

substance: Heb. *yesh* has the numerical value of 310.

May the Lord: Psalms 29:11.

Appendix: Money, Weights, and Measures

Reprinted from Herbert Danby, *The Mishnah: Translated from the Hebrew with Introduction and Brief Explanatory Notes* (Oxford: Oxford University Press, 1963).

A. Money

1 *perutah* (the smallest copper coin).

8 *perutah*—1 *issar.*

2 *issar*—1 pondion.

2 *pondion*—1 *ma'ah* (the smallest silver coin current. It is sometimes referred to simply as 'a piece of silver'; *Bava Metsi'a* 4:3. Its weight is given as 16 barleycorns).

3 *issar*—1 *teresit* (*Shevu'ot* 6:3).

12 *pondion*—1 *dinar* or *zuz.*

6 *ma'ah*—1 *dinar* or *zuz.*

5 *asper*—1 *dinar* or *zuz* (*Eduyot* 1:10; *Ma'aser Sheni* 2:9).

2 tr*opaic*—1 *dinar* or *zuz.*

2 *dinar*—1 *sheqel.*

2 *sheqel*—1 *sela.*

25 *dinar*—1 gold *dinar* or *zahuv.*

100 *dinar*—1 *mina.*

For the purchasing power of money at the time of the Mishnah, cf. *Bava Batra* 5:1 (a yoke of oxen), *Bava Metsi'a* 5:1 (price of wheat), *Bava Metsi'a* 5:2 (rent of a courtyard), *Ketubbot* 5:8 (a woman's annual dressing allowance), *Ma'aser*ot 2:5 (fruit in small quantity), *Eruvin* 8:2 (price of bread and flour), *Menahot* 13:8 (young bullocks, rams, and lambs), *Bava Qamma* 10:4 (an ass), *Me'ilah* 6:4 (mantle and shirt).

B. Weights

1 *zuz*

2 *zuz*—1 common *sheqel.*

2 *sheqel*—1 *sela* (but cf. *Ketubbot* 5:9; *Hullin* 11:2)

4 *zuz*—1 *sheqel* of the Sanctuary.

50 *zuz*—1 *tartemar*

100 *zuz*—1 Italian *mina.*

160 *zuz*—1 *mina.*

6,000 *zuz*—1 *talent.*

37.5 *minas*—1 *talent.*

C. Distance

1 fingerbreadth.

4 fingerbreadths—1 handbreadth.

2 handbreadths—1 *sit* (the distance between the tips of the outstretched thumb and index finger).

3 handbreadths—1 span.

2 spans—1 cubit (but cf. *Kelim* 17:9, 10).

266.67 cubits—1 *ris.*

2,000 cubits—1 mile (or Sabbath-day's journey).

7.5 *ris*—1 mile (*Yoma* 6:4).

D. Liquid and Dry Measure

64 *qurtov*—1 *log* (the contents of 6 eggs).

2 *litra*—1 *log.*

4 *log*—1 *qav*

3 *qav*—1 *hin*

6 *qav*—1 *se'ah*

3 *se'ah*—1 *ephah* (Cf. *Menahot* 6:6).

30 *se'ah*—1 *kor* (or 1 *homer*).

2 *letekh*—1 *kor.*

E. Measurement of Area

1 *kor*'s area—75,000 square cubits.

1 *se'ah*'s area—2,500 square cubits.

1 *qav*'s area—416.67 square cubits.

(That is, such ground as suffices for the sowing of a *kor*, *se'ah*, or *qav* of seed respectively. Cf. *Arakhin* 3:2; Leviticus 27:16.)

Glossary of Untranslated Hebrew Terms

Robert Goldenberg and Leonard Gordon

Adar The twelfth month, early spring. A second Adar (Adar Sheni) is periodically added before *Nisan* to align the solar and lunar years. *Rosh Hashanah* 1:1.

aleph First letter of the Hebrew alphabet.

alpha First letter of the Greek alphabet. *Sheqalim* 3:2, *Menahot* 8:1.

am ha'arets "The people of the Land." Jews who were not scrupulous in observing the laws of purity and/or the laws of tithes. Contrast *haver*; see also introduction to *Demai*. *Demai* 2:5.

androgynos A dually sexed person; from Greek "andro-" (man), and "gyno-" (woman). They are treated like men in certain legal contexts and like women in others, but the Mishnah occasionally develops unique stipulations for them when designations of "male" or "female" prove untenable. Neither the concept nor the word itself appear in the Hebrew Bible. See *tumtum* below; *Bikkurim* 4:1–5.

apiqoros Derived from the name *Epicurus*, in rabbinic parlance the term denotes a skeptical unbelieving Jew. *Avot* 2:14, *Sanhedrin* 10:1.

asherah In the Hebrew Bible either a sacred pole or tree, but in the Mishnah either a tree that is worshipped or a tree under which is an idol. Even incidental benefit from an *asherah* is proscribed for both ritual and everyday purposes. *Sukkah* 3:1.

Atseret Better known as the Festival of Weeks, *Shavu'ot*; celebrated fifty days after Passover, hence sometimes called in English "Pentecost" (from Greek meaning fiftieth).

Av The fifth month, midsummer. The annual fast commemorating the loss of the Temple falls on the ninth day of this month. *Ta'anit* 4:6.

Av Bet Din "Father of the court." The phrase denotes either the head of a rabbinic tribunal or the second-ranking member of the rabbinic conclave, after the *Nasi*. *Ta'anit* 2:1, *Hagigah* 2:2.

aylonit (Paradoxically) "a female ram." A barren woman, hence the etymology. Barrenness has marital implications, limiting the range of possible husbands, proscribing levirate marriage and *halitsah*, and, in some cases, terminating the *aylonit*'s rights to her *ketubbah*. *Gittin* 4:8.

Beit Avtinas A chamber in the Temple where the spices for the incense were compounded. It is named after the priestly family that carried out this function. *Yoma* 3:11, *Sheqalim* 5:1.

Beit Hamoqed "The fire chamber." A room in the Temple in which fire was perpetully maintained. Each morning, the altar was ignited by fire from here after having been swept clean of the previous day's ashes. *Tamid* 1:1.

Beit Hanitsots "The spark chamber." It is unclear what purpose this room served, although one can imagine that it provided kindling either to the *Beit Hamoqed* or to the altar itself. *Tamid* 1:1.

Beit Haperas A plowed-up field which may contain corpse fragments. *Tohorot* 4:5.

Berakhot Plural of *Berakha* or benediction; the first tractate of the Mishnah.

bet Second letter of the Hebrew alphabet. *Sheqalim* 3:2.

beta Second letter of the Greek alphabet.

birah "Palace" or "fortress." Medieval commentators generally follow the Amoraic opinion that *ha-birah* refers to *the* Temple or to a particular location within the Temple complex. Certain practices must take place within the *Birah*. *Pesahim* 3:8.

dalet Fourth letter of the Hebrew alphabet. Cited in connection with *Adonai*, the usual circumlocution for the unspeakable name of God. *Shevu'ot* 4:13.

darkonot A denomination of coinage. A gold coin corresponding to the Persian daric or the Greek *drakhma*. *Sheqalim* 2:1, see also Ezra 8:27.

demai Produce obtained from an *am ha'arets* and not certainly tithed. See introduction to tractate *Demai*.

dinar (or *denar*). A basic unit of money, between *issar* and *sheqel*, equal to *zuz*. *Ketubbot* 6:3, *Keritot* 1:7.

dupondius See *pondion*. A Roman denomination.

Elul The sixth month, early fall.

ephah A biblical dry measure, equal to three *se'ah*, no longer in common use by the time of the Mishnah. *Menahot* 7:1.

eruv (pl. *eruvin*). "Mixture" or "combination." A deposit of food allowing one to travel beyond boundaries otherwise restricted on the Sabbath.

(*a*) One may not travel more than 2,000 cubits beyond the boundaries of one's town on the Sabbath. However, if before the Sabbath someone deposits two meals' worth of food in an accessible place within the prescribed 2,000 cubits' distance, this spot constitutes a temporary abode, thereby allowing a range of up to 2,000 cubits beyond the common Sabbath limit.

(*b*) An *eruv* may also be arranged between residences that share a common courtyard. See *Eruvin* chapter 6.

etrog (pl. *etrogim*). A citron—the rabbinic interpretation of the biblical "fruit of *hadar* trees" used during the festival of Sukkot (see Leviticus 23:40). *Hadar* is usually understood as requiring that the fruit be beautiful. *Sukkah* 3:5–7.

Gehinom Derived from scattered biblical references to "the valley of ben-Hinnom." The term became the standard rabbinic name for Hell, the place where the wicked receive their just punishment. *Avot* 1:5, 5:19.

genizah The related verb means to put something away, to withdraw it from circulation or availability. This noun indicates a place where such materials are put in storage. In later times the notion lost its derogatory overtones and *genizah* came to designate something more like an archive. *Shabbat* 17:1, *Sheqalim* 6:2.

get (sing.), gittin (pl.) The term can designate a variety of legal documents, but most often refers to a bill of divorce. See tractate *Gittin*.

gimel Third letter of the Hebrew alphabet. *Sheqalim* 3:2.

givlit, gizrah Architectural terms of unclear meaning. *Oholot* 14:1.

haggadah (pl. *haggadoth*). Interpretation of Scripture to an end other than legal clarification. Also refers to the text read at the Passover Seder.

halakhah "Way" or "path" or "received tradition" (*Keritot* 3:9). The body of rules governing practical behavior, or any such rule. The Mishnah is mostly concerned with such matters, but there are several tractates—*Yoma*, *Sukkah*, *Sanhedrin*, and others—that feature narrative or homiletical elaboration as well.

halal (fem. *halalah*; pl. *halalim*). "Profaned" or (in other contexts) "defiled." A woman who has had sexual relations with a man to whom she may not legally be married becomes a *halalah* and may not be married to a priest. A divorcee who is married to a priest produces offspring who are not reckoned as priests and may not serve in the Temple or be married into the priesthood. *Qiddushin* 4:1.

halitsah "Drawing-off" (of the shoe). The ceremony performed when a man refuses to marry the widow of his childless brother. Deuteronomy 25, *Yevamot* 12:1.

hallah (pl. *hallot*). "Loaf" but translated here as "dough offering." Numbers 15:17–21 mandates that a small portion of each batch of dough in the land of Israel be given "to the Lord." Like *terumah*, *hallah* was given to priests.

Hallel From the Hebrew root denoting praise, *Hallel* is the name for the liturgical recitation of Psalms 113–118. Major themes include rejoicing in and gratitude for divine redemption, which is why it was reserved for holidays—Passover, Sukkot, Hanukkah, the New Month—that are distinctly joyful occasions. *Pesahim* 10:7.

halutsah A woman who performed the *halitsah* ceremony. A *halutsah* is deemed to have the legal status of a divorcee (that is, she may not be married to a *kohen*).

hamets "Leaven," made from wheat, barley, spelt, rye, or oats. On Passover, eating *hamets*, deriving any secondary benefit from it, and even having it within one's household are all prohibited. Hence, one must search for and "eliminate" all *hamets* products before the Passover holiday officially begins. *Pesahim* 1:1.

haroset A side dish consisting of fruits, honey, and nuts in various combinations that was served at the Passover feast. There was dispute as to whether this was a ritually necessary inclusion or just a pleasant counterpart to the bitterness of the *maror*. *Pesahim* 10:3.

hasid A charitable, patient, God-fearing person. Often contrasted with *rasha*—a wicked person. *Berakhot* 5:1, *Avot* 2:5, 5:14.

Havdalah "Separation," "distinction." A ceremony marking the end of a Sabbath or Festival day. The actual text of the ceremony does not appear in the Mishnah. *Berakhot* 5:2.

haver (pl. *haverim*). Associate or Fellow. Jews who were scrupulous in observing the laws of purity and in separating tithes properly. Contrast *amha'arets*; see introduction to *Demai*.

havurah Group. Chiefly either a group dedicated to consuming their meals in purity (see previous entry), or a group assembled for the purpose of consuming the Passover sacrifice. *Pesahim* 9:9.

heyl A structure within the Temple complex marking off the sacred domain. *Pesahim* 5:10, *Middot* 2:3. Also rendered "ledge."

hin A Biblical unit of liquid measure seen as archaic in the Mishnah. *Menahot* 9:2, *Eduyot* 1:3.

homer A measure of grain. See *Arakhin* 7:1, based on Leviticus 27:16.

hullin Nonsacred foodstuffs. *Tevul Yom* 3:5.

issar A small unit of money, equivalent to one half pondion. *Bava Qama* 8:6.

Iyyar Second month of the year, late spring.

kapporet "Propitiatory," i.e. the cover of the Ark, upon which the High Priest on the Day of Atonement (*Yom Kippur*) would sprinkle the blood of the sacrificial bull and ram, and atone for the sins of the Israelites. *Sheqalim* 6:5, *Middot* 1:1. During the Second Temple period there was no Ark and no *kapporet*. *Yoma* 5:2.

karet Often translated as "extirpation," literally "cutting off." The divinely inflicted punishment for those who intentionally violate certain prohibitions in the Torah. Unintentional violations of these same rules normally incur a purgation offering. Rabbinic sources are unclear about what *karet* actually entails, later materials suggest childlessness or premature death. See tractate *Keritot*.

karmelit An area that is considered by virtue of its size or location neither private property nor public space. Though it is prohibited to carry an object on the Sabbath into a *karmelit*, unintentional violation is not punished. *Eruvin* 9:2.

ketubbah "Written document." The word is used (*a*) for a document in which the groom promises a payment to the bride in the event of his death or their divorce; and (*b*) for the amount of money so designated. *Ketubbot* 4:7, 5:1.

Kislev The ninth month, winter. *Ta'anit* 1:5.

kohen (pl. *kohanim*). Priest(s). Male descendants of Aaron the Priest who officiated in the Temple of Jerusalem and constituted a marriage caste of their own. They are mentioned frequently throughout the Mishnah.

kohl Cosmetic ointment for the eyes. *Kelim* 13:2.

kor The largest common unit of volume or area. *Eruvin* 2:6, *Bava Metsi'a* 5:4.

kortab The smallest common unit of liquid or dry measure. *Miqva'ot* 7:5.

koy Probably some type of antelope. The *koy* does not fit into the binary of domestic/undomestic animals. For a sample of the implications of those categories, and the degrees to which the *koy* adheres to each, see *Bikkurim* 2:8.

Kutim Samaritans. As a result of the censorship of Jewish books, our printed editions occasionally have *Kutim* when the intent is "gentiles." *Gittin* 1:5.

letekh A unit of liquid or dry measure between a *se'ah* and a *kor*. *Bava Metsi'a* 6:5.

litra A small unit of liquid or dry measure between a *kortab* and a *log*. *Terumot* 4:10.

log A unit of liquid or dry measure between a *litra* and *qav*. *Yadayim* 1:1.

lulav "Palm branch." A bundle of branches used in the celebration of the Festival of Booths (Sukkot); alternatively, a palm branch by itself. Leviticus 23:40; *Sukkah* 4:1.

ma'ah A small unit of money between an *issar* and a *zuz*. *Hagigah* 1:2.

ma'amad (pl. *ma'amadot*). "Post," lit. "station." A group of people that accompanied any one of the twenty-four *mishmarot* ("courses") of the priests. The priests and Levites of the *ma'amad* went up to the Temple as witnesses to the offering of the sacrifices, and the Israelites of the *ma'amad* assembled in their own towns to recite suitable passages of Scripture. *Ta'anit* 4:2.

Ma'amad U-Moshav "Standing and sitting": gestures of mourning and consolation. *Megillah* 4:3.

ma'aser Tithe; an Israelite farmer was to give ten percent of his produce to a Levite; see Numbers 18. Found very frequently; see tractates *Ma'aserot* and *Ma'aser Sheni.*

madaf impurity. Impurity transmitted by overhang. A relatively mild degree of impurity. *Zavim* 4:6.

mamzer (pl. *mamzerim*). Commonly but inaccurately translated "bastard." In rabbinic law the offspring begotten from a severely prohibited sexual union. *Yevamot* 4:13. *Mamzerim* may not marry into the general Israelite population. *Qiddushin* 4:1.

maneh A unit of money, equal to 100 *zuz*. *Yoma* 3:7.

Marheshvan The eighth month, early to midautumn. *Ta'anit* 1:3.

maror "Bitter herbs." One of the foods required for the Passover feast. *Pesahim* 10:5.

matsah (pl. *matsot*). "Unleavened bread" made from wheat, spelt, rye, barley, or oats. The only bread product that may be consumed throughout Passover. *Pesahim* 10:5.

melog A type of property brought by a wife into a marriage. The husband has use of *melog* property and its produce throughout the life of the marriage but bears no responsibility for any reduction in its value or any loss, damage, or deterioration which the property may suffer from his use. Contrast *tson barzel* below. *Yevamot* 7:1.

menorah "Lampstand" or "candelabrum," but almost exclusively used as a proper noun to describe the lampstand in the Temple. *Menahot* 3:7.

metsora One afflicted with *tsara'at,* scale-disease ("leper"). See tractate *Nega'im.*

mezuzah (pl. *mezuzot*). "Doorpost." A small rolled-up piece of parchment on which are written two passages from the Torah and which is fastened to the doorpost of a house or city gate. See Deuteronomy 6:9. *Pesahim* 9:5.

midras impurity. Impurity conveyed by pressure (sitting, lying, riding). *Hagigah* 2:7, *Kelim* 18:7.

midrash (pl. *midrashim*). "Inquiry" into Scripture beyond its obvious surface meaning. In later times the word also came to denote an exposition designed to solve an exegetical problem. *Ketubbot* 4:6.

mil Unit of distance ("mile"). *Yoma* 6:8.

mina A large unit of money, between a golden *dinar* (= twenty-five *zuz*) and a talent.

minhah "Offering." The afternoon Prayer, and also the afternoon Temple grain offering that it replaced. *Pesahim* 10:1.

mishmar (pl. *mishmarot*). See *ma'amad* above.

mishnah (pl. *mishnayot*). "Teaching," or "repetition." The term can designate (*a*) a book edited by R. Judah the Patriarch whose translation lies before you, or (*b*) the body of teaching ascribed to a particular Sage (e.g. "the mishnah of R. Aqiva"), or (*c*) a single paragraph or item in either of these bodies of material.

Mo'ed Any of the festivals mandated in the Torah. In the Mishnah the word regularly refers to the intermediate days of the festivals of Sukkot and Passover. The word is also the name of the second Order of the Mishnah.

Musaf "Additional." The added Prayer (and, in Temple times, offering) special to Sabbaths and Festival days. *Ta'anit* 4:4, *Megillah* 4:2.

Nasi "Prince" or "Patriarch." The head of the rabbinic movement in the Land of Israel during the first few centuries CE. The most famous carrier of the title was "R. Judah the Patriarch," credited with having assembled the Mishnah. The term also designated the heads of the tribes during the period of desert wandering. *Nedarim* 5:5, *Horayot* 2:6, *Hagigah* 2:2.

natin (fem. *netinah*; pl. *netinim*). Descendants of the Gibeonites whom Joshua "gave" to the Temple—that is, made into Temple slaves (Joshua 9:27). Like *mamzerim*, they had a low status in the Israelite community and were only allowed to marry into groups of similarly low status. *Qiddushin* 4:1.

nazir (fem. *nezirah*; pl. *nezirim*). One who vows a special level of personal holiness, marked by abstinence from products of the vine, from cutting the hair, or from contact with the dead. See Numbers 6, tractate *Nazir*.

ne'ilah Lit. "Locking up." Once the closing prayer of any fast day, now retained only on Yom Kippur. *Ta'anit* 4:4. The term also appears in a more literal sense elsewhere.

nevelah "Carrion," the corpse of an animal that died otherwise than by ritual slaughter.

nezirut The state of being a *nazir*, or the duration of a *nazir*'s vow.

niddah A menstruating woman, also the name of a tractate dealing with such persons. Leviticus 15:19–24.

Nisan The first month, occurring in spring. The Passover sacrifice takes place on the fourteenth of Nisan. *Ta'anit* 1:2.

omer "Sheaf." Before the new harvest could be consumed, an *omer* of barley had to be reaped and its resulting flour offered as a meal-offering in the Temple on 16 Nisan, the second day of Passover. Only after it had been offered was the rest of the produce of the new harvest permitted for common use. *Menahot* 10:10.

onen A mourner before the burial. *Pesahim* 8:8.

orlah Lit. "foreskin." The fruit of young trees, forbidden during the first three years of the tree's productive life. Leviticus 19:23–25, tractate *Orlah*.

pe'ah Lit. "the corner," of a planted field that is left unharvested for the poor to glean. The name of a tractate of the Mishnah.

Perushim In the Mishnah the word refers to the Pharisees (*Yadayim* 4), but more broadly the word can designate a variety of ascetics.

perutah (pl. *perutot*). The smallest unit of money. *Qiddushin* 1:1, *Bava Qamma* 9:6.

piggul Lit. "unfit, loathsome." A sacrifice brought to the altar with the intention of consuming the meat at an inappropriate time or inappropriate place; the sacrifice is invalid at once, even before that time limit has been reached. Leviticus 19:7, *Zevahim* 2:3.

pondion A unit of money. *Bava Metsi'a* 4:5.

prozbul A word derived from the Greek, meaning "to the court." A document transferring debts to the court for the duration of the Seventh Year when debts would otherwise be remitted. *Shevi'it* 10:3.

psykter A large vessel. *Eruvin* 10:15, *Tamid* 5:5.

Purim Lit. "lots." A festival mandated in the book of Esther marking the deliverance of the Jews of Persia during the month of Adar. *Megillah*; *Eduyot* 7:7.

qav An intermediate unit of liquid and dry measure, between *log* and *se'ah*. *Pe'ah* 8:5.

Qiddush "Sanctification." A prayer recited at the inaugural meal of a Sabbath or Festival. See *Berakhot* chapter 8. Or the process of mixing the "lustration water" for removing corpse impurity. *Parah* chapter 7.

qonam A term introducing a vow of abstinence or a vow denying a second party enjoyment of a particular benefit. See tractate *Nedarim*. At *Nedarim* 1:2 a list of alternative formulations is provided.

qolbon (pl. *qolbonot*). A fee for converting *sheqel* payments from foreign currency. *Sheqalim* 1:7.

qorban "Sacrifice." The word is used to formalize a vow. *Nedarim* 1:4.

qurtov The smallest unit of dry or liquid measure. *Miqva'ot* 7:4.

Rabban Lit. "our rabbi," a title given to the Patriarch, by the third century CE the administrative head of the Jewish community in the Land of Israel. See also *Nasi*.

regel (pl. *regalim*). "Foot." Any of the three pilgrimage festivals—Passover, Sukkot, and the Feast of Weeks. *Pesahim* 8:1.

re'iyyah "Appearance." Offering made by pilgrims during the three pilgrimage festivals, Passover, the Feast of Weeks, and Sukkot. *Hagigah* 1:1.

revi'it "Quarter." Part of a *log*, a liquid measure. *Nazir* 7:1. *ris*. A unit of distance. *Yoma 6:4*.

se'ah A unit of liquid or dry measure and by extension a unit of area, between *qav* and *letekh*. *Terumot* 5:6.

sela A large unit of money or weight, between *sheqel* and *mina*. *Shevu'ot* 6:7.

seraq Unproductive, said of a tree that produces no fruit. *Kilayim* 6:5.

Sha'atnez Mixture of linen and wool, forbidden by the Torah (Deuteronomy 22:11). *Kilayim* 9:8.

Shaharit "Morning," said of the first prayer of the day, or by extension any early-morning activity. *Berakhot* 1:2, *Rosh Hashanah* 2:8.

Shema Lit. "Hear," the first word of the passage (Deuteronomy 6:4–9) around which the morning and evening services are built. *Berakhot* 1:1.

sheqel (pl. *sheqalim*). A unit of money or weight. In particular the annual contribution to the Temple. *Sheqalim* 1:6.

sherets The translation "vermin" corresponds to *sherets*, lit. "swarming thing." Dead vermin are a primary source of impurity (*Kelim* 1:1). *Shabbat* 14:3 limits the category to the eight species mentioned in Leviticus 11:29–30. Depending on context, *sherets* may refer to a single animal or to the class.

Shevat The eleventh month of the year, early spring. *Rosh Hashanah* 1:1.

shevut An action forbidden on the Sabbath or Festivals by rabbinic decree but not forbidden in the Torah. *Eruvin* 10:3, *Betsah* 5:2.

shittuf "Association" or "partnership." The occupants of a common courtyard may jointly contribute to a putative common meal that binds their homes into a single unit and so may carry items from one home to another. See *eruv* above. *Eruvin* 6:8.

shofar (*a*) The ram's horn blown in the Temple and during the synagogue service on Rosh Hashanah. (*b*) The chests (shaped like a *shofar*?) into which contributions for the upkeep of the Temple were placed. *Sheqalim* 6:5, *Rosh Hashanah* 3:3.

siqariqon Confiscation of previously Jewish-owned property after the defeat of Bar Kokhba. *Gittin* 5:6.

sit A unit of length, exact size uncertain. *Orlah* 2:3.

si'ur Partly leavened dough. *Pesahim* 3:5.

sotah A woman whose husband suspects her of infidelity. See tractate *Sotah*.

sukkah (pl. *sukkot*). Lit. "booth." The temporary dwelling where meals are eaten during Sukkot, the fall harvest festival. See tractate *Sukkah*.

talmud Lit. "learning." The general sense of the word is study. It is more common in the narrower sense of the comments and discussions (the *Gemara*) on the text of the Mishnah by the rabbinic Sages of the Land of Israel and Babylonia from the third to the fifth centuries CE, but in the Mishnah itself the word does not yet have this meaning.

Tammuz The fourth month, early summer. *Ta'anit* 4:6.

tanna (pl. *tannaim*). A rabbinic teacher from the period of the Mishnah. The word does not appear in the text.

tarpe'iq Unit of coinage, half a *dinar*. Often rendered "tropaic." *Ketubbot* 5:7.

tartemar See *tritomer*.

tav The final letter of the Hebrew alphabet.

tekhelet The blue-green color of the fringes on a garment prescribed by Numbers 15:38. *Berakhot* 1:2, *Qinnim*, end.

tefillah Lit. "prayer." (*a*) Strictly speaking the most important prayer in the rabbinic liturgy, an anthology of petitions and benedictions recited several times a day. *Berakhot* 4:1. (*b*) Singular of *tefillin*.

tefillin "Phylacteries." Small boxes of leather, worn on the arm and the forehead, containing verses from the Torah. In ancient times they were often worn all day; now use is generally limited to the time of the weekday morning prayer. *Mo'ed Qatan* 3:4.

terefah Lit. "torn." Meat that has been killed other than by intentional slaughter for consumption. The term mostly designates an animal found to have had a fatal defect. *Zevahim* 12:4.

teresith A unit of money of intermediate value. *Shevu'ot* 6:3.

terit A type of fish or recipes prepared from fish. *Avodah Zarah* 2:6.

terumah Lit. "heave offering." A portion of each year's crop that is a priestly entitlement based on Numbers 18. In tractate *Sheqalim*, the term more broadly designates funds taken out of the Sheqel chamber in the Temple.

teqi'ah, teru'ah Sounds produced by a *shofar* (ram's horn), especially on fast days and the New Year. *Tamid* 7:3, *Rosh Hashanah* 4:1–2.

teva'in A unit of money. *Sheqalim* 2:4.

Tevet The tenth month, winter.

tevul yom (fem. *tevulat yom*). One who has immersed for purification that day. Such a person is no longer impure but for certain purposes remains restricted until the sun has set.

tevusah blood. Blood that has oozed from a corpse. *Oholot* 3:5.

Tishre The seventh month, fall. The month in which fall Rosh Hashanah, Yom Kippur, and Sukkot.

tritomer A unit of weight, fifty *zuz*. *Sanhedrin* 8:2.

tsara'at Skin affliction often rendered (incorrectly) "leprosy." See tractate *Nega'im*.

tsitsit Lit. "fringe." In particular the fringe commanded at Numbers 15:38.

tumtum A person with no identifiable sex characteristics. *Yevamot* 9:6.

tson barzel Lit. "iron sheep," that is inalienable property. The term refers to a wife's property which the husband, in the case of her death or divorce, must restore in full. Compare *melog*, above. *Yevamot* 7:1.

urim v'tumim Priestly instruments of divination, no longer used in Second Temple times. *Shevuot* 2:2.

Yom Tov Religious festival, in particular Rosh Hashanah, Yom Kippur, and the pilgrimage festivals of Passover, Sukkot, and Shavuot. See tractates *Rosh Hashanah, Yoma, Betsah, Mo'ed Qatan.*

Yovel The fiftieth, Jubilee year. *Qiddushin* 1:2.

zav (fem. *zavah*; pl. *zavim, zavot*). A person rendered impure by an irregular sexual discharge. See tractate *Zavim.* Leviticus 15.

zikhronot "Remembrances." One of the central portions of the *Rosh Hashanah* liturgy. More particularly the biblical passages that constitute this portion. *Rosh Hashanah* 4:5.

zivah The discharge that makes one a *zav*.

zonah Lit. "harlot." In rabbinic law, a woman whose sexual history disqualifies her from being married to a priest. *Yevamot* 7:5.

zuz A unit of weight or money. Another name for the *dinar*.

Index of Biblical Passages

Adapted from Herbert Danby, *The Mishnah: Translated from the Hebrew with Introduction and Brief Explanatory Notes* (Oxford: Oxford University Press, 1963).

Index of Names and Subjects